The McGavocks
of
Carnton Plantation

BOOKS BY LOCHLAINN SEABROOK

Everything You Were Taught About the Civil War is Wrong, Ask a Southerner! - Correcting the Errors of Yankee "History"
Encyclopedia of the Battle of Franklin - A Comprehensive Guide to the Conflict that Changed the Civil War
Carnton Plantation Ghost Stories: True Tales of the Unexplained from Tennessee's Most Haunted Civil War House!
The McGavocks of Carnton Plantation: A Southern History - Celebrating One of Dixie's Most Noble Confederate Families and Their Tennessee Home
A Rebel Born: A Defense of Nathan Bedford Forrest - Confederate General, American Legend
Abraham Lincoln: The Southern View - Demythologizing America's Sixteenth President
Nathan Bedford Forrest: Southern Hero, American Patriot - Honoring a Confederate Icon and the Old South
Lincolnology: The Real Abraham Lincoln Revealed in His Own Words - A Study of Lincoln's Suppressed, Misinterpreted, and Forgotten Speeches and Writings
The Caudills: An Etymological, Ethnological, and Genealogical Study - Exploring the Name and National Origins of a European-American Family
The Blakeneys: An Etymological, Ethnological, and Genealogical Study - Uncovering the Mysterious Origins of the Blakeney Family and Name
UFOs and Aliens: The Complete Guidebook
Britannia Rules: Goddess-Worship in Ancient Anglo-Celtic Society - An Academic Look at the United Kingdom's Matricentric Spiritual Past
Christmas Before Christianity: How the Birthday of the "Sun" Became the Birthday of the "Son"
The Book of Kelle: An Introduction to Goddess-Worship and the Great Celtic Mother-Goddess Kelle, Original Blessed Lady of Ireland
The Goddess Dictionary of Words and Phrases: Introducing a New Core Vocabulary for the Women's Spirituality Movement
Aphrodite's Trade: The Hidden History of Prostitution Unveiled

Thought Provoking Books For Smart People

www.SeaRavenPress.com

THE McGAVOCKS
of
Carnton Plantation

A Southern History

Celebrating One of Dixie's Most Noble
Confederate Families and Their Tennessee Home

Lochlainn Seabrook

Introduction by Dr. Michael R. Bradley
Foreword by Sue A. Thompson

Franklin, Tennessee

THE McGAVOCKS OF CARNTON PLANTATION
A SOUTHERN HISTORY

Published by
Sea Raven Press, P.O. Box 1054, Franklin, Tennessee 37065-1054 USA
www.searavenpress.com • searavenpress@nii.net
Thought Provoking Books For Smart People

Copyright © 2008, 2011 Lochlainn Seabrook
in accordance with U.S. and international copyright laws and regulations, as stated and protected under the Berne Union for the Protection of Literary and Artistic Property (Berne Convention), and the Universal Copyright Convention (the UCC).
All rights reserved under the Pan-American and International Copyright Conventions.

First Sea Raven Press edition: July 2008
Second Sea Raven Press edition: July 2011

ISBN: 978-0-9827700-8-5
Library of Congress Catalog Number: 2011923521

This work is the copyrighted intellectual property of Lochlainn Seabrook and has been registered with the Copyright Office at the Library of Congress in Washington, D.C., USA. No part of this work (including text, covers, drawings, photos, illustrations, maps, images, diagrams, etc.), in whole or in part, may be used, reproduced, stored in a retrieval system, or transmitted, in any form or by any means now known or hereafter invented, without written permission from the publisher. The sale, duplication, hire, lending, copying, digitalization, or reproduction of this material, in any manner or form whatsoever, is also prohibited, and is a violation of federal, civil, and digital copyright law, which provides severe civil and criminal penalties for any violations.

The McGavocks of Carnton Plantation: A Southern History - Celebrating One of Dixie's Most Noble Confederate Families & Their Tennessee Home, by Lochlainn Seabrook. Introduction by Dr. Michael R. Bradley; Foreword by Sue A. Thompson. Includes bibliographical references and index. (Portions of this book have been adapted from the author's other works.)

Front and back cover design, book design and layout, by Lochlainn Seabrook
Cover images: copyright © Lochlainn Seabrook
Typography: Sea Raven Press Book Design
Sketch of the author on "About the Author" page copyright © Tracy Latham

The views on the American "Civil War" documented in this book *are* those of the publisher.

The paper used in this book is acid-free and lignin-free. It has been certified by the Sustainable Forestry Initiative and the Forest Stewardship Council and meets all ANSI standards for archival quality paper.

Printed and manufactured in occupied Tennessee, former Confederate States of America

Dedication

To my cousins the McGavocks

Epigraph

The South produced statesmen and soldiers, planters and doctors, and lawyers and poets, but certainly not engineers and mechanics. Let Yankees adopt such low callings.

> Margaret Mitchell, *Gone with the Wind* (1936)

CONTENTS

Foreword, by Sue A. Thompson - 9
Preface, by Lochlainn Seabrook - 11
Acknowledgments - 19
Notes to the Reader - 21
Introduction, by Dr. Michael R. Bradley - 23

❧{ PART ONE }❧
THE CARNTON McGAVOCKS

1: Surname Etymology & Distribution - 27
2: Early McGavock History - 32
3: Randal & Sarah - 41
4: John & Carrie - 48
5: The McGavocks & Slavery, Part 1 - 65
6: The McGavocks & Slavery, Part 2 - 94
7: The McGavocks & Slavery, Part 3 - 131
8: The McGavocks & Slavery, Part 4 - 185
9: The War for Southern Independence - 232
10: The McGavocks & Lincoln's War, Part 1 - 278
11: The McGavocks & Lincoln's War, Part 2 - 323
12: Carnton's Role in the Battle of Franklin II - 370
13: The End of the McGavock Era at Carnton - 385
14: Life at Carnton After the McGavocks - 429

❧{ PART TWO }❧
A TOUR OF CARNTON PLANTATION

15: Carnton: Front & Back Exterior - 435
16: Carnton's Interior: First Floor - 458
17: Carnton's Interior: Second Floor - 479

⋅⁂{ PART THREE }⁂⋅
THE McGAVOCK CONFEDERATE CEMETERY
18: Where Some of the South's Finest Rest in Faded Glory - 501

⋅⁂{ PART FOUR }⁂⋅
McGAVOCK GENEALOGY
19: The McGavock Family Tree: Carnton Plantation Line Only - 513
20: A Royal McGavock Family Tree: From Robert the Bruce King of Scotland to Colonel John W. McGavock - 521

APPENDICES
Appendix A: A Complete McGavock Family Tree - 531
Appendix B: A Complete Winder Family Tree - 579
Appendix C: Some Well-Known Relations and Ancestors of the McGavocks, the Winders, and the Author - 589
Appendix D: McGavock and Winder Astrology - 591
Appendix E: The Sons of Confederate Veterans - 593
Appendix F: Company H Twentieth Tennessee Infantry - 597
Appendix G: Colonel Buckner's Mint Julep Recipe - 605

Illustrations - 607
Notes on the Bibliography - 957
Bibliography - 961
Index - 993
About the Author - 1040
The Author's Genealogy - 1042
About the Introduction Writer - 1045
About the Foreword Writer - 1047

FOREWORD
Sue A. Thompson

Cotton was "King" and the "livin' was easy" for the Southern plantation owners and their families in the early 1800s. Daily life was heaped with a gracious dollop of grandeur during that brief window of time on the South's great antebellum estates.

The landed gentry were leaders in fashion, manners, and entertaining, and Tennessee's upper class McGavock family was no exception. They were among the premiere trend setters in Southern propriety, style, and taste.

In his exceptional new book, *The McGavocks of Carnton Plantation*, Southern historian Lochlainn Seabrook, a former Carnton tour guide and a cousin of the marvelous McGavock clan, generously allows the reader a wide glimpse both of the lineage of this colorful and upright family and their absorbing legacy.

In Part One we learn of the McGavocks' history, from their birth in distant Scotland all the way to the present day. Included is a cast of fascinating characters, personal histories, and stories of both their victories and tragedies—including the death of beloved family members. Of insightful interest is the accounting of how the McGavocks felt about and dealt with slavery, secession, the Civil War, and abolition. Seabrook provides authentic facts that will enlighten and educate you.

Part Two is an outside and inside tour of Carnton Plantation, one that is detailed and inclusive. Far from dreary, as one might expect from room-by-room descriptions of furnishings, you will find yourself riveted by the incredible history of every detail and piece.

This perceptive look at the decorative arts of Carnton will give each "guest" a wonderful view into the bygone era that is the grand Old South. Your visual visit will be generously peppered with McGavock portraits, recovered antiques, moving personal dramas, and charming family narratives.

Your imagination will soar at the description of the McGavocks'

The McGavocks of Carnton Plantation

lavish parties, the hooped skirts, the top hats, the expert corn shucking and chicken plucking of the servants, and festive tea parties in the courtyard—complete with croquet and cigars, cornbread and glazed ham, and silver trays loaded down with mint juleps in frosted crystal goblets.

Part Three gives us an inside look at the awe inspiring McGavock Confederate Cemetery, where nearly 1,500 of Dixie's bravest sons rest to this day. Part Four covers the Carnton Plantation family tree branch by branch.

The latter half of the book is comprised of hundreds of amazing illustrations, many with captions containing valuable information not found in the main chapters. There are also sections devoted to the complete McGavock and Winder genealogical records, and scholarly types will enjoy the nearly 1,700 footnotes of well researched citations.

Seabrook, whose love and enthusiasm for Carnton Plantation exudes from every page, lives by that unwritten rule known so well to the historian, archaeologist, and antique collector: "A life is told through objects." You will never forget your literary tour of exquisite Carnton Plantation with the author as your own private docent.

And when your "tour" is over, you will have this detailed and delightful book to remember it by and to refer back to, which is only right and proper. For at the home of the McGavocks it was a tradition that "no guest ever left without a gift to take home with them."

The McGavocks of Carnton Plantation, is an unforgettable memorial to a heroic Confederate family. Well done Mr. Seabrook, and thank you indeed for your superb contribution to the South's history. The chronicles of Williamson County are now much richer.

Sue Armstrong Thompson
Master Curator and Decorative Arts Director
The Lotz House Museum
Franklin, Tennessee

PREFACE

Lochlainn Seabrook

❧ QUESTIONS

As a former Carnton Plantation tour guide, many have asked me about the authentic history of those who founded this beautiful antebellum home. How and when did they build it, and how long did they live there? Why did they eventually sell it and move out? Why is the house a mixture of so many different architectural styles? When did these changes take place, and what happened to the barns, the five-bay carriage house, the countless outbuildings, the greenhouse, gardens, corrals, horse paddocks, fruit orchards, large trees, and the many servants' houses that once dotted the property?

Where did the McGavocks come from originally and what does their name mean? What were their lives really like at the famous mansion in Franklin, Tennessee? Who are their ancestors, and is it true that they descend from European royalty, are related to a number of modern day celebrities, and have a connection with the powerful, secret, mysterious, and controversial ancient Christian society, the Knights Templar?

(Photo © Lochlainn Seabrook)

Why were the McGavocks die-hard Confederates and why did they proudly fly the Confederate Flag over their home, the same flag that is so misunderstood and detested across the U.S. today? Why did they side against the North and Lincoln, the same man who today is continually voted America's favorite, best, and most popular president?

Why did Lincoln attack the South to begin with? Was his invasion of Dixie legal, right, or necessary? How did the McGavocks perceive Lincoln? How did they feel about Lincoln's War, and what role did Colonel John W. McGavock, his wife Caroline E. Winder, and Carnton Plantation play in the conflict?

THE McGAVOCKS OF CARNTON PLANTATION

Why did the McGavocks love and respect men like Rebel chieftain General Nathan Bedford Forrest, a man who today's liberals and the politically correct consider a sadistic racist and a violent illiterate redneck from the backwoods of Tennessee?

How did the Battle of Franklin II affect the McGavocks? Why was it fought? Should it have been fought at all? Why was it so disastrous for the South, who or what was responsible for the debacle, and what did this Rebel loss mean for the Confederacy?

What about the McGavock Confederate Cemetery? When was it established and why, and who is buried there? Why are there so many less men interred in the cemetery than died at 2nd Franklin? And what about Carnton's ghosts? Is Carnton really haunted and, if so, what kind of paranormal activities occur at the plantation?

Why did the McGavocks own servants (wrongly called "slaves" in the North), and how could they use the Bible to justify the institution? How did they treat their black bondsmen and bondswomen and what was their overall attitude toward African-Americans? What about Southern "slavery" itself? Was it really the institution portrayed by anti-South Yankees like Harriet Beecher Stowe?

These questions and many others will be answered in the following pages.

But if you are used to the North's highly skewed, self-serving version of the "Civil War" and the New South's traitorous view of the McGavocks, Carnton, and the Old South, be prepared to have your mind greatly expanded. The answers to these questions will not be the ones you expect, for this is the McGavocks' history written from their point of view: the Southern perspective.

❧ PRESERVING THE McGAVOCKS' HERITAGE

As a Southern historian, author, descendant of numerous Confederate soldiers, and a 14th-generation Southerner, I have a great interest in my cousins the McGavocks, and in the majestic estate they built and owned, Carnton Plantation.

Many of us who descend from, or who are related to, the McGavocks feel as if Carnton is our "family home." This is only natural for it is indeed a part of our heritage. As such it is our responsibility to keep its true history alive.

THE MCGAVOCKS OF CARNTON PLANTATION

To this end, as a McGavock relation, I offer the following history, the true and untold story of the Carnton McGavocks, which includes their family tree (royal and non-royal), and hundreds of photos, drawings, maps, and diagrams.

This book is not just for those of us who are related to the McGavocks, however. This family and their home are part of both Tennessee's history and America's history. This makes it a work for all Americans, and for anyone interested in authentic Southern history as told by a Southerner. It is only when Northern mythology, anti-South Civil War propaganda, and New South disinformation are stripped away, that we will be able to see the Carnton McGavocks for who they really were: one of America's most noble, patriotic, Christian families.

(Photo © Lochlainn Seabrook)

But, critics of the South will argue, how can anyone who sided against Lincoln and owned slaves be considered "noble, patriotic, and Christian"? If you read this book in its entirety—from cover to cover—you will discover the truth for yourself, a truth that is far different from what our schools and society have long taught us.

❧ JUDGING THE PAST USING MODERN VALUES
It is never right to judge our ancestors by the standards of our day, an all too common practice known as presentism. Instead we must approach them with an open and enquiring mind, and with a thorough understanding of the time and place they lived in. This is only fair and correct, for it is the scientific and scholarly way. Without this approach one is dealing only with opinion, which is not historically valuable.

❧ SETTING THE RECORD STRAIGHT
When we do look at the past objectively, we learn that the world the McGavocks and other Southern Victorians lived in was not as black and white as many would like us to believe.

For example, contrary to Northern mythology: the Southern

THE MCGAVOCKS OF CARNTON PLANTATION

Founding Fathers originally intended the United States to be a confederacy; both the American slave trade *and* American slavery started in the North; the American abolition movement began in the South; the South did not "rebel" against the U.S. (the U.S. rebelled against the Constitution and so the Constitution-loving South had no choice but to leave the Union); Southerners did not want slavery (and in fact very few owned human chattel); Northerners considered slaves to be property, while Southerners considered them to be human beings; before the War the South was racially integrated while the North was racially segregated; Lincoln—who promoted the ideas of American apartheid and the mass deportation of blacks—was the archenemy, not the friend, of African-Americans; the U.S. government was created primarily by Southerners, not Northerners (the Declaration of Independence, for example, was written by a Southerner,[1] the framework of the Constitution was laid out by two Southerners and a Scotsman,[2] the location of the nation's capital was selected by Southerners,[3] and it was mainly Southerners who called for a Bill of Rights to be added to the Constitution); and the Southern Confederacy itself was merely an attempt to continue the constitutional government, a Confederate Republic, originally created by the Founders,[4] most who, like the McGavocks, were Southerners.[5]

❧ THE BEACON OF TRUTH

The McGavocks of Carnton Plantation, written with love and esteem for this distinguished family, intends to both set the record straight and to preserve it. This is vital because the real story about the McGavocks has been both rewritten by Yankee mythologists and censored by New South thought police. There is much they would rather you not know.

As we will see, however, when the beacon of truth is thrown on this fascinating family there is nothing about them that modern day Americans, Southerners, or McGavock relations need be ashamed of. Actually, there is

---

1. Thomas Jefferson (1743-1826).
2. James Madison (1751-1836) of Virginia, Charles Pinckney (1757-1824) of South Carolina, and James Wilson (1742-1798) of Scotland (who later died in North Carolina).
3. Southerners Jefferson and Madison pushed the idea through, while Southerner George Washington (1732-1799) and various Southern Congressmen selected the actual site for America's capital in what would later become Washington, D.C.
4. See Rable, passim.
5. Other Southerners who helped make the United States largely a Southern creation were George Mason (1725-1792), Patrick Henry (1736-1799), John Marshall (1755-1835), and James Monroe (1758-1831).

THE McGAVOCKS OF CARNTON PLANTATION

everything to be proud of. For they were part of a magnificent social, cultural, and political tradition that can be traced back to George Washington and Thomas Jefferson, James Monroe and William Henry Harrison, John Tyler and James Knox Polk, John C. Calhoun and Jefferson Davis, Charles Lindbergh and Henry Ford, right into the present day with individuals like Ron Paul, Sarah Palin, Clyde Wilson, Michael Williams, Eric Cantor, Laura Ingraham, Thomas J. DiLorenzo, Sean Hannity, Monica Crowley, Herman Cain, Pat and Bay Buchanan, Michele Bachmann, Andrew Napolitano, Rush Limbaugh, and many others.

(Photo © Lochlainn Seabrook)

In the late 1700s this libertarian-like movement—based on states' rights and individual freedom—was known as Jeffersonianism (after the author of the Declaration of Independence, Thomas Jefferson). Today we call it paleoconservatism, or Tea Partyism, a political system that derives from the very heart and soul of the traditional Southern Founding Fathers over 230 years ago.[6]

If the McGavocks of Carnton Plantation could see the U.S. today they would be stunned to see how far America has strayed from the path intended by these ingenious social and political pioneers.

❧ JUSTIFYING THE UNJUSTIFIABLE

Despite this awe-inspiring American heritage, simply because the McGavocks were Southerners, Confederates, and "slave owners," their name and reputation have often suffered at the hands of the uninformed, the biased, and the mean-spirited. Sometimes the libel is subtle, other times overt.

Traditional Southerners know exactly what I am speaking of. We deal with it every day in a myriad of ways, from South-insulting TV commercials and South-demeaning TV shows, to open attacks on our emblems, lifestyle, and history.

---

6. Plano, Greenberg, Olton, and Riggs, s.v. "Jeffersonianism."

THE MCGAVOCKS OF CARNTON PLANTATION

The McGavocks were daily exposed to this same sort of ignorance and hostile treatment by Northern journalists, writers, and politicians, who used false words like "arch traitors" to describe Confederates, and who referred to the legal act of the secession of the Southern states as "the foulest, most heinous, and gigantic instance of crime recorded in history."[7] The "Civil War" itself was, in great part, the result of this very type of Northern arrogance, her bias toward Southerners, and her lack of understanding of or respect for Southern culture.

Sadly, this unwarranted prejudice has crept southward: unbelievably, to this very day, if you attend a Civil War reenactment at Carnton, you are more likely to see an Abraham Lincoln impersonator than a Jefferson Davis impersonator. Meanwhile, unenlightened New South and Northern authors still regularly put out books that assail and disparage the McGavocks. Why? What is the purpose of all the animosity aimed at this Franklin clan and other wonderful Confederate families of the Old South?

The answer is simple. It is a continuation of the North's and the New South's 150 year old attempt to justify the unjustifiable: the North's illegal invasion of Dixie and the senseless persecution, pillage, arrest, imprisonment, torture, rape, murder, and wanton deaths of millions of Southerners between 1861 and 1877.[8]

Despite the fact that in the South we are taught to "be polite" and keep our mouths shut, most of us have grown impatient seeing our unique region maligned and degraded by the ignorant and the malicious. Many of us are now standing up for Southern Truth. This book is one small part of that movement.

❧ A FAIR & HONEST HISTORY FROM THE SOUTHERN PERSPECTIVE

Unlike what you will read in many other books on the McGavocks and on

---

7. "Civil War Sesquicentennial: 150 Years Ago This Month," *The Nashville Retrospect*, July 2011, p. 7.
8. "Reconstruction," which began unofficially at Appomattox (with Lee's "surrender") on April 9, 1865, and officially at Washington, D.C. with Lincoln's "Proclamation of Amnesty and Reconstruction" on December 8, 1863 (this was followed up, after Lincoln's death, with the first of President Andrew Johnson's Reconstruction Acts on March 2, 1867), did not end until March 4, 1877, with the inauguration of President Rutherford B. Hayes (who finally terminated Lincoln's madness when he began pulling Union troops out of the South, beginning with South Carolina on April 10, 1877). In this way, the North needlessly and cruelly prolonged Lincoln's War for another twelve years. Clearly punishment, vengeance, and the idea of "Northernizing" the South, were the real motivations behind Yankee "Reconstruction."

THE MCGAVOCKS OF CARNTON PLANTATION

Carnton Plantation, nothing in this one has been fabricated to embarrass them, to ridicule their lifestyle, or slander their good name. There will be no criticism of the South based on Yankee folklore, no defamation of the Confederacy built on the agendas of the politically correct, no vilification of servant owning Southern families—white or black—founded on Northern propaganda, or what Edward A. Pollard rightly called the "ingenious falsehoods of the enemy," and "the misrepresentation and hypocrisy of the North."[9]

What you will find in this book is a fair and honest history of the McGavocks as seen through the eyes of the South. In short, this is a positive and respectful tribute to a royal Confederate family, penned by a blood relative with deep Southern roots.

❧ THE McGAVOCKS' STORY TOLD THEIR WAY

If the McGavocks were alive today this is their story as they would tell it. Since they are not, we will carry the banner of Southern Truth forward for them. For as even the Lincoln-loving Yankee poet Walt Whitman once wisely observed: "The real war will never get in the books."[10]

It is my hope that *The McGavocks of Carnton Plantation* will aid in both the preservation of this family's genuine history and that of the Confederacy, for thousands of Southern men and women perished—including several McGavocks and Winders—fighting for freedom from a Northern-based political, cultural, and social tyranny that is not only with us still, but is now stronger than ever.

(Photo © Lochlainn Seabrook)

Lochlainn Seabrook
July 2011, Civil War Sesquicentennial
Franklin, Williamson County, Tennessee

---

9. Pollard, LC, pp. 503, 405.
10. Whitman, CPW, p. 80.

(Photo © Lochlainn Seabrook)

Acknowledgments

Special thanks to:

My wife Cassidy
My daughters Fiona and Dixie
Dr. Michael R. Bradley, former U.S. history professor at Motlow College, Sons of Confederate Veterans chaplain, popular lecturer, and award winning author
Sue A. Thompson, Master Curator, the Lotz House Museum, Franklin, Tennessee
The Tennessee State Library and Archives (TSLA)
Ann Toplovich, Executive Director, The Tennessee Historical Society
Williamson County Public Library
Frances Hall, former President of the Franklin Chapter 14 United Daughters of the Confederacy
Ronny Mangrum, Adjutant for Roderick, Forrest's War Horse Camp 2072, Sons of Confederate Veterans
Betty Jane Carl
The Van Rens family
Harpeth River Watershed Association
Zach Petty

THE MCGAVOCKS OF CARNTON PLANTATION

(Photo © Lochlainn Seabrook)

Notes to the Reader

• This book is in no way connected with the Carnton Association, its members, or the plantation's staff and employees. As a Southern historian and freelance writer I wrote this work out of admiration for my relatives the McGavocks, an interest in their beautiful antebellum home, and a belief in the Jeffersonian (that is, Confederate) ideals to which they faithfully adhered.

• As Carnton's furnishings are often moved from one room to another or removed entirely to make way for new items, some of the interior furnishings described in this book may now be in different locations than when I worked there.

• In any study of the "Civil War" it is vitally important to bear in mind that the two major political parties were then the opposite of what they are today. The Democrats of the 19th Century were conservatives, akin to the Republican Party of today, while the Republicans of the 19th Century were liberals, akin to the Democratic Party of today. Thus the Confederacy's Democratic president, Jefferson Davis, was a conservative (with libertarian leanings); the Union's Republican president, Abraham Lincoln, was a liberal (with socialistic leanings).

• Contrary to popular opinion, there were three "Battles of Franklin," though generally only one is recognized by most "Civil War" scholars. The conflict commonly, and inaccurately, known as simply the Battle of Franklin was actually the second, and so is more correctly called the Battle of Franklin II, or 2nd Franklin. It is this particular conflict with which this book is primarily concerned.

Unfortunately for the town of Franklin, the state of Tennessee, and the South itself, the North won all three battles. They occurred in the following sequence:

1. Battle of Franklin I, or 1st Franklin, April 10, 1863
2. Battle of Franklin II, or 2nd Franklin, November 30, 1864
3. Battle of Franklin III, or 3rd Franklin, December 17, 1864

The Confederate Memorial in Franklin Center proudly honors those who donned Rebel Gray and fought and fell in the defense of personal liberty, political freedom, the Constitution, and self-government.

• As many have asked me about my relationship to the McGavocks and other Victorian Confederates, I have made note of my kinship where appropriate.

• All Bible quotations are from the King James Version (KJV).

L.S.

The McGavocks of Carnton Plantation

(Photo © Lochlainn Seabrook)

INTRODUCTION

Dr. Michael R. Bradley

Carnton Plantation has been many things. It began as a working farm on the developing frontier when Middle Tennessee was still considered to be "the west" and not "the south." From a working farm Carnton developed into a large plantation which provided a comfortable standard of living for its owners, the McGavock family.

The high point of drama in Carnton's history came on November 30, 1864, when the house and its grounds became a field hospital for the Army of Tennessee during the Battle of Franklin. In the months after that blood-drenched day part of the grounds became a hallowed spot as the McGavock family saw to the burial of many of the Confederate dead from that engagement. The patriotism and love of country, namely the South, portrayed by the McGavock family is a sterling example of dedication to place, cause, and country.

As the years passed Carnton became yet other things. Slowly, it ceased to be the home of the McGavocks and was inhabited by tenant farmers, and was even used to store hay! But then Carnton was rescued from oblivion and began to be restored to portray its days as a plantation home. But the path of restoration has not been smooth.

Shall Carnton be a hallowed place, a place where the sacrifice of hundreds of young Southern men is remembered; or shall it be a venue for social gatherings? Is Carnton to be portrayed as a Confederate field hospital, of which there are few; or is Carnton to be presented to the public as a plantation house, of which there are many? Which history of Carnton will be preserved, what aspect of its past emphasized?

The McGavock family is one of the oldest and most influential of Middle Tennessee families. They have produced leaders in politics, business, and community affairs for generations. They have been the friend and confidant of governors and presidents. One of them, Carrie, established a reputation for charity, piety, and service so that she was known as "the Good Samaritan of Williamson County." She is also the

THE MCGAVOCKS OF CARNTON PLANTATION

Southern patriot who saw to the honorable reburial of the Confederate cemetery which is now owned by the United Daughters of the Confederacy.

In Lochlainn Seabrook's latest work, *The McGavocks of Carnton Plantation: A Southern History*, you will learn many things about the McGavock family and about Carnton which are omitted from more popular accounts of the family and their historic home. You will gain an insight into the turbulent times in which the family lived and the contributions they made. And you will come to see Carnton as a symbol of all these things.

Dr. Michael R. Bradley
Chaplain, Dr. J. B. Cowan Camp #155, SCV
Commander, Tennessee Division, SCV (2006-2010)
Tullahoma, Tennessee

PART ONE

The Carnton McGavocks

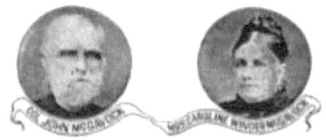

Surname Etymology & Distribution

❧ McGAVOCK ETYMOLOGY

LET US START AT THE beginning: what is the origin and meaning of the surname McGavock? McGavock is a Celtic name that is made up of two words: Mac, which means "a descendant of the clan of," and Gavock, which is an English corruption of *Daibhidh*, *Daibheid*, or *Dhabhóig*, all Gaelic words for David. Therefore, McGavock is a Celtic name that means "one of the clan of David." The early spelling was probably *Mac Dabhóc*, or something similar.

The name David, of course, is not Celtic. It is the English spelling of the Hebrew name *Daviyd*, meaning "beloved one," and has no connection to the Gaelic language. However, ancient Scots and Irish often named their children after biblical figures, like King David of Israel (2 Samuel 5:3), just as many Americans would later do. In fact, for many centuries David was the most popular name in Scotland.[11]

Bible names themselves were, and still are, immensely popular. David, the Patron Saint of Wales (b. about 500), is one of the better known examples of this tradition in Welsh culture. Throughout Scotland's history there have also been many Davids of note, from King David I (1084-1153), son of King Malcolm III (1031-1093), to King David II (1322-1369), son of Robert the Bruce (1274-1329). As we will see, the McGavocks are descendants of all of these Scottish royals.

---

11. Dorward, s.v. "MacDade/MacDaid."

The McGavocks of Carnton Plantation

But how did "Gavock" derive from David? An early variation of the Gaelic spelling of David (*Daibhidh*) was *Dabhóǵ* or *Dabóc*, which became "Davock" in English, a language periodically and violently forced on Celtic peoples of the British Isles over the centuries. Over time, with the repeated pronunciation of MacDavock, a linguistic corruption took place: the "d" mutated into a "g," creating the name "Gavock."

Try quickly repeating MacDavock five times and you will see how this happened: the "c" in Mac eventually silences the "D" in Davock, transforming it into a "G," and sometimes also a "C." In fact, the name is sometimes spelled MacCavock.[12] In Ireland the anglicized and corrupted version of *Dabhóǵ*, that is Gavock, became McGavock, while in Scotland it became McGuffock.

Two English spellings that appear related to McGavock are MacGavic or MacGavick. Actually, these are variants of the Scottish surname MacVicar ("of the clan of the vicar"), and are thus not truly related to the McGavock surname or family.[13]

In modern American English, McGavock would be written MacDavid, McDavid, or simply Davidson (though the Scottish Davidsons, early on known as Clan Dhai—after their first chief, David Dubh of Invernahaven—appear to have no true connection with the Scottish McGavocks).[14] Ancient Scottish civil records spell the surname Davidson variously as *Davisoun* and *David Filius*.[15]

In modern Ireland and Scotland one may still find the Davidson surname spelled MacDade or MacDaid,[16] or even MacDevitt and MacDavitt, all which are also variations of MacDaibheid ("son of David").[17] Davis, sometimes used as a synonym for MacDavid or

---

12. Another cognate of Davock or MacDavock is MacCooke. According to some authorities, the Irish families of MacDavock, MacCavock, and MacCooke are not connected to the Carnton McGavocks of Antrim, Ireland, but instead belong to an unrelated Irish branch of the Burkes of Connacht.
13. Dorward, s.v. "MacVicar"; Philip Smith, p. 91.
14. Scarlett, p. 24.
15. Clan Davidson was virtually wiped out at the Battle of Invernahaven in 1370. All that is left to mark the site today are a few stones. Enough descendants remained, however, to carry on the line into modern times. The Clan Davidson Association, formed in 1909, was recently reactivated. Its goal is to find and unite Davidsons in all parts of the world. Way and Squire, s.v. "Davidson," pp. 381-382.
16. Dorward, s.v. "MacDade/MacDaid."
17. MacLysaught, s.v. "Mac Daid."

THE MCGAVOCKS OF CARNTON PLANTATION

MacDavymore, is found in Wales.[18]

Though all of these spellings are somewhat common, none, that we know of, have ever been used by the Southern branch of the early American McGavocks.[19]

❧ FAMILY ORIGINS

The earliest McGavocks came from Scotland, but we know little or nothing about them. Their Scottish origins, however, entitle all McGavock descendants to wear the traditional McGavock family tartan known as the "Davidson Tartan."[20]

The next stage we do know about, for it takes us to Northern Ireland, to the area of County Antrim and the town of Glenarm, and more specifically to the small township of Cairntun or Carntown nearby. This is where the first McGavocks that can be positively identified originated.

Despite their Celticness, there are English McGavocks as well, though no doubt they are descendants of the Gaelic McGavocks. Most of the English relations come, not surprisingly, from Cumberland County, which is in northern England, on the border with Scotland. One thousand years ago Cumberland was, in fact, a part of southwest Scotland, a section, as we will see, of the same region in which the earliest known McGavocks arose.

❧ SURNAME & FAMILY DISTRIBUTION

While large scale Scots-Irish emigration to America began in the early 1700s, McGavock emigration specifically began in the mid-1700s. This wave of hardy, self-reliant, ingenious Scots-Irish pioneers would prove to be among the first to identify themselves as "Americans."[21] By the early 1900s there were McGavocks in all fifty states. However, most were concentrated in the state of the Carnton McGavocks: Tennessee.

---

18. MacLysaught, s.v. "Davis"; "Mac David."
19. The Cornish spelling of David, *Dewy*, is preserved in the English town of Davidstow (original spelling: *Dewystōw*). The name means, "the Holy Place of Saint David."
20. P. D. Smith, pp. 49, 88.
21. Garraty, p. 94.

THE MCGAVOCKS OF CARNTON PLANTATION

The following list shows how the McGavocks are distributed among America's fifty states today. The majority still remain in the South and the Midwest, the two original regions of early McGavock settlement.

1. Tennessee: 18 percent
2. Illinois: 13 percent
3. Kentucky: 12 percent
4. Missouri: 7 percent
5. Virginia: 7 percent
6. Arkansas: 4 percent
7. Indiana: 3 percent
8. Minnesota: 3 percent
9. New Jersey: 3 percent
10. Washington: 3 percent
11. Wisconsin: 3 percent
12. California: 2 percent
13. Colorado: 2 percent
14. Michigan: 2 percent
15. Oklahoma: 2 percent
16. Alabama: 1 percent
17. Alaska: 1 percent
18. Arizona: 1 percent
19. Connecticut: 1 percent
20. Maine: 1 percent
21. Nebraska: 1 percent
22. North Carolina: 1 percent
23. North Dakota: 1 percent
24. Ohio: 1 percent
25. Pennsylvania: 1 percent
26. Texas: 1 percent
27. Delaware: less than 1 percent
28. Florida: less than 1 percent
29. Georgia: less than 1 percent
30. Hawaii: less than 1 percent
31. Idaho: less than 1 percent
32. Iowa: less than 1 percent
33. Kansas: less than 1 percent
34. Louisiana: less than 1 percent
35. Maryland: less than 1 percent
36. Massachusetts: less than 1 percent
37. Mississippi: less than 1 percent
38. Montana: less than 1 percent
39. Nevada: less than 1 percent
40. New Mexico: less than 1 percent
41. New York: less than 1 percent
42. New Hampshire: less than 1 percent
43. Oregon: less than 1 percent
44. Rhode Island: less than 1 percent
45. South Dakota: less than 1 percent
46. South Carolina: less than 1

THE MCGAVOCKS OF CARNTON PLANTATION

      percent
47. Utah: less than 1 percent
48. Vermont: less than 1
      percent
49. West Virginia: less than 1
      percent
50. Wyoming: less than 1
      percent

Early McGavock History

❧ TWO EARLY BRANCHES

THERE WERE TWO MAIN EARLY American branches of the McGavocks: a Northern one and a Southern one. This is not unusual. Many European-American families have similar regional divisions in their history.

It is not currently known where and how these two branches connect, but we can be sure they are ultimately from the same Scottish McGavock ancestor, probably Hugh McGavock of Galloway, Scotland. Both the surname McGavock, and this specific spelling, are rare, and both branches hail from the same time period and from the same Irish county: Antrim. So it is apparent we are dealing with different lines of the same family.

It is my theory that the Southern and Northern branches descend from two of Hugh's sons, James (Southern branch) and a hypothetical Randal (Northern branch). The times, places, and names all match up. But as of yet there is no empirical evidence to prove this proposal.

❧ THE AMERICAN NORTHERN McGAVOCK BRANCH

The American Northern McGavock branch came to America from Ireland in the mid-1800s, settling mainly in the central and northern Midwestern region. This branch used alternate spellings of the name, such as McGuffock, McGaffick, McGavic, McGavick, and MacGavock.

The earliest known ancestor of this branch is Patrick

THE MCGAVOCKS OF CARNTON PLANTATION

MacGavock, born possibly around 1780, in Ireland. His son, Alexander McGavock (b. about 1805, in County Antrim, Ireland), and Alexander's wife Sarah Ann Devlin and their six children, emigrated to America in 1847, settling in Fox Lake, Illinois. From here their descendants spread out into Wisconsin and Minnesota. To this day, a majority of McGavocks from the Northern branch call these three states home.

☙ THE AMERICAN SOUTHERN McGAVOCK BRANCH

The American Southern McGavock branch, also from Ireland, emigrated 100 years earlier, in the mid-1700s, coming through Pennsylvania, then Virginia, finally settling primarily in Tennessee.

As we saw in the previous chapter, the American McGavocks are widely dispersed: there is at least one McGavock family in every state. But there is something even more interesting about the McGavock distribution list.

Though the McGavocks began arriving in America in the mid 1700s, we can still see the original pattern of emigration of the Northern and Southern branches: the two states with the most McGavocks are Tennessee with 18 percent, and Illinois with 13 percent, more than any other states. Despite our modern transient world, most families tend to stay rooted to their place of origin. Thus we can be sure that these figures have changed little over time.

Throughout this book we will be focusing on the Southern branch, since these are the immediate ancestors of the Carnton McGavocks.

☙ EARLY CELTIC ANCESTORS: SCOTSMAN HUGH McGAVOCK

The Carnton McGavocks were one of the wealthiest and most influential families in the American South, with a long and noble history that includes royal European ancestry.

Although he himself is not believed to be of royal blood, the earliest known ancestor from this line is the Scottish Presbyterian, Hugh McGavock, the great-grandfather of Colonel John W. McGavock of Carnton Plantation. Hugh seems to have been born about 1700 in

THE MCGAVOCKS OF CARNTON PLANTATION

Galloway, Scotland, located in the southwestern part of the country on the boundary with Cumberland County, England, England's northwest border. In fact, as mentioned, one thousand years ago, at the time of the *Domesday Book* (written by Norman scribes in the year 1086), much of Cumberland County was part of the Dumfries and Galloway region of Scotland.[22]

Today rainy rugged Galloway, famous for its horse and cattle, is part of Dumfries and Galloway (in Gaelic, *Dùn Phris agus an Gall-Ghaidhealaibh*), a "Council Area," or local authority region, comprising the former counties of Wigtownshire (in the west), Kirkcudbrightshire (in the middle), and Dumfriesshire (in the east). Kirkcudbright and Wigtown together are now referred to as Galloway.

At some point (possibly about 1720), Hugh emigrated to Ireland, settling in the township of Cairntun or Carntown, near Glenarm, County Antrim. Cairntun is in the province of Ulster, now a part of troubled modern day Northern Ireland.

Hugh came to own the township of Cairntun, though it is not known when or by what means. He was also probably the founder of the McGavock estate named after the township, and thus called Carntown, Cairntun, or Cairntown, located in Tickmacrevan Parish. It would be from this Irish township and home that Carntown Plantation in America would derive its name one hundred years later.

❧ THE McGAVOCKS OF GLENARM, IRELAND

Glenarm, which remains primarily an agricultural area, is located on the northeastern coast of Ireland, on Highway A2, just south of the town of Carnlough and just north of Drumnagreagh Port. Geographically, it is one of the closest Irish towns to Scotland, which is just across the North Channel of the Irish Sea, about 200 miles distance.

Hugh must have traveled by boat from Scotland to Ireland on

---

22. The word Galloway probably comes from the name *Gallgaidhill*, a group of mercenary warriors of Norse and Gaelic heritage. This Scottish people got its name for its use of an unusual form of the Gaelic language. Seeming like outsiders, they were called the *Gallgaidhill*, meaning "stranger Gaels," or "foreign Gaels." Scotland, as well as the Scots themselves, derived their name from the ancient Celtic ancestor-goddess known across Europe as Scotia. Seabrook, BK, p. 65.

THE MCGAVOCKS OF CARNTON PLANTATION

this, or a similar, route. So close are the two Celtic nations at this exact point that modern ferry lanes have been opened to carry passengers back and forth from ports near Glenarm.

Home of the world famous natural wonder, the Giant's Causeway, as well as numerous castles of note, Ireland's County Antrim has an interesting ancient history. According to Christian legend, as a Pagan youth, Ireland's patron saint, Saint Patrick (b. 4th Century), was held as a slave in this region for seven years before escaping to England. He is said to have been a livestock herder, working around what is now known as the Hill of Slemish, a dormant volcano only a dozen or so miles from what was to become the McGavocks' estate in Glenarm.

Hugh and his wife Margaret (maiden name unknown) never emigrated to America. Both died at the McGavocks' Cairntun Manor near Glenarm, probably sometime around 1750. Hugh's occupation is unknown, as are the number of children he and Margaret bore. We believe that at least two of his sons were named James and Randal.

❧ JAMES "THE EMIGRANT" McGAVOCK

The former son, James "Dada" McGavock, Colonel John's grandfather, was born in Glenarm in 1728, almost certainly at Cairntun, the Irish township owned by his parents Hugh and Margaret. Finding life increasingly difficult in the mountainous terrain of his 30-acre farm, in 1754 he sailed to America as a young adult, looking for a better life.

James first stepped ashore in America at the port of Philadelphia, Pennsylvania, where he settled for a time. Around 1757 he moved to Augusta (now Rockbridge) County, Virginia, where he purchased a parcel of land for about $75.00, today's equivalent of $2,500. Also that year he served with Colonel Francis Nash (b. 1742)—after whom Nashville, Tennessee, is named—in the fight against Native-Americans in Ohio.

Sometime after 1760 James purchased Fort Chiswell, in Wythe County, Virginia, not far from the city of Wytheville, where he settled and opened up a tavern inn on the busy frontier highway known at the time as "Wilderness Road." The enterprising Irishman subsequently turned the palisaded garrison into a family home. Then, between 1779 and 1780, he built a log cabin called the Mansion House at Max Meadows, a town just a few miles north of the fort.[23] A number of other moves seem to have been made as James sought new land for his commercial enterprises, none of which were to succeed.

That James' constantly changed residences is somewhat surprising since 18th-Century frontiersmen generally settled in one place for most of their lives. A closer study, however, reveals that his many relocations were prompted by numerous and extremely violent "Indian incursions." While fighting off hostile Native-Americans and building log homes, he also tried, but failed, to turn Fort Chiswell into Wythe County's courthouse town. Early chronicles state that he established at least one Virginia settlement "along the upper waters of the New River and on the Holstein . . ."[24]

❧ BLUE BLOODED MARY CLOYD

On February 20, 1760, in Augusta County, Virginia, James married Mary "Sally" Cloyd (1741-1827), no doubt completely unaware that she descended from European royalty. She herself was probably innocent of the fact as well. Nonetheless, of regal descent she was. It was Mary who would bring blue blood into the Southern McGavock branch.[25]

❧ MARY'S ROYAL ANCESTRY

More specifically, it is Mary's mother, and my cousin, Irishwoman Margaret Campbell (c. 1704-1764) of Rockbridge County, Virginia, who connects James' and Mary's descendants to regal DNA.[26] For not only were these early Campbells royals themselves, they also descended from other famed royal Scots, including Robert Stewart II, Robert "the

---

23. Max Meadows takes its name from an early German settler in the area, Wilhelm Mack, who owned a large parcel of meadows there known as "Mack's Meadows." After Mack's death (around 1745), the spelling gradually mutated to Max Meadows.
24. D. E. Johnston, p. 61.
25. I descend from the same Campbell family as Mary's mother Margaret Campbell (making me cousins with all of Mary's descendants, just one of the many ways I connect to the McGavocks. For more on the European and royal relations of the McGavocks, the Winders, and myself, see Appendix C.
26. Margaret, like her daughter's husband, James McGavock, was born in Northern Ireland, in this case in Drumboden, Kilmacrenan, County Donegal, Ulster Province.

THE MCGAVOCKS OF CARNTON PLANTATION

Regent" Stewart III, Robert the Bruce, David I, Malcolm III, Duncan I, and a number of other Scottish kings.[27]

There are also English royals in Mary's family tree, English Kings such as Egbert (England's first), Ethelwulf, Alfred the Great, Edward I, Edmund I, Edgar the Peaceful, Athelred II, and Edmund II.[28]

Mary has a long line of French and Frankish royals in her background as well, dating from her 33rd great-grandfather, Emperor Charlemagne.[29] This line includes truly ancient kings such as Pepin, Clodion, Childeric I, Clovis I "the Great," Clotaire I, Pharamond, Walter, Clodius III, Bartherus, Hilderic, Sunno, Farabert, Clodomir IV, Marcomir IV, Odomir, Richemer, Rathberius, Antenor IV, and Clodomir III, just to name a few. This line is said to go back to the legendary Alexander, King of Troy (born 747 B.C.E.). Mary also descends from a host of royal Norman ancestors, beginning with her 21st great-grandfather, William the Conqueror.[30]

Naturally Mary has royal Irish ancestors, one of the earliest known being the redoubtable Niall of the Nine Hostages, an Irish king who lived in the 4th Century.[31] Other Irish kings in Mary's family tree include, Mortogh O'Brien, Torlogh O'Brien, Dounough O'Brien, Teige O'Brien, Ceinneidigh, and Erchad MacMurchada.

In all, the Cloyd line includes thousands of kings and queens, princes and princesses, dukes and duchesses, barons and baronesses, counts and countesses, earls, lords and ladies, sirs and knights, and even a few saints, all far too numerous to name. These lines definitively date back to such places as ancient Rome and Mary's 31st great-grandfather the great Roman orator and historian, Tacitus,[32] and to his cousin, Emperor Marc Anthony, Mary's 64th great-grandfather.[33] Though Mary descends from Marc's first wife, Octavia Major Tiberius of Rome (born

---

27. J. Burke, "Kings of Scotland," pp. lxxx -lxxxv.
28. J. Burke, "Kings of England," pp. lix -lxxix.
29. Charlemagne is my 37th great-grandfather.
30. William is my 29th great-grandfather.
31. Niall is my 50th great-grandfather.
32. Tacitus is my 50th great-grandfather.
33. Marc Anthony is my 60th great-grandfather.

THE MCGAVOCKS OF CARNTON PLANTATION

64 B.C.E.),[34] students of history will recall that Marc's second wife was the notorious Queen of Egypt, Cleopatra VII (born 60 B.C.E).

We will note here that William the Conqueror, the Stewarts, and the Bruces all descend from the Vikings of Denmark and Sweden, many of them also blue blooded kings. This makes the descendants of James McGavock and Mary Cloyd the offspring of royal Scottish, royal Irish, royal Norman, royal French, and royal Scandinavian heritage.[35]

❧ NATIVE-AMERICANS KILL McGAVOCKS

An experienced mountain girl from Virginia, Mary Cloyd knew all too well the dangers of frontier life before she married James McGavock. But it was at age twenty-four, shortly after they became a couple, that she experienced one of the most horrific events in her life, one she could not possibly have been prepared for.

In March 1764 the wife of her brother Joseph Cloyd (b. about 1728), their child John (b. about 1750), along with Mary's mother, Margaret (Campbell) Cloyd, were all savagely murdered by Shawnee Indians about five miles west of the town of Fincastle, Virginia.

Unfortunately in the early history of America, as Europeans and Natives[36] came into contact for the first time, such incidents were all too common. (McGavock relative, Felix Grundy, himself had watched as Indians killed and scalped members of his own family.)[37] Forty-nine years later, in 1813, Virginian, Founding Father, and future U.S. president, Thomas Jefferson (1743-1826), was still discussing "the cruel massacres that the aboriginal inhabitants in our vicinities have committed

---

34. Octavia is my 60th great-grandmother.
35. In all actuality, Mary Cloyd and her McGavock descendants derive from and are related to the royal families of virtually every European nation dating back to earliest European history.
36. The term "Native-American" (indicating early Americans of Asian descent) is used throughout this book as a mere custom since scientists have recently discovered early American artifacts that appear to have been made by Europeans. It is not known yet whether these truly ancient Caucasians came to North America by boat or land bridge. What is known is that the presence of whites in the Americas thousands of years before the Vikings (in the year 1000 CE) and Columbus (in 1492) throws open the title of "First Americans" and puts into question just who the real Native-Americans are. For more on this topic see the National Geographic Website: http://ngm.nationalgeographic.com/ngm/0012/feature3/index.html.
37. Coit, p. 69.

THE MCGAVOCKS OF CARNTON PLANTATION

on the women and children of our frontiers taken by surprise . . ."[38]

✒ MILITARY MAN & REVOLUTIONARY

James McGavock and Mary Cloyd had ten children, one named Randal, who is of special interest to us, for it was he who would inaugurate the Tennessee McGavocks. James was a captain in the Seven Years War, also known as the French and Indian War (1754-1760).

The Scottish-Irish-American mountain man was also one of the "Freemen of Fincastle County (Virginia)" who, on January 20, 1775, signed the first state declaration of independence (from Britain) in America. Threatening to rebel against the crown unless their demands were met, the Freemen ended the letter to their British overlords with this ominous postscript: "These are real though unpolished sentiments of liberty, and in them we are resolved to live or die."[39]

Just four months later, on April 19, 1775, America's first War of Secession, the Revolutionary War, would launch with the Battles of Lexington and Concord (Massachusetts). James, a true Jeffersonian lover of liberty and self-government, fought with the American colonies, America's first European-American Confederacy, against British tyranny, just as his descendants, such as Lieutenant Colonel Randal William McGavock, would fight eighty-six years later against Yankee tyranny.[40]

James, Irish immigrant, frontiersman, adventurer, Revolutionary War hero, Indian fighter, entrepreneur, businessman, military man, settler, and traditional Southerner, died March 22, 1812, in his log Mansion House at Max Meadows, and was buried at the McGavock Cemetery in Chiswell, Wythe County, Virginia.[41]

---

38. Foley, p. 422.
39. D. E. Johnston, p. 56.
40. The term "European-American Confederacy" is used because there was a confederacy in America prior to the arrival of the first Europeans. We are speaking here, of course, of Native-Americans, whose nations were organized into our continent's first confederacy. The second Confederacy was the original U.S.A., formed in 1776 and fully functioning by 1781, while America's third Confederacy was the C.S.A., formed in 1861. For the purposes of simplicity and focus, however, throughout this book we will concentrate only on the latter two, the two European-American Confederacies.
41. Due to his service in the American Revolutionary War, all female descendants of James McGavock are entitled to become members of the Daughters of the American Revolution (DAR), while all male descendants are qualified for membership in the Sons of the American Revolution (SAR). For more information on these

The McGavocks of Carnton Plantation

ᘓ JAMES McGAVOCK'S DISAPPEARING HOUSE
If you travel to Max Meadows today you will not find James' original home, the Mansion House, or McGavock House, as it was also known. This is because it is no longer in Virginia, or even in the U.S. It is now in Ireland.

ᘓ JAMES' LOG HOME TO EDUCATE EUROPEANS
In 1989 James' log house was traded for a trailer by the non-McGavock owners, who had purchased it earlier from McGavock descendants. This important piece of American heritage was then swapped with the Ulster American Folk Park, located near the city of Omagh in County Tyrone, Northern Ireland.

    This one-of-a-kind open air museum, which like America's Colonial Williamsburg, uses costumed demonstrators, is about seventy miles southwest of the original Irish McGavock estate, Cairntown, in Glenarm. The park's goal is to promote the many contributions of Northern Ireland's American emigrants, one of whom is James McGavock. And herein lies the clue as to why James' American house has been relocated near to where he was born in 1728, some 5,000 miles away from Max Meadows.

    In 1989 a team of historical experts from the Ulster American Folk Park traveled from Ireland to Virginia where they dismantled his house log by log, and took the entire structure back to Omagh. It was kept in storage until 2008, when it was unpacked, reconstructed, and put on public display. James' restored log home is now part of the park's living history experience, providing a valuable learning tool for Europeans interested not only in early Irish-American architecture, but also in how the people of Northern Ireland helped shape 18th-Century Appalachia in the U.S.[42]

---

two organizations, visit their Websites. The DAR: www.DAR.org. The SAR: www.SAR.org.
42. For more information on the Ulster American Folk Park in Omagh, Ireland, visit their Website at: www.folkpark.com.

Randal & Sarah

⌘ THE CROCKETTS, POLKS, & FRANKLINS

WHEN THEY CAME OF AGE, James' and Mary's children, all born in Virginia, began intermarrying into numerous American families of note, including the families of Davy Crockett (1786-1836) of Green County, Tennessee, President James Knox Polk (1795-1849) of Sugar Creek, North Carolina, and Benjamin Franklin (1706-1790) of Boston, Massachusetts.

Alberta Pugsley McGavock (1841-1878), for example, the daughter of Dr. David Turner McGavock (1813-1866) and Caroline Elizabeth Pugsley (1815-1863)—all of Nashville, married Dr. Dallas Bache (1838-1902), a great-grandson of Benjamin Franklin.

Dr. Bache's famous brother, Alexander Dallas Bache (1806-1867), also a great-grandson of Franklin, attended West Point, where after graduation he acted as assistant professor, then served as a lieutenant in the U.S. Army Corps of Engineers. Later he became a professor of philosophy and natural history at the University of Pennsylvania, then spent several years in Europe studying their educational system. In 1843 he was named superintendent of the U.S. Coastal Survey, a post under which he helped complete a survey of the American coast. He passed away in Newport, Rhode Island, in 1867, two years after the end of Lincoln's War.

Both Dr. Dallas Bache and Alexander Dallas Bache are the sons of Richard Bache, Jr. (1784-1848) and Sophia Burrell Dalles (1784-1860), of Philadelphia. Richard, Jr. is the son of Richard Bache, Sr. (1737-1811), of Settle, Yorkshire County, England, and Sarah "Sally" Franklin (1743-1808), Benjamin Franklin's only daughter.

THE McGAVOCKS OF CARNTON PLANTATION

Little could James McGavock, Sr. and Mary Cloyd have known that some of their descendants would later live in a small Tennessee town named after Dr. Bache's great-grandfather, and that thousands of visitors a year would travel from around the globe just to visit their celebrated home, Carnton Plantation.

❧ THE McGAVOCKS & THE McDOWELLS

The Virginia McGavocks also married into one of my ancestral lines, the McDowells, a family of royal descent who lived in Rockbridge and Wythe Counties, Virginia.

James McGavock's son David (1763-1838), for instance, married Elizabeth McDowell (1761-1805), the 4th great-granddaughter of Scotsman Uchtred McDowell (b. 1546), my 12th great-grandfather.[43] It is through Uchtred's wife, Euphemia Dunbar (b. 1555 in Scotland), my 12th great-grandmother, that the McDowells descend from royalty, including from such kingly families as the Bruces and the Stewarts.[44]

❧ ELIZABETH McDOWELL'S ROYAL ANCESTRY

Since, like Mary Cloyd, Elizabeth also brought blue blood into the McGavock family, let us look at a few of her more notable royal ancestors.

One of the most interesting of these is Edward I "Longshanks" King of England, Elizabeth's 18th great-grandfather, considered by many to be England's greatest Medieval ruler.[45] Other European kings from Elizabeth McDowell's line include Edward II, Edward III, Henry Plantagenet II, Henry Plantagenet III, John "Lackland" I, Stewart I, James Stewart II, James Stewart III, James "Iron Belt" Stewart IV, Christian Oldenberg I, Ferdinand II, Alfonzo IX, and Fernando III.

---

43. Elizabeth's brother James McDowell (1770-1835) is the father of Elizabeth Preston McDowell (1794-1854), the wife of noted U.S. senator and onetime Franklin resident, Thomas Hart Benton (1782-1858). Benton's daughter, Southern belle Jessie Ann Benton (1824-1902), married Union General John C. Frémont (1813-1890), who was relieved of his command by President Lincoln for emancipating slaves in Missouri.
44. Magdalene McDowell (b. about 1606) of Rockbridge, Virginia, the half great-grandaunt of Elizabeth McDowell (b. 1761)—also of Rockbridge, Virginia—wife of David McGavock the surveyor (1763-1838), brother of Randal McGavock founder of Carnton Plantation, is my 10th great-grandmother.
45. Edward I is my 21st great-grandfather.

THE MCGAVOCKS OF CARNTON PLANTATION

Since royal families intermarry, often with those from neighboring countries, the McDowells, and through them some of the McGavocks, can count ancestry in nearly every royal European house. The result of this is that Elizabeth McDowell and Mary Cloyd were cousins, as were Colonel John and his wife Carrie Winder, another descendant of European royalty.

One of the most intriguing ancestors of the McDowells, the Cloyds, and the McGavocks, is the French King Merovée "the Young" (b. c. 415), the man after whom the celebrated long-haired Merovingian line of rulers was named. Colonel John W. McGavock's 46th great-grandfather, Merovée, (or Merovech, as he is also known) has been made even more famous in modern times by such books as *Holy Blood, Holy Grail*; *The Templar Revelation*; and *The Da Vinci Code*.[46]

A few other well-known cousins of the Carnton McGavocks are Queen Elizabeth II, Prince Charles, the late Princess Diana, their two sons, Princes William and Harry, Prince Andrew, Duchess Sarah Ferguson, Prime Minister Sir Winston Churchill, actor Patrick Macnee (*The Avengers*), actress Helena Bonham Carter, actor René Auberjonois ("Odo" on *Star Trek: Deep Space Nine*), actor Thomas Cruise Mapother, IV ("Tom Cruise"), President George Washington, and Prince of Walachia Vlad III (also known as "Count Dracula").[47]

ॐ RANDAL McGAVOCK

Another one of James and Mary's sons, the one we are most interested in, was Randal McGavock, born in Rockbridge County, Virginia, June 20, 1766. In his mid to late twenties Randal attended school at Dickinson College in Carlisle, Pennsylvania, where he studied law and was a member of a debate team that included future chief justice of the Supreme Court, Roger Brooke Taney (1777-1864).[48] Randal graduated in 1794 and returned to his family's home in Virginia.

---

46. Merovée is my 48th great-grandfather.
47. From my personal family tree.
48. Taney would become famous for writing the majority opinion in the Dred Scott case of 1856, which stated that black servants were property and not citizens. He would also become known, as we will see, for a run-in with Abraham Lincoln, who illegally tried to have Chief Justice Taney arrested and imprisoned.

43

THE MCGAVOCKS OF CARNTON PLANTATION

Earlier, in 1786, James urged Randal's elder brother David (future husband of Elizabeth McDowell above), to head west. It was this parental exhortation that would give birth to the McGavocks of Carnton Plantation, for in compliance with his father's instructions David traveled to what was then called Fort Nashborough, a rough-and-tumble frontier town on the Cumberland River in an area that was still part of North Carolina. The town that would become Nashville was then little more than a group of crude log cabins hastily built on the Cumberland bluffs. David spent his summers here raising crops, returning to Wytheville each Winter.

Ten years later, in the Summer of 1796, Randal journeyed to Nashville to join his elder brother and help establish the McGavock family in the area. "In the name of their father," the two purchased over 2,000 acres of the best land they could find. Randal fell in love with the region and decided to settle here permanently. Under America's first president, George Washington, Tennessee achieved statehood that same year. Randal and David were now Tennesseans.

James' friend, Andrew Jackson (1767-1845), began encouraging him to invest additional money in the new state, which needed financing for the development of roads, towns, and railroads. With James' two sons now residents of Nashville, he was happy to oblige.

To this end James sent his sons southward toward Williamson County and the small Tennessee town of Franklin—founded in 1799 when the county was formed from Davidson County.[49] Here James asked his boys to look into purchasing additional property, particularly useful farmland. While they were in the area he also asked Randal and David to inspect a 640-acre land grant that had been given to him by the state of North Carolina for his services in the Revolutionary War.

Randal, whose background was in law and politics, and David, who was a shrewd land speculator, expert surveyor, and talented cartographer, made an excellent team. Elected to the Tennessee legislature in 1806, David gained further experience when he drew up

---

49. Hale and Merritt, Vol. 3, p. 837.

THE MCGAVOCKS OF CARNTON PLANTATION

the boundaries for Davidson County and then became the registrar of the Land Office, an occupation he held until his death. His main job as registrar was to distribute land grants throughout Middle Tennessee. David's grandson, David Harding McGavock (1826-1896), would go on to build the beautiful Two Rivers Mansion in Nashville, not far from Andrew Jackson's home, the Hermitage.

Family tradition states that Randal was able to acquire every bit of land inside a bend in the Harpeth River located three miles to the south of Franklin, from an Indian by swapping a shotgun and a pony.[50] There are no records of this transaction.

What we do know is that innate good sense combined with fine mapmaking skills and real estate acumen allowed Randal and David to buy up more prime acreage surrounding their father's Franklin land grant, swelling the property to 1,420 acres. This parcel, situated on the broad flat Plain of Franklin, was one of the choicest properties in Williamson County. It was soon to become the site of Carnton Plantation.

❧ SARAH DOUGHERTY RODGERS

Randal's wife, twenty years his junior, was Sarah Dougherty Rodgers, born April 1, 1786, in Wythe County, Virginia—ten years before the thirty year old McGavock realtor arrived in Nashville. The couple married on February 28, 1811, in what would later become known as the world's country music capital: Music City. Randal and Sarah are the parents of Colonel John W. McGavock of Carnton Plantation.

Sarah's sister, Ann Phillips Rodgers (1787-1847), married Felix Grundy (1777-1840), a leading Tennessee senator and a cabinet member under America's eighth president, Martin Van Buren (1782-1862). Both Sarah and Ann were the daughters of American Revolutionary War soldier John Rodgers (b. 1747). As is the Southern custom of naming children after their grandparents, Colonel John was probably named after John, his grandfather.

---

50. V. M. Bowman, p. 63.

THE MCGAVOCKS OF CARNTON PLANTATION

❦ EARLY TENNESSEE

In 1796, less than two decades after the Revolutionary War, there were still few Europeans in Williamson County, or, in fact, anywhere west of Tennessee. The Lewis and Clark Expedition (1804-1806), whose goal was to find the Western source of the Missouri River, was still eight years in the future, and little was known of the lands west of the Mississippi River, which runs along what is now Tennessee's western border.

To get an idea of how primitive and unmapped America was at the time, the 3,472 square-mile area we today call Yellowstone National Park, which extends over vast sections of Wyoming, Idaho, and Montana, would not be discovered (by European-Americans) until 1870, seventy-four years after Randal and David McGavock settled in Nashville.

Tennessee itself formed the Western border of the U.S. well into the late 1700s. This made Western and Middle Tennessee, a region with few white pioneer families, a part of the "Old Wild West." This is why, before Tennessee became the sixteenth state on June 1, 1796, it was called simply, along with the rest of the as yet unformed Western states, the "Western Territory," and it is why Tennesseans were referred to as "Westerners" at the time.

Even after 1800, Native-Americans, like the Chickasaw, Shawnee, and Cherokee, still dominated much of Tennessee. Their love for this area was so great that they would all go on to fight loyally for the Confederacy in 1861.[51] In fact, the state owes its name to the latter: Tennessee was named by Andrew Jackson[52] after the Cherokee capital Tanase or Tanasi, a cluster of Cherokee villages once located on the Tanase River (now the Little Tennessee River), near the present-day city of Vonore, Monroe County, Tennessee.[53]

---

51. The last Confederate officer to capitulate to the Yanks was a Georgia Cherokee chief named Degataga, better known as Stand Watie (1806-1871), who served as brigadier general of the Cherokee Mounted Rifles. Watie bravely refused to give up his weapons and forces until June 23, 1865, two months after Lee's official surrender at Appomattox, April 9, 1865.
52. Garrett and Goodpasture, p. 16.
53. Vonore, located near the Smoky Mountains, is about 200 miles southeast of Franklin, Tennessee.

THE MCGAVOCKS OF CARNTON PLANTATION

It was the very presence of the "large aboriginal population" that occupied the area that kept European-Americans from settling sooner in what was to become Franklin, Tennessee.[54] One of the earliest white settlers was David McEwin (or McEwen), who, in 1798, located his family in the area known as Roper's Knob, a 994-foot mountain that served as a signal station for Union troops during Lincoln's War.[55]

Between 1797 and 1810 numerous other white pioneers settled in Williamson County as well, such as Ewen Cameron, who is said to have built Franklin's first house in 1797. Other early county settlers were: Samuel Crockett, III (1772-1827), John Aulson, Andrew Goff, George Neely, Thomas H. Perkins, Mathew Johnson, William Edmondson, Thomas McKay, Solomon Brent, William Hulmey, Zion Hunt, Robert Caruthers, R. P. Currin, John Harness, Timothy Demonbruen, Thomas Hart Benton, Edmund Wall, Byrd Bramlett, Nicholas Perkins Stephen Childress, Abram Poindexter Maury (Franklin's founder), and of course, the McGavocks.

As late as 1835 the town of Franklin had a population of only 1,500 people, and included a mere "four churches, three male and two female academics, eight physicians and seven lawyers."[56]

Despite the relative primitiveness of the region at the time, the visionary McGavocks had chosen their new western land wisely. The backwater village of Franklin happened to be located in the heart of the Middle Tennessee Basin, an extravagantly fertile agricultural area that would one day transform itself into the pride and wealth of the South.

---

54. Archaeological evidence of Franklin's original inhabitants is extensive, for long before the founding of the town by European-Americans the region was the home of a wide number of First Nation peoples. Archaeologists are still uncovering the remains of large fortified Native-American cities, settlements, pyramidal mounds, earth works, stone graves, foot trails, and burial mounds in and around Franklin, particularly along the Harpeth River. Thruston, pp. 35-41.
55. Yankee signals from atop Roper's Knob could be seen for at least six miles in every direction.
56. Hale and Merritt, Vol. 3, pp. 837-839.

John & Carrie

❧ THE BIRTHS OF JOHN & ELIZABETH McGAVOCK

ON APRIL 2, 1815, RANDAL'S and Sarah's third son was born in Nashville. His name was John W. McGavock.[57] In a few short decades he would become a famous Confederate colonel and the owner of Carnton Plantation during Lincoln's illegal war against states' rights.

It was probably in the following few years 1816, 1817, or 1818, that Randal began construction of Carnton Plantation, an enormous project that would take between eight and ten years to complete. For help with the design Randal hired a Virginia architect surnamed Swope, who drew up the plans and helped guide the McGavock workers and servants in building the home.[58] Swope integrated several different architectural styles into what would eventually come to be viewed as one of the most graceful and attractive homes in Tennessee.[59]

Just a few years later, on May 17, 1819, Randal and Sarah's second daughter came into the world. Named Elizabeth Irwin McGavock, she would grow up to marry my close cousin General William Giles Harding (1808-1886), the man who owned beautiful Belle Meade Plantation in Nashville, then considered one of the finest horse

---

[57]. John's middle name was probably William, or perhaps Williamson, the middle names given to some of his McGavock cousins, men who also bore the first name John.
[58]. Wilkerson, p. 253.
[59]. V. M. Bowman, p. 62.

breeding farms in America.[60] The union of this couple, who were married in the guest parlor at Carnton Mansion, created an inextricable link between the two families, and it is the reason Belle Meade is today considered the sister plantation to Carnton.

❧ HINCHEYVILE CONNECTIONS

Early that same year, 1819, Randal and his relation Felix Grundy—along with James Irwin, James Trimble, and Alfred Balch—helped develop Franklin's first subdivision, Hincheyville. Named for Virginian, Hinchea Petway (b. 1785), a wealthy Franklin business owner whose house once stood on Main Street, the Hincheyville District was comprised of ninety acres that ran from Bridge Street to 11th Avenue near what is today Old Franklin center. The fifty-nine lots also enclosed areas of Main and Fair Streets and is now listed on the National Register of Historic Places.[61]

Petway's wife, Susanna Caroline Parrish (1789-1858), is the daughter of Susan Maury (1764-1819), of the noted Maury family who gave their name to Maury County, Tennessee. Susan's brother is Abram Poindexter Maury (1766-1825), a Virginia frontiersman and surveyor who moved west to Tennessee, bought land (an area then known as Poplar Grove) in Williamson County, donated a parcel of it to the state, then designed and laid out the town of Franklin on the site. Abram, the founder of Franklin,[62] who would later become a well-known Tennessee politician, is buried in Franklin at the Maury Family Cemetery.[63]

Abram's son, my cousin Abraham Poindexter Maury (1801-1848), married into a royal European line through his wife Mary Eliza Terrell Claiborne (1806-1852), of Nashville. Mary descends from my

---

60. I am 5th cousins with General Harding through a mutual pair of ancestors: my 10th great-grandparents, Thomas Harding (1639-1674) and his wife Anne Mosley (b. 1648), are the general's 5th great-grandparents. My 6th great-grandmother is Nancy Margaret Harding, born 1743 in Shenandoah, Warren County, Virginia, died 1819 in Vico, Perry County, Kentucky. Nancy's husband, my 6th great-grandfather, is John Combs, Sr. (1735-1819).
61. Petway's historically important brick house was eventually, and unthinkingly, torn down.
62. I am related to Abram through marriage, via his wife Martha Branch Worsham (1775-1844), my 4th cousin.
63. The Maury Family Cemetery is located in a modern subdivision called Founders Pointe, named for the Franklin founder. In 1799 this area, in west Franklin, was known as Poplar Grove on account of the large forest of poplar trees once located there.

THE MCGAVOCKS OF CARNTON PLANTATION

21st great-grandfather, Edward I, "Longshanks," the 31st King of England. King Edward is Mary's 18th great-grandfather, making her not only a relative of mine, but also of the Carnton McGavocks.[64]

Another one of Mary's ancestors, her 4th great-grandfather, William Terrell (1629-1729) of Reading, Berkshire County, England, had a descendant named Sarah Rush (1778-1858), whose son, my 4th cousin Major Nathaniel Francis Cheairs (1818-1914), built Rippavilla Plantation in Spring Hill, Tennessee. Confederate patriot Major Cheairs would later become notable for serving under another one of my cousins, General Nathan Bedford Forrest (1821-1877), at the Battle of Thompson's Station (March 5, 1863), and for surrendering to Union war criminal Ulysses S. Grant at the tragic Battle of Fort Donelson (on February 16, 1862).

Another famous son of Abram P. Maury is my cousin Matthew Fontaine Maury (1796-1808), "the Pathfinder of the Sea."[65] A prodigious and ingenious inventor, also known as the "Father of Mine Warfare," he served as an officer in both the U.S. Navy (before Lincoln's War) and the C.S. Navy (after the secession of the Southern states), in which he commanded the Confederate Torpedo Bureau in Richmond.[66] He lived just west of what is now Mount Hope Cemetery in Franklin.

❧ MAYORSHIP & RETIREMENT

Two years after the founding of the Franklin subdivision Hincheyville in 1819, two of John W. McGavock's siblings perished just months apart: an unnamed younger sister who was born and died in April 1821, and one of John's older brothers, William McGavock (b. July 23, 1813), who passed away at age seven on June 10, 1821.

In 1824 Randal became the eleventh (and first officially elected) mayor of Nashville, serving for one term, from 1824 to 1825. While in office he became familiar with a number of powerful people, including

---

64. Along with future U.S. president James Knox Polk, Franklin resident Abraham was a Tennessee representative in the Twenty-fourth and Twenty-fifth Congresses. Heiskell, Vol. 1, p. 307.
65. As noted, I am related to Matthew and his brother Abraham through the Worshams, the maternal side of their family.
66. Pritchard, p. 119.

THE McGAVOCKS OF CARNTON PLANTATION

his father's friend Andrew Jackson, soon to become America's seventh president (in 1829). Randal also became friends with Felix Grundy, James Knox Polk, the future eleventh president (in 1845), and Sam Houston (1793-1863), the future first governor of Texas and a relative of Mary Ann Montgomery (1826-1893), the wife of General Nathan Bedford Forrest.

In 1826, after his term ended, Randal moved his family from Nashville to the more tranquil life at Carnton in Franklin. The beautiful, sprawling plantation was completed that year and made a wonderful and restful place for the sixty year old to spend his golden years. He would devote much of his remaining time to turning Carnton into one of the finest thoroughbred horse farms in the South.

❧ REVOLUTIONARY WAR HEROS IN FRANKLIN

Randal McGavock was not the first man with connections to the first American Revolutionary War to move to Franklin, "Tennessee's most handsomest town." Years before, my cousin Guilford Dudley, Sr. (1756-1833) and his wife Anna Bland Eaton (1763-1847), both from Virginia, had made the move to Franklin from Halifax County, North Carolina, where they were living at the time.

Dudley was a colonel in the Revolutionary War and fought at the battles of Camden and Hobkirk Hill. He applied for his war pension in Franklin on October 12, 1832, and died there just five months later. Dudley—along with three other Revolutionary War veterans, Moses Priest, David Squier, and Miles Priest—is buried beside his wife Anna in Franklin's earliest European burial ground, the old City Cemetery, site of the churchyard of the McGavock's place of worship, what was then called the First Presbyterian Church.[67]

---

67. Today, relocated at the corner of 5th Ave. North and Main St., the church is called Historic Franklin Presbyterian Church. Note: There is also a McGavock buried in Franklin's City Cemetery: Eliza McDowell McGavock (1801-1876), wife of Dr. Andrew B. Ewing (1796-881). The couple rest together in the now decaying and forlorn burial ground. Eliza, a descendant of European royalty and a cousin of the author through mutual Virginia and English ancestors, is the daughter of Hugh McGavock (1761-1844) and Nancy Kent (1763-1835).

51

The McGavocks of Carnton Plantation

❧ JOHN'S PERSONALITY & CHARACTER

Randal's son John deeply admired men like Colonel Guilford Dudley for their willingness to fight against England's despotic King George III. John himself would one day enthusiastically rally against America's despotic "King Abraham" in the nation's second Revolutionary War.

What was John like? He was shy, dignified, disliked public life, and had a pleasing manner and disposition. People often said that he reminded them of "a gentleman of the olden time," which the conservative, gentle, and kindly Southerner would certainly have taken as a compliment. John's father-in-law, Colonel Van Perkins Winder (1809-1854), born in Somerset County, Maryland, once referred to the soft-spoken Franklinite as "a well educated and refined gentleman of amiable and affectionate disposition and feelings."

John, his fellow Tennesseans noted, was an "old school Southerner . . . manly and chivalrous," who possessed "courtly manners and [the] stately bearing of olden times." A "most charming and loveable character," he was a "good and noble man" who was "courteous and kind to every one with whom he came in contact." In fact, he was known to address his black servants the same way he would address the president of the United States.

John was an individual, it was said, "whose neighbors and all who knew him admired, respected and loved. In manner, mind and face he was a true Southern gentleman. Dignified of mein, full of information, warm in his friendships, lovely in his hospitality; he was a type of the old school the South will always be proud to call its own."[68]

❧ JOHN AS CIVILIAN AIDE TO GOVERNOR POLK

No doubt through earlier connections his father Randal had established with the Polk family, sometime between 1839 and 1841 John became an aide-de-camp (a military assistant to a superior) to then Tennessee Governor James Knox Polk. Some say that at this time John was made a colonel, though this is debated.[69]

---

68. From one of Col. John W. McGavock's many obituaries.
69. Others maintain that he was not made a colonel until the start of Lincoln's War in 1861.

The McGavocks of Carnton Plantation

About this time, on December 19, 1840, John's wife's grandfather, Felix Grundy, passed away in Nashville, and was buried not far from the McGavock Family Vault in Mount Olivet Cemetery. The famed Virginian had been a successful attorney, served in the U.S. House of Representatives and the Tennessee House of Representatives, assisted in establishing the Tennessee-Kentucky state line in 1820, was appointed attorney general by President Van Buren, and lived out his final days as a U.S. senator.[70]

❧ THE PASSING OF CARNTON'S FOUNDER

Three years later, on September 27, 1843, Randal, the Virginia-born farmer who conceived of and built Carnton Plantation, passed away peacefully at the Mansion he had so lovingly envisioned nearly three decades earlier. He was laid to rest in the McGavock Family Cemetery (now located at the eastern head of the McGavock Confederate Cemetery),[71] just yards from the rear of Carnton Mansion. His funeral card reads:

> The friends and acquaintances of Mr. Randal McGavock are respectfully invited to attend his funeral at his late residence, tomorrow, Friday morning, at half past ten o'clock. Sermon by the Rev. Mr. [. . .]. Thursday, Sept. 28, 1843.[72]

❧ MODERNIZING CARNTON

That same year, in 1843, as children are often inclined to do, John set about updating his late father's estate. He probably considered the house somewhat old-fashioned, as it was over a generation old by then.

His ultimate plan was to transform the mansion from a Federal style to a Greek Revival style, the one most popular in Middle Tennessee at the time. Also incorporating Georgian features, he started modestly, repainting the woodwork in new, brighter colors, hanging florid French

---

70. Sobel, s.v. "Grundy, Felix."
71. Having been established after Lincoln's War, the McGavock Confederate Cemetery did not exist at the time of Randal's death.
72. Funeral card courtesy of the Williamson County Public Library.

wallpaper, and installing imposing double doors in the front entranceway.

❧ POLK & THE MEXICAN-AMERICAN WAR

On April 28, 1845, John's first cousin once removed, Anne Eliza McGavock (1820-1868), married Judge Henry Dickinson, I (1806-1872). Their son, Jacob McGavock Dickinson, Sr. (1851-1928), born in Mississippi, went on to become U.S. assistant attorney general under President Stephen Grover Cleveland (1837-1908),[73] and secretary of war under President William Howard Taft (1857-1930).[74]

Two months later, on June 8, 1845, former President Andrew Jackson, close friend of Carnton's founder, Randal McGavock, died at his country estate, the Hermitage, where he was interred in Hermitage Gardens. It was under "Old Hickory" that Thomas Jefferson's "classless pastoral republic" became a "class-ridden industrial democracy," initiating the transformation of America from an agricultural nation into an industrial one.

With Jackson's death Old America too was now dead. The frontier era had come to end, the Wild West largely subdued. Jackson had presided over the birth of a new country, modern America, opening the door for the materialistic, industry-based presidency of big government, big spending liberal, Abraham Lincoln (1809-1865), soon to become the agrarian South's arch nemesis.[75]

The year 1845 marked another milestone in American history: John's former boss Governor Polk became America's eleventh president. It was during Polk's administration that the idea of "Manifest Destiny"—perfectly embodied in the figure of Jackson[76]—helped push two powerful nations into war, a war that would have serious consequences for the McGavocks and every other Southern family.

Against the wishes of such Southern leaders as John Caldwell

---

73. Cleveland is the only U.S. president to have been elected to two non-consecutive terms: 1885-1889 and 1893-1897.
74. Sobel, s.v. "Dickinson, Jacob McGavock."
75. Coit, pp. 406-407.
76. J. W. Ward, pp. 133-135, 143-144, 148-149.

The McGavocks of Carnton Plantation

Calhoun (1782-1850), this conflict, the Mexican-American War, was fought from 1846 to 1848, taking the lives of as many as 14,000 American men. The U.S. was victorious, however, adding vast new lands to the nation that would later become the states of California, Nevada, Utah, Arizona, and New Mexico. Texas, also once part of Mexico, had seceded earlier, in 1836, during the Texas Revolution. Since the McGavocks have connections with this conflict, let us review it briefly.

The Texans' bloody battle for independence included the Battle of the Alamo, fought from February 23 to March 6, 1836, at the famous Spanish mission-fort located in what is now the city of San Antonio. Here, 4,000 Mexicans, under General Antonio López de Santa Anna (1794-1876), killed all 200 of the American defenders, including McGavock relation, frontiersman Davy Crockett.

Nonetheless, Mexico lost its fight with the Texas revolutionaries a month later at the Battle of San Jacinto (April 21, 1836), where Santa Anna was captured by General Sam Houston, friend of Randal McGavock. Texas was now an independent republic, with Houston as its first and only president. Nine years later, on December 29, 1845, Texas achieved statehood, becoming America's twenty-eighth state.[77]

While increasing America's size, power, status, and natural resources, her acquirement of these new Western territories also threw fuel on an already simmering fire between the South and the North over the issue of states' rights (which Northern and New South historians inaccurately portray as the issue of slavery). President Polk could not have guessed that his efforts to expand the U.S. would help lead the country into a far bloodier conflict within thirteen years, one that would pit brother against brother, father against son, sister against sister, mother against daughter.

The enormous stress and work load required of Polk during his time as chief executive took its toll on his health. Within a few months after he left office on June 15, 1849, the McGavocks' good friend passed

---

77. Houston, who dressed as a Native-American, went on to become the governor of Texas from 1859 to 1861, but was removed from office when he refused to side with the Confederacy.

THE MCGAVOCKS OF CARNTON PLANTATION

away in Nashville. He was buried on the grounds of Nashville's State Capitol, where he was joined forty-eight years later by his wife Sarah Childress (b. September 4, 1803), who died on August 14, 1891. Said to be intensely haunted, the couple's beautiful burial site remains one of Music City's leading tourist attractions.

❧ MORE REMODELING & A DEATH
While the Mexican-American War was raging John had more domestic thoughts on his mind. In 1847, while continuing his modernization of Carnton Mansion, he added a small Greek Revival porch to the front, entirely altering the appearance of the facade.

On July 6, 1848, sad news arrived at the plantation: a daughter of John's younger sister, Elizabeth Irwin McGavock, had died that day. John's niece, Sarah Susan Harding (b. October 15, 1847), was less than a year old.

❧ THE MARRIAGE OF JOHN & CARRIE
Six months later to the day, John was in Louisiana. Here a momentous event occurred, one that would change Franklin history forever. According to the December 23, 1848, issue of *The Christian Record*, on December 6 of that year Reverend McNari performed a wedding between thirty-three year old John W. McGavock and nineteen year old Caroline Elizabeth Winder, the daughter of a wealthy English-American family from Louisiana.

❧ THE CONFEDERATE WINDERS
The Winders, whose earliest ancestor is to be traced to Lorton, Cumberland County, England,[78] are descendants of European royalty who were already well established in Tennessee, and had already married into the Polk and Grundy families, by the time Carrie and John wed. Just as the Winders had provided superlative soldiers, such as Lieutenant Colonel Levin Winder (1757-1819), in the First Revolutionary War

---

78. From my personal family tree. As we will see, there were also Winders in Lincolnshire and Devonshire Counties, England, as early as the 13th Century, and quite probably much earlier.

THE MCGAVOCKS OF CARNTON PLANTATION

against Britain,[79] they also supplied a number of stalwart, intelligent, and courageous men in the fight against Lincoln and the North during the Second Revolutionary War: the War for Southern Independence (1861-1865), still wrongly referred to as the "Civil War" by the uninformed.

Among them was Carrie's brother, Felix Grundy Winder (1839-1863), who was killed while fighting bravely at the Battle of Vicksburg, Mississippi, which took place between May 18 and July 4, 1863.

There was also Carrie's 2nd cousin once removed, Brigadier General John Henry Winder (1800-1865)[80]—who is mentioned in the famous journal of my cousin, South Carolina belle Mary Chesnut (1823-1886),[81] and Carrie's 2nd cousin once removed, Brigadier General Charles Sidney Winder (1829-1862),[82] whose death at the Battle of Cedar Mountain, Virginia (on August 9),[83] was personally lamented by both General Robert Edward Lee (1807-1870) and General Thomas "Stonewall" Jackson (1824-1863).[84]

At the beginning of Lincoln's War, General John Henry Winder, a West Point graduate (class of 1820), served as inspector of general military camps in Richmond, a position that was enlarged in 1864 when he was made commissary general of prisoners east of the Mississippi River. As provost marshal general, it was Winder's job to maintain law and order among troops in southeast Virginia.

---

79. In his letter to Lafayette, dated February 14, 1815, Thomas Jefferson makes reference to a "Winder" (see Foley, p. 925; M. D. Peterson, TJ, p. 1363). This is Gen. William Winder (1714-1792), the 2nd great-grandfather of Carrie Winder of Carnton, and the father of Levin Winder (mentioned above)—the sixteenth governor of Maryland (1812-1816), who earlier had served as an officer in the Fourth Maryland Regiment during the First American Revolutionary War. From my personal family tree.

80. John Henry Winder is one of the few men who died of "other" causes during Lincoln's War. In his case the cause of death was listed as "exhaustion."

81. See e.g., Chesnut, DD, p. 343. Mary also mentions a "Miss Winder" in her diary. See Chesnut, DD, p. 113. I am 6th cousins with Mary Chesnut. We are related through both the Conway family of Virginia and mutual royal European ancestors.

82. See Warner, GG, s.v. "Charles Sidney Winder."

83. I am cousins with Carrie and with both Gen. John Winder and Gen. Charles Winder. All four of us descend from King Edward I, "Longshanks" of England (1239-1307), my 21st great-grandfather, Carrie's 17th great-grandfather. Gen. Lee is my 5th cousin. For a fuller treatment of Gen. Charles Sidney Winder's role in the Battle of Cedar Mountain, see Wood, pp. 34-78.

84. For the official Confederate notice of Charles' death on the battlefield, see ORA, Ser. 1, Vol. 12, Pt. 2, p. 191. Note: I am cousins with Stonewall Jackson through a mutual ancestor, the Saint Leger family of England and Normandy, France. From my personal family tree.

THE MCGAVOCKS OF CARNTON PLANTATION

Among the functions he and his staff of civilian detectives performed was the tracking and arrest of spies, issuing passports for those traveling North, and closing down illegal bars and pubs.[85] The position made him quite unpopular with the local citizens of Richmond, who did not like having their freedom to consume alcohol curtailed.[86]

It seems that a Confederate military hospital, one of two of the South's largest (the other was Camp Chimborazo Hospital), was named after John: Camp Winder Hospital, in Richmond, Virginia. Both the Winder and the Chimborazo (also located in Richmond) possessed some 7,800 beds.[87]

General John Henry Winder did indeed have a reputation for being tough on both Yanks and on his Confederate brethren. In her journal, dated February 10, 1865, Mary Chesnut—a cousin of modern Nashvillian, actress Reese Witherspoon[88]—writes that General Mansfield Lovell dined at her home, then left to attend General John Henry Winder's funeral. Now that he is dead, Chesnut noted, at least Winder was safe from the coming violence. For as Lovell told Mary, if the Yanks ever captured Winder they would not be easy on him, for he had not been easy on Yankee prisoners—who complained loudly and often about the Rebel prison inspector.[89]

After Winder's death that month his position as commissary general of prisoners was taken over by another one of my cousins, General Gideon Johnson Pillow (1806-1878) of Williamson County, Tennessee.[90]

---

85. Katcher, CWSB, p. 209; Eaton, HSC, p. 61.
86. Warner, GG, s.v. "John Henry Winder."
87. Eaton, HSC, p. 103.
88. One of Mary Chesnut's closest living Witherspoon relations at the time was John Witherspoon (1818-1902), her 2nd cousin. John's wife, Mary Serena Chesnut Williams (1821-1887), is a niece of Mary Chesnut's husband, James Chesnut, Jr. See Muhlenfeld, p. 28. For references to these individuals in Mary's diary see e.g., Chesnut, DD, pp. 129, 155, 250, 251. My cousin actress Reese Witherspoon descends from a signer of the Declaration of Independence, clergyman John Witherspoon (1723-1794)—the 3rd cousin of John Witherspoon (1818-1902) above. John the signatory, born in Scotland, was once the president of Princeton University and the school has commemorated him with his own statue. He also has a street, a public school, and a Princeton dormitory named after him in the town. He is referred to several times in the writings of Thomas Jefferson, a true hero to traditional Southerners, conservatives, Tea Partyists, and libertarians.
89. Chesnut, MCCW, p. 712.
90. I am cousins with Pillow through mutual Virginia ancestors.

THE MCGAVOCKS OF CARNTON PLANTATION

❧ MAY-DECEMBER COUSINS
Born on September 9, 1829, at Natchez, Adams County, Mississippi, Caroline, nicknamed "Carrie," was fourteen years younger than her husband.[91] This was not unusual for the time period. We will recall that John's father Randal was twenty years older than his wife Sarah.

How did John and Carrie meet when they lived several states apart? They were kin, and in their younger days no doubt often came into contact with one another at family get-togethers, both in Tennessee and in Louisiana.

How were they cousins? Carrie's mother, Martha Ann Grundy (1812-1891)[92] is the sister of John's grandmother, Ann Phillips Rodgers, which makes John and Carrie 1st cousins once removed.

❧ CARRIE WINDER
Like her husband John, Carrie was a fascinating person with many wonderful and unique characteristics. One of the more interesting of these was her love of the color black. Carrie perplexed family and friends alike with her lifelong compulsion to wear all black, even at her wedding.

Her family name is also unusual, for it has two distinct etymologies. The first, held by many modern day Winder family members, states that the name is pronounced WIND-er, as in the "wind that blows," and that it comes from the Old English word *vindr*, meaning "wind," and the word *erg*, meaning "hut."

According to this etymology the earliest Winders inhabited Northern England, where the cold winds required sheltering inside for long periods. Such locations were called *Vindrerg*, or in contemporary English, "Winder." In fact there is still at least one town in England called Winder (in Cumbria County). As the Tennessee Winders originally hailed from Lorton, Cumbria County, a county that is bordered on its northern edge by Scotland, this etymology seems to

---

91. Some modern researchers assert that Carrie was born Dec. 9, 1829. This date contradicts her own gravestone, as well as numerous obituaries from Feb. 1905, all which state that Carrie was born Sept. 9.
92. Martha's middle name is sometimes spelled Anne.

make the most sense.

The second etymology for the name is as follows. Like the surnames Farmer, Gardner, Hooper, Slater, Tyler, Baker, Skinner, Glover, Carter, Plummer, Cooper, Hunter, Plowwright, and Taylor, Winder can also be an English occupational surname: in the 19th Century a winder (pronounced WHINE-der) was the person who wound the wool during the process of making yarn.[93]

In this case the name is a derivative of the Old English word *windan*, meaning "to wind." Thus some of the earliest Winders might have spelled the surname *le Windere* ("the winder").[94] In fact, the oldest known mention of the surname is for one *John le Windere*, found in 1275 in the records of Lincolnshire and Devonshire Counties, England.[95]

Whatever the true origins of her surname, either way it fit Carrie well. The young Mississippi girl, who would one day be compared to the likes of British Queen Boadicea,[96] French saint Joan of Arc, and Confederate heroine Emma Sansom,[97] would go on to become a faithful, hard working, industrious wife who held her family together through thick and thin; a literal whirlwind of energy, one in charge of overseeing all of Carnton's domestic chores, child rearing, the upkeep of the gardens, and the plantation's social life.

In fact, during the halcyon days of Carnton Carrie would be considered a "woman of the highest type," an "earnest Christian," and a "devoted mother and wife" who "exemplified the sweetest virtues of her sex." As a friend and neighbor Carrie would come to be called "thoughtful and charitable," a woman who "was true in every relation of life."

---

93. Bardsley, p. 399.
94. Lower, s.v. "Winder."
95. Reaney and Wilson, s.v. "Winder." Winder should not be confused with the surnames Winders, Windus, and Windes, which derive from the Old English surname *Wyndhouse*, meaning "a worker (in threads and yarns) at the winding-house."
96. Boadicea is my 40th great-grandmother.
97. I am a direct descendant of the Sansom family of Virginia and West Virginia.

The McGavocks of Carnton Plantation

❧ A STEAMBOAT TO MEMPHIS, A COACH & FOUR TO FRANKLIN

As mentioned, on December 6, 1848, John W. McGavock and Carrie Winder tied the knot in a humble Louisiana wedding ceremony at her parents' sugar farm, known as Ducros Plantation, in Houma, Terrebonne Parish, roughly sixty miles southwest of New Orleans.

After much festivities, filled with excitement at their new union, they rode a steamboat up the Mississippi to Memphis, in awe of the sights and sounds of travel on the "Great River," also popularly known as "Moon River," the "Big Muddy," and "Old Man River." From Memphis they took a "coach and four" (horses), with accompanying baggage wagons and outriders, to Carnton Plantation in Franklin, Tennessee, where they went to live with John's widowed mother Sarah. The couple would spend the rest of their lives together here.

But as they settled in, the wealthy, refined, and composed pair of traditional Southerners could not have known that their future would be far from what they envisioned in those early days of matrimonial bliss. In fact, due to the illegal and senseless war instigated by an uncouth, violent, and politically driven liberal Northerner named Lincoln, history would come to loudly proclaim them as one of America's most famous couples. This was something they never dreamed of, or wanted. But fame often comes to those who least expect it.

❧ CHILDREN OF JOHN & CARRIE

Within ten months of their marriage John and Carrie bore their first child: Martha Winder (b. September 25, 1849). Four more children followed in fairly rapid succession, making five in all: Mary Elizabeth (b. March 28, 1851), John Randal (b. June 05, 1854), Harriet "Hattie" Young (b. July 02, 1855), and Winder (b. July 13, 1857).

Meanwhile, on June 21, 1851, Carrie's nine-month old brother, William Shields Winder (b. August 1, 1850), passed away. Soon after, on February 18, 1852, one of Carrie's sisters, Malvina Bass Winder (b. March 30, 1841), died. Malvina, who succumbed at their parents' home in Louisiana, was ten years old. Malvina's funeral card reads:

THE MCGAVOCKS OF CARNTON PLANTATION

> The friends of V. P. Winder are requested to attend the funeral of his daughter Malvina—to proceed from his Residence to the private Burial Ground 4 G. S. Guion, Thursday morning at 10 o'clock. Terrebonne, La., Wednesday, Feb. 18th, 1852.[98]

Another one of Carrie's sisters died a little over a year later: Martha Ann Grundy Winder (b. February 10, 1837) passed away on August 8, 1853, at the Winder residence in Terrebonne Parish. Martha was just sixteen. Her funeral card reads:

> The friends of Col. and Mrs. V. P. Winder are invited to attend the Funeral of their Daughter MARTHA, [. . .] Wednesday morning at 8 o'clock from the 1st Presbyterian Church. Funeral Service by Rev. Dr. Edgar. Thursday, August 9th, 1853.[99]

Next came Carrie's father, Colonel Van Perkins Winder, who passed away on December 8, 1854, at his home in Houma, Terrebonne Parish, Louisiana. Colonel Winder's funeral card reads:

> The friends and acquaintances of Col. Van P. Winder, deceased, are invited to attend his Funeral, from his residence to-morrow morning, Thursday, at 9 o'clock. Ducros, Wednesday, November 8, 1854.[100]

Though sorrowful, Carrie could not have been shocked at any of this. Three of her young sisters and one of her young brothers had passed away even before she married John in 1848. In the Victorian Era death was as common as birth on America's Western frontier.

Of their five children, only John and Carrie's two oldest children would themselves live into adulthood. The first three perished of various diseases, all before the age of thirteen, two of them before Lincoln's War.

---

98. Funeral card courtesy of the Williamson County Public Library.
99. Funeral card courtesy of the Williamson County Public Library.
100. Funeral card courtesy of the Williamson County Public Library.

The McGavocks of Carnton Plantation

❧ DEATH & INHERITANCE

The first of these deaths was not long in coming. On September 11, 1854, only five years after their Louisiana marriage, the couple's oldest son John Randal died of intestinal problems.

A few months later, on December 28, 1854, John's mother Sarah also passed away at Carnton. Young John Randal and his grandmother Sarah were both buried in Carnton's McGavock Family Cemetery, next to Carnton founder, Mayor Randal McGavock, her husband and little John's grandfather.

According to Randal's will, with Sarah's death, ownership of the plantation was to be passed on to John, now thirty-nine years old. This important transition was tempered by more death, however.

On March 18, 1855, another child of John's sister, Elizabeth Irwin McGavock, passed away. William R. Harding (b. September 16, 1854) was eight months old. Then yet another of John's and Carrie's children died: Mary Elizabeth passed away on Tuesday, January 26, 1858, while she was visiting the family's Winder relatives at Ducros Plantation, in Houma, Louisiana. The cause of Mary's death was quite common at the time: yellow fever.

Below is Mary Elizabeth's obituary from a Louisiana newspaper that week. The original spelling and punctuation have been retained. A bracket and ellipsis indicate a lacuna (a missing or unintelligible part of the text). We will note that mention is made that Mary Elizabeth died "at the residence of her father." This would indicate that John W. McGavock had a home in Terrebonne Parish, Louisiana, in 1858. If so, I have no knowledge of it; although, because John and Carrie were so closely related, we can be quite sure that the McGavocks owned land and other holdings in the area. So this is quite possible, even probable.

On the other hand, this statement could be an error of the writer of the obituary. If so, he should have written that Mary Elizabeth died "at the residence of her *grandfather* . . ." This would be accurate for, as we have seen, her maternal grandfather, Colonel Van Perkins Winder, Sr., indeed owned a home (a plantation) in Houma, Louisiana: his daughter Carrie and her husband John W. McGavock were married there in 1848.

The McGavocks of Carnton Plantation

On to Mary Elizabeth McGavock's obituary. The name of the newspaper and the date of the article are unknown. But it was probably a New Orleans newspaper, and the article was no doubt penned in late January or early February 1858:

> DIED—At the residence of her father, in the parish of Terrebonne, Tuesday, the 26th of January, MARY ELIZABETH; second daughter of John and Caroline Winder McGavock, in the sixth year of her age.
>
> It is with a trembling hand that I touch the chord, which vibrates so painfully in the hearts of those who loved and mourn for sweet little Mame. But remembering that He said 'of such is the kingdom of Heaven,' let us look up with the eye of Faith to that blessed company of angels, where [. . .] her childish voice to sounds of praise she sings with them around the throne of the Lamb—safe from sin and sorrow, safe from broken hopes and hearts grown cold, safe from the world and worldly things, safe for Time and Eternity. Believing parents let this great theme [. . .] with gratitude to Him who has been so good to your darling as to take her to himself. I know your heartstrings will often be tightened by a child's laugh; a voice will make echoes, a step speak of the life, health and hope of her who is gone before; but remember, that her laugh is changed to the sound of thanksgiving, her voice rings in Heaven, her step treads the Courts of the Home of our God.
>
> > 'She is no dead, the child of our affection,
> > But gone into that school,
> > Where she no longer needs our poor
> >   protection,
> > And Christ himself doth rule.'[101]

A few months later, on August 5, 1855, Colonel John's famous 1st cousin, Lysander McGavock, founder of the equally famous Midway Plantation, passed away at his home at the age of fifty-four. He was buried in the family plot just north of his beautiful home in Brentwood.

---

101. Mary Elizabeth McGavock's obituary transcribed by the author. Obituary courtesy of the Williamson County Public Library.

The McGavocks & Slavery

Part 1

◈ THE FARMING LIFE

DESPITE THE McGAVOCKS' SORROWS, LIFE went on as usual at Carnton Plantation. There was little choice. Farms must operate 365 days a year, whatever human drama takes place on and around them. That Spring, in 1858, there were fields to hoe, crops to plant, and animals to tend to. Much of this work fell, of course, to Carnton's servants, wrongly known as "slaves" by Northerners and New South Southerners.

Just how did "slavery" work at Carnton? Was it really the hideously cruel and barbaric institution we have been taught it was? Did the McGavocks whip their slaves? Did their servants really have no rights?

The McGavocks were intelligent, sensitive, highly educated people. How could they be so inhumane as to be slave owners? How could they use the Bible to justify slavery? Were not Jesus, the prophets, and even God himself, against it? When I worked as a docent at Carnton, these were among the most common questions I received from my guests.

Since "slavery" is so tightly wound into the fabric of Carnton's history, and since this is also one of the topics that is both most

The McGavocks of Carnton Plantation

misunderstood and of most interest to those who visit the plantation, this is an ideal place to pause from our study of the McGavock family to discuss it more thoroughly.

We will note here that the following is obviously in no way a defense of slavery: I consider it one of the most immoral, monstrous, and reprehensible institutions ever created by humanity. For it violates both the Golden Rule (the basis of nearly every known religion, from Wicca, Judaism, and Buddhism, to Christianity, Deism, and Hinduism) and Natural Law (the God-given right to live free, the very foundation of the U.S. Constitution).[102] What the following four chapters will be devoted to is a discussion of slavery as it was understood and experienced by European-Americans, African-Americans, and Native-Americans living in the Old South in the 17th, 18th, and 19th Centuries.

❧ BENJAMIN FRANKLIN: EXAMINING AUTHENTIC RACISM

Because they were slave owners, many today consider the McGavocks "racists." This is not technically true, at least not if we judge them by the standards of their day instead of ours. This is only right, fair, and historically accurate, for labeling the McGavocks racist for owning human chattel is a product of both a basic misconception of 19th-Century America and 21st-Century political correctness gone mad.

If we choose to judge early Southerners by today's mores and ideas, then we must judge early Northerners by the same ones. For, as we will see, both the American slave trade and American slavery got their start in the North. What is more, the institution was practiced across Yankeedom right up to and into the "Civil War."

How odd then that in the Carnton McGavocks' hometown of Franklin, Tennessee, some city authorities today regard the Confederate Flag as a symbol of bigotry (and have even talked of banning it from public parades), while the town itself was named after a Yankee slave owner, one who would now be considered an overt white supremacist,

---

102. Napolitano, p. xvi. For an excellent modern discussion of Natural Law, and how it has been eroded by big-government liberals like Lincoln, see Napolitano, passim.

The McGavocks of Carnton Plantation

Benjamin Franklin.[103] How can it be *inappropriate* for the Confederate Flag to be flown in what was once a Confederate city, in a Confederate state, in a Confederate nation, while it is considered *appropriate* for that same city to be named after an anti-South, slave-owning Northern racist?

The famous Boston inventor and statesman detested slavery, but not because it hurt blacks, but because it hurt whites. How? By forcing an "unnatural intermingling" of the two races, whereby the white race was thought to be diluted and diminished by the black one.

In Franklin's view whites were a civilized, light, happy, righteous, forgiving, Christian people, while the majority of blacks, he said, "are of a plotting Disposition, dark, sullen, malicious, revengeful, and cruel in the highest Degree."[104] Because of these perceived differences, Franklin came to believe in maintaining the "racial purity" of the European-American race, a goal that was threatened by the introduction of black slavery into the U.S., which he feared would make whites darker.

Franklin, who as a newspaper publisher had printed advertisements for slave sales,[105] noted with revulsion how "the introduction of slaves" always "greatly diminished the whites," and how slaves always "pejorate the families that use them; the white children become proud, disgusted with labor, and, being educated in idleness, are rendered unfit to get a living by industry."[106]

While advocating the banning of slavery, Franklin felt that it was also proper to be biased toward one's own race, making him what we would call today an abolitionist-racist. Franklin was no isolated character in this regard.[107]

Studies of 19th-Century society show that nearly all white Northerners were of the same mind as the famed printer and writer. In fact, Franklin could have been speaking for most Yankees and

---

103. Hale and Merritt, Vol. 3, p. 838.
104. Website: www.historycarper.com/resources/twobf3/slavery.htm.
105. K. C. Davis, p. 37.
106. B. Franklin, LWBF, Vol. 2, p. 422.
107. Franklin was so Anglocentric and xenophobic that he even complained about Germans immigrating to Pennsylvania. Adams and Sanders, p. 327.

THE McGAVOCKS OF CARNTON PLANTATION

Northerners when he voted to prohibit the institution while at the same time complaining about the problem of disappearing whites in the face of an ever increasing population of blacks.[108] It is a fact, Franklin wrote, that

> the number of purely white people in the world is proportionably very small. All Africa is black or tawny; Asia chiefly tawny; America (exclusive of the new comers) wholly so. And in Europe, the Spaniards, Italians, French, Russians, and Swedes, are generally of what we call a swarthy complexion; as are the Germans also, the Saxons only excepted, who, with the English, make the principal body of white people on the face of the earth. I could wish their numbers were increased. And while we are, as I may call it, scouring our planet, by clearing America of woods, and so making this side of our globe reflect a brighter light to the eyes of inhabitants in Mars or Venus, why should we, in the sight of superior beings, darken its people? Why increase the sons of Africa, by planting them in America, where we have so fair an opportunity, by excluding all blacks and tawnys, of increasing the lovely white and red? But perhaps I am partial to the complexion of my country, for such kind of partiality is natural to mankind.[109]

The McGavocks may have been slave owners, but being Southerners they never looked at other races the way Yankees, such as Franklin, did. In fact, there is no record, written or verbal, of this type of racism, or any other kind, at Carnton Plantation. Quite the contrary.

While the McGavocks were not public abolitionists prior to the War, at the same time it can be accurately said that unlike Franklin, and later Lincoln, they were true friends of American blacks. As we will see, there was good reason for this.

❧ TRUE ABOLITIONISM WAS RARE IN THE NORTH
The case of Benjamin Franklin highlights an uncomfortable truth for those who embrace Northern mythology: authentic abolitionism—that

---

108. Goodman, pp. 332, 333, 334, 336.
109. Sparks, Vol. 2, pp. 320-321.

THE MCGAVOCKS OF CARNTON PLANTATION

is, believing that slavery should be abolished *and* that blacks should be accepted into American life as equals—was actually quite rare in the North, with true abolitionists never representing more than the tiniest percentage of the northern population.[110] In 1858 Lincoln himself admitted as much when he discussed abolition with an Illinois audience. After emancipating America's black servants, what then?, he asked rhetorically:

> Free them, and make them politically and socially, our equals? My own feelings will not admit of this; and if mine would, we well know that those of the great mass of white people will not.[111]

As our future sixteenth president intimates here, abolitionists were detested by nearly all Northern whites, who saw them as troublemakers, malcontents, agitators, and revolutionaries who threatened white hegemony. This is why a furious New England mob attacked abolitionist William Lloyd Garrison (1805-1879) in Boston, Massachusetts, and tried to lynch him; it is why he was arrested in 1829, tried and convicted by a Northern jury and sent to prison for several months;[112] and it is why subscriptions for his weekly abolitionist periodical, *The Liberator*, never exceeded 3,000 and were bought mainly by blacks, not whites.[113]

As hard evidence for the widespread existence of anti-abolitionist sentiment in the North prior to Lincoln's War, we need look no further than the story of Prudence Crandall (1803-1890).

Crandall was a white New England teacher who founded the "High School for Young Colored Ladies and Misses" in Canterbury, Connecticut, in 1834. One would think that fellow Yanks would have applauded her efforts. Instead, for trying to offer blacks a free education in New England, Crandall, a Quaker and abolitionist, was harassed, arrested (three times), and imprisoned, while Northern white mobs

---

110. Adams and Sanders, pp. 144, 148-149.
111. Nicolay and Hay, ALCW, Vol. 1, p. 288.
112. McKissack and McKissack, p. 170.
113. Furnas, p. 408; Rosenbaum and Brinkley, s.v. "Liberator, The."

attacked and stoned her school, eventually shutting it down and driving her out of the state.[114]

Here is her story, according to fellow Quaker Jessie Gidley Carter:

> People who tried to establish schools for the negroes at first found this a very hard thing to do. Many slaveholders said that the negroes were not bright enough to learn, or else that if they were taught they would become dangerous to the country. . . . the Friends [that is, the Quakers] and others were steadily and faithfully working for better things. The story of Prudence Crandall shows how earnest the friends of the slaves were and how much they were willing to suffer for their ideas.
>
> Prudence Crandall was a young Quaker schoolteacher in Connecticut. In the summer of 1832, she bought a house in the town of Canterbury, where she opened a boarding and day school for girls. The school had the support of the leading townspeople, until a colored girl, Sarah Harris, became one of its pupils. Sarah was a bright student, who wanted to fit herself to be a teacher of her own race. She was a good girl, she had pleasant manners, she had been through the district school, and both teacher and pupils of the little boarding school were willing to have her stay and study with them. The parents of the other girls, however, were deeply offended.
>
> "If Sarah Harris stays," they declared, "we will take our daughters out."
>
> This put Prudence Crandall into a very hard place. She could not afford to lose the money from her richer pupils. She was already in debt. And yet, as she thought of the great need of Sarah Harris and of many other colored girls, ready and eager to learn, although there was no one to teach them, her duty seemed clear. She took courage and said that if the white girls were taken out, she would open her school for girls of the negro race. This made the people of the town very indignant. A town-meeting was called, where more than a thousand excited people met to protest against the bold action of this one little Quaker woman.
>
> "That nigger school shall never be allowed in Canterbury nor in any other town in this State!" cried out one of the angry

---

114. Buckley, p. 62.

The McGavocks of Carnton Plantation

men.

The friends of Prudence Crandall were not allowed to say anything, and the meeting broke up with much noise and confusion.

Prudence Crandall did not show any fear. She received fifteen or twenty colored pupils from New York, Philadelphia, Providence, and Boston. This was in Fourth Month, 1833. In a little less than a year and a half, the school had to be given up; and during that time the teacher and the students patiently bore many hardships. The stores of the town would sell them nothing; and people insulted the colored girls on the street and tried to make their life miserable at the school itself. Not satisfied with such things as this, the leading men of the town influenced the State Legislature to pass a law called the "Black Law," which said that no one should set up any school in Connecticut for teaching any colored person not a native of the State. When the people of Canterbury heard that the law was passed, they were wild with excitement, ringing bells and firing cannon to show their joy.

For breaking this law, Prudence Crandall was then taken to jail and shut up in a murderer's cell, as this happened to be the only one empty. The courageous young teacher was very willing to bear the disgrace for the sake of the cause. The next day, her friends gave bonds for her and the jailer let her go; but the story of her unfair imprisonment quickly spread over the country and roused much interest and sympathy. Twice her case was tried in court, but the juries could not agree, and the decision was never given. All this time the little school had been going on; but soon after the trials in court, some of Prudence Crandall's enemies tried to set fire to her house, and, a few nights afterward, a number of persons attacked the place with iron bars and clubs and broke the windows. It is hard to believe that people who pretended to be Christians could be so cruel to a houseful of frightened girls. In the face of such danger, Prudence Crandall saw that she must at last give up her school. This was in Ninth Month, 1834. Four years later, the "Black Law" was repealed. It seems a strange law to have been made at this time in the North, for the Northern States had been "free States" for years . . . [115]

None of Connecticut's white population shed a tear for

---

115. *Quaker Biographies*, Vol. 5, pp. 140-143.

THE MCGAVOCKS OF CARNTON PLANTATION

Crandall. Instead, the state (in particular her politicians) was quite happy to see her, and her school, disappear. Their smug parting comment sums up the North's feelings perfectly at the time: "Once open this door, and New-England will become the Liberia of America," they shrieked as Crandall left Connecticut for the last time.[116]

More proof that abolitionists were widely detested in the North comes from the grim story of white abolitionist publisher Elijah Parish Lovejoy (1802-1837), who was shot to death in Alton, Illinois, by a white gang. Prior to Lovejoy's murder at the hands of his fellow Illinoisans, his printing office had been destroyed three times by Northern anti-abolitionists. He died trying to protect it during their fourth attempt.

We should not be surprised at the Prairie State's attitude toward blacks. As we will see, Illinois, Lincoln's adopted home state, was one of the most anti-black states in the nation, in great part because of Lincoln himself.

The reason for the North's open animosity toward abolitionists was simple: not only was racism toward blacks at its deepest and darkest in the North, but the slavery business itself began and was headquartered in the North.

New York City, the capital of the North's economy, was also the capital of American slavery right up to the end of Lincoln's War, and for good reason: the two were inextricably linked. And it was for this very reason, that is, pure economic interest, that the North was far more interested in maintaining the institution than the South. As one wealthy New York businessman said to abolitionist Reverend Samuel J. May in 1835:

> Mr. May, we are not such fools as not to know that slavery is a great evil, a great wrong. But it was consented to by the founders of our Republic. It was provided for in the Constitution of our Union. A great portion of the property of the Southerners is invested under its sanction; and the business of the North as well as

---

116. Garrison and Garrison, Vol. 1, p. 323.

The McGavocks of Carnton Plantation

the South has become adjusted to it. There are millions upon millions of dollars due from Southerners to the merchants and mechanics of New York alone, the payment of which would be jeopardized by any rupture between the North and the South. We cannot afford, sir, to let you and your associates succeed in your endeavor to overthrow slavery. It is not a matter of principle with us; it is a matter of business necessity. We cannot afford to let you succeed; and I have called you out to let you know, and to let your fellow-laborers know, that we do not mean to allow you to succeed. "We mean, sir," said he with increased emphasis,—"we mean, sir, to put you Abolitionists down— by fair means if we can, by foul means if we must."[117]

❧ THE SOUTH'S CENTRAL ISSUE: SELF-GOVERNMENT NOT SLAVERY

The South also went to war over economics. But it was not over the economics of slavery, as Northern mythologists have been misleading the public for the past 150 years. For slavery was only practiced by a tiny handful of mainly wealthy Southerners. And neither was slavery either a racist institution meant to "keep blacks in their place" or the foundation of the South's economy.[118] This is why Dixie would not, and did not, go to war to preserve the "peculiar institution."

The truth is that the South fought to preserve its economic, social, political, and psychological freedom from a tyrannical, liberal Northern government, one intent on crushing everything the South believed in and held dear.[119] Southerners, being naturally conservative, wanted to "conserve" authentic American tradition, a way of life embedded in the original Constitution as laid down by the Southern Founding Fathers. Thus, when the Southern Confederacy created its own Constitution in 1861, it was, with a only a few minor exceptions, a near exact reproduction of the original 1787 U.S. Constitution.[120]

Tragically, that year, 1861, the North appointed itself despotic

---

117. O. Johnson, pp. 184-185.
118. For more on this topic see Seabrook, L, pp. 471-475.
119. See Kennedy and Kennedy, NT, passim.
120. Nivola and Rosenbloom, p. 510.

ruler over this freedom loving sovereign nation, the Confederate States of America (C.S.A.). Ensconcing a liberal tyrant on the throne at Washington, D.C., it then invaded her.

How else could the conservative South herself respond but defensively?

Mustering armed forces to defend hearth and home against Lincoln's aggressive and illegal action then was, in great part, a matter of honor, Southern honor, a regional pride built around Dixie's passion for liberty, independence, and self-determination.

But there was something more.

As we have said, maintaining slavery was never the central issue in the South. It was the right to decide when and how slavery should be abolished in their region that was important to Southerners. No one likes to be told what to do and what not to do, especially by foreigners, and more particularly by hostile foreigners, as Lincoln was seen by Southerners at the time.

And was it not the height of Yankee hypocrisy that while the U.S. Constitution continued to protect slavery between the years 1861 and 1865, and while the institution was still being practiced in the North,[121] Lincoln sought to destroy it in the South before either whites or blacks were ready to deal with the issue of complete and sudden emancipation?

In response the South relied on the Constitutional guarantees of self-government and secession to try and slow things down, in order to give themselves time to prepare for abolition. The impatient North went on to assure the South that it would strip it of these rights at gunpoint.

Thus it was that Southerners viewed the North's threats not as an attempt to destroy slavery, but as a promise to economically and politically subjugate Dixie.[122] How would you feel if a foreigner living a thousand miles away violently and illegally threatened to take away

---

121. Despite the fact that slavery had been "abolished" in the North in the late 1700s and early 1800s, the practice of keeping slaves continued unabated, which is why there were between 500,000 and 1 million slaves in the North in the 1860s. Eaton, HSC, p. 93; Hinkle, p. 125.
122. W. C. Davis, JD, p. 167.

THE MCGAVOCKS OF CARNTON PLANTATION

your right to govern your own life?

ଛ THE McGAVOCKS, LINCOLN, & SLAVERY
One of the millions of Southern families who supported the idea of self-government were the McGavocks, who believed that the Federal government did not possess the right to appropriate their rights, their property, or their servants, by any means, especially by force. For Southerners these were local state issues, not national ones. The McGavocks, like all Southerners, just wanted to be left alone to manage their own personal and local affairs, a sentiment clearly articulated by Southern leaders from John C. Calhoun to Jefferson Davis (1808-1889).[123]

Had Lincoln done just that, the McGavocks and other Southern servant owners would have eventually ended the institution in their own time and way, peacefully, legally, and without bloodshed, just as the North had allowed itself the privilege to do between the late 1700s and early 1800s: when slavery became unprofitable in the region at this time, Northern merchants and bankers simply pushed the institution southward.[124] As we saw above concerning the comments made to Reverend May, Yankee businessmen did not want to permanently end slavery across the U.S., however, for they were still capitalizing on it.

The problem Northerners faced regarding slavery in their own region was threefold:

1) Due to a short growing season, largely rocky sandy soil, and an increasingly industrial economy, it was decided that it was no longer beneficial for them to try and sustain the institution in their region.[125]

2) A near completely racist white Northern population did not want to work alongside blacks in the newly opening factories or have to compete with them for jobs.[126]

3) Since, like perishable foods, slaves tended to "wilt and die"

---

123. Coit, p. 452.
124. Rosenbaum and Brinkley, s.v. "Slavery."
125. P. M. Roberts, pp. 195-196.
126. U. B. Phillips, pp. 119-120.

THE MCGAVOCKS OF CARNTON PLANTATION

with increasing regularity the longer they were kept on board ships, it was advantageous for slavers to off-load their human cargo as quickly as possible. Sailing from Africa, nearly all Yankee slave ships first stopped off in the Caribbean Islands where still "fresh" African slaves were sold to sugar plantation owners. A journey from the Caribbean to New England, however, a trip of a week or two, would have certainly killed off much of the slaver's cargo. Thus, he stood to make more money by instead sailing to the next closest ports: those in the South along the Atlantic seaboard. (Those Africans who were not sold in Southern ports, and survived, were taken back to the Northeast and sold to wealthy Yankee families.)[127]

For these reasons, throughout the 1700s and 1800s Northerners began to regard slavery as largely unprofitable.[128]

Despite this fact, it was still advantageous for Northerners to maintain slavery, for they were making millions of dollars a year from the institution. But if it could no longer be maintained advantageously in the North, where then was it to go? The obvious choice was to move it Southward.[129]

As Chesnut attests in her voluminous and fascinating Victorian journals, the North sold their slaves to the South when they discovered that it did not pay to keep them there anymore. Then the Yanks "freed them," and gradually pushed them down South. At the same time they gave themselves decades to rid their region of blacks, using methods that would wreak the least amount of financial damage.[130]

This is all too true, for Lincoln was anxious to force his political agenda (which was to install the liberal big government concept known as the American System in Washington, D.C.) on the South and was not above using violence to do it. His War was the result. Sadly for America, he would not give Dixie the honor of ending slavery in her own way and time as the North had given itself.

---

127. Furnas, pp. 119, 121.
128. P. M. Roberts, p. 198; Garraty and McCaughey, p. 81.
129. Lott, p. 6.
130. Chesnut, MCCW, p. 196.

The McGavocks of Carnton Plantation

In the end it was Northern greed and geography that sealed the South's doom in the War between the Confederacy and the Union. After all, it was Mother Nature who dealt the fateful hand by giving Dixie lush, sprawling, green, fertile lands, and long hot summers, perfect for the outdoor businesses of agriculture and commerce; and it was she who gave to the North hilly terrain, poor sandy soil, and long cold winters, ideal for the indoor businesses of manufacturing and finance. As the authors of the *History of Tennessee* state it, eventually the commercial section of the U.S. (the North) naturally became slave dealers, while America's agricultural area (the South) became slave purchasers.[131]

During his seventh and final debate with Lincoln at Alton, Illinois, on October 15, 1858, Illinois Senator Stephen A. Douglas (1813-1861) pointed out that the U.S. Constitution, along with the concept of states' rights, themselves had been constructed around the geography of North America. This, in turn, impacted where slavery would endure and where it would die out:

> This government was made upon the great basis of the sovereignty of the States, the right of each State to regulate its own domestic institutions to suit itself, and that right was conferred with the understanding and expectation that inasmuch as each locality had separate interests, each locality must have different and distinct local and domestic institutions, corresponding to its wants and interests. Our [Founding] fathers knew, when they made the government, that the laws and institutions which were well adapted to the green mountains of Vermont were unsuited to the rice plantations of South Carolina. They knew then, as well as we know now, that the laws and institutions which would be well adapted to the beautiful prairies of Illinois would not be suited to the mining regions of California. They knew that in a republic as broad as this, having such a variety of soil, climate, and interest, there must necessarily be a corresponding variety of local laws—the policy and institutions of each State adapted to its condition and wants. For this reason this Union was established on

---

131. Garrett and Goodpasture, p. 44.

THE McGAVOCKS OF CARNTON PLANTATION

the right of each State to do as it pleased on the question of slavery, and every other question, and the various States were not allowed to complain of, much less interfere with, the policy of their neighbors.[132]

With slavery being more compatible with Southern weather and soil than Northern, naturally slavery eventually ended up being more profitable in the South.

Why then should the South be blamed for her own topography and climate, bestowed on her by God himself? Lincoln never bothered to answer this question. He did not even think to ask it. And for this 3 million Americans would perish.[133]

Carnton's founder, Randal McGavock, who died eighteen years before Lincoln's War, was blissfully unaware of what was to come. He had no way of knowing that in 1861 a Northern tyrant would send "Yankee devils" right to his front door; that they would threaten to burn down his entire plantation and even threaten to murder his son John; that they would literally steal millions of dollars of his children's inheritance and possessions; and that finally they would foment one of the bloodiest battles in world history just a mile and a half away, part of it even overlapping onto his own land.

And neither could Randal have possibly imagined that his son would have to send all of Carnton's servants further south to escape the dangers of this illegitimate incursion of foreign soil, one we Southerners still rightly call the "Grand Invasion."

❧ THE McGAVOCK SERVANTS

In the early 1800s all of this was still nearly a half century in the future, and Randal had a plantation to build. With Northerner Eli Whitney's invention of the cotton gin in 1793 (a piece of technology that decreased

---

132. Nicolay and Hay, ALCW, Vol. 1, p. 487.
133. Timothy D. Manning, Sr., personal correspondence. Some Southern historians, like Manning, estimate that Lincoln's War took the lives of as many as 1 million Northerners and 2 million Southerners. These figures include all races and both non-combatants and black slaves, men, women, and children.

THE MCGAVOCKS OF CARNTON PLANTATION

labor but increased the need for manpower),[134] and a severe white labor shortage all across America at the time, he naturally turned to the institution of slavery for help.[135] For it was the Yankee invention of the cotton gin that resuscitated, and continued to perpetuate, the entire institution of slavery, as even Lincoln admitted on October 13, 1858:

> Mr. [Preston Smith] Brooks, of South Carolina, once said, and truly said, that when this government was established, no one expected the institution of slavery to last until this day; and that the men who formed this government were wiser and better than the men of these days; but the men of these days had experience which the fathers had not, and that experience had taught them the invention of the cotton-gin, and this had made the perpetuation of the institution of slavery a necessity in this country.[136]

As we will see, it was this need for manpower, not racism, that was the real purpose behind American slavery after all.[137]

Being affluent, Randal was one of the few men in Tennessee who could afford black servants, and who actually owned them. At the time of his death in 1843 Carnton Plantation had twenty-two. When John inherited the estate after his mother's death in 1854, Carnton's million-dollar community of servants was passed on to him as well. In the ensuing years John acquired another twenty-two, making a total of forty-four black servants at the plantation's peak. In 1860, however, one year before the War, that number had dropped to thirty-nine.

One of the remnants of the McGavock servant period, which lasted a mere thirty-nine years (from 1826 to 1865), is the lone brick house on the eastern side of the property, quarters for Carnton's house servants.

As mentioned, at the plantation's peak there were between thirty-nine and forty-four servants at Carnton. The McGavocks paid

---

134. W. B. Garrison, CWTFB, p. 106.
135. This shortage was particularly felt in early New York City, where white labor was said to be difficult to secure, overpriced, and unreliable. O. Williams, p. 6.
136. Nicolay and Hay, ALCW, Vol. 1, p. 480.
137. Green, EWBAT, pp. 4, 61-62.

THE MCGAVOCKS OF CARNTON PLANTATION

between $1,500 and $2,500 for each individual. At an average cost of $2,000 a piece in 1860 ($55,000 a piece in today's currency), this means they owned about $88,000 in black domestics, the equivalent of $2,400,000 today. To put this number in perspective, currently the average cost of a house in the U.S. is $250,000. The McGavocks invested over nine times that amount in black servants alone.

❧ A CLOSER LOOK AT AMERICAN "SLAVERY"

The type of "slavery" practiced by families like the McGavocks was very different than what has been taught in our Northern-biased school texts and Yankee-slanted history books.

Let us consider Southern servants themselves.

During the Great Depression of the 1930s, the Work Projects Administration gathered together the oral histories of surviving former black slaves and published them in what is commonly called the "Slave Narratives." In all, some 80 percent of the African-American authors of these accounts spoke positively about their lives as servants, about their owners, and about their owners' families.[138] How do anti-South crusaders respond to this fact today? They simply ignore it, or bury it along with the rest of the authoritative facts about Southern slavery.

As a result, when you mention the word slavery today, the image that comes to most people's minds is that of a terrified African bound in cold iron chains, living in a squalid cage, wearing tattered filthy rags, working tirelessly in the hot sun without pay, and being beaten and whipped both day and night, his or her flesh raw with open wounds and writhing maggots. In the North these colorful images were further exaggerated by referring to Southern slave owners as the "lords of lash and loom," a notorious phrase usually accompanied by unspeakable descriptions of bare-backed blacks crying and screaming as they "groaned beneath the lash."[139]

Anti-South propaganda expert Abraham Lincoln contributed to this fiction with statements like the following. The slave owner, he

---

138. Kennedy, p. 91.
139. McKissack and McKissack, p. 102.

The McGavocks of Carnton Plantation

claimed,

> sits in the shade, with gloves on his hands, and subsists on the bread that Sambo is earning in the burning sun.[140]

Was this kind of slavery ever *routinely* practiced anywhere in America? Absolutely not, and for several simple reasons, the least of which was that no business could sustain itself if its workers—enslaved or free—were treated in such a cruel manner. What boss today, after all, brutalizes his or her workers? The very thought of it is contrary to all reason.

Bosses were no different in earlier times. For evidence of this we must look, not to the North, the birthplace of both American slavery and anti-South mythology, but to the South.

❧ SOUTHERN "SLAVE REBELLIONS"

To begin with, if black servants were treated cruelly there was literally nothing to prevent them from rising up on their farms and plantations, overthrowing their owners, and leaving.[141] Southern plantations were not armed concentration camps with barbed wire, security guards, and white racist militias specially trained to maintain law and order over blacks, as these large farms have been painted by the North.

On the contrary, by and large Southern plantations were, in typical Southern fashion, relaxed, flexible, and informal, with few set rules and with both masters and servants coming and going, sometimes for days and even weeks at a time.

Mary Chesnut, as just one example, writes of how she often left her servants on their own to do as they pleased, something they were well used to.[142] Such historical facts reveal that a great deal of mutual trust and respect existed between servants and their owners, hardly the

---

140. Nicolay and Hay, ALCW, Vol. 1, p. 414.
141. There were fugitive slave laws meant to protect slave owners from such incidents, but in most cases they were essentially ineffectual: by the time local law enforcement found out about the servants' escape, they had usually disappeared into thin air.
142. Chesnut, MCCW, p. 716.

THE MCGAVOCKS OF CARNTON PLANTATION

type of atmosphere that would foster rebellion, rioting, mayhem, and murder.

One must also consider that there was a great disparity in population. On the average large Southern plantation, for instance, there were commonly 100 blacks to six whites, a European-American family that typically consisted of a father, mother, and four children. That is a ratio of about seventeen to one. The ratio on such plantations between *adult* slaves and *adult* white males was even greater: about thirty to one.[143] A force contemplating revolt with these types of odds on their side could be completely confident of victory. Why not rise up and mutiny then if life under slavery was in every way unbearable?

Even on a smaller plantation like Carnton, where there were as many as forty-four blacks and only a handful of white adults present, the McGavocks' servants could have effortlessly overpowered Randal and Sarah, or John and Carrie, at any time, particularly at night.

The fact is they never did.

In many antebellum Southern towns, blacks equaled whites in population; in others they actually outnumbered whites. While they were never the majority in the South, blacks once made up a huge percentage of the overall population: according to the 1860 U.S. Census, of the South's 12 million inhabitants in 1860, exactly one third of them, or 4 million, were black.[144] Of these, 3.5 million were servants, 500,000 were free.[145]

Just as revealing is the fact that a majority of the Southern states had black populations that were nearly equal to the white population in 1860, and two Southern states, Mississippi and South Carolina, actually possessed more blacks than whites that year. The former had 436,696 blacks to only 354,700 whites, the latter with 402,541 blacks to only 301,271 whites. Some states like Florida, with 61,753 blacks to 78,686 whites, and Louisiana, with 333,010 blacks and 376,280 whites, were

---

143. Fogel and Engerman, p. 242.
144. Buckley, p. 81.
145. Seabrook, EYWTACWW, p. 158. Also see Stephenson, ALU, p. 168; Cooper, JDA, p. 378; Quarles, p. xiii; Ransom, pp. 214-215.

THE MCGAVOCKS OF CARNTON PLANTATION

nearly dead even.[146] Furthermore, in the rice-growing regions of the South blacks outnumbered whites two to one.[147]

The point is that had Southern blacks wished to arm themselves and fight, they could have easily overthrown and killed their owners, wrecked Southern plantations, burned Southern cities to the ground, and emancipated themselves. And yet, there were virtually no major, and scarcely any minor, slave insurrections in any city in Dixie at any time between 1619 and 1865, despite the North's numerous cruel attempts to incite such revolts in the South.[148]

Most important to our discussion is the fact that none occurred during Lincoln's War.[149] In fact, as we will see in a moment, over a period of hundreds of years, only three so-called "slave revolts" were significant enough to have been given the names of their instigators.[150]

The racist North attributed the dearth of slave rebellions to "the natural docility, laziness, and imbecility of the Negro." But Southerners like the McGavocks, who lived in constant daily close contact with African-Americans, well knew that blacks possessed none of these attributes, and that their "low state" was not their natural condition. It was caused by the "degrading environment" of slavery.[151]

Thus, contrary to the Northern white view of blacks, the average Southern white regarded the average Southern black as ambitious, hard working, skilled, and highly intelligent, which is why, after Lincoln's War, former Confederates, such as General Nathan Bedford Forrest, wanted to help repopulate the South with African immigrants.[152] Of his Southern black brothers and sisters, Forrest said:

> They are the best laborers we have ever had in the South. . . . there is no need for a war of the races. I want to see the whole country

---

146. Katcher, CWSB, p. 225.
147. Garraty and McCaughey, p. 159.
148. M. M. Smith, p. 37.
149. C. Johnson, p. 239.
150. Rosenbaum and Brinkley, s.v. "Slave Revolts."
151. Garraty and McCaughey, p. 81.
152. Hurst, p. 330.

THE MCGAVOCKS OF CARNTON PLANTATION

prosper.[153]

One would have to search long and hard to find an example of a Yankee officer, or any Northerner for that matter, expressing similar sentiments.

So the question remains: in the 250 years that slavery existed in Dixie, why, when it would have been so simple to do so, did slaves not rise up, overtake the South, and free themselves? This question is particularly interestingly in light of the fact that during Lincoln's War, white women, children, and seniors were left alone on their farms for four years, sometimes outnumbered ten to one by their black servants. Why did the slaves on these estates not rise up en masse and either revolt or simply walk away? It would have been ridiculously easy to do.

❧ THE PROSSER AND VESEY "SLAVE REBELLIONS"

There were indeed a few black insurrections in the South, but scarcely enough to be counted on one hand. And of these some were actually instigated by anti-South whites, not Southern blacks.

Moreover, most were so insignificant that they were never even reported. Of the three most important slave revolts, two do not even deserve the name "rebellion," for no rebellion ever actually took place. Let us look at these.

The Gabriel Prosser Rebellion: In 1800 Virginia slave and Methodist, Gabriel Prosser (1776-1800), set out to form a posse and "kill all the whites" in the name of God. But inclement weather delayed his massacre and he was never able to reassemble his mob.

The Denmark Vesey Rebellion: In 1822 South Carolina slave and black racist, Denmark Vesey (1767-1822), also a Methodist, planned to assail the city of Charleston and murder as many whites as possible. Before he could begin his attack, however, his scheme was discovered and he and thirty-four of his fellow black accomplices were hanged.[154]

---

153. Seabrook, NBF, p. 67.
154. Rosenbaum and Brinkley, s.v. "Slave Revolts."

The McGavocks of Carnton Plantation

࿇ THE NAT TURNER "REBELLION"

The Nat Turner Rebellion: This, the third important slave "revolt," only received publicity because of the exceptionally heinous crimes that the psychotic Turner, again a Methodist, and his henchmen committed. For it was not a rebellion in the true sense of the word. It lasted only twelve hours, covered only a few square miles, and in no way advanced the cause of blacks.

Indeed, it reversed it: in its aftermath whites passed new exceptionally harsh slave codes, and abolitionist sentiment, once strong across the entire South, was considerably dampened for several years. Despite these facts, pro-North historians have had little choice but to admit that Turner's was "the most serious uprising in the history of American slavery."[155]

Additionally, this incident cannot be attributed specifically to *Southern* slavery. Why? Because it occurred thirty years before the "Civil War," when both slavery and the slave trade were still being openly practiced by tens of thousands of people in the North. In fact, much if not all of the responsibility for the Nat Turner Rebellion must lie with William Lloyd Garrison's Northern newspaper, *The Liberator*, which was read primarily by blacks, not whites.[156]

The Yankee paper's articles were filled with antislavery and anti-South propaganda of the most inaccurate, overly embellished, vituperative, and absurd kind. Sadly, Turner and his followers, inflamed by this nonsense, sought their revenge on a white society almost wholly innocent of Garrison's accusations and lies.[157] Since we are striving to learn the truth about Southern slavery, as well as the McGavocks' role in the institution, a brief overview of this "slave revolt" will be beneficial.

At 2:00 A.M., on August 21, 1831, Turner (1800-1831), an escaped servant operating under a series of obscure and dubious "signs from Heaven," led a fifty-member gang of vicious blacks on a murderous rampage through Jerusalem, Southampton County, Virginia. Using axes,

---

155. Rosenbaum and Brinkley, s.v. "Slave Revolts."
156. Furnas, p. 408; Rosenbaum and Brinkley, s.v. "Liberator, The."
157. Seabrook, L, pp. 345-346.

The McGavocks of Carnton Plantation

hatchets, and knives rather than firearms (to avoid detection), they tortured, butchered, and killed entire European-American families, mostly women and children, almost none who owned slaves or who even had slave owning relatives.

Under Turner's racist orders to "kill all whites," Caucasian men, women, children, and even newborn infants, were all slain with equal and unmerciful ferocity, usually while asleep in their beds. As their victims slumbered peacefully, Turner and his butchers sank freshly sharpened axes deep into their skulls. Most never woke up. Those who did were greeted with scenes of horror beyond all description. Of this diabolical massacre one historian notes that all that was left afterward were pillaged homes and headless bodies strewn across the town.[158]

Turner later gleefully bragged of his foul deeds. At a plantation owned by the Whitehead family, for example, he boasted that he grabbed a struggling Margaret Whitehead, "and after repeated blows with a sword, I killed her by a blow on the head, with a fence rail."[159]

During Turner's psychopathic killing spree nearly sixty innocent defenseless whites died, many who were, like a majority of Southerners, ardent abolitionists.

Four weeks later Turner and most of his fellow murderers were captured. The violent outlaw never showed any remorse for his crimes, and on November 11, he and some twenty of his followers were hanged for their senseless outrages. "Senseless" because Virginia was the most zealous antislavery state in the South, perhaps even in the entire nation at the time, with a strong abolition movement that dated back to before the formation of the U.S. Indeed, the entire American abolition movement had begun in Virginia.[160]

❧ THE JOHN BROWN "SLAVE REBELLION"

The next "slave rebellion" of any consequence has also been misnamed, for it was not instigated by slaves, or even by free blacks, but by a white

---

158. Blassingame, p. 129.
159. T. R. Gray, p. 13.
160. Kennedy, p. 91.

The McGavocks of Carnton Plantation

Northerner.

This particular "revolt" occurred twenty-eight years after Turner's debacle and was headed by New Englander John Brown (1800-1859), an antislavery-obsessed madman from Torrington, Connecticut.

To Brown, Southern blacks, for reasons he and many other Northerners could not comprehend, were unwilling to mutiny, overturn their plantations, and kill their white owners and their families. Brown decided that a white man needed to goad them into action.

The fanatic began his insane escapade when pro-states' rights forces (known wrongly by Northerners as "pro-slavery" forces) burned down the town of Lawrence, Kansas, on May 21, 1856, in anger over increasing anti-states' rights sentiment (known wrongly by Northerners as "antislavery" sentiment) in the area. The "Sacking of Lawrence," as it is called, outraged Brown, who immediately called for revenge.[161]

On the evening of May 24, during a surprise night attack, he hacked five unarmed, pro-states' rights men to death with swords at Pottawatomie Creek, Kansas. Brown's innocent victims were: William Sherman, Allen Wilkinson, William Doyle, James Doyle, and Drury Doyle. Instead of helping his cause, however, Brown's pointless and bloody binge only further incited Southern whites against him, heightening tensions in the Kansas Territory guerrilla war that would one day become known as "Bleeding Kansas."[162]

Not surprisingly, Southern blacks did not support Brown either. Indeed, while he did his best to galvanize African-Americans to turn against their owners and join him, after several years he managed to interest only five former black servants in enlisting in his mob. The other sixteen men in his twenty-two man team were white, many of them his own family members.

Brown next intended to capture the Federal armory at Harpers Ferry, Virginia (in what is now part of Jefferson County, West Virginia), then emancipate all the servants in the area. He assumed that learning of his "noble crusade," thousands of freed blacks would unite with him,

---

161. Current, TC, s.v. "Bleeding Kansas."
162. Boatner, s.v. "Bleeding Kansas"; Rosenbaum, s.v. "Brown, John."

after which he would lead the resulting army across the South, liberating the region's remaining bondsmen and bondswomen as he went.

The plan was so absurd, so unworkable, so impossible, that even black abolition leaders, like Frederick Douglass (1817-1895), tried to dissuade him from going through with it, calling the scheme suicidal.[163]

Brown was not one to be reasoned with, however. Like Turner, he claimed to have had numerous visions in which God appointed him to "free the slaves." The Bible-thumping Connecticuter could not have been very familiar with the Good Book, however, because, as we will see, throughout the Old and New Testaments, far from condemning slavery, God overtly encourages it, Jesus ignores it, and Saint Paul condones it.

With delusional un-biblical reveries filling his head, and with thousands of dollars in support money from other wrong-headed Northerners, on October 16, 1859, the serial-killer led his tiny band of mercenaries on an attack against the arsenal buildings at Harpers Ferry.[164] A two-day skirmish ensued, which ended on the 18th with Brown's capture.

The ill-informed Yankee was tried and convicted, and on December 2 he was executed by hanging for treason against the state of Virginia.[165] In the crowd was a cousin of mine, a man soon to become known as "Stonewall Jackson," who no doubt retained the memory of this bizarre episode in American history until the day he himself died a

---

163. Born Frederick Augustus Washington Bailey in Talbot County, Maryland, Douglass was the son of a white father and a black mother. After freedom he adopted the surname Douglass, which he borrowed from James Douglas, the hero of Sir Walter Scott's (1771-1832) poem, *Lady of the Lake*. Douglass' two marriages, the first to a black woman (Anna Murray), the second to a white woman (Helen Pitts), caused considerable controversy at the time. After purchasing his freedom he went on to become the most famous black civil rights leader and orator in early American history. His impassioned antislavery lectures, books, and his newspaper, the *North Star*, aided the movement to finally abolish the "peculiar institution" that had begun years earlier in the North. However, unlike pacifist William Lloyd Garrison, feminist-abolitionist and former Northern slave Sojourner Truth, and many others, Douglass eventually began advocating violence as a means to end servitude, one of the few beliefs he had in common with his so-called "friend" President Lincoln. Wilson and Ferris, s.v. "Douglass, Frederick."

164. One of Brown's more famous supporters was Allan Pinkerton, who gave his moniker to the famous detective agency of the same name. Pinkerton donated $500 to Brown, the equivalent of about $13,000 dollars today. Shenkman and Reiger, p. 100.

165. Boatner, s.v. "Brown, John."

few years later, on May 10, 1863. Ironically, General Jackson passed away in the middle of Lincoln's own failed attempt to start a black insurrection in the South.

South-hating Northerners, such as Henry David Thoreau (1817-1862), Ralph Waldo Emerson (1803-1882), Horace Greeley (1811-1872), Louisa May Alcott (1832-1888), William Cullen Bryant (1794-1878), William Henry Seward (1801-1872), Henry Wadsworth Longfellow (1807-1882), Franklin Benjamin Sanborn (1831-1917), and James Russell Lowell (1819-1891)—some of these individuals who had actually bankrolled Brown—hailed him as a martyred saint, one who had died, like Jesus, to save mankind from sin.[166]

But what was the South's sin? Slavery? As we will discuss in more detail shortly, this "sin" started in the North which then pushed it southward, a fact Thoreau, Emerson, Greeley, and the others never discussed let alone acknowledged.

Despite Brown's deification in the North, even Lincoln, whose favorite song was now *John Brown's Body*,[167] pronounced the radical's "slave revolt" a failure, as he noted on February 27, 1860, during his Cooper Union Speech:

> John Brown's effort was peculiar. It was not a slave insurrection. It was an attempt by white men to get up a revolt among slaves, in which the slaves refused to participate. In fact, it was so absurd that the slaves, with all their ignorance, saw plainly enough it could not succeed.[168]

Our sixteenth president was rarely ever so honest and accurate.

Ironically, one of the five people Brown and his men killed

---

166. To their credit not all Yankees idolized Brown. Of the anti-South madman, Massachusettsian Nathaniel Hawthorne (1804-1864), author of *The Scarlet Letter* (1850), *The House of the Seven Gables* (1851), and *The Blithedale Romance* (1852), said: "Nobody was ever more justly hanged." N. Hawthorne, Vol. 12, p. 327.
167. Not all Northerner's appreciated the macabre, overtly anti-South tone of *John Brown's Body*. One, U.S. General George B. McClellan, found it so offensive he tried to have it banned, unsuccessfully. It remained popular enough in the North, however, that the music from the song—by composer William Steffe (1830-1890)—was later used to support the lyrics of the American patriotic anthem, *The Battle Hymn of the Republic*, written by Northern abolitionist Julia Ward Howe (1819-1910). McKissack and McKissack, p. 131.
168. Nicolay and Hay, ALCW, Vol. 1, p. 609.

during their "uprising" to save blacks from slavery, was a free Southern black man named Heyward Shepherd, who had refused to join his band of hair-brained assassins.[169]

❧ WHY SOUTHERN BLACKS REMAINED IN THE SOUTH

But not even Brown's futile attempt at fanning the flames of racial hatred and his ignoble death on the gallows could inspire 3.5 million black Southern servants to rebel. As has been pointed out by Northern historians, despite the fact that the number of blacks moving from south to north was "mysteriously tiny in number," this certainly was not due to cowardice. Blacks had fought courageously in nearly every American war up until 1860.[170]

No doubt one of the reasons for the Southern slave's antipathy toward freedom lay in his own pre-American "utter familiarity" with the institution. For the average Southern black slave's African forebears were almost certainly either slaves or slave owners and slave-traders themselves.

Thus to newly arriving blacks in New York, Rhode Island, or Massachusetts, the concept of slavery in America was by and large taken for granted. In fact, in the antebellum period few blacks were even aware that there were parts of the world where slavery did not exist, and so scarcely gave any thought to striving for emancipation. This is why, up until 1860, only a mere one two-thousandth, or about .05 percent, of the South's total slave population of 3.5 million, fled North in anticipation of freedom.[171]

Little changed after Lincoln launched his illicit war against the South in 1861. Even then 95 percent of all Southern black servants chose to remain in the South,[172] on their masters' plantations, where safety and certainty reigned.[173]

Southern blacks were indeed, by and large, completely

---

169. Grissom, p. 129.
170. Furnas, p. 400.
171. Furnas, pp. 400, 401.
172. Gragg, p. 88.
173. Current, LNK, p. 228.

The McGavocks of Carnton Plantation

uninterested in leaving their Dixie homeland and heading North, before, during, or after the War. This explains why, though the Underground Railroad functioned throughout most of the conflict, only about 4,000 total (just 1,000 Southern slaves a year) out of 3.5 million availed themselves of it—a mere 0.11 percent of the total.[174] The rest voluntarily stayed at home, defending both their owners' farms, and the owners themselves, from marauding Yanks.[175]

It was this same loyal, stay-at-home group—representing 95 percent of all Southern blacks (a group even recognized by Lincoln)[176]—that eventually inspired the concept of sharecropping: as nearly all slaves refused to leave their plantations after emancipation, the owners simply subdivided their land into small plots and turned them over to their new freedmen and freedwomen. This saved blacks from having to seek employment elsewhere (or worse, try and raise money to buy their own land), while it saved plantation owners the trouble of trying to find new employees.[177]

There was something far deeper going on here than just mere practicality, however. Former slaves quite rightly considered themselves true Americans and true Southerners. After all, by 1860, 99 percent of all blacks were native-born Americans, a larger percentage than for whites.[178] As 19th-Century African-Americans saw it, they had been born in the South, lived their whole lives in the South, and would die in the South, just as had all of their known ancestors—who lay buried in cemeteries all across Dixie. In short, the South was their home and they would not leave it; not for John Brown, not for freedom, not for money.

Obviously we are not trying to diminish the immorality and hardships of slavery here. However, it must be said that had there been universal misery and unrest among black servants across the South, many more than a mere 5 percent would have "escaped" North. Even those few who did, almost always ran by themselves, or with just one other,

---

174. Rosenbaum and Brinkley, s.v. "Underground Railroad."
175. Gragg, pp. 191-192.
176. See e.g., Nicolay and Hay, ALCW, Vol. 2, pp. 473-474.
177. White, Foscue, and McKnight, p. 212.
178. Fogel and Engerman, pp. 23-24.

and none fled from the stereotypical large gangland-style plantations.[179]

This black apathy toward liberty, of course, worked against the Yankees' liberal political agenda. And so in 1863, five years later, one more attempt would be made to incite a nationwide African uprising, this time by America's own highest leader, the states' rights-loathing, Southerner-turned-Northerner, Abraham Lincoln.

❧ ABRAHAM LINCOLN'S "SLAVE REBELLION"

On January 1, 1863, halfway through his War, as Northern support for the conflict was plunging, Lincoln calculatingly issued his Final Emancipation Proclamation in the South in the hope of redirecting the character of the War from "preserving the Union," his original publically proclaimed motivation, to ridding the nation of the "evils of Southern slavery."

We know this was a sinister plot and a political ploy of the lowest kind for several reasons; and the South knew it too, which is why, agreeing with Jefferson Davis, the Richmond *Examiner* called it the most shocking crime perpetuated by a politician in the history of the U.S.[180]

There was good reason for this statement: Lincoln's Emancipation Proclamation was unconstitutional, and therefore unlawful, for a country cannot issue laws in another. A joke circulated in the South at the time: in retaliation for Lincoln's edict, President Davis would now issue an "Enslavement Proclamation" that would declare all blacks in the North slaves on January 1, 1864.[181]

Lincoln's Emancipation Proclamation was abhorred over much of Europe as well. London's newspaper, the *Spectator*, called it "a very sad document," and "a hypocritical sham,"[182] one the London *Standard* said was meant to intentionally "deceive England and Europe." The London *Times* denounced it as "the wretched makeshift of a pettifogging lawyer," one who was doing his best to "excite a servile war in the States

---

179. Furnas, pp. 400, 401.
180. Current, TC, s.v. "African-Americans in the Confederacy."
181. Wiley, SN, p. 39.
182. W. B. Garrison, CWTFB, p. 93.

THE MCGAVOCKS OF CARNTON PLANTATION

he cannot occupy with his armies."[183] On October 11, 1862, the *Spectator* supported this view, adding:

> The [U.S.] Government liberates the enemy's slaves as it would the enemy's cattle, simply to weaken them in the coming conflict. . . . The principle asserted is not that a human being cannot justly own another, but that he cannot own him unless he is loyal to the United States.[184]

How true! And what rank hypocrisy all of this was, for at the time not only was slavery still unofficially legal (and practiced) in the North,[185] but Northern free blacks were still subject to strict Jim Crow laws that prohibited them from riding alongside whites, voting, sitting on juries, attending white churches, being buried in white cemeteries, marrying whites, or even becoming U.S. citizens.[186]

In 1861, just before he himself launched the War at Fort Sumter on April 12, Lincoln promised Confederate Vice President Alexander Hamilton Stephens (1812-1883) that his administration would never "directly or indirectly interfere" with Southern slavery. On March 4, he had uttered the same words in his First Inaugural Address, and even threw his support behind the Fugitive Slave Law (which made it a crime to harbor runaway servants or prevent their arrest, and required them to be returned to their owners).[187] Around the same time he also pushed through Congress an amendment to the Constitution proclaiming that the federal government would forever be denied the power to abolish or interfere with slavery in any way, in any state.[188]

---

183. Foster, pp. 392-393.
184. Bancroft, Vol. 2, p. 339.
185. Farrow, Lang, and Frank, pp. 131-132; Kennedy, pp. 104-105. See also Stampp, p. 271; Meltzer, Vol. 2, pp. 247-248; C. Johnson, pp. 126-128; Rosenbaum and Brinkley, s.v. "Slave Trade"; Durden, p. 288.
186. McKissack and McKissack, p. 151.
187. The Fugitive Slave Law also permitted freedmen and freedwomen to be forcibly returned to their previous owners, and runaways could be legally removed to a state where slavery was still legal and re-sold.
188. Beard and Beard, Vol. 2, pp. 64-65.

The McGavocks & Slavery

Part 2

❧ LINCOLN SHIFTS THE FOCUS OF HIS WAR

WHY DID LINCOLN GO BACK on his word in 1863 and not only interfere with slavery but violently try to abolish it? Because his political ambitions took priority over everything else, even the civil rights of blacks.

Halfway through the conflict, as Northern public support for the president and his War was rapidly declining, and as Northern re-enlistment was plummeting, he saw his political dream slipping away. Issuing the Emancipation Proclamation, he thought, could rekindle support for his War by recasting the conflict from a political one into a moral one.

For Lincoln it was vital that the South be put in the position of the "bad guy," for this would give the North the moral advantage. The most expedient way for the Yanks to do this at the time of course was to transform the motivation behind their War from one being fought against states' rights (which Lincoln deceptively called "preserving the Union") into one begin fought against the preservation of slavery.[189]

America's twenty-eighth president, Woodrow Wilson (1856-

---

189. Scruggs, p. 8.

THE MCGAVOCKS OF CARNTON PLANTATION

1924), concurs with this view, noting that during the first half of the conflict Lincoln had promoted the idea that his War was only about "preserving the Union."[190] But by September 1862, Wilson goes on to say, he had decided that it would help re-energize flagging support for the conflict if he now made it one that was both for the Union *and* against slavery. Simultaneously, the guileful president understood, it would make the South look evil in the eyes of the world and halt any possibility of European recognition of the Confederacy.[191]

Amazingly, Lincoln's scheme to resuscitate the War worked. Buoyed by the recent Yankee "win" at the Battle of Sharpsburg (September 17, 1862),[192] Northerners, unaware of their president's devious intrigue, accepted this unaccountable shift in focus. Hatred of the South was renewed for another two years, which gave Lincoln additional time to grind down the Confederacy.

Of course, as we will see, from the beginning Lincoln's true aim for initiating the War was to extinguish the concept of states' rights in the South so that he could replace the Founder's government, a Confederate Republic, with the extreme liberal, federalist system of government that he preferred, one known as the "American System."

❧ THE REAL REASONS LINCOLN WAS AGAINST SLAVERY

Lincoln's intention behind the abolishment of slavery was just as cynical and self-serving. For him it was never about black civil rights, for he was not even concerned about white civil rights.

No, at first abolition for him was primarily about preventing the

---

190. See e.g., Nicolay and Hay, ALCW, Vol. 2, p. 103.
191. W. Wilson, DR, pp. 226-227.
192. Only Lincoln could have possibly seen what the Yanks call the Battle of Antietam as a Yankee win. The truth is that mainstream historians (i.e., pro-North ones), have long considered Sharpsburg "a draw," with neither side scoring a victory. We in the South would beg to differ, however, with both Lincoln and Northern writers. We see the battle as a Confederate win. Examples: General Robert E. Lee (1807-1870) fought more aggressively and gallantly than the overly cautious Union General George Brinton McClellan (1826-1885), who possessed superior numbers; Rebel General Ambrose Powell Hill (1825-1865) successfully drove back Union General Ambrose Everett Burnside (1824-1881), ending the battle; the Yanks lost far more men than the Confederacy; McClellan did not pursue Lee after he left the field, allowing Lee to safely withdraw his troops back to Virginia, reorganize, and fight another day; finally, shortly after the conflict Lincoln relieved McClellan of his command and sent him home to New Jersey. Confederate victory.

institution from spreading back into the North, and also out into the Western Territories (the as of yet unformed Western states). Indeed, this topic consumed the majority of his time and energy during the famous 1858 senatorial debates between he and Stephen A. Douglas.[193]

The question is why was Lincoln against the expansion of slavery?

The answer is that he and other European-Americans in the North feared that blacks would pour northward and intermix with their children, dilute and corrupt the white race, add an "unwholesome colored population" to the region, endanger racial purity, spread disease, threaten prosperity, lower moral standards, scare off visitors and tourists, frighten away new students of local colleges, encourage further Negro immigration, drive down property values and wages, instigate a massive crime wave, thwart colonization, "abolitionize" and "Africanize" the local white populace, and most important of all, take away jobs from whites.[194]

For Lincoln and his Northern constituents Southern slavery also served as an ideal method of "race control": keeping blacks in bondage in Dixie meant that Northerners need not worry about a "flood of darkies" coming over the Mason-Dixon Line any time soon, with whites "tied down and helpless, and run over like sheep," as Lincoln bluntly put it.[195] With slavery confined to the South Yanks could continue to promote antislavery views without fear of having to actually deal with the "unthinkable horror" of how to handle 3.5 million newly freed, hungry, homeless, and jobless blacks, many of them illiterate, armed, and angry.

This is why for Lincoln the issue was never about permanent and total emancipation. Rather it was about containing the spread of slavery so that racist whites like himself would not have to intermingle with blacks.[196] "If we do not let them [blacks] get together in the [Western] Territories," he said publicly on July 10, 1858, "they won't mix [with

---

193. See e.g., Nicolay and Hay, ALCW, Vol. 1, pp. 221-224.
194. Litwack, NS, pp. 113-152; Garraty and McCaughey, p. 254.
195. Nicolay and Hay, ALCW, Vol. 1, p. 556.
196. Seabrook, L, pp. 353-475; Ransom, p. 173.

THE MCGAVOCKS OF CARNTON PLANTATION

whites] there."[197]

More specifically, as President Wilson writes, in Lincoln's mind it was not a question of slavery continuing in the South or anywhere else. It was a question of keeping it out of the newly developing Western Territories.[198]

On this issue in particular Lincoln had the "almost unanimous" support of the North, nearly all of whose inhabitants agreed with the president that the territories should remain "as white as New England."[199] One of Lincoln's own senators, Lyman Trumbull (1813-1896), summed up the president's feelings on the matter perfectly when he referred to their political party as "the white man's party."[200]

Lincoln was not the first to want to prevent the spread of slavery because, as his group asserted, it would both harm and compete with white society. In fact, he was merely following in the footsteps of a long list of Northerners who had preceded him.

Years before, for example, in 1846, Northern Representative David Wilmot (1814-1868) of Pennsylvania, introduced his Wilmot Proviso to try and prevent the spread of slavery into Western lands acquired from Mexico in the Mexican-American War (1846-1848). His proposition, later known as the "free-soil" position, was not for the sake of blacks, however, as Northern historians insist. It was for the sake of whites.[201]

We will note here that the Free-Soilers, a short-lived coalition party formed in New York in 1848, were not abolitionists demanding free land giveaways from the government, as Yankee propaganda has always portrayed them. To Free-Soilers the term "free-soil" actually meant "soil that is free of black people."[202] For their objection to slavery was not due to a sympathy for blacks, but a sympathy for their own race: they did not want African-Americans settling in the Western Territories

---

197. Nicolay and Hay, ALCW, Vol. 1, p. 257.
198. W. Wilson, DR, pp. 130-131.
199. DiLorenzo, LU, p. 101.
200. *The Congressional Globe*, 36th Congress, 1st Session, p. 58; Carey, p. 181.
201. Woods, p. 45.
202. DiLorenzo, LU, p. 101.

The McGavocks of Carnton Plantation

where they would compete with whites for jobs and land.[203] Wilmot himself declared:

> I have no squeamish sensitiveness upon the subject of slavery, no morbid sympathy for the slave. I plead the cause and the rights of white freemen. I would preserve to free white labor a fair country, a rich inheritance, where the sons of toil, of my own race and own color, can live without the disgrace which association with negro slavery brings upon free labor. I stand for the inviolability of free territory. It shall remain free, so far as my voice or vote can aid in the preservation of its free character. . . . The white laborer of the North claims your service; he demands that you stand firm to his interests and his rights, that you preserve the future homes of his children, on the distant shores of the Pacific, from the degradation and dishonor of negro servitude. Where the negro slave labors, the free white man cannot labor by his side without sharing in his degradation and disgrace.[204]

Wilmot, who once commented that he had spent much of his adult life (like Lincoln) fighting against Northern Abolitionists,[205] later remarked to a colleague:

> By God, sir, men born and nursed of white women are not going to be ruled by men who were brought up on the milk of some damn Negro wench![206]

Lincoln could not have agreed more. On October 16, 1854, during a speech at Peoria, Illinois, he said:

> Whether slavery shall go into Nebraska, or other new Territories, is not a matter of exclusive concern to the people who may go there. The whole nation is interested that the best use shall be made of the Territories. We want them for homes of free white people. This cannot be, to any considerable extent, if slavery shall

---

203. Ransom, p. 173.
204. *Appendix to the Congressional Globe*, 29th Congress, 2nd Session, February 8, 1847, p. 317.
205. Ransom, p. 97.
206. Klinkner and Smith, p. 42.

The McGavocks of Carnton Plantation

be planted within them.[207]

Four years later, on October 16, 1858, at his Alton, Illinois, debate with Stephen A. Douglas, Lincoln reasserted his own views on the matter, this time even more forcefully and clearly:

> Now, irrespective of the moral aspect of this question as to whether there is a right or wrong in enslaving a negro, I am still in favor of our new Territories being in such a condition that white men may find a home—may find some spot where they can better their condition—where they can settle upon new soil, and better their condition in life. I am in favor of this not merely (I must say it here as I have elsewhere) for our own people who are born amongst us, but as an outlet for free white people everywhere, the world over—in which Hans, and Baptiste, and Patrick, and all other men from all the world, may find new homes and better their condition in life.[208]

With such evidence at hand, how long can we continue to call Lincoln the "Great Emancipator"?

❧ THE TRUTH BEHIND LINCOLN'S EMANCIPATION PROCLAMATION

Though you will never read this in a Northern or New South history book, the fact is that Lincoln's Emancipation Proclamation was never intended to be permanent, for he was quite willing to allow the Southern states to reestablish slavery after the War.[209]

More than once Lincoln even suggested that he might not issue any proclamation to free the slaves.[210] Even after it was issued, originally, by his own orders, the Emancipation Proclamation was supposed to be temporary, not permanent, for it would cease when the South (or individual states) surrendered, he maintained.[211] To back up

---

207. Nicolay and Hay, ALCW, Vol. 1, p. 197.
208. Nicolay and Hay, ALCW, Vol. 1, p. 508.
209. Current, LNK, pp. 242-246; W. C. Davis, AHD, p. 164; Weintraub, p. 73.
210. Current, LNK, p. 225.
211. W. B. Garrison, LNOK, p. 181.

THE McGAVOCKS OF CARNTON PLANTATION

his promise he then offered the Confederacy "liberal terms on . . . substantial and collateral points."[212] What were these points?

At least one of them was allowing any Southern state returning to the Union to continue practicing slavery within their borders. Lincoln demanded only one thing: slaves who were already free could not be reenslaved (for eventually he wanted to be able to deport them to Liberia in Africa). As for those still under slavery, he said he would leave their fate to their individual state governments,[213] a states' right he had been defending for many years prior to the War.[214]

In essence, in the Summer and Fall of 1864 complete and full emancipation was not absolutely necessary to Lincoln if a Confederate state would simply surrender peacefully, rejoin the Union,[215] and pay its taxes.[216] After all, his main worry concerning the loss of the Southern states was financial in nature, as he so openly and strongly asserted in his "Message to Congress in Special Session" on July 4, 1861.[217]

Lincoln's Secretary of State Seward confirmed his boss' commitment to allowing slavery to continue in loyal Southern states, stating that the effect of the Emancipation Proclamation and other "war measures" would end with the fighting. It is patently clear then that Lincoln originally intended that the institution of slavery would be reestablished after the South's defeat, or if and when it capitulated.[218]

Further evidence of this is supplied by Lincoln's "Ten Percent Plan," issued in December 1863.[219] Here a Confederate state could be "readmitted" to the Union if just 10 percent of its citizens took an oath of allegiance to the U.S. Afterward, according to the liberal U.S. president, that state could reestablish slavery if it so desired.[220]

On June 9, 1864, Lincoln made reference to his Ten Percent

---

212. Nicolay and Hay, ALCW, Vol. 2, p. 550.
213. Current, LNK, p. 245.
214. Litwack, NS, p. 277.
215. Nicolay and Hay, ALCW, Vol. 2, p. 296.
216. Nicolay and Hay, ALAH, Vol. 10, p. 123.
217. Nicolay and Hay, ALCW, Vol. 2, p. 63. Also see Seabrook, L, pp. 215-246.
218. L. H. Johnson, NAS, p. 141.
219. W. S. Powell, p. 144.
220. See Current, LNK, pp. 223, 239, 240, 241.

The McGavocks of Carnton Plantation

Plan in his "Reply to the Committee Notifying President Lincoln of his Renomination":

> I will say now . . . I approve the declaration in favor of so amending the Constitution as to prohibit slavery throughout the nation. When the people in revolt [that is, in the Confederacy], with a hundred days of explicit notice that *they could within those days resume their allegiance without the overthrow of their institution*, and that they could not so resume it afterward, elected to stand out, such amendment of the Constitution as now proposed became a fitting and necessary conclusion to the final success of the Union cause [emphasis added].[221]

In 1864, according to Confederate Secretary of State Judah Benjamin (1811-1884), far from demanding complete and immediate abolition, Lincoln let it be known that he was willing to allow the issue of slavery to be decided on by a general vote in both the South and the North.[222]

On August 24 of that year Lincoln drafted the following unsent and unused instructions to Henry Jarvis Raymond of the *New York Times*:

> Sir: You will proceed forthwith and obtain, if possible, a conference for peace with Honorable Jefferson Davis, or any person by him authorized for that purpose. You will address him in entirely respectful terms, at all events, and in any that may be indispensable to secure the conference. At said conference you will propose, on behalf of this government, that upon the restoration of the Union and the national authority, the war shall cease at once, all remaining questions to be left for adjustment by peaceful modes. If this be accepted, hostilities to cease at once. If it be not accepted, you will then request to be informed what terms, if any, embracing the restoration of the Union would be accepted. If any such be presented you in answer, you will forthwith report the same to this government, and await further instructions. If the presentation of any terms embracing the restoration of the Union be declined, you will then request to be informed what terms of

---

221. Nicolay and Hay, ALCW, Vol. 2, p. 529.
222. Harwell, p. 307.

peace would be accepted; and, on receiving any answer, report the same to this government, and await further instructions.[223]

Lincoln states unwaveringly here that as long as the Southern states rejoin the Union they can continue slavery; or as he put it more obliquely, "upon restoration of the union . . . all remaining questions [are] to be left for adjustment by peaceful modes." Where is the evidence here that Lincoln was an abolitionist?

What is more, his Emancipation Proclamation did not free slaves in *every* state, that is, in both the North and the South. It liberated them only in the Southern states where he had no legitimate power, for the Confederacy had been a legally separate and independent nation since early 1861.

Why did Lincoln commit this criminal act, and why did he wait so long to do it? The answer to these questions was offered by the president himself.

In a September 2, 1863, letter to Salmon P. Chase, Lincoln admitted that his Emancipation Proclamation was illegal, except as a tactical maneuver.[224] "The original proclamation has no constitutional or legal justification, except as a military measure," he told his secretary of the treasury.[225]

In plain terms, freeing the slaves was, as even Yankee historians are forced to point out, militarily beneficial to the North.[226]

And herein lies a clue to the many authentic reasons Lincoln issued this remarkable document: not only was his supply of white soldiers being quickly depleted—necessitating the need for blacks to enlist (up until then he had been vehemently against the idea), he was also hoping that by announcing that all black servants in the South were free, that they would turn on their owners and overthrow the plantations. The ensuing bloody rebellion would so weaken the Confederacy, Lincoln hoped and predicted, that the South would quickly

---

223. Nicolay and Hay, ALCW, Vol. 2, p. 568.
224. Fehrenbacher, ALSW, pp. 500-501.
225. Nicolay and Hay, ALCW, Vol. 2, pp. 402-403.
226. Hansen, p. 267.

The McGavocks of Carnton Plantation

surrender, bringing the War to an immediate end. This, in turn, would allow him to get back to his original business: installing the American System, this despite the fact that well over 50 percent of the nation (the entire South and much of the North) was against the un-American idea.

Incredibly, Lincoln knew that hundreds of thousands, perhaps millions, would die in the process. But he showed no concern whatsoever. His only interest was to subdue the South in pursuit of his political agenda: to get his party—the liberal party of the industrial, mercantile North—into power so it could establish its business program, one that benefitted Northern businessmen and hurt Southern farmers.[227]

Even many Northerners were horrified at the inhumanity of Lincoln's emancipation plan. Illinois Senator Stephen A. Douglas, for example, introduced a bill that would punish anyone seeking to instigate revolts and riots among Southern slaves. But Lincoln laughed Douglas' recommendation off, calling his entire speech "seditious." When Lincoln himself was questioned about the motivations behind his "war measure," his response was as cold as an Illinois Winter:

> Nor do I urge objection of a moral nature in view of possible consequences of insurrection and massacre at the South.[228]

The wording of Lincoln's Emancipation Proclamation itself suggests an open invitation to Southern blacks to mayhem and murder:

> . . . the Executive Government of the United States, including the military and the naval authority thereof, will recognize and maintain the freedom of such persons, and will do no act or acts to repress such persons, or any of them, in any efforts they may make for their actual freedom.[229]

As history has shown, despite Lincoln's aggressive and callous posturing, his hopeful prognostication turned out to be dead wrong. Not a single

---

227. Simpson, p. 74.
228. Nicolay and Hay, ALCW, Vol. 2, p. 235.
229. Nicolay and Hay, ALCW, Vol. 2, pp. 237, 287.

The McGavocks of Carnton Plantation

slave uprising occurred after his infamous proclamation was issued.

Years before, on April 20, 1848, on the U.S. Senate floor Jefferson Davis had hinted at the reason: I am not afraid that our servants will ever riot, the future Confederate president asserted, for they are cheerful and carefree.[230]

Of course today we know that Southern slaves were not what we would consider happy in the full and true sense of the word. However, according to numerous studies over the years we know that many were at least content, the reasons for which we will examine shortly.

Despite growing support in the North for Lincoln's seemingly humanitarian emancipation plan, Southerners were not fooled by his devious Machiavellian Diplomacy.[231] On January 18, 1863, only seventeen days after he issued his proclamation, here is what one Confederate, my cousin Brigadier General Gideon Johnson Pillow, had to say about the "tyrant and usurper" and his nefarious edict. In search of new recruits, Pillow's letter was addressed to "the people of Tennessee and the Confederate States":

> Having been directed by General [Braxton] Bragg to organize a volunteer and conscript bureau for the purpose of recruiting and strengthening his army and making it self-sustaining, I appeal to you to come promptly to its support.
>
> Upon that army depends the safety of your homes and all that you hold dear. We are no longer in doubt as to the character of the Lincoln despotism. The ruin and desolation which is everywhere left in the track of its armies attests to its vandalism.
>
> The late proclamation of the tyrant and usurper, proposing to free all our slaves and taking them into his Army, and inciting the slaves to insurrection and massacre of their owners and their families, places him and his Government without the pale of civilization. Men who will not resist such a despotism do not deserve to be freemen.[232]

---

230. W. C. Davis, JD, p. 176.
231. Plano, Greenberg, Olton, and Riggs, s.v. "Machiavellian Diplomacy."
232. ORA, Ser. 4, Vol. 2, p. 362.

The McGavocks of Carnton Plantation

The very idea that the North's megalomaniacal leader was willing to exchange the lives of millions of white and black Southerners for political expediency was ghastly to all thinking people. But neither General Pillow or any other Southerner need have worried. No black Southern servants were ever "incited to insurrection and massacre" by Lincoln, or by anyone else, as he himself later grudgingly admitted.[233]

❧ YANKEE BRIBERY, FRAUD, & INTIMIDATION

Even the failure of his Emancipation Proclamation to stir up race riots and initiate the mass murder of millions of Southern whites did not stop Lincoln from pushing forward with his political agenda, however. He had one final trick up his sleeve.

Aside from the many thousands who were captured and forcibly driven North, some blacks did indeed leave their Southern homes during the War in anticipation of freedom in the North. But they did so not in revolt, or out of malevolent anger toward their white overseers. Most left because they were bribed, defrauded, and intimidated by Lincoln's officers, who held out false promises of a better life. The North's intention? An attempt once again to incite slave insurrections in Dixie.

How dismayed many of these particular blacks must have been when upon their "emancipation" they discovered that Lincoln's promise of "forty acres and a mule" was a lie[234] (there were no mules,[235] and Lincoln's "black land giveaways" were only meant to be temporary,[236] and most ultimately went to rich white Northerners anyway),[237] and that the Yanks were freeing them, not out of a humanitarian concern or for black civil rights, but out of purely practical self-interested concern: they needed someone to do the army's drudge work (laundry, cooking, washing dishes, chopping firewood, watering horses, mucking out stalls, road building), forced labor that was little different from what many had

---

233. Nicolay and Hay, ALCW, Vol. 2, p. 454.
234. Mullen, p. 33; Rosenbaum and Brinkley, s.v. "Forty Acres and a Mule."
235. J. H. Franklin, p. 37.
236. Foner, R, pp. 70-71.
237. Thornton and Ekelund, p. 96.

THE MCGAVOCKS OF CARNTON PLANTATION

experienced as bonded servants.²³⁸ Lincoln actually sent many of them back to work on plantations, the very situation he had promised to free them from.²³⁹

In fact, as Yankee General Benjamin F. "the Beast" Butler's word "contraband" for all Southern blacks reveals, even after emancipation, the North still regarded blacks as inferior to whites, and as the legitimate property of whites.²⁴⁰ Likewise, Lincoln and his cohorts never referred to liberated blacks as "freemen." Instead they called them "freedmen": one who has been emancipated but who is not quite truly free.

What does this all of this tell us about so-called "Southern slavery" in the mid-1800s?

❧ THE SOUTHERN BLACK WAR EFFORT

Whatever horrors were inherent to the institution, the form of "slavery" that was practiced by the McGavocks and other Southerners was so mild and benign that few if any blacks were impelled to insurrection, violence, murder, or flight. This is why, throughout Lincoln's War, the vast majority of blacks stayed with their owners in their own homes, and on their own farms and plantations.

Nearly 50 percent of the 200,000 blacks who eventually fought for Lincoln were not "emancipated" Southern black slaves at all, but rather were free Northern blacks,²⁴¹ many no doubt who had been "emancipated" from the pool of 500,000 to 1 million black slaves who lived in the North in 1860.²⁴² As we will see shortly, many more Southern blacks than that stayed at home and fought for the South in one capacity or another.

Indeed, along with the 1 million European-Americans,²⁴³ 70,000

---

238. Furnas, p. 750. For more on the brutal, even murderous slave-like treatment of freed Southern blacks by Yankees, see Wiley, SN, pp. 175-259.
239. Wiley, SN, p. 185.
240. Wiley, SN, p. 175.
241. C. Johnson, p. 170.
242. Eaton, HSC, p. 93; Hinkle, p. 125.
243. Katcher, CWSB, p. 46.

The McGavocks of Carnton Plantation

Native-Americans, 60,000 Hispanic-Americans,[244] 50,000 foreigners,[245] 12,000 Jewish-Americans,[246] and 10,000 Asian-Americans[247] who also fought for the South, an estimated 300,000 Southern black men armed themselves, enlisted, and served heroically under the Rebels' Stars and Bars, tens of thousands more *Southern* blacks than served under the Yanks' Stars and Stripes.[248] This number is even more impressive when we consider that Southern blacks were exempt from the draft: though many were impressed into service, the rest volunteered.[249]

It is clear from raw percentages alone that far more blacks fought for the Confederacy than for the Union. The Confederacy had about 1 million soldiers. Of these an estimated 300,000 were black,[250] 30 percent of the total. The Union had about 3 million soldiers. Of these an estimated 200,000 were black, just 6 percent of the total.[251] Thus the South had 24 percent more black soldiers in its armies than the North.[252]

And these numbers are conservative if we use the definition of a "private soldier" as determined by German-American Union General August Valentine Kautz (1828-1895) in 1864:

> In the fullest sense, any man in the military service who receives pay, whether sworn in or not, is a soldier, because he is subject to military law. Under this general head, laborers, teamsters, sutlers, chaplains, etc., are soldiers.[253]

---

244. Hinkle, p. 108. See also Quintero, Gonzales, and Velazquez, passim.
245. Lonn, p. 218.
246. Rosen, p. 161.
247. Hinkle, p. 108; Blackerby, passim.
248. Barrow, Segars, and Rosenburg, BC, p. 97; *The United Daughters of the Confederacy Magazine*, Vols. 54-55, 1991, p. 32. Some believe the number was closer to 93,000. See Shenkman and Reiger, pp. 105-106; R. M. Brown, p. xiv.
249. E. M. Thomas, p. 236. There are no records of the exact number of blacks that served on either the Confederate side or the Union side, but reliable estimates are still possible.
250. Barrow, Segars, and Rosenburg, BC, p. 97; *The United Daughters of the Confederacy Magazine*, Vols. 54-55, 1991, p. 32.
251. Greenberg and Waugh, p. xi.
252. The exact number of Billy Yanks and Johnny Rebs, by some estimates, was 2,898,304 of the former, 1,234,000 of the latter. Livermore, p. 63. Also see Katcher, CWSB, p. 46.
253. Kautz, p. 11. Using Kautz' definition of a "private soldier," some 2 million Southerners fought in the Confederacy: 1 million whites and perhaps as many as 1 million blacks.

The McGavocks of Carnton Plantation

As most of the 4 million blacks living in the South at the time of Lincoln's War remained loyal to the Confederacy, and as at least 500,000 to 1 million of these either worked in or fought in the Rebel army and navy in some capacity, Kautz's definition raises the percentage of Southern blacks who defended the Confederacy as literal soldiers to as many as 50 percent of the total Confederate soldier population!

Among the list of loyal Southern African-Americans who fought for states' rights were Jacques Esclavon, Gabriel Grappe, Charles Lutz, Jean Baptiste Pierre-August, Levin Graham, Peter Vertrees, Lufray Pierre-August,[254] Henry Love, Hiram Kendael, Joe Warren, Dan Humphreys, George Briggs, Hardin Blackwell, Lewis McConnell, Daniel Robinson, Fielding Rennolds,[255] and Louis Napoleon Nelson,[256] just a few of untold thousands. Most are unnamed and so are destined to be forever unknown. At least 30,000 alone served as faithful body servants to their white Confederate masters.[257]

The numbers were overwhelming. Even anti-South historians have been forced to admit that a "puzzling" number of Southern blacks were ready and willing to fight against Lincoln, the North, and "those damned abolitionists," many blacks even going so far as to buy Confederate bonds,[258] donate money, food, and livestock, sew uniforms, sponsor auctions and bake sales, hold balls, fairs, and parties, and sell off property and anything else that might help advance the Confederate Cause.[259]

From every corner of the new Confederacy were heard accounts of both free and enslaved blacks who were anxious to contribute in some way to the new nation.[260] There were so many black Rebels on the battlefield that Northern soldiers, most who were overtly racist, were

---

254. *The Civil War Book of Lists*, p. 169.
255. Segars and Barrow, BSCA, pp. 48, 99, 142, 200, 221.
256. Louis' grandson is African-American educator and SCV member Nelson W. Winbush, a friend of mine and the foreword writer for my book *Everything You Were Taught About the Civil War is Wrong, Ask a Southerner!*
257. Barrow, Segars, and Rosenburg, BC, p. 71.
258. L. H. Johnson, NAS, p. 180.
259. Quarles, p. 37; Greenberg and Waugh, pp. 372-373.
260. W. C. Davis, LA, p. 142.

THE MCGAVOCKS OF CARNTON PLANTATION

completely dumbstruck at the sight. We should not be surprised to learn then that the first Northerner killed in the War, Major Theodore Winthrop (1828-1861) of the Seventh Regiment, New York State Militia, was brought down by a black Confederate sharpshooter, Private Sam Ashe of the First North Carolina Infantry.[261] General Stonewall Jackson's army alone contained some 3,000 black soldiers, an image that froze Yankees in their tracks in fear and revulsion.[262]

On September 10, 1862, a Union doctor caught sight of Jackson's troops and recorded the following entry in his diary:

> At four o'clock this morning the Rebel army began to move from our town, Jackson's force taking the advance. The movement continued until eight o'clock P.M., occupying sixteen hours. The most liberal calculation could not give them more than 64,000 men. Over 3,000 Negroes must be included in the number. These were clad in all kinds of uniforms, not only in cast-off or captured United States uniforms, but in coats with Southern buttons, State buttons, etc. These were shabby, but not shabbier or seedier than those worn by white men in the rebel ranks. Most of the negroes had arms, rifles, muskets, sabres, bowie-knives, dirks, etc. They were supplied, in many instances, with knapsacks, haversacks, canteens, etc., and they were manifestly an integral portion of the Southern Confederacy Army. They were seen riding on horses and mules, driving wagons, riding on caissons, in ambulances, with the staff of generals and promiscuously mixed up with all the rebel horde.[263]

Countless numbers of Southern blacks voluntarily enlisted in the Confederate army and the Confederate navy, many in brigades that had their own voluntarily all-black musical bands.[264] Thousands more ran away from their plantations, not to join the Yankees and kill Rebels, but

---

261. Winthrop was killed at the Battle of Bethel Church, Virginia, June 10, 1861. Through his father he was a descendant of Englishman John Winthrop (1587-1649), a governor of Massachusetts, while through his mother he descended from the puritanical fire-and-brimstone preacher and famed Yankee theologian, Jonathan Edwards (1703-1758).
262. Hinkle, p. 106.
263. L. H. Steiner, pp. 19-20.
264. See e.g., Salley, Vol. 1, pp. 218-219.

to join the Rebels and kill Yankees. In Charleston, South Carolina—the "cradle of secession," as the Yanks derogatorily called the city[265]—it was noted that there were thousands of blacks building fortifications for the Confederacy. Their main interest was not insurrection and flight northward, but the chance to take up arms and shoot Union soldiers.[266]

In Memphis, Tennessee, hundreds of enthusiastic free blacks marched in a soldierly parade. As the *Memphis Avalanche* "joyously proclaimed":[267]

> "A procession of several hundred stout Negro men, members of the 'domestic institution,' marched through our streets yesterday in military order, under command of Confederate officers. They were all armed and equipped with shovels, axes, blankets, etc. A merrier set were never seen. They were brimful of patriotism, shouting for Jeff. Davis and singing war songs." And four days later it again said: "Upward of one thousand Negroes, armed with spades and pickaxes, have passed through the city within the past few days. Their destination is unknown; but it is supposed that they are on their way to the other side of Jordan." The drafting of colored men, and especially of slaves, by thousands to work on Confederate fortifications, was, in general, rather ostentatiously paraded through the earlier stages of the war. A paper published at Lynchburg, Virginia, had as early as April, chronicled the volunteered enrollment of seventy of the free Negroes of that place to fight in defense of their State; closing with, "Three cheers for the patriotic free Negroes of Lynchburg."[268]

If more proof of Southern black support for the Confederacy is required we need look no further than a letter written by former Northern slave Frederick Douglass to Lincoln in 1862. In it the black civil rights leader used the example of the overwhelming number of blacks in the Confederate army to urge the president to allow blacks to officially enlist in the Union army (Lincoln had steadfastly refused up

---

265. Pollard, LC, p. 434.
266. Rogers, AGA, p. 151.
267. See the *Memphis Avalanche*, September 3, 1861.
268. Alexander, p. 338.

THE McGAVOCKS OF CARNTON PLANTATION

until that time). Wrote Douglass to the president:

> There are at the present moment, many colored men in the Confederate Army doing duty not only as cooks, servants and laborers, but as real soldiers, having muskets on their shoulders and bullets in their pockets, ready to shoot down loyal [Yankee] troops, and do all that soldiers may do to destroy the Federal government and build up that of the traitors and rebels. There were such soldiers at Manassas, and they are probably there still. There is a negro in the [Confederate] army as well as in the fence, and our Government is likely to find it out before the war comes to an end. That the negroes are numerous in the rebel army, and do for that army its heaviest work, is beyond question.[269]

Douglass was highly desirous of a military commission himself, in this case as an assistant adjutant to Yankee General Lorenzo Thomas. But he was ignored, and the invitation he "fondly hoped" for (to become a member of Lincoln's armed forces) never came.[270] Douglass, a "friend" of Lincoln's, rightly accused the president of fighting with his "white hand" while keeping his "black hand" tied and bound.[271]

It was not just male blacks who "did duty" in the Rebel military as soldiers. We also know of black female Rebel soldiers,[272] some, like "Confederate Mary," who served as spies; some, like Hattie Carter, who served as ammunition runners; others who disguised themselves as males in order to get a shot at Lincoln's men and proudly defend Dixie, their beloved homeland. As part of their training many all-black Confederate military units set up a dummy of Lincoln and practiced running it through with swords. The brag among black Confederate soldiers was: a Southern Negro can whip any Northern Negro—and the white Yankee to boot.[273]

When my cousin General Richard Taylor (1826-1879), the son

---

269. *Douglass' Monthly*, September, 1861, Vol. 4, p. 516.
270. Douglass, LTFD, p. 805.
271. Buckley, p. 89.
272. Barrow, Segars, and Rosenburg, BC, p. 95.
273. Greenberg and Waugh, pp. 373, 382, 387, 393.

The McGavocks of Carnton Plantation

of former U.S. President Zachary Taylor (1784-1850), met up with some black Rebel troops in Mobile, Alabama, in late 1864, he found them hard at work on fortifications. When the conversation turned to the Confederate African-American war effort, one of the black soldiers told Taylor:

> If you will give us guns we will fight for these works, too. We would rather fight for our own white folks than for strangers.[274]

Likewise, when James Chesnut, Jr. (1815-1885) spoke to his black servants about enlisting in the Confederate military, his wife Mary noted that nearly all were keen to enlist and fight.[275] They were happy, the famed diarist continued, to serve in the Confederate army if James would only give them arms and in return grant them land and their freedom.[276]

Confederate Secretary of State Judah Benjamin had a similar experience. One day his slaves came to him and declared:

> Master, set us free, and we will fight for you. We had rather fight for you than for the Yankees.[277]

On July 4, 1861, one of the many thousands of slaves who joined the Confederate army, Thomas A. Phelps, wrote from Virginia to his mother at home, saying:

> I take this opportunity of writing to you to let you know that I am well and doing well, and I hope that this letter will find you as well as I am now in Yorktown. I will leave at 4 o'clock p. m. today for a scout about the woods for the Yankees. . . . We are looking out for a fight on the 5th of July by the 5th Regiment Louisiana volunteers. Give my love to Mistress and Master Jim Phelps, and to all of them in New Orleans. You must excuse this bad writing.

---

274. R. Taylor, p. 249.
275. Foote, Vol. 3, p. 755.
276. Chesnut, MCCW, p. 313.
277. Lubbock, p. 561.

The McGavocks of Carnton Plantation

> I am writing in a hurry; have not time to write. I am about to leave for the Mill. So good by all. No more at present.
> Your devoted son, THOMAS A PHELPS
> P. S. — Good by to the white folks until I kill a Yankee.[278]

Unfortunately, letters like this do not conform to Northern and New South myths about Southern blacks and slavery, and so they have been disregarded or even suppressed.

Many postwar Southern whites credited Southern blacks with literally saving the South from complete and utter destruction. How?

With the bulk of the young and middle-aged white males away on the battlefield, it was primarily the work, intelligence, bravery, and talents of Southern African-American servants—who remained at home and kept the farms going, provided food and supplies for the Confederate armies, and who protected white females and their children against the ravages of Lincoln's blue-coated meddling invaders—that spared Dixie from utter annihilation.

Indeed, Yankee commanders on the battlefield frequently complained of this very reality, which is one of the reasons they suggested "freeing" Southern black slaves. Not to give them freedom and equal rights with whites, but to eliminate the Confederacy's primary support system: millions of loyal Southern blacks who had refused to leave their homes, farms, and plantations. For by staying at home in the South, they helped maintain Southern resolve, supported Confederate troops, and protected Southern families.

Lincoln himself recognized this fact, which is one of the main reasons he issued his Emancipation Proclamation: he believed that freeing Southern slaves would cause them to flee North, disrupting the foundation of both Southern society and the Confederacy's military.[279]

Yankee Quartermaster-General Montgomery Cunningham Meigs (1816-1892) was of the same mind, as he grumbled in an official report on November 18, 1862:

---

278. Wallcut, p. 20.
279. See Lapsley, Vol. 7, pp. 337-338.

THE MCGAVOCKS OF CARNTON PLANTATION

> The labor of the colored man supports the rebel soldier, enables him to leave his plantation to meet our armies, builds his fortifications, cooks his food, and sometimes aids him on picket by rare skill with the rifle.[280]

Meigs then recommends liberating Southern blacks; again, not for the purpose of civil rights. He, like Lincoln, merely wanted to employ them in the Northern army, and then only if segregated from whites and "put under strict military control." As the Union officer wrote:

> In all these modes it [that is, the labor of Southern blacks] is available to assist our Army, and it is probable that there will be less outrage, less loss of life, by freeing these people, if put under strict military control, than if left to learn slowly that war has removed the white men who have heretofore held them in check, and to yield at last to the temptation to insurrection and massacre.[281]

Like Lincoln's, Meigs' wish for "insurrection and massacre" also failed to materialize, and Southern blacks, in their millions, remained at home where they continued to support the Confederate Cause in whatever way they could. Indeed, this is how the Southern tradition of sharecropping began: after the War planters subdivided their land into small plots, known as "fragmented plantations," that were then tilled by millions of former black servants. Where did they come from? They never left. When Lincoln illegally invaded the South in 1861 they had refused to leave.[282]

The numbers were enormous. Even the most virulent South-hating scholars and authors admit that at least 80 percent of all Southern black servants stayed in Dixie with their white families.[283] But the actual

---

280. ORA, Ser. 3, Vol. 2, p. 809.
281. ORA, Ser. 3, Vol. 2, p. 809.
282. White, Foscue, and McKnight, p. 212. It should be pointed out that there were also white sharecroppers. Wilson and Ferris, s.v. "Plantations."
283. Genovese, p. 97.

The McGavocks of Carnton Plantation

percentage was much higher: of the South's 3,500,000 black servants, only one in twenty, or just 5 percent, joined the Yanks. The other 95 percent maintained their loyalty to Dixie.[284] Those thousands who marched off to war against Lincoln proudly wore Confederate gray, with placards on their hats reading: "We will die by the South."[285]

In May 1865, one month after War's end, Chesnut remarked that in her region there was not a single case of a servant betraying their master or mistress, and that on most plantations "things looked unchanged." Blacks, now free laborers known as "plantation hands," were still working in the fields of their original white families, as if not one of them had ever seen a Yankee or even knew they existed.[286]

Out of the hundreds of her father-in-law's "slaves," only one left the plantation to be with the Yankees, Chesnut records. A black butler named Eben fled to the other side under the assumption that the invading Northern forces had come to "save niggers." But he soon eagerly returned to his station in the Chesnuts' kitchen after unscrupulous Federal soldiers stole his favorite belonging: a watch and chain.[287]

Thus it could truly be said that while white Southern soldiers lost on the battlefield, Southern black servants won the War on the home front by helping to preserve families and their agricultural holdings across Dixie. Except for the many Southern lives themselves that were expended in the fight against the North, no single greater contribution to the South's War effort can be named. Europe never came close to providing even a fraction of this type of support to the Confederacy. Noted African-American historian Benjamin Quarles considers the Southern black's contribution to the Confederate Cause beyond measure.[288]

❧ SLAVERY IN THE 21st CENTURY

Today no sensible person supports the idea of authentic slavery, which

---

284. Current, LNK, p. 228; Gragg, p. 88. See also Barney, p. 141.
285. Barrow, Segars, and Rosenburg, BC, pp. 8, 25.
286. Chesnut, MCCW, pp. 801, 834, 835.
287. Chesnut, MCCW, pp. 803, 823-824.
288. Quarles, p. 273.

The McGavocks of Carnton Plantation

contradicts all of our modern concepts of civil and natural rights. Pure and simple, the concept of one human being the legal property of another is a degrading horror and a wretched evil. Without question most modern Americans would agree with the black servant Linda Brent who, in 1861, wrote of the institution that it is a "deep, and dark, and foul . . . pit of abominations."[289] Like nearly all other Southerners past and present, I could not agree more.

The truth, however, is that this "pit of abominations," far from being a 19th-Century Southern phenomenon, was one that began long before in far off lands, in particular in Africa herself,[290] where tribal wars and inter-tribal raids helped enrich African chiefs through the capture and selling of fellow Africans into bondage.

The slaves created from this thriving industry were sold not only by Africans to other Africans, but later also to Arabian and European slave traders.[291] In fact, not only does the trade and the practice of slavery continue worldwide to this day—both in Africa and in numrous other nations, including the U.S.—but there are more slaves now than ever before in human history.[292]

While most Americans assume that Lincoln's War ended slavery everywhere in 1865, the tragic fact is that it has always existed—and still does. At this very moment there are an estimated 200 million people in bondage around the globe (two-thirds of the entire population of the U.S.), part of the flourishing worldwide slave industry that, along with Africa, also includes countries such as India, Haiti, the Dominican Republic, Thailand, and Pakistan.

The Thirteenth Amendment did not even manage to end slavery in the U.S., for America continues to be home to a major portion of the international slavery business. According to a 1999 CIA study, some 50,000 people a year, mostly women and children, are brought to America as slaves and set to work as farmhands, sweatshop laborers,

---

289. Brent, p. 6.
290. Civil War Society, ECW, s.v. "Slavery."
291. Blassingame, pp. 3, 5-6, 10, 14.
292. "CNN Newsroom," CNN News, June 10, 2008.

prostitutes, and private house servants.[293]

The situation has grown so serious that it has spawned a 21st-Century abolitionist movement across the U.S., and organizations like the Los Angeles-based Coalition to Abolish Slavery and Trafficking, are forming to assist those caught up in the web of the modern-day American slave trade.[294]

While Africa was practicing slavery on her own people long before the arrival of Arabic, European, and American slave traders, as mentioned, it continues there today as well. An estimated 200,000 African children alone are sold into slavery each year by other Africans, while in the region of North Africa, as just one example, some 90,000 adults are currently enslaved, human chattel that sell for a mere $15.00 a person.[295]

This is far below the value assigned to black servants by American Southerners in the 1800s. The average price for a black servant in the Victorian South was $2,000, about $55,000 in today's currency. As the War progressed and inflation rose, so too did the price of Southern servants, until near the end of the conflict they were selling in Richmond, Virginia, for $10,000 each,[296] the equivalent of about $250,000 today—the price of the average modern American house.

❧ UNCLE TOM'S CABIN

All Western societies today recognize the immorality of slavery and condemn it as an affront to civilized humanity. At the same time it must be acknowledged that the idea that every aspect of Southern "slavery" as it was practiced in the 17th, 18th, and 19th Centuries was hideously cruel and barbaric, is an invention of anti-South propagandists.

Indeed, this particular stereotype derives almost wholly from one of the North's most infamous anti-South propagandists, Yankee author Harriet Beecher Stowe (1811-1896). An abolitionist from

---

293. Website: www.pbs.org/newshour/bb/law/jan-june01/slavery_3-8.html.
294. See Website: www.castla.org.
295. Website: www.infoplease.com/spot/slavery1.html.
296. Litwack, BSSL, p. 35; Wiley, PPC, p. 97.

THE MCGAVOCKS OF CARNTON PLANTATION

Connecticut who moved to Ohio, Stowe worked tirelessly to rid the nation of slavery by writing such provocative books as *Uncle Tom's Cabin*. We can certainly applaud her for her efforts.

There was just one problem with Stowe's antislavery works: they were all based on information she had gained secondhand, and that from unreliable biased sources.[297] For Stowe never stepped foot on a Southern plantation, had no firsthand knowledge of slavery, and never even visited the South.[298] In fact, like most Northerners then as now, she had no idea what a plantation was or how slavery was practiced, and even less knowledge of what life was like outside Cincinnati, where her notorious book was written.[299]

So she made up stories based on how she wanted to think Southern "slavery" was practiced, chronicling what she believed the institution to be rather than what it actually was. Her characters, drawn from her vivid imagination and from slanted and vitriolic South-loathing abolitionist tracts, were little more than two-dimensional cartoon-like stereotypes that never existed in Dixie.[300]

President Woodrow Wilson rightly asserts that the abuses portrayed in Stowe's book "were in every sense exceptional" in the South,[301] calling her book the "product of the sympathetic imagination, which the historian must reject as quite misleading."[302]

In her diaries Chesnut describes *Uncle Tom's Cabin* as

---

297. Rosenbaum and Brinkley, s.v. "Uncle Tom's Cabin."
298. Garraty and McCaughey, p. 230.
299. Northern propaganda has long defined a plantation as "a large, Southern cotton estate, ruled by racist, indolent whites, and worked by black slave labor." In reality, a plantation is nothing more than a term for a large farm, and has nothing to do with the South, cotton, white planters, or black slavery. Indeed, in the 1700s and early 1800s, plantations, with and without slaves, were common across the North as well. See Seabrook, EYWTACWW, pp. 91-94. The origins of the plantation predates even the voyages of Columbus, with a history that extends over five continents, enduring long after the American "Civil War" was over. Curtin, RFPC, p. xiii. Webster thus correctly defines a plantation as simply "a place that is planted or under cultivation; an agricultural estate usually worked by resident labor." Mish, s.v. "plantation." Rhodes Island's original name, for example, was "Rhode Island and Providence Plantations," a carryover from the 1600s when the slave-heavy state was first named. J. B. Scott, pp. 84-85. See also pp. 86-87.
300. Civil War Society, ECW, s.v. "Stowe, Harriet Beecher."
301. W. Wilson, DR, pp. 126-127.
302. W. Wilson, DR, p. 181.

THE MCGAVOCKS OF CARNTON PLANTATION

"sickening,"³⁰³ and Stowe herself as "nasty" and "coarse."³⁰⁴ As for the woman's highly inventive mind, Chesnut calls it detestable and repugnant. Stowe writes her books by making things up out of thin air,³⁰⁵ the diarist penned, a common and accurate complaint across the South.

Understandably besieged by overwhelming criticism from both Southerners and Northerners for her wildly embellished tales, Stowe later admitted that her book was not meant to be taken literally, and that it was more a work of art than fact—this despite her strange claim that God had commanded her to write it.³⁰⁶

Unbeknownst to most of those who are familiar with her highly fictitious tale, the extremely cruel slave owner in her book, Simon Legree (whose surname she misspells),³⁰⁷ along with all of the other evil folks brought forth from her overwrought imagination, are *Northerners*, whose poor, exploited, and mistreated slaves live and work on imaginary farms in states Stowe never visited.³⁰⁸ Furthermore, while Legree himself was a transplanted Yankee from Connecticut, most of the *Southern* characters in Stowe's book are portrayed as outstanding and empathetic individuals.³⁰⁹

The reality is that *Uncle Tom's Cabin* was a work of Yankee propaganda, a political fiction full of both misinformation and disinformation, meant to rouse Northern passions against the institution of slavery, a common ploy of Northern abolitionists. Stowe, in fact, knew literally nothing about blacks, slavery, the South, plantation life, or African-American culture. And the violence, unethical treatment, and immorality she portrayed between black slaves and their masters and mistresses was not only rare, but was in fact illegal in the South,

---

303. Chesnut, DD, p. 184.
304. Chesnut, DD, p. 189.
305. Chesnut, MCCW, pp. 583, 730.
306. Lewis, p. 292.
307. Stowe named her lead character, the much-hated fanciful figure, Simon Legree, after a real slave owner in South Carolina with the surname Legare. Chesnut, MCCW, p. 168.
308. Rosenbaum and Brinkley, s.v. "Uncle Tom's Cabin."
309. Garraty and McCaughey, p. 230.

punishable by law, and condemned by all good Southern people.[310] Her portrait of plantation life was, in the end, highly distorted and irrational, while her black characters were atypical.[311]

It is important to note that Stowe's novel was actually inspired by the book *Truth Is Stranger Than Fiction*, the autobiography of Josiah Henson (1789-1883), a *Northern* slave.[312] In her appeal to end slavery Stowe tried to incite Northern hatred toward the South by denigrating the people of Dixie. But in fact she revealingly based most of her story on the behavior of *Northern* slave owners from Maryland, Henson's birthplace. So much for this disreputable piece of anti-South fiction.

We have other evidence that Southern slavery was not what we have been taught by Northern and New South historians and textbooks.

In the 1850s a Boston minister named Nehemiah Adams (1806-1878) traveled to the South to examine the phenomenon of "cruel slave owners" for himself. Dr. Adams was shocked to discover that there was no truth in the Northern anti-South myths he had heard for so long. In the fascinating account of his journey, entitled, *A Southside View of Slavery*, Adams writes of the whip:

> The white overseers have it in their power, of course, to perpetuate many tyrannical and cruel acts . . . [But] [t]here is a public sentiment to which they are amenable; a cruel, neglectful master is marked and despised; and if cruel or neglectful by proxy, he does not escape reprobation. . . . This is a brand upon a man which he and his family are made to feel deeply.[313]

In 1835 James Madison (1751-1836) was paid a visit by English author Harriet Martineau (1802-1876), at which time he

> mentioned the astonishment of some strangers, who had an idea that slaves were always whipped all day long, at seeing his negroes

---

310. Fox-Genovese, p. 360.
311. Garraty and McCaughey, p. 230.
312. Stowe admitted as much, which is why Henson later republished his autobiography under the title: *The Memoirs of Uncle Tom*.
313. N. Adams, p. 97.

THE MCGAVOCKS OF CARNTON PLANTATION

go to church one Sunday. They were gayly dressed, the women in brightly-coloured calicoes; and, when a sprinkling of rain came, up went a dozen umbrellas. The astonished strangers veered round to the conclusion that slaves were very happy . . .[314]

These and a thousand other facts destroy the dark, heartless, anti-South fantasy world Stowe created.

Nonetheless, she accomplished her goal, for the best-selling 1852-book, which was translated into twenty-three languages and sold millions of copies, was instrumental in ending slavery by shaping public opinion.[315] And happy she must have been, for Stowe, like her liberal heroes Abraham Lincoln[316] and Horace Greeley[317] (and, at one time William Lloyd Garrison),[318] was an ardent colonizationist who looked forward to the day when all blacks would be shipped out of America. And this could not be accomplished until all slaves (then considered personal property) were freed.[319]

Yet even pro-North writers have had to admit that it was *Uncle Tom's Cabin* that allowed abolitionists to finally win the propaganda war.[320] According to Yankee legend, after meeting her in 1862, midway through the South-North conflict, Lincoln himself referred to Stowe as "the little lady who started this big war,"[321] a statement as fictitious as her book!

Stowe's words were indeed highly inaccurate, and as such, they inflicted tremendous damage on the South's image, a negative image that, unfortunately, has endured to the present day—even at historic Confederate homes in Middle Tennessee.

---

314. Martineau, Vol. 2, pp. 7-8.
315. Weintraub, p. 65.
316. See Seabrook, L, p. 584-633.
317. Fogel, p. 254.
318. During the time Garrison supported and "approved" of the ACS, he considered it a "praiseworthy association." W. L. Garrison, p. 3.
319. Burlingame, p. 50.
320. Buckley, p. 71.
321. Skidmore, p. 114; Isaacson, p. 154; McKissack and McKissack, p. 177.

The McGavocks of Carnton Plantation

❧ PSYCHOPATHY & SLAVERY

The truth is that the horrific, bestial, and sickening form of slavery depicted in *Uncle Tom's Cabin* never existed in everyday life anywhere in America. It came from the overly agitated imagination of a sentimental novelist and South-loathing, antislavery activist who cared more about abolishing slavery than the facts.

Were there inhumane Southern slave owners and slave traders? Of course. There are unthinking vicious people in every type of business. Were there slave owners who were racists? No question. Racists of every color exist in every occupation. Were their atrocities committed on Southern farms? Absolutely. Some blacks were mistreated and some even suffered torture, rape, and death at the hands of their deranged owners. These incidents are well-known and have been repeated in thousands of anti-South books for generations. And they are still being peddled today by rabid South-haters.

What the readers of these works are not told is that such incidents were the exception rather than the rule, just as they are in today's business world. For as Chesnut wisely intimated, a man who was cruel to his servants was a man who was capable of being cruel to anyone.[322] After all, the type of person who commits such crimes is suffering from an illness known as antisocial personality disorder (APD), or what is popularly known as sociopathy or psychopathy, a mental disease that is rare in every time period and in every society.

APD is a disease in which the afflicted individual (a sociopath or psychopath) operates without a conscience, without empathy, and subsequently without remorse, viewing other people as mere objects to be exploited and manipulated for personal gain and pleasure. To re-emphasize, this serious sickness of the mind is uncommon today, just as it was uncommon in the mid-1800s.

Those few psychopaths who were involved in inhumane slaving practices in the South were strongly condemned by all thinking Southerners and, whenever possible, were arrested, tried, convicted,

---

322. Chesnut, MCCW, p. 642.

THE McGAVOCKS OF CARNTON PLANTATION

and imprisoned.

We should also bear in mind that white-on-white violence (like black-on-black violence) was far more common than white-on-black violence. In other words, psychopathic whites were far more likely to physically abuse other whites than they were blacks.[323] To believe otherwise, as Northern myth has asserted for decades, is not only ridiculous, it is illogical.

❧ THE TRUTH ABOUT PHYSICAL FORCE

When a Southern slave owner was put in a position where force was needed (such as with a violent servant)—which for the average slaver was seldom if at all—it was not motivated by innate cruelty, by sadistic tendencies, or by APD. It was motivated by the same thing that motivates modern free labor bosses: the desire for maximum profits.

While today's supervisors use the threat of demotion and termination for inferior work or bad behavior, Victorian slavers used the threat of force, for this was then the accepted approach to discipline. One of the instruments of force sometimes resorted to, of course, was the infamous whip.

But whipping was not a corrective tool created specifically for the Southern slave trade. It was the standard form of punishment in the U.S. from the 1600s to the 1800s for law-breakers of every kind, whether black, white, brown, or red. Indeed, this particular penal custom was a gift of the English, who left us records of "rogues" being "graciously whipped" from as early as the late 1500s. The practice was then brought to America with the very first wave of Anglo immigrants.[324]

As early as 1698, for example, Pennsylvanian Gabriel Thomas (1661-1714) wrote that:

> Thieves of all sorts, are oblig'd to restore four fold after they have been Whipt and Imprison'd, according to the nature of their Crime; and if they be not of Ability to restore four fold, they must

---
323. Garraty and McCaughey, p. 25.
324. Hacker, p. 35.

THE MCGAVOCKS OF CARNTON PLANTATION

be in Servitude till 'tis satisfied.³²⁵

Here we see that at the time Northern criminals were not only whipped for their misdeeds, but were also sentenced to a form of bondage known as servitude, the exact same type that millions of black "slaves" would later serve under in the American South.

The truth, contrary to Northern folklore, is that from New England to the Deep South, the whipping post was the centerpiece of the village green in hundreds of towns and cities across early America. The standard punishment for horse thieves, for instance, nearly all who were white, was "three good whippings," each one consisting of thirty-nine lashes.³²⁶

Whipping was a standard military punishment at the time as well. During the Revolutionary War, while the "father of the nation," George Washington, served as general of the Continental Army, he regularly whipped his white soldiers for a host of offences ranging from drunkenness to desertion. Indeed, his floggings were so violent that Congress had to create a rule regulating the number of times a whip could be applied to a soldier's bare back.³²⁷

In 1812 an enlightened and more humane Congress made courts-martial whippings entirely unlawful (in one of the more outrageous cases a soldier had been branded, had his head shaved, and was given fifty lashes). Military officers, however, believed it was the only sure means of enforcing discipline. Congress had no choice but to later lift its ban and whipping was reinstated in 1833.³²⁸

During Lincoln's War white farmers in the South risked being whipped for violating the governmental ban on growing cotton instead of food.³²⁹ And it is well-known that both white and black Yankee soldiers used the whip on "stubborn" captured Southern blacks between

---

325. G. Thomas, p. 47.
326. Coit, pp. 37, 48.
327. Jensen, NN, p. 33.
328. Alotta, p. 3.
329. Channing, p. 29.

The McGavocks of Carnton Plantation

1861 and 1865.[330] Black Union soldiers were even known to whip white civilians during the War.[331]

The whip then was the normal American penalty for bad behavior. Thus it was only natural that it was also used to enforce authority on plantations. In fact, black slaves themselves, such as those who worked in positions of power (for example, mammies, overseers, and drivers), regularly used the whip on other black slaves when the situation warranted it.[332] And we will note that there were extremely cruel *black* slave owners who occasionally used it on their black chattel as well.[333]

Such intimidation was not imposed to create submissive and docile slaves, as Northern mythologists have long claimed. Rather it was used to create the largest and best product at the lowest cost in the most efficient manner.

Let us bear in mind that while today even shoving a person can result in arrest for "assault and battery," in the 1800s physical punishment of all kinds was regarded as the norm. This sentiment lasted well into the 20th Century, and there are no doubt people reading this book who will recall being "whipped" with a belt or spanked with a paddle as a child. President Jimmy Carter, for instance, (whose great-grandfather Littleberry Walker Carter fought for the Confederacy in Lincoln's War), was whipped as a child.[334]

In 18th-Century America then the whipping of a slave was considered no more exceptional or barbaric than the whipping of an unruly child by its parents.[335] Southern hero General Nathan Bedford Forrest, like most Victorian Southern children, was routinely whipped for bad behavior as a schoolboy,[336] so it was only natural that later in life, as a slave trader and slave owner, he sometimes used the whip on his

---

330. Wiley, SN, pp. 213, 244, 245.
331. Henry, ASTF, p. 246.
332. Genovese, pp. 356, 368, 371, 374, 378-380.
333. Genovese, p. 408.
334. DeGregorio, s.v. "Jimmy Carter."
335. Horn, IE, p. 68.
336. Lytle, p. 14; Parks, p. 82.

THE MCGAVOCKS OF CARNTON PLANTATION

black servants. Does this appall us today? It does. But perhaps not quite as much when we learn that as a military officer in the Confederate army he also whipped his white soldiers for insubordination.[337]

It is also important to note that the U.S. judicial system expected slave owners (Northern and Southern) to attend to disciplinary matters themselves, and not clog up the courts with petty grievances concerning disobedient slaves.[338] As such, use of the whip was an accepted and recognized form of penalizing black servants.[339]

In the end physical discipline on Southern plantations was about pure economics. Too much force would have increased rather than decreased the cost of labor, which is just one of the many reasons why African-American, Native-American, and European-American slave owners did not use physical coercion on their human chattel unless absolutely necessary.[340]

Yes, threat of punishment was also important in sustaining the power hierarchy on the early plantation. But it is for this very same reason that it is also vital today in the modern office. Obviously the balance between a superior and his or her subordinates cannot be achieved, however, if the former resorts to brute violence.

Slave owners, most who were experienced, professional, and highly intelligent businessmen, understood this, as did the authors of a variety of Victorian plantation books, all which strongly discouraged farm managers from using any kind of corporal punishment.

Here is what one such work, the popular 19th-Century *Instructions to Managers* had to say on the subject: the most vital ingredient in managing servants is how their superiors act toward them and treat them. It is true that there needs to be a certain amount of discipline on a farm. However, remember that when a servant's work is finished it is only right to treat him with humanity, sympathy, and even permissiveness. Kindness and rewards are much more effective than

---

337. Wyeth, TDF, p. 279.
338. O. Williams, pp. 42-43.
339. Horn, IE, p. 68.
340. Fogel and Engerman, pp. 232, 238-239.

THE MCGAVOCKS OF CARNTON PLANTATION

punishment, the author wrote.[341] These were words that nearly all Southern slave owners, black, white, brown, or red, understood and agreed with.

❧ AUTHENTIC SLAVERY WAS NEVER PRACTICED IN THE OLD SOUTH

We can see from these few examples alone that most everything we have been taught about American slavery is largely Yankee and New South folklore. What then was American slavery like?

Edward A. Pollard (1831-1872), Virginian, staunch Confederate, and editor of the Richmond *Examiner* during the War, said it best: there was never such a thing as "slavery" in the Old South. What North and New South writers conveniently and slanderously call Southern "slavery" was actually, Pollard rightly asserts, a "well-guarded and moderate system of negro servitude."[342]

The first blacks brought to British North America (in 1619) were not regarded as slaves, but as indentured servants, laborers with the same rights as white indentured servants.[343] Though this status would eventually change from voluntary servitude to involuntary servitude, most Southerners, unlike Northerners, correctly referred to bonded blacks as "servants" (not "slaves") right up to and after Lincoln's War.[344] As such, Southerners seldom used the phrase "African slavery." Like Jefferson Davis they used the term "African servitude."[345]

What is the difference between slavery and servitude?

❧ THE DISTINCTION BETWEEN SERVITUDE & SLAVERY

Slavery is the state of working under the control, ownership, or absolute dominion of another, without pay, and often for life. Additionally, slaves have no rights of any kind, are generally debased and disenfranchised, and cannot purchase their freedom. In short, a true

---

341. Fogel and Engerman, p. 240.
342. Pollard, SHW, Vol. 2, pp. 202, 296-297, 562.
343. Ransom, p. 41.
344. Grissom, p. 128.
345. Cooper, JDA, p. 666.

slave is seen by his or her owner as little different than a cow or a horse, just another piece of livestock to be owned and worked.[346]

Servitude, on the other hand, is for a limited duration, the individual is not "owned"—his boss is not his "owner" or "master" but rather his employer—and he or she is paid a wage. Servants also possess a wide variety of personal and civil rights that are both recognized and protected by society and tempered by religious sentiment. (In this way, under servitude a person's right to comfort and happiness are taken for granted and he or she is treated with common respect and decency.) Finally, servants have the right and the power to buy their freedom.

It is clear from these facts alone that the South practiced servitude not slavery.

This truth is acknowledged even by the U.S. government: when the Thirteenth Amendment was ratified on December 6, 1865, and slavery in every state was finally officially abolished, the writers, knowing that it was servitude not slavery that was practiced in the South, used both the word "servitude" (for historical accuracy) and the word "slavery" (to please abolitionists):

> Neither slavery nor involuntary servitude . . . shall exist within the United States, or any place subject to their jurisdiction.[347]

The use of the injurious and false word "slavery" instead of "servitude" for the type of bondage that was practiced in the Old South has been forced on us by Northern influences and by New South political correctness. For this word, like the equally fallacious and deleterious Northern terms "copperhead," "rebel," "pro-slavery," and "slave state," are all pieces of Lincolnian propaganda that have helped justify the Yankee president's unjust War and, during the War itself, aided the liberal North in its victory over the conservative South.[348]

To make sure Europe supported the Union, Lincoln lied to her

---

346. Drescher and Engerman, p. 192.
347. Findlay and Findlay, p. 226.
348. The Southerner's attitude toward being called a "rebel" later reversed. From then on it was capitalized and viewed as a badge of honor.

THE McGAVOCKS OF CARNTON PLANTATION

about the true nature of the War and the South, then ordered his secretary of state, William Henry Seward, to threaten war against European nations who recognized the Confederacy,[349] in particular Britain and France,[350] both who, a number of times, were quite prepared and willing to support the Southern Rebels.[351] Indeed, France was in the process of building warships for the South, and England actually provided one that sailed to America and destroyed U.S. property, before both nations dropped their sponsorship out of fear of Lincoln's threatening reprisals. (One European nation did manage to continue its support of the Confederacy throughout the War, however: the Duchy of Saxe-Coburg-Gotha. God bless her.)[352]

Tragically for Dixie, the leaders of Britain and France, misled by Lincoln's falsehoods, never fully understood the true nature of so-called "Southern slavery." But those Southerners who lived through this period, and those today who have researched the institution objectively, understand that it was, in all actuality, a form of servitude not slavery.

This fact is overtly preserved in the Latin words for the Western form of slave: *servus* (male), *serva* (female).[353] So-called Southern "slaves" then were actually servants, not slaves in the literal, technical, or traditional sense.

In short, there was no such thing as "slavery" or a "slave state" in the Old South. This politicized nomenclature is an invention of anti-South partisans whose aim has been to defile the South in the eyes of the world and, as noted, to excuse Lincoln's unholy war on the Confederacy.

The truth is that Southerners who were labeled "proslavery," and Southern states that were labeled "slave states," were merely pro-states' rights. For, as we will see, only a tiny minority of Southerners actually owned servants. The South's ultimate goal was always the preservation

---

349. P. J. Buchanan, p. 131.
350. For examples of Lincoln's various dire warnings, threats, and promises to wage war on any European nation that impeded his assault on the South, see Owsley, pp. 309, 401, 516-517, 539-540.
351. D. H. Donald, WNWCW, pp. 55-78.
352. *The Civil War Book of Lists*, p. 204.
353. Traupman, s.v. "slave."

THE MCGAVOCKS OF CARNTON PLANTATION

of the right of self-determination (self-government), not the continuation of black servitude, no matter what the North chooses to believe or what name they choose to call the institution.

In point of fact, if one were to take pro-North history books and replace the word "proslavery" with the words "pro-states' rights" one would have a much more accurate and honest portrait of the South-North conflict.

The McGavocks & Slavery

Part 3

ॐ THE TRUTH ABOUT LIFE UNDER SERVITUDE

NOW THAT WE UNDERSTAND THE distinction between slavery and servitude, it is time to look at how the latter was actually practiced in the Old South. In doing so we will see what life was really like for blacks at Carnton Plantation, not what anti-South crusaders want the world to believe.

As for the 250 year old institution of *Northern* slavery, we will let the North defend it.[354] Our focus will be on the institution as practiced in the South.

ॐ MARRIAGE, CHILDREN, HOMES, & FARMS

To begin with, nearly all Southern servants were allowed, even encouraged, to marry and have children, for as modern studies show, in nearly all cases the married are happier, healthier, more productive, and more stable than the unmarried.

Countless examples of legal slave marriages exist in the historical record, one of the most famous, of course, being the marriage between

---

354. For information on Northern slavery see my book *Everything You Were Taught About the Civil War is Wrong, Ask a Southerner!*

The McGavocks of Carnton Plantation

Northern slave, abolitionist, and feminist, Sojourner Truth (1797-1883), and a fellow Northern black slave named Tom.[355]

Victorian blacks, like Victorian whites, needed little encouragement to "walk down the aisle," for marriage was practically a religion among them. Of this phenomenon, Chesnut, who makes note of numerous legal Southern slave marriages in her diaries,[356] writes that it was routine for black servants to marry, and that afterward they behaved just like any other married couple. For marriage was one of their great pleasures and the primary focus of their lives.[357] Why is it that Northern and New South writers never mention this fact?

Marriage was just the beginning of a litany of civil, social, and human rights that were accorded to black servants in the South. They were also free to build their own homes, plant their own gardens, own their own livestock, clothes, and furniture, and farm their own parcels of land. Indeed, a number of freedmen reported that as servants nearly all of them had owned property, and that they loved nothing better than to amass wealth, property, and belongings.[358]

We have numerous records of black servants owning real estate, hogs, horses, cows, jewelry, buggies, and wagons, and whose personal products included corn, rice, fowl, beehives, peanuts, fodder, syrup, hay, mules, butter, sugar, tea, and sheep, among hundreds of other items. Many black servants became wealthy selling their goods, had excellent credit, and owned more land than whites living in the same area.[359]

❧ WAGES & EARNINGS

Another great Northern slavery myth is that Southern servants were not

---

355. McKissack and McKissack, p. 32. Sojourner Truth, originally named Isabella Baumfree, was born in 1797 in Ulster Country, New York, on the estate of Northern slave owners, the Dutch-American Hardenberghs. Truth gave her biography orally to a European-American woman named Olive Gilbert, who recorded the story, resulting in the book, *Narrative of Sojourner Truth*. It was first published in 1850. Truth, pp. iii, v.
356. See e.g., Chesnut, MCCW, p. 465.
357. Chesnut, DD, p. 114.
358. M. M. Smith, p. 182.
359. M. M. Smith, pp. 175-179.

THE MCGAVOCKS OF CARNTON PLANTATION

paid by their masters, but "slaved away" for nothing. To the contrary, not only were Southern servants financially compensated, they were also encouraged to own their own businesses. And not only this, the extra money they earned from plying their own trades, added to their basic daily income, could be quite substantial,[360] and greatly contributed to a thriving "black commerce" across the South.[361]

At Carnton Plantation one can still see evidence of the Southern practice of paying black servants ("slaves"): outside, on the east wall of the Mansion, the doorstep (on the left) that leads into the McGavocks' office, is worn down from thousands of scuffling shoes that passed over it between 1826 and 1909. Most of the shoes that ground away this stone between 1826 and 1865 specifically belonged to the McGavocks' black servants, who lined up here for both their daily work orders and their weekly pay packets.

While the average Southern servant's income seems to have been around $48 a year (or about $1,300 in today's currency, a substantial wage at the time), many ambitious blacks earned from $60 to over $300 a year ($1,600 to $8,000 in today's currency respectively), many drawing "considerably higher wages" than whites doing the same type of labor.[362]

Servants who hunted and fished in their free time could earn, along with the raising of livestock and the production of foodstuffs, an appreciable income, which they funneled into their internal economy. Adding to their economic stability was the fact that a black servant could bequeath or inherit property from other servants.[363]

A huge percentage of Southern blacks were foremen and managers on their owners' farms and plantations, and many more were skilled artisans and craftsmen, such as woodworkers and basketmakers, occupations by which a stable financial independence could easily be achieved.[364] Those among the latter two categories did their own

---

360. Fogel and Engerman, pp. 127, 128.
361. M. M. Smith, p. 189.
362. Fogel and Engerman, pp. 151, 241.
363. M. M. Smith, pp. 180-181.
364. Wilson and Ferris, s.v. "Black Life."

advertising, hired themselves out, wrote up and settled their own contracts, collected their own money, paid their own bills, and rented or purchased their own homes and shops. The employers (misleadingly called "owners" or "masters" by Northerners) of this class of servants took a small fixed percentage from their income (to offset the cost of their upkeep). Other than that, there was little, if any, distinction between servile artisans and free artisans.[365]

All of these occupations brought in excellent wages, not only basic plantation income, but in extra income, money that was often saved up and used to purchase one's freedom, or the freedom of relatives and friends. As a reminder: one cannot buy one's self out of slavery; only out of servitude. And as history has recorded, thousands of "slaves" bought their freedom both before and during the War.

One of the most famous in the latter category, of course, was Northern servant Frederick Douglass, whose independence was purchased by British sympathizers. Another was South Carolina servant Denmark Vesey, who bought his freedom in 1800 using money he had won in a lottery.[366] Arguably the best known example was President Lincoln's modiste, Elizabeth Keckley, a former Virginia slave who not only bought her freedom, but did so using money she earned from hiring herself out as a dressmaker.[367] No true slave has ever possessed this right.

Selling products from his own land, a field servant could easily earn $300 a year above his base income, the equivalent of about $8,000 today, while a skilled black artisan, making his own products, could earn an extra $500 a year, the equivalent of about $13,500 today. Employers (that is, "owners" or "masters") also often invited their servants to become participants in a variety of profit sharing schemes, and along with financial bonuses and gifts of land for good service and performance, a servant's money earning potential was quite spectacular.[368] Sometimes

---

365. Fogel and Engerman, pp. 151, 241.
366. Garraty and McCaughey, p. 159; Rosenbaum, s.v. "Vesey, Denmark."
367. C. Johnson, pp. 131, 188-189.
368. Fogel and Engerman, p. 56.

these cooperative business ventures were operated on a smaller scale, such as when plantation owners, like James and Mary Chesnut, shared the profits from their gardens with their servants.[369]

All told, a skilled hard working Southern black servant could easily earn today's equivalent of $25,000 annually. This was considered "great wealth" in 1840: the average American income for whites that year was $100, or only about $2,400 in today's currency. And as the employers ("owners") of servants only expropriated an average of about 12 percent of a servant's yearly income, a considerable sum could be saved up. Shrewd and enterprising servants used this money wisely, either for self-purchase, additional business investments, or for improving their quality of life.[370]

Southern blacks themselves testified to their economic and social freedom under the institution of servitude. In 1860, after observing blacks and whites working closely together on an Alabama plantation, British author Laurence Oliphant interviewed the farm's black servants, who told him that they could earn more as servants than as freemen, and that "slaves" who were poor had only themselves to blame.[371]

The South's black servant economy flourished for decades under the sagacious control of hard working African-Americans, who acquired, exchanged, and bartered real estate at market for such commodities as blankets, whiskey, and sugar. We know of a number of these individuals from archival state records, for some servants accumulated substantial debts between themselves and ended up in court.

One of the most common paths black servants took toward financial stability and even wealth was cotton production. Both males and females grew and sold their own cotton, individually or collectively, often selling larger bales and bigger crops, and at higher prices, than many white cotton farmers.

South Carolina servants noted that during this period many fellow blacks walked around with large rolls of money, money that was

---

369. Chesnut, MCCW, p. 285.
370. Fogel and Engerman, pp. 148, 153.
371. M. M. Smith, p. 185.

The McGavocks of Carnton Plantation

later depleted by Lincoln's War. If we had not been set free in 1865, they opined, you would have discovered wealthy black slaves laden with the money we had made from our extra crop production. So great was the wealth produced by black servants that many amassed a significant amount of property, ranging from homes, land, and cattle ranches, to boats, carriages, and entire stables of horses.[372]

Working on their own land in cooperative units and collective family groups, producing and selling their own goods, practicing bequeathment and inheritance, all gave Southern black servants, particularly those of the low-country of South Carolina and Georgia, a great degree of autonomy, power, and prestige, both within and without the servant community. And in fact, in many ways they were much more similar to what we would now term "proto-peasants"[373] than they were even to servants.[374]

Hence Chesnut noted that what Northerners and scallywags called Southern "slaves" were actually known by most Southerners as "operatives," "tenants," and "peasants." This is why Chesnut, like countless other Southerners, often referred to the institution of Southern black servitude as "peasantry."[375]

❧ SERVILE OCCUPATIONS

As plantation workers, Southern black servants were generally divided into two broad categories: house servants and field servants. House servants were occupied with cleaning, cooking, sewing, washing, weaving, and tending children.

Field servants, a more diverse group, were organized by skill, experience, aptitude, and intelligence, and were assigned various occupations that included: managers, foremen, drivers, plowmen, hoe hands, harrowers, seed sowers, coverers, sorters, ginners, packers, milkmaids, gardeners, stock minders, carpenters, coopers, rakers,

---

[372]. M. M. Smith, pp. 186, 188-191.
[373]. A proto-peasant is an early or primitive type of (free) farmer, yeoman, or agricultural laborer.
[374]. M. M. Smith, p. 182.
[375]. Chesnut, MCCW, pp. 246, 428.

THE MCGAVOCKS OF CARNTON PLANTATION

drillers, droppers, still operators, masons, rail-splitters, and blacksmiths.

But servants did not just clean house, muck out stalls, milk cows, construct barrels, make horseshoes, and till the soil. Far from being merely "meek, illiterate cotton pickers," as the North prefers to label them, early 19th-Century records reveal that the occupations of Southern black servants covered a spectacularly wide spectrum of professionalism, including: highly skilled craftsmen and craftswomen, weavers, seamstresses, musicians, nurses, stewards, teamsters, coachmen, furniture makers, and even highly technical architects and engineers. Even "lowly" field hands were required to have a vast number of skills ranging from a detailed knowledge of farming (planting, cultivating, and harvesting), land management, and dairying, to the use and maintenance of farm machinery and building construction.[376]

❧ WORK HOURS, FREE DAYS

Just like their free-laboring white and black counterparts at the time, the normal work week for Southern black servants was about 70 to 75 hours a week, with Sundays off. On Saturdays, the day traditionally set aside for servants to work their own land, they labored either a half day, or had the entire day free. Each year they also had about a week's worth of work free holidays (such as Christmas, Good Friday, Independence Day, and the post harvest period), with odd days off as rewards.[377]

On Sundays they could attend their own black-only "Negro churches" and at night they could participate in all-black promenades and other types of social gatherings.[378] With about twelve days a year lost due to sickness, the average servant ended up working about 265 days a year, slightly less than today's 21st-Century office worker.[379]

On their days off servants had near complete freedom. They could hunt, fish, nap, rest, play games, garden, spend time with their families, take weekend jaunts into town, almost anything they desired.

---

376. Fogel and Engerman, pp. 38-41.
377. Rosenbaum and Brinkley, s.v. "Slavery"; M. M. Smith, p. 189.
378. Chesnut, MCCW, pp. 458, 607, 734.
379. Fogel and Engerman, p. 208.

THE MCGAVOCKS OF CARNTON PLANTATION

They could also continue working for the plantation and receive extra pay and bonuses.

But many chose to use their free days to work at their own businesses, earning additional extra money and raising their status, not only on the plantation, but in the community around them. A host of highly respected black servants rose up the economic ladder in just this fashion, earning their way to increased social freedom and financial prosperity and independence.[380]

❧ HOW SOME BLACKS BENEFITTED FROM PLANTATION LIFE

Today in the 21st Century we have nothing good to say about 19th-Century servitude ("slavery" to Yanks), for there was truly nothing good about it. For one thing, in the long run it hurt both employer ("owner") and servant, community and city, state and nation. For did it not go against the very foundation of both American religion and the Constitution? For another, the loss of personal freedom is arguably the worst fate that can befall a person, as any prisoner or former convict can tell you.

And it is certainly true that the time and energy of black servants was exploited, and it is just as true that they did not have the same rights or freedoms that their employers or free blacks had.

By the same token it is an implacable reality that in comparison to free laborers, life on the plantation, in fact, benefitted Southern servants in some ways. How?

According to modern day cliometricians (economic historians), due to the well-known superior quality of black labor, large slave plantations were 34 percent more efficient than free labor Southern farms, and 40 percent more efficient than Northern free labor farms.[381] The extra wealth derived from this increased productivity was passed onto the servants in the forms of higher wages, greater independence, and better quality housing, food, clothing, and health care.

---

380. Fogel and Engerman, p. 149.
381. Fogel and Engerman, pp. 192-193, 209-210.

THE MCGAVOCKS OF CARNTON PLANTATION

In addition, though the plantation was unquestionably a for-profit business, as we have just seen, it also functioned, on some levels, as a communal enterprise. For example, servile blacks paid less for their clothes than did free blacks, and servants could also save on interest charges: a free black could expect to pay exorbitant rates, while a servant could take advantage of the far lower rates offered by his employer.[382]

❧ HOW SOME BLACKS BENEFITTED FROM SERVITUDE

Just as ancient Rome's white slaves often had far better social, political, and financial opportunities than Europe's free laborers,[383] so too did black Southern servants compared with many of their free white neighbors. In fact, servitude benefitted Southern blacks in a number of different ways.

For instance, in comparison to free blacks, and even in comparison to many free whites, black Southern servants lived longer, had lower suicide rates, earned more money, had better diets, suffered less illness, were better skilled, lived in bigger and better houses, had superior health care, had lower death rates and lower maternal death rates in childbearing.[384]

There was also the fact that it was impossible for a servant to ever experience homelessness or joblessness, or suffer from starvation or neglected health problems. Why? Because their Southern owners were legally obligated to care for them at all times and through any type of hardship, from the cradle to the grave.

When a black servant became too old or too ill to work, or if a black child became orphaned, for instance, their employers ("masters" and "mistresses") bore the legal responsibility of looking after their welfare until the day of their deaths—or freedom, whichever came first.[385] As Chesnut said, Southern servants employed their own time, meaning that they worked as employees under their owners, who in turn

---

382. Fogel and Engerman, pp. 156-157.
383. Muller, p. 207.
384. Fogel and Engerman, pp. 84, 109-123, 124-125, 241, 261.
385. Thornton and Ekelund, p. 96.

paid their medical bills and provided their food and clothing.[386] The diarist herself hired and paid several servants during the War.[387] Servants in this category, most who could read and write, lived basically as free blacks did.[388]

Hired out slave hands could earn considerable sums for themselves and their employers. In Virginia in 1863, as one example, it cost $30 a month to hire a slave (about $800 today), while a Confederate soldier earned only $11 a month (about $250 today).[389]

After the War some slave owners were so in debt to their former slaves that there was no possibility of ever repaying them.[390] The weight of the responsibility for caring for servants was such that a universal joke arose in the South: it was not the servants that one need fear would run away. It was their employers. English novelist William M. Thackeray (1811-1863) characterized slave ownership this way: it is similar to owning an elephant when all that is needed is a horse.[391]

Chesnut writes that nearly all Southerners considered slaves an annoyance rather than a benefit, one that never came close to paying off. It is far simpler and cheaper, she noted, to hire a free laborer than to own a man whose father, mother, wife, and numerous children have to be fed, clothed, houses, nursed, and have their taxes and doctor's bills paid throughout their entire lives.[392]

Thousands of Southern servant owners, such as fire-eating die-hard Confederate Rebel Edmund Ruffin (1794-1865),[393] agreed. Ruffin, like thousands of others, eventually auctioned off his black servants; not

---

386. Chesnut, MCCW, p. 243.
387. Chesnut, MCCW, p. 589.
388. Genovese, pp. 392, 393.
389. Eaton, HSC, p. 104.
390. Chesnut, MCCW, p. 792.
391. Thackeray, p. 127. A modern analogy would be owning a four-wheel drive pickup truck when all that is needed is a regular car.
392. Chesnut, MCCW, p. 803.
393. Ruffin, a professional agriculturist who pioneered crop rotation and who is said to have been the person who fired the first shot at the Battle of Fort Sumter I, committed suicide after the War rather than live in ignoble humiliation under Yankee rule. To this day Ruffin is considered an archetypal Confederate hero among traditional Southerners, one typifying Dixie's age old love of personal liberty, states' rights, and political independence.

THE MCGAVOCKS OF CARNTON PLANTATION

because they were poor producers, but because they were excellent consumers, making the expense of maintaining them nearly impossible.[394]

Contrast this with Victorian free laborers who, just like employees today, had no one to care for them during times of want and difficulty, no protection against joblessness, ill-health, homelessness, or starvation.

Servitude then functioned much like a social welfare program with built-in health and life insurance, operating in some ways like an early form of socialism. Yes, servants helped defray these costs through their work and through monthly percentage payments to their employers. But they earned wages at the same time as well, both through their regular work and also through their personal extracurricular labors. In all, most Southern servants were highly indulged and protected by their "owners," so much so that "slavery" itself often became a sort of status symbol among blacks.

Would servile blacks have given all these benefits up for freedom? Some would have, and some certainly did. A few fled north on the Underground Railroad,[395] while others purchased their freedom with their hard earned savings.

But, after contemplating the quasi-freedom of living in the North, where the anti-African Black Codes were strictly enforced and where white racism was far more deeply entrenched, many Southern blacks reconsidered. When War came, this group, most of whom were third, fourth, and fifth generation Southern Americans, quite consciously chose to remain in the South, in their own homes, on the plantations with their "white families."

Then, when Lincoln freed them, and he and the North tried to deport them back to Africa, with one voice this group cried "no!" For they quite rightly considered themselves true Americans and true Southerners. After all, by 1860, 99 percent of all blacks were native-

---

394. Channing, p. 128.
395. Rosenbaum and Brinkley, s.v. "Underground Railroad."

THE MCGAVOCKS OF CARNTON PLANTATION

born Americans, a larger percentage than for whites.[396] As black educator and former Southern servant Booker T. Washington (1856-1915) wrote:

> I was born in the South. I have lived and labored in the South. I wish to be buried in the South.[397]

Thus it was that a majority of Southern blacks would not be removed from their homes, or their home nation, the place of their birth and that of all their known ancestors. Most, if not all, of the McGavocks' servants were in this category.

❧ THE MYTH OF ABUSE

We have all heard and read of the horrible abuses of slaves on Southern plantations. Thousands upon thousands of Northern and New South authors have delighted, and continue to delight, in regaling the world with these tales. Yes, abuse did occur between whites and blacks (on both sides), but it was extremely rare, and, we should note, such abuses also took place on Northern plantations.

What these anti-South authors have conveniently left out, however, is the bold fact that on the typical Southern plantation black servants were not chained up, whipped, beaten, tortured, mistreated, or separated from their families. Quite the opposite. Their owners invested enormous time and money into purchasing and caring for them, and they were thus handled very carefully. The result was, as we have seen, that their basic welfare was almost always more than amply taken care of.

Chesnut cites an example of Dick, the black butler of the Miller family, and Hetty, the black maid of the Anderson family. When the two servants fell in love, the Millers sold Dick to the Andersons so that he and Hetty could get married and live together as husband and wife.[398]

---

396. Fogel and Engerman, pp. 23-24.
397. Scott and Stowe, p. 321. Dr. Washington's expectation was fulfilled. He was buried in Tuskegee, Alabama, on November 17, 1915.
398. Chesnut, DD, p. 225.

THE MCGAVOCKS OF CARNTON PLANTATION

Such incidents were the rule across the South, though Northern "histories" of the War completely ignore them.

❧ THE TYPICAL AMERICAN BLACK SERVANT

The average American black "slave" was clean, well-groomed, well-mannered, and well-fed, and wore fresh clothing each day. As Chesnut and millions of other Southerners did, their employers sometimes taught them to read and write; or just as often the servants taught themselves.[399]

The Northern myth that slave owners purposefully prevented their servants from learning to read and write for fear of them becoming "too smart," "impudent," and "uppity" is just that, a Northern myth. While there were certainly some Southern owners who bought into this absurd concept, again, these were the exception rather than the rule.

Actually, the more abilities and talents a servant had, the more valuable he was (in financial worth and productivity), not only to his employer, but also to himself, to his family, and to society. With this, his personal power and station in life increased, allowing him potential for greater advancement in life. This truly benefitted everyone on the Southern plantation, from the lowliest field hand to the wealthiest and largest land owner.[400]

❧ BLACK CRAFTSMEN

In essence, in the Victorian South the average American black servant worked for his room and board, which was provided to him by his employers. Intelligent servants, and those with special skills, could easily advance, and were often placed in occupations of status, which in turn allowed them to earn an income that quite often led to prosperity, and even freedom, if they chose it.

In Franklin, Tennessee, alone, for instance, we have records of

---

[399]. Chesnut, MCCW, p. 263.
[400]. Much has been made of a 19th-Century American law that prohibited teaching slaves to read and write. South-loathers maintain that the thinking behind this counterproductive regulation was to keep black servants in a permanent state of ignorance and docile subservience, a hopelessly irrational interpretation. The fact is that most Southern servant employers ("slave owners" to Northerners) wisely disregarded the law, for reasons given in the associated paragraph.

servants who were highly sought after, and highly paid, for their work as artisans and furniture makers. The McGavocks owned a number of items that they purchased from just such craftsmen. An example is the small wooden chair located in the girls' bedroom upstairs, made by African-American artisan and freedman, Richard "Dick" Poynor, (1802-1882) which was highly prized by the McGavock family.[401]

⁂ APPRENTICESHIP

It is apparent from the foregoing that early American black servitude had little or nothing in common with actual slavery, but was far more similar to apprenticeship, another form of servitude in which one is legally bound to work for an employer for a predetermined amount of time in return for training in a specific trade.[402] This was why, after all, anti-abolitionist and black colonizationist Abraham Lincoln—who opposed the spread of slavery, not slavery itself—suggested that servants be "subject to apprenticeship" after emancipation.[403]

Thus the Chesnuts, like many other Southern "slave owners," apprenticed their black servants, even issuing them "degrees" for attaining various levels of achievement, just as in a regular school.[404]

⁂ SOUTHERN "SLAVERY" WAS MILD

It was because of the true nature of Southern "slavery" that in 1781 Virginian Thomas Jefferson made reference to "the mild treatment our slaves experience,"[405] while in 1866, another Virginian, Edward A. Pollard, described Southern "slavery" as "altogether, one of the mildest and most beneficent systems of servitude in the world."[406]

---

401. Dick's surname is sometimes spelled Poyner.
402. Fogel and Engerman, pp. 36, 150.
403. Nicolay and Hay, ALCW, Vol. 2, p. 91. As we will see, Lincoln was never interested in abolishing slavery. An advocate of American apartheid, his main goal was to limit the spread of slavery outside the South and deport willing blacks to Africa, South America, or the Carribean. This is why American slavery was not abolished until eight months after Lincoln died. For more on these topics see my books *Abraham Lincoln: The Southern View*, and *Lincolnology: The Real Abraham Lincoln Revealed in His Own Words*.
404. Chesnut, DD, p. 167.
405. Foley, p. 815.
406. Pollard, SHW, Vol. 2, p. 562.

The McGavocks of Carnton Plantation

President Woodrow Wilson held the same view. In his book *Division and Reunion: 1829-1889*, he writes that in the South, black servants were almost always overindulged, and with great affection, by their masters.[407] Southern slaves were even allowed to choose their own work schedule and workload, which they did by carefully limiting their output so as not to overstress themselves.[408]

Chesnut notes that across the South black servants were almost universally considered to be the most comfortable, most indolent, the fattest, and the happiest "peasantry" that ever graced the earth. Indeed, they were so well situated and so coddled by their white owners that it was easy for Mary and her peers to forget that slavery was an evil.[409]

The South Carolina diarist added that most Southerners were not afraid of their servants fleeing to the other side during Lincoln's War, for they were simply too contented where they were. Writes Mary:

> General Lee and Mr. Davis want the negroes put into the army. Mr. Chesnut and Major Venable discussed the subject one night, but would they fight on our side or desert to the enemy? They don't go to the enemy, because they are comfortable as they are, and expect to be free anyway.[410]

Southern black servants were so well taken care of that they not only had better appetites than free blacks,[411] but, according to census records, they were the same height as whites (and an inch taller than the average British Royal Marine of the day). Height, of course, is one of the standard measures of one's nutritional history.[412]

In 1888, twenty-three years after Lincoln's War, William S. Speer wrote the following about my cousin General William Giles

---

407. W. Wilson, DR, p. 126.
408. Blassingame, pp. 180, 182.
409. Chesnut, MCCW, p. 428.
410. Chesnut, DD, p. 224.
411. See Fogel, pp. 137, 138-140.
412. C. Johnson, p. 130. American females, for example, are much taller today than ever before in the nation's history, due almost solely to healthier diets in childhood.

THE MCGAVOCKS OF CARNTON PLANTATION

Harding of Belle Meade, the sister plantation to Carnton. Before the War, Speer noted, General Harding

> was opposed, as his father before him had been, to purchasing slaves, and also opposed to trusting his slaves to the charge of an overseer. Consequently he would never invest in a cotton or sugar plantation, but kept his slaves under his immediate supervision, a course generally thought to be a less profitable method of working slave labor, but by him considered the more humane. During the civil war his slaves remained faithful to him, and a goodly number remain with him at this writing. He cares for them in sickness and in health as formerly. They are contented, happy set; well fed; well clothed; fat, sleek and merry.[413]

Virginian and social theorist George Fitzhugh (1806-1881) contrasted the comparatively moderate version of American slavery with that of Africa, where there are found extremely barbaric forms of bondage.[414]

The stark contrast between the Northern view of Southern "slavery" and the reality of Southern servitude was noted even by some Northerners. One Yank who visited the South in 1844 was genuinely surprised to find that:

> On principle, in habit, and even on grounds of self-interest, the greater part of the slave-owners were humane in the treatment of their slaves,—kind, indulgent, not over-exacting, and sincerely interested in the physical well-being of their dependents.[415]

Even many anti-South writers have had to grudgingly concede that just prior to Lincoln's War slavery in the South had attained its most gentle and civilized level for such an institution.[416] So lax were Southern "slave owners" toward their "sable charges" that, as Chesnut writes, she and other white masters and mistresses often took orders from their

---

413. Speer, p. 2.
414. McKissack and McKissack, p. 119.
415. W. Wilson, DR, p. 126.
416. M. M. Smith, p. 32.

THE MCGAVOCKS OF CARNTON PLANTATION

servants![417]

Little wonder that so few blacks ever tried to escape the plantations, trading the relatively easy life of a "contented peasant" for the difficult life of a runaway, chased from town to town both day and night by lawmen, bounty hunters, and hound dogs. As we have seen, as Chesnut and other Southern servant owners often jokingly complained, it was so costly and labor intensive, so complicated and difficult owning and maintaining black servants, that it was usually the owner, not the servants, who most often considered running away from the plantation.

Again we are not defending, or even trying to mitigate the evils of, either slavery or servitude. We are simply explaining why the McGavocks, like nearly all other slave owning Southerners, called the blacks who worked for them "servants," "domestics," "maids," "butlers," "menservants," "womenservants," "hands," "operatives," "tenants," and "peasants," but almost never "slaves." Indeed, most bonded blacks referred to themselves as "servants."[418]

Whites also often referred to their black chattel either by their Christian names (Maggie, Bill, etc.), or by their occupational titles: "washerwoman,"[419] "body servant,"[420] "housekeeper,"[421] "chambermaid,"[422] and "dairy maid."[423] As a race most Southern whites simply called them "Negroes,"[424] while they usually referred to their form of servitude as "the domestic institution."[425]

In short, the word "slave" and the concept of authentic slavery were all but unknown in the South. Only in the North, where anti-South mythology and propaganda were accepted as fact, were these erroneous terms used on a daily basis for servitude in Dixie.

---

417. Chesnut, MCCW, p. 721.
418. See e.g., Chesnut, MCCW, p. 491.
419. Chesnut, DD, p. 397.
420. Chesnut, DD, p. 84.
421. Chesnut, DD, p. 169.
422. Chesnut, DD, p. 169.
423. Chesnut, MCCW, p. 350.
424. Chesnut, DD, p. 181.
425. M. M. Smith, p. 191.

THE MCGAVOCKS OF CARNTON PLANTATION

❧ SLAVE HOMES

There is another Northern myth we need to dispel while on this topic, and that is the stereotype that the abodes of American servants were filthy, poorly-made hovels, filled with lice and rats.

When you visit Carnton next, take a close look at the brick servants' house on the property. Notice the high quality of the design and of the materials that were used. This was no accident. The house was built by Randal McGavock's black servants themselves, experts in the crafts of masonry, carpentry, and general construction.

At about 1,000 square feet, some may consider it small. But the home was cozy and well made, and we can be sure that its inhabitants kept it clean and tidy. President Wilson noted that, contrary to Northern generalities about Old Dixie, Southern servants were quite "comfortably quartered."[426]

Of course looking back from today's perspective, we wish that the black occupants of the McGavocks' servants' houses were free citizens, with the same rights as whites. Nonetheless, at the time, these dwellings were highly prized by those who lived in them. There were free blacks, and free whites, living in Franklin with far less. Indeed, there are Franklinites of all races today living in smaller, less well built homes, as any objective construction expert will tell you.

Both Northern and foreign visitors to the South in the 1800s reported that most slave houses were of a much higher standard than the homes of poor and even many middle class whites. In fact, Southern servants' quarters compared very favorably with those of the average working class family around the world.

Right into the early 1900s, for instance, entire families from among London's laboring poor existed in tiny, single-room flats that were not even fit for livestock. Indeed, the rural and urban poor in most countries have always lived in what we today would consider squalor, most in filthy dilapidated shacks that are far below the level of the Victorian South's clean, fairly spacious, well constructed slave

---

426. W. Wilson, DR, p. 126.

THE MCGAVOCKS OF CARNTON PLANTATION

housing.[427]

Southern slaves themselves were well aware of the difference between their standard of living and that of many whites around them—the poorest whites who, as blacks often noted, lived in rude windowless huts made of mud and sticks.[428]

The result of such comparisons was enormous pride and appreciation among servants for what they had. After the War former slaves reminisced sympathetically about how poor whites would often come to their door begging for handouts and assistance, recalling that the suffering of many whites rivaled, or even far exceeded, their own.[429]

❧ FREE BLACKS IN THE SOUTH

Speaking of free blacks, by now, it should not surprise us to learn that not all blacks in the South were "slaves," that is, bonded servants. In fact, there were at least 250,000 known free blacks living across Dixie in the early to mid 1800s.[430] By 1860 there were some 500,000,[431] more than double the number of free blacks living in the North.

That same year nearly 11 percent of Virginia's black population was free, numbering 58,042 individuals. Officially Tennessee had 7,300 free blacks in 1860, though there were no doubt thousands more, not only in the Volunteer State, but across the rest of the South as well, who went unrecorded.[432]

❧ BLACK SLAVE OWNERS

We should also not be shocked to discover that many free Southern blacks were extremely wealthy slave owners themselves,[433] black masters and mistresses who bought and sold others of their race with the same

---

427. Genovese, pp. 526-527, 533-534.
428. Gragg, pp. 87-88.
429. Genovese, p. 24.
430. Rosenbaum and Brinkley, s.v. "Free Blacks."
431. Seabrook, EYWTACWW, p. 158. Also see Ransom, pp. 214-215; Cooper, JDA, p. 378; Quarles, p. xiii; Stephenson, ALU, p. 168.
432. *The Civil War Book of Lists*, pp. 193, 195.
433. Long and Long, p. 702.

THE MCGAVOCKS OF CARNTON PLANTATION

commercial mindedness that white slave owners did.[434] Many, like early African-American servant owner Anthony Johnson, even owned white slaves.[435]

In the deep South, just one specific region of Dixie, nearly 25 percent of free blacks owned black servants.[436] This is in stark contrast to white Southern servant owners, who made up only 1 percent of the entire total U.S. population in 1860! The Census for that year alone shows that 10,000 black servants were owned by other blacks.[437]

One of these was the Metoyer family of Louisiana, an African-American slave holding clan who owned 400 black servants, over eight times as many as the McGavocks of Carnton Plantation. At about $2,000 a piece in 1860, their servants were worth a total of $22,000,000 in today's currency, making the Metoyer's one of the most affluent families in all of American history, black or white.[438]

The third largest slaveholder in South Carolina was William Ellison, a former black slave who owned ninety-seven African servants, worth a total of about $5,250,000 today.[439] One of the richest men in the state, he was wealthier than 90 percent of his white neighbors.[440] The Ellison family became the social core of Charleston's many black slave owners and was a staunch supporter of the Southern Cause.[441] Of the clan it was written: they were the epitome of loyal Rebels.[442]

One of Ellison's fellow South Carolinians, John Stanley, was a black man who owned 163 black slaves, worth about $9,000,000 today. In 1860 the African-American women of Charleston, who owned 70 percent of the town's black-owned slaves, used the wealth they accumulated from the so-called "peculiar institution" to start up their

---

434. Genovese, pp. 406-408.
435. C. Johnson, p. 81-85.
436. Greenberg and Waugh, pp. 376-377.
437. Kennedy and Kennedy, SWR, pp. 64-65.
438. Greenberg and Waugh, p. 376.
439. Greenberg and Waugh, p. 376.
440. C. Johnson, pp. 133-134.
441. Greenberg and Waugh, pp. 386-387.
442. Johnson and Roark, p. 208.

THE McGAVOCKS OF CARNTON PLANTATION

own prosperous businesses.[443]

Born into slavery, Horace King of Russell County, Alabama, was later freed, after which he founded a highly lucrative bridge building company using slave labor. King, a generous Confederate benefactor, donated money and purchased uniforms for Rebel soldiers throughout the War.[444] In 1905 it was noted that he had been

> a constant and liberal contributor to the support of the Confederacy. He also furnished clothes and money to the sons of his former master who were in the army, and erected a monument over the grave of their father.[445]

Andrew Durnford of Louisiana was a free black millionaire who owned seventy-five black slaves. Durnford complained about both the price of his slaves and their poor work ethic, calling them "rascally negroes." Unlike George Washington, Thomas Jefferson, Nathan Bedford Forrest, and thousands of other white Southern slave owners, Durnford never freed any of his slaves (except one body servant who he favored). Indeed, he never expressed any misgivings about the institution at all.[446]

Countless other examples of black slavers abound, such as the Virginia black who owned seventy-one slaves; the Louisiana black who owned seventy-five; and two in South Carolina who each owned eighty-four slaves.[447] All were black planters of great wealth and influence in their communities.

Then there was William Johnson of Natchez, Mississippi. A free African-American, Johnson saved up his money, purchased a plantation, and bought fifteen black slaves. His famous farm, called "Hardscrabble,"

---

443. Greenberg and Waugh, p. 376.
444. Greenberg and Waugh, p. 377.
445. Fleming, p. 208.
446. J. C. Perry, p. 178.
447. Stampp, p. 194.

THE McGAVOCKS OF CARNTON PLANTATION

is today part of the Natchez National Historical Park.[448]

When Lincoln's invaders began their illicit raid on the South, they were appalled to often come across entire plantations without a single white person. Both the owners and the servants were black. This was something new and radical to the Northern mind. But it was well-known and accepted in the South, where race relations were normalized by constant and close association.[449]

✤ BLACK OVERSEERS ON WHITE PLANTATIONS

In fact, even on white-owned Southern plantations a vast majority of them were headed by black overseers. In her journals, for example, Chesnut makes frequent reference to James Team, the married black overseer of her father-in-law's numerous plantations, a position Team held his entire life. Of him Mary writes that he had the support and esteem of the whole world. The highly regarded African-American overseer was also a planter himself, one worth $13,500 in 1860,[450] about $350,000 in today's currency. Many other black servants operated at even higher levels of supervision, such as general manager. This position was only one rung down from actual ownership.[451]

Let us break these numbers down more specifically. On small white-owned plantations (with one to fifteen servants), almost all overseers were black. On moderate sized white-owned plantations (sixteen to fifty servants), more than five out of six used black overseers. On large white-owned plantations (over fifty servants), 75 percent of the overseers were black. And on extra large white-owned plantations (over 100 servants), 70 percent employed black overseers.[452]

It was in this way that blacks played a vital role not only in plantation management, but also in the financial success of both

---

[448]. J. C. Perry, p. 173. For more on the Natchez National Historical Park, see Website: www.nps.gov/natc/index.htm. For more on black slave owners, see Koger, passim; Johnson and Roark, passim.
[449]. J. C. Perry, p. 175-176.
[450]. Chesnut, MCCW, pp. 75, 255.
[451]. Fogel and Engerman, pp. 210-212.
[452]. Fogel and Engerman, pp. 200-201.

individual farms and of the Southern economy as a whole. Such interracial business relationships were virtually unheard of in the North before or after the War.

❧ WHITE RACISM WAS FAR WORSE IN THE NORTH

Southern race relations are to be contrasted with those in the North, where whites had less contact with blacks, making racism far more ingrained. Jim Crow laws, along with both legal and customary segregation, for instance, were "universal" in all of the Northern states, but were "unusual" in the South.[453] Indeed, during the antebellum period there was no segregation anywhere in Dixie, yet it was endemic to America's northeastern states right up to, and far beyond, the 1860s.[454]

The North's onerous Black Codes forbade, among many other things, black immigration and black civil rights, and even banned blacks from attending public schools. Little wonder that those blacks who managed to survive in the North were generally less educated and less skilled than Southern blacks. Up to 1855 it was this very type of oppression that prevented blacks from serving as jurors in all but one Northern state: Massachusetts,[455] the birthplace of both the American slave trade (in 1638)[456] and American slavery (in 1641).[457]

Even after Lincoln's fake and illegal Emancipation Proclamation was issued (on January 1, 1863), literally nothing changed for African-Americans living north of the Mason-Dixon Line. When former slaves managed to make economic progress there, they found themselves blocked at every turn by a hostile racist Northern government, the very body that had "emancipated" them. This blockage was accomplished not only by Black Codes, by also through the implementation of severe Jim Crow laws and public segregation laws.[458]

---

453. Rosenbaum and Brinkley, s.v. "Jim Crow Laws."
454. C. Johnson, pp. 206-207.
455. Rosenbaum and Brinkley, s.v. "Free Blacks."
456. Meltzer, Vol. 2, p. 139.
457. G. H. Moore, pp. 5, 11, 17-19.
458. H. C. Bailey, p. 155; DiLorenzo, RL, pp. 26-27, 257-258.

THE MCGAVOCKS OF CARNTON PLANTATION

Trade unions and a highly discriminatory legal system further undermined black efforts to merge into Northern society.[459] All of this was done under the auspices of President Lincoln, and later, after his assassination, with the authorization of his cabinet, all of whom he had carefully hand-picked.[460]

While on the topic of our sixteenth president and Northern racism, we should point out that "The Land of Lincoln," Illinois, Lincoln's adopted home state, was one of the most anti-black Jim Crow states in America at the time,[461] in large part because of his work to restrict black civil rights there. White Illinoisans, for instance, arguably among the most racist Northerners in the 1850s and 60s, threatened to start "a war of extermination" if blacks were given equal rights in their state.[462] It was said that Illinois' Black Codes were so stringent that the civil rights of African-Americans were "virtually nonexistent" there.[463]

On November 14, 1864, Lincoln himself admitted that Louisiana was less racist than his own state, saying:

> A very fair proportion of the people of Louisiana, have inaugurated a new state government, making an excellent new constitution—better for the poor black man than we have in Illinois.[464]

What Lincoln deceptively does not mention here is that Illinois' blacks were largely "poor" (that is, devoid of basic civil rights) because of he himself!

In 1857, for instance, Lincoln aided in the white supremacist movement in his state by asking the Illinois legislature to appropriate funds for the deportation of all blacks out of the state. Why? To help prevent one of his greatest fears: the dilution of the white race through

---

459. Thornton and Ekelund, pp. 95-98.
460. D. H. Donald, L, pp. 261-267.
461. See e.g., Litwack, NS, pp. 70-72.
462. Woodard, p. 15.
463. Nye, p. 49.
464. Nicolay and Hay, ALCW, Vol. 2, p. 597.

THE MCGAVOCKS OF CARNTON PLANTATION

interracial breeding.[465]

Whites from central Illinois in particular had little use for blacks, considering them, not human beings, but lowly creatures, little more than livestock "with wool on their heads."[466] Wrote one newspaper editor from the area, who could not abide the idea of free blacks moving to Illinois: We don't want any Negroes around here. Send them all to the Northeast![467]

An Illinois senator, Joseph Kitchell, was of the same mind as the rest of the whites in his state, including Lincoln. The residence of Negroes among us, he announced,

> even as servants . . . is productive of moral and political evil. . . . The natural difference between them and ourselves forbids the idea that they should ever be permitted to participate with us in the political affairs of our government.[468]

Illinoisans passed countless anti-integration and anti-immigration laws to prevent blacks from settling in or even traveling through their state, with punishments ranging from whipping to being sold back into slavery at public auction.[469] In 1862 Illinois voters adopted a constitutional provision that barred the further admission of blacks into their state,[470] a Black Code that Lincoln allowed to remain on the books until 1865, the year his War finally came to an end.[471]

In 1863, for instance, eight blacks were arrested and convicted for entering Illinois unlawfully. Of these, seven were sold back into slavery (temporarily) to pay off their fines[472]—all under Lincoln's watch.

Black Illinois residents complained bitterly of their treatment. One of these, John Jones, a wealthy African-American living in Chicago,

---

465. Berwanger, p. 4-5.
466. DeCaro, p. 17.
467. Berwanger, p. 30. Note that Illinois was considered a Western state at the time.
468. N. D. Harris, pp. 233-234.
469. Litwack, NS, p. 70.
470. W. B. Garrison, CWTFB, p. 179.
471. Litwack, NS, p. 71.
472. J. M. McPherson, NCW, p. 252.

sent the following to Governor Richard Yates: We, the colored people of Illinois, it began, are highly displeased with the degradation we are suffering under in our State. Though we were born here, we are viewed as strangers. A black man cannot even buy a burial plot in Chicago for himself. The hatred toward us all comes from the anti-Negro laws passed by the whites of Illinois.[473]

All of the Northern states had similar Black Codes on their books at the time, a social phenomenon that did not go unnoticed by foreign visitors.

As early as 1831 individuals like French aristocrat Alexis de Tocqueville (1805-1859), who toured the South and the North that year, noticed that Southerners were "much more tolerant and compassionate" toward blacks than Northerners. This fact was also remarked on by British journalists, even in the middle of Lincoln's War.

In 1862, as just one example, the *North British Review* noted that in the North, "where slavers are fitted out by scores . . . free Negroes are treated like lepers."[474] This was the same year Lincoln issued his Preliminary Emancipation Proclamation, which, of course, called for the deportation of all freed blacks out of the U.S.[475]

After a thorough examination of both the South and the North, Tocqueville summed up his observations this way:

> Whosoever has inhabited the United States must have perceived that in those parts of the Union in which the negroes are no longer slaves, they have in nowise drawn nearer to the whites. On the contrary, the prejudice of the race appears to be stronger in the States which have abolished slavery than in those where it still exists; and nowhere is it so intolerant as in those States where servitude never has been known.
>
> It is true that in the North of the Union marriages may be legally contracted between negroes and whites; but public opinion would stigmatize a man who should connect himself with a negress as infamous, and it would be difficult to meet with a single instance

---

473. *Anglo-African*, January 14, 1865.
474. *The North British Review*, p. 240.
475. See Nicolay and Hay, ALCW, Vol. 2, pp. 237-238.

of such a union. The electoral franchise has been conferred upon the negroes in almost all the States in which slavery has been abolished; but if they come forward to vote, their lives are in danger. If oppressed, they may bring an action at law, but they will find none but whites among their judges; and although they may legally serve as jurors, prejudice repulses them from that office. The same schools do not receive the child of the black and of the European. In the theatres, gold can not procure a seat for the servile race beside their former masters; in the hospitals they lie apart; and although they are allowed to invoke the same Divinity as the whites, it must be at a different altar, and in their own churches with their own clergy. The gates of Heaven are not closed against these unhappy beings; but their inferiority is continued to the very confines of the other world; when the negro is defunct, his bones are cast aside, and the distinction of condition prevails even in the equality of death. The [Northern] negro is free, but he can share neither the rights, nor the pleasures, nor the labour, nor the afflictions, nor the tomb of him whose equal he has been declared to be; and he can not meet him upon fair terms in life or in death.

In the South, where slavery still exists, the negroes are less carefully kept apart; they sometimes share the labour and the recreations of the whites; the whites consent to intermix with them to a certain extent, and although the legislation treats them more harshly, the habits of the [Southern] people are more tolerant and compassionate. In the South the master is not afraid to raise his slave to his own standing, because he knows that he can in a moment reduce him to the dust at pleasure. In the North the white no longer distinctly perceives the barrier which separates him from the degraded race, and he shuns the negro with the more pertinacity, since he fears lest they should some day be confounded together.

Among the Americans of the South, Nature sometimes reasserts her rights, and restores a transient equality between the blacks and the whites; but in the North pride restrains the most imperious of human passions. The American of the Northern States would perhaps allow the negress to share his licentious pleasures if the laws of his country did not declare that she may aspire to be the legitimate partner of his bed; but he recoils with horror from her who might become his wife.

Thus it is, in the United States, that the prejudice which repels the negroes seems to increase in proportion as they are emancipated, and inequality is sanctioned by the manners while it

THE MCGAVOCKS OF CARNTON PLANTATION

is effaced from the laws of the country. But if the relative position of the two races which inhabit the United States is such as I have described, it may be asked why the Americans have abolished slavery in the North of the Union, why they maintain it in the South, and why they aggravate its hardships there? The answer is easily given. It is not for the good of the negroes, but for that of the whites, that measures are taken to abolish slavery in the United States.[476]

What Tocqueville refers to as "those States where servitude never has been known" is a reference to what were then called the Western Territories (today the Western states), at the time an area with the least number of blacks and where slavery had never been practiced. It was here that he found white racism toward blacks the strongest.

To emphasize these facts, the Frenchman goes on to point out that while slaves had been freed in the North and now had so-called "full equal rights," Northern white society continued to strongly discourage blacks, often with the threat of death, from voting, sitting on juries, or attending white schools or white churches. According to Tocqueville blacks in the "abolitionist North" were not even permitted to sit next to whites in theaters, take a sick bed next to them in Northern hospitals, or be buried next to them in death.

In the 1840s English writer James Silk Buckingham (1786-1855) wrote that "the prejudice of colour is not nearly so strong in the South as in the North."[477] Here is how Robert Young Hayne (1791-1839), a South Carolina senator, described the treatment of those few Southern blacks who fled to the North:

> . . . there does not exist on the face of the whole earth, a population so poor, so wretched, so vile, so loathsome, so utterly destitute of all the comforts, conveniences, and decencies of life, as the unfortunate blacks of Philadelphia, and New York and Boston. Liberty has been to them the greatest of calamities, the heaviest of curses. Sir, I have had some opportunities of making comparison

---

476. Tocqueville, Vol. 1, pp. 383-385.
477. Buckingham, Vol. 2, p. 112.

between the condition of the free negroes of the North, and the slaves of the South, and the comparison has left not only an indelible impression of the superior advantages of the latter, but has gone far to reconcile me to slavery itself. Never have I felt so forcibly that touching description, 'the foxes have holes, and the birds of the air have nests, but the Son of Man hath not where to lay his head,' as when I have seen this unhappy race, naked and houseless, almost starving in the streets, and abandoned by all the world. Sir, I have seen, in the neighborhood of one of the most moral, religious and refined cities of the North, a family of free blacks driven to the caves of the rocks, and there obtaining a precarious subsistence from charity and plunder.[478]

Only a few years later, in 1835, Virginian James Madison met with English author Harriet Martineau and regaled her with stories about how the Northern states erected numerous barriers in an attempt to thwart Negro emigration.[479] In 1841, after traveling through Philadelphia, an English Quaker, Joseph Sturge (1793-1859), met with former Illinois Governor Edward Coles (1786-1868). Writes Sturge:

In the course of conversation, the Governor spoke of the prejudice against colour prevailing here as much stronger than in the slave States [the South]. I may add, from my own observation, and much concurring testimony, that Philadelphia appears to be the metropolis of this odious prejudice, and that there is probably no city in the known world, where dislike, amounting to hatred of the coloured population, prevails more than in the city of brotherly love![480]

After a visit to New York City, English writer Edward Dicey (1832-1911) recorded his observations concerning Yankee racism and Northern blacks. In the North, Dicey noted:

Everywhere and at all seasons the coloured people form a separate

---

478. J. Hawthorne, Vol. 2, pp. 109-110.
479. M. D. Peterson, JM, p. 377.
480. Sturge, p. 40.

THE MCGAVOCKS OF CARNTON PLANTATION

community. In the public streets you hardly ever see a coloured person in company with a white, except in the capacity of servant. . . . On board the river steamboats, the commonest and homeliest of working [white] men has a right to dine, and does dine, at the public meals; but, for coloured passengers, there is always a separate table. At the great [Northern] hotels there is, as with us [in England], a servants' table, but the coloured servants are not allowed to dine in common with the white. At the inns, in the barbers' shops, on board the steamers, and in most hotels, the servants are more often than not coloured people. . . . White [Northern] servants will not associate with black on terms of equality. . . . I hardly ever remember seeing a black employed as shopman, or placed in any post of responsibility. As a rule, the blacks you meet in the Free [that is, Northern] States are shabbily, if not squalidly dressed; and, as far as I could learn, the instances of black men having made money by trade in the North, are very few in number.[481]

Compare all of this to the South, where whites and blacks worked in close association with one another on a daily basis, creating race relations that, on the whole, were friendlier and warmer than in any other region in America, as the following example illustrates.

In the early 1800s Northern landscape architect Frederick Law Olmsted (1822-1903) traveled to Virginia, where he witnessed something that he found absolutely shocking.[482] In his book *The Cotton Kingdom*, the stunned Yankee racist[483] wrote:

> I am struck with the close cohabitation and association of black and white—negro women are carrying black and white babies together in their arms; black and white children are playing together . . .; black and white faces are constantly thrust together out of the doors, to see the train go by. . . . A fine-looking, well-dressed, and well-behaved coloured young man sat, together with a white man, on a seat in the cars. I suppose the man was his master; but he was much the less like a gentleman of the two. The railroad company

---

481. Dicey, Vol. 1, pp. 70-72.
482. Olmsted, an anti-South author of numerous books, including, *A Journey in the Seaboard Slave States* (1856), is best known for being the designer of New York City's Central Park.
483. See Fogel and Engerman, pp. 179-180.

THE McGAVOCKS OF CARNTON PLANTATION

> advertise to take coloured people only in second-class trains; but servants seem to go with their masters everywhere. Once, to-day, seeing a lady entering the car at a way-station, with a family behind her, and that she was looking about to find a place where they could be seated together, I rose, and offered her my seat, which had several vacancies round it. She accepted it, without thanking me, and immediately installed in it a stout negro woman; took the adjoining seat herself, and seated the rest of her party before her. It consisted of a white girl, probably her daughter, and a bright and very pretty mulatto girl. They all talked and laughed together; and the girls munched confectionary out of the same paper, with a familiarity and closeness of intimacy that would have been noticed with astonishment, if not with manifest displeasure, in almost any chance company at the North.[484]

But this scene would have astonished or displeased few white Southerners, nearly all who were accustomed to, and even enjoyed, the company of blacks, as this incident clearly shows.

Mary Chesnut writes of an incident that too reveals the true state of race relations in the South. One hot August day during the War, she found herself traveling on a river boat in Alabama, one overseen, not by a white deck hand, but by a black one, as was the norm in the South. Writes Mary:

> Montgomery, July 30th.—Coming on here from Portland there was no stateroom for me. My mother alone had one. My aunt and I sat nodding in armchairs, for the floors and sofas were covered with sleepers, too. On the floor that night, so hot that even a little covering of clothes could not be borne, lay a motley crew. Black, white, and yellow disported themselves in promiscuous array. Children and their nurses, bared to the view, were wrapped in the profoundest slumber. No caste prejudices were here. Neither [abolitionists] Garrison, John Brown, nor Gerrit Smith ever dreamed of equality more untrammeled.[485]

Naturally such scenes contradict Yankee myth so they are ignored by

---

484. Olmsted, CK, Vol. 1, p. 39.
485. Chesnut, DD, p. 226.

THE MCGAVOCKS OF CARNTON PLANTATION

pro-North historians.

And let us not forget that it was a Southern state, Virginia, that would later vote the first black into its highest office: in 1989, Lawrence Douglas Wilder, the grandson of Southern black servants, became the first elected black governor in the U.S. Even the first *non-elected* African-American governor was from a Southern state: as lieutenant governor of Louisiana, Pinckney B. S. Pinchback (1837-1921) succeeded to the position in 1872 when Governor Henry Clay Warmoth (1842-1931) was impeached and forced to step down.

The first two blacks to serve in the U.S. Congress were also from the South: Hiram Rhodes Revels (1827-1901) of Mississippi entered the Senate February 23, 1870; Joseph Hayne Rainey (1832-1887) of South Carolina entered the House of Representatives December 12, 1870. Despite these bold facts, it is the South, not the North, that continues to be unfairly associated with racism.

European-American revulsion toward blacks was so deeply rooted in the North that many white Yanks, even those who considered themselves "friends of the Negro," promoted the idea of using whites as slaves rather than their "sable-skinned" fellow Americans. One of these was Puritan abolitionist Samuel Sewall (1652-1730), who was a judge at the infamous Salem Witch Trials in 1692.[486] Though he hated slavery, he could not abide the thought of free blacks living among New England whites. Wrote Sewall:

> And all things considered, it would conduce more to the Welfare of the Province, to have White Servants for a Term of Years, than to have Slaves for Life. Few can endure to hear of a Negro's being made free; and indeed they can seldom use their freedom well; yet their continual aspiring after their forbidden Liberty, renders them Unwilling Servants. And there is such a disparity in their Conditions, Colour & Hair, that they can never embody with us, and grow up into orderly Families, to the Peopling of the Land: but

---

[486]. Sewall later recognized his error in helping to condemn dozens of innocent people to death as "witches," and spent the rest of his life repenting.

The McGavocks of Carnton Plantation

still remain in our Body Politick as a kind of extravasat Blood.[487]

Northern white racism was severe enough that it actually helped spawn the phenomenon of all-black churches, still with us today. As early Northern whites could not bear to sit next to African-Americans in church, blacks had little choice. In 1787, in Philadelphia, Pennsylvania, for example, two former Northern slaves, Richard Allen (1764-1835) and Absalom Jones (1746-1818), started what was probably the first African-American-only church, the Mother Zion African Methodist Episcopal Church, when white members at nearby Saint George's Church denied them the right to worship there.[488]

Over a century later Northern racism was, if anything, even more unyielding and firmly established.

When Lincoln illegally instituted the first military draft in U.S. history, for instance, 50,000 Northerners took to the streets in New York in protest. They did not vent their anger in peaceful demonstrations against the government, however. These so-called Northern "humanitarians and abolitionists" turned on the blacks of their state, chasing, beating, and even lynching them. Many were hanged from trees and lampposts, while the bodies of dead blacks were burned in the streets. At least 100 people were killed and damage was estimated to be at least $1.5 million ($33.5 million in today's currency).[489]

So deep was the racism of white New Yorkers that these same mobs attacked and flogged white abolitionists, even destroying their homes and businesses. The "New York Draft Riots," as they are still deceptively called by Northern and New South historians, lasted four days (July 12-16, 1863) and were finally only quelled when Lincoln sent in Union troops returning from the Battle of Gettysburg (fought July 1-3, 1863).[490]

This type of white racism in the North, compared to that in the

---

487. Sewall, Vol. 2, pp. 17-18.
488. McKissack and McKissack, p. 56.
489. LeVert, s.v. "New York Draft Riots."
490. Simmons, s.v. "Draft Riots."

THE McGAVOCKS OF CARNTON PLANTATION

South, was observed by many others, including the above mentioned James Silk Buckingham. After traveling across the U.S. he noted that in Dixie

> it is not at all uncommon to see the black slaves of both sexes, shake hands with white people when they meet, and interchange friendly personal inquiries; but at the North I do not remember to have witnessed this once; and neither in Boston, New York, or Philadelphia would white persons generally like to be seen shaking hands and talking familiarly with blacks in the streets.[491]

Racism was so firmly fixed in Northern culture that many abolitionist-minded Northerners and politicians were forced to promote emancipation using racist arguments, otherwise no one would listen to them. Knowing that Northern blacks would have preferred to live in the more tolerant South, some radical Republicans called for abolition because it would offer the benefit of starting a mass migration of blacks out of the North and into the South! And indeed, after Lincoln issued the Emancipation Proclamation a fearful U.S. government (no doubt with Lincoln's blessing) inaugurated the policy of "containment,"[492] in which it was attempted to prevent freed blacks from coming North by keeping them "hemmed in," as Stephen A. Douglas put it, across the South.[493]

All of this helps explain why Nat Turner, John Brown, and Lincoln could not manage to instigate even a tiny slave insurrection in the South, for even if blacks chose to leave Dixie where would they go? Certainly not North! And it is also why the infamous "Southern" Black Codes (which restricted the advancement of black civil rights) actually originated in the North, where they existed long prior to those adopted later by Southerners.[494]

We will note that rampant Northern racism endured well into

---

491. Buckingham, Vol. 2, p. 112.
492. Garraty and McCaughey, p. 254.
493. Nicolay and Hay, ALCW, Vol. 1, p. 241.
494. DiLorenzo, RL, pp. 26-27, 257-258.

THE McGAVOCKS OF CARNTON PLANTATION

the 20th Century. When 750,000 Southern blacks headed North to join in the prosperity of the labor boom in the early 1900s, for instance, Northern whites, far from welcoming them, instead regarded them as "dangerous and loathsome competition." As a result, between June and December 1919 alone twenty-six race riots exploded across America, the worst one occurring in the nation's capital city, Washington, D.C. Terribly violent racially based riots, such as those witnessed in recent years in Detroit, Harlem, Jersey City, and Philadelphia, continue in the North into the present day,[495] along with an ever increasing rate of hate crimes.

Some of the most recent of these have included the appearance of nooses (an anti-black symbol) and swastikas (an anti-Jewish symbol) in police stations, U.S. Coast Guard stations, post offices, and college campuses in New York and Connecticut.[496]

❧ RED SLAVE OWNERS

Along with the tens of thousands of America's black slave owners there were countless Native-American slave owners as well,[497] many who were planters and owned cotton plantations, particularly in the Lower South.[498]

It is impossible to know the exact number because most of these individuals were never accurately counted in the Censuses (those that are listed represent only a tiny fraction of the total). But we know there were thousands of Indian peoples, among them the Choctaw, Chickasaw, Seminole, Cherokee, and the Creek,[499] who possessed African-American slaves,[500] because they are mentioned in the reports, journals, and diaries of those whites who came in contact with them.[501]

---

495. Wade, pp. 151, 343.
496. Website: www.foxnews.com/story/0,2933,301403,00.html.
497. Civil War Society, ECW, s.v. "Watie, Stand."
498. Simpson, p. 183.
499. Rosenbaum and Brinkley, s.v. "Five Civilized Tribes."
500. Simmons, s.v. "Indians, in the War."
501. See Jahoda, pp. 85, 148, 154, 225, 241, 246, 247, 249; J. C. Perry, pp. 96, 99, 101; Grissom, p. 182. Native-Americans also made slaves out of some of the earliest whites to land on North America's shores. Among these were European-Americans like Virginia Dare, the first child born of English parents in America.

THE MCGAVOCKS OF CARNTON PLANTATION

Fortunately for Southern historians, the 1860 Census listed how many slaves were owned by the various Indians tribes. However, these figures must be considered vastly undercounted due to the many inherent errors of the enumeration process:

Choctaw: 385 red slave owners, 2,297 black slaves
Cherokee: 384 red slave owners, 2,504 black slaves
Creek: 267 red slave owners, 1,651 black slaves
Chickasaw: 118 red slave owners, 917 black slaves[502]

While the average European-American slaveholder owned five or less slaves,[503] the average Native-American slaveholder owned six. One Choctaw slaver owned 227.[504] Thus, it was non-white slave owners who individually owned the most slaves, not whites.

The Confederacy certainly had knowledge of red slave owners because officers like Yankee-turned Rebel, Brigadier General Albert Pike (1809-1891), who, in 1861, was acting as special commissioner in charge of treaty-making, noted hundreds of them among the Confederate Indian troops in the Indian Territories (later to become Oklahoma) and in various Southern states like Missouri and Texas.[505]

One of the more famous examples of Native-American slave owners are to be found among the supporters of Cherokee chief Stand Watie (1806-1871),[506] the last Confederate officer to surrender to the Yank invaders (on June 23, 1865). His strongest allies were the southeastern Indian slave owners who had been relocated to the West by a callous United States army.[507]

None of this should be surprising as the institution of slavery was part and parcel of Native-American culture, with Indians enslaving other

---

Furnas, p. 28. Most pro-North histories fail to mention this fact.
502. J. C. Perry, p. 99.
503. Gragg, p. 84; DiLorenzo, LU, p. 174.
504. J. C. Perry, p. 101.
505. Katcher, CWSB, p. 226.
506. Warner, GG, s.v. "Stand Watie."
507. Simmons, s.v. "Watie, Stand."

THE McGAVOCKS OF CARNTON PLANTATION

Indians for hundreds, if not thousands, of years prior to the introduction of African slavery in the Americas[508] by Columbus and other Hispanics.[509]

In the pre-Columbian Americas, for example, slavery was an integral part of such Native-American peoples as the Maya, Aztec, and Inca, who depended on large scale slave labor in warfare and farming.[510]

Other Indian peoples who once practiced slavery include the Cherokee, Iroquois, Navaho, Seminole, Choctaw, Creek, Chickasaw, Cheyenne, Natchez, Comanche, Arapaho, Kiowas, Paiute, Chinook, Yuchie, Pima, Nootka, Papago, Carib, Halchidhoma, Guarani, Shasta, and Klamath. Some of the forms of slavery employed were particularly brutal, involving torture and even cannibalistic rituals. It is said that slavery was as economically important to many of these Native-American tribes as it was to European-American slavers prior to the "Civil War."[511]

❧ BROWN SLAVE OWNERS

Of course, neither red, black, or white American slave owners would have ever even had the opportunity to become involved in this occupation had it not been for their brown brethren, the Hispanics and Latinos.[512]

Both the European and the American slave industries got their start with a Portuguese explorer Henry the Navigator (1394-1460) who, while searching for gold along the West African coast in the early 1400s, happened upon a vast indigenous slave industry run by local African slave owners and slave traders. Henry wasted no time in involving Portugal in the sordid business. This resulted in the first African slaves being brought to the New World in 1503. The owners, captains, and crews on these ships were all Hispanic-Europeans.[513]

---

508. Furnas, p. 118.
509. Garraty and McCaughey, p. 7.
510. R. S. Phillips, s.v. "Slavery."
511. Meltzer, Vol. 2, pp. 61-73.
512. "Hispanics" here is used to indicate those born in, or deriving ancestry, from Spain or Portugal. "Latinos" refers to those of Latin-American origin; that is, those of mixed European and Native-American heritage. The former were responsible for bringing slavery to the New World, while the latter were responsible for expanding it across the Americas.
513. Lott, p. 18.

THE MCGAVOCKS OF CARNTON PLANTATION

Over the next few centuries African and Hispanic slavers were responsible for the capture, sale, and shipment of literally millions of blacks from Africa to Latin-American colonies and nations, such as Hispaniola, Brazil, and Cuba, the latter being one of the last Western nations to ban slavery, in 1886, twenty-one years after the Thirteenth Amendment (not Lincoln) outlawed it across the U.S.[514] The very word *negro* is a legacy of those dark days: because Portuguese and Spaniards were the first Europeans to involve themselves in the slave business, the word *negro*, Spanish for "black," was later adopted by the English as the logical word for Africans.[515]

Here is evidence that American slavery was not a creation of the South. American slavery was a creation of Europe, and more specifically of Hispanic Europe, which introduced the institution to Latin America long before it was introduced to the American South by Yankees. Neither were these early African slaves first used on cotton plantations in the South, as Northern folklore asserts. They were first sent to work on sugar plantations in the West Indies.

Under the auspices of the Spanish government, the Hispanic slave industry persisted, as mentioned, with the arrival of Italian explorer Christopher Columbus (1451-1506) in the Caribbean islands in 1492, who historians credit with the founding of American slavery itself.[516] At Hispaniola, Columbus enslaved thousands of the native Indian inhabitants, reducing their free population from 1 million to a mere 60,000, in just fifteen years. Contrast this with the black slave population of America's South which, far from diminishing in numbers, increased by millions from the beginning of the institution in Georgia in 1749 (the Peach State was the first Southern state to start using slaves), to its end in 1865.

---

514. In 1526 Hispanics also tried to introduce slavery into what is now the Southern United States. It was in that year that a Spanish Colonial judge, Lucas Vásquez de Ayllón (1475-1526), sent 500 Spaniards and a "few Negro slaves" to try and establish a settlement somewhere between what are now the coasts of Virginia and Georgia. The experiment ended when the entire group perished from local diseases. Had they lived, Hispanics would also have been directly responsible for being the first to introduce black slaves into the Southern states. Furnas, p. 27.
515. Garraty and McCaughey, p. 25.
516. Meltzer, Vol. 2, p. 4.

The McGavocks of Carnton Plantation

Brown slave trading and brown slave ownership were further augmented with the Spanish Conquest of the Americas, and in particular as a result of the efforts of the Spanish priest Bartolomé de Las Casas (1484-1566), who recommended to Spain's Queen Isabella (1451-1504) that the native Indian slaves of Hispaniola be replaced with African slaves. The Spanish monarch agreed, for it was found that Indians did not do as well under slavery as Africans. Why? Because slavery in the Americas primarily surrounded agriculture, and Native-Americans were mainly nomadic hunter-gatherers, while Africans were mainly farmers, with an agricultural tradition that dated back thousands of years.

There followed an Hispanic-induced flood of thousands of enslaved Africans to the New World, one that both nearly destroyed the Native-American population and which opened the door to the slave industry across what would one day become the United States of America.[517]

❧ AFRICA'S ROLE IN AMERICAN SLAVERY

Of course, the full responsibility for American slavery cannot be laid at the feet of either Latinos, Europeans, or Middle Easterners. Some of it must fall on Africa herself, a continent that was practicing slavery on her own people back to at least the African Iron Age (about 2,200 years ago), a full 1,600 years before the arrival of Arab, and later European, slave ships on Africa's shores.[518]

After examining the facts even American historians with no love for the South have been forced to admit that domestic slavery existed among the Negroes of preconquest Africa since time immemorial.[519] Experts in the study of comparative slavery agree that in pre-colonial Africa slavery was widespread and commonplace,[520] and that it was so ancient there that it had "no distinct beginning."[521]

This is why few if any of those Africans later purchased by

---

517. Kennedy, pp. 21-23.
518. Davidson, pp. 30, 32.
519. Rozwenc, p. 253.
520. Drescher and Engerman, p. 29.
521. U. B. Phillips, p. 6.

The McGavocks of Carnton Plantation

Europeans to be slaves started off as free men. They were brought to America already in bondage.[522]

Let us examine this for a moment.

Native Africans were never actually hunted down and captured directly by the crews of visiting slave ships. Rather, they were captives who had already been taken during intertribal raids and then enslaved by enterprising African kings, who quite eagerly traded them to non-African slavers for rum, gunpowder, and textiles.[523] Wars were often started on purpose by greedy Negro chiefs in order to obtain slaves, a practice that eventually became "endemic" across many parts of the continent.[524]

Thus, as objective historians now admit, nearly every one of the Africans brought to America on Yankee slave ships had already been enslaved in their home country, after which they were sold to whites by fellow Africans.[525] Whites played no role whatsoever in the actual enslaving process that took place in the interior, and hence had no idea what went on beyond the coastal areas.[526] Even Lincoln admitted as much, saying:

> . . . the African slave trader . . . does not catch free negroes and bring them here. He finds them already slaves in the hands of their black captors, and he honestly buys them at the rate of about a red cotton handkerchief a head. This is very cheap, and it is a great abridgement of the sacred right of self-government to hang men for engaging in this profitable trade![527]

Likewise, in 1908 J. Clarence Stonebraker wrote:

> Slave dealers only obtained their slaves by one tribe conquering another and delivering same into the hands of the slave dealers, or by the consent of parents, getting up their children and selling them. The very false stories that a vessel's crew could go into the

---

522. Lott, pp. 17, 19.
523. Furnas, p. 115.
524. Blassingame, p.14.
525. Garraty, p. 77.
526. J. Thornton, p. 307.
527. Nicolay and Hay, ALCW, Vol. 1, p. 197.

The McGavocks of Carnton Plantation

jungles and drive out as many negroes as they wished is grossly vile, and was hatched along with many others by the unconscionable and incorrigible prejudice of [Northern] partisans, and for an equally vile purpose. Such things are still being taught and believed to an extent in the frigid [Yankee] section of our country . . . [528]

Africa herself then must be held accountable for taking part in the enslavement and forced deportation of some 10 million of her own people between the 16th and the 19th Centuries.[529]

In short, it was African chiefs who first enslaved other Africans,[530] and it was African slave dealers who then carried them to the coast and sold them to Arabs, Europeans, and eventually Yankees.[531] And it was on this walk to the coast, forced violently along by their African owners, that most African slaves died—not on the infamous Middle Passage to the Americas, as Yankee mythology has long maintained.[532]

Some early African peoples, such as the Efik kingdom of Calabar, based their entire economy on the indigenous African slave trade. Large scale kidnaping expeditions were common, while many Africans garnered slaves through intertribal warfare or simple marauding or gang fighting. Early African slave merchants in Timbuktu exported their slaves to places like the Moorish kingdoms north of the Sahara. Eventually Africa began selling her slaves to such Europeans as the Portuguese, the English, the French, the Dutch, and the Danish. It was through these avenues that slavery eventually made its way to the American South.[533]

But contrary to Northern history, slavery did not take a direct route from Africa to Dixie; nor in the beginning was slavery desired or requested by the South. It came first through her Northern neighbor, the Yankee, the true founder of so-called "Southern slavery."

---

528. Stonebraker, pp. 50-51.
529. Blassingame, p. 3.
530. Hacker, p. 18.
531. Shillington, pp. 174, 175.
532. Drescher and Engerman, p. 34.
533. Garraty, p. 77.

THE MCGAVOCKS OF CARNTON PLANTATION

❧ HOW & WHY AMERICAN SLAVERY BEGAN IN THE NORTH

As mentioned, none of this is meant to excuse, condone, or justify either servitude or slavery. The South, unlike the North, has both repeatedly acknowledged its role in slavery and repeatedly apologized for it—neither, we will note here, which the North has done. It is only to point out that the so-called "slavery" practiced by the South was nothing like the image created by Northern abolitionists in the 1800s, or by the politically correct today.

In defense of the McGavocks and other Southern families it is time that we point out that both the North American slave trade *and* North American slavery got their start in the North, and that right up until the middle of Lincoln's War both were fueled by Northern money. How and why this occurred is vital to our study of slavery at Carnton Plantation.

Black slavery had taken root in the North due to a severe shortage of white labor. Two problems were the high cost and the difficulty of finding white labor.[534] The main issue, however, was that during the colonial period land was so cheap, often free, that there was no need for whites to work for a wage under an employer. Instead they could simply claim a piece of land and become independent farmers and tradesmen, owning and running their own businesses and farms.[535]

Still, as Thomas Jefferson pointed out in 1811, assistance was needed to clear forests, cultivate the soil, and harvest crops on these new huge tracts of land, acreage that was out of proportion to the small amount of labor available.[536]

For help early American colonists turned to Native-Americans, but found, like Spain's Queen Isabella, that they did not do well under servitude. Additionally, indentured white slaves (mainly Englishmen and women) were not only scarce in numbers, but those who could be found were prone to buying their freedom as soon as they reached America's

---

534. See e.g., O. Williams, p. 6.
535. Smelser, ACRH, p. 59.
536. Foley, p. 323.

The McGavocks of Carnton Plantation

Western frontier (as we will see in our next chapter).

Along with white slaves, white European convicts had once been a source of American labor as well, but the British government eventually began to cut back on their importation to the New World. For these reasons a large inexpensive work force was needed. And so in the early 1600s, America's North, as Europe had already done, turned to Africa.[537]

Thus it was that the American slave trade got its start in 1638, when Boston began importing African slaves: it was in that year that Captain William Pierce brought New England's first shipload of Africans from the West Indies aboard the Salem vessel *Desire*.[538] By 1676 Boston slavers were routinely coming home with shiploads of human cargo from East Africa and Madagascar.[539] By the 1700s Massachusetts had 5,000 black slaves and 30,000 bondservants.[540]

By 1639 Connecticut had slaves,[541] and by 1645 New Hampshire had them as well. The largest slave concentrations in New England were in Rockingham County, New Hampshire; Essex, Suffolk, Bristol, and Plymouth Counties, Massachusetts; New London, Hartford, and Fairfield Counties, Connecticut; and Newport and Washington Counties, Rhode Island. There were so many slaves in Rhode Island's Narragansett region that they made up half the population.[542] At one time the state's slave traders owned and operated nearly 90 percent of America's slave trade.[543]

By the early 1700s black slavery had evolved into the literal heart of New England's economy, and by the mid-1700s, New York had the largest slave force of any Northern colony, with slaves making up over

---

537. White, Foscue, and McKnight, p. 38.
538. Meltzer, Vol. 2, p. 139. Also see Cartmell, p. 26. The 120-ton *Desire* was built at Marblehead, Massachusetts, in 1636. Norwood, p. 31.
539. McManus, BBN, pp. 9, 10, 11.
540. Bowen, p. 217.
541. B. Steiner, passim.
542. McManus, BBN, pp. 6-7.
543. For more on the topic of slavery in Rhode Island, as well as in other New England states, see Website: www.boston.com/bostonglobe/ideas/articles/2010/09/26/new_englands_hidden_history/?page=1.

The McGavocks of Carnton Plantation

35 percent of the population.[544] Slavery was so integral to the North's culture, society, and economy that even the South-hating Harriet Beecher Stowe had to acknowledge that:

> The Northern slaveholder traded in men and women whom he never saw, and of whose separations, tears, and miseries he determined never to hear.[545]

Indeed, the first state in the U.S. to legalize slavery was not Tennessee, South Carolina, or Mississippi. It was Massachusetts, in 1641.[546] And the capital of the American slavery business was not Nashville, Atlanta, or New Orleans. It was New York City. Slavery would not begin in the South for another 108 years: in 1749, Georgia, the last of the thirteen original colonies, was the first Southern state to begin using slaves. This was over a century *after* the North began using slaves.[547]

Slavery took root in New York at the very beginning, when the region, then called New Netherland, was established by the Dutch in 1624. When the British took over in 1664, and renamed it New York, slavery increased greatly. Between 1697 and 1790, for example, Albany's slave population grew from 3 percent to 16 percent. Influential Albany plantation owners, like the Schuyler and Van Rensselaer families, made vast fortunes using black slaves to build up their estates. A number of their well-known homes stand in New York's capital city to this day,[548] including Ten Broeck Manor,[549] Cherry Hill Mansion,[550] and the Schuyler Mansion.[551]

By the year 1700 New York Harbor was teeming with slave ships and slavery had become the foundation of the state's economy. New

---

544. McManus, BBN, pp. 1-17.
545. Rice, NAR, p. 607.
546. G. H. Moore, pp. 5, 11, 17-19.
547. McKissack and McKissack, p. 3.
548. Williams-Meyers, pp. 22, 54. See also pp. 87-93.
549. Website: www.sites.google.com/site/tenbroeckmansion/Home.
550. Website: www.historiccherryhill.org.
551. Website: www.nysparks.state.ny.us/historic-sites/33/details.aspx.

THE MCGAVOCKS OF CARNTON PLANTATION

Yorkers believed that their "peculiar institution" was so vital to the North's economy that they blocked and delayed emancipation for over 100 years, until 1827.

New Yorkers loved their black slaves so dearly that later, in December 1860, when the Southern states began seceding on the eve of the "Civil War," New York City's mayor Fernando Wood advocated that his city secede as well, for it was primarily King Cotton that was keeping it economically stable.[552] Little wonder that when Lincoln's War finally erupted, New York was one of the last states to recruit African-Americans: the state's governor, Horatio Seymour, refused to enlist them until he was forced to by the U.S. War Department.[553]

New York's slave owners were a brutal lot, engaging in a myriad of cruel practices, from disenfranchisement and the separation of families to whipping and even murder.[554] New York City's booming slave market was inhumane enough that it inspired the very first antislavery book in America: *The Selling of Joseph*, written and published in 1701 by the aforementioned Salem Witch Trial judge, Samuel Sewall.

To protect their human investment, New York insurance companies sold insurance policies to Yankee slave owners: in 1853, for example, a New York slave was insured for $550 by a Northerner named John Yellmann.[555] New Yorkers were loathe to give up the lucrative institution,[556] which is why they continued it right through Lincoln's War, though by then it was often a clandestine affair. New York City is today America's largest and most affluent metropolis because of slavery.[557]

New York City was far from being the only huge Northern slave port. New Jersey, Massachusetts, and Rhode Island became veritable epicenters of the trade as well, with vast fortunes being made by New England bankers, manufacturers, shipowners, and merchants, even long

---

552. Farrow, Lang, and Frank, p. xxvii.
553. Buckley, p. 103.
554. Stewart, p. xxvi.
555. McKissack and McKissack, pp. 3, 4, 23.
556. See Stewart, passim.
557. Seabrook, EYWTACWW, pp. 79-80.

THE McGAVOCKS OF CARNTON PLANTATION

after it had been banned in 1808 by U.S. president and Southerner, Thomas Jefferson.[558]

Rhode Island boasted not only black slaves, but Native-American slaves as well, forced to work alongside one another in the fields of the Narragansett planters. By 1770 New England alone possessed some 11,000 African slaves.[559]

One of Rhode Island's more notable slave traders was the wealthy Portuguese-born Jew, Aaron Lopez (d. 1782). Lopez, who possessed twenty-seven slaves and owned at least thirty slave ships, believed that blacks were subhuman animals who were best kept in leg irons and handcuffs. He routinely outfitted slave ships at Newport and was friends with a number of other famous New England slave traders, among them William English, Peleg Clarke, Nathaniel Waldron, and Nathaniel Briggs. Far from being criticized for his occupation, fellow Northerners lauded Lopez for his work, his very name becoming a synonym for scrupulousness, morality, and good character.[560]

So great were the profits made by slave traders like Lopez at Newport, Rhode Island,[561] that it has been said that the city was literally constructed over the graves of thousands of Africans.[562] By 1790, when Liverpool had become England's primary slave port, her only serious competition was from the Yankee slave ship owners of Bristol and Newport, Rhode Island.[563]

Rhode Island's state flag still bears a ship's anchor, an apt reminder of her days as the nation's largest slave trader, one that imported 100,000 African slaves—20 percent of all those brought into the U.S.[564]

The slavers of Rhode Island and those of Massachusetts combined to make New England the leading slave-trading center in

---

558. Rosenbaum and Brinkley, s.v. "Slavery."
559. Furnas, pp. 117, 119.
560. Friedman, pp. 123-127.
561. K. C. Davis, p. 7.
562. M. M. Smith, p. 25.
563. Garraty, p. 77.
564. C. Johnson, p. 125.

THE MCGAVOCKS OF CARNTON PLANTATION

America and slavery "the hub of New England's economy." Two-thirds of Rhode Island's fleets and sailors alone were devoted to the trade. Even the states' governors participated in it, such as Jonathan Belcher (of Massachusetts) and Joseph Wanton (of Rhode Island). So integral was slavery to New England that without it she would have collapsed into financial ruin.[565]

Vestiges of New England's "peculiar institution" are still obvious to this day, one of the more conspicuous being the pineapple. Though it is now seen as a "welcome" sign across the Northeast, this is a corruption of its original meaning: when New England slave traders returned from their ocean expeditions to the tropics to pick up slaves, they would stick a pineapple on their fencepost to let everyone in town know that they were "welcome" to come in and shop for slave products, as well as for slaves themselves.[566] The pineapple motif, that great symbol of Yankee slavery, is still commonly seen all over the U.S., not just in the North, but in the South as well.

It was not just slave trading that Rhode Island was involved in. The state also possessed thousands of crop and cattle plantations which depended almost exclusively on slave labor.[567] In fact, due to the number of plantations that once dotted the Renaissance City, to this day the official name of the state of Rhode Island is "Rhode Island and Providence Plantations," a remnant from the 17th Century when it was first christened.[568]

Many notable New England families owe their present-day wealth and celebrity to the Northern slave trade.[569] Among them: the Cabots (ancestors of Massachusetts Senators Henry Cabot Lodge, Sr. and

---

565. McManus, BBN, pp. 6-7.
566. Manegold, pp. 132-134.
567. Hacker, pp. 19, 25.
568. "America Live," FOX News, October 25, 2010. For early evidence of Rhode Island's official full name, "Rhode Island and Providence Plantations," see Article 1 of *The Treaty With Great Britain*, the famous secession contract between England's King George III and America's original thirteen colonies, signed at Paris, France, November 30, 1782. J. Williams, p. 365; Rouse, pp. 78-79. Rhode Island's true official name was also mentioned in the first draft of the Preamble to the U.S. Constitution, written about August 1787. J. B. Scott, pp. 84-85. See also pp. 86-87.
569. K. C. Davis, pp. 20, 23.

THE MCGAVOCKS OF CARNTON PLANTATION

Henry Cabot Lodge, Jr.), the Belchers, the Waldos (ancestors of Ralph Waldo Emerson), the Faneuils (after whom Boston's Faneuil Hall is named), the Royalls, the Pepperells (after whom the town of Pepperell, Massachusetts, is named), the DeWolfs (the largest slave-trading family in Rhode Island), the Champlains (after whom Lake Champlain is named), the Ellerys, the Gardners (after whom Boston's Isabella Stewart Gardner Museum is named), the Malbones, the Robinsons, the Crowninshields (after whom Crowninshield Island, Massachusetts, is named), and the Browns (after whom Rhode Island's Brown University is named).[570]

The slave trading Royall family, who made millions from their slave plantations in Antigua, donated money and land to what would become the Harvard Law School. The educational center still uses a seal from the Royall family crest.[571]

At least one half of the land in Brookline, Massachusetts, was once in the possession of slave owners, while in the town of Concord, Massachusetts, 50 percent of its government seats were occupied by slave owners. In this quaint New England borough, where slavery continued well into the 1830s (decades after the official "abolition" of slavery there), those blacks fortunate enough to be freed were then, unfortunately, exiled to the woods surrounding Walden Pond, where they struggled for survival in fetid squatter camps.[572]

Even after slavery was abolished in the North, both Rhode Island and Massachusetts continued to amass huge profits from the slave trade,[573] the same profits that would later help Lincoln fund his "Civil War" on the South.[574]

Not to be outdone, America's Northern capital city, Washington, D.C., boasted one of the nation's largest slave marts, one

---

570. Meltzer, Vol. 2, pp. 145, 148; C. Johnson, pp. 125-126.
571. The Royall's original home and slave quarters have been turned into a museum located in Medford, Massachusetts. See Website: www.royallhouse.org.
572. See Lemire, passim. For more on the topic of slavery in Brookline, Massachusetts, see Website: www.boston.com/bostonglobe/ideas/articles/2010/09/26/new_englands_hidden_history/?page=1.
573. Rosenbaum and Brinkley, s.v. "Slavery."
574. Spooner, NT, No. 6, p. 54.

The McGavocks of Carnton Plantation

located in full view of Northern members of Congress,[575] as even Lincoln mentioned.[576] Apparently the sight of Africans "slaving away" did not disturb our sixteenth president or any other Yankee politicians.[577] Indeed, it was these slaves, the *Northern* slaves from this very market, who built the White House, the U.S. Capitol, and numerous other Federal buildings in the city, along with many of her city streets.[578]

Slavery was so accepted in Northern society that Lincoln allowed it to continue in the District well into the War for Southern Independence: citizens of Washington, D.C. were allowed to own slaves and trade in slaves right up until the passage of the District of Columbia Emancipation Act, approved on April 16, 1862, which effectively prohibited the practices.[579]

Abolitionists were overjoyed that slavery was finally banned from the Union's capital city. But because of the anti-abolitionist president, it had not come easily.[580] In fact, he stalled and deferred month after month, until over a year passed. As he himself said just a few months prior to his inauguration:

> I have no thought of recommending the abolition of slavery in the District of Columbia, nor the slave-trade among the slave States.[581]

Actually, the entire process of ridding the District of the North's "peculiar institution" had taken hundreds of years, in part because of

---

575. W. Wilson, DR, p. 126.
576. Nicolay and Hay, ALCW, Vol. 1, p. 185.
577. Green, W, p. 180.
578. De Angelis, pp. 12-18; Lott, p. 65; J. J. Holland, passim.
579. J. C. Perry, p. 191.
580. Though earlier in his presidency Lincoln had promised that he would never interfere with slavery in Washington, D.C., as usual, when it benefitted him he changed his mind. In this case, he needed the abolitionist vote for his upcoming bid for reelection. Additionally, freeing Washington's slaves allowed him to press Congress harder for black deportation and colonization—a goal he mentioned, as we are about to see, in the District of Columbia Emancipation Act itself.
581. Nicolay and Hay, ALCW, Vol. 1, p. 659. Lincoln made this statement in a "strictly confidential" letter to North Carolinian John A. Gilmer, on December 15, 1860. The president-elect was interested in appointing Gilmer secretary of the treasury. Desperate to have a Southerner in his cabinet, in his letter Lincoln laid out his position on slavery, hoping to allay any fears Gilmer might have about the future of the institution. Gilmer saw through it and the ploy failed. New Englander Salmon P. Chase became Lincoln's first secretary of the treasury.

THE MCGAVOCKS OF CARNTON PLANTATION

Lincoln![582]

The president's "humanitarian" act was tainted, however, by several things.

One was the fact that Lincoln's emancipation proclamation in Washington, D.C. turned out to be for the benefit of colonizationists like himself, not for the benefit of the slaves. For he had included a clause in the bill calling for their immediate deportation upon liberation.[583] The day the bill was signed into law, April 16, 1862, the president even wrote a letter to the House and Senate applauding them for recognizing his call for the deportation of the city's newly freed blacks and for setting aside funds for their colonization in foreign lands.[584]

There was also the anger of the city's whites, most who had no taste for abolition to begin with.[585] At the same time, antislavery advocates fumed over Lincoln's concomitant demand of Congress that it appropriate funding to deport, to Liberia and Haiti, the very blacks he had just freed. (Though the crafty president finally liberated the city's slaves, cleverly he had never promised that he would not attempt to colonize them outside the U.S.)[586]

Legalized white racism continued all the way into the 1940s in Washington, and it was not until the early 1950s that legislation was passed barring the city's restaurants from refusing to serve black patrons. It was not until 1956 that the District finally became fully and legally racially integrated.[587]

The North was also responsible for creating the infamous "Cotton Triangle," or "Slave Triangle," as it is also known.[588] Here

---

582. J. C. Perry, p. 191. This did not end segregation, of course. If anything it exasperated the problem of Northern white racism. Indeed, total integration was not achieved in Washington, D.C. until 1956. Weintraub, p. 147.
583. Seabrook, L, pp. 600-601.
584. Nicolay and Hay, ALCW, Vol. 2, p. 144.
585. Lincoln and the abolitionists, Caucasian Washingtonians complained, were determined to make the city a literal nightmare for the town's whites. Leech, pp. 295, 298. Such individuals apparently did not realize that Lincoln was not an abolitionist.
586. Buckley, p. 86; Leech, p. 298.
587. Weintraub, p. 147.
588. Weintraub, p. 54.

THE MCGAVOCKS OF CARNTON PLANTATION

Yankee slave ships sailed to Africa where rum (made in Northern distilleries) was traded for African slaves (already enslaved by other Africans). These individuals were brought back to America through northeast ports, then sold to the South, where they were used in the cotton growing industry on Dixie's expansive plantations. The harvested cotton was then sold to New England's textile mills, whose products were peddled worldwide at huge profits. These profits were then used to fund more Northern slave expeditions to Africa, completing the Triangle.[589]

It is clear from this description alone that every American slave ship that ever sailed to Africa left and returned from, not a Southern C.S. port, but a Northern U.S. port. This is why the only person ever arrested, tried, and executed for slaving was a Northerner, Captain Nathaniel Gordon (1826-1862) of New York—one of the many Northern states that openly continued to trade in slaves and practice slavery long after it had been officially abolished.[590]

Gordon's execution occurred on February 21, 1862, fifty-four years after the U.S. Congress under Thomas Jefferson prohibited the trade, in 1808, as a crime punishable by death.[591] But it was not Southerner President Jefferson who killed Gordon (Jefferson died in 1826). It was Northerner President Lincoln, who issued the order for the slave trader's execution on February 4, 1862.[592]

The fact is that the South owned no slaving ships and did not engage in the traffic of human beings. Hence, the last slave ship to be captured and closed down was a Northern slave ship, the *Nightingale*, on April 21, 1861, over a week after the start of Lincoln's War. The ship, known fondly to Northerners as the "Prince of Slavers," was made in New Hampshire, sailed from Massachusetts, and had a New York captain. At the time of its seizure the *Nightingale* had 900 manacled Africans on board and was proudly flying the U.S. flag from her mast.[593]

---

589. For more on the Cotton and Slave Triangles, see Farrow, Lang, and Frank, pp. 48-49, 50.
590. O. Williams, p. 83.
591. Kennedy, p. 208.
592. See Nicolay and Hay, ALCW, Vol. 2, pp. 121-122.
593. Kennedy, pp. 104-105.

THE MCGAVOCKS OF CARNTON PLANTATION

No slave ship ever flew under the Confederate Flag, yet it is this same flag that is today universally viewed as a "symbol of slavery"!

We must ask ourselves then: is it the flag of the U.S.A. or the flag of the C.S.A. that deserves to be called "America's true slave flag"? And is it the U.S. capital city (Washington, D.C.) or the C.S. capital city (Richmond, Virginia) that deserves the title of "America's true slave capital"?[594]

Now we can better understand the words of U.S. Senator Jefferson Davis, soon to become the Southern Confederacy's first and only president, who, in 1848, rightly chastised his Northern brethren on the Senate floor for their abolitionist hypocrisy:

> You were the men who imported these negroes into this country; you enjoyed the benefits resulting from their carriage and sale; and you reaped the largest profit accruing from the introduction of slaves.[595]

ॐ HOW & WHY SLAVERY ENDED IN THE NORTH

We will recall that slavery was limited from the beginning in the North by the region's short growing season, sandy rocky soil, ever growing industrial economy,[596] widespread racism among the white Northern population,[597] and finally the North's enormous distance from both Africa (where slaves were picked up) and the tropics (where slaves were needed on sugar plantations). This last factor made it much more profitable to sell slaves in the American South (which was a much shorter distance from Africa and the Caribbean).[598] All of these elements contributed to the death of Northern slavery.

But the final nail in the coffin of Yankee slavery was the skyrocketing birth rate of whites in that region after 1750. This huge new supply of free workers destroyed the Yankee slave economy and

---

594. Lott, pp. 65-68.
595. Dunbar, Vol. 1, p. 218.
596. P. M. Roberts, pp. 195-196.
597. U. B. Phillips, pp. 119-120.
598. Furnas, pp. 119, 121.

The McGavocks of Carnton Plantation

wage rates fell, making slavery unnecessary, cumbersome, inefficient, uneconomical, and finally obsolete across the North.[599]

One by one the Northern states abolished slavery, *slowly*, *voluntarily*, and *gradually*: Vermont in 1777; Pennsylvania in 1780; Massachusetts in 1780; Connecticut in 1784; Rhode Island in 1784; New Jersey in 1804; New York in 1827.[600] Northern states like New Hampshire and Delaware did not fully rid themselves of slavery until the passage of the Thirteenth Amendment, December 6, 1865. In short, the North gave itself nearly 100 leisurely years to eliminate slavery from within its borders.

Unfortunately, Lincoln and his liberal cohorts did not allow the same natural process to unfold in the South as it had in their own region. Instead, in Dixie they abolished slavery abruptly and by using force, and all within a period of two short years: 1863 to 1865. We will discuss the consequences of Lincoln's actions in more detail in a moment.

If slavery started in the North, was maintained in the North, and was fueled by Northern money right up until the end of the War, where did the McGavocks' servants come from? They were purchased—either directly or indirectly—from Northern slave traders.[601] Slavery was, in fact, forced on the South, and became entrenched there due to pressure from Northern businessmen and from Southern fears of violent slave uprisings, a fear fabricated and reinforced by Yankee abolitionists, many who wanted to free the slaves, not for blacks themselves, but to humiliate the South[602] and financially injure Southern slave owners.[603]

By this time, however, in 1860, there was no way that the South could give up slavery overnight as the North expected it to. It would now require a long, complex, well thought out process, one an intolerant, racist, and impatient Lincoln was not willing to wait for. By

---

599. McManus, BBN, pp. 175-179.
600. The Northwest Ordinance, issued in 1787, banned slavery throughout the Northwest Territory, an area that included what would soon become the Midwestern states of Illinois, Wisconsin, Ohio, Michigan, and Indiana.
601. Tilley, FHLO, p. 29.
602. Coit, pp. 298-299; White, Foscue, and McKnight, p. 211.
603. Garraty and McCaughey, p. 253.

refusing to give up Thomas Jefferson's Constitutional principle of states' rights (see the Tenth Amendment), the agrarian South was standing in the way of Northern industrial progress, and Lincoln and his radical liberal party members would make the South pay.[604]

Despite these bold facts, it is the South which was, and continues to be, unfairly held responsible for the institution of American slavery.

---

604. Simpson, pp. 78-91.

The McGavocks & Slavery

Part 4

❧ THE SOUTHERN ABOLITION MOVEMENT

CONTRARY TO NORTHERN MYTHOLOGY, NOT only did the Old South not invite slavery into its region, it never fully "embraced" it either. In fact, up until the year 1800 nearly all Southerners were abolitionists.

In late 1861 slave owner Mary Chesnut wrote that both she and her husband James Chesnut, Jr. (President Jefferson Davis' aide-de-camp) literally detested all forms of slavery, in particular African slavery. And I will never get used to the word "nigger," she wrote emphatically.[605]

All Southerners detest the institution more than Harriet Beecher Stowe ever could; we hate slavery, know that it is doomed, and are happy for it, Mary goes on to assert. She then describes a letter she had written to her husband while he was on their plantation in Mississippi in 1842. It is the most ardent abolitionist document, the diarist noted, one she kept so that the South's haughty opponents to the North might one day learn the truth about so-called "Southern slavery."[606]

---

605. Chesnut, MCCW, p. 729.
606. Chesnut, MCCW, pp. 245, 246.

THE MCGAVOCKS OF CARNTON PLANTATION

In her entry for June 29, 1861, the Southern belle included the following words: "slavery has got to go, of course!"[607] Such statements are all but ignored, or even suppressed, by Northern and New South writers. But we traditional Southerners are well aware of them.

Early Southerners like the Chesnuts, being innately humanitarian, abhorred the institution of slavery and felt that they had, quite rightly, unwillingly inherited it from their Northern neighbors, who in turn had inherited it, by force, from Great Britain.[608] Hence, in the early 1800s Virginia's eccentric antislavery senator John Randolph (1773-1833) could truthfully say that slavery was never something the South sought out. Rather, it was "imposed" upon her against her choosing.[609] Likewise, Virginia Senator John Taylor (1753-1824) declared that slavery is a disaster thrust upon the South; one that must be endured rather than praised.[610]

In 1820 Thomas Jefferson perfectly captured the slavery situation in Dixie at the time:

> We have the wolf by the ears, and we can neither hold him, nor safely let him go.[611]

But not knowing how or when to free the slaves did not mean that Southerners found slavery good or even acceptable. To the contrary, as we are about to see, throughout the early decades of the U.S., much of the South's time and energy was directed almost solely on how to deal with the "wolf." Indeed, most white Southerners had by then recognized the fact that they themselves had become slaves of the North's slavery system, one that in turn required them to become slave owners.[612]

---

607. Chesnut, DD, p. 74.
608. Simpson, pp. 77-78, 85.
609. Coit, p. 166.
610. Woods, p. 33. John Taylor "of Caroline," a die-hard Jeffersonian and vehement anti-Federalist, would later inspire the supporters of states' rights (like John C. Calhoun), as well as members of the libertarian movement, with his strict constructionist views of the Constitution.
611. Foley, pp. 811-812.
612. Van Loon, p. 353.

The McGavocks of Carnton Plantation

Personally, 17th-Century Southerners, now "saddled" with slavery, would have preferred that it had never come to America's shores to begin with. This is why both the civil rights movement and the abolition movement began in, and were so strong in, Dixie from the earliest days of the nation. And this is why the South tried to ban slavery long before the North did.

As President Wilson writes, nowhere in America were there more sincere, more openly declared denunciations of the "evil influence" of slavery on both whites and blacks than in the South:

> A mild antislavery sentiment, born of the philanthropic spirit, had existed in all parts of the country from the first. Nowhere were there to be found clearer or more plainly spoken condemnations of its evil influence at once upon masters and slaves and upon the whole structure and spirit of society than representative southern men had uttered.[613]

In fact, the first colony to try and stop the American slave trade was not a Northern one, but a Southern one: Virginia.[614] Among the Virginians who were behind the antislavery movement was America's first president, George Washington (1732-1799), who was so against the institution that he beseeched God to help bring about emancipation in both the South and the North as soon as possible. Said the Southerner in 1798:

> Not only do I pray for it on the score of human dignity, but I can clearly foresee that nothing but the rooting out of slavery can perpetuate the existence of our union by consolidating it in a common bond of principle.[615]

Since the American abolition movement got its start in the South, and more specifically in Virginia, we should not be surprised to learn that it was in the Old Dominion State that voluntary emancipation

---

613. W. Wilson, DR, pp. 119-120.
614. Kennedy, p. 91.
615. Garrison and Garrison, Vol. 3, p. 100.

THE MCGAVOCKS OF CARNTON PLANTATION

found its greatest success: between 1782 and 1790 some 10,000 black servants were voluntarily freed by white Virginian slave owners. In contrast, slave owners in many Northern states showed much greater reluctance to give up their black chattel. New Jersey, for example, did not pass its emancipation act until 1804, which is why it still had over 3,500 slaves as late as 1830.[616]

After the American Revolutionary War ended in 1783, though the Federal government had not yet even given citizenship to blacks, many Southern states were passing laws allowing African-Americans to own property, testify in court, vote, and travel without restrictions.[617]

Shortly thereafter, a Southerner, St. George Tucker (1752-1827), one of the earliest abolitionists in the U.S., was formulating ideas for permanently ending slavery in Virginia in 1796, as were Southerners James Madison and Thomas Jefferson. In 1807, under President Jefferson, the Southern states enthusiastically voted to end the slave trade by 1808, the year the Constitution had set as the earliest date Congress could decide on the issue.[618]

But, as we have seen, and as even Lincoln was forced to acknowledge,[619] Northerners ignored the ban and continued the trade illegally,[620] right through to the end of the War for Southern Independence.[621]

A myriad of other early Southerners stepped forward to push the abolitionist cause. Among them were Calvin A. Wiley of North Carolina and the Reverend James Lyons of Mississippi. Both men campaigned for legal reforms that would lift the ban on educating slaves, help protect slave marriages, ban the splitting up of slave families, and allow slaves to testify in court.[622]

---

616. Garraty and McCaughey, p. 81.
617. Adams and Sanders, p. 118.
618. W. Wilson, DR, p. 124.
619. Nicolay and Hay, ALCW, Vol. 2, p. 6.
620. Faust, s.v. "slavery."
621. See Stampp, p. 271; Meltzer, Vol. 2, pp. 247-248; C. Johnson, pp. 126-128; Rosenbaum and Brinkley, s.v. "Slave Trade"; Durden, p. 288.
622. Eaton, HSC, pp. 237-238.

THE MCGAVOCKS OF CARNTON PLANTATION

A friend of Chesnut's, Confederate General James Johnston Pettigrew (1828-1863), wrote an antislavery essay in 1862. Mary not only read it but highly approved of Pettigrew's words and ideas, and told him so, much to the officer's pleasure.[623] Sadly the North Carolinian died shortly after the Battle of Gettysburg and never saw the fruition of his dream of ending of slavery in the South.[624]

Of the 130 abolition societies established before 1827 by Northern abolitionist Benjamin Lundy (1789-1839), over 100, comprising four-fifths of the total membership, were in the South.[625] Early North Carolina had a number of well-known "forceful" antislavery leaders, such as Benjamin Sherwood Hedrick (1827-1886) and Daniel Reaves Goodlow,[626] and in South Carolina the famed Quaker sisters, Sarah Grimké (1792-1873) and Angelina Grimké (1805-1879), were just two among millions of Southerners fighting for the cause of abolition.[627]

In the early 1800s Madison and Jefferson were still discussing, and fully expecting, their home state of Virginia to move toward abolishing slavery,[628] and by the mid 1800s the Southern abolition movement was in full swing.

In 1854, the aforementioned Yankee minister Nehemiah Adams took a trip into the South. He found, contrary to all that he had heard about "racist Southerners," a vast and thriving abolition movement, especially against the slave trade. Adams noted that white Southerners everywhere wanted to abolish the institution, "till no wrong, no pain, should be the fruit of it which is not incidental to every human lot."[629]

"As a general rule," wrote anti-South, antislavery advocate Hinton Rowan Helper (1829-1909), in the South "poor white persons are regarded with less esteem and attention than negroes," with the

---

623. Chesnut, MCCW, p. 357.
624. Warner, GG, s.v. "James Johnston Pettigrew."
625. Cash, p. 63.
626. H. C. Bailey, p. 197.
627. Oates, AL, p. 29.
628. M. D. Peterson, JM, p. 371; Ellis, AS, pp. 102, 173.
629. N. Adams, p. 77.

THE MCGAVOCKS OF CARNTON PLANTATION

condition of "vast numbers" of whites being "infinitely worse off."[630]

This truth was so obvious that many 19th-Century Northerners came to admit that Southern slavery was far from the miserable institution that radical Yankee abolitionists tried to portray. Union officer Charles Francis Adams, Jr. (the great-grandson of famed U.S. Founder, President John Adams), wrote the following to his father Charles, Sr.,[631] Lincoln's ambassador to Great Britain:

> I'm gradually getting to have very decided opinions on the negro question; they're growing up in me as inborn convictions and are not the result of reflection. I note what you say of the African race and 'the absence of all appearance of self reliance in their own power' during this struggle. From this, greatly as it has disappointed me, I very unwillingly draw different conclusions from your own. The conviction is forcing itself upon me that African slavery, as it existed in our slave states [the South], was indeed a patriarchal institution, under which the slaves were not, as a whole, unhappy, cruelly treated or overworked. I am forced to this conclusion.[632]

On November 9, 1862, the young Confederate diarist Sarah Morgan wrote sarcastically of Lincoln and the North's erroneous views of "Southern slavery." Sarah mingled, laughed, played, and worked with her family's black servants and knew the truth that the Yankee president dare not admit:

> If Lincoln could spend the grinding season on a [Southern] plantation, he would recall his proclamation.[633] As it is, he has only proved himself a fool, without injuring us. Why last evening

---

630. Helper, ICS, p. 42.
631. As a Yankee diplomat in England, Charles Francis Adams, Sr. created numerous problems for the Confederacy. One of his most monstrous actions was issuing Lincoln's order to threaten Great Britain with war should she aid the American South in any way. Such tactics were, of course, hypocritical since the U.S. herself had aided and supported "belligerent" nations in the past. For more on Adams and this topic, see Owsley, pp. 401-412.
632. W. C. Ford, Vol. 2, p. 215.
633. Sarah is referring here to Lincoln's *Preliminary* Emancipation Proclamation (as opposed to the one best known to the public today, the *Final* Emancipation Proclamation). Calling for abolition then black deportation, the president issued the preliminary version on September 22, 1862.

THE MCGAVOCKS OF CARNTON PLANTATION

> I took old [slave] Wilson's place at the baggasse chute, and kept the rollers free from cane until I had thrown down enough to fill several carts, and had my hands as black as his. What cruelty to slaves! And black Frank thinks me cruel, too, when he meets me with a patronising grin, and shows me the nicest vats of candy, and peels cane for me. Oh! very cruel![634]

Fashionably and expensively dressed black servants "promenading" through town on Sundays almost always appalled Northern visitors to the South, for this image was the opposite of what they had been told to expect.[635] After fighting for some time in Virginia, one of Lincoln's soldiers, a private from New Hampshire, wrote: after now having seen Southern slavery for myself, I firmly believe that we Yanks have been fooled. It is nothing like we were taught. Why just the other day I saw slaves going to church who were as happy and cheerful as can be.[636]

When Northern landscape architect Frederick Law Olmsted traveled through Virginia in the early 1800s, he was stunned by the incongruity of what he had believed about Southern "slavery" and the reality of Southern servitude: the slaves he saw working in the fields were either whistling or singing.[637]

During his travels to America's Southland, English novelist William M. Thackeray (1811-1863) had a similar experience, as he discusses in his work, *Roundabout Papers*:

> How they sang; how they laughed and grinned; how they scraped, bowed, and complimented you and each other, those negroes of the cities of the Southern parts of the then United States! My business kept me in the towns; I was but in one negro-plantation village, and there were only women and little children, the men being out a-field. But there was plenty of cheerfulness in the huts, under the great trees—I speak of what I saw—and amidst the dusky bondsmen of the cities. I witnessed a curious gaiety; heard

---

634. Dawson, pp. 277-278.
635. Stampp, p. 289.
636. Wiley, LBY, p. 43.
637. Stampp, p. 164.

amongst the black folk endless singing, shouting, and laughter; and saw on holidays black gentlemen and ladies arrayed in such splendor and comfort as freeborn workmen in our towns seldom exhibit.[638]

Around the same time, in 1856, seven years before Lincoln's War, here is what one famous antislavery Virginian, Robert E. Lee (1807-1870), had to say about the institution:

> There are few, I believe, in this enlightened age, who will not acknowledge that slavery as an institution is a moral and political evil. It is idle to expatiate on its disadvantages. I think it is a greater evil to the white than to the colored race.[639]

Long before Lee spoke these words, white Southerners everywhere were already adopting evermore liberal reforms that, along with the forces of industrialization, urbanization, and the Enlightenment, would have inevitably led to eventual abolition and emancipation all across the South. That is, if Lincoln had not interfered by illegally invading what was by then a constitutionally formed foreign country.[640]

After the War started Southerners in their thousands continued to come out against the "peculiar institution." Among them, of course, was Lee, who had turned down an offer to lead Northern armies at the start of the conflict with this statement:

> If I owned the four million slaves of the South I would sacrifice them all to the Union . . .[641]

The true irony of all this, of course, is that the North ended up using slavery as justification for this invasion, and yet it was the North who sold these same slaves to the South to begin with.[642]

---

638. Thackeray, p. 127.
639. H. A. White, p. 50.
640. E. M. Thomas, p. 242.
641. *The Independent* (New York), Vol. 71, July-December 1911, p. 697.
642. Kennedy and Kennedy, SWR, p. 73.

THE MCGAVOCKS OF CARNTON PLANTATION

How different Southern truth is from Northern myth!

❧ JEFFERSON: U.S. PRESIDENT, FOUNDING FATHER, SOUTHERN ABOLITIONIST

Since ardent antislavery advocate Jefferson so aptly contradicts the Northern myth about "Southern slavery," it is worth taking a moment to look at this fascinating Southerner and his views on the "peculiar institution" more closely.

Jefferson's attack on slavery began even long before the formation of the U.S., while the states were still colonial possessions of England. As a member of the House of Burgesses in 1769, for instance, he asked the British crown for permission to emancipate all slaves in the American colonies (his request was rejected). This was nearly a century (ninety-six years) before the Thirteenth Amendment abolished slavery in the North in December 1865.[643]

In 1776, now a member of the Continental Congress, Jefferson referred to slavery as a "wickedness" and again tried to get rid of the trade, this time by adding a condemnation of England (for forcing slavery on the original thirteen colonies) to his rough draft of the Declaration of Independence. The document, written between June 12 and 27, reads:

> [King George III] . . . has waged cruel war against human nature itself, violating it's most sacred rights of life & liberty in the persons of a distant [African] people who never offended him, captivating & carrying them to slavery in another hemisphere, or to incur miserable death in their transportations thither. This piratical warfare, the opprobrium of infidel powers, is the warfare of the Christian king of Great Britain. Determined to keep open a market where MEN should be bought & sold, he has prostituted his negative for suppressing every legislative attempt to prohibit or to restrain this execrable commerce, and that this assemblage of horrors might want no fact of distinguished die, he is now exciting those very people to rise in arms against us, and to purchase that liberty of which he has deprived them, by murdering the people upon whom he also obtruded them; thus paying off former crimes

---

643. Foley, pp. 816-817.

THE MCGAVOCKS OF CARNTON PLANTATION

which he urges them to commit against the lives of another.[644]

Why are these powerful antislavery words (Clause 20 in Jefferson's draft)—written by a Southerner—not in the Declaration of Independence as we know it today? According to an extremely irritated Jefferson, his denunciation of slavery was removed by committee from the final draft, in part, because it would have angered not only Northern slave traders,[645] but also Northern businessmen,[646] nearly all who were deeply involved in the slave industry,[647] the same Yankee industry, as we have seen, whose profits were later used by Lincoln to fund his "Civil War."[648]

While his antislavery clause was withdrawn from the first draft of the Declaration of Independence, the final version, adopted on July 4, 1776, did retain Jefferson's belief that ". . . all men are created equal, that they are endowed by their Creator with certain unalienable Rights, that among these are Life, Liberty and the pursuit of Happiness."[649]

We will note here that Northern liberal Lincoln did not agree with Southern conservative Jefferson on this point. As Lincoln himself stated on June 26, 1857, during a speech in Springfield, Illinois:

> There is a natural disgust in the minds of nearly all white people at the idea of an indiscriminate amalgamation of the white and black races; . . . [Yet my opponent Judge Stephen A. Douglas] . . . finds . . . [my political party] insisting that the Declaration of Independence includes all men, black as well as white, and forthwith he boldly denies that it includes Negroes at all, and proceeds to argue gravely that all who contend it does do so only because they want to vote, and eat, and sleep, and marry with Negroes! He will have it that they cannot be consistent else.

---

644. Foley, p. 970.
645. Bowen, pp. 600-601.
646. Foley, p. 246.
647. K. C. Davis, pp. 10, 30. John Adams' favorite part of Jefferson's draft of the Declaration of Independence was his attack on King George for foisting slavery on the American colonies. J. C. Miller, p. 8. Primarily opposites on the political spectrum, Southerner Jefferson and Northerner Adams at least had abolition in common.
648. See Spooner, NT, No. 6, p. 54.
649. Foley, p. 399.

THE McGAVOCKS OF CARNTON PLANTATION

> Now I protest against the counterfeit logic which concludes that, because I do not want a black woman for a slave, I must necessarily want her for a wife. I need not have her for either. I can just leave her alone. In some respects she certainly is not my equal; but in her natural right to eat the bread she earns with her own hands without asking leave of anyone else, she is my equal and the equal of all others. . . .
>
> I think the authors of that notable instrument [the Declaration of Independence] intended to include all men, but they did not intend to declare all men equal in all respects. They did not mean to say all were equal in color, size, intellect, moral developments, or social capacity. . . .
>
> I have now briefly expressed my view of the meaning and object of that part of the Declaration of Independence which declares that 'all men are created equal.'[650]

Again in 1776, now a member of the Virginia House of Delegates, Jefferson's draft of the Virginia Constitution contained a clause calling for the total emancipation of all slaves in that state. This was eighty-nine years prior to Lincoln's bogus and felonious Emancipation Proclamation.

In 1777 Jefferson assisted in creating America's first Constitution, known as the Articles of Confederation.[651] In doing so he said: "It is our duty to lay every discouragement on the importation of slaves."[652] But the final document, ratified on March 1, 1781, was not allowed to say anything about the trade.

In 1778 he introduced a bill to Congress to prevent the further "evil" of the importation of slaves, which temporarily halted the trade, though not the institution itself.[653] The bill must have soon been overturned, or ignored, because it was not long before he was once again trying to push through new antislavery proposals.

In 1781, his last year as governor of Virginia, Jefferson began penning his famous booklet *Notes on the State of Virginia*, in which he

---

650. Nicolay and Hay, ALCW, Vol. 1, pp. 231-233.
651. See Jensen, AC, passim.
652. Foley, p. 973.
653. Foley, p. 812.

called slavery a "tyranny," a "blot in our country," and "a great political and moral evil," further adding that "the minds of our citizens may be ripening for a complete emancipation . . ."[654] Nearly every Southerner agreed.

In 1784, having by this time been elected to Congress under the Articles of Confederation,[655] Jefferson wrote a report on the temporary government of the Western Territory which included a clause that read: ". . . after the year 1800 of the Christian era, there shall be neither slavery nor involuntary servitude in any of the said states . . ."[656] Congress again ultimately deleted this sentence from the document.

Once more, this time in 1786 as U.S. minister to France, Jefferson attempted to divest Virginia of the burden of slavery by proposing gradual emancipation. His manumission clause was rejected.

In 1787, while the U.S. was still a Confederacy (and was in fact called "the Confederacy" by Americans),[657] Jefferson authored the Northwest Ordinance, which established rules regarding how states were to be created from the Western Territories and admitted to the Union. In it he included a clause completely prohibiting slavery in the new Western states that were to be created. It read: "There shall be neither slavery nor involuntary servitude in the said territory . . ."[658] At the time, of course, slavery was still legally practiced in all of the Northern states.

---

654. Jefferson, NSV, pp. 145, 146.
655. Sobel, s.v. "Jefferson, Thomas."
656. Foley, p. 811.
657. The U.S.A. was first created as a confederacy (a weak central government in compact with powerful, fully independent nation-states), and existed in this form from 1781 to 1789. As such, it was called "the Confederacy" by all early Americans between these years. Thomas Jefferson's writings alone contain dozens of references to "the Confederacy" during this period. Likewise, our first Constitution was known as the "Articles of Confederation." Despite the renaming of our nation as the "United States of America" after 1789, many Americans, both South and North, continued to refer to her as the Confederacy, some right up until the time of Lincoln's War in 1861. Lincoln himself publicly referred to the U.S. as "the Confederacy" that very year. Here is more evidence that the South fought, not over slavery, as Yankee myth asserts, but to maintain the original Confederacy of the Founding Fathers, most who were Southerners and true believers in confederation. This is why the seceded states called themselves "the Confederacy." For more information on Jefferson, Lincoln, and the original American Confederacy, see my books, *Abraham Lincoln: The Southern View*; *Lincolnology: The Real Lincoln Revealed in His Own Words*; and *Everything You Were Taught About the Civil War is Wrong, Ask a Southerner!* For more on the period of the U.S. Confederacy, see Jensen, NN, passim.
658. Cluskey, p. 186.

THE McGAVOCKS OF CARNTON PLANTATION

In 1796 Jefferson created a bill on the subject of slavery, saying: "Nothing is more certainly written in the book of fate than that these people are to be free."[659] The bill, however, was "kept back."[660]

In 1800, in a memorandum outlining his "services to my country," Jefferson, now vice president of the U.S. under President John Adams (1735-1826), proudly and rightfully noted that he was responsible for formulating the "act prohibiting the importation of slaves." But his plan to end slavery by that year failed.[661]

Thus it was on December 2, 1806, now as America's third president, that he addressed the Senate and the House of Representatives in his Sixth Annual Message to bring a special reminder to the American people: on January 1, 1808, the American slave trade would come to an end, Jefferson stated authoritatively. In the meantime, he encouraged citizens everywhere to try to prevent new slave expeditions from leaving for Africa and to "interpose your authority constitutionally" by withdrawing "from all further participation in those violations of human rights which have been so long continued on the unoffending inhabitants of Africa."[662]

Due to resistance from wealthy Northern industrialists, who would become known as the "Wall Street Boys," most who were heavily involved in the slave trade and had absolutely no interest in black civil rights, President Jefferson's promise never materialized.[663] Nonetheless, it should be emphasized that this particular Southern attempt to end American slavery occurred fifty-five years before Lincoln's Emancipation and fifty-seven years before the passage of the Thirteenth Amendment, which finally and officially ended all aspects of American slavery.

❧ THE CONFEDERACY OUTLAWED THE FOREIGN SLAVE TRADE FIRST

Even the C.S.A. (Confederate States of America) banned the foreign

---

659. Foley, p. 816.
660. P. L. Ford, Vol. 1, p. 76.
661. Foley, p. 442.
662. Foley, p. 811.
663. Ransom, p. 253.

THE MCGAVOCKS OF CARNTON PLANTATION

slave trade before the U.S.A. did. Upon the C.S.A.'s formation in 1861 the Confederate Congress included a clause in its Constitution forbidding foreign trade in human chattel. Here, from the C.S. Constitution, Article 1, Section 9, Clause 1, is the exact wording:

> The importation of negroes of the African race, from any foreign country, other than the slaveholding States or Territories of the United States of America, is hereby forbidden; and Congress is required to pass such laws as shall effectually prevent the same.[664]

This was five years before the U.S. banned the foreign slave trade. Indeed the original U.S. Constitution, also Article 1, Section 9, Clause 1, allowed the

> ... importation of such Persons as any of the States now existing shall think proper to admit ...[665]

Those referred to here as "such Persons" were, of course, slaves.

It can truly be said then that the South, not the North, initiated the abolition movement, and that no slave ship ever sailed under a Southern or Confederate Flag. It is any wonder that the South was well-known to have treated its black servants better than the North treated its free blacks?[666]

❧ VERY FEW SOUTHERNERS OWNED SLAVES

Land and black servants were costly in the 1800s, so invariably slavery was a rich man's business. Yet nearly all 19th-Century Southerners were poor farmers. This alone proves that in all actuality very few Southerners owned black servants. And we have statistics to back this up.

According to the 1860 U.S. Census, Randal McGavock of Carnton Plantation was one of only 4.8 percent (or 385,000 individuals

---

664. F. Moore, Vol. 2, p. 323.
665. E. McPherson, PHUSAGR, p. 93.
666. Kennedy, p. 91.

out of 8 million) of Southerners who owned slaves.[667] Of these most owned less than five.[668] What this means is that on the eve of Lincoln's War, *95.2 percent Southerners did not own slaves!*[669]

Thus there was no "slave owning majority," as Northern myth consistently maintains. Quite the opposite. The large slaveholding families of the South numbered only about 10,000, this out of literally millions of Southern families.[670] This was only 0.6 percent of the 1.5 million families who lived across the South in 1860.[671] They were so rare that most Southerners, being indigent rural farmers, probably did not even personally know a slave owning family.

Correcting for the mistakes of Census takers—which would include wrongly counting slave hirers as slave owners and counting more than once those thousands of slave owners who annually moved the same slaves back and forth across multiple states—this figure, 4.8 percent, is no doubt much smaller. Either way, Southerners themselves believed that only 5 percent of their number owned slaves, which is slightly high, but roughly accurate.[672]

---

667. Seabrook, EYWTACWW, p. 90.
668. Gragg, p. 84; DiLorenzo, LU, p. 174.
669. M. M. Smith, pp. 4-5.
670. Long and Long, p. 702.
671. E. M. Thomas, p. 6.
672. B. S. Parker, p. 343. Important note: in an attempt to tarnish the South, anti-South proponents like to artificially inflate the numbers of white Southern slave owners (they completely ignore black and red slave owners) by calculating using the number of *households* ("families") instead of the *total number of white Southerners*. Using the lower number of households as opposed to the higher number of total whites, of course, gives a higher number of slave owners, which is why they use this method: it puts the South in the worst light possible, and gives further justification for Lincoln's unjustifiable War. For example, anti-South Yankee historian and socialist, Kenneth M. Stampp, who Northerners and scallywags consider the "authority" on slavery figures, states that in 1860, there were 385,000 Southern slave owners, about 1,500,000 free Southern families, and a total of 8,000,000 whites. Stampp, pp. 29-30. All of this is true, up to this point. Enemies of the South, however, compute the number of Southern slave owners by calculating what percentage 385,000 (the number of Southern slave owners) is of 1,500,000 (the number of Southern households). This gives a result of about 25 percent, the pro-North claim being then that "25 percent of all Southern whites were slave owners in 1860." This, indeed, is the exact figure and calculation formula Stampp and his ilk use (see e.g., Stampp, p. 30). Unfortunately, as "households," women, and children did not (and could not) own slaves, this formula is not only disingenuous and misleading, it is mathematically incorrect. The correct calculation, the one I and other traditional Southerners use, is to compute the number of Southern slave owners by calculating what percentage 385,000 is of 8,000,000 (the total number of Southern whites). This gives a result of 4.8 percent. When we correct for enumeration errors (see the following footnote), this number comes down to about 4 percent or less. Hence, we can safely *and*

THE MCGAVOCKS OF CARNTON PLANTATION

Going back in time, the number of Southern slave owners decreases precipitously. In 1850, for example, of the 8,039,000 whites living in the Southern states, only 186,551 were slave owners, a mere 2.3 percent of the total white population. Thus, 97.7 percent of Southern whites that year were non-slave owners.[673] Of these same whites only 46,274 owned twenty or more servants (0.5 percent), only 2,500 owned thirty or more (0.03 percent), and a mere handful (0.02 percent) owned 100 or more.[674]

This last group, the so-called "Aristocratic Planters," eventually numbered about 150,000, but still comprised only 3 percent of the total number of slaveholders.[675] In fact, the extremely wealthy planters, and thus those who owned the most servants, made up only one-half of 1 percent of the total population of the South.[676]

To put these numbers in perspective, the South's 300,000 white slave owners made up only 1 percent of the total U.S. white population of 30,000,000 people in 1861, and only 3 percent of the South's 9,150,000 whites.[677] If America's 4,000,000 black slaves (North and South) are added to this figure, the South's white slave owners comprised only 0.8 percent of the total white and black population of

---

accurately say that only about 4 percent of Southern whites were slave owners in 1860. The other 96 percent were not. Be aware of this cowardly and treacherous pro-North trick, one found in nearly every anti-South book.

673. For the number of Southern whites in 1850, see Wilson and Ferris, s.v. "Plantations"; Bradley, NBFES, p. 33. For the number of slave owners in 1850, see Helper, ICS, p. 148. How the total number of slave owners was arrived at: while "official" records state that there were 347,525 slave owners in the South in 1850, this is a gross error. Professor James Dunwoody Brownson DeBow (1820-1867), famed publisher and statistician, and Superintendent of the U.S. Census at the time, stated that this number wrongly includes slave hirers, a profession entirely different than that of a slave owner. Additionally, when slaveholders owned slaves in different states, or moved the same ones from state to state, they were erroneously counted more than once. Adjusting for these mistakes, we find the following: from 347,525 we must subtract 158,974 (the number of Southern slave hirers) and 2,000 (the number of slave owners who were entered more than once). Thus the total number of individual slave owners in the South in 1850 was 186,551, about 4 percent of the white population. See Helper, ICS, pp. 146-148.
674. Wilson and Ferris, s.v. "Plantations"; Bradley, NBFES, p. 33.
675. Kennedy and Kennedy, SWR, p. 83.
676. Channing, p. 8.
677. See Foner, FSFLFM, pp. 87-88.

The McGavocks of Carnton Plantation

America in 1861.[678]

With only 5 percent of Southerners as slave owners, what about the other 95 percent? They were non-servant owning, yeoman farmers, small landholders who operated without labor assistance,[679] and who thus had no need for outside labor and no interest in the institution of slavery.[680]

In fact, there had been enormous tension between slaveholders and non-slaveholders from the very beginning, for the latter group resented the very existence of black servant labor in the South.[681] Even Northern slave owner, and later U.S. president, Ulysses S. Grant, admitted that:

> The great bulk of the legal voters of the South were men who owned no slaves; . . . [thus] their interest in the contest [to abolish slavery] was very meagre . . .[682]

Southern scholar Shelby Foote correctly calls this group "the slaveless majority," a phrase never heard, discussed, or even acknowledged by pro-North writers.[683] Yet it made up the foundational bulk (95 percent) of the population of the Old South.

❧ THE McGAVOCKS, THE BIBLE, & SLAVERY

Many people today find it particularly distressing to learn that the McGavocks and many other servant owning Southerners used the Bible

---

678. In 1861 there were 20,750,000 million whites in the North, and 9,150,000 whites in the South (Hacker, p. 581), making the total American white population 29,900,000; or rounded off, 30,000,000. In 1861 there were 3,500,000 black slaves in the South (Quarles, p. xiii; T. A. Bailey, p. 341; Weintraub, p. 70; Cooper, JDA, p. 378; Rosenbaum and Brinkley, s.v. "Civil War"), and 500,000 black slaves in the North. Eaton, HSC, p. 93), making a total of 4,000,000 slaves nationwide. (Some estimates indicate that there were as many as 1,000,000 slaves in the North in the 1860s. See Hinkle, p. 125.) We will note here that these figures do not include the millions of Native-Americans (many who were also slave owners) who inhabited vast areas of North America, as well as other ethnic groups, such as Asian-Americans and Hispanic-Americans.
679. White, Foscue, and McKnight, p. 209.
680. Kennedy and Kennedy, SWR, p. 83.
681. Ransom, p. 174.
682. U. S. Grant, Vol. 1, p. 223.
683. Foote, Vol. 3, p. 755.

to defend black servitude. Northern historians have indeed painted a bleak picture of Southerners in this regard, and shame on them for doing so.

In order to correct these false stereotypes let us examine this phenomenon more closely. Even a brief objective look will reveal that this piece of anti-South folklore is false, one-sided, and disingenuous. After all, it is merely just one more arrow in the South-hater's quiver, one meant to further hurt, anger, and humiliate Dixie and her people.

❧ THE EARLY CHRISTIAN CHURCH EMBRACED SLAVERY

To begin with, using the Bible to justify slavery was not specifically a Southern tradition, or even an American one. Both the North and the South engaged in the practice before, during, and even after the War. And it was not just Americans who used the Good Book to support slavery. This was a worldwide custom dating back to the earliest days of Christianity.[684]

In early Medieval times, for instance, the Church itself upheld the laws of feudalism, which was little more than a slave state in which serfs were bought and sold with the land. Though serfs had no civil rights and lived or died at the mercy of their owners, their plight was completely ignored by the Church. Why? Because the Bible makes no mention of serfdom or feudalism.[685] Since both were legal, and because Jesus commanded his followers to obey the laws of the land,[686] the Church backed away from the entire issue.

While we modern Christians understandably condemn slavery, many of the early Church Fathers perceived it quite differently. Both Saint Gregory of Nazianzus (329-389) and Saint Augustine (354-430) saw the institution as a consequence of Original Sin and the Fall of Man. Saint Thomas Aquinas (c. 1225-1274) taught that it was a punishment from God,[687] while Saint Ambrose (339-397), the Bishop of Milan,

---

684. Muller, p. 154.
685. Walker, s.v. "Slavery."
686. Mark 12:16-17.
687. Cross and Livingstone, s.v. "Slavery."

argued that slaves should be happy because their condition gave them an opportunity to perfect the Christian ideals of patience, humility, and forgiveness.[688]

With such Christian luminaries and the Bible supporting slavery it is hardly surprising that centuries later most Victorian Christians argued that slavery must be a divinely sanctioned institution.

❧ THE NEW TESTAMENT & SLAVERY

The Bible was not used to justify African servitude because of prevailing sentiments about white superiority. In fact, the Holy Scriptures say nothing about race and slavery. Rather it was because both Jesus, Christianity's founder, and Saint Paul, Christianity's greatest apostle, mention servitude and slavery numerous times without ever speaking out against them.[689]

In the Epistle of Philemon, for example, we find Paul returning a runaway (white) slave, named Onesimus, to his master, Philemon, with no comment about the injustices or evils of slavery.[690] This is hardly the action of an abolitionist. Rather it is the action of a law-abiding, proslavery advocate, as Paul's own words to the slaves at Colossae (located in what is now southeast Turkey) testifies:

> Servants, obey in all things your masters according to the flesh; not with eyeservice, as menpleasers; but in singleness of heart, fearing God.[691]

Paul tolerated slavery in part because of his mystical belief that merely being a Christian obliterated the social, ethnic, and even gender lines that separate people from one another. Wrote Paul:

> There is neither Jew nor Greek, there is neither bond nor free, there is neither male nor female: for ye are all one in Christ

---

688. Muller, p. 186.
689. See e.g., Matthew 8:5-13; Matthew 10:24-25; Luke 12:47; Ephesians 6:5; I Timothy 6:1; Titus 2:9-10.
690. Philemon 1:1-25.
691. Colossians 3:22.

Jesus.[692]

Saint Peter agreed with Paul on the topic of slavery and even issued the same command for slaves to be obedient to their owners, again without condemnation of the institution. Wrote Peter:

> Servants, be subject to your masters with all fear; not only to the good and gentle, but also to the froward.[693]

In fact, there is no unequivocal admonition against slavery anywhere in the New Testament. Jesus himself demands that one who desires to be his chief disciple should be the slave of all,[694] and later, after Jesus' resurrection, the apostles are called "slaves of the Lord."[695] In today's totalitarian environment of political correctness how many Christians would be willing to publically refer themselves as "slaves of the Lord"?

Why did neither Jesus or his apostles denounce slavery? Slavery was so accepted, so integral to ancient Roman and Near Eastern society, that even espousing the idea of abolition would have caused widespread violence, resulting in massive social disorder and financial upheaval. Abolition then, in this particular situation, would not have agreed with the teachings of Jesus and the Christian Church.[696] This exact sentiment would be echoed 2,000 years later by good Christians across the South.

❧ THE OLD TESTAMENT & SLAVERY

The Old Testament (or Torah) is also completely silent on the evils of slavery. Instead it offers many examples of both the backhanded approval of slavery and its full sanction by God.[697] Indeed, the institution was openly practiced by the early Hebrews throughout their era, with

---

692. Galatians 3:28.
693. 1 Peter 2:18.
694. Matthew 20:27; Mark 10:44.
695. Acts 4:29; 16:17; Galatians 1:10.
696. T. C. Butler, s.v. "Slave/servant."
697. See e.g., Exodus 21:26-27; Proverbs 29:19.

one of the more famous of them, Joseph, shown being sold into slavery by his own brothers.[698]

If this was not enough to rationalize slavery, Christian supporters of the institution could always turn to the book of Genesis and read of the idea that Africans bore the "mark of Cain," a people cursed by Noah to be the "servants of servants," meaning the "lowest of slaves."[699]

Also known as the "curse of Ham" (actually the curse of Ham's son, Canaan, and his descendants), early Americans, like the Mormons, construed these passages to mean that Africans had inherited the "affliction" of black skin and a life of servitude under white rule.[700] As the Old Testament authors state it:

> And Ham, the father of Canaan, saw the nakedness of his father,

---

698. Genesis 37:26-28.
699. Genesis 4:1-15; 9:25. See Metzger and Coogan, s.v. "Slavery and the Bible."
700. The non-Bible based Mormons, or more officially, the members of the Church of Jesus Christ of Latter-Day Saints (LDS), have long embraced a belief in the "mark of Cain," though understandably this fact has been largely kept from the general public. As such, early Mormon laws did not prohibit slavery. Rather they sanctioned them. Mormon leader Brigham Young (1801-1877), for example, not only welcomed white slave owners into his church, he settled the Salt Lake Valley area in Utah using Mormon slave owners and their slaves. And in 1852, as the first territorial governor of Utah, Young asked the legislature to legalize slavery, making it the only territory west of the Missouri River and north of the Missouri Compromise line to allow the institution. B. H. Johnson, p. 140; Olson, p. 148. All Mormons once held that blacks would continue to be an "inferior race" in the "Next World." Not surprisingly, blacks, being of the "lineage of Cain," were not allowed to join the Mormon priesthood or participate in Temple ordinances until 1978, 148 years after the church's founding in 1830 by Yankee polygamist and former Mason, Joseph Smith (1805-1844). The change only came after decades of severe criticism, condemnation, and charges of racism from around the world. Little wonder that in the early 1900s the Utah branch of the new KKK (as separate from the original racially inclusive KKK) flourished with the membership of Mormon ministers. Wade, p. 143. Despite the church's modern 1978 concession, the belief in the "Curse of Ham" survives among many individual Mormons and Mormon groups. But this is not the pseudo-Christian church's only politically incorrect, non-biblical dogma. It still embraces beliefs in both a Father-God and a Mother-Goddess (as well as a "plurality" of other deities), the secret ritual of baptism for the dead (condemned in 1 Cor. 15:29 by Saint Paul as a Pagan practice), the belief that Jesus and Satan are brothers, the posthumous attainment of self-godhood (in order to rule other planets after earthly death), and the continuance of male polygamy after death—a tenant particularly distressing to many female LDS members. For more on these topics from an LDS perspective, see the church's excellent publication: *Encyclopedia of Mormonism*, by Daniel H. Ludlow, s.v. "Cain," "Race, Racism," "Blacks," "Devils," "Priesthood," "Mother in Heaven," "Godhood," "Baptism for the Dead," passim. For a non-Mormon Christian view of the LDS church see: *Mormonism Unmasked*, by R. Philip Roberts. Revealingly, the scandalous non-Christian Joseph Smith, murdered in an Illinois jail by an angry Christian mob, was an admirer of the equally scandalous non-Christian Abraham Lincoln of Illinois. See e.g., Nicolay and Hay, ALAH, Vol. 1, p. 182. For more on Lincoln's anti-Christian atheism, see Seabrook, L, pp. 918-938.

and told his two brethren without. And Shem and Japheth took a garment, and laid it upon both their shoulders, and went backward, and covered the nakedness of their father; and their faces were backward, and they saw not their father's nakedness. And Noah awoke from his wine, and knew what his younger son had done unto him. And he said, Cursed be Canaan; a servant of servants shall he be unto his brethren. And he said, Blessed be the LORD God of Shem; and Canaan shall be his servant. God shall enlarge Japheth, and he shall dwell in the tents of Shem; and Canaan shall be his servant.[701]

❧ WHITE SLAVERY

These and other scriptures were used by early Americans to defend the institution of servitude, not just for blacks, but for all races. As just mentioned, the Bible does not speak in terms of race in the passages mentioned above, and neither did most 19th-Century Southerners see slavery in terms of race, in part, because enslavement was a common punishment for criminals of all races at the time.[702]

This is also why neither tens of thousands of African-American slave owners, Hispanic-American slave owners, or Native-American slave owners were considered an anomaly in the South. Even the practice of owning European-American slaves and servants was once accepted in America.

The truth is that the vast majority of white immigrants who came to America's original thirteen English colonies—at least two-thirds[703]—came as white servants.[704] In fact, *white indentured servitude, being much preferred over African slavery (Africans were considered "alien" by early white colonialists,[705] their skin color a symbol of death and evil),[706] was the institution that paved the way for black slavery in*

---

701. Genesis 9:22-27.
702. Kennedy, p. 105.
703. Drescher and Engerman, p. 239.
704. Stampp, p. 16.
705. Garraty and McCaughey, p. 26.
706. Hoffer, p. 12.

THE MCGAVOCKS OF CARNTON PLANTATION

America.[707]

Even in the McGavocks' day (1800s) the memory of white servitude in the U.S. was still fresh. One of Randal McGavock's fellow classmates at Dickinson College, for instance, had come from a family of early American white slaves and servants: Roger Brooke Taney, Chief Justice of the U.S. Supreme Court, descended from ancestors who, in the mid-1600s, emigrated from England to the British colony in Maryland as indentured servants.[708]

Many Europeans who could not afford to purchase their passage to America, sold themselves into indentured servitude to ship captains. After arriving in America, the captain, in turn, sold the servant's work contract (known as an indenture) to a local farmer.[709] At least two known signers of the Declaration of Independence arrived in America in this manner,[710] while the European ancestor of at least one American president, Martin Van Buren (1782-1862), is known to have emigrated to America as an indentured servant.[711]

Thirteen of the thirty members of Virginia's House of Burgesses came across the Atlantic as indentured servants, as did Adam Thoroughgood (1604-1640), the founder of the city of Norfolk, Virginia.[712] So many whites arrived in America from Europe as retainers that writer Hulbert Footner (1879-1944) commented on it: many of America's earliest European families proudly traced their beginnings to an indentured servant, he penned in the early 1900s.[713]

It was also not uncommon for wealthy Europeans to accrue

---

707. Wilson and Ferris, s.v. "Plantations." Many Northern whites, like Yankee judge Samuel Sewall, disliked blacks so much that they advocated using white slaves instead. See Sewall, Vol. 2, pp. 17-18.
708. Roger's wife, Anne Phoebe Charlton Key (1783-1855), was a sister of Francis Scott Key (1799-1843), who wrote the U.S. National Anthem, *The Star Spangled Banner*. Like Lincoln, lawyer-poet Francis Scott Key detested abolitionists and the abolition movement. Indeed, he was a co-founder of the American Colonization Society (ACS), a Yankee organization dedicated to the idea of deporting all freed American blacks out of the country, preferably to Liberia, Africa—a colony set up in 1822 by the ACS for this express purpose. Lincoln mentioned Liberia many times in his speeches and writings as the best solution to the "race problem." See Seabrook, L, pp. 584-633.
709. Higginbotham, pp. 392-393.
710. Smelser, ACRH, p. 58.
711. DeGregorio, s.v. "Martin Van Buren."
712. See Website: www.virginiabeachhistory.org/thoroughgoodhouse.html.
713. Furnas, p. 108.

THE MCGAVOCKS OF CARNTON PLANTATION

property in the American British colonies via the headright system. Here an individual paid for the oceanic passage of indentured white servants from England in exchange for land. An ancestor of America's fourth president, James Madison, did just this, acquiring some 2,000 acres of property by 1664.[714]

Several U.S. presidents themselves began their adult lives as enslaved servants. One of these, our thirteenth president, Millard Fillmore (1800-1874), was indentured to a cloth maker. After "slaving away" for a number of years, Fillmore managed to purchase his freedom for $30, a fortune in the early 1800s (the equivalent of about $500 today).[715]

President Martin Van Buren's third great-grandfather, Cornelius Maesen Van Buren (1612-1648), emigrated from the Netherlands to New York as an indentured servant.[716] Henry Wilson (1812-1875), President Ulysses S. Grant's second vice president and a cofounder of the Free-Soil Party, worked as an indentured slave for eleven years, from age ten to twenty-one.[717] Even one of Lincoln's ancestors, an early relation who was part of the Massachusetts Bay Colony, came to America as an indentured servant.[718]

One of the reasons politician and Tennessee Unionist Andrew Johnson (1808-1875) was somewhat conciliatory toward the South after Lincoln's War was that he himself had been enslaved in his youth.[719] Unlike Fillmore, however, Johnson did not wait to earn his way out of the institution. He simply ran away. His master, a tailor, posted a $10 reward in the Raleigh (North Carolina) *Gazette* for the young servant's capture and return, but never collected. Johnson escaped permanently, later to become America's seventeenth president.[720]

While, thanks to whites like Lincoln, there is no denying that a

---

714. DeGregorio, s.v. "James Madison."
715. Furnas, p. 108.
716. DeGregorio, s.v. "Martin Van Buren."
717. DeGregorio, s.v. "Ulysses S. Grant."
718. Furnas, p. 108.
719. DeGregorio, s.v. "Andrew Johnson."
720. Shenkman and Reiger, p. 96.

THE McGAVOCKS OF CARNTON PLANTATION

culture of white supremacy dominated 19th-Century America, Victorian whites were very familiar with the fact that ancient Egyptian, Phoenician, Philistine, Persian, Assyrian, Canaanite, Babylonian, Israelite, Hebrew, Greek, Roman, and Jewish slaves were Caucasian, as were the slaves of more modern Europeans nations, such as Normandy, Italy, Cyprus, Crete, and Sicily. Thus slavery was not as shocking to early American whites as we have been led to believe.

Indeed, also well-known to them was the fact that the word slave itself derives from the Slavs,[721] a Caucasian people from the area of Salonika (Thessaloniki), Greece, who, in Medieval times, were enslaved by other European peoples, such as the Vikings, who became wealthy trafficking in their fellow whites.[722] In fact, from the beginning of the history of European slavery, it was primarily a white institution, with white slaves being captured, owned, and sold by fellow whites.

Historically speaking, of course, both the earliest known slave traders and the earliest known slaves were Caucasians: the Babylonians, Assyrians, Sumerians, Mesopotamians, Egyptians, Arabians and Hebrews—at some point in their history—all either enslaved other whites or were themselves enslaved by other whites. Many others from the same period, such as the Greeks and Romans, were slaves of European extraction, enslaved by other Europeans.[723] Greek society itself was built upon and around white slavery.[724]

In the early years of the Roman Empire three out of four residents of what we now call Italy were slaves, some 21 million in total. Both the slavers and their chattel were white.[725] (Contrast this number with the much smaller figure 3.5 million, the total number of black slaves in the American south in 1860,[726] an area many times the size of

---

721. Mish, s.v. "slave."
722. The Vikings, who carried on a European-wide slave trade for many decades, captured and enslaved untold numbers of whites from Ireland all the way to what is now Slovakia. Males were sold as slave laborers while females were sold into harems.
723. Meltzer, Vol. 1, pp. 9-201; Nye, p. 46.
724. Muller, pp. 121, 134.
725. Fogel, p. 17.
726. Cooper, JDA, p. 378.

THE MCGAVOCKS OF CARNTON PLANTATION

Italy.)[727]

White slavery was so common in ancient Rome that even the poorest families had at least one or more slaves. A historian living at the time wrote that when one particular Roman experienced a financial setback, leaving him nearly bankrupt, he complained that he was left with *only* 4,116 slaves—all white, of course.[728] This was more slaves than the entire city of Nashville, Tennessee, possessed in 1860.[729]

Ancient Europe's view of slavery was summed up by Aristotle (384-322 B.C.E.) in the 4th Century. According to the famed Greek philosopher a certain percentage of society are born to be slaves,[730] "tools with voices," as he referred to them—natural born servants who need to be enslaved for their own good.[731]

European slavery was such a dominant aspect of the region that it eventually spilled over into both Asia and the Arabic world. Swedish Vikings, for example, enslaved whites from the northern forests of Russia (once literally known as the "nation of slaves"),[732] then traded them to Muslims for Oriental goods.[733]

White slavery was not just a phenomenon of the ancient world or the Middle Ages. Soviet dictator Joseph Stalin enslaved an estimated 12 million[734] to 18 million Caucasians during his reign of terror in the 1930s,[735] as many as 14.5 million more white slaves than the entire American South's 3.5 million black slaves.

Between 1941 and 1945 nearly 8 million Caucasians were enslaved across Europe under Nazi Germany, including children as young as six years of age. This means that the Nazis owned 4.5 million

---

727. To put these numbers into perspective: Italy is 116,345 square miles. The Confederacy was 850,000 square miles. Thus, while the American South was 87 percent larger than Italy, ancient Italians owned 84 percent more slaves than Southerners.
728. Celeste, pp. 141-142.
729. J. M. McPherson, NCW, p. 319.
730. Muller, p. 116.
731. Drescher and Engerman, pp. 195, 230.
732. Radzinsky, p. 33.
733. Boorstin, pp. 208-209.
734. Rayfield, p. 180.
735. Montefiore, p. 643.

more white slaves than the American South owned black slaves.

Under Nazi leader Adolf Hitler (a socialist), white European families were routinely separated and forced to work in factories, fields, and mines, where they were dehumanized, beaten, whipped, and starved by their German overlords.[736] White Nazi slavery was the largest revival of the institution in the 20th Century, and one of the fastest and most monumental expansions of slavery in world history.[737] This occurred a mere sixty-six years ago.

ꙮ ABRAHAM THE SLAVE OWNER

Slavery then was not a racial white-black issue in the early to mid 1800s. It was often more a religious one. And it was for just this reason that books, like Albert Taylor Bledsoe's (1809-1877) *An Essay on Liberty and Slavery* (1856), were owned, read, and embraced by families like the McGavocks.

Bledsoe, a brilliant unreconstructed Southerner, observed in his book, for example, that Abraham, the father of Judaism, owned over 1,000 (white) slaves, but was not condemned by God. Rather he received God's greatest blessing: an eternal covenant. How, then, Bledsoe asked "could these professing [Northern] Christians proceed to condemn and excommunicate a poor brother [that is, a Christian, Southern servant owner] for having merely approved what Abraham had practiced?"[738]

ꙮ GOD ON SLAVERY

Abraham was not the only early Jew who practiced slavery with the consent and even the encouragement of God. According to the Bible, the Hebrew people, spiritual precursors to the Christian faith, had the full sanction of the Almighty behind them in their acceptance of the institution. Here, in the Book of Leviticus, is what God himself has to say on the matter:

---

736. Meltzer, Vol. 2, pp. 270-277.
737. Drescher and Engerman, p. 289.
738. Bledsoe, ELS, p. 142.

The McGavocks of Carnton Plantation

> I am the Lord your God, which brought you forth out of the land of Egypt, to give you the land of Canaan, and to be your God . . .
>
> Both thy bondmen [male slaves], and thy bondmaids [female slaves], which thou shalt have, shall be of the heathen that are round about you; of them shall ye buy bondmen and bondmaids.
>
> Moreover of the children of the strangers that do sojourn among you, of them shall ye buy, and of their families that are with you, which they begat in your land: and they shall be your possession.
>
> And ye shall take them as an inheritance for your children after you, to inherit them for a possession; they shall be your bondmen [slaves] for ever . . . .[739]

The Bible not only permits Hebrews to enslave foreigners permanently,[740] it even allows a father to sell his children into slavery.[741] Early Hebrew laws ordained that a slave had no human rights, and that slaves could not marry, but only "mate." The children from these unions were considered the property of the owner.

According to Exodus 21:3, if a male slave was freed, his wife and children had to remain behind in slavery if the woman had been given to him by the owner.[742] And while some early Christians were already discussing the incompatibility between slavery and Jesus' message of brotherly love, according to the Talmud, God sanctioned slavery among the Jews up until at least the year 400.[743]

While today we rightly argue these ideas and practices away in defense of civil and natural rights, in the 17th, 18th, and 19th Centuries Americans took the Bible more literally, and as with passages like those above, at face value.

And so it was in the extremely religious world of Victorian Tennessee. Who are we to judge it? As Victorian Southerner Mary

---

739. Leviticus 25:38, 44-46.
740. T. C. Butler, s.v. "Slave/servant."
741. Exodus 21:1-6; Deuteronomy 15:12.
742. McKenzie, s.v. "Slave, slavery."
743. Metzger and Coogan, s.v. "Slavery."

THE MCGAVOCKS OF CARNTON PLANTATION

Chesnut herself knowingly said in defense of the existence of servitude in the Old South: we are creatures of our own time and place, of the 19th Century.[744]

❧ THE ENTIRE WORLD ONCE SUPPORTED SLAVERY
When it came to the "peculiar institution" our Southern predecessors and ancestors were in good company.

For thousands of years, from ancient times to the dawn of the formation of the U.S., few, except a small number of Quakers, spoke out against the institution. And even among this normally highly conscientious religious community overt racism toward blacks was often witnessed,[745] with some, like atheist Lincoln (whose ancestors were Quakers),[746] supporting the American Colonization Society.[747] Still others were even slave owners—slave owners who believed that blacks were inherently flawed.[748] New England Quakers in particular were known to be busily engaged in the slave trade throughout the 1700s.[749]

But let us not judge the Quakers too harshly. For nearly every known major writer, philosopher, politician, and theologian of every race and creed who lived during this time period supported the idea of slavery.

As just noted, Aristotle believed that "from the hour of their birth some are marked out for subjection, others for rule."[750] Protestant reformer Martin Luther (1483-1546) heartily agreed. Thus when a group of European slaves asked for their freedom in 1525, like Saint Paul, Luther unsympathetically replied that those in bondage needed to accept their lot in life, for in order for the world to function, both free men and enslaved men were needed.[751]

---

744. Chesnut, MCCW, p. 246.
745. Litwack, NS, pp. 205-208, 221.
746. Barton, pp. 236-237.
747. M. Perry, p. 85.
748. Garraty and McCaughey, p. 29.
749. Furnas, p. 120.
750. A. J. Grant, p. 221.
751. Fogel and Engerman, p. 31.

THE MCGAVOCKS OF CARNTON PLANTATION

Long before Luther's time the Catholic Church, indeed all of Christendom itself, was actively involved in slavery,[752] which is why Catholic philosophers, like Thomas More (1477-1535), thought it befitting for menial laborers, the poor, and criminals to be made into slaves.[753]

Early Christians also defended slavery as a form of evangelism, one that introduced the saving grace of the Gospel of Christ to "ignorant African savages," none who, they believed, would see Heaven without a proper baptism. This particular defense was especially aggravating to 19th-Century black civil rights leaders, like former Northern slave Frederick Douglass, who wrote:

> ... I can see no reason, but the most deceitful one, for calling the religion of this land Christianity. I look upon it as the climax of all misnomers, the boldest of all frauds, and the grossest of all libels.[754]

❧ CARNTON'S ONE RUNAWAY SERVANT

Many blacks lived and worked at Carnton during the McGavocks' eighty-six year ownership of the plantation, and only one is known to have run away. This gives us great insight into how the McGavocks viewed and treated the blacks who worked for them.

Why, many have asked, did this particular servant, named Dick, feel the need to escape Carnton Plantation? We do not know for sure. But beyond the obvious answer that he simply desired his freedom, it could have been for any number of reasons, none of them having to do directly with the McGavocks.

Sometimes servants did not get along with each other. Other times a love affair went bad or a marriage became intolerable. It was also not unusual for a servant to run off for a few weeks in order to visit loved ones on other plantations.

There are endless possibilities. Perhaps this particular individual

---

752. L. M. Graham, pp. 459-461.
753. Fogel and Engerman, pp. 29-31.
754. Douglass, NLFD, pp. xi, 118.

THE MCGAVOCKS OF CARNTON PLANTATION

was merely an "habitual runaway." Every plantation had one. In fact, so common was this type of individual that plantation owners built the loss into their yearly calculations.[755]

Still it is unlikely that Dick ran away for the specific purpose of being free. In 1852, when this incident occurred, there was no such thing as complete and authentic liberty for blacks anywhere in the U.S., particularly, as we have seen, in the North. Free blacks often had as many, and in many cases even more, restrictions placed on them than servile blacks.

❧ SLAVERY WAS LEGAL WORLDWIDE IN THE 1800s

Even if Dick did run away in an attempt to gain his freedom, however, is it fair to blame his situation on Colonel John?

Absolutely not.

For one thing, both slavery and the slave trade were still being legally practiced across the North in 1852, as the institution was still protected by the U.S. Constitution. More to the point, while today slavery is unimaginable, it was perfectly lawful across America for 246 years:

- It was legal in the American colonies from 1619 (when the first African servants were brought by the Dutch to the English settlers at Jamestown, Virginia) and 1641 (when Massachusetts became the first state to legalize it),[756] to 1776 (the year the U.S.A. was formed).
- It was legal from 1776 to 1789 (the period of the American Confederacy lasted from 1781 to 1789).
- It was legal in the U.S.A. from 1789 to 1865, and in the C.S.A. from 1861 to 1865, the year the Thirteenth Amendment was ratified on December 6, finally ending the institution in every state. This is one reason why Northern slave owners, such as General Ulysses S. Grant (1822-1885), kept their slaves until after the

---

755. Genovese, pp. 649, 653.
756. G. H. Moore, pp. 5, 11, 17-19.

THE MCGAVOCKS OF CARNTON PLANTATION

War ended,[757] and why other Yankees, like Lincoln, editor Horace Greeley, Union officer Nathaniel Prentiss Banks (1816-1894), and Union officer Benjamin F. "the Beast" Butler (1818-1893), approved of the idea of black colonization outside the U.S.[758]

It should be remembered that slavery was also legal in Europe, Asia, Latin America, and Africa, and indeed in every other nation on earth at the time the McGavocks owned black servants. As we have seen, pre-European Africa had been practicing slavery, servitude, vassalage, and serfdom on its own people for thousands of years[759] (often in forms far more brutal than anything found in the American South),[760] dating back at least 2,200 years ago to the continent's Iron Age.[761]

Entire African kingdoms were built on indigenous slavery and routinely engaged in the mass subjugation of neighboring tribes (chiefly through raiding). Among the early African peoples who engaged in slavery were the Yoruba of western Nigeria, the Fon of Dahomey, and the Fanti and Asante (or Ashanti) of Ghana.[762]

Slavery was so imbedded in African culture that native peoples often gave their towns names that were associated with the institution. An example is the village of Atorkor, located today in what is the Volta region of Ghana. As controllers of the local slave supply, the main source of income among early Atorkorians was slave trading, hence the rough meaning of their village name: purchase and leave.[763]

It was just such facts that made the institution so understandable to many American black civil rights leaders. One of these was the great African-American educator, intellectual, and author William E. B. Du

---

757. Wallechinsky, Wallace, and Wallace, p. 11; Woods, p. 67. Grant did not free his slaves until he was forced to by the ratification of the Thirteenth Amendment on December 6, 1865, eight months after Lincoln's War ended.
758. Adams and Sanders, pp. 215-216.
759. Lott, pp. 17, 19.
760. See Davidson, pp. 120-121, 123-124.
761. Davidson, p. 30.
762. Davidson, pp. 229, 242, 251.
763. A. C. Bailey, p. 82.

The McGavocks of Carnton Plantation

Bois (1868-1963), who wrote that he could forgive slavery for it "is a world-old habit."[764]

❧ UNFAIRLY JUDGING OUR ANCESTORS

The point is that we should not judge our predecessors by the standards, values, and morals of our day (presentism). It is not fair, scientific, or historically accurate. After all, how will our hopefully more enlightened descendants evaluate us 150 years from now? If they judge us the way many people today judge our Victorian ancestors, especially our *Southern* Victorian ancestors, we will not stand up very well.

Southerners like the McGavocks were, after all, a product of their times, just as we are. And like nearly all 19th-Century Americans, they were taught by their society, parents, church, school, and the science of the day, that servitude was inherent to human society, that it was, as we have just seen, an institution decreed by God himself.

How could it have been any different? At the time there was not a single egalitarian, nonracist, co-racial society on earth that early Americans could have used as a model. In every nation on earth, one race, whether it was white, black, red, yellow, or brown, dominated all others, usually in what we would now think of as an inhumane and racist manner.

More to the point, *forced labor* has been the rule since the dawn of time.[765] On the other hand, *unforced labor*, if there truly is such a thing, has always been the exception.[766] And as of the mid 1800s there had never been a single known instance of a purely nonracist society in all of recorded history.[767]

---

764. Du Bois, p. 172.
765. Drescher and Engerman, p. 204.
766. Since all humans, no matter what their race, nationality, or socioeconomic background, *have* to work to survive, many slavery scholars correctly consider all labor "forced."
767. Ellis, FB, p. 107. To this day there is still no completely egalitarian society on earth, for most people around the globe, whatever their skin color, seem unable to accept the fact that "race" is an illusion, a sociological theory that has no real basis in biology. We are all one species and descend from a single common prehistoric ancestor (symbolized in the pre-biblical Babylonian creation myth as the "first man" Adapa, in the pre-biblical Sumerian creation myth as Adamu, and in the later biblical Jewish creation myth as Adam). In reality the apparent physical differences among us stem solely from one thing: where on the planet our distant ancestors originated. Dark skinned people tend to evolve in hot equatorial regions, light

The McGavocks of Carnton Plantation

Knowing these facts gives us a much better understanding of those blacks, whites, browns, and reds who practiced slavery during America's past.

While we can certainly disagree with the ancient belief that slavery is an inherent element of human society, we are in no position to condemn early Americans for embracing it. What deeds are we committing today that we will be severely castigated for in the year 2161?

Let us hope that our future critics are fair in their assessment of us, and that they take into account our current social, political, and religious beliefs, as well as our level of scientific knowledge. For in all of these fields we will look extremely primitive to 22nd-Century Americans living 150 years from now.

❧ SLAVE ABUSE AT CARNTON?

We do know one thing about Dick's case: he did not run away because of any type of abuse at Carnton.

None of the McGavocks, especially Colonel John, ever mishandled their black servants. Not only were they good, gentle, and moral Christians, and thus not the type to engage in such activities, if they had, there would be both personal and civil records of their arrest and trial.

We are dealing with Southern fact here, not Northern myth.

❧ COLONEL JOHN'S $50 REWARD FOR DICK'S CAPTURE

Shortly after Dick fled Carnton, John ran an ad in the local newspaper on January 11, 1853, offering a reward of $50 (today the equivalent of about $1,350) for his capture and return. It read:

---

skinned people tend to evolve in cool boreal regions. Thus, as Ashley Montagu (1905-1999) postulated decades ago, when speaking of modern *Homo sapiens* it would be more accurate to replace the word "race" with the word "variety."

THE MCGAVOCKS OF CARNTON PLANTATION

$50 REWARD

Run away from the undersigned, about the 26th of December last, a negro man named Dick, 21 years old, about 6 feet high, of black complexion, with a mark or wart on the side of his face, rather stooped shouldered. He wore when he left, a black pilot clothcoat lined with red flannel, jean pants and a black cloth cape. I will give twenty dollars if taken in the state, or fifty if taken out.

January 11, 1853
JNO. McGAVOCK

John has been criticized by modern anti-South advocates for this ad, allegedly because they believe it proves that the McGavocks were cruel, unjust, and racist toward blacks. But nothing could be further from the truth. John's servant Dick, who under U.S. law was considered "private property" at the time, was worth today's equivalent of about $60,000. What would you have done in John's situation?

It is easy, from today's perspective, to vilify John for this action and to think that we would have simply allowed Dick to go free. But if we could look at the situation through his eyes in 1853, we would see things very differently. For not only was slavery constitutionally legal all across the U.S., but as a whole, American society, both North and South, accepted it as a necessary and even God-ordained institution.

Additionally, not only was the American Fugitive Slave Law in effect at the time (legally requiring the capture and return of runaway servants in all states), but $60,000 (in today's currency) was at stake. Even for multimillionaires like the conservative law-abiding McGavocks, this was a costly investment, one not to be squandered.

Finally we must bear in mind that black, red, and brown slave owners also ran ads in local papers for the capture and return of their runaway slaves.

This was not a racial issue. It was a legal and financial one.

☙ THE McGAVOCK'S TREATMENT OF THEIR SERVANTS

How then did the McGavocks view their own servants?

We know from family journals that like most Southerners they referred to them as "servants," not "slaves," and that they considered them "a part of the family." The McGavocks were far from alone in this particular practice. Contrary to what our Northern influenced text books teach, this was the norm across the South. Mary Chesnut said that their black housekeeper and children's nurse, Mammy Baldwin, was always loved, cared for, and looked upon as one of the family.[768]

This sentiment was nearly always mutual and returned in kind. Colonel John's personal body servant once called his employer (that is, his "owner") "the politest man that ever was," and most Southerners, both European and African, came to feel that they had two families: a white one and a black one, a relationship often marked by the most heartfelt tenderness and authentic love.[769]

This type of relationship existed from the earliest days of colonial America right up until Lincoln's War. On June 8, 1845, for instance, as President Andrew Jackson lay near death at his Tennessee home, the Hermitage, anguished family members and weeping black servants surrounded his bed, listening intently as the dying Southerner uttered his last wish: "I hope to meet you all again one day in Heaven: both white and black."[770]

Many of the letters that white Southern servant owners sent home from the battlefield were addressed to both their white biological family and their black servant family. Indeed, it was perfectly normal for a white Reb to tenderly inquire as to the general well-being of the African-Americans back at his farm, my black family, as he would commonly refer to them.[771] Similarly, Southern white civilians used the phrase, my family—black and white, on a routine basis.[772]

Even pro-North, anti-South writers have been forced to acknowledge that intimate bonds of affection did in fact develop between the two races;[773] that typically servants were made to feel like members

---

768. Chesnut, MCCW, p. 250.
769. Wiley, LJR, p. 328.
770. *Andrew Jackson*, History Channel, June 26, 2008.
771. Garraty and McCaughey, p. 254.
772. Fox-Genovese, p. 133.
773. Rosenbaum and Brinkley, s.v. "Slavery."

THE MCGAVOCKS OF CARNTON PLANTATION

of the family, essentially becoming part of their owners' white kinship group[774]—that is, as part of the owner's extended family;[775] and that there were innumerable cases of lifelong relationships built around love and mutual respect between owners and servants.[776]

Such relationships help explain why in so many instances when Union armies invaded a Southern town, black servants fled with their white families rather than into the arms of the enemy. Even in those rare situations where blacks did seek refuge with the advancing Union armies, loyalty and devotion to their white "brothers and sisters" often continued. In one such incident, at the Battle of Sharpsburg (Antietam to Yanks) on September 17, 1862, eyewitnesses reported a Southern black servant who pulled his injured white owner to safety before sprinting across a field through gunfire and into the Federal line.[777]

❧ MARIA OTEY REDDICK

We have other clues as to the relationship between whites and blacks at Carnton. One "mulatto" female servant named Maria Otey (1832-1922),[778] the personal maid of Carrie (Winder) McGavock, raised three generations of McGavock children, then voluntarily returned to Carnton from Alabama after the War to continue working for the family, this time as a paid employee. The freedwoman would hardly have come back to the McGavocks' plantation had she been abused or seen other servants abused there.

Maria, who married "mulatto" Bolling Reddick (b. 1833 in Virginia)[779] and was thereafter known as "Maria Reddick," bore eight children at the plantation.[780] Indeed, she had her own long and interesting history at Carnton. As late as 1971 there were still living individuals who could recall the image of Maria quietly sewing, sitting

---

774. M. M. Smith, pp. 37, 194.
775. Drescher and Engerman, p. 175.
776. Garraty and McCaughey, p. 217.
777. Channing, p. 129.
778. Maria was born in Mississippi.
779. Bolling's first name is also spelled Boling and Bowling in some records.
780. Some sources refer to her as Mariah Reddick.

and talking with other Franklin women, or reminiscing about the good old days before the "late unpleasantness," as many Southerners still refer to Lincoln's War.[781]

Maria had begun as a servant of Carrie Winder's father Colonel Van Perkins Winder, Sr. in Louisiana.[782] On Carrie's marriage to John W. McGavock in 1848, Mr. Winder gave the sixteen-year old African-American from Mississippi to Carrie as a wedding gift.[783]

Maria was so devoted to the McGavock family that she gave the eulogy at Carrie's funeral in 1905, then stayed on to work for the family until 1919, eight years after the last McGavock sold Carnton and moved out. Maria, who is buried in Franklin's Toussaint L'Ouverture (African-American) Cemetery,[784] dedicated seventy-one years of her life to serving the McGavocks, longer than most of the McGavocks themselves lived.[785]

ᴥ RACIST LINCOLN, RACIST ILLINOIS

Middle Tennessee was a good place for 19th-Century blacks to reside. The region was liberal by Yankee standards, for in the mid-1800s most of the Northern states had tough "Black Codes," laws that severely restricted the movements and rights of blacks. As we have discussed, Illinois, Lincoln's adopted state, possessed some of the most stringent anti-black laws in America, in great part because of the president

---

781. V. M. Bowman, p. 62.
782. As noted earlier, the wife of Col. Van Perkins Winder, Sr., Carrie's mother, was Martha Ann Grundy, a daughter of Tennessee senator, Felix Grundy. Van's genealogy: born in Maryland, he is the great-grandson of Gen. William Winder (1714-1792) and Esther Gillis (1724-1767), the 2nd great-grandson of John Winder (1676-1716) and Jane Dashiel (1675-1696), and the 3rd great-grandson of John "the Immigrant" Winder (1635-1698) and Bridget Meador (b. 1634) of Lorton, Cumberland County, England. From my personal family tree.
783. V. M. Bowman, p. 62.
784. This Franklin cemetery was named after François Dominique Toussaint ©. 1745-1803), a self-educated slave who led the black Haitian Rebellion in 1791. Taking the name of a series of hard-hitting campaigns to free his fellow servants, L'ouverture (meaning "the opening"), he conquered Santo Domingo in 1801 and took over governorship. In the ongoing conflict with France he was captured and sent to a prison at Fort-de-Joux in the French Jura. Toussaint L'ouverture died in a dungeon there in 1803, becoming a martyr for the cause of universal black emancipation. The Negro Haitian Rebellion was still a daily topic of discussion by white Americans in the mid-1800s and was no doubt occasionally brought up at the McGavocks' dinner table.
785. According to her gravestone, Maria passed away in 1922.

THE McGAVOCKS OF CARNTON PLANTATION

himself.

In 1862, Lincoln, who as an attorney had once defended a slave owner in court (and lost), helped the citizens of Illinois amend their state constitution to include a passage that read, "no negro or mulatto shall immigrate or settle in this state."[786] He even urged the Illinois legislature to set aside funding to deport all free blacks from the state in order to prevent miscegenation (that is, racial interbreeding),[787] a racist word invented, not by Southerners, but by Northerners.[788]

With men like Lincoln serving in its government it is certainly no surprise that Illinois was so anti-black. After all, it was old Abe himself who, on July 17, 1858, made a public speech at Springfield, Illinois, that included the following words: "What I would most desire would be the separation of the white and black races."[789]

A year earlier, on June 26, 1857, during another address at Springfield, here is what the die-hard colonizationist said to his Northern audience about the horrors of race-mixing and the benefits of "separating" the races. In this statement he reveals one of the main reasons he was against slavery and in favor of black deportation: his absolute dread of miscegenation, or amalgamation, as it was also known. Stated Lincoln to his Northern audience:

> Judge [Stephen] Douglas is especially horrified at the thought of the mixing of blood by the white and black races: agreed for once—a thousand times agreed. There are white men enough to marry all the white women, and black men enough to marry all the black women; and so let them be married. . . . In 1850 there were in the United States 405,751 mulattoes. Very few of these are the offspring of whites and *free* blacks; nearly all have sprung from the black *slaves* and white masters. A separation of the races is the only perfect preventive of amalgamation. . . . [because] statistics show

---

[786]. Kennedy, p. 165.
[787]. Berwanger, pp. 4-5.
[788]. Wilson and Ferris, s.v. "Miscegenation." The names of the three men who invented the word miscegenation are David G. Croly (from New York), George Wakeman (also from New York), and Samuel S. Cox (a congressman from Ohio).
[789]. Nicolay and Hay, ALCW, Vol. 1, p. 273.

THE MCGAVOCKS OF CARNTON PLANTATION

that slavery is the greatest source of amalgamation.[790]

Lincoln was clear: by nature, slavery forces the races to intermingle, which in turn brings about the undesirable birth of "mullatos." Only a "separation of the races" could fully prevent this, he maintained. Thus one of Lincoln's party members, Illinois Senator Lyman Trumbull, noted that:

> There is a great aversion in the West—I know it to be so in my state—against having free Negroes come among us. Our people want nothing to do with the Negro.[791]

After Lincoln's death Illinois continued to ignore the issue of black suffrage, even refusing to put it to the vote. Little wonder that even Union generals, like Carl Schurz (1829-1906),[792] referred to 19th-Century Illinois as being nearly completely Negrophobic.[793]

Even after the War white Illinoisans continued to discriminate against blacks. One Illinois law, for example, required that free blacks possess a "certificate of freedom" and post a bond of $1,000 to reside in the state. Those who violated these conditions were subject to arrest after which they were hired out as a laborer (what Yankees would call a slave) for one year.[794]

Illinois was far from being the only Northern state that issued these types of Black Codes. In fact, at one time all of the Northern states had rigorous laws on the books that restricted the movements of blacks and black civil rights. Michigan, whose Black Laws strongly suggested that blacks traveling through the state not stop but continue on to Canada, banned blacks from voting because, as they saw it, blacks belong

---

790. Nicolay and Hay, CWAL, Vol. 1, p. 234.
791. Curry, p. 79.
792. Schurz, born near Cologne, Germany, in 1829, moved to the U.S. in August 1852, where he made several significant contributions to American government and society. Among them were: the development of national parks, more humane treatment of Native-Americans, and the preservation of the public domain. Sobel, s.v. "Schurz, Carl."
793. P. Smith, pp. 339, 974.
794. Woods, p. 81.

THE MCGAVOCKS OF CARNTON PLANTATION

to a disgraced race of humans.[795] Another example is Iowa, where, in 1857, the white populace rejected black suffrage by a vote of 49,000 to 8,000.[796]

Naturally, New York City, America's slavery capital for decades, had its own set of strict Black Codes, all of them considered particularly hostile. Offences by black servants could garner punishments ranging from beatings and whippings to deportation and even execution. In 1741 the mere hint of a slave revolt resulted in the public killing of twenty-seven slaves, all who died by hanging or burning at the stake.[797]

Hundreds of such examples from the racist Old North could be given.

❧ TENNESSEE & ITS BLACK RESIDENTS

The Carnton McGavocks' home state had few such laws and what restrictions it did have regarding blacks were largely ignored. Indeed, in Tennessee blacks were free to live and work on their own, and on most Tennessee plantations black servants and their white owners worked together, side-by-side in the fields, a yeoman farming tradition, in fact, in all of the Old Southern states.[798]

In 1860 Tennessee's 7,300 free blacks (a state with one of the highest number of free blacks in America)[799] enjoyed particular liberties and civil rights, placing them on, or quite near, the same level as free, lower- and working-class whites. In 1796, for instance, the Tennessee Constitutional Convention gave free blacks the right to vote, a law that remained on the books until 1835.[800]

White Tennessee was so liberal in comparison to white Yankeedom that it became the first state, South or North, to authorize the enlistment of free blacks in its military (C.S.A.). This occurred in June 1861, a year and three months *before* the Union officially sanctioned

---

795. Berwanger, pp. 32, 33.
796. Garraty and McCaughey, p. 253.
797. O. Williams, pp. 48, 70.
798. Simpson, p. 218; Garraty and McCaughey, p. 214.
799. Jordan, p. 370.
800. Genovese, pp. 401-402.

the recruitment of blacks in August 1862.[801]

That June the Tennessee legislature passed an act allowing the governor to receive into the military service "all male free persons of color, between the ages of 15 and 50 . . ."[802] Tennessee's black soldiers, unlike Lincoln's segregated black soldiers, were integrated and treated, clothed, paid, and fed on an equal basis with Tennessee's white soldiers.[803]

What is more, since the fall and bloodless capture of Nashville by Union troops February 23-25, 1862,[804] Tennessee had labored under Yankee domination. To Northerners Tennessee was, after all, as Lincoln referred to it, the "Shield of the South," while he called Middle Tennessee the "heart of the Confederacy." Hence the state's capital city had been attacked and occupied early on in the conflict. Indeed, it was the first Confederate capital to fall,[805] becoming a major Union base of operations throughout the remainder of the War.[806]

That same year, 1862, Andrew Johnson, a Southern pro-Union man, was appointed military governor of Tennessee by Lincoln.[807] Permanently sealing Tennessee's fate as an ex-Confederate state, the Confederacy-hating preacher, William Gannaway "Parson" Brownlow (1805-1877), was later elected governor of the state (in 1865).[808]

Finally, the Volunteer State was so ambivalent about states' rights and slavery that it was the last Southern state to leave the Union (June 8, 1861) and the first one to rejoin it (July 24, 1866).[809] It was also the only Southern state to ban slavery by popular vote, which occurred when Tennessee adopted a new constitution on February 22,

---

801. Jordan, pp. 218, 266.
802. ORA, Ser. 4, Vol. 1, p. 409; Wiley, SN, p. 147.
803. Jordan, pp. 218-219.
804. Henry, SC, p. 87; R. L. Mode, p. 31.
805. W. B. Garrison, CWTFB, pp. 116, 138.
806. Long and Long, p. 175.
807. J. H. Franklin, pp. 24, 25.
808. As governor (from 1865-1869) the mean-spirited, caustic Brownlow ruled Tennessee with an iron fist, ushering in Reconstruction in the Volunteer State with Hitler-like efficiency. He continued his war against Tennessee Confederates as the state's U.S. senator from 1869 to 1875. Over a century and a half later Brownlow's name is still uttered with contempt and disgust by educated Tennesseans.
809. Cromie, p. 248.

The McGavocks of Carnton Plantation

1865.[810] Thus Tennessee freed its slaves two months before the end of the War for Southern Independence and ten months before the ratification of the Thirteenth Amendment on December 6, 1865, which for the first time prohibited slavery in every state.[811]

Aiding this New South movement along in Tennessee was the fact that Lincoln had also (illegally, it should be added) instituted a Reconstruction government in the state, hoping to coalesce support among former Southern Whigs (liberals), many who had been against secession.[812]

While all of these factors helped make Tennessee a safer and more comfortable place for blacks than the highly racist and restrictive Northern states at the time, it was Southern whites themselves who contributed most to this transition. For the people of Dixie, the veritable birthplace of American abolitionism, had always been in the vanguard of the move to end the Northern-created "peculiar institution."

❧ AFRICAN-AMERICAN CULTURAL CONTRIBUTIONS

Both free and servile African-Americans made incredible cultural contributions to the entire South, including to Carnton, though revealingly none of these gifts were ever acknowledged or even mentioned by the so-called "Great Emancipator." (Indeed, Lincoln never once thanked American blacks for anything, including their courageous service in the Union army and navy. He never even sent condolences to the thousands of black families whose sons had died in his War.)[813]

For example, it was the McGavocks' servants who built Carnton itself. They constructed (or sometimes helped construct) the Mansion and all of the outbuildings, including the barns, the greenhouse, the five-bay carriage house, sheds, fences, and corrals. They planted the gardens,

---

810. Tennessee's new 1865 state constitution not only abolished slavery, it also repudiated secession, much to the anger of pro-Confederate supporters, mainly in Middle and Western Tennessee.
811. The Thirteenth Amendment was the first Federal law to inhibit the power of the states in defining the status of their own residents. Hall, s.v. "Thirteenth Amendment." Interestingly, though it finally and completely abolished slavery across the U.S., the Thirteenth Amendment allowed slavery as a punishment for convicted criminals.
812. Rosenbaum and Brinkley, s.v. "Reconstruction."
813. Seabrook, AL, p. 467.

THE McGAVOCKS OF CARNTON PLANTATION

orchards, and trees, took care of the livestock, tilled the soil, and harvested the crops. The wood used to build all of these structures was cut in the McGavock sawmill, and the bricks were all handmade in the family's kiln by these same highly skilled artisans. The sawmill and kiln themselves were also probably made by the black servants.

Inside Carnton Mansion one can still see many examples of superb African craftsmanship, such as the ornamental gingerbread wood pattern running up along the side of the staircase. What was true at Carnton was true for nearly every other servant owning family across the South.

None of this was unusual, though pro-North historians would have us believe otherwise. The truth is that early black architects, craftsmen, iron workers, and woodcarvers were responsible for much of the South's beautiful homes, buildings, artwork, furnishings, and even her boats, bridges, and graveyard decorations. Early blacks also gave America the banjo (a true African instrument in both name and design), countless new foods, dances, manners, folkways, and words, such as "boogie," "gumbo," "tote," "goober," "okra," "jazz," "mumbo-jumbo," and "un-huh" and "unh-uh." They also bequeathed to the world a voluminous body of superlative African-American literature.[814]

Such architectural features as steep hip roofs, central fireplaces, broad porches with wide overhanging roofs, and the use of dirt (and sometimes moss) to build walls, were all elements of African origin, introduced to America by both free and bonded blacks. According to old building records most of the plantations of Louisiana, as just one example, were built almost exclusively by African architects. In the 1800s Yankee architect Olmsted visited the Pelican State during his travels through the South, and wrote that the best houses and most beautiful grounds he found there actually belonged to black, not white, owners.[815] Much of the beauty and majesty of Carnton herself can be attributed to these same incredibly talented local black craftsmen and women.

---

814. Wilson and Ferris, s.v. "African Influences."
815. Wilson and Ferris, s.v. "Architecture, Black."

The McGavocks of Carnton Plantation

❧ THE MAMMY: A POSITIVE IMAGE IN THE SOUTH, A NEGATIVE ONE IN THE NORTH

The African-Americans at Franklin's most haunted Civil War house contributed in more mundane but equally important ways as well. Under Sarah's, and later Carrie's, tutelage and direction, they helped clean house and wash clothes, assisted in cooking and serving meals, and aided in raising and tending generations of Southern white children. The primary person in charge of this particular duty was the mammy, an individual with whom many youngsters were more familiar than their own biological mothers.

The mammy was no fictional anti-black stereotype, as the North falsely asserts. An actual foster mother rather than just a type of "nurse," many a white Southern youngster grew from childhood into adulthood under her eagle-eyed daily supervision. Fans of Margaret Mitchell's (1900-1949) book and film, *Gone With the Wind*, will be very familiar with the indispensable African-American mammy, one integral to 19th-Century Southern culture and much beloved by Victorian white Southerners.

The mammy, who typically lived in a cabin near the "big house," was chosen for her loving, maternal, even-tempered personality, and was considered by her white owners to be a virtual member of their family, as we saw in the case of Mary Chesnut.[816]

So close was the mammy to the master's and mistress' offspring that it was usually she who they would turn to for love and security, not their real mother. For the mammy not only socialized the children, but she also often ran the household, interceded with parents on the children's behalf, punished the children for misbehaving, washed and dressed them, told them bedtime stories, sang them songs, rocked them to sleep, and even breast-fed them when necessary.[817] Little wonder that white children often voluntarily spent more time with their mammy than with their biological mothers.[818]

---

816. C. Johnson, p. 15.
817. Blassingame, p. 167.
818. Cash, p. 51.

THE MCGAVOCKS OF CARNTON PLANTATION

So common was the need for lactating mammies (known as "black wet nurses") that white families routinely ran ads in local newspapers for them. And the lack of prejudice ran both ways: white Southern mistresses, many from the middle- and upper-classes, were also known to breast-feed the infant children of their black servants. Like the white children who were nursed by black mammies, blacks who were breast-fed by whites also referred to them as "Ma." This sharing in the role of infant nurturer enabled Southern white and black women to form female bonds wholly unknown among whites and blacks in the North. Much of the world Mitchell depicted was indeed real, not a wishful dream world as anti-South proponents proclaim.[819]

Though today she is considered a racist stereotype from a dark chapter in America's past, at least up until the year 1923 the black mammy was still held in high esteem by many Southern whites.

It was in that year that several Southern senators proposed the erection of a monument called "The Black Mammy of the South," in Washington, D.C. The reasoning behind the statue was wholly positive: to honor the mammy's many contributions to the South, as well as her image as the embodiment of love, devotion, and faithfulness. But Washington, D.C.'s Black Mammy statue was never realized. Soon after the monument's proposal the idea was permanently shelved out of respect for the sensitivities of African-Americans, most who apparently see her as a disgraceful reminder that they descend from slaves owned by whites.[820]

This is unfortunate. For while it is perhaps understandable that some blacks today harbor a deep resentment toward whites over slavery, (given the universal dissemination of the skewed Northern version of the "Civil War"), it is not fully justifiable. For one thing, such individuals completely ignore the reality of America's tens of thousands of black, brown, and red slave owners. They also disregard their own native African ancestors, without whose contributions American slavery could have never been created in the first place.

---

819. M. M. Smith, pp. 33, 262-265. See also C. Johnson, pp. 14-15.
820. Adams and Sanders, p. 249.

THE MCGAVOCKS OF CARNTON PLANTATION

Also, as I have often pointed out in my writings, the earliest recorded slavers and slaves were both white. And let us not forget that the entire world once operated on and around slavery, an institution that has been endemic to nearly every known people, race, and society since the beginning of time. This is why, in 1927, pro-North historian Hendrik Willem Van Loon urged his fellow Yankees to stop condemning Southerners for keeping "slaves." For slavery has existed, he rightly asserted, across the entire globe since humans first became bipedal.[821]

In short, no matter what our skin color, we all the descendants of slaves. Why, then, pick on the whites of the Old South?

Modern African-Americans would also do well to consider the manner in which their own 19th-Century American ancestors saw the situation. It was quite different!

On September 29, 1865, for instance, just five months after Lincoln's War came to an end at Appomattox, a group of North Carolina blacks held a "Negro Convention" that issued the following declaration:

> Born upon the same soil and brought up in an intimacy of relationship unknown in any other state of Society, we have formed attachments for the white race which must be as enduring as life.[822]

---

821. Van Loon, p. 350.
822. Ashe, p. 40.

The War for Southern Independence

❧ THE McGAVOCKS & LINCOLN'S WAR

NOW THAT WE HAVE A more balanced and authentic view of the McGavocks and Southern black servitude, we will continue with our history of the family itself.

We left off with the death of John's and Carrie's second daughter, Mary Elizabeth, in 1858, at the age of six. Two years later, another one of John's sister's children died. Four year old M. Louise Harding (b. January 2, 1856), the daughter of Elizabeth Irwin McGavock, passed away on October 30, 1860.

This brings us to that pivotal point in both American and McGavock history: the beginnings of the actual formation of the Southern Confederacy, December 20, 1860 (the day the first Southern state, South Carolina, voted to secede), and the start of the War for Southern Independence just a few months later on April 12, 1861.

What role did the McGavocks play in this war? Who started it, and why? What is the reason the McGavocks sided with the Confederacy, and what is their connection to the Battle of Franklin II? Over the next two chapters we will address these inquiries, beginning with a look at the causes of Lincoln's useless, bloody, and illegal $100

THE McGAVOCKS OF CARNTON PLANTATION

billion dollar War[823] and its 10,455 battles and skirmishes.

❧ SOUTH VERSUS NORTH
From the very beginning of the birth of the American colonies, South and North were manifesting sharp cultural, religious, social, and political differences. They were like two distinct nations even then, and the differences only became more evident with joining of the Southern and Northern colonies into Thomas Jefferson's American Confederacy in 1781, later to become known as the United States of America. Southern historian Frank Lawrence Owsley (1890-1956) rightly considered this the merger of two completely different civilizations.[824]

The North was mainly industrial, nationalistic, liberal, agnostic, Catholic, progressive, business oriented, and publically schooled. To the Yankee mind the Union was a purely commercial entity, a single monolithic democracy by which that region could profit through tariffs, bounties, and "sectional aggrandizement." In contrast, the South was primarily agricultural, localistic, conservative, highly religious, Protestant, traditional, family oriented, and home-schooled. To Confederates the Union was a moral social order, a "friendly association" of states held together by trust, fairness, harmony, and the concept of states' rights.[825]

Furthermore, as the South saw it, Northerners were discourteous and reserved, while they themselves were well mannered and emotional. Northerners were greedy, shrewd, and materialistic, while Southerners were generous, hospitable, and spiritual. Northern society was prim, proper, and fast-paced, Southern society was relaxed, informal, and leisurely.[826]

Jefferson himself believed that Northerners were "cool, sober,

---

823. The cost of Lincoln's War in 1865 was as follows: Confederacy, $3.5 billion. Union, $3.750 billion. The combined total that year was $7.250 billion. Pollard, LC, p. 420. The equivalent today would be: Confederacy, $48.3 billion. Union, $51.8 billion. The total cost of Lincoln's War in 2010 currency: $100 billion.
824. Simpson, p. 72.
825. Rozwenc, pp. 10-11.
826. McWhiney and Jamieson, pp. 171-172.

The McGavocks of Carnton Plantation

laborious, perservering, chicaning, and superstitious and hypocritical in their religion," while Southerners were "fiery, voluptuary, indolent, unsteady, generous, candid, and without attachment or pretensions to any religion but that of the heart."[827]

Speaking of religioisity, the following example alone aptly illustrates the broad chasm separating South and North: the U.S. Constitution does not contain the word God. The C.S. Constitution, however, not only mentions God, it calls him "Almighty God."[828]

Could any two regions have been more culturally, politically, spiritually, and socially opposite? Conservative Southerner Patrick Henry was commenting on this phenomenon as early as 1787, when he observed that the South and the North were two completely unique and contrasting peoples, and that the agricultural South would end up being dominated by the industrial North if they formed a union together.[829]

Understanding these aspects of early American culture certainly gives us a better understanding of why Southerners so willingly picked up arms to defend their homeland against the North, and why they could make comments like the following, by Confederate Lieutenant Colonel R. A. Alston:

> There are a hundred thousand men in the South who feel as I do, that they would rather an earthquake should swallow the whole country than yield to our oppressors—men who will retire to the mountains and live on acorns, and crawl on their bellies to shoot an invader wherever they can see one.[830]

There are some indications that the Old South and the Old North were also divided by a certain amount of ethnicity, primarily Gaelic versus Anglo-Saxon.[831] Dixie, which later designed its Confederate Battle Flag chiefly around Scotland's Saint Andrew's Cross

---

827. Beveridge, LJM, Vol. 1, p. 279.
828. Lang, pp. 215, 216.
829. Kennedy and Kennedy, NT, p. 188.
830. Pollard, LC, p. 444.
831. Horwitz, pp. 68-69.

THE MCGAVOCKS OF CARNTON PLANTATION

and on Ireland's Saint Patrick's Cross, had a noticeable Celto-cavalier flavor,[832] while the upper Northeast, steeped in centuries of Anglo-Puritanism, was more English in color, and is indeed still called "New England." Even the Confederate army was more like a gathering of clans headed by a warrior-chieftain than a standard military force headed by a commander-in-chief.[833]

It could be said then that the War was waged, in part, between Gaelic Southern cavaliers and Anglo Northern Puritans.[834]

The animosity between the primary Celtic nations (Ireland, Scotland, and Wales,) and England are well-known and have existed for centuries right into the present day. This ethnic animus was already quite evident in America in the 1700s and 1800s, the time period in which the very Celtic McGavocks lived at Carnton, a family who, if they were alive today, would be very proud of their Gaelic, Southern "redneck" roots.[835]

Added to these built-in differences was the fact that the North had long been forcing high tariffs on the South, all which unduly benefitted the North's financial and commercial groups. Why? Because tariffs help impede the import of foreign goods, which were, at the time, a boon to the largely manufacturing North.[836]

But these same tariffs hurt Southern farmers. Why? Because Dixie was largely an agrarian consumerist region. Northern-imposed tariffs raised the prices the South had to pay for finished imported goods,[837] especially manufactured goods purchased from the North. Because of her own tariff protection, the North was able to charge the South greatly inflated prices.[838]

This sectional shell game, for decades wholly dominated by the

---

832. Cannon, pp. 18, 25, 60.
833. E. M. Thomas, p. 117.
834. McWhiney and Jamieson, pp. 170-191; M. M. Smith, pp. 112-113. Despite this apparent ethnic divide, it remains true that in 1860 there were many Britons in the South and many Celts in the North.
835. Bultman, pp. 23-24, passim.
836. Rosenbaum and Brinkley, s.v. "Jefferson Republican Party."
837. Thornton and Ekelund, pp. xiv, 16; Weintraub, pp. 55, 58.
838. Woods, p. 53.

THE McGAVOCKS OF CARNTON PLANTATION

North, prompted many Southerners, like Thomas Cooper, the president of South Carolina College, to ask: Are we in the South not tired of playing slave to the Northern master? Is it not time we consider leaving the Union?[839]

Cooper's question is understandable. For the Southern states had come to feel that they were now mere colonies of the empirical North, just as the early American colonies came to feel they were living under the thumb of the British Empire and her insufferably unfair taxes.

This economic tyranny of one section over another, however, was only one small part of a much larger political *weltanschauung* that the North was trying to impose on Dixie, one that the liberal Whig, Henry Clay (1777-1852), called "the American System."

❧ JEFFERSONIANS, REPUBLICANS, & THE CONFEDERACY

The American System went against everything Southerners believed in. But this was intentional: Northern politicians had made their political platform as anti-South as possible. Why?

We all know that the first U.S. government was created by the Founding Fathers. What many people do not realize is that most of the Founders were Southerners and, as such, were educated in Jeffersonianism (also known as Republicanism or Antifederalism), a distinctly Southern school of political thought, then as now.[840]

---

839. J. S. Bowman, CWDD, p. 11.
840. In the 21st Century, as the Republican and Democratic Parties have continued to moderate their views and platforms, the two are now so similar that there are few differences between them. In Jefferson's day, however, his Republican Party (the Jeffersonians) and the opposition Federalist Party (the Hamiltonians) were as different as night and day. The result is that today, what was 18th-Century Jeffersonianism, would be more correctly called paleoconservatism, Tea Partyism, or even libertarianism. To avoid confusion, it should be noted that by the time of Lincoln, the parties had switched platforms, so that the conservative Republicans of Jefferson's day were by then called Democrats, while the liberal Federalists (Democrats) of Jefferson's day became known as Republicans. Hence, during the presidential campaign of 1860, the McGavocks and other traditional Southerners were Democrats (in that period, conservatives, as they called themselves) while Lincoln and most Northerners were Republicans (in that period, liberals, as they referred to themselves). See e.g., J. H. Franklin, pp. 111, 130, 149. This is why, at least until the mid-19th-Century, historians and Lincoln scholars, like Professor James Garfield Randall, referred to our sixteenth president as the "liberal statesman." See Randall, ALTLS, passim. The parties have since switched back to their original platforms, though, as mentioned above, in highly diluted forms. Modern paleoconservatism, libertarianism, and Tea Partyism are attempts to retain the original conservative republican doctrines and beliefs of the Southern Founding Fathers. Woods, p. 47.

The McGavocks of Carnton Plantation

Jeffersonianism (or Tea Partyism or Libertarianism as it is also known), has been most recently and publically espoused by Ron Paul, a Northerner turned Southerner. The name derives from our third U.S. president, Thomas Jefferson.[841]

Jefferson was the champion of constitutionalism: a small, limited, weak, decentralized government that was to be supported and controlled by a loose union of strong sovereign nation-states.[842] In this, a confederate nation—that is, a confederacy—the only real power given to the central government was to protect these individual nation-states against "domestic violence" and "invasion." Other than that, each state was to retain all the powers and rights of a sovereign country, with the central (or Federal) government being entirely subservient to their will.[843]

Overt proof that this was the intention of the Founders is to be found in the Ninth and Tenth Amendments of the U.S. Constitution. They read:

> The enumeration in the Constitution, of certain rights, shall not be construed to deny or disparage others retained by the people (Ninth Amendment).[844]

> The powers not delegated to the United States by the Constitution, nor prohibited by it to the States, are reserved to the States respectively, or to the people (Tenth Amendment).[845]

A description of the powers and responsibilities of the "United States" (that is, the Federal government at Washington, D.C.) is found in Article 4, Section 4, Paragraph 1 of the U.S. Constitution. It reads:

> The United States shall guarantee to every State in this Union a republican form of government, and shall protect each of them

---

841. Plano, Greenberg, Olton, and Riggs, s.v. "Jeffersonianism."
842. Plano, Greenberg, Olton, and Riggs, s.v. "Constitutionalism." See also s.v. "Confederation."
843. Nivola and Rosenbloom, p. 67.
844. Findlay and Findlay, p. 212.
845. Findlay and Findlay, p. 214.

against invasion; and, on application of the Legislature, or of the Executive (when the Legislature cannot be convened), against domestic violence.[846]

In other words, the central government of the U.S. has only one real power: protecting its citizens from internal violence and external invasion. *All* other powers lie with the people and their individual states.

More evidence of the Founders' original intent (that the states were to remain sovereign nations) is that, to this day, it is the states which elect the president (via the Electoral College), not the majority vote of the people.[847] (Lincoln himself was elected president, both in 1860 and in 1864, by the Electoral College.)[848]

Likewise, when America finally severed all ties with Great Britain, King George III (1738-1820) signed a treaty of peace in Paris in 1783, recognizing America, not as a single monolithic nation, but as a confederation of individual nation-states. The document even named them individually, referring to each one as "a free, sovereign, and independent State."[849]

That the original thirteen American colonies began life as separate nation-states, that is as a Confederacy, is the same reason early Americans pledged their allegiance to their native states rather than to the U.S.:[850] they considered the states their countries, not the United States or the national government.[851]

Hence the majority of Southerners, like Robert E. Lee, literally referred to their home states as "my country." Though admitting that he

---

846. Findlay and Findlay, p. 214.
847. Ashe, pp. 22-23.
848. Lincoln was a minority president. Garraty and McCaughey, p. 241. That is, he was elected both times with less than 50 percent of the American vote. In 1860 he won with only 39.8 percent of the popular vote. In 1864 he did manage to garner 55 percent of the popular vote. However, a large number of these votes were obtained illicitly. Seabrook, AL, pp. 270-274; Seabrook L, pp. 860-882. Furthermore, the Southern states did not vote in the U.S. elections that year. If they had, Lincoln would have lost by a landslide. Hacker, p. 589; D. H. Donald, LR, p. 65; L. H. Johnson, NAS, p. 127; C. Adams, p. 58; W. B. Garrison, LNOK, pp. 193-197.
849. Ashe, p. 25.
850. Rosenbaum and Brinkley, s.v. "Antifederalists."
851. Adams and Sanders, p. 56.

THE MCGAVOCKS OF CARNTON PLANTATION

was a citizen of the United States, antebellum Jefferson Davis observed that "my allegiance is first due to the State I represent."[852] Thomas Jefferson too called Virginia "my country."[853]

John Randolph of Virginia took note of the North's desire to exact allegiance from the Southern states, saying:

> When I speak of my country, I mean the Commonwealth of Virginia. I was born in allegiance to [the English King] George III. . . . My ancestors threw off the oppressive yoke of the mother country, but they never made me subject to New England in matters spiritual or temporal; neither do I mean to become so voluntarily.[854]

Thus in the Old South one would refer to himself as a Tennessean, a South Carolinian, a Floridian, a Virginian, or a Texan, while a Northerner would refer to himself as a "citizen of the United States."[855]

It was because we were a Confederate Republic,[856] a confederation (that is, a league of independent nation-states),[857] not a nation, that Jefferson literally referred to our new country as "the Confederacy,"[858] and called our first constitution "the Articles of Confederation."[859] Though this particular important period in American history only lasted from 1781 to 1789,[860] Americans, including Lincoln, continued to call the U.S. "the Confederacy" well into the 1800s.[861]

The foundation of the U.S. Confederacy was built on the

---

852. Rowland, Vol. 1, p. 509.
853. See e.g., Foley, pp. 399, 900.
854. Garland, p. 103.
855. Henry, SC, p. 16. The question of loyalty to state or nation was debated as early as 1787, at the Constitutional Convention in Philadelphia. Collier and Collier, p. 264. While most Northerners pledged their allegiance to the nation, well into the 1800s most Southerners chose to give their allegiance to their home states. This tradition lives on across Dixie to this day among traditional Southerners.
856. See Stephens, CV, Vol. 1, pp. 504-505; Rable, passim.
857. Plano, Greenberg, Olton, and Riggs, s.v. "Confederation."
858. Foley, p. 699.
859. Foley, p. 167.
860. See Jensen, NN, passim; AC, passim.
861. Nicolay and Hay, ALCW, Vol. 1, p. 606. In referring to the United States of America, Lincoln used the word Confederacy many dozens of times throughout his political career. See e.g., Nicolay and Hay, ALCW, Vol. 1, pp. 168, 181, 611, 616, 624, 628, 691.

republican concepts of states' rights, the right of both accession *and* secession, freedom of religion, speech, and press, and a system of governmental checks and balances held in place by complete independence between the executive, judicial, and legislative branches. Confederate Jefferson called this separation of powers "the leading principle of our Constitution."[862]

Jefferson's original Confederate Republic, created only as a tenuous "league of friendship" between the states, also called for a policy of non-expansionism and non-interventionism, with an emphasis on free trade. Additionally, the Confederalists were against the idea of a national bank, internal improvements, tariffs, income tax, and subsidies, all which the South rightly believed led to greed, corruption, and a host of other political evils.[863]

Today we can certainly understand the fears of the Victorian Southerners who lived later, during the 19th Century: only a few decades earlier, their grandfathers had fought and died trying to break away from a powerful empire, a monarchical government, that had oppressed the Southern colonies using some of these very same political and economic instruments of control.[864]

❧ HAMILTONIANS, FEDERALISTS, & THE AMERICAN SYSTEM

But there was one Northern Founding Father in particular who was violently opposed to Jefferson and his Republican Confederate ideals: British government-loving Alexander Hamilton (1755-1804), a staunch monarchist whose followers were called the Hamiltonians or Federalists.[865]

Even as the U.S. itself was being formed, the Hamiltonians wanted the American Confederacy overturned and replaced with a

---

862. Foley, p. 194.
863. Weintraub, pp. 40-41.
864. Burns and Peltason, pp. 40-41.
865. Today, Hamilton's Federalists would most closely associated with the liberal left-wing of the Democratic Party, and in some cases even with certain aspects of socialism.

THE MCGAVOCKS OF CARNTON PLANTATION

government based on a European mercantilist system.[866] Its leader would be a king-like president with tyrannical powers. The government, which was to be based on expansionism and imperialism, would control the money supply, grant subsidies to corporations, engage in protectionism, nationalize the banking system, issue soaring protective tariffs, create paper money and easy credit, allow monopolies and public works, engage in colonialism, offer federally financed internal improvements, intervene in foreign affairs, and establish the nation's first income tax.[867]

Furthermore, states' rights, the very bedrock of the Jeffersonian Confederacy, would be thrown out to make way for the Hamiltonian concept of a fully federated, all-powerful, empire-like central government that would lord over the now weak subjugated states.[868] Little wonder that Jefferson referred to the Hamiltonian Federalists as an "Anglican monarchical and aristocratical party."[869]

This, in essence, was what would later be called the American System, a political platform that could not have been more foreign, contrary, and offensive to the South's way of thinking.

❧ A DICTATOR IN THE WHITE HOUSE

Henry Clay, a rabid 19th-Century Hamiltonian, happened to be the political idol of a then largely unknown Southerner-turned-Northerner named Abraham Lincoln.[870] Lincoln embraced everything his hero believed in, including not only black colonization, but also Clay's American System, a Victorian form of Hamilton's monarchist governmental views.

Thus, when he began running for the highest office in the land, Lincoln campaigned on the ideas of the American System, horrifying Southerners all across Dixie. It was clear that he had every intention of

---

866. DiLorenzo, RL, pp. 56-60.
867. Thornton and Ekelund, p. 100; Weintraub, p. 49; DiLorenzo, RL, pp. 59-61, 67, 73, 233-234.
868. Weintraub, p. 40.
869. Foley, p. 546.
870. It would be no exaggeration to say that anti-abolitionist Lincoln worshiped slave owner Clay, even referring to him publicly as "my beau ideal of a statesman." Nicolay and Hay, ALCW, Vol. 1, p. 299.

THE MCGAVOCKS OF CARNTON PLANTATION

replacing their beloved Jeffersonian Confederate Republic with a Hamiltonian federal government, then ensconcing himself at its head as a sort of dictator. As President Wilson writes of Dixie at the time, in the eyes of Southerners, Lincoln's ascension to the Oval Office meant the establishment of a party determined to destroy the "Southern System," one that would demolish southern interests and even assist in fomenting slave rebellions across the South.[871]

Is it any wonder that the Southern states began talking of seceding from the U.S. on November 6, 1860, the day that the big spending liberal from Illinois—today still widely known as the most politically corrupt state in the Union[872]—was elected president? Should we be surprised that the first state to secede, South Carolina, did so only two weeks later, on December 20, and that by the time Lincoln took office only a few months later, seven Southern states had already split from the Union, or that more would shortly follow?

What many do not realize today is that the Confederacy the South formed was not a rebellion against the U.S.A. For staunch and loyal Southerners, from John C. Calhoun, Jefferson Davis, Robert E. Lee, and Alexander H. Stephens, to Nathan Bedford Forrest, John Singleton Mosby, Stephen R. Mallory, and Edmund Ruffin, adored the Union and were extremely resistant to the idea of breaking away from her.

Indeed, this is one reason why, during the construction of the new Confederacy, Southerners were so adamant about creating a national flag that retained elements of the old U.S. flag. (It was only after several months of War against a despotic, aggressive, cruel, and meddlesome U.S. that they began to change their minds and demand a flag that was as dissimilar to the U.S. flag as possible.)[873]

In truth, the split was the South's noble attempt to continue Jefferson's original U.S. Confederacy, a nation forged in the crucible of

---

871. W. Wilson, DR, p. 208.
872. "A Brief History of Illinois Corruption," Suddath Claire, *Time*, December 11, 2008, Website: www.time.com/time/nation/article/0,8599,1865681,00.html.
873. Cannon, pp. 7, 11, 14.

The McGavocks of Carnton Plantation

the country's first Revolutionary War against Great Britain. This is why, in 1860, Southerners named their new league of states "the Confederacy."

In early 1861, in the South's mind then, it was clearly the North that had rebelled. For it had revolted against the Founders' Constitution and their Confederate ideals. Because of this the South could only see the coming battle with the North as America's "Second Revolutionary War"; that is, a second war of secession in which an oppressed nation would seek to legally break away from a despotic, venal, excessive, and corrupt monarchical power.[874]

❧ REASONS LINCOLN DID NOT START THE WAR

The War for Southern Independence (incorrectly known as the "Civil War" in the North),[875] was launched by Lincoln on April 12, 1861, a piece of tactical chicanery in which he scandalously tricked the South into firing the first shot at Fort Sumter in order to make it appear that she was the aggressor.[876]

The real question is, why did Lincoln inaugurate a war against the South, against a people he regarded as citizens of his own country, the U.S.A.?[877]

It was not over slavery, for in 1860, as we have seen, only 4.8 percent of Southerners owned slaves. It was not essential to either the South's agrarian system or to her economy, and thus life in the South would not have been very different without it.[878]

---

874. Dean, p. 162.
875. The word "civil" denotes something that occurs "between the states of one nation." Indeed, Webster defines civil war as "a war between opposing groups or citizens of the same country." Mish, s.v. "civil war." The Southern states, however, were not part of the U.S.A. at the start of Lincoln's War. They belonged to a separate and legally formed independent country, the C.S.A. (Confederate States of America). This is why the term "Civil War" is not used by either traditional Southerners or informed individuals. In the South the correct term, the War for Southern Independence, is preferred. Seabrook, EYWTACWW, pp. 25-27.
876. Seabrook, EYWTACWW, pp. 35-39.
877. Lincoln never recognized the legitimacy of the Southern Confederacy, which makes it even harder to understand why he went to battle against her: throughout his entire War he regarded the people of the South as citizens of the U.S.A. Under what circumstances does a nation's leader justify making war on a segment of his own people, a people that is peacefully and legally pursuing its constitutional rights? In Lincoln's case it was about money, greed, ego, revenge, and hunger for political power.
878. Simpson, pp. 73-74, 76.

THE MCGAVOCKS OF CARNTON PLANTATION

The main reason we know the War was not over slavery, however, is because Lincoln specifically said so. The War, he incessantly repeated to the public, was to restore and preserve the Union, not to emancipate Southern slaves.[879] He said the same thing to Confederate politicians, and he maintained this position throughout his entire four-year War.

For instance, there is the February 3, 1865, comment he made just two months before the Confederacy stacked arms for the last time at Appomattox. It was on this day that Lincoln met with three Confederate commissioners to discuss a "negotiated peace" at Hampton Roads, Virginia. For both sides the issue on the table was cut and dry: Lincoln would only call for a halt to the fighting if the Confederacy would agree to "reunion." The South would only agree to stop the bloodshed if its "independence" was recognized.

Yet, while anti-South propagandists continue to claim otherwise,[880] on numerous occasions, including at Hampton Roads,[881] Lincoln made it perfectly clear that abolition was not a requirement for ending the War or reviving the Union.[882] According to Confederate Vice President Alexander H. Stephens, Lincoln told him personally that

> . . . the [Emancipation] Proclamation was a war measure, and would have effect only from its being an exercise of the war power, as soon as the war ceased, it would be inoperative for the future.[883]

In essence Lincoln instigated his War over "national integrity," not antislavery sentiment.[884] If it were otherwise why did he call the conflict the "War of Rebellion"? We can be sure that if it had been about slavery he would have termed it the "War of Slavery." In fact, from the very beginning he went out of his way to make sure the nation, and in

---

879. J. M. McPherson, MFO, p. 206.
880. See e.g., Civil War Society, ECW, s.v. "Hampton Roads Conference."
881. Seabrook, L, pp. 684-690.
882. D. H. Donald, L, p. 559.
883. Nicolay and Hay, ALAH, Vol. 10, p. 123.
884. Parry, s.v. "Lincoln, Abraham."

The McGavocks of Carnton Plantation

particular the South, understood that he had no intention of "interfering" with the institution.

On March 4, 1861, shortly after taking office, the new U.S. commander-in-chief drove the point home in his First Inaugural Address:

> Apprehension seems to exist among the people of the Southern States that by the accession of a Republican administration their property and their peace and personal security are to be endangered. There has never been any reasonable cause for such apprehension. Indeed, the most ample evidence to the contrary has all the while existed and been open to their inspection. It is found in nearly all the published speeches of him who now addresses you. I do but quote from one of those speeches when I declare that 'I have no purpose, directly or indirectly, to interfere with the institution of slavery in the States where it exists. I believe I have no lawful right to do so, and I have no inclination to do so.' Those who nominated and elected me did so with full knowledge that I had made this and many similar declarations, and had never recanted them.[885]

After this speech, several months passed. The War was in full swing and pressure from abolitionists was increasing. Still Lincoln would not even consider emancipation let alone enact it.

In the Summer of 1861, after angrily revoking an attempt by one of his officers to emancipate slaves in Missouri, he had a conversation with abolitionist Reverend Charles Edward Lester. The president expressed his impatience with Lester and other Northern abolitionists who were pushing for abolishing slavery.[886] Said Lincoln:

> I think [Massachusetts Senator Charles] Sumner and the rest of you would upset our applecart altogether if you had your way.... We didn't go into the war to put down slavery, but to put the flag back, and to act different at this moment, would, I have no doubt, not only weaken our cause but smack of bad faith; for I never should have had votes enough to send me here if the people had supposed

---

885. Nicolay and Hay, ALCW, Vol. 2, p. 1.
886. Oates, AL, p. 100.

THE MCGAVOCKS OF CARNTON PLANTATION

> I should try to use my power to upset slavery. Why, the first thing you'd see, would be a mutiny in the army. No, we must wait until every other means has been exhausted. This thunderbolt will keep.[887]

We will note that Lincoln admits here that the Northern people would never have elected him and that Northern soldiers would have mutinied if he had tried to "use his power to upset slavery." In other words, neither Northern citizens or Northern soldiers were interested in black civil rights in the Summer of 1861.

Most of Lincoln's military officers were of the same mind. Yankee General Ulysses S. Grant, an Ohio slave owner[888] and black colonizationist[889] who kept his slaves until eight months *after* the War was over,[890] spoke for nearly all Federal soldiers when he said:

> The sole object of this war is to restore the union. Should I be convinced it has any other object, or that the government designs using its soldiers to execute the wishes of the Abolitionists, I pledge to you my honor as a man and a soldier. I would resign my commission and carry my sword to the other side.[891]

Just prior to the conflict Lincoln had even gone so far as to defend the South's right to practice slavery, admitting that it would be illegal for he or anyone else to interfere. On August 21, 1858, for example, during his public debate with Senator Stephen A. Douglas at Ottawa, Illinois, candidate Lincoln said:

---

887. Lester, pp. 359-360.
888. Hinkle, p. 125.
889. Adams and Sanders, pp. 215-216.
890. Grant did not free his slaves until he was forced to by the ratification of the Thirteenth Amendment on December 6, 1865, eight months after Lincoln's assassination and the War had ended. Rutherford, FA, p. 38; Wallechinsky, Wallace, and Wallace, p. 11; Woods, p. 67. Other famous Northerners who were associated with slavery, either through actual ownership or through marriage, were: General Winfield Scott, Admiral David G. Farragut, General George H. Thomas, and Lincoln's wife, Mary Todd. McElroy, p. 357. Lincoln himself made reference to a slave owning Yankee, the Honorable George Robertson, in a November 26, 1862, letter. See Nicolay and Hay, ALCW, Vol. 2, p. 259.
891. Meriwether, p. 219.

THE MCGAVOCKS OF CARNTON PLANTATION

> I will say here, while upon this subject [of Negro equality], that I have no purpose, directly, or indirectly, to interfere with the institution of slavery in the States where it exists. I believe I have no lawful right to do so, and I have no inclination to do so.[892]

Lincoln then goes on to reveal the real reason he would never meddle with slavery:

> I have no purpose to introduce political and social equality between the white and the black races. There is a physical difference between the two, which in my judgement will probably forever forbid their living together on terms of respect, social and political equality, and inasmuch as it becomes a necessity that there must be a superiority somewhere, I . . . am in favor of the race to which I belong having the superior position. I have never said anything to the contrary . . .[893]

Lincoln's white supremacist views are not the only reasons we know that the War was not over slavery. Both before and during the War the vast majority of Northerners and Southerners stated in the strongest language possible that they would never risk their lives or fight against their fellow Americans over such an institution. This is not surprising, for in 1860 only a tiny fraction of Southerners owned black servants, while the number of Northerners who owned them was even less. Two years into the War Mary Chesnut makes mention of the fact that in reality, when it came to the conflict, neither the Confederates or the Yankees really cared about their black servants. Either side would sacrifice them in an instant if it meant winning the fight, she wrote.[894]

The U.S. Congress agreed with Lincoln as to the purpose of the War. Shortly after the start of the conflict, on July 22, 1861, it released a declaration stating that the Union's intention for going to war with the South was not for the

---

892. Nicolay and Hay, ALCW, Vol. 1, p. 539.
893. Nicolay and Hay, ALCW, Vol. 1, p. 539.
894. Chesnut, DD, p. 224.

purpose of overthrowing or interfering with the rights or established institutions [that is, slavery] of those States; but to defend and maintain the supremacy of the Constitution and to preserve the Union with all the dignity, equality, and rights of the several States unimpaired; that as soon as these objects are accomplished, the war ought to cease.[895]

For those who are not yet convinced that the "Civil War" was *not* over slavery, consider the following exchange between Lincoln and Yankee abolitionist Horace Greeley.

On August 19, 1862, Greeley published an open letter to Lincoln in his New York newspaper, the *Tribune*, assaulting the president's abysmal civil rights record and accusing of him of prolonging the War by refusing to abolish slavery. Those who voted for you, Greeley, began,

> are sorely disappointed and deeply pained by the policy you seem to be pursuing with regard to the slaves of the rebels. . . We think you are strangely and disastrously remiss in the discharge of your official and imperative duty with regard to the emancipating provisions of the new Confiscation Act. . . . Had you, sir, in your Inaugural Address, unmistakably given notice that . . . you would recognize no loyal person as rightfully held in slavery by a traitor, we believe the rebellion would therein have received a staggering, if not fatal blow.[896]

This stinging criticism, along with many others, went on for several pages.

Four days later, on August 22, 1862, an arrogant Lincoln responded to the withering public attack with his own. Dear Mr. Greeley, he wrote to the celebrated antislavery advocate:

> If there be those who would not save the Union unless they could at the same time save slavery, I do not agree with them. If there be those who would not save the Union unless they could at the same

---

895. E. McPherson, PHUSAPR, p. 16.
896. Brockett, pp. 308, 309, 311.

THE MCGAVOCKS OF CARNTON PLANTATION

> time destroy slavery, I do not agree with them. My paramount object in this struggle is to save the Union, and is not either to save or destroy slavery. . . . If I could save the Union without freeing any slave, I would do it . . . What I do about slavery and the colored race, I do because I believe it helps save the Union . . .[897]

This letter was written exactly one month before he issued his Preliminary Emancipation Proclamation (in which he calls for deporting all blacks out of the U.S.),[898] and just four months before issuing his Final Emancipation Proclamation (in which he refers to his edict, not as a civil rights measure, but as a temporary "war measure").[899]

All doubts as to how Lincoln viewed his War completely evaporate when we read the following words, uttered by our sixteenth president on August 15, 1864:

> My enemies pretend I am now carrying on this war for the sole purpose of abolition. So long as I am President, it shall be carried on for the sole purpose of restoring the Union. . . . Let my enemies prove to the country that the destruction of slavery is not necessary to a restoration of the Union. I will abide the issue.[900]

Yet another reason we know Lincoln's War was not over slavery is because, as we have already seen, Negrophobia was much worse in the North than in the South.[901] But just as importantly, we know from Lincoln's public statements about African-Americans that he was no abolitionist and thus no real friend of blacks.[902] And not only did he hate and mistrust abolitionists as a group, but they hated and mistrusted him in return, and for good reason.[903]

Once he was asked if it bothered him that there were abolitionists in his party. That's fine, he replied, "as long as I am not

---

897. Nicolay and Hay, ALCW, Vol. 2, pp. 227-228.
898. See Nicolay and Hay, ALCW, Vol. 2, pp. 237-238.
899. See Nicolay and Hay, ALCW, Vol. 2, p. 287.
900. Nicolay and Hay, ALCW, Vol. 2, p. 562.
901. Ransom, p. 172-174.
902. Seabrook, EYWTACWW, pp. 122-123.
903. W. B. Garrison, CWC, p. 97.

tarred with the Abolitionist brush."[904] So great was the animosity between Lincoln and Northern abolitionists that one reason he thought he would lose his bid for reelection in 1864 is because they had sided so completely against him.[905]

Indeed, most abolitionists were hesitant to vote for him in the 1860 election. Why? Because not once in all of his public speeches had he called for the immediate destruction of slavery.[906] In fact, right up until the day he issued his Final Emancipation Proclamation, January 1, 1863, he was still hedging, delaying, and obfuscating on the topic.

Lincoln may have detested the abolitionist movement so vehemently, in part, because its foundation rested primarily on blacks, not whites,[907] a race that, by his own admission, he did not like, understand, or want to live with.[908] Anti-South writers have tried to hide these facts for decades, but proof is proof, as Lincoln's own words amply attest. "What I would most desire would be the separation of the white and black races," he stated publicly on July 17, 1858, at Springfield, Illinois.[909]

During the Lincoln-Douglas debates, while Douglas often attacked his tall lanky opponent for wanting social equality for blacks, the reality is that this was something Lincoln had no interest in whatsoever. In fact, he shared the view of nearly all other white Northerners, namely, that blacks were inherently inferior and so could never be their social or political equals.[910]

In essence, when it came to American blacks Lincoln was not concerned with abolition. His only goal was to prevent the growth of slavery outside the Southern states.[911]

---

904. C. Adams, p. 135; DiLorenzo, GC, p. 255; Johannsen, p. 55.
905. Simmons, s.v. "Lincoln, Abraham."
906. McKissack and McKissack, p. 134.
907. Civil War Society, ECW, s.v. "Abolitionists."
908. See e.g., Nicolay and Hay, ALCW, Vol. 1, pp. 197, 254, 289, 370, 406-407, 483, 508.
909. Nicolay and Hay, ALCW, Vol. 1, p. 273.
910. See e.g., Nicolay and Hay, ALCW, Vol. 1, pp. 187-188.
911. Rosenbaum and Brinkley, s.v. "Lincoln and Douglas."

The McGavocks of Carnton Plantation

❧ THE RACISM BEHIND THE EMANCIPATION PROCLAMATION

There is also the overt fact that Lincoln cynically delayed issuing the Emancipation Proclamation for as long as possible, much to the infuriation of black leaders (like Frederick Douglass) and abolitionists (like Horace Greeley). Then when he finally did issue it he only freed blacks in the South, as he called it, "in states in rebellion," where he had no legal power,[912] and where the Federal government had no control.[913] In the border states, where he had the legal ability to enforce abolition, he did nothing.[914] In other words, his proclamation had no "teeth,"[915] freed no one, and in fact, nothing happened.[916]

In short, not a single slave was freed by Lincoln's edict.[917] It was after all, as he repeatedly called it, simply a "fit and necessary war measure,"[918] a "military measure,"[919] a temporary order that would end with the War.[920] The one thing it was not was a civil rights measure.[921]

Thus years later, shortly after the end of "Reconstruction" in 1877, Yankee abolitionist Lydia Maria Child (1802-1880) could reveal a truth few pro-North supporters would care to admit today: the real tragedy of Lincoln's Emancipation Proclamation is that it did not spring from a moral purpose. It was merely the result of "military necessity" and nothing more.[922] Here are the president's exact words:

> . . . upon this act, sincerely believed to be an act of justice, warranted by the Constitution upon military necessity, I invoke the considerate judgement of mankind and the gracious favor of

---

912. Neilson, s.v. "Lincoln, Abraham."
913. R. S. Phillips, s.v. "Lincoln, Abraham."
914. T. A. Bailey, p. 341.
915. Simmons, s.v. "Emancipation Proclamation."
916. Denney, p. 248; Long and Long, p. 306.
917. Garraty and McCaughey, p. 253.
918. Nicolay and Hay, ALCW, Vol. 2, p. 287.
919. Long and Long, p. 404.
920. Nicolay and Hay, ALAH, Vol. 10, p. 123.
921. DiLorenzo, RL, pp. 35-38.
922. P. Smith, p. 975.

THE MCGAVOCKS OF CARNTON PLANTATION

Almighty God.[923]

It is no surprise that many of Lincoln's own cabinet members—some of them, unlike Lincoln, who were genuine abolitionists—were shocked and confused by the decree. One of them, Lincoln's secretary of state, William Henry Seward, wrote accurately of his boss' liberation order:

> We show our sympathy with slavery by emancipating slaves where we cannot reach them, and holding them in bondage were we can set them free.[924]

Lincoln never tried to hide the fact that his War was not about slavery or black civil rights, nor did he try to conceal the real reason for issuing his Emancipation Proclamation. In early 1863, shortly after the edict was published, he told his friend Frank Carpenter about how his famous proclamation came to be:

> Things had gone from bad to worse until I felt that we had reached the end of our rope on the plan of operations we had been pursuing [that is, to quickly and efficiently crush the South]—that we had played our last card and must change our tactics, or lose the game. I determined on the Emancipation Proclamation, and . . . called a Cabinet meeting upon the subject.[925]

No mention by Lincoln here of black civil rights, no humanitarian gestures, no great sweeping oratory on the evils of slavery. Just the desperate talk of the U.S. commander-in-chief at "the end of his rope," playing his "last card" in a tactical, political-military "game."

With Northern support for his War now drying up, it is not surprising that Union recruitment continued to decrease while desertions continued to increase (at a rate of 1,250 a week between 1863 and

---

923. Nicolay and Hay, ALCW, Vol. 2, p. 288.
924. Piatt, p. 150.
925. Coffin, pp. 330-331.

THE MCGAVOCKS OF CARNTON PLANTATION

1865),[926] forcing Lincoln to call for 500,000 new volunteers while at the same time threatening to draft the reluctant.[927]

During the same two years he spent desperately trying to postpone the Emancipation Proclamation, 1861 and 1862, he was also working hard to continue to prohibit blacks from enlisting in the U.S. army and navy, which is why, at the start of the War, when thousands of Northern blacks showed up to fight, Lincoln turned them all away,[928] saying he had no use for their services.[929]

Blacks would never serve in any U.S. military outfit, Lincoln had at first pledged. For when it came to enlisting African-Americans Lincoln had always agreed with the man who was soon to become his most famous officer, William T. Sherman, who said: "All the Congresses on earth can't make the Negro anything else than what he already is."[930]

What the black man "already was" only white supremacists like Lincoln and Sherman could answer. Whatever Sherman meant, it is obvious that blacks were not wanted in the U.S. armed forces by either this high ranking officer or his boss.

Perhaps what "Uncle Billy" was hinting at was the overt racism of Northerners, including his own, which promised to forever forbid the enrollment of blacks in the U.S. military.

In May 1862 the Chicago *Tribune* stated that only a "traitor" would entertain the belief that whites needed blacks in the Federal army to subdue the Confederacy. Washington, D.C.'s main newspaper, the *National Intelligencer*, questioned the ability of the "primitive" African to handle firing weapons, noting that Yankee abolitionist John Brown had been wise to select spears rather than guns to hand out to Virginia slaves. Besides, cried the New York *Times*, enlisting blacks would certainly arouse nothing but revulsion across the North, for no whites would ever

---

926. W. B. Garrison, CWTFB, p. 158. By the end of Lincoln's War some 200,000 Yankee soldiers deserted. Alotta, p. 188.
927. Daugherty, pp. 169, 210-211.
928. McKissack and McKissack, p. 134.
929. Mullen, p. 19.
930. C. Johnson, p. 170.

voluntarily serve under a black officer.[931]

With such Northern racist resistance blocking the way, blacks were only finally officially admitted in July 1862 when, with dwindling white enlistments, increasing desertion and defection rates, and a mounting white death toll, it became clear to Lincoln that he would need more manpower in order to defeat the South.[932] Even then there was no real followup on this authorization until he issued the Final Emancipation Proclamation in January 1863, at which point Lincoln was literally forced to allow black enlistment.[933] This is, after all, why he repeatedly referred to the proclamation as a "military necessity."

In a August 17, 1864, letter to Charles D. Robinson the double-talking racist statesman conceded that he had allowed blacks to become soldiers, not due to "sentiment or taste," but because of a need of "physical force," a force that is measured "as horse-power and steam-power are measured." Without that "physical force," Lincoln assured Robinson, the North would not be able to win the War.[934] As with so many Northerners at the time, for our sixteenth chief executive it was all about skin color, numbers, and political and military dominance.

In contrast, even before it began drafting whites, the Confederacy had signed up blacks at the very start of the War to work as military laborers and unofficially even as soldiers. Black Confederate regiments were seen, for example, in Richmond, Virginia, in February, 1861, two months *before* the War started.[935]

Such facts prompted black civil rights leaders, like Frederick Douglass, to put even more pressure on Lincoln to allow African-Americans to enroll in the U.S. military. We saw earlier that Douglass sent the following to the anti-black Yankee president in 1862:

> There are at the present moment, many colored men in the Confederate Army doing duty not only as cooks, servants and

---

931. Cornish, pp. 41, 42-43.
932. Garraty and McCaughey, p. 254.
933. Mullen, pp. 18, 19, 21.
934. Nicolay and Hay, ALCW, Vol. 2, p. 564.
935. Jordan, p. 219.

THE MCGAVOCKS OF CARNTON PLANTATION

laborers, but as real soldiers, having muskets on their shoulders and bullets in their pockets, ready to shoot down loyal [Yankee] troops, and do all that soldiers may do to destroy the Federal government and build up that of the traitors and rebels. There were such soldiers at Manassas, and they are probably there still. There is a negro in the [Confederate] army as well as in the fence, and our Government is likely to find it out before the war comes to an end. That the negroes are numerous in the rebel army, and do for that army it heaviest work, is beyond question.[936]

But Lincoln would have none of it. Neither Douglass or the pleas of thousands of other Northern black and white abolitionists could move him on this issue. "This is a white man's war," his officers and the U.S. War Department stalwartly announced, refusing to entertain the idea of men of African heritage serving in the Union military at any time and in any position.[937] Pro-North historians admit that, up until that point, Northerners believed that recruiting blacks into the U.S. military would backfire, not only because of white racism, but because blacks were not courageous enough to take up arms.[938]

Here then was yet another one of Lincoln's many motivations for issuing the Emancipation Proclamation: blacks could not be enlisted in the army because they were still considered "property." The Emancipation Proclamation gave them a new legal status, that of free human beings, which in turn, for the first time in the Victorian period, made them acceptable for military enrollment. Still, even after emancipation Lincoln continued to refuse blacks citizenship.

We will note here that blacks had served in official capacities in all of America's wars prior to 1861, all the way back to the first Revolutionary War against the British Empire in 1775. In fact, the first person killed by British troops during the Boston Massacre in 1770 was an American black (named Crispus Attucks), while black soldiers were present thereafter at nearly all of the Revolutionary battles including

---

936. *Douglass' Monthly*, September 1861, Vol. 4, p. 516.
937. Quarles, p. 31; Buckley, p. 81.
938. N. Bradford, p. 572.

THE MCGAVOCKS OF CARNTON PLANTATION

those at Lexington, Concord, Ticonderoga, White Plains, Bennington, Brandywine, Saratoga, Savannah, and Yorktown. Two heroic blacks even made the famous crossing with George Washington over the Delaware River on December 25, 1776. Blacks also served in the War of 1812 and under Andrew Jackson at the Battle of New Orleans in 1814.[939]

It was only under Lincoln, forty-seven years later, that the United States of America completely barred blacks from enlisting in the armed services, questioning their intelligence, stamina, and courage. Thus, it was Lincoln who injected white racism and racial integration in the U.S. military for the first time, a situation that lasted well into the 1940s.

Little wonder that for nearly two years into Lincoln's presidency he and his administration continued to refuse to even consider the idea of black U.S. soldiers. Instead they maintained that the war did not in any way involve either free or enslaved blacks, only whites.[940]

The real reason was, of course, that Lincoln and most of his officers and soldiers were racists and did not want to intermingle with blacks—on or off the battlefield. As Sherman said:

> I would prefer to have this a white man's war . . . With my opinions of negroes and my experience, yea prejudice, I cannot trust them yet. Time may change this but I cannot bring myself to trust negroes with arms in positions of danger and trust.[941]

❧ LINCOLN'S CIVIL RIGHTS RECORD

No, the "Civil War" was not about slavery, or even black civil rights. These were not even ancillary issues, though this is what Northern folklorists would have us believe. For the South the conflict was always about states' rights and self-determination, and to a lesser degree personal pride and Southern honor. Nothing more, nothing less.

Considering Lincoln's white supremacist views, we must also

---

939. Mullen, pp. 9-15.
940. Mullen, p. 18.
941. M. A. D. Howe, pp. 252-253.

THE MCGAVOCKS OF CARNTON PLANTATION

ask why, if he was indeed the "father of black civil rights," he was not also in favor of equal rights for women and other minorities, such as Native-Americans and children. There were few if any laws to protect youngsters, for example, who could be found working under atrocious conditions in factories across the U.S. Lincoln's lack of concern in this area prolonged the suffering of children for decades. In fact, it was not until 1938, under President Franklin Delano Roosevelt (1882-1945) and the passage of his Fair Labor Standards Act, that child labor under sixteen years of age was prohibited.[942]

There was also the issue of women's rights, a major topic of discussion during Lincoln's presidency. Yet he virtually ignored it, even though both black civil rights leaders, such as Sojourner Truth[943] and Frederick Douglass[944] (both personal friends of the president), and white abolitionists, such as Wendell Phillips (1811-1884) and William Lloyd Garrison, also considered themselves feminists and fully supported the women's movement.[945] Indeed, the motto of the Victorian women's movement was: "Equality before the law, without distinction of sex or color."[946]

And here is the reason women's rights leaders (most who were also abolitionists), such as Elizabeth Cady Stanton (1815-1902) and Susan B. Anthony (1820-1906), were outraged by Lincoln's Emancipation Proclamation.[947] It left wealthy educated white women with far less civil rights than poor illiterate blacks. (Feminist leaders would have a similar reaction to the anti-South Fourteenth Amendment in 1868—which primarily sought to secure civil rights for former slaves but said nothing about the civil rights of women,[948] and the Fifteenth Amendment, also

---

942. Weintraub, p. 119.
943. McKissack and McKissack, p. 97.
944. Simmons, s.v. "Douglass, Frederick."
945. Weintraub, p. 58.
946. Stanton, Anthony, and Gage, p. 219.
947. Civil War Society, ECW, s.v. "Abolitionists."
948. Foner, R, pp. 255-256. The hated Fourteenth Amendment, "ratified" on July 9, 1868, was never officially approved by ten Southern states. Why? Because one of its main intentions was to fully transform Jefferson's Constitutional Confederacy into a strongly centralized Federation, something the traditional South was wholly against. Its constant references to the South's "insurrection" and "rebellion" also understandably irritated Southerners. Therefore, without approval by the ten Southern states, the amendment's "ratification"

issued in 1868—which gave black males the right to vote, but completely ignored women's suffrage.)[949]

In part, because of Lincoln's apathy on the issue of women's rights, during his administration women continued to be prohibited from holding public office, serving on juries, or managing their own finances. Even slaves had more rights. In the case of divorce, Lincoln displayed the same utter lack of concern: when a Victorian marriage came to an end a husband retained rights over his ex-wife's money and was even given custody of the children.[950]

A stroke of Lincoln's pen could have changed all of this. Instead, as just one example, women were not allowed to vote until 1920 (with the ratification of the Nineteenth Amendment), fifty-five years after the president's death.

Racism and sexism were utterly abhorrent to all rational people in the mid-1800s, both in the South and in the North. Thankfully these "isms" were rapidly disappearing due to the new consciousness brought about by the "Age of Enlightenment" then spreading around the world. Yet strangely, even in the midst of all these positive social changes, Lincoln was never able to rid himself of his own racism and sexism.

❧ BEHIND LINCOLN'S CONFISCATION ACTS

In looking at Lincoln's civil rights record we must also consider his several Confiscation Acts, the second one which he signed on July 17, 1862. This allowed, illegally we should add, Union soldiers to seize property belonging to the South, including her servants. The U.S. Congress interpreted the document as an act of emancipation, and it

---

was never legal, and to this day it remains technically unratified. Kennedy and Kennedy, SWR, pp. 170-171. The passage of the Fourteenth Amendment in Tennessee was particularly vexing to traditional Constitutionalists. The anti-South, Southern-born governor at the time, William Gannaway Brownlow, convened a special session of the Tennessee Legislature to ratify the amendment. Fifty-six members were needed for the necessary quorum, but only fifty-four attended, and of these only three-fourths voted to ratify. Thus technically the Fourteenth Amendment is still not legal in Tennessee, or in any other state. P. Smith, p. 710.
949. An angry Anthony ignored the prohibition and voted in the 1872 presidential election. She was arrested and fined. McKissack and McKissack, pp. 153, 166-167.
950. McKissack and McKissack, pp. 95-96.

THE MCGAVOCKS OF CARNTON PLANTATION

was. But it was not for the purpose of setting blacks free and giving them equal rights and American citizenship, something Lincoln had long been against.[951]

Its real purpose was to liberate Southern blacks then deport them out of the country, and as far away as possible. As Lincoln worded the act, it would authorize him to provide for colonization

> in some tropical country beyond the limits of the United States, of such persons of the African race, made free by the provisions of this act, as may be willing to emigrate.[952]

❧ LINCOLN'S PERSONAL WAR AGAINST BLACKS

There is another important reason we know that Lincoln's War was not over slavery and that it had nothing to do with black civil rights.

We have Lincoln's many racist comments about white superiority and black inferiority, his not infrequent use of the "n" word,[953] his statements about not opposing slavery but only the extension of slavery (and that only because it would degrade white society), his opposition to black equality, his personal revulsion toward the idea of a white and black melting pot society,[954] and his reference to "all colored people" as "inferior races"—including Mexicans, who he often called "greasers"[955] and "mongrels."[956]

It is also vitally important in our discussion of the Carnton McGavocks to remind ourselves that Lincoln consistently blocked the progress of black civil rights; detested the abolition movement and its members; was opposed to both interracial marriage and the right of blacks to vote or sit on juries; blocked black enlistment; then even when

---

951. See e.g., Nicolay and Hay, ALCW, Vol. 1, pp. 406-407.
952. Nicolay and Hay, ALAH, Vol. 6, pp. 356-357.
953. See e.g., Nicolay and Hay, CWAL, Vol. 11, pp. 105-106; Nicolay and Hay, ALCW, Vol. 1, pp. 292, 298; Holzer, pp. 22-23, 67, 318, 361. Contrast this with millions of white Southerners, like Mary Chesnut, who refused to use the "n" word. See Chesnut, MCCW, p. 729.
954. As just one example of many that could be given, see the transcript for the first debate between Lincoln and Douglas at Ottawa, Illinois, on August 21, 1858. Nicolay and Hay, ALCW, Vol. 1, pp. 286-300.
955. Nicolay and Hay, ALCW, Vol. 1, p. 524; Neely, p. 213.
956. See e.g., Nicolay and Hay, ALCW, Vol. 1, p. 449.

he finally allowed it, ordered that white and black soldiers be segregated and that black soldiers be paid almost half that of whites.[957] Lincoln also refused to give black soldiers bonuses, pensions, or support for dependents, all which were routinely accorded to white soldiers.[958] He would not even allow black soldiers equal medical treatment. Medicines and emergency care were to go to whites first, blacks second.[959]

Lincoln's other racial crimes are almost too numerous to mention, such as, for example, the fact that his military officers often kept Southern blacks penned up in corrals like common livestock. General Forrest once came upon one of these Yankee "black camps" near Pulaski, Tennessee. Disgusted, he immediately freed the unfortunate inmates (probably enlisting them into his own already integrated forces), then set fire to their "miserable hovels."[960]

President Jefferson Davis, who adopted and raised a black orphan named Jim Limber during the War,[961] commented frequently on the Yankee penchant for violating the rights of blacks. On December 7, 1863, at the fourth session of the Confederacy's First Congress, Davis denounced Lincoln and the Union for the "savage ferocity" they were using to wage war against the South and her black citizens:

> Nor has less unrelenting warfare been waged by these pretended

---

957. Unlike in Lincoln's army, there was never any segregation in the Confederate military, or anywhere else in the Old South for that matter. C. Johnson, pp. 206-207. Southern blacks fought under the Rebel flag from day one, side-by-side with their white Southern brothers. And when the Confederacy finally officially authorized black enlistment in 1865, it unhesitatingly continued its integration policy. In contrast, the U.S. government did not sanction the integration of white and black troops until 1948, when President Harry Truman (1884-1972) issued Executive Order 9981. The U.S. government did not end the segregation of children in schools on army posts until 1954, by order of then Secretary of Defense Woodrow Wilson (a traditional Southerner). Weintraub, p. 146. Overt white racism in the U.S. armed forces, initiated in 1861 by Lincoln and his administration, continues to this day: currently, for example, though blacks comprise 17 percent of the American military, only 9 percent are officers. "CNN Newsroom," CNN News, July 25, 2008.
958. Current, TC, p. 4.
959. Cartmell, pp. 144, 145.
960. ORA, Ser. 1, Vol. 39, Pt. 1, p. 545. Serving under my cousin General Forrest were forty-five of his own slaves, all who he emancipated prior to War's end. He had set all of his house servants free even before the War started, years before Lincoln issued his fake Emancipation Proclamation. For more on Forrest and Southern servitude, see my book *A Rebel Born: A Defense of Nathan Bedford Forrest*.
961. C. Johnson, pp. 187-188.

THE McGAVOCKS OF CARNTON PLANTATION

friends of human rights and liberties against the unfortunate negroes. Wherever the enemy have been able to gain access they have forced into the ranks of their army every able-bodied black that they could seize; and have either left the aged, the women, and the children to perish by starvation, or have gathered them into camps where they have been wasted by a frightful mortality. Without clothing or shelter, often without food, incapable, without supervision, of taking the most ordinary precautions against disease, these helpless dependents, accustomed to have their wants supplied by the foresight of their masters, are being rapidly exterminated, wherever brought in contact with the invaders. There is little hazard in predicting that in all localities where the enemy have gained a temporary foothold, the negroes, who under our care increased sixfold in number since their importation into the colonies by Great Britain, will have been reduced by mortality during the war to not more than one-half their previous number.

A Union official reported in 1864 that the mortality in the negro camps was "frightful"; most competent judges place it at not less than twenty-five per cent in the last two years.[962]

What is Davis referring to here?

One example is Lincoln's use of black soldiers as shock troops, advance units who took the brunt of enemy fire in order to spare white lives, usually in engagements where the outcome was in doubt.[963] Though nearly all of these soldiers were led by white officers, many who did not like blacks and were not concerned for their welfare, pro-North historians continue to blame "racist" Confederate soldiers for the extremely high black mortality rate, which was 40 percent higher than the white mortality rate.[964] However, with the facts now at hand, can there really be any question that it was primarily Lincoln and *his* racist white soldiers who were responsible?

On April 14, 1876, here is how Lincoln's black "friend," Frederick Douglass, described the sixteenth president to other blacks during a speech in Washington, D.C.:

---

962. Fite, SICNDCW, pp. 293-294.
963. Cornish, pp. 87, 269; Jordan, p. 229.
964. Current, TC, p. 4.

THE MCGAVOCKS OF CARNTON PLANTATION

It must be admitted, truth compels me to admit, even here in the presence of the monument we have erected to his memory, Abraham Lincoln was not, in the fullest sense of the word, either our man or our model. In his interests, in his associations, in his habits of thought, and in his prejudices, he was a white man.

He was preeminently the white man's President, entirely devoted to the welfare of white men. He was ready and willing at any time during the first years of his administration to deny, postpone, and sacrifice the rights of humanity in the coloured people to promote the welfare of the white people of this country. In all his education and feeling he was an American of the Americans. He came into the Presidential chair upon one principle alone, namely, opposition to the extension of slavery. His arguments in furtherance of this policy had then motive and mainspring in his patriotic devotion to the interests of his own race. To protect, defend, and perpetuate slavery in the States where it existed, Abraham Lincoln was not less ready than any other President to draw the sword of the nation. He was ready to execute all the supposed constitutional guarantees of the United States Constitution in favour of the slave system anywhere inside the slave States. He was willing to pursue, recapture, and send back the fugitive slave to his master, and to suppress a slave rising for liberty, though his guilty master were already in arms against the Government. The race to which we belong were not the special objects of his consideration.[965]

❧ LINCOLN'S PLANS FOR FREED BLACKS: DEPORTATION & COLONIZATION

Lincoln was also an enthusiastic supporter of the American Colonization Society (ACS), founded in 1816 in Washington, D.C., by a Northerner, New Jerseyan Reverend Robert Finley.[966] The organization—one of whose most influential members was Lincoln's political idol, slave owner Henry Clay—promoted the idea of making America white coast to coast through the racial cleansing of the U.S.

This was to be accomplished by shipping all American blacks, as our American apartheid supporting president put it, "to Liberia—to their

---

965. Douglass, LTFD, p. 872.
966. Fogel, p. 252.

own native land" (that is, Africa).⁹⁶⁷ This explains why Lincoln was a leader of the Illinois chapter of the ACS, a state whose legislature he had personally convinced to finance the deportation of free blacks.⁹⁶⁸

Indeed, early on, the ACS had the full support of the U.S. Congress, which appropriated $500,000—the equivalent of $12 million today—for its use.⁹⁶⁹ It was this money, along with private donations, that the ACS used to found Liberia, an African colony specifically developed for deported American blacks.⁹⁷⁰

Among the early leaders, officers, and supporters of the ACS were such noted Yankees as New England statesman Daniel Webster (after whom the town of Webster, Massachusetts, was named), New Yorker William H. Seward (Lincoln's secretary of state and the man after whom Seward, Alaska, was named), and Maryland poet Francis Scott Key (author of the U.S. National Anthem, *The Star-Spangled Banner*).⁹⁷¹ The nation's largest and most enthusiastic ACS chapter was in Boston, Massachusetts, where both antislavery and anti-black sentiment was high (as we have seen, the two were not mutually exclusive in New England).⁹⁷²

We will note here that the Confederacy never supported, funded, or showed the slightest bit of interest in Liberia, the Union's first colony abroad. It was strictly a Northern (Yankee) affair, which is why Liberia's flag, a simplified Stars and Stripes, was directly patterned on the U.S. flag, not the C.S. flag.⁹⁷³

Also, contrary to Northern myth, Liberia's name was not meant to symbolize the "liberation" of blacks from American slavery. It was meant to symbolize the liberation of blacks from American soil. Prior to Lincoln's War most Yankees wanted nothing to do with their African-American counterparts, as the very existence of the Northern-created

---

967. Nicolay and Hay, ALCW, Vol. 1, p. 288.
968. W. B. Garrison, LNOK, p. 186; DiLorenzo, LU, p. 28.
969. D. H. Donald, L, p. 355.
970. Rosenbaum and Brinkley, s.v. "Colonization."
971. Website: www.slavenorth.com/colonize.htm.
972. Nye, p. 20.
973. Furnas, p. 319.

The McGavocks of Carnton Plantation

ACS and Liberia prove.

Oddly, however, while most Southerners, like the Grimké sisters, detested the ACS,[974] and while most Northerners eventually and reluctantly gave up their dream of cleansing America of black-skinned people as hopelessly impractical and too expensive, there was one man who persisted in trying to keep the dream alive: the big spending, big government Northern liberal, Abraham Lincoln.

Indeed, as will become increasingly clear, throughout his entire life Lincoln was keenly interested in, even obsessed with, black colonization, actually becoming more so with the passage of time.[975] In fact, he was widely regarded as the most outspoken and enthusiastic black colonizationist in America in the mid-1800s.

As the leading proponent of black deportation, Lincoln was fond of quoting Thomas Jefferson on the topic, as he did in New York during his famed Cooper Union speech on February 27, 1860. In the process, Lincoln reveals his true incentive for wanting to emancipate and deport American blacks:

> In the language of Mr. Jefferson, uttered many years ago, 'It is still in our power to direct the process of emancipation, and deportation, peaceably, and in such slow degrees, as that the evil will wear off insensibly; and their places be . . . filled up by free white laborers.'[976]

Though Radicals (the 19th-Century term for Northern abolitionists) like John Parker Hale (1806-1873)—the first antislavery advocate elected to the U.S. senate—correctly felt that colonization was

---

974. South Carolinians Angelina and Sarah Grimké called the very idea of black colonization "the monster Prejudice, which could [only] love the colored man *after* he got to Africa." Grimké, p. 40.

975. Some 12,000 American blacks were eventually deported to Liberia. But their "liberation" was short-lived: conditions there were so horrid that hundreds died before they could find a way back to the U.S. To this day the descendants of these early inhabitants are still called "Americo-Liberians," and make up 10 percent of the nation's population. This group is to be contrasted with the other 90 percent, the native, indigenous population of Africans, with whom they share ongoing rivalries and disputes in this, Africa's oldest black republic. Rosenbaum, s.v. "Liberia."

976. Nicolay and Hay, ALCW, Vol. 1, p. 608. Jefferson's words are from his autobiography, written in 1821, when he was seventy-seven years old. See Foley, p. 816.

The McGavocks of Carnton Plantation

perhaps the most impossibly ridiculous notion ever created, Lincoln embraced it with a burning passion, fostering it at every opportunity.[977] In fact, he lobbied feverishly for the colonization of American blacks until the day he died, as General Benjamin F. "the Beast" Butler attests.

According to Butler, in early April, 1865, just a few days before Lincoln was shot (on April 14) by Northerner John Wilkes Booth (1838-1865), the president called the Yankee officer to the White House to discuss the practicalities of deporting all blacks out of America.[978] Butler remembers Lincoln's exact words:

> But what shall we do with the negroes after they are free? I can hardly believe that the South and North can live in peace, unless we can get rid of the negros. . . . I believe that it would be better to export them all to some fertile country with a good climate, which they could have to themselves.[979]

Earlier in his presidency, in 1862, midway through his War, one of the bargaining chips Lincoln used to pressure the border states into siding with the Union (and freeing their slaves) was his assurance that after emancipation, freed blacks could all be quickly gotten rid of by shipping them out of the country. "Room in South America for colonization [of blacks] can be obtained cheaply," he solemnly promised.[980]

For Lincoln it truly was all about race and politics, which is why he excluded black slaves in the Border States and those in Yankee occupied areas in the South, from his Preliminary Emancipation Proclamation, issued on September 22, 1862.[981] And it is why his colonization plan was included in this document. After stating his intention to recommend to Congress the adoption "of a practical measure" that would aid in abolishing slavery, he goes on to say that

---

977. Foner, FSFLFM, p. 280.
978. Current, LNK, p. 230. Also see Furnas, p. 320.
979. B. F. Butler, p. 903. See also Pickett, p. 326; M. Davis, pp. 147-148.
980. Nicolay and Hay, ALCW, Vol. 2, p. 205.
981. T. A. Bailey, p. 339.

The McGavocks of Carnton Plantation

> . . . the effort to colonize persons of African descent with their consent upon this continent or elsewhere, with the previously obtained consent of the governments existing there, will be continued.[982]

Lincoln's pledge to continue to work toward the goal of deporting all blacks out of America never made it into his Final Emancipation Proclamation (issued a few months later, on January 1, 1863). Why? Because his cabinet feared that it might alienate Northern abolitionist voters in the upcoming 1864 election, a group that was already angry at him for having delayed emancipation for nearly three years. Lincoln agreed with this ploy, and the colonization clause was struck from the final version.[983] After all, he wanted and needed every vote he could get, and he had already proven that he would do anything to insure that he succeeded in this endeavor, including ignoring the plight of American black servants in order to achieve his political ends.

Again, this was a fact he never tried to conceal, as we will remember from his public response to Free-Soiler Horace Greeley on August 22, 1862:

> If there be those who would not save the Union unless they could at the same time save slavery, I do not agree with them. If there be those who would not save the Union unless they could at the same time destroy slavery, I do not agree with them. My paramount object in this struggle is to save the Union, and is not either to save

---

982. Nicolay and Hay, ALCW, Vol. 2, p. 237.
983. In fairness to Lincoln and other early whites, North and South, the idea of racial separatism was not unique to European-Americans. In the 1920s, for example, a black-sponsored "Back to Africa" movement emerged. Its founder, Jamaican-born black nationalist, Marcus Garvey (1887-1940), promoted the ideas of black pride, economic independence from whites, and the establishment of a black-only state in Africa. Unfortunately for supporters of the Back to Africa movement, Garvey was later convicted of fraud, imprisoned, and eventually deported. Even earlier, in the 19th Century, African-American abolitionist Martin Delany (1812-1885) advocated a separation of the races, with an emphasis on black separatism specifically. Delany and Garvey were not the first, nor the last, to push for black separatism. The idea continues today among a number of African-American groups. Unfortunately, they are virtually unknown to the public: the liberal mainstream media, which feeds off the Lincolnian ploy of stirring up imaginary racial hatred, refuses to report on them and their nefarious activities. Like the NAACP and other hate groups (as even many blacks refer to them), the liberal media would go out of business if the truth got out: the vast majority of whites, blacks, browns, and reds are *not* racists. For more on the NAACP as a hate group, see Seabrook, AL, pp. 341-343.

or destroy slavery. If I could save the Union without freeing any slave, I would do it . . . What I do about slavery and the colored race, I do because I believe it helps save the Union . . .[984]

That same month, August 1862, an incredulous, disappointed, and disgusted delegation of prominent blacks came to the White House to try and convince the president of the importance of issuing an emancipation decree (Lincoln was still stiffly resisting the idea), and dissuade him from going forward with his colonization plan. White supremacist Lincoln's reply was predictable. Looking the black committee straight in the eye, he said:

> You and we are a different race. We have between us a broader difference than exists between any other two races. . . . As I think your race suffers greatly . . . by living with us, ours suffers by your presence. . . . [O]n this broad continent, not a single man of your race is made the equal of a single man of ours. . . . [Because] there is an unwillingness on the part of our people [that is, white Northerners], harsh as it may be, for you free colored people to remain with us . . . it is better for us both, therefore, to be separated.[985]

The recipients of these words were the first free blacks ever to be invited to the White House. Unfortunately for them, the visit was not a welcoming one.

Lincoln went on to tell the group that: "The ban is still upon you," and strongly suggested that they embrace the idea of colonization.[986] There was an area in Central America he would be happy to send them to, he added—with the support and protection of the U.S. government, of course.[987]

When news of this meeting got out, blacks nationwide were outraged, in particular black civil rights leaders. One of these, Frederick

---

984. Nicolay and Hay, ALCW, Vol. 2, pp. 227-228.
985. Nicolay and Hay, ALCW, Vol. 2, pp. 222-225.
986. Nicolay and Hay, ALCW, Vol. 2, p. 223.
987. Nicolay and Hay, ALCW, Vol. 2, p. 224.

THE MCGAVOCKS OF CARNTON PLANTATION

Douglass, long considered a "friend" of Lincoln, openly condemned the president for displaying

> all his inconsistencies, his pride of race and blood, his contempt for negroes and his canting hypocrisy. . . . The tone of frankness and benevolence which he assumes in his speech to the colored committee is too thin a mask not to be seen through. The genuine spark of humanity is missing in it, no sincere wish to improve the condition of the oppressed has dictated it.[988]

Another offended black penned the following to the president: What makes you think you have more of a right to live in the United States than we do?[989]

Lincoln never replied to this question, and did not need to. His answer was already well-known. Just in case some had missed it, he made it clear once again on December 1, 1862, in his Second Annual Message to Congress. After promising the "slave states" (the derogatory Yankee term for the pro-states rights Southern states) that they would be financially compensated if they freed their slaves by the year 1900, he said:

> Congress may appropriate money and otherwise provide for colonizing free colored persons, with their own consent, at any place or places without the United States.[990]

What Lincoln failed to realize was that, although he fiercely believed that whites and blacks could not live together, they had been doing just that for several centuries, from the very first days of European settlement, in fact, when the Dutch brought the first African servants to colonists in Virginia in 1619.[991] Between that year and 1860, across America literally millions of both free and bonded blacks had lived in close, and usually peaceful, proximity with Europeans, with blacks in the

---

988. *Douglass' Monthly*, September, 1862, Vol. 5, pp. 707-708.
989. Current, LNK, p. 223.
990. Nicolay and Hay, ALCW, Vol. 2, p. 271.
991. M. Perry, p. 49.

THE MCGAVOCKS OF CARNTON PLANTATION

South often considered veritable "family members."

To his credit Lincoln was against *compulsory* deportation of blacks, even declaring that the government must foot the bill for their eviction from America. Still, he remarked, if no place could be found for them in Africa or Central America, he was willing to settle them almost anyplace—as long as it was, as he said, "without the United States."[992]

These remarkable passages, largely disregarded by history and wholly suppressed by Lincoln apologists and Northern textbook and mainstream publishers, are today thus largely unknown to the general public. Nonetheless, it was well-known during Lincoln's War that he did not initiate the conflict over slavery, or to instigate black civil rights.

Southerners were well aware of this fact, and agreed. In his fantastic autobiographical history of Lincoln's War, *The Rise and Fall of the Confederate Government*, President Jefferson Davis wrote:

> The truth remains intact and incontrovertible, that the existence of African servitude was in no wise the cause of the conflict, but only an incident. In the later controversies that arose, however, its effect in operating as a lever upon the passions, prejudices, or sympathies of mankind, was so potent that it has been spread like a thick cloud over the whole horizon of historic truth.[993]

After all, had the South truly wanted to maintain slavery, the most obvious means by which to achieve this would have been simply to remain within the U.S., a nation in which slavery was perfectly legal until December 1865.[994]

Indeed, up until that time the U.S. Constitution had protected the institution, a safeguard that the South lost when it seceded.[995] Thus, if all Dixie cared about was slavery, why did she leave the Union, where both slavery and the slave trade had been vigilantly protected under the

---

992. Nicolay and Hay, ALCW, Vol. 2, p. 271.
993. J. Davis, RFCG, Vol. 1, p. 80.
994. Horwitz, pp. 290-291.
995. Ransom, p. 173.

269

THE MCGAVOCKS OF CARNTON PLANTATION

U.S. flag for centuries?[996] Northern President Lincoln himself, as we have seen, was prepared to keep slavery until the year 1900,[997] or even permanently, if the Southern states would only return to the Union[998] and pay their taxes.[999]

Additionally, we know that Davis' statement is true because when it came to blacks, Lincoln's self-confessed number one goal was always deportation, not civil rights. As even pro-North historians admit, many Northern abolitionists were just as ready to deport blacks as they were to free them. Lincoln was just one member of this group of millions, one that consistently pushed to create a workable resettlement plan. Replant the Negro in Central America, in Africa, or even on the planet Mars, anywhere but America, they cried. It was in this way that even the so-called "enemies of slavery" played a role in keeping the embers of slavery burning.[1000]

But this was not authentic abolitionism, and Lincoln knew it. Still there was no shame in it, which is why he never tried to hide it.

Not surprisingly, most of his military officers were not true abolitionists either. Indeed, some, like Lincoln's favorite commander, U.S. Grant, went so far as to say that: "I never was an abolitionist, not even what could be called antislavery."[1001] This is why, after the War and the issuance of Lincoln's fake and illegal Emancipation Proclamation, Grant happily wrote that Americans are still "just as free to avoid the social intimacy with the blacks as ever they were . . ."[1002]

None of this should shock us. While Grant and his wife were ardent slave owners before, during, and after the "Civil War,"[1003] Lincoln's days as a lawyer included defending slave owners, and even participating in a case that involved the selling of black slaves, a case for

---

996. Coit, p. 469.
997. Nicolay and Hay, ALCW, Vol. 2, p. 270.
998. Nicolay and Hay, ALCW, Vol. 2, p. 296.
999. Nicolay and Hay, ALAH, Vol. 10, p. 123. See also Current, LNK, pp. 242-246; W. C. Davis, AHD, p. 164; W. B. Garrison, LNOK, p. 181; Weintraub, p. 73.
1000. Catton, Vol. 1, p. 86.
1001. Foote, Vol. 2, p. 638. Grant uttered this remark in a letter to Elihu B. Washburne, August 30, 1863.
1002. U. S. Grant, Vol. 1, p. 215.
1003. Rutherford, FA, p. 38; Wallechinsky, Wallace, and Wallace, p. 11; Woods, p. 67.

The McGavocks of Carnton Plantation

which he was well paid.[1004]

Modern Americans who believe that their early American leaders intended the nation to be a "Melting Pot," a rainbow of various races, colors, and cultures, are of course grossly mistaken. Lincoln is the most obvious example of just one of millions of Northerners who devoted their entire lives to creating what President Wilson called the "Unmelted Pot."[1005] So much for the fiction that Lincoln was a civil rights activist and that he inaugurated his War to end slavery.

What was his motivation for waging destruction, fire, and death on the South then?

❧ THE TRUE CAUSES OF LINCOLN'S WAR

For one thing, Lincoln and the Union could not afford to lose the South's most valuable natural resources: her 3,549 miles of coastline, her 189 ports and port towns, inlets, rivers, immense, fertile farmlands, abundant agricultural products, and her 12 million hardworking people. Her major seaports alone—New Orleans, Louisiana; Mobile, Alabama; Pensacola, Florida; Fernandina, Florida; Savannah, Georgia; Charleston, South Carolina; Wilmington, North Carolina; New Bern, North Carolina; and Norfolk, Virginia—were worth untold millions of dollars to the North.[1006]

Indeed, in early 1861, the Southern Confederacy—where per capita wealth was double that of the North, where 60 percent of America's wealth lay,[1007] where per capita income was growing 30 percent more rapidly than in the North—was the fourth richest nation on earth, even wealthier than Germany, France, Italy, Belgium, Spain, or Denmark. In fact, there was only one European country richer than the C.S.A. that year, and that was England.[1008]

Aside from not wanting to lose Dixie's 850,000 square miles of territory, her 3,549 miles of coastline, her 189 ports, her 36,000 miles

---

1004. Manning, p. 26.
1005. Wade, p. 148; Ashmore, Jussim, and Wilder, pp. 105-106; F. King, p. 141.
1006. Seabrook, AL, p. 76.
1007. Current, TC, p. 429.
1008. Fogel and Engerman, pp. 249, 251.

271

of internal water line (rivers), her 12 million people, and her agricultural products (in 1850 worth the equivalent of nearly $10 billion in today's currency), Lincoln and his "Wall Street Boys" also did not want to forfeit the enormous tax revenues the North derived from the South: over 90 percent of these came from the Yankee tariff imposed on Dixie.[1009]

Obviously, based on economics alone, Lincoln could not afford to let the South secede. For the North the "Civil War" was indeed, in great part, a conflict built around business and finance. While modern pro-North historians have tried hard to obscure this fact, Lincoln knew it and so did nearly everyone else, even foreigners. In 1862, for example, English novelist Charles Dickens (1812-1870) wrote the following about America's "War Between the States":

> The Northern onslaught upon slavery is no more than a piece of specious humbug disguised to conceal its desire for economic control of the United States. Union means so many millions a year lost to the South; secession means loss of the same millions to the North. The love of money is the root of this as many, many other evils. The quarrel between the North and South is, as it stands, solely a fiscal quarrel.[1010]

The South was rich in countless resources. Therefore her "economic control" was absolutely vital to Northern interests. It is easy to see then why Lincoln and his Wall Street Boys considered Dixie the ultimate money prize, one they could not afford to lose.[1011]

In short, as Southern agrarian Andrew Nelson Lytle (1902-1995) noted in 1931, at its root Lincoln's War was a conflict between a nearly purely agrarian people and a people devoted almost totally to commercialism and industrialism. With the North in power, Lytle notes, Yankees naturally demanded that all of America's citizens, North and South, pursue not the right to "life, liberty, and the pursuit of

---

1009. Scruggs, p. 13.
1010. Dickens, Charles. "American Disunion," *All the Year Round*, December 21, 1861, p. 299.
1011. Ashe, p. 24.

THE MCGAVOCKS OF CARNTON PLANTATION

happiness," but a heedless consumption of Northern products.[1012]

But even if the South had remained in the Union it would have still posed a problem for Lincoln, because he could not install his vaunted American System of government as long as the concept of states' rights was alive in the South. For, in his dictatorial mind, if the South were allowed to go its own way to become a free-trading independent nation, his plan would backfire, seriously impeding the economic progress of the North.[1013]

The Southern conservative concept of states' rights and the Northern liberal concept of the American System were in complete opposition to one another. One had to go and as far as Lincoln was concerned, it would be the former. The Southern Confederacy had to be crushed into dust then, and for Lincoln only a full-scale total "war of extermination,"[1014] using a scorched earth approach, could achieve this.[1015] Indeed, he was the first American leader to institute a policy of total war. Unfortunately, it was on his own people![1016]

Nearly 100 years later another socialistic dictator would seek to crush states' rights, this time in Germany. In his autocratic quest for world domination this individual cited none other than the false ideas of Abraham Lincoln in order to justify his own insane plan. His name was Adolf Hitler (1889-1945),[1017] and the book was called *Mein Kampf* ("My Struggle").[1018]

For some reason, which will be forever unknown, when it came to the South's secession Lincoln the attorney did not think to do battle in the courtroom, just as nearly every other civilized nation has done in time of internecine conflict. What happened to the long-standing tradition of using arbitration to settle international disputes?[1019] It ended

---

1012. Lytle, pp. 30-31.
1013. C. Adams, p. 25.
1014. Pollard, LC, p. 509.
1015. Oates, AL, p. 136.
1016. Manning, p. 149.
1017. DiLorenzo, LU, pp. 81-84.
1018. See Hitler, Vol. 2, pp. 830-831.
1019. Henry, ATSF, p. 223.

THE MCGAVOCKS OF CARNTON PLANTATION

with Lincoln.

Instead, he pitted Americans against one another in a needless and illegal four year conflict that killed three million of his own citizens. Among those officially known to have been killed, wounded, or maimed for life, were 359,528 Yankee soldiers and 329,000 Rebel soldiers.[1020] Untold thousands more—mostly non-combatants, and practically all of these Southern civilians, primarily women, children, and seniors, both white and black—also perished.

❧ A PERSONAL CONNECTION: ELIAS JENT, SR.

My 3rd great-grandfather, Confederate cavalryman Elias Jent, Sr. (1810-1864), who served in the First Regiment of the Thirteenth Kentucky Cavalry (known as "Caudill's Army"), was murdered by Yankee soldiers while at home in Knott County, Kentucky, on furlough. Elias, on authorized leave, had been unarmed at the time of his capture, making his execution illegal, immoral, and unethical.[1021]

❧ LINCOLN BLAMES GOD FOR HIS WAR

In the end, when his idea of faulting the South for starting the War (because she "rebelled" against the Union and practiced "slavery"), was rejected by most Americans, Lincoln tried to avoid taking the blame by placing responsibility for the entire conflict on the Almighty.

In his Second Inaugural Address, on March 4, 1865, one month before Lee surrendered at Appomattox, Lincoln said that God

> gives to both North and South, this terrible war . . . Fondly do we hope—fervently do we pray—that this mighty scourge of war may speedily pass away. Yet, if God wills that it continue . . . so still it must be said 'the judgments of the Lord, are true and righteous

---

1020. Katcher, CWSB, pp. 45-46.
1021. My 3rd great-grandmother Rachel Cornett was also killed during the incident. Elias and Rachel had been out walking from Hindman to Lott's Creek sometime in 1864. They had stopped at a relative's house, when marauding Yankee troops arrived and dragged the couple from the house. Shots in the yard were heard from inside. A few moments later they were both found hanging from a nearby tree, just two victims out of thousands of Yankee criminality and Northern inhumanity. From the author's personal family tree.

THE McGAVOCKS OF CARNTON PLANTATION

altogether.'[1022]

We will bear in mind that about this time, early 1865, Lincoln arrogantly rejected the South's offer to peacefully and honorably rejoin the Union, asserting that the South must instead unconditionally surrender to the "national authority."[1023] President Jefferson Davis protested, asserting that the Confederacy had already agreed to end slavery and now only wanted Lincoln to cease all violence so that the Southern states could return, under their own self-governing power,[1024] to the U.S. The Yankee leader would not be moved and Davis' plea was coldly dismissed.[1025]

Lincoln's inhumane and illogical refusal to deal equitably with Dixie continued the War, the suffering, the pain, and the anguish for several more weeks, while thousands more perished. Yet the self-confessed anti-Christian atheistic world leader[1026] had the impudence to end his Second Inaugural Address with these words:

> With malice toward none; with charity toward all . . . let us strive on to . . . do all which may achieve and cherish a just and lasting peace . . .[1027]

For four years Lincoln had shown almost nothing but malice toward the South, and even toward those Northerners who had disagreed with him. And he had rejected and scoffed at all those who had attempted to bring about a peaceful resolution to his War. In fact, it was he who had ended any possibility of a "just and lasting peace" with his criminal and devious shenanigans at Fort Sumter, and it was he who prevented peace from returning for the next four years. For at any time he could have called his troops home and let the Confederacy go.

1022. Nicolay and Hay, ALCW, Vol. 2, p. 657.
1023. Nicolay and Hay, ALCW, Vol. 2, pp. 614, 633.
1024. That is, Davis wanted states' rights to be maintained and respected by the U.S. if the Southern states agreed to reunionize. Being a big government liberal, Lincoln was vehemently against states' rights.
1025. Ashe, p. 56.
1026. See Seabrook, L, pp. 918-938.
1027. Nicolay and Hay, ALCW, Vol. 2, p. 657.

THE MCGAVOCKS OF CARNTON PLANTATION

Lincoln's inhumanity, rhetorical sophistry, outrageous treachery, and shrewd political cunning knew no bounds.[1028]

❧ DID LINCOLN'S WAR PRESERVE THE UNION?
The real tragedy of Lincoln's War is that it did not "preserve the Union," which is the reason the president himself continually gave for fighting the conflict to begin with. Instead, he destroyed it. For the very definition of a union is a *voluntary* association between two or more people, groups, or states. This is why, when the Founders created the U.S., they first called it a Confederacy (a voluntary union of nation-states) rather than a nation (an *involuntary* union of states).

After killing hundreds of thousands of her people and bombing her cities into rubble, Lincoln forced the South back into the Union at gunpoint, smashing the concept of states' rights and overturning the constitutional government of the Founding Fathers. This was, after all, his true intention from the beginning, for both stood in the way of realizing his beloved anti-South agenda: the installation of Henry Clay's liberal American System at Washington, D.C.

The supreme irony of all this was, of course, that it was Davis (and the C.S.A.) who stood for true democracy, not Lincoln (and the U.S.A.), the latter who behaved more like a fascist leading an authoritarian nation. This is why, when Lincoln's minister to Russia, Cassius Marcellus Clay (1810-1903), defended the North's militaristic intentions as a battle for "nationality and liberty," the London *Times* replied that it was impossible to understand how the North could refer to itself as the advocate of freedom while at the same time physically forcing the South to remain in the Union. The South was fighting for liberty. The North was fighting for tyranny, the paper correctly observed.[1029]

But why, we might ask, would any sane person want to control the lives of millions of other people? The answer is that no sane person would want to. In Lincoln's case only a psychologist willing to devote

---

1028. Dean, pp. 171-172.
1029. D. H. Donald, WNWCW, p. 76.

THE McGAVOCKS OF CARNTON PLANTATION

years of study to his life, deeds, and words could possibly begin to determine why our sixteenth president would want to impose his political ideals on, and totally control the destinies of, twelve million Southerners, four million who were black.

Whatever the truth behind Lincoln's motivations, it is clear that he was one of the most dishonest men ever to serve in political office. The McGavocks, who later angrily sued Lincoln's government, would have agreed. And so would President Thomas Jefferson. As the conservative Libertarian-Republican stated in 1813: "An honest man can feel no pleasure in the exercise of power over his fellow citizens."[1030] "Dishonest Abe," however, did.

As a result, to this day Americans continue to labor under the monolithic, bloated, oversized behemoth known as "big government"—along with the corrosive influence of modern liberalism[1031]—Lincoln's primary, true, and lasting legacies. And yet, as President Woodrow Wilson observes, the Constitution was meant to be an instrument of Confederation, not of Federation—that is, of national consolidation.[1032]

Jefferson and the other Southern Founders, the architects of the first American Confederacy and its small limited government, have been turning over in their graves ever since.

1030. Foley, p. 708.
1031. Bork, p. 4.
1032. W. Wilson, DR, pp. 241-242.

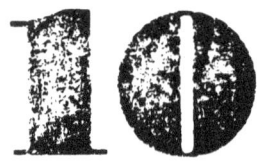

The McGavocks & Lincoln's War

Part 1

➢ WAR COMES TO TENNESSEE

IN 1861 FEW IF ANY traditional Southerners supported Lincoln's progressive, ultra-liberal, anti-South political beliefs, just as few traditional Southerners would support them were he alive today. And even fewer of them tolerated his white supremacist ideas. This resistance toward Lincoln, not the United States of America, is how and why the "Civil War" came to Tennessee in the Spring of that year.

Though Tennesseans, like all Southerners, truly loved the Union and had held out desperate hope for reconciliation with the North, the election of the first sectional president (one who happened to be pro-North) in American history was just too much.[1033]

For decades the North had been meddling in the South's affairs, stirring up emotions, fears, and animosities, treading on the honor of a proud, unique, and separate people. By 1860 the South had, in many ways, become a mere colony of the North, with most of her profits winding up in the pockets of Yankee businessmen.

Even Southern slavery benefitted the Yanks far more than it did

---

1033. C. Adams, p. 89. Lincoln contributed several other "firsts" to American history: he was the first president born beyond the boundaries of the original thirteen colonies, and the first to be assassinated. Sobel, s.v. "Lincoln, Abraham."

THE MCGAVOCKS OF CARNTON PLANTATION

the Rebs. As South Carolinian Mary Chesnut poignantly noted in her diary on July 8, 1862:

> This war was undertaken by us to shake off the yoke of foreign invaders. So we consider our cause righteous. The Yankees, since the war has begun, have discovered it is to free the slaves that they are fighting. So their cause is noble. They also expect to make the war pay. Yankees do not undertake anything that does not pay. They think we belong to them. We have been good milk cows—milked by the tariff, or skimmed. We let them have all of our hard earnings. We bear the ban of slavery; they get the money. Cotton pays everybody who handles it, sells it, manufactures it, but rarely pays the man who grows it. Second hand the Yankees received the wages of slavery. They grew rich. We grew poor. The receiver is as bad as the thief. That applies to us, too, for we received the savages they stole from Africa and brought to us in their slave-ships. As with the Egyptians, so it shall be with us: if they let us go, it must be across a Red Sea—but one made red by blood.[1034]

Chesnut is right. The South had born all of the evils of the Yankee-created institution of slavery, while the North had taken most of the earnings. Thus the North grew increasingly fat and wealthy while the South grew increasingly thin and poor. In the process the North was exonerated, its title as the founder of American slavery forgotten. The South meanwhile was found "guilty" by association, and is still unfairly punished to this day for the crime of practicing the North's "peculiar institution."

For Tennesseans and all other Southern states, Lincoln's ascendancy to the Oval Office meant an end to any chance for Dixie's economic independence.[1035] Indeed, to them it spelled increased hardships, deprivations, and humiliation under the "colonial rule" of the North and a tyrannical anti-South leader. And so on June 8, 1861, by a huge majority vote, the Volunteer State reluctantly seceded from the

---

1034. Chesnut, DD, pp. 200-201.
1035. M. M. Smith, p. 37.

THE MCGAVOCKS OF CARNTON PLANTATION

United States of America, almost sixty-five years to the day from when it had joined on June 1, 1796.[1036]

❧ THE McGAVOCKS: AVID CONSERVATIVES & CONFEDERATES

The Carnton McGavocks were among those who voted for secession. Dyed-in-the-wool Jeffersonians, states' righters, and traditional Southerners who loved both the Constitution and the Union, they wanted nothing more than to be left alone to live their lives in peace, and end black servitude ("slavery") in their own time and way. Lincoln's illegal invasion of the South after Fort Sumter made all of that impossible.

Naturally, John and Carrie sided with the Confederacy, as did the rest of the Southern McGavock branch.[1037] In fact, until modern political correctness made the word "Confederacy" a taboo, the McGavocks were well-known, well respected, and well loved in Franklin and across Middle Tennessee for being staunch Confederates. And like most true Southerners of their day, they flew the Confederate Battle Flag at their home in Franklin, a beautiful symbol (designed by my cousin, Southern hero General P. G. T. Beauregard) representing Christianity (the design was based on both Saint Andrew's Cross and Saint Patrick's Cross), their homeland Dixie, family, independence, courage, and Southern military valor, honor, and pride.[1038]

Yet today, just as you will not see a Confederate Flag flying in any Franklin parade (town authorities consistently display their displeasure at the once everyday custom, and are even trying to make it illegal), you will also not see a Confederate Flag flying at Carnton Plantation, a tragic and unnecessary concession to New South/scallywag

---

1036. Phelan, p. 440.
1037. The Northern McGavock branch, of course, sided with Lincoln and the Union. The two family lines undoubtedly and unknowingly fired at each across many a battlefield.
1038. The origins of the Confederacy's Battle Flag can still be seen in the flags of Scotland and Ireland, with their prominent display of Saint Andrew's and Saint Patrick's diagonal crosses. Cannon, pp. 18, 25, 60.

The McGavocks of Carnton Plantation

values,[1039] an anti-South, anti-Confederate mind set embraced by those who have been inculcated by the North to be ashamed of their own heritage.[1040]

If they were alive today Colonel John and Carrie would be extremely offended to learn that their beloved Confederate symbol is now banned from their own Confederate home. And so should any true-blooded modern day American, for half of the nation fought for the "the Stainless Banner," as traditional Southerners lovingly refer to their flag. Much of Europe at one time also stood behind this emblem of strict constitutionality, self-determination, and states' rights.

Here is what President Jefferson Davis, speaking after Lincoln's War, said about New South Southerners (scallywags) decades before the term was coined:

> Nothing fills me with deeper sadness than to see a Southern man apologizing for the defense we made of our inheritance. Our cause

---

1039. A scallywag (or scalawag) is a Southerner who has "gone back on their raisin'"; that is, one who denies their Southern heritage and embraces the North's version of the "Civil War," along with all of its anti-South myths, lies, and slanders. The scallywag is still extremely disliked in the South and traditional Southerners consider him/her a traitor to their homeland, Dixie.

1040. I have often been told that the reason for this prohibition against the Confederate Flag here in Franklin (and elsewhere across the South) is because "it might offend someone." Yet, an individual who would be offended by the sight of the Confederate Flag is the exact type of uninformed person who needs to be reeducated, and this cannot happen unless the flag is displayed. What the politically correct who now run most of our nation's historic sites neglect to grasp is that millions of people today *do* understand the real meaning of the Confederate Flag—and they are not offended by it. And among those who do not, the vast majority are open-minded and *want* to learn the truth. Recent polls suggest that nearly half of all Southerners still love, honor, and cherish the flag as a genuine symbol of individual freedom and of America's beautiful, unique, multicultural, multiracial Southern heritage. Thus, those Southern historic homes and battle sites that refuse to display the Confederate Flag (and refuse to carry Civil War books written from the South's perspective), are offending the majority of their guests only to spare the sensitivities of a few, the very ones who need to learn the truth the most desperately. Our historic home and museum directors also fail to realize that by not flying, selling, and displaying the Confederate Flag (and by selling *only* pro-North books on the War), they are offending at least 76 percent of the guests who come through their doors, for only 20 percent of Americans label themselves "liberal" ("Tom Sullivan Show," FOX Business News, July 4, 2011), while according to a 2009 Gallup Poll, 40 percent consider themselves "conservative" and 36 percent call themselves "moderates." See Website: www.gallup.com. Please do your part in helping to preserve and honor our Southern heritage: ask the Southern Civil War sites you visit to fly the Confederate Flag and to carry books, like this one, written by *Southern* historians and authors. Let them know that you are offended by the absence of our national symbol, the "Starry Cross," and by the presence of the pro-North books they carry—nearly all which continue to unfairly, and often viciously, smear Dixie using 150 year old anti-South pro-Yankee propaganda.

was so just, so sacred, that had I known all that has come to pass, had I known what was to be inflicted upon me, all that my country was to suffer, all that our posterity was to endure, I would do it all over again.[1041]

Colonel John would have agreed most emphatically with Davis. How do we know? Because the shy but fiery states' righter was a lifelong and ardent member of the State Association of the United Confederate Veterans (UCV), a precursor to today's group, the Sons of Confederate Veterans (SCV), a multicultural, multiracial organization of which I myself am a member. Representatives from the UCV were present at John's funeral, and after the sermon, men like George W. Jackson of the UCV "testified in touching words to the love which Col. McGavock had felt to the Confederate cause and to the Confederate soldiers."[1042]

In addition, John's funeral procession was escorted by a local group of Confederate veterans known as the "McEwen Bivouac" (of which John was an honorary member), who carried his casket to the grave site and lowered it into the ground.

Though a stalwart Democrat, John was actually what we today would call a Libertarian: one who embraced far-right conservatism. Thus it was said of him that: "In early life . . he accepted its [conservative] principles as the surest for the perpetuation of . . . [Southern] rights and liberties . . ."[1043] As a "pure-hearted patriot" for the South and the Confederacy: "Confederate soldiers respected, honored and loved him . . . The Southern Confederacy and its soldiers never had a more generous, true, and unwavering friend."[1044]

Colonel John's wife Carrie, also what we would call a conservative old school Republican, was no less enthusiastic about the Confederate Cause. Of her it was written:

From the beginning of the civil war until its close her devotion to

---

1041. C. Johnson, p. 188.
1042. From one of Col. John W. McGavock's obituaries.
1043. From one of Col. John W. McGavock's obituaries.
1044. From one of Col. John W. McGavock's obituaries.

The McGavocks of Carnton Plantation

the Southern Confederacy was unfaltering, and at the end of that struggle until her death she maintained a deep and active interest in the Confederate veterans.[1045]

Another writer said of Carrie:

For her unwavering loyalty to the Confederate cause, both in war and in peace, her benefactions to the soldier boys living and honor paid to them in death, a spirit which she shared with her noble husband, she will be ever remembered in this County and section. The Confederate cemetery which bears her husband's name, where sleep hundreds of fallen heroes, was the object of her unwavering and tender devotion.[1046]

The couple's children were also profoundly involved in the Confederate Movement. Their daughter Hattie (McGavock) Cowan was not only an active and influential member of the Franklin Chapter of the United Daughters of the Confederacy (UDC), No. 14, she also served as its president on several occasions. After her death one writer revealed the depth of Hattie's involvement in the Southern Cause:

Born of parents whose lives were so closely identified with the history and welfare of Williamson county, and who donated so much of their time and means to the Confederacy, Mrs. Cowan was reared in an atmosphere of loyalty to 'The Lost Cause,' and her deep devotion to patriotic work was one of the main factors in her long and useful life.[1047]

Hattie's husband was Lieutenant Colonel George Limerick Cowan (1842-1919), a courageous Confederate soldier and a member of both General Nathan Bedford Forrest's staff and his famed Escort. During the postbellum period Lieutenant Cowan served as the treasurer of the "Association of Lt. Gen. Nathan Bedford Forrest Escort and Staff," and later was elected president of the beloved (Confederate) Veterans

---

1045. From one of Col. John W. McGavock's obituaries.
1046. From one of Carrie McGavock's obituaries.
1047. From one of Carrie McGavock's obituaries.

THE McGAVOCKS OF CARNTON PLANTATION

Association, a group devoted to aiding former Confederate soldiers and their families.[1048]

Unlike today under Lincoln's involuntary "Union," the McGavocks' world was a sharply contrasted one in which the South was forever pitted against the much reviled North. As such, all of these individuals would have certainly agreed with Chesnut, who, after the War, noted that the South had taken up arms to rid its region of Yankees and Yankee rule. For Southerners had no use for Yankees in Dixie, nor did they find their company pleasurable.[1049] Writes Mary on April 19, 1865:

> How different from ours of them is their estimate of us. How contradictory is their attitude toward us. To keep the despised and iniquitous South within their borders, as part of their country, they are willing to enlist millions of men at home and abroad, and to spend billions, and we know they do not love fighting per se, nor spending money. They are perfectly willing to have three killed for our one. We hear they have all grown rich, through "shoddy," whatever that is.[1050] Genuine Yankees can make a fortune trading jackknives.[1051]

❧ LT. COL. RANDAL McGAVOCK: CONFEDERATE HERO

The Carnton McGavocks were not the only members of this noble family who swore allegiance to the Rebel flag and the Southern Cause. Some of them even gave their lives for the Confederacy. One of the more illustrious of these was John's 1st cousin, Lieutenant Colonel Randal William McGavock.

Randal was born on August 10, 1826 (the year Carnton Plantation was completed) in Nashville, Tennessee. He was the fifth of thirteen children born to Jacob McGavock (1790-1878)—clerk, Nashville's Superior Court, Metro District (to 1812), and Davidson

---

1048. Bradley, NBFES, pp. 139-140, 164.
1049. Chesnut, MCCW, p. 789.
1050. Mary may be speaking here of either a fabric made from reclaimed wool of inferior quality or, more likely, of cheap imitative products, both which are known by the noun shoddy.
1051. Chesnut, DD, pp. 378-379.

THE MCGAVOCKS OF CARNTON PLANTATION

County Court (1816)—and Louisa Caroline Grundy (1798-1878). Louisa was the daughter of two famed Tennesseans: Senator Felix Grundy and Ann Phillips Rodgers. Ann was a sister of Sarah Dougherty Rodgers, the wife of Randal McGavock (1766-1843), who founded and built Carnton.

At an early age Randal evinced a precocious and inquiring mind that would one day serve him well in both politics and on the battlefield. In 1836 Randal attended the Classical and Mathematical Seminary in Nashville, and from 1843 to 1846 he studied at the University of Nashville. From 1847 to 1848 he attended Harvard Law School, which led to a successful career as an attorney that began on May 10, 1849, in Nashville.

On March 20, 1851, out of mere curiosity, the twenty-four year old began a two year tour of Europe, Asia, and Africa. During his time in the British Isles he visited some of his McGavock relatives in Ireland.

In 1854 he became a published author with his book, *A Tennessean Abroad*. The next year, on August 23, 1855, he married Seraphine Deery (1835-1918), a daughter of William Deery (of County Derry, Ireland) and Elizabeth Allison. The newlyweds moved to Allisona, a small country town about twenty miles southeast of Franklin center. Their house was known as the "Deery Family Home."[1052]

From 1858 to 1859, like his granduncle and namesake, Randal served as mayor of Nashville. In May of 1861, just one month before Tennessee seceded from the Union, Randal enlisted in the Tennessee Home Guard and was elected captain. In September of 1861 the Home Guard was turned into Company H of the Tenth Tennessee Regiment, at which point he was promoted to Lieutenant Colonel.[1053]

Randal was captured in February 1862 at the Battle of Fort Donelson and was sent north to the Yankee prison at Fort Warren on Georges Island (Boston Harbor), Boston, Massachusetts. He spent five miserable months there, from March 6 to July 31, 1862. During that time he endeared himself to the Union officers and was released early.

1052. Today beautiful Allisona is the home of a number of country music artists, such as Josh Turner.
1053. Ridley, p. 43.

THE MCGAVOCKS OF CARNTON PLANTATION

Like thousands of other Rebel soldiers discharged from Federal prisons during Lincoln's War, he then returned to the battlefield to proudly continue fighting for his country, the C.S.A.

Just one year later, however, on May 12, 1863, Randal was shot down and killed at the Battle of Raymond, Mississippi, fearlessly leading his men in a charge against Lincoln's Northern interlopers. His body was brought home to Nashville for burial and laid next to his relations in the McGavock family plot at Mount Olivet Cemetery, where his grave can still be seen to this day.

His wife Seraphine remarried twice after Randal passed into the better land. First to Connally F. Trigg (in 1868), and second to Union Major, Ohioan, and U.S. Congressman Augustus Herman Pettibone (in 1898). Seraphine died in Nashville on March 20, 1918, one of the last surviving Confederate widows.

Randal was a fascinating individual with a keen, educated, and inquisitive mind. He traveled purely for enjoyment and proved himself a talented writer by recording his worldwide jaunts in a series of intriguing journals. The McGavocks and all their relatives can be justly proud of the brave, intelligent, and talented Confederate, Lieutenant Colonel Randal William McGavock.[1054]

❧ JOHN BECOMES A CONFEDERATE COLONEL

Randal's 1st cousin John, the owner of Carnton Plantation in 1861, was commissioned a colonel for helping to organize and fund local Confederate regiments.[1055]

Colonel John gladly permitted Company H of the Twentieth Tennessee Regiment Voluntary Infantry to hold their enrollment ceremony at McGavock's Grove on the Mansion's front lawn in May of 1861. Among those who were proudly mustered in that day at Carnton was twenty-one year old Theodrick "Tod" Carter (1840-1864), a local Franklin boy who we will meet again shortly. A few months later, on

---

1054. See Gower, passim.
1055. Some say that he was made colonel earlier, when he worked as an aide-de-camp for then Governor James Knox Polk. The matter is debated.

THE McGAVOCKS OF CARNTON PLANTATION

September 28, 1861, Company F of the Eighth Tennessee Cavalry Battalion was also raised in the beautiful wooded area at Carnton.[1056]

Company H was particularly associated with the town of Franklin, as Confederate soldier, Nashville alderman, and president of the Tennessee State Board of Health, Dr. William Josiah McMurray, noted in 1904:

> Company H of the Twentieth Tennessee Infantry, was raised in and around Franklin, Williamson County, in the early spring of 1861. We believe there were only a few in this company that were not from this grand old county, which was settled almost entirely by the sons and daughters of Virginia and North Carolina, as good and patriotic people as ever supported any government. It was here that lived the McGavocks, McEwins, McMurrays, Mortons, Perkins, Ewins, Fosters, Caruthers, Marshalls, DeGraffenreids and a host of other families equally as true. This county voted in 1860, 1,800 votes, and in 1861 and 1862 sent 2,200 Volunteers into the Confederate armies. With the ancestry that she had, could she have been anything else but Southern to the core?[1057]

Jefferson Davis, the Confederacy's first and only president, then personally asked John if his home could be designated a Rebel field hospital, and if he would be willing to remain at home during the War, in case he and his plantation were needed. Naturally the proud colonel, "Southern to the core" and a Confederate loyalist of the most ardent type, said yes.[1058] No one could know at the time that it would be this very role that would soon make Carnton one the most famous antebellum houses, *and* the most famous haunted Civil War house, in Tennessee.

❧ HOME-SCHOOLING AT CARNTON
As Lincoln's War progressed local schools were suspended due to lack

---

1056. Crutchfield and Holladay, p. 133.
1057. McMurray, p. 164.
1058. If deemed necessary, John was commanded to run the field hospital at Carnton, which explains why he did not lead Rebel troops or fight on the battlefield during Lincoln's War.

of students and teachers, invasion and pillage by Yankees, and simple inflation, all which sapped the life blood from the South's educational system. Thus Southern parents everywhere were forced to return to the practice of home-schooling, since the earliest days of the colonies, a popular American tradition.

The wealthy too, which included the McGavocks, were not immune to school closings across the South. Fortunately for most in this socioeconomic class, tutors were available.

John's and Carrie's surviving children, Martha, Hattie, and Winder, were given their school lessons by Carnton's live-in governess, Elizabeth Field "Lizzy" Clouston (christened in, and probably born about, 1846 in Franklin, Tennessee). Elizabeth would later become locally renowned for marrying one of the wounded Rebel soldiers of the Battle of Franklin II, Roland W. Jones, who she helped nurse back to health at Carnton through the Winter of 1864-1865.[1059]

❧ EARLY CONFEDERATE VICTORIES

The closing of Southern schools was only one of many signs that the War was truly on. Tens of thousands of Southern boys and men eagerly enlisted, encouraged by the hope-filled kisses, carefully packed rucksacks, and lovingly made homespun uniforms bestowed on them by adoring Confederate mothers, sisters, girlfriends, wives, and faithful servants.

Believing that "one Johnny Reb could whip five Billy Yanks," and that the War would be over within a few weeks, it is not surprising that early on enthusiastic Confederate soldiers scored a number of major and minor victories. Among these were a variety of skirmishes, engagements, raids, and battles, including (in chronological order):

Fort Sumter I (April 12-14, 1861)
Cole Camp (June 19, 1861)
Carthage (July 5, 1861)

1059. Elizabeth and Roland married in Williamson County, Tennessee, December 14, 1865.

THE MCGAVOCKS OF CARNTON PLANTATION

Blackburn's Ford (July 18, 1861)
Manassas I (July 21, 1861)
Oak Hills or Wilson's Creek (August 10, 1861)
Kessler's Cross Lanes (August 26, 1861)
Dry Wood Creek (September 2, 1861)
Lexington I (September 13-20, 1861)
Liberty or Blue Mills, or Blue Mills Landing (September 17, 1861)
Barbourville (September 19, 1861)
Greenbrier River (October 3, 1861)
Ball's Bluff (October 21, 1861)
Round Mountain (November 19, 1861)
Chusto-Talasah (December 9, 1861)
Chustenahlah (December 26, 1861)
Sacramento (December 28, 1861)

❧ YANK ATROCITIES: WHY COLONEL JOHN SENT HIS BLACK SERVANTS SOUTH

In early 1862, however, Confederate progress began to lose strength as the Yank invaders closed in on Tennessee from nearly all sides. That year some ten thousands bales of cotton were burned in and around Franklin to prevent it from falling into the hands of the enemy (Lincoln would have sold it and used the money to purchase more military supplies).[1060]

Then, with the capture of Nashville on February 23, 1862—the first major Southern capital to fall in the War[1061]—Colonel John decided to move his thirty-nine black servants to Alabama, and also to Louisiana, where he and his McGavock and Winder relations owned land. This procedure, known as refugeeing,[1062] was far more than the mere desire to protect his multimillion dollar human investment, as critics of the McGavocks contend. It was a grand humanitarian gesture, one that was

---

1060. In Memphis some 100,000 bales of cotton were burned on the approach of the Federal armies. Owsley, p. 47.
1061. R. L. Mode, p. 31.
1062. E. M. Thomas, p. 240.

THE MCGAVOCKS OF CARNTON PLANTATION

for the good of the McGavock servants themselves.

White Yankee soldiers were well-known for their racism and utter intolerance of blacks. Chesnut remarked on an incident in which a Southern friend of hers, Mary Kirkland, and her black servants were confronted by white Union soldiers during the War:

> Mary Kirkland has had experience with the Yankees. She has been pronounced the most beautiful woman on this side of the Atlantic, and has been spoiled accordingly in all society. When the Yankees came, Monroe, their negro manservant, told her to stand up and hold two of her children in her arms, with the other two pressed as close against her knees as they could get. Mammy Selina and Lizzie then stood grimly on each side of their young missis and her children. For four mortal hours the soldiers surged through the rooms of the house. Sometimes Mary and her children were roughly jostled against the wall, but Mammy and Lizzie were staunch supporters. The Yankee soldiers taunted the negro women for their foolishness in standing by their cruel slave-owners, and taunted Mary with being glad of the protection of her poor ill-used slaves. Monroe meanwhile had one leg bandaged and pretended to be lame, so that he might not be enlisted as a soldier, and kept making pathetic appeals to Mary.
>
> "Don't answer them back, Miss Mary," said he. "Let 'em say what dey want to; don't answer 'em back. Don't give 'em any chance to say you are impudent to 'em."
>
> One [Yankee] man said to her: "Why do you shrink from us and avoid us so? We did not come here to fight for negroes; we hate them. At Port Royal I saw a beautiful white woman driving in a wagon with a coal-black negro man. If she had been anything to me I would have shot her through the heart." "Oh, oh!" said Lizzie, "that's the way you talk in here. I'll remember that when you begin outside to beg me to run away with you."
>
> Finally poor Aunt Betsy, Mary's mother, fainted from pure fright and exhaustion. Mary put down her baby and sprang to her mother, who was lying limp in a chair, and fiercely called out, "Leave this room, you wretches! Do you mean to kill my mother? She is ill; I must put her to bed." Without a word they all slunk out ashamed. "If I had only tried that hours ago," she now said. Outside they remarked that she was "an insolent rebel huzzy, who thinks herself too good to speak to a soldier of the United States," and one of them said: "Let us go in and break her mouth." But the

THE MCGAVOCKS OF CARNTON PLANTATION

better ones held the more outrageous back. Monroe slipped in again and said: "Missy, for God's sake, when dey come in be sociable with 'em. Dey will kill you."
"Then let me die."[1063]

Chesnut's story of Mary Kirkland and the Union soldiers aptly illustrates one of the many reasons Lincoln would not permit blacks to serve as active combatants in the U.S. military during the first half of his War: Yankee racism was so severe that enlisting blacks in the Union forces would have actually endangered them more than being on the battlefield.

Yet Lincoln himself had long been vehemently against enlisting blacks. On July 21, 1862, for instance, he met with his cabinet and stated: "I am averse to arming the negroes,"[1064] just one of dozens of times in which, for obviously racist reasons, he flatly refused to even entertain the idea.

Despite his foolhardy resistance, at the start of the War thousands of blacks begged to be allowed to enlist to fight for the Union.[1065] In April 1861, as just one example, Jacob Dodson, an experienced and well respected black soldier, offered himself and 300 other African-Americans for military service. Lincoln was not interested, however, and had his secretary of war, Simon Cameron, send back the following brusque reply to a stunned Dodson:

> This Department has no intention at present to call into the service of the Government any colored soldiers.[1066]

On August 6, 1862, Lincoln's War Department sent a similar message to Edward Salomon, the governor of Wisconsin that read: "The President declines to receive Indians or negroes as troops."[1067] Or as Secretary of War Cameron put it even more indelicately, the present

---

1063. Chesnut, DD, pp. 385-386.
1064. Tyler, PH, p. 12.
1065. Faust, s.v. "black soldiers"; Quarles, p. 29.
1066. ORA, Ser. 3, Vol. 1, p. 133.
1067. ORA, Ser. 3, Vol. 2, p. 314. See also Dee Brown, pp. 179-180.

conflict "forbids the use of savages."[1068] And so tens of thousands of blacks (and Native-Americans) were turned away by Lincoln during the first two years of the War.

Blacks who managed to enlist without being noticed, were soon caught and "honorably discharged." White clergyman Moncure D. Conway wrote: "At Washington I found that the mere mention of a Negro made the President nervous . . ."[1069] Thus, in Cincinnati, Ohio, a black recruiting office was shut down by police, who told the blacks who had shown up to fight for Lincoln: this is the white man's war, and you damned niggers are not needed or wanted![1070]

When, in January 1863, Lincoln was finally forced to give into "military necessity" and began allowing full-fledged black recruitment,[1071] the reaction of his white troops was predicable: they hissed and booed, desertions increased, and a general "demoralization" set in across the entire Federal military.[1072]

One of the more demoralized of Lincoln's commanders was General Joseph "Fighting Joe" Hooker (1814-1879), head of the Army of the Potomac. Hooker wrote a scathing report about the president's Emancipation Proclamation, noting that:

> At that time [early 1863] . . . a majority of the officers, especially those high in rank, were hostile to the policy of the [U.S.] Government in the conduct of the war. The emancipation proclamation had been published a short time before, and a large element of the [Union] army had taken sides antagonistic to it, declaring that they would never have embarked in the war had they anticipated the action of the government.[1073]

The mere mention of the idea of "black enlistment" brought

1068. ORA, Ser. 3, Vol. 1, p. 184. We will note here that though Lincoln and the Union at first refused to allow Indians to serve in the Federal armies, Native-Americans, like Stand Watie and tens of thousands of others, were welcomed into the Confederate armies from day one.
1069. Conway, p. 108.
1070. Reid, p. 2; Barney, pp. 127-128.
1071. See Nicolay and Hay, ALCW, Vol. 2, p. 288.
1072. P. Smith, p. 308.
1073. Henderson, Vol. 2, p. 411.

many white regiments close to insurrection. A Yankee soldier with the Ninetieth Illinois reported on the general feeling among his fellow Union compatriots at the time: Not a single one of us wants to fight with Negroes. This is *our* war. Blacks should stay out of it![1074]

Northern Catholics were just as displeased with Lincoln's new focus on enrolling black soldiers and the abolition of slavery. New York's Archbishop John Hughes declared that he and his flock, along with the overwhelming majority of Union troops, had no intention of fighting a bloody and costly war just to satisfy a group of rabid Yankee abolitionists.[1075]

Northern white outrage was somewhat mitigated when Lincoln ordered the army and navy to be racially segregated, but newly recruited blacks were not happy with the president's command that all colored troops were to be officered by whites.[1076] As such, most objective historians have had to concede that many Northern soldiers were irrationally vicious toward black soldiers.[1077]

White Yankee racism continued throughout the War. During inclement weather, for example, white Northern soldiers were known to throw black Yankee soldiers out of their tents using derogatory language and raised fists.[1078]

Most white Union officers never completely accepted leading black troops as there was no status or honor in it. In fact, so few white officers could be found who were willing to "lower" themselves to leading blacks that white privates, induced with the promise of promotion,[1079] finally had to be coerced into taking the positions.[1080]

The situation got so hostile that Federal officers had to literally be ordered to treat black soldiers the same as white soldiers, and the "n" word, along with degrading disciplinary action and offensive language

---

1074. P. Smith, p. 308.
1075. Foote, Vol. 1, p. 538.
1076. Katcher, CWSB, p. 159; Foote, Vol. 2, p. 393.
1077. Eaton, HSC, p. 263.
1078. Catton, Vol. 3, p. 24.
1079. W. B. Garrison, CWC, p. 105.
1080. Simmons, s.v. "Negro Troops."

aimed at blacks, had to be banned with the promise of harsh punishments for violators.[1081] Meanwhile white Union soldiers continued to put on minstrel shows that satirized and humiliated African-Americans, a not uncommon form of entertainment, particularly aboard U.S. warships.[1082]

But Northern white racism in the U.S. army often manifested in far more serious and diabolical ways. Southern diaries, letters, and journals are replete with reports of incredible Yankee brutality against not only white Southern women they came across, but black Southern women as well, even those that had at first cheered them on as liberators. Yankee crimes against black females included robbery, pillage, beatings, torture, rape, and even murder.[1083]

Southern black males were treated just as badly by their Northern "emancipators." Those who survived such crimes were taken, at gunpoint and against their will, from their peaceful, healthy, and safe lives of service and domesticity on the plantation, to the filth, hardships, and dangers of life on the battlefield, where at least 50 percent of them died alone in muddy ditches fighting for the Yanks against their own native homeland, the South.[1084]

Those who resisted "involuntary enlistment" were sometimes shot or bayoneted on the spot. When black soldiers rebelled against the abuse of the white Yankee soldiers, they were whipped.[1085] Both white and black Union soldiers mistreated Southern slaves who remained loyal to Dixie, entering their homes, shooting bullets through the walls, overturning furniture, and stealing various personal items.[1086]

As mentioned, many newly "freed" black males were used as shock troops: driven onto the battlefield first in an effort to save white soldiers, they died in large numbers, mowed down by Confederate iron, lead, and steel.[1087] This type of usage is almost certainly what racist

---

1081. P. Smith, p. 309.
1082. ORA, Ser. 3, Vol. 4, p. 1029; Katcher, CWSB, pp. 128, 158-159.
1083. Gragg, p. 192.
1084. Pollard, SHW, Vol. 2, pp. 196-198.
1085. Wiley, SN, pp. 241, 309-310, 317.
1086. Henry, ATSF, p. 248.
1087. Jordan, p. 229; Cornish, pp. 87, 269.

THE MCGAVOCKS OF CARNTON PLANTATION

Lincoln was intimating in his August 26, 1863, letter to James C. Conkling, when he wrote:

> ... whatever negroes can be got to do as soldiers, leaves just so much less for white soldiers to do, in saving the Union.[1088]

Lincoln's reluctant concession to black enlistment was not at all what either abolitionists or African-Americans had hoped it would be. For in the beginning he turned nearly all freed black men into common U.S. army laborers, doing drudgery work little different from what they had experienced as slaves (for example, construction, serving officers, cooking, cutting firewood, and washing).[1089]

Lincoln's Emancipation Proclamation itself spells out the future role of the black Union soldier—*and it was not combat*. It was simple guard duty, as the January 1, 1863, edict plainly states:

> I further declare and make known that such [black] persons of suitable condition will be received into the armed service of the United States to garrison forts, positions, stations, and other places, and to man vessels of all sorts in said service.[1090]

Lincoln's Emancipation Proclamation was followed to the letter, which is why the first black soldiers in the U.S. military were not allowed to serve as active combatants. Rather they were signed up specifically to work as ordinary grunts, teamsters, blacksmiths, carpenters, masons, scouts, longshoremen, pioneers, wheelwrights, medical assistants, orderlies, laundry workers, spies, and of course, "slaves,"[1091] almost anything but armed fighters.[1092]

This so-called "Freedmen's labor system," overseen by Yankee General Nathaniel Prentiss Banks, was so blatantly racist that he was roundly criticized across the North for doing nothing more than putting

---

1088. Nicolay and Hay, ALCW, Vol. 2, p. 398.
1089. Simmons, s.v. "Negro Troops."
1090. Nicolay and Hay, ALCW, Vol. 2, p. 288.
1091. Wiley, SN, p. 321.
1092. Buckley, p. 82.

blacks back into slavery. The brutal U.S. government program was also rife with corruption and fraud: freed blacks were regularly whipped while their already paltry wage was often "withheld" by unscrupulous and inhumane Northerners who pocketed the money then disappeared.[1093]

The fact that one of Lincoln's top officers, the cross-eyed General Benjamin F. "the Beast" Butler, insisted on referring to freed Southern blacks as "contraband" (meaning "illegal property") certainly did not help the cause of black civil rights. But Lincoln never objected to the dehumanizing title. In fact he approved it. The name stuck and even continued to be widely used in the North after the War.

Southern blacks, in fact, were far from being truly free after Lincoln's Emancipation Proclamation. Indeed, this is why Lincoln and the rest of the North referred to them as "freedmen" rather than as "freemen": they had been freed from the "shackles of slavery," but they were not yet free from the shackles of Northern racism.

Lincoln's own racism was seemingly infinite. Not only did he refuse to grant Northern black soldiers equal treatment in any way,[1094] he also gave them half the pay of white soldiers.[1095] *White* U.S. privates were paid thirteen dollars per month, while *black* U.S. privates were paid just seven dollars per month.[1096] (Contrast this with the Confederacy: in some Southern states blacks were actually paid up to three times the rate of whites for military service.[1097])

Three of the seven dollars of the black soldiers' monthly pay was a deduction for clothing, a deduction not imposed on white Union soldiers. Often even this small amount was withheld from black recruits by Yank officers, who sometimes simply stole the money, only one of dozens of ways the U.S. defrauded African-Americans during the War.[1098]

To add to the insult, blacks could not officially be promoted

---

1093. Wiley, SN, pp. 201-202, 212-213.
1094. W. B. Garrison, LNOK, p. 176.
1095. J. M. McPherson, BCF, pp. 788-789.
1096. Mullen, p. 25.
1097. Channing, p. 23.
1098. Wiley, SN, pp. 322-323.

THE MCGAVOCKS OF CARNTON PLANTATION

beyond the level of non-commissioned officer.[1099] And even when they were, black officers were paid the same as white privates. At least eighteen blacks who protested Lincoln's inequitable wages were charged with "mutiny" and executed by hanging or firing squad. These executions went on even after Lincoln's death and the War had ended. As late as December 1, 1865, six black privates accused of mutiny (that is, for protesting Lincoln's racist pay scale) were rounded up and killed by musketry at Fernandina, Florida. This was a full year and a half after the U.S. Congress authorized retroactive equal pay for black soldiers in June 1864.[1100] Lincoln, an outspoken and self-admitted anti-Christian "infidel," had not been the forgiving type, and neither were many of his officers and soldiers.

A war correspondent for the New York *Evening Post* described what he witnessed in a typical Yankee army camp: most of the white Yankee soldiers and their officers routinely approached black soldiers in the harshest, most vulgar, and most inhumane manner, only speaking to them with depraved curse words and vicious criticisms.[1101]

In 1862 an eyewitness living on Hilton Head Island, South Carolina, reported that the occupying white Yankee soldiers there spoke horribly to the blacks, using the most insulting words, while in Norfolk, Virginia, a freed black woman wrote of seeing other blacks being severely and regularly abused by Union men. Yankee crimes in the Palmetto State included the destruction of property, pillage, assault and battery, and even rape, against innocent black females who had fled to them, believing them to be liberators. This same African-American woman forlornly penned: it looks like I'm Master Lincoln's slave from now on.[1102]

It is obvious that even after reluctantly allowing blacks into the

---

1099. Wiley, SN, pp. 323-324. Out of the 200,000 blacks who served in the U.S. military during the War for Southern Independence, only about 100 eventually held officer commissions. But even these were ultimately replaced by white officers because, as Yankee General Nathaniel P. Banks reported, "the appointment of colored officers is detrimental to the service." ORA, Ser. 3, Vol. 3, p. 46.
1100. Alotta, pp. 26-28.
1101. Channing, p. 129.
1102. Channing, p. 131; Jimerson, p. 81; J. D. Fowler, p. 317.

The McGavocks of Carnton Plantation

Union army and navy, Lincoln and his military men continued to see them as little more than servile laborers and cannon-fodder.[1103]

Black civil rights leaders, like Sojourner Truth, complained to Lincoln about his pitiful treatment of black soldiers, but to no avail.[1104] Frederick Douglass rightly asked the president: if blacks were good enough to serve under General George Washington, why are they not now good enough to serve under General George McClellan?[1105]

Most black men probably did not want to serve under (George Brinton) McClellan (1826-1885) anyway. Like many other Northern officers, McClellan spent much of his time enforcing the Fugitive Slave Law of 1850, returning runaway servants to their owners. This was the same law that Lincoln promised to strengthen in his First Inaugural Address,[1106] despite the fact that overturning it, or even ignoring it, would have helped bring slavery to an end much sooner.[1107]

Southern female servants and their children, meanwhile, could expect little better in the way of treatment from their "Northern emancipators." Driven from their homes in cattle-like droves, they were set to work on "U.S. government plantations," so-called "abandoned" Southern farms.[1108]

In reality these were Confederate plantations whose original owners had been chased off or killed, replaced by Yankee bosses who often withheld food, clothing, bedding, and medicine from their new charges, resulting in an appalling death toll.[1109] Though their numbers were never recorded, eyewitnesses testify that the vast majority of blacks rounded up and put in "contraband camps" died as well, the U.S. government apparently placing little importance on their survival.[1110]

Southern blacks were so frightened of Lincoln's soldiers that

---

1103. Simmons, s.v. "Negro Troops."
1104. McKissack and McKissack, pp. 138-139.
1105. N. A. Hamilton, p. 120; Förster and Nagler, p. 207; Masur, p. 110; J. M. McPherson, NCW, p. 163.
1106. Nicolay and Hay, ALCW, Vol. 2, p. 1.
1107. DiLorenzo, RL, p. 21.
1108. L. H. Johnson, NAS, p. 135.
1109. Pollard, SHW, Vol. 2, p. 198.
1110. Wiley, SN, p. 202.

The McGavocks of Carnton Plantation

they went to almost any length to avoid being taken away by them, for they knew that the Yanks were likely to torture them, force them into labor camps, or even kill them. Some simply wanted to escape hearing the Yanks' "ungodly speech" or having to gaze upon their "hideous faces."

One of the most ingenious methods Southern blacks came up with to escape being "freed" by Yankees was to malinger or feign illness. Many a Southern black, for instance, was spared "a fate worse than death" by faking a limp, wearing a perfectly good arm in a sling, or taking to bed with a host of alarming moaning sounds.[1111]

The dread of Northern racism was horrendous enough in Dixie that during the War most black servants did not have to be sent South. They went voluntarily, requested to be moved, or simply moved by themselves. The reality of this fact was brought to life by Chesnut. In 1862 she noted in her journal that after my cousin General Richard Taylor's home had been attacked and looted by foraying Yanks, his black servants then moved themselves southward to the city of Algiers, not far from New Orleans. Apparently the white Yankee penchant for intimidating and abusing Southern blacks was contagious. According to Chesnut, black Union soldiers treated Southern blacks even worse than white Union soldiers.[1112]

Yanks viewed Southern blacks no better after the War than they did during the conflict. We have record of an incident in South Carolina of a black man running up to thank a white Federal soldier for Lincoln's emancipation. The grateful former servant threw his arms around the Union general, embracing him affectionately. But the Yank violently pulled himself away, then quickly pulled a gun and shot the innocent man dead. He wanted nothing to do with such ridiculous falderal, he screamed. He then calmly walked away.[1113]

It was not just Southern blacks who feared white Yankees. Tens of thousands of Northern blacks had experienced the horrors of "Yankee rule" between 1641—the year it was legalized in the first Northern state

---

1111. P. Smith, pp. 362-363.
1112. Chesnut, DD, pp. 227-228, 386.
1113. Chesnut, MCCW, p. 798.

THE MCGAVOCKS OF CARNTON PLANTATION

(Massachusetts),[1114] and 1862—the year New York state officially finally ceased trading in slaves (we will remember that it was in that year that Lincoln had New York ship captain and Yankee slave trader, Captain Nathaniel Gordon, executed for trafficking in human chattel).

As the instigators of the American slave trade, Northern blacks certainly had much to fear from their Yankee masters. Former Northern slave Sojourner Truth, for example, once referred to the U.S. flag, not as the "Stars and Stripes," but as the "Scars and Stripes."[1115]

On another occasion, in 1864, over a year after the Emancipation Proclamation had been issued, Truth discovered, to her horror, that whites near Washington, D.C. were kidnaping the black children of freed Southern servants right under Lincoln's nose, and forcing them back into Northern slavery. The small community the freed blacks lived in, ironically called "Freedman's Village," had been set up by the U.S. army to help newly emancipated African-Americans adjust to living in free white society. Truth used the justice system to have the children released and returned to their parents. But not before her own life was threatened by the violent and unrepentant Yankee slavers.[1116]

With such information at hand, can there be any doubt that Colonel John's altruism in refugeeing his servants by sending them further South during the War saved their lives? And is it any wonder that even though most Southern slaves had been "freed" by Lincoln on January 1, 1863, that John's servants went willingly with him further south for safety, and voluntarily remained there until after the War?

❧ THE McGAVOCKS & THE HAND OF FATE

As Lincoln's War progressed the hand of fate soon dealt several more blows to the McGavock family. On January 27, 1862, twenty-three year old Josephine P. Southall (b. February 12, 1839), a daughter of Colonel John's younger sister Mary Cloyd McGavock, passed away. A few days

---

1114. G. H. Moore, pp. 5, 11, 17-19.
1115. Gilbert, p. 254.
1116. McKissack and McKissack, pp. 142, 143, 144.

THE MCGAVOCKS OF CARNTON PLANTATION

later, on January 31, 1862, Elizabeth Crockett died. Elizabeth, of the famed Crockett family, is the wife of John's 1st cousin, Lysander McGavock, founder of Midway Plantation in nearby Brentwood.[1117]

On February 12, 1862, Colonel John's older brother, James Randal McGavock (b. January 9, 1812), died at the age of fifty, leaving behind his wife Louisa C. Chenault (1813-1885) and their beautiful plantation Riverside, located just across the Harpeth River. Louisa's mother, Mary Eleanor Rodgers (b. about 1790), is the sister of Ann Phillips Rodgers, who married Felix Grundy. (John had already lost one brother: an unnamed male who came into the world, and left it, on September 25, 1816.)

The next wave of death was particularly bitter. On March 19, 1862, nearly one year after Tennessee broke away from the Union, the Colonel's and Carrie's oldest child, twelve and a half year old Martha Winder, died of complications related to a heart problem. She was buried in the McGavock Family Cemetery at Carnton, where her grave can still be seen.

Soon after, the end came for another one of James Randal McGavock's daughters: thirteen year old Ann Louise McGavock (b. September 9, 1849) died on October 7, 1862. Just weeks later, on October 23, 1862, John's younger sister, forty-five year old Mary Cloyd McGavock (b. September 4, 1817), herself died.

A few months afterward, one of James Randal McGavock's daughters, Colonel John's niece, passed away on September 29, 1863: twenty-six year old Sarah "Sallie" McGavock (b. March 12, 1837). Sarah, of Riverside Plantation, was the owner of the McGavocks' shamrock-emblazoned family Bible, which is sometimes on display at Carnton (usually in the ladies' parlor).

ॐ LINCOLN, WAR CRIMINAL

While the Grim Reaper was busy knocking on Carnton's door, as well

---

[1117]. Elizabeth's 1st cousin, Samuel Crockett, III (1772-1827), was the founder of the famous rifle making homestead known as Forge Seat, in Brentwood, Tennessee.

THE MCGAVOCKS OF CARNTON PLANTATION

as those of several other McGavock relations,[1118] Lincoln's bloody, needless, and illegal War proceeded unabated.

The U.S. president did not sit idly by as his troops were invading the new foreign nation to the south. He was busy making sure that his fight against states' rights would end with a Northern triumph and the total subjugation of Dixie.

To begin with Lincoln had sheer numbers on his side: the North, with a booming population of 19,798,866 people, sent 2,898,304 soldiers out onto the field. The South, in contrast, with its much smaller (white) population of 7,215,525 people, could only manage to send 1,228,000 soldiers into battle.[1119]

But just in case this was not enough, Lincoln decided to prevent all possibility of Union defeat by committing a truly stunning number of well chronicled constitutional, civil, political, ethical, social, and moral crimes. These atrocities included:

- Completely subverting (and perverting) the Constitution.[1120]
- The ruling of the American people by "arbitrary power."[1121]
- Arresting and deporting Yankee antiwar advocates, like Ohio Congressman Clement L. Vallandigham, who, though a civilian, was illegally tried by a military court.[1122]
- Indiscriminately arresting and trying (by military commission) civilian draft resistors and others suspected of "disloyalty."[1123]
- Seizing rail and telegraph lines leading to the capital.[1124]
- Suppressing and shutting down over 300 hundred pro-peace Northern

---

1118. Infant mortality was extraordinarily common during the Victorian era. One of John's close cousins, Harriet Russel McGavock (1828-1903), after whom he named his daughter Harriet ("Hattie"), had nine children with her husband William A. Goodwyn (1824-1898). All nine died young (before reaching adulthood) from various diseases. One died in 1859, four died in 1860, two died in 1863, and two died in 1875.
1119. Katcher, CWSB, p. 46.
1120. Crocker, p. 59.
1121. Dean, p. 154.
1122. Scruggs, p. 24; Napolitano, p. 69.
1123. Neely, pp. 172-175.
1124. Tatalovich and Daynes, p. 322.

The McGavocks of Carnton Plantation

    newspapers, and arresting their owners.[1125]
- Censoring telegraph communications.[1126]
- Torturing both Northern soldiers (accused of desertion) and Northern citizens (accused of espousing antiwar sentiment, which Lincoln referred to as "treason");[1127] the preferred methods were "violent cold water torture" and being suspended by handcuffed wrists.[1128]
- Murdering unarmed Confederate prisoners, even in Southern states (like Kentucky), that had not joined the Confederacy.[1129]
- Prohibiting former Confederates and supporters of the Confederacy from voting in the 1864 election, thereby helping to guarantee that he would be reelected.[1130]
- Using spies, detectives, "secret agents,"[1131] fraud, and bribery to insure his reelection in 1864, resulting in "the foulest corruptions," said to have been obvious at every level of his party.[1132]
- Forcing foreigners (that is, citizens of the Confederate States of America) to take an oath of allegiance to the United States of America, or face arrest and imprisonment.[1133]
- Illegally suspending the writ of *habeas corpus* across the entire U.S.,[1134] and for the first time in U.S. history.[1135]
- Assuming the extraordinary right of "extraordinary powers"[1136]

1125. L. H. Johnson, NAS, p. 125. See e.g., Nicolay and Hay, ALCW, Vol. 2, p. 416.
1126. DiLorenzo, LU, p. 52.
1127. See e.g., Nicolay and Hay, ALCW, Vol. 2, p. 521.
1128. Neely, pp. 109-112.
1129. Pollard, LC, p. 413.
1130. See e.g., Nicolay and Hay, ALCW, Vol. 2, p. 417.
1131. See e.g., Nicolay and Hay, ALCW, Vol. 2, pp. 486, 489-490.
1132. Mitgang, p. 402; D. H. Donald, L, p. 385.
1133. Nicolay and Hay, ALCW, Vol. 2, pp. 442-444.
1134. Nicolay and Hay, ALCW, Vol. 2, pp. 541-542.
1135. Burns and Peltason, p. 192. For other examples of Lincoln's suspension of *habeas corpus*, see Nicolay and Hay, ALCW, Vol. 2, pp. 39, 54, 85, 93, 239, 406-407.
1136. See Nicolay and Hay, ALCW, Vol. 2, pp. 60, 124. Lincoln believed, without proof, that during civil disruption the president possessed certain powers not available to him during times of peace. As he himself said: "*I think* the Constitution invests its Commander-in-Chief with the law of war in time of war" [emphasis added]. Nicolay and Hay, ALCW, Vol. 2, p. 397.

(unconstitutional and therefore illegal).[1137]
- Prohibiting the emancipation of slaves by his cabinet members and Union military officers, such as General John. C. Frémont,[1138] General David Hunter,[1139] John W. Phelps,[1140] Jim Lane,[1141] and General Simon Cameron[1142] (which proves once and for all, if nothing else does, that Lincoln did not wage war against the South over slavery).[1143]
- Unlawfully ordering a naval blockade of Southern ports (unlawful because Lincoln never recognized the Confederacy as a separate nation and war had not yet been officially declared).[1144]
- Completely removing every inhabitant living in certain counties, "*en masse*," as Lincoln put it, in the Southern states.[1145]
- "Checking" (that is, arresting) clergymen who "become dangerous to the public interest" (that is, who contradicted Lincoln).[1146]
- Declaring all medicines contraband of war (which helped kill countless thousands of Southerners, both soldiers and civilians, not to mention thousands of Yankee soldiers held in Confederate prisons).[1147]
- Threatening war on any nation, particularly England and France, if they in any way supported, aided, or recognized the Confederacy (not necessarily illegal but highly unethical as the U.S. herself had long insisted on the right to assist "belligerent"

1137. Christian, p. 13.
1138. Leech, p. 151; Black, p. 165. Lincoln later stripped Frémont of his command for freeing slaves in his assigned military area. K. C. Davis, p. 439.
1139. R. W. Black, p. 165; Wiley, SN, pp. 296-298; Leech, pp. 305-306.
1140. Quarles, pp. 115-116.
1141. Quarles, pp. 113-114.
1142. D. H. Donald, L, p. 363; Leech, p. 155.
1143. Lincoln admitted that he nullified the emancipation proclamations of his officers because, as he put it, there was no "indispensable necessity." Nicolay and Hay, ALCW, Vol. 2, p. 508. The nation's 4 million slaves (North and South) must have wondered what he meant by this.
1144. W. B. Garrison, CWC, p. 13; Findlay and Findlay, pp. 84-85; C. Adams, p. 39; Owsley, pp. 79-80, 229-267; K. L. Hall, s.v. "Lincoln, Abraham"; "Civil War."
1145. Nicolay and Hay, ALCW, Vol. 2, p. 416.
1146. Nicolay and Hay, ALCW, Vol. 2, pp. 464, 491.
1147. Tyler, PH, pp. 13-14; Bailyn, Dallek, Davis, Donald, Thomas, and Wood, p. 5; Grissom, pp. 126-127; C. Adams, p. 57.

nations, for example, in 1793, 1841, and 1855. As recently as the 1860s, Lincoln's Secretary of State Seward had declared that the U.S. be allowed to sell arms to Mexico, which was then at war with France. Such facts, however, did not suit Lincoln's purposes, so he chose not to remind the world of them).[1148]

- Proclaiming Confederate privateersmen "insurgents"[1149] and "pirates,"[1150] subject to the death penalty[1151] (privateering, that is, working on an armed privately-owned vessel, was and is a legal profession).[1152]
- Intimidating judges.[1153]
- Closing the post office in an effort to prevent anti-Lincoln, antiwar mail from being sent or delivered.[1154]
- Forcing all Federal employees to contribute 5 percent of their annual income to his 1864 reelection campaign.[1155]
- Refusing to exchange prisoners (which aided in the deaths of thousands of soldiers, both Confederate and Federal).[1156]
- Defying the Supreme Court.[1157]
- Refusing to officially acknowledge Jefferson Davis as the president of the Confederacy.[1158]
- Instituting the largest number of military drafts in U.S. history.[1159]
- Fabricating heretofore unknown offices, such as "military governor," in conquered Southern states.[1160]
- Shutting down the governments of entire Northern states and arresting

---

1148. Owsley, pp. 405, 401-412. For one of Lincoln's and Seward's war threats against England, see Nicolay and Hay, ALCW, Vol. 2, pp. 48-51.
1149. Nicolay and Hay, ALCW, Vol. 2, p. 146.
1150. See Nicolay and Hay, ALCW, Vol. 2, p. 95.
1151. Gragg, p. 73; Tyler, PH, pp. 13-14.
1152. Mish, s.v. "privateer."
1153. J. Davis, RFCG, Vol. 2, pp. 460-468.
1154. Tatalovich and Daynes, p. 322.
1155. W. B. Garrison, LNOK, p. 281.
1156. C. Adams, pp. 57, 208-209; Grissom, pp. 126-127.
1157. Burns and Peltason, p. 437.
1158. Pollard, LC, p. 413.
1159. D. H. Donald, L, pp. 429, 450, 489, 510, 539.
1160. See e.g., Nicolay and Hay, Vol. 2, p. 131.

members of their state legislatures (usually for suspicion of advocating peace with the South); one of the more notable of these was the state of Maryland, which originally had hoped to join the Confederacy.[1161]
- Establishing U.S. military rule in a foreign nation (the C.S.A.), and even within states still part of the Union (such as Missouri).[1162]
- Inaugurating America's first federal monetary monopoly.[1163]
- Imprisoning some 38,000 to 50,000 Northern civilians (men, women, and children),[1164] without trial, many for as long as four years.[1165]
- Incarcerating civilians, like Rebel Vice President Alexander H. Stephens, in military prisons.[1166]
- Levying the first personal income tax, launching what would later become the Internal Revenue Service (IRS).[1167]
- Preventing governmental debate over secession.[1168]
- Ordering the first and only mass execution (and that of his own citizens) by a president in U.S. history.[1169]
- Changing the meaning of the "United States" from plural to singular.[1170]
- Establishing provisional courts in conquered Southern states[1171] (this was illegal because Dixie's own civilian courts remained open

---

1161. J. Davis, RFCG, Vol. 2, pp. 460-468. For more on Lincoln's illegal subjugation of Maryland, see Pollard, LC, pp. 123-125.
1162. See e.g., Nicolay and Hay, ALCW, Vol. 2, p. 416.
1163. DiLorenzo, LU, p. 137.
1164. Lott, p. 158.
1165. Neely, pp. 113-114.
1166. Stephens, RAHS, pp. 356-357, passim.
1167. Hacker, p. 584; Napolitano, p. 74.
1168. Christian, p. 14; Hacker, p. 581.
1169. Nicolay and Hay, ALCW, Vol. 2, p. 267; D. H. Donald, L, 392-395; W. B. Garrison, CWTFB, p. 62; C. Adams, p. 210.
1170. DiLorenzo, LU, pp. 75, 89, 90.
1171. Lincoln lied to the American public, telling them that the courts in *all* of the Confederate states had been "suppressed," giving him alleged justification for imposing military rule and committing countless other crimes in the South. See Nicolay and Hay, ALCW, Vol. 2, p. 99. Actually, the courts in the Southern states remained open throughout the War. Any that were "suppressed" were suppressed by Lincoln himself. For an example of Lincoln's illegal establishment of a provisional court in a foreign country, in this case, the Confederate States of America, see Nicolay and Hay, ALCW, Vol. 2, pp. 248-249.

The McGavocks of Carnton Plantation

during the War).[1172]
- Illegally creating the state of West Virginia from the state of Virginia[1173] (Lincoln encouraged the western area of Virginia to secede while he was at war with the South because she had seceded).[1174]
- Stationing U.S. soldiers at polling places in order to intimidate voters into casting their votes for him.[1175]
- Rigging Northern elections to skew the outcome in his favor.[1176]
- Bribing voters, soldiers, and fellow politicians to vote for his party.[1177]

Lincoln even signed an order for the arrest of the Supreme Court's Chief Justice Roger B. Taney, simply because Taney had told him that suspending *habeas corpus* was unconstitutional and therefore illegal. Little wonder that even pro-North writers say that the Lincoln administration represented not only the worst period for civil liberties up until then, but it also ranks as one of the worst in all of American history.[1178] Some 19th-Century Northerners, like Constitution-loving Henry Clay Dean (1822-1887)—who was arrested by the president for promoting peace, called "Lincoln's reign" a "vibration between anarchy and despotism."[1179]

Lincoln later tried to justify his criminal activities with this bizarre declaration, sounding more like a megalomanic madman than a U.S. president:

> I felt that measures otherwise unconstitutional might become lawful by becoming indispensable to the preservation of the

---

1172. E. M. Thomas, p. 152.
1173. Lincoln knew this was unconstitutional, which is why he brought the issue up with his cabinet members on December 23, 1862. Nicolay and Hay, ALCW, Vol. 2, p. 283.
1174. It is illegal for a section of a state to secede from the parent state without the parent state's approval. Virginia never authorized the secession of West Virginia, thus she is not legally a state today. C. Adams, p. 58. See also W. B. Garrison, LNOK, pp. 193-197; D. H. Donald, L, pp. 300-301, 405; DiLorenzo, RL, pp. 148-149.
1175. Mitgang, pp. 403, 404.
1176. L. H. Johnson, NAS, pp. 123-124; Horn, IE, p. 217; DiLorenzo, LU, p. 52; Simpson, p. 62.
1177. W. B. Garrison, ACW, pp. 194-195; DeGregorio, s.v. "Abraham Lincoln"; D. H. Donald, L, p. 249.
1178. Neely, p. 53.
1179. Dean, p. 11. See also Randall, CPUL, passim.

THE MCGAVOCKS OF CARNTON PLANTATION

Constitution through the preservation of the nation. Right or wrong, I assumed this ground and I now avow it.[1180]

Believing that he was "preserving" the Constitution when in fact he was destroying it, reveals the true depth of Lincoln's distorted thinking.

Some of Lincoln's crimes were more unethical and immoral than illegal, such as when he became the first president to "pack" the Supreme Court with his own hand-picked justices,[1181] or when he became the president who fired more appointees from previous administrations than any other in history,[1182] or when he ordered the largest mass execution in U.S. history.[1183]

We must also mention an incident that occurred on October 31, 1864, a mere eight days before the upcoming presidential election (on November 8, 1864). It was on Halloween that his supporters in Congress, at his backroom prompting, intentionally admitted Nevada to the Union, at the last moment, in order to secure three extra electoral votes for their president.[1184]

But Lincoln committed other far more serious violations and outrages. For four years he virtually ignored the pleas of numerous Confederate peace commissions while simultaneously sanctioning the pillaging and destruction of non-military structures, such as Southern homes, shops, mills, prisons, gins, pubs, churches, libraries, and universities, even Catholic convents. All of this while the more well-bred, considerate, and humanitarian Rebel soldier often called out "down Yank!" before opening fire.[1185]

Why would an army want to bomb a school, a library, or a

1180. Ingersoll, p. 22; Nicolay and Hay, ALCW, Vol. 2, p. 508.
1181. W. B. Garrison, CWC, pp. 12-13.
1182. Shenkman and Reiger, p. 103. During his first year in office alone Lincoln threw out 1,457 men (leaving a mere 200 from former administrations), replacing them with his own hand-selected appointees.
1183. W. B. Garrison, CWTFB, p. 62. On December 26, 1862, Lincoln ordered the hanging of thirty-eight Sioux Indians for fighting against U.S. troops. The Native-Americans had simply been resisting the breaking of numerous treaties by the U.S. government, and for this they lost their lives. Lincoln had wanted to hang hundreds more, but decided against it for fear of losing European support for the Union. Seabrook, L, pp. 765-768; D. H. Donald, L, pp. 392-395; DiLorenzo, RL, pp. 157-158.
1184. Oates, AL, p. 79.
1185. Catton, Vol. 3, p. 264.

THE MCGAVOCKS OF CARNTON PLANTATION

house of God into dust?[1186] Why would Lincoln's most highly esteemed officers order the hanging of Confederate soldiers "without trial?"[1187] Why would a U.S. president order the murder of dozens of Native-Americans because they challenged the government for breaking her treaties? Only Lincoln and his henchmen, such as Grant, Sherman, Philip Sheridan, David Hunter, Edward Hatch, and Butler "the Beast" (also known in the South as "Spoons," for his proclivity for stealing silverware from Confederate families)[1188] know the answers to these questions.[1189]

It was also Lincoln who authorized the wholesale murder of perhaps a million Southern white civilians (most who were defenseless seniors, women, and children) and as many as a million Southern blacks. And it was he who then issued the Emancipation Proclamation in an effort to start a massive slave revolt in the South while,[1190] at the same time, campaigning to deport from the U.S. the very blacks he intended to liberate.[1191]

"Honest Abe's" greatest crimes, however, were calling up militia into federal service, initiating a war against both individual states and a foreign nation, spending $2,000,000 (about $55,000,000 in today's currency) to fund it, and instituting unconstitutional reconstruction

---

1186. In her diary, February 26, 1865, an incredulous Mary Chesnut asked a similar question of Sherman and his Yankee forces: "Why stop to do so needless a thing as burn [the] . . . courthouse, the jail, and the tavern?" Chesnut, DD, p. 357.
1187. See e.g., ORA, Ser. 1, Vol. 43, p. 811.
1188. Channing, p. 114; *The Civil War Book of Lists*, p. 149.
1189. According to international rules of warfare, as laid down by Swiss philosopher and jurist Emerich de Vattel (1714-1767), during war, private property cannot be taken unless paid for. This, and nearly every other rule of military conduct formulated by the Geneva Convention, was wholly disregarded by Lincoln and his officers between April 12, 1861 and April 9, 1865.
1190. See Nicolay and Hay, ALCW, Vol. 2, p. 287.
1191. See Nicolay and Hay, ALCW, Vol. 2, p. 237. Although it is true that, as far as we know, Lincoln did not directly order the killing of Southern civilians, he must still be held accountable for their deaths. Why? Because he never ordered his officers not to commit such acts, even when he knew full well these atrocities were being committed. Indeed, he often stood by and said nothing, completely aware that his soldiers were pillaging, raping, burning, and murdering their way across the South, all with their officers' blessings, and sometimes even under their direct orders. What is more, Lincoln personally thanked, rewarded, and promoted men like Sherman and Grant for their battlefield performances, and often met with them, as he did on March 27, 1865, to excitedly hear about their "achievements" and congratulate them in person. Finally, Sherman, Grant, and Sheridan, along with numerous other Yank war criminals, received official thanks from Congress "for gallantry," either at Lincoln's suggestion or with his permission.

THE MCGAVOCKS OF CARNTON PLANTATION

measures in seceded states occupied by Yankee troops. None of these actions, like most of those listed above, were legal without congressional approval, and he knew it. In fact, in response to Lincoln's dramatic and unheard of "extension of executive power," on December 22, 1862, the U.S. Supreme Court went even further, publically noting that:

> Under the Constitution, Congress has no right to make war on any state, and the President has no right to make any war.[1192]

Lincoln ignored this and countless other condemnations of his actions, not only by those in his own administration, but also by the Northern public. And yet in one of the greatest ironies of world history, it was Lincoln's criminal activities and complete and utter disregard for civil rights that won the War. How?

By strangling personal, legal, and Constitutional liberties for four years Lincoln was able to suppress the Northern peace movement, whose numerical strength and powerful antiwar voice would have certainly brought an end to the conflict long before his second term in 1864. At the same time, in the Confederacy, Jefferson Davis' respect for civil rights prompted him to allow full freedom of the press, freedom of speech, and freedom from arbitrary arrest, throughout the conflict, even when the Confederacy was actually hurt by these same rights.[1193] As a result, the Southern peace movement, made up mainly of Southern pro-Unionists, grew exponentially.

In the South, anti-Confederate societies, like The Order of the Heroes of America and The Peace and Constitutional Society, agitated aggressively against Davis, the War, even the military, undermining every Rebel victory with a myriad of subversive tactics. These included suggesting that citizens not serve and encouraging active duty soldiers to desert. Additionally, they influenced the home folks to write their relations on the battlefield and ask them to "lay down their guns and come home." Southern peacemongers handed out leaflets on every

---

1192. Ashe, p. 57.
1193. D. H. Donald, WNWCW, p. 84.

street corner, spreading antiwar sentiment with countless horror stories of privation, disease, and death. Some actually infiltrated the Rebel army and navy, disseminating discouragement, discontent, and disenchantment wherever they went.[1194]

With the Confederate forces sabotaged from within it was only a matter of time before desertion and absenteeism levels skyrocketed (General Robert E. Lee, for example, ended the War with but a skeleton of his original army). By the beginning of 1865 the Rebel military force had ebbed to ineffective levels.

Had Davis operated as Lincoln had with regard to civil rights, how different the outcome of the War would have been. The South had scruples and lost. The North had none and won!

In great part then the Confederacy was defeated because it nurtured democracy; the North was victorious because it killed democracy.[1195]

By April 9, 1865, the day of Lee's surrender at Appomattox, Lincoln's misdeeds had seriously impacted the South's infrastructure and left the entire region in ruin, poverty, and desolation, with damage estimated to be $20 billion (the equivalent of $260 billion today).[1196] Most importantly, to Lincoln and his followers, his War permanently destroyed the once Constitutionally legal act of secession (which he wrongly called "the essence of anarchy"),[1197] along with the Jeffersonian idea that the U.S. was to be a confederation of strong, sovereign, nation-states with a weak central government.[1198]

In its place Lincoln implanted a new, radical, anti-Founding Fathers concept: the U.S. was now a single nation of weakened, dependent states, operating under an all-powerful, central, nationalized government, overseen by a president possessed of unprecedented,

---

1194. Simmons, s.v. "Civil Rights in the Confederacy"; "Heroes of America, The Order of the"; "Peace and Constitutional Society."
1195. Simmons, s.v. "Peace Societies"; "Peace Society, The."
1196. Ashe, p. 64.
1197. Nicolay and Hay, ALCW, Vol. 2, p. 5.
1198. Plano, Greenberg, Olton, and Riggs, s.v. "Jeffersonianism."

THE MCGAVOCKS OF CARNTON PLANTATION

tyrannical powers.[1199] With Henry Clay's American System now fully functional, Lincoln opened the door to big government, big business, big spending, and Big Brother, a socialistic dynamic that would reach its zenith in the early 1930s with President Franklin Delano Roosevelt's ultra left-wing, "New Deal" programs.[1200]

It is no surprise to learn then that the term "New Deal" was not an invention of the Roosevelt administration. Rather, it dates back to 1865, when it was coined to describe Lincoln's socialist domestic policies.[1201] A partial list of items from Lincoln's own "New Deal" program includes: the Morrill Tariff (1861); the first income tax (1861); an expanded postal service (1861); the Homestead Act (1862); the Morrill Land-Grant College Act (1862); the Department of Agriculture (1862); the Bureau of Printing and Engraving (1862); Transcontinental Railroad land grants (1862, 1863, 1864); National Banking Acts (1862, 1863, 1864, 1865, 1866); comptroller of the currency (1863); the National Academy of Science (1863); free urban mail delivery (1863); the Yosemite nature reserve land grant (1864); the Contract Labor Act (1864); the Office of Immigration (1864); railway mail service (1864); and the money order system (1864)[1202]

How similar Lincoln and Roosevelt were! If the Lincoln years represent the Second American Revolution, then the Roosevelt years were truly the "Third American Revolution." For it was during this period that the concept of the national government underwent a complete transformation, from passive and aloof to aggressive and interventionist.[1203]

But that was not all. Lincoln's anti-confederate political aspirations also left nearly 3 million American citizens dead, deteriorating race relations, unremitting hatred and misunderstandings

---

1199. Rosenbaum and Brinkley, s.v. "Civil War."
1200. Critics of Roosevelt's New Deal noted that, among other things, it allowed the federal government too much power, which led to growing interference with free enterprise and fears of the country becoming socialistic. Weintraub, p. 121.
1201. Thornton and Ekelund, p. 99.
1202. Thornton and Ekelund, p. 99.
1203. Hacker, pp. 1125-1126.

on both sides, the destruction of the South's laissez-faire economy and agrarian lifestyle (replaced by rank Northern industrialism and materialism), and a permanent emotional scar running along the Mason-Dixon Line. As of 2011, the year this book was published, the South has yet to completely recover from Lincoln's "Civil War." Is it any wonder that to hide its war crimes, Lincoln's government, that is the U.S. government, censored photographs of the battlefield dead for almost eighty years?[1204]

The West had not seen a dictator like this in power since the days of the Roman Empire, hence one of his many Southern nicknames: "Emperor Lincoln." At least this is how most Americans saw him at the time, particularly Southern Americans. After Lincoln's reelection in 1864, one Confederate newspaper called him a revolting clown, one who had given himself more power than Caesar.[1205] One of Lincoln's own officers, George B. McClellan, referred to the president as a "well meaning baboon"[1206] and "the original gorilla";[1207] that is, someone with more power than brains.

Lincoln's true character was recognized by other Northerners of note as well, even thirty-six years later. On September 8, 1900, in Grand Rapids, Michigan, New Yorker and future American president, Theodore Roosevelt (1858-1919), declared that during the War,

> on every hand Lincoln was denounced as a tyrant, a shedder of blood, a foe to liberty, a would be dictator, a founder of an empire.[1208]

Early Americans had fought to the death to be free of an empire, the British Empire. In just a few short years Lincoln turned the U.S. itself into one.

1204. Horwitz, pp. 208, 227.
1205. D. H. Donald, L, p. 547.
1206. DeGregorio, s.v. "Abraham Lincoln"; Beschloss, p. 113; K. C. Davis, p. 219; Flood, p. 37; D. H. Donald, L, p. 319.
1207. Minor, p. 49.
1208. Ashe, p. 60; Minor, p. 35.

THE MCGAVOCKS OF CARNTON PLANTATION

॰ LINCOLN'S UNPOPULARITY AS SEEN IN THE 1860 & 1864 ELECTIONS

The actual depth of Lincoln's unpopularity among Americans at the time can be seen at the voting booth.

Some will protest, however, that he won both of his elections. This is correct. But his wins were not evidence of popularity. Quite the contrary: in the first he was clearly a minority president, while both his first and second wins were attained by highly controversial and often illegal methods, with half the nation, the South, not even voting.[1209] Let us look at this topic more closely for a moment.

In his first election, on November 6, 1860, he won via the Electoral College only, not by popular vote, and few people, if anyone, in the South voted for him.[1210] In fact, in ten of the fifteen Southern states he was considered so dangerous and inept that he was not even put on the ballot. Thus he received not a single vote in Dixie that year.[1211]

There that can be little question that bribery, lying, and cheating took place on Lincoln's behalf during the 1860 election, as well, and that prime administrative positions and other political favors were traded for votes. This all occurred, no doubt, under Lincoln's supervision,[1212] for his convention managers later admitted that they had promised "anything and everything" to anyone who would vote for him.[1213] (Lincoln would pay for this double-dealing: his sordid campaign promises necessitated appointing a myriad of individuals with opposing viewpoints, a split cabinet that he was forced to do battle with throughout his entire first term.)[1214]

Overall, of the 4,685, 561 ballots cast that November, Lincoln received only 39.8 percent (1,865,908, votes) of the popular vote, while his opponents received a combined total of 60.2 percent (2,819,653 votes). Even his electoral win was marginal: while 152 electoral votes

---

1209. Dean, pp. 212-213.
1210. In the 1860 election Lincoln won 180 electoral votes. His opponents combined won 123.
1211. Garraty, p. 298.
1212. Current, LNK, p. 200.
1213. W. B. Garrison, LNOK, p. 75.
1214. Simmons, s.v. "Lincoln, Abraham."

THE MCGAVOCKS OF CARNTON PLANTATION

(out of 303) were needed to win, Lincoln received a mere 180 (or 59.41 percent). His opponents received the other 123. It was only by a slim margin of twenty-eight electoral votes that Lincoln was elected, and all 180 were from Northern states.

Thus his first presidential victory was strictly a sectional, narrow, Northern electoral one. Clearly, in 1860, by far the vast majority of Americans, both North and South, did not want him to be president. In fact if we go by the popular vote alone, 61 percent of Northerners and 100 percent of Southerners wanted someone else to be president!

With the bulk of the American populace obviously against him, during his bid for reelection in 1864 Lincoln decided not to take any chances, so he rigged votes,[1215] arrested and imprisoned tens of thousands of Northern peace advocates and anti-Lincoln Yankees (some for nothing more than making "disloyal remarks"),[1216] posted soldiers at polling stations in order to intimidate voters,[1217] closed down hundreds of Northern newspapers that printed anti-Lincoln or pro-peace articles,[1218] and deported Yankee antiwar politicians like Clement L. Vallandigham[1219]—a man who Southerners called "the most talented and prominent representative" of the Northern conservatives.[1220]

Also, in violation of Article 4, Section 3, of the U.S. Constitution,[1221] Lincoln illegally created the state of West Virginia (to accrue more electoral votes).[1222] This he did by pushing the region that would become West Virginia, to secede from Virginia at a time when he had pronounced the secession of the Southern states unlawful.[1223] Again,

---

1215. DiLorenzo, LU, p. 52.
1216. Neely, p. 55.
1217. Christian, p. 26.
1218. L. H. Johnson, NAS, p. 125.
1219. Napolitano, p. 69.
1220. Pollard, LC, p. 465.
1221. As noted, it is illegal for a section of a state to secede from the parent state without its approval. Clearly, Virginia never authorized the secession of West Virginia. C. Adams, p. 58.
1222. W. C. Davis, HD, pp. 79-80.
1223. W. B. Garrison, LNOK, pp. 193-197.

his double standard did not concern him.[1224]

Lincoln also managed to force millions of Yankee soldiers to vote for his party by creating the holiday we now call "Thanksgiving Day." By presidential order he established its observation on the last Thursday of each November. The purpose? Soldiers would be furloughed in late October, arriving home just in time to vote in the elections in early November.[1225]

Unofficially, Union soldiers were sent home for Thanksgiving Day with the stern admonition: Soldiers, you fight for the Union. Now vote for the Union![1226] A stunning majority of Yankee soldiers, 116,887 out of 150,635, did just that.[1227] Lincoln later admitted that he would not have won in 1864 "without the soldiers' vote."[1228] Among these, of course, were thousands of newly liberated black soldiers, craftily and intentionally freed by Lincoln's Final Emancipation Proclamation on January 1, 1863, just in time to gratefully cast their votes for the "Great Emancipator" in the upcoming 1864 election.

That November 6, again, no Southern votes counted for or against him, this time because the Southern states had broken away and formed a separate country. Thus of the thirty-five states then in existence, only twenty-four, those in the U.S.A., participated. The other eleven, including Tennessee, did not as they were now part of the C.S.A., losing Lincoln some eighty odd potential electoral votes.[1229]

We will note here that Lincoln had illegally, and unnecessarily, prohibited the Confederate states from voting in the '64 election. "Unnecessarily" because the Confederate states were busy constructing and maintaining their own sovereign government—one of whose

---

1224. As mentioned, Lincoln knew this was unconstitutional. Why else would he feel the need to discuss the issue with his cabinet on December 23, 1862? Nicolay and Hay, ALCW, Vol. 2, p. 283. See also Nicolay and Hay, ALCW, Vol. 2, pp. 285-287, where Lincoln resorts to his usual tortured logic to justify his actions regarding the secession of West Virginia.
1225. W. B. Garrison, LNOK, p. 214.
1226. Daugherty, p. 214.
1227. Ransom, p. 210. Only a tiny percentage, 33,748 soldiers, risked voting for Lincoln's opponent, General George McClellan.
1228. Hesseltine, pp. 381, 382, 384. See also D. H. Donald, LR, p. 80; Simmons, s.v. "Lincoln, Abraham."
1229. Kane, p. 168.

THE MCGAVOCKS OF CARNTON PLANTATION

members was America's tenth president, John Tyler (1790-1862), the only U.S. president to serve in the Confederate government.[1230] But Lincoln no doubt saw his anti-South decree as necessary in order to avoid a blistering humiliation: why allow eleven states to vote when it was clear they would not?[1231]

Lincoln's chicanery and illegalities served him well that year: of 233 possible electoral votes available in the 1864 election, he received 212, while just one of his opponents, General George Brinton McClellan, received the other twenty-one. Either way, as Henry Clay Dean pointed out in 1869, if the seceded Southern states are taken into account, "Lincoln at no time had the support of more than one-third of the electoral vote of the country."[1232]

In spite of all this Lincoln barely won the popular vote that year: 45 percent of Northerners, the only people who voted in the 1864 U.S. election, voted against him. Among the 55 percent who voted for him were hundreds of thousands of Yankee soldiers who, as we just saw, the president had purposefully furloughed just in time to travel home and vote. The additional "strong recommendation" of their officers, suggested by Lincoln himself, that they vote for the president and his party, was not lost on them.[1233] Again, it is certain that he would have been defeated in the 1864 election without this highly questionable deception.[1234]

But even with 55 percent of the popular vote in 1864, Lincoln's second-term win was not as sweeping as one might think. Of the total 4,031,877 votes cast that November, he received 2,218,388, just over half, with the remaining votes, 1,8134,499 going to his opponents. He won by a mere 404,889 votes. If only 80,000 people, or 2 percent, had

---

1230. Shenkman and Regier, p. 103.
1231. The eleven Southern states who did not vote in the 1864 U.S. election were: Alabama (with 8 electoral votes), Arkansas (with 5 electoral votes), Florida (with 3 electoral votes), Georgia (with 9 electoral votes), Louisiana (with 7 electoral votes), Mississippi (with 7 electoral votes), North Carolina (with 9 electoral votes), South Carolina (with 6 electoral votes), Tennessee (with 10 electoral votes), Texas (with 6 electoral votes), and Virginia (with 10 electoral votes).
1232. Dean, p. 65.
1233. Oates, AL, pp. 80-81.
1234. D. H. Donald, LR, pp. 79-80.

voted against him in certain areas of the North, Lincoln would have lost the race.[1235] And if the South had voted, he would have certainly lost by the greatest landslide in American history. Either way, Lincoln won both elections with less than 50 percent of the popular vote.

Do the results of either of these elections show what one would call a unified ringing endorsement by the American people? Hardly.

While the North celebrates their beloved President Lincoln to this day in literature and film, and with parades and Paganistic statuary, 150 years later traditional Southerners still twinge at the mere mention of his name, as well as the appearance of his face on the U.S. penny, the five-dollar bill, the Illinois license plate, and Mount Rushmore. He is not loved here in Dixie; at least not by anyone who is familiar with authentic Southern history.

In 1911 Captain Samuel A'Court Ashe, the last surviving commissioned officer of the Confederacy, summed up Southern sentiment toward Lincoln and his illegal invasion this way:

> This unnecessary war was Lincoln's real gift to posterity, his contribution as a citizen—all else was accidental. So Mr. Lincoln stands in history as one who did more evil than any man known to the world.[1236]

No true lover of liberty and the Constitution could have put it better.

❧ THE AFTERMATH OF LINCOLN'S EMANCIPATION PLAN

Why so many African-Americans today worship Lincoln is even more of a mystery.

We have already seen that he was not their friend. But what many do not realize is that one of the primary consequences of his victory over the South was that the quality of life for blacks immediately plummeted, then remained below slavery levels for nearly the next 100 years.

1235. Current, LNK, p. 212.
1236. Ashe, p. 64.

The McGavocks of Carnton Plantation

After Lincoln's War, for instance, black life span dropped 10 percent, diets and health deteriorated, disease and sickness rates went up 20 percent, the number of skilled blacks declined, and the gap between white and black wages widened, trends that did not even begin to reverse until the onset of World War II seventy-five years later, in 1939.[1237]

Of life after "liberation" Adeline Grey, a black South Carolina servant, wrote that when "liberation" came she could still vividly remember it, while slavery was but a dim memory. Why? Because life was much more difficult and painful after emancipation than before.[1238]

The pain of emancipation was due, in great part, to the fact that Lincoln never pushed through any kind of organized, gradual, or compensated emancipation plan, as nearly every other Western nation had done when it abolished slavery.[1239] And Lincoln's promise to freedmen of "forty acres and a mule" was little more than a carrot on the end of a stick, used to lure blacks into a false sense of governmental protection after emancipation (as we will recall, Lincoln's so-called "black land giveaways" were never meant to be permanent,[1240] and what little of these were dispersed went primarily to wealthy white Northerners).[1241]

In truth, prior to emancipation Lincoln set up no effectual homestead act, no substantive support plans, and no land redistribution program. As such, freed blacks were literally cast out on the street with no education, no jobs, no housing, no job training, no grants or loans, to simply "root, pig, or perish," as Lincoln callously put it.[1242]

Where was the plan for a smooth transition from captivity to freedom? There was not one. As a former female slave later recollected of those times: We had no idea what to do. There was no place to go

---

1237. Fogel and Engerman, p. 261.
1238. Hurmence, p. 102.
1239. To his credit, Lincoln had at first crusaded for gradual compensated emancipation. But the Radicals (that is, abolitionists) in his party wanted immediate non-compensated emancipation. Under pressure to secure votes for his 1864 reelection campaign, Lincoln caved into the abolitionists and issued his disastrous and illegal Final Emancipation Proclamation on January 1, 1863.
1240. Foner, R, pp. 70-71.
1241. Thornton and Ekelund, p. 96.
1242. Stephens, RAHS, pp. 83, 137; Stephens, CV, Vol. 2, p. 615.

after we were freed. We were just turned loose with no direction and no assistance, she bemoaned.[1243]

Under Lincoln's "root, pig, or perish" emancipation plan, blacks who as servants had lived quality lives equal to and often superior to many whites and free blacks, now found themselves living out in the open or in makeshift tents, begging for food and work. There was now less work for them under freedom than there had been under servitude, and thus the black economy plummeted.[1244]

Disease, homelessness, starvation, beggary, prostitution, poverty, and thievery now became the lot of untold thousands of former black servants. Even many of those who managed to become sharecroppers eventually found themselves in a state of peonage (a debt that tied them to the land), living in crude filthy shacks, suffering from illiteracy, ill health, and malnutrition. All of this was a far cry from the quality of life experienced by Southern blacks when they had lived under servitude.[1245]

Black house servant Sarah Debro of North Carolina was "freed" then put to work by her Yankee "emancipators" as a field hand, a job she had never done before. Here, in 1937, is what Sarah, who worked for the Cain family, had to say about Lincoln's "emancipation": After the War Yankees came round orderin' us Negroes about like slaves, even though we was "free." The Yanks gave us houses they had built. They told us to go live in 'em. But they were horrible little things, with no windows, and made of mud and sticks, like poor white folks live in. We was used to much better. As servants we had had warm dry houses made of wood, with nice brick chimneys and glass windows. I told my Mammy that I didn't want to live in the Yankees' house. She beat me and sent me to bed. I laid there and looked up at the ceilin'. I could see the stars through the cracks in the roof. I cried myself to sleep. I always had plenty to eat when we worked for Master. But under Yankee freedom we was always starvin'. It was a horrible time, so bad that I

1243. Bailyn, Dallek, Davis, Donald, Thomas, and Wood, p. 11.
1244. Thornton and Ekelund, p. 96.
1245. Wilson and Ferris, s.v. "Cotton Culture."

would have much rather been a slave than a freed girl. In between doin' slave work and tryin' to find something to eat, I had to fight off dem Yankee mens. They was always tryin' to have their way with me. Dem Yanks are cruel people. When I look back in time I still think fondly of my days as a slave.[1246]

She did not realize it, but Sarah Debro was among the fortunate. Most freed black servants were given neither a home or a job, and many were not able to fight off the sexual advances and violent treatment of Yankee soldiers. As Chesnut said of Lincoln's emancipation debacle, the Yanks have let loose Satan himself, and have no idea how to handle him.[1247]

The man behind all of this is the one many Americans, both black and white, tenderly call the "Great Emancipator"! With such a legacy, what many in the South really want to know is why, year after year, Lincoln is continually voted America's "favorite," "best," and "greatest president"?[1248] And why do Northerners sometimes refer to him as "Father Abraham," equate him with men like Moses and even Jesus, and liken his mother Nancy Hanks (a relative of actor Tom Hanks)[1249] to the Virgin Mary?[1250] Lincoln did not even end slavery, as pro-North historians pretend. The Thirteenth Amendment ended it eight months after he died.[1251]

The man himself repeatedly said he was not qualified to be the nation's highest leader. In a letter to Thomas J. Pickett of Rock Island, Illinois, for example, dated April 16, 1859, Lincoln wrote:

> I do not think myself fit for the presidency. I certainly am flattered, and grateful that some partial friends think of me in that connection.[1252]

1246. Gragg, pp. 87-88.
1247. Chesnut, MCCW, p. 834.
1248. R. S. Phillips, s.v. "Lincoln, Abraham."
1249. Davenport, p. 25.
1250. Lewis, pp. 92-93, 325.
1251. Weintraub, p. 74.
1252. Nicolay and Hay, ALCW, Vol. 1, p. 533.

The McGavocks of Carnton Plantation

To this day, millions of traditional Southerners agree with this sentiment and only wish that Lincoln had followed his own judgement.

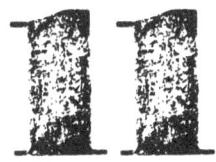

The McGavocks & Lincoln's War

Part 2

❧ MORE CONFEDERATE VICTORIES

WITH A DESPOT LIKE LINCOLN in the U.S. White House, with the superficial support of Europe, and with far more financial backing, military supplies, and railroad mileage (21,679 miles in the North, 8,947 miles in the South), it is little wonder that Union wins were becoming more and more commonplace as the War drew on.

And the United States of America had other advantages as well:
- The Union had more iron production (951,000 tons in the North, 37,000 tons in the South).
- The Union had over twice the food production (the North with 717 million bushels, the South with 316 million bushels).
- The Union had twice the industry of the South (the North had 110,000 manufacturing plants and 1.3 million industrial workers, the South had only 18,000 plants and 110,000 industrial workers).
- The Union had more than twice the number of states (the North with twenty-three, the South with eleven).[1253]

1253. While the Confederate Battle Flag contains thirteen stars representing the Confederacy's thirteen states, two of these, Kentucky and Missouri, were not full-fledged members as only portions of their territories seceded. Thus the Confederacy had only eleven official member states.

THE MCGAVOCKS OF CARNTON PLANTATION

- The Union had nearly three times Dixie's manpower (22 million whites in the North to 8 million whites in the South).[1254]
- By the end of the war the Union had three times the military forces of the South.[1255]

Despite the incredible odds stacked against her, however, the Confederacy continued to score victories against Lincoln, keeping hope alive across the South. Among the Rebel wins during this period were (in chronological order):

Valverde (February 20-21, 1862)
Tampa (June 30-July 1, 1862)
Murfreesboro I (July 13, 1862)
Cedar Mountain (August 9, 1862)
Independence I (August 11, 1862)
Lone Jack (August 15-16, 1862)
Manassas Station Operations (August 25-27,1862)
Thoroughfare Gap (August 28, 1862)
Manassas II (August 28–30, 1862)
Richmond (August 29-30, 1862)
Mile Hill (September 2, 1862)
Harpers Ferry (September 12-15, 1862)
Munfordville (September 14-17, 1862)
Shepherdstown (September 19-20, 1862)
Clark's Mill (November 7, 1862)
Cane Hill (November 28, 1862)
Hartsville (TN) (December 7, 1862)
Fredericksburg I (December 11-15, 1862)
Jackson (TN) (December 19, 1862)
Parker's Cross Roads (December 31, 1862)
Galveston (January 1, 1863)

1254. The Southern population statistic includes Kentucky and Missouri. Katcher, CWSB, p. 225. See also Weintraub, p. 70; Rosenbaum and Brinkley, s.v. "Civil War."
1255. Livermore, p. 63. While at the beginning of Lincoln's War Federal forces were twice as strong as the South, by April 1865 they had tripled. Eaton, HSC, p. 94.

THE MCGAVOCKS OF CARNTON PLANTATION

Hartville (MO) (January 9-11, 1863)
Thompson's Station (March 5, 1863)
Kelly's Ford (March 17, 1863)
Brentwood (March 25, 1863)
Miskel Farm (April 1, 1863)
Charleston Harbor (April 7, 1863)
Chancellorsville (April 30-May 6, 1863)
Salem Church (May 3-4, 1863)
Winchester II (June 13-15, 1863)
Fairfield (July 3, 1863)
Lebanon (July 5, 1863)
Corydon (July 9, 1863)
Manassas Gap or Wapping Heights (July 23, 1863)
Fort Sumter II (August 17- 23, 1863)
Lawrence or Quantrill's Raid (August 21, 1863)
Baxter Springs (October 6, 1863)
Charlestown (October 18, 1863)
Buckland Mills (October 19, 1863)
Sabine Pass II (September 8, 1863)
Chickamauga (September 18-20, 1863)
Stirling's Plantation (September 29, 1863)
Rogersville (November 6, 1863)
Bean's Station (December 14, 1863)
Dandridge (January 17, 1864)
Olustee (February 20, 1864)
Okolona (February 22, 1864)
Rio Hill (February 26, 1864)
Walkerton (March 2, 1864)
Paducah (March 25, 1864)
Mansfield (April 8, 1864)
Fort Pillow (April 12, 1864)
Poison Spring (April 18, 1864)
Marks' Mills April 25, 1864
Calcasieu Pass (May 6, 1864)
Chester Station (May 10, 1864)

The McGavocks of Carnton Plantation

Proctor's Creek (May 12-16, 1864)
New Market (May 15, 1864)
Ware Bottom Church (May 20, 1864)
New Hope Church (May 25-26, 1864)
Pickett's Mill (May 27, 1864)
Cold Harbor II (May 31-June 12, 1864)
Petersburg I (June 9, 1864)
Patients and Penitents (June 9, 1864)
Brices Cross Roads (June 10, 1864)
Petersburg II (June 15-18, 1864)
Staunton River Bridge (June 25, 1864)
Ream's Station I (June 29, 1864)
Kernstown II (July 24, 1864)
Kennesaw Mountain (June 27, 1864)
Monocacy (July 9, 1864)
The Crater (July 30, 1864)
Brown's Mill (July 30, 1864)
Deep Bottom II (August 13-20, 1864)
Gainesville (FL) (August 17, 1864)
Lovejoy's Station (August 20, 1864)
Memphis (August 21, 1864)
Glasgow (October 15, 1864)
Lexington II (October 19, 1864)
Little Blue River (October 21, 1864)
Independence II (Oct 22, 1864)
Fair Oaks and Darbytown Road (October 27-28, 1864)
Johnsonville (November 4-5, 1864)
Bull's Gap (November 11-13, 1864)

Southerners like Colonel John and Carrie were ecstatic over these Rebel wins, and could not heap enough praise on President Davis and the Confederate soldiers who were fighting and dying to maintain states' rights, Southern unity, and the Constitution.

But all of that was about to change.

With the Confederate victory at the Battle of Columbia,

The McGavocks of Carnton Plantation

Tennessee, November 24-29, 1864, the stage was set for the upcoming show of horrors that was to become known as the Battle of Franklin II (or the 2nd Battle of Franklin), one of the last of 298 officially recognized battles fought on Tennessee soil during the War.[1256] Colonel John did not fight in this conflict, and did not need to. It came to his front door.

❧ HOOD & THE DISASTROUS BATTLE OF FRANKLIN II

It was Wednesday afternoon, November 30, 1864, about 2:30 P.M.[1257] The Battle of Franklin II was about to commence within a mile or so of Carnton Plantation. Rebel commander General John Bell Hood (1831-1879)[1258] was getting ready to throw his 27,000-man Army of Tennessee into a futile suicide mission against the 27,000-man Army of the Ohio,[1259] led by his former West Point roommate, the ever controversial Union General John McAllister Schofield (1831-1906).[1260]

Meanwhile most of Schofield's men were well entrenched on the southern side of downtown Franklin,[1261] while others were stationed at nearby Fort Granger, a Union stronghold centered atop a natural defensive position, Figuers' Bluff, situated on the Harpeth River just

---

1256. The only state with more battles fought within its borders was Virginia, with 519. Cartmell, p. 17. Actually, many more than 298 conflicts were waged on Tennessee soil. According to historian Thomas Cartwright, including skirmishes and other types of action, there may have been as many as 1,000. Also of interest is the fact that Tennessee provided one-sixth of all the soldiers in the Confederate armies. Strangely, however, one-sixth of all the Union dead are buried in Tennessee. Morton, pp. 328-329.
1257. Though there is no direct connection with Franklin II, November 30 is celebrated by Scots around the world as Saint Andrew's Day, after the Patron Saint of Scotland. Coincidentally, the Confederate Battle Flag (a blue diagonal cross with thirteen stars on a field of red) happens to have been partly designed on Scotland's national flag, which is emblazoned with Saint Andrew's Cross (a white diagonal cross on a field of cobalt blue).
1258. I am cousins with Gen. Hood through our mutual ancestors, the Meriwether family of Virginia.
1259. Estimates of the numbers of Confederate and Union troops at the Battle of Franklin II vary widely, ranging from 20,000 Rebels and 17,000 Yankees to 27,000 Rebels and 35,000 Yankees. As even the experts disagree, it is probably safe to say that there were roughly about 27,000 on each side. It is considered by most to be one of the more evenly matched battles of Lincoln's War. See *The Civil War Book of Lists*, p. 65.
1260. As just one example of the contention that surrounded Schofield: he created a furor among Northern officers over his actions in Missouri, leading to charges that he was an "imbecile," and that he had sided with Southern sympathizers while withholding protection from Union loyalists. The situation became so acrimonious that a number of Yankee officers called for Schofield's removal. Lincoln used up a lot of ink defending Schofield—and not very convincingly. See e.g., Nicolay and Hay, ALCW, Vol. 2, pp. 419-423.
1261. J. C. Bradford, p. 91.

THE MCGAVOCKS OF CARNTON PLANTATION

northeast of Franklin center.[1262]

To reach them the Rebels were being ordered to cross a two-mile wide piece of flat land known as the "Plain of Franklin." Under the circumstances Hood's outrageous plan of attack, a full-on frontal assault, practically guaranteed a one-way ticket to Heaven, and every Confederate knew it. The area was quickly dubbed "the Valley of Death."

Assuming they were about to perish on the bluegrass fields before them, Hood's soldiers cleaned themselves up in preparation for burial, then sought out army chaplain, James H. McNeilly.[1263] They wanted to give him their watches, jewelry, letters, photographs, and other valuables, to be sent home to their loved ones after the battle. But McNeilly was also fighting that day and sadly had to refuse them.[1264]

❧ CLEBURNE'S SUGGESTION

Hood's division commanders were no less pessimistic. To a man all pleaded with the general to discard his hair-brained strategy for one more suited to the terrain and situation.

One of those who questioned his superior was the brilliant infantry commander General Patrick Ronayne Cleburne (1828-1864), from Ovens Township, County Cork, Ireland. Cleburne, known as the "Stonewall Jackson of the West"[1265] (and one of the many Southerners who advised enrolling blacks in the Confederate military then freeing them),[1266] suggested moving the Rebel troops at Franklin forward in life-saving columns rather than in death-defying rows, an ingenious tactic that would have spared many limbs and lives.[1267] As did Confederate General Benjamin Franklin "Frank" Cheatham (1820-1886), the Irishman went on to argue with his superior about the indefensible bloodshed that

---

1262. Fort Granger, the center of various earlier more primitive and unfinished Confederate fortifications, was built up by Federal troops between February 1862 and April 1863. Today a small park, located behind Pinkerton Park off Route 96, marks the spot, with walking trails and interpretive wayside exhibits.
1263. McNeilly's surnames is spelled M'Neilly in some documents.
1264. Thomas Cartwright, personal interview.
1265. Pollard, LC, p. 449.
1266. Seabrook, EYWTACWW, pp. 164-166.
1267. McDonough and Connelly, p. 73.

THE MCGAVOCKS OF CARNTON PLANTATION

would occur if the full frontal attack plan was undertaken.[1268]

Despite such logical pleas, the hard-headed Hood refused to listen. His command was to be carried out as ordered.

❧ FORREST AT CARNTON

Meanwhile, learning of Hood's intended mad scheme, famed Southern hero General Nathan Bedford Forrest paid a visit to Carnton Plantation to ask a star-struck McGavock family if he could use their second-floor porch as an observation deck in order to survey the battlefield.[1269] The surviving McGavock children, Winder and Hattie, in particular must have been in awe at the appearance of the celebrated Confederate chieftain at their door,[1270] the man Southerners then lovingly referred to as "the great cavalry chief of the West."[1271]

Looking northward Forrest was not happy with what he saw from Carnton's upper portico: across the Franklin Plain, an enormous flat field that swept up into the hills of downtown Franklin, lay 27,000 Yanks in wait, hiding behind a near solid wall of abatis, peering over hundreds of feet of fortified entrenchments. Forrest was familiar with the terrain of course: he had fought at the Battle of Franklin I on April 10, 1863, where the Rebels had been defeated.[1272] He was determined that they would not lose a second time on the same ground. Only one thing stood in the way of absolute victory: Hood's preposterous battle plan.

Furious, the charismatic cavalryman stormed off to his commander's headquarters at Winstead Hill[1273]—named after local

---

1268. McDonough and Connelly, p. 63.
1269. It was Carrie who later recalled the upper porch being used as an observation post.
1270. While it is well attested that Forrest visited Carnton in late November 1864, it is not known how long the famous Rebel commander remained at the plantation.
1271. Pollard, LC, p. 492.
1272. Mathes, p. 306.
1273. Part of Winstead Hill Park is today owned by the Sons of Confederate Veterans (SCV) and by the United Daughters of the Confederacy (UDC), which is why it is one of the only public places in all of Franklin where you will see a Confederate Battle Flag flying. The site hosts an automobile pull-off with interpretive signs, important Confederate monuments, memorials to the fallen generals at Franklin II, and a walking trail. For more information, see the official city Website: www.franklin-gov.com/index.aspx?page=380. See also Website: http://tennessee-scv.org/Camp1293/winstead.htm.

THE MCGAVOCKS OF CARNTON PLANTATION

Virginia planter Samuel Winstead (1778-1851)[1274]—where he proposed crossing the Harpeth River north of Franklin in a flanking maneuver or a turning movement (rather than a forward movement),[1275] that would put him on the enemy's rear.[1276] According to nearly all military historians today, this was Hood's only chance of winning.[1277] Still the battle hardened general would not budge and the two argued bitterly as they often did.[1278]

❧ A GRAND & NOBLE SIGHT

While this was going on, thousands of hungry freezing Confederate soldiers, many of them without weapons or boots, were marching across Carnton's yards that brisk November day, toward downtown Franklin and their well-fed, well-armed, well-supplied, "blue-bellied" enemies. Among those who the McGavocks watched file through their backyard were the divisions of General William W. Loring (1818-1886), General Edward C. Walthall (1831-1898), and General Samuel G. French (1818-1910), all from my cousin General Alexander Peter "Old Straight" Stewart's (1821-1908) corps.[1279]

The Army of Tennessee's band was playing Southern favorites, *Bonnie Blue Flag*,[1280] *Dixie*, *Ben Bolt*, and *The Girl I Left Behind*, as the Rebels lined up, awaiting their next order. The color bearers proudly held their war worn Confederate battle flags high for all the world to see, as excited and nervous mumbling passed through the throng.

Looking out of their windows that day the McGavocks witnessed a truly grand and noble sight, a pageant of humanity never to be forgotten: in the haze of the late afternoon Autumn sun, there stood a vast sea of gray-clothed and butternut-colored men, gun barrels

---

1274. Winstead's surname is also sometimes spelled Winsted.
1275. Sword, SI, p. 300.
1276. Horn, DBN, p. 19.
1277. Henry, SC, p. 429.
1278. Civil War Society, CWB, p. 42.
1279. Thomas Cartwright, personal interview. I am related to Stewart through mutual royal Scottish ancestors.
1280. This tune is still used to this day as the fight song for Atlanta's Georgia Institute of Technology (or Georgia Tech, as she is more popularly known).

THE McGAVOCKS OF CARNTON PLANTATION

glistening, bayonets bristling; an ocean of Southern bravery punctuated here and there with bright red flags patterned on the symbols of the patron saints of two Celtic nations: Scotland's Saint Andrew's Cross and Ireland's Saint Patrick's Cross.

Even the Yanks across the field sat in silence, awestruck before the stunning spectacle. One later remembered the view from the Union side as he sat waiting nervously in his trench: We had never seen anything like that Rebel line—and never would again.[1281]

❧ THE BATTLE OPENS

It was 3:30 P.M., and the sun was sinking rapidly in the western sky. This late in the year there were not more than a few hours of light left. The moment had arrived to welcome the Yankee intruders to the Rebel town of Franklin with some cold Confederate steel.

Much of Hood's artillery, however, nearly 100 guns, along with General Stephen Dill Lee's (1833-1908) 9,700-man infantry corps, had not yet arrived from Spring Hill.[1282] Hood had left Lee's corps in the rear on the south bank of the Duck River in Columbia[1283] to create the impression of an imminent attack from the South.[1284] But by now this strategy had become pointless, as the Yanks had already slipped North of the Rebels the day before (November 29) during what has become known as the "Spring Hill Affair," a debacle some historians call perhaps the most important "bloodless" battle of the whole conflict.[1285]

Why had Hood allowed Lee to remain behind, and why was he now about to go into battle with a partial army, minus 9,700 men and his largest and most powerful weapons? These are two more questions lost

---

1281. B. C. Miller, p. 154; Woodworth, p. 300.
1282. Sword, SI, p. 300. See also McDonough and Connelly, p. 65. I, like Robert E. Lee, am cousins with Gen. Stephen Dill Lee.
1283. Horn, DBN, p. 16.
1284. J. S. Bowman, CWDD, p. 186.
1285. Long and Long, p. 602. Though it has long been considered a "non-fighting event," in truth the Rebels suffered between 800 and 1,000 casualties that day at Spring Hill.

THE MCGAVOCKS OF CARNTON PLANTATION

to history.[1286]

Hood placed General Cheatham—whose brother Felix R. Cheatham married Ophelia Clay McGavock (the 1st cousin once removed of Colonel John of Carnton)—on the far left, General Stewart on the right, and General Forrest and his cavalry on the far right flank, along the Harpeth River.[1287] Since Hood had nixed Forrest's brilliant idea of a turning or flanking maneuver, the weight of the battle was about to fall primarily on the two infantry corps of Cheatham and Stewart.[1288]

At 4:00 P.M., despite immense odds, Hood gave the order and the bugle sounded the opening charge.[1289] Of this moment Sam Watkins of Confederate Company H writes that they marched down across a huge open field "toward the rampart of blood and death."[1290] There was no turning back now.

As the bloodcurdling Rebel Yell let loose across the hills of Franklin, the first unprotected advance line of Hood's men surged north onto the field, breaking into a desperate but brave run. Firing their guns as they went they valiantly hurled themselves straight at their well covered, blue coated opponent. Among the Union ranks looking down his barrel at the approaching Confederates that day was the "Boy Colonel," twenty-one-year old Arthur MacArthur (1843-1912), with the Twenty-fourth Wisconsin Volunteer Infantry, the father of World War II hero General Douglas MacArthur (1880-1964).[1291]

Hood had managed to get twenty-four guns on the field, each

1286. Lee and his corps arrived soon after the fighting began. However, Hood never utilized them to their full potential. Why? The Kentuckian, who had a reputation for neglecting detail and for ambiguous planning, seemed confused from the start. Handing out vague orders to his officers was yet another way in which the brave but unfocused Hood helped lose Franklin II.
1287. Fisher, p. 160. On a personal level Forrest was fortunate that Hood positioned him miles from the core battle, as he was spared the intense fighting, and the death and destruction that followed, around the Carters' cotton gin. However, in terms of military strategy it turned out to be yet another one of Hood's many blunders. One can only imagine how the tide of Franklin II might have turned had Hood placed the War's most ingenious and successful cavalryman on the Columbia Pike instead of sending him in the opposite direction to needlessly scout the Harpeth River. One thing we can be sure of: Forrest would have much preferred to be at the center of the action!
1288. Henry, SC, p. 429.
1289. Ridley, p. 417.
1290. Watkins, p. 210.
1291. W. B. Garrison, ACW, pp. 244-245.

sending an ear-splitting boom echoing around the valley as the cannon launched their deadly volleys toward downtown Franklin.[1292]

After bloodily tearing through the abatis, the brave Confederate troops bounded up the slopes toward the Union works where they managed to make a few breaks in the Federal line. The blue coats began to fall back in panic and for a brief second Johnny Reb could smell victory. But the moment passed quickly as Billy Yank regrouped and began pouring a galling fire into the ranks of Confederates. The first line was now down, nearly every man fatally wounded or already dead.

Quickly a second Confederate line was launched. But it too fell. A third, fourth, and fifth line was sent off toward oblivion, each suffering the same fate.

Still the brave Rebels kept coming.

Sprinting across the wide open flat Plain of Franklin, on which Carnton itself sits, thousands of Confederate soldiers were falling like ducks in a shooting gallery as protected Union troops easily cut them down with repeating rifles and enfilading cannon fire.

In all, nine Rebel lines attacked the Army of the Ohio's stronghold that day, and all nine were repulsed in some of the bloodiest fighting ever seen on American soil. Federal officers later reported that their lines had received as many as thirteen distinct attacks.[1293] Of this moment Confederate soldier Watkins later wrote:

> The air [was] loaded with death-dealing missiles. Never on this earth did men fight against such terrible odds. It seemed that the very elements of heaven and earth were in one mighty uproar. Forward, men! And the blood spurts in a perfect jet from the dead and wounded. The earth is red with blood. It runs in streams, making little rivulets as it flows. Occasionally there was a little lull in the storm of battle, as the men were loading their guns, and for a few moments it seemed as if night tried to cover the scene with

---

1292. Contrary to popular Carnton Plantation legend, twenty year old Anson Tyler Hemingway (1844-1926) of the Seventy-second Illinois Volunteer Infantry Regiment—the grandfather of noted American novelist Ernest Hemingway (1899-1961)—was not present at the Battle of Franklin II. Thomas Cartwright, personal interview.
1293. Henry, SC, p. 430.

her mantle. The death angel shrieks and laughs and old father Time is busy with his sickle, as he gathers in the last harvest of death, crying, More, more, more! while his rapacious maw is glutted with the slain.[1294]

At 4:30 P.M. Lee arrived with his 100-gun artillery and the Divisions of General Carter L. Stevenson (1817-1888), General Henry D. Clayton (1827-1889), and General Edward Johnson (1816-1873). But it was already too little too late. With the sun setting at 5:15 P.M. that Fall day, darkness was fast approaching. This hampered but did not halt the bloodshed. In fact, "the battle that should never have been fought" lasted well until after midnight and was, in fact, one of the only night battles of the War.[1295]

Strangely, maddingly, Hood stayed far in the rear, never once considering a change of plan, or putting a stop to the insane and unnecessary slaughter of his men.[1296]

❧ DEATH & DESTRUCTION

Caught up in the "hottest" fighting, Cleburne died, pierced through the left side of his chest by a single bullet near the Carter cotton gin house just off Columbia Road. Additionally, three other generals were killed, along with sixty-seven regimental commanders.[1297] A fifth fatally wounded general would die within hours, while the sixth would perish in less than two weeks. Out of a total of 425 officers in the Confederacy, these were six of the seventy-seven Confederate generals who were killed or mortally injured during Lincoln's War. In fact, the Rebels lost more major officers at Franklin II than in any other single action.[1298] To add insult to misery, thirty-two Rebel battle flags were captured by the Yanks, symbols of all the South held dear.[1299]

Among the wounded were Major General John Calvin Brown

1294. Watkins, p. 210.
1295. Wood, pp. 204-205.
1296. Woodworth, p. 300.
1297. Thomas Cartwright, personal interview.
1298. Hansen, p. 566.
1299. McMaster, p. 481.

THE MCGAVOCKS OF CARNTON PLANTATION

(1827-1889), Brigadier Generals Arthur Middleton Manigault (1824-1886),[1300] William Andrew Quarles (1825-1893), Thomas Moore Scott (1829-1876), and Francis Marion Cockrell (1834-1915). Cockrell's Brigade was hit especially hard, with a 60.2 percent loss of men, the sixth highest Confederate loss of any Rebel brigade in a single action during the entire War.[1301]

At least one Confederate officer was captured: Brigadier General George Washington Gordon (1836-1911).[1302] The ranks had been so thinned of major officers that many units had to be commanded by junior officers or even enlisted men.[1303]

Naturally this had a highly deleterious effect on both the troops and the outcome of what was soon to be known as the "Battle of Nashville": most of the lower-ranked Confederate officers were purposefully chosen from the local population because they were well-known and respected in their region.

Now, after Franklin II, however, nearly every brigade, regiment, and company in Hood's army had to be taken over by new officers, most of whom were both inexperienced and unknown to the men they were to command. The new officers thus lacked any personal understanding of their troops. This lack of leadership was passed onto the men as a lack of confidence in their superiors, something that could only hurt the South's chances of success.[1304] And it did.

When it was all over the Army of Tennessee had wasted some 7,000 of the South's finest (nearly one-fifth of its forces) at Franklin II alone: officially these included 1,750 dead, 4,500 wounded, and 702 taken prisoner,[1305] though some modern Southern historians think these numbers were probably much higher, for these startling figures do not include those missing in action (many of whom later died), or those only

---

1300. I am cousins with Gen. Manigault, in part through mutual royal European ancestors.
1301. *The Civil War Book of Lists*, p. 92.
1302. Morton, p. 276. I am cousins with Gen. Gordon through mutual European ancestors.
1303. Sword, SI, p. 301.
1304. Horn, DBN, p. 32.
1305. McDonough and Connelly, p. 157.

THE MCGAVOCKS OF CARNTON PLANTATION

slightly wounded and thus still able to fight and march.[1306] (By comparison the Army of the Ohio's losses were minimal: 189 killed, 1,030 wounded, and 1,104 missing.)[1307]

On December 14, Mary Chesnut picked up her pen and wrote the following in her diary:

> Hood and . . . [Schofield] have had a fearful fight, with carnage and loss of generals excessive in proportion to numbers. That means they were leading and urging their men [right] up to the enemy.[1308]

The Battle of Franklin II, sometimes known as the "Gettysburg of the West,"[1309] turned out to be the tomb of the Army of Tennessee, a survivor noted bitterly years later.[1310]

A Yankee woman named Carrie Snyder (of Indianapolis, Indiana) happened to be visiting friends in Franklin as the battle commenced. What follows is her description:

> I had been sitting on the back porch playing at backgammon with Mrs. Rainney, as was our custom after dinner. A few shots from the infantry had been heard; then, as it became quiet, I began to think there would be no fight after all. Young and foolish thing that I was, I began to fear there would be no fight. I wanted to see a battle, or hear one; but I got enough of it, sooner than I expected. We kept on playing backgammon until about three o'clock, then the firing began to get thicker and sounded more like a snapping roar than anything I could otherwise describe. We got up and walked about the house and yard; bullets occasionally whistled over our heads. We did not fear them much if we had the brick house between us, but presently a cannon ball or shell came screeching over the house from the Confederate side. I think I grew short

---

1306. Thomas Cartwright, personal interview.
1307. Hansen, p. 566. Confederate historians think these numbers are too small as well, for in fact the Federals actually had no idea how many of their men perished at Franklin II. Why? Because they struck out for Nashville the night of the battle, November 30, 1864, leaving most of their dead and wounded on the field. Thomas Cartwright, personal interview.
1308. Chesnut, DD, p. 339.
1309. Pois and Langer, p. 99.
1310. Sword, CLH, p. 266.

quicker than anything you ever saw. Oh—my! but I just thought I was hit sure. What did I do? Well you'd better believe I got down low and wasn't long in following the old folks into the cellar. Then the noise began in dead earnest. I hadn't seen anything, but I had heard more than I wanted to. I wanted them to quit right off, but they wouldn't; they just kept up a roar, and rumble, and screeching that fairly stopped my heart from beating. We thought, down there in that cellar, that a shell would come through those walls, explode inside of the house and blow us all into 'Kingdom come,' the next minute. Just think of us three women and one old man curled up on that coal bin, in that dark cellar, from four o'clock in the afternoon until four o'clock in the morning—no light, no fire, no sleep, and the old lady bewailing the fact that we had not caught up some bedding and brought down with us. She thought more of those old quilts than she appeared to think of our lives and wanted us to go up stairs and get them. Not much. There had been rumors among the special friends of the Confederates that if the Federals fell back they had said they would burn Franklin. There was a young lady of our party whose friends were in the Southern army and she had given this report circulation. Suddenly a bright light turned darkness into day and her fears were apparently about to be realized. 'Fire!' she screamed. 'There, what did I tell you? Now we've escaped the battle to be burned alive in this horrid old cellar. Oh, my God, what will become of us!'

It seems the Federal army had thought best to keep up the appearance of fright or great haste in their evacuation (for Schofield evidently intended to draw Hood on to Nashville), and had set fire to the government stables, in which there was nothing left but a few tons of hay and some worthless saddles, harness, etc. That was the only building destroyed, unless by accident, or if in the way.

Then the firing had entirely ceased and steps were heard over head, and Mr. R., lifting the trap door, calls out 'Who's there—friends?' We went up out of our dismal prison, with limbs cramped, and fairly shaking, as in fact we had been all night, and Confederate soldiers told us they 'had the town, and the Yanks are gone.' So we began to move about more freely, but what do you suppose were my feelings as I thought I was among the enemy, cut off; did not know where my husband was nor how long I must remain where I felt that I must keep my mouth shut and no sympathizing ear to pour my troubles into?

The McGavocks of Carnton Plantation

Well, in the morning we went out upon the battle field, and O, horror upon horrors! what a sight. God forgive me for ever wishing to see or hear a battle. They said that beside the wounded the Federals had carried away in their ambulances, there were over 6,000 dead and wounded soldiers—blue and gray—all mixed up together; you had to look twice as you picked your way among the bodies to see which were dead and which were alive and often a dead man would be lying partly on a live one, or the reverse—and the groans; the sickening smell of blood! That sight and the sounds I then heard were with me in my dreams for months, startling me with their horrid nightmare vision. I noticed while wandering along the earthworks that all or nearly all of the Union soldiers were shot in the foreheads . . . . They came up in the very worst place they could have come, for them (the Confederates), and ought to have known what the result would have been. There were twelve or thirteen of Hood's best generals dead on the Union breastworks, and in front the ground was covered with bodies, and pools of blood that it was no fiction to call 'fields of gore.' The cotton in the old cotton gin was shot out all over the ground and looked as if it had been scattered there by some designing hand, and the small grove of locusts to the right of the Carter's creek pike was cut off by bullets as clean as if cut by a knife. Mr. Carter's son (a Confederate soldier) was found dead in his own father's yard next morning. The family had stayed in the cellar all through the fight, and all night. Our soldiers [that is, the Yanks] had all been stripped of everything but their shirts and drawers; but the Confederate soldiers could not be blamed much for that, for they were half clothed, half barefoot and many of them bareheaded; but I saw one thing I thought contemptible. A fine looking Union soldier had been stripped of all but his shirt and drawers. He was lying off by himself at the roadside near the depot. He was apparently an officer. His shirt was fine flannel. 'H'yar,' says a big Confederate, calling to some of his men—'boys, h'yar's a mighty fine shut on this ere dead Yank' (giving him a kick). I thought it was bad enough to strip him of hat, coat, pants, boots and socks; they might at least give him a single garment to bury him in. When I went past one of their hospitals there were several wagon loads of limbs in a pile that had been amputated.

It was several days before they knew that I was a northern woman, but when they did they seemed to respect my helpless condition and treated me kindly. And I shall never forget one of the men, a nurse and cook for the wounded—a Mr. Hicks, from

THE MCGAVOCKS OF CARNTON PLANTATION

Mississippi. He had no confidence in Hood's forward movement, and tried to comfort me as we walked among the flowers, and talked in whispered words. 'Be comforted,' said he; 'it is only for a few days, and you will be among your friends again. This cannot last.' And sure enough, sooner than I thought, the fierce cannonading eighteen miles away, at Nashville, told me that something would happen soon. I overheard an officer say, 'We are going to cut the bridge.' Then I knew that the Confederates were falling back. And there they came. Barefoot; bareheaded; half of them without guns; running; and as the rear guard of the Confederates passed through and scattering shots were heard, I jumped to my feet and went out. I could stand it no longer. Among the first men to enter town were some railroad men that I knew, and I rushed out and caught them in my arms. I was a prisoner no longer. I expect I acted like a crazy woman. But do you wonder at it?[1311]

❧ THE BATTLE OF NASHVILLE

As Mrs. Snyder notes, by midnight, even as sporadic fighting and scattered gunfire continued, the Yanks, who had escaped with relatively few casualties, were crossing the Harpeth River northward over repaired bridges, burning them as they went. Covering the eighteen mile trip quickly and quietly, the Army of the Ohio arrived in Nashville by dawn, where Schofield joined Southerner-turned-Northerner, Union General George Henry Thomas (1816-1870).

Thomas, nicknamed the "Rock of Chickamauga" for his stalwart performance at the battle of that name,[1312] was already a seasoned veteran before Lincoln's War, having fought alongside Robert E. Lee and Albert Sidney Johnston (1803-1862) in the Mormon War of the 1850s. Under Thomas the Federals, now with a combined force of 55,000 men

---

1311. Thatcher, pp. 309-313.
1312. Thomas, born in Virginia, switched sides and fought for the North, in great part, because his wife was a New Yorker. But he earned few accolades for this decision. In fact, it permanently tainted his military career and injured his private life, for he was never again completely trusted by either Northerners or Southerners. Even Thomas' Virginia relations disowned him: they burned his letters, turned his picture to the wall, and strongly advised him to change his name. Thomas did not advance his reputation among former Confederates when, after the War, he went on to serve as commander of Louisiana and Texas, one of the five military districts set up by Radical Republicans to physically force "Reconstruction" on an unwilling South. Warner, GB, s.v. "George Henry Thomas"; Sword, SI, p. 33; Cartmell, p. 35; J. H. Franklin, p. 79.

THE MCGAVOCKS OF CARNTON PLANTATION

stationed in what would become "Music City," set about fortifying the town in preparation for the inevitable "final showdown."[1313]

A defensive system was immediately instigated, one based around three of the town's larger forts: Fort Negley, Fort Morton, and Fort Houston, along with several smaller structures, Hill (Number) 210, Fort Gillem (later called Fort Sill), Fort Garesché, and Battery Donaldson. Nashville's beautiful capitol building, early on commandeered by the meddlesome Yanks and turned into Fort Johnson, was reinforced with earth parapets, cedar log stockades, and breastworks made of cotton bales, manned by a regiment of infantry and fifteen mounted guns.[1314] Thomas' defenses would prove to be nearly impregnable.

The need to repair river bridges and regroup his men, along with a sudden onslaught of sleet, ice, snow, and generally miserable, frigid weather, delayed Hood's pursuit. But he arrived in Nashville with 23,000 men shortly thereafter and settled in to await Thomas' next move,[1315] earnestly hoping for reinforcements from the trans-Mississippi.[1316]

Naturally reinforcements never came: by now no one could afford to give up any men; the Confederacy was already stretched too thin as it was. Still, when the thaw arrived on December 15, the two armies were as prepared as they could be to meet up one last time.[1317]

1313. The exact number of Yanks who fought at Nashville is not known, but the most reliable lists put the number at 54,881. Horn, DBN, p. 3.
1314. Fort Houston was later renamed Fort McCook in honor of Union Gen. Dan McCook. Fort Negley would later be renamed Fort Harker, though locally it is still known by its original moniker. The Yanks did more than strengthen their defenses when they built Fort Negley: the original site, with its beautiful oak tree covered slopes, had been a favorite picnic spot of local families. Lincoln made fast work of the breathtaking groves when he sent in 2,000 impressed slaves with axes to clear the forest. Nashville's best picnic grounds were not the only casualty of the fort's construction: Tennesseans had recently erected the Asylum for the Blind nearby, at a cost of $40,000 (in today's currency $1 million). Because the building was in the path of Fort Negley's guns, the Yanks unsentimentally blew it up and cleared it away. Horn, DBN, pp. 25-26. Nashville has never been the same since the megalomaniac tyrant Lincoln took it over in February 1862.
1315. As with the Union side, the precise number of Confederates who took part in the Battle of Nashville has never been established. The official returns of the Army of Tennessee on December 10, 1864, however, show that Hood had a total combination (infantry, cavalry, and artillery) of 23,053 men "present effective." Horn, DBN, p. 3.
1316. Henry, SC, pp. 430-431.
1317. Simmons, s.v. "Nashville, Tennessee."

THE MCGAVOCKS OF CARNTON PLANTATION

(The inclement weather had delayed Thomas' plans as well. He had hoped to attack Hood days earlier but was held up when the weather changed and the ground became covered with ice and slush, and the roads turned to freezing mud.[1318] Union General Ulysses S. Grant, who still bore a grudge against Thomas from the past, and who did not fully appreciate "the Rock's" situation, became extremely upset over what he saw as stalling and hesitancy.[1319] Several times he threatened to demote Thomas and come to Nashville and take over command of Federal forces himself. Only warmer temperatures on the morning of December 15 prevented this.)[1320]

We will note here that unaccountably, and in hindsight, tragically, after 2nd Franklin Hood sent one of his most valuable warriors, General Forrest, along with three cavalry divisions and one infantry division (some 6,500 men), to Murfreesboro, Tennessee, thirty miles to the southeast, with the express order to destroy railroads, railroad bridges, and blockhouses along the way. (Pro-South author Stanley F. Horn—a friend of the McGavocks—correctly referred to the move as a self-destructive mistake of unimaginable magnitude.)[1321]

Hood's ultimate objective seems to have been for Forrest to take the relatively small city of Murfreesboro, or at least surround the Yankee garrison there and prevent it from getting supplies or reinforcements.[1322] But why at that specific moment?[1323] Hood was about to go up against

---

1318. Weeks, p. 126.
1319. C. R. Hall, p. 159.
1320. See Horn, DBN, pp. 43-72. It is unfortunate that Grant did not take over Thomas' command. To this day, I, like many other Southerners, feel that Hood would have had much better odds against Grant, whom 19th-Century Southerners considered inept and "stupid" (see e.g., Pollard, LC, p. 509), than against the more militarily talented Thomas.
1321. Horn, DBN, pp. 36, 41. The blunder was doubly egregious because, as it turned out, the Federal cavalry at Nashville was the deciding factor in the outcome of the conflict. Even as Union officers, like cavalry commander Brig. Gen. James Harrison Wilson (1837-1925), later admitted, if Forrest and his fearsome and famous cavalry escort had been present at the scene to greet the Yankee horsemen, how different might the Battle of Nashville turned out. Seabrook, ARB, p. 417.
1322. Sword, CLH, pp. 283-284, 344.
1323. Military critics continue to see Forrest's detachment to Murfreesboro as one of Hood's greatest mistakes, for at the time it was a city of relatively little importance in comparison to Nashville. And besides, at Nashville Thomas' cavalry was expecting Forrest, and indeed was already preparing to "contend" with him. See e.g., ORA, Vol. 45, Ser. 1, Pt. 2, pp. 17-18. It is possible, as some Confederate soldiers later stated, that Hood had not originally planned on fighting the Yanks in Nashville, but rather had intended to capture

THE MCGAVOCKS OF CARNTON PLANTATION

an army over twice his size, one deeply entrenched in a seven mile wide arc in and around Tennessee's largest city, its very capital.[1324]

That day during a sharp engagement, Thomas battered Hood's left, then forced the Rebels south, back onto Franklin Pike and Granny White Pike, toward Overton Hill. The fighting, which also pushed west, then spilled over into the area of Belle Meade Plantation, Carnton's sister plantation, where an intriguing incident took place.[1325]

A cousin of mine, Selene Harding (1846-1892),[1326] daughter of General William Giles Harding and Elizabeth Irvin McGavock, ran out and stood on the stone arm of the front steps waving her handkerchief at the Rebel cavalry as it came flying through her yard.

According to a Confederate officer at the scene, Lieutenant James Dinkins, bullets were sizzling in all directions, some tearing off shrubbery and hitting the mansion. Despite being urged by the men to get back into the house, the fearless Southern belle refused to move, gallantly shouting encouragement until all of the troops had passed. Dinkins, who caught up her handkerchief as he galloped past, later wrote that she appeared like a beautiful Greek goddess amidst the powder smoke, and was the bravest person on the scene.[1327]

But Selene's uplifting feminine support did little to change the tide of events that day. By evening the Yanks had driven the Rebels back some two miles, sacred Southern ground that they would never

---

Murfreesboro in order to establish Winter quarters there. Nonetheless, the question remains: now that he knew he soon would be facing far superior forces in Nashville, why was Hood even thinking about the small Union complement stationed at Murfreesboro? And why send Forrest, of all people, the man who Sherman and many others considered one of the Confederacy's finest and most fearsome officers, there to engage it? Horn, DBN, pp. 69-70.

1324. Woodworth, p. 301.

1325. During the Battle of Nashville, Belle Meade Plantation served as a headquarters for the Confederacy, while its (horse) race track was used to park Confederate wagon trains.

1326. Selene is my 6th cousin.

1327. Horn, DBN, p. 85. Selene later married Confederate Gen. William Hicks "Red" Jackson (1835-1903) who, during the Battle of Nashville, had commanded a cavalry brigade under Forrest. After the War Jackson helped turn Belle Meade Plantation into one of the top horse breeding farms in the South. The president of the National Agricultural Congress and the Tennessee Bureau of Agriculture, Jackson passed away at the Harding estate on March 30, 1903, and was laid to rest at Mount Olivet Cemetery in Nashville. Warner, GG, s.v. "William Hicks 'Red' Jackson."

THE MCGAVOCKS OF CARNTON PLANTATION

recover.[1328]

The next day, December 16, 1864, dawned foggy, wet, and cold. But this did not prevent thousands of Nashville spectators from thronging into the nearby hills to watch the event. And neither did the weather stop Thomas who, now tasting victory, struck the hill again, this time with additional attacks on Shy's Hill (which contained Confederate artillery).

As the Federals—among them, Colonel Benjamin Harrison (1833-1901), future U.S. president[1329]—bore down on the Rebels with their superior Spencer repeating rifles, Hood's right and center collapsed. With Stephen Dill Lee's right fully exposed, the Confederates had little option: flee or perish. As the rain continued, darkness was now closing in "like a pall" over both the conqueror and the defeated.

It was all over, except for the official reports. Horn calls the Yanks' successful assault on Shy's Hill the pivotal determinant in the decisive Battle of Nashville.[1330]

A heavy freezing rain helped cover Hood's hasty and disorganized withdrawal into the Brentwood Hills, back south toward Franklin. But not before Thomas had captured thousands of Rebel prisoners, dozens of cannon, and thousands of small arms.

For the record, despite the severe thrashing it dealt the Confederacy, the Union did not escape unharmed at Nashville. It suffered some 2,140 casualties, just slightly less than half that of the Rebels. A high percentage of those killed outright, particularly during

---

1328. McMaster, p. 482.
1329. Col. Harrison was commander of the First Brigade, Provisional Detachment (District of the Etowah), under Maj. Gen. James Blair Steedman (1817-1883). Horn, DBN, 172. Harrison, who was elected America's twenty-third president in 1889, fought in the Atlanta campaign and helped score a major Yank victory at the Battle of Peach Tree Creek, Georgia, July 20, 1864. DeGregorio, s.v. "Benjamin Harrison." Besides Harrison, five other U.S. presidents also served in the War for Southern Independence, like Harrison, all on the wrong side; that is, with the Union: James A. Garfield (1831-1881), Ulysses S. Grant (1822-1885), Rutherford B. Hayes (1822-1893), Chester A. Arthur (1829-1886), and William McKinley (1843-1901). One U.S. president did get it right: Virginian John Tyler (1790-1862), who, though he did not fight in Lincoln's War (being too old at the time), served as a member of the Provisional Congress of the Confederacy. He was later elected to the Confederate House of Representatives, but passed away before taking his seat.
1330. Horn, DBN, pp. 129, 138.

THE MCGAVOCKS OF CARNTON PLANTATION

the skirmish at Peach Orchard Hill,[1331] were black Yanks (from the First and Second Colored Brigades),[1332] who, like all of Lincoln's military, were segregated from white Union soldiers[1333] and led by white Union officers.[1334]

While this fact, that Unionized blacks fought against the South at Nashville, is endlessly repeated by Northern propagandists, what is never mentioned is that there were dozens, perhaps even hundreds, of blacks fighting unofficially under Hood on the Confederate side at Nashville.[1335]

As the one and only defeat of a principal Rebel army,[1336] it is for good reason that the Battle of Nashville has been called the most complete demolition of any major Confederate force during Lincoln's War.[1337] And because of Thomas' near total domination of the conflict, military researchers have voted it third in the top ten list of "best commanded battles of the War."[1338]

Once more Hood had unnecessarily put his troops in harm's way, losing an additional 4,462 men before fleeing southward through fog, rain, and sleet with the barefooted, hatless, jacket-less, starving, rag-tag remnants of his once mighty army. One eyewitness recalls prints of

---

1331. The side of Peach Orchard Hill was said to be so deep with Yankee bodies that one could walk all the way down to the bottom without touching the ground. Horn, DBN, p. 123. Many of these men, who were from Lincoln's segregated black brigades, must have been jealous as they looked across the battlefield and saw Confederate blacks fighting side-by-side with white Rebel soldiers.
1332. See Horn, DBN, pp. 74, 76, 120, 172.
1333. Barrow, Segars, and Rosenburg, BC, p. 4; Mullen, p. 31.
1334. L. H. Johnson, NAS, p. 134.
1335. As few official records of Confederate black soldiers still exist (many were certainly purposefully destroyed by anti-South proponents), we have no ironclad numbers. What we do know is that numerous Confederates, men like the Army of Tennessee's Gen. Nathan Bedford Forrest, were well-known to have commanded blacks. Some sixty-five African-Americans, for instance, served under Forrest throughout the entire War, forty-five from his own plantations. As we will see, Forrest officially liberated his black house servants even before the War, while he freed his servant-soldiers shortly after the Battle of Chickamauga (September 18-20, 1863). This was only months after Lincoln issued his phony Emancipation Proclamation (which freed no slaves), and over two years before all American black slaves were officially emancipated under the Thirteenth Amendment. See Seabrook, ARB, pp. 160, 165, 274.
1336. Henry, SC, p. 434.
1337. Sword, SI, p. 304.
1338. The Civil War Book of Lists, p. 63.

THE McGAVOCKS OF CARNTON PLANTATION

blood left in the snow by Hood's barefooted men.[1339]

Some were able to wrap burlap cloth around their feet in order to protect them from ice and sharp stones.[1340] However, the luckiest among them wore handcrafted shoes made from highly protective pieces of rawhide from beeves (which were simply wrapped around their feet), or from caps and coat sleeves.[1341]

❧ HOOD'S RETREAT

The victorious Union soldiers went in hot pursuit, nipping at Hood's heels south back through Franklin (where the Battle of Franklin III took place on December 17) and Spring Hill and on to Columbia, Tennessee. The Rebels' escape route, from Nashville down Granny White Pike toward Brentwood and Franklin, is today marked with historical signs indicating the cheerless path of "Hood's Retreat."

Of this sad episode Captain Thomas J. Key noted that it was one of the most shocking and inglorious beatings an army had ever received.[1342] Watkins stated that he had "never seen an army so confused and demoralized."[1343] Hood himself later wrote of the incident: "I beheld for the first and only time a Confederate army abandon the field in confusion."[1344] Swedish-American poet and historian, Carl Sandburg (1878-1967), observed that in the entire War no defeat was so complete as Hood's at Nashville. His army had utterly disappeared.[1345]

Even then Hood and his remaining troops were only saved from complete destruction by "the Wizard of the Saddle," General Forrest, who rejoined Hood just north of Columbia and the Duck River on

---

1339. Horn, DBN, p. 154.
1340. Eaton, HSC, p. 95.
1341. Wiley, LJR, p. 121; Horn, DBN, p. 44. Lack of footwear was a common problem for the Confederacy throughout Lincoln's War. It has been said, for example, that Lee might have won the Battle of Sharpsburg (Antietam to Yanks)—fought September 16-18, 1862—had his men had shoes. By some estimates Lee needed some 40,000 pairs. Many of his men were not able to fight that day because of the raw condition of their bare feet. Eaton, HSC, p. 95.
1342. Wiley, LJR, pp. 87-88.
1343. Watkins, p. 213.
1344. Hood, p. 303.
1345. Sandburg, SOL, p. 342.

THE MCGAVOCKS OF CARNTON PLANTATION

December 18.[1346] From there Forrest and his barefoot men gallantly and violently defended the army's rear as it made its way south,[1347] where it arrived in Tupelo, Mississippi, in late December.[1348] (The Yanks finally broke off the chase on December 27, allowing the remaining 15,000 fleeing Rebel troops to withdraw across the Tennessee River in peace.)[1349]

Pro-South writer Andrew Nelson Lytle put the situation this way: Hood rolled the dice and lost; Sherman won. Why? Because Hood was not up to the task he had been assigned. Thus in a mere thirty-five days he literally obliterated the Army of Tennessee.[1350]

If only Hood had listened to Forrest, or Cleburne, or any of his other officers on the afternoon of November 30. How different things might have turned out. Instead, the West's mighty Confederate force, the 51,000- man Army of Tennessee, had been decimated.[1351] The fight for freedom from Yankee tyranny in the West was finished.

For all practical purposes the War of Southern Independence itself was over, lost at Atlanta, Spring Hill, Franklin II, and now Nashville. There were no other engagements of any major consequence after Nashville, and within 120 days Lincoln's illegal bloodbath to violently force the Confederacy back into the Union came to an end.

Here is how General Grant saw it years after the War:

> If Hood had been an enterprising commander, he would have given us a great deal of trouble. Probably he was controlled from Richmond [by President Davis]. As it was he did the very thing I wanted him to do. If I had been in Hood's place I would never have gone near Nashville. I would have gone to Louisville, and on north until I came to Chicago. What was the use of his knocking his head against the stone walls of Nashville? If he had gone north, Thomas never would have caught him. We should have had to

---

1346. Sword, CLH, p. 406.
1347. Browning, pp. 88-89.
1348. McDonough and Connelly, p. 178.
1349. Horn, DBN, p. 163.
1350. Lytle, p. 370.
1351. Chesnut, MCCW, p. 698.

THE MCGAVOCKS OF CARNTON PLANTATION

raise new levies. I was never so anxious during the war as at that time.[1352]

Indeed, according to Yankee top brass on the battlefield and in Washington, D.C., at the time the Union was nearing bankruptcy, the War Department was demoralized, the U.S. civilian population was war weary, Federal soldiers—who had not been paid in five months—were exhausted, and the nation's commercial and financial affairs were crumbling.

On December 15, 1864, the first day of the Battle of Nashville, the North had been on the verge of giving up! Hood could have stretched the Union to the breaking point by merely veering around Nashville and attacking Northern cities. But the stubborn Kentucky general seems to have had something to prove, and so ignored what more rational military men would have done in his situation.[1353]

As Horn wrote of the "decisive Battle of Nashville," Hood's dream of a triumphant Confederate army marching up to the Ohio River was to remain just that: a dream. There would be no Confederate flags waving in Chicago after all, as Grant had feared. All had been decided by the Battle of Nashville, and that decided by Hood. Thus in the end it was Hood who had decided the fate of the Confederacy.[1354]

Now, as thousands of Hood's humiliated and tired stragglers and deserters began to disperse across the South, they spread despondency and discontent to both the public and other soldiers, further hurrying along the end of the Confederacy and the ultimate destruction of the Southern Cause.[1355]

❧ WHY DID HOOD ORDER A FRONTAL ATTACK?

The question is still being asked, of course: Why did Hood, a West Point graduate (already displaying superb leadership qualities) with U.S. army

---

1352. J. R. Young, p. 294. Grant's assumption is wrong. Davis had originally planned for Hood to stay on top of Sherman. See Horn, DBN, p. 7
1353. Horn, DBN, pp. ix-xi.
1354. Horn, DBN, p. 166.
1355. McMaster, p. 483.

THE McGAVOCKS OF CARNTON PLANTATION

experience fighting Native-Americans in Texas, send underfed, underclothed, worn-out men to their deaths at Franklin and Nashville using outdated and inappropriate offensive tactics?

Why, even after four years of hard earned know-how on the field of action during Lincoln's War, and being personally appointed general by President Davis himself, did he doom thousands of his own troops and the Confederacy herself?

Many theories have been put forth by Hood's critics and his admirers alike. And the debate still rages.

❧ WOUNDS, LAUDANUM, & STRONG DRINK

On July 21, 1857, deep in the wilds of the Texas frontier, Hood, then a U.S. army lieutenant, was engaged in fierce hand-to-hand combat with hostile Indians. During the melee an arrow ripped through the back of his left hand, nailing it to his saddle. Breaking off the shaft, he quickly tore his hand away and continued fighting. Hood recovered from the wound, but it left his hand weakened and tender. Other far more serious wounds were to follow, however.

At the Battle of Gettysburg, Pennsylvania (July 1-3, 1863), enemy fire permanently paralyzed his left arm, which he wore in a sling for the rest of his life. Then, while at the Battle of Chickamauga, Georgia (September 18-20, 1863), Hood's right leg was so badly damaged that he had to have it amputated close to the trunk. From then on he had to be lifted onto his saddle and strapped in, his missing limb replaced with a $5,000 cork leg made in France.[1356] Propped upright, with his crutch tied to his saddle, his arm in a sling, and his "dead" leg hanging limply in his stirrup, Hood made a heroic if heartrending sight.

Some speculate that he controlled the severe pain of these injuries through the use of laudanum (a tincture of opium), a drug that may have affected his mental acuity at times.[1357] Others postulate that Hood may have imbibed alcoholic spirits to relieve his suffering and that he may have indeed been drunk at Franklin II. This particular rumor,

---

1356. W. B. Garrison, CWC, p. 27.
1357. Black, p. 191.

THE MCGAVOCKS OF CARNTON PLANTATION

which is without foundation, was still floating around the South when Chesnut mentioned it four months later in February 1865.[1358]

❧ HOOD & THE PETER PRINCIPLE

Another theory for Hood's actions and behavior is that he simply was not cut out to be a high ranking officer and lead men into battle. In fact, as advocates of this hypothesis hold, Hood was a perfect example of the Peter Principle, which states that in a hierarchy one tends to rise to the level of one's incompetence. In plain English, Hood was promoted to a position beyond his skills, intelligence, and experience.[1359]

This is not a modern view. In 1879 Confederate General Richard Taylor looked back and wrote:

> It is painful to criticise Hood's conduct of this campaign. . . . he was a splendid leader in battle, and as a brigade or division commander unsurpassed; but, arrived at higher rank, he seems to have been impatient of control, and openly disapproved of [Gen. Joseph Eggleston] Johnston's conduct of affairs between Dalton and Atlanta. Unwillingness to obey is often interpreted by governments into capacity for command.[1360]

In 1882 Watkins was even more succinct:

> Hood was a good man, a kind man, a philanthropic man, but he is both harmless and defenseless now. He was a poor General in the capacity of Commander-in-Chief. Had he been mentally qualified, his physical condition would have disqualified him. His legs and one of his arms had been shot off in the defense of his country. As a soldier, he was brave, good, noble, and gallant, and fought with the ferociousness of the wounded tiger, and with the everlasting grit of the bull-dog; but as a General he was a failure in every particular.[1361]

1358. Chesnut, MCCW, p. 731.
1359. See Peter and Hull, passim.
1360. R. Taylor, p. 257.
1361. Watkins, p. 218.

THE MCGAVOCKS OF CARNTON PLANTATION

Surely most then, as today, would agree with General Wade Hampton III (1818-1902) that Hood had been pushed up the ranks too quickly.[1362]

❧ A WEST POINT RIVAL

Yet another possibility for why Hood ordered a suicide mission at 2nd Franklin concerns an old school rivalry.

Hood and his Franklin nemesis, Union General Schofield—just one of millions of white Yanks who later, as U.S. secretary of war (1868-1869) under President Andrew Johnson, would vote against enfranchising blacks during Reconstruction[1363]—had been roommates at West Point. Here, in 1853, Schofield graduated fourth out of a class of fifty-five and was considered a successful military scholar who later taught, as an assistant professor, at the school.

In contrast, Hood, who also graduated that year (along with future Yank officers Philip Sheridan and William Sooy Smith),[1364] left near the bottom of his class (forty-fourth out of fifty-five), and while there earned 196 demerits for bad behavior (four shy of expulsion). Little wonder that in his day Hood was considered by many to be a West Point failure, a humiliation that he carried the rest of his life.[1365]

Perhaps, even after a decade, Kentuckian Hood was still infuriated at New Yorker Schofield for besting him at the famed military academy. Perhaps, as the Battle of Franklin II opened on the afternoon of November 30, Hood saw it as a golden opportunity to finally get even with the one who beat him in education by beating him on the battlefield.

❧ OLD SCHOOL HOOD

Others speculate that when it came to fighting, Hood was old school.

1362. Chesnut, MCCW, p. 710.
1363. DeGregorio, s.v. "Andrew Johnson."
1364. *The Civil War Book of Lists*, p. 125.
1365. In all fairness to Hood, it should be noted that Schofield too racked up a number of demerits during his time at West Point, 196 to be exact, the same number as Hood. The difference is that between demerits Schofield was apparently able to study and pass exams, while Hood was not.

THE MCGAVOCKS OF CARNTON PLANTATION

According to this hypothesis Hood held to the belief that "real men" do not fight from behind trees, barricades, walls, or from inside pits. They "stand up and fight" in the open, in plain view of the enemy. And such men do not attack from the flanks or rear either. Instead, they attack only from the front, marching straight at their foe.

This form of combat, common in ancient times among the Greeks, Celts, and Romans, was also used during America's first Revolutionary War in 1775, right up until the beginning of her second Revolutionary War in 1861, the War for Southern Independence.

But by the end of the first year of that conflict, improvements in ordnance technology and new military attitudes were calling for fresh, more modern forms of fighting on the battlefield, such as the use of trenches, breastworks, earthworks, underground bombproofs, embrasures, and other types of elaborate fortifications, including anti-personnel entanglements, such as wire, abatis, and fallen trees. The days of the massed frontal assault were over. Trench warfare had begun.[1366]

Most Confederate leaders took to it at once. Confederate Chief of Ordnance Josiah Gorgas, for example, noted in June of 1864 that by then most Rebel troops were fighting behind multiple rows of ditches,[1367] while General Robert E. Lee became known as the "King of Spades" for requiring his men to dig temporary trenches prior to battle.[1368]

Unfortunately for the Army of Tennessee, Hood seemed to want nothing to do with this "newfangled" form of fighting, despite the fact that both the Federal army and the rest of the Confederate army had adopted it, modernizing themselves almost from the start of the War. Hood, stuck in the past, preferred the ancient "barbaric" Celtic method of combat, the aggressive and offensive type epitomized by the likes of McGavock cousin and Scottish hero Sir William "Braveheart" Wallace (1272-1305), at the Battle of Sterling Bridge in 1297.

Hood himself said as much. In his military memoir, *Advance and*

1366. Pritchard, pp. 97-98.
1367. Eaton, HSC, p. 101.
1368. Sorrel, p. 128.

THE MCGAVOCKS OF CARNTON PLANTATION

Retreat, the Kentuckian wrote:

> The troops of the Army of Tennessee had for such length of time been subjected to the ruinous policy pursued from Dalton to Atlanta, that they were unfitted for united action in pitched battle. They had, in other words, been so long habituated to security behind breastworks that they had become wedded to the 'timid defensive' policy, and naturally regarded with distrust a commander likely to initiate offensive operations.[1369]
>   . . . A soldier cannot fight for a period of one or two months constantly behind breastworks, with training that he is equal to four or five of the enemy by reason of the security of his position, and then be expected to engage in pitched battle and prove as intrepid and impetuous as his brother who has been taught to rely solely upon his own valor. The latter, when ordered to charge and drive the enemy, will—or endeavor to—run over any obstacle he may encounter in his front; the former, on account of his undue appreciation of breastworks and distinct remembrance of the inculcations of his commanding officer, will be constantly on the look-out for such defences. His imagination will grow vivid under bullets and bombshells, and a brush-heap will so magnify itself in dimension as to induce him to believe that he is stopped by a wall ten feet high and a mile in length. The consequence of his troubled imagination is that, if too proud to run, he will lie down, incur almost equal disgrace, and prove himself nigh worthless in a pitched battle.
>   A somewhat similar result is to be observed in engagements, in the open field, with the red men of the forest. Those who are familiar with their mode of warfare well know that, whenever they are attacked away from such shelter as trees and boulders, they at once become confused, and scatter in all directions. I concede that five hundred, in the open field, would overpower one hundred men, howsoever well trained; but two hundred and fifty properly trained soldiers should always prove the equal of five hundred Indians, mainly because of the difference in the manner of handling forces, practiced by the respective combatants. On the one hand, shelter is invariably sought in time of battle; on the other, reliance is placed upon boldness and valor.
>   In accordance with the same principle, a cavalryman

1369. Hood, p. 162.

proper cannot be trained to fight, one day, mounted, the next, dismounted, and then be expected to charge with the impetuosity of one who has been educated in the belief that it is an easy matter to ride over infantry and artillery, and drive them from the field. He who fights alternately mounted and dismounted, can never become an excellent soldier of either infantry or cavalry proper. Moreover, the highest perfection in the education of troops, well drilled and disciplined, can only be attained through continued appeals to their pride, and through incitement to make known their prowess by the substantial test of guns and colors, captured upon the field of battle. Soldiers thus educated will ever prove a terror to the foe.

  The continued use of breastworks during a campaign, renders troops timid in pitched battle; and the employment of such defences is judicious and profitable alone when resorted to at the proper time. They should be used not unto excess, and only in such instances as I have already mentioned, and in such as I shall hereafter specify. The result of training soldiers to rely upon their own courage, we behold in the achievements of Lee's troops. Long will live the memory of their heroic attempt to scale the rugged heights of Gettysburg; of their gallant charge over the breastworks at Gaines's Mills, and again over the abatis and strong entrenchments at Chancellorsville; of the many deeds of equal daring, which history will immortalize.[1370]

Hood's beliefs as described here certainly explain much of what occurred at Franklin II.

They also explain why an erratic and indecisive Davis replaced General Joseph Eggleston Johnston (1807-1891) with Hood on July 19, 1864.[1371] Johnston had been fighting defensively, patiently wearing down the Union troops and wasting Yankee time and munitions by protecting men and territory rather than by using aggressive movements. Davis wanted an offensive fighter, however, and at that time there was only one man he would consider for the job: his "gallant friend Hood"[1372]

1370. Hood, pp. 131-132.
1371. In one of the War's more bizarre twists of fate, Johnston died after catching a cold while marching bareheaded in the funeral procession of his old Yankee enemy Sherman. Warner, GG, s.v. "Joseph Eggleston Johnston."
1372. J. Davis, RFCG, Vol. 2, p. 488.

THE MCGAVOCKS OF CARNTON PLANTATION

of Kentucky.[1373]

Tragically for Dixie, after the War Union officers admitted that if the South had fought defensively throughout the conflict, in the manner of Johnston (not to mention Forrest and others), she would have won. One of these men, Grant, wrote:

> For my own part, I think Johnston's tactics were right. Anything that could have prolonged the war a year beyond the time that it did finally close, would probably have exhausted the North to such an extent that they might then have abandoned the contest and agreed to a separation. . . .[1374] I think his policy was the best one that could have been pursued by the whole South—protract the war, which was all that was necessary to enable them to gain recognition in the end.[1375]

In fact, as Grant rightly observes, taking out the defensive Johnston and replacing him with the offensive Hood was exactly what the Yanks wanted. Hood's sometimes reckless offensive tactics turned the tables, allowing the North to take the defensive and wear down the South, which is precisely what occurred.

❧ BLAMING & PUNISHING SUBORDINATES

Another theory maintains that Hood, who often blamed his subordinates for his mistakes, was mad over the Spring Hill Affair, in which he felt his officers had let General Schofield slip past the Rebel encampment on Tuesday night, November 29, 1864 (the day before Franklin II), while he slept at Oaklawn Mansion.[1376] Indeed, modern day military tacticians

---

[1373]. Black, p. 65. Ironically, it was in great part Hood's leg wound that created a strong bond of friendship between he and fellow Kentuckian Davis, one that would later help put an end to the Confederacy: after surgery Hood was sent to convalesce in Richmond, Virginia, the Confederacy's capital. While there he came under Davis' spell and influence, even becoming the president's protégée. Hood had entered the hospital a lieutenant general. By the time he recovered he had been promoted to a corps commander in the Army of Tennessee. Horn, DBN, p. 5.
[1374]. U. S. Grant, Vol. 2, p. 167.
[1375]. U. S. Grant, Vol. 2, p. 345.
[1376]. Oaklawn, built in 1835 by Absalom Thompson, and Hood's headquarters during what is also known as the "Spring Hill Blunder," later became the home of country music legends George Jones and Tammy Wynette (1942-1998). In 2005 the film *Daltry Calhoun*, starring Johnny Knoxville and Juliette Lewis, was

THE McGAVOCKS OF CARNTON PLANTATION

have determined that the consequences of this "great lost opportunity" led directly to the disaster of Franklin II the next day.[1377]

That morning, November 30, still fuming at what he considered cowardice and ineptitude, Hood and his officers breakfasted at Rippavilla Plantation, where he gave the men a thorough dressing down. Infuriated, the officers refused to be Hood's scapegoat, and rigorously challenged their commander's accusations.[1378]

Forrest in particular was not happy with this latest incrimination, and stormed out in a rage. Hood hobbled angrily after his dashing cavalry officer, following him out to the front porch. As he was about to mount his horse the lanky but powerful Forrest turned to his physically challenged superior and growled: "Sir, if you was a whole man I'd whip you to within an inch of yer life!"[1379]

The squabble ended with breakfast, but the rancorous feelings continued on the battlefield at Franklin later that day where, many surmise, Hood punished the "insubordination" by ordering his men to

---

filmed at Oaklawn, and in June 2008 the estate was featured in an episode of HGTV's hit series *Design Star*. A side note: I am related to Ms. Wynette by marriage, through her husband and my close cousin, famed songwriter Don Chapel (Lloyd Franklin Amburgey) and his daughter Donna Chapel, Tammy's stepdaughter. Don wrote a number of hit songs, including *When the Grass Grows Over Me* (recorded by George Jones, Conway Twitty, Ernest Tubb, Liz Anderson, Kitty Wells, and Johnny Paycheck), *Joey*, *All Night Long*, *My Heart is Soakin' Wet*, and *Together We Stand Divided We Fall*, all also recorded by Ms. Wynette. In the late 1960s Donna went on to sing backup vocals for Tammy in her newly formed band with Don. I am also cousins with Don's famous sisters Martha Carson (Irene Ethel Amburgey) of Neon, Letcher County, Kentucky—known as the "First Lady of Gospel Music," and Jean Chapel (Opal Jean Amburgey), a popular Nashville songwriter and singer who was known as the "Female Elvis Presley."
1377. Weeks, p. 128; Wood, p. 203.
1378. Brandt, pp. 194-195.
1379. Rippavilla was built between 1851 and 1853 by Maj. Nathaniel Francis Cheairs (1818-1914), my 4th cousin. It was Cheairs who surrendered Confederate forces to Grant at the Battle of Fort Donelson on February 16, 1862. After he was exchanged later that year, Cheairs served as an aide under Forrest and fought with him at the Battle of Thompson's Station on March 5, 1863. Like so many antebellum homes in Middle Tennessee, Rippavilla Plantation has an intriguing history. Its founder Maj. Cheairs married Susan Peters McKissack (1821-1883), the sister of Jessie Helen McKissack (1838-1921), who became infamous for her fling with Confederate Maj. Gen. Earl "Buck" Van Dorn (1820-1863). When Jessie's husband, Dr. George Boddie Peters (1814-1888), uncovered the illicit affair, he stormed into Van Dorn's headquarters down the road at what is now known as Ferguson Hall, and executed the unsuspecting general with a shot through the head, cutting short a brilliant military career. Dr. Peters was later captured, tried, and acquitted. After Van Dorn's death, at Confederate Gen. Braxton Bragg's orders, Forrest took over Van Dorn's command of the cavalry on the left wing of the Army of Tennessee. Both Rippavilla and Ferguson Hall exist to this day, the former which is open for public tours.

THE MCGAVOCKS OF CARNTON PLANTATION

make a full frontal attack across the Plain of Franklin. According to this premise, by forcing them to "fight like real men," Hood was hoping to both punish them and build their courage and confidence back up.[1380]

None of these theories answer every question. Yet all may contain a grain of truth.

In the end, we will never know definitively why Hood sent his men out onto an open grassy field to face a better equipped enemy that was safely dug in behind a multitude of elevated, well protected fortifications.

❧ THE NEAR DEMISE OF AN ARMY

Whatever the reasoning behind his decision, the fact remains that Hood had acted rashly at Franklin and Nashville, helping to drive his own military force, the Army of Tennessee, into the ground.[1381]

It is true that some 15,000 men arrived in Tupelo weeks later, hardly constituting a "destroyed army." But this was less than half the number, fifty-one thousand, he started out with when he took over command a mere six months earlier in July 1864. Of this remaining minority, most were exhausted, freezing, starving, shoeless, blanketless, and depressed, or as one Confederate aide phrased it: We were by now dispirited, dispersed, crushed, and misplaced.[1382]

Many others were wounded and naked, or were by now wearing grimy Federal uniforms taken from captured or dead Yanks.[1383] As we have seen, their situation was so desperate that Hood's men were fashioning cowhide, hats, and even sleeves torn from jackets, into foot wrappings.[1384]

This was an army that was in no condition to march let alone fight. Thus the remaining troops disbanded to convalesce and reform,

---

1380. Woodworth, p. 299.
1381. Civil War Society, CWB, pp. 60-61.
1382. Chesnut, MCCW, pp. 698, 709-710.
1383. Hood's soldiers were far from being the only Johnny Rebs who suffered due to lack of provisions and supplies. The complaint of one soldier was typical of many across the Confederacy: The back of my trousers is gone, my one pair of socks is threadbare, and my only shirt is decomposin' on my very back, he lamented. Pritchard, p. 12.
1384. Henry, SC, p. 434; Horn, DBN, p. 44.

THE MCGAVOCKS OF CARNTON PLANTATION

and Hood resigned in dishonor on January 23, 1865. His command was taken over by General Richard Taylor, the brother of Sarah Knox Taylor (1815-1835), the first wife of Confederate President Jefferson Davis.[1385] On May 4, 1865, Taylor and his men became the last Confederate force to surrender east of the Mississippi River.[1386]

❧ HOOD'S FINAL DAYS

Hood was demoted and served out the remainder of the War as a lieutenant general, finally surrendering to Union authorities at Natchez, Mississippi, on May 31, 1865. He then retired to New Orleans, where he worked in the cotton and insurance businesses. Marrying Anna Marie Hennen (1838-1879) on April 30, 1868, he fathered eleven children (among them, three sets of twins), then lost his fortune in the yellow fever epidemic that hit southern Louisiana in the Winter of 1878-1879.[1387]

Hood himself died of that same disease on August 31, 1879, along with his wife Anna and their eldest daughter Lydia. He was buried in the Hennen family tomb at the Metairie Cemetery in New Orleans.[1388]

This was a sad end to what I consider the potentially promising military career of a truly courageous man. Hood's retreating army sang the following words to the tune of *The Yellow Rose of Texas*:

> And now I'm going southward, for my heart is full of woe,
> I'm going back to Georgia to find my Uncle Joe,
> You may sing about your dearest maid, and sing of Rosalie,
> But the gallant Hood of Texas played hell in Tennessee.[1389]

Others, however, have not been so kind in their estimation of the headstrong Rebel officer.

1385. McDonough and Connelly, p. 178. I am cousins with both Gen. Richard Taylor and his sister, Sarah Knox "Knoxie" Taylor. The Taylors, like the McGavocks and myself, descend from both Virginians and from European royalty, many from identical ancestors.
1386. Warner, GG, s.v. "Richard Taylor."
1387. Warner, GG, s.v. "John Bell Hood."
1388. Boatner, s.v. "Hood, John Bell."
1389. Ridley, p. 439.

The McGavocks of Carnton Plantation

♣ SUMMARIZING FRANKLIN II

How does the Battle of Franklin II go down in history?

In *Gone With the Wind*, author Margaret Mitchell not only portrays one of her lead characters, Rhett Butler, as having fought at 2nd Franklin, but in a revealing conversation in Atlanta between Scarlett O'Hara, Melanie Hamilton, and Frank Kennedy, she also encapsulates the Southern feeling about Hood's questionable fitness for generalship.

After Frank tells the women that Hood has been fighting up in Tennessee in an attempt to lure the Yanks out of Georgia, he receives this acid reply from the Peach State's most famous and feisty heroine: Hood's plan didn't turn out very well, did it? cried Scarlett sarcastically. Marching away to Tennessee he left us with no protection, and the damn Yankees were able to pick us off like fish in a barrel![1390]

The archetypal Southern belle speaks for many Southerners, both then and now. For example, in her diary, dated January 7, 1865, Mary Chesnut mentions a rumor she had heard that Hood had been killed. The response across the South? Immense happiness, she wrote sadly, for she considered herself a friend of the controversial Kentuckian.[1391]

Wartime letters from Confederate soldiers reveal the depth of disdain for Hood, not only by many of his own men, but by those who had never served under him. Dated July 18, 1864, this letter, from a lieutenant from Mississippi to his wife is typical: The most hated officer in the Confederate army is, without question, John Bell Hood, which is why many of the men say they refuse to serve under him[1392]

After walking over the bloody battlefield the following morning, the aforementioned Yankee, Carrie Snyder, wrote of Hood:

> ... any general that would order men to march across such an open field to drive men, protected by such an earthwork as that, must have been a heartless wretch.[1393]

1390. Mitchell, pp. 889, 475.
1391. Chesnut, MCCW, p. 700.
1392. Wiley, LJR, p. 241.
1393. Thatcher, p. 311.

THE MCGAVOCKS OF CARNTON PLANTATION

Famed fire-eater and Texas Senator Louis Trezevant Wigfall (1816-1874), known for his savage wit, had similar feelings toward Hood. He would have had a wonderful military career, Wigfall wrote, if only President Davis had not tried to make a general out of him.[1394]

Confederate officer Captain Foster of Granbury's Brigade summed up what would be Hood's legacy in the eyes of many: General Hood proved that he is a murderer of Confederate soldiers, one who will burn in hell for all eternity.[1395]

Not surprisingly for a man like Hood, he declared 2nd Franklin a Confederate victory (since his troops had penetrated Union lines near the Carter House and had driven the Yanks from town),[1396] and was even planning a second attack the next morning. No one but old school Hood, obsessed with the manly romance of ancient Celtic military techniques, could have possibly viewed the outcome of the battle in such a manner.

Yet, he was not immune to the tragic immensity of what had occurred under his watch. On the morning of December 1 Hood was seen sitting on his horse overlooking the Franklin battlefield, sobbing silently like a little boy.[1397]

Two weeks later a similar scene played out after the Battle of Nashville, when an injured Watkins slogged through rain and freezing mud to Hood's headquarters to request a "wounded furlough." There to

---

1394. D. H. Donald, WNWCW, p. 33.
1395. Sword, SI, p. 302.
1396. Cisco, SRG, p. 143. Actually, Hood did not come close to "driving" the Yanks from Franklin. On the contrary, Schofield never planned on stopping in "Tennessee's handsomest town" to begin with. He only meant to pass through it on his way to Nashville to meet Thomas. Hood's suicidal attack at Franklin was merely an interference, and only slowed, but did not halt, Schofield's northern progress toward Music City. As mentioned, the same could be said of the Battle of Nashville: it was an unnecessary conflict for the Confederacy, one that was not winnable and which wasted valuable time and resources (Nashville had, after all, been securely in Union hands for nearly three years, since February 1862). Hood would have been better off staying in Georgia and pursuing Sherman, President Davis' original plan. This would have both prevented Sherman's infamous "March to the Sea" (see Horn, DBN, p. 7), which dealt the death blow to the Confederacy in the Eastern theater, and spared the Army of Tennessee what would soon become its premature death in Nashville. At the very least, as Grant declared, after Hood decided to leave Georgia he should have bypassed Nashville and headed north into Louisville, then Chicago, where he could have delivered a fatal blow to an already weakened, dispirited, and nearly bankrupt Union that admitted it was on the verge of giving up.
1397. Lowry, p. 583.

his surprise he found his superior in a "much agitated" condition, pulling at his hair with his one hand and "crying like his heart would break." The young soldier never saw Hood again, and later forgave him with these words: "Mercy has erased all his errors and flaws."[1398]

It is true that Hood's critics have underestimated the impact his last two battles had on him. On February 5, 1865, two months before the end of Lincoln's War, Hood visited one of Chesnut's friends, the Prestons. Mary and her husband James Chesnut, Jr. were invited to meet with the famous Confederate officer, after which Mary wrote the following in her diary:

> Hood came yesterday. He is staying at the Prestons' with Jack. They sent for us. What a heartfelt greeting he gave us. He can stand well enough without his crutch, but he does very slow walking. How plainly he spoke out dreadful words about "my defeat and discomfiture; my army destroyed, my losses," etc., etc. He said he had nobody to blame but himself.[1399]

While we can certainly sympathize with Hood's anguish and applaud his daring, perseverance, and dedication to the Confederate Cause, at the same time we must make an honest assessment of his actions on November 30, 1864. It is simply this: there can be little question that Franklin II (along with Nashville) shattered the last remaining hope for a Confederate win against Lincoln by bringing an end to Rebel strength, and thus control, in the Western theater.[1400]

Some go as far as to say that it was Hood who lost the War itself.[1401] Looking back from the perspective of 1882, Watkins wrote of Franklin II:

> Kind reader, right here my pen, and courage, and ability fail me. I shrink from butchery. Would to God I could tear the page from these memoirs and from my own memory. It is the blackest page

---

1398. Watkins, p. 217.
1399. Chesnut, DD, p. 342.
1400. J. C. Bradford, p. 91.
1401. Lytle, pp. 359-360.

THE MCGAVOCKS OF CARNTON PLANTATION

in the history of the war of the Lost Cause. It was the bloodiest battle of modern times in any war. It was the finishing stroke to the independence of the Southern Confederacy. I was there. I saw it. My flesh trembles, and creeps, and crawls when I think of it to-day. My heart almost ceases to beat at the horrid recollection. Would to God that I had never witnessed such a scene![1402]

Indeed, it is now commonly held by all but the most ardent Hood supporters that the Confederacy lost the War, not in the East under Robert E. Lee, but in the West, under the command of John Bell Hood. President Davis himself later called Hood's entire Tennessee campaign misguided, distancing himself as best he could from the debacle.[1403]

❧ WHY THE SOUTH LOST LINCOLN'S WAR

Was Hood solely responsible? Absolutely not. In fact, there are innumerable reasons why the South lost and the Confederacy collapsed, and not all of them even military-related.

Among them there was President Davis' outrageous cronyism; his lack of innovation, his orthodox, old school, conservative approach to the War; his inability to admit when he was wrong and thus adapt and grow; his decision to run both the war office and all military operations (in essence, he became his own secretary of war); his refusal (or inability) to see the big picture; his countless economic restrictions; his policies of dispersing his military forces (instead of concentrating them) and departmentalizing the military (instead of conjoining it); his obsession with bureaucracy and detail rather than with fighting and winning the War; and his failure to learn how to get along with other Confederate leaders.[1404]

Then there was Confederate Vice President Alexander H. Stephens' dislike of and apathy toward Davis; Southern loyalty to state

---

1402. Watkins, pp. 208-209.
1403. Cooper, JDA, p. 540.
1404. D. H. Donald, WNWCW, pp. 91-112; Henry ATSF, p. 218.

THE MCGAVOCKS OF CARNTON PLANTATION

government over national government;[1405] a haphazardly run commissary under General Lucius Bellinger Northrop (1811-1894);[1406] the lack of a Confederate Supreme Court; lack of an official presidential cabinet; lack of separate Confederate political parties (which would have either provided alternatives to the Davis administration or forced it to focus more stringently on the important matter at hand: winning the War); an inadequate Quartermaster Department; the illegal military draft of workers engaged in war industries; varying (that is, non-standardized) railroad track widths across the South; non-connecting railroad lines; an inconsistent and sporadic postal service;[1407] a lack of good business sense among those running the Confederate government;[1408] and a Subsistence Department that was, illogically, made independent of the control of military commanders.[1409]

There was also the fiasco of postponing *official* Confederate enlistment of blacks as active combatants;[1410] endless and needless squabbling among supercilious Rebel officers; the lack of a true military general-in-chief;[1411] the election of military officers (which undermined authority and fostered insubordination); Yankee General Winfield Scott's (1786-1866) Anaconda Plan;[1412] Lincoln's illegal naval blockade; lack of European support and her failure to officially recognize the South, intervene or mediate;[1413] the overall industrial and economic weakness

---

1405. While this loyalty was proper and constitutionally correct, it did interfere with the C.S.A.'s ability to fight the U.S.A. at the time. This is, in great part, because the Confederacy was a newly born republic in 1861, and had not had time to fully learn how to marshal and unify its eleven independent member states.
1406. Pollard, LC, pp. 480-489. Later, evidence revealed that Northrop had done his best under nearly impossible circumstances. See Warner, GG, s.v. "Northrop, Lucius Bellinger."
1407. Channing, pp. 22, 25, 26-27.
1408. Pollard, LC, pp. 488-489.
1409. Jordan and Pryor, p. 462.
1410. As noted earlier, the Confederacy had enlisted blacks into the military even before the start of the War, and long before Lincoln reluctantly decided to do so. However, these early and brave African-American combatants were not considered "official" soldiers since their enrollment had not yet been sanctioned by President Davis and his cabinet.
1411. In early 1865 the Confederate government created the new rank of commander-in-chief for Gen. Robert E. Lee, but the effort came just prior to the South's surrender at Appomattox. Channing, p. 162.
1412. J. C. Bradford, p. 62.
1413. In fairness to Europe, a majority of her people had wanted to both acknowledge and aid the South. However, she was prevented from doing so by war threats from Lincoln. Seabrook, L, p. 761.

of the South compared to the North; and increasing disloyalty and desertion among Confederates due to the influence of Southern antiwar organizations.

Other reasons for the South's loss include the North's overwhelming resources in comparison to the South's (for example, twenty-three Northern industrial states against eleven Southern agricultural states); the South's refusal to engage in trade with the North during the War;[1414] Lee's lost "Special Orders Number 191" (which was retrieved by the enemy and used against the South); Dixie's libertarian emphasis on democratic and personal rights; the highly pugnacious and individualistic tendencies of the liberty-loving Southern people, who had an inherent dislike of authority, structure, and discipline; the Confederate government's insistence on raising money for the War by borrowing instead of taxing;[1415] governmental interference with the South's free market (which discouraged agricultural and industrial production); a self-imposed cotton embargo; and the Confederacy ignoring Vice President Stephen's brilliant cotton-export plan.

And let us not forget the loss of New Orleans—the Confederacy's financial center—to the Yanks just one year into the fight (May 1, 1862); the loss of Nashville two years into the fight (February 23-25, 1862)[1416]—which split the Confederacy and gave Lincoln control over the vital Cumberland, Tennessee, and Mississippi Rivers; ongoing loss of Southern territory and with it currency depreciation, reduction of the labor supply, intensifying inflationary trends,[1417] the sharp and drastic decline of Confederate currency, and general economic disorganization;[1418] older, less flexible officers in the Confederacy than in the Union; a Confederate military mindset that was often too strictly Jominian (that is offensive rather than defensive); an overly traditional Southern generalship that did not learn and grow as the more progressive

---

1414. Pollard, LC, pp. 481-487.
1415. See Pollard, LC, p. 428.
1416. R. L. Mode, p. 31; Henry, SC, p. 87.
1417. Unlike the inhabitants of the South, Northerners actually flourished under the increasingly high prices during the War. Chesnut, DD, p. xiv.
1418. Pollard, LC, pp. 415-428.

thinking Northern generalship did throughout the War;[1419] the lack of a "grand military strategy" like Grant's;[1420] the premature deaths of brilliant Confederate warriors like Stonewall Jackson, Albert Sidney Johnston, and Turner Ashby (1828-1862); not giving General Nathan Bedford Forrest command of larger forces; inconsistent leadership of an under-equipped, hastily formed army and navy; a largely displaced and terrified civilian population reduced to refugee status; the lack of a Confederate treasury; and perhaps worst of all, runaway inflation.

All of these things, which Edward A. Pollard rightly referred to as "a policy of blunders,"[1421] heavily contributed to the gradual weakening of the Southern Confederacy.

Despite all of this, Hood stands out as the one who lost Atlanta, Franklin, and Nashville, arguably the most significant battles during the latter half of the War, each a major turning point that inevitably spelled doom for the Confederacy.[1422]

However one chooses to look at it, Hood ranks high on the list of the Confederacy's worst generals for having been "the only man on either side to lose an entire army." Being placed at the bottom of the 425 Rebel generals and 583 Yankee generals who fought in Lincoln's War (not to mention the thousands of lower ranked officers on both sides), this is not certainly not how the incredibly brave but hardheaded Hood would have wanted to be remembered.[1423]

I myself, a cousin of the General, do not like to remember him in this way either, though it is difficult not to when one personally surveys the Franklin and Nashville landscapes and recalls those two bitter weeks between November 30 and December 16, 1864.

❧ LAST WORDS ON FRANKLIN II

What final words can a 21st-Century writer offer on 2nd Franklin?

In 1903 here is how William R. Garrett and Albert V.

1419. D. H. Donald, WNWCW, pp. 5-10, 15, passim.
1420. Lytle, p. 306.
1421. Pollard, LC, p. 487.
1422. Black, pp. 8-9.
1423. *The Civil War Book of Lists*, pp. 143, 144.

THE MCGAVOCKS OF CARNTON PLANTATION

Goodpasture put it:

> The Battle of Franklin was the most pathetic of the Tennessee battles. In the midst of homes and friends, with scarce time to receive from their parents the kiss of welcome after their protracted absence, the flower of the Tennessee youth went into battle, full of ardor and resolution—many of them never to return. The fearful havoc in their ranks inflicted a pang in every household in Middle Tennessee.[1424]

It certainly was a pathetic and fearful battle—"one of the bloodiest" of the War, Jefferson Davis called it.[1425] Yet, it was one that did not need to be, indeed, should not have been, fought.

For one thing, Schofield never intended to fight Hood at Franklin on November 30. His goal all along had been to march northward from Columbia straight to Nashville to join forces with Thomas. Had Hood destroyed Schofield's army at Spring Hill, where it had been in a vulnerable and endangered position,[1426] instead of letting him pass by during the night of November 29, Schofield's plans would have been wrecked and the Battle of Franklin II would never have taken place.

Hood could then have marched into Nashville himself and there delivered the fatal blow against a much diminished Yankee fighting force. As it was, Hood lost 7,000 men at Franklin, then detached his finest cavalryman, Forrest, with another 6,500 men to Murfreesboro before attacking a refreshed, well entrenched army twice his size under Schofield and Thomas in Nashville two weeks later. For his total and unquestioned victory, Thomas was given a new nickname: "the Sledge of Nashville."[1427]

Yes, Franklin II should have never occurred, and not only because of "lost opportunities" at Spring Hill. There is also the bold fact

---

1424. Garrett and Goodpasture, pp. 230-231.
1425. J. Davis, RFCG, Vol. 2, p. 575.
1426. Henry, SC, p. 428.
1427. Steele and Steele, Vol. 2, p. 567.

that the outcome of Lincoln's War had already been clearly decided by November 1864. By then all of the major Confederate cities had already been captured, with Virginia, North Carolina, and South Carolina being the only Southern states still under effective control of the Confederacy.[1428]

Last and perhaps most importantly, by the end of 1864, Rebel army funds, ammunition, clothing, food, and morale were at their lowest ebb, and were in fact nearing total depletion.[1429] And there were the desertion rates, which were at an all-time high.

Despite all of this, hundreds of thousands of brave Confederate men fought on in an effort to preserve Southern honor, Southern unity, Southern rights, and Southern independence, and for this they can never be faulted. We can only eulogize them as everlasting heroes.

❧ FINAL CONFEDERATE VICTORIES

After the Battles of Franklin II and Nashville, the Rebels continued to rack up sporadic victories here and there. The primary Confederate wins during the final days of the War were:

Fort Fisher I (December 7-27, 1864)
Natural Bridge (March 6, 1865)
Dinwiddie Courthouse (March 31, 1865)
Cumberland Church (April 7, 1865)
Palmito Ranch or Palmito Hill (May 12-13, 1865)

Unfortunately for the South these last few victories had little impact. For as we have seen, by now the outcome of the War had been decided.

1428. Channing, p. 152.
1429. Johnny Reb was often given more supplies from family, friends, and Southern sympathizers than from his own government. In fact, without these extra provisions many Confederate soldiers would have died and their units would have disbanded long before the War ended. Pollard, LC, p. 480.

The McGavocks of Carnton Plantation

❧ THE BATTLE OF FORT DONELSON

Indeed, far earlier, the three Battles of Franklin, as well as Nashville, had been the final nails in a coffin that had been well under construction since the Battle of Fort Donelson, Tennessee, February 11 through 16, 1862.

It was here that Confederate officers needlessly surrendered (except the dauntless General Forrest), forcing Rebel General Albert Sidney Johnston to relinquish Kentucky and most of Middle and Western Tennessee, all which had been controlled by the Confederacy up until that time. This allowed further strengthening of Union control at Nashville (by now a primary Federal nerve center), which by December 15, 1864, the day Hood threw his broken-down forces against Thomas there, had become a near unconquerable Yankee city.

The Confederate capitulation at Donelson had other dire consequences for the future of the South. At the time Grant was about to be arrested, tried, and imprisoned by his commander-in-chief, U.S. Major General Henry Wagner Halleck (1815-1872), for "gross insubordination."[1430] The unnecessary Rebel surrender, however, handed Grant a major win, one he had not earned. This in turn caused Halleck to drop all charges, while catapulting the general to the status of national hero in the North.[1431]

Grant was then promoted and over the next three years went on to cause the deaths of hundreds of thousands of Southerners. He even delivered the final blow of Southern humiliation, writing out the terms of the Confederacy's surrender at Appomattox Court House on April 9, 1865.

Now an international symbol of victory, strength, power, and success, he was quite naturally elected president of the U.S. in 1868. As head of the second most corrupt administration in American history (the first was Lincoln's), one widely known as "the nadir of national disgrace," for two long terms Grant continued to wound and demean the South, supporting and maintaining the hellish "Reconstruction" period

---

1430. Hansen, pp. 120-124.
1431. Wyeth, LGNBF, pp. 40-42.

with brute military force.[1432]

The Battle of Franklin II was indeed the inevitable outcome of a series of Confederate mistakes and needless disasters, all which led directly to the equally ruinous Battle of Nashville. As Southern historians have long noted, the bloodbath at Franklin II sprang from the breakdown at Spring Hill, the loss at Nashville from both.[1433]

The question is, could 2nd Franklin have been prevented? Not with Hood in command of the Army of Tennessee.

❧ HOW HOOD'S LOSS AT ATLANTA LOST THE WAR

Arguably, as Scarlett O'Hara intimated, Hood's greatest blunder came months before, at the Battle of Atlanta, July 22 through September 1, 1864. Here Hood lost the region to Yankee war criminal General William Tecumseh Sherman (1820-1891), a victory that allowed Lincoln to get reelected.

Up until then the president's popularity in the North had been decreasing daily, and by the Summer of that year even Lincoln himself was resigned to losing his bid for a second term. With the North growing evermore war weary over rising death tolls and a shrinking treasury it seemed almost certain that a peace candidate would secure the next election.

Sherman's impressive win and Hood's equally impressive loss at Atlanta changed all of that virtually overnight. With renewed war fever and a revitalized belief in their leader, Northerners, helped along by Lincoln's shady backroom deals and illegal shenanigans, handily voted Lincoln into office a second time.[1434] This permitted the warmongering Illinoisan to continue the conflict long enough to wear down the Confederacy by April of 1865.[1435]

1432. Weintraub, p. 76. The scandals that occurred under Grant's presidency could fill a small volume. Some of the best known are the Tweed Ring Scandal, the Credit Mobilier Scandal, and the Whiskey Ring Scandal.
1433. Henry, SC, p. 430.
1434. N. Bradford, p. 490.
1435. Union wins that Summer by Yankee war criminals Grant, Thomas, George Meade (1815-1872), and Philip Sheridan (1831-1888), also helped get Lincoln reelected.

The McGavocks of Carnton Plantation

Had Hood not ignored Jefferson Davis' original game plan (to stay on top of Sherman), and had he not repeatedly taken the offensive (he should have fought defensively),[1436] he would have won Atlanta, Lincoln would have been defeated in the '64 election, and, more than likely, his opponent, George Brinton McClellan, who believed in states' rights and was conciliatory toward the South, would have become the nation's seventeenth president. McClellan, who called Lincoln's War a failure, whose platform writer was peacenik Clement Laird Vallandigham, and whose running mate, George Hunt Pendleton (1825-1889), was an Ohioan peace candidate, would have immediately negotiated a peaceful end to the War, sparing thousands of lives and the near ruin of the South.

The Confederacy itself may have survived, and today 120 million Southerners would be living in their own nation, the fourth richest in the world, under the original Constitution of the Founding Fathers; the same men who called the United States "the Confederacy" between 1781 and 1789,[1437] and who wrote out America's first constitution and named it "The Articles of Confederation."[1438]

1436. W. B. Garrison, CWTFB, p. 31.
1437. See Jensen, NN, passim.
1438. See Jensen, AC, passim.

Carnton's Role in the Battle of Franklin II

◆ CARNTON AS A CONFEDERATE FIELD HOSPITAL

IT WAS NOW ABOUT 6:00 P.M., Wednesday, November 30, 1864. The Battle of 2nd Franklin had been raging for nearly three hours and already hundreds were dead. But it was far from over.

Meanwhile, as fast as Hood's men were mowed down by Union fire they were brought to Carnton, for there were no conventional hospitals in Franklin in 1864. Besides Carnton, some forty-three other buildings in town were used as field hospitals during Franklin II (in total, forty-one for the Rebs and three for the Yanks), including other private homes, schools, the courthouse, the Masonic Lodge, shops, and several churches. Poignantly, thanks to Lincoln's unconstitutional War, Franklin itself had become one huge field hospital—a town whose peaceful agrarian inhabitants had never once posed a threat to either Lincoln or the North.

At Carnton Carrie ordered the carpets pulled back and the furniture shoved to the walls, after which the most severely wounded were carted to the McGavocks' home and brought inside. These numbered about 300. The less seriously injured, as many as 1,500, were treated in the spacious yards outdoors in makeshift areas under the trees.

According to eyewitnesses, every available square inch inside and outside the home was packed with the injured, all except the

The McGavocks of Carnton Plantation

parents' master bedroom, which was set aside for the family's private use. Even the tiny closet under the stairway was utilized for the placing of the wounded. Family legend says that up to three men were kept there at a time.

Over the next six months dozens of Rebel soldiers gasped their final breath in and around Carnton. But it was in the first two days that the most horrors were experienced.

Thursday December 1 and Friday December 2, screams could be heard both day and night, as the surgeon's saw cut off damaged limbs and bullets were extruded with scalpels, all without anaesthesia. A dirty rag with traces of chloroform, some opium, or a few quick shots of whiskey might help dull the pain. Otherwise, soldiers bit down on bullets, leather, cloth, or pieces of wood to stifle their shrieks as the doctors' saws cut through raw flesh, sinew, ligaments, and bone.

Blood stains still cover the floors of Carnton's upstairs bedrooms where these ghastly operations took place, enduring emblems of Confederate courage and the South's unconquerable love of liberty. Those of us who honor the bravery of these fearless American patriots carefully step over and around these stains out of respect, gratitude, admiration, and even veneration.

❧ HATTIE REMEMBERS

Years later, in a newspaper interview, John and Carrie's daughter Hattie would recall her memories as a nine year old of the sights and sounds of hundreds of wounded and dying soldiers being brought to Carnton that night, beginning about dinnertime. In particular she could still visualize the bodies of several famous Confederate generals laid out on her families' back porch.

She would also remember the terrible effects of the battle, including the smell of the blood coming off the fields around Carnton, as well as the aroma of powder smoke blowing around and into the house. And though Franklin II had occurred years before, Hattie could still recollect how their frightened and confused cattle charged home from the fields, seeking protection in the McGavocks' barn.

The McGavocks of Carnton Plantation

❧ JOHN & CARRIE PITCH IN

As Hattie and her younger brother Winder hid in their parents' bedroom upstairs (as mentioned, the only room off limits to the military), Colonel John and Carrie, along with their loyal black servant Maria Reddick and her son Theopolis, helped all they could in those dark hours.[1439] Carrie, in particular, showed what Southern women are made of.

Confederate Captain William D. Gale, who was present at Carnton at the time (and who, in a few short weeks, would act as assistant adjutant general of Stewart's Corps at the Battle of Nashville), penned one of the most memorable accounts of the conditions at the plantation on Wednesday November 30, and on Thursday December 1. In it he included a description of Carrie's sterling humanitarianism. Mrs. McGavock's mansion, Gale wrote,

> was in the rear of our line. The house is one of the large old-fashioned houses of the better class in Tennessee, two stories high, with many rooms. . . . This was taken as a hospital, and the wounded, in their hundreds, were brought to it during the battle, and all the night after. Every room was filled, every bed had two poor, bleeding fellows, every spare space, niche, and corner under the stairs, in the hall, everywhere—but one room for her family.
>
> And when the noble old house could hold no more, the yard was appropriated until the wounded and the dead filled that, and all were not yet provided for.
>
> Our doctors were deficient in bandages, and she began by giving her old linen, then her towels and napkins, then her sheets and tablecloths, then her husband's shirts and her own undergarments.
>
> During all this time the surgeons plied their dreadful work amid the sighs and moans and death rattle. Yet, amid it all, this noble woman . . . was very active and constantly at work. During all the night neither she nor any of the household slept, but dispensed tea and coffee and such stimulants as she had, and that, too, with her own hands. . . . She walked from room to room, from man to man, her skirts stained in blood, the incarnation of pity and mercy. Is it strange that all who were there praise and call

---

1439. M. Moore, p. 93.

her blessed?[1440]

❧ THE GOOD SAMARITAN OF WILLIAMSON COUNTY

Carrie personally nursed some of the wounded at Carnton for long periods, such as General William Andrew Quarles, who remained at the plantation for two months. Little wonder that Confederate soldiers referred to Carrie as an "Angel of Mercy." But her strong sense of compassion and concern for the less fortunate did not begin with Lincoln's War.

Far earlier she was known to periodically take in two or three orphans from the orphanage in New Orleans to act as household servants at Carnton. She would raise them at the Mansion, educate them, and give them religious training, then later pay to find them suitable homes and employment.

For her unselfish service to the Confederacy, kind heart, Christ-like ways, loving generous nature, and lifelong faithfulness to her husband, children, and relatives, she would later be called "the Good Samaritan of Williamson County," putting to shame all of the mean-spirited attacks on her character by heartless Northerners and cruel New South scallywags that continue to this day.[1441]

Following is an article that mentions Carrie and her many wonderful attributes:

> CHRISTMAS OF THE LONG AGO IN THE GOOD COUNTY OF WILLIAMSON, by Anna Bland [name of newspaper and date of publication unknown]
>
> Mrs. McGavock, member of one of the most prominent and, at one time, wealthiest families of this section, was mistress of the beautiful and historic Carnton estate, situated near Franklin. She was particularly noted for her charity, and reared in her own

---

1440. *Confederate Veteran*, Vol. 30, p. 448.
1441. Many have asked me why pro-North supporters and scallywags have long delighted in slandering conservative Carrie McGavock— an anti-South tradition that continues to this day. The answer is that Carrie is, and always has been, a beloved icon of the traditional South. This has made her, like Nathan Bedford Forrest and other loyal Confederates, a perfect target for South-loathers, most who are of a liberal political persuasion. The object, in my opinion, seems to be to further embarrass and humiliate the South in a futile attempt to direct attention away from Lincoln's illegal and unnecessary war on the Confederacy.

The McGavocks of Carnton Plantation

home a number of orphan children. It is said that she once gave shelter at one time to seven little waifs. Mrs. McGavock was devoted to the Confederate cause, and did a great deal for its soldiers. The two acres occupied by the Confederate cemetery are on the original McGavock place, and were given by Carnton's mistress and Colonel McGavock for the purpose.[1442]

❧ THE SIX CELEBRATED CONFEDERATE GENERALS OF FRANKLIN II

That night and the next morning, December 1, the bodies of several Confederate generals were brought to Carnton and laid in the breezeway section of the back porch in "pathetic dignity," so their troops and local townsfolk could walk past and pay their final respects. Of this appalling scene local historian Virginia McDaniel Bowman writes: The ghastly images of the icy wind playing through their hair, and beams from lanterns falling on bloodied but pallid faces, cause the mind to reel at the price Dixie paid for its short independence.[1443]

Much debate has been generated as to the exact number of deceased generals laid out at Carnton. Some say four, some five, others claim there were six. We know for a fact, however, that only four died during the battle, while two others perished later from wounds suffered during the battle. Thus the corpses of only four generals could have been, and were, displayed on Carnton's rear gallery that morning.

The names of the six generals who died from wounds received at Franklin II are recorded here as immortal Southern heroes:

1. General John Adams (1825-1864)
2. General Patrick Ronayne Cleburne (1828-1864)
3. General Otho French Strahl (1832-1864)
4. General Hiram Bronson Granbury (1831-1864)
5. General States Rights Gist (1831-1864)[1444]

1442. Article transcribed by Lochlainn Seabrook, which was provided courtesy of the Williamson County Public Library.
1443. V. M. Bowman, p. 63.
1444. I am cousins with Gen. Gist through mutual Dudley family ancestors.

THE MCGAVOCKS OF CARNTON PLANTATION

6. General John Carpenter Carter (1837-1864)

☙ THE FOUR GENERALS ON CARNTON'S BACK PORCH
It was the first four of these who died during 2nd Franklin, and whose bodies were displayed on Carnton's back portico:

1. General Adams: his body was discovered on Thursday morning, December 1. Struck by as many as nine bullets, he had fallen about 100 yards east of Columbia Road (now Columbia Avenue, also known as Route 31), near the Carter cotton gin house (which no longer exists). His remains were taken to Carnton that same morning.
2. General Cleburne: also found on the morning of December 1, Cleburne died in the same vicinity as Adams, from a single shot in the chest. His body was also taken to Carnton that morning, where Carrie McGavock carefully set aside his kepi (cap), sword, and other personal items not stolen from his corpse by Yanks during the night. Carrie kept these articles hidden under her mattress in the master bedroom and later gave them to Cleburne's relatives.[1445]
3. General Strahl: his body was discovered on the battlefield on Wednesday night, November 30. He had been shot three times and had expired in a ditch just west of Columbia Road. His remains were taken to Carnton that evening.
4. General Granbury: killed from a shot that entered beneath his right eye, his body was discovered in a ditch to the east near Columbia Road, also near the Carter cotton gin house, after which it was brought to Carnton on the morning of December 1.[1446]

A newspaper article from the 19th Century reveals how this

1445. Cleburne's kepi is today on display at the Tennessee State Museum in downtown Nashville. For more information on the museum, visit their Website: www.tnmuseum.org.
1446. McDonough and Connelly, pp. 158-161.

THE MCGAVOCKS OF CARNTON PLANTATION

macabre display of Southern generalship was viewed over 100 years ago:

> This remarkable scene of so many distinguished officers lying dead, side by side, was perhaps never before witnessed in any battle of the world.[1447]

❧ THE TWO GENERALS WHO NEVER MADE IT TO CARNTON
The bodies of the two remaining generals, Gist and Carter, were not taken to Carnton:

5. General Gist, who was shot in the chest (close to the heart) near Strahl on November 30, was carried, still breathing, to a Confederate field hospital to the left of the Rebel line, where he died later that night. His body was then taken to the home of William White on Boyd Mill Road (about two miles west of the Carter House), and buried under a cedar tree. On December 2, Gist's body servant, "Uncle" Wiley Howard, removed the general's corpse and took it to the Gist plantation in South Carolina, Gist's home state. Here his remains were re-interred at Trinity Episcopal Churchyard in the city of Columbia.

    Gist's death was important enough to be noted by Chesnut, who referred to it in her journal in December 1864.[1448] This was, in part, because General Gist's 1st cousin, William Henry Gist (1807-1874), was the governor of South Carolina (Chesnut's home state) from 1858 to 1860, when he left office because of Lincoln's accession to the presidency. On December 20, 1860, Governor Gist signed his state's "Ordinance of Secession," which officially and legally dissolved the union between South Carolina and the U.S.[1449] The son of

---

[1447]. The name of the newspaper, as well as the author and date of the article, are unknown. Article courtesy of the Williamson County Public Library.
[1448]. Chesnut, DD, p. 339.
[1449]. South Carolina's Ordinance Of Secession reads: "We, the people of the State of South Carolina, in convention assembled, do declare and ordain, and it is hereby declared and ordained, That the ordinance adopted by us in convention on the twenty-third day of May, in the year of our Lord one thousand seven hundred and eighty-eight, whereby the Constitution of the United States of America was ratified, and also

THE MCGAVOCKS OF CARNTON PLANTATION

Nathaniel Gist and Elizabeth Lewis McDaniel, General Gist's first and middle names, States Rights, perfectly embody the foundation of the Confederate Cause for which hundreds of thousands of Southerners gave their lives.[1450]

6. General Carter, shot in the stomach, fell near the Carter House (no relation) at twilight on November 30, trying to reinforce Gist during the first Rebel assault. That night, still living, Carter was carried back southward along Columbia Avenue to the William Harrison House (just south of Winstead Hill), where he died ten days later on December 10. The general was subsequently buried at Rose Hill Cemetery in Columbia, Tennessee, where his grave can still be observed.

Just before his death, Army Chaplain Charles Todd Quintard (1824-1898) asked the mortally wounded man if he had any last words. Tell my wife, Carter moaned, that I have always faithfully loved her and that there are no words to express how sad I am to leave her.[1451]

❧ THE HARRISON HOUSE

The site of Carter's death, the Harrison House, has its own fascinating history, one connected to the McGavocks and Carnton, for two months earlier another Rebel cavalryman died here.

After being wounded at a skirmish at nearby Parry Station, General John Herbert Kelly (1840-1864) was taken to the Harrison House, where he perished about September 4, 1864. Kelly was buried in the Harrison Family Cemetery, but later, in 1866, his body was re-interred at Magnolia Cemetery, Mobile, Alabama.

The Harrison House is also notable for a famous wartime

---

all acts and parts of acts of the General Assembly of this State ratifying amendments of the said Constitution, are hereby repealed; and that the union now subsisting between South Carolina and other States, under the name of the 'United States of America,' is hereby dissolved. Done at Charleston the twentieth day of December, in the year of our Lord one thousand eight hundred and sixty." And so began the life of the infant Confederate States of America.
1450. For more on General Gist, see Cisco, SRG, passim.
1451. Logsdon, TATG, p. 45.

THE MCGAVOCKS OF CARNTON PLANTATION

incident. Used as Hood's first battle headquarters for the upcoming debacle at Franklin II, it was here that Hood planned his fateful attack, and where he argued with General Forrest about his strategy during their last staff conference before the momentous conflict.

Forrest, who had grown up in Chapel Hill not far from Franklin, and who, unlike Hood, had fought at the Battle of Franklin I (on April 10, 1863), was very familiar with the area, and knew well that Hood's plan could not succeed.[1452] More arguments would ensue between the two before Hood would order his men to march across an open field near Carnton, without artillery, against the well entrenched Yanks.

❧ FUNERAL SERVICES & FINAL BURIALS

On Friday December 2, the bodies of Cleburne, Granbury, and Strahl, were taken to the home of William Polk at Columbia, Tennessee, where a moving funeral service was held, led by Chaplain Quintard.

Later that day their remains were hurriedly buried at Rose Hill Cemetery in paupers' graves, in a part of the cemetery known as the "potter's field." Many Southerners, including Quintard, were outraged at this, and at the fact that they had been buried so close to the graves of detested Union soldiers.

The egregious error was corrected the next day, Saturday December 3, by re-interring the three bodies at the Gothic Saint John's Episcopal Church on present-day Highway 43 (between the town's of Columbia and Mt. Pleasant). Cleburne's burial here, at the Polks' brick plantation church, is especially noteworthy.

On the original November march north, up from Florence, Alabama, through Columbia, Spring Hill, and Franklin, Tennessee, Cleburne had reined his horse in while passing St. John's, remarking that

---

1452. Forrest was not present at the Battle of Franklin III, which took place on December 17, 1864—but not by choice. Though the Rebels had re-taken control of the town after Franklin II on November 30, several weeks earlier, after the Battle of Nashville, as the Army of Tennessee was fleeing southward during "Hood's Retreat," Federal troops caught up with the Confederates at Franklin where a violent fight ensued. The numbers of Confederate casualties are unknown, but they may numbered in the hundreds. Forrest was absent because, illogically, as mentioned, Hood had sent him to Murfreesboro, some thirty miles to the southeast, just prior to the Battle of Nashville.

THE MCGAVOCKS OF CARNTON PLANTATION

he would almost be willing to die just to be buried in such a lovely place.[1453] How prophetic those words would turn out to be. But his stay in the cold ground at St. John's was to be brief. Cleburne's body was later re-interred in the Confederate Cemetery, at Helena, Arkansas, the Irishman's adopted home town.

On Monday December 5, at her family's home in Mobile, Alabama, Cleburne's fiancee, Susan Tarlton, heard a newsboy on a nearby street yelling out that Cleburne had died at the Battle of Franklin II. The young Confederate woman fainted dead away.[1454]

Strahl—an Ohio-born Yankee who later courageously adopted Tennessee as his home state and joined the Confederate army—was also later re-interred, in this case at Old City Cemetery, Dyersburg, Tennessee, while Granbury was later re-buried in the Lone Star State graveyard and city named after him: Granbury Cemetery, Granbury, Texas. Adams was buried at Maplewood Cemetery, Pulaski, Tennessee.

In the end, none of the famous six generals who died from wounds suffered at Franklin II were buried in the McGavock Confederate Cemetery. Nonetheless, their names remain immortalized in Franklin in the streets named after them, located near where each of the generals fell on the battlefield.

❧ CARNTON: A FITTING MONUMENT TO FRANKLIN II

It was out of devotion to his Irish roots that in the early 1800s Randal McGavock had named his beautiful Franklin home Carnton, meaning "the homestead located near a stone monument memorializing a significant event, or the burial site of a great commander."

As one of the War's bloodiest and most needless battles took place a mere mile and a half away (indeed, during the conflict Carnton was situated at the rear of General Stewart's line),[1455] it turned out to be a most appropriate moniker. The McGavocks' obituaries would remark on the fact that the "beautiful old Southern mansion . . . stands on

---

1453. Woodworth, p. 298.
1454. McDonough and Connelly, pp. 166-168.
1455. Groom, p. 210.

The McGavocks of Carnton Plantation

historic ground, the battlefield of Franklin." Thus Carnton became the living stone monument of Franklin II, and to the six generals, and hundreds of others, who perished fighting for freedom against dictator Lincoln and Northern tyranny.[1456]

❧ YANKEE CRIMES, CRUELTY, & BRUTALITY AT CARNTON

As the dust from the battle settled gloomily over the village of Franklin in those early weeks of December 1864, work turned from caring for the dead to caring for the wounded.

The Yankees now literally "owned" the town (illegally), and thus the wounded Rebel soldiers at Carnton were considered Federal prisoners of war. As soon as a wounded Johnny was deemed well enough to travel, he was arrested, chained, and taken to the nearest Federal prison, usually a rat-infested, dungeon-like structure, located in the frigid North, surrounded by hostile Yanks. One of these, of course, was Lincoln's notorious Camp Douglas (commonly known as "Eighty Acres of Hell") in Chicago, where nearly 6,000 Confederate prisoners were tortured then purposefully starved to death during the War under Yankee Colonel Benjamin J. Sweet.

Not surprisingly—having been captured by a Union army whose battle cry was "kill all Southerners!"[1457]—many of the injured Rebs at Carnton were treated inhumanely by their Northern captors and were removed before they had sufficiently healed.

An example of this particular Yankee atrocity was Colonel William Lavel Butler, of the Twenty-fifth Alabama. Butler, who had been seriously wounded by a Union bullet that had passed through his body, was recovering at the Figuers' home on West Main Street. After being examined by a Yank doctor and proclaimed healthy enough to be sent to prison, the half-dead Confederate commander was handcuffed and dragged toward the door. The desperately injured man was about

---

[1456]. Union soldiers who died at 2nd Franklin now lie in the National Cemetery at the Stones River National Battlefield, Murfreesboro, Tennessee. Union soldiers who were fatally wounded at 2nd Franklin were later buried in the National Cemetery in Nashville, Tennessee.
[1457]. Pollard, LC, p. 435.

THE MCGAVOCKS OF CARNTON PLANTATION

to be taken out into a raging snowstorm and thrown into an open cattle car with no overcoat or blanket, and shipped North by rail.[1458]

Butler began cursing his arresting Union officer, adding: You will kill me if you take me out of here! But the unfeeling Northerner was not to be swayed by pity, humanity, or common sense. You're a Federal prisoner!, he yelled back at the dying man, and away Butler went.[1459] One can only guess how many other Confederate wounded were treated in a similar manner across town at Carnton Plantation.

As foreign occupiers the Union troops also showed little mercy to the town's civilian inhabitants, including the McGavocks, who they badgered, even threatening to burn their house down. Carnton was only spared the torch because earlier, in 1862, Colonel John had taken the Union's Oath of Allegiance at gunpoint.

The McGavocks were fortunate. Earlier, after the Battle of Franklin I (April 10, 1863), ten Franklin houses were burned to the ground by vengeful, unthinking Yankee soldiers "as per order of Major-General [David] Stanley."[1460]

Not even the area's schools were safe from Lincoln's henchmen. One of Franklin's finest educational establishments, Harpeth Academy—owned by Carnton founder Randal McGavock in the early 1820s[1461]—was damaged so severely by Union men that it had to be closed in 1863, shortly after the Battle of Franklin I.

That same year Yankees also burned down Triune's magnificent school, Porter Female Academy (later rebuilt by McGavock relation Dr. Jonathan Smith Bostick, b. 1794). With humane and law-abiding Christian generals like Robert E. Lee and Stonewall Jackson leading them, our Confederate soldiers never engaged in such heartless, illegal, and unnecessary activities as the torching of U.S. schools.

While Lincoln's soldiers somehow managed to restrain themselves from demolishing Carnton, they did in fact seize the entire

---

1458. McDonough and Connelly, pp. 173, 177.
1459. Logsdon, EBF, pp. 102-103.
1460. ORA, Ser. 1, Vol. 23, Pt. 1, p. 237.
1461. Hale and Merritt, Vol. 3, p. 839.

THE McGAVOCKS OF CARNTON PLANTATION

plantation, stealing everything they could from the McGavocks. Their plunder included livestock and thousands of bushels of grain, along with furniture, jewelry, food, family heirlooms, and countless other unknown possessions.

The rampaging malicious Feds took some $8,000 worth of timber alone, nearly $205,000 in today's currency. And though Carnton had once been a thriving thoroughbred breeding farm, with prize horses valued in the millions, it was said that Yankee raiders took everything from the McGavocks' "splendid stables," except for two mule colts.[1462] (As Middle Tennessee—prime horse-breeding country—was gradually taken over by Lincoln and his soldiers, such thievery as occurred at Carnton greatly contributed to the Confederate cavalry's war-long dearth of horses and, in turn, to the collapse of the Confederacy itself; for the cavalry was supposed to act as the army's primary offensive force.)[1463]

McGavock legend says that the family hid their best silverware under the front "turtle walkway" for safekeeping. But as this was the standard place to conceal small valuables of this kind, it is probable that the Yanks pried up the bricks and discovered this treasure as well.[1464]

❧ POSTWAR DEVASTATION: THE DECLINE OF CARNTON

Union soldiers stationed in Franklin eventually made off with the equivalent of millions of dollars of the McGavocks' personal belongings, livestock, and goods, and after the War Colonel John sued the U.S. for damages. Like so many other Southerners who took Uncle Sam to court, however, he lost his case.[1465]

1462. V. M. Bowman, p. 63.
1463. Eaton, HSC, pp. 107-108.
1464. The McGavocks were indeed lucky. Yankee soldiers completely occupied Arlington House, the extraordinary home of Mary Anna Randolph Custis (1808-1873), the wife of Gen. Robert. E. Lee. Their family heirlooms were looted, along with invaluable items belonging to such men as President George Washington, Mary's step great-grandfather. After Lincoln's War, instead of returning the home to the Lee family, the U.S. government confiscated the property and turned the mansion into a tourist attraction. Lee's land was transformed into what is now known as "Arlington Cemetery." While today all true Americans rightly pay homage to Arlington Cemetery, it is important to understand that it began as a Yankee insult upon Southern honor and dignity.
1465. Seabrook, CPGS, pp. 44-45.

The McGavocks of Carnton Plantation

Even those who "won," however, were usually cheated by the U.S. government out of most of what was owed them, and then reimbursed long after their deaths. One of these was McGavock neighbor Fountain Branch Carter (1797-1871), father of the famous Tod Carter (1840-1864).

During the War Fountain kept detailed records of the losses he suffered due to the Yankee invasion of Franklin. His computations even included $2 he was owed for three bushels of corn that had been stolen by insolent Union soldiers. The total of his claim came to $20,061.10, the equivalent of $262,625 today. With callous disregard for the Carter family, the U.S. government only paid them back $335, with a loss of $19,726. But perhaps fortunately, Fountain was not aware of the offence: when the U.S. finally cleared its debt with the Carters in 1886 Fountain had been dead for fifteen years.[1466]

As it turned out, the pillage of the McGavocks' plantation by cruel Yanks would be just one of the many factors that led to the final closure and sale of Carnton in 1911. There were other factors that contributed to Carnton's decline as well.

The War, which turned the Southern economy upside-down, devastated the McGavocks financially, marking the beginning of the breakup of the entire antebellum plantation system. In the five cotton states alone the number of large farms had by now dropped off by 50 percent.[1467]

Under the North's new carpetbag-scallywag regime, Carnton herself began to languish, once rich crop lands went fallow, and livestock and even land had to be sold off in an effort to pay bills and ever mounting debts.[1468] Eventually the McGavocks had to issue both crop liens and even tenant contracts to newly freed blacks just to survive through the following year.

Though the plantation continued temporarily under a sharecropping agreement with a few of their former servants, the end

---

1466. W. B. Garrison, ACW, p. 72.
1467. Ransom, pp. 234-235.
1468. Rosenbaum and Brinkley, s.v. "Reconstruction."

was plainly in sight. Yet the family, deeply Christian, maintained a positive attitude.

About this time the McGavocks might have recalled the last words of Southern hero John C. Calhoun, as he lay dying in his bed in Washington, D.C., March 31, 1850: "The South, the poor South! God knows what will become of her!"[1469]

Decades before Lincoln's War Calhoun had accurately and uncannily predicted the South-North bloodbath, and had spoken of a "deep-seated disease, which threatens great danger" to the South. That "danger" was Northern tyranny, greed, materialism, and industrialism.[1470] The Carolinian had even envisioned Dixie smoldering beneath burning rubble, subjugated, in tatters, the result of a "bitter" conflict between the two sections.[1471] How prophetic.

But not even Calhoun could have known just how truly devastating the War would be for the South, and for good Confederate families like the McGavocks.

1469. Sobel, s.v. "Calhoun, John C."
1470. Benton, Vol. 1, p. 734.
1471. Coit, p. 475.

The End Of the McGavock Era at Carnton

❧ TWO McGAVOCK MARRIAGES

THE YEAR WAS 1883. WITH the War now nearly twenty years in the past, John's and Carrie's only surviving son, twenty-five year old Winder, married nineteen year old Susan Lee "Susie" Ewing, a local Brentwood girl (b. April 4, 1863), on February 5.

Eleven months later, on January 3, 1884, John's and Carrie's only surviving daughter, twenty-eight year old Hattie, married forty-one year old Confederate Lieutenant Colonel George Limerick Cowan, a Celt born on October 15, 1842, in County Derry, Ireland. They then moved into Windermere, the brown house at the bottom of Carnton's driveway.[1472]

As an eight year old, George had come to America in 1850 with his parents, Robert Cowan (b. about 1820) and Margaret Limerick (b. about 1822). The family eventually settled in Bedford County, Tennessee, not far from the home of one of the most celebrated Southern heroes of all time, Confederate cavalryman and superlative Rebel chieftain General Nathan Bedford Forrest, whose parents named

---

1472. Windermere, located at 1344 Carnton Lane (across the street from Carnton), has recently been restored to its 1860s appearance.

THE MCGAVOCKS OF CARNTON PLANTATION

him after the county he was born in.[1473]

Eleven years on, at the start of Lincoln's War, nineteen year old George enlisted under Nathan Boone (a relative of frontiersman Daniel Boone and contemporary singer Pat Boone), and fought with General Forrest's deadly and greatly feared Escort Company.

Lieutenant Cowan not only served his nation bravely on the battlefield, but he later became the president of the Veterans Association, an organization that was inaugurated on July 27, 1877, in order to support former Confederate soldiers who had served in Forrest's Escort and on his staff.[1474]

❧ THE REAL NATHAN BEDFORD FORREST

The McGavocks have been roundly criticized for their association with Forrest, due, in part, to the fact that Colonel John's son-in-law, Lieutenant Cowan, served in the General's Escort, and also because he led the group at Forrest's funeral in Memphis in 1877.[1475]

Additionally, at least one family member, Dr. Felix Grundy McGavock (1832-1897), worked with Forrest (in Memphis) after the War,[1476] while at the same time Carnton herself is closely associated with Forrest: we will remember that he used the upper rear porch as an observation post during the Battle of Franklin II.[1477]

Because Forrest is no longer here to defend himself it is only proper that we speak up in the General's defense and reveal the true man. For he helped shape the history of both Carnton and the city of Franklin.

1473. Bedford County was later reorganized. Today Chapel Hill, Forrest's birth city, is in Marshall County, Tennessee.
1474. Bradley, NBFES, p. 139.
1475. Henry, FWMF, p. 461.
1476. B. S. Wills, p. 339.
1477. Dr. McGavock's wife is Mary Manoah Bostick (1832-1862), who is the 1st cousin once removed of Dr. Jonathan Smith Bostick of Triune, Tennessee. As previously mentioned, in 1863, during Lincoln's War, Yankee troops wantonly, maliciously, and illegally burned down the famous Porter Female Academy at Triune. Dr. Bostick donated the money to rebuild the school, after which it was renamed Bostick Female Academy. The school is today a private residence.

The McGavocks of Carnton Plantation

❧ DEFAMING A SOUTHERN HERO
Few have been more unjustly maligned than the Wizard of the Saddle. Even this wonderfully melodious nickname has been used by his enemies as a indictment against him (for his alleged time as "Grand Wizard" of the KKK). Northerners, who have created their own names for him—such as that horrid monster in human form—to this day still delight in referring to him derogatorily as that "Grand Wizard Forrest."[1478]

Naturally, from the very beginning of the War for Southern Independence, the Northern press had a field day concocting and printing absurd stories about him. The U.S. government also participated in this yellow journalistic slander, using anti-Forrest tales as wartime propaganda intended to galvanize anti-South sentiment in the North. These inventions were picked up by the masses and disseminated as fact.

Today the liberal left, the politically correct, and other progressive groups have latched onto these ridiculous 19th-Century fictions, which they use to continue to berate, taunt, and abuse the South and her people. One of their main targets, of course, is Forrest.

❧ SOUTHERNERS WHO HATE THE SOUTH
Even many Southerners—having allowed themselves to be Northernized and brainwashed by Yankee mythology—misunderstand Forrest. This breed, known as the good "New South" (as opposed to the "bad" Old South), have turned against their own people, history, symbols, and heritage, and have taken sides with the very region that tried to destroy their homeland only 150 years ago.

It is for good reason that those among this group were known as scallywags, "the local lepers of the community," during "Reconstruction." The term is still as popular as ever in the South. Here in Franklin, for example, where the scallywag population grows exponentially each year, this group continues to be shunned by traditional Southerners. For just as Old South families once asserted,

---

1478. Wade, pp. 40, 59.

The McGavocks of Carnton Plantation

those who betray their own homeland can never be relied on or honored.[1479]

ꙮ THE CHARGES AGAINST FORREST

What disturbed the Old North most about Forrest was:
1) his occupations as a slave owner and slave trader.
2) his role at the Battle of Fort Pillow—where he is alleged to have ordered the murder of surrendering white and black Yanks.
3) his position in the Ku Klux Klan—which Northerners maintain he founded and headed.

Forrest has also been branded a violent and irrational madman (even though he never spent a single night in jail and was never convicted of a single crime), an unfaithful husband (even though he only married once, remained faithful for life, and never even looked at another woman), a corrupt politician (even though he was elected *and* reelected to office numerous times, and once threatened to quit when he discovered fraud in his department), a drunken lout (though he was an ardent teetotaler), a miserly curmudgeon (even though he gave generously to the needy throughout his life, financially helped support a wide circle of family members, paid for his brothers' schooling, raised a battalion of mounted infantry using his own money, and at death gave nearly his entire estate to Confederate charities), and an unscrupulous businessman (even though he was a honest, self-made multimillionaire and one of the most successful and wealthiest men in the U.S.).

Despite the obvious falsity of such charges, they remain the primary reasons Forrest is detested and vilified today by the New North and the New South.

That he was widely respected and loved by fellow Southerners during his lifetime is clear from an article in the Memphis *Avalanche* newspaper, written upon Forrest's promotion to Lieutenant Colonel in the Summer of 1861. Wrote the author: "No better man could have been selected for such a duty of known courage and indomitable

---

1479. Foner, R, p. 297.

perseverance. He is a man for the times."[1480] Sadly, while Forrest's contemporaries knew the truth about him, that truth has been thoroughly suppressed and is thus unknown to most modern day people.

In an effort to reestablish authentic Southern history and clear Forrest's name, let us take a brief look at these three accusations against him.

❧ FORREST AS SLAVE TRADER

Forrest—who, in his day usually went by his middle name Bedford—is painted as a sadistic slave trader, even though, in reality, he was so well-known as a humanitarian that blacks at auction actually asked to be purchased by him over others. He also never sold servants to unsavory characters and went out of his way to make sure he did not divide up black families. Indeed, he was known to have brought several black families back together by buying up the scattered children and parents from various other homes, farms, and plantations.[1481]

And he was not a slave trader his entire life, as the North charges. Though he was the wealthiest and largest trader in Memphis in the mid-1800s (one year he made the equivalent of $2,600,000),[1482] he only worked in this occupation for seven years. He started in 1852 and quit in 1859, happily abandoning the business three years *before* Lincoln's War because he, like nearly all Southerners at the time, realized that the institution of slavery was on its way out.[1483]

❧ FORREST AS SLAVE OWNER

The North labels Forrest a cruel slave owner who beat, tortured, and even killed innocent blacks under his care. But in fact he was quite liberal with his servants for the time period. For example, he made sure they were always thoroughly bathed, well groomed, and wore immaculately clean highly starched clothing.[1484] He also encouraged

---

1480. Strain, p. 52.
1481. Henry, FWMF, p. 26.
1482. Stampp, p. 265.
1483. Wyeth, LGNBF, p. 22.
1484. Sheppard, p. 25.

them to learn to read and write, and after the War he allowed his black employees to buy, own, and carry firearms, something for which he was roundly criticized by the U.S. government, the very nation whose president had issued the Emancipation Proclamation![1485]

As previously mentioned, even before the War Forrest had begun freeing his slaves, liberating not only his own personal house servants, but also those for sale through his slave trading business.[1486] It is not surprising to learn then that at the start of the conflict, while Lincoln was prohibiting eager African-Americans from enlisting in the U.S. military, the general was signing up every able-bodied black man he could find, even enlisting forty-five of his own servants in the Confederate Cause.

All were promised freedom for their service, and in late 1863, shortly after the Battle of Chickamauga (September 18-20, 1863), he emancipated all of the survivors for their heroic service.[1487] This was only a few months after Lincoln reluctantly published his Emancipation Proclamation and over two years before the U.S. finally ratified the Thirteenth Amendment on December 6, 1865, which abolished slavery across the entire country for the first time.[1488]

Forrest's beneficence was known far and wide, which is why many of his former black servants eagerly returned to work for him after the War, this time as paid employees.[1489] And when, in April 1866, he offered to let 200 of his black employees out of their work contracts, nearly all of them chose to stay on with him.[1490]

According to an African-American soldier who served with Forrest at the Battles of Shiloh and Brice's Cross Roads, the general had seven armed black guards, steadfast soldiers who protected him both day and night. If Forrest detested blacks, as South-haters assert, why did he insist on having African-American guards specifically, and how was he

---

1485. Hurst, pp. 38-41, 274.
1486. Seabrook, ARB, p. 160.
1487. Wyeth, TDF, p. xxi.
1488. Foner, R, p. 37.
1489. Sheppard, p. 283.
1490. Hurst, p. 273.

THE MCGAVOCKS OF CARNTON PLANTATION

able to sleep peacefully at night in their presence?[1491]

Is any of this what one would expect if Forrest were truly a vicious racist?

❧ FORREST & FORT PILLOW

The North and the New South accuse Forrest of a host of atrocities at the Battle of Fort Pillow, Tennessee, on April 12, 1864, including ordering the slaughter of "surrendering" Yanks. In particular he is reviled for his alleged mistreatment of black Union soldiers stationed at the fort.[1492] The more uninformed South-hating historians even assert that he murdered every single black Yankee soldier here.[1493]

As Forrest himself stated, however, these stories were nothing more than preposterous fictions created by "dastardly Yankee reporters,"[1494] fictions that were then later exaggerated by the North's overtly slanted Wade-Gooch Report. As not a single Union soldier (white or black) ever surrendered at Fort Pillow,[1495] even many Northerners were forced to admit that the report was one of the finest examples of anti-South disinformation and propaganda produced during the War.[1496]

The on-site conditions, along with the behavior of the Union troops, at Fort Pillow that day certainly contributed to the Confederate win and the high Yankee death count: a poorly designed fort; a weak and inexperienced Union commander (Major William F. Bradford); widespread drunkenness among the Union soldiery; refusal to surrender; retreat of the Union garrison without lowering its fort flag; confusion over the truce; unarmed pro-Union civilians in the fort; a complex topography (the fort was located on a steep hill at the junction of the Mississippi River and Coal Creek); a mass drowning of fleeing Yanks;

1491. Ashdown and Caudill, pp. 184-185.
1492. See in particular the thoroughly anti-South, anti-Forrest work by A. Ward.
1493. Wade, p. 16.
1494. Wyeth, LGNBF, p. 428.
1495. Jordan and Pryor, p. 448.
1496. *Ohio Archaeological and Historical Quarterly*, Vol. 48, 1939, p. 40.

The McGavocks of Carnton Plantation

and lack of promised U.S. naval reinforcement.[1497]

All of this was exacerbated by an already potentially explosive situation: the garrison had become a "nest" of white and black Yankee thieves, thugs, rapists, and mercenaries who had been preying on and terrorizing the local citizenry for weeks. In addition, many of these blue coats were former Rebel soldiers from the area, so-called "galvanized Yanks" (that is, Northernized Unionized Southerners),[1498] and were considered traitors by Forrest's men. The General, with nothing else pressing at the moment, decided to rid the fort of this pestilence at the request of the local populace. Forrest, who was nothing if not thorough in his approach to clearing the South of Yanks, was simply performing his duties as a Confederate officer that April 12.

We will note a supreme irony here: Forrest led a racially integrated soldiery, with many of his own black servants fighting at his side.[1499] The Union soldiers he went up against at Fort Pillow, however, as Lincoln had ordered, fought in racially segregated units.[1500] And yet it is Forrest who is labeled a racist by uninformed critics of the South!

Lincoln, Grant, Sherman, and U.S. Secretary of War Edwin M. Stanton (1814-1869), all promised retaliation if Forrest was found guilty of war crimes at Fort Pillow. But revealingly none ever followed, for after an intense investigation by the U.S. government—whose report on the incident, by the Yankees' Committee on the Conduct of the War, was later shown to be laden with errors, filled with hearsay used as "evidence," overtly conflicting testimonies, and "exaggerations in style and content obviously designed more to stir human emotions than to convince human reason"[1501]—the general was cleared of all charges.[1502] Years later, Sherman, who ended up siding with Forrest in the affair,[1503]

1497. Seabrook, ARB, pp. 351-352.
1498. Watts, s.v. "galvanized Yankee"; Faust, s.v. "Galvanized Yankees."
1499. J. C. Perry, pp. 218, 223.
1500. A. Ward, pp. 78, 161.
1501. Cornish, p. 173.
1502. Foote, Vol. 3, p. 112; J. M. McPherson, BCF, p. 794; Chesnut, MCCW, p. 596.
1503. Sherman, Vol. 2, pp. 12-13.

THE MCGAVOCKS OF CARNTON PLANTATION

called him the most outstanding military man of the entire War.[1504]

The truth about Fort Pillow is this: no atrocities occurred and for the rest of their lives Forrest and his men would rightfully testify that "all allegations to the contrary are mere malicious inventions, started, nurtured, and accredited at a time, and through a sentiment of strong sectional animosity."[1505] Forrest himself later succinctly (and humorously) explained the entire battle this way: "The damned Yankees kept firin' horizontally right up into the air!"[1506]

The whole event has been best summed up by Lieutenant William Witherspoon (a relation of the author and actress Reese Witherspoon), who fought with the Seventh Tennessee, Company L. Wrote Witherspoon: The Yankee version of what occurred at Fort Pillow is nothing remotely similar to what actually took place. We Southerners have already expressed more than enough regret, and the truth is that no apology is needed—not now or in the future.[1507]

❧ FORREST POSTBELLUM

Incredibly, even Forrest's post-War activities are criticized by the North, but only by those ignorant of the facts.

After Forrest reluctantly laid down his arms and surrendered to Federal authorities on May 3, 1865, he returned to Memphis where he attempted to rebuild the shattered remains of his life. Lincoln's War had bankrupted Forrest, as it had so many other faithful Confederate families (one of Lincoln's intentions to begin with). In the late 1860s Forrest asserted that he had gone into the army worth the equivalent of $35 million in today's currency, but had come out a pauper.[1508] Forrest now had no choice but to start over—from scratch.

He began by inviting his former enemies, Northern officers, to head South and become business partners. One of these partnerships, with Union Major B. E. Diffenbacher, was hugely successful and by the

---

1504. Wyeth, TDF, p. xxxi.
1505. Jordan and Pryor, p. 440.
1506. Pollard, LC, p. 499.
1507. Henry, ATSF, p. 125.
1508. Hurst, p. 342.

THE McGAVOCKS OF CARNTON PLANTATION

end of 1867 it had produced stunning profits.[1509]

Forrest also became president of the Selma, Marion, and Memphis Railroad, his attempt to open up trade with, and heal the breach with, the North. While heading the railroad, my cousin Forrest went into business with another one of my relations: Confederate Colonel Edmund Winchester Rucker (1835-1924), who led Rucker's Brigade at the Battle of Franklin II and lost an arm while fighting gallantly at the Battle of Nashville.[1510]

As part of his plan to resuscitate the South, Forrest called for a Dixie-wide effort to employ former black servants, as well as bring in new blacks from Africa to repopulate the South, for he thought they made better workers than whites. There is no longer any need for racial conflict. Let's work together to make our nation prosperous once again, the charismatic Southerner stated publically.[1511]

How different this was from white supremacist and black colonizationist Abraham Lincoln who, right up until his death, campaigned incessantly to rid the country of blacks altogether, saying, as he did on July 17, 1858: "What I would most desire would be the separation of the white and black races."[1512] His own generals, such as Benjamin F. Butler, later attested to Lincoln's lifelong campaign to "cleanse" America of its black population.[1513]

❧ FORREST'S ROLE IN THE KKK

The North also likes to denounce Forrest for his role as the "founder and head of the Ku Klux Klan,"[1514] neither charge which is true. The six Pulaski, Tennessee, men who established the KKK on Christmas Eve in

---

1509. Sheppard, p. 284.
1510. Forrest and Rucker worked together in Memphis from 1869-1874. Rucker is my 3rd cousin. My 4th great-grandmother is Phoebe Rucker (b. 1776), Edmund's 1st cousin.
1511. Hurst, p. 330. There is some scholarly research suggesting that, at the time, Forrest was correct in his belief that blacks were more productive workers than whites. See e.g., Genovese, pp. 296, 301.
1512. Nicolay and Hay, ALCW, Vol. 1, p. 273.
1513. See e.g., B. F. Butler, p. 903. Many other famous Northerners also did not believe in abolition or equality of the races, such as General William T. Sherman. "A nigger as such is a most excellent fellow," the red haired war criminal once stated arrogantly, "but he is not fit to marry, associate, or vote with me or mine." Seabrook, L, p. 907.
1514. See e.g., Highsmith and Landphair, p. 28.

The McGavocks of Carnton Plantation

1865 are well-known, and Forrest did not join the organization until two years later, in 1867.[1515]

As for the General's alleged role as the "Grand Wizard" of the KKK, there is no evidence for this other than hearsay and Yankee folklore, for Klan members never recorded anything on paper, and as such, no official records exist stating that he was their leader.[1516] To the contrary, most evidence indicates that it was George Washington Gordon[1517] (captured at the Battle of Franklin II) who was Grand Wizard during the time Forrest was a member, as Gordon's own wife later testified.[1518] At most Forrest may have been some kind of advisor or recruiter, but even this is not known for sure.[1519]

In 1871 Forrest was put on the witness stand before a government investigative committee on Klan activities.[1520] The general not only denied being the leader of the KKK, but he also disclaimed even being a member (though he did state that he was "in sympathy" with the Klan).[1521] The KKK was nothing more than a defensive body, he rightly asserted, organized to counter the nefarious work of the North's Freedmen's Bureau, Union League,[1522] and various Loyal Leagues, all anti-South organizations.[1523]

After a severe grilling the committee found Forrest innocent of all charges in association with the organization, and he was never bothered by U.S. authorities again.[1524] Despite this, to this day anti-Forrest proponents routinely ignore their own government's decision in the case!

1515. The six founders of the first official KKK were comprised of three ex-Confederate officers and soldiers: Capt. John C. Lester, Capt. John B. Kennedy, Capt. James R. Crowe, Frank O. McCord, Richard R. Reed, and J. Calvin Jones. Seabrook, EYWTACWW, p. 195.
1516. Horn, IE, p. 37.
1517. I am cousins with Gordon through mutual royal European ancestors.
1518. B. S. Wills, p. 336.
1519. Mathes, p. 373.
1520. Seabrook, NBF, p. 57.
1521. Hurst, p. 315.
1522. Ridley, pp. 649-650.
1523. *Reports of the Committees of the Senate of the United States (for the Second Session of the Forty-second Congress)*, pp. 22, 33, 34.
1524. Henry, FWMF, p. 448.

The McGavocks of Carnton Plantation

⁂ THE REAL KKK

Since the McGavocks have been "tainted" by their association with KKK associate Forrest, in the interest of Southern truth (as opposed to Northern fiction) let us take a brief look at the Klan itself.

The original KKK was not what is commonly thought or taught. It must be remembered that in the days following the War, lawlessness was widespread across the South. Not because of former Confederates, but because of carpetbaggers: greedy Yankees who had come South in order to prey on the ravaged citizens of Dixie.

There were also roaming bands of angry, freed blacks, stirred up by Northern government officials, Northern soldiers, and even Northern ministers, to seek revenge on their former employers ("owners"). Scallywags, "New South" Southerners who had turned against their own kind for profit, were also committing many atrocities and crimes.

The North added further degradation and insult to the South by illegally imposing military rule on an already subjugated people. This, along with a repressive, corrupt, and often violent scallywag-carpetbag regime (sometimes known as carpetbaggism), was more than any Southerner could be expected to bear.[1525]

During this same period the U.S. War Department established the Freedmen's Bureau, an agency intended to provide welfare relief to freed former slaves dispossessed by Lincoln's illegal, cruel, sudden, and unplanned emancipation. We will note here that no U.S. government agency was ever formed to aid dispossessed Southern whites, nor was any money ever allocated by the U.S. government to assist disenfranchised Southern whites.

Unfortunately, the Bureau quickly deteriorated into a tool of militant carpetbaggers and scallywags, who used it to inculcate freed slaves in Northern anti-South propaganda,[1526] and train them to use weapons and military tactics to taunt, punish, riot, rob, rape, and even murder their former employers.[1527] It was due to this very corruption,

---

1525. Simpson, pp. 62-64.
1526. Simpson, p. 62.
1527. Sheppard, p. 288.

THE MCGAVOCKS OF CARNTON PLANTATION

along with "stirring up the blacks," that caused the Freedmen's Bureau to finally be shut down July 1, 1869, another in a long list of Northern blunders that eventually led to the complete failure of Reconstruction itself.[1528]

Meanwhile, under Reconstruction former Confederates were disarmed, disenfranchised, and barred from the ballot box and from holding political office, while newly freed blacks, many of them illiterate and inculcated with hateful anti-South propaganda, were given the right to vote, then purposefully placed in office.[1529] As Southern historian Frank Lawrence Owsley correctly said of this time, the South had been conquered by war and was now being humiliated and impoverished by peace.[1530]

It was in the midst of this period of sorrow, pain, fury, and anarchy, of carpetbag-scallywag rule, which the North still arrogantly calls "Reconstruction," that the first KKK was born. If there was ever a time for a loyal Southern body of officials to keep the peace and defend their families, homes, and businesses, it was then.[1531] Even the U.S. Congress would later accept the creation of the Klan as a logical and understandable reaction to the North's horrid anti-South laws, official ineptitude, and general immorality.[1532]

The Klan's sole purpose at this time was to act as a self-policing, relief-and-aid society for the protection and care of all Southern families, particularly those made homeless and jobless by Lincoln's War.[1533] Forrest himself accurately called it a "protective, political, military organization."[1534]

And the "protection" provided by the Klan was not just for whites, but for blacks as well, for contrary to Northern folklore the

---

1528. Rosenbaum and Brinkley, s.v. "Freedmen's Bureau."
1529. Weintraub, pp. 75-76.
1530. Simpson, p. 63.
1531. Sheppard, p. 287.
1532. *Report of the Joint Select Committee to Inquire into the Condition of Affairs in the Late Insurrectionary States*, pp. 453-454. See also Adams and Sanders, p. 217.
1533. See e.g., Pollard, LC, p. 413.
1534. *Reports of the Committees of the Senate of the United States (for the Second Session of the Forty-second Congress)*, p. 33.

THE MCGAVOCKS OF CARNTON PLANTATION

original KKK was not an anti-black organization. It was an anti-Yankee organization,[1535] which is why there were thousands of black members in this the original KKK.[1536] We even have evidence of an all-black KKK that operated for some time in the Nashville area.[1537]

The original KKK's Creed read, in part:

> This is an institution of Chivalry, Humanity, Mercy, and Patriotism, embodying in its genius and its principles all that is chivalric in conduct, noble in sentiment, generous in manhood, and patriotic in purpose; its peculiar objects are:
> 1. To protect the weak, the innocent, and the defenseless from the indignities, wrongs, and outrages of the lawless, the violent, and the brutal; to relieve the injured and oppressed; to succor the suffering and unfortunate, and especially the widows and orphans of Confederate soldiers.[1538]

The original KKK and her affiliate groups (such as the Knights of the White Camellia) were so popular in postbellum Dixie that they eventually attained a combined membership of some 600,000.[1539] It is well-known, however, that nearly the entire white Southern population counted itself among the organization's unofficial supporters and secret sympathizers.[1540]

In March 1869, when the original Klan eventually had begun to take on white racist leanings (in reaction to ever increasing black hate crimes against whites, instigated by corrupt Northern officials), and with the power of Reconstruction now weakening, the Freedmen's Bureau now dissolving, and a number of state governments now repossessed by the South, Forrest, the organization's most famous, influential, and

---

1535. Morton, p. 343; Horwitz, pp. 200-201.
1536. Hurst, p. 305; Lester and Wilson, p. 26; Rogers, p. 34.
1537. Horn, IE, pp. 362-363. We will note that at one time (1920s-1930s) even the modern KKK—though it has no connection with the original KKK—possessed African-American members, and treated both whites and blacks the same. See Terkel, p. 239. In Indiana, for example, white klansmen decided to broaden their racial base by organizing a "colored division" whose uniform was white capes, blue masks, and red robes. See Blee, p. 169.
1538. Morton, p. 338.
1539. Lester and Wilson, p. 30.
1540. Sheppard, p. 289.

THE MCGAVOCKS OF CARNTON PLANTATION

engaging supporter ordered the group to disband.[1541] Thus the original (that is, the real) KKK lasted only three years, from 1865 to 1869.[1542]

The North's attempt to fully subject the South through "peaceful Reconstruction" had failed. Lincoln had won the War, but ultimately lost the battle, for as soon as the North ended Reconstruction in 1877 and Union troops were removed, the South began to hastily regroup by first installing former Confederate officers into political office.

The heretofore nonexistent racial discord created in the once integrated South by Lincoln and his radical successors would last for another eighty-seven years, at which time President John F. Kennedy introduced the Civil Rights Act of 1964. This act finally outlawed discrimination based on "race, religion, color, sex, or national origin." (We will note here that this was the first time whites were included in an American civil rights bill).

❧ THE ORIGINAL KKK AS DISTINGUISHED FROM THE MODERN KKK

The KKK would reemerge in 1915 in a new and altogether different form than the original, with its largest membership, not in the South, but in the North. In 1923, for example, Indiana hosted the biggest gathering of modern Klansmen in U.S. history.[1543] (Not surprisingly, the state's second largest college, Purdue University, was still racially segregated well into the 1940s).[1544]

The two organizations therefore should not be confused, the first KKK being simply a non-racial fraternity of former Confederate soldiers devoted to law-enforcement and the assistance of Southern orphans, widows, and seniors, as well as the poor and disenfranchised of all races. As such, the members of original KKK, as distinct from those belonging to the modern KKK, are still rightly considered by many traditional

---

1541. Lytle, p. 385; Morton, p. 345; Hurst, p. 327.
1542. Ridley, p. 639; Mathes, p. 373.
1543. See Wade, pp. 215-247, 364. Note that Indiana, a *Northern* state, is the only state where the KKK elected the governor and both U.S. senators. In fact, after 1960, the KKK grew in strength all across the North, a region journalists at the time referred to as displaying signs of "white backlash."
1544. See e.g., Higginbotham, pp. vii-ix.

THE MCGAVOCKS OF CARNTON PLANTATION

Southerners to be Southern patriots.[1545]

❧ FORREST'S LAST DAYS

In the last years of his life battle hardened Forrest softened up considerably. Feeling the sting of past sins and regrets, he asked his attorney to drop his lawsuits (even though all of them were winnable). He also turned intensely religious, becoming a born-again Christian and a member of the Cumberland Presbyterian Church in Memphis, much to his wife Mary Ann's eternal happiness (she had been a member herself for many years).[1546]

Succumbing to a host of physical ailments brought on by his war service, Forrest passed away on October 29, 1877, at the age of fifty-six, the year Reconstruction ended across the South. He had lived to see his beloved Dixie freed from Northern military tyranny at least. That day, suffering from complications due to diabetes, he took his last breath at the home of his brother Jesse in Memphis. Today his burial site in Forrest Park is marked by a large and impressive equestrian statue.[1547]

At his funeral on October 31, some 10,000 people came to pay their final respects to the illustrious Tennessean who gave his entire estate to Confederate charities, and who was widely known as a "tender-hearted, kindly man."[1548] As if to mock Northern folklore, one-third of the mournful guests at Forrest's funeral were African-American.[1549] We will note that this was far less than those who were at Lincoln's interment twelve years earlier. Why? Because white Northerners strictly prohibited blacks from attending the "Great Emancipator's" funeral![1550]

1545. C. Adams, p. 164.
1546. Mathes, p. 374.
1547. Forrest Park is located on Union Ave., between South Manassas Street and South Dunlap Street, Memphis, Tennessee. The GPS coordinates are: Latitude: 35.1397, Longitude: -90.0346.
1548. R. Taylor, p. 200.
1549. Seabrook, NBF, p. 60.
1550. Seabrook, ARB, p. 12.

The McGavocks of Carnton Plantation

❧ FORREST'S LEGACY

Forrest's presence is still felt strongly in Franklin: countless city streets have been named after him, and the area of the town known as Forrest's Crossing commemorates the place where the general forded the Harpeth River in an eastern flanking movement against the Yanks during the Battle of Franklin II. There is even a subdivision in Franklin named after Forrest's most famous and beloved warhorse, Roderick.

The epitome of the Southern gentleman and the standard by which all Confederate heroes are judged, Forrest embodies the all-American son (he paid off his mother's debts), sibling (he put his younger brothers through school), bread-winner (he supported not only his own family, but a wide assortment of friends and relatives), patriot (he gave four years of his life to his country), and husband (faithful to Mary Ann to the end).

It is little wonder that so many Southern parents name their sons after Forrest, that State parks, local parks, streets, roads, highways, libraries, schools, businesses, golf courses, cemeteries, apartment complexes, subdivisions, and office buildings across America are named after him, that countless literary characters, like those created by William Faulkner, were inspired by Forrest, or that author Winston Groom named the lead character in his film *Forrest Gump* after him. A street only yards from Carnton still bears the General's name, while the state of Mississippi named an entire county after him: "Forrest"!

During his lifetime Forrest truly was, as Lytle called him, "the spiritual comforter" of the people of the South.[1551] Some 150 years later, he still is.

On the battlefield the long-haired steely-eyed Forrest, esteemed for his almost supernatural good fortune (which he himself attributed to his wife's prayers),[1552] reckless bravery, and brilliant leadership,[1553] and for his countless wins throughout Tennessee, Alabama, and

---

1551. Lytle, p. 390.
1552. Sheppard, p. 298.
1553. Rosenbaum, s.v. "Forrest, Nathan Bedford."

THE McGAVOCKS OF CARNTON PLANTATION

Mississippi,[1554] defeated such Yank generals as Benjamin H. Grierson, William Sooy Smith, Samuel D. Sturgis, and Edward Hatch, all veteran soldiers and West Point graduates.

Forrest held special contempt for the militarily schooled, who he called "West Pinters." His innate military genius and intuitive grasp of both tactics and strategy actually set him above most in this category, which is why he took extra enjoyment trouncing them in battle.[1555] Of "West Pinters" he once said:

> Whenever I met one of them fellers that fit by note, I generally whipped hell out of him before he got his tune pitched.[1556]

But Forrest did not particularly appreciate having "West Pinters" on his side either. During Lincoln's War he would have no doubt agreed with South Carolinian James H. Hammond who complained that West Point would be the death of the South,[1557] and after the War with General Robert Augustus Toombs (1810-1885), who declared that the epitaph of the Confederate army should read: Deceased. Cause: West Point.[1558]

The largely unschooled Forrest (he had only six months of formal education), who never smoked, drank, or womanized, who once single-handedly thrashed four men in a pre-War fight (killing one), and who completely ignored the by-the-book military rules of drilling, discipline, saluting, standing to attention, and engagement, captured far more enemy supplies than he could ever use, helped refine the concept of mobile warfare, always went on the offensive, greatly delayed the Yank's victory, and was the only man out of nearly 4 million soldiers, South and North, to rise from the rank of private to lieutenant general.[1559]

1554. R. S. Phillips, s.v. "Forrest, Nathan Bedford."
1555. Woodworth, p. 132.
1556. Morton, pp. 12-13.
1557. E. M. Thomas, p. 140.
1558. Warner, GG, s.v. "R. A. Toombs."
1559. Seabrook, ARB, passim; Morton, pp. 12-17; Black, p. 198.

The McGavocks of Carnton Plantation

He and his men, who each carried two Colt Navy revolvers, were known for their unorthodox tactics, such as using decoys to confuse the enemy (for example, Forrest would often have the same two or three cannon wheeled round and round a surrounded Yankee unit in order to make them think they were far outgunned and outmanned). Almost always outnumbered himself, Forrest also utilized ingenious bluffs, learned as a child on the American frontier, to score victories against much bigger armies. He would, for instance, sometimes pose as a Yankee soldier in order to escape the clutches of a confused Federal unit that had surrounded him; or he would boldly send some of his men into a Yankee camp, pretending to be Confederate deserters, in order to gather enemy intelligence.

After winning a battle Forrest did not simply leave the field. He pursued and decimated his opponent whenever possible, exploiting all the advantages of the rapid mobility of the cavalry. So admired was "Old Bedford" for his military successes that leaders of both sides adopted many of his strategies and tactics.[1560]

Idolized by his men, Forrest had twenty-nine horses shot out from under him, was shot at himself 179 times, killed thirty-one Union soldiers in personal combat (and wounded hundreds more), was wounded four times, and captured some 31,000 prisoners. Impressive statistics for a soldier of any time period.

Had Jefferson Davis and his officers recognized Forrest's genius earlier and given him control of larger forces, who knows what direction Lincoln's War might have taken.[1561] We in the South will always believe that the Confederacy could have won under the leadership of a General-in-Chief Forrest.[1562]

At Forrest's funeral Halloween day, 1877, Davis indeed expressed regret that he had not realized how great a military man Forrest truly was until he read the Tennessean's wartime reports years

---

1560. Strain, p. 52.
1561. Sheppard, p. 301.
1562. Shenkman and Reiger, pp. 118-119.

later. Enlightenment had come too late.[1563]

Davis was only partly to blame for this tragic oversight, however. Many of Davis' officers, such as Braxton Bragg (1817-1876), with whom Forrest frequently argued, had always presented Forrest to the Confederate president as little more than an audacious looter.[1564]

Still, posthumous fame has made Forrest an eternal Southern hero. When General Lee was asked who he thought should be named the finest soldier in the Confederacy, he said, "A man I never met: Forrest." General Joseph Eggleston Johnston called Forrest "the greatest soldier of the war," while General Beauregard noted that "Forrest's capacity for war seemed only to be limited by the opportunities for its display."[1565]

The European military elite were of the same mind. In an 1892-magazine article, Lord Garnet Joseph Wolseley (1833-1913), commander-in-chief of the British army, said:

> Panic found no resting place in that calm brain of his, and no danger, no risk, appalled that dauntless spirit. Inspired with true military instincts, he was verily nature's soldier.[1566]

Union officers were equally enamored of Forrest, the chivalric Southern gentleman who loved children and was the self-appointed protector of women.[1567] One of them, an awed Sherman, was so frustrated by Forrest's ability to appear from nowhere, destroy armies three times his size, then instantly disappear into thin air, referred to the Celtic Confederate chieftain as "that Devil Forrest."[1568] Sherman's annoyance finally reached the point where he was ready to bankrupt the U.S. Treasury to have the "Devil" hunted down and killed. Later Sherman grudgingly but admiringly said:

1563. J. Davis, RFCG, Vol. 2, pp. 696-697.
1564. Woodworth, p. 265.
1565. B. A. C. Emerson, p. 116.
1566. Wyeth, LGNBF, p. 636.
1567. Hurst, pp. 216, 379.
1568. ORA, Ser. 1, Vol. 38, Pt. 4, p. 480.

The McGavocks of Carnton Plantation

> I think Forrest was the most remarkable man our Civil War produced on either side . . . [with] a genius for strategy which was original and . . . to me incomprehensible.[1569]

Little wonder he has been voted the number one best Confederate general by military scholars, which on most lists places him even above the incomparable Robert E. Lee.[1570]

?• WHY FORREST WAS LOVED BY THE McGAVOCKS
As is clear from this abbreviated portrait of Nathan Bedford Forrest, Lieutenant Cowan's association with him was not something the McGavocks would have been ashamed of. Quite the opposite.

Forrest, whose recruitment slogan was "join up lads and have some fun killin' Yanks!,"[1571] who preferred hand-to-hand combat, who (against the rules) sharpened his sword on *both* sides, and who was the very personification of Southern manliness, and of conservative, traditional Southern values, was idolized by nearly every Southerner from Texas to Virginia. Forrest's Dixie-wide group of admirers and supporters was comprised of both white and black Southerners,[1572] including, of course, nearly all of those who lived in his home state, Tennessee.[1573]

?• THE PASSING OF CARRIE'S BROTHER
On February 23, 1886, at the young age of thirty-three, Carrie's brother Van Perkins Winder, Jr. (b. September 11, 1852) passed away in Terrebonne Parish, Louisiana, twenty-four years to the day after Nashville was captured by the Yanks. The namesake of their father, Van Perkins the younger had been a great land owner across the Pelican State. His obituary reads as follows:

1569. Wyeth, LGNBF, p. 635.
1570. *The Civil War Book of Lists*, p. 162.
1571. Bedwell, p. 38.
1572. To this very day one will still see both whites and blacks at events honoring General Forrest, such as the Forrest Boyhood Home Fundraiser, held at Chapel Hill, Tennessee, every June.
1573. For a detailed *positive* study of Forrest, see my book, *A Rebel Born: A Defense of Nathan Bedford Forrest*. Also see my condensed version of the above book: *Nathan Bedford Forrest: Southern Hero, American Patriot*.

THE MCGAVOCKS OF CARNTON PLANTATION

(**A New Orleans newspaper, obituary by T. R. M., dated March 2, 1886**)
IN MEMORIAM - Died—On Tuesday, February 23, 1886, of acute pneumonia, Van P. Winder, at his late residence in Houma, Terrebonne Parish, La.

    One of the best of that class who, 'because they are strong,' invest the future of the land with hope, his early death gives sincere and general grief. Along the Lafourche and the Terrebonne, in the communities where he grew [. . .] his clear promise of excellence and eminence, and throughout the State and elsewhere, in the circles, social and professional, in which he mingled and labored, he will be greatly missed and mourned.

    Sprung from the best stock, reared amid [. . .] associations, and nurtured in a Christian home, his fine spirit, generous nature and warm heart made him a centre of affection and interest, the qualities developed in his opening manhood foretokening an honorable and successful career.

    May the God of all comfort send 'sufficient grace' and 'strength as their day,' to the venerable mother, the young wife, and the stricken hearts and homes sitting in the shadow of this unspeakable sorrow. T. R. M. New Orleans, March 2, 1886.[1574]

❧ THE PASSING OF JOHN & CARRIE

Seven years later Colonel John passed away at Carnton at age seventy-eight on June 7, 1893, nine years after his daughter's Hattie's marriage to Lieutenant Cowan. He had been confined to bed suffering from "bowell trouble" for several days, which was listed as the "immediate cause of dissolution."

John's reputation in Franklin was such that every shop closed that day to honor him, and local newspapers mournfully sang his praises, calling him a "venerable friend" and "a true, old time Southern gentleman." His funeral, held at Carnton, was one of the largest ever witnessed in Middle Tennessee.

After John's death Carrie inherited the plantation, by then a dubious gift. For thanks to Lincoln the once stunning 1,420-acre farm was now barely ten acres and worth a mere one-fifth of its original value.

1574. Obituary courtesy of the Williamson County Public Library.

THE McGAVOCKS OF CARNTON PLANTATION

Some ten and half years on, around August 1903, Carrie, the Colonel's wife and the "queen of that beautiful old Southern mansion," began to experience "failing health." It was nothing serious, the family doctor reported, just old age.

Eighteen months later, on February 22,1905, the seventy-five year old matron followed her husband to the grave on the fortieth anniversary of Tennessee's prohibition against slavery and the adoption of its new Constitution. The Colonel had died at Carnton while Carrie passed away at their daughter Hattie's house at the end of the driveway. Both are buried in the McGavock Family Cemetery at Carnton, near John's parents, Randal and Sarah.

≥ COLONEL JOHN W. McGAVOCK'S OBITUARIES

At the time of the couple's deaths Tennessee newspapers, particularly those in Williamson County, were filled with obituaries and tender memorials to the McGavocks, as the following examples show.

Note that brackets surrounding an ellipsis [. . .] indicate a lacuna (a blank space or missing part of the text). Words within the lacuna brackets are my guesses or statements. Words within plain brackets are my additional comments. I transcribed all obituaries, which were provided courtesy of the Williamson County Public Library, Special Collections Department. The original spelling, format, and punctuation of the articles have been retained.

> **(A Franklin newspaper, name unknown, date probably June 7 or 8, 1893)**
> We are pained to hear of the severe illness of our venerable friend, Col. John McGavock, whose condition has been lately such as to cast a cloud of discouragement over his family and friends. We hope it may prove, however, not quite so bad as feared, and that we may soon see his familiar face and figure on our streets again.
>
> Later: Just on going to press, and too late for extended notice, we learn with deep regret that Col. McGavock has passed. A truly excellent man has gone from us. We will have more to say next week.

THE MCGAVOCKS OF CARNTON PLANTATION

(A Franklin newspaper, June 9, 1893)
LATE COL. JOHN M'GAVOCK
A Large Number of Friends Attend His Funeral
Franklin, June 9 [1893] - (Special) - The largest funeral seen here in years was that of Col. John McGavock to-day. All business houses were closed during the hour for services, which took place at the residence, one mile from town. Rev. Mr. Kennedy of this place and Rev. Mr. Chester of Nashville, officiated at the grave. The services were conducted by McEwen [. . .] Bivouac and Col. Thos. Claiborne, of Nashville, and Rev. Mr. Fisher, Chaplain of the bivouac. The distinguished dead was an honorary member of the State Association of the U.C.V. [United Confederate Veterans], which had representatives present. A large delegation of friends and relatives came from Nashville. Among them were Justice Howell E. Jackson, Gen. W[illiam]. H[icks]. Jackson, Capt. Garnett, John M. Bass [married Mary Melvina Grundy, b. 1809, a sister of John's wife's mother, Martha Ann Grundy], Capt. Steger and others. The services were simple in accord with the wish of the deceased.

(A Franklin newspaper, name unknown, date probably June 7 or 8, 1893)
The death of Col. John McGavock of Williamson County, removes from its walks one of the men most intimate with the proud history of that good county, and a man whose neighbors and all who knew him admired, respected and loved. In manner, mind and face he was a true Southern gentleman. Dignified of mein, full of information, warm in his friendships, lovely in his hospitality; he was a type of the old school the South will always be proud to call its own. A man of learning, wealth, usefulness and influence, he might easily have stood at any time for public honors, but preferred instead the private walks of life and the sweet companionship of his lovely family. He died in the fullness of years, after a life well spent, and leaves behind him a proud [. . .]

(A Franklin newspaper, name unknown, date probably sometime in June 1893)
COL. JOHN M'GAVOCK
[. . . It was?] announced in our local columns [. . . this week that?], this aged citizen and estimable gentleman has paid the final account and gone to his reward. He [. . . had?] been confined to his room [. . . for?] a few days, bowell trouble [. . . being the?] immediate

THE MCGAVOCKS OF CARNTON PLANTATION

cause of dissolution; [. . . and?] for many months he has been feeling more and more feeble, and his friends for some time had realized [. . . that?] the pins of his tabernacle were [. . . failing?] and that the fall of the structure was only a matter of short time. His death closes a long, useful and [. . .] life, and removes from our midst a most charming and loveable character whose entire life of a [. . .] over 78 years had been spent [. . .] and spotlessly in the very community where he was born, having been born and reared at the same home where he died. Perhaps no one ever lived or died in the community [. . . who was?] loved and mourned by a larger number of people. Although a man [. . . of?] positive traits of character, he commanded the respect and admiration of [. . .] his noble, manly and chivalrous [. . .]. He was the true type of the old time Southern gentleman, and [. . . more?], perhaps, than any other man [. . . dead or?] living, linked the present with [. . .] age and order of things in the [. . .]. He was reared in the days of "Old Hickory," whose acquaintance [. . . and?] personal relationship he enjoyed [. . . and?] whose character he very much [. . . admired?] and in many respects resembled. To the day of his death he kept [. . . in?] his house the chair that Jackson occupied while acting as Chief Magistrate of the nation.

Colonel McGavock was a born gentleman, and could not possibly have [. . . done?] a small or ignoble act if he had [. . . tried?]. He was courteous and kind to every one with whom he came in contact and his high breeding and culture showed themselves in his manner towards the humblest negro scullery [. . . maid?] as much as towards the greatest [. . . man?] in the Nation. He was a man of scholarly attainments and his conversation was pleasing and prepossessing [. . .] degree while being perfectly free [. . . from?] pedantry. Possessing a splendid [. . .], he gave with unsparing hand [. . . to?] every worthy cause and object. In [. . . the?] qualities of head and heart, an [. . .], he was in manner and sympathies a democrat [that is, what today would be called a conservative Republican]. A man of superb [. . . knowledge?], he was kind and gentle as a [. . . man?] in his family and social relations. Taking no part in spoils-hunting [. . . and?] political scrambles, he ever upheld with voice and vote the standard of the Democratic Party [today the Republican Party]. Full of remembrances and traditions of the shadowy past, he was brim full of the spirit and progress of the present, and perfectly free from the cant that can [. . .] no habitation for virtue save [. . .] the things that were.

THE MCGAVOCKS OF CARNTON PLANTATION

Entering freely into the present order of things, he inspired respect [. . .] men and institutions of the good old days in which the splendid virtues [. . . which?] characterized his Life, were [. . .] to the youth of the laud as [. . .] dearer than life itself. He was a [. . . very?] good and noble man in all that [. . . here several missing sentences] . . . dear esteem in which he was held, and we do not suppose there is a man, woman or child in the county who knew him but loved him and mourns him. We offer his noble life as the best balm of consolations to his stricken family and friends, and propose a peace to his memory. The writer is proud that it has been his good fortune to have known such a grand character as Col. McGavock was.

(A newspaper, name unknown, date probably June 8 or 9, 1893)
His Remains Sadly Laid at Rest on Yesterday in the McGavock Family Burying Ground Adjoining the Beautiful Confederate Cemetery.

A large number of the citizens of Williamson County and other friends of the late Col. John McGavock, from various portions of the State, gathered yesterday at the residence of the deceased, near Franklin, to pay the last tribute of respect to their departed friend.

The funeral sermon was preached by Rev. Mark Kennedy, pastor of the Presbyterian Church at Franklin. Prayer was offered and a few remarks were made by Rev. Mr. Chester, after which Gen. W[illiam]. H[icks]. Jackson, on behalf of the Confederate veterans, testified in touching words to the love which Col. McGavock had felt to the Confederate cause and to the Confederate soldiers.

The body was then conveyed to the hearse by the following active pall-bearers: J[acob]. M[cGavock]. Dickinson [Sr.], W. R. Garrett, F. F. McGavock [probably Francis F. McGavock, 1840-1921, the Colonel's 1st cousin once removed], John M. Bass, Walter A. Roberts, F. G. Ewing and Henry Kenning, accompanied by the following honorary pall-bearers: Howell E. Jackson, Dr. Wm. Reid, W. G. N. Perkins, W[illiam]. H[icks]. Jackson, Jas. L. Parkes, E. F. Glass, Dr. John S. Park, R. J. Gordon, R. C. Webb, John B. McEwen, J. G. Wallace, Dr. Harding, John Harding, David McGavock [probably David Harding McGavock, 1826-1896, founder of Two Rivers Plantation in Nashville], and T. M. Steger.

A large procession escorted the remains to the cemetery,

The McGavocks of Carnton Plantation

headed by McEwen Bivouac of Confederate Veterans. Arrived at the grave, the remains were cosigned to McEwen Bivouac for burial. The following pall-bearers of McEwen Bivouac conveyed the body from the hearse and lowered it into its last resting place: John Atwood, Judge Cook, John M. Nevils, N. N. Cox, Geo. W. Smithson, Jas. Neely, Jas. P. Hanner, W. J. Petway.

Prof. S. V. Wall, President of the Bivouac, spoke as follows:

Col. Jno. McGavock spent his entire life of 78 years in the community of Franklin, on the farm where he was born and reared. His long and beautiful life was full of honor, usefulness, charity and good works. He [. . . built?] a character of so much beauty, strength and symmetry that all who love the true and good admire his virtues, cherish his memory and lament his death. The generosity, hospitality, kindness and love of the pure-hearted patriot for the Confederate soldiers have bound their hearts to him in indissoluble ties of affection. Confederate soldiers respected, honored and loved him, and he honored and loved the Confederate soldiers and their cause. In the name of McEwen Bivouac I read the following resolutions adopted by the bivouac:

'Whereas, Col. John McGavock was an honorary member of the McEwen Bivouac, and also a member of the Confederate State Association, loved the Confederate soldiers, ministered to their wants while living, and donated the beautiful grounds where so many noble and brave heroes lie buried.

'Resolved, that Tennessee has lost a peerless citizen, the country at large one of its purest and brightest lights, and the McEwen Bivouac one of its most estimable and honored members.

'Resolved, that the McEwen Bivouac will ever cherish his memory, love his family, and honor his brave and unsullied name. Respectfully submitted. S. V. Wall, Jas. P. Hanner, Geo. W. Smithson, Committee.'

Col, Thos. Claiborne followed with an eloquent and beautiful tribute of respect. The services were closed with prayer by Rev. T. B. Fisher, Chaplain of McEwen Bivouac. The grave was then covered with flowers, and the assembly dispersed.

John McGavock now lives in the hearts of his friends and fellow-citizens, and will be held in cheerful memory as the ideal of Southern manhood.

[The article continues]

THE MCGAVOCKS OF CARNTON PLANTATION

The intelligence of the death of Col. John McGavock, of Williamson County, saddened many hearts not only in Tennessee but throughout the entire South. He never held nor sought public office, and thus did not challenge public notice, in the way that makes many men conspicuous; and yet Tennessee has had but few sons who have so profoundly impressed their personality upon so many people. Without seeking leadership he, nevertheless, by the intensity of his nature, the clearness and soundness of his intellect, the transparent honesty of his purposes and a courage that never flinched, reinforced by a character that constrained reverence was the moulder of the thoughts and actions of others, and this [. . . several missing sentences here] . . . but no thoughtful person who knew the brave heart and pure character of Col. McGavock would feel for a moment that it was any extravagance to ascribe to him these shining qualities in their highest degree. He exemplified in his bearing and character all that we revere in the old school Southerners. They have been portrayed as follows:

Prodigal in their generosity, with a sense of personal honor that preferred death to an impeachment of character, holding it a sacred duty.

'To right such wrong, where it is given,
Though in the very court of heaven.'

Bred to the courtly manners and stately bearing of olden times, deeply imbued with religious reverence, born with the instinct of command, trained in all manly accomplishments with a courage as keen, but as polished as a sword, boundless in their hospitality, and offering to women a devotion and courtesy not excelled by the paladins of old, they were a race of men who, in the splendor of their characteristics, were equal to the best that any time has produced.

Col. McGavock would have been a model for this character picture of the South.

He was a Democrat [today what would be called a Republican] who never wavered. He bitterly deplored some of the measures of his party and chafed under its leadership, but never in its greatest adversities nor in its bitterest schisms did he for an instant falter in his support. In early life he accepted its principles as the surest for the perpetuation of our rights and liberties, and while he boldly opposed party men and party measures, it was always within the party, and he no more thought of effectuating his

THE McGAVOCKS OF CARNTON PLANTATION

desires by abandoning his party than a Calvinist would of leaving his church in order to get rid of leaders in whom he had lost faith, or heresies that held temporary sway. He took a large view of the life and mission of the Democratic party [now the Republican Party] and subordinated present discontents in order to conserve and not paralyze a power whose usefulness in the eyes of a nation's life would more than compensate for the injuries inflicted by temporary disorders. The Southern Confederacy and its soldiers never had a more generous, true, and unwavering friend.

Since the war it was his self-imposed mission to protect their graves and keep their memories ever fresh. When such men die it is right that we should pause in our active pursuits and contemplate their virtues and garner from their lives the rich harvest of in- [. . . last line of article is missing].

࿔ CAROLINE WINDER McGAVOCK'S OBITUARIES

The press was no less effusive and complimentary of Carrie at her passing at age seventy-six. The following are several examples of her obituaries:

> **(A Tennessee newspaper, dated February 22, 1905)**
> Mrs. Caroline Winder McGavock
> FRANKLIN, Tenn., Feb. 22—(Special.)—Mrs. Caroline Winder McGavock, widow of Col. John McGavock, died this morning at the home of her daughter, Mrs. George L. Cowan [Hattie], on the Lewisburg pike. She had been in failing health for about eighteen months, and her death was not unexpected, being caused by old age. Mrs. McGavock was born Sept. 9, 1829, at Natchez, Miss., and was married to the late Col. McGavock Dec. 6, 1848. Five children were born to them, of who two survive, Mrs. George L. Cowan and Winder McGavock. Mrs. McGavock was a granddaughter of the great Felix Grundy. The funeral services will be held at 11 o'clock to-morrow morning at Carnton, the old homestead, conducted by Rev. J[ames]. H. McNeilly, of Nashville, and local divines. The family had a large acquaintance in Tennessee, Texas and Louisiana. The McGavock home place figured prominently during the Civil War, when one Major and four Brigadier Generals lay dead at one time on the front porch during the battle of Franklin, and the Confederate Cemetery, in which over eighteen hundred of the heroes of the war now sleep, is located there, the ground being donated by Col. McGavock for that purpose.

The McGavocks of Carnton Plantation

For the record we will note a number of errors in this obituary: only four generals were laid on the porch at Carnton; the porch was not at the front of the house, but at the rear; since there were two major battles and one minor one fought at Franklin, the correct name for the second one is "the Battle of Franklin II"; and there were never "over eighteen hundred" deceased in the McGavock Confederate Cemetery, for the number of dead did not exceed 1,750.

(A Tennessee newspaper; obituary probably written near the end of February 1905)
Funeral of Mrs. McGavock.
The funeral of Mrs. Carrie E Winder McGavock, widow of Col. John McGavock occurred last Thursday morning at Carnton, the historical homestead. A large concourse, representative of every part of the country, from Nashville and elsewhere, assembled to pay respect to the venerable lady. The floral tributes were superb, many coming from distant points.

Pursuant to written request of Mrs. McGavock, the obsequies were simple, there being no formal eulogy. A choir rendered old-time hymns, "Jesus Lover of My Soul," "We'll Never Say Goodbye in Heaven," "Nearer, My God to Thee," "Goodnight," prayers were said by Rev. J[ames]. H. McNeilly and J. W. Hanner, a scripture lesson was read by Rev. W. J. McMillin [McMillan], and the remains were then carried to the family burial ground and deposited in the same grave with her husband. A more impressive funeral service was never held in this county.

(A Franklin newspaper, name unknown, dated February 23, 1905)
FRANKLIN, TENN., THURSDAY, FEBRUARY 23, 1905
BEAUTIFUL CHRISTIAN CHARACTER CALLED HOME.
Thousands of loved ones in Franklin and Williamson County will learn with tear-dimmed eyes of the peaceful ending of the earth life of Mrs. Caroline E. McGavock, and friends throughout this beautiful southland will mourn the departure of the noble Christian woman.

Surrounded by daughter, son, sister, and other relatives, the end came peacefully yesterday at 6:57 o'clock am, at the historic McGavock homestead, 'Carnton,' a short distance south of Franklin, in her 76th year. Since her illness a few years ago Mrs.

THE MCGAVOCKS OF CARNTON PLANTATION

McGavock had continued the loveable, sweet ministry that had characterized the entire life of the modest, retiring, Godly character, and she accomplished much in the amelioration of the wants of the needy, though enfeebled by years and disease.

While the war raged fiercely about her home, and after the fight, the wide piazzas were covered with dead and wounded Confederates, notably, the bodies of five generals—Cleburne, Gist, Strahl, Adams, and Granberry [Granbury]—who had been killed in the fight, and Gen. Cockrell, who was wounded.

Since the death of her distinguished husband, Col. John McGavock, some years since, she had continued to reside at the handsome and imposing mansion of antebellum days, whose hospitable doors were ever opened to all who visited the scene of the conflict.

She had given her personal supervision and care of the Confederate cemetery, [. . . one?] of the most beautiful burying grounds.

The ground, near the family homestead, was donated by Mrs. McGavock and her [. . . husband?] the southern gentleman and ardent [. . . Confederate Colonel?]. It was largely through their efforts [. . . that the?] bodies of 1484 Confederate veterans [. . . now?] rest.

[. . .] with the numerous noble deeds [. . .] womanhood, her memory is cherished [. . .] throughout the land whom she [. . .] own home since the war and instilled [. . .] will live long after those who profited [. . . from the?] generosity of the ministering angel shall [. . .] peacefully into that sleep that knows [. . .]

Mrs. McGavock was a devoted member of the Presbyterian Church, and her daily walk was consistent with that of [the] highest type of Christianity. She was one of the sweetest, grandest, simplest characters the world has ever known, and her memory will be cherished by thousands who came within her salutary influence.

She was the daughter of the late Van P. Winder of Natchez, Miss., and later of Louisiana. In the year 1848 (December) she was united in marriage to Col. John McGavock.

Surviving are a son—Winder McGavock—and one daughter—Mrs. Hattie Cowan; also two sisters—Mrs. Louise [McGavock Winder] Campbell of Franklin and Miss Sallie [Guion] Winder of Louisiana—and one brother, Thos. [Levin] Winder of California.

Funeral services will be conducted at 'Carnton' this

THE MCGAVOCKS OF CARNTON PLANTATION

morning at 11 o'clock, by Revs. J[ames]. H. McNeilly, W. J. McMillan and J. W. Hanner.

The interment will be in the family burying ground.

The pall-bearers are: F. F. McGavock, J[acob]. M[cGavock]. Dickinson [Sr.], F. G. Ewing, Jno. M. Bass, F. G. Ewing, W. A. Roberts, Harry [Henry] Kenning, F[rancis]. M[cGavock]. Ewing, Capt. T. M. Stegar, W. W. Campbell.

(A newspaper, name and date unknown)
MRS. McGAVOCK
By Mrs. S. E. R. Rose, West Point, Miss.
The pages of history contain the names of many warriors of the so-called 'weaker sex.'

To their praise be it said that women, as a sex, are devoted to peace. However, they have proved that they can fight if occasion demands it. In Holy Writ we find the names of women who have led great armies. Deborah, at the head of the troops of Israel, was an inspiration, and Semiramis, the Assyrian queen, led her armies forth to conquer the nations of the world.

Boadicea, with stirring words, appealed to the Britons to throw off the Roman yoke, and Joan of Arc, inspired Maid of Orleans, defeated the invaders of France.

The American revolution developed a Molly Pitcher to stand at the cannon's mouth, and the war between the states gave us an Emma Sansom, who braved the Federal sharpshooters, guiding Gen. Forrest to the ford, enabling him to overtake the enemy and gain a wonderful victory.

But who can tell the countless deeds of heroism of the women of the Confederacy from 1861-65?

Not half can ever be written on history's pages, but in the book of life, where golden deeds are recorded, they have all been written by the recording angel in letters of living light.

The annals of the war between the states record so many great deeds of heroic women that it is difficult to single out one from the rest, but the name mentioned here is only the type of the many grand and noble women of the South. In deeds of heroism none exceed and few equal in true merit the courage and devotion of Mrs. John McGavock of Franklin, Tenn., who for her many charitable deeds obtained the sobriquet "The Good Samaritan of Williamson County."

Caroline Elizabeth Winder McGavock, wife of Col. John McGavock, is recalled by many friends as the queen of that

THE MCGAVOCKS OF CARNTON PLANTATION

beautiful old Southern mansion that stands on historic ground, the battlefield of Franklin.

During that bloody battle her home was converted into a hospital and she was the ministering angel to the sick and wounded soldiers. Every room in the large two-story house was filled, and the yard as well. Amid the groans and death rattles, all night long, she aided the surgeons giving her towels, bed linen and garments for bandages, and with her own hands dispensing coffee and stimulants. Even her skirts were stained with blood from the gaping wounds of dying men. She was the personification of love, tenderness and sympathy as she moved among the suffering soldiers. By her thoughtfulness a list of the dead was kept and over 2,000 soldiers sleep in the cemetery, a gift from her and her husband. Faithful to the Confederate soldiers in life, they were not forgotten beneath the sod.

To-day the Southland rises up and calls her 'blessed,' together with all that noble army of Southern women, who counted no sacrifice too costly to be laid on the altar of their country.

(A Tennessee newspaper; obituary written February 23, 1905)
A NOBLE MATRON Joins a Noble Husband on the Eternal Shores.
The Venerable Widow of Col. John McGavock Peacefully Passes Away in her 76th Year.
At 7 o'clock yesterday morning Mrs. Caroline E. Winder McGavock, widow of Col. John McGavock, died at the home of her daughter Mrs. George L. Cowan, near Franklin. She had been [. . . in?] failing health for eighteen months, [. . . but?] only within the last week had an [. . . early?] termination of her earthly career been anticipated. She suffered [. . .] no malady, save a general failing of her physical powers due to advancing age. Her mind was clear to the [. . . last?]. She was conscious until a very [. . . few?] minutes before the end came, quietly passing from time to eternity in the midst of sorrowing loved ones from whom every affectionate ministration had been rendered.

Mrs. McGavock was born Sept. 9, 1829, at Natchez, Miss., her father moving when she was a year old to Houma, Terra Bonne Parish, La. She was, therefore, in her seventy-sixth year.

She was a daughter of Col. Winder, a distinguished and wealthy gentleman, and was married to the [. . .] Col. McGavock,

THE MCGAVOCKS OF CARNTON PLANTATION

Dec. 6, 1848. Five children were born to them, of them two survive, Mrs. Geo. L. Cowan and Winder McGavock, She had two surviving sisters, Mrs. Louise Campbell [Louise McGavock Winder, b. 1845] of this place, and Miss Sallie Winder [Sallie Guion Winder, b. 1854], of Louisiana, and one living brother Thomas [Thomas Levin Winder, b. 1848], who resides in California. Mrs. McGavock was a granddaughter of Felix Grundy, the greatest [. . .] the southwest ever knew.

The funeral services will be held at 11 o'clock this morning at Carnton, the old homestead, conducted by Rev. J[ames]. H. McNeilly, W. J. McMillin [McMillan], and J. W. Hanner [his family once owned Wyatt Hall],[1575] the interment to [. . .] the family grave-yard, in the same grave with her beloved husband. The pallbearers will be F. F. McGavock, J[acob]. M[cGavock]. Dickinson [Sr.], F. G. Ewing, J. M. Bass, W[alter]. A. Roberts, Harry [Henry] Kenning, Frank M. Ewing [Francis McGavock Ewing?], W. W. Campbell and Capt. T. M. Stegar.

Mrs. McGavock was a woman of the highest type. An earnest Christian, a devoted member of the Presbyterian church, as wife and mother she exemplified the sweetest virtues of her sex; as friend and neighbor, thoughtful and charitable, she was true in every relation of life.

For her unwavering loyalty to the Confederate cause, both in war and in peace, her benefactions to the soldier boys living and honor paid to them in death, a spirit which she shared with her noble husband, she will be ever remembered in this County and section. The Confederate cemetery which bears her husband's name, where sleep hundreds of fallen heroes, was the object of her unwavering and tender devotion.

(A Nashville newspaper; obituary written February 23, 1905)
DEATH CLAIMS A GOOD WOMAN
MRS. CLARA [Caroline] W. M'GAVOCK, GOOD SAMARITAN OF WILLIAMSON COUNTY.
Her Life Had Been a Beautiful Benediction to the Community.

Mrs. Carrie Winder McGavock, widow of Col. John McGavock, died yesterday at 7 o'clock [AM] at the residence of her

---

1575. Members of the Hanner family of Franklin lived at the noted house Wyatt Hall on Franklin Road from 1852 to 1856.

THE MCGAVOCKS OF CARNTON PLANTATION

daughter, Mrs. George Cowan, near Franklin, Tenn., after a long illness. For more than half a century she had been a well-known figure in Middle Tennessee, zealous not only in the work of the Presbyterian Church at Franklin, but in all public politics and benevolent measures. So [. . . great?] was her hospitality that it was rare [. . . that her?] house was without guests, and her character so uniform that it is probable [. . . that no?] deserving person was ever turned away from her door.

From the beginning of the civil war until its close her devotion to the Southern Confederacy was unfaltering, and at the end of that struggle until her death she maintained a deep and active interest in the Confederate veterans. This, whenever possible, took a practical direction and many old soldiers through her efforts had found employment or other [. . . means?] to [. . . survive?].

[. . . an entire missing paragraph here]

The [. . .] Confederate cemetery at Franklin where many thousands of soldiers [. . . rest?] was given by the McGavocks, [. . .] for years kept it [. . .]. She was [. . .] as the Good Samaritan of Williamson County. [. . .] had been a beautiful benediction to the community where she lived, and her home, 'Cairnton,' named for the old McGavock home in Scotland, was known far and wide for its hospitality. Mrs. McGavock was 76 years old and was the daughter of Van Perkins Winder [Sr.] of Terrebonne Parish, La. She married Col. John McGavock in 1846 [actually 1848], had since that date been a resident of Franklin. Her mother was the daughter of Judge Felix Grundy of this city [Nashville], [. . . she?] being the sister of the late Mrs. Louisa McGavock [Louisa Caroline Grundy, 1798-1878, wife of Jacob McGavock, 1790-1878], Lawrence McGavock [?], Mrs. Felicia Porter [Felicia Grundy, 1820-1889] and Mrs. John M. Bass [Mary Melvina Grundy, b. 1809], [. . . all?] eminent women of this day.

Mrs. McGavock had two living sisters, Mrs. Samuel Campbell of Franklin and Miss Sallie [Guion] Winder of Louisiana. Her one surviving brother is Mr. Thomas [Levin] Winder of San Francisco, one of the preeminent physicians of the Pacific [. . .]. Her oldest brother, Capt. Felix Grundy Winder, was killed at the siege of Vicksburg [Mississippi, which took place May 18-July 4, 1863]. The Federals had charged the Confederates and were repulsed. [. . .] Winder's company led the charge and then jumped upon the fortifications, where he waved his cap at the fleeing Federals. While standing thus he was shot and killed by a sharp shooter.

The McGavocks of Carnton Plantation

Mrs. McGavock leaves two children, Winder McGavock and Mrs. Hattie Cowan, both of Franklin.

The funeral took place to-day at 11 o'clock at Cairnton, followed by interment at the family burial ground.

❧ DEATH OF WINDER McGAVOCK

After Carrie's death Carnton was passed down to her son Winder. The forty-nine year old died at the Mansion only two years later, on June 3, 1907. Two of Winder's obituaries follow:

(A Franklin newspaper, name unknown, date sometime around June 5 or 6, 1907.)
WINDER McGAVOCK

At 3:48 P.M., Monday June 3, 1907, at Carnton, the family residence, Winder McGavock died. He was born July 13, 1857. Funeral services were held at the residence on Tuesday afternoon at 4 o'clock, conducted by Revs. W. J. McMillan and W. T. Haggard. Interment was in Mt. Hope Cemetery. The pall-bearers were: Jno. H. Henderson, E. E. Green, Brown Campbell, Geo. H. Armistead, Harry [Henry] Cenning [Kenning], Alex Titcomb, J. W. Reid, D. J. Kenneday.

(A Franklin newspaper, name unknown, date June 6, 1907.)
DEATHS

McGAVOCK—At 3:48 o'clock last Monday afternoon Winder McGavock passed away at Carnton, the historic homestead, near Franklin. He was born July 13, 1857, and was, therefore, nearly fifty years old. Though it had been known for a long time that his health was precarious, there had not been immediate danger of a fatal termination to his malady until last Friday when there was a sudden change for the worse. It was seen that the end was not far distant; and with his devoted family gathered about him, the husband and father, whose life had been gentle and loving, and the esteemed citizen, whose worth had won a universal respect, serenely awaited the summons to exchange life for immortality.

When the intelligence reached Franklin Sunday that there was no hope for his recovery there were those manifestations of regret and sympathy for the sorrowing loved ones, which strikingly attested their hold upon the regard of the community; and the obsequies which ensued the next afternoon were a further and

THE MCGAVOCKS OF CARNTON PLANTATION

impressive tribute to the high esteem in which he was held. His friends were legion; of enemies, he had none; a worthy scion of a noble parentage whose memory will ever abide in the affectionate remembrance of the people of this county, to whom Col. John McGavock and his noble wife were striking figures of an old and honored regime.

Winder was a man of the highest verse of honor, modest yet manly, warm hearted and true in all the relations of life.

The tribute which was paid him in the vast concourse which attended his obsequies was one of the most impressive seen in this community for many years. The services at the home were simple, as was his expressed desire. 'Asleep in Jesus' was sung by a choir of several voices, after which the Rev. W. J. McMillan, pastor of the Presbyterian Church, of which he had long been a member, read a scripture lesson, the same which had been read at the funeral of his mother. 'Some Sweet Day' was rendered as a solo by Mr. Green; then came a prayer by Rev. W. T. Haggard, pastor of the Methodist Church, and the hymn, 'We'll Never say Goodbye in Heaven.'

The cortege was one of the longest ever seen here, being over a half mile in length, and at Mt. Hope, as the sun was slowly setting, the casket which contained all that was mortal of the honored citizen and gentleman, was deposited in its last earthly resting place. Above it rose a mound which was literally covered with beautiful floral remembrances from friends far and near, fragrant with the incense of affection and friendship. It is understood that in the near future the remains of Col. McGavock and his wife and their three children who are buried at Carnton will be removed to Mt. Hope.

The immediate family of the deceased consisted of his wife [Susan Lee "Susie" Ewing, 1863-1931], who is the elder daughter of Mr. H. S. Ewing [Herbert Ewing, b. 1837], three daughters [Hattie, Sara, and Martha], two sons [John and Winder, Jr.] and a sister, Mrs. George L. Cowan [Hattie McGavock, 1855-1932]. Besides these there is a large connection among the leading families of Middle Tennessee. His father, Col. John McGavock, as is well known, was born on the farm which he inherited and was one of nature's real noblemen. His mother was a Winder, of the prominent Louisiana family of that name. She was survived by two sisters, Mrs. Louise W. Campbell, of Franklin, and Miss Winder, of Homer, La. [Claiborne Parish].

To the stricken wife and widow, beloved of the entire

THE MCGAVOCKS OF CARNTON PLANTATION

community, to the bereaved children and devoted sister, a heartfelt sympathy is offered from a multitude of sorrowing friends who knew the worth of him whose departure [. . . is now mourned?].

ॐ THE LAST OF THE McGAVOCKS LEAVE CARNTON

After Winder's death, his wife Susan Lee "Susie" (Ewing) moved to downtown Franklin and sold the house in 1911. There was no money left and no heart to continue running the large empty farm by then anyway. Thus ended the nearly 100 year reign of the McGavocks at one of Tennessee's most beautiful and famous plantations.[1576]

That same year Winder's and Susie's daughter Sara "Sallie" Ewing McGavock (b. December 7, 1885) passed away at 6:15 A.M. "at the home of her mother, Mrs. Susie Lee McGavock," on December 11. Young Sara was just twenty-six years of age.

Funeral services were held at the Presbyterian Church in Franklin, and she was buried in Mount Hope Cemetery on December 12, 1911. The pallbearers at Sara's funeral were: Dave Kenneday, Newton Cannon, Jr., Lawrence Ayres, J. F. Eggleston, John Cowan, R. B. North, and John White.

ॐ DEATH OF LIEUTENANT COWAN, THE KNIGHTS TEMPLAR, & THE HOLY GRAIL

Seven years later, Hattie's husband, Lieutenant George Limerick Cowan, passed away at his Franklin home at age seventy-six on September 18, 1919. The funeral was held the next day, September 19, 1919, at the First Presbyterian Church in Franklin at 2:30 P.M. Services were conducted by Dr. E. D. McDougall and Dr. J. I. Armstrong. Pallbearers were the Confederate Veterans and the Elders and Deacons of the Presbyterian Church.

Services at the grave were conducted by the Knights Templar (that is, the "Knights of the Temple"), a clandestine Christian military order that has officially existed since the 12th Century, but which has

---

[1576]. We are assuming here that Randal purchased, or took control of, the land Carnton Plantation was built on around 1810 or so.

THE MCGAVOCKS OF CARNTON PLANTATION

roots that date back many thousands of years earlier.[1577] And here begins a strange mystery.

It is not known if Lieutenant Cowan was a member of the Knights Templar. If he was, I have not been able to corroborate it. And if he was not, why was this mysterious, wealthy, extremely powerful, and highly secretive holy order at his grave side? They would not turn up at someone's funeral without good reason. Whether Cowan was a member or not, there is indeed an explanation, though deeply cryptic, for their presence at Mount Hope Cemetery that cool September day.

As a professional genealogist I have discovered, through many years of research, that the Lieutenant's wife, Hattie McGavock, is the 55th great-granddaughter of Merovée (b. about 415), the first of the famed dynastic line of long-haired kings of France, who take their name from him: the Merovingians.[1578] Though I understand that the following is not accepted by mainstream Christianity, for the moment let us objectively examine this intriguing topic in a genuine spirit of open scientific and genealogical inquiry.

According to ancient Gnostic Christian legend, Jesus and Mary Magdalene were married and had a daughter named Sarah (revealingly, a Jewish name meaning "princess"). Thus Mary Magdalene, being the carrier of the royal bloodline of Jesus, is the literal "Holy Grail" of early Celtic and British myth.[1579] As the story is related in early apocryphal

---

1577. Paull and Culwell, pp. 163-168.
1578. I myself am the 49th great-grandson of King Merovée.
1579. For more on the early Christian beliefs about the relationship between Jesus and Mary Magdalene, see R. J. Miller, passim. In the *Gospel of Mary*, for example, Peter the Apostle says to Mary Magdalene: "Sister, we know that the Savior loved you more than any other woman. Tell us the words of the Savior that you know, but which we haven't heard." Mary 6:1-2 (R. J. Miller, p. 363). The *Gospel of Philip* states: "There were three who always walked with the Lord: Mary his mother and her sister and Magdalene, the one who was called his companion." Haskins, p. 33. In this same Gospel can be found the following remarkable passage concerning Mary Magdalene: "But Christ loved her more than all the disciples and used to kiss her often on the mouth." Haskins, p. 40. While works like the *Gospel of Mary* and the *Gospel of Philip* are rejected by modern mainstream orthodox Christianity, they were widely accepted by most early Christians right up to the 4th Century, when they were pronounced heretical—for political purposes—by the Catholic Church. Unlike the mainstream branch of the Church, Gnostic groups like the Knights Templar, however, retained the earlier mystical Pagan traditions of the primitive Christian Church, an act for which they were ruthlessly punished for many centuries by Catholic authorities. For more on early Christianity, see my book *Christmas Before Christianity: How the Birthday of the "Sun" Became the Birthday of the "Son."*

THE MCGAVOCKS OF CARNTON PLANTATION

texts, after Jesus' death, Mary and their baby daughter Sarah escaped by boat to France, where Sarah later grew up and married into the French royal family.

Several hundred years later, in the 5th Century, a male descendant of Sarah allegedly had a secret child with Merovée's mother, Queen Basina of France (b. 398),[1580] an event noted in ancient royal family trees and Gnostic Christian charts by, not a human, but a fish, to this very day, the sacred emblem of Jesus Christ. The famed Italian mystic, artist, and inventor, Leonardo da Vinci (1452-1519), himself a Gnostic Christian (and perhaps connected to the Knights Templar), is said to have recorded various aspects of the sacred mysteries of the Divine Feminine in his paintings, such as *The Last Supper* and the *Mona Lisa*.[1581]

Thus it was, according to this ancient mystical tradition, that the Holy Blood of Jesus was passed on to all of Merovée's descendants, which includes many of the McGavocks and the Winders. Hattie herself happens to be in this line, as both her father, Colonel John McGavock,

---

1580. Queen Basina's husband is King Clodion "Le Chevelu," the Long-Haired King of France, born about 395 in Westphalia, Germany. The couple are my 48th great-grandparents.
1581. IXOYE, the Greek letters within the "Jesus Fish" above, spell *ichthys*, the Greek word for fish (the modern branch of science devoted to the study of fish is called ichthyology). Early Christians used the stylized fish emblem as a secret symbol of the Christian Church. Why? Partly for protection from the Roman government, deeply suspicious of the newly established, ever growing religion. But there were other reasons. 1) Jesus was a "Fisher of men," born in what was then the sign of Pisces (the fish). 2) The Greek word *ixoye* (in English *ichthys*), meaning "fish," is also an acronym for the words "Jesus Christ God's Son Savior." 3) The fish was one of the sacred animals of the early Gnostic Christian Virgin-Mother-Goddess, who wore a crown of twelve astrological stars and rode through the heavens on the crescent Moon. Also a Moon- and Triple-Goddess variously known across the ancient world as Ma, Ma Ma, Mar, Maria, Mariah, Mariam, Marie, Marina, and Myrrh, her name derives from the Latin word *mare*, meaning "sea," itself a symbol of the Divine Feminine. To help attain political supremacy, mainstream Christianity adopted this Pagan deity, absorbing her into the figure of the Virgin Mary, which is why, despite her Christianization, Mary retains many of the Goddess Marie's Pagan elements. Among them is Marie's primitive Gnostic title, *Stella Maris* ("Star of the Sea"), by which Mary is still known. The New Testament also retains in Mary vestiges of the Pagan deity's role as a Triple-Goddess (see e.g., the "Three Marys," John 19:25; see also Haskins, p. 33), along with her pre-Catholic image as a Moon-Goddess (see e.g., Revelation 12:1). All of this would have been very familiar to the mystical Knights Templar, who venerated the Virgin Mary in her Latin Gnostic form as Maria the Virgin-Moon-Triple-Goddess—who later emerged as "Maid Marian" in the Robin Hood legends. Why this mysterious, powerful, and ancient Goddess-worshiping Christian group was present at Lt. Cowan's funeral remains a mystery. For more on Goddess-worship and Christianity, see my books *Britannia Rules*; *The Book of Kelle*; *The Goddess Dictionary of Words and Phrases*; and *Aphrodite's Trade*.

THE MCGAVOCKS OF CARNTON PLANTATION

and her mother, Caroline Elizabeth "Carrie" Winder, are direct descendants of King Merovée.

One of the chief stated functions of the Knights Templar is to honor, protect, and maintain Jesus' royal bloodline, particularly among the well-known. Is it possible that they were at Lieutenant Cowan's grave on September 19, 1919, because both the Confederate officer's wife and their children (Carrie Winder Cowan, John McGavock Cowan, Leah Cowan, Samuel Kincaid Cowan, and Winder McGavock Cowan) are of Merovingian heritage?

As a Christian, out of respect for all of Christianity's tens of thousands of denominations, sects, and cults and their widely varied belief systems, I neither condone or condemn this theory. I merely include it here for interest's sake and for posterity, and in the hope that additional information may become available to future McGavock researchers regarding this very interesting connection between the Carnton McGavocks and early Christianity.

❧ DEATH OF HATTIE McGAVOCK COWAN

Some thirteen years after her husband's death, Hattie herself passed away. Strangely, her death occurred on November 30, 1932, the sixty-eighth anniversary of the Battle of Franklin II, which she herself had experienced firsthand at Carnton as a nine year old girl. Hattie was seventy-seven years old at the time of her passage into the better world.

The following are two of Hattie's obituaries. The first is from a local newspaper (name and author unknown), dated July 20, 1932:

> MRS. COWAN, 77, DIES AT FRANKLIN
> Member of One of State's Most Prominent Families Succumbs.
> FRANKLIN, Tenn., July 20—(Spl)—Mrs. Hattie McGavock Cowan, 77, a member of one of Tennessee's most famous families, died at her home on Bridge Street here last night at 9:45 o'clock.
>   Mrs. Cowan, widow of Capt. George L. Cowan, was reared in the famous McGavock 'Carnton' home near Franklin. She was a daughter of Col. John R. [W.] McGavock and Mrs. Caroline Winder McGavock and was a great-granddaughter of Judge Felix Grundy.
>   She lived her entire life in Williamson County, taking an

The McGavocks of Carnton Plantation

active part in community activities from the time her home, 'Carnton,' was used as a hospital after the Battle of [2nd] Franklin, when she was a child of 9, until she became ill several months ago.

Mrs. Cowan was a lifelong member of the Franklin Presbyterian Church. She was chairman of the local chapter for the Monroe Harding Children's Home in Nashville, a charter member of Old Glory Chapter of the Daughters of the American Revolution and of the Franklin Chapter of the United Daughters of the Confederacy, No. 14, of which she was past president.

She was a member of Women's Auxiliary to the John E. Stephen[s] Post, American Legion, and was a member of the Franklin Garden Club.

She is survived by two daughters, Miss Carrie Cowan [1884-1961] and Miss Leah Cowan [1888-1950], and three sons, John [1886-1954] and Sam [Kincaid] Cowan [1890-1963] of Franklin and Winder McGavock Cowan [b. 1892] of Daytona Beach, Fla.

Funeral services will he beld at the residence on Bridge Street Thursday morning at 10:30 o'clock. Rev. W. Humphrey Armistead, pastor of the Franklin Presbyterian Church, will officiate. Burial will be in Mt. Hope Cemetery.

(A local Franklin newspaper, name and date unknown)
BELOVED WOMAN CALLED HOME
Mrs. Hattie McGavock Cowan Succumbs To Long Illness Thursday Night.

Mrs. Hattie McGavock Cowan, aged 77 years, died at 9:45 p.m. Tuesday at her home on Bridge street, following an illness of several months. Funeral services were from the residence at 10:30 Thursday morning, conducted by Rev. W. Humphrey Armistead, pastor of the Presbyterian church. Interment in Mt. Hope cemetery.

In the death of Mrs. Cowan, Franklin and Williamson county have lost one of their most widely known and greatly beloved women. Although she had been in failing health since last November, her passing came as a shock to her host of friends.

She was born July 2, 1855, at 'Carnton,' the famous McGavock home and one of the most historic spots in Middle Tennessee. In this home, which had been in the McGavock family for five generations and which was used as a hospital the day after the great Battle of Franklin [II], Hattie McGavock Cowan spent her girlhood. She was the daughter of Col. John and Mrs. Caroline

THE MCGAVOCKS OF CARNTON PLANTATION

Winder McGavock, and a great-granddaughter of Judge Felix Grundy. She was a member of a pioneer Williamson county family and was prominently connected over the State. McGavock Cemetery, given by her father, the only private Confederate cemetery in Tennessee, was lovingly cared for by the family and remained a part of 'Carnton' until the estate was sold about 20 years ago, at which time a deed to the cemetery was made to the State of Tennessee.

Born of parents whose lives were so closely identified with the history and welfare of Williamson county, and who donated so much of their time and means to the Confederacy, Mrs. Cowan was reared in an atmosphere of loyalty to 'The Lost Cause,' and her deep devotion to patriotic work was one of the main factors in her long and useful life. She was a charter member of Franklin chapter No. 14 [the United Daughters of the Confederacy] and several times served as its president. She was also a charter member of Old Glory Chapter, D. A. R. [Daughters of the American Revolution], organized in 1877. She was deeply interested in the woman's auxiliary of the John E. Stephens Post of the American Legion [. . . several missing sentences here].

She was always active [. . .] auxiliary and in the Sunday School, where for years she taught; a great deal of her work being among the children, and many prominent Franklin citizens of today learned the catechism under the ennobling influence of her tutelage, and at the time of her death she was chairman from the local church for the Monroe-Harding Children's Home.

Though a leader in public endeavors, Mrs. Cowan was greater still as a home-maker. She was a devoted wife and mother and especially gifted in culinary arts, upon which she had become an authority. Hospitality was a foreword in her home and its doors were ajar all the time to neighbors and friends. Having spent a life replete with good work, always busy, it was fitting that she should fall asleep just at the bedtime hour, as one who had finished a day well spent; in the midst of her family circle, to whom the sympathy of the community goes out.

Mrs. Cowan was the widow of Capt. George L. Cowan, a gallant Confederate soldier. She is survived by two daughters, and three sons: Misses Carrie and Leah Cowan, John and Sam K. Cowan, all of Franklin; and Winder McGavock Cowan of Daytona

The McGavocks of Carnton Plantation

Beach, Florida.[1582]

The last of the original Carnton adults, Susie (Ewing) McGavock, died at age sixty-eight on October 25, 1931. Hattie, Lieutenant Cowan, Winder, and Susie are all buried at Mount Hope Cemetery in downtown Franklin: Hattie and her husband in the Cowan family plot, Winder and his wife in the McGavock family plot.

1582. I transcribed both of these obituaries, which were provided courtesy of the Williamson County Public Library.

14

Life at Carnton After the McGavocks

❧ CARNTON MANSION AS A BARN

CARNTON WAS OWNED BY FIVE private individuals after it was sold by Susie in 1911. Almost immediately it began to go to rack and ruin. At one point it was completely abandoned and its owner turned the Mansion into a barn where livestock food was stored, and where farm animals themselves were sometimes housed.

During this period the upper floor was used as a hay loft, while pigs and chickens had free run of the downstairs. One local Franklin resident recalled children riding their horses through the central passageway: in through the back door and out through the front door!

By the early 1970s there were several holes in the roof, "big enough for a cat to walk through," and the rain that poured through them was beginning to cause serious damage to the house's structure.

❧ BIRTH OF THE CARNTON ASSOCIATION

In 1976, just as Carnton was nearing complete dilapidation, a group of Franklinites, concerned over the fate of the plantation, formed a non-profit organization known as the Carnton Association, to help raise money for its purchase.

Two years later, the owners at that time, Dr. and Mrs. W. D. Sugg of Bradenton, Florida, generously donated the entire ten acre estate to the private foundation, with the deed being signed on September 22, 1978. Though they had never lived at Carnton, they had owned it since

The McGavocks of Carnton Plantation

the 1950s.

Since then the Association has acquired an extra thirty-eight acres from the state as a barrier to further incursion from the modern world. Nearby, numerous subdivisions, shopping centers, churches, and strip malls have sprung up over the past few years. Urban sprawl is pushing in on all sides.

The Carnton Association's goal was, and continues to be, to restore and preserve the McGavocks' once lovely antebellum home for future generations.

❧ CARNTON'S GHOSTLY INHABITANTS

No history of the Carnton McGavocks would be complete without mention of the plantation's spectral residents.

The death and carnage that occurred in and around Carnton left an indelible mark in the atmosphere, and even in her very walls. Indeed, Carnton is possessed of so much paranormal activity that it is known today as "Tennessee's most haunted Civil War House."

You may or may not personally believe in ghosts, but hundreds of individuals have witnessed a variety of supernatural phenomena here, including everything from General Cleburne's ghost walking along the back porch to a lady in a white Victorian dress standing on the upper balcony. Phantom smells, sounds, mists, unaccountable cold spots, strange astral beings, odd lights, and other peculiar "bumps in the night" have also been experienced.

In the dining room, for example, the sound of clattering pots and pans have been heard, along with the sound of breaking dishes. Objects have been known to move throughout the house for no apparent reason, and a woman's severed head has been seen floating up and down the staircase (possibly the victim of a murderous rampage between two black servants said to have taken place at Carnton many years ago).

A floating needle was once observed in the ladies' parlor, female guests sometimes have their hair stroked by an unseen hand, and footsteps have been heard in almost every part of the Mansion when no one else was in or near the building. Naturally, the sounds of battle—horses, guns, screaming, yelling, crying, cannon, and marching

THE MCGAVOCKS OF CARNTON PLANTATION

troops—have all been heard outside at Carnton, the most common sight being the wraithlike appearance of long dead Confederate soldiers standing, walking, and sitting. When alive these same men would have been quite amused at these tales, since the telling of stories of the supernatural around an evening campfire was one of their favorite pastimes.

One of the more common sightings, backed up by the testimonies of numerous eyewitnesses, is that of a Confederate cavalry official. Clad in a long gray officer's coat, he paces up and down the lower back porch, his spurs jangling as his heavy boot heels hit the floorboards. He has also been spotted sitting on this same veranda, staring eerily out from beneath a general's hat. Most feel that this is the ghost of General Cleburne, whose body was brought to this very spot for public viewing on the morning of December 1, 1864. As he died young, violently, and before his time, he is the most likely type of soul (a grounded spirit) to remain attached to the material plane, haunting the area where he perished.

I myself had several paranormal experiences while working at Carnton, and have photographed unexplainable bright orbs of light outside under the front windows that were not visible to the naked eye. On my tours so many people asked me about Carnton's ghostly side that I wrote a book on the topic called, *Carnton Plantation Ghost Stories: True Tales of the Unexplained from Tennessee's Most Haunted Civil War House!* It has become a bestseller.

PART TWO

A Tour of Carnton Plantation

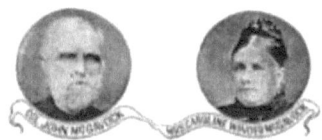

Carnton: Front & Back Exterior

ꙮ THE FIRST STRUCTURE: A CRYPTIC DWELLING

WE HAVE TAKEN A TOUR of the history of the Carnton McGavocks and we have seen Lincoln's War and the world of black servitude through their eyes. Now it is time to take a tour of the plantation itself, beginning with the pre-Carnton land, buildings, and residents.

In the early 1800s there was virtually nothing of European origin in the Franklin area except a few scattered farms and small country houses. One of these was the first structure known to have stood on the Carnton property, near what was to become the northwest corner of the plantation's modern garden.

Who built it and when was it built? The answers to these questions are unknown. As the first European home in Franklin is said to have been constructed in 1797 by Ewen Cameron, an educated guess would be that Carnton's first house was a rather primitive dwelling, constructed by an early pioneer family between 1798 and 1800.

We do know that they must have been an intrepid group to have ventured so far West at that time. For they would have been among the only European-Americans in a region that was still nearly completely dominated by Native-Americans. And, as we have seen, some were extremely hostile toward early white settlers like the McGavocks.

Carnton's first structure has long since vanished. Hopefully in the near future additional archaeology will be done where it once stood,

The McGavocks of Carnton Plantation

so that we can learn more about this building's mysterious origins, function, appearance, and inhabitants.

❧ THE SECOND STRUCTURE: THE TWO-STORY BRICK HOUSE

The second known structure on the Carnton property was a small two-story, four-room brick house, probably constructed between 1800 and 1815—most likely in 1811.[1583] This was still standing firm when Randal McGavock bought the land that it was sitting on. In fact it was in such excellent condition that he would later build his Mansion around it.

Some believe that this second structure, the two-story brick house, may have been made by, or was owned by, the family of the woman who would soon become Randal's wife, Sarah Dougherty Rodgers. This seems likely since members of her clan, the Rodgers, lived in the house well into the 1830s. There is no definitive evidence for this theory, however.

This 1,800 square-foot structure, which had a family dining room, kitchen, and workroom on the first floor, and three bedrooms on the second, no longer exists. But the imprint of where it once stood can still be seen in the ground, as it ran from the Mansion all the way to the smokehouse. An idea of its shape and size can be gleaned from the "ghost" contour of its roof line, which remains visible on the east outer wall of the Mansion.

On this same wall there are two doors which, strangely, seem to open out into midair. Facing the wall, the door on the left leads into the men's parlor (or office), while the door on the right leads into the dining room. More on these shortly.

What happened to the original 1811 house?

In 1909 it was so heavily damaged by a tornado that it had to be torn down. In 2002 archaeologists started digging in the foundation and began uncovering artifacts such as kitchen utensils, children's marbles, and arrowheads. When the archaeology is complete Carnton Association

---

[1583]. From this point on we will refer to this structure as the 1811 house.

THE McGAVOCKS OF CARNTON PLANTATION

plans to restore the original house, then turn it into a small museum with artifacts on display.

❧ THE THIRD STRUCTURE: CARNTON MANSION
According to Carnton historian James Redford, it is not known exactly when Randal built Carnton Mansion, also referred to as the "big house," but it was probably before 1820, perhaps as early as 1815—though an even earlier date cannot be ruled out. If the house took eight to ten years to build, as one might expect, however, construction probably began sometime between 1816 and 1818, for it was completed in 1826.

Despite its early 18th-Century, pre-Victorian birth, Carnton is today being restored as a mid-19th-Century Victorian home, the time period in which Colonel John owned the property and in which the War for Southern Independence was fought not far from Carnton's door.

❧ AN AMERICAN TREASURE
Its importance as an American treasure has earned Carnton Plantation a designation as a National Historic Landmark (NHL), one of less than 2,500 places listed as such in the U.S. According to the National Park Service, which hosts the NHL Program:

> National Historic Landmarks are nationally significant historic places designated by the Secretary of the Interior because they possess exceptional value or quality in illustrating or interpreting the heritage of the United States.[1584]

Like so many antebellum homes and buildings in Williamson County, and even like old downtown Franklin itself, Carnton is also listed on the National Register of Historic Places, an organization that describes itself as the "Nation's official list of cultural resources worthy of preservation."[1585]

1584. For more information on the National Historic Landmark Program, visit their Website: www.cr.nps.gov/nhl.
1585. For more information on the National Register of Historic Places, visit their Website: www.cr.nps.gov/nr.

The McGavocks of Carnton Plantation

❧ THE 1811 HOUSE BECOMES A KITCHEN

Randal was an extraordinarily wealthy man and wanted a house that reflected his station in life. He had his Federal-style, 10,000 square-foot, three-story Mansion put on an elevated foundation that was built up against the original two-story 1811 brick house, which then became the east wing of the "big house."

After construction of Carnton was completed in 1826 and the Rodgers family finally moved out of the 1811 house, sometime in the mid-1830s this smaller structure was converted into the McGavocks' kitchen. Why?

Early Victorians cooked their meals over an open fire, which created numerous hazards. The main dangers were from smoke, flames, sparks, soot, and heat, although the dirt, insects, and mice that came in with tinder and logs also created problems. Thus kitchens were kept separate from the main house.

❧ MEANING & ORIGINS OF THE NAME CARNTON

Randal named his home Carnton after their 18th-Century family estate in Glenarm, Ireland, called Cairntown, Carntown, or Cairnton House. In American English Cairntown became Cairnton, the spelling used until the early 1900s. Today the modernized spelling is Carnton.

A cairn is a pile of stones created to memorialize an important event or person. One well-known American cairn, for example, is located at Walden Pond, Concord, Massachusetts, and is dedicated to individualist, author, and naturalist Henry David Thoreau (1817-1862). Thoreau's cairn is quite large, having been built up over a period of many years by visitors to the site.[1586]

[1586.] I have visited beautiful Walden Pond on numerous occasions and tossed stones onto Thoreau's enormous cairn there. It is not commonly known due to suppression by Northern historians, but Walden was once the site not only of Thoreau's famous cabin, but of filthy rundown squatters camps where Concord's "freed" black slaves were forced to live after "emancipation." See Lemire, passim. It is also interesting to note that Yankee Thoreau was a libertarian, as were most Southerners at the time. Unfortunately, he, like so many other early New Englanders, such as Ralph Waldo Emerson, was blinded by Northern anti-South propaganda—much of it fabricated by Lincoln (see my book *Lincolnology*). Thus, Thoreau became a rampant anti-South advocate who idolized other South-loathers, like Yankee madman and serial killer John Brown.

The McGavocks of Carnton Plantation

The suffix "ton" in Carnton is from the Old English word *tun*, meaning a farmstead or village. From it we get our modern word "town." Thus *cairntun* literally means "the farm near a stone memorial."

❧ THE CARNTON FACADE
Carnton's front face—oriented toward the south to take advantage of the light and heat of the Sun, particularly in Winter—is an elegant example of early 18th-Century Federal design, with its symmetrical Georgian dimensions and eight beautifully proportioned windows. Over the front door is a semicircular fanlight window while on the left and right of the door can be seen the sidelight windows, both features common to Federal architecture.

❧ THE FRONT GREEK REVIVAL PORTICO
The front porch, added in 1847, is primarily a miniature version of the back one, which will be discussed in detail. A couple of notes here will suffice.

Situated on the southern side of the house, the limestone floor of the lower front portico is in contrast to the floor of the back porch, which was made of wood. The stone, which cost $400, the equivalent of $10,000 today, adds an aura of Grecian stateliness to the facade.

The upper front porch is entered through the jib window in the sitting room at the top of the second-floor stairs. It once offered a stunning panoramic view of the McGavocks' property, which would have included farmland, horse paddocks, rolling green hills, crop fields, and verdant meadows.

This south-facing porch, however, is quite small and it is doubtful it got very much use, especially in the Summertime when the Tennessee sun beats down with unremitting vigor.

❧ FLEMISH BOND BRICKWORK
Looking closely at the brickwork on the front of the Mansion from a mason's eye reveals something of interest: the original bricks were laid in a style known as Flemish Bond. To understand the importance of this it is helpful to know a little bit about brickwork masonry.

The McGavocks of Carnton Plantation

The long end, or side, of a brick is called the "stretcher," the short end the "header." Bricks are laid in rows called "courses," and the way they are laid is called a "bond."

In Flemish Bond a stretcher is alternated with a header all the way across one course of bricks. On the next course the header is laid in the middle of the stretcher of the brick in the course below it. Since the bricks all have to be perfectly aligned from course to course, Flemish is the most difficult to lay. However, this also makes it the most aesthetically pleasing to the eye.

The most popular types of brickwork are Stretcher Bond, Common or American Bond, English Bond, Running Bond, Herringbone Bond, Stack Bond, and Flemish Bond. Stretcher, the style used on most homes and buildings, is the commonest of the three because of the ease of laying it and its lower cost.

The fact that Randal had Flemish Bond, the most expensive, difficult, and beautiful type of brickwork, built into Carnton Mansion's outer front wall tells us a lot about who he was and what kind of image he wanted to project to the world.

ॐ CARNTON'S WALLS

While we are on the topic of Carnton's walls we should note that her bricks were made by the McGavocks' African-American servants on site, and that Randal had the walls built three-bricks thick.

This latter piece of construction was quite unusual for that day due to the expense and time-intensive labor that was involved. Indeed, this would be unusual, if not unheard of, even today when the walls of modern homes are typically a single brick thick.

It is probable that Randal did this both because of the severe wind conditions common to Middle Tennessee, and because thicker walls mean better insulation: the house stayed cooler during the hot Summer months and warmer during the frigid Winter months.[1587]

Whatever his precise motivations were, we can be glad he did

1587. Tennessee Winters were harsher in the past than they are today.

THE MCGAVOCKS OF CARNTON PLANTATION

because it is likely that Carnton would not be standing today otherwise. We will recall that in 1909 a tornado took out the original 1811 house that stood on the east side of the property. This structure, built by a far less affluent family, would have had walls only one brick deep and so would not have had the durability of Randal's house.

❧ CARNTON'S WINDOWS: SOME NUMERICAL TRIVIA

Randal's Mansion has twenty-one windows (whose casings, sashes, jambs, stools, muntins, and sills are all made from ash tree wood): nine on the facade of the house, eight on the back, two on each end, and two dormers on the front roof. Eight of the windows are on the first floor, nine are on the second floor, and four are on the third floor.

On the facade each of the four first floor windows has twenty-eight panes of glass set in a twelve over fourteen sash; that is, there are twelve panes in the upper sash, sixteen in the lower sash (total: 112 panes). The five second story windows on the front each contain twenty-four panes set in a twelve over twelve sash (total: 120 panes). This gives the entire facade a total of 232 panes in nine windows.

On the back of the Mansion, each of the four first floor windows have twenty-eight panes of glass set in a twelve over fourteen sash (total: 112 panes). The four second story windows on the rear of the house each contain twenty-four panes set in a twelve over twelve sash (total: ninety-six panes). The entire back of the house has 208 panes of glass in eight windows.

The four attic windows on each end of the house's third floor, have fifteen window panes each and are set in a six over nine sash (total: sixty panes). The front dormers (there are none on the back of the house) each contain twelves panes and are set in a six over six sash (total: twenty-four panes). This gives the third floor a total of eighty-four panes of glass in six windows.

Excluding the basement windows, the front fanlight window, and the sidelight windows around the front door, Carnton's twenty-one windows have a total of 524 panes of glass.

Incredibly, after nearly 200 years and a major war on her doorstep, some of Carnton's original panes of glass remain intact and serviceable. These particular panes can be distinguished by observing the bubbles, waves, and ripples in the glass, a result of the uneven 18th-Century hand-making process. The other non-original panes have been replaced at various times over the past two centuries, with some being quite modern.

The pintle hinges around the windows, on which the restored shutters now hang, are original to the building.

❧ CARNTON'S TREES

On the original plantation there were a number of enormous, stately, and beautiful trees situated around the house. While some of these were blown down during the 1909 tornado event, sadly, many were later intentionally cut down, some quite recently. It has been suggested that this was done to "update" Carnton, to make it look more "modern." Others say that someone on Carnton's Board of Directors simply did not like the trees and wanted them removed.

Not surprisingly, unnecessarily cutting down most of the large trees near the Mansion has created tremendous controversy. Not only did this strip Carnton of much of its original appearance, appeal, and ambiance, but it ruined a natural habitat that took decades, perhaps even over a century, for Nature to create.

Humans once enjoyed the beauty and shade the trees provided as well, and animals used the branches, leaves, and bark for protection, nesting, and feeding. Many people are still talking about this environmental debacle to this day. Even Carnton's ghosts, who react negatively to any physical changes on the property, are said to be up in arms over the removal of the McGavocks' trees.

❧ McGAVOCK'S GROVE

Had the trees been left standing we would still be able to see what was called McGavock's Grove, a large wooded area near the house that included cedar and boxwood rows on each side of the front walkway.

Unlike his father and many of his other relations, Colonel John never had an interest in entering politics and never held any political office. Nonetheless, he was a staunchly political, Jeffersonian

THE MCGAVOCKS OF CARNTON PLANTATION

Confederate (similar to today's Tea Partyists), and was a delegate to the 1860 Democratic National Convention (the conservatives of the day). Thus before and during the War he enjoyed holding political rallies in McGavock's Grove.

    Standing in Carnton's spacious front yard one can easily imagine the happy comradery of the McGavock family and their guests, and the rousing patriotic speeches about states' rights and Southern unity and independence as they stood beneath the tall shade trees. Prominent voices that were heard in McGavock's Grove include Andrew Jackson, Felix Grundy, Sam Houston, and James Knox Polk, among many others.[1588]

❧ HOW CARNTON'S FACADE ONCE LOOKED

Carnton Mansion no longer appears as it did when it was built in the early 1800s, for many changes have taken place since then. However, we can see what the front of the big house originally looked like by imagining it without dormers on the roof, bars on the basement windows, or the upper and lower Greek Revival porches—the latter which we will be discussing in further detail. We would also need to visualize the roof with walnut shake shingles instead of tin sheeting. All of these items were added much later.

    Stripping all of this away in our mind's eye, we will see a simple yet exquisite early 19th-Century home, a symmetrical brick rectangle, with double end chimneys, whose beautiful lines form an elegant monument to a once important and wealthy Williamson County family.

❧ THE FRONT WALKWAY

The front brick sidewalk, laid in a Herringbone Bond design, is called a "turtleback walkway" because it was made with a concave surface to drain off rainwater. It is the oldest sidewalk in Tennessee and is now protected by conservation laws. According to McGavock legend the family hid their silverware under the front walk during the War to hide

---

1588. V. M. Bowman, p. 62.

The McGavocks of Carnton Plantation

it from Lincoln's blue-coated invaders. As we have seen this was a wise decision.

We have noted that originally there were rows of both boxwood and tall stately cedar pines running along each side of the walkway leading from the driveway up to the front of the Mansion. Modern cedars have been replanted in their place, although these are not nearly as large as the cedars that would have been here during the McGavock era. A Franklin newspaper photo of the front walkway from 1905 shows a number of towering and imposing cedars on either side.

❧ THE FRONT DRIVEWAY

Originally Carnton's dirt front driveway seems to have been part of an actual town road that ran past the front of the house. Or perhaps the driveway connected the plantation to this road. Either way, the name of the road is unknown, for it was abandoned long ago. The driveway is all that remains to mark this mysterious street.[1589]

Also in the past, the driveway encircled the entire Mansion, from front to back, winding around the east side to the backyard, and then around the west side to the front yard. A remnant of this original configuration remains today, but only at the front of the house. While currently the drive is made of dirt, the original was probably "paved" with gravel, as was the custom among the well-to-do.

Stepping from their carriages at the front of the house, visitors would pass through the gate and walk up the turtleback walkway to the front door. Servants would then lead the guests' horses, buggies, or carriages around the back to the barn area, or perhaps to the five-bay carriage house, located on the east side of the Mansion, where they would be tied up, watered, and fed as needed.

❧ THE CARRIAGE HOUSE

Speaking of the carriage house, little is known of this building.

In my private collection, however, I have a drawing of Carnton

---

1589. V. M. Bowman, p. 62.

The McGavocks of Carnton Plantation

by a man named Clyde Sears. It shows the carriage house attached to the east wall of the house near where the office (or library) door is located. Perhaps this door once led directly into the carriage house, just as modern homes have doors that lead directly from the house into the garage. The origins and demise of this structure are not known.

Unfortunately Mr. Sears' artwork is of an indeterminate date.

❧ THE MYSTERIOUS ELL

Other Carnton architectural enigmas abound. According to Williamson County historian Virginia McDaniel Bowman, an early photo shows a "long brick ell of many rooms" on the east side of the house (an ell is an extension of right angles to the length of a building).

What the function of this brick structure was, and who built it and when, are also mysteries. It was torn down many years ago, with seemingly no chronicle of its existence.[1590]

❧ THE GREENHOUSE

Reference is also made in old Carnton records of a greenhouse on the property. On the same Sears drawing mentioned above, the greenhouse is shown located on the southeastern quadrant of the property, out near the front road. As far as I know, no specific archaeology has been done in either this area or on the sites of the ell and the carriage house.

The McGavocks would have used their greenhouse just the way we do today: as an enclosure to cultivate and protect young plants year-round. We can be sure they grew various ornamental flowers in their greenhouse, and quite probably herbs and even experimental plants, grasses, vegetables, and grains. Carnton was, after all, a plantation with hundreds of acres devoted to food crops. There can be little doubt then that the McGavocks, along with the farm's black managers and overseers, were enthusiastic and scientifically-minded agriculturalists.

1590. V. M. Bowman, p. 62.

The McGavocks of Carnton Plantation

❧ THE BACK OF CARNTON
What many people think of as the "front" of Carnton Mansion is actually the rear of the house. The two are often mistaken because of the sweeping grand Greek Revival porch at the back, which has come to symbolize Carnton Plantation.[1591] But if you walk all the way around the house, you will see a distinct front and back.

Originally there was a large circular gravel driveway situated in the back yard, near the rear entrance. Horses and carriages were ridden up to this area and the passengers unloaded, after which servants would lead the horses away to be temporarily cared for.

During the McGavocks' residence there were also fruit orchards, great fields of cotton, hemp, tobacco, and small grains, large stands of statuesque trees, barns, a five-bay carriage house,[1592] sheds, a greenhouse, paddocks, and corrals located across the back of the property. Modernization, human interference, weather, and time have divested Carnton of nearly all of these.

As with Carnton's facade, the back looks quite different from how Randal originally envisioned it. To understand how Carnton's rear side first appeared we must, as with the front, imagine it without any porch or tin sheeting on the roof. Also the bricks on the back wall were not painted white, but would have been left their natural color.

Penny-pinching Scots-Irishman Randal saved money by laying the bricks at the back of the house using an economic English Bond design. This is in contrast to the front bricks, which, as discussed, were laid in the more ornate and expensive Flemish Bond pattern.

❧ THE BACK GREEK REVIVAL PORTICO
Between 1847 and 1850 John and Carrie added dormers to the roof and replaced the original walnut roof shakes with tin sheeting. Sometime soon thereafter, in the 1850s, they also added the stunning Greek

---

1591. Indeed, Carnton's rear Greek Revival portico is the emblem used by Carnton Association on all of its promotional material.
1592. A large carriage house can still be seen at Carnton's sister plantation in Nashville: Belle Meade. Carnton's five-bay carriage house was no doubt similar.

THE MCGAVOCKS OF CARNTON PLANTATION

Revival back porch, also known as the gallery or veranda, to Carnton Mansion.

It is impossible not to notice that the bricks on the back of the house have been painted white. As mentioned, this is not original, as in 1826 all of the masonry would have been left its natural brick color.

Why and when these bricks were painted over is not known. It must have been done between the 1840s (the beginning of Colonel John's modernization process) and 1909 (the year the 1811 house was torn down), however, because an old pre-1909 photo reveals that the bricks at the back of the Mansion were, by that time, painted white. Perhaps the postbellum McGavocks simply wanted the brickwork to match the color of their new rear Greek Revival portico.

❧ THE LOWER BACK PORCH

The lower back porch is famous for being the spot where the bodies of the four dead Confederate generals were laid on the morning of December 1, 1864, and for being the location of a mysterious spectral figure seen and heard roaming there.

As we have seen, tradition asserts that this is the ghost of General Patrick Cleburne, for it is wearing the uniform of a Confederate officer. Over the years many have witnessed his ethereal pensive form here as if in deep thought, while others have heard the sounds of his boots and spurs striding back and forth across the wooden deck boards.

Many people have asked me if the wood floor on the lower back porch is original. It is not. These boards are recently added reproductions; although the balustrade (small support posts, or balusters) which support the upper railing, is original. The two columns at the west end of the porch are reproductions.

❧ THE UPPER BACK PORCH

For the rest of her days Carrie loved to sit on the upper deck of the back porch during Tennessee's long hot summers, taking in the cooling breezes that passed over the fields surrounding Carnton. We can picture her relaxing peacefully here, perhaps reading Augusta Jane Evans' *Macaria or Altars of Sacrifice*, the most popular and widely read novel in

The McGavocks of Carnton Plantation

the Confederacy during the War.

In particular Carrie enjoyed the breezeway, the open end on the western side of the upper deck overlooking the plantation's windswept landscape, which was specially made for this purpose. Carrie had a hammock installed here, and a hole and a remaining hook, where it was attached to a porch column and the back wall, can still be seen.

The breezeway (on both the upper and lower porches) provided an additional benefit to the inhabitants of Carnton: it faces southwest where it catches maximum daylight, making it an ideal spot for such activities as reading and sewing.

❧ A SLOPING FLOOR

The floor on the back upper deck slopes downward, from back to front, quite extraordinarily. This is not because the porch is "settling with age," although some of the tilt must be attributed to this. It was built at an angle intentionally so that rain water would flow off it, preventing rot and mildew.

❧ BLUE CEILINGS, PINK FLOORS

Many have asked me about the ceiling and floor colors on the back porch. The blue ceiling and the pink floor are the original colors. The question is, why these hues in particular?

In Old Southern tradition the colors blue and pink were supposed to keep the "haints and hags" away, that is, unwanted ghosts and witches. Unless we are to believe that ghosts and witches disliked blue and pink, the reasoning behind the association between these two colors and paranormal entities remains unclear. It is probable that elements of this superstition began in Africa, and were brought to America by servile blacks aboard Yankee slave ships. These later became intertwined with European-America superstitions, finally becoming a part of Southern culture.

Whatever its true origins, there is at least one known reason for the use of these specific colors at Carnton.

The Victorians were enamored with ancient Greek culture, and Greek Revival fever was sweeping America at the time. This is, after all,

THE MCGAVOCKS OF CARNTON PLANTATION

why Colonel John added the front Greek Revival portico to the house in 1847 and why he and Carrie added the back one in 1850.

We will note here that Southerners as a whole have always been enamored with Classical culture, which is why so many Southern cities have been given Classical names. Among these we have: Memphis, Tennessee; Sparta, Tennessee; Carthage, Tennessee; Antioch, Tennessee; Troy, Tennessee; Cairo, Georgia; Athens, Georgia; Corinth, Mississippi; and Alexandria, Virginia.

Victorian Nashvillians were so obsessed with the Classical period that in 1897 they built an exact replica of Greece's famous temple, the Parthenon. The structure still stands today as an art museum, complete with a forty-foot statue of the Greek Goddess Athena—the female deity who gave her name to Athens, Greece.[1593]

But what does blue and pink have to do with the early Greeks?

The primary colors found by 19th-Century archaeologists in ancient Greek ruins were pink (associated with sea shells) and blue (associated with the ocean), both which are in turn connected to ancient Goddess-worship. For the primary female deities were believed to have come from the sea.[1594]

It is for these reasons that the ceilings on the front and back porches were painted blue, while the floors on the back portico were painted pink (the floor of the earlier front porch is natural stone).

❧ CARNTON'S OUTBUILDINGS: THE SERVANTS' HOUSE
There were originally a total of eleven servants' quarters on the property, all constructed by Carnton's black masons and carpenters. Today only one remains: a single brick house set off to the east of the Mansion. The other ten, made of wood, were log cabins lined up along

---

1593. For more on the Nashville Parthenon, see Website: www.nashville.gov/Parthenon.
1594. As we have seen, ancient goddesses such as Ma, Mar, Maria, Mariam, Marie, Marina, Myrrh, and the Virgin Mary, all take their name from the Latin word *mare*, meaning "sea." Mare probably derives from an ancient and lost Indo-European word, perhaps *ma* or *mar*, meaning "mother" or "sea" or "mother-sea." Catholics still call Mary by her original Pagan title: *Stella Maris*, "The Star of the Sea." The name of the goddess Aphrodite, who gave her name to the continent of Aphro-ka—that is, Africa—is revealing: her name literally means "(born) of the sea foam." Seabrook, AT, pp. 58-59; Seabrook, BK, pp. 38-41.

THE MCGAVOCKS OF CARNTON PLANTATION

the river, or more likely, out in the field on the south (front) side of the house. All of these have long since deteriorated due to weather.

The remaining brick house was used by the domestics or house servants, who were higher in rank than the field servants who occupied the log cabins. We will note here that this was not a cruel hierarchy forced on black servants, as anti-South writers have asserted. For African-American bondsmen and bondswomen themselves had a complex and extraordinarily harsh caste system of "lower," "middle," and "upper classes," one far more rigid and artificial than any that could have been imposed on them by European-American society.[1595]

The upper floor of the brick house served as the servants' home and would have housed one family on each side. Downstairs on the bottom floor was a workshop for weaving cloth and for doing repairs on chairs, tables, and other furnishings in need of mending.

❧ MODERN PUMP HOUSE

On the eastern edge of Carnton's property, on the hill behind the servants' quarters, toward the river, there is a small, gray stone, box-like structure, with an aging shake roof. Looking very much like a miniature house, this is a modern pump house and is in no way connected to the original Carnton landscape.

❧ THE SPRINGHOUSE

Near the pump house is the McGavocks' springhouse, probably built in the early 1820s. This structure, like the fresh spring it sat on, was an integral part of nearly all 19th-Century homes because it protected the family's drinking water from animals, and because it cooled the water and air inside.

The McGavocks' springhouse was constructed on a small stream running along the eastern side of the property, a body of water appropriately called McGavock Creek. The building contains a shelf and stairs that lead down into water. These steps provided a place to set

---

1595. Stampp, pp. 331-340.

The McGavocks of Carnton Plantation

perishable foods such as bottles of milk, butter, eggs, fruit, meats, and vegetables. Sometimes baskets were filled with food items and lowered into the water on ropes.

Now more a trickling stream than a fast flowing creek, the tiny body of water still winds through dense vegetation that is shielded from the sun, helping to keep its waters cool. As such, McGavock Creek was ideal for keeping the family's foods fresh. The springhouse then was an early form of refrigeration. Laundry was also probably done inside the springhouse, particularly on hot Summer days.

❧ THE SMOKEHOUSE

Like the 1811 house, the small brick smokehouse on the east side of Carnton was built between 1800 and 1815. As its name indicates it was used for smoking (cooking and drying) foods, and so special holes were created in the upper walls to allow the smoke to vent.

The smokehouse was used primarily in the Autumn months to salt and smoke hog meat for preservation. This was done by rolling and packing pieces of meat in large wooden troughs filled with brine salt. These strips of salted flesh were then hung over smoking fires made of hickory chips.

The dried, salted, hickory-smoked meat created from this process could be stored for long periods of time in the smokehouse, functioning much like our modern day freezer. The family could then eat or sell this meat at their leisure. Some of the original wooden salt troughs remain inside the building, with the original brine salt still in them.

Lard, used for cooking, and for making soap and candles, was also produced in the smokehouse. The process involved boiling the fat off hog carcasses using large iron kettles, examples of which have been placed in the smokehouse for Carnton's visitors to view.

Hogs were one of the many types of livestock raised on the McGavock farm. The 1850 Census for Williamson County shows that the family owned 250 that year.

The McGavocks of Carnton Plantation

❧ WORK & PLAY AT THE SMOKEHOUSE

The McGavocks used to sit under the trees near the smokehouse and hold tea parties and various types of gatherings. At these Victorian get-togethers, family and friends would sit in lawn chairs, sip lemonade and tea, chat, and play games. No doubt some guests brought fiddles, prompting young and old to jump up and dance the Virginia Reel on the soft grass.

One can still imagine the children laughing and playing croquet, the men in their black broadcloth talking politics and smoking cigars, and the women in their bonnets, crinoline hooped skirts, ribbons, lace, and flowers, chatting in the shade of the giant trees beneath dainty parasols, whisking bugs away with their peacock feather fly brushes.

Tables were brought out by the servants and classic summery Southern foods, like lettuce salad, melons, ices, collard greens, cornbread, whiskey punches, glazed ham, claret cups, and terrapin stew, were served. The hot weather favorite was a tray of mint juleps, served in ice-frosted glass goblets.

This little "courtyard," situated directly in front of the smokehouse, served other uses as well. Work oriented activities, such as corn shucking and chicken plucking, were performed by the McGavock servants here.

❧ THE PRIVY

There were few homes with indoor bathrooms in the 19th Century. Even the wealthy had at least one outhouse or privy on their property, and the McGavock family was no exception.

Carnton's outhouse was located in the backyard, about where the flower bed now stands. Archaeology has been done here and, as early families also often used their privy as a garbage can or waste dump, many interesting artifacts have been found.

This was a long way to walk on cold Winter night, which is why McGavock family members relied mainly on chamber pots, especially in the Winter. Chamber pots of all sizes and designs were kept next to the bed, an example of which can be seen in the girls' bedroom upstairs.

THE MCGAVOCKS OF CARNTON PLANTATION

❧ THE McGAVOCK GARDEN

One of more outstanding features of Carnton was its enormous ornamental garden. This is just as true today as it was in the 1800s.

It is not known exactly where the original McGavock garden was laid out. An early drawing of the estate shows it located on the southeast corner of the house (to the right of the front porch), the opposite of where it is now positioned. In fact its current location is just a guess by modern restorers.

There may have been two gardens, a vegetable garden (for food) and a formal garden (for pure aesthetics). The latter, situated in the front yard, was laid out in a stylized pattern of boxwood and holly trees. These were combined with ornamental flowers, such as roses. A vestige of the original ornamental garden can still be seen: three holly trees in the front yard.

The original designs of Carnton's gardens are not known either. The present one is a reproduction of an 1847-style garden that was used in the area by upperclass Tennesseans, such as close McGavock friend President Andrew Jackson. The ornamental flower garden in the front yard was plotted out by Randal McGavock's wife, Sarah (Dougherty Rodgers) McGavock, and her good friend Rachel Donelson (1767-1828), Andrew Jackson's wife, just before Rachel's death in 1828.[1596]

We do know what the McGavocks grew in their vegetable garden, because they left us detailed lists. Among the foodstuffs grown were standards like lettuce, tomatoes, corn, squash, onions, string beans, and melons.

In the mid-1800s the garden was not just a family hobby. It was an essential aspect of nearly every Southern home, rich or poor. You could not go to a grocery store and buy a wide variety of freshly picked vegetables as you can today. The Victorian garden supplied a family with most of its nutrients and food, and so was indispensable to survival.

The McGavocks were also connoisseurs of herbs, which they grew for their medicinal properties and for use as condiments and tea.

[1596]. V. M. Bowman, pp. 61-62.

THE MCGAVOCKS OF CARNTON PLANTATION

Another popular group of items grown in the garden were ornamental flowers, probably used as Spring and Summer table decorations in the house. Some of these were also undoubtedly grown in Carnton's greenhouse.

Naturally, the McGavocks would have supplemented their garden diet with both the meat from their hogs, cows, sheep, and chickens, and also with local wild foods, such as strawberries, mushrooms, hickory nuts, and huckleberries. Fish, turtles, and watercress came from the nearby creeks and rivers, such as McGavock Creek, and the Harpeth and West Harpeth Rivers, and wild game from the surrounding forests and meadows, such as turkey, opossum, squirrel, duck, boar, and deer, helped round out their diet.

Not all food was fresh. Canned foods played an important role on early farms and plantations, and the McGavocks and their servants stored much of what was grown in their gardens in airtight canning jars for use throughout the cold Winter months. One of the four cool dark rooms in the rough unfinished basement may have been used as a root cellar and storage area for this purpose.

During my time as a docent at Carnton I was often asked: "What becomes of the vegetables that are grown in the McGavock garden today?" The answer is that some are eaten by the employees, and also occasionally by members of the Carnton Association. Franklin's wild animals get the rest.

❧ THE GARDEN FENCE

The large high board white fence now surrounding the garden deserves mention. This is a modern addition, a guess based on the tall garden fences that were in common usage in Tennessee in the early 1800s. Not only would such a fence have protected the plants from inclement weather and animals, but it would have also served to provide some privacy for the McGavock family.

The planking fence has proven to be a controversial addition to the grounds, with some maintaining that it is a necessary aspect of authentic restoration, and others arguing that it is an unattractive barrier that blocks one's view of the house.

THE MCGAVOCKS OF CARNTON PLANTATION

❧ THE VERSATILE OSAGE ORANGE TREE

There are several notable objects in today's garden at Carnton. One is the large osage orange (*Maclura pomifera*) on the southeast side, near the Mansion. This gnarled and twisted tree—named for a Native-American people, the Osage Nation, that originated in what is now Kentucky—is known to have been standing during the Battle of Franklin II, which makes it well over 150 years of age. In fact it is so old that it is now protected by law as an historic tree.

The osage orange, also known as the hedge tree, is a member of the mulberry family, and was extremely popular among farmers before the invention of barbed wire. For being tough, limber, strong, and amazingly resistant to decay, rot, termites, disease, and ice, it proved to be ideal as a windbreak and shelterbelt, and more especially as a living fence (called a hedge fence) for enclosing livestock. Even after the advent of barbed wire the osage orange continued to be used by Western farmers, this time as fence posts for attaching the wire.

Native-Americans also found its wood perfect for making war clubs and bows, hence another one of its nicknames, the bodark tree, from the French words *bois d'arc*, meaning "bow wood." Osage orange wood is still used by archers to this day.

Still another nickname, the hedge apple tree, derives from its large yellowish fruits, known as hedge apples, which give off an orange-like aroma, hence its most common name, osage orange.

During Lincoln's War soldiers found a more nefarious use for the osage orange trees they discovered growing around Franklin. Using techniques dating back to ancient times, they felled the trees and carved their branches into sharp dagger-like points. These obstacles, known as abatis, from the Old French word *abateis* (meaning "a pile of things thrown down"), were laid in front of the approaching enemy with the sharp ends pointing forward. The idea was to slow him down long enough to make him an easy target; or to give one time to flee.

Many a Rebel soldier was cut to pieces by Yankee abatis at Franklin II, while many more, pausing to figure out a way around it, were shot and died on the awful spear-like branches.

The McGavocks of Carnton Plantation

❧ THE PECAN TREE & A YANKEE BOMB
The McGavocks' garden had one other tree of note, though it is no longer visible.

A pecan tree near the center of the garden once had a twin, which fell down during a storm many years ago. When the workers came to dig the tree up and remove it, they discovered an unexploded Yankee bomb in its roots, a cold and cruel vestige of Franklin's darkest day, when foreign intruders from the North illegally invaded the town on Wednesday, November 30, 1864. The artillery device, a 3-inch Hotchkiss shell, was diffused and is now on display in Carnton's gift shop.

❧ THE BASEMENT
Although Carnton's four-room basement is located under the Mansion, it is only accessible through a sunken outside door (on the east wall near the back porch), so we will include it here in our chapter on Carnton's exterior.[1597]

Guests to the plantation are understandably curious about the basement, but there is not much to see. It is small, cramped, musty, dirty, dark, and full of cobwebs, with crumbling walls and a partial dirt floor. Some have called it "creepy." It is not a place that most people would want to spent the night in, or even briefly visit during the day.

Carnton currently uses it for storage. But, as mentioned, it may have begun life as a root cellar, an integral aspect of early American homes in the days before refrigeration.

❧ THE McGAVOCK FAMILY CEMETERY
Off to the northwest of the property, a few hundred yards from the Mansion, is the McGavock Family Cemetery. Several dozen individuals are buried here from both the McGavock and the Rodgers family, the latter who lived on the property prior to the McGavocks' ownership. A few of the grave sites, markers, and stones are suffering from neglect,

---

1597. A storm door (a swinging metal hatchway) leading to the basement exists on the northern side of the house. Its origins, which seem to be fairly modern, and its functions are not known to the author.

weather, and age, and the individuals' personal information is unreadable or nonexistent.

Most notable among those interred here are Carnton founder Randal McGavock and his wife Sarah Dougherty Rodgers, and Colonel John W. McGavock and his wife Caroline Elizabeth "Carrie" Winder, along with their three eldest children, all who perished before the age of thirteen: Martha, Mary, and John, Jr. The couple's other two surviving children, Winder and Hattie, are buried a few miles away at Mount Hope Cemetery, in downtown Franklin. As we just saw, according to the unknown author of one of Winder McGavock's obituaries:

> It is understood that in the near future the remains of Col. McGavock and his wife and their three children who are buried at Carnton will be removed to Mt. Hope.

Who conceived this plan and why is not known. But it never came to pass, and the bodies of these five individuals were allowed to rest in peace at their original burial place at Carnton.

❧ CARNTON'S SERVANTS' CEMETERY

A few yards to the west of the family plots, abutting the McGavock Confederate Cemetery, lies the servants' cemetery, which the uninformed refer to as the "slave cemetery." Most of the graves are unmarked and the occupants are unknown.

One of the tombstones has the following mysterious inscription on it: "Isaiah & Winder Redicks, died June 13, 1877." These are most likely Isaiah Reddick and Winder Reddick, probable relatives of Maria (Otey) Reddick, Carnton's most famous house servant.

Much more archaeological and geneaological research needs to be done on the entire servants' cemetery.

This completes our tour of Carnton's exterior features and outbuildings.

16

Carnton's Interior: First Floor

❧ INSIDE CARNTON: DOWNSTAIRS

MOVING INTO THE INTERIOR OF the Mansion, it should be noted that all of the woodwork is original, and that all of the furnishings are either authentic antiques or actually belonged to the McGavocks. There are no fakes or reproductions.

One of the most common questions asked by Carnton's modern guests concerns the origins of the genuine family furnishings at Carnton. Many were donated by, or are on loan from, McGavock descendants. These make up a tiny fraction of Carnton's furnishings, however. Most are antiques purchased to match the time period, style, and region that the McGavocks lived in.

Carnton Mansion contains a total of seventeen rooms, not including the closets (two in every bedroom). The first floor has five rooms (including the hallway), the second floor consists of six rooms (including the hallway), the attic has two rooms, and the basement contains four rooms.

The house's well laid out symmetrical interior has eight primary rooms, four downstairs and four upstairs.

On the first floor we have:
1. The dining room
2. The men's parlor (also known as the office or library)
3. The ladies' parlor (also known as the family parlor or back parlor)

The McGavocks of Carnton Plantation

    4. The guest parlor (also known as the front parlor or best parlor)

On the second floor we have:
    5. The master bedroom (also known as the parents' bedroom)
    6. The children's nursery
    7. The girls' bedroom (also known as the front guest room)
    8. The guest bedroom

The two bedrooms on the right-hand side of the second floor were originally meant for guests, the two bedrooms on the left were reserved for the family. This plan was later abandoned as the family increased in size.

There is a very small room located at the front of the house in the middle on the second floor, sometimes referred to as the sitting room, which we will discuss momentarily.

Like a feature from Margaret Mitchell's classic novel *Gone With the Wind*, an imposing staircase connects the first, second, and third floors.

❧ THE CENTRAL PASSAGEWAY

The downstairs is notable for its grand central passageway, or what we would today call a hallway, an outstanding element of the Federal, Georgian, and Greek Revival styles. But passageway is a more accurate name for it because it bisects the entire Mansion, creating a literal passage from the front to the back. This was more functional than aesthetic and was in fact one aspect of a form of Victorian air conditioning. How did it work?

❧ VICTORIAN AIR CONDITIONING

On hot Summer days both Carnton's front and back doors were opened to allow a free flow of air through the building, helping to keep the house cool. The staircase's design, connecting all three floors, aided in this process by moving the air from the passageway to the second and even third floors.

The McGavocks of Carnton Plantation

To augment the air movement even further, the McGavocks opened the windows in the attic, which helped draw the hot air upwards from the first floor and out the attic windows on the third floor.[1598]

❧ STANDARD FEDERAL FEATURES

Standard Federal architectural features of the central passageway include twelve-foot ceilings, buttonhole molding patterns in the wooden door casings, and the fanlight window over the front door, which is mirrored in the center ceiling arch.

❧ THE WALLPAPER

While the wallpaper is not original, it *is* an exact reproduction of the pattern that was on the walls of the passageway in the 1850s. How do we know what was there at that time? On the third floor several layers of modern paint and wallpaper were removed, revealing two original wallpaper swatches. These can still be seen at the top of the third floor stairs.

❧ RAILS & GINGERBREAD

The passageway once had chair rails, another common Federal feature. But these were removed, probably by Colonel John during his "modernization" period in the 1840s and 1850s when, during renovation, he substantially altered the appearance of the interior and exterior of the house.

Also interesting is the gingerbread design running up along the side of staircase, lovingly made by some of the McGavock servants, expert craftsmen in woodworking and design.

❧ LARD & WHALE OIL

In the middle of the passageway ceiling one might expect to see a sumptuous chandelier draped with crystals. However, not only was there no electricity at the time, but even kerosene was not widely

---

1598. The temperature inside Carnton Mansion is today controlled using a geothermal air system located in the ceilings.

The McGavocks of Carnton Plantation

available until the 1850s.

Thus the earliest McGavocks at Carnton used a much more primitive form of lighting in the passageway called a passage lamp, which burned whale oil or lard. It did not give out much light, though mechanically it was an ingenious invention: it was lowered and raised on a pulley so it could be more easily lit and blown out. The passage lamp is the only known location in the house where McGavocks had a hanging light fixture.

❧ TWO McGAVOCK TABLES

In the center of the passageway sits a marble-topped table that once belonged to the McGavocks. The candle stand at the foot of the staircase is also a family heirloom.

A common feature in Victorian homes before the advent of electric light bulbs, the hallway candle table played an important role in day-to-day life at Carnton: in the morning, the first one downstairs would light the candle; in the evening, the last one to go upstairs would blow it out.

❧ VICTORIAN LINOLEUM

On the floor of the passageway is a covering called floor cloth. A thin piece of canvas that has been stretched, painted, and covered with twelve to fifteen layers of varnish, this was the Victorian precursor to modern linoleum. If you look closely, the canvas is so thin that imprints of the floorboards can be seen underneath it.

Floor cloth, which acts like a sealant, was ideal for use in high-traffic, heavily traveled areas like the passageway and the dining room. While the McGavocks no doubt purchased new canvas for their floor cloth, the less affluent would have bought used sails from old ships.

❧ ASH FLOORS

The original wood floor in the passageway, which is now under the floor cloth, is ash, the same wood that is used on all of the floors throughout the house, except for the dining room and ladies' parlor.

The McGavocks of Carnton Plantation

❧ A WEALTHY BUT PENNY-PINCHING SCOTS-IRISH FAMILY

The Carnton McGavocks were an upperclass family of extreme wealth, one of the richest in Tennessee. While, for example, the property of the average Victorian family was worth about $10,000, the equivalent of $230,000 today, in 1850 the Carnton property alone was worth $150,000, which has a current value of $4 million. The McGavocks' servants, livestock, house, and outbuildings were worth untold millions more.

Still, as we have seen, the McGavocks were Scottish-Irish penny-pinchers, constantly looking for ways to cut costs, yet maintain a lavish appearance. One example of this can be seen beneath the arches in the passageway. Here you will find poplar columns that were painted to look like marble. It is so expertly done that this expensive looking faux marble finish has fooled many a trained eye.

❧ THE DINING ROOM

Moving into the downstairs area we first come to the dining room. Like the passageway, the floor in this room is also covered with floor cloth. This helped protect the wooden floorboards against constant foot traffic, dropped food, spilled drinks, and scuff marks from chairs.

In the eastern corner of the room is a door, now sealed off. This once led into the kitchen, located in the east wing (originally the 1811 two-story brick house, owned and probably built by the Rodgers family). Over the decades the McGavocks and their servants tread a well-worn path between these two rooms. Standing outside where the 1811 house was once located, one can see that the doorsteps to both rooms have been ground down from decades of shoe leather.

What kinds of food did the McGavocks eat in this room? Some of them were, no doubt, the same, or similar, to those foods mentioned as Southern favorites by the wealthy South Carolinian, Mary Chesnut: sandwiches, gumbo, fish, fried oysters, mushrooms, wild game (turkey, duck, venison, and partridge), apple toddy, tea, boiled ham, various salads (such as chicken salad), salad dressings, homemade breads, eggs, fruit, wine sauce, bacon, olives, cranberries, muffins, yellow butter,

THE MCGAVOCKS OF CARNTON PLANTATION

pound cake, pound cake pudding, preserves, sausages, chocolate jelly cake, spareribs, hot coffee, melons, Madeira, beef, ice cream, green peas, hotcakes, stuffed peppers, pickles, stuffed tomatoes, claret soup, custard, truffles, toddies, *suprême de volaille* (a rich *velouté*, or white sauce, made with chicken stock, cream, and egg yolks), chickens in jelly, sweet potatoes, lemonade, ices, rice, asparagus, gravy, rolls, juleps, sweets, Rhine wine, sugarplums, biscuits, strawberries, sherry, champagne, brandy, trays of "innumerable delicacies," and in the Winter, eggnog.

❧ ORIGINAL FAMILY HEIRLOOMS

There are a number of interesting items in the dining room that belonged to the McGavocks: the dining room table, the cruet set (made around 1855), the serving tray, the glass cake stand, the mixing stand or ham stand, as it was also known (used for storing and mixing liquors), two of the dining room chairs, and the large chest known as a sideboard.[1599]

This last item is made of cherry and was constructed in Philadelphia, Pennsylvania, around 1800. Some have postulated that it may have been given to the McGavocks as a gift by the founder of the city of Franklin: Virginia pioneer and surveyor, Abraham Poindexter Maury. As we will recall, Maury, whose family also gave their name to Maury County, Tennessee, donated the land Franklin now sits on, and designed and mapped out the town.

As part of their penny-pinching, the McGavocks had their oak dining room table, which was made about 1855, painted over, or hand-inked, to look like more expensive rosewood. During the Battle of Franklin II it took on a second function: it was used as an operating table for wounded Confederate soldiers.

The dining room chairs are quite small by today's standards, but this was intentional: their size allowed more people to fit around the dining room table, helpful when entertaining large numbers of guests. The fireplace mantel is original to the house and, like all of the other mantel's in the mansion, is made from poplar tree wood.

1599. The McGavocks' cruet set was used for salt, pepper, oils, and condiments.

THE MCGAVOCKS OF CARNTON PLANTATION

❧ WALLPAPER & RESTORATION

The wallpaper in the dining room deserves special mention. Though we do not know what was on the original McGavock walls of this room, a reproduction entitled *El Dorado*, appropriate to the time and place, has been hung.

At a cost of $60,000, the 1849-panoramic mural, located on the west wall, was hand-stamped by the famed French wallpaper company Zuber, using the original 1,350 wood blocks and some 250 different colors.[1600] There are twenty-four panels of wallpaper.

As part of Carnton's ongoing restoration process, the colors of the dining room's woodwork and ceiling have been re-painted in their original hue.[1601]

❧ FRENCH CHINA & A PORTRAIT

Another family item is the French porcelain china displayed on the dining room table. This stunning collection did not belong to the Carnton McGavocks, however. It was the property of closely related McGavock cousins.

What is unique about this set, made in Paris about 1850, is that each piece was hand-painted. Not only hand-painted, but amazingly, each piece has a different design on it. Looking over to the cupboard one will notice the rest of the 200-piece collection (which includes serving dishes). A set of china of this type is literally priceless.

Above the dining room fireplace is a fine portrait of Randal's and Sarah's third-born son, Colonel John W. McGavock. The painting was made by the itinerant portrait painter, Washington Bogart Cooper (1802-1889), probably around 1850, when John was about thirty-five

---

1600. Zuber, founded by Frenchman Jean Zuber, is still in business and advertises itself as "the last factory in the world to produce wood block printed wallpapers and furnishing fabrics." Zuber's grandson, French realist painter Jean Henri Zuber (1844-1909), was a talented artist in his own right, and is known for his sensitive landscapes and urban scenes. For more information on the Zuber company, visit their Website: www.zuber.fr.

1601. The original paint colors were uncovered through paint analysis.

The McGavocks of Carnton Plantation

years old.[1602]

❧ THE MENS' PARLOR
We now move into the next room over, to the south of the dining room.

The 19th-Century version of the modern "man cave," the men's parlor certainly has a strong and distinctly masculine ambiance about it, and for good reason. Just as men today enjoy getting together at the home of a friend to watch sports events on TV, 19th-Century men also occasionally relished male companionship, and the men's parlor was used in just this way by the men of Carnton.

Though there was no electricity, Carnton's menfolk had no shortage of entertainment. Favored pastimes included playing cards (such as old maid, cribbage, bridge, faro, and whist) and board games (such as chess, dominoes, Fox and Geese, and draughts or checkers) before a roaring fire—the pleasure of which was augmented with liquor and cigars. A spittoon was provided for those who enjoyed chewing their tobacco instead of smoking it.

We can also be sure that many an hour was passed in more serious pursuits in the men's parlor. Colonel John, for instance, an ardent traditional Southerner and states' rights advocate, led countless political discussions in this room, also known as the library.

❧ BOOKKEEPING AT CARNTON
But the men's parlor was not just fun and games, reading, politics, and socializing. It also doubled as Carnton's office, for it was here that the plantation's male owners did their bookkeeping and general accounting.

There was certainly a lot to keep track of, for Carnton was like a small self-contained city. As we have seen, there were a number of large crops (such as Irish and sweet potatoes, wheat, oats, and Indian corn), vegetables, fruits, and ornamental flowers grown on Carnton's

---

1602. Cooper, who lived with his wife and children in Nashville, created some of his most brilliant work during his famous "painting trips," which included a journey on the Mississippi River from 1838 to 1839, and trips to New York City, New York, Philadelphia, Pennsylvania, and Cincinnati, Ohio, between 1841 and 1842. In 1858 he could be found painting in the Tennessee cities of Knoxville, Memphis, and Chattanooga.

THE MCGAVOCKS OF CARNTON PLANTATION

original 1,420 acres, along with countless head of livestock, including: thirty-seven horses, 300 sheep, thirty mules, four oxen, fifty cattle, 200 hogs, and twenty-four dairy cows.

There were also children to be tended to and taught, clothes to be washed, and food to be cleaned, cooked, and served. Additionally, there were many adults, immediate family and close relations, staying at Carnton at any one time.

Behind all of this was the muscle power that fueled Carnton's once thriving commercial industry: nearly four dozen black servants, all who lived in eleven houses on Carnton's property, where they and their families were cared for, clothed, and fed seven days a week. The servants' employer ("owner"), as we will recall, was responsible for all of his bondsmen's needs, from food and clothing to housing and medical care.

Recording the cash flow of Carnton's grain sales alone would have been a daunting task. Tabulating the numbers of the entire multimillion dollar enterprise would have taken enormous focus and intelligence, not to mention a keen knowledge of mathematics.

Looking at the McGavocks' original secretarial desk in the men's parlor, one can almost imagine Randal or Colonel John sitting here before a flickering candle, studiously itemizing the many obtuse sales figures of the day, going over and over piles of receipts, bills, and new orders. Such businesslike scenes, however, would have been counterbalanced by the sights and sounds of the men's boisterous daytime parties and late-night revelries.

❧ SCOTCH, CIGAR HOLDERS, & A DOOR TO NOWHERE

Like most of Carnton's rooms, the floor of the men's parlor was also carpeted. The pattern of the carpet here is called "Scotch." Though this is a reproduction of what might have been on the floor of this room, with its Celtic theme, the Scottish-Irish McGavocks would have heartily

THE MCGAVOCKS OF CARNTON PLANTATION

approved of it.[1603] (The carpet is so delicate that the room has been roped off to prevent damage from shoes.)

The house's chair rails were later removed from some rooms. But the men's parlor retains them, no doubt a conscious choice to maintain an aspect of early Victorian Southern tradition in this particular room. And while the wallpaper pattern and wooden window blinds are not original, the McGavocks would have had something similar (Venetian blinds were quite common at the time), and the colors of the woodwork are accurate for the period.

The restored ceiling was painted using horsehair brushes, just like those used originally. This gives modern Carnton's guests an accurate idea of how the finished product would have actually looked in the early 1800s.

Other family heirlooms in the men's parlor are Colonel John's cigar holder, some of his books on the book shelves (such as *Webster's Dictionary*),[1604] Carrie's complete collection of poetry books (on the top shelf), the portrait of John's father, Carnton founder Randal McGavock, over the mantel, and a surveying kit that belonged to David, Randal's older brother (the wooden box on the table at the back of the room). David, we will recall, surveyed and drew up the first map of Davidson County, whose main city is Nashville.

On the east wall, to the left of the fireplace, is the original door to the east wing, or kitchen. It was through this entrance that Carnton's tradesmen, temporary hands, and servants came and went to get their work orders for the day, and to receive their pay from Randal or Colonel John at the end of each week. The well-worn doorstep outside attests to the tremendous number of people who passed between the kitchen and the main house between 1826 and 1909.

Since the destruction of the 1811 house in the latter year, there is nothing on the other side of this door but the outer wall, and so it has

---

1603. They might not have approved of the name "Scotch," however. True Scots prefer not to be called Scotch, which is, after all, understandable: Scotch is the name of Scotland's most famous alcoholic beverage. Likewise, American terms such as "Scotch-American" and "Scotch-Irish" are not appreciated in Scotland, where the correct name for these branches of Celts is respectively, Scottish-American and Scots-Irish.
1604. John had a particular interest in history and geography.

THE McGAVOCKS OF CARNTON PLANTATION

been closed off to protect the public.

❧ ANDREW JACKSON'S CURIOUS "GIFT"
A notable item belonging to the McGavocks is the rocking chair in the men's parlor. According to both family legend and family obituaries it was a present from Andrew "Old Hickory" Jackson (1767-1845). Why would America's seventh president give such a gift to the McGavocks?

Randal and Jackson were best friends, as were Randal's wife Sarah and Jackson's wife Rachel Donelson, whose father, John Donelson (1725-1785), was one of the founders of the city of Nashville, originally called Fort Nashborough.[1605] A town and a road near Nashville are named after the Donelson family.[1606]

The two couples enjoyed each other's company and were known to have visited one another, probably quite regularly.[1607] The Jacksons in particular loved having friends drop by to see them at their sumptuous Nashville home known as the Hermitage.

As the story goes, Jackson found the seating at Carnton Plantation rather uncomfortable, formal, and stiff. Eventually, on one of his visits, he brought an unpretentious and simple, but comfortable rocking chair along with him, giving it to the McGavocks as a present.

Of course, the family was deeply honored. But subsequently they must have wondered about his true motivations: every time Old Hickory came to visit, the only chair he would sit in was his "gift" to the McGavocks!

❧ JACKSON, A SOUTHERN MAN'S MAN
As best friends, the McGavocks would probably have displayed a portrait of President Jackson, and one can still be seen on the south wall of the men's parlor. Voted in for two consecutive terms (1828 and 1832),

---

[1605]. Nashville was named in honor of Virginian, Francis Nash, a brigadier general who died fighting in America's first Revolutionary War on October 7, 1777, as a result of wounds suffered at the Battle of Germantown, Pennsylvania.
[1606]. The Donelson family name is very popular in Middle Tennessee. Even Franklin has a road named after them: Donelson Creek Parkway.
[1607]. Randal McGavock and Andrew Jackson were probably not aware of it, but they were cousins.

THE MCGAVOCKS OF CARNTON PLANTATION

Jackson, the only president to pay off the entire national debt while in office, was so popular in Tennessee that he was elected the state's first U.S. representative (in 1796) without any opposition.

Indeed, Southerners from all over Dixie loved the gaunt and charismatic backwoodsman, despite his support for certain types of internal improvements and his stand against nullification. After all, he was an "everyday Joe," one who had survived an assassination attempt; who was hated by Yankees and other anti-South factions; was a War Hawk; was a true Democrat (in the 1800s a conservative) who stood up for the "little guy" and the working man; and who made John C. Calhoun his vice president (Calhoun was the principle spokesman for states' rights, a sacred doctrine in the South).

Not only was "Old Hickory" a true representative of the American people, he was also a national war hero who, like all traditional Southerners, was against political patronage, a national bank, and life tenure. As such he had battled against Federalist Whigs (liberals) like Henry Clay and Daniel Webster (1782-1852), two anti-Jeffersonians whose views later greatly influenced Federalist Lincoln in his left-wing, progressive dream of destroying states' rights in the South.[1608]

Thin-skinned Jackson was widely known for other things as well, among them his hair-trigger temper and violent adherence to the South's manly code of honor. He was, for example, involved in a number of fist fights, and once, when a man slandered his good wife Rachel, he challenged him to a duel, killing the foolhardy offender.

1608. One of Daniel Webster's more notable "contributions" to history was his idea that the "Union created the states." Nothing could have been further from the truth. For it was the states, that is, the original thirteen colonies, that created the Union, a body which, at the time, was called "the Confederacy," the first name of the U.S.A. Years later Lincoln would embrace Webster's outrageous falsehood and use it as a sledge hammer to beat the South into submission. DiLorenzo, RL, p. 259. Indeed, the entire reason he gave for initiating the bloodiest war on American soil was to "preserve the Union." What Lincoln completely disregarded was the fact that the Founding Fathers had intended that the Union be wholly subservient to the states, which were originally considered separate and independent nations. In an effort to advance their agenda (that is, to establish a strong central federalist government), Webster, and later Lincoln, reversed this, claiming that the Union was superior to the states, older than the states, and that it, in fact, had created the states, and therefore must be preserved. Lincoln himself knew he was deceiving the public because later, in his famous "Gettysburg Address," he made reference to the American nation as "that government of the people, by the people, and for the people . . ." His lie led to the deaths of nearly three million Americans between 1861 and 1865.

THE McGAVOCKS OF CARNTON PLANTATION

Still, here was a plain, simple, generous, and loyal frontiersman from the rugged woodlands of South Carolina, a true defender of states' rights that Southerners like the liberty-loving McGavocks could admire and appreciate.

Jackson would not be the last South Carolinian to fight against the Hamiltonian monarchists. On Lincoln's ascension to power, Jackson's home state would become the first to secede from the Union and vote to form a Southern Confederacy. God bless the Palmetto State!

❧ GEORGE WASHINGTON: SOUTHERN IDOL

There is another picture hanging in the men's parlor that many of Carnton's guests asked me about during my tours.

The portrait of George Washington on the east wall is not original to the room, but it is almost certain that his image hung on one of Carnton's walls at one time or another. Because of their love of states' rights and the Constitution, their lifelong dedication to the Southern Cause, and their charge to free America from British tyranny, the Southern Founding Fathers were heros to traditional Southerners like the McGavocks.

Washington was certainly at the top of this list of luminaries in the Old South, which is why an equestrian portrait of the large, powerful, and dignified Virginian was chosen as the emblem on the Great Seal of the Confederacy in 1862. Selecting America's first president to symbolize the Confederacy was highly appropriate, for under his leadership the United States was first known as "the Confederacy," and its first Constitution was known as "the Articles of Confederation."

It was also for these very reasons that a great equestrian statue of Washington was erected in Richmond's Capital Square in 1858 (the one copied on the Confederate Seal); it is why Washington's image was engraved on Confederate money; it is why he was known across the South literally as "the Father of the Confederacy";[1609] it is why the

---

1609. Channing, pp. 13, 69.

THE MCGAVOCKS OF CARNTON PLANTATION

inauguration of the permanent (as opposed to the provisional) Confederate government was purposefully set to take place on Washington's birthday (February 22, 1862); and it is why many Southerners, such as Thomas R. R. Cobb of Georgia, suggested that the new Confederacy be called "The Republic of Washington" rather than the Confederate States of America.[1610]

In late April 1864 the designer of the Great Seal of the Confederacy, Louisiana Senator Thomas J. Semmes of New Orleans, gave his reason for choosing the somber and serious-minded Washington as the symbol's centerpiece:

> Washington has been selected as the emblem for our shield, as a type of our ancestors, in his character of *princeps majorum* ["premier leader"]. In addition to this, the equestrian figure is consecrated in the hearts of our own people by the local circumstance that on the gloomy and stormy 22nd of February, 1862, our permanent government was set in motion by the inauguration of President [Jefferson] Davis under the shadow of the statue of Washington.[1611]

Under Washington's image are the words *Deo Vindice*, Latin for "God Will Vindicate." The strongly pro-Confederate McGavocks knew very well what these words on the Great Confederate Seal meant, and were in full agreement with them.

To this day thousands of good and faithful Southerners continue to stand behind this Latin pronouncement, whose meaning could only possibly be understood by a people who have been invaded, occupied, humiliated, exiled, arrested, tortured, raped, executed, and murdered by a foreign nation led by a dictatorial, socialistic, tyrant. In this case his name was Abraham Lincoln.[1612]

❧ THE LADIES' PARLOR

While many modern Americans are busy trying to blur the lines between

---

1610. Henry, SC, pp. 25-26, 446; Cannon, p. 2.
1611. *Southern Historical Society Papers*, Vol. XVI, Richmond, VA., January-December, 1888.
1612. For examples of Yankee crimes against the South, see Pollard, LC, pp. 404, 635.

THE MCGAVOCKS OF CARNTON PLANTATION

men and women (feminizing the former, masculinizing the latter), Victorians understood, accepted, and even emphasized the many innate differences between the two sexes. And so, in the early 1800s, it was only natural that men and women were free, even encouraged, to have their own gender-specific rooms. Thus, just as the men of Carnton had their parlor, the women of Carnton had theirs as well.

The ladies' parlor, also known as the family parlor, family sitting room, or back parlor, is located at the rear of the house on the north side. Here Carnton's women and girls would gather to chat, gossip, sew, read alone or to one another, play games, or just relax. A true family room that was not used for company, this parlor also served as a casual place for family gatherings.

During parties and social events, however, it functioned as a second dining room. This was achieved by opening the large moveable walls, actually folding doors, that formed a temporary barrier between the ladies' parlor and the guest's parlor. The space of each room was thus doubled, allowing family and guests more freedom of movement.

❧ UPSIDE DOWN WALLPAPER

There are many special aspects of the ladies' parlor, one of the most noticeable being the wallpaper. It is an exact reproduction of the original wallpaper, previously mentioned, found in the hallway at the top of the stairs on the third floor's east wall.

For some unknown reason, the McGavocks hung it upside down there, so when the copy was brought in during restoration of the room, it too was hung upside down.

It may be that the McGavocks simply liked the look of the motif in the wallpaper better wrong side up; or perhaps it reminded them of a Celtic or religious design they were familiar with. We will never know for sure. But it is fun to theorize.

❧ WINDOW SHADES & THE FAMILY BIBLE

The painted designs on the window shades in the ladies' parlor are from an 1827 decorators' guidebook. The McGavocks would have owned something very similar to these.

THE McGAVOCKS OF CARNTON PLANTATION

Original family heirlooms in the room include the sewing stand (owned by Randal's great-niece), a gilded framed print on the wall called "Noah's Sacrifice" (from about 1850),[1613] and the family Bible (from about 1856), which later was owned and kept by Sarah "Sallie" McGavock (1837-1863), a daughter of James Randal McGavock (Colonel John's brother) and Louisa C. Chenault of nearby Riverside Plantation.

The marble-topped table in the center of the room also once belonged to the Riverside McGavocks. Mirrors and crystals were placed strategically throughout the room in order to magnify light coming in from the windows.

❧ FAMILY PORTRAITS

On the east wall of the ladies' parlor are several portraits of interest. Over the door is a painting of young Harriet "Hattie" McGavock, the only surviving daughter of Colonel John and Carrie (Winder) McGavock. The painting, which belonged to the McGavocks, was made around 1868 by artist George Dury, when Hattie was thirteen years old.

On either side of the door on the same wall are portraits of two McGavock relatives: Randal McGavock (1803-1890) and his second wife and 1st cousin, Cynthia E. McGavock (1820-1882), both from Wythe County, Virginia, and both descendants of European royalty.

This particular Randal is the son of Hugh McGavock (1761-1844) and Nancy Kent (1763-1835), another relative of mine. Nancy descends from the same family as American frontiersman Davy Crockett. Hugh was a deputy sheriff in Montgomery County, Virginia, and a collector of revenue for Wythe County, Virginia, in 1790. In 1799 he served as quartermaster of the Western Battalion, and as a captain in Colonel Joseph Crockett's regiment in Virginia. He also fought Shawnee Indians in Pennsylvania.

Cynthia is the daughter of Joseph McGavock (1780-1833), of Fort Chiswell, Wythe County, Virginia (who is the brother of Hugh

---

1613. The frame is original as well.

above), and Margaret Graham (1784-1868), a Scottish-Irish descendant of North Carolina Presbyterians.

Randal, son of Hugh and Nancy, is the nephew of Randal McGavock, founder of Carnton, and a 1st cousin of Colonel John of Carnton. His wife Cynthia is the niece of Randal McGavock, founder of Carnton, and also a 1st cousin of Colonel John of Carnton.

❧ CARRIE'S BLACK WEDDING DRESS

On the opposite wall, over the fireplace mantel in the ladies' parlor, is a beautiful and famous painting of Hattie's mother Carrie, who would one day come to be known as "the Good Samaritan of Williamson County." The portrait, another McGavock family heirloom, was probably done on or near her wedding day, December 6, 1848, at her parents' home, Ducros Plantation in Houma, Louisiana, when she was just nineteen years old.

There is something strange about the portrait that many people do not notice at first glance, however: Carrie is wearing a black dress. Since modern tradition dictates that first-time brides wear white at their marriage ceremony, people today are understandably inquisitive about Mrs. McGavock's unusual wedding attire.

To begin with, Carrie had a predisposition toward the color black and could be found wearing it nearly everywhere, at all occasions, in all seasons. This seems to have been nothing more than an eccentric, if obsessive, color preference.

But there may have been a more down-to-earth reason for wearing black on her wedding day. What Carrie is wearing is not a wedding dress after all. She and Colonel John planned on leaving Louisiana immediately after the ceremony. With no time to change clothing or pack another suitcase, she simply wore what necessity dictated, and that was a stout black traveling dress. It just so happened that it was also her favorite color.

❧ CARRIE'S WINDOWS

Carrie had a strong emotional attachment to the ladies' parlor, one that went far beyond that of the other women who lived at Carnton.

THE McGAVOCKS OF CARNTON PLANTATION

To begin with, she spent many cheery and pleasant hours in this room surrounded by her family, relatives, and friends, creating pleasant memories that she would lovingly dwell on for the rest of her life. There was something else that drew her to the back parlor again and again, however.

In 1883 her youngest and only surviving son, Winder, married Susie Ewing. And though the couple remained at Carnton, the following year, in 1884, her youngest and only surviving daughter Hattie married and left the plantation for her own home, Windermere, located at the end of the Carnton driveway (across Carnton Lane). Nine short years later, in 1893, Carrie's husband Colonel John passed away.

Used to having her children and husband about the house, the highly sociable and maternal Carrie must have found the loneliness almost unbearable. To help with her depression she had two holes knocked out in the west wall, to the left and right of the fireplace, in the ladies' parlor, where large matching windows were installed, letting in more light. In her later years Carrie had a bed set up in front of the right window where she could gaze down the drive at her daughter and son-in-law's house. In the last months of her life Carrie rarely left this room, and in fact, according to local legend, it was in this very bed, in this very room, that Carried passed away on February 22, 1905.[1614]

Later, during restoration, the two windows were removed and the holes bricked back up, so that the house would appear as it did in the 1860s. However, the outlines of "Carrie's windows" can still be seen on the outer west wall of the Mansion.

To this day many people have had unnerving paranormal experiences in the ladies' parlor, including seeing strange orbs of light and grey floating mists, and smelling fragrant perfumes. Does Carrie's spirit refuse to leave the room where she once experienced such happiness? Many people think so, and, having had some of these same experiences, I am one of them.

[1614]. According to her obituary, however, Mrs. McGavock passed away at her daughter Hattie's house, Windermere.

THE MCGAVOCKS OF CARNTON PLANTATION

❧ THE GUEST PARLOR

Moving into the room to the south is the guest parlor.

The guest parlor was reserved for entertaining, and the highly social McGavocks are known to have held many formal affairs, receptions, weddings, and parties here. Among the many guests said to have visited the guest parlor are Presidents James Knox Polk and Andrew Jackson, as well as lesser statesmen like Felix Grundy and Sam Houston.

It is also said that on January 2, 1840, Randal's daughter (Colonel John's sister), Elizabeth Irwin McGavock, married her husband, the founder of Belle Meade Plantation, my cousin General William Giles Harding, in this parlor.[1615]

We will note here that one of General Harding's daughters, Willie Elizabeth Harding (1832-1895), married her 1st cousin David Harding McGavock (1826-1896), who built the elegant Two Rivers Mansion in Nashville. David is the grandson of David McGavock the surveyor, brother of Randal McGavock, who built Carnton Plantation.

❧ UPMARKET FURNISHINGS

In a desire to impress their guests and provide a superlative ambiance of Southern luxury and hospitality, the McGavocks spent more lavishly on decorating this room than any other. Thus the guest parlor, also known as the best parlor, front parlor, or company parlor, located on the south side of the Mansion, would have been filled with the finest furnishings and decor money could buy.

Among the more spectacular of these was the *étagère* (a piece of light furniture, often with a mirror, on which small ornamental items, like statuettes, are displayed),[1616] and enormous mirrors, purposefully placed to reflect maximum light—an attempt to "brighten" up the room. The ceiling paint, known as "Prussian Blue," was intended to have a similar effect while imparting an atmosphere of stateliness and beauty.

1615. As mentioned, my 6th great-grandmother is Nancy Margaret Harding, born 1743 in Shenandoah, Warren County, Virginia. Nancy is Gen. Harding's 3rd cousin. I am his 5th cousin.

1616. At the time I worked at Carnton the *étagère* was located in the corner of the guest parlor.

THE MCGAVOCKS OF CARNTON PLANTATION

Reinforcing the ceiling color is the solar lamp with its mesmerizing blue globe, situated on the table in the middle of the room. At night its bluish light would have merged with the overhead color, making the ceiling "disappear." This gave the room a more open and spacious feeling.

Today, with its expensive, formal, matching furniture suite, intricate window treatments, large costly mirrors, and stunning Greek Revival mantel, the latter which was installed by Colonel John in the 1850s, the restored room truly reflects its original function as a posh entertaining parlor.[1617]

The window shades, unlike the informal ones in the ladies' parlor, have an intentionally opulent design. Though we do not know what the guest parlor shades looked like when the McGavocks lived at Carnton, these are a good guess since they match the time, place, and status of the family.

The colors of the woodwork and ceiling are believed to be authentic to the 1850s, Colonel John's modernization period, at which time he also removed the room's chair rails.

❧ FAMILY HEIRLOOMS & LAVISH PARTIES

The family heirlooms in the guest parlor include the Rococo writing table (probably from the Riverside McGavocks), and the 19th-Century flute, which belonged to Lysander McGavock (1800-1855) and his wife Elizabeth Crockett (1795-1862), of Midway Plantation, in Brentwood, Tennessee (originally located near the Good Springs Post Office). Elizabeth is the 3rd cousin of my cousin, famed American frontiersman Davy Crockett.[1618]

The Carnton McGavocks, known for their charm, grace, and hospitality, were great lovers of music, socializing, and entertaining, and in fact they owned a number of musical instruments for these very

---

1617. The other fireplace mantels throughout the house, all in the Federal style, were never altered. Note that all of Carnton's fireplaces once burned wood, but were later changed over to coal burning fireboxes.
1618. I am related to the Crockett family, in part, through the royal Stewart family of Scotland.

The McGavocks of Carnton Plantation

purposes. These included a square grand piano-forte,[1619] a wooden flute, a melodeon (a type of accordion popular among the Scottish and the Irish), and a harp, each regularly played by both family members and guests. (The piano-forte now located in the guest parlor is not original to the McGavocks, but an authentic instrument from the same period, made in Boston, Massachusetts, in the 1850s.)

Widely known for holding lavish parties, the McGavocks practiced a traditional Southern custom among the wealthy: no guest ever left the estate without a small gift to take home with them.

All of the doors in the house, normally kept closed, were flung open to provide more space and to allow guests to flow from room to room. This was important because sometimes the festivities would become quite raucous, with dancing guests occasionally spilling out into the central passageway, which doubled as a ballroom.

The third floor was also used for ballroom space on occasion. Such parties often lasted into the wee hours of the morning, as late as 3:00 A.M. in some cases.

1619. Piano-forte was the original name for what we know today simply as the piano. The instrument was given the name piano-forte, meaning "soft-loud" in Italian, because it was the first keyboard instrument that could be played at different volume levels, depending on how gently or hard one struck the keys. This was due to the invention of the piano-forte's hammer system, which could strike the strings at varying velocities. Earlier keyboard instruments, like the harpsichord, typically plucked the strings, resulting in a single volume level. This made the piano-forte a truly revolutionary musical invention, allowing composers like Ludwig von Beethoven (1770-1827), who was still alive when Randal McGavock moved into Carnton (in 1826), to write some of the most sublime, poignant, and subtle music ever created.

Carnton's Interior: Second Floor

❧ THE STAIRWAY

AS WE CONTINUE ON OUR tour of Carnton we now leave the first floor and move up to the second. The stairway that takes us there is entirely original to the house and is nearly 200 years old.

The gingerbread design that runs along the grand staircase was designed, cut, and installed by some of Carnton's African-American servants, many who were, like the creators of this particular wood decoration, highly skilled artisans.

The poplar railing on the staircase is another example of the McGavocks' Scots-Irish penny-pinching: it has been painted over to look like more expensive cherry wood.

❧ THE SECOND-FLOOR HALLWAY

We now come to the second-floor hallway.

We do not know what the McGavocks had on the floor here, but historical restorers at Carnton have laid a reproduction of a beautiful Italian wool carpet. The design, known as "Venetian," was typical for a plantation house in Middle Tennessee in the 1860s, and would have matched the 19th-Century Southern obsession with Classical European culture.

There were other reasons this design would have been an ideal choice for a family like the McGavocks. Not only was it fashionably decorative, but it would have also amply withstood the intense foot

THE MCGAVOCKS OF CARNTON PLANTATION

traffic in the hallway.

ॐ THE MASTER BEDROOM

To the immediate left is the master bedroom, also known as the parents' bedroom. Originally, in the early 1800s, this was Randal's and Sarah's bedroom. When Sarah passed away in 1854 (Randal died eleven years earlier, in 1843), ownership of the house passed to Colonel John, at which time it became he and Carrie's master bedroom.

The wash basin and stand in the corner of the master bedroom are original. Also notable in this room are the wooden baseboards, painted to look like marble (a sign of affluence).

The restored bed (originally owned by the Riverside McGavocks), with its luxuriant feather tick[1620] and its soft curtains (meant to keep heat in during the Winter and keep insects out during the Summer), looks short by modern standards. Indeed, it is only 72 inches long, while today's mattresses range from 75 to 84 inches. Why so short then, especially when we know that Victorians were actually slightly taller than we are today?

During the 1800s people slept upright, so the length of beds was necessarily shortened, saving money on materials. More importantly, however, the shorter length allowed the sleeper's feet to be placed against the footboard, making it easier to prop himself up in bed. This custom was based on the then scientific belief that if a person laid prone at night, fluids would drain into the lungs, literally "drowning" one in his sleep.

ॐ A SORROWFUL PAINTING

Over the mantel of the master bedroom hangs a painting of Colonel John's and Carrie's first three children, all who died before the age of thirteen. On the left is Mary Elizabeth McGavock (1851-1858)—who

---

1620. Victorians called feather mattresses feather ticks, after the name of the cotton fabric known as ticking, used to make the outer bag into which the feathers were placed. This bag, the mattress, was called a tick. The ticking was often rubbed with soap or wax to make it more durable. The soft tick was then laid on top of a firm under-mattress, which helped support the basically shapeless tick.

THE MCGAVOCKS OF CARNTON PLANTATION

passed away just before her seventh birthday;[1621] in the middle is Martha Winder McGavock (1849-1862)—who passed away at age twelve;[1622] and on the right is John Randal McGavock (June 1854-September 1854)—who passed away at only three months old.[1623] The images of the two daughters were made from a photo showing them holding hands, while John's was made from memory and from descriptions by the family.[1624]

Set in clouds with rays of light entering from the upper left, the painting has an ethereal, almost heavenly quality to it that is quite intentional. This type of work is known as a "mourning portrait," for it memorializes the tragic deaths of its subjects.

The idea that all three youngsters were now in Heaven with their Maker was no doubt very comforting to the McGavocks, and over the years they spent many hours staring wistfully at this stunning work of art.

❧ STRANGE CLOSETS

Since there appears to be two wall closets in the master bedroom, one on either side of the fireplace, many of my tour guests used to ask me why there is also an armoire in the room. There were indeed no clothes closets in early Victorian homes, and so these large, portable wooden closets, or wardrobes, as they are also known, were an essential item in every home. What then were the two wall closets in this room used for?

Opening one of closet doors reveals an extremely shallow cupboard-like space, less than a foot deep from the front to the back, with a few shelves and wall hooks. The appearance is very peculiar, almost comical to us, for we are used to huge, modern, walk-in closets.

But the Victorians were an ingenious lot, and the tiny dimensions of these little "cupboards" were intentional.

When returning from outside, clothing was hung or folded up and stored in them. The fire in the fireplace, just a foot away, heated the

---

1621. As mentioned, Mary died of yellow fever.
1622. Martha died, presumably, from a heart condition.
1623. John is said to have perished from "inflammation of the bowels."
1624. Some Victorian artists refused to paint infants, considering them unworthy of their time and attention. This is probably the reason John was portrayed as a three year old rather than as a baby.

abutting walls of the closets, which in turn warmed the belongings inside. The next time these pieces of clothing were put on, usually the following morning, they were dry and warm, perfect for cool or frigid weather.

These then were clothes-warming closets, brilliant devices that served their purpose well, but became obsolete with the advent of indoor central heating.

❧ JIB WINDOWS

The window toward the east wall of the master bedroom is what is known as a jib window, since the bottom half has been cut to open and move laterally, like the jib sail on a sailboat.

Carrie had jib windows put in the two back second-floor bedrooms (that is, the master bedroom and the guest bedroom), so that she and Colonel John, and their guests, would have access to the back upper floor of the beautiful Greek Revival porch that the couple added in 1850. Jib windows were used instead of regular doors in order to preserve the symmetry of the house.

Here is how they work.

The upper sash opens up and locks in place, then the two small lower doors are swung open. One then crouches down before passing out onto the porch. Carrie walked through the jib window in the master bedroom hundreds of times during her years at Carnton.

❧ THE CHILDREN'S NURSERY

Moving east we come to what was probably the young children's bedroom. There is some architectural evidence for this: unlike the other three second-floor bedrooms, originally, this room had no door to the second-floor hallway. Instead its single door led directly into the master bedroom, a traditional design in early Victorian homes. The idea behind this will seem quaint, even strange, to many modern parents.

❧ VICTORIAN DISCIPLINARIANS

As we know, in earlier times parents were far more authoritarian when it came to raising children than today. By omitting the nursery's door to

THE MCGAVOCKS OF CARNTON PLANTATION

the hallway and constructing one that was connected only to the master bedroom, Victorian parents were better able to keep a close watch on their children. This provided several benefits.

For one thing youngsters could not sneak out of their room, for their only exit led directly into their parents' bedroom. Second, parents could efficiently attend to any problems their children might encounter during the night. A coughing spell, for instance, would bring a quick response from mother, who had only to fly through the doorway connecting the two bedrooms instead of having to go out into the hallway before gaining access to the children's room.

❧ MODERN CHILD REARING COMES TO CARNTON

In the 1850s Colonel John and Carrie must have begun to view child rearing through more modern eyes; that is, they no longer wanted to be disturbed by their children at night.

And so a door was added to the nursery that led directly into the hallway, allowing the children to come and go as they pleased without bothering mom and dad in the next room. At that point the original connecting door, which remains, was probably locked permanently. The modern idea of privacy had come to Carnton!

Close inspection of the "new" doorway reveals that it does not match the other bedroom doors in size and construction.

As a safety precaution, the closet door in the nursery led to the 1811 kitchen wing—that is, the two-story brick house—where Carnton's live-in nanny, Elizabeth Field "Lizzy" Clouston, had a room on the second floor. The door was bricked over after the 1909 tornado destroyed the 1811 house. However, the "ghost" impression of the door can still be seen on the east end of Carnton Mansion. It is located up near the "ghost" line at the top of the kitchen roof, just above the men's parlor door.

❧ THE BATTLE OF FRANKLIN I

The children's nursery provided many happy moments for the McGavocks. And yet, it also came to symbolize one of the most horrific events in American history.

THE MCGAVOCKS OF CARNTON PLANTATION

It all began on April 10, 1863, when Lincoln's invaders fought their Confederate brethren at Franklin in what is now known as the Battle of Franklin I, or simply 1ˢᵗ Franklin. The Union was victorious, and continued to dominate the city for the rest of the War, much to the disgust of Confederate families like the McGavocks.

❧ THE UNION OCCUPATION OF NASHVILLE

The Carnton McGavocks in Franklin were not the only ones affected by Yankee domination in the area, of course. A year earlier, on February 23, 1862, Nashville had been the first Southern capital to fall into Union hands.[1625] It did not regain full rights to govern itself again until Lincoln's illegal foreign occupation completely ended in 1877, the last year of the North's unconstitutional "Reconstruction" period.[1626]

Many close relations of the Carnton McGavocks lived in Nashville during this fifteen-year period of Yankee military rule, making it unquestionably one of the most painful chapters in McGavock family history.

❧ JOHN SIGNS THE YANKEE OATH OF ALLEGIANCE

It was in the year 1862, however, the year Nashville was captured by Union forces, that Colonel John, under the threat of arrest and imprisonment, was forced to "turn Yankee"; that is, sign the Yankees' "Oath of Allegiance."[1627] Federal troops promised to burn down Carnton Mansion and all of its outbuildings, dooming his family to bankruptcy and homelessness, if he did not sign.

Lincoln had already turned millions of Southern civilians into exiled refugees: Southern roads, rivers, and rails were packed with thousands of itinerant Confederate families fleeing the smoking countryside in search of shelter and safety. John knew what might await his own family. What choice did he have?

But even if he did sign, he knew this would not necessarily

1625. R. L. Mode, p. 31.
1626. See Rosenbaum and Brinkley, s.v. "McCardle, Ex Parte."
1627. Channing, p. 109.

THE MCGAVOCKS OF CARNTON PLANTATION

protect him and his property from abuse. Chesnut makes note of a resident of New Orleans who, *after* taking the Yankee oath, was beaten and dragged through the streets, had his house robbed, and who was then forced to guide the Union soldiers through the town before he was freed.[1628] Such stories were no doubt on Colonel John's mind when he was confronted by his Northern adversaries.

Conflicted by his undying allegiance to both the Confederacy and his family and home, we can only imagine how distasteful and difficult it was for him to sign this piece of paper. Yankee pistols cocked at his ears no doubt expedited matters.

Many are curious about this illegal, evil, vindictive, and oppressive document, intentionally issued by Lincoln to humiliate the South. Below is a typical example of the type that Colonel John and thousands of other Confederate family members were forced to autograph throughout the War. It was written by none other than our sixteenth president, the Constitutuion-loathing liberal, Abraham Lincoln:

UNION OATH OF ALLEGIANCE

I _____ of the county of _____, state of _____, do solemnly swear, in presence of Almighty God, that I will henceforth faithfully support, protect, and defend the Constitution of the United States, and the Union of the States thereunder; and that I will bear true faith, allegiance and loyalty to the same, any ordinance, resolution or law of any State, convention or legislature to the contrary notwithstanding; and further, that I do this with a full determination, pledge and purpose, without any mental reservation or evasion whatsoever; and that I will, in like manner, abide by and faithfully support all acts of Congress passed during the existing rebellion with reference to slaves, so long and so far as not repealed, modified or held void by Congress, or by decision of the Supreme Court; and that I will, in like manner, abide by and faithfully support all proclamations of the President made during the existing rebellion having reference to slaves, so long and so far

---

1628. Chesnut, MCCW, p. 467.

THE MCGAVOCKS OF CARNTON PLANTATION

as not modified or declared void by decision of the Supreme Court: So help me God.[1629]

There were variations on this oath, such as the ludicrous "Ironclad Oath," which required Confederates to swear loyalty to the U.S., not only in the future, but also in the past.[1630] How many Southerners pretended that they had always been faithful to the Union while signing these obscene documents is of course unknown, but a fair guess would be 100 percent!

✥ SUPPORTING, PROTECTING, & DEFENDING THE CONSTITUTION

One of the many ironies of the U.S. Oath of Allegiance was that it demanded the signer to "faithfully support, protect, and defend the Constitution of the United States," something that Lincoln himself clearly was not doing at the time, and never had any intention of doing. In fact, it was only because Lincoln so thoroughly subverted the U.S. Constitution that he was able to finally subdue the South. If he had been a law-abiding president and followed the dictates of the Constitution, how different the outcome of the War would have been.

There was an even more stunning incongruity about the Yankee oath, however. It was the Southern Confederacy, the C.S.A., not the U.S.A., that was trying to "faithfully support, protect, and defend the Constitution." Not the Constitution as Lincoln saw it in 1861, but the original one that had been adopted by the Founding Fathers in 1787.[1631]

Because it stood in the way of installing Clay's American System, however, Lincoln, like other liberal progressives, had no patience with the Founder's conservative Constitution. And so he simply ignored those articles and clauses he disliked, while forcing the ratification of new constitutional amendments he did like. As Lincoln said shortly after winning his first presidential election, when I get to the Oval Office,

---

1629. Nicolay and Hay, ALCW, Vol. 2, p. 443.
1630. Siepel, p. 169.
1631. Plano, Greenberg, Olton, and Riggs, s.v. "Constitutional Convention of 1787."

THE MCGAVOCKS OF CARNTON PLANTATION

> I shall take an oath to the best of my ability to preserve, protect, and defend the Constitution. This is a great and solemn duty. With the support of the people and the assistance of the Almighty I shall undertake to perform it. I have full faith that I shall perform it. *It is not the Constitution as I would like to have it*, but as it is that is to be defended [emphasis added].[1632]

Thus the document that Lincoln demanded his enemies sign was not truly an oath of allegiance to the Constitution. It was an oath of allegiance to his anti-South political agenda, thrust on the unwilling people of a foreign country at the tip of a bayonet.

In truth, Lincoln himself would not have signed his own oath, yet he expected oppressed foreigners to sign it! Is it any wonder that the McGavocks and millions of other Southerners regarded the Yankee president's unlawful pledge with outrage and revulsion?

❧ THE BATTLE OF FRANKLIN II

As we have seen, on November 30, 1864, Lincoln's marauders once again used Franklin as a human chessboard in their effort to destroy states' rights and close down the constitutionally formed Southern Confederacy. This marked the onset of the Battle of Franklin II.

❧ THE NURSERY AS OPERATING THEATER

That night thousands of wounded and dying Confederate soldiers were brought to Carnton, which had been designated a Rebel field hospital by President Jefferson Davis prior to the War. Our Confederate leader must have had a premonition: Carnton turned out to be the house closest to the Confederate lines, making it a truly convenient battle side infirmary.

In the rapidly dying light of that Fall afternoon, doctors hurriedly set up their makeshift operating tables (typically a board or a door placed on top of two sawhorses) in the rooms on the south side of the house,

---

1632. Coffin, p. 235. Lincoln devotee and left-wing liberal, President Barack Hussein Obama, recently made a similar statement, calling the U.S. Constitution "an imperfect document." "Glenn Beck," FOX News, September, 17, 2009 (Constitution Day, 222nd anniversary).

THE MCGAVOCKS OF CARNTON PLANTATION

where there would be the most daylight for the longest period of time. (There were no windows on the western side of the house at the time, except two small ones in the attic.)

The windows had the added benefit of offering fresh air for those rare times when chloroform was used. Normally there was no painkiller to numb the cutting of the surgeon's blade, except perhaps a quick slug of whiskey.

This brings us back to the children's nursery, for being located on the south (front) side of the Mansion, it happened to be one of the few rooms in the house with ideal window positioning for medical procedures.

We do not know how many operations took place in this room, but we do know what kind they were: amputations.

❧ AMPUTATIONS, ENDLESS SCREAMS, & PILES OF LIMBS

In transforming the nursery into an instant operating theater, the furniture was hurriedly removed, the carpet was rolled back, and hay was spread over the floor to soak up the blood. Doctors then quickly went at their horrific occupation: sawing off hundreds of irreparable hands, arms, feet, and legs. The shrieks of the soldiers echoed throughout Carnton Mansion that night, and in the days that followed.

Once a limb was removed, it was unceremoniously tossed out of the children's nursery window to the ground below, to make ready for the next patient.[1633] With horror, an injured eyewitness later said that he saw a mountain of amputated limbs piled nearly as high as the second-floor outside Carnton's southern windows, realizing that soon his own limb would be added.

Soldiers hauled these macabre remnants away for burial on a buckboard. But the heap of bloody arms and legs soon grew into mountainous proportions again.

1633. Surgeons worked on soldiers outside on Carnton's grounds as well.

The McGavocks of Carnton Plantation

❧ BUCKET RINGS & POOLS OF BLOOD

Tragically, nothing was known about hygiene at the time, and so dirty bandages were often used, and in between operations doctors simply rinsed their blood-soaked hands in buckets of water placed near the operating table: not to clean them, but to make them less slippery for holding their surgical instruments!

These medical tools, of course, were never sterilized but instead were dipped into the same buckets of water, then wiped down with dirty sponges.[1634] The circular marks left by these bloody pails full of odious, bacteria-laden fluids, called "bucket rings," can still be seen on the floor of Carnton's children's nursery.

Also still visible on the floor in this room are numerous reddish-brown stains from blood that drained off the operating tables. Seeping into the wooden floor over the next few weeks, they left permanent reminders of the horrors of November 30, 1864. As I often pointed out to my tour guests, there is even what looks like a bloody footprint near one of the windows.

❧ DOCTORS: THE REAL KILLERS AT FRANKLIN II

To make matters worse for the wounded Confederate soldiers who were taken to Carnton, bullets and shrapnel pierced sweaty grime-laden clothing, pushing the germs from these bits of cloth directly into their wounds.

With no knowledge of the role of bacteria, filthy wounds were never properly cleaned. Metal projectiles were simply dug from the entrance wounds with begrimed bullet-forceps and other various types of dirt-incrusted probes. The opening was then sewn up with unhygienic needles and thread, then bandaged over, often with bloody pre-used cloth.

With routine sanitation all but unknown, the wounded were then transferred in never-before-cleaned ambulances—or manure carts if none were available; hands were not washed with soap between

---

1634. Katcher, CWSB, p. 86.

THE MCGAVOCKS OF CARNTON PLANTATION

operations; fingers were not gloved; bedding was fouled and seldom laundered; and wounds were constantly dug at with dirty hands and filthy instruments, preventing healing.

Furthermore, surgeon's uniforms and gowns were heavily soiled, the recovered soldiers often left the hospital wearing the same wretched rags they had arrived in, and the operating table, sometimes with a dirt-encrusted rubber groundcloth thrown over it, was almost never cleaned between surgeries.

There were other problems that beset "Civil War" medicine as well.

Having received little training, many of the Confederacy's doctors and surgeons scarcely deserved the title. Indeed, overall, the Southern armies suffered from an appalling lack of medical staff. At the start of Lincoln's War, for example, the Confederate military had only twenty-four medical officers[1635] (this figure grew to a mere 3,400 by the end of the War). Additionally, unlike the Federal government, the Confederate government possessed no sanitary commission, a body that would have helped establish field hospitals on trains, formed women's medical aid societies, and distributed health and sanitation leaflets.[1636]

Not surprisingly patients received almost no post-operative care or attention. In those rare instances when water was used to wash out a wound, it was never boiled. Instead it was usually taken directly from a local creek or river, thoroughly contaminated with bacteria and water-borne parasites. Thus, instead of initiating the healing process, a large percentage of surgeries resulted in various infections, including gangrene, erysipelas, and pyemia, the latter affliction which killed nearly 100 percent of its victims.[1637]

Scalpels were usually dull, medical quarters rickety and temporary (often located right on the battlefield), and diagnosis was typically made by "intuition." In addition, painkillers were largely unavailable and medical supplies woefully inadequate (all due to Lincoln

---

1635. Civil War Society, ECW, s.v. "Medical Care, Battle Wounds and Disease."
1636. Eaton, HSC, 103.
1637. Katcher, CWSB, p. 86.

THE MCGAVOCKS OF CARNTON PLANTATION

and Yankee General Winfield Scott's "Anaconda Plan," part of which comprised his illegal blockade of Southern ports beginning on April 19, 1861).[1638]

It was no accident that Confederate doctors were known as "butchers," making a visit to a wartime hospital understandably more feared than a stint on the battlefield. Little wonder that at any one time at least 50 percent (or more) of a unit was "out of commission." Not due to battle wounds, but from bacterial infections of one kind or another.

Southerners rightly heaped abuse on Lincoln for his complicity in the villainous ill treatment of Confederate soldiers and citizens. One Rebel official, Captain Alfred W. Bell of the Thirty-ninth North Carolina Regiment, wrote: It is horrifying to witness the pain and agony visited on my people by Abraham Lincoln. I sincerely pray that he will rot in the fires of Hell for all eternity.[1639]

The families of the countless Southern boys and men who died unnecessarily from infections and sickness between 1861 and 1865 would have concurred.

None of this was helped by the fact that prior to being wounded, most Johnny Rebs were already suffering from inadequate nutrition and exposure to cold, wet, and heat.

Needless to say, it was not war wounds that killed most Confederate troops (injuries from swords and bayonets, for example, amounted to a mere one half of 1 percent of all wounds during the War).[1640] It was the bacterial infections that were spread from patient to patient by the doctors themselves. In fact, for every soldier injured on the field, five times that many became sick from infection. In short, three times as many soldiers died from disease than died from battle.[1641] Among Confederate troops at least two out of three perished, not from a Yankee bullet, but from illness, much if not most of it brought on by a trip to a military medical facility.[1642]

1638. Pritchard, pp. 104-105.
1639. Wiley, LJR, p. 244.
1640. Horwitz, p. 178.
1641. Eaton, HSC, p. 102.
1642. Civil War Society, ECW, s.v. "Medical Care, Battle Wounds and Disease."

THE MCGAVOCKS OF CARNTON PLANTATION

Unfortunately, thanks to the Yankee custom of bombing Southern courthouses and governmental buildings (where military records were kept), statistics on Confederate deaths are scarce and often inaccurate.[1643] Nonetheless, those from the Union side are helpful in understanding the role played by diseases caused by infections.

After the War Yankee authorities reported that while 41,238 U.S. soldiers died in battle and another 49,205 died from wounds, a staggering 186,216 perished from disease. This is over four times the number of the other two groups combined.[1644] Only God himself knows how many Southern men died from unsanitary conditions and unhygienic medical procedures. It was certainly in the many hundreds of thousands.

What we know for sure is that countless men had a limb amputated in Carnton's children's nursery who would have otherwise lived—except for one thing: the introduction of disease laden microbes into their bodies by well-meaning military surgeons; men armed not only with limited medical supplies due to Lincoln's illegal naval blockade, but with limited scientific knowledge as well.

❧ BULLETS 101

To highlight the nursery's role as a "Civil War" operating theater, a modern display has been placed in the room. The glass and wooden case contains various types of bullets used in 1864, a Yankee amputation kit, and a portable medical kit that was carried in one's pocket on and off the battlefield.

The bullets used in the War for Southern Independence were quite different from those we are familiar with today. Modern bullets are made of hard metals, and are elongated, smooth, and pointed at the tip. This is because they are designed for speed, accuracy, and penetration power; that is, for the purpose of making a fast clean kill.

Most "Civil War" bullets were designed with the opposite idea in mind. They traveled slowly in order to more easily hit a broad target, and also so they would stop as soon as they encountered any resistance.

1643. See e.g., Henry, ATSF, p. 188.
1644. Katcher, CWSB, p. 120.

The McGavocks of Carnton Plantation

The idea here was to halt one's opponent by seriously injuring him. To this end 19th-Century bullets were often:

- grooved with rings to diminish their speed.
- short and rounded to create drag and produce the largest wound possible.
- made of soft metals so they would mushroom upon penetrating the skin.

The sinister intention behind the unwieldy design of these bullets was to do the most damage to the enemy's body as possible; in other words, to maim then infect, rather than kill outright.[1645]

This truly evil design worked flawlessly, which is one reason why infections, not bullets themselves, killed the vast majority of men during Lincoln's War. At Carnton, for example, hundreds died during Franklin II while at least another 123 died inside Carnton's walls or on the grounds of the plantation of these exact types of infectious wounds.

❧ CARNTON'S INTERIOR WALLS

Near the corner of the children's nursery, behind the doorway, can be found a curious hole in the wall. This has been intentionally cut out to reveal the hardy brick structure of the interior walls.

On close examination one can see what appears to be bits of hair inside the plaster. Horse (and sometimes pig) hair was used as a cohesive medium to strengthen the plaster bond, very typical for the period.

❧ THE GIRLS' BEDROOM

Moving across the hall we come to what is known as the front guest room, although it is more likely that this room was originally used as a bedroom for the young girls in the family.

Because it is situated on the southern side of the house (in the southwest corner), where the light of day lasted the longest, it too was

---

1645. Katcher, CWSB, p. 59.

used as an operating theater on the afternoon of the Battle of Franklin II.

As such, blood stains can also be seen on the floor of this room by the windows and closets, and especially near the fireplace, where those recovering from surgery were no doubt placed to keep them warm. If you look closely you can see the bloody outline of an amputated leg permanently stained into the floorboards.

❧ DOLL BED, POYNOR CHAIR, & WASHSTAND

Among the notable Carnton McGavocks' items in this room are the doll bed and the small children's ladder-back chair, the latter which was probably made by master craftsman and former black servant, Richard "Dick" Poynor (1802-1882). Poynor's well-made furniture was a popular seller in the 1800s, and today is considered quite valuable, particularly as an example of fine 19th-Century African-American workmanship.

Other McGavock heirlooms can also be seen in the girls' bedroom, such as the bed, the marble-topped dresser and mirror, and the marble-topped washstand, all from the McGavocks at Riverside Plantation, located southeast a short distance across the Harpeth River.

The bed has a unique feature that was highly appreciated by the McGavocks and other Victorians: the headboard can be removed. The purpose? To allow greater air movement around the bed on hot Summer nights.

The blanket chest at the foot of the bed was made around 1800, while the chest on the southern wall cleverly serves a dual function as both a dresser and a writing desk.

❧ THE RELIGIOUS LESSON IN CARNTON'S DOORS

Carnton's interior doors were originally painted by Randal to look like more expensive mahogany wood. But as part of Colonel John's modernization in the late 1840s and early 1850s, most of them were eventually painted over in solid colors. The paint on the door of the girl's bedroom, however, has been removed so the original 1830s woodgrain is once again visible.

While on the topic of Carnton's doors, it is interesting to note that most of them bear what is known as the Cross and Bible Motif, and the door on the girls' bedroom is no exception. Even a casual look at the door will show a large cruciform design in the upper half and what looks like an open Bible in the lower one.

Religious conservative Victorians, like the McGavocks, not only wanted to maintain an aura of godliness in their homes, they also wanted to remind family members and guests to keep their minds on "the things of the Lord." What better way to accomplish this than to carve into each and every doorway two of the most vital Christian symbols: the crucifix of Jesus and the Good Book.

The Cross and Bible Motif did not fade away with the end of the Victorian Period in 1901.[1646] Look around your own home. Odds are, even in the 21st Century, you will find that one or more of your doors also contain this well-known and much beloved Christian pattern.

❧ THE GUEST BEDROOM

At the back of the house, at the northwestern corner, lies the guest bedroom, also known as the back guest room. Here overnight visitors could freshen up, rest, read, and sleep in splendiferous luxury in one of the South's most magnificent antebellum homes. One of the luxuries provided here were chamber pots, so guests would not have to journey to the outhouse in the middle of the night.

While it is said that Andrew Jackson may have slept in this room, other events were not so happy, such as when Colonel John's mother Sarah Dougherty Rodgers passed away here in 1858.

Like all of the furniture on the second floor the guest room furniture is from the antebellum period. The arrowback Windsor chairs, for example, date from about 1825, while the room's table is from around 1790. The only original piece is the cherry chest, built around 1830.

The room contains a curious item that often goes unnoticed by most: the original door lock. It has been installed upside down. Why?

1646. The Victorian Period generally follows the birth and death of England's Queen Victoria, who was born in 1819 and died in 1901. All of the Carnton McGavocks were Victorians.

THE MCGAVOCKS OF CARNTON PLANTATION

The construction workers who built Carnton ran out of the proper locks by the time they reached this part of the house. There was one left, but it could only be fitted to the door upside down.

❧ THE PROBLEM OF LIGHT

Because light was scarce in this rear north-facing room, the McGavocks probably utilized a traditional interior decorator's trick to counteract the problem.

On the wall today there is a reproduction of period wallpaper that is meant to capture light and reflect it back into the room. In this way even the minimal amount of natural light coming in through the windows is mirrored outward, illuminating the entire bedroom in a soft hue. On a sunny afternoon it is a truly amazing sight.

❧ CARRIE'S CEMETERY JOURNAL & ANOTHER JIB WINDOW

Carrie's Confederate cemetery journal is usually kept here in the guest bedroom in a glass display case. Considered the plantation's most precious item, it is a record of the re-burials of nearly 1,500 Rebel soldiers in the graveyard at the northwest corner of Carnton's property in April 1866.

Contrary to myth, Carrie played no role in the actual re-interment of the soldiers. And though family tradition states otherwise, she also did not record the data in what is now known as her "Cemetery Journal." A Franklinite, George W. Cuppet, who headed the reburial effort, chronicled the information in "Carrie's book," and later passed the sacred work onto the McGavocks for safekeeping.[1647]

The little book got its name from the fact that Carrie eventually became the one primarily responsible for maintaining both the cemetery and its records. (All of the information in Carrie's Cemetery Journal, including a complete list of the dead, can be found in my book *Carnton Plantation Ghost Stories*.)

1647. George W. Cuppet's surname is sometimes also spelled Cuppett or Cuppert.

THE MCGAVOCKS OF CARNTON PLANTATION

Like the children's nursery, the guest bedroom also possesses one of Carrie's jib windows leading out to the back porch. An original Carnton McGavock item in this room is the 1830s cherry chest. The cherry worktable, made in Tennessee, probably once belonged to the Riverside McGavocks.

ᴥ THE SITTING ROOM

There is a small room located on the south side (front) of the house in the middle of the second floor, variously referred to as the ladies' sitting room, the sitting room, or simply the second-floor study. The only jib window at the front of the Mansion is located here (it was added during Colonel John's modernization process), allowing admission to the small second-floor Greek Revival porch on the house's facade.

It is not known what the exact function of this room was, but over the decades it was no doubt used for a variety of purposes, including sewing, storage, reading, relaxing, dressing, napping, studying, and writing. There are some indications that at one point Carrie used this space as an office. It is also quite likely that the McGavock children were given their educational lessons in the sitting room during the War, when Franklin's schools were suspended.

The smallest proper room at Carnton Mansion, it is the only one without a fireplace. The two side chairs here are original to the house.

ᴥ THE ATTIC

Carnton's guests are quite curious about the attic on the third floor, but are forbidden from entering it. At their request I used to take some of my more inquisitive tour guests to this floor after hours. The attic actually contains nothing more that two unfinished rooms that today are used for storage.

What did the McGavocks use it for? As mentioned earlier, there are indications that it sometimes served as a ballroom for entertaining, dancing, and music. A smaller room set in the back seems to be have been used as a gentlemen's "drinking and refreshment room." After Carnton's halcyon days had passed with the death of Colonel John in 1893, the attic was probably transformed into a permanent storage area.

The McGavocks of Carnton Plantation

❧ THE MYSTERY OF THE UNFINISHED THIRD FLOOR

As far as we know, the McGavocks never completed decorating and furnishing the third floor, and it has remained in a rather crude state ever since. This could indicate that originally they never intended it to be used for anything but storage.

There is evidence to support this: not only does the attic contain no fireplaces (making it unsuitable for bedrooms), but the McGavocks only hung wallpaper on the eastern wall of the third floor, from the top of the stairs to the left doorway. The purpose? When someone looks up at the third floor while climbing the stairway from the first to the second floor, the attic looks finished. More Scottish-Irish penny-pinching.

The remnants of this upside down wallpaper, which can still be seen, are original, and, as discussed, an exact reproduction has been hung, also upside down, in the ladies' parlor downstairs on the first floor.

While the unfinished third floor would seem to be quite benign, some who have visited it say that it has an eerie, even sinister feeling about it. I myself have experienced the same thing in the attic on more than one occasion. One wonders if something terrible occurred here many years ago. A psychic walk-through could be revealing.

This ends our tour of both the interior of Carnton Mansion and of the plantation itself.

PART THREE

The McGavock Confederate Cemetery

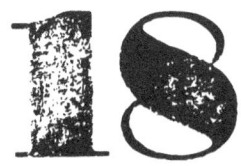

Where Some of the South's Finest Rest in Faded Glory

❧ REMEMBERING THOSE LOST AT THE BATTLE OF FRANKLIN II

THE 2nd BATTLE OF FRANKLIN left deep scars in Williamson County, a trauma that has lasted to this day. For not only did literal Hell come to Franklin that Fall afternoon in 1864, many of those who fell at Franklin II were the sons, husbands, brothers, fathers, uncles and grandfathers of local families, literally shot and killed in front of their own homes. Those "noble and brave spirits" who gave their lives for the Southern Cause that day, Watkins called them.[1648]

The McGavocks did their part to help heal the psychological and emotional trauma left over from these deaths, as the following story illustrates.

❧ THE STORY OF TOD CARTER

One Franklinite who perished that day was a youth named Captain Theodrick "Tod" Carter, like myself, a cousin of General Robert E.

1648. Watkins, p. 212.

THE MCGAVOCKS OF CARNTON PLANTATION

Lee.[1649] On Wednesday, November 30, 1864, after two years of service in the Confederate army, the young officer was finally nearing home again, though it was not the homecoming he would have preferred.

Instead, he was charging uphill toward his parents' house on Columbia Pike amid a hail of whistling Minié balls, his throat burning from acrid powder smoke, his eyes blinded by haze, his ears deafened by the powerful booms of cannon.[1650] Despite this, Tod was no doubt cheered by the sight of his childhood domicile in the murky distance.

Inside his family's Franklin house, which, unfortunately *and illegally*, had been commandeered by the Union as its temporary headquarters,[1651] were seventeen people, including his father, Fountain Branch Carter,[1652] an elder brother, Colonel Moscow Branch Carter (C.S.A.), four of his sisters, a daughter-in-law, a number of grandchildren, and several female servants. Members of the family of Johann Albert Lotz[1653] from across the street had also fled to the Carter House.[1654]

Reassured by an arrogant Yankee commander, General Jacob Dolson Cox (1828-1900) of the Twenty-third Army Corps, that Hood would never be foolish enough to attack over an open field, the entire group remained instead of seeking safer ground. They would come to regret their decision.

Between 3:30 and 4:00 P.M. that afternoon, Hood both infuriated his troops and dumbfounded the enemy by launching an unexpected offensive assault across the Franklin Plain. As the conflict exploded into life, the left Confederate flank inevitably began to surge northwest, toward the Carter House, Cox's headquarters, in an attempt

---

1649. From my personal family tree. Gen. Robert E. Lee has a number of other famous relations, among them the actor Lee Marvin (1924-1987), who was named after Gen. Lee, and famed 1930s-1940s screen legend, Margaret Sullavan (1911-1960). Davenport, pp. 120-127.
1650. The Minié ball was named after its co-designer, French army officer, Captain Claude-Etienne Minié (1804-1879). The surname, like the ball, is pronounced minn-YAY.
1651. Cox, p. 53.
1652. Tod's mother, Mary Armistead Atkinson (b. 1806), was not present, having died twelve years earlier, in 1852.
1653. The German surname Lotz rhymes with "oats."
1654. The Lotz House remains standing to this day. Considered to be Franklin's most beautifully restored and preserved antebellum home, it is open for public tours. Website: www.lotzhouse.com.

THE MCGAVOCKS OF CARNTON PLANTATION

to cut off the Yankee command.

Culminating around the Carter family's nearby cotton gin house just to the southeast, the shooting and shelling lasted well into the early evening, leaving terrible carnage on both sides. The Yanks savagely dismantled the thirty-six square foot Carter gin and used the materials in the making of their breastworks. But most of the other buildings on the Carters' property survived, and to this day the bullet holes from that terrible day and night are still visible.[1655]

❧ DECEMBER 1, 1864

At dawn the next morning, Thursday, December 1, Franklin's citizens, and what was left of the Confederate Army of Tennessee, awoke to begin the sorrowful task of searching the battlefield for the wounded and dead. What a horrific scene greeted their eyes, as they peered through tears at the devastation, the ground stained red for miles in every direction, rivulets and even streams of blood flowing off the battlefield.

The author's cousin, Hardin Perkins Figuers (1849-1912),[1656] who was fifteen at the time, and who watched much of the battle from a tree in his front yard, later noted that there were so many injured and deceased soldiers on the ground that one could walk across the entire battlefield without ever setting foot on soil.[1657]

A soldier from Alabama wrote: Of all the battlefields I have seen not one of them compares to Franklin II. The ground is blanketed with the dead and the breastworks are overflowing with them.[1658] The Alabamian was, if anything, understating the situation, for other eyewitnesses report that many of the ditches around Franklin were piled with Rebel bodies seven deep.[1659]

After the battle Yankee Captain John K. Shellenberger wandered the field seeking wounding Union soldiers. Years later he wrote of the incident in this horrific account:

1655. Weeks, pp. 128-129.
1656. Hardin descends from my Harding family, of Belle Meade Plantation.
1657. Brandt, p. 117.
1658. McMurry, p. 176.
1659. Woodworth, p. 301.

The McGavocks of Carnton Plantation

> . . . as I stepped up into the embrasure, the sight that met my eyes was most horrible even in the dim starlight. The mangled bodies of the dead rebels were piled up as high as the mouth of the embrasure, and the [Union] gunners said that repeatedly when the lanyard was pulled the embrasure was filled with men, crowding forward to get in, who were literally blown from the mouth of the cannon. Only one rebel got past the muzzle of that gun and one of the gunners snatched up a pick leaning against the breastwork and killed him with that. Captain Baldwin of this battery [Sixth Ohio] has stated that as he stood by one of his guns, watching the effect of its fire, he could hear the smashing of the bones when the missiles tore their way through the dense ranks of the approaching rebels.
>
> While I was cautiously making my way around one side of that heap of mangled humanity, a wounded man lying at the bottom, with head and shoulders protruding, begged me for the love of Christ to pull the dead bodies off him. The ditch was piled promiscuously with the dead and badly wounded and heads, arms, and legs were sticking out in almost every conceivable manner. The ground near the ditch was so thickly covered with bodies that I had to pick my steps carefully to avoid treading on some of them. The air was filled with the moans of the wounded; and the pleadings for water and for help of some of those who saw me were heartrending.[1660]

In his book *Company Aytch*, Watkins' bone-chilling description of that "dark and dismal day" has understandably gone down in history as the most famous of all. Watkins noted that, though a writer, he had no words to accurately describe Franklin II, and wished that he did not have to write about it, let alone remember it:

> I cannot describe it. It beggars description. I will not attempt to describe it. I could not. The death-angel was there to gather its last harvest. It was the grand coronation of death. Would that I could turn the page. But I feel, though I did so, that page would still be there, teeming with its scenes of horror and blood.[1661]

[1660]. Shellenberger, pp. 33-34.
[1661]. Watkins, p. 209.

THE MCGAVOCKS OF CARNTON PLANTATION

One of the bodies Watkins may have spotted as he scoured the blood-soaked Plain of Franklin that day was that of twenty-four year old Tod Carter, who was found a mere 150 yards from his house, pierced by nine bullets, one over his left eye. Though unconscious, he was still breathing. He was carried back to his home where he died the next day surrounded by grieving family members.

Tod was one of the few veterans of the Battle of Franklin II who was not buried at the McGavock Confederate Cemetery (he was interred across town in Franklin's Rest Haven Cemetery).[1662] Yet his story was typical of hundreds of boys and men who fought and died in the senseless clash between the two old enemies, one a foreign and illicit invader on sovereign Southern land.

❧ BURYING & RE-BURYING THE DEAD

The morning Tod Carter was discovered was especially cold. The hard ground was in no condition for burying hundreds of mangled bodies. But the townspeople, along with men from Hood's army, had no choice but to dig as deep as they could. Over two days some 1,750 shallow graves were excavated during the darkest forty-eight hour period in Franklin's history.

❧ DISAPPEARANCE OF THE WOODEN GRAVE MARKERS

Of necessity many corpses were buried where they lay. Others were buried in long trenches, each grave spread over with a thin layer of dirt, along the south end of downtown Franklin.

A primitive wooden headboard, with what information was known about the deceased, was hammered into the frozen soil to serve as a marker. Everything was soon covered in a fine sheet of ice and snow as Nature purified the scene with her Winter garment of white.

The wooden plaques did not remain long, however. That Winter the weather was exceptionally frigid and Franklin's poor needed fire wood.[1663] According to Hattie McGavock's husband, Captain

---

[1662]. Rest Haven Cemetery's seven acres was donated by Franklin attorney John Marshall in 1855.
[1663]. V. M. Bowman, pp. 60-61.

THE MCGAVOCKS OF CARNTON PLANTATION

George L. Cowan, local blacks made numerous attacks on the headboards over the following weeks,[1664] and the soldiers' grave markers gradually began to disappear. It was in this way that many men who had formerly been identified became "unknowns."

❧ ORIGINS OF THE McGAVOCK CONFEDERATE CEMETERY

Nearly two years later, in April 1866, Colonel John decided that something needed to be done about the situation. To this end he donated two acres at what is now the northwest corner of Carnton, next to the McGavock family cemetery, to be used as an eternal resting place for the fallen Rebel heroes.[1665] John, along with various citizens of Franklin, helped raise the money to fund the reburial project.[1666]

A portion of an article from an old newspaper reveals some of the details of the process. The name of the newspaper and its date of publication are unknown:

> ... States, informing them of what was being done, and stating that all States who desired to contribute in honoring the memory of the brave dead were welcomed to send the association the cost—$2—of marking the graves of those from their State who fell in the battle and that these contributions would be used to form a fund for maintaining the cemetery in good order.
>
> Missouri's assessment, according to this plan, was $260, as her dead numbered 130. Through voluntary subscriptions, this sum was readily raised, the donators being as follows:
>
> Jasper County Camp, by Halliburton; R. R. Hutchinson, St. Louis; Edward Barton, Linneus Vincent Marmaduke, Sweet Springs; A. E. Asbury, Higginsville; R. H. Kieth, Kansas City; R. H. Stockton, St. Louis; Steve Cooper, Boonsboro; Robert McCulloch, St. Louis; J. N. Games, Triplett; S. M. Kennard, St. Louis...[1667]

1664. Logsdon, TATG, pp. 40-41.
1665. Crutchfield and Holladay, pp. 194-195.
1666. Logsdon, TATG, p. 40.
1667. This article, transcribed by the author, was provided courtesy of the Williamson County Public Library.

The McGavocks of Carnton Plantation

Similar fund-raising "associations" were no doubt formed in other Southern states represented at Franklin II.

Digging up the remains of nearly 2,000 corpses and carting them to Carnton for re-interment was a gargantuan and complex undertaking, especially since they had been in the ground for nearly a year and a half. Today we can scarcely imagine the horror of it. But the work went on. By the time the project was completed each new grave had been fitted with a fresh cedar headboard, with the graves themselves arranged by state.

On March 22, 1890, a committee, of whom one of the members was Captain Cowan, was put in charge of the cemetery. One of their first goals was to replace the already aging wooden headboards with granite headstones. This was accomplished by raising money from local contributions and from the various states whose men had perished at Franklin II.

The beautiful iron fence and gates surrounding the cemetery were later erected through the generous efforts of Mary Ann Gay of Macon, Georgia (whose step-brother is buried here).[1668] May her name, and those of the other contributors, be forever remembered.[1669]

❧ A CIVILIAN IS BURIED AT THE REBEL CEMETERY

One man who helped manage the project was Marcellus Cuppet (b. January 16, 1841), a brother to the reburial supervisor, George W. Cuppet. George was assigned this task because he was the son-in-law of William C. Collins (1823-1895), Carnton's manager during Lincoln's War, 1861-1865.[1670] Contrary to Carnton legend, Marcellus was not black, nor was he a former McGavock servant.[1671]

On April 26, 1866, Marcellus died of a heart attack in the middle of the work effort. Buried in the graveyard himself (in the Texas

---

1668. V. M. Bowman, p. 61.
1669. While a $2.00 per grave donation was requested from the other (twelve) Southern states to help bear the expenses, only four contributed: Missouri, Louisiana, South Carolina, and Mississippi.
1670. The wife of William W. Collins is Lucy Ellen Birch (1824-1909). The couple lived at Collins' Farm, located on what was once the northeastern edge of Carnton Plantation.
1671. Marcellus Cuppet's surname is also sometimes spelled Cuppett or Cuppert.

THE MCGAVOCKS OF CARNTON PLANTATION

section), he is the only civilian interred in the McGavock Confederate Cemetery.

❧ THOSE WHO WERE LOST

Tragically, not all of the Confederate soldiers who died at the Battle of Franklin II found their way into Carnton's burial ground. After the Battle of Nashville, where Hood racked up another 4,500 casualties, the Yankees, who had been occupying Franklin since the first engagement there on April 10, 1863, did a detailed survey of the town's battlefield and recorded 1,750 Rebel graves. Yet, today there are only 1,481 graves in the McGavock Confederate Cemetery. Why?

Excluding five generals who were buried elsewhere, at least two men who were subsequently removed by relatives, and at least one soldier who was buried in the cemetery later, at least 265 bodies were never found. The remains of these men still lay in the ground somewhere between Carnton Plantation and downtown Franklin.

Of the 1,481 men buried in the cemetery, only 780 are identifiable. Of the remaining 701, there are 558 unknowns and 143 with partial information, but not enough to positively identify the remains.

When the cemetery was completed in 1866 it was dedicated and opened to the public. It is unique in that it survives as the largest privately owned Confederate cemetery in the U.S. To this day the graveyard continues to be a popular pilgrimage site for traditional Southerners and Neo-Confederates, a role it took on even before the end of the 19th Century.[1672]

❧ THE UDC & SCV

Today the Confederate Cemetery at Carnton is owned by the McGavock Confederate Cemetery Corporation. Elected members of Franklin Chapter 14, United Daughters of the Confederacy (UDC), serve as trustees. The goal of the UDC trustees is to "preserve the cemetery and

---

1672. Crutchfield and Holladay, p. 220.

THE MCGAVOCKS OF CARNTON PLANTATION

to honor the soldiers buried there."[1673] The grounds of the cemetery are maintained by the Sons of Confederate Veterans (SCV), of which I am a member.[1674]

Note that while Mississippi contributed the most lives at Franklin II (a total of 424), you will not see a single marker for soldiers from Virginia, the only Southern state not represented. Why? At the time of the battle they were off fighting with Lee against the "Nero of the 19th Century," Yankee war criminal General William T. Sherman, in the Eastern theater.[1675]

In the 1903 book *History of Tennessee*, we find an elegant summation of the McGavock Confederate Cemetery:

> Col. John McGavock, one of the noblest of men, on whose magnificent estate the battle was partly fought, not only made his house a hospital for the wounded, but also gathered the dead and interred them with decent obsequies in a beautiful site adjoining his family cemetery, and in his will, devised the ground to be forever dedicated as a Confederate Cemetery. In all these offices of mercy, he was aided and inspired by his wife. Here sleep the heroes of Franklin, honored and lamented by friend and foe, while McGavock Cemetery, their resting place, remains, likewise, a monument to John McGavock and his honored wife.[1676]

1673. Mrs. Louise Beauchamp, President of Franklin Chapter 14, United Daughters of the Confederacy, personal correspondence.
1674. I descend from dozens of Confederate soldiers, one of whom was my 3rd great-grandfather, Elias Jent, Sr. (1810-1864). Elias fought with the Confederacy's First Regiment of the Thirteenth Kentucky Cavalry. As mentioned earlier, he and his wife, Rachel Cornett, my 3rd great-grandmother, were murdered in 1864 by Yankee soldiers while he was on furlough.
1675. For the complete indexed list of those buried at the McGavock's Confederate Cemetery, see my book: *Carnton Plantation Ghost Stories: True Tales of the Unexplained from Tennessee's Most Haunted Civil War House!*
1676. Garrett and Goodpasture, p. 231.

PART FOUR

McGavock Genealogy

The McGavock Family Tree

Carnton Plantation Line Only

Researched, Compiled, Written, and Edited by Lochlainn Seabrook
Copyright © 2008, 2011 Lochlainn Seabrook

KEY:
1) A cross (+) *after* a name indicates descent from European royalty.
2) A cross (+) *before* a name indicates a partner of the individual listed above.
3) Underlined names indicate individuals known to have lived at Carnton Plantation; others may have, but evidence is scarce or nonexistent.
4) abt: about
5) m: marriage
6) d: died
7) Bef: before

Note: For the complete McGavock family tree, see Appendix A. For the complete Winder family tree, see Appendix B.

Descendants of Randal McGavock

Founder of Carnton Plantation

Four Generations

1 **Randal McGavock**,+ Carnton Founder, b: June 20, 1766 in Rockbridge Co., VA; d: September 27, 1843 at Carnton Plantation, Franklin, Williamson Co., TN; Number of children: 7; Gender: Male; Burial: September 1843, McGavock Family Cemetery, Carnton Plantation, Franklin, TN (Note: Randal, a friend of President Andrew "Old Hickory" Jackson, was one of the wealthiest men in Middle TN; he was the 11th mayor of Nashville 1824-1825; came to Nashville in 1796 with his brother David, a surveyor, who laid out the border lines for Davidson County)
....+**Sarah Dougherty Rodgers**, b: April 01, 1786 at Max Meadows, Wythe Co., VA, or TN; m: February 28, 1811 in Nashville, TN (or Rockbridge, VA?); d: December 28, 1854 at Carnton Plantation, Franklin, Williamson Co., TN; Number of children: 7; Father: John Rodgers (b. 1747; served in the American Rev. War; buried at McGavock Family Cemetery, Carnton Plantation); Mother: Anne Phillips; Gender: Female; Burial: December 1854, McGavock Family Cemetery, Carnton Plantation, Franklin, TN (Note: Sarah was the sister-in-law of Felix Grundy; she was also a good personal friend of Rachel (Donelson) Jackson, the wife of President Andrew Jackson)

......2 **James Randal McGavock**,+ b: January 09, 1812 in TN; d: February 12, 1862; Number of children: 10; Gender: Male (Note: James owned beautiful Riverside Plantation, located just across the Harpeth River not far from Carnton; although James died before the Battle of Franklin II in November, 1864, his family watched the conflict from the windows of their home; Riverside still stands but is now privately owned)
.........+**Louisa C. Chenault**, b: August 07, 1813 in Bardstown, KY; m: November 01, 1832; d: February 12, 1885; Number of children: 10;

THE MCGAVOCKS OF CARNTON PLANTATION

Father: Stephen Chenault; Mother: Mary Eleanor Rodgers; Gender: Female (Note: Louisa's Mother was a sister of Ann Phillips Rodgers, wife of Felix Grundy, and of Sarah Dougherty Rodgers, wife of Mayor Randal McGavock, founder of Carnton)

............3 **Mary Ellen McGavock**,+ b: September 23, 1833; d: June 16, 1891; Number of children: 4; Gender: Female (Note: Mary and her husband Randal Milton Ewing were cousins)
...............+**Randal Milton Ewing**, b: June 01, 1829 in Williamson Co., TN; m: September 13, 1853; Number of children: 4; Father: Dr. Andrew B. Ewing; Mother: Eliza McDowell McGavock,+ Gender: Male

...................4 **Carrie Eliza Ewing**,+ b: September 17, 1854; Gender: Female
...................4 **Charles Andrew Ewing**,+ b: September 25, 1857; Gender: Male
....................+**Sarah Elizabeth Owen**, b: Abt. 1859; m: November 02, 1887; Gender: Female
...................4 **Francis McGavock Ewing**,+ b: December 26, 1861; Gender: Male
....................+**Eliza M. Marshall** b: Abt. 1863; m: January 19, 1892; Gender: Female
...................4 **William Frierson Ewing**,+ b: February 20, 1864; Gender: Male

...............3 **Sarah "Sallie" McGavock**,+ owned family Bible; b: March 12, 1837 d: September 29, 1863 Gender: Female
..................+**William Frierson**, b: Abt. 1835; m: June 05, 1830; Father: Hon. Irving Frierson; Gender: Male
...............3 **Maria Louisa McGavock**,+ b: May 09, 1839; d: June 26, 1842; Gender: Female
...............3 **Randal McGavock**,+ b: August 24, 1841; d: March 13, 1842; Gender: Male
...............3 **William Chenault McGavock**,+ b: March 04, 1843; Gender: Male
...............3 **Elizabeth Harding McGavock**,+ b: July 18, 1845; d:

THE MCGAVOCKS OF CARNTON PLANTATION

February 17, 1871; Gender: Female

................+**Edwin H. Douglas**, b: Abt. 1843; m: July 29, 1869; Father: Benjamin Douglass; Gender: Male

................3 **James Randal McGavock**,+ b: October 21, 1847; d: May 01, 1869; Gender: Male

................3 **Ann Louise McGavock**,+ b: September 09, 1849; d: October 07, 1862; Gender: Female

................3 **Stephen Chenault McGavock, Dr.**,+ b: December 18, 1851; d: December 04, 1881; Gender: Male (Note: he never married)

................3 **Van Winder McGavock, Sr.**,+ b: June 10, 1855 in Wythe Co., VA; d: 1934; Number of children: 10; Gender: Male

...................+**Cynthia Rodes Pointer**, b: June 30, 1863 in Williamson Co., TN; d. 1907; m: November 17, 1880; Number of children: 10; Father: Samuel Pointer; Mother: Cynthia R. Holland; Gender: Female

..................4 **James Randal McGavock**,+ b: August 15, 1881; Gender: Male

..................4 **Sallie Pointer McGavock**,+ b: January 25, 1883; Gender: Female

..................4 **Louisa McGavock**,+ b: June 12, 1884; Gender: Female

..................4 **Randal Ewing McGavock**,+ b: April 02, 1886; Gender: Male

..................4 **Van Winder McGavock, Jr.**,+ b: December 03, 1887; Gender: Male

..................4 **Samuel Pointer McGavock**,+ b: June 14, 1890; Gender: Male

..................4 **William McGavock McGavock**,+ b: August 15, 1892; Gender: Male

..................4 **Thomas Pointer McGavock**,+ b: July 23, 1893; Gender: Male

..................4 **Mary Ellen McGavock**,+ b: December 12, 1894; Gender: Female

..................4 **Cynthia Holland McGavock**,+ b: August 03, 1897; Gender: Female

THE MCGAVOCKS OF CARNTON PLANTATION

.......2 **William McGavock**,+ b: July 23, 1813 in TN; d: June 10, 1821; Gender: Male

.......2 **John W. McGavock, Col.**,+ Civil War Soldier, C.S.A.,+ b: April 02, 1815 in TN; d: June 07, 1893 in Franklin, Williamson Co., TN; Number of children: 5; Gender: Male; Burial: June, 1893, McGavock Family Cemetery, Carnton Plantation, Franklin, TN. (Notes: John owned Carnton during the Battle of Franklin II, Nov. 30, 1864; earlier he was an aide-de-camp to Gov. James K. Polk, who later became 11th President of US; John was a Col. of the TN militia during Lincoln's War; he saw no combat because he was assigned to run the Confederate Field Hospital at Carnton; a shy farmer but very political (he was a delegate to the 1860 Democratic National Convention); a die-hard Confederate, Southern traditionalist, and conservative; inherited Carnton at his Mother Sarah's death in 1854; his middle name was probably William or Williamson)

...........+**Caroline Elizabeth "Carrie" Winder**,+ b: September 9 (some sources say December 9), 1829, in MS, or Terrebonne Parish (sugar plantation near Thibodaux, La Fourche, or New Orleans), LA; m: December 06, 1848 at Ducros Plantation, Houma, Terrebonne Parish, LA; d: February 22, 1905, at her daughter Hattie's house, Franklin, Williamson Co., TN; Number of children: 5; Father: Van Perkins Winder, Sr.,+; Mother: Martha Ann Grundy; Gender: Female; Burial: February 1905, McGavock Family Cemetery, Carnton Plantation, Franklin, Williamson Co., TN. (Notes: Carrie was living at Carnton during the Battle of Franklin II, Nov. 30, 1864, at which time she cared for the wounded and dying; known as the "Good Samaritan of Williamson County" for her deep Christianity and her many good deeds; John and Carrie were 1st cousins, once removed)

..................3 **Martha Winder McGavock**,+ b: September 25, 1849 at Carnton Plantation, Franklin, Williamson Co., TN; d: March 19, 1862, at Carnton Plantation, Franklin, Williamson Co., TN, age twelve, of heart problems; Gender: Female; Burial: McGavock Family Cemetery, Carnton House Plantation, Franklin, Williamson Co., TN

..................3 **Mary Elizabeth McGavock**,+ b: March 28, 1851; d: January 26, 1858, while visiting relatives at Ducros Plantation, Houma, Terrebone Parish, LA, age six, of yellow fever; Gender: Female; Burial:

THE MCGAVOCKS OF CARNTON PLANTATION

McGavock Family Cemetery, Carnton House Plantation, Franklin, Williamson Co., TN

...............3 **John Randal McGavock**,+ b: June 05, 1854 at Carnton Plantation, Franklin, Williamson Co., TN; d: September 11, 1854, at Carnton Plantation, Franklin, Williamson Co., TN, age three months, of intestinal problems; Gender: Male; Burial: McGavock Family Cemetery, Carnton House Plantation, Franklin, Williamson Co., TN

...............3 **Harriet Young "Hattie" McGavock**,+ b: July 02, 1855, at Carnton Plantation, Williamson Co., TN; d: November 30, 1932 in Franklin, Williamson Co., TN? Number of children: 5; Gender: Female; Burial: Mt. Hope Cemetery, Franklin, Williamson Co., TN (Note: Hattie, her husband G. L. Cowan, and their children, lived in the little brown house, "Windermere," across the street from Carnton; it can still be seen to this day)

...................+**George Limerick Cowan, Lt.**, Civil War Soldier, C.S.A.; b: October 15, 1843 in Derry County, Ireland; m: January 03, 1884 in TN; d: September 18, 1919; Number of children: 5; Father: Robert Cowan; Mother: Margaret Limerick; Gender: Male; Burial: Mt. Hope Cemetery, Franklin, Williamson Co., TN (Note: the McGavock family Bible states that he was born Oct. 15, 1842, though other sources disagree with this date; George served under the famous Confederate Gen. Nathan Bedford Forrest)

........................4 **Carrie Winder Cowan**,+ b: October 12, 1884 in TN; d: Abt. 1950 in TN; Gender: Female

........................4 **John McGavock Cowan**,+ b: July 11, 1886 in TN; d: Abt. 1950 in TN; Gender: Male

........................4 **Leah Cowan**,+ b: August 18, 1888; Gender: Female

........................4 **Samuel Kincaid Cowan**,+ b: December 20, 1890 in TN; d. 1963; Gender: Male

........................4 **Winder McGavock Cowan**,+ b: August 18, 1892 in TN; Gender: Male

...............3 **Winder McGavock**,+ b: July 13, 1857 at Carnton Plantation, Franklin, Williamson Co., TN; d: June 03, 1907 at Carnton

THE MCGAVOCKS OF CARNTON PLANTATION

Plantation, Franklin, Williamson Co., TN; Number of children: 5; Gender: Male; Burial: June 1907, McGavock Family plot, Mt. Hope Cemetery, Franklin, Williamson Co., TN (Note: Winder inherited Carnton Plantation at his Mother Carrie's death in 1905)

................+**Susan Lee "Susie" Ewing**, b: April 04, 1863 in Brentwood, Williamson Co., TN; m: February 05, 1883 in TN; d: October 25, 1931, in Franklin, Williamson Co., TN? Number of children: 5; Father: Herbert Ewing; Mother: Sally Hughes; Gender: Female; Burial: October 1931, McGavock Family plot, Mt. Hope Cemetery, Franklin, Williamson Co., TN (Note: after Winder died in 1907 Susie moved with her remaining children to downtown Franklin; she sold Carnton Plantation in 1911, thus ending the McGavocks' 100 year ownership)

........................4 **Hattie McGavock**,+ b: April 06, 1884 in TN; Gender: Female

........................4 **Sallie Ewing McGavock**,+ b: December 07, 1885 in TN; Gender: Female

........................4 **John McGavock**,+ b: November 24, 1887 in TN; Gender: Male

........................4 **Martha Winder McGavock**,+ b: December 26, 1890 in TN; Gender: Female

........................4 **Winder McGavock, Jr.**,+ b: April 01, 1894 in TN; Gender: Male

..........2 _____ **(unnamed) McGavock**,+ b: September 25, 1816; d: September 25, 1816; Gender: Male

..........2 **Mary Cloyd McGavock**,+ b: September 04, 1817 in TN; d: October 23, 1862; Number of children: 2; Gender: Female

..............+**Joseph Branch Southall**, b: Abt. 1815 in NC; m: September 22, 1836; Number of children: 2; Father: _____ Southall; Mother: Patience Branch; Gender: Male

..................3 **Randal McGavock Southall**,+ b: July 17, 1837; d: 1866; Gender: Male (Note: he never married)

..................3 **Josephine P. Southall**,+ b: February 12, 1839; d: January 27, 1862; Gender: Female (Note: she never married)

THE MCGAVOCKS OF CARNTON PLANTATION

..........2 **Elizabeth Irwin McGavock**,+ b: May 17, 1819 in TN; d: August 09, 1867; Number of children: 6; Gender: Female

..............+**William Giles Harding, Gen.**, b: September 15, 1808 in Nashville, Davidson Co., TN; d: December 15, 1886 in Nashville, Davidson Co., TN; m: January 02, 1840 at Carnton Plantation, Franklin, TN; Number of children: 7; Father: John Harding; Mother: Susannah Shute; Gender: Male (Note: William built and owned the beautiful thoroughbred farm, Belle Meade Plantation, near Nashville, TN, which had a national reputation for raising the best blooded livestock, especially horses; to this day Belle Meade is considered a sister plantation to Carnton)

......................3 **Selene Harding**,+ b: April 05, 1846; d: December 13, 1892; Gender: Female

...........................+**William Hicks "Red" Jackson, Gen.** C.S.A., b: October 1, 1835; d: March 30, 1903; m: December 15, 1868; Gender: Male

......................3 **Sarah Susan Harding**,+ b: October 15, 1847; d: July 06, 1848; Gender: Female

......................3 **Mary Elizabeth Harding**,+ b: February 05, 1850; Gender: Female

..........................+**Howell E. Jackson**, b: Abt. 1848; m: April 30, 1874; Gender: Male

......................3 **William R. Harding**,+ b: September 16, 1854; d: March 18, 1855; Gender: Male

......................3 **M. Louise Harding**,+ b: January 02, 1856; d: October 30, 1860; Gender: Female

......................3 _____ **(unnamed) Harding**,+ b: October 09, 1860; d: October 30, 1860; Gender: Female

................2 _____ **(unnamed) McGavock**,+ b: April 1821 in TN; d: April 1821; Gender: Female

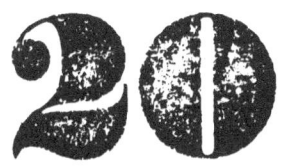

A Royal McGavock Family Tree

From Robert the Bruce King of Scotland to Colonel John W. McGavock

Carnton Plantation Line Only

Researched, Compiled, Written, and Edited by Lochlainn Seabrook
Copyright © 2008, 2011 Lochlainn Seabrook

NOTES:

1) A cross (+) *after* a name indicates descent from European royalty.

2) The McGavocks and the Winders descend from multiple royal families, thousands in fact, far too many to list in a book of this nature. The following royal McGavock tree, showing Colonel John W. McGavock's direct descent from Robert the Bruce King of Scotland, is just one example. What is more, the colonel descends from most of his royal lines in more than one way, in some cases, many dozens of times.

3) The number of children listed is not always accurate (for many are unknown), particularly for earlier parents.

Direct Line of Descent

Nineteen Generations

1 **Robert I (& VIII) "the Bruce" Bruce, King of Scotland**,+ b: July 11, 1274, in Writtle, Turnberry Castle, near Chelmsford, Essex Co., England; d: June 07, 1329, in Cadross, Dunbartonshire, Scotland (of leprosy); Number of children: 3; Father: Robert the Bruce VII, Earl Carrick of Scotland (1243-1304); Mother: Margaret, Countess Carrick of Scotland (1256-1290); Gender: Male; Burial: 1329 Abbey Church, Dunfermline, Fifeshire, Scotland

…+**Isabelle Lady Matilda, Queen of Scotland**,+ b: 1278 in Castle Kildrummy, Aberdeenshire, Scotland; m: 1296; d: 1320; Number of children: 1; Father: Donald 6th Earl of Mar Scotland,+ Mother: Elen (Helen) Verch Llewelyn of Wales+; Gender: Female

..2 **Marjorie Bruce, Princess of Scotland**,+ b: 1297 in Scotland; d: March 02, 1315/16 in Knock between Renfrew and Paisley, Scotland; Number of children: 1; Gender: Female; Burial: Paisley Abbey

….+**Walter Stewart, "the Young" VI High Stewart Scotland**,+ b: 1293 in Dundonald, Kyle, Ayrshire, Scotland; m: March 02, 1314/15 in Scotland; d: April 09, 1326 in Bathgate Castle, Bathgate, West-Lothian, Scotland; Number of children: 2; Father: James Stewart, 5th Steward of Scotland,+ Mother: Cecilia De Burgh, of Dunbar; Gender: Male; Burial: Paisley, Scotland

…3 **Robert II Stewart "the Bruce" King of Scotland**,+ b: March 02, 1315/16 in Paisley, Scotland; d: May 13, 1390 in Dundonald Castle, Dundonald, Ayrshire, Scotland; Number of children: 10; Gender: Male; Burial: 1390; Scone Abbey, Scone,

The McGavocks of Carnton Plantation

Perthshire, Scotland
..... +**Elizabeth Muir Queen of Scotland**, b: 1317 in Rowallan, Argyll, Scotland; m: November 22, 1337 in Kyle, Argyll, Scotland; d: 1355 in Rowallan, Argyll, Scotland; Number of children: 7; Father: Adam Muir, Knight; Mother: Joanna Danzielstour; Gender: Female; Burial: 1355 Paisley Chapel, Renfrew, Scotland

....4 **Robert "the Regent" Stewart, III King of Scotland**,+ b: 1337 in Dundonald, Ayrshire, Scotland; d: April 04, 1404 in Rothsay Castle, Dundonald, Ayrshire, Scotland; Number of children: 12; Gender: Male; Burial: Dunfermline, Fifeshire, Scotland
.......+**Muriella Keith**, b: Abt. 1351 in Argyllshire, Scotland; Number of children: 3; Father: William Keith; Gender: Female

.....5 **Marjory (Marcellina) Stewart, Lady**,+ b: Abt. 1375 in Lorn, Argyllshire, Scotland; d: Bef. January 1422/23; Number of children: 1; Gender: Female
........+**Duncan "Na Adh" Campbell, Sir**, b: 1400 in Lochow, Argyllshire, Scotland; m: February 06, 1391/92 in Lorn, Argyllshire, Scotland; d: 1453; Number of children: 1; Father: Colin "Iongantach" Campbell; Mother: Margaret (Mary, Mariota) Campbell; Gender: Male; Burial: Kilmun, Argyllshire, Scotland

......6 **Archibald Campbell, I**, **Master of Lochawe, Scotland**+ b: Abt. 1400 in Lochow, Argyllshire, Scotland; d: Aft. April 1431; Number of children: 1; Gender: Male; Burial: Kilmun, Argyllshire, Scotland
.........+**Elizabeth Somerville**, b: Abt. 1413 in Carnwath, Lanarkshire, Scotland; m: Abt. 1430 in Lanarkshire, Scotland; d: 1440; Number of children: 1; Father: John Somerville, II Lord Somerville Carnwarth; Mother: Helen Hepburn, of Hailes; Gender: Female

THE MCGAVOCKS OF CARNTON PLANTATION

.......7 **Colin Campbell**,+ b: Abt. 1433 in Lochow, Argyllshire, Scotland; d: May 10, 1493; Number of children: 3; Gender: Male

..........+ **Elizabeth Stewart**,+ b: Abt. 1430 in Lorn, Argyllshire, Scotland; m: Abt. 1455 in Argyllshire, Scotland; d: October 26, 1510 in Dunbartonshire, Scotland; Number of children: 3; Father: John "Mourach" Stewart, Sir,+ Mother: Isabel De Ergadia,+ Gender: Female; Burial: Kilmun, Argyllshire, Scotland

........8 **Archibald Campbell 2nd Earl of Argyl**,+ b: Abt. 1466 in Lochow, Argyllshire, Scotland; d: September 09, 1513 in battle of Floden, Kirknewton, Northumberland, England; Number of children: 4; Gender: Male; Burial: Kilmun, Argyllshire, Scotland

...........+ **Elizabeth Stewart**,+ b: Abt. 1456 in Inchmurrin Castle, Inchmurrin Isle, Dunbartonshire, Scotland; m: Abt. 1474 in Lennox, Scotland; Number of children: 4; Father: John Stewart, Lord Darnley,+ Mother: Margaret Montgomery; Gender: Female

.........9 **Dugal Campbell, I**,+ b: Abt. 1475 in Inverary, Argyleshire Co., Scotland; Number of children: 1; Gender: Male

............+ **Clara Sedalia Campbell**, b: Abt. 1480 in Glenorchy, Argyleshire Co., Scotland; m: Abt. 1499 in Inverary, Argyleshire Co., Scotland; Number of children: 1; Gender: Female

..........10 **Duncan Campbell**,+ b: Abt. 1500 in Inverary, Argyleshire Co., Scotland; Number of children: 1; Gender: Male

...............+ _____ _____?; b: Abt. 1502; Number of children: 1; Gender: Female

THE MCGAVOCKS OF CARNTON PLANTATION

............11 **Patrick Campbell**,+ b: Abt. 1530 in Drumbroden, Londonderry, Ireland; d: in Inverary, Argyleshire Co., Scotland; Number of children: 1; Gender: Male
................+ _____ _____?; b: Abt. 1532; Number of children: 1; Gender: Female

.............12 **Hugh Campbell**,+ b: Abt. 1560 in Drumbroden, Londonderry, Ireland; d: in Inverary, Argyleshire Co., Scotland; Number of children: 1; Gender: Male
.................+ **Mary Graham**, b: Abt. 1562; Number of children: 1; Gender: Female

.............13 **Andrew Campbell**,+ b: 1609 in Drumbroden, Londonderry, Ireland; d: in Inverary, Argyleshire Co., Scotland; Number of children: 1; Gender: Male
.................+ **Mary Rice**, b: Abt. 1612 in Belfast, County Antrim, Ireland; Number of children: 1; Gender: Female

...............14 **Duncan Campbell**,+ b: 1645 in Inverary, Argyleshire Co., Scotland; d: Abt. 1705 in Ulster, Ireland   Number of children: 1; Gender: Male
...................+**Mary McCoy**, b: 1648 in Inverary, Argyleshire Co., Scotland; m: 1672; d: Abt. 1705; Number of children: 1; Gender: Female

................15 **John Campbell**,+ b: November 16, 1674 in Drumboden, Kilmachrenan, Donegal, Northern Ireland; d: 1741 in Augusta Co., VA; Number of children: 2; Gender: Male
....................+**Grizella Hay**, b: Abt. 1677 in County Antrim, Northern Ireland; m: 1695 in Ulster, Northern Ireland; Number of children: 2; Father: Patrick Hay; Mother: _____ _____? Gender: Female

THE MCGAVOCKS OF CARNTON PLANTATION

................16 **Margaret Campbell**,+ (the author's Campbell line) b: Abt. 1707 in Drumboden, Kilmacrenan, County Donegal, Ulster Province, Northern Ireland; d: March 1764, murdered by Shawnee Indians, along with her son Joseph's wife and her & Joseph's son John, about 5 miles west of the town of Fincastle, VA; Number of children: 3; Gender: Female

...................+**David Cloyd, Sr.**, b: 1710 in New Castle Co., DE, or Ulster, Northern Ireland; m: 1726 in Rockbridge Co., VA; d: April 04, 1792 in Rockbridge Co., VA; Number of children: 3; Father: James Cloyd; Mother: _____ _____? Gender: Male; Burial: Back Creek, Pulaski Co., VA

................17 **Mary "Sally" Cloyd**,+ (the author's 8th cousin) b: March 14, 1740/41 in Rockbridge Co., VA, or New Castle, DE; d: 1827 in Reed Creek, Wythe Co., VA; Number of children: 10; Gender: Female

...................+**James "Dada" McGavock, Sr., Capt.**, American Rev. War; b: 1728 in Near Glenarm, County Antrim, Northern Ireland; m: February 20, 1760 in Augusta Co., VA; d: March 22, 1812 in log "Mansion House" at Max Meadows, Wythe Co., VA; Number of children: 10; Father: Hugh McGavock; Mother: Margaret _____? Gender: Male; Burial: 1812 McGavock Cemetery, Ft. Chiswell, Wythe Co., VA

................18 **Randal McGavock**,+ Founder of Carnton Plantation, 11th Mayor of Nashville+ b: June 20, 1766 in Rockbridge Co., VA; d: September 27, 1843 in Carnton Plantation, Franklin, Williamson Co., TN; Number of children: 7; Gender: Male; Burial: September 1843 McGavock Family Cemetery, Carnton Plantation, Franklin, TN

...................+**Sarah Dougherty Rodgers**, b: April 01, 1786 in Max Meadows, Wythe Co., VA, or TN; m: February 28, 1811 in Nashville, Tennessee (or Rockbridge, VA?); d: December 28, 1854 in Carnton Plantation, Franklin, Williamson Co., TN; Number of children: 7; Father: John Rodgers, served in

THE MCGAVOCKS OF CARNTON PLANTATION

American Revolutionary War; Mother: Anne Phillips; Gender: Female; Burial: December 1854 McGavock Family Cemetery, Carnton Plantation, Franklin, TN

..................19 **John W. McGavock, Col.**, War for Southern Independence, C.S.A.+ b: April 02, 1815 in Nashville, Davidson Co., TN; d: June 07, 1893 in Carnton Plantation, Franklin, Williamson Co., TN; Number of children: 5; Gender: Male; Burial: June 1893 McGavock Family Cemetery, Carnton Plantation, Franklin, Williamson Co., TN

..........................+**Caroline Elizabeth "Carrie" Winder**,+ b: September 9 (some sources say December 9), 1829, in MS, or Terrebonne Parish (sugar plantation near Thibodaux, La Fourche, or New Orleans), LA; m: December 06, 1848 at Ducros Plantation, Houma, Terrebonne Parish, LA; d: February 22, 1905, at her daughter Hattie's house, Windermere, Franklin, Williamson Co., TN; Number of children: 5; Father: Van Perkins Winder, Sr., +; Mother: Martha Ann Grundy; Gender: Female; Burial: February 1905, McGavock Family Cemetery, Carnton Plantation, Franklin, Williamson Co., TN.

THE MCGAVOCKS OF CARNTON PLANTATION

Stone marker for one of the hundreds of unknown Rebel soldiers buried at the McGavock Confederate Cemetery, Franklin, Tennessee. (Photo © Lochlainn Seabrook)

APPENDICES

Appendix A

A Complete McGavock Family Tree

Researched, compiled, and edited by Lochlainn Seabrook
Copyright © 2011 Lochlainn Seabrook

Notes: Living generations have been excluded to protect their privacy. Only primary McGavock individuals and their spouses in this family tree are listed in the book's Index.

KEY:
1) A cross (+) *after* a name indicates descent from European royalty.
2) A cross (+) *before* a name indicates a partner of the individual listed above.
3) abt: about
4) m: marriage
5) d: died
6) Bef: before

Descendants of Hugh McGavock

Eight Generations

1 Hugh McGavock, progenitor (earliest known McGavock ancestor), b: 1686 in Donegore, County Antrim, Ireland; Number of children: ?
+ _____ _____? b: abt. 1690, Ireland?
....2 Hugh McGavock, McGuffock, MacDaibhidh, b: Abt. 1700 in Galloway, Scotland (or near Glenarm, County Antrim, Northern Ireland); d: Bef. 1750 in Carntown/Carnton, near village of Glenarm, County Antrim, Northern Ireland; Number of children: ?
......+Margaret _____? b: Abt. 1705 in near Glenarm, County Antrim, Northern Ireland; d: in Carntown/Carnton, near village of Glenarm, Tickmacrevan Parish, County Antrim, Ireland; m: Abt. 1725; Number of children: ?

THE MCGAVOCKS OF CARNTON PLANTATION

......3 James "Dada" McGavock, Sr., Capt. in the Revolutionary War b: 1728 in Near Glenarm, County Antrim, Northern Ireland (came to America about 1757); d: 22 Mar 1812 in log "Mansion House" at Max Meadows, Wythe Co., VA (emigrated to Philadelphia, PA about 1755; moved to Augusta (now Rockbridge) Co., VA about 1757; settled at Fort Chiswell, Wythe Co., VA after 1760; fought in Revolutionary War); Number of children: 10

..........+Mary "Sally" Cloyd,+ b: 14 Mar 1741 in Rockbridge Co., VA, or New Castle, DE; d: 1827 in Reed Creek, Wythe Co., VA m: 20 Feb 1760 in Augusta Co., VA m: 20 Feb 1760 in Augusta Co., VA; Number of children: 10; Father: David Cloyd, Sr. Mother: Margaret Campbell,+

..........4 Hugh McGavock, Capt. Rev. War,+ b: 25 Sep 1761 in Max Meadows, Wythe Co., VA, or Rockbridge Co,. VA; d: 02 Apr 1844 in at his home at Max Meadows, Wythe Co., VA; Number of children: 12

...............+Nancy Kent,+ b: 11 Dec 1763 in Edgehill, Montgomery Co., VA; d: 10 Feb 1835 m: 29 Mar 1785 in Franklin, Williamson, Co., TN; Number of children: 12; Father: Jacob Kent; Mother: Mary Crockett,+

...............5 Joseph McGavock, Captain War of 1812,+ b: 14 Jun 1787 in Wythe Co., VA; d: 15 Jun 1853 in Carroll Co., KY; Number of children: 2

...................+Sally Hay, b: 18 Mar 1801 in Wytheville, Wythe Co., VA; d: 05 Mar 1837 m: Abt. 1835; Number of children: 2; Father: William Hay; Mother: Martha Buchanan

...................6 Martha McGavock,+ b: Abt. 1835; d: Abt. 1835
...................6 Sally McGavock,+ b: 1837; d: 1841

...............5 Mary "Aunt Polly" McGavock,+ b: 31 Aug 1788 in Wythe Co., VA; d: 15 Feb 1866; Number of children: 4

...................+Thomas Cloyd, b: 21 Aug 1774; d: 27 Jul 1849; m: 21 Sep 1809; Number of children: 4; Father: Joseph Cloyd, Col.; Mother: Elizabeth Gordon

...................6 Thomas Cloyd,+ b: 10 Apr 1815; d: 24 Sep 1817
...................6 Lucinda Cloyd,+ b: 21 Jul 1818; d: 18 Dec 1843
........................+Gordon C. Kent,+ b: 29 Jun 1806; d: 18 Sep 1869; m: Abt. 1840; Father: Joseph Kent, Col.,+; Mother: Margaret McGavock,+
...................6 Nancy Cloyd,+ b: 21 Mar 1820; d: 25 Apr 1825
...................6 David Cloyd,+ b: 27 Jan 1824 in Pulaski Co., VA; d: 07 Sep 1863 in Dunker Bottom, Pulaski Co., VA; Number of children: 3
........................+Elizabeth McDowell McGavock,+ b: 05 Oct 1826 in near Nashville, Davidson Co., TN; m: 20 Dec 1848; Number of children: 3; Father: Randal McGavock,+; Mother: Almira Haynes
........................7 Lucy T. Cloyd,+ b: 04 Jul 1850; d: July 1895
...............................+ Robert Barton, b: Abt. 1848; m: 25 Nov 1875
........................7 Catherine McGavock Cloyd,+ b: 07 Jul 1852; d: 09 May 1895

THE MCGAVOCKS OF CARNTON PLANTATION

..........................+ Haven B. Howe, b: Abt. 1850; m: 16 Apr 1873
.....................7 Mary David Cloyd,+ b: 01 Nov 1858; d: 22 Jun 1864
...............5 James McGavock,+ McGavock House, Nashville b: 28 Mar 1790 in Wythe Co., VA; d: 23 Jan 1841—brutally murdered near Nashville, Davidson Co., TN; Number of children: 14 (with two wives)
..................+ Lusinda Ewing, b: 10 Dec 1792 in Williamson Co., TN; d: 21 Apr 1848 m: 18 Dec 1810; Number of children: 8; Father: Alexander Ewing, Captain in the American Revolutionary War; Mother: Sally Smith (Note: although researchers spell her first name Lucinda, her gravestone spells it Lusinda)
..................6 Nancy Kent McGavock,+ b: 13 Nov 1813 in Williamson Co., TN; d: 29 Jan 1863; Number of children: 11
.....................+ Eldrige N. Claud, b: 03 Feb 1804; d: 01 Feb 1848 m: 17 Nov 1831; Number of children: 10; Father: Philip Claud; Mother: Susan Nusom
.....................7 Sarah Ann Claud, b: 15 Aug 1832
.....................7 Susan L. Claud, b: 10 Dec 1833
.....................7 Amanda M. Claud, b: 22 Dec 1835
.....................7 James William Claud, b: 12 Jan 1837
.....................7 Joshua D. Claud, b: 06 Jun 1838
.....................7 Nancy Tennessee Claud, b: 20 Dec 1839
.....................7 Mary Frances Claud, b: 05 Feb 1841
.....................7 Elizabeth J. W. Claud, b: 29 Mar 1842
.....................7 Philip Eldridge Claud, b: 21 Dec 1844
.....................7 Mary Tennessee Claud, b: 31 Dec 1846
..................*2nd Husband of Nancy Kent McGavock,+
.....................+William L. Buford, b: 05 Sep 1808; d: 1884 m: 24 Aug 1854; Number of children: ?
.....................7 Frances Helen Buford, b: 13 Sep 1855
..................6 Sarah M. McGavock,+ b: 11 Dec 1815 in Davidson Co., TN; d: 23 Dec 1836; Number of children: 2
.....................+Jonathan Bateman, b: 28 Apr 1805 in Williamson Co., TN; m: 28 Mar 1830; Number of children: 2; Father: William Bateman; Mother: Elizabeth Bateman
.....................7 Nancy T. Bateman, b: 13 Jan 1835
.....................7 Virginia F. Bateman, b: 05 Nov 1836
..................6 Melinda Winder McGavock,+ b: 19 Dec 1817; d: 23 Oct 1846; Number of children: 6
.....................+ James Smith, Jr., b: Abt. 1815; d: in near Franklin, Williamson Co., TN; m: 02 Oct 1833; Number of children: 6; Father: James Smith, Sr.; Mother: Mildred Turner
.....................7 Lucinda Ann Smith, b: 18 Jun 1834

The McGavocks of Carnton Plantation

..................7 Sarah M. Smith, b: 22 Jan 1837
..................7 Amanda Malvina Smith, b: 15 Jun 1839
..................7 Eliza Margaret Smith, b: 13 Feb 1841
..................7 James Joseph Smith, b: 25 May 1843
..................7 William Turner Smith, b: 19 Aug 1846
................6 Alexander Ewing McGavock,+ b: 25 Sep 1820; d: 01 May 1833
................6 Amanda M. McGavock,+ b: 02 Nov 1822; d: 31 Aug 1847; Number of children: 3
....................+Turner Smith, b: Abt. 1820; d: 25 Nov 1880 m: 08 Aug 1839 m: 08 Aug 1839; Number of children: 3; Father: James Smith, Sr.; Mother: Mildred Turner
..................7 James Alexander Smith,+ b: 02 Jun 1840
..................7 Lucinda J. Smith,+ b: 04 Sep 1842; d: 12 May 1869
........................+Robert F. Cotton, b: Abt. 1840; m: 19 Sep 1865
..................7 Amanda Mildred Smith,+ b: 05 Jan 1845; d: 12 Dec 1852
................6 Oscar Hugh McGavock,+ b: 03 Apr 1825 in Williamson Co., TN; d: 20 Feb 1860 in TN; Number of children: 7
....................+America N. Bryant, b: 15 Mar 1827 in TN; d: 26 Aug 1893 m: 22 May 1845; Number of children: 7; Father: William Bryant; Mother: America Williams
..................7 Lucinda Elizabeth McGavock,+ b: 22 Apr 1846; Number of children: 8
........................+R. L. Hamil, b: 30 Oct 1839; d: in Izard Co., AR? m: 20 Apr 1862; Number of children: 8; Father: William Hamil; Mother: Minerva Conyers
........................8 William O. Hamil, b: 27 Dec 1863
........................8 John Hamil, b: Abt. 1862
........................8 Olivia E. Hamil, b: 11 Apr 1868
........................8 Caroline Hamil, b: 18 Dec 1869
........................8 Elizabeth Hamil, b: 29 Jul 1872
........................8 Newton Hamil, b: 18 Mar 1875
........................8 Nannie L. Hamil, b: 08 Jul 1877
........................8 James S. Hamil, b: 25 Oct 1879
..................7 William McGavock,+ b: 18 Nov 1847
..................7 Hugh W. McGavock,+ b: 06 Jan 1850; Number of children: ?
........................+Joanna Howard, b: Abt. 1852; m: 16 Oct 1873; Number of children: ?
........................8 Ester Maud McGavock, b: 28 Jul 1875
..................7 Joseph C. McGavock,+ b: 13 Mar 1852; Number of children:

THE MCGAVOCKS OF CARNTON PLANTATION

3
..........................+H. A. Evans, b: 19 Jul 1856; m: 29 Jan 1874; Number of children: 3; Father: Malachi Evans; Mother: Elizabeth Scarborough
.........................8 James W. McGavock,+ b: Abt. 1874
.........................8 Emeline A. McGavock,+ b: 24 Sep 1876
.........................8 Robert E. Lee McGavock,+ b: 28 Dec 1879
......................7 George McGavock,+ b: 17 Dec 1853
......................7 James P. McGavock,+ b: 12 Jul 1856; Number of children: ?
..........................+ Tinnie _____? b: 22 Apr 1875; d: 11 May 1906; Number of children: ?
.........................8 Hugh McGavock, b: 1884 in Granite, Greer Co., OK; d: in Granite, Greer Co., OK
......................7 Oscar Hugh McGavock,+ b: 25 Dec 1859
..................6 Eliza Jane McGavock,+ b: 12 Dec 1827 in Williamson Co., TN; d: 14 Jun 1868; Number of children: 8
......................+ George Washington Armstrong, b: 02 Jun 1812; d: 04 Sep 1880 m: 16 Sep 1847; Number of children: 8; Father: William Armstrong
......................7 Lucinda Ellen Armstrong,+ b: 04 Nov 1848
......................7 James William Armstrong,+ b: 08 Jun 1851
......................7 Virginia Ann Armstrong,+ b: 11 Jun 1854
......................7 George Turner Armstrong,+ b: 11 Jul 1857; d: 28 Jan 1858
......................7 Sally Armstrong,+ b: Sep 1859
..........................+ J. T. Burnham, b: Abt. 1857; m: 12 Dec 1878
......................7 John Oscar Armstrong,+ b: 20 Apr 1862
......................7 Amanda White Armstrong,+ b: 17 Apr 1865
......................7 Eliza Jane Armstrong,+ b: 04 Jun 1868
..................6 Lucinda Ewing McGavock,+ b: 15 Feb 1830 in Davidson Co., TN; d: 05 Feb 1861; Number of children: 6
......................+John H. Graham, b: 09 Oct 1825; d: 30 Apr 1848 m: 20 May 1847 (Note: they had no children) m: 20 May 1847; Father: John Graham; Mother: Jane Horton
..................*2nd Husband of Lucinda Ewing McGavock,+
......................+ William A. Graham, b: 30 Jan 1827 in Franklin, Williamson Co., TN; m: 24 Sep 1848; Number of children: 6; Father: John Graham; Mother: Jane Horton
......................7 William Graham,+ b: 24 Mar 1850; d: 29 Oct 1854
......................7 John Graham,+ b: 11 Jan 1852; d: 06 Aug 1855
......................7 Hugh Graham,+ b: 23 Dec 1853; d: 24 Jul 1855
......................7 William T. Graham,+ b: 13 Jan 1856

THE MCGAVOCKS OF CARNTON PLANTATION

.........................+Narcissa Mitchell, b: Abt. 1858; m: 04 Feb 1877
....................7 Lysander Graham,+ b: 26 Feb 1858; d: 11 Apr 1876
......................7 Sallie Graham,+ b: 26 Jun 1860
.........................+ W. J. Wright, b: Abt. 1858; m: 01 Jan 1879
..............2nd Wife of James McGavock,+ McGavock House, Nashville:
..................+ Mary Kent,+ b: 28 Dec 1788; d: 05 Apr 1827 m: 12 Mar 1812; Number of children: 6; Father: Joseph Kent, Col.,+; Mother: Margaret McGavock,+
..................6 Margaret K. McGavock,+ b: 03 Jun 1813; d: 21 Mar 1835; Number of children: 1
......................+ Hardy Wilkerson Bryan, LA State Rep. b: 13 Feb 1811; d: 16 Oct 1855 in Edgefield, TN m: 23 Jul 1833; Number of children: 1; Father: Hardy S. Bryan; Mother: Catherine Young
......................7 James Hardy Bryan,+ b: 17 Mar 1835; d: 01 Sep 1845 in Concordia Parish, LA
..................6 Sarah Jane McGavock,+ b: Abt. 1815; d: Abt. 1815
..................6 Lucinda McGavock,+ b: 18 Feb 1817 in Nashville, Davidson Co., TN; d: 23 Jun 1847; Number of children: 2
......................+ Jeremiah George Harris, journalist b: 23 Oct 1809 in Groton, CT; d: 1901 m: 05 May 1842; Number of children: 2; Father: Richard Harris; Mother: Mary Avery
......................7 Joseph Ewing Harris,+ b: 02 May 1843; d: 28 Aug 1865 in London, England (while making a tour of Europe)
......................7 Lucie Harris,+ b: 26 Oct 1846
.........................+ Van S. Lindsley, Dr. b: Abt. 1844; m: 16 Apr 1868
..................6 Wiley McGavock,+ b: Abt. Nov 1818; d: 1838
..................6 Joseph Kent McGavock,+ b: 20 Sep 1820; d: 10 Sep 1845
..................6 Mary Kent McGavock,+ b: 1826 in Davidson Co., TN; d: 09 Mar 1867; Number of children: 5
......................+Albert Gallatin Wilcox, b: 27 Nov 1816 in Montgomery Co., TN; d: 23 Mar 1880; m: 10 Jan 1849; Number of children: 5 Father: John Earl Wilcox; Mother: Elizabeth _____?
......................7 Joseph Ewing Wilcox,+ b: 25 May 1850; d: 29 Mar 1868
......................7 Mary Alberta Wilcox,+ b: 09 Oct 1851; d: 29 Dec 1861
......................7 John Earl Wilcox,+ b: 10 Feb 1854
......................7 James McGavock Wilcox,+ b: 10 Feb 1856
......................7 Gerald Hiter Wilcox,+ b: 02 May 1863; d: 14 Sep 1868
..............5 Jacob McGavock,+ Clerk Superior Court b: 23 Sep 1790 in Max Meadows, Wythe Co., VA; d: 15 Dec 1878 at his son-in-law's house, Dr. J. Berrian Lindsley, Nashville, Davidson Co., TN; Number of children: 13

THE MCGAVOCKS OF CARNTON PLANTATION

............+Louisa Caroline Grundy, b: 10 Feb 1798 in Bardstown, or Springfield, Washington Co., KY; d: 21 Jan 1878 in Nashville, Davidson Co., TN m: 11 May 1819; Number of children: 13; Father: Felix Grundy, TN Senator, Statesman, Lawyer; Mother: Ann Phillips Rodgers

............6 Anne (or Anna) Eliza McGavock,+ b: 02 Apr 1820 in Nashville, Davidson Co., TN; d: 25 Jun 1868; Number of children: 2

............+Henry Dickinson, I, Judge b: 06 Sep 1806; d: 27 Mar 1872 in Nashville, Davidson Co., TN; m: 28 Apr 1845; Number of children: 2; Father: A. Dickinson

............7 Louise Grundy Dickinson,+ b: 07 Sep 1848

............+Philip Lindsley, b: Abt. 1846; m: 28 Apr 1869; Father: Philip Lindsley, D. D., Rev.; Mother: Margaret E. Lawrence

............7 Jacob McGavock Dickinson, Sr., Judge,+ b: 30 Jan 1851 in Columbus, MS; d: 13 Dec 1928 in Nashville, Davidson Co., TN; Jacob was U.S. assistant attorney general under President Stephen Grover Cleveland and secretary of war under President William Howard Taft; of children: 4

............+Martha Overton, b: 03 June 1853 at Traveller's Rest Plantation, Nashville, TN; d: 08 Mar 1917 in Nashville, Davidson Co., TN; m: 20 Apr 1876 in Nashville, Davidson County, Tennessee; Number of children: 4; Father: Col. John Overton, Jr. (1821-1898), who built the Maxwell House Hotel in Nashville and named it after his wife; Mother: Harriet Virginia Maxwell (1831-1899); Note: Martha's grandfather, Judge John Overton, Sr. (1766-1833), was the owner of Travellers Rest, Nashville, TN (used as headquarters by Confederate General John Bell Hood between the battles of Franklin II and Nashville); along with Andrew Jackson and General James Winchester (the grandfather of Col. Edmund Winchester Rucker, who was at Franklin II), Judge Overton founded Memphis, TN

............8 _____ Dickinson, b: Abt. 1877
............8 _____ Dickinson, b: Abt. 1879
............8 _____ Dickinson, b: Abt. 1881
............8 Jacob McGavock Dickinson, Jr., Gen. b: 04 Feb 1891 in Nashville, Davidson Co., TN (or Chicago, IL); d: Aft. 1933

............+Margaret Adams Smith, b: 1893; d: 1987 m: 10 Jun 1916 in Cincinnati, OH; Father: Rufus Smith; Mother: Edith Harrison

............6 Margaret Jane McGavock,+ b: 02 Jun 1821; d: 05 Nov 1822
............6 Felix Hugh McGavock,+ b: 22 Mar 1823; d: 07 Jun 1824
............6 Hugh Felix McGavock,+ b: 04 Feb 1825; d: 14 Nov 1825
............6 Randal William McGavock, Lt. Col.,C.S.A.,+ b: 10 Aug 1826 in Nashville, Davidson Co., TN; d: 12 May 1863 during the War for Southern Independence, at Battle of Raymond, MS

THE MCGAVOCKS OF CARNTON PLANTATION

..................+Seraphine Deery, b: 1835 in Sullivan Co., TN; d: 20 Mar 1918 in Nashville, Davidson Co., TN; m: 23 Aug 1855 in Deery Family Home, Allisona, Williamson Co., TN; Father: William Deery; Mother: Elizabeth Allison
..................6 Edward Jacob McGavock,+ b: 17 Dec 1828 in Nashville, Davidson Co., TN; d: 07 Apr 1880; Number of children: 5
..................+Ella Young, b: Abt. 1830; d: 28 Mar 1861; m: 05 May 1857; Number of children: 3; Father: Alexander Young; Mother: Elizabeth Davis
..................7 Louisa Grundy McGavock, b: 15 Feb 1858; d: 31 Jan 1885
..................+T. J. Tyner, Dr. b: Abt. 1856; m: Nov 1880
..................7 Frank McGavock, b: 08 Jun 1859; Number of children: 2
..................+Theresa Ewin Perkins, b: 03 Feb 1865 in Franklin, Williamson Co., TN; m: 15 Oct 1884; Number of children: 2; Father: Samuel Perkins; Mother: Theresa Ewin
..................8 Theresa Perkins McGavock, b: 28 May 1885
..................8 Louisa Grundy McGavock, b: 03 Jun 1890
..................7 Ella Young McGavock, b: 12 Aug 1860 in Pecan Point, AR; Number of children: ?
..................+Sheldon Wilson, b: 04 Oct 1849 in Pittsburg, PA; m: 14 Feb 1882; Number of children: ?; Father: Anthony Wilson; Mother: Laura Leare
..................8 Louise McGavock, Wilson b: 22 Nov 1882
..................2nd Wife of Edward Jacob McGavock,+:
..................+Elizabeth Scott Eskridge, b: 29 Nov 1835 in Columbus, MS; d: 09 Feb 1903 in Hot Springs, AR m: 25 Jun 1866; Number of children: 2; Father: T. P. Eskridge, Judge; Mother: Mary Bynum
..................7 Edward Jacob McGavock,+ b: 24 Jun 1868; d: 03 Feb 1922; Number of children: 1
..................+Louisa Trimble Reid, b: 12 Nov 1881; d: 15 Dec 1950; Number of children: 1
..................8 Edward Jacob McGavock,+ b: 30 Apr 1910; d: 13 Nov 1978
..................7 Mary Eskridge McGavock,+ b: 14 Dec 1872; d: 23 Nov 1946
..................+M. D. Russel, b: Abt. 1870; m: 15 May 1894
..................6 Sarah M. "Sallie" Bass McGavock,+ b: 17 Jul 1830 in Nashville, Davidson Co., TN; d: Jul 1903; Number of children: 6
..................+John Berrian Lindsley, Dr., Rev., b: 24 Oct 1822 in Princeton, NJ; d: 07 Dec 1897 m: 09 Feb 1857; Number of children: 6; Father: Philip Lindsley, D. D., Rev.; Mother: Margaret E. Lawrence
..................7 Louisa Grundy Lindsley, b: 11 Mar 1858
..................7 Jacob McGavock Lindsley, b: 30 Mar 1860
..................+Kitty Kline, b: Abt. 1862

THE MCGAVOCKS OF CARNTON PLANTATION

..............7 Mary McGavock Lindsley, b: 12 Jun 1861
....................+Robert C. Kent, b: Abt. 1859; m: 28 Oct 1886
..............7 Margaret Elizabeth Lindsley, b: 26 Feb 1863; Number of children: 1
.... +Percy Warner (Percy Warner Park, Nashville, TN, named after him), b: 1861; d: 1927 in Nashville, Davidson Co., TN? m: 28 Oct 1884; Number of children: 1 Father: James C. Warner
...........................8 Percie Warner, b: Abt. 1886
...........................+Luke Lea, b: Abt. 1884
..............7 Annie Dickinson Lindsley, b: 03 Sep 1864
.... +C. C. Walden, Dr. b: Abt. 1862; m: 01 Jun 1898
..............7 Randal McGavock Lindsley, b: 23 Jul 1870; d: 30 May 1871
...............6 Felix Grundy McGavock, Dr.,+ b: 22 Apr 1832 in Nashville, Davidson Co., TN; d: 06 Dec 1897 in AR?; Number of children: 2
.... +Mary Manoah Bostick, b: 1832 near Triune, Williamson Co., TN; d: 08 Jun 1862 in Memphis, TN; m: 08 Jan 1855 in near Triune, Williamson Co., TN; Number of children: 2 Father: John C. Bostick; Mother: Mary T. "Polly" Hyde (Note: Mary Manoah Bostick is the 1st cousin once removed of Dr. Jonathan Smith Bostick (b. 1794), who gave the funds for the reconstruction of the famous Porter Female Academy in Triune, TN., which was burned by Yankee soldiers during Lincoln's War. The rebuilt school was renamed the Bostick Female Academy.)
..............7 Mary Louisa McGavock,+ b: 18 Aug 1857; d: 16 Jun 1877
.......................+Louis B. McWhirter, b: Abt. 1855 m: 20 Feb 1877
..............7 Manoah McGavock,+ b: 21 Jul 1859 in Williamson Co., TN; d: 08 May 1932; Number of children: 1
.......................+William S. Bransford, b: 06 Aug 1851 in Glasgow, KY; d: 08 Apr 1938 in Nashville, Davidson Co., TN? m: 08 Nov 1877; Number of children: 1 Father: Thomas L. Bransford; Mother: Lucinda Settle
...................8 Mary Louise Bransford, b: 28 Oct 1878
...............6 Mary Louise McGavock,+ b: 08 Jan 1838 in Nashville, Davidson Co., TN; d: ?; Number of children: 2
......................+James Todd, b: 26 Feb 1821 in Ireland; d: 09 Feb 1890 in KY? m: 16 May 1865; Number of children: 2 Father: John Todd; Mother: Martha _____?
..............7 Louise Grundy Todd, b: 04 Apr 1867
..........................+Frederick Joy, b: Abt. 1865; m: 20 Dec 1892
..............7 James Ross Todd, b: 29 Mar 1869
..........................+Margaret J. Menefee, b: Abt. 1871; m: 01 May 1901
...............6 John Jacob McGavock,+ b: 03 Jun 1835 in Nashville, Davidson

The McGavocks of Carnton Plantation

Co., TN; d: Aft. 1865 in AR; Number of children: 4
.................+Sally D. Martin, b: 20 Apr 1844; m: 25 May 1865; Number of children: 4 Father: James Martin, Rev.; Mother: Nancy R. Gillespie
....................7 Mary Todd McGavock, b: 21 Jun 1866
....................7 Nannie Martin McGavock, b: 11 Mar 1869
....................7 Louise McGavock, b: 08 Nov 1870
....................7 Randal William McGavock, b: 12 Dec 1872
................6 Martha Winder McGavock,+ b: 26 Jun 1839; d: 10 Jan 1840
................6 Hugh Albert McGavock,+ b: 04 Jan 1842 in Nashville, Davidson Co., TN; d: 30 Jul 1854 in Nashville, Davidson Co., TN
............5 Jane McGavock,+ b: 19 Sep 1792; d: 03 May 1795
............5 Robert McGavock,+ b: 20 Oct 1794 in Max Meadows, Wythe Co., VA; d: 16 Oct 1872 in MO; Number of children: 11
................+Ann Hickman, b: 12 May 1805 in Bourbon Co., KY; d: 17 Oct 1881; m: 09 Mar 1819 in Howard Co., MO; Number of children: 11 Father: Thomas Hickman, Col.; Mother: Sarah Prewitt
................6 Randal H. McGavock,+ b: 23 Jul 1820 in Howard Co., MO; d: 07 Apr 1894; Number of children: 8
.... +Anne Hite (the author's family line),+ b: 06 Oct 1826 in Jefferson, KY; d: 07 Apr 1894 in Hancock, KY m: 12 Dec 1850; Number of children: 8 Father: James Henning Hite+; Mother: Harriet Ramsay, Ramsey
....................7 Robert H. McGavock, b: 06 Sep 1851; Number of children: 7
........................+Bettie Dean, b: 04 Jan 1852 in Cloverport, KY; m: 17 Feb 1876; Number of children: 7 Father: Thomas Dean; Mother: Mary E. Miller
........................8 Malcolm McGavock, b: 21 Mar 1877
........................8 Stella McGavock, b: 17 Dec 1878
........................8 Roberta McGavock, b: 22 Mar 1881
........................8 Alvin Lee McGavock, b: 21 Jul 1883
........................8 Marie Anna McGavock, b: 02 Sep 1885
........................8 Hugh Dean McGavock, b: 06 Oct 1887
........................8 Pearl McGavock, b: 29 Jan 1891
....................7 Thomas Elmore McGavock, b: 29 Aug 1853; Number of children: 6
........................+Emma Newton, b: 24 Jan 1854; d: 22 Dec 1899 m: 11 Oct 1877; Number of children: 6
........................8 Annie D. McGavock, b: 06 Nov 1878
........................8 Emma Lee McGavock, b: 02 Aug 1880
........................8 Susan Newton McGavock, b: 17 Feb 1884
........................8 John Hugh McGavock, b: 24 Nov 1885

THE MCGAVOCKS OF CARNTON PLANTATION

.............................8 Daniel L. McGavock, b: 31 Dec 1889
.............................8 Vera E. McGavock, b: 12 Oct 1893
........................7 Frances E. H. McGavock, b: 04 Sep 1855; d: 05 Jul 1896; Number of children: 5
.............................+ John Long, b: 08 Jan 1857; d: 04 Nov 1898 m: 05 Oct 1878; Number of children: 5
.............................8 Oscar Richard Long, b: 11 Aug 1879
.... +Susan Early, b: Abt. 1880 m: 02 Nov 1899
.............................8 Mary Bertha Long, b: 27 May 1884; d: 22 Jul 1919
.................................+Michael Hendrick, b: Abt. 1882 (Note: they did not have children)
.............................8 Margaret Forrest Long, b: 18 Feb 1887
................................+William Benton Ireland, b: Abt. 1885; m: 28 Oct 1891
.............................8 Allen Thomas Long, b: 24 Nov 1890
.............................+Mary Aline Zix, b: Abt. 1892; m: 21 Jun 1916
.............................8 John William Long, b: 02 Jul 1896; d: 02 Jul 1896
........................7 William R. McGavock, b: 1858; d: 24 Mar 1863
........................7 Oscar W. McGavock, b: 22 Sep 1860
........................7 Maggie B. McGavock, b: 30 Dec 1862
........................7 Lillie Hite McGavock, b: 26 Nov 1864
........................7 Annie Hay McGavock, b: 12 Jan 1869; Number of children: 1
.............................+Hilary Harding, Hardin, b: Abt. 1867 m: 09 Feb 1899; Number of children: 1
.............................8 Julius Randal Harding, Hardin b: 01 Aug 1902
...................6 Thomas Cloyd McGavock,+ b: 01 Feb 1823 in Howard Co., MO; d: 13 Oct 1860; Number of children: 7
........................+Mary Lightfoot, b: 23 Oct 1822; d: 14 Feb 1860 m: 25 Jun 1846; Number of children: 7 Father: Philip Lightfoot; Mother: Eliza Lander
........................7 David Cloyd McGavock, Civil War Soldier b: 25 Mar 1847; d: 14 Feb 1865, in the War for Southern Independence
........................7 Rosa Delia McGavock, b: 17 Mar 1849; d: 05 Oct 1877; Number of children: 1
.............................+George Barrett Exall, b: 07 Aug 1845 in Northhampton Co., VA; m: 23 Oct 1873; Number of children: 1
.............................8 Joseph Kenneth Exall, b: 10 Apr 1876
........................7 Ann Eliza McGavock, b: 12 Apr 1851 in Breckinridge Co., KY; Number of children: 3
.............................+John D. Ryan, b: 24 Oct 1852 in Perry Co., IN m: 23 Jan 1876; Number of children: 3

THE MCGAVOCKS OF CARNTON PLANTATION

..........................8 Mary L. Ryan, b: 18 Nov 1876
..........................8 Rosa A. Ryan, b: 05 Apr 1879
..........................8 Charles E. Ryan, b: 08 Jul 1881
....................7 Hugh Lander McGavock, b: 20 Jun 1853; d: 07 Jul 1870
....................7 Ada Frances McGavock, b: 19 Apr 1855
..........................+Henry Richards, b: Abt. 1853 m: 08 Nov 1898
....................7 Mary Emma McGavock, b: 14 Mar 1857; d: Abt. 1858
....................7 Thomas McGavock, b: 27 Jan 1860; d: 28 Jan 1860
................6 Jacob McGavock,+ b: 06 May 1824 in Howard Co., MO; d: 28 Aug 1877 in Athens, AL; Number of children: 8
......................+Elizabeth Haynes, b: 11 Mar 1827; d: 25 Jan 1879 in Athens, AL m: 06 Mar 1845; Number of children: 8 Father: William Haynes
....................7 Sarah A. McGavock, b: 01 Jan 1846 in Breckinridge Co., KY; Number of children: 3
..........................+James H. Jones, b: Abt. 1844 in Limestone Co., AL m: 10 Feb 1872; Number of children: 3
..........................8 Jacob McGavock Jones, b: 08 Nov 1873
..........................8 Frederick Jones, b: 04 Feb 1880
..........................8 Francis Jones, b: 04 Feb 1880
....................7 Mary J. McGavock, b: 13 Dec 1847 in Breckinridge Co., KY; Number of children: 1
..........................+Clarence Fredericks, b: 26 Jul 1842; d: 13 Apr 1883 m: 30 Dec 1874; Number of children: 1
..........................8 Marie Doane Fredericks, b: 04 Nov 1880
....................2nd Husband of Mary J. McGavock:
..........................+Edward Ragland, Cap. b: Abt. 1845 m: 21 Dec 1892
....................7 James F. McGavock, b: 16 Dec 1851
..........................+Fannie E. Young, b: Abt. 1853; m: Abt. 1873
....................2nd Wife of James F. McGavock:
..........................+Mattie B. Watts, b: Abt. 1860; m: Abt. 1880
....................7 Lula E. McGavock, b: 22 Jul 1860
..........................+John Long, b: Abt. 1858; m: 08 Mar 1898
....................2nd Husband of Lula E. McGavock:
..........................+ John Long, b: 08 Jan 1857; d: 04 Nov 1898; m: 08 Mar 1898; Number of children: 5
....................7 Morgan Forest McGavock, b: 22 Sep 1862; d: 23 Mar 1892
....................7 Ida Belle McGavock, b: 23 Jan 1865; d: 20 Oct 1890
..........................+Jacob Deaton, b: Abt. 1863; m: 14 Dec 1888
....................7 William Robert McGavock, b: 06 Apr 1866; Number of children: 3

THE MCGAVOCKS OF CARNTON PLANTATION

...............+Belle Ragsdale, b: Abt. 1868; m: 27 Jul 1892; Number of children: 3
...............8 Leon Ragsdale McGavock, b: 07 Oct 1893
...............8 Montrose H. McGavock, b: 05 Mar 1896
...............8 Belle McGavock, b: 29 Aug 1902
............7 Kate Eugenie McGavock, b: 21 Nov 1867
...............+James Blair, b: Abt. 1865 m: 25 Feb 1886
............6 Robert Emmet McGavock,+ b: 07 Jul 1826 in Breckinridge Co., KY; d: 04 May 1875; Number of children: 6
............+Matilda Bondurant, b: Abt. 1828; d: 04 Jan 1856 m: 05 Mar 1855 (Note: They had no children)
............2nd Wife of Robert Emmet McGavock,+:
............+Sally A. Crews, b: 08 Aug 1839 in Madison Co., KY m: 14 Apr 1857; Number of children: 6 Father: Milton Crews; Mother: Rhoda Fox
............7 Robert M. McGavock, b: 13 Aug 1860; d: 31 Jan 1863
............7 William C. McGavock, b: 02 Feb 1862
............7 James E. McGavock, Dr., b: 19 Nov 1863; d: in Bay City, MI?
............7 Rhoda F. McGavock, b: 24 May 1865; Number of children: 4
...............+Logan H. Taylor, Dr. b: Abt. 1863; m: Aug 1888; Number of children: 4
...............8 Lawson Taylor, b: 1889
...............8 Robert McGavock Taylor, b: Aug 1890
...............8 Hunton Taylor, b: Apr 1892
...............8 Elizabeth Taylor, b: Sep 1893
............7 Anne H. McGavock, b: 09 Nov 1869
............7 Robert E. McGavock, b: 21 May 1874
...............+Gertrude Morcum, b: Abt. 1876 m: Mar 1898
............6 James H. McGavock, farmer,+ b: 25 Jan 1828 in Breckinridge Co., KY; d: 25 Mar 186 in Howard Co., MO; Number of children: 6
............+Martha Talbot, b: 16 Jan 1838; m: 06 Nov 1856; Number of children: 6 Father: Williston J. Talbot; Mother: Elizabeth Hays
............7 Anne Louisa McGavock, b: 18 Oct 1858; d: 09 Sep 1865
............7 Charles T. McGavock, b: 05 Jun 1863
............7 Catherine McGavock, b: 10 Dec 1865
............7 Robert L. McGavock, b: 24 Jun 1869
............7 Williston McGavock, b: 23 Aug 1871 in Howard Co., MO; Number of children: 3
...............+Anna Watkins, b: Abt. 1873; Number of children: 3
...............8 Claud T. McGavock, b: Nov 1896

THE MCGAVOCKS OF CARNTON PLANTATION

...........................8 Martha McGavock, b: Jul 1899
...........................8 Williston McGavock, b: Sep 1902
......................7 James R. McGavock, b: 23 Jan 1874
..................6 Gordon Cloyd McGavock,+ b: 12 Nov 1829 in Breckinridge Co., KY; d: in near Franklin, Howard Co., MO?; Number of children: 6
.......................+Lucy M. Lewis, b: 05 May 1836; m: 14 Dec 1859; Number of children: 6 Father: Addison Lewis; Mother: Sarah Minor
......................7 John L. McGavock, b: 08 Jan 1861; Number of children: 3
...........................+Dora Bibb, b: Abt. 1863; m: 12 Sep 1889; Number of children: 3
...........................8 Mary L. McGavock, b: 11 Jul 1894
...........................8 Florence B. McGavock, b: Aug 1897
...........................8 Gordon C. McGavock, b: Dec 1900
......................7 Sarah McGavock, b: 28 Feb 1863
......................7 Mary C. McGavock, b: 23 May 1867
......................7 Louisa McGavock, b: 17 Nov 1869
...........................+Roger Woods, b: Abt. 1867 m: 10 Apr 1901
......................7 Hugh K. (Kent?) McGavock, b: 29 Nov 1871
......................7 Robert E. McGavock, b: 03 Sep 1876
..................6 David McGavock,+ b: 20 May 1832; d: Abt. 1832
..................6 John Hickman McGavock,+ farmer, b: 01 Mar 1834 in Breckinridge Co., KY; Number of children: 9
...........................+Elizabeth Skillman, b: 04 Aug 1834 in Breckinridge Co., KY; m: 18 Jan 1860; Number of children: 9 Father: Richard Skillman; Mother: Nancy Board
......................7 Leon McGavock,+ b: 29 Oct 1860; Number of children: 4
...........................+Jenny H. Ireland, b: 14 Jan 1873; m: 28 Oct 1891; Number of children: 4
.... 8 Virginia McGavock,+ b: 29 Mar 1893; Number of children: 1
...............................+R. Perry Davis, b: Abt. 1891 m: May 1916; Number of children: 1
.... 8 Leonora Elizabeth McGavock,+ b: 04 Jan 1895
.... 8 Mary Florence McGavock,+ b: 09 Jun 1897; Number of children: 2
...............................+James B. Fitch, b: Abt. 1895; m: 12 Nov 1921; Number of children: 2
.... 8 Addie Donelson McGavock,+ b: 06 Feb 1899
...........................+Frank Allen Heinzle, b: Abt. 1897; d: Apr 1950 m: Dec 1929 (Note: they did not have children)

THE MCGAVOCKS OF CARNTON PLANTATION

...............7 Marion McGavock,+ b: 30 Sep 1862
...............7 Gordon S. McGavock,+ b: 24 Jan 1865
...............7 Lucy F. McGavock,+ b: 03 Nov 1867
...............7 John Kent McGavock,+ b: 27 Oct 1869; Number of children: 6
........................+Margaret Jane Wilson, b: 23 Mar 1875; m: 09 Feb 1899; Number of children: 6
........................8 Elizabeth Skillman McGavock,+ b: 30 Aug 1902
........................8 John Hickman McGavock, II,+ b: 04 Aug 1904; Number of children: 2
.............................+Francine Caroline Emanuelson, b: Abt. 1906 m: 16 Jul 1927; Number of children: 2
........................8Forrest Wilson McGavock,+ b: 13 Feb 1907
........................8 Richard McGavock,+ b: Abt. 1909
........................8 David McGavock,+ b: Abt. 1911
........................8 Margaret McGavock,+ b: Abt. 1915
...............7 Eva McGavock,+ b: 16 Feb 1872; d: 20 Oct 1872
...............7 Melissa M. McGavock,+ b: 26 Jun 1873; d: 1881; Number of children: 3
........................+Zachary Harding, Hardin b: Abt. 1871; m: Abt. 1896; Number of children: 3
........................8 Lucille Harding, Hardin b: 11 Jun 1897
........................8 Virgil Hickman Harding, Hardin b: 21 Jul 1902
........................8 Marion Harding, Hardin b: 10 Jul 1905
...............7 Francis L. McGavock,+ b: 06 Jun 1876; d: 1881
...............7 Abraham Skillman McGavock,+ b: 20 Dec 1879
............6 Cloyd McGavock,+ b: 19 Jan 1836; d: Abt. 1836
............6 Joseph McGavock,+ b: 06 Jan 1838; d: Abt. 1838
............6 Francis F. (Fenelon or Fenlon) McGavock,+ b: 14 Apr 1840 in Cloverport, Breckinridge Co., KY; d: 26 Feb 1921 in Columbia, Maury Co., TN; Number of children: 9
...............+Margaret (Margretta) Cunningham, b: 01 Jul 1843 in Greenville, TN; m: 19 Dec 1865; Number of children: 9 Father: A. N. Cunningham, Rev.; Mother: Margaretta Eason
...............7 William L. McGavock,+ b: 28 Apr 1867; d: 11 Jan 1886
...............7 Lula A. McGavock,+ b: 22 Mar 1869
........................+Andrew Ewing,+ b: 25 Jul 1851; m: 22 Feb 1899; Father: William Ewing,; Mother: Margaret Lucinda McGavock,+
...............7 Maggie C. McGavock,+ b: 02 Nov 1871; Number of children: 2

THE MCGAVOCKS OF CARNTON PLANTATION

.............................+J. T. Mitchell, b: Abt. 1869; m: 02 Jun 1893; Number of children: 2
............................8 Margaret Rebecca Mitchell, b: 16 May 1895
............................8 John Tilman Mitchell, b: 27 Apr 1899
.......................7 Francis McGavock,+ b: 06 Jan 1874
.......................7 Robert McGavock,+ b: 22 Oct 1876
.......................7 Lillian McGavock,+ b: 19 Dec 1878
.......................7 Julia C. McGavock,+ b: 27 Mar 1881
............................+Oliver H. Shields, b: Abt. 1879 m: 22 Jan 1902
.......................7 Charles Alexander McGavock,+ b: 20 Dec 1883 in near Franklin,TN on Spencer's Creek; d: Jan 1864; Number of children: 4
............................+Mary McCord Ezell, b: 12 Dec 1883 in Pulaski, TN m: Abt. 1905; Number of children: 4
............................8 Lillian McGavock,+ b: Abt. 1906
............................8 Martha McGavock,+ b: Abt. 1908; Number of children: 1
.................................+_____ Neel, b: Abt. 1905; m: Abt. 1935; Number of children: 1
............................8 Mary McGavock,+ b: Abt. 1911
............................8 Margetta McGavock,+ b: Abt. 1915
.......................7 Frederick McGavock,+ b: 05 Jul 1887
...............5 Hugh McGavock,+ b: 04 Sep 1796 in Max Meadows, Wythe Co., VA; d: 10 Oct 1880 in Punento, Vigo Co., IN; Number of children: 9
....................+Elizabeth Hay, b: 20 Feb 1798; m: Abt. 1818; Number of children: 9 Father: William Hay; Mother: Martha Buchanan
....................6 Nancy M. McGavock,+ b: 05 Feb 1819; d: Aft. 1903 in Wing, AR?; Number of children: 13
........................+Richardson Vanderslice, b: 16 Feb 1809 in Montgomery Co., PA or Wythe Co., VA; d: 03 Jan 1883; m: 04 Jan 1838; Number of children: 13; Father: Jacob Vanderslice; Mother: Amelia Shannon
.......................7 Frances A. Vanderslice, b: 05 Dec 1838; d: 02 Dec 1899
............................+William W. Johnson, b: Abt. 1835 m: 01 Jan 1860
.......................7 Mary Vanderslice, b: 17 Feb 1840
............................+Richard C. Henson, b: Abt. 1838 m: 23 May 1858
.......................7 John Vanderslice, b: 23 Apr 1842
............................+Mattie Milam, b: Abt. 1844 m: 09 Oct 1870
.......................2nd Wife of John Vanderslice:
............................+D. J. Wilson, b: Abt. 1855 m: Abt. 1875
.......................7 Elizabeth Vanderslice, b: 28 Jan 1844
............................+Thomas J. Rice, b: Abt. 1842; m: 18 Sep 1867

THE MCGAVOCKS OF CARNTON PLANTATION

...............7 James Vanderslice, b: 21 Nov 1845
...................+Ella Thompson, b: Abt. 1847; m: 07 Jan 1873
...............7 William Vanderslice, b: 07 Oct 1847
...................+Alice M. Garmany, b: Abt. 1849; m: 26 Jan 1881
...............7 Thomas M. Vanderslice, b: 04 Sep 1949; d: 04 Jul 1853
...............7 Robert Vanderslice, b: 25 Aug 1852
...................+Dora M. Adams, b: Abt. 1854 m: 12 Jun 1890
...............7 Louisa Vanderslice, b: 17 Jul 1854
...................+Elmore Hill, b: Abt. 1852
...............7 Sally Vanderslice, b: 21 Jul 1856
...................+John M. Nall, b: Abt. 1854 m: 14 Feb 1889 m: 14 Feb 1889
...............7 Ada Vanderslice, b: 20 Sep 1858; d: 11 Dec 1882
...................+George W. Drummond, b: Abt. 1856; m: 11 Nov 1880
...............7 Lacy Vanderslice, b: 23 Sep 1860
...............7 Nannie Vanderslice, b: 21 Nov 1862; d: 09 Dec 1897
...................+Ben DeLanghter, b: Abt. 1860 m: 07 Jun 1896
............6 Sarah H. McGavock,+ b: 22 Jan 1822; d: 02 Sep 1874; Number of children: 5
...................+Thomas Leake, b: Abt. 1820; m: 18 Apr 1843; Number of children: 5
...............7 Elizabeth Leake, b: Abt. 1844
...............7 Martha Leake, b: Abt. 1846
...............7 William Leake, b: Abt. 1848
...............7 John Leake, b: Abt. 1850
...............7 Louisa Leake, b: Abt. 1852
............6 Elizabeth C. McGavock,+ b: 06 Aug 1825; d: 22 Feb 1857; Number of children: 5
...................+William Morris, b: Abt. 1823 m: 06 Jul 1848; Number of children: 5
...............7 Mary Morris, b: Abt. 1849
...............7 Maria Morris, b: Abt. 1851
...............7 Emily Morris, b: Abt. 1853
...............7 John Morris, b: Abt. 1855
...............7 William Morris, b: Abt. 1857
............6 Louisa G. McGavock,+ b: 13 Apr 1827; d: 29 Oct 1866; Number of children: 6
...................+James W. Scott, b: Abt. 1825; m: 22 Oct 1844; Number of children: 6
...............7 James Scott, b: Abt. 1845

THE MCGAVOCKS OF CARNTON PLANTATION

..............7 Nancy Scott, b: Abt. 1847
..............7 Cyrus Scott, b: Abt. 1849
..............7 Marshall Scott, b: Abt. 1851
..............7 Franklin Scott, b: Abt. 1853
..............7 Marshall (2) Scott, b: Abt. 1855
............6 Martha H. McGavock,+ b: 17 Jul 1830 in Wythe Co., VA; Number of children: 13
..................+Jeremiah Morris, farmer b: 17 Jun 1822 in Green Co., KY; d: in Linn Co., MO? m: 24 Nov 1846; Number of children: 13 Father: John Morris; Mother: Susannah Sharp
..............7 Hugh Morris, b: 05 Nov 1847
..............7 Susan Morris, b: 02 Apr 1849
....................+Samuel Williams, b: Abt. 1847 m: 05 Oct 1870
..............7 Thomas Morris, b: 14 Jun 1851
....................+Isabella Brown, b: Abt. 1853 m: 20 Aug 1876
..............7 Elizabeth Morris, b: 12 May 1853
....................+J. Gooch, Dr., b: Abt. 1850; m: 17 Jan 1874
..............7 Zecharia Morris, b: 23 Mar 1855
..............7 Nancy Morris, b: 27 Feb 1856
....................+L. McIntyre, b: Abt. 1854; m: 25 Dec 1877
..............7 Sarah Morris, b: 16 Oct 1860
..............7 Robert L. Morris, b: 16 Aug 1863
..............7 Martha Morris, b: 08 Oct 1865
..............7 Mary Morris, b: 03 Nov 1868
..............7 Cordelia Morris, b: 25 Aug 1870
..............7 Hulda Morris, b: 13 Sep 1872
..............7 Jane Morris, b: 11 Jul 1875
............6 James W. McGavock,+ b: 27 May 1832; Number of children: 5
..................+Julia Ann Pickerell, b: Abt. 1834; m: Abt. 1855; Number of children: 5
..............7 Mary Eliza McGavock, b: Abt. 1855
..............7 Jane McGavock, b: Abt. 1857
..............7 Stephen McGavock, b: Abt. 1859
..............7 George McGavock, b: Abt. 1861
..............7 Ann McGavock, b: Abt. 1863
............6 Jane B. McGavock,+ b: 09 May 1834 in Larue Co., KY; Number of children: 7
..................+Charles H. Moore, b: 12 Sep 1831 in Jefferson Co., KY; m: 12 Feb 1852; Number of children: 7
..............7 William Thomas Moore, b: 16 May 1853

The McGavocks of Carnton Plantation

..........................+Josephine Ring, b: Abt. 1855 m: 10 Oct 1878
....................7 Sallie E. Moore, b: 10 Nov 1854
..........................+Marion McGlone, b: Abt. 1852 m: 06 Sep 1877
....................7 Hugh Franklin Moore, b: 12 Aug 1857
....................7 James M. Moore, b: 20 Mar 1860
....................7 Susan R. Moore, b: 29 Mar 1862
....................7 John Burton Moore, b: 08 Oct 1865
....................7 Louisa G. Moore, b: 27 Nov 1868
..................6 Frances A. McGavock,+ b: 06 May 1836 in Larue Co., KY; d: 09 Feb 1865; Number of children: 1
......................+Henry Ratchford, b: Abt. 1834 m: 15 Mar 1853; Number of children: 1
....................7 Hugh Robert Ratchford, b: Abt. 1854
..................6 Susan R. McGavock,+ b: 14 Mar 1838 in Larue Co., KY; d: 26 Jun 1859; Number of children: 2
......................+Francis Beard, b: Abt. 1836 m: 31 Jan 1854; Number of children: 2
....................7 James Beard, b: Abt. 1855
....................7 Thaddeus Beard, b: Abt. 1857
..............5 David McGavock,+ b: 06 May 1798; d: 25 Aug 1801
..............5 Margaret McGavock,+ b: 12 Mar 1800 in Max Meadows, Wythe Co., VA; d: 19 Jul 1845 in Rockville, IN; Number of children: 9
..................+Samuel McNutt, Rev., b: 1790 in Rockbridge Co., VA; d: 21 Jan 1869 in Rockville, IN; m: 02 Oct 1819; Number of children: 9
..................6 Margaret A. McNutt, b: 1820; d: 30 Nov 1855
......................+Robert N. Allen, b: Abt. 1818; m: 06 Jul 1837
..................6 Hugh McGavock McNutt, b: Abt. 1822; d: Abt. 1822
..................6 Mary McNutt, b: Abt. 1824; d: 1845
......................+James Brown, Rev. b: Abt. 1820
..................6 Sarah K. McNutt, b: Abt. 1825; d: 12 Apr 1846
......................+Levi Sidewell, b: Abt. 1824 m: 1842
..................6 James A. McNutt, b: 13 Feb 1826; d: 27 Jun 1874
......................+Sally Hines, b: Abt. 1828 m: 20 Jul 1854
..................6 Samuel D. McNutt, b: 05 Jan 1827; d: 26 Feb 1860
......................+Sarah E. Milligan, b: Abt. 1829; m: 27 Dec 1853
..................6 Robert McNutt, twin b: Abt. 1829
..................6 Maria McNutt, twin b: Abt. 1829
..................6 Frances E. McNutt, b: 01 Oct 1833; d: 21 Dec 1858
......................+James McGavock Cloyd,+ b: 18 Jun 1828; d: 03 Mar 1892 m: 05 Nov 1853; Father: David Cloyd; Mother: Sally McGavock,+

THE MCGAVOCKS OF CARNTON PLANTATION

...............5 Eliza McDowell McGavock,+ b: 04 Dec 1801 in Max Meadows, Wythe Co., VA; d: 06 Jan 1876 in Franklin, Williamson Co., TN; Number of children: 9
...................+Andrew B. Ewing, Dr. b: 27 Jul 1796 in Barton's Station, Davidson Co., TN; d: 15 May 1881 in Franklin, Williamson Co., TN; m: 01 May 1821; Number of children: 9 Father: William Ewing; Mother: Margaret Love
....................6 William Ewing, b: 03 May 1823 in Williamson Co., TN; d: 27 Apr 1863; Number of children: 5
........................+Margaret Lucinda McGavock,+ b: 20 Jul 1829 in Max Meadows, Wythe Co., VA; d: 10 Jul 1855; m: 24 Sep 1850; Number of children: 3 Father: Joseph McGavock,+; Mother: Margaret Graham
.......................7 Andrew Ewing,+ b: 25 Jul 1851
...........................+Lula A. McGavock,+ b: 22 Mar 1869; m: 22 Feb 1899 Father: Francis F. (Fenelon or Fenlon) McGavock,+; Mother: Margaret (Margretta) Cunningham
.......................7 Joseph William Ewing,+ b: 17 Feb 1853; d: 16 Jan 1889
.......................7 Lucy Elizabeth Ewing,+ b: 24 Mar 1855
...........................+William J. Brown, b: Abt. 1853; m: 25 Oct 1882
...................2nd Wife of William Ewing,:
........................+Lida Hooker Withers, b: 27 Apr 1835; d: 02 Nov 1865 in Franklin, Williamson Co., TN; m: 15 Aug 1859 in Hudson, OH; Number of children: 2 Father: John W. Withers, Dr.; Mother: Mary Porter
.......................7 Mary Withers Ewing, b: 04 Oct 1860; d: 30 Aug 1862
.......................7 William Milton Ewing, b: 09 Dec 1862
...........................+Margaret D. Mills, b: Abt. 1864 m: 18 May 1886
....................6 Hugh McGavock Ewing, b: 11 Dec 1824; d: 30 Apr 1899
....................6 Margaret Ewing, b: 09 Nov 1826; d: 31 Dec 1832
....................6 Randal Milton Ewing, b: 01 Jun 1829 in Williamson Co., TN; Number of children: 4
........................+Mary Ellen McGavock,+ b: 23 Sep 1833; d: 16 Jun 1891 m: 13 Sep 1853; Number of children: 4 Father: James Randal McGavock,+ of Riverside Plantation; Mother: Louisa C. Chenault
.......................7 Carrie Eliza Ewing,+ b: 17 Sep 1854
.......................7 Charles Andrew Ewing,+ b: 25 Sep 1857
...........................+Sarah Elizabeth Owen, b: Abt. 1859 m: 02 Nov 1887
.......................7 Francis McGavock Ewing,+ b: 26 Dec 1861
...........................+Eliza M. Marshall, b: Abt. 1863 m: 19 Jan 1892
.......................7 William Frierson Ewing,+ b: 20 Feb 1864
....................6 _____ (unnamed) Ewing, b: 01 Jun 1832; d: Abt. 1832
....................6 Andrew J. Ewing, b: 19 May 1835; d: 28 Dec 1887

THE MCGAVOCKS OF CARNTON PLANTATION

................6 Sarah Amanda Ewing, b: 09 Oct 1838; d: 23 Jan 1846
................6 Susan Mary Ewing, b: 20 Jan 1841
................6 Ann Eliza Ewing, b: 01 Aug 1843; d: 05 Aug 1895
.............5 Randal McGavock,+ (his portrait hangs in Carnton's ladies' parlor); b: 19 Jun 1803 in Max Meadows, Wythe Co., VA; d: 19 Mar 1890 in Max Meadows, Wythe Co., VA; Number of children: 7
................+Maria Reed, b: Abt. 1805; m: 17 Oct 1826 in Springfield, KY; Number of children: 2
................6 _____ (unnamed) McGavock, twin b: 26 Jul 1827; d: Abt. 29 Jul 1827
................6 Reed McGavock, twin b: 26 Jul 1827; d: 07 Jan 1828
.............2nd Wife of Randal McGavock,+ (his portrait hangs in Carnton's ladies' parlor)
................+ Cynthia E. McGavock,+ (her portrait hangs in Carnton's ladies' parlor); b: 29 Feb 1820 in Max Meadows, Wythe Co., VA; d: 10 Jun 1882 in Max Meadows, Wythe Co., VA; m: 13 Dec 1845; Number of children: 5 Father: Joseph McGavock,+; Mother: Margaret Graham
................6 Hugh Ewing McGavock,+ b: 07 Jul 1849
................6 Sally M. McGavock,+ b: 05 Nov 1851 in Max Meadows, Wythe Co., VA; d: 14 Oct 1875; Number of children: 2
....................+Walter H. Robertson, Rev., b: Abt. 1850 in Amelia Co., VA; d: 02 Jul 1903 m: 02 Aug 1871; Number of children: 2 Father: William H. Robertson; Mother: Martha Holcombe
....................7 Lizzie Robertson,+ b: 24 Jul 1872
........................+Alex Crockett, Dr., b: Abt. 1870 m: 07 Jun 1893
....................7 Holcombe McGavock Robertson,+ Surgeon, US Navy b: 24 Oct 1874
................6 Joseph Randal McGavock,+ b: 28 Mar 1854 in Max Meadows, Wythe Co., VA; Number of children: 4
....................+Elizabeth "Lizzie" L. Hager, b: 01 Aug 1864 in Wythe Co., VA m: 01 Feb 1888; Number of children: 4 Father: John W. Hager; Mother: Mary Williams
....................7 Nannie Lee McGavock,+ b: 19 Oct 1888
....................7 Mary Williams McGavock,+ b: 12 May 1890
....................7 Joseph Randal McGavock,+ b: 08 Jul 1891
....................7 Cynthia Elizabeth McGavock,+ b: 25 May 1894
................6 Jacob Cloyd McGavock,+ b: 23 Jun 1856 in Max Meadows, Wythe Co., VA; d: in Max Meadows, Wythe Co., VA?; Number of children: 5
....................+Amanda Billups, b: 21 Nov 1861 in Norfolk, VA?; d: in Max Meadows, Wythe Co., VA? m: 02 Oct 1883; Number of children: 5 Father: Cealy

The McGavocks of Carnton Plantation

Billups; Mother: Elizabeth Anne Summers
..................7 Eulalie McGavock,+ b: 08 Jul 1885
..................7 Randal McGavock,+ b: 20 Nov 1887
..................7 Cecil McGavock,+ b: 19 Mar 1890
..................7 Jacob C. McGavock,+ b: 08 Jul 1893
..................7 Ezra Summers McGavock,+ b: 12 Dec 1897
..............6 Lucy Nancy McGavock,+ b: 10 Apr 1858 in Max Meadows, Wythe Co., VA; Number of children: 7
....................+John Brown Kent, b: 04 Sep 1849; m: 05 Apr 1882; Number of children: 7 Father: Joseph F. Kent; Mother: Frances Peyton
..................7 Randal McGavock Kent,+ b: 28 Feb 1883
..................7 Fanny Brown Kent,+ b: 08 Oct 1884
..................7 Cynthia McGavock Kent,+ b: 13 Feb 1886
..................7 Jennie Lewis Kent,+ b: 11 Oct 1887
..................7 Lucy McGavock Kent,+ b: 15 Oct 1891
..................7 Emily Roberta Kent,+ b: 31 Jan 1893
..................7 Joseph Francis Kent,+ b: 20 Jul 1895
............5 Sally McGavock,+ b: 04 Aug 1805; d: 19 Feb 1872
................+John H. Otey, b: Abt. 1803 m: 10 Oct 1848 in (Note: they did not have children)
..........2nd Wife of Hugh McGavock, Capt. Rev. War,+:
............+_____ Campbell, b: Abt. 1762 in Cripple Creek, Wythe Co., VA; d: Abt. 1783 in Cripple Creek, Wythe Co., VA? m: 1786 in Cripple Creek, Wythe Co., VA
..........4 David McGavock, surveyor,+ b: 06 Feb 1763 in Max Meadows, Rockbridge/Wythe Co., VA; d: 07 Aug 1838 in Nashville, Davidson Co., TN; Number of children: 11
............+Elizabeth McDowell,+ b: 1761 in Rockbridge Co., VA; d: Bet. 1803 - 1807 in Nashville, Davidson Co., TN (some say Rockbridge Co., VA, during a visit in 1807); m: 16 Jun 1789 in VA; Number of children: 9 Father: James McDowell, Gov. of VA,+; Mother: Elizabeth Cloyd,+
............5 James McGavock,+ McGavock House, Nashville b: 28 Mar 1790 in Wythe Co., VA; d: 23 Jan 1841—brutally murdered near Nashville, Davidson Co., TN; Number of children: 14 (with two wives)
................+Lusinda Ewing, b: 10 Dec 1792 in Williamson Co., TN; d: 21 Apr 1848; m: 18 Dec 1810; Number of children: 8 Father: Alexander Ewing, Captain, American Revolutionary War; Mother: Sally Smith
................6 Nancy Kent McGavock,+ b: 13 Nov 1813 in Williamson Co., TN; d: 29 Jan 1863; Number of children: 11
....................+Eldrige N. Claud, b: 03 Feb 1804; d: 01 Feb 1848 m: 17 Nov

THE MCGAVOCKS OF CARNTON PLANTATION

1831; Number of children: 10 Father: Philip Claud; Mother: Susan Nusom
...............7 Sarah Ann Claud, b: 15 Aug 1832
...............7 Susan L. Claud, b: 10 Dec 1833
...............7 Amanda M. Claud, b: 22 Dec 1835
...............7 James William Claud, b: 12 Jan 1837
...............7 Joshua D. Claud, b: 06 Jun 1838
...............7 Nancy Tennessee Claud, b: 20 Dec 1839
...............7 Mary Frances Claud, b: 05 Feb 1841
...............7 Elizabeth J. W. Claud, b: 29 Mar 1842
...............7 Philip Eldridge Claud, b: 21 Dec 1844
...............7 Mary Tennessee Claud, b: 31 Dec 1846
.... 2nd Husband of Nancy Kent McGavock,+:
...............+William L. Buford, b: 05 Sep 1808; d: 1884 m: 24 Aug 1854; Number of children: 1
...............7 Frances Helen Buford, b: 13 Sep 1855
............6 Sarah M. McGavock,+ b: 11 Dec 1815 in Davidson Co., TN; d: 23 Dec 1836; Number of children: 2
...............+Jonathan Bateman, b: 28 Apr 1805 in Williamson Co., TN m: 28 Mar 1830; Number of children: 2 Father: William Bateman; Mother: Elizabeth Bateman
...............7 Nancy T. Bateman, b: 13 Jan 1835
...............7 Virginia F. Bateman, b: 05 Nov 1836
............6 Melinda Winder McGavock,+ b: 19 Dec 1817; d: 23 Oct 1846; Number of children: 6
...............+James Smith, Jr. b: Abt. 1815; d: in near Franklin, Williamson Co., TN; m: 02 Oct 1833; Number of children: 6 Father: James Smith, Sr.; Mother: Mildred Turner
...............7 Lucinda Ann Smith, b: 18 Jun 1834
...............7 Sarah M. Smith, b: 22 Jan 1837
...............7 Amanda Malvina Smith, b: 15 Jun 1839
...............7 Eliza Margaret Smith, b: 13 Feb 1841
...............7 James Joseph Smith, b: 25 May 1843
...............7 William Turner Smith, b: 19 Aug 1846
............6 Alexander Ewing McGavock,+ b: 25 Sep 1820; d: 01 May 1833
............6 Amanda M. McGavock,+ b: 02 Nov 1822; d: 31 Aug 1847; Number of children: 3
...............+Turner Smith, b: Abt. 1820; d: 25 Nov 1880 m: 08 Aug 1839; Number of children: 3 Father: James Smith, Sr.; Mother: Mildred Turner
...............7 James Alexander Smith,+ b: 02 Jun 1840
...............7 Lucinda J. Smith,+ b: 04 Sep 1842; d: 12 May 1869

THE MCGAVOCKS OF CARNTON PLANTATION

................+Robert F. Cotton, b: Abt. 1840 m: 19 Sep 1865
............7 Amanda Mildred Smith,+ b: 05 Jan 1845; d: 12 Dec 1852
..........6 Oscar Hugh McGavock,+ b: 03 Apr 1825 in Williamson Co., TN; d: 20 Feb 1860 in TN; Number of children: 7
............+America N. Bryant, b: 15 Mar 1827 in TN; d: 26 Aug 1893 m: 22 May 1845; Number of children: 7 Father: William Bryant; Mother: America Williams
............7 Lucinda Elizabeth McGavock,+ b: 22 Apr 1846; Number of children: 8
................+R. L. Hamil, b: 30 Oct 1839; d: in Izard Co., AR? m: 20 Apr 1862; Number of children: 8 Father: William Hamil; Mother: Minerva Conyers
.... 8 William O. Hamil, b: 27 Dec 1863
.... 8 John Hamil, b: Abt. 1862
.... 8 Oilva E. Hamil, b: 11 Apr 1868
.... 8 Caroline Hamil, b: 18 Dec 1869
.... 8 Elizabeth Hamil, b: 29 Jul 1872
.... 8 Newton Hamil, b: 18 Mar 1875
.... 8 Nannie L. Hamil, b: 08 Jul 1877
.... 8 James S. Hamil, b: 25 Oct 1879
............7 William McGavock,+ b: 18 Nov 1847
............7 Hugh W. McGavock,+ b: 06 Jan 1850; Number of children: 1
................+Joanna Howard, b: Abt. 1852; m: 16 Oct 1873; Number of children: 1
.... 8 Ester Maud McGavock, b: 28 Jul 1875
............7 Joseph C. McGavock,+ b: 13 Mar 1852; Number of children: 3
................+H. A. Evans, b: 19 Jul 1856; m: 29 Jan 1874; Number of children: 3 Father: Malachi Evans; Mother: Elizabeth Scarborough
.... 8 James W. McGavock,+ b: Abt. 1874
.... 8 Emeline A. McGavock,+ b: 24 Sep 1876
.... 8 Robert E. Lee McGavock,+ b: 28 Dec 1879
............7 George McGavock,+ b: 17 Dec 1853
............7 James P. McGavock,+ b: 12 Jul 1856; Number of children: 1
................+Tinnie _____? b: 22 Apr 1875; d: 11 May 1906; Number of children: 1
.... 8 Hugh McGavock, b: 1884 in Granite, Greer Co., OK; d: in Granite, Greer Co., OK

THE MCGAVOCKS OF CARNTON PLANTATION

..................7 Oscar Hugh McGavock,+ b: 25 Dec 1859
..................6 Eliza Jane McGavock,+ b: 12 Dec 1827 in Williamson Co., TN; d: 14 Jun 1868; Number of children: 8
..................+George Washington Armstrong, b: 02 Jun 1812; d: 04 Sep 1880 m: 16 Sep 1847; Number of children: 8 Father: William Armstrong
..................7 Lucinda Ellen Armstrong,+ b: 04 Nov 1848
..................7 James William Armstrong,+ b: 08 Jun 1851
..................7 Virginia Ann Armstrong,+ b: 11 Jun 1854
..................7 George Turner Armstrong,+ b: 11 Jul 1857; d: 28 Jan 1858
..................7 Sally Armstrong,+ b: Sep 1859
..................+J. T. Burnham, b: Abt. 1857 m: 12 Dec 1878
..................7 John Oscar Armstrong,+ b: 20 Apr 1862
..................7 Amanda White Armstrong,+ b: 17 Apr 1865
..................7 Eliza Jane Armstrong,+ b: 04 Jun 1868
..................6 Lucinda Ewing McGavock,+ b: 15 Feb 1830 in Davidson Co., TN; d: 05 Feb 1861; Number of children: 6
..................+John H. Graham, b: 09 Oct 1825; d: 30 Apr 1848 m: 20 May 1847 (Note: they had no children); Father: John Graham; Mother: Jane Horton
..................2nd Husband of Lucinda Ewing McGavock,+:
..................+William A. Graham, b: 30 Jan 1827 in Franklin, Williamson Co., TN; m: 24 Sep 1848; Number of children: 6 Father: John Graham; Mother: Jane Horton
..................7 William Graham,+ b: 24 Mar 1850; d: 29 Oct 1854
..................7 John Graham,+ b: 11 Jan 1852; d: 06 Aug 1855
..................7 Hugh Graham,+ b: 23 Dec 1853; d: 24 Jul 1855
..................7 William T. Graham,+ b: 13 Jan 1856
..................+Narcissa Mitchell, b: Abt. 1858 m: 04 Feb 1877
..................7 Lysander Graham,+ b: 26 Feb 1858; d: 11 Apr 1876
..................7 Sallie Graham,+ b: 26 Jun 1860
..................+W. J. Wright, b: Abt. 1858 m: 01 Jan 1879
..................2nd Wife of James McGavock,+ McGavock House, Nashville:
..................+Mary Kent,+ b: 28 Dec 1788; d: 05 Apr 1827 m: 12 Mar 1812; Number of children: 6 Father: Joseph Kent, Col.,+; Mother: Margaret McGavock,+
..................6 Margaret K. McGavock,+ b: 03 Jun 1813; d: 21 Mar 1835; Number of children: 1
..................+Hardy Wilkerson Bryan, LA State Rep. b: 13 Feb 1811; d: 16 Oct 1855 in Edgefield, TN; m: 23 Jul 1833; Number of children: 1 Father: Hardy S. Bryan; Mother: Catherine Young
..................7 James Hardy Bryan,+ b: 17 Mar 1835; d: 01 Sep 1845 in

THE MCGAVOCKS OF CARNTON PLANTATION

Concordia Parish, LA
................6 Sarah Jane McGavock,+ b: Abt. 1815; d: Abt. 1815
................6 Lucinda McGavock,+ b: 18 Feb 1817 in Nashville, Davidson Co., TN; d: 23 Jun 1847; Number of children: 2
....................+Jeremiah George Harris, journalist b: 23 Oct 1809 in Groton, CT; d: 1901; m: 05 May 1842; Number of children: 2 Father: Richard Harris; Mother: Mary Avery
....................7 Joseph Ewing Harris,+ b: 02 May 1843; d: 28 Aug 1865 in London, England (while making a tour of Europe)
....................7 Lucie Harris,+ b: 26 Oct 1846
........................+Van S. Lindsley, Dr. b: Abt. 1844 m: 16 Apr 1868
................6 Wiley McGavock,+ b: Abt. Nov 1818; d: 1838
................6 Joseph Kent McGavock,+ b: 20 Sep 1820; d: 10 Sep 1845
................6 Mary Kent McGavock,+ b: 1826 in Davidson Co., TN; d: 09 Mar 1867; Number of children: 5
....................+Albert Gallatin Wilcox, b: 27 Nov 1816 in Montgomery Co., TN; d: 23 Mar 1880; m: 10 Jan 1849; Number of children: 5 Father: John Earl Wilcox; Mother: Elizabeth _____?
....................7 Joseph Ewing Wilcox,+ b: 25 May 1850; d: 29 Mar 1868
....................7 Mary Alberta Wilcox,+ b: 09 Oct 1851; d: 29 Dec 1861
....................7 John Earl Wilcox,+ b: 10 Feb 1854
....................7 James McGavock Wilcox,+ b: 10 Feb 1856
....................7 Gerald Hiter Wilcox,+ b: 02 May 1863; d: 14 Sep 1868
............5 John McGavock,+ b: 30 Jan 1792 in Wythe Co., VA; d: 07 Jul 1877 in Edgefield, TN; Number of children: 7
................+Cynthia Kent,+ b: 28 Jun 1797 m: 1816 m: 1816; Number of children: 1 Father: Joseph Kent, Col.,+; Mother: Margaret McGavock,+
................6 _____ (unnamed) McGavock b: Abt. 1817
............2nd Wife of John McGavock,+:
................+Sally Shall, b: 1794 in Hagerstown, MD; m: Abt. 1820; Number of children: 1 Father: George Shall, Cap.; Mother: Margaret Crebs
................6 Elizabeth McGavock,+ b: Abt. 1821 in Davidson Co., TN; Number of children: 2
....................+Napoleon Young, b: Abt. 1820; m: Abt. 1840; Number of children: 2 Father: John Young; Mother: Nancy Boyd
....................7 Elizabeth Young,+ b: Abt. 1841
....................7 Boyd M. Young,+ b: 26 Dec 1843
........................+Eudora Thompson, b: Abt. 1845 m: 11 Aug 1867
............3rd Wife of John McGavock,+:
................+Elizabeth B. Hinton, b: 07 Dec 1803; d: 01 May 1861 m: 06 Nov

THE MCGAVOCKS OF CARNTON PLANTATION

1823; Number of children: 5 Father: Jeremiah Hinton; Mother: Sallie Boyd
............6 Mary Ann Kent McGavock,+ b: 11 Sep 1824 in Davidson Co., TN; d: 05 Sep 1864; Number of children: 2
............+Ewing P. McGinty, b: 08 Sep 1817; d: 21 Sep 1855 m: 23 Nov 1848; Number of children: 2 Father: William A. McGinty; Mother: Eliza Hyre
............7 Mary Elizabeth McGinty,+ b: 25 Apr 1851; d: 11 Aug 1868
............7 Johnnie Ewing McGinty,+ b: 20 Jun 1853; d: 14 Jan 1881
............+William H. Pearce, b: Abt. 1851 m: 03 Oct 1876
............6 Sarah A. McGavock,+ b: 15 Mar 1826
............+John S. Hart, b: Abt. 1824 m: 02 Oct 1873
............6 Cynthia Tennessee McGavock,+ b: 26 Jul 1827 in Davidson Co., TN; Number of children: 3
............+John Berry McFerrin, Rev., b: 15 Jun 1807 in Rutherford Co., TN; d: 10 May 1887 in Edgefield, TN; m: 12 Nov 1855; Number of children: 3 Father: James McFerrin; Mother: Jane Campbell Berry
............7 Catherine Louisa McFerrin,+ b: 24 Dec 1856
............+William R. Bryan, b: Abt. 1854 m: 15 Feb 1882
............7 Mary McGinty McFerrin,+ b: 01 Mar 1857; d: 17 Aug 1858
............7 Bettie McGavock McFerrin,+ b: 23 Jul 1861
............+James Henry Yarbrough, b: Abt. 1859 m: 15 Jun 1881
............6 Catherine Louisa McGavock,+ b: 28 Jun 1830; d: 21 Sep 1855
............6 John William McGavock,+ farmer, b: 27 May 1832 in Nashville, Davidson Co., TN; d: 01 May 1899 in Nashville, Davidson Co., TN; Number of children: 5
............+Emily Batte, b: 03 Aug 1836 in Giles Co., TN m: 29 Jan 1856; Number of children: 5 Father: Thomas Batte; Mother: Marianna _____?
............7 Hugh W. McGavock,+ b: 26 Nov 1856; Number of children: 5
............+Eliza Harris, b: 12 Oct 1857 m: 07 Oct 1880; Number of children: 5 Father: Elijah Harris; Mother: Virginia M. Watkins
.... 8 William Allen McGavock,+ b: 16 Aug 1881
.... 8 Elijah Harris McGavock,+ b: 10 May 1883
.... 8 Loulie McGavock,+ b: 10 Mar 1885
.... 8 Charles Grandison McGavock,+ b: 04 Jun 1887
.... 8 Virginia Watkins McGavock,+ b: 25 Jun 1897
............7 John Augustus McGavock,+ b: 27 Sep 1857; d: 02 Feb 1891 in CA
............7 Edwin A. McGavock,+ b: 07 Aug 1860 in Nashville, Davidson Co., TN?; d: 11 Feb 1891 in CA
............7 Annie Lou McGavock,+ b: 11 Dec 1866; Number of children:

The McGavocks of Carnton Plantation

2
............................+Benjamin B. Gillespie, b: 01 Feb 1860 m: 30 Nov 1887; Number of children: 2
............................8 Nellie G. Gillespie,+ b: 23 Sep 1890
............................8 Frank W. Gillespie,+ b: 03 Oct 1891
........................7 Frank W. McGavock,+ b: 29 Jun 1869; d: 23 Jan 1900
................5 Francis McGavock,+ of Clifflawn Plantation; b: 31 Jan 1794 in Wythe Co., VA, or Clifflawn Plantation, Nashville, TN; d: 23 Dec 1866 in Cliff Lawn Plantation, Nashville, TN; Number of children: 5
....................+Amanda P. Harding, McGavocks, Belle Meade Plantation, b: 23 Oct 1807 in Belle Meade Plantation, Nashville, Davidson Co., TN; d: 24 Oct 1873 in Nashville, Davidson Co., TN m: 23 Oct 1823; Number of children: 5 Father: John Harding, Belle Meade Plantation; Line; Mother: Susannah Shute
....................6 John Harding McGavock,+ b: 03 Oct 1824 in Davidson Co., TN; d: 12 Apr 1861 in AR; Number of children: 4
........................+Georgia A. Moore, b: 24 Aug 1833 in Oglethorpe Co., GA m: 01 Dec 1853; Number of children: 4 Father: Joseph T. Moore; Mother: Eliza W. Gregory
........................7 Lida Carey McGavock,+ b: 27 Sep 1854; d: 15 Nov 1854
........................7 John Harding McGavock,+ b: 30 Sep 1855; d: 27 Feb 1862
........................7 Susan John McGavock,+ b: 23 May 1857; Number of children: 3
............................+William Henry Grider, b: 01 Feb 1855 m: 25 Feb 1880; Number of children: 3 Father: John H. Grider; Mother: Maria L. Morris
............................8 Georgia Douglas Grider,+ b: 02 Aug 1881
............................8 Josephine Louise Grider,+ b: 18 Mar 1886
............................8 John McGavock Grider,+ b: 28 May 1892
........................7 Joseph Moore McGavock,+ b: 22 Mar 1859; d: 09 Jun 1861
................6 David Harding McGavock,+, Two Rivers Plantation; b: 01 Sep 1826 in Nashville, Davidson Co., TN; d: 20 Mar 1896 in Nashville, Davidson Co., TN; Number of children: 2
........................+Willie Elizabeth Harding, Belle Meade Plantation, b: 28 Sep 1832 in Spring Place, Nashville, Davidson Co., TN; d: 23 Dec 1895; m: 23 May 1850; Number of children: 2 Father: William Giles Harding, Gen., Belle Meade Plantation; Mother: Elizabeth Hoggatt Clopton; note: Willie and David are 1st cousins
........................7 Frank Owens McGavock,+ b: 25 Sep 1851 at Two Rivers Plantation, Nashville, Davidson Co., TN; Number of children: 3
............................+Lula Spence, b: 21 Sep 1853 in Murfreesboro, TN; d: 11 Jan 1882 m: 16 Sep 1875; Number of children: 3 Father: David H. C. Spence;

THE MCGAVOCKS OF CARNTON PLANTATION

Mother: Sally Aiken
.................8 Spence McGavock,+ b: 26 Jul 1876; d: 04 Dec 1936
.... 8 Louisa B. McGavock,+ b: 28 Oct 1878; d: 22 Nov 1965
.... 8 Willie McGavock,+ b: 26 Jan 1880; d: 30 Aug 1881
............2nd Wife of Frank Owens McGavock,+:
................+Clara C. Plimpton, b: Abt. 1855; m: 18 Aug 1896
............7 Elizabeth Clopton "Bessie" McGavock,+ b: 18 Aug 1864; d: Jun 1870
...........6 Susannah Elizabeth McGavock,+ b: 27 Nov 1829; d: 04 Jan 1894
..............+William Henry Smith, b: Abt. 1827 m: 21 Feb 1850
...........6 Amanda McGavock,+ b: 17 Jan 1832 in Davidson Co., TN; d: 29 Aug 1899; Number of children: 3
..............+Archer Cheatham, Merchant b: 11 Dec 1828; d: 15 Aug 1879 in Nashville, Davidson Co., TN? m: 04 Sep 1851 m: 04 Sep 1851; Number of children: 3 Father: John Long Cheatham; Mother: Melissa Saunders
............7 William Bolling Cheatham,+ b: 26 Jun 1852 in Nashville, Davidson Co., TN
................+Hattie Armstrong, b: 1856 in Nashville, Davidson Co., TN m: 19 Jul 1902
............7 Amanda F. Cheatham,+ b: 05 May 1855
................+Christian S. Pearce b: Abt. 1853 m: 09 Dec 1875
............7 Mary D. Cheatham,+ b: 19 May 1861
................+Thomas H. Lipscomb, b: Abt. 1859
...........6 Elizabeth Virginia McGavock,+ b: 15 Jun 1836; d: 24 Jul 1841
.........5 Randal McGavock,+ b: 27 Mar 1796 in Wythe Co., VA (some say Nashville, Davidson Co., TN); d: 11 Jun 1864 in Dunker Bottom, Pulaski Co., VA; Number of children: 9
............+Almira Haynes, b: 18 Oct 1802 in Knoxville, TN or Nashville, Davidson Co., TN; d: 31 Aug 1874 in Pulaski Co., VA m: 24 Mar 1818; Number of children: 9 Father: Stephen Haynes; Mother: Catherine Blackwell
...........6 David Shall McGavock,+ b: 21 Dec 1818 in near Nashville, Davidson Co., TN; d: 08 Aug 1866 in farm at Spring-Dale, Pulaski Co., VA; Number of children: 6
..............+Cynthia M. Cloyd,+ b: 18 Feb 1820; d: 15 Aug 1847 m: 31 Jul 1844; Father: David Cloyd; Mother: Sally McGavock,+
...........2nd Wife of David Shall McGavock,+:
..............+Pauline Ligon, b: 19 Jan 1828 in Powhatan Co., VA m: 09 Dec 1851 in Petersburg, VA; Number of children: 6 Father: James Ligon; Mother: Judith Archer Bentley
............7 Henry Bentley McGavock,+ b: 19 Sep 1852

THE MCGAVOCKS OF CARNTON PLANTATION

..........................+Grace Goodwyn,+ b: 15 Oct 1850 m: 03 Oct 1876; Father: Philo Hiram Goodwyn, Jr.; Mother: Martha Shall McGavock,+
....................7 James Randal McGavock,+ b: 25 Feb 1855
....................7 William Ligon McGavock,+ b: 02 Jul 1858
....................7 Myra Lee McGavock,+ b: 01 Apr 1861
..........................+Thomas Ellis, b: Abt. 1859 m: 02 Dec 1886
....................7 Pauline Archer McGavock,+ b: 11 Nov 1863 in Pulaski Co., VA; Number of children: 1
..........................+George Gretter Moseley, b: 20 Apr 1864; d: in Columbia, SC? m: 23 Oct 1895; Number of children: 1 Father: Robert D. Moseley; Mother: Jane Gretter
..........................8 David Gretter Moseley,+ b: 15 Jan 1898
....................7 David Ellen McGavock,+ b: 22 Aug 1865; d: 10 Sep 1875
................6 Martha Shall McGavock,+ b: 10 Sep 1820 in near Nashville, Davidson Co., TN; d: 14 Oct 1880; Number of children: 11
......................+Philo Hiram Goodwyn, Jr. b: 25 Aug 1802 in Bridgewater, NY; d: 28 Mar 1860; m: 20 Jan 1841; Number of children: 11 Father: Philo Hiram Goodwyn, Sr.; Mother: Hannah Merrill
....................7 McGavock Goodwyn, Col.,+ War for Southern Independence, C.S.A., b: 23 Nov 1841; d: 21 Jun 1875
....................7 Frank Wills Goodwyn,+ b: 06 May 1843; d: 03 Dec 1875
....................7 Clara Leslie Goodwyn,+ b: 11 Mar 1845; d: 29 Apr 1847
....................7 Philo Hiram Goodwyn,+ b: 14 Dec 1846; d: 22 Nov 1862
....................7 George Coons Goodwyn,+ b: 16 Nov 1848; d: 25 Jun 1851
....................7 Grace Goodwyn,+ b: 15 Oct 1850
..........................+Henry Bentley McGavock,+ b: 19 Sep 1852 m: 03 Oct 1876; Father: David Shall McGavock,+; Mother: Pauline Ligon
....................7 Mary Lizzie Goodwyn,+ b: 18 Nov 1752
....................7 David McGavock Goodwyn,+ b: 16 Nov 1854
..........................+Jessie Vincent, b: Abt. 1856 m: 22 Nov 1882
....................7 Frederick Stringer Goodwyn,+ b: 28 Nov 1856; d: 24 Mar 1860
....................7 Martha Goodwyn,+ b: 05 Sep 1858; d: 10 Jun 1859
....................7 Philo Hiram Goodwyn,+ b: 30 Nov 1860
..........................+Isadore Cantrell, b: Abt. 1862 m: 10 Oct 1883
................6 Catherine Blackwell McGavock,+ b: 30 Jul 1822 in near Nashville, Davidson Co., TN; d: 29 Nov 1898; Number of children: 10
......................+George Philips Bowers, Jr. b: 24 Aug 1819 in Scituate, MA; d: 1890; m: 03 Feb 1844 in OIberville Parish, LA; Number of children: 10 Father: George Philips Bowers, Sr.; Mother: Laura Eugenia Florian

The McGavocks of Carnton Plantation

..............7 George Florian Bowers,+ b: 03 Feb 1845
...................+Eliza P. Pike, b: Abt. 1847 m: 12 Jan 1870
..............7 Kate McGavock Bowers,+ b: 24 Jul 1846; d: 15 Dec 1848 in New Orleans, LA
..............7 Pattie Virginia Bowers,+ b: 09 Jun 1848
...................+Bogart Shall, b: Abt. 1846 m: 20 Feb 1866
..............7 Randal McGavock Bowers,+ b: 23 Dec 1849 in New Orleans, LA
..............7 David Cloyd Bowers,+ b: 02 May 1851 in New Orleans, LA; d: 28 Oct 1884
..............7 Wilhelmus Bogart Bowers,+ b: 25 Jun 1853
...................+Flora Evans, b: Abt. 1855
..............7 William H. Avery Bowers,+ b: 02 May 1855 in New Orleans, LA; d: 25 Sep 1858 in New Orleans, LA
..............7 Annie Bowers,+ b: 09 Jun 1857
...................+Espy H. Williams, b: Abt. 1855 m: 15 Apr 1879
..............7 Nellie Bowers,+ b: 31 Dec 1858
...................+W. E. Philips, b: Abt. 1856; m: 10 Jun 1881
..............7 Laura Eugenie Bowers,+ b: 15 Apr 1862
...................+J. D. Ford. Dr., b: Abt. 1860
............6 Mary Ann Scott McGavock,+ b: 24 Oct 1824 in near Nashville, Davidson Co., TN; d: 06 Apr 1852 in New Orleans, LA; Number of children: 1
..............+William Murphy Greenwood, b: 16 Jan 1819 in New York, NY; d: 1853 in San Francisco, CA; m: 05 Nov 1849; Number of children: 1 Father: Richard Greenwood; Mother: Mary Murphy
..............7 Mary Ann McGavock Greenwood,+ b: 31 Mar 1852 in San Francisco, CA?
...................+Charles Josselyn, b: Abt. 1850 m: 27 Apr 1875
............6 Elizabeth McDowell McGavock,+ b: 05 Oct 1826 in near Nashville, Davidson Co., TN; Number of children: 3
..............+David Cloyd, b: 27 Jan 1824 in Pulaski Co., VA; d: 07 Sep 1863 in Dunker Bottom, Pulaski Co., VA; m: 20 Dec 1848; Number of children: 3 Father: Thomas Cloyd; Mother: Mary "Aunt Polly" McGavock,+
..............7 Lucy T. Cloyd,+ b: 04 Jul 1850; d: Jul 1895
...................+Robert Barton, b: Abt. 1848 m: 25 Nov 1875
..............7 Catherine McGavock Cloyd,+ b: 07 Jul 1852; d: 09 May 1895
...................+Haven B. Howe, b: Abt. 1850 m: 16 Apr 1873
..............7 Mary David Cloyd,+ b: 01 Nov 1858; d: 22 Jun 1864
............2nd Husband of Elizabeth McDowell McGavock,+:
..............+Andrew Moore, b: 16 Jul 1833 in Rockbridge Co., VA m:

THE MCGAVOCKS OF CARNTON PLANTATION

02 Oct 1866 (Note: They had no children); Father: David Moore; Mother: Elizabeth Harvey

..................6 Harriet Russel McGavock,+ 9 children died young b: 05 Nov 1828 in near Nashville, Davidson Co., TN; d: 22 Mar 1903; Number of children: 9

........................+William A. Goodwyn, b: 13 Nov 1824; d: 13 Oct 1898 in Nashville, Davidson Co., TN; m: 20 Dec 1848 in Iberville Parish, LA (Note: all 9 of their children died young of scarlet fever or diptheria); Number of children: 9 Father: Philo Hiram Goodwyn, Sr.; Mother: Harriet Rice

........................7 Willie McGavock Goodwyn,+ b: 20 Dec 1849; d: 13 Aug 1860

........................7 Myra Goodwyn,+ b: 29 Feb 1852; d: 02 Aug 1860

........................7 Harry Russel Goodwyn,+ b: 10 Jan 1854; d: 16 Oct 1860

........................7 David Cloyd Goodwyn,+ b: 28 Feb 1857; d: 27 Aug 1860

........................7 Randal McGavock Goodwyn,+ b: 22 Jun 1859; d: 18 Aug 1859

........................7 Martha Goodwyn,+ b: 23 Jul 1860; d: 12 Mar 1863

........................7 Annie Goodwyn,+ b: 03 Feb 1862; d: 07 Mar 1863

........................7 William Rice Goodwyn,+ b: 14 Feb 1866; d: 03 Sep 1875

........................7 Hugh McGavock Goodwyn,+ b: 01 Jun 1871; d: 16 Sep 1875

..................6 George Shall McGavock,+ b: 22 Oct 1830; d: 22 Aug 1832

..................6 Jane Ellen McGavock,+ b: 08 Nov 1832 near Nashville, Davidson Co., TN; d: 20 Jun 1865; Number of children: 2

........................+James R. Christian, Dr., b: 10 Apr 1818 in Hopkins Co., KY; d: 08 Jun 1881 in Holly Springs, MS; m: 18 May 1852; Number of children: 2 Father: Matthew Christian; Mother: Lucy _____?

........................7 Randal McGavock Christian,+ b: 20 Mar 1853; d: 03 Oct 1860

........................7 James Russel Christian,+ b: 08 Aug 1861

..............................+Mattie Humphreys, b: Abt. 1863

..................6 Myra McGavock,+ b: 02 Oct 1843

...............5 Emily McGavock,+ b: 29 Jul 1798; d: 26 Dec 1798

...............5 _____ (unnamed) McGavock,+ b: 04 Oct 1799; d: 11 Oct 1799

...............5 Lysander McGavock,+ founder of Midway Plantation; b: 22 Oct 1800 in Nashville, Davidson Co., TN; d: 05 Aug 1855 at Midway Plantation, Brentwood, Williamson Co., TN; Number of children: 6

........................+Elizabeth Crockett; b: 07 Sep 1795 in Wythe Co., VA; d: 31 Jan 1862 m: 05 Dec 1822; Number of children: 6 Father: James Crockett; Mother: Mary Drake; Note: Midway was built largely on land owned originally by Elizabeth's family; Samuel Crockett, III (1772-1827), her famous rifle making 1st

THE MCGAVOCKS OF CARNTON PLANTATION

cousin, built Forge Seat, Brentwood, TN; Elizabeth's uncle, Lt. Andrew Crockett (1745-1821)—who built the Andrew Crockett House in Brentwood—was a well regarded officer in the American Rev. War

............6 Ephraim C. McGavock,+ b: 25 Mar 1825; d: 07 Jul 1840

............6 Cynthia McGavock,+ b: 06 Apr 1827; d: 04 Jan 1882; Cynthia remained at her parent's home, Midway Plantation, and never married

............6 Sally E. McGavock,+ b: 28 Oct 1828; d: 29 May 1899

....................+Thomas Pointer, b: 4 Aug 1826; d: 25 Dec 1904 m: 12 Feb 1852

............6 Emily (or Emilie) McGavock,+ b: 02 Apr 1830 in Williamson Co., TN; d: 26 July 1920; Number of children: 3; Emily and her husband Oliver built a house north of Midway Plantation which they named Hayesland. It burned down while they were on their honeymoon in Europe, and they later rebuilt it; the home is today called Boxwood Hall

....................+Oliver Bliss Hayes, II, Jr. b: 17 Oct 1825 in Nashville, Davidson Co., TN; d: 16 Aug 1868; m: 06 Jul 1852; Number of children: 3 Father: Oliver Bliss Hayes, Sr., Rev.; Mother: Sarah Clements "Sallie" Hightower

..................7 Lysander McGavock Hayes,+ b: 03 May 1853; d: 1921; Number of children: 2

........................+Hortense Cocke, b: 20 Feb 1856; d: 8 May 1917; m: 10 Jan 1888; Number of children: 3; Father: Daniel Fenton Cocke; Mother: Margaret Roberson

.... 8 Margaret Hayes,+ b: 1889; d: 1970; Number of children: 3; Note: Margaret graduated from Ward's Seminary in Nashville, and later attended the Horace Mann School in NY

..............................+Ferdinand Powell, b: Abt. 1885 in Johnson City, TN m: Abt. 1910; Number of children: 3

.... 8 McGavock Hayes,+ b: 1895; d: 1956; Number of children: 2; Note: he attended both the Duncan School and the University of TN, toured the Grand Canyon, and served in World War I; McGavock and Ella's two daughters, Mary Elizabeth Hayes and Margaret Hayes, were the fifth and last generation of the Hayes family to live at Midway Plantation

..............................+Ella Blanton Smith, b: 1904 in Atlanta, GA; d: 1990 m: 1927; Number of children: 2

..................7 Thomas Pointer Hayes,+ b: 17 Jun 1858; d: 01 Aug 1862

..................7 Elizabeth "Bettie" Hayes,+ b: 26 Dec 1863

........................+W. W. Martin, b: Abt. 1861 m: 05 Sep 1889

............6 Hugh Lysander McGavock,+ b: 30 Mar 1833 at Midway Plantation, Brentwood, Williamson Co., TN; d: unexpectedly on 13 Nov 1852, at the age of nineteen of pneumonia, while attending Cumberland University in

The McGavocks of Carnton Plantation

Lebanon, TN

................6 Margaret Elizabeth "Betsie" or "Maggie" McGavock,+ b: 03 Feb 1836; d: 1923; Margaret remained at her parent's home, Midway Plantation, and never married

...............5 Hugh L. White McGavock, twin,+ b: 09 Aug 1804 in Nashville, Davidson Co., TN; d: 01 Jul 1853; Number of children: 1

..................+Mary Wilson Hagen, b: 22 Oct 1824 in Nashville, Davidson Co., TN; m: 25 Jul 1843; Number of children: 1 Father: Henry Hagen; Mother: Catherine Talbot

..................6 Hugh Frank McGavock,+ b: 04 Oct 1844; d: 31 Dec 1891

........................+Belle Story b: Abt. 1846 m: 1889

...............5 Sally McGavock, twin,+ b: 09 Aug 1804 in Nashville, Davidson Co., TN; d: 22 Aug 1857; Number of children: 3

..................+Joseph Love Ewing, b: 30 May 1798 in Davidson Co., TN; d: 16 May 1860; m: 11 Nov 1824; Number of children: 3 Father: William Ewing; Mother: Margaret Love

..................6 James McGavock Ewing,+ b: 20 Nov 1825; d: 24 Mar 1826

..................6 John O. Ewing,+ b: 30 Mar 1833

........................+Fannie E. Wilkinson, b: Abt. 1835 m: 29 Jun 1854

..................2nd Wife of John O. Ewing,+:

........................+Sarah A. Lightfoot, b: Abt. 1836 m: 13 Feb 1861

..................6 Hugh F. Ewing,+ b: 28 Jun 1836

........................+Pattie J. Pointer b: Abt. 1838; m: 14 Mar 1861

..................2nd Wife of Hugh F. Ewing,+:

........................+Lizzie _____? b: Abt. 1838; m: 01 Aug 1872

..................3rd Wife of Hugh F. Ewing,+:

........................+Bettie _____? b: Abt. 1840 m: 01 Oct 1878

..........2nd Wife of David McGavock, surveyor,+:

...............+Mary Turner, b: 1773 in NC; d: 1834 in Nashville, Davidson Co., TN; m: 1812 in Nashville, Davidson Co., TN?; Number of children: 2

...............5 David Turner McGavock, Dr.,+ b: 19 Apr 1813 in Nashville, Davidson Co., TN; d: 09 Jan 1866 in Nashville, Davidson Co., TN; Number of children: 9

..................+Caroline Eliza Pugsley, b: 12 May 1815 in England; d: 07 Dec 1863 in Nashville, Davidson Co., TN m: 04 Dec 1832 m: 04 Dec 1832; Number of children: 9 Father: Charles Pugsley, Dr.; Mother: Eliza Rooke

..................6 Mary T. McGavock,+ b: 04 Dec 1833 in Probably Nashville, Davidson Co., TN; d: 1842 in Nashville, Davidson Co., TN

..................6 Eliza L. McGavock,+ b: 08 Oct 1836 in Nashville, Davidson Co., TN; d: 30 Nov 1862; Number of children: 2

THE MCGAVOCKS OF CARNTON PLANTATION

.................+Emmet Cockrill b: Dec 1832 in AL; d: 1870 m: 17 Feb 1857; Number of children: 2 Father: Sterling H. Cockrill; Mother: Ann MacDonald, McDonald

....................7 Sterling R. Cockrill,+ b: 27 Jan 1858

....................7 Emmet Minor Cockrill,+ b: Oct 1859; d: 1890

.................6 Ophelia Clay McGavock,+ b: 16 Jun 1839 in Nashville, Davidson Co., TN; d: 04 Apr 1865; Number of children: 3

....................+Felix R. Cheatham b: 30 Apr 1824; d: 22 Jan 1893 m: 17 Feb 1857; Number of children: 3 Father: Leonard Pope Cheatham; Mother: Elizabeth Davis Robertson

....................7 Felix R. Cheatham,+ b: 09 Nov 1857; d: 28 Oct 1883

....................7 Frank James Cheatham,+ b: 20 Dec 1860; d: 1896

........................+E. L. Cheatham b: Abt. 1862 m: 10 Feb 1891

....................7 Caroline McGavock Cheatham,+ b: 23 Sep 1862; d: 19 Feb 1864

.................6 Alberta Pugsley McGavock,+ b: 10 Feb 1841 in Nashville, Davidson Co., TN; d: 04 Jun 1878; Number of children: 4

....................+Dallas Bache, Dr. (great-grandson of Benjamin Franklin); b: 23 Jun 1838 in Washington, D.C.; d: 02 Jun 1902 in San Diego, San Diego Co., CA; m: 19 Apr 1864 in Davidson Co., TN; Number of children: 4 Father: Richard Bache, Jr.; Mother: Sophia Burrell Dalles

....................7 Harriet Bache,+ b: Abt. 1865

........................+Charles Clapp, b: Abt. 1863

....................7 Caroline Pugsley Bache,+ b: Abt. 1867

....................7 Alberta Bache,+ b: Abt. 1869

....................7 Dallas Bache,+ b: Abt. 1871

........................+Bertha E. Clarkson, b: Abt. 1873 m: Apr 1893

.................6 Charles Pugsley McGavock,+ b: 1843; d: 1843

.................6 Caroline Pugsley McGavock,+ b: 22 May 1845 in Nashville, Davidson Co., TN; Number of children: 7

....................+Samuel Marmaduke Whitside, Gen., b: 09 Jan 1839 in Canada m: 24 Nov 1868; Number of children: 7 Father: William H. Whitside; Mother: Martha Murray

....................7 McGavock Whitside,+ b: 26 Jul 1870; d: 07 Oct 1870

....................7 Samuel Marmaduke Whitside,+ b: 20 Aug 1872; d: 29 Jan 1877

....................7 Effie Whitside,+ b: 24 Apr 1874; d: 07 Aug 1876

....................7 Warren Whitside,+ b: 02 Nov 1875

....................7 Dallas W. Whitside,+ b: 22 Apr 1879; d: 1879

....................7 Madeline Whitside,+ b: 1882

THE MCGAVOCKS OF CARNTON PLANTATION

..................7 Victor M. Whitside,+ b: 1886

..................6 Annie Rooke McGavock,+ b: Oct 1847; d: 1849

..................6 David Ella McGavock,+ b: 10 May 1855 in Nashville, Davidson Co., TN; Number of children: 3

....................+Frances Conrad, b: Abt. 1857; d: Abt. 1875; m: Sep 1872; Number of children: 1

..................7 Francis C. Conrad,+ b: 1873

..................2nd Husband of David Ella McGavock,+:

....................+Francis M. Coxe, b: Abt. 1860 in Philadelphia, PA; d: in San Francisco, CA?; m: Aug 1879; Number of children: 2

..................7 Ella Coxe,+ b: 1882

..................7 Mabel Coxe,+ b: 1884

..................6 David Albert McGavock,+ b: 14 Jul 1857; d: 30 Oct 1862

..............5 Albert McGavock,+ b: 1814 in Nashville, Davidson Co., TN; d: 28 Oct 1836 in Nashville, Davidson Co., TN

..........4 James McGavock, Jr., Rev. War Soldier,+ b: 10 Jun 1764 in Max Meadows, Wythe Co., VA; d: 12 May 1838 in Fort Chiswell, Wythe Co., VA; Number of children: 12

..............+Mary Drake Crockett, b: 23 May 1778 in Wythe Co., VA; d: 27 Nov 1826; m: 24 Apr 1799 in Wythe Co., VA; Number of children: 12 Father: James Crockett; Mother: Mary Drake

..............5 Cynthia McGavock,+ b: 09 Apr 1800; d: 01 Jun 1874

..............5 Randal McGavock,+ b: 08 May 1802 in Fort Chiswell, Wythe Co., VA; d: 25 Oct 1826

..............5 James McGavock,+ b: 26 May 1804 in Wythe Co., VA; d: 23 Oct 1839; Number of children: 3

..................+Agnes Crockett,+ b: 05 May 1813 in Wythe Co., VA m: 15 Apr 1830; Number of children: 3 Father: Robert Crockett, Major; Mother: Jennie Lewis Stewart, Stuart,+

..................6 Mary McGavock,+ b: 22 May 1834 in Wythe Co., VA; Number of children: 7

....................+John R. Richardson, Jr., b: 1828; d: 21 Feb 1898; m: 16 Jul 1851; Number of children: 7 Father: John R. Richardson, Sr.; Mother: Anne Powel

..................7 Agnes L. Richardson,+ b: 08 Jul 1852

..................7 John R. Richardson,+ b: 01 Mar 1857

..................7 Sarah McGavock Richardson,+ b: 11 Nov 1860

..................7 William McGavock Richardson,+ b: 23 Apr 1863

..................7 Nisbet P. Richardson,+ b: 06 Jul 1866; d: 17 Nov 1886

..................7 Jane L. Richardson,+ b: 04 Jul 1868

..................7 Cynthia Cloyd Richardson,+ b: 16 Mar 1875

THE MCGAVOCKS OF CARNTON PLANTATION

................6 Jane Lewis McGavock,+ b: 29 Sep 1836 in Wythe Co., VA; d: Apr 1883; Number of children: 4
......................+Henry Woodson Richardson, b: 02 Feb 1831 m: 15 Apr 1850; Number of children: 4 Father: John R. Richardson, Sr.; Mother: Anne Powel
....................7 Ann Smith Richardson,+ b: 02 Dec 1857
....................7 James McGavock Richardson,+ b: 16 Mar 1860
....................7 Henry Woodson Richardson,+ b: 27 Aug 1863; d: 10 Dec 1898
....................7 Mary Susan Richardson,+ b: 16 Jul 1869
................6 Sarah McGavock,+ b: 12 May 1839
.............5 Ephraim McGavock,+ b: 12 Dec 1805 in Wythe Co., VA; d: 12 Jan 1876; Number of children: 8
..................+Abbie Jouett Williamson, b: 02 Mar 1812 in NY; d: 05 Aug 1877 m: 17 Nov 1840; Number of children: 8
..................6 James Hampton McGavock, b: 16 Feb 1842 in Wythe Co., VA; Number of children: 6
......................+Elizabeth Pointer, b: 14 Jun 1843; d: 01 May 1893 m: 22 Jul 1867; Number of children: 5 Father: William H. Pointer; Mother: Sarah Buford
....................7 Edward Pointer McGavock, b: 15 Sep 1868
....................7 Stephen McGavock, b: 25 May 1873; d: 22 Jul 1873
....................7 William Pointer McGavock, b: 28 Nov 1876
..........................+Flora McDowell Stokes b: Abt. 1878; m: 11 Jul 1894
....................7 James Hampton McGavock, b: 11 Jul 1878; d: 12 Nov 1878
....................7 Cloyd McGavock, b: 02 Mar 1880
..........................+Annie L. Jordan, b: Abt. 1882 m: 30 Jul 1902
................2nd Wife of James Hampton McGavock:
......................+Eveline Moore Prescott b: 05 Mar 1868 in Wythe Co., VA? m: 23 Jun 1900; Number of children: 1
....................7 John Fulton McGavock, b: 28 Feb 1902
................6 Francis Ella McGavock, b: 02 Aug 1843; d: 24 Nov 1843
................6 Sarah Jackson McGavock, b: 13 Feb 1845; d: 02 Feb 1901
................6 John Williamson McGavock, b: 25 Oct 1846 in Wythe Co., VA; d: Aft. 1928 in Wythe Co., VA; Number of children: 15
......................+Emily Graham b: 22 Sep 1848; d: 18 Aug 1889; m: 21 Nov 1871 Father: David Graham; Mother: Martha Pearce
................2nd Wife of John Williamson McGavock:
......................+Jane Byrd Pendleton, b: 26 Jun 1869; m: 17 Jun 1891; Number of children: 15 Father: Gurdon H. Pendleton; Mother: Jane Page
....................7 David Graham McGavock, b: 08 Oct 1872
....................7 John Williamson McGavock, b: 21 Nov 1873

THE MCGAVOCKS OF CARNTON PLANTATION

................7 Ephraim McGavock, b: 25 Nov 187
................7 Martha P. McGavock, b: 26 Jul 1876
................7 Abigail Jouett McGavock, b: 19 Nov 1877
................7 James H. McGavock, b: 03 Dec 1878
................7 Henry Parish McGavock, b: 01 May 1880
................7 Margaret Matthews McGavock, b: 14 Apr 1884
................7 Mary Bell McGavock, b: 11 Jul 1886
................7 Unnamed McGavock, b: 17 Feb 1889
................7 Emily Maria Graham McGavock, b: 16 Jun 1892
................7 Byrd Page McGavock, b: 09 Jul 1894
................7 Sarah Jackson McGavock, b: 06 Jun 1896 in Wythe Co., VA
......................+John Allison, b: Abt. 1895 in Wythe Co., VA m: Abt. 1920
................7 Gurdon Pendleton McGavock, b: 15 Nov 1898
................7 Stephen McGavock, b: 25 Nov 1901
..............6 Cynthia McGavock, b: 21 Aug 1848 in Wythe Co., VA; Number of children: 1
................+John H. Fulton, Capt. C.S.A. Civil War b: 18 Jul 1837 m: 06 Jun 1876; Number of children: 1
................7 Fannie Jouet Fulton, b: 10 Mar 1877
............6 Francis Hargrave McGavock, b: 14 Aug 1850; d: 16 Jan 1889
............6 Mary Jouet McGavock, b: 13 Aug 1852; d: 20 Aug 1853
............6 Margaret M. McGavock, b: 15 Apr 1854
..........5 Stephen McGavock,+ b: 08 Nov 1807; d: 20 Jul 1880
..........5 Mary McGavock,+ b: 08 Oct 1809; d: 11 Nov 1859
..........5 Elizabeth McGavock,+ b: 06 May 1811; d: 21 Oct 1859
................+Alexander Chaffin, b: Abt. 1809
..........5 Joseph Cloyd McGavock,+ b: 17 Dec 1813; d: 10 Oct 1886
..........5 Andrew J. McGavock,+ b: 20 Nov 1814; d: 14 Sep 1838
..........5 Sarah McGavock,+ b: 30 Sep 1817; d: 13 Sep 1839
..........5 William McGavock,+ b: 27 Dec 1819; d: 10 Sep 1849
..........5 Margaret McGavock,+ b: 22 Oct 1821 in Wythe Co., VA; d: 11 Mar 1900 in Wytheville, Wythe Co., VA; Number of children: 2
................+Harold Smythe Matthews, b: 24 Oct 1818 in Wythe Co., VA; d: 11 Jun 1863; m: 16 Dec 1840; Number of children: 2 Father: John P. Matthews; Mother: Malvina Smythe
................6 Sarah Matthews, b: 18 Oct 1843; d: 26 Aug 1900
................+Vincent C. Huff, Dr. b: Abt. 1841 m: 06 Oct 1863
................6 Malvina Matthews, b: 01 Oct 1845; d: 04 Jun 1881
..........4 Cynthia McGavock,+ b: Abt. 1766

THE MCGAVOCKS OF CARNTON PLANTATION

..........4 Randal McGavock, Eleventh Mayor of Nashville,+ b: 20 Jun 1766 in Rockbridge Co., VA; d: 27 Sep 1843 in Carnton Plantation, Franklin, Williamson Co., TN; Number of children: 7

..............+Sarah Dougherty Rodgers, b: 01 Apr 1786 in Max Meadows, Wythe Co., VA, or TN; d: 28 Dec 1854 in Carnton Plantation, Franklin, Williamson Co., TN; m: 28 Feb 1811 in Nashville, TN (or Rockbridge, VA?); Number of children: 7 Father: John Rodgers, American Revolutionary War vet.; Mother: Anne Phillips

...............5 James Randal McGavock,+ Riverside Plantation, Franklin, TN; b: 09 Jan 1812 in Nashville, Davidson Co., TN; d: 12 Feb 1862 in Probably TN; Number of children: 10

...................+Louisa C. Chenault, b: 07 Aug 1813 in Bardstown, Nelson Co., KY; d: 12 Feb 1885 in Probably TN; m: 01 Nov 1832; Number of children: 10 Father: Stephen Chenault; Mother: Mary Eleanor Rodgers

...................6 Mary Ellen McGavock,+ b: 23 Sep 1833; d: 16 Jun 1891; Number of children: 4

........................+Randal Milton Ewing, b: 01 Jun 1829 in Williamson Co., TN m: 13 Sep 1853; Number of children: 4 Father: Andrew B. Ewing, Dr.; Mother: Eliza McDowell McGavock,+

........................7 Carrie Eliza Ewing,+ b: 17 Sep 1854

........................7 Charles Andrew Ewing,+ b: 25 Sep 1857

............................+ Sarah Elizabeth Owen b: Abt. 1859 m: 02 Nov 1887

............................7 Francis McGavock Ewing,+ b: 26 Dec 1861

............................+Eliza M. Marshall, b: Abt. 1863 m: 19 Jan 1892

........................7 William Frierson Ewing,+ b: 20 Feb 1864

..................6 Sarah "Sallie" McGavock,+ owned family Bible b: 12 Mar 1837; d: 29 Sep 1863

........................+William Frierson, b: Abt. 1835; m: 05 Jun 1830   Father: Irving Frierson, Hon.

..................6 Maria Louisa McGavock,+ b: 09 May 1839; d: 26 Jun 1842

..................6 Randal McGavock,+ b: 24 Aug 1841; d: 13 Mar 1842

..................6 William Chenault McGavock,+ b: 04 Mar 1843

..................6 Elizabeth Harding McGavock,+ b: 18 Jul 1845; d: 17 Feb 1871

........................+Edwin H. Douglas, b: Abt. 1843; m: 29 Jul 1869   Father: Benjamin Douglass

..................6 James Randal McGavock,+ b: 21 Oct 1847; d: 01 May 1869

..................6 Ann Louise McGavock,+ b: 09 Sep 1849; d: 07 Oct 1862

..................6 Stephen Chenault McGavock, Dr.,+ b: 18 Dec 1851; d: 04 Dec 1881

..................6 Van Winder McGavock, Sr.+ b: 10 Jun 1855 in Wythe Co., VA; d: 1934; Number of children: 10

The McGavocks of Carnton Plantation

..................+Cynthia Rodes Pointer, b: 30 Jun 1863 in Williamson Co., TN; d. 1907; m: 17 Nov 1880; Number of children: 10 Father: Samuel Pointer; Mother: Cynthia R. Holland
......................7 James Randal McGavock, b: 15 Aug 1881
......................7 Sallie Pointer McGavock, b: 25 Jan 1883
......................7 Louisa McGavock, b: 12 Jun 1884
......................7 Randal Ewing McGavock, b: 02 Apr 1886
......................7 Van Winder McGavock, Jr., b: 03 Dec 1887
......................7 Samuel Pointer McGavock, b: 14 Jun 1890
......................7 William McGavock McGavock, b: 15 Aug 1892
......................7 Thomas Pointer McGavock, b: 23 Jul 1893
......................7 Mary Ellen McGavock, b: 12 Dec 1894
......................7 Cynthia Holland McGavock, b: 03 Aug 1897
...............5 William McGavock,+ b: 23 Jul 1813 in Nashville, Davidson Co., TN; d: 10 Jun 1821
...............5 John W. McGavock, Col., War for Southern Independence, C.S.A.,+ b: 02 Apr 1815 in Nashville, Davidson Co., TN; d: 07 June 1893 at Carnton Plantation, Franklin, Williamson Co., TN; Number of children: 5
...................+Caroline Elizabeth "Carrie" Winder,+ b: 09 Sept 1829 in Natchez, MS (some say Terrebone Parish), on her parents' sugar plantation near Thibodaux, La Fourche, LA); d: 22 Feb 1905 at her daughter Hattie's house "on the Lewisburg Pike," Franklin, Williamson Co., TN; m: 06 Dec 1848 in Ducros Plantation, Houma, Terrebonne Parish, LA; Number of children: 5 Father: Van Perkins Winder, Sr., Colonel,+; Mother: Martha Ann Grundy
...................6 Martha Winder McGavock,+b: 25 Sep 1849 in Carnton Plantation, Franklin, Williamson Co., TN; d: 19 Mar 1862 in Carnton Plantation, Franklin, Williamson Co., TN, age 12 of heart problems
...................6 Mary Elizabeth McGavock,+ b: 28 Mar 1851; d: 26 Jan 1858 in while visiting relatives at Ducros Plantation, Houma, Terrebone Parish, LA, age 6 of yellow fever
...................6 John Randal McGavock,+ b: 05 Jun 1854 in Carnton Plantation, Franklin, Williamson Co., TN?; d: 11 Sep 1854 in Carnton Plantation, Franklin, Williamson Co., TN, age 3 months of intestinal problems
...................6 Harriet Young "Hattie" McGavock,+ b: 02 Jul 1855 in Carnton Plantation, Franklin, Williamson Co., TN; d: 19 Jul 1932 in at her home on Bridge St., Franklin, TN; died on the 68th anniversary of the 2nd Battle of Franklin, perhaps at "Windermere," Franklin, Williamson Co., TN?; Number of children: 5
......................+George Limerick Cowan, LT., C.S.A., rode in Gen. Nathan Bedford Forrest's Escort; b: 15 Oct 1842 in County Derry, Ireland; d: 18 Sep 1919 in "Windermere," Franklin, Williamson Co., TN?; m: 03 Jan 1884 in Williamson

The McGavocks of Carnton Plantation

Co., TN; Number of children: 5 Father: Robert Cowan; Mother: Margaret Limerick

..............7 Carrie Winder Cowan,+ b: 12 Oct 1884 in TN; d: 1961 in TN

..............7 John McGavock Cowan,+ b: 11 Jul 1886 in TN; d: 1954 in TN

..............7 Leah Cowan,+ b: 18 Aug 1888 in Franklin, Williamson Co., TN?; d: 1950 in Franklin, Williamson Co., TN?

..............7 Samuel Kincaid Cowan,+, Pvt. World War I b: 20 Dec 1890 in TN; d: 18 Apr 1963

..............7 Winder McGavock Cowan,+ b: 18 Aug 1892 in TN

............6 Winder McGavock,+ b: 13 Jul 1857 in Carnton Plantation, Franklin, Williamson Co., TN?; d: 03 Jun 1907 at Carnton Plantation, Franklin, Williamson Co., TN (Lived at Carnton with his wife Susie until his death in 1907); Number of children: 5

....................+Susan Lee "Susie" Ewing, b: 04 Apr 1863 in Brentwood, Williamson Co., TN; d: 25 Oct 1931 in Franklin, Williamson Co., TN?; m: 05 Feb 1883 in TN; Number of children: 5 Father: Herbert Ewing; Mother: Sally Hughes

..............7 Hattie McGavock,+ b: 06 Apr 1884 in TN; d: 28 Jul 1955 in Franklin, Williamson Co., TN?; Number of children: 1

........................+Elijah Hanes Ayres, Sr., b: Abt. 1882; Number of children:

.... 8 Elijah Haynes Ayres, Jr., World War II b: 1913; d: 03 Feb 1943 (lost in the North Atlantic Sea while serving on board the U.S. "Dorchester"; sunk by an enemy sub)

..............7 Sara "Sallie" Ewing McGavock,+ b: 07 Dec 1885 in TN; d: 11 Dec 1911 in "at the home of her mother, Mrs. Susie Lee McGavock"

..............7 John McGavock,+ b: 24 Nov 1887 in TN; d: 25 Nov 1955 in Franklin, Williamson Co., TN?

........................+Mary Gillespie, b: 10 Sep 1889; d: 17 May 1951

..............7 Martha Winder McGavock,+b: 24 Dec 1890 in TN; d: 03 Jan 1909

..............7 Winder McGavock, Jr., Sgt. World War I,+ b: 01 Apr 1894 in TN; d: 02 Feb 1948

............5 _____ (unnamed) McGavock,+ b: 25 Sep 1816 in Nashville, Davidson Co., TN; d: 25 Sep 1816

............5 Mary Cloyd McGavock,+ b: 04 Sep 1817 in Nashville, Davidson Co., TN; d: 23 Oct 1862; Number of children: 2

....................+Joseph Branch Southall, b: Abt. 1815; m: 22 Sep 1836; Number of children: 2 Father: _____ Southall; Mother: Patience Branch

....................6 Randal McGavock Southall,+ b: 17 Jul 1837; d: 1866

The McGavocks of Carnton Plantation

............6 Josephine P. Southall,+ b: 12 Feb 1839; d: 27 Jan 1862
............5 Elizabeth Irwin McGavock,+ b: 17 May 1819 in Nashville, Davidson Co., TN; d: 09 Aug 1867 in Nashville, Davidson Co., TN?; Number of children: 6
............+William Giles Harding, Gen., Belle Meade Plantation (the author's family line); b: 15 Sep 1808 in Nashville, Davidson Co., TN; d: 15 Dec 1886 in Nashville, Davidson Co., TN m: 02 Jan 1840 in the guest parlor (?), Carnton Plantation, Franklin, Williamson Co., TN; Number of children: 7 Father: John Harding, Belle Meade Plantation line; Mother: Susannah Shute
............6 Selene Harding,+, Belle Meade Plant. Line b: 05 Apr 1846; d: 13 Dec 1892
............+William Hicks "Red" Jackson, Gen. C.S.A., b: October 1, 1835 at Paris, TN; d: March 30, 1903 at Belle Meade Plant. (Note: Jackson commanded a cavalry brigade under Forrest at the Battle of Nashville) m: 15 Dec 1868
............6 Sarah Susan Harding,+, Belle Meade Plantation line; b: 15 Oct 1847; d: 06 Jul 1848
............6 Mary Elizabeth Harding,+, Belle Meade Plantation line; b: 05 Feb 1850; d: 1913; Number of children: 1
............+Howell Edmunds Jackson, b: 08 Apr 1832 in Paris, Henry Co., TN; d: 08 Aug 1895 m: 30 Apr 1874: Number of children: 1 Father: Alexander Jackson; Mother: Mary Hunt
............7 Elizabeth Jackson, b: 1876; d: 1947; Number of children: 1
............+Matthew Gardner Buckner, b: Abt. 1875; Number of children: 1
.... 8 Mary Harding Buckner, b: 1898; d: 2003; Number of children: 1
............+Stuart Ragland, Sr. b: Abt. 1895; Number of children: 1
............6 William R. Harding,+, Belle Meade Plantation line; b: 16 Sep 1854; d: 18 Mar 1855
............6 M. Louise Harding,+, Belle Meade Plantation line; b: 02 Jan 1856; d: 30 Oct 1860
............6 _____ (unnamed) Harding,+ b: 09 Oct 1860; d: 30 Oct 1860
............5 _____ (unnamed) McGavock,+ b: Apr 1821 in Nashville, Davidson Co., TN; d: Apr 1821
.........4 Margaret McGavock,+ b: 10 Dec 1769; d: 17 Feb 1837; Number of children: 14
............+Joseph Kent, Col.,+ b: 07 Nov 1765 in Montgomery Co., VA?; d: 20 Oct 1843; m: 1787; Number of children: 14 Father: Jacob Kent; Mother: Mary

THE MCGAVOCKS OF CARNTON PLANTATION

Crockett,+
............5 Mary Kent,+ b: 28 Dec 1788; d: 05 Apr 1827; Number of children: 6
............+ James McGavock,+ McGavock House, Nashville b: 28 Mar 1790 in Wythe Co., VA; d: 23 Jan 1841—brutally murdered near Nashville, Davidson Co., TN; m: 12 Mar 1812; Number of children: 14 Father: David McGavock, surveyor,+; Mother: Elizabeth McDowell,+
............6 Margaret K. McGavock,+ b: 03 Jun 1813; d: 21 Mar 1835; Number of children: 1
....................+Hardy Wilkerson Bryan, LA State Rep. b: 13 Feb 1811; d: 16 Oct 1855 in Edgefield, TN; m: 23 Jul 1833; Number of children: 1 Father: Hardy S. Bryan; Mother: Catherine Young
....................7 James Hardy Bryan,+ b: 17 Mar 1835; d: 01 Sep 1845 in Concordia Parish, LA
............6 Sarah Jane McGavock,+ b: Abt. 1815; d: Abt. 1815
............6 Lucinda McGavock,+ b: 18 Feb 1817 in Nashville, Davidson Co., TN; d: 23 Jun 1847; Number of children: 2
....................+Jeremiah George Harris, journalist b: 23 Oct 1809 in Groton, CT; d: 1901; m: 05 May 1842; Number of children: 2 Father: Richard Harris; Mother: Mary Avery
....................7 Joseph Ewing Harris,+ b: 02 May 1843; d: 28 Aug 1865 in London, England (while making a tour of Europe)
....................7 Lucie Harris,+ b: 26 Oct 1846
........................+Van S. Lindsley, Dr., b: Abt. 1844 m: 16 Apr 1868 m: 16 Apr 1868
............6 Wiley McGavock,+ b: Abt. Nov 1818; d: 1838
............6 Joseph Kent McGavock,+ b: 20 Sep 1820; d: 10 Sep 1845
............6 Mary Kent McGavock,+ b: 1826 in Davidson Co., TN; d: 09 Mar 1867; Number of children: 5
....................+Albert Gallatin Wilcox, b: 27 Nov 1816 in Montgomery Co., TN; d: 23 Mar 1880; m: 10 Jan 1849; Number of children: 5 Father: John Earl Wilcox; Mother: Elizabeth _____?
....................7 Joseph Ewing Wilcox,+ b: 25 May 1850; d: 29 Mar 1868
....................7 Mary Alberta Wilcox,+ b: 09 Oct 1851; d: 29 Dec 1861
....................7 John Earl Wilcox,+ b: 10 Feb 1854
....................7 James McGavock Wilcox,+ b: 10 Feb 1856
....................7 Gerald Hiter Wilcox,+ b: 02 May 1863; d: 14 Sep 1868
............5 Jacob Kent, Captain in War of 1812,+ b: 22 Apr 1790 in Bedford Co., VA?; d: 24 Apr 1858 in at his home in Montgomery Co., VA; Number of children: 1

THE MCGAVOCKS OF CARNTON PLANTATION

................+Mary M. Buford, b: 14 Jul 1795 in VA; d: 20 Dec 1850; m: 07 Sep 1814; Number of children: 1 Father: Henry Buford; Mother: Mildred Blackburn
...............6 Margaret L. Kent,+ b: 06 Apr 1817; d: 19 Dec 1891
......................+John A. Langhorne, b: Abt. 1815; m: 07 May 1839
..............5 Jane D. Kent,+ b: 19 Jul 1791 in Wythe Co., VA; d: 14 Jul 1830
.................+John McCandlass Taylor, Jr., Major,+ b: 22 Aug 1780 in Montgomery Co., VA; d: 29 Sep 1856; m: 14 Apr 1813; Father: John McCandlass Taylor, Sr.; Mother: Elizabeth Campbell,+
..............5 James R. Kent,+ b: 23 Oct 1792; d: 29 May 1867
.................+Mary Cloyd, b: 17 Feb 1800; d: 05 Feb 1858; m: 31 Mar 1818 Father: Gordon Cloyd, Gen.; Mother: Elizabeth McGavock,+
..............5 Sally Kent,+ b: 26 Jun 1794; d: 24 Feb 1822
..............5 Robert Kent,+ b: 01 Jan 1796; d: 14 Sep 1852
.................+Elizabeth M. Craig, b: Abt. 1798 m: 15 Apr 1819
..............5 Cynthia Kent,+ b: 28 Jun 1797; Number of children: 1
.................+John McGavock,+ b: 30 Jan 1792 in Wythe Co., VA; d: 07 Jul 1877 in Edgefield, TN; m: 1816; Number of children: 7 Father: David McGavock, surveyor,+; Mother: Elizabeth McDowell,+
.................6 _____ (unnamed) McGavock b: Abt. 1817
..............5 Hugh McGavock Kent,+ b: 12 Apr 1800; d: 31 May 1870
.................+Ann Christian Bratton, b: Abt. 1802; d: 04 Aug 1876 m: 04 Jul 1822
..............5 Joseph Karolleman Kent,+ b: 02 May 1803 in Wythe Co., VA; d: 28 Jul 1835
.................+Jane Trigg, b: Abt. 1805 in Bedford Co., VA; d: 31 Aug 1843; m: Oct 1830; Father: Alanson Trigg; Mother: Lucy Quarles
..............5 Ann Frances Kent,+ b: 02 Jan 1805; d: 03 Apr 1852
.................+Alfred C. Moore b: Abt. 1803 m: 09 Mar 1830
..............5 Gordon C. Kent,+ b: 29 Jun 1806; d: 18 Sep 1869
.................+Margaret Cloyd,+ b: 06 Mar 1812; d: 23 May 1833; m: 14 Mar 1832; Father: David Cloyd; Mother: Sally McGavock,+
..............2nd Wife of Gordon C. Kent,+:
.................+Lucinda Cloyd,+ b: 21 Jul 1818; d: 18 Dec 1843 m: Abt. 1840; Father: Thomas Cloyd; Mother: Mary "Aunt Polly" McGavock,+
.... 3rd Wife of Gordon C. Kent,+:
.................+Jane L. McKee b: Abt. 1815 m: Abt. 1845
..............5 David F. Kent,+ b: 24 Dec 1807; d: 28 Jan 1850
.................+Elizabeth Cloyd b: 24 Aug 1816; d: Feb 1869; m: 02 Jan 1834; Father: Gordon Cloyd, Gen.; Mother: Elizabeth McGavock,+

THE MCGAVOCKS OF CARNTON PLANTATION

..............5 Margaret E. Kent,+ b: 06 Oct 1809; d: 04 Aug 1862
..............5 Lucinda E. Kent,+ b: 01 Mar 1811; d: 13 Oct 1829
..........4 Mary McGavock,+ b: Abt. 1772; d: Abt. 1800
..............+Philip Gaines, b: Abt. 1770 m: 1798 in (Note: they had no children)
..........4 Elizabeth McGavock,+ b: 05 Jul 1776; d: 05 Sep 1830; Number of children: 6
..............+Gordon Cloyd, Gen., b: 09 Mar 1771; d: 04 May 1833 m: Mar 1797; Number of children: 6 Father: Joseph Cloyd, Col.; Mother: Elizabeth Gordon
..............5 _____ (unnamed) Cloyd, b: 1797; d: 1797
..............5 Mary Cloyd b: 17 Feb 1800; d: 05 Feb 1858
..................+James R. Kent,+ b: 23 Oct 1792; d: 29 May 1867 m: 31 Mar 1818; Father: Joseph Kent, Col.,+; Mother: Margaret McGavock,+
..............5 _____ (unnamed) Cloyd, b: 1802; d: 1802
..............5 Peggy Cloyd, b: 24 Dec 1812; d: 31 Jul 1906
..............5 Louisa Cloyd, b: 18 Aug 1812; d: Jun 1816
..............5 Elizabeth Cloyd, b: 24 Aug 1816; d: Feb 1869
..................+David F. Kent,+ b: 24 Dec 1807; d: 28 Jan 1850; m: 02 Jan 1834; Father: Joseph Kent, Col.,+; Mother: Margaret McGavock,+
..........4 Joseph McGavock,+ b: 01 Mar 1780 in Fort Chiswell, Wythe Co., VA; d: 26 Dec 1833; Number of children: 5
..............+Margaret Graham, b: 30 Dec 1784 in Wythe Co., VA; d: 21 Mar 1868 in Wythe Co., VA; m: 02 Jun 1812 in Wythe Co., VA; Number of children: 5 Father: Robert Graham; Mother: Mary Craig
..............5 Mary Haller McGavock,+ b: 23 Nov 1813 in Max Meadows, Wythe Co., VA; d: 04 Apr 1893 in Max Meadows, Wythe Co., VA; Number of children: 2
..................+Samuel Rush Crockett, b: 27 Jun 1810 in Crockett's Cove, Wythe Co., VA; d: 08 Nov 1879 in Max Meadows, Wythe Co., VA; m: 02 Jul 1840; Number of children: 2 Father: John Crockett; Mother: Nancy Agnes Graham
..................6 Joseph McGavock Crockett,+ farmer, b: 07 Nov 1841 in Wythe Co., VA
......................+Elizabeth Malvina "Lizzie" Crockett, b: 05 Feb 1843; d: 23 Mar 1871 m: 02 Jan 1868 in (Note: they did not have children)
..................2nd Wife of Joseph McGavock Crockett, Farmer,+:
......................+Mary Agnes Wood, b: 23 Mar 1845; m: 03 Sep 1873 Father: Thomas Wood; Mother: Margaret E. Crockett
..................6 Mary R. Crockett,+
..............5 Sally Cloyd McGavock,+ b: 24 Apr 1815; d: 13 Mar 1824
..............5 Nancy Crockett McGavock,+ b: 25 Mar 1817; d: Oct 1861
..............5 Cynthia E. McGavock,+ (her portrait hangs in Carnton's ladies'

THE MCGAVOCKS OF CARNTON PLANTATION

parlor) b: 29 Feb 1820 in Max Meadows, Wythe Co., VA; d: 10 Jun 1882 in Max Meadows, Wythe Co., VA; Number of children: 5
................+Randal McGavock,+ (his portrait hangs in Carnton's ladies' parlor) b: 19 Jun 1803 in Max Meadows, Wythe Co., VA; d: 19 Mar 1890 in Max Meadows, Wythe Co., VA m: 13 Dec 1845; Number of children: 7 Father: Hugh McGavock, Capt. Revolutionary War,+; Mother: Nancy Kent,+
................6 Hugh Ewing McGavock,+ b: 07 Jul 1849
................6 Sally M. McGavock,+ b: 05 Nov 1851 in Max Meadows, Wythe Co., VA; d: 14 Oct 1875; Number of children: 2
.....................+Walter H. Robertson, Rev., b: Abt. 1850 in Amelia Co., VA; d: 02 Jul 1903; m: 02 Aug 1871; Number of children: 2 Father: William H. Robertson; Mother: Martha Holcombe
....................7 Lizzie Robertson,+ b: 24 Jul 1872
..........................+Alex Crockett, Dr., b: Abt. 1870 m: 07 Jun 1893
....................7 Holcombe McGavock Robertson,+ Surgeon, US Navy b: 24 Oct 1874
................6 Joseph Randal McGavock,+ b: 28 Mar 1854 in Max Meadows, Wythe Co., VA; Number of children: 4
.....................+Elizabeth "Lizzie" L. Hager, b: 01 Aug 1864 in Wythe Co., VA m: 01 Feb 1888; Number of children: 4 Father: John W. Hager; Mother: Mary Williams
....................7 Nannie Lee McGavock,+ b: 19 Oct 1888
....................7 Mary Williams McGavock,+ b: 12 May 1890
....................7 Joseph Randal McGavock,+ b: 08 Jul 1891
....................7 Cynthia Elizabeth McGavock,+ b: 25 May 1894
................6 Jacob Cloyd McGavock,+ b: 23 Jun 1856 in Max Meadows, Wythe Co., VA; d: in Max Meadows, Wythe Co., VA?; Number of children: 5
.....................+Amanda Billups, b: 21 Nov 1861 in Norfolk, VA?; d: in Max Meadows, Wythe Co., VA? m: 02 Oct 1883; Number of children: 5 Father: Cealy Billups; Mother: Elizabeth Anne Summers
....................7 Eulalie McGavock,+ b: 08 Jul 1885
....................7 Randal McGavock,+ b: 20 Nov 1887
....................7 Cecil McGavock,+ b: 19 Mar 1890
....................7 Jacob C. McGavock,+ b: 08 Jul 1893
....................7 Ezra Summers McGavock,+ b: 12 Dec 1897
................6 Lucy Nancy McGavock,+ b: 10 Apr 1858 in Max Meadows, Wythe Co., VA; Number of children: 7
.....................+John Brown Kent, b: 04 Sep 1849; m: 05 Apr 1882; Number of children: 7 Father: Joseph F. Kent; Mother: Frances Peyton
....................7 Randal McGavock Kent,+ b: 28 Feb 1883

The McGavocks of Carnton Plantation

..................7 Fanny Brown Kent,+ b: 08 Oct 1884
..................7 Cynthia McGavock Kent,+ b: 13 Feb 1886
..................7 Jennie Lewis Kent,+ b: 11 Oct 1887
..................7 Lucy McGavock Kent,+ b: 15 Oct 1891
..................7 Emily Roberta Kent,+ b: 31 Jan 1893
..................7 Joseph Francis Kent,+ b: 20 Jul 1895
..............5 Margaret Lucinda McGavock,+ b: 20 Jul 1829 in Max Meadows, Wythe Co., VA; d: 10 Jul 1855; Number of children: 3
..................+William Ewing, b: 03 May 1823 in Williamson Co., TN; d: 27 Apr 1863; m: 24 Sep 1850; Number of children: 5 Father: Andrew B. Ewing, Dr.; Mother: Eliza McDowell McGavock,+
..................6 Andrew Ewing,+ b: 25 Jul 1851
..................+Lula A. McGavock,+ b: 22 Mar 1869; m: 22 Feb 1899; Father: Francis F. (Fenelon or Fenlon) McGavock,+; Mother: Margaret (Margretta) Cunningham
..................6 Joseph William Ewing,+ b: 17 Feb 1853; d: 16 Jan 1889
..................6 Lucy Elizabeth Ewing,+ b: 24 Mar 1855
..................+William J. Brown, b: Abt. 1853 m: 25 Oct 1882
..........4 Sally McGavock,+ b: 22 Apr 1787 in Fort Chiswell, Wythe Co., VA; d: 08 Nov 1853; Number of children: 5
..................+David Cloyd, b: 01 May 1776; d: 13 Mar 1848; m: 22 May 1811; Number of children: 5 Father: Joseph Cloyd, Col.; Mother: Elizabeth Gordon
..............5 Margaret Cloyd,+ b: 06 Mar 1812; d: 23 May 1833
..................+Gordon C. Kent,+ b: 29 Jun 1806; d: 18 Sep 1869; m: 14 Mar 1832; Father: Joseph Kent, Col.,+; Mother: Margaret McGavock,+
..............5 Joseph Cloyd,+ b: 11 May 1813; d: 19 Jul 1884
..................+Mary E. Byars, b: Abt. 1815 m: 23 May 1838
..............5 Gordon Cloyd,+ b: 03 Oct 1816; d: 01 Mar 1869
..............5 Cynthia M. Cloyd,+ b: 18 Feb 1820; d: 15 Aug 1847
..................+David Shall McGavock,+ b: 21 Dec 1818 in near Nashville, Davidson Co., TN; d: 08 Aug 1866 in farm at Spring-Dale, Pulaski Co., VA m: 31 Jul 1844; Number of children: 6; Father: Randal McGavock,+; Mother: Almira Haynes
..............5 James McGavock Cloyd,+ b: 18 Jun 1828; d: 03 Mar 1892
..................+Frances E. McNutt, b: 01 Oct 1833; d: 21 Dec 1858 m: 05 Nov 1853; Father: Samuel McNutt, Rev.; Mother: Margaret McGavock,+
..............2nd Wife of James McGavock Cloyd,+:
..................+Harriet J. Ernest, b: Abt. 1840 m: Abt. 1860 m: Abt. 1860

THE MCGAVOCKS OF CARNTON PLANTATION

UNPROVEN LINE

......3 "Randal McGavock," a hypothetical person that I created to help explain the origins of the Northern, that is Yankee, American branch of the McGavocks. It is my theory that this Randal was the brother of James "Dada" McGavock, Sr. (1728-1812), and was thus possibly the progenitor of the Northern branch, so I have tentatively included him and his descendants here (much more research needs to be done on this line); b: Abt. 1730 in Near Glenarm, County Antrim, Northern Ireland; Number of children: ?
...........+_____ _____? b: Abt. 1735; m: Abt. 1760; Number of children: ?
..........4 Patrick McGavock, b: Abt. 1780 in Ireland; d: Abt. 1865 in Ireland; Number of children: ?
...............+_____ _____? b: in Ireland; d: in Ireland; Number of children: ?
...............5 Alexander McGavock, b: Abt. 1805 in County Antrim, Ireland; d: 1861 in Beloit, WI; Number of children: 6
....................+Sarah Ann Devlin, b: Abt. 1807 in County Antrim, Ireland; d: 1854 in Beloit, WI? m: Abt. 1827; Number of children: 6
....................6 Hugh McGavock, b: 26 Jan 1828 in County Antrim, Ireland; d: 02 Jun 1908 in Beloit, WI; Number of children: 9
.........................+Catharine "Kate" Buckley, b: Abt. 1830 in Janesville, WI; m: 01 Feb 1857; Number of children: 9
........................7 Alexander McGavock, b: Abt. 1858
........................7 Hugh McGavock, b: Abt. 1860
........................7 Charlotte McGavock, b: Abt. 1862
........................7 Mary McGavock, b: Abt. 1864
........................7 Tom McGavock, b: Abt. 1866
........................7 John McGavock, b: Abt. 1868
........................7 Joseph McGavock, b: Abt. 1870
........................7 Edward McGavock, b: Abt. 1872
........................7 Patrick McGavock, b: Abt. 1874
....................6 Charlotte McGavock, b: Abt. 1830
....................6 Sarah Ellen McGavock, b: Abt. 1832
....................6 Patrick McGavock, b: Abt. 1834
....................6 Alexander McGavock, b: Abt. 1836
....................6 William John McGavock, b: Abt. 1838

Appendix B
A Complete Winder Family Tree

Researched, compiled, and edited by Lochlainn Seabrook
Copyright © 2011 Lochlainn Seabrook

Notes: Living generations have been excluded to protect their privacy. Only primary Winder individuals and their spouses in this family tree are listed in the book's Index.

KEY:
1) A cross (+) *after* a name indicates descent from European royalty.
2) A cross (+) *before* a name indicates a partner of the individual listed above.
3) abt: about
4) m: marriage
5) d: died
6) Bef: before

Descendants of Capt. John "The Immigrant" Winder

1 John "the Immigrant" Winder, Capt. (progenitor, earliest known Winder ancestor); b: 1635 in Lorton, Cumberland, England;; d: 23 Sep 1698 in Somerset Co., MD; Number of children: 6
..+Bridget Meador; b: 1634 in (Lorton, Cumberland?) England; m: Bet. 1663 - 1664 in England; Number of children: 6
..2 Susan Winder; b: 09 Dec 1664 in Nansamond, VA; d: Jul 1674
..2 Thomas Winder; b: 26 Apr 1666 in Manokin, VA; d: Apr 1705 in Northumberland Co., VA
......+Elizabeth Brereton, probably a royal line; b: Abt. 1670 in Manokin, VA
..2 Elizabeth Winder; b: 04 Jan 1668 in Somerset Co., MD; Number of children:

THE MCGAVOCKS OF CARNTON PLANTATION

4
......+Joseph Venables; b: Apr 1662 in New Kent Co., VA; d: 1758 in Snow Hill, MD; Number of children: 4; Father: Abraham Venables; Mother: Sarah _____?
......3 Elizabeth Venables; b: Abt. 1690 in Somerset Co., MD
......3 John Venables; b: Abt. 1692 in Somerset Co., MD
......3 William Venables; b: Abt. 1694 in Somerset Co., MD
......3 Benjamin Venables; b: Abt. 1708 in New Kent Co., VA
..2 Meriam Winder; b: 27 Mar 1673 in Somerset Co., MD
......+Simon Perkins; b: Abt. 1669
..2 John Winder; b: 07 Mar 1676 in Wicomico, Somerset Co., MD; d: 13 Jul 1716 in Wicomico, Somerset Co., MD; Number of children: 6
......+Jane Dashiel; b: 30 Jul 1675 in Somerset Co., MD; d: 1696 in Somerset Co., MD; Number of children: 6; Father: James Dashiel, Sr.; Mother: Ann Cannon
......3 Bridget Winder; b: Bet. 1696 - 1697 in Somerset Co., MD; d: Abt. 1730 in Somerset Co., MD; Number of children: 6
..........+James Dashiel; b: 03 Oct 1690 in Somerset Co., MD; d: Abt. 1736 in Somerset Co., MD; m: Abt. 1717 in Somerset Co., MD; Number of children: 6; Father: James Dashiel, Jr.; Mother: Mary Waters
..........4 James Dashiel; b: 1714 in Somerset Co., MD
..........4 Jesse Dashiel; b: 1716 in Somerset Co., MD
..........4 Winder Dashiel; b: 1718 in Somerset Co., MD
..........4 Benjamin Dashiel; b: 1720 in Somerset Co., MD
..........4 Mary Dashiel; b: 1722 in Somerset Co., MD
..........4 Sarah Dashiel; b: 1724 in Somerset Co., MD
......3 John Winder; b: Abt. 1699 in Somerset Co., MD; d: Abt. 1730 in Somerset Co., MD
......3 Elizabeth Winder; b: 1701 in Somerset Co., MD; d: Abt. 1750 in Somerset Co., MD; Number of children: 2
..........+Christopher Dashiel; b: 1694 in Somerset Co., MD; d: 1727 in Somerset Co., MD; m: Abt. 1721 in Somerset Co., MD; Number of children: 2; Father: James Dashiel, Jr.; Mother: Mary Waters
..........4 Elizabeth Dashiel; b: Abt. 1721 in Somerset Co., MD
..........4 Mary Dashiel; b: 1723 in Somerset Co., MD
......*2nd Husband of Elizabeth Winder:
..........+Walter Jacobs; b: Abt. 1700 in Somerset Co., MD; d: Abt. 1750 in Somerset Co., MD; m: Abt. 1730 in Somerset Co., MD
......3 Rachel Winder; b: 1703 in Somerset Co., MD; d: Abt. 1750 in Somerset Co., MD
......3 Thomas Winder; b: 1706 in Somerset Co., MD; d: in Somerset Co., MD
..........+Eleanor _____?; b: Abt. 1706 in Somerset Co., MD; m: Abt. 1726 in

THE MCGAVOCKS OF CARNTON PLANTATION

Somerset Co., MD
......3 William Winder, Gen. and Judge, Rev. War soldier; b: 16 Mar 1714 in Somerset Co., MD; d: 07 Jul 1792 in Princess Anne, Somerset Co., MD; Number of children: 4
..........+Esther Gillis,+; b: 06 Oct 1724 in Somerset Co., MD; d: 09 Oct 1767 in Somerset Co., MD; m: 22 Sep 1743 in Somerset Co., MD; Number of children: 4; Father: Thomas Gillis; Mother: Prisilla Denwood,+
..........4 John Winder, Dr., American Rev. War,+; b: 19 Jan 1746 in Somerset Co., MD; d: 01 Dec 1822 in Northampton Co., VA; Number of children: 2
...............+Elizabeth "Betty" Jones; b: Abt. 1750 in VA; m: 31 Jan 1770 in Northamption Co., VA; Number of children: 2
...............5 Thomas Jones Winder, Dr.,+; b: 16 Dec 1762 in Somerset Co., MD; d: 19 Dec 1818 in Concordia Parish, LA; Number of children: 7
...................+Harriet Handy; b: 18 Sep 1786 in Somerset Co., MD; d: 28 Nov 1821 in Concordia Parish, LA; m: 01 Oct 1802 in Somerset Co., MD; Number of children: 7; Father: Levin Handy; Mother: _____ _____?
...................6 Elizabeth Jones Winder,+; b: 04 Apr 1807 in Somerset Co., MD; d: 28 Nov 1821 in Somerset Co., MD
...................6 John Jones Winder,+; b: 28 Apr 1808 in Somerset Co., MD; d: 29 Aug 1808 in Somerset Co., MD
...................6 Van Perkins Winder, Sr., Colonel,+; b: 03 Jun 1809 in Somerset Co., MD; d: 07 Nov 1854 in of yellow fever at Ducros Plantation, Houma, Terrebonne Parish, LA; Number of children: 15
........................+Martha Ann Grundy; b: 25 Jun 1812 in Nashville, Davidson Co., TN; d: 16 Dec 1891 in New Orleans, Orleans Parish, LA; m: 06 Dec 1828 in Winchester, Franklin Co., TN; Number of children: 15; Father: Felix Grundy, TN Senator, Statesman, Lawyer; Mother: Ann Phillips Rodgers
........................7 Caroline Elizabeth "Carrie" Winder,+; b: 09 Sept 1829 in Natchez, MS (some say Terrebone Parish (sugar plantation near Thibodaux, La Fourche [or New Orleans], LA); d: 22 Feb 1905 in at her daughter Hattie's house "on the Lewisburg Pike," Franklin, Williamson Co., TN; Number of children: 5
............................+John W. McGavock, Col., War for Southern Independence, C.S.A.,+; b: 02 Apr 1815 in Nashville, Davidson Co., TN; d: 07 Jun 1893 in Carnton Plantation, Franklin, Williamson Co., TN; m: 06 Dec 1848 in Ducros Plantation, Houma, Terrebonne Parish, LA; Number of children: 5; Father: Randal McGavock, 11th Mayor of Nashville,+; Mother: Sarah Dougherty Rodgers
............................8 Martha Winder McGavock,+; b: 25 Sep 1849 in Carnton Plantation, Franklin, Williamson Co., TN; d: 19 Mar 1862 in Carnton Plantation, Franklin, Williamson Co., TN, age 12 of heart problems
............................8 Mary Elizabeth McGavock,+; b: 28 Mar 1851; d: 26 Jan

THE MCGAVOCKS OF CARNTON PLANTATION

1858 in while visiting relatives at Ducros Plantation, Houma, Terrebone Parish, LA, age 6 of yellow fever

...............................8 John Randal McGavock,+; b: 05 Jun 1854 in Carnton Plantation, Franklin, Williamson Co., TN?; d: 11 Sep 1854 at Carnton Plantation, Franklin, Williamson Co., TN, age 3 months of intestinal problems

............................8 Harriet Young "Hattie" McGavock,+; b: 02 Jul 1855 in Carnton Plantation, Franklin, Williamson Co., TN; d: 19 Jul 1932 in at her home on Bridge St., Franklin, TN; died on the 68th anniversary of the 2nd Battle of Franklin, perhaps at "Windermere," Franklin, Williamson Co., TN?; Number of children: 5

................................+George Limerick Cowan, LT., C.S.A., Forrest's Escort; b: 15 Oct 1842 in County Derry, Ireland; d: 18 Sep 1919 in "Windermere," Franklin, Williamson Co., TN?; m: 03 Jan 1884 in Williamson Co., TN; Number of children: 5; Father: Robert Cowan; Mother: Margaret Limerick

................................9 Carrie Winder Cowan,+; b: 12 Oct 1884 in TN; d: 1961 in TN

................................9 John McGavock Cowan,+; b: 11 Jul 1886 in TN; d: 1954 in TN

................................9 Leah Cowan,+; b: 18 Aug 1888 in Franklin, Williamson Co., TN?; d: 1950 in Franklin, Williamson Co., TN?

................................9 Samuel Kincaid Cowan,+, Pvt. World War I; b: 20 Dec 1890 in TN; d: 18 Apr 1963

................................9 Winder McGavock Cowan,+; b: 18 Aug 1892 in TN

............................8 Winder McGavock,+; b: 13 Jul 1857 in Carnton Plantation, Franklin, Williamson Co., TN?; d: 03 Jun 1907 in Carnton Plantation, Franklin, Williamson Co., TN (Lived at Carnton with his wife Susie until his death in 1907); Number of children: 5

................................+Susan Lee "Susie" Ewing; b: 04 Apr 1863 in Brentwood, Williamson Co., TN; d: 25 Oct 1931 in Franklin, Williamson Co., TN?; m: 05 Feb 1883 in TN; Number of children: 5; Father: Herbert Ewing; Mother: Sally Hughes

................................9 Hattie McGavock,+; b: 06 Apr 1884 in TN; d: 28 Jul 1955 in Franklin, Williamson Co., TN?; Number of children: 1

....+Elijah Hanes Ayres, Sr.; b: Abt. 1882; Number of children: 1

....................................10 Elijah Haynes Ayres, Jr., World War II; b: 1913; d: 03 Feb 1943 in Lost in the North Atlantic sea while serving on board the US "Dorchester"; sunk by an enemy sub

................................9 Sara "Sallie" Ewing McGavock,+; b: 07 Dec 1885 in TN; d: 11 Dec 1911 "at the home of her Mother, "Mrs. Susie Lee McGavock"

................................9 John McGavock,+; b: 24 Nov 1887 in TN; d: 25 Nov

THE MCGAVOCKS OF CARNTON PLANTATION

1955 in Franklin, Williamson Co., TN?
................+Mary Gillespie; b: 10 Sep 1889; d: 17 May 1951
................9 Martha Winder McGavock,+; b: 24 Dec 1890 in TN; d: 03 Jan 1909
................9 Winder McGavock, Jr., Sgt. World War I,+; b: 01 Apr 1894 in TN; d: 02 Feb 1948
..........7 Harriet Ann Grundy Winder,+; b: 06 Nov 1830 in Terrebonne, LA; d: 21 Aug 1831 in Terrebonne, LA
..........7 Margaret Rawlins Winder,+; b: 01 Jul 1832 in Terrebonne, LA; d: 30 Aug 1844 in Terrebonne, LA
..........7 Elizabeth Rowan Winder,+; b: 05 Apr 1834 in Terrebonne, LA; d: 01 Aug 1842 in Terrebonne, LA
..........7 John Davidson Smith Winder,+; b: 28 May 1835 in Terrebonne, LA; d: 31 May 1838 in Terrebonne, LA
..........7 Martha Ann Grundy Winder,+; b: 10 Feb 1837 in Terrebonne Parish, LA; d: 08 Aug 1853 in Terrebonne Parish, LA
..........7 Felix Grundy Winder, War for Southern Independence, C.S.A.,+; b: 22 May 1839 in Terrebonne, LA; d: Bet. 18 May - 04 Jul 1863, killed at the Battle of Vicksburg, MS
..........7 Malvina Bass Winder,+; b: 30 Mar 1841 in Terrebonne, LA; d: 18 Feb 1852 in Terrebonne, LA
..........7 George Guion Winder,+; b: 07 Apr 1843 in Terrebonne, LA; d: Abt. 1900 in Terrebonne, LA
..........7 Louise McGavock Winder,+; b: 04 Jun 1845 in Terrebonne, LA; d: Abt. 1905 in Terrebonne, LA; Number of children: 4
................+Patrick Campbell; b: Abt. 1845 in AL; d: Abt. 1910 in AL; Number of children: 4
................8 William W. Campbell; b: 16 Jul 1868 in AL; d: Abt. 1920 in AL
................8 Martha G. Campbell; b: 15 Apr 1871 in AL; d: Abt. 1920 in AL
................8 John S. Campbell; b: 09 Apr 1873 in AL; d: Abt. 1920 in AL
................8 Sallie W. Campbell; b: 23 Sep 1875 in AL; d: 18 Apr 1876 in AL
..........7 John Bay Winder,+; b: 09 Apr 1847 in Terrebonne, LA; d: Aug 1889 in Terrebonne, LA; Number of children: 4
................+Louise McNair; b: Abt. 1853 in LA; d: 1882 in LA; m: Abt. 1875; Number of children: 4
................8 Fay C. Winder; b: 10 Aug 1877 in Terrebonne, LA; d:

THE MCGAVOCKS OF CARNTON PLANTATION

Abt. 1920 in Terrebonne, LA
..............................8 Louise C. Winder; b: 11 Dec 1879 in Terrebonne, LA; d: Abt. 1920 in Terrebonne, LA
..............................8 Nina McNair Winder; b: 12 Feb 1882 in Terrebonne, LA; d: Abt. 1920 in Terrebonne, LA
..............................8 Sarah Winder; b: 12 Feb 1882 in Terrebonne, LA; d: Abt. 1920 in Terrebonne, LA
........................7 Thomas Levin Winder,+; b: 10 Dec 1848 in Terrebonne Parish, LA; d: Abt. 1905 in Terrebonne Parish, LA or CA
..............................+Cornelia Williams; b: Abt. 1850 in Los Angeles, CA; m: 26 Nov 1872 in Los Angeles, CA
........................7 William Shields Winder,+; b: 01 Aug 1850 in Terrebonne, LA; d: 21 Jun 1851 in Terrebonne, LA
........................7 Van Perkins Winder, Jr.,+; b: 11 Sep 1852 in Terrebonne Parish, LA; d: 23 Feb 1886 in Terrebonne Parish, LA
..............................+Bettie Goode; b: Abt. 1855; m: 02 Jan 1883 in Houma, Terrebonne Parish, LA
........................7 Sallie Guion Winder,+; b: 20 Dec 1854 in Terrebonne Parish, LA; d: Abt. 1905 in Terrebonne Parish, LA
....................6 Lucretia Perkins Winder,+; b: 18 Aug 1810 in Somerset Co., MD; d: 14 Sep 1810 in Somerset Co., MD
....................6 John Winder,+; b: 26 Aug 1812 in Somerset Co., MD; d: 14 Sep 1812 in Somerset Co., MD
....................6 Caroline Lucretia Winder,+; b: 22 Feb 1814 in Somerset Co., MD; d: 24 Dec 1855 in Somerset Co., MD
..........................+George S. Guion; b: Abt. 1814 in Somerset Co., MD; d: Abt. 1870 in Concordia, LA; m: Abt. 1834 in Somerset Co., MD
....................6 John Winder,+; b: 24 Dec 1816 in Somerset Co., MD; d: 20 Jul 1817 in Somerset Co., MD
................5 William Winder,+; b: 10 Jun 1771 in VA; d: 08 Oct 1796
............*2nd Wife of John Winder, Dr., American Rev. War,+:
................+Susannah Harmonson; b: Abt. 1764 in VA?; m: 17 Jul 1783 in Northampton Co., VA
............4 William Winder, Capt.,+; b: 1747 in Somerset Co., MD; d: 1808 in MD; Number of children: 2
................+Charlotte Henry; b: Abt. 1751 in Somerset Co., MD; Number of children: 2; Father: John Henry; Mother: Dorothy Rider
................5 William H. Winder, Sr.,+; b: 18 Feb 1775 in Somerset Co., MD; d: 24 May 1824 in Baltimore, MD; Number of children: 6
....................+Gertrude Polk,+ (related U.S. Pres. James Knox Polk); b: 13 Apr

THE McGAVOCKS OF CARNTON PLANTATION

1781; d: 28 Dec 1872; m: 09 May 1799; m: 09 May 1799; Number of children: 6; Father: William Polk; Mother: Esther "Hetty" Winder,+

................6 John Henry Winder, Brig. Gen. C.S.A.,+; b: 21 Feb 1800 in Rewston, Somerset Co., MD; d: 08 Feb 1865 in Florence, SC; Number of children: 5

....................+Elizabeth Shepherd; b: Abt. 1804 in Rewston, Somerset Co., MD; d: 1825; m: 1823; Number of children: 1

....................7 William A. Winder,+; b: 1824 in Rewston, Somerset Co., MD; Number of children: 1

.........................+Abby Goodwin; b: Abt. 1828; Number of children: 1

.........................8 William John C. Winder,+; b: Abt. 1850

................*2nd Wife of John Henry Winder, Brig. Gen. C.S.A.,+:

....................+Caroline A. Cox; b: Abt. 1804 in Rewston, Somerset Co., MD; m: Aft. 1825; Number of children: 4

....................7 John C. Winder; b: Abt. 1826 in Rewston, Somerset Co., MD

....................7 William Sidney Winder; b: Abt. 1828 in Rewston, Somerset Co., MD

....................7 Thomas P. Winder; b: Abt. 1830 in Rewston, Somerset Co., MD

....................7 Gertrude Winder; b: Abt. 1832 in Rewston, Somerset Co., MD

................6 William H. Winder, Jr.,+; b: Abt. 1802 in Rewston, Somerset Co., MD

................6 Charlotte Winder,+; b: Abt. 1804 in Rewston, Somerset Co., MD

................6 Gertrude Winder,+; b: Abt. 1812 in Rewston, Somerset Co., MD

................6 William Tasker Winder,+; b: Abt. 1814

................6 Aurelia Winder,+; b: Abt. 1822 in Rewston, Somerset Co., MD

..........4 Jane Winder,+; b: 21 Oct 1749 in Somerset Co., MD; d: 27 Sep 1803 in Somerset Co., MD; Number of children: 8

..............+Henry Dashiel Handy; b: 07 Mar 1747 in Somerset Co., MD; d: 26 Mar 1787 in Somerset Co., MD; m: 24 Oct 1770 in Somerset Co., MD; Number of children: 8; Father: Isaac Handy; Mother: Anne Dashiel

..............5 Esther Handy; b: 04 Oct 1771 in Somerset Co., MD; d: 30 Jul 1834 in Louisville, KY

................+George Dashiel; b: 14 Mar 1770 in Somerset Co., MD; d: 04 Mar 1852 in Somerset Co., MD; m: 31 May 1791 in Somerset Co., MD; Father: George Dashiel; Mother: Rose Fisher

..............5 Anne Handy; b: 21 Jun 1773 in "Pemberton," Somerset Co., MD; d: 02 Dec 1802 in Somerset Co., MD

THE MCGAVOCKS OF CARNTON PLANTATION

................+Hugh Gemmill; b: 25 Dec 1766 in Irwin, Scotland; d: 29 Nov 1822 in Newcastle Co., DE; m: 22 Apr 1775 in Somerset Co., MD
..............5 Henry Dashiel Handy; b: 16 Feb 1775 in Somerset Co., MD; d: 14 Sep 1803 in Somerset Co., MD
................+Nancy Campbell; b: Abt. 1775 in Somerset Co., MD; d: Abt. 1840 in Somerset Co., MD; m: Abt. 1795 in Somerset Co., MD; Father: Zacharias Campbell; Mother: _____ _____?
..............5 Thomas Winder Handy; b: 17 Mar 1777 in "Pemberton," Somerset Co., MD; d: 27 Jun 1851 in Somerset Co., MD
................+Matilda Henry; b: 23 Sep 1779 in Somerset Co., MD; d: 14 Apr 1810 in Somerset Co., MD; Father: Isaac Henry; Mother: Dorothy Henry
..............5 George Day Scott Handy; b: 28 Oct 1779 in Somerset Co., MD; d: 21 Dec 1849 in Somerset Co., MD
................+Mary Frisby Tilden; b: Abt. 1785 in Somerset Co., MD; d: 1850 in Somerset Co., MD; m: 1804 in Somerset Co., MD
..............5 Peter Handy; b: 20 Oct 1781 in Somerset Co., MD; d: 17 Sep 1802 in Somerset Co., MD
..............5 Hugh Henry Handy; b: 18 Nov 1783 in Somerset Co., MD; d: 1784 in Somerset Co., MD
..............5 William Winder Handy; b: 12 Jan 1785 in Philadelphia, PA; d: 27 Jan 1864 in Somerset Co., MD; Number of children: 9
................+Elizabeth Tyson; b: 02 Mar 1791 in Philadelphia, PA; d: 1840 in Somerset Co., MD; m: 27 Aug 1811 in Philadelphia, PA; Number of children: 8
..................6 Jesse Tyson Handy; b: 17 Aug 1813 in Somerset Co., MD
..................6 Jane Winder Handy; b: 26 Aug 1816 in Somerset Co., MD
..................6 Jane Winder Handy; b: 16 Oct 1816 in Somerset Co., MD
..................6 Margaret Handy; b: 19 Sep 1819 in Somerset Co., MD
..................6 Henry Handy; b: 14 Dec 1821 in Somerset Co., MD
..................6 Elizabeth Ann Handy; b: 23 Jul 1823 in Somerset Co., MD
..................6 William Winder Handy; b: 28 Mar 1825 in Somerset Co., MD
..................6 Charles Handy; b: 17 Jan 1827 in Somerset Co., MD
..............*2nd Wife of William Winder Handy:
................+Mary Ann Poultney; b: Abt. 1810 in Somerset Co., MD; m: Abt. 1843 in Somerset Co., MD; Number of children: 1
..................6 Thomas Poultney Handy; b: 19 Dec 1843 in Somerset Co., MD
..........4 Esther "Hetty" Winder,+; b: 09 Oct 1751 in Coventry, Parish, Somerset Co., MD; d: 14 Dec 1790 in Coventry, Parish, Somerset Co., MD; Number of children: 8
................+Isaac Handy; b: 19 Dec 1743 in Coventry, Parish, Somerset Co., MD; d: 14 Jul 1772 in Coventry, Parish, Somerset Co., MD; Number of children: 2;

THE MCGAVOCKS OF CARNTON PLANTATION

Father: Isaac Handy; Mother: Anne Dashiel
.... 5 Margaret "Peggy" Winder Handy,+; b: 30 Sep 1768; Number of children: 2
.... +John Whittington Rowand; b: 1768 in Coventry, Parish, Somerset Co., MD; d: 1795 in Coventry, Parish, Somerset Co., MD; Number of children: 2
.... 6 Charlotte Henry Rowand, Roundes,+; b: 10 Mar 1794
.... 6 Esther Winder Rowand, Roundes,+; b: 01 Sep 1789
.... 5 Richard Henry Handy,+; b: 11 Aug 1771 in Coventry, Parish, Somerset Co., MD; d: 30 Jun 1826 in Coventry, Parish, Somerset Co., MD
.... +Elizabeth Campbell; b: 1772 in Coventry, Parish, Somerset Co., MD; m: 06 Jan 1795 in Somerset Co., MD; Father: Zacharias Campbell; Mother: _____ _____?
.... *2nd Husband of Esther "Hetty" Winder,+:
.... +William Polk, related to U.S. Pres. James Knox Polk; b: 11 Dec 1752 in Somerset Co., MD; d: 1814 in MD; m: Feb 1775 in MD; Number of children: 6; Father: David Polk,+; Mother: Betsy Gillis
.... 5 Gertrude Polk,+ related U.S. Pres. James Knox Polk; b: 13 Apr 1781; d: 28 Dec 1872; Number of children: 6
.... +William H. Winder, Sr.,+; b: 18 Feb 1775 in Somerset Co., MD; d: 24 May 1824 in Baltimore, MD; m: 09 May 1799; Number of children: 6; Father: William Winder, Capt.,+; Mother: Charlotte Henry
.... 6 John Henry Winder, in the War for Southern Independence, Brig. Gen. C.S.A.,+; b: 21 Feb 1800 in Rewston, Somerset Co., MD; d: 08 Feb 1865 in Florence, SC; Number of children: 5
.... +Elizabeth Shepherd; b: Abt. 1804 in Rewston, Somerset Co., MD; d: 1825; m: 1823; Number of children: 1
.... 7 William A. Winder,+; b: 1824 in Rewston, Somerset Co., MD; Number of children: 1
.... +Abby Goodwin; b: Abt. 1828; Number of children: 1
.... 8 William John C. Winder,+; b: Abt. 1850
.... *2nd Wife of John Henry Winder, Brig. Gen. C.S.A.,+:
.... +Caroline A. Cox; b: Abt. 1804 in Rewston, Somerset Co., MD; m: Aft. 1825; Number of children: 4
.... 7 John C. Winder; b: Abt. 1826 in Rewston, Somerset Co., MD
.... 7 William Sidney Winder; b: Abt. 1828 in Rewston, Somerset Co., MD
.... 7 Thomas P. Winder; b: Abt. 1830 in Rewston, Somerset Co., MD
.... 7 Gertrude Winder; b: Abt. 1832 in Rewston, Somerset Co.,

The McGavocks of Carnton Plantation

MD
................6 William H. Winder, Jr.,+; b: Abt. 1802 in Rewston, Somerset Co., MD
................6 Charlotte Winder,+; b: Abt. 1804 in Rewston, Somerset Co., MD
................6 Gertrude Winder,+; b: Abt. 1812 in Rewston, Somerset Co., MD
................6 William Tasker Winder,+; b: Abt. 1814
................6 Aurelia Winder,+; b: Abt. 1822 in Rewston, Somerset Co., MD
.............5 Charlotte Polk,+; b: Abt. 1785 in Coventry, Parish, Somerset Co., MD
.............5 Hetty Polk,+; b: 09 Apr 1779 in Coventry, Parish, Somerset Co., MD; Number of children: 2
................+Nehemiah King; b: Abt. 1775; m: 01 Apr 1797; m: 01 Apr 1797; Number of children: 2
................6 Charlotte King,+; b: Abt. 1801
................6 Henry King,+; b: Abt. 1803
.............5 Betsy Polk,+; b: 19 May 1776 in Coventry, Parish, Somerset Co., MD; d: 06 Oct 1822
.............5 William Polk,+; b: 09 Aug 1786 in Coventry Parish, Somerset Co., MD
................+Almy Townsend; b: Abt. 1790; d: 13 Feb 1856; m: 29 Nov 1811
.............5 Josiah Polk,+; b: 17 Nov 1783 in Coventry, Parish, Somerset Co., MD; d: 1814
................+Rebecca Troup; b: Abt. 1787
..2 William Winder; b: 20 Oct 1679 in Wicomico, Somerset Co., MD; d: 1710 in Northumberland Co., VA
.........4 Levin Winder, (governor of MD 1812-1816).+; b: 04 Sep 1757 in Somerset, MD; d: 01 Jul 1819 in Baltimore, MD (Note: he was a lieutenant colonel in the American Revolutionary War); Number of children: ?
..............+Mary Stoughton Sloss; b: 1759-1765 in Somerset, MD; d: Bef. 13 May 1822; m: Abt. 1797 in Somerset, MD; Number of children: ?
..............5 Edward Stoughton Winder,+; b: 21 Sep 1798 in Somerset, MD; d: 07 Mar 1840; Number of children: ?
......................+Elizabeth Taylor Lloyd; b: Abt. 1800; m: 1820 in MD; Number of children: ?
................6 Charles Sidney Winder, Brig. Gen. C.S.A.,+; b: 07 Oct 1829 in Easton, Talbot Co., MD; d: 09 Aug 1862

Appendix C

Some Well-Known Relations & Ancestors of the McGavocks, the Winders, & the Author

Queen Victoria
Queen Elizabeth II
Prince Charles
Prince Andrew
Duchess Sarah Ferguson
Princes William and Harry
Princess Diana
Sir Winston Churchill
Davy Crockett
George Washington
James Knox Polk
Benjamin Franklin
Dr. Dallas Bache
Alexander Dallas Bache
William the Conqueror
Edward I "Longshanks"
Henry the VIII
Tacitus
Lord Alfred Tennyson
Jane Austen
Emperor Marc Antony
Octavia Major Tiberius
Charlemagne
Count Dracula
Lady Godiva
Queen Boadicea (or Boudicca)
Sir William "Braveheart" Wallace
Louis the XIV
Knut Eriksson
Princesses Caroline and Stephanie of Monaco
Grace Kelly
Robert the Bruce
James VI (King James Bible named after)
Saint Edward II
Robert Stewart II
Robert "the Regent" Stewart III
David I
Malcolm III
Duncan I
Egbert
Ethelwulf
Alfred the Great
Edmund I
Edgar the Peaceful
Athelred II
Edmund II
Alexander, King of Troy
Niall of the Nine Hostages
Mortogh O'Brien
Torlogh O'Brien
Dounough O'Brien
Teige O'Brien
Ceinneidigh
Erchad Mac Murchada
Edward II
Edward III
Henry Plantagenet II
Henry Plantagenet III

THE MCGAVOCKS OF CARNTON PLANTATION

John "Lackland" I
James Stewart I
James Stewart II
James Stewart III
James "Iron Belt" Stewart IV
Christian Oldenberg I
Ferdinand II
Alfonzo IX
Fernando III
Merovée "the Young"
Pepsin
Clodion
Childeric I
Clovis I "the Great"
Clotaire I
Pharamond
Clodius III
Bartherus
Hilderic
Sunno
Farabert
Clodomir IV
Marcomir IV
Odomir
Richemer
Rathberius
Antenor IV
Clodomir III
Helena Bonham Carter
Patrick Macnee (*The Avengers*)
René Auberjonois ("Odo," *Star Trek: Deep Space Nine*)
Thomas Cruise Mapother, IV ("Tom Cruise")

Appendix D

McGavock & Winder Astrology

Note: For beginners who are interested in astrology and wish to look up the interpretations of each planetary position, I have provided the primary aspects in the captions.

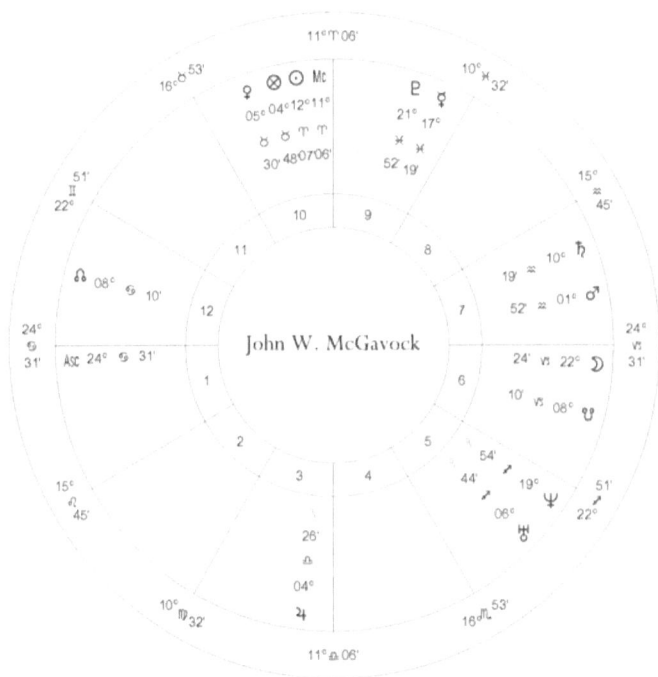

The natal horoscope of Colonel John W. McGavock, born April 2, 1815, at Franklin, Tennessee (time of birth unknown). Sun in Aries in the 10th House; Moon in Capricorn in the 6th House; Cancer rising (1st House); Mercury in Pisces in the 9th House; Venus in Taurus in the 10th House; Mars in Aquarius in the 7th House; Jupiter in Libra in the 3rd House; Saturn in Aquarius in the 7th House; Uranus in Sagittarius in the 5th House; Neptune in Sagittarius in the 5th House; Pluto in Pisces in the 9th House; North Node in Cancer in the 12th House; South Node in Capricorn in the 6th House; Midheaven in Aries in the 10th House. (Chart © Lochlainn Seabrook)

THE MCGAVOCKS OF CARNTON PLANTATION

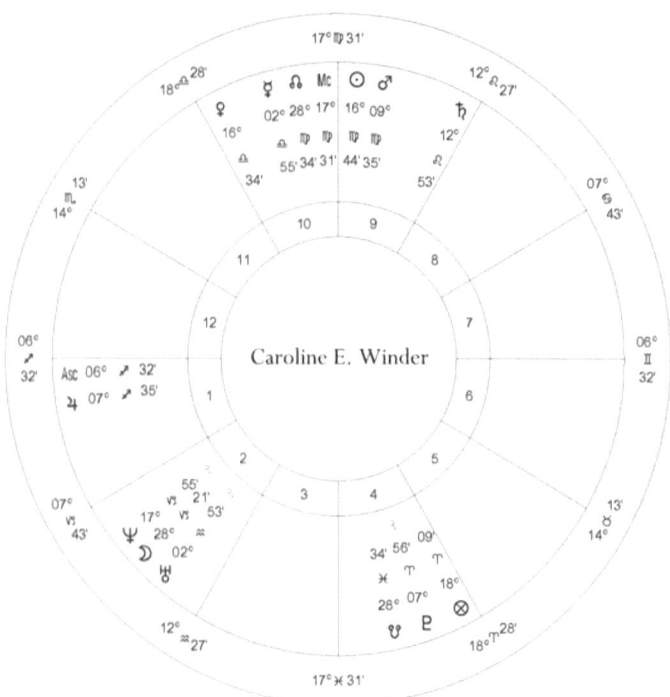

The natal horoscope of Caroline Elizabeth "Carrie" Winder, born September 9, 1829, at Natchez, Mississippi (time of birth unknown). Sun in Virgo in the 9th House; Moon in Capricorn in the 2nd House; Sagittarius rising (1st House); Mercury in Libra in the 10th House; Venus in Libra in the 10th House; Mars in Virgo in the 9th House; Jupiter in Sagittarius in the 1st House; Saturn in Leo in the 9th House; Uranus in Aquarius in the 2nd House; Neptune in Capricorn in the 2nd House; Pluto in Aries in the 4th House; North Node in Virgo in the 10th House; South Node in Pisces in the 4th House; Midheaven in Virgo in the 10th House. (Chart © Lochlainn Seabrook)

Appendix E

The Sons of Confederate Veterans

Defending the South, particularly the Old South, is today considered a social misdemeanor by many. Some look on it as a veritable crime. Even the very words "Confederacy" and "confederate" are seen as offensive (it is much more acceptable, for instance, to make reference to New York's *Yankee* Stadium than to Alabama's *Confederate* Stadium), and the topic of slavery can no longer be discussed objectively without accusations of "racism."[1677] The term "pro-South" is considered by the more ill-informed to literally mean "white racism," while the word "Confederate" is being hastily removed from public view because of its alleged "negative connotations."

What is more, the Confederate Battle Flag has been taken down from the South's many public squares, streets with the names of Confederate soldiers are being changed, NASCAR has prohibited the display of any Confederate symbols, and the song *Dixie* has been banned at sporting events. Those with Confederate ancestors are made to feel ashamed and the monuments and grave sites of the Confederate war dead are regularly desecrated.

[1677]. I myself, along with hundreds of noted scientists worldwide, including Paul R. Ehrlich, C. Loring Brace, Ashley Montagu, Robert T. Anderson, Nigel Barnicot, Lancelot Hogben, Jean Hiernaux, Richard W. Holm, Frank B. Livingstone, and S. L. Washburn, do not embrace the concept of race, holding it to be scientifically unviable. There is just one "race": the human race. For more on this topic see Montagu's works, passim.

THE MCGAVOCKS OF CARNTON PLANTATION

Yet half the United States, along with much of Europe (including France's Emperor Napoleon III and nearly all of the British Parliament), once supported the Confederacy, and at least 25 percent of all 19th-Century Southerners died fighting under her beautiful blue-crossed, Christian-inspired flag.

The McGavocks of Carnton Plantation, who were Confederates of the highest standing, who proudly flew the Confederate Flag at their home in Franklin, Tennessee, and who were nonracist servant ("slave") owners, would be appalled at the rise of the anti-South movement and its liberal, left-wing, politically correct agenda to suppress and finally obliterate all traces of the Old South. Traditional Southerners today should be no less alarmed.

Thankfully there are numerous organizations dedicated to preserving both America's Southern heritage and her Confederate history. One of these is the Sons of Confederate Veterans (SCV), a successor to the United Confederate Veterans (UCV), the organization to which Colonel John W. McGavock of Carnton enthusiastically belonged during the latter half of the 1800s. I myself am a member of the SCV, and am proud to follow in the footsteps of my cousin Colonel McGavock. Like all of our members—from the 19th Century to the 21st Century—I am deeply committed to educating the public concerning authentic Southern history, while at the same time preserving it for future generations.

Despite what anti-South groups proclaim, neither the Victorian UCV or the modern SCV are "racist organizations." Quite the contrary. In fact, if the SCV was a biased group I would certainly not be a member, and neither would my good friends Dr. Michael R. Bradley (who wrote the Foreword to this book)[1678] and African-American educator Nelson W. Winbush, the living grandson of a black Confederate soldier.[1679]

In truth, I know of no pro-South or neo-Confederate groups that are prejudicial. The SCV, for example, is strictly non-racial, and has anti-

---

[1678]. Dr. Bradley, former commander of the Tennessee Division of the SCV (2006-2010), is currently the Chaplain of Dr. J. B. Cowan Camp #155, SCV, Tullahoma, Tennessee. For more information, visit their Website: www.tennessee-scv.org/camp155.
[1679]. Nelson, the grandson of Louis Napoleon Nelson (who served proudly under General Nathan Bedford Forrest and was the Confederacy's only known black chaplain), wrote the Foreword to my bestselling book, *Everything You Were Taught About the Civil War is Wrong, Ask a Southerner!* Nelson is a member of Jacob Summerlin Camp #1516, SCV, Kissimmee, Florida. Website: www.jacobsummerlin.org.

THE MCGAVOCKS OF CARNTON PLANTATION

defamation, anti-racism clauses built into its constitution.

Michael, Nelson, and I are justly proud of our multicultural membership and of the fact that the SCV is interracial, that is, intentionally designed for members of all races. The group's only requirement is that one has an ancestor who fought for or aided the Confederacy during Lincoln's War.

Since not only 1 million European-Americans,[1680] but 300,000 (to as many as 1 million) African-Americans,[1681] 70,000 Native-Americans, 60,000 Hispanic-Americans,[1682] 50,000 foreigners (including Irish, Welsh, German, Italian, Spanish, Australian, Cuban, Polish, Hungarian, French, West Indian, Belgian, Prussian, Mexican, English, Swedish, Canadian, Scottish, and countless racially mixed individuals),[1683] 12,000 Jewish-Americans,[1684] and 10,000 Asian-Americans,[1685] defended the Southern Cause, we are truly a multiracial organization, just as the Confederate Army and the Confederate Navy were between 1861 and 1865.[1686] There were at least twelve foreign soldiers of royal birth in the Confederate military, as well as a host of foreign-born Rebel officers.[1687]

Anti-South writers, scholars, teachers, museum directors, organizations, publishers, bookstores, and libraries, of course, would rather you not know these things, so they suppress them. But we boldly print the facts here for all to see! (Since, according to Gallup, only 20 percent of Americans consider themselves "liberals,"[1688] it is hoped that one day the politically correct owners and directors of our nation's historic places will begin catering to the conservative majority—rather than the liberal minority—who walk through their doors.)[1689]

1680. Katcher, CWSB, p. 46; Eaton, HSC, p. 93.
1681. Barrow, Segars, and Rosenburg, BC, p. 97; Hinkle, p. 106; *The United Daughters of the Confederacy Magazine*, Vols. 54-55, 1991, p. 32.
1682. Hinkle, p. 108. See also Quintero, Gonzales, and Velazquez, passim.
1683. Lonn, p. 218.
1684. Rosen, p. 161.
1685. Hinkle, p. 108; Blackerby, passim.
1686. One Confederate outfit alone, the First Louisiana, was comprised of men of thirty-seven different nationalities. *All* of the descendants of these individuals qualify for membership in the SCV.
1687. *The Civil War Book of Lists*, pp. 172-174.
1688. "Tom Sullivan Show," FOX Business News, July 4, 2011.
1689. Some 40 percent of the people visiting Civil War sites and historic homes are conservative and 36 percent are moderates, while only 20 percent are liberal. Thus at least 76 percent of Civil War tourists are open-minded individuals who are interested in genuine Southern history, rather than the fake sugar-coated

THE MCGAVOCKS OF CARNTON PLANTATION

For those non-Southerners and New South Southerners who are interested in learning more about the Southern version of the War, the book you now hold in your hands is a good place to start. Excellent companions include my books, *Everything You Were Taught About the Civil War is Wrong, Ask a Southerner!*; *A Rebel Born: A Defense of Nathan Bedford Forrest*; *Abraham Lincoln: The Southern View*; *Lincolnology: The Real Abraham Lincoln Revealed in His Own Words*; and *Carnton Plantation Ghost Stories*.

The best full-length Southern histories of the War are Edward A. Pollard's aptly named two-volume work, *Southern History of the War*, and President Jefferson Davis' two-volume work, *The Rise and Fall of the Confederate Government*. For those Southerners who are unaccountably ashamed of their heritage, or for Yankees contemplating moving to the South, my friend Clint Johnson's *The Politically Incorrect Guide to the South* is highly recommended.

I remain dedicated to fulfilling the charge made to the SCV by my cousin General Stephen Dill Lee[1690] in New Orleans, in 1906:

> To you, Sons of Confederate Veterans, we submit the vindication of the cause for which we fought; to your strength will be given the defense of the Confederate soldier's good name, the guardianship of his history, the emulation of his virtues, the perpetuation of those principles he loved and which made him glorious and which you also cherish. Remember it is your duty to see that the true history of the South is presented to future generations.

May this book, *The McGavocks of Carnton Plantation: A Southern History*, play a small role in vindicating the cause for which my Southern ancestors and relatives fought and died: the preservation of the original Jeffersonian government ("the Confederacy") and Constitution (the "Articles of Confederation") as created by the Founding Fathers.

L.S.

"history" penned by pro-North writers. For more information on the percentages of political groups, see Website: www.gallup.com/poll/124958/conservatives-finish-2009-no-1-ideological-group.aspx.

1690. Lee, who fought at the Battles of Atlanta, Franklin II, and Nashville, was not just a loyal Confederate veteran after the War. He later also became a staunch women's rights advocate, unlike Lincoln and many others in the North.

Appendix F

Company H
Twentieth Tennessee Infantry

by Dr. William Josiah McMurray
- 1904 -

Author's note: As Company H Twentieth Tennessee Regiment Voluntary Infantry was formed in Franklin, Tennessee, and had such an impact on life here, I have included this brief history (exactly as McMurray wrote it) to honor its members. My notes are in brackets. Be aware that McMurray's soldiers' list is not precisely alphabetized. Lochlainn Seabrook

The boys who made up this [Williamson County] company, in their childhood's days played marbles over the ground on which was fought one of the bloodiest battles of ancient or modern days, and in this battle, Company H of the Twentieth Tennessee Infantry did its full share.

Company H was organized by electing Moscow B. Carter, Captain; M. Fount DeGraffenreid, First Lieutenant; R. Swanson, Second Lieutenant; P. H. Eelbeck, Third Lieutenant; Thos. Parkes, Orderly Sergeant; F. M. Lavender, Second Sergeant; Felix G. Allen, Third Sergeant; and John E. Smith, Fourth Sergeant.

This company was mustered into the State Service May 28th, 1861, and sent to Camp Trousdale for instructions in the duties of the soldier, and when the Twentieth Regiment of Volunteers was formed, this Company took the letter H and was given a place of honor, as the left color Company of the Regiment.

The roll of this noble band of men and what became of each, as far as we can learn, is as follows:

Captain Moscow B.[ranch] Carter. Elected Lieutenant Colonel at organization of Regiment, captured at Battle of Fishing Creek, Jan. 19th, 1862. His post office is now Franklin, Tenn.
First Lieutenant, M. F.[ount] DeGraffenreid. Promoted to Captain at

The McGavocks of Carnton Plantation

  organization of Regiment; resigned April 1862, lives in Kentucky.
R. Swanson. Second Lieutenant, resigned after the battle of Shiloh. Post office, West Harpeth, Tenn.
P. H. Eelbeck. Resigned 1861. Died after the war in Franklin, Tenn.
Anglin, Daniel. Lives at Union Valley, Williamson County, Tenn.
Armstrong, Ben. F. Wounded at battle of Murfreesboro, December 31, 1862, and died from his wound.
Alexander, Jas. L. Died in Hospital, Knoxville, August, 1861.
Andrews, John. Killed in Breckinridge's charge at Murfreesboro, Jan. 2, 1863.
Andrews, Frank M. Died in Hospital, in 1863.
Bennett, Wm. Killed in the battle of Shiloh, April 7th 1862.
Bennett, W. S. Lives in Williamson County, Texas.
Bennett, J. A. Lives in Williamson County, Texas.
Berry, Johnson. Wounded at battle of Nashville, 1864, and captured and died of wounds while in prison.
Boyd, W. E. Died in Hospital at Knoxville, August 1861.
Boyd, John. Wounded at Shiloh, April 6th, 1862; died from wound.
Boxley, Philip H. Wounded at Shiloh, Chickamauga, and Franklin [II]; lives at Franklin, Tenn.
Beech, Paul B. Captured at Missionary Ridge, Nov., 25th, 1863. Post office, Williamson County, Tenn.
Beech, Fred B. Wounded at Chickamauga, captured at Missionary Ridge; died in West Tenn.
Byrd, Thos. H. Wounded at Murfreesboro. Post office Basin Springs, Tenn.
Butts, J. L. Killed in Breckinridge's charge at Murfreesboro, Jan., 2nd, 1863.
Butts, C. C. Died since the war.
Butts, Daniel. Died in Hospital, April 3rd, 1863.
Buchanan, Thos. Discharged 1861; lives in Texas.
Cliffe, Dr. Dan. Lives in Franklin, Tenn.
Cartwright, Joseph. Discharged 1862; underage.
Campbell, Jas. A. Killed at battle of Hoover's Gap, June 24th, 1863.
Carter, Theo. ["Tod"]. Promoted to Captain in Quartermaster's Department. Captured Missionary Ridge, Nov., 25, 1863; made

The McGavocks of Carnton Plantation

his escape and was Aide on the staff of Gen. Thos. Benton Smith, and was killed in front of his father's house at the battle of Franklin, Tenn., Nov. 30th, 1864. [This is an error. Tod died several days later, on December 2.]

Carter, Wad. Promoted to color guard; wounded at Shiloh, lives in Texas.

Cunningham, H. R. Captured Missionary Ridge. Post office Williamson County, Tenn.

Cook, N. P. Transferred to Thirty-second Tenn. Regiment. Lives in Arkansas.

Crenshaw, Thos. Wounded at Murfreesboro in Breckinridge's charge.

Crenshaw, Hardin. Wounded at Fishing Creek [known as the Battle of Mill Springs to Yankees], Jan. 19th, 1862. Post office, Nashville.

Caruthers, Thos. Elected First Lieutenant at re-organization of Regiment, May 8th, 1862. Promoted to Captain, 1863. Wounded at Murfreesboro, Dec, 31, 1862, and at Franklin, Nov. 30th, 1863. Post office, Franklin, Tenn.

Canada, Allen. Captured Missionary Ridge. Lives in Williamson County, Tenn.

Canada, Wm. C. Captured Missionary Ridge; died since war.

Canada, Jos. A. Wounded in a ditch on the Kennesaw Line while broiling a piece of bacon. Post office, Davidson County.

Castleman, Chas. Died 1902.

Castleman, Jas. D. Lost an arm at Hoover's Gap; now an inmate of Confederate Soldier's Home.

Davis, Jas. A. Wounded at Murfreesboro. Post office, Dickson, Tenn.

Davis, Jasper. Died in Hospital, 1863.

Davidson, Wm. Lives in Texas.

Davis, John. Discharged in 1862. Post office, West Harpeth.

Davis, Buster. Discharged under age; died since war.

Eelbeck, Frank. Promoted to Commissary Sergeant, 1861. Post-office, Nashville, Tenn.

Edney, Turner. Died in hospital, April, 1863.

Edney, Robert. Died in hospital, 1863.

Fox, Joe. Lost an arm July 22, 1864, near Atlanta; now a minister of the gospel; Post-office, Maury County.

Fox, Bryant E. Lost a leg May 22, near New Hope Church, Ga.;

THE MCGAVOCKS OF CARNTON PLANTATION

post-office, White Oak, Williamson County, Tenn.

Foster, Jos. A. Discharged May 28, 1861; Post-office, Rutherford County, Tenn.

Flein, Frank. Went fishing and never returned.

Givens, Ben M. Wounded and captured at Fishing Creek; also wounded at Hoover's Gap; died in Georgia, 1863.

Givens, John. Discharged in 1861; died since the war.

Givens, Sharp. Lives in Kentucky.

Gresham, Jos. A. Lives in Williamson County [Tennessee].

Gee, W. H. Discharged since war in Hickman County.

Giles, C. Y. Elected Orderly Sergeant at re-organization of Regiment; wounded at Resaca, Ga.; was one of the six of Company H who surrendered with Gen. Jos. E. Johnston at Greensboro, N. C.

Giles, Thos. J. Elected Fourth Sergeant at re-organization of Regiment; killed at battle of Nashville, 1864.

Garrett, Wash. Discharged under conscript law as over age, 1862. Lives in Texas.

George, W. R.

Harvey, Robert H. Promoted to Ordinance Sergeant; Postoffice, Lawrenceburg, Tenn.

Harrison, Harvey. Died at Corinth, 1862.

Harrison, Jas. Post-office, Basin Springs, Tenn.

Harrison, Dock. Lives in Kentucky.

Harrison, Dan. Wounded and captured at Fishing Creek; made escape from prison; lives at Jingo, Tenn.

Hughes, R. B. Elected Lieutenant at re-organization of Regiment; wounded at Murfreesboro, and Jonesboro, Ga.; postoffice, Nashville, Tenn.

Hughes, W. P. Discharged 1862; Post-office, Nashville, Tenn.

Hutchinson, Alfred. Lost an arm at Chickamauga. Lives in Texas.

Hughes, Jas. Post-office, Nashville, Tenn.

Hampton, John. One of the six of Company H at General Johnston's surrender in North Carolina.

Harbison, W. J. (Butch). Post-office, Dickson, Tenn.

Hay, Jesse K. Died in 1862.

Ham, Isaac. Post-office, Basin Springs, Tenn.

Ham, Fred. Died in 1863.

The McGavocks of Carnton Plantation

Ham, Jesse D. Wounded at Shiloh and at Chickamauga in the same hand; was one of the six of Company H who surrendered at Greensboro, N. C.
Hume, Wm. M. Wounded at Hoover's Gap; died since the war.
Huff, Sam.
Ivy, A. Killed at Fishing Creek, being the first man of Company H killed in the war.
Ivy, W. L. Died in Florida in 1868.
Ivy, W. R. Died in hospital in 1863 at Newnan, Ga.
Ivy, John W. Wounded at Murfreesboro; Post-office, Basin Springs.
Inman, Reuben. Discharged 1862; post-office, Terrill, Texas.
Inman, Jos. Discharged 1862; Post-office, Basin Springs.
Inman, Jeff. Discharged 1862; died since war.
Jones, Jas. Killed in a falling house in Nashville in 1863.
Jones, John. Killed at Jonesboro, Ga., 1864.
Jamison, Sam. Died since the war.
King, William. Killed at Shiloh, April 6, 1862.
King, Robert. Died at Mill Springs, Ky., 1862.
Knight, Thos. M. Killed at Hoover's Gap, June 24, 1863.
Kirby, Mack D. Discharged 1862; Post-office, Terrill, Tex.
Lewis, Kelly. Post-office, Fernvale Springs, Tenn.
Lavender, F. M. Second Sergeant. Promoted to Lieutenant January, 1862; promoted to Captain, 1862; promoted to Major at reorganization of Regiment; promoted to Lieutenant Colonel, 1862; wounded at Shiloh, and captured in Breckinridge's charge at Murfreesboro. Resigned in 1863 on account of disability; died since the war.
Morris, Nathan E. Wounded at Peach Tree Creek, near Atlanta; made turnip greens out of briars and "buck bushes." Post-office, Grassland, Tenn.
Mcintosh, John. Wounded at Hoover's Gap; Post-office, Hickman County, Tenn.
Moss, Newton J. Post-office, Basin Springs.
Marr, Ben F. Wounded at Chickamauga and died soon after.
McNeal, Young. P. O., Fernvale Springs.
McFadden, Robt. Discharged, 1861.
Murphy, John. Killed July 22, 1864, near Atlanta, Ga.

THE McGAVOCKS OF CARNTON PLANTATION

Marshall, John. Transferred to quartermaster department, 1861; killed in R. R. [railroad] wreck at Harpeth River on N. Western Railroad, July 4, 1870.

McAllister, Jas. M. Killed at Shiloh, April 6, 1862.

Mangrum, Wesley. Wounded in Breckinridge Charge at Murfreesboro, 1863; wounded at Nashville, 1864; lives in Cheatham County.

Mangrum, Wiley. P. O., Williamson Co. [Tennessee].

Mangrum, John W. Wounded at Murfreesboro; P. O., Franklin, Tenn.

Mangrum, W. B. Died, 1879.

Mauley, Jas. Discharged, 1861.

McKay, R. H. Wounded at battle of Shiloh, April 7, 1862; P. O. Franklin, Tenn.

Newcomb, Nelson. Killed at Fishing Creek, Jan. 19, 1862.

Nolen, F. C. Discharged under age; died since the war.

Norman, Jack A. Killed after the war.

Ormes, Wm. Discharged, 1862; over age.

Overton, Jas. Wounded at Shiloh; discharged as under age, 1862; died 1872.

Ogles, Levi. P. O., Perry County [Tennessee].

Owen, Joshua. Died since the war.

Pinkerton, Jack. Killed at battle of Nashville, Tenn., 1864.

Pritchard, Wash. Died in his tent at Knoxville, Oct., 1862.

Pritchard, Isaac. Lives in Kentucky.

Pritchard, John. Died in 1863.

Parker, D. C. Lost a leg at Chickamauga; P. O., Franklin, Tenn.

Parkes, Thos. Lieutenant; detached at Decatur, Ala., 1861, and placed on duty in Secret Service department; later received appointment on Staff of General [Joseph] Wheeler; died since our last Reunion at his residence in Nashville.

Prewitt, Wm. P. O., South Harpeth, Tenn.

Prewitt, Adam. P. O., South Harpeth, Tenn.

Prewitt, Thos. Died since war.

Rodes, Wm. G. Elected Lieutenant at re-organization of regiment; died 1863.

Reams, W. R. Discharged 1861; died 1864.

Reid, Peter H. Discharged 1862; P. O., Brentwood, Tenn.

The McGavocks of Carnton Plantation

Short, Jesse. Elected Sergeant; wounded at Chickamauga, Resaca, and Jonesboro; P. O., Franklin, Tenn.

Short, Henry M. Wounded at Shiloh and battle of Franklin, and surrendered at Greensboro, N. C. with "Old Joe," April, 1865; P. O., Union City, Tenn.

Sayers, Harvey. Killed at Fishing Creek.

Sayers, W. D. Wounded at Murfreesboro; P. O., Franklin, Tenn.; died since the war.

Southall, Phil. Promoted to Sergeant; wounded at Resaca, and surrendered with General Joe Johnston at Greensboro, N. C.

Smith, Jos. J. Sergeant; wounded at Shiloh, Chickamauga, and Franklin; P. O., Franklin, Tenn.

Smith, Geo. C. Lives in West Tennessee.

Stovall, Thos. Wounded at Murfreesboro; captured at Missionary Ridge; P. O., Franklin, Tenn.

Stovall, Martin. Wounded at Kennesaw Mtn.; died since the war.

Smith, Dub. Wounded at Chickamauga and Resaca; died since the war.

Smart, Hiram. Died since war.

Smith, John C. Elected Sergeant; discharged 1861; P. O., Franklin, Tenn.

Shy, W. M. Appointed to Color Guard, 1861; elected Lieutenant, 1862; elected Captain, 1862, at re-organization of regiment; promoted to Major in 1863 to Lieutenant Colonel in 1863, and to Colonel in 1864: killed at battle of Nashville, while in command of the regiment.

Stevens, Thos. Killed at Shiloh.

Sellars, Thos. S. Died in 1863.

Sexton, Jas. Discharged as under age, 1862.

Shelton, G. M. Killed by falling from train, July, 1861.

Smith, Sam. Wounded at Shiloh; lives in Humphrey's Co., Tenn.

Tomlin, Geo. Captured in Tennessee, 1863; died since the war.

Truett, Frank. Died in Knoxville, 1861.

Truett, Jas. T. Died since the war.

Tally, Thos. J. Died since the war.

Tanner, Thos. A. Captured at Missionary Ridge; died, 1901.

Taylor, Wm. E. P. O., Maury Co., Tenn.

Tierce, J. P. Wounded at Murfreesboro; lives in Georgia.

The McGavocks of Carnton Plantation

Vowel, Jones. Wounded at Chickamauga and Jonesboro, Ga.; killed in a personal difficulty in 1874.
Vaught, G. M. P. O. Nashville, Tenn.
Vaughn, Thos. R. Lives in West Tenn.
Vaughn, J. R. P. O. Nashville, Tenn.
Vaughn, Geo. W. P. O. Nashville, Tenn.
White, John. Wounded at Fishing Creek and killed at Shiloh.
White, Jas. H. Elected Lieutenant, 1861; wounded July 22, 1864, near Atlanta, Ga. Paroled May 22, 1865; died as Commandant of Tennessee Confederate Soldier's Home in 1896.
White, Ben E. Killed at Chickamauga.
Withers, Jas. H. Surrendered with General Johnston at Greensboro, N. C. Died in Nashville, Tenn., 1880.
Withers, Ben. Killed at Chickamauga.
Whitfield, Thos. Discharged 1852; lives in Williamson County.
Watson, Thos. J. Discharged 1861; died since war.
Wray, Major I. Discharged 1861. Died since war.
Wray, Frank. Killed at Fishing Creek.
York, Thos. J. Killed at Shiloh.

This splendid Company of 167 men did their whole duty as their casualties will show:

Killed in battle 25
Wounded in battle 50
Died from disease 21
Transferred, discharged and resigned 40
Captured 14
Died since war 30
Lost sight of 6

The following were the noted 6 that surrendered with Gen. Joe Johnston at Greensboro, N. C, 1865: C. Y. Giles, Jesse D. Ham, Henry M. Short, John Hampton, Philip Southall, Jas. H. Withers.[1691]

[1691]. McMurray, pp. 164-172.

Appendix G

Colonel Buckner's Mint Julep Recipe

> To aid in the effort to preserve Southern culture, I have included below a copy of a wonderful letter containing an authentic Southern recipe for mint julep. It is from Colonel (later Lieutenant General) Simon Bolivar Buckner, Jr., U.S. Army, to Major General William D. Connor, superintendent of the United States Military Academy at West Point. Buckner, born July 18, 1886, in Kentucky, is the son of the famous Confederate General Simon Bolivar Buckner, Sr., who surrendered to Yankee war criminal General Ulysses S. Grant at the Battle of Fort Donelson, February 16, 1862. Colonel Buckner, the author of the letter below, was killed during World War II on Okinawa, June 18, 1945, and is buried at the Buckner family plot in Frankfort, Kentucky.

March 30, 1937

My dear General Connor:

Your letter requesting my formula for mixing mint juleps leaves me in the same position in which Captain Barber found himself when asked how he was able to carve the image of an elephant from a block of wood. He said that it was a simple process consisting merely of whittling off the part that didn't look like an elephant.

    The preparation of the quintessence of gentlemanly beverages can be described only in like terms. A mint julep is not a product of a formula. It is a ceremony and must be performed by a gentleman possessing a true sense of the artistic, a deep reverence for the ingredients and a proper appreciation of the occasion. It is a rite that must not be entrusted to a novice, a statistician nor a Yankee. It is a heritage of the Old South!; an emblem of hospitality, and a vehicle in which noble minds can travel together upon the flower-strewn paths of a happy and congenial thought.

    So far as the mere mechanics of the operation are concerned, the procedure, stripped of its ceremonial embellishments, can be described as

The McGavocks of Carnton Plantation

follows:

    Go to a spring where cool, crystal-clear water bubbles from under a bank of dew-washed ferns. In a consecrated vessel, dip up a little water at the source. Follow the stream thru its banks of green moss and wild flowers until it broadens and trickles thru beds of mint growing in aromatic profusion and waving softly in the Summer breeze. Gather the sweetest and tenderest shoots and gently carry them home. Go to the sideboard and select a decanter of Kentucky Bourbon distilled by a master hand, mellowed with age, yet still vigorous and inspiring. An ancestral sugar bowl, a row of silver goblets, some spoons and some ice and you are ready to start.

    Into a canvas bag pound twice as much ice as you think you will need. Make it fine as snow, keep it dry and do not allow it to degenerate into slush. Into each goblet, put a slightly heaping teaspoonful of granulated sugar, barely cover this with spring water and slightly bruise one mint leaf into this, leaving the spoon in the goblet. Then pour elixir from the decanter until the goblets are about one-fourth full. Fill the goblets with snowy ice, sprinkling in a small amount of sugar as you fill. Wipe the outside of the goblets dry, and embellish copiously with mint.

    Then comes the delicate and important operation of frosting. By proper manipulation of the spoon, the ingredients are circulated and blended until nature, wishing to take a further hand and add another of its beautiful phenomena, encrusts the whole in a glistening coat of white frost. Thus harmoniously blended by the deft touches of a skilled hand, you have a beverage eminently appropriate for honorable men and beautiful women.

    When all is ready, assemble your guests on the porch or in the garden where the aroma of the juleps will rise heavenward and make the birds sing. Propose a worthy toast, raise the goblets to your lips, bury your nose in the mint, inhale a deep breath of its fragrance and sip the nectar of the gods.

    Being overcome with thirst, I can write no further.

Sincerely,
S. B. Buckner, Jr., Colonel

ILLUSTRATIONS

The McGavocks of Carnton Plantation

Artistic rendering of what the rear of Carnton Mansion may have looked like after the back porch was added in 1850. Includes the now missing 1811 two-story brick house (located on the left between the mansion and the smokehouse). Converted by the McGavocks into their kitchen, it was blown down by a tornado in 1909. (Drawing courtesy and © The Wills Company, Nashville, Tennessee)

THE MCGAVOCKS OF CARNTON PLANTATION

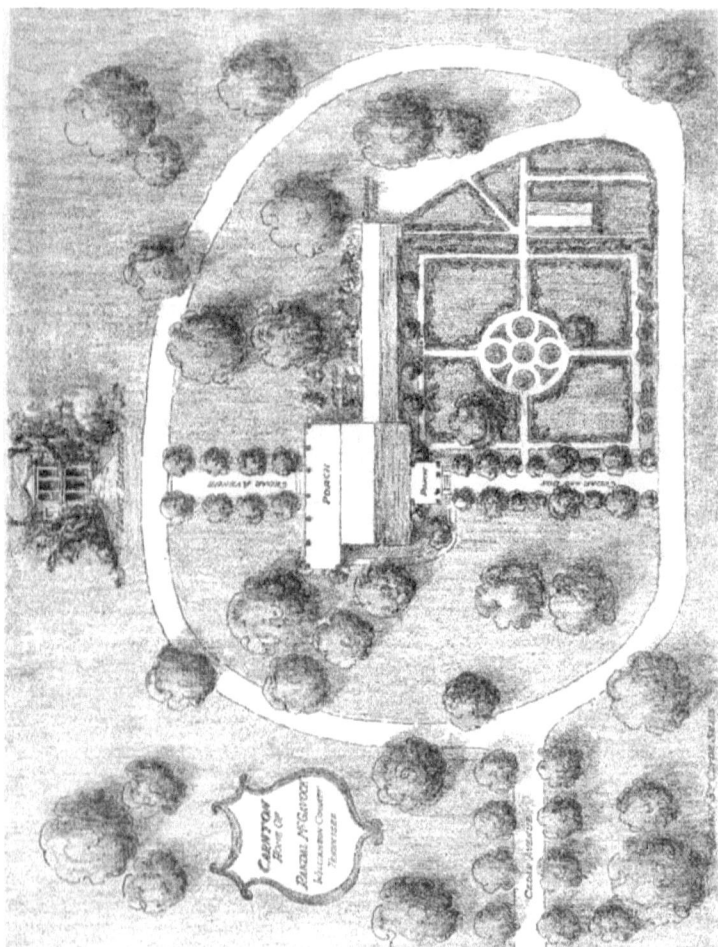

Carnton Plantation, Franklin, Tennessee. Left, the back of the house, is north. Aerial view of mansion and surrounding grounds (barns, paddocks, crop fields, servants' quarters, etc., not included). Drawing by Clyde Sears, date unknown. Top of illustration is north (the back of the house); bottom is south (the front of the house). McGavock Creek and the brick servants' house are to the right (not shown); Franklin Center is toward the upper left corner (not shown). At the time of this drawing note several important features: the garden is located in front of the house at the southeast corner (the opposite of where it is now); the driveway encircles the entire house; the carriage house was once attached to the east side of the mansion—next to the men's parlor; the greenhouse (lower right) was located next to the garden; there was a "cedar avenue" leading up to the property from the west (left); "cedar and box" trees lined the front walk; "holly" was planted along the south side of the carriage house; and a "cedar avenue" led up to the back porch from the rear driveway. (Image courtesy Tennessee State Library and Archives—henceforth written TSLA)

THE McGAVOCKS OF CARNTON PLANTATION

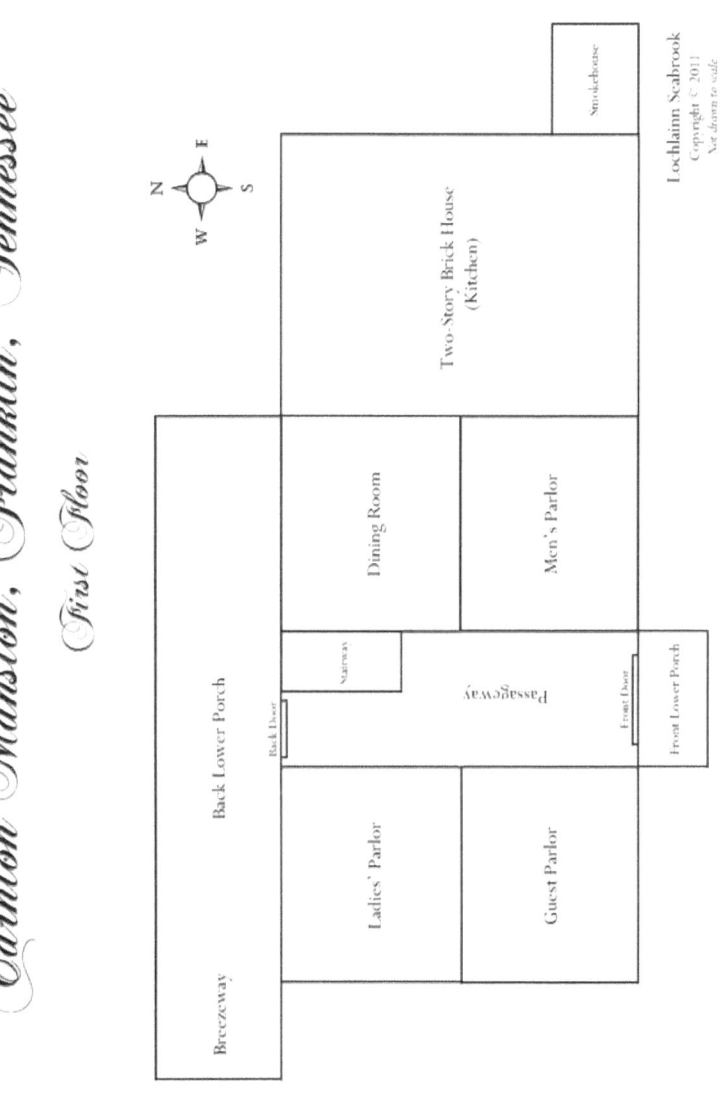

THE MCGAVOCKS OF CARNTON PLANTATION

Carnton Mansion, Franklin, Tennessee
Second Floor

- Breezeway
- Back Upper Porch
- Guest Bedroom
- Girls' Bedroom
- Stairway
- Stairway
- Hallway
- Sitting Room
- Front Upper Porch
- Master Bedroom
- Children's Nursery
- Two-Story Brick House (Kitchen)
- Smokehouse

Lochlainn Seabrook
Copyright © 2011
Not drawn to scale

THE MCGAVOCKS OF CARNTON PLANTATION

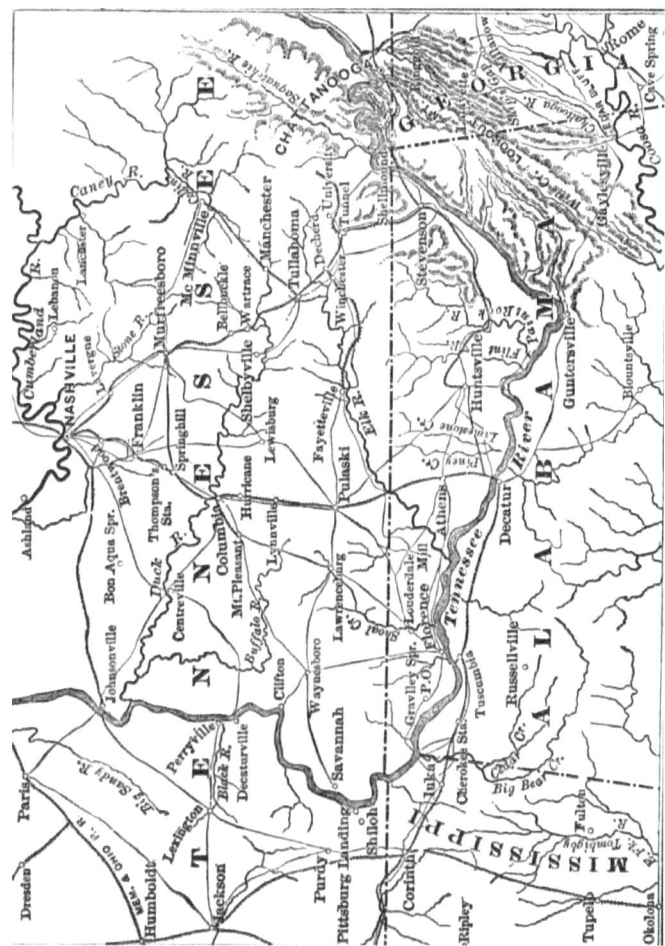

Map showing the path of Confederate General John Bell Hood and the Army of Tennessee after the Battle of Atlanta on July 22, 1864. In early November of that year, Hood advanced northward from Florence, Alabama, into Columbia, Tennessee, where he met up with Union General John McAllister Schofield and the Battle of Columbia took place between the 24th and the 29th. Hood then followed Schofield to Spring Hill, Tennessee, where the Battle of Spring Hill was fought on the 29th. Schofield and his men slipped past Hood during the evening, reaching Franklin, Tennessee, on November 30th. Here the disastrous Battle of Franklin II ignited later that day, with Schofield fleeing north towards Nashville that night, arriving the next day. Hood pursued Schofield into Nashville, where fighting was delayed several weeks due to inclement weather. After the skies cleared the two armies met for the last time, culminating in the Battle of Nashville, December 15-16, 1864. The conflict finished off what was left of the Army of Tennessee, breaking the back of the Confederacy in the West. General Robert E. Lee surrendered in Virginia four months later. (Map from Cox's *The Battle of Franklin, Tennessee*)

THE MCGAVOCKS OF CARNTON PLANTATION

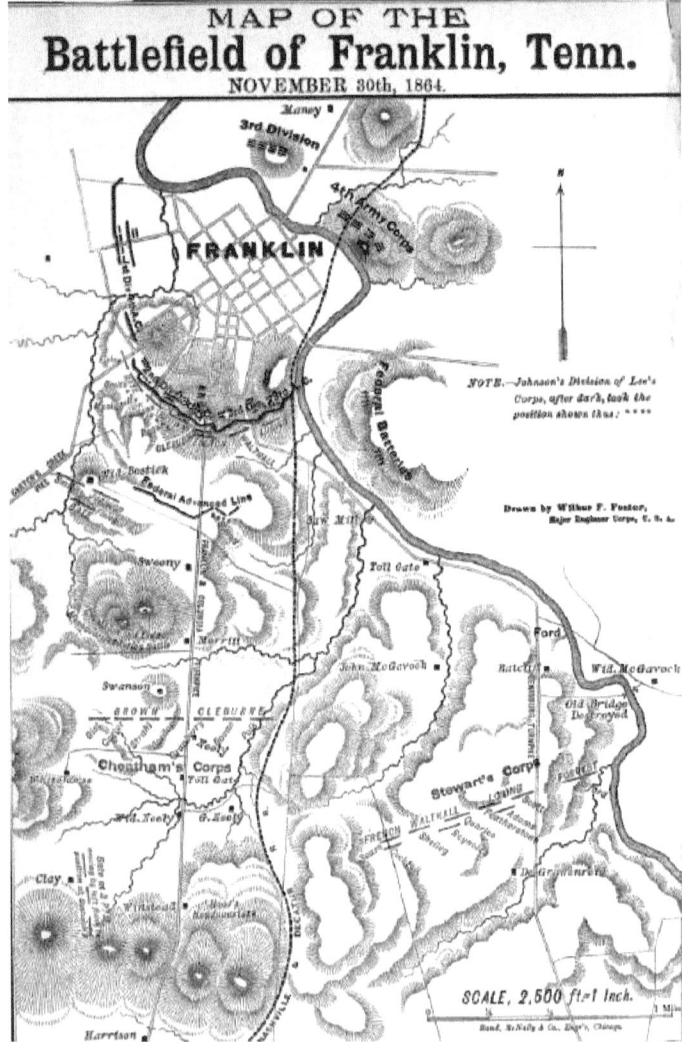

Map of the Battle of Franklin II. Note the location of Carnton Plantation, listed as "John McGavock," right lower middle. The location of his brother's plantation, James Randal McGavock's Riverside, can be seen on the right side across the Harpeth River, listed as "Wid. McGavock," for James' wife Louisa C. Chenault (James passed away in the winter of 1862). The "hottest" fighting of the battle took place around the "Franklin & Columbia Turnpike" (now Columbia Ave.), left center. Franklin II took place within the area bordered by the Carter House in the North, Winstead Hill in the South, Carters Creek Pike in the West, and the Harpeth River in the East. (Map from *The Southern Bivouac* magazine, Vol. 1, June 1885-May 1886, Louisville, Kentucky, p. 9.)

THE MCGAVOCKS OF CARNTON PLANTATION

Sign at the entrance to Carnton Plantation. (Photo © Lochlainn Seabrook)

THE McGAVOCKS OF CARNTON PLANTATION

Carnton Plantation Mansion, Franklin, Tennessee, front view, as it looks today. (Photo © Lochlainn Seabrook)

THE MCGAVOCKS OF CARNTON PLANTATION

Signage at Carnton Plantation entrance, wide shot. (Photo © Lochlainn Seabrook)

THE MCGAVOCKS OF CARNTON PLANTATION

Entrance gate, Carnton Plantation. (Photo © Lochlainn Seabrook)

The McGavocks of Carnton Plantation

Historical marker at the entrance of Carnton Plantation. (Photo © Lochlainn Seabrook)

THE MCGAVOCKS OF CARNTON PLANTATION

Front driveway approach to Carnton Plantation, looking east. (Photo © Lochlainn Seabrook)

The McGavocks of Carnton Plantation

Colonel John W. McGavock (1815-1893), Confederate officer and owner of Carnton Plantation during Lincoln's War. John is the son of Randal McGavock, founder of Carnton Plantation, and Sarah Dougherty Rodgers. He is the husband of Caroline E. "Carrie" Winder. Photo from a newspaper, probably from around 1885. (Image courtesy Williamson County Public Library)

The McGavocks of Carnton Plantation

Colonel John W. McGavock, a later newspaper photo, probably from just before his death in 1893. (Image courtesy Williamson County Public Library)

THE MCGAVOCKS OF CARNTON PLANTATION

Caroline Elizabeth "Carrie" Winder (1829-1905), daughter of Van Perkins Winder and Martha Ann Grundy, and wife of Colonel John W. McGavock of Carnton Plantation. Carrie was known as "the Good Samaritan of Williamson County," for her charitable nature and many kind acts, such as taking in orphans, aiding the poor, and helping nurse the wounded at Carnton after the Battle of Franklin II. (Image from Ridley's *Battles and Sketches of the Army of Tennessee*)

THE MCGAVOCKS OF CARNTON PLANTATION

Carnton Mansion, front view. Colonel John and Carrie owned and lived at Carnton Plantation during Lincoln's War. Prior to the conflict the house was designated a Confederate field hospital by President Jefferson Davis, a function for which it admirably served on November 30, 1864. (Photo © Lochlainn Seabrook)

The McGavocks of Carnton Plantation

Carnton Mansion, rear view. (Photo © Lochlainn Seabrook)

THE McGAVOCKS OF CARNTON PLANTATION

Carnton Mansion, southeast view, looking northwest. (Photo © Lochlainn Seabrook)

THE McGAVOCKS OF CARNTON PLANTATION

Carnton Mansion, showing back (right) and east (left) side. Note the dark "ghost" line running up and down the left brick wall of the house, a vestige of the roof line of the original 1811 Rodgers' family house. This small two-story structure was damaged by a tornado in 1909 and torn down. (Photo © Lochlainn Seabrook)

THE MCGAVOCKS OF CARNTON PLANTATION

Windermere, Franklin, Tennessee. This recently restored home belonged to Hattie McGavock (daughter of Colonel John of Carnton Plantation) and her husband Confederate Lieutenant George L. Cowan. Windermere is located west of Carnton, at the end of the driveway across the street. (Photo © Lochlainn Seabrook)

THE MCGAVOCKS OF CARNTON PLANTATION

Carnton Mansion, front view, before the recent restoration of the window shutters. (Photo © Lochlainn Seabrook)

THE MCGAVOCKS OF CARNTON PLANTATION

A more recent view of the Carnton Mansion facade, looking northeast. The shutters have been replaced. (Photo © Lochlainn Seabrook)

THE MCGAVOCKS OF CARNTON PLANTATION

Carnton Mansion, south side, front view with front walkway. (Photo © Lochlainn Seabrook)

THE MCGAVOCKS OF CARNTON PLANTATION

Carnton Mansion, south side, front view, as it looked in 2008. (Photo © Lochlainn Seabrook)

THE MCGAVOCKS OF CARNTON PLANTATION

Carnton Mansion, northwest side, back and side view, from the garden. (Photo © Lochlainn Seabrook)

THE MCGAVOCKS OF CARNTON PLANTATION

Carnton Mansion as it looked at the time of publication, 2011. (Photo © Lochlainn Seabrook)

THE MCGAVOCKS OF CARNTON PLANTATION

Carnton Mansion, east side view. (Photo © Lochlainn Seabrook)

THE MCGAVOCKS OF CARNTON PLANTATION

Carnton Mansion, back, facing southeast. (Photo © Lochlainn Seabrook)

THE MCGAVOCKS OF CARNTON PLANTATION

Carnton Mansion, northwest side, back and side view with the controversial board garden fence. (Photo © Lochlainn Seabrook)

THE MCGAVOCKS OF CARNTON PLANTATION

Carnton Mansion, east side view, showing a closeup of the sloping "ghost" roof line of the original 1811 brick house, which later became the McGavocks' kitchen. The black horizontal lines over the two doors may be the roof lines of the carriage house (when this particular structure was built and removed is unknown). Also note the second floor "ghost" door (darker bricks) above the men's parlor door (on left). This doorway once led from the children's nursery in the mansion directly into the bedroom of Carnton's nanny Elizabeth Clouston, located on the second floor of the 1811 house. After the 1909 tornado destroyed the latter, the doorway was bricked over. The door on the right leads to the family dining room. (Photo © Lochlainn Seabrook)

THE MCGAVOCKS OF CARNTON PLANTATION

Carnton Mansion, front view, showing Tennessee's oldest walkway. Note the curvature for draining off rain, giving it the name "turtleback" walkway. Many famous early Americans trod over these bricks. (Photo © Lochlainn Seabrook)

THE MCGAVOCKS OF CARNTON PLANTATION

Carnton's smokehouse. (Photo © Lochlainn Seabrook)

THE MCGAVOCKS OF CARNTON PLANTATION

Smokehouse, showing the site of the original 1811 brick house alongside. (Photo © Lochlainn Seabrook)

SMOKEHOUSE
c. 1815

Before modern refrigerators, much of the livestock, particularly hogs, were cured for preservation. Animals were slaughtered in the late fall, salted and smoked over hickory chips, and then hung and stored throughout the year in the smokehouse. Animal fat was rendered into lard and used for cooking, making soap, and candles.

Sign in Carnton's smokehouse. (Photo © Lochlainn Seabrook)

The McGavocks of Carnton Plantation

Closeup of Carnton's smokehouse door. (Photo © Lochlainn Seabrook)

THE MCGAVOCKS OF CARNTON PLANTATION

Iron kettle, Carnton's smokehouse, used for making lard from hog fat. (Photo © Lochlainn Seabrook)

THE MCGAVOCKS OF CARNTON PLANTATION

Original wooden salt trough, located in Carnton's smokehouse. The trough was partially filled with brine salt and hog meat was rolled in it to prepare it for smoking. (Photo © Lochlainn Seabrook)

THE MCGAVOCKS OF CARNTON PLANTATION

Another view of the smokehouse, facing southwest. (Photo © Lochlainn Seabrook)

THE MCGAVOCKS OF CARNTON PLANTATION

Site of the original 1811 brick house, probably built and owned by the Rodgers' family, which married into the McGavock family. Now an archaeological dig, the house was located between the smokehouse and Carnton Mansion. (Photo © Lochlainn Seabrook)

Another view of the site of the original 1811 brick house and the archaeological dig. (Photo © Lochlainn Seabrook)

THE MCGAVOCKS OF CARNTON PLANTATION

Carnton's basement door. (Photo © Lochlainn Seabrook)

THE MCGAVOCKS OF CARNTON PLANTATION

Carnton's house servants' quarters, front view. (Photo © Lochlainn Seabrook)

THE McGAVOCKS OF CARNTON PLANTATION

Carnton's house servants' quarters, rear side view. Note the two doors at the back, which lead into the first floor or basement, the location of two of the plantation's workshops. (Photo © Lochlainn Seabrook)

THE MCGAVOCKS OF CARNTON PLANTATION

Carnton's house servants' quarters, interior view. (Photo © Lochlainn Seabrook)

THE McGAVOCKS OF CARNTON PLANTATION

Carnton's servants' quarters, another interior view. Furnishings are a guess by modern historians. (Photo © Lochlainn Seabrook)

The McGavocks of Carnton Plantation

First floor or basement of the house servants' quarters, used as a workshop for repairing furniture and other household items. (Photo © Lochlainn Seabrook)

THE MCGAVOCKS OF CARNTON PLANTATION

Another front view of Carnton Plantation's servants' quarters. Referred to as a "slave house" by the uneducated, Southern servants often had a much higher standard of living than free blacks and even many whites at the time. This well made, roughly 1,000 square-foot brick home, built by Randal McGavock's talented black servant craftsmen themselves, is just one example of this fact. To this day, the durable 200-year old house is far superior in quality, construction, craftsmanship, materials, size, and aesthetics, to many modern houses in Franklin. (Photo © Lochlainn Seabrook)

THE MCGAVOCKS OF CARNTON PLANTATION

Eastern view with Carnton's smokehouse, the now empty site of the 1811 brick house, and Carnton Mansion in the background. (Photo © Lochlainn Seabrook)

THE MCGAVOCKS OF CARNTON PLANTATION

Carnton's attic windows, west side. (Photo © Lochlainn Seabrook)

THE MCGAVOCKS OF CARNTON PLANTATION

Carnton's attic windows, east side. (Photo © Lochlainn Seabrook)

THE MCGAVOCKS OF CARNTON PLANTATION

Carnton's breezeway, back lower porch, the area where the four Confederate generals who were killed at the Battle of Franklin II were laid out on the morning of December 1, 1864. Walking past single file, mournful troops paid their final respects to the brave Rebel officers who fell while leading their men against meddlesome Yankee soldiers and their aggressive commander-in-chief, big government liberal President Abraham Lincoln. (Photo © Lochlainn Seabrook)

THE McGAVOCKS OF CARNTON PLANTATION

Carnton's breezeway, back upper porch. Spectral figures are often sighted here by stunned eyewitnesses. (Photo © Lochlainn Seabrook)

THE MCGAVOCKS OF CARNTON PLANTATION

Carnton Mansion's imposing lower and upper Greek Revival porches, added to the front facade years after the original house was built. (Photo © Lochlainn Seabrook)

THE MCGAVOCKS OF CARNTON PLANTATION

Carnton's front doors before they were changed from white to brown. (Photo © Lochlainn Seabrook)

THE MCGAVOCKS OF CARNTON PLANTATION

Carnton Mansion, front view, southwest corner. The garden is on the left, the smokehouse is on the right. (Photo © Lochlainn Seabrook)

THE MCGAVOCKS OF CARNTON PLANTATION

Carnton Mansion, front walk view, facing north. According to family legend, the McGavocks wisely buried their valuables under this walkway during the War for Southern Independence to protect them from Lincoln's men—many who had a well-known and much feared penchant for theft. Yankee soldiers, who thought nothing of tearing bracelets from the wrists of little girls, wedding rings from the fingers of wives, and pendants from the necks of elderly women, were even seen digging up the graves of Southerners in order to loot their corpses of jewelry. (Photo © Lochlainn Seabrook)

THE MCGAVOCKS OF CARNTON PLANTATION

Carnton Mansion, east wall, where the 1811 brick house once attached to the main house. The door on the left leads to the men's parlor. The door on the right leads to the dining room. (Photo © Lochlainn Seabrook)

THE MCGAVOCKS OF CARNTON PLANTATION

Carnton's front turtleback walkway. Closeup showing Herringbone Bond design. (Photo © Lochlainn Seabrook)

THE MCGAVOCKS OF CARNTON PLANTATION

Back brick wall of Carnton Mansion showing English Bond design. (Photo © Lochlainn Seabrook)

The McGavocks of Carnton Plantation

Carnton Mansion's front facade brickwork showing Flemish Bond design. (Photo © Lochlainn Seabrook)

THE MCGAVOCKS OF CARNTON PLANTATION

Back and side view of Carnton Mansion, facing southeast. (Photo © Lochlainn Seabrook)

THE MCGAVOCKS OF CARNTON PLANTATION

Carnton Mansion, looking northwest, as she appears today. (Photo © Lochlainn Seabrook)

THE MCGAVOCKS OF CARNTON PLANTATION

East view of the Mansion with the smokehouse on the right. (Photo © Lochlainn Seabrook)

THE MCGAVOCKS OF CARNTON PLANTATION

The west end of the guest parlor, Carnton Mansion. Located on the first floor at the southwest corner of the house, this sumptiously appointed room was used by the McGavocks for entertaining. Note the blue globed solar lamp and the flute on the center table (to the right). In the back the ladies' parlor, situated at the rear of the home, can be seen through the open doorway. During parties these doors were opened to make the house feel larger and to give guests the ability to flow from room to room more easily. (Photo © Lochlainn Seabrook)

THE MCGAVOCKS OF CARNTON PLANTATION

The east end of the guest parlor, Carnton Mansion. While the piano-forte in the right foreground was not owned by the McGavocks, it is an original instrument from the same period. During social gatherings where music was performed, guests sometimes used the central passageway (through the door on the right) as a ballroom. Not infrequently, dancing and celebrations were known to continue well into the wee hours of the morning. (Photo © Lochlainn Seabrook)

The McGavocks of Carnton Plantation

Back lower porch looking east across the "courtyard," toward Carnton's house servants' quarters and the smokehouse. The top of the springhouse can just be seen at the bottom of the hill. McGavock Creek runs through the woods in the distance. (Photo © Lochlainn Seabrook)

The McGavocks of Carnton Plantation

Carnton Mansion's front walkway leading to front driveway, looking south across what used to be McGavock pasture and crop land. (Photo © Lochlainn Seabrook)

THE MCGAVOCKS OF CARNTON PLANTATION

Carnton's "courtyard" in front of the smokehouse. (Photo © Lochlainn Seabrook)

THE MCGAVOCKS OF CARNTON PLANTATION

A wide angle view of Carnton's "courtyard" looking southeast. (Photo © Lochlainn Seabrook)

Dining room door (east outer wall) of Carnton Mansion, showing the worn down step that once led into the now missing 1811 two-story brick house—which was converted into the family's kitchen. (Photo © Lochlainn Seabrook)

THE MCGAVOCKS OF CARNTON PLANTATION

Ornamental flowers (tiger lilies), Carnton's garden. (Photo © Lochlainn Seabrook)

THE MCGAVOCKS OF CARNTON PLANTATION

Carnton's springhouse sitting on McGavock Creek. (Photo © Lochlainn Seabrook)

Carnton's springhouse, interior, showing moss-covered creek water intentionally flooding the floor. During Carnton's active plantation years this water would have been kept clean and free of debris by the servants, as perishable foods (e.g., eggs, fruit, vegetables, milk, cream, butter, etc.) were kept on the steps and stone shelves beneath the surface of the water—an early form of refrigeration. (Photo © Lochlainn Seabrook)

THE MCGAVOCKS OF CARNTON PLANTATION

A section of Carnton's vegetable garden. (Photo © Lochlainn Seabrook)

THE MCGAVOCKS OF CARNTON PLANTATION

Another area of Carnton's vegetable garden. (Photo © Lochlainn Seabrook)

Ornamental flowers (daisies) in Carnton's garden. (Photo © Lochlainn Seabrook)

THE MCGAVOCKS OF CARNTON PLANTATION

Northwest section of the garden, the site of the earliest known house on the property (perhaps pre-1800). (Photo © Lochlainn Seabrook)

THE MCGAVOCKS OF CARNTON PLANTATION

Carnton's southeast yard. The Mansion is to the right. The log cabin homes of the plantation's field servants were probably located along the forest line in the background. Unlike Carnton's house servants' quarters (made of brick), the less durable wooden houses of the field servants have long since vanished. (Photo © Lochlainn Seabrook)

THE MCGAVOCKS OF CARNTON PLANTATION

Another view of the garden, this one facing east toward Carnton's backyard. (Photo © Lochlainn Seabrook)

THE MCGAVOCKS OF CARNTON PLANTATION

McGavock Creek, which runs along the modern eastern boundary of Carnton. Though it was once a clear running stream, or even a small river, today this portion of it is sluggish and algae-covered, possibly due, in part, to urbanization. (Photo © Lochlainn Seabrook)

THE MCGAVOCKS OF CARNTON PLANTATION

A sidelight window, Carnton's front door. (Photo © Lochlainn Seabrook)

Original two-hundred year old pane of glass on the back of Carnton Mansion. Note the ripples and bubbles from the 19th-Century hand-making process. (Photo © Lochlainn Seabrook)

THE MCGAVOCKS OF CARNTON PLANTATION

Men's parlor windows, front first floor, southeast corner. (Photo © Lochlainn Seabrook)

THE MCGAVOCKS OF CARNTON PLANTATION

Children's nursery windows, front second floor, southeast corner. (Photo © Lochlainn Seabrook)

THE MCGAVOCKS OF CARNTON PLANTATION

Girls' bedroom windows, front second floor, southwest corner. (Photo © Lochlainn Seabrook)

The McGavocks of Carnton Plantation

Guest parlor windows, front first floor, southwest corner. (Photo © Lochlainn Seabrook)

Men's outer parlor door (east outer wall), showing the worn down step that once led to the now absent 1811 house. (Photo © Lochlainn Seabrook)

THE MCGAVOCKS OF CARNTON PLANTATION

Flower bed in Carnton's "courtyard," site of the McGavocks' privy. (Photo © Lochlainn Seabrook)

THE MCGAVOCKS OF CARNTON PLANTATION

Carnton's famous and legally protected osage orange tree, named after the Osage, a living Native-American people whose early ancestors have been traced back to the region now known as Kentucky. (Photo © Lochlainn Seabrook)

THE MCGAVOCKS OF CARNTON PLANTATION

Closeup of the hammock hook on the lower back porch. (Photo © Lochlainn Seabrook)

THE MCGAVOCKS OF CARNTON PLANTATION

Ghostly phenomena at Carnton. I caught these three bright orbs on camera outside the men's parlor windows, first floor, in the summer of 2005. (In the color verison of this photo they are bright white.) They were not visible to the naked eye when I took the picture, and they were not in the photo I took immediately after from the same location. These white unearthly spheres are hovering over the spot where hundreds of amputated limbs were thrown from the children's nursery windows on the second floor (directly above) during the Battle of Franklin II, when the Mansion was used as a Confederate field hospital. Are these strange self-luminous balls of light the energy fields of Rebel soldiers who perished at Carnton in late Fall of 1864? Having personally experienced other paranormal phenomena at the plantation, I believe they are. This photo is from my bestselling book *Carnton Plantation Ghost Stories*. (Photo © Lochlainn Seabrook)

THE McGAVOCKS OF CARNTON PLANTATION

Another haunting presence at Carnton. I captured this luminescent orb (the white blurry circle near the top edge of the photo) on camera in the summer of 2005. This one is quite large and almost transparent. Again, it was not visible to me at the time I snapped off the shot. When I took the photo I was standing outside Carrie's window (first floor), now bricked over, near the lower breezeway (left), facing the west wall of the mansion. See following image. (Photo © Lochlainn Seabrook)

THE MCGAVOCKS OF CARNTON PLANTATION

Different colored bricks and mortar show the outline of one of Carrie's two tall windows on the west wall of the house. After Carrie's death the windows were removed and bricked over, perhaps in an effort to restore the house to its original 19th-Century appearance. The lower breezeway is just visible on the left. (Photo © Lochlainn Seabrook)

THE MCGAVOCKS OF CARNTON PLANTATION

Pintle hinge, back lower porch window, on which Carnton Mansion's shutters sit. (Photo © Lochlainn Seabrook)

THE MCGAVOCKS OF CARNTON PLANTATION

Historical marker at the entrance of the McGavock Family Cemetery, located on the modern northern edge of the Carnton property. (Photo © Lochlainn Seabrook)

THE MCGAVOCKS OF CARNTON PLANTATION

McGavock Family Cemetery, Carnton Plantation, Franklin, Tennessee. (Photo © Lochlainn Seabrook)

THE MCGAVOCKS OF CARNTON PLANTATION

Gravestone of Randal McGavock (1768-1843), founder of Carnton Plantation, McGavock Family Cemetery, Carnton Plantation, Franklin, Tennessee. (Photo © Lochlainn Seabrook)

The McGavocks of Carnton Plantation

Gravestone of Sarah Dougherty Rodgers (1786-1854), wife of Randal McGavock, founder of Carnton Plantation, McGavock Family Cemetery. (Photo © Lochlainn Seabrook)

The McGavocks of Carnton Plantation

Gravestone of Confederate Colonel John W. McGavock (1815-1893), owner of Carnton Plantation during Lincoln's War, McGavock Family Cemetery. John is the husband of Caroline Elizabeth "Carrie" Winder. (Photo © Lochlainn Seabrook)

Gravestone of Caroline Elizabeth "Carrie" Winder (1829-1905), wife of Colonel John W. McGavock, McGavock Family Cemetery. Carrie is the granddaughter of the celebrated Tennessee senator, Felix Grundy, and his wife Ann Phillips Rodgers. Ann is the sister of Sarah Dougherty Rodgers, the wife of Randal McGavock—Colonel John's father and the founder of Carnton. This makes Carrie and John 1st cousins once removed. (Photo © Lochlainn Seabrook)

THE MCGAVOCKS OF CARNTON PLANTATION

Gravestone of John Randal McGavock (b. 1851), son of Colonel John and Carrie, McGavock Family Cemetery. Little John lived for only three months and six days. (Photo © Lochlainn Seabrook)

Gravestone of Martha Winder McGavock (1849-1862), daughter of Colonel John and Carrie, McGavock Family Cemetery. Martha died nearly one year into Lincoln's War at about twelve and a half years of age. (Photo © Lochlainn Seabrook)

Gravestone of Mary Elizabeth McGavock (1851-1858), daughter of Colonel John and Carrie, McGavock Family Cemetery. Mary did not live to see her seventh birthday. (Photo © Lochlainn Seabrook)

Gravestone of Cynthia Rodes Pointer (1863-1907), wife of Van Winder McGavock, Sr. (1855-1934), McGavock Family Cemetery. Van Winder is the nephew of Colonel John of Carnton. (Photo © Lochlainn Seabrook)

THE MCGAVOCKS OF CARNTON PLANTATION

Gravestone of Elizabeth Harding McGavock (1845-1871), McGavock Family Cemetery. Elizabeth is the niece of Colonel John of Carnton, and the wife of Edwin H. Douglas. (Photo © Lochlainn Seabrook)

Gravestone of Van Winder McGavock, Sr. (1855-1934), nephew of Colonel John of Carnton, and husband of Cynthia Rodes Pointer (1863-1907), McGavock Family Cemetery. (Photo © Lochlainn Seabrook)

THE MCGAVOCKS OF CARNTON PLANTATION

Carnton Plantation Servants' Cemetery, Carnton Plantation, Franklin, Tennessee. The McGavock Family Cemetery is only yards away (to the right). Nearly all Southern white servant owners, like the McGavocks, regarded their black employees as "part of the family," which is why the practice of burying black servants next to their white masters and mistresses dates back to the very beginning of so-called "Southern slavery." While across Dixie one can still find hundreds examples of antebellum European-American and African-American cemeteries situated side by side, it is far more difficult to find such graveyards in the North. This is because the Old North, well-known to have been far more racist than the Old South, was racially segregated before Lincoln's War, a prejudice that extended all the way to the grave. I have personally toured a number of Yankee cemeteries, and their black slaves (when they were even given a proper burial) are nearly always interred far away from their white owners. (Photo © Lochlainn Seabrook)

THE MCGAVOCKS OF CARNTON PLANTATION

The Cowan family plot, Mount Hope Cemetery, Franklin, Tennessee. (Photo © Lochlainn Seabrook)

Gravestone of Confederate Lieutenant Colonel George Limerick Cowan (1842-1919), Cowan family plot, Mount Hope Cemetery, Franklin, Tennessee. George, the husband of Hattie McGavock (1855-1932)—daughter of Colonel John of Carnton, was a proud member of both General Nathan Bedford Forrest's staff and his celebrated Escort. (Photo © Lochlainn Seabrook)

Gravestone of Harriet Young "Hattie" McGavock (1855-1932), wife of Lieutenant George L. Cowan, daughter of Colonel John and Carrie of Carnton, Cowan family plot, Mount Hope Cemetery, Franklin, Tennessee. Hattie and George lived at Windermere, at the foot of Carnton's driveway. Hattie was nine years old when the "Civil War" came to Carnton's door in November of 1864. (Photo © Lochlainn Seabrook)

THE MCGAVOCKS OF CARNTON PLANTATION

McGavock family plot, Mount Hope Cemetery, Franklin, Tennessee. It is located a few hundred yards from the Cowan family plot. Other people of note buried at Mount Hope include: country comedienne Sarah Ophelia (Colley) Cannon—better known by her stage name, Minnie Pearl; country singer Mary Ann Ward—better known as Marion Worth; Elvis Presley's music producer, Felton Jarvis; U.S. Congressman Nicholas Cox; U.S. Congressman William Wirt Courtney; U.S. Congressman Wynne F. Clouse; and Confederate soldier and U.S. Congressman Hendley Stone Bennett. Besides the McGavocks, I have Rucker, Grigsby, and Crockett relations buried at Mount Hope. (Photo © Lochlainn Seabrook)

Gravestone of Winder McGavock (1857-1907), husband of Susie Ewing (1863-1931), son of Colonel John and Carrie of Carnton, McGavock family plot, Mount Hope Cemetery, Franklin, Tennessee. Winder briefly inherited Carnton Plantation after the death of his mother in 1905, only to die himself two years later at the age of fifty. The estate was then turned over to Winder's wife Susie, who moved to downtown Franklin and sold Carnton in 1911, finally ending the 100 year period of McGavock ownership. (Photo © Lochlainn Seabrook)

THE MCGAVOCKS OF CARNTON PLANTATION

Carnton's back door. (Photo © Lochlainn Seabrook)

The McGavocks of Carnton Plantation

Carnton's back porch, looking west toward the modern day garden. (Photo © Lochlainn Seabrook)

THE MCGAVOCKS OF CARNTON PLANTATION

Looking east at Carnton's west side from the garden. The lower and upper back porches, as well as the shuttered third floor windows, stand out in bold relief. (Photo © Lochlainn Seabrook)

THE MCGAVOCKS OF CARNTON PLANTATION

East entrance to the McGavock Confederate Cemetery, Carnton Plantation, Franklin, Tennessee. (Photo © Lochlainn Seabrook)

The McGavocks of Carnton Plantation

Historical marker at the west entrance to Carnton's McGavock Confederate Cemetery, with Carnton Mansion just visible in the morning haze on the left in the distance. Note that the number of generals "brought to the house" was four, not five. (Photo © Lochlainn Seabrook)

THE MCGAVOCKS OF CARNTON PLANTATION

McGavock Confederate Cemetery, western end looking east. Carnton Mansion is on the right. (Photo © Lochlainn Seabrook)

THE MCGAVOCKS OF CARNTON PLANTATION

Stone marker, McGavock Confederate Cemetery, memorializing 225 of the unidentifiable bodies of Confederate soldiers who died at the Battle of Franklin II. (Photo © Lochlainn Seabrook)

THE MCGAVOCKS OF CARNTON PLANTATION

Stone marker, McGavock Confederate Cemetery, memorializing the 230 native Tennessee Confederate soldiers who are known to have died at the Battle of Franklin II. (Photo © Lochlainn Seabrook)

THE MCGAVOCKS OF CARNTON PLANTATION

The fading gravestone of one of Franklin's most famous sons: twenty-four year old Theodrick "Tod" Carter, Rest Haven Cemetery, Franklin, Tennessee. Promoted to the rank of captain on May 1, 1862, Tod fought with the Confederacy's Twentieth Tennessee Regiment. During the conflict he became a Middle Tennessee war correspondent for *The Chattanooga Daily Rebel*, writing under the pseudonym "Mint Julep." On November 30, 1864, Captain Carter was shot down just yards from his family home, Carter House, at the Battle of Franklin II, defending his town against Lincoln's invaders and Northern tyranny. He died from his wounds three days later. His epitaph above reads: "In memory of Theodrick 7th son of F. B. and M. A. Carter, born March 24th 1840. Died Dec. 2nd 1864." "F. B." is Tod's father, Fountain Branch Carter (1797-1871). "M. A." is his mother, Mary Armistead Atkinson (1806-1852). (Photo © Lochlainn Seabrook)

THE MCGAVOCKS OF CARNTON PLANTATION

Oaklawn Mansion, Spring Hill, Tennessee. In November 1864 Oaklawn served as Confederate General John Bell Hood's headquarters during the Battle of Spring Hill, one day prior to Franklin II. Later the house was purchased by current Franklin, Tennessee, resident George Jones and his wife at the time, Tammy Wynette (to whom I am related through marriage). The day I took this photo in 2005, the movie *Daltry Calhoun*, with Johnny Knoxville and Juliette Lewis, was being filmed at Oaklawn. (Photo © Lochlainn Seabrook)

THE MCGAVOCKS OF CARNTON PLANTATION

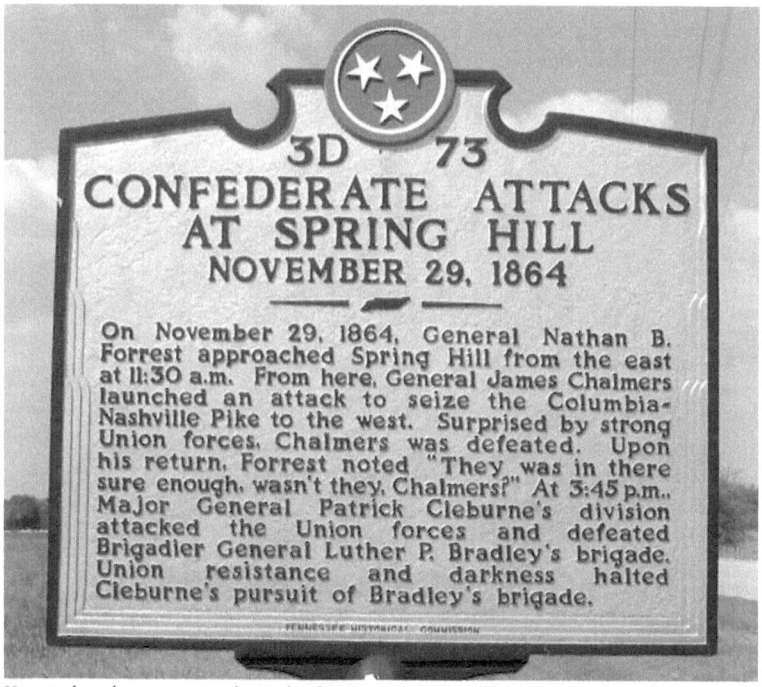

Historical marker concerning the Battle of Spring Hill, Spring Hill, Tennessee. Note the mention of Rebel General Cleburne, who perished the next day at the Battle of Franklin II and whose body was laid on Carnton Mansion's back porch. My cousin General Forrest is also mentioned. (Photo © Lochlainn Seabrook)

THE MCGAVOCKS OF CARNTON PLANTATION

Battle of Nashville Monument, Nashville, Tennessee. The Battle of Nashville took place December 15-16, 1864, just two weeks after the Battle of Franklin II. Confederate General John Bell Hood is widely held to have destroyed what was left of the Army of Tennessee at Nashville. (Photo © Lochlainn Seabrook)

The McGavocks of Carnton Plantation

Franklin, Tennessee, street signs honoring Confederate Generals John Adams and Patrick Cleburne, both who died at the Battle of Franklin II. This corner sign is located in the general vicinity where the two officers fell for the last time. (Photo © Lochlainn Seabrook)

THE MCGAVOCKS OF CARNTON PLANTATION

Belle Meade Mansion, Nashville, Tennessee, sister plantation to Carnton. Belle Meade was the home of Confederate General William Giles Harding (1808-1886), a close cousin of the author's and the husband of Elizabeth Irwin McGavock (1819-1867)—the sister of Colonel John of Carnton. (Photo © Lochlainn Seabrook)

THE MCGAVOCKS OF CARNTON PLANTATION

The Carter family cotton gin house—where the "hottest fightin'" took place at the Battle of Franklin II—was located some 300 feet east of what is now the corner of Columbia Avenue and Cleburne Street. The Yanks had a gun battery set up in front of the gin, which they used to mow down the Confederate ranks approaching from the South. Both the Carter gin house and the Carter House are the two landmarks most commonly referenced by eyewitnesses at Franklin II. As such, the section between the two structures is considered the core battlefield area by military authorities. While the brick Carter House managed to survive the War, the wooden gin has long since disappeared. However, a small memorial park has been set up in Franklin in the general area where it once stood (see next image). (Drawing from Ridley's *Battles and Sketches of the Army of Tennessee*)

Carter's Cotton Gin Memorial Park on Columbia Avenue, Franklin, Tennessee, site of the most intense fighting at Franklin II. Saved from commercial development, this small parcel of lawn is one of the few authentic remnants of the Battle of Franklin II battleground that has been preserved. In 2004 the Civil War Preservation Trust listed the Franklin Battlefield in the top ten of the nation's most endangered battlefields. (Photo © Lochlainn Seabrook)

THE MCGAVOCKS OF CARNTON PLANTATION

Carter House, Franklin, Tennessee, once the home of Fountain Branch Carter and his famous son, Confederate Captain Tod Carter. During the Battle of Franklin II the house was illegally commandeered by Union General Jacob D. Cox for use as his headquarters. Bullet holes can still be seen in the buildings on the property, vestiges from that fateful day when the family was forced to flee into the basement and their twenty-four year old son Tod, a young Rebel officer serving under Hood, was mowed down only yards away by Yankee fire. (Photo © Lochlainn Seabrook)

Historical marker indicating the site of the Carter House, near the epicenter of the Battle of Franklin II. The first name of Fountain B. Carter's son "Tod" is misspelled as "Theodoric." The correct spelling is Theodrick. (Photo © Lochlainn Seabrook)

THE MCGAVOCKS OF CARNTON PLANTATION

Irish-born Confederate Major General Patrick Ronayne Cleburne (1828-1864), the first of the six generals who perished at the Battle of Franklin II, headed Cleburne's Division at the conflict. Like nearly all Southerners, Cleburne hated slavery and pushed for both abolition and the official enlistment of blacks in the Confederate army and navy. Known as the "Stonewall Jackson of the West," his ghost is said to haunt the lower back porch of Carnton Mansion, where his lifeless body was laid on the morning of December 1, 1864. (Image courtesy Library of Congress)

THE MCGAVOCKS OF CARNTON PLANTATION

Confederate Brigadier General States Rights Gist (1831-1864), the second of the six generals who died as a result of fighting at the Battle of Franklin II, led Gist's Brigade at the conflict. A cousin of the author, Gist also fought bravely at the battles of Manassas I, Chickamauga, and Chattanooga. He is the 1st cousin of William Henry Gist (1807-1874), the governor of South Carolina. Governor Gist signed South Caronlina's December 20, 1860, "Ordinance of Secession," making the Palmetto State the first of the Southern states to officially and legally secede from the Union. This led to a domino effect in which other Southern states immediately began to break from the U.S.A., launching the formation of the Confederate States of America, or C.S.A., in February 1861. (Photo from Scofield's *The Retreat From Pulaski to Nashville, Tenn.*)

THE MCGAVOCKS OF CARNTON PLANTATION

Confederate Brigadier General John Carpenter Carter (1837-1864), the third of the six generals who died as a result of fighting at the Battle of Franklin II, led Maney's Brigade at the conflict. A native Georgian, Carter was a successful lawyer before the War. He also fought at the battles of Shiloh, Perryville, Murfreesboro, and Chickamauga. Mortally injured at Franklin II, he died from his wounds on December 10, 1864, at the Harrison House in Franklin. (Image from Scofield's *The Retreat From Pulaski to Nashville, Tenn.*)

THE MCGAVOCKS OF CARNTON PLANTATION

Confederate Brigadier General Hiram Bronson Granbury (1831-1864), the fourth of the six generals who perished at the Battle of Franklin II, led Granbury's Brigade at the conflict. A native Mississippian, before the War Granbury was a lawyer and a chief justice in Texas. He was one of the unfortunate Rebels who was captured at the Battle of Fort Donelson, but was exchanged and went on to fight at the battles of Chickamauga Chattanooga, Atlanta, and finally, Franklin II. The town of Granbury, Texas, where his body is buried, is named after him. (Image from Scofield's *The Retreat From Pulaski to Nashville, Tenn.*)

THE MCGAVOCKS OF CARNTON PLANTATION

Confederate Brigadier General Otho French Strahl (1831-1864), the fifth of the six generals who perished at the Battle of Franklin II, led Strahl's Brigade at the conflict. An Ohio lawyer before the War, Strahl correctly sided with the South against liberal Lincoln, also serving with distinction at the battles of Shiloh, Chickamauga, and Murfreesboro. As he lay dying on the Franklin battlefield one of his men asked him desperately, "What do we do now gineral?", to which he replied: "Keep on firing!" These were his last words. His corpse was later placed on Carnton's back porch for viewing by his troops. It is said that Strahl knew beforehand that Franklin II would be his last battle on earth. (Photo from Ridley's *Battle and Sketches of the Army of Tennessee*)

THE MCGAVOCKS OF CARNTON PLANTATION

Confederate Brigadier General John Adams (1825-1864), the sixth of the six generals who perished at the Battle of Franklin II, led Adams' Brigade at the conflict. Born of Irish parents, Adams fought in numerous campaigns, including those in Tennessee and Mississippi. He is shown here leading his men against the blue-coated enemy at Franklin on November 30, 1864. According to eyewitnesses, even with his right arm severely injured, he continued to ride forward in a courageous attempt to surmount the Yankee breastworks. As he prepared his horse to leap the fortifications, both were shot down in a hail of bullets. Adams' noble steed died mid jump, its lifeless body remaining grotesquely frozen astride the wall until the next day. The general's body was taken to Carnton, where it was laid out on the McGavocks' back porch before his burial at Maplewood Cemetery, Pulaski, Tennessee. (Image from Ridley's *Battles and Sketches of the Army of Tennessee*)

THE MCGAVOCKS OF CARNTON PLANTATION

"Old Straight," Confederate Lieutenant General Alexander Peter Stewart (1821-1908), who led Stewart's Corps at the Battle of Franklin II. Although a successful and well respected military man, Stewart was more at home in the classroom than on the battlefield. A cousin of the author, the native Tennessean was a professor at numerous universities before and after Lincoln's War, and served as the chancellor of the University of Mississippi until 1886. (Photo from Ridley's *Battle and Sketches of the Army of Tennessee*)

THE MCGAVOCKS OF CARNTON PLANTATION

A late photo of Confederate officer Stephen Dill Lee (1833-1908), the Confederacy's youngest lieutenant general. A cousin of the author and General Robert E. Lee, he led Lee's Corps at the Battle of Franklin II. After the War Lee settled in Mississippi where he became the president of Mississippi State College and lived the life of a gentleman farmer. He also headed the United Confederate Veterans (today known as the Sons of Confederate Veterans), the organization to which Colonel John McGavock of Carnton Plantation belonged. (Image from Ridley's *Battles and Sketches of the Army of Tennessee*)

THE MCGAVOCKS OF CARNTON PLANTATION

The then sparsely populated and peaceful bucolic town of Franklin, Tennessee, as it looked to Confederate General John Bell Hood before the Battle of Franklin II on November 30, 1864. This photo was presumably taken from Winstead Hill, overlooking Columbia Pike (now Columbia Avenue). Note the flat expanse where the battle was fought, known as the Plain of Franklin, and the surrounding hills. The Confederates marched in from the South (from the lower right) up the pike to meet the entrenched Yankee forces waiting in and around downtown Franklin (at the top of the picture). (Photo from Ridley's *Battles and Sketches of the Army of Tennessee*)

THE MCGAVOCKS OF CARNTON PLANTATION

Confederate Monument, Franklin, Tennessee, honoring the brave and loyal men who fought for the Confederacy at the Battle of Franklin II. Erected November 30, 1899 (thirty-five years after the conflict), by the proud descendants of Confederate soldiers, tragically—and absurdly—today Confederate flags are not allowed to be displayed. (Photo © Lochlainn Seabrook)

The McGavocks of Carnton Plantation

Elm Springs Mansion, Columbia, Maury County, Tennessee, modern headquarters of the Sons of Confederate Veterans (SCV), the same organization Colonel John W. McGavock of Carnton belonged to after the War, when it was called United Confederate Veterans (UCV). Like his cousin John before him, the author is also a proud member of this noble organization. Rebel commander Hood engaged Yankee commander Schofield near Elm Springs November 24-29, 1864, at the Battle of Columbia, which led to the fateful and unnecessary Battles of Spring Hill (November 29), Franklin II (November 30), and Nashville (December 15-16). (Photo © Lochlainn Seabrook)

THE MCGAVOCKS OF CARNTON PLANTATION

Figuers family home, Franklin, Tennessee. On the afternoon of November 30, 1864, the author's cousin, fifteen year old Hardin Perkins Figuers (1849-1912), climbed one of these oak trees in his front yard and watched in amazement as the Confederate and Union armies took their positions on the Plain of Franklin. What unfolded was a scene of horror that he would remember until the day he died. (Photo © Lochlainn Seabrook)

THE MCGAVOCKS OF CARNTON PLANTATION

The title of this engraving, made about 1866, is "The first reading of the Emancipation Proclamation before the cabinet." This momentous event took place on July 22, 1862. This was only the first of four versions of the now infamous document. The final version, the one best known to the public, was issued on January 1, 1863. Then as today, Southerners considered it to be one of the greatest pieces of political trickery in the history of the U.S., a cynical ploy that Lincoln himself admitted was illegal, except as a "war measure." He later confessed that he only reluctantly issued it because "we had reached the end of our rope . . . and had about played our last card . . ." The card game he is referring to here did not concern abolition or black civil rights. It was about his plan to unconstitutionally force the South back into the Union at gunpoint. Let us note here that what is known as the preliminary version of the Emancipation Proclamation (issued September 22, 1862) contained Lincoln's black colonization plan for immediately deporting all freed blacks out of the country, preferably to Africa or Central America. His cabinet members wisely talked "Honest Abe" out of including this clause in the final draft. Despite his repeated call for American apartheid, the self-confessed white supremacist and white separatist continues to be called the "Great Emancipator," the "black man's best friend," and "America's Greatest President" by Lincolnites and the ill-informed. From left to right: (seated) Edwin M. Stanton, Lincoln's second secretary of war; (standing) Salmon P. Chase, Lincoln's first secretary of the treasury; (seated) Abraham Lincoln, America's sixteenth president; (seated in back) Gideon Welles, Lincoln's secretary of the Navy; (seated in front) William H. Seward, Lincoln's secretary of state; (standing in back) Caleb B. Smith, Lincoln first secretary of the interior; (standing in back) Montgomery Blair, Lincoln's first postmaster general; and (seated far right) Edward Bates, Lincoln's first attorney general. (Image courtesy Library of Congress)

The McGavocks of Carnton Plantation

Fort Granger (located behind Pinkerton Park), Franklin, Tennessee, occupied by Union troops during the Battle of Franklin II. Set strategically atop Figuers' Bluff on the Harpeth River, all that is left today of the garrison—originally constructed by Confederate troops—are earthen ramparts, overgrown trails, and grassy clearings. Interpretive wayside exhibits provide visitors with information on the original layout and history of the fort. (Photo © Lochlainn Seabrook)

THE MCGAVOCKS OF CARNTON PLANTATION

General Nathan Bedford Forrest (1821-1877), beloved Tennessean and Southern icon. Forrest was present at the Battle of Franklin II, November 30, 1864. That day he used the upper back portico at Carnton Plantation as an observation deck shortly before the fight began. Two weeks later he singlehandedly saved what was left of the Army of Tennessee as it fled southward after the equally disastrous Battle of Nashville. Forrest was the only man in either the Yankee or Rebel army to rise from private to lieutenant general. Much has been written about the good General by anti-South writers, all of it malicious, false, and absurd. Sherman, who spent four years unsuccessfully hunting down the lanky charismatic Rebel chieftain, later pronounced him "the most remarkable soldier the war produced." See my books *A Rebel Born: A Defense of Nathan Bedford Forrest* and *Nathan Bedford Forrest: Southern Hero, American Patriot*. (Photo courtesy U.S. Army Military History Institute)

The McGavocks of Carnton Plantation

General Nathan Bedford Forrest's boyhood home, Chapel Hill, Tennessee. Forrest was not born here (that location, a cabin a couple of miles distant, disappeared long ago), but he did live here for several years before his father William (1801-1837) moved the Forrest family to Mississippi. The entire property (including out buildings) is being restored and will soon be open to the public for guided tours. To this day, each summer the Forrest Boyhood Home is the site of an annual fundraiser, complete with merchants, food, music, pro-South readings, Forrest reenactments, period dress, an auction, animals, and living exhibits and displays of 19th-Century Tennessee life. Among the many guests at the 2011 fundraiser was Tennessee Senator Bill Ketron. (Photo © Lochlainn Seabrook)

Sign outside Forrest's boyhood home, Chapel Hill, Tennessee. (Photo © Lochlainn Seabrook)

Name of the area (and also of a large subdivision) in Franklin where Forrest and his men crossed a bend in the Harpeth River during Franklin II. (Photo © Lochlainn Seabrook)

THE MCGAVOCKS OF CARNTON PLANTATION

Duck River sign, Columbia, Tennessee. Confederate General John Bell Hood crossed here (from south to north) with his troops in late November, just prior to the debacle at Franklin, November 30, 1864. A few weeks later he retreated south back across the Duck (heading for Mississippi) after the Battle of Nashville, December 15-16. (Photo © Lochlainn Seabrook)

THE MCGAVOCKS OF CARNTON PLANTATION

Downtown Franklin, Tennessee, still looks much as it did during the Battle of Franklin II in the Fall of 1864. (Photo © Lochlainn Seabrook)

THE MCGAVOCKS OF CARNTON PLANTATION

Many unenlightened Southerners are offended by the Confederate flag (a symbol of self-determination) but show no revulsion whatsoever toward genuine symbols of Northern slavery in Dixie, such as this pineapple motif atop a street light post in Franklin, Tennessee. Why the town allowed this emblem of the Yankee-African slave trade to be placed around its environs is even more of a mystery. Many innocently believe it to be a "welcome" sign. But this is just another example of the North suppressing the truth about its past as the founder of both the American slave trade and American slavery. In fact, Yankees have intentionally reinterpreted the true meaning of the pineapple in an effort to hide its origins: after *Northern* slave captains (there was no such thing as a *Southern* slave captain) returned to New England, New York, and Maryland from their slaving journeys to Africa and the Caribbean, they impaled a pineapple on their front fence posts, a sign to passersby that fresh slaves were now available and that they were "welcome" to come in and make a purchase. (Photo © Lochlainn Seabrook)

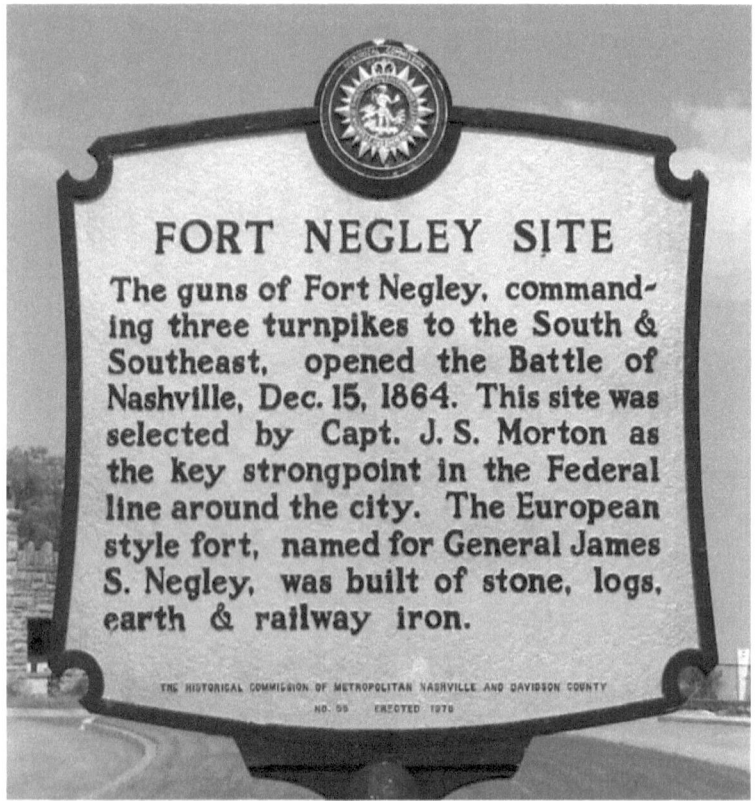

Historical marker at the entrance of Fort Negley, Nashville, Tennessee. The fort was crucial to the Yankee win against Hood at the Battle of Nashville, two weeks after Franklin II. (Photo © Lochlainn Seabrook)

THE MCGAVOCKS OF CARNTON PLANTATION

Storefront, Nashville, Tennessee. Unlike many other large cities, modern Nashville has managed to retain some of its 19th-Century flavor and charm. The McGavocks of Carnton Plantation were very familiar with the town's streets, sites, and scenes, many which were unnecessarily destroyed by Lincoln and his armies during the War for Southern Independence. (Photo © Lochlainn Seabrook)

THE MCGAVOCKS OF CARNTON PLANTATION

Court House, Franklin, Tennessee, used as a field hospital during and after the Battle of Franklin II. It sits across from the Confederate Monument in Franklin Center. Strangely, the cannon surrounding the monument were recently discovered to be Yankee guns from Massachusetts. (Photo © Lochlainn Seabrook)

THE MCGAVOCKS OF CARNTON PLANTATION

Decorative street banner, Franklin, Tennessee, noting the establishment of the town in 1799, thirty-three years after the birth of Randal McGavock, the founder of Carnton Plantation. (Photo © Lochlainn Seabrook)

THE MCGAVOCKS OF CARNTON PLANTATION

Franklin, Tennessee, wooden marker indicating where Confederate General Patrick Cleburne fell during Franklin II. The Carter's Cotton Gin Memorial site is in the background. (Photo © Lochlainn Seabrook)

THE MCGAVOCKS OF CARNTON PLANTATION

Franklin street sign honoring States Rights Gist (1831-1864), one of six Confederate generals who perished as a result of wounds received at the Battle of Franklin II. He was not, however, one of the four generals laid on Carnton's back lower portico. South Carolina Governor William Henry Gist (1807-1874), States Rights' 1st cousin, was well-known to the famous Southern belle and South Carolina diarist Mary Chesnut. All three are cousins of the author. (Photo © Lochlainn Seabrook)

Franklin street sign honoring Hiram Bronson Granbury (1831-1864), one of six Confederate generals who perished as a result of wounds received at the Battle of Franklin II. His body was laid out on Carnton's back porch so that his troops could pay their respects. (Photo © Lochlainn Seabrook)

THE MCGAVOCKS OF CARNTON PLANTATION

Andrew "Old Hickory" Jackson (1767-1845), family friend of the McGavocks of Carnton Plantation. President Jackson, who lived at the Hermitage just outside Nashville, visited Carnton on a number of occasions, and even gave the family a special gift: a comfortable rocking chair still on display in the men's parlor. Carnton's garden is a reproduction of an 1847-style garden used by Jackson and other wealthy Tennesseans. (Image courtesy Library of Congress)

THE MCGAVOCKS OF CARNTON PLANTATION

The Hermitage, Andrew Jackson's home, Hermitage, Tennessee. Confederate General Nathan Bedford Forrest and his men stopped here on July 21, 1862, for about an hour to rest and water their horses. (Forrest was also hoping that Jackson's memory would inspire his soldiers.) It just so happened that a party was in full swing at the Hermitage that day, a one-year anniversary celebration of the Battle of Manassas I (the Battle of First Bull Run to Yanks), an early Confederate win. The charismatic Rebel chieftain was, no doubt, the center of attention for that brief sixty minutes, before ordering his troops back on the road to hunt down Lincoln's invaders. (Photo © Lochlainn Seabrook)

Historical marker at the entrance of the Hermitage, the home of President Andrew Jackson, Hermitage, Tennessee. (Photo © Lochlainn Seabrook)

THE MCGAVOCKS OF CARNTON PLANTATION

Grave site of President Andrew Jackson and his wife Rachel Donelson (1767-1828), Hermitage Gardens, the Hermitage, Hermitage, Tennessee. Rachel was a close friend of Sarah Dougherty Rodgers, the wife of Randal McGavock, the founder of Carnton Plantation. (Photo © Lochlainn Seabrook)

Historical marker, Confederate Circle, Mount Olivet Cemetery, Nashville, Tennessee. Lieutenant Colonel Randal William McGavock (close cousin of Colonel John of Carnton) and General Benjamin F. Cheatham (the latter who fought at the Battle of Franklin II) are mentioned. Randal's first name is misspelled. (Photo © Lochlainn Seabrook)

THE MCGAVOCKS OF CARNTON PLANTATION

Above, the Confederate Monument at Arlington National Cemetery, Arlington, Virginia, original site of Gen. Robert E. Lee's home, Arlington House—before it was stolen and ruthlessly plundered by the Yanks. Note the man second from the right: not merely a black slave or a body servant, but a real armed black Confederate soldier, marching proudly side-by-side with his white Confederate brothers. The memorial was designed by Southern artist Moses Ezekiel, one of 12,000 Jewish Confederate soldiers who routinely witnessed thousands of blacks in the Rebel armed forces firsthand—which is why, after all, he included an African-American in this typical Civil War scene as experienced by Southerners. About the time this monument was erected, in 1908, the North began suppressing the truth about the reality of black Confederate soldiers because it exposed the supreme lie of Lincoln's War; namely, that it had been fought to "free the slaves" in the "evil slave-ridden South." Contrary to this contrived Yankee nonsense, slavery was still being practiced in the North in 1861, the very birthplace of American slavery (in Massachusetts in 1641). What is more, of the South's 4,000,000 blacks, an estimated 300,000 served as combatants in the Confederate army and navy, far more than went North and fought for Lincoln (many who did so with great regret). At least 95 percent of the remaining 3,700,000 Southern blacks stayed in their homeland, Dixie (ignoring Lincoln's fake Emancipation Proclamation), where they supported the Confederacy in a myriad of ways—as the Arlington Confederate Monument, there for all to see, silently and stubbornly attests.

THE MCGAVOCKS OF CARNTON PLANTATION

McGavock Mausoleum and Burial Ground, Mount Olivet Cemetery, Nashville, Tennessee. On the left can be seen some of the graves of various family members. The McGavocks of Carnton are closely related to the Nashville McGavocks, and those buried here (some twenty miles north of Franklin) would have been very familiar with the Franklin plantation. At the time of this photo (summer 2006) the grounds, structures, and gravestones here were all in varying degrees of decay and disrepair. A later visit, however, showed signs of restoration. (Photo © Lochlainn Seabrook)

The McGavocks of Carnton Plantation

McGavock Monument, Mount Olivet Cemetery, Nashville, Tennessee. (Photo © Lochlainn Seabrook)

THE MCGAVOCKS OF CARNTON PLANTATION

Cemetery plaque honoring some of the Nashville McGavocks buried in the McGavock family plot, Mount Olivet, Nashville, Tennessee. Jacob McGavock (1790-1878) is the 1st cousin of Confederate Colonel John of Carnton. Jacob's wife, Louisa Caroline Grundy (1798-1878), is the aunt of Colonel John's wife, Caroline "Carrie" Winder. Confederate Lieutenant Colonel Randal William McGavock (1826-1863) is the 1st cousin once removed of Colonel John of Carnton. (Photo © Lochlainn Seabrook)

Gravestone of Dr. Felix Grundy McGavock (1832-1897), McGavock family plot, Mount Olivet Cemetery, Nashville, Tennessee. The brother of Lieutenant Colonel Randal William McGavock and the husband of Mary Manoah Bostick, of Triune, Tennessee, after Lincoln's War Felix went into business with Confederate icon General Nathan Bedford Forrest in Memphis. Of royal European heritage, Felix is the son of Jacob McGavock and Louisa Caroline Grundy, and the 1st cousin once removed of Colonel John of Carnton. (Photo © Lochlainn Seabrook)

The McGavocks of Carnton Plantation

Gravestone of Confederate Lieutenant Colonel Randal William McGavock (1826-1863), Mount Olivet Cemetery, Nashville, Tennessee. Randal, a known guest at Carnton, died at the Battle of Raymond (Mississippi), May 12, 1863, bravely fighting for states' rights against the North's illicit intruders. (Photo © Lochlainn Seabrook)

THE MCGAVOCKS OF CARNTON PLANTATION

Another view of the McGavock Burial Ground and Mausoleum, Mount Olivet Cemetery, Nashville, Tennessee. (Photo © Lochlainn Seabrook)

Gravestone of Confederate Major General Benjamin Franklin Cheatham (1820-1886), Mount Olivet Cemetery, Nashville, Tennessee. "Frank," as he was affectionately known, fought at the Battle of Franklin II and was a friend of the McGavocks of Carnton Plantation. The Cheathams, another Virginia family to whom I am related, later settled in Robertson County, Tennessee, and married into the Nashville McGavock clan. (Photo © Lochlainn Seabrook)

THE MCGAVOCKS OF CARNTON PLANTATION

Gravestone, Ewing family plot, City Cemetery, Franklin, Tennessee. Mentioned is Eliza McDowell McGavock (1801-1876), the daughter of Revolutionary War officer, Captain Hugh McGavock (1761-1844), and his wife Nancy Kent (1763-1835). Eliza is the wife of Dr. Andrew B. Ewing (1796-1881), and the 1st cousin of Colonel John McGavock of Carnton Plantation. A number of other notable Revolutionary War soldiers are also buried in this cemetery, such as Virginia Colonel Guilford Dudley, Sr. (1756-1833), a cousin of the author. (Photo © Lochlainn Seabrook)

THE MCGAVOCKS OF CARNTON PLANTATION

The Maury Family Cemetery, Franklin, Tennessee. The Maury family, friends of the McGavocks of Carnton Plantation, was a major player in the development and history of Franklin and the War for Southern Independence. (Photo © Lochlainn Seabrook)

Grave of Abram Poindexter Maury (1766-1825), founder of Franklin, Tennessee, Maury Family Cemetery, Franklin, Tennessee. Connections: Abram's wife, Martha Branch Worsham (1775-1844), is the 2nd great-grandniece of my 8th great-grandmother Sarah Worsham (b. 1644) of Virginia, making Martha and me 4th cousins. Sarah's husband, my 8th great-grandfather, Abraham Womack (1644-1732), is the 9th great-grandfather of another one of my cousins, country artist Lee Ann Womack. One other note of interest: Abraham Womack is the grandfather of John W. Mosby, Jr. (1710-1801), the 1st cousin four times removed of my 5th cousin Confederate Colonel John Singleton Mosby (1833-1916). (Photo © Lochlainn Seabrook)

THE MCGAVOCKS OF CARNTON PLANTATION

Gravestone of Brigadier General John Carpenter Carter (1837-1864), Rose Hill Cemetery, Columbia, Tennessee. Carter was one of the six Confederate generals who perished from wounds received at the Battle of Franklin II. (Photo © Lochlainn Seabrook)

THE MCGAVOCKS OF CARNTON PLANTATION

Confederate Monument and Burial Ground, Rose Hill Cemetery, Columbia, Tennessee. Dedicated to "Our Fallen Heroes, 1861-1865," the beautiful stone memorial is surrounded by small plain headstones marked "Unknown." A number of civilian McGavocks (male and female) are buried at Rose Hill as well. (Photo © Lochlainn Seabrook)

THE MCGAVOCKS OF CARNTON PLANTATION

Harrison House, Franklin, Tennessee. Confederate General John Bell Hood planned the Battle of Franklin II here. His army marched past the home on the morning of November 30, 1864, following the Battle of Spring Hill. The Harrison House is the death place of Confederate General John Carpenter Carter, who perished on December 10, 1864, from wounds received at the Battle of Franklin II. (Photo © Lochlainn Seabrook)

Historical marker in front of the Harrison House, Franklin, Tennessee. (Photo © Lochlainn Seabrook)

THE MCGAVOCKS OF CARNTON PLANTATION

Lotz House, Franklin, Tennessee. German immigrant Johann Albert Lotz built the home in 1858 on property he purchased from Fountain Branch Carter, the owner of the Carter House (across the street) and the father of famed Confederate Captain Theodrick "Tod" Carter. During the Battle of Franklin II, Johann, his wife Margaret, and their three children, fled to the Carter House cellar for safety. Like Carnton, Lotz House was used as a field hospital during the battle (indicated by the display of a large red flag out front), after which the Lotz family packed up and moved to California. The most beautifully restored and decorated of all Franklin's antebellum homes, Lotz House is today one of our town's most popular Civil War attractions. (Photo © Lochlainn Seabrook)

THE MCGAVOCKS OF CARNTON PLANTATION

The Harpeth River, downtown Franklin, Tennessee. The river played a pivotal role in the Battle of Franklin II, aiding the Yanks, hampering the Rebs. (Photo © Lochlainn Seabrook)

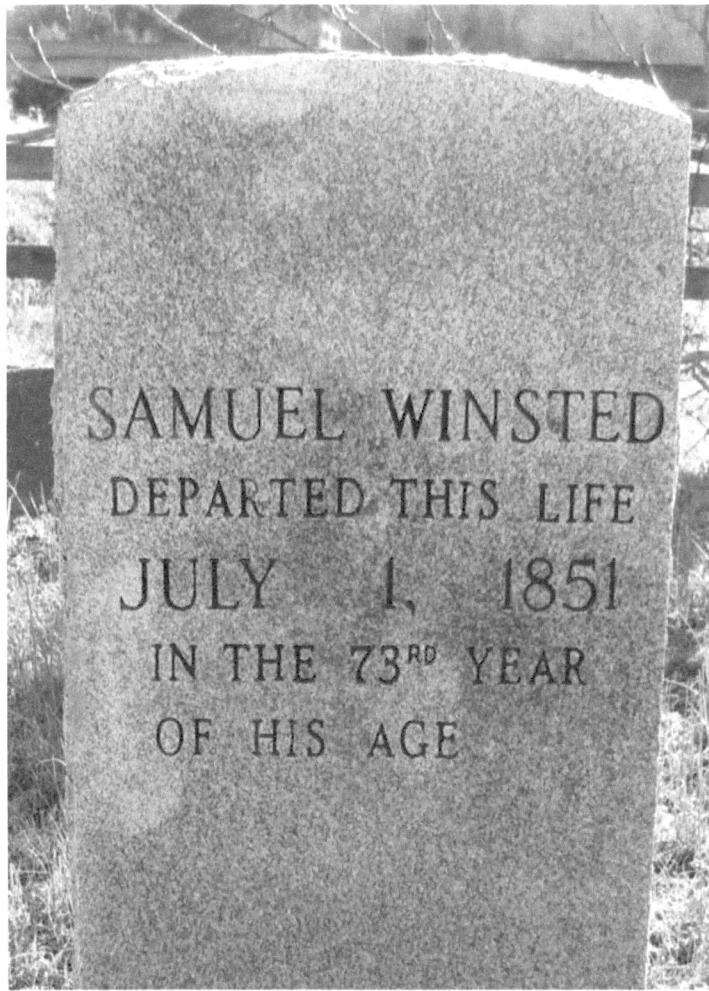

Gravestone of Samuel Winsted (1778-1851), Franklin, Tennessee. Winsted, who died ten years before Lincoln's War, gave his name to Winstead Hill, the site of General John Bell Hood's command post during the Battle of Franklin II. Born in Virginia during the American Revolutionary War, Winstead's ancestors hail from York, England. (Photo © Lochlainn Seabrook)

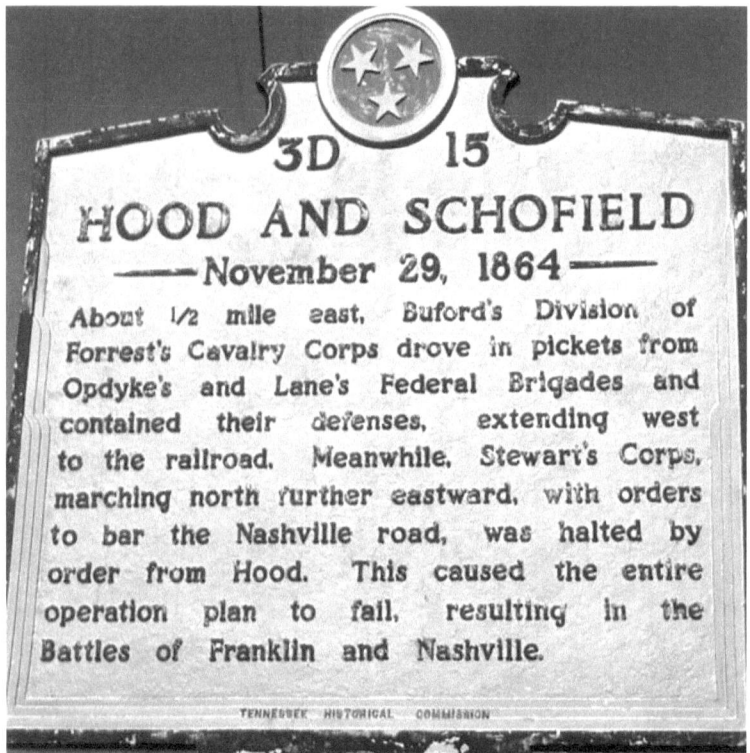

Historical marker located between Spring Hill and Franklin describing events one day before the Battle of Franklin II. As many do, the writer faults Hood for mismanaging the Middle Tennessee campaign—which led to the downfall of the Confederate Army of Tennessee, the close of the Western theater, and ultimately the loss of the War. (Photo © Lochlainn Seabrook)

Historical marker indicating "Hood's Retreat," Brentwood, Tennessee, one day after the catastrophe known as the Battle of Nashville, December 15-16, 1864 (two weeks after Franklin II). This sign had been knocked over and was set back up by the author. (Photo © Lochlainn Seabrook)

The McGavocks of Carnton Plantation

Kentuckian John Bell Hood (1831-1879), commander of Confederate forces (the Army of Tennessee) at the Battle of Franklin II, November 30, 1864. Hood, along with his love interest during the War, Sally Buchanan "Buck" Preston (1842-1880), were good friends of South Carolinian Mary Chesnut. The author is a cousin of the general. (Photo from Ridley's *Battles and Sketches of the Army of Tennessee*)

THE MCGAVOCKS OF CARNTON PLANTATION

New Yorker John McAllister Schofield (1831-1906), commander of Union forces (the Army of the Ohio) at the Battle of Franklin II, November 30, 1864. Earlier, Schofield and Hood had been classmates at West Point, graduating the same year, in 1853. (Photo courtesy Library of Congress)

The McGavocks of Carnton Plantation

Virginian-turned-Yank, George Henry "Rock of Chickamauga" Thomas (1816-1870), commander of Union forces at the Battle of Nashville, December 15-16, 1864. After joining Lincoln to fight against his homeland Thomas was repudiated by his Virginia relations, who burned his letters and strongly suggested he change his name. To this day Southerners wonder what the outcome of the War might have been had this outstanding military man remained loyal to Dixie. (Photo courtesy Library of Congress)

THE MCGAVOCKS OF CARNTON PLANTATION

Tennessean Benjamin Franklin "Frank" Cheatham (1820-1886), Confederate corp commander at the Battle of Franklin II, November 30, 1864. Two weeks after leading Cheatham's Corps at Franklin, the general fought at the Battle of Nashville. The Cheathams intermarried with the McGavocks. (Photo courtesy Library of Congress)

THE MCGAVOCKS OF CARNTON PLANTATION

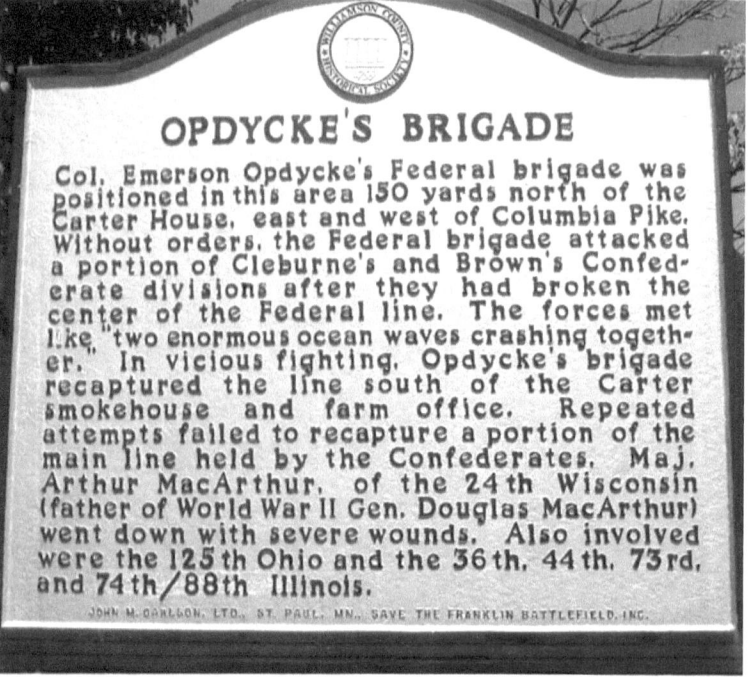

Yet another one of the numerous Yankee-oriented historical markers in Franklin, Tennessee (sadly, there are very few Confederate-oriented historical markers in our once Confederate town). The one above, situated just south of the Carter House, outlines Union activity in the area during the Battle of Franklin II. Yankee Major Arthur MacArthur, the father of World War II hero General Douglas MacArthur, is mentioned. (Photo © Lochlainn Seabrook)

THE MCGAVOCKS OF CARNTON PLANTATION

Midway Plantation, Brentwood, Tennessee, named for its location "midway" between Franklin and Nashville. The fourteen-room mansion was constructed about 1829, on what was originally a prehistoric Native-American site, by Lysander McGavock (1st cousin of Colonel John of Carnton) and his wife Elizabeth Crockett (3rd cousin of Davy Crockett). A number of the Indian artifacts discovered here are today stored at the Smithsonian Institution. A good portion of Midway's 1,000 acres was inherited by Elizabeth from her family. This included her parents, James Crockett and Mary Drake, who had migrated to Williamson County, Tennessee, from Wythe County, Virginia, settling in Brentwood about 1799 on land James received from a Revolutionary War grant. The original mansion partially burned down in 1846, after which Lysander rebuilt it on the foundation of the first structure. The reconstructed antebellum house (above) was completed sometime between 1847 and 1849. An 1850 agricultural census valued Midway Plantation at $25,000, or $720,000 in today's currency. A large and ancient spring flowed behind the plantation, and later the local post office and a stagecoach tavern were named after it: Good Springs (a modern street nearby, Good Springs Road, retains their memory). At its zenith some forty black servants worked at Midway, where Lysander grew tobacco, corn, oats, wheat, and cotton, and held equine sporting events on his horse racing track. A number of "Civil War" skirmishes were fought around Midway, which served as both a field hospital and an officer's command post. A Yankee soldier is said to have been buried on the property. Some of the breastworks, swales, and trenches from Lincoln's War could still be seen up until quite recently when Midway's land was divided up and developed. The architectural style of Midway has many similarities to Carnton Mansion. Midway Mansion, and the surrounding McGavock land, was leased by the family to the Brentwood Country Club in 1956, at which time Lysander's spacious crop fields were transformed into a golf course and his house became the "clubhouse." Once known as the "countriest country club" in America, famous members have included country music legends Faron Young, Billy Walker, and the Gatlin Brothers. Another member of note, country comedienne Minnie Pearl, was once a common sight on the club's tennis courts. In the past few decades most of Midway's remaining original land has been sold off to real estate developers and turned into sprawling subdivisions. (Photo © Lochlainn Seabrook)

THE MCGAVOCKS OF CARNTON PLANTATION

Entrance to the McGavock-Hayes Cemetery, Midway Plantation, Brentwood, Tennessee. (Photo © Lochlainn Seabrook)

THE MCGAVOCKS OF CARNTON PLANTATION

Gravestone of Lysander McGavock (1800-1855), McGavock-Hayes Cemetery, Midway, Brentwood, Tennessee. Lysander is the founder of Midway Plantation and the 1st cousin of Colonel John of Carnton. (Photo © Lochlainn Seabrook)

THE MCGAVOCKS OF CARNTON PLANTATION

Gravestone of Elizabeth Crockett (1795-1862), wife of Lysander McGavock, founder of Midway, McGavock-Hayes Cemetery, Midway, Brentwood, Tennessee. Elizabeth is the 3rd cousin once removed of noted Tennessean, American frontiersman, and hero of the Alamo, Davy Crockett (1786-1836). She is the 1st cousin of the renown rifle maker Samuel Crockett, III (1772-1827)—the founder of Forge Seat in Brentwood, Tennessee—and the niece of Samuel's father, noted American Revolutionary War hero Lt. Andrew Crockett (1745-1821), both of Wythe County, Virginia. Elizabeth passed away during the first year of Lincoln's War. (Photo © Lochlainn Seabrook)

THE MCGAVOCKS OF CARNTON PLANTATION

Gravestone of Emily McGavock (1830-1920), McGavock-Hayes Cemetery, Midway, Brentwood, Tennessee. Emily is the wife of Oliver Bliss Hayes, Jr. (1825-1868), and with Oliver the co-founder and original owner of Boxwood Hall, Brentwood, Tennessee. She is the 1st cousin once removed of Colonel John of Carnton. (Photo © Lochlainn Seabrook)

THE MCGAVOCKS OF CARNTON PLANTATION

Boxwood Hall, Brentwood, Tennessee, owned by Oliver Bliss Hayes, Jr. (1825-1868) and his wife Emily McGavock (1830-1920), a close cousin of the Carnton McGavocks. The original home, known as Hayesland, and constructed on Midway Plantation property, burned down while the couple were on their European honeymoon. They rebuilt the house and renamed it Boxwood Hall. Some 150 years later it remains one of Williamson County's most magically beautiful homes. (Photo © Lochlainn Seabrook)

The McGavocks of Carnton Plantation

A community in Brentwood, Tennessee, named after the McGavocks of Williamson County. (Photo © Lochlainn Seabrook)

THE MCGAVOCKS OF CARNTON PLANTATION

Street sign, Brentwood, Tennessee, showing local streets named after Lysander McGavock, founder of Midway Plantation and 1st cousin of Colonel John of Carnton. (Photo © Lochlainn Seabrook)

THE MCGAVOCKS OF CARNTON PLANTATION

State Capitol, Nashville, Tennessee. Completed in 1859, it was captured by Lincoln's military henchmen February 23, 1862, and renamed Fort (Andrew) Johnson. The South never recovered from the Yankee occupation of their capital city, which marked the division of the Confederacy and the loss of Rebel control of the strategically vital Mississippi, Cumberland, and Tennessee Rivers. (Photo © Lochlainn Seabrook)

THE MCGAVOCKS OF CARNTON PLANTATION

Nashville's State Capitol in 1864, during the War for Southern Independence. Yankee cannon, covered with canvas tarps to protect them from the rain, can be seen strategically placed across the front of the building, with the city and hills across the background. (Photo courtesy Library of Congress)

The McGavocks of Carnton Plantation

Outer Union lines at the time of the Battle of Nashville, December 1864. By then, much of the land had been denuded of vegetation and turned to mud, while the city of Nashville proper had lost numerous homes, shops, and buildings, many of them needlessly plundered and burned down by heartless Yankee troops. (Photo courtesy Library of Congress)

THE MCGAVOCKS OF CARNTON PLANTATION

Equestrian statue of President Andrew Jackson (1767-1845), State Capitol grounds, Nashville, Tennessee. "Old Hickory" was said to be a frequent visitor at Carnton Plantation, whose current garden has been patterned after the Jackson family garden at the Hermitage. (Photo © Lochlainn Seabrook)

THE MCGAVOCKS OF CARNTON PLANTATION

The man behind the madness, cruelties, horrors, and illegalities of the so-called American "Civil War," President Abraham Lincoln (1809-1865), shown here in the field with famed future detective Allan Pinkerton (1819-1884) on the left, and Union Major General John Alexander McClernand (1812-1900) on the right. Both Lincoln and Pinkerton were known to have donated money to abolitionist madman John Brown (1800-1859), one of the most virulent anti-South Yankees in American history. Photo taken at Antietam, Maryland, around October 1862. (Photo courtesy Library of Congress)

Gravestone of John Rodgers, McGavock Family Cemetery, Carnton Plantation, Franklin, Tennessee. John, born January 23, 1747, is the father of Sarah Dougherty Rodgers (1786-1854), the wife of Randal McGavock (founder of Carnton), and the grandfather of Colonel John of Carnton (who was probably named after him). John Rodgers may have been the owner, and perhaps the builder, of the 1811 two-story brick house that became Carnton's kitchen, which was later destroyed by a tornado in 1909. (Photo © Lochlainn Seabrook)

THE MCGAVOCKS OF CARNTON PLANTATION

President James Knox Polk (1795-1849), North Carolinian, eleventh U.S. president, friend of the McGavocks, and guest at Carnton Plantation. It was during his presidency that the U.S. won the Mexican-American War (1846-1848), opened the Smithsonian Institution, and printed the nation's first postage stamps. Depleted by his short but demanding term in the White House, James died at Polk Place, his Nashville home, at the young age of fifty-three. (Image courtesy Library of Congress)

THE MCGAVOCKS OF CARNTON PLANTATION

Home of President James Knox Polk (during his youth), Columbia, Tennessee. The historical marker in front of the house reads: "James Knox Polk: The parents of the eleventh President of the United States occupied this property in 1816, at which time young Polk was 21. From that time, except for periods of absence due to holding public office, or his extensive law practice, this was his home until he was inaugurated into the Presidency." (Photo © Lochlainn Seabrook)

THE MCGAVOCKS OF CARNTON PLANTATION

Forge Seat, the home of Samuel Crockett, III (1772-1827), Brentwood, Tennessee. The house, built by Samuel in 1808, takes its name from an iron forge on the property, which was used by Samuel and his son, Andrew Crockett (1793-1852), to make rifles. Samuel's father, Revolutionary War vet Lt. Andrew Crockett (1745-1821)—who founded the Andrew Crockett House (also known as the Crockett-Knox House), in Brentwood—was one of the 250 signers of the Cumberland Compact in 1780, a simple state constitution meant to help govern early settlers immigrating to the Cumberland River area that was to become Nashville, Tennessee. The Crockett rifles, still known for their excellent craftsmanship, bear the letters "S. & A. C." According to local legend, on his way to the Indian Wars, America's future seventh president and McGavock family friend, Andrew Jackson (1767-1845), stopped at Forge Seat to purchase rifles for his soldiers. The Crocketts, whose most famous member is frontiersman Davy Crockett (1786-1836), intermarried numerous times with the McGavocks and were widespread across Williamson County in the 1800s. Davy's 3rd cousin once removed, Samuel of Forge Seat is the 1st cousin of Elizabeth Crockett (1795-1862), the wife of Midway Plantation's Lysander McGavock (1800-1855)—the 1st cousin of Colonel John of Carnton Plantation. (Photo © Lochlainn Seabrook)

THE MCGAVOCKS OF CARNTON PLANTATION

Rippavilla Plantation, Spring Hill, Tennessee. Confederate General Nathan Bedford Forrest and his men camped here in 1863 prior to the Battle of Franklin I (April 10). Over a year later Confederate General John Bell Hood and his officers, including Forrest, breakfasted here on the morning of November 30, 1864, where they argued about the controversial events of the preceding night in what has become known as the "Spring Hill Affair." The founder of Rippavilla, Confederate Major Nathaniel F. Cheairs (1818-1914), a close cousin of the author, carried the flag of surrender to Yankee General Ulysses S. Grant at the unfortunate Battle of Fort Donelson, February 16, 1862. (Photo © Lochlainn Seabrook)

THE MCGAVOCKS OF CARNTON PLANTATION

Riverside Plantation, Franklin, Tennessee. Located across the Harpeth River, a stone's throw from Carnton, Riverside was built in the 1830s by James Randal McGavock (1812-1862)—the brother of Colonel John of Carnton (1815-1893)—on land owned by their father, Randal McGavock (1766-1843), the founder of Carnton Plantation. Upon his death in 1843 Randal willed the Riverside property to James. While the large plantation house was being built, James and his wife Louisa C. Chenault (1813-1885) lived in a rustic log cabin James had constructed in the backyard. It was at this time that Randal's good friend Andrew Jackson stopped by and planted several young cedar trees on the property, which grow there to this day. Sallie (1837-1863), the daughter of Riverside founders James and Louisa, owned the McGavock family Bible, which can still be seen on display at Carnton, as can numerous other household items from the Riverside McGavocks. Like Carnton, Riverside was once famous for its beautiful stables and fine horses. It even had its own race track. During the Battle of Franklin II horrified members of the family watched the conflict from the relative safety of their hilltop location (the center of the fighting took place several miles to the northwest). Having passed away in 1862 James was spared the terrible scene. The beautiful home pictured above is not James and Louisa's original house, which partially burned down in 1905. This new neo-classical home was constructed afterward around the solid brick remains of the first Riverside Manor house. Riverside is today privately owned. (Photo © Lochlainn Seabrook)

THE MCGAVOCKS OF CARNTON PLANTATION

Riverside log cabin, Franklin, Tennessee. Built around 1832 by James Randal McGavock on property willed to him by his father Randal McGavock (founder of Carnton Plantation), it is located behind the present day Riverside Manor house. The two-story double-pen cabin was used by James and his wife Louisa as their temporary residence while the original big plantation house was under construction. It was later used as the servants' quarters ("slave house" to Yanks and scallywags). The architectural design, known as "glorified pioneer," features a hall or "dog run" in the middle of the structure with fireplaced rooms at each end. The family's smokehouse, built around 1840, remains standing as well (situated just out of frame). (Photo © Lochlainn Seabrook)

THE MCGAVOCKS OF CARNTON PLANTATION

One of the aged cedars (center) donated and planted nearly 200 years ago by McGavock friend and political ally, Andrew Jackson, at Riverside Plantation, Franklin, Tennessee. (Photo © Lochlainn Seabrook)

THE MCGAVOCKS OF CARNTON PLANTATION

Franklin, Tennessee, street sign honoring Maria (or Mariah) Reddick and her family, beloved black servant at Carnton Plantation. Maria worked for the McGavocks both under servitude and as a free woman for many decades, and gave the eulogy at Carrie (Winder) McGavock's funeral in Franklin in 1905. (Photo © Lochlainn Seabrook)

Franklin, Tennessee, street sign honoring Otho F. Strahl (1832-1864), one of the six Confederate generals who perished from wounds received at the Battle of Franklin II. (Photo © Lochlainn Seabrook)

THE MCGAVOCKS OF CARNTON PLANTATION

Nashville, Tennessee, street sign paying homage to Edmund Winchester Rucker (1835-1924), the author's 3rd cousin. Colonel Rucker led Rucker's Brigade at the battles of both Franklin II and Nashville, the latter at which he was captured and lost an arm. After the War Rucker became business partners in Memphis with another one of the author's cousins, General Nathan Bedford Forrest. (Photo © Lochlainn Seabrook)

THE MCGAVOCKS OF CARNTON PLANTATION

Two Rivers Plantation, Nashville, Tennessee. Built in 1859 in the Italianate style by David Harding McGavock (1826-1896) and his wife Willie Elizabeth Harding (1832-1895) of Belle Meade Plantation, Two Rivers remains one of the most impressive antebellum homes in the South. The land it sits on was originally owned by the author's family, the Hardings of Belle Meade Plantation. David is the 1st cousin once removed of Colonel John of Carnton Plantation. (Photo © Lochlainn Seabrook)

THE MCGAVOCKS OF CARNTON PLANTATION

Sketch of Two Rivers Mansion, Nashville, Tennessee, at its peak operating period. Illustration from W. Woodford Clayton's *History of Davidson County, Tennessee, With Illustrations and Biographical Sketches of its Prominent Men and Pioneers*. Date and artist unknown. (Image courtesy TSLA)

THE McGAVOCKS OF CARNTON PLANTATION

Two Rivers Mansion, Nashville, Tennessee, second floor hallway. Date: 1970, photographer Jack E. Boucher. The last of the elaborate antebellum homes built in Middle Tennessee, it was named for its location between the Stones River and the Cumberland River. (Photo courtesy TSLA)

SCV sign at Winstead Hill, Franklin, Tennessee. Colonel John of Carnton Plantation, a member of the United Confederate Veterans (UCV)—the precursor of today's SCV, would have heartily approved of this park dedicated to the memory of the Southern Confederacy. (Photo © Lochlainn Seabrook)

THE MCGAVOCKS OF CARNTON PLANTATION

Street sign, Franklin, Tennessee, honoring the town's long and distinguished Confederate history. Scallywags, liberals, and displaced Yankees, ignorant of the uniqueness, importance, and beauty of our Southern heritage, continue the scandalous practice of trying to get the names of such street signs changed to suit their politically correct vision of America. At the time of this writing state capitols across the South are being forced to take down the Confederate Flag, Southern universities are forbidding their students from singing *Dixie*, the words "Rebel" and "Confederates" are being dropped from the names of sports teams (NASCAR recently banned the display of the Confederate Flag), and the South's Civil War monuments are regularly defaced. If the Left and South-haters have their way, America will one day be stripped of every last vestige of Southernness, pro-South historians (like the author) will be blacklisted, and Dixie herself will become an exact duplicate of the progressive North. This was, after all, part of liberal Lincoln's plan from the beginning, the big spending, warmongering, Constitution-loathing president in whose footsteps his political descendants now defiantly walk. May this book help halt this villainous anti-South process—one that may someday cause the above street to be renamed "Union Drive." The McGavocks of Carnton Plantation, proud Confederates all, would not have wanted their heritage diminished in any way. The majority of today's Southerners are of the same mind. Those who read this book will understand why and, it is hoped, join in the movement to preserve genuine Southern history, along with the South's wonderfully diverse society and culture. (Photo © Lochlainn Seabrook)

Cultural signage at Winstead Hill, Franklin, Tennessee. (Photo © Lochlainn Seabrook)

Historical marker at Winstead Hill, Franklin, Tennessee, Confederate General John Bell Hood's military center during the Battle of Franklin II. (Photo © Lochlainn Seabrook)

THE MCGAVOCKS OF CARNTON PLANTATION

Panoramic view from Winstead Hill, Franklin, Tennessee, overlooking the Plain of Franklin and distant hills—some, like Roper's Knob, Cedar Hill, and Figuers' Bluff, that were used as signal posts or artillery batteries by the Yankees before and during the Battle of Franklin II. Minus the modern buildings and most of the trees (the area was primarily farmland in the mid 1800s), this is the view Confederate commander John Bell Hood would have had on November 30, 1864, the day of the conflict. The general used Winstead Hill, as well as Breezy Hill across the street (east, to the right), to stage and deploy his troops northward (from right to left) up Columbia Pike (now Columbia Ave.)—which can be seen cutting across the middle of the photo. Carnton Plantation is located a few miles to the right. The core battlefield area is out of frame to the upper left, a mile or so up Columbia Ave., with the "hottest fightin'" occurring around the Carter House and the family's cotton gin (the latter which was situated about 300 feet east of the corner of present-day Cleburne St. and Columbia Ave.). (Photo © Lochlainn Seabrook)

THE MCGAVOCKS OF CARNTON PLANTATION

Carnton Plantation, front view, date and photographer unknown. Note Carrie (Winder) McGavock's two windows on the lower left of the house (west side), which have since been removed and bricked over. (Photo courtesy TSLA)

THE MCGAVOCKS OF CARNTON PLANTATION

Carnton Mansion, rear view, photographer unknown, date about 1890. Elements of note: Carrie's windows on the lower right side of the house; horseshoes nailed to second front column from right; numerous trees (now missing); original 1811 two-story brick house on far left, before it was destroyed by a tornado in 1909; and several dogs on the front steps. Someone has scribbled what appears to be "Winder McGavock" at the bottom middle of the photo, and "Geo. L. Cowan" in the bottom right corner. The numbers 1 through 6 appear under the six people sitting on the back porch. Whether or not Winder and George were among them is not known for sure. However, it is possible since Winder died in 1907 and George passed away in 1919. It is also possible, and very likely, that both Colonel John (who died in 1893) and Carrie (who died in 1905) are in this picture. Under the photo's bottom border (not shown) the same mysterious writer penned, incorrectly: "The long veranda where five Confederate generals, amid the drifting smoke of the Battle of Franklin, lay dead." (Only four were laid here.) (Image courtesy TSLA)

THE MCGAVOCKS OF CARNTON PLANTATION

Fort Warren, George's Island, Boston Harbor, Boston, Massachusetts. Aerial view from 700 ft. Date: 1958. Photographer J. T. O'Toole. Confederate Lieutenant Colonel Randal William McGavock, 1st cousin of Colonel John of Carnton Plantation, was captured at the disastrous Battle of Fort Donelson in February 1862 and sent here, where he was imprisoned from March 6 to July 31, 1862. Now a National Historic Landmark, the pentagonal fort, built continuously between 1831 and 1861, also illegally housed civilian political prisoners, such as Confederate Vice President Alexander H. Stephens—yet another one of Lincoln's many war crimes. (Photo courtesy TSLA)

THE MCGAVOCKS OF CARNTON PLANTATION

While Lincoln's armies were racially segregated (by his order), Southern armies were racially integrated, with whites and blacks fighting side-by-side throughout the entire conflict. These facts still shock many Northerners and scallywags. Yet, 150 years later they are well-known and accepted in Dixie—which is why so many African-American reenactors regularly attend Civil War shows across the South. Not to portray Union soldiers, but to portray Rebel soldiers. The two young Confederate friends above, at the Nathan Bedford Forrest Boyhood Home Fundraiser, at Chapel Hill, Tennessee, June 2011, came armed and ready to fight the Yanks. The Southern armies contained between 300,000 and 1 million blacks, depending on how one defines a "soldier." Northern armies were comprised of a little less than 200,000 blacks, many who were forced to "enlist" at gunpoint, or be shot where they stood. As eyewitnesses later testified, many Southern blacks were so repulsed by the idea of fighting for racist Lincoln that they selected the latter choice: for these individuals death was preferable to serving in the Yankee military machine, where they knew they would be treated like lepers due to the color of their skin. You will never read about these courageous African-American men in any pro-North history book. (Photo © Lochlainn Seabrook)

THE MCGAVOCKS OF CARNTON PLANTATION

Historical marker, Boiling Spring Indian Settlement, Brentwood, Tennessee. Williamson County was once the home of a prehistoric Native-American people known to archaeologists as the Mound Builders, or Mississippians. At this particular site the remains of a large enclosed village, whose inhabitants fed mainly on deer and corn, was discovered. The Tennessee Mound Builders, who had begun far earlier as hunter-gatherers, eventually settled into an agrarian lifestyle, transforming into sedentary farmers across what was to become the American South. Ceremonial structures, fire pits, and alters are evidence that this sophisticated people had a rich spiritual life. Preferring to live alongside rivers, they buried their dead inside large earthen mounds, and later in stone-slab graves. All of the McGavocks' homes, such as Carnton, Riverside, Midway, Two Rivers, Clifflawn, and Boxwood Hall—as well as those of their relatives, such as Forge Seat and Belle Meade Plantation—sit on what was once Native-American territory. Much of this land was purchased from its Indians owners, not stolen, as popular legend teaches. (Photo © Lochlainn Seabrook)

THE MCGAVOCKS OF CARNTON PLANTATION

Carnton Mansion, rear view. Date: April 17, 1960, photographer unknown. This photo provides an excellent view of Carrie's two windows on the west side of the house (lower right) before they were bricked over. Note the 1950s car on left, the circular rear driveway that goes right up to the back porch, the screen door on the back of the house, trees that are now gone, and both the missing balustrade and the missing breezeway section on the lower porch. (Photo courtesy TSLA)

THE MCGAVOCKS OF CARNTON PLANTATION

Front view of Carnton Mansion. Date: April 17, 1960, photographer unknown. Note again Carrie's windows on the west wall, as well as missing shutters, numerous trees since cut down or blown down, the TV antennae on right roof line, and the missing breezeway and balistrade on back porch (left rear of house). (Photo courtesy TSLA)

THE MCGAVOCKS OF CARNTON PLANTATION

Seraphine Deery (1835-1918), wife of Lieutenant Colonel Randal William McGavock, date and photographer unknown. The couple married in 1855 and moved into the Deery Family Home in Allisona, Tennessee, twenty miles southeast of Franklin. (Photo courtesy TSLA)

The McGavocks of Carnton Plantation

Seraphine Deery, a later image. Seraphine was the first and only wife of Confederate Lieutenant Colonel Randal William McGavock. At the time of this photo, taken at the Jackson Day Ball, Hotel Tulane, Nashville, Tennessee (post 1898, exact day unknown), Seraphine was in her third marriage—to attorney Augustus Herman Pettibone (1835-1918) of Ohio, a liberal U.S. Congressman and a major in the Union army. (Photo courtesy TSLA)

THE MCGAVOCKS OF CARNTON PLANTATION

Ferguson Hall, Spring Hill, Tennessee. Owned by Martin Terrell Cheairs (1804-1891)—the brother of Confederate Major Nathaniel Francis Cheairs (1818-1914), the founder of Rippavilla Plantation (both cousins of the author)—this lovely antebellum home was the site of one of the many tragic dramas of Lincoln's War. In the Spring of 1863 Confederate General Earl Van Dorn (1820-1863), serving as the head of cavalry in the Army of Tennessee under commander General Braxton Bragg (1817-1876), selected Ferguson Hall (then known as the Cheairs Home) as his headquarters. On May 7 of that year, a local doctor, George Boddie Peters (1814-1888), walked into Van Dorn's office and shot him through the head, allegedly for having an affair with his wife, the beguiling Jessie Helen McKissack (1838-1921). This murder in turn affected the town of Franklin as well as the Battle of Franklin II. After Van Dorn's death, General Bragg turned the left wing of his cavalry over to the daring horseman, fearsome Yankee hunter, and ingenious military leader, General Nathan Bedford Forrest (1821-1877). Bragg was subsequently replaced by Rebel General Joseph E. Johnston (1807-1891), who was then replaced by General John Bell Hood (1831-1879), who launched his Tennessee Campaign after the Confederate loss at the Battle of Atlanta against Union General William T. Sherman (1820-1891) on July 22, 1864. Four months later Forrest would stand on Carnton's upper deck to view the battlefield before riding into history at the catastrophic conflict that would become known as the Battle of Franklin II. To this day an entire region of Franklin is called "Forrest's Crossing," named for the bend where Forrest forded the Harpeth River on the afternoon of November 30, 1864. Ferguson Hall, an 1853 Greek Revival house that is on the National Register of Historic Homes, is today owned and managed by the Tennessee Children's Home, an institution that serves "abused, neglected, abandoned, wayward, or orphaned children and youth, as well as their families, in a Christian manner." (Photo © Lochlainn Seabrook)

THE MCGAVOCKS OF CARNTON PLANTATION

Jacob McGavock Dickinson, Sr. (1851-1928), U.S. assistant attorney general under U.S. President (Stephen) Grover Cleveland (1837-1908) and secretary of war under President William H. Taft (1857-1930). Jacob married Martha Overton (1853-1917), the granddaughter of Judge John Overton (1766-1833), founder of Travellers Rest Plantation in Nashville, and the cofounder of Memphis, Tennessee. Jacob, the 1st cousin twice removed of Colonel John of Carnton, is the grandson of Jacob McGavock (1790-1878) and Louisa Caroline Grundy (1798-1878). Date of photo: 1909. (Photo courtesy Library of Congress)

The McGavocks of Carnton Plantation

Photo of a portrait of David McGavock (1763-1838), surveyor and brother of Randal McGavock (1766-1843), founder of Carnton. An early Nashville settler, David drew up the boundaries for Davidson County, Tennessee, out of which Williamson County was later formed. Date and artist unknown. (Image courtesy TSLA)

THE MCGAVOCKS OF CARNTON PLANTATION

Mary Turner (1773-1834), second wife of surveyor David McGavock (1763-1838), the brother of Randal McGavock, founder of Carnton Plantation. Portrait date: 1830. Artist: Ralph E. W. Earl. (Image © The Tennessee Historical Society)

THE MCGAVOCKS OF CARNTON PLANTATION

Dane Hall, Harvard Law School, Cambridge, Massachusetts, as it looked during Confederate Lieutenant Colonel Randal William McGavock's residence, 1847-1849. Date and artist unknown. (Image courtesy TSLA)

THE MCGAVOCKS OF CARNTON PLANTATION

Architect's sketch of Clifflawn Plantation, the home of Francis McGavock (1794-1866), 1st cousin of Colonel John of Carnton. Francis' father is David McGavock, surveyor, brother of Randal McGavock, founder of Carnton. Francis' wife is Amanda P. Harding (1807-1873) of Belle Meade Plantation, a member of the author's Harding family. Clifflawn, built about five miles west of Nashville, was once, like Carnton and Belle Meade Plantations, a famous thoroughbred breeding farm. (Image courtesy TSLA)

THE MCGAVOCKS OF CARNTON PLANTATION

Felix Grundy (1777-1840), noted Southern statesman, as well as a friend and relation of the Carnton McGavocks. Colonel John's wife, Caroline Elizabeth "Carrie" Winder (1829-1905), is his granddaughter. Felix, a conservative Tennessee senator, later served as the U.S. attorney general under President Martin Van Buren (1782-1862). Date of drawing: unknown. Artist: unknown. (Image courtesy Library of Congress)

THE MCGAVOCKS OF CARNTON PLANTATION

Anne Eliza McGavock (1820-1868), wife of Judge Henry Dickinson, I (1806-1872). Anne, the daughter of Jacob McGavock and Louisa Caroline Grundy, is the 1st cousin once removed of Colonel John of Carnton Plantation. (Image courtesy TSLA)

THE MCGAVOCKS OF CARNTON PLANTATION

The McGavock Confederate Cemetery at Carnton Plantation as it looked in 1870. Photographer: S. J. Terry, of Franklin, Tennessee. (Photo courtesy TSLA)

THE MCGAVOCKS OF CARNTON PLANTATION

Sarah M. Bass "Sallie" McGavock (1830-1903), the wife of Dr. Reverend John Berrian Lindsley (1822-1897). Sarah, the daughter of Jacob McGavock and Louisa Caroline Grundy, is the 1st cousin once removed of Colonel John of Carnton Plantation. Date and creator unknown. (Image courtesy TSLA)

THE MCGAVOCKS OF CARNTON PLANTATION

Dead Confederate soldiers along Hagerstown Road, Antietam, Maryland, September 1862. Southern historians estimate that President Lincoln was directly responsible for the deaths of as many as 2 million Southerners, white and black. To this day Southerners are still asking the obvious question: for what purpose did our brave ancestors sacrifice their lives? Lincoln neither preserved the Union or ended slavery. It is these bold impermeable facts that have forced pro-North authors and scholars to re-write history and suppress the truth, all in an effort to justify Lincoln's unjustifiable War. The result is that American school textbooks today teach only one version of the so-called "Civil War": the North's. What they do not teach is that this version is almost completely based on anti-South propaganda, hyperbole, lies, and slander. Their students are never even told that there is a far more accurate and objective version of the War: the South's. It is up to us to educate our children at home and to put pressure on schools to start teaching the Southern version of Lincoln's pointless and illegal war on Dixie. (Photo courtesy Library of Congress)

THE MCGAVOCKS OF CARNTON PLANTATION

Thanks to Lincoln and his unconstitutional invasion of the South, by April 1865 beautiful Richmond, Virginia, lay in charred smouldering ruins. Deceptively, devilishly, and cruelly, the Northern president had spoken of "the better angels of our nature" in his first Inaugural Address, March 4, 1861. (Photo courtesy Library of Congress)

THE MCGAVOCKS OF CARNTON PLANTATION

James "Dada" McGavock (1728-1812), husband of Mary "Sally" Cloyd (1740-1827). Born in Northern Ireland, James emigrated to Philadelphia, Pennsylvania, about 1755. He moved to Virginia around 1757. He served with Colonel Francis Nash (1742-1777) against the Indians in Ohio in 1757. He settled at Fort Chiswell, Virginia, in 1772. James was a captain in the American Revolutionary War. He acquired land in Tennessee, which he gave to his sons David and Randal, the latter who was the founder of Carnton Plantation. James is the grandfather of Colonel John of Carnton. Date and artist unknown. (Image courtesy TSLA)

THE MCGAVOCKS OF CARNTON PLANTATION

Mary "Sally" Cloyd (1741-1827), wife of Captain James "Dada" McGavock (1728-1812). A relative of the author, Mary introduced European royal blood into several of the McGavock family lines. She is the grandmother of Colonel John of Carnton Plantation. Date and artist unknown. (Image courtesy TSLA)

THE MCGAVOCKS OF CARNTON PLANTATION

McGavock Confederate Cemetery, Carnton Plantation, Franklin, Tennessee. Photo (taken from a postcard) shows Victorian women from the Scobey family tending graves at a Confederate reunion in 1890. (Image courtesy TSLA)

THE MCGAVOCKS OF CARNTON PLANTATION

Jacob McGavock (1790-1878), clerk, Superior Court, Metro District (Tennessee) to 1812; Davidson County (Tennessee) Court 1816-1878. Jacob is the husband of Louisa Caroline Grundy (1798-1878), the father of Confederate Lieutenant Colonel Randal William McGavock (1826-1863), and the 1st cousin of Colonel John of Carnton. Date of portrait unknown. Artist: possibly Washington B. Cooper. (Image courtesy TSLA)

THE MCGAVOCKS OF CARNTON PLANTATION

Louisa Caroline Grundy (1798-1878), wife of Jacob McGavock (1790-1878), and the daughter of two celebrated Tennesseans: Felix Grundy (1777-1840) and Ann Phillips Rodgers (1787-1847), the latter a sister of Sarah Dougherty Rodgers (1786-1854), the wife of Randal McGavock (1766-1843), founder of Carnton Plantation. Date of painting unknown, artist unknown. (Image courtesy TSLA)

THE MCGAVOCKS OF CARNTON PLANTATION

Emily (or Emilie) McGavock (1830-1868), the daughter of Lysander McGavock (1800-1855) and Elizabeth Crockett (1795-1862). Born in Williamson County, Tennessee, she is the wife of Oliver Bliss Hayes, II (1825-1868) of Boxwood Hall, and the 1st cousin once removed of Colonel John of Carnton. Date of portrait, about 1846. Artist unknown. (Image © The Tennessee Historical Society)

The McGavocks of Carnton Plantation

Emma Sansom (1847-1900) of Social Circle, Georgia, famous for leading Confederate General Nathan Bedford Forrest (1821-1877) to a hidden river ford following the Battle of Day's Gap near Gadsden, Alabama, in the Spring of 1863. Both Forrest and his young female scout came under Yankee fire during their bold foray along the swollen waterway known as Black Creek, but the general soon returned her unharmed to her terrified mother. In recognition of Emma's bravery and defense of the South, a monument has been erected to her at Gadsden and the town's high school was named after her. In her obituaries in 1905, Colonel John's wife Carrie Winder was favorably compared to Emma. To this day both women are honored as Confederate heroines who devoted their lives to the Southern Cause: self-government. (Image from *Battles and Sketches of the Army of Tennessee*)

THE MCGAVOCKS OF CARNTON PLANTATION

The 1820 William County (Tennessee) Census, showing resident Randal McGavock (1766-1843), founder of Carnton Plantation, and his family. Randal is the thirteenth name down the list. (Image public domain)

857

The McGavocks of Carnton Plantation

Map of Scotland showing the area of Dumfries and Galloway in the southwest (darkened section at bottom). One of the earliest known McGavock ancestors, Hugh McGavock, was probably born in this area around the year 1700.

THE MCGAVOCKS OF CARNTON PLANTATION

Map of England showing historic Cumberland County in the northwest (darkened section in the upper left), which today borders the Dumfries and Galloway region of Scotland, birthplace of Hugh McGavock. The English branch of the McGavocks are from the Cumberland area, as are the earliest known ancestors of the Winders, who intermarried into the McGavocks of the American South.

THE MCGAVOCKS OF CARNTON PLANTATION

Sally E. McGavock (1828-1899), daughter of Lysander McGavock and Elizabeth Crockett (3rd cousin of frontiersman Davy Crockett). This portrait is from about 1858. Sally is the 1st cousin once removed of Colonel John McGavock of Carnton Plantation. She and her husband Thomas Pointer (1826-1904) lived for a time at Midway Plantation, Brentwood, Tennessee. (Image © The Tennessee Historical Society)

THE MCGAVOCKS OF CARNTON PLANTATION

An earlier portrait of Sally E. McGavock (1828-1899), daughter of Lysander McGavock and Elizabeth Crockett, from about 1846. (Image © The Tennessee Historical Society)

The McGavocks of Carnton Plantation

William Giles Harding (1808-1886), founder of Belle Meade Plantation, Nashville, Tennessee, and a close cousin of the author (who descends from the Hardings of Virginia). This portrait with signature is from the 1870s. William's second wife was Elizabeth Irwin McGavock (1819-1867), daughter of Randal McGavock (1766-1843) and Sarah Dougherty Rodgers (1786-1854), and the sister of Colonel John McGavock of Carnton (1815-1893). (Image © The Tennessee Historical Society)

THE McGAVOCKS OF CARNTON PLANTATION

Lysander McGavock (1800-1855), founder and owner of Midway Plantation, Brentwood, Tennessee. Portrait from about 1846. Lysander is the 1st cousin of Colonel John of Carnton. (Image © The Tennessee Historical Society)

THE MCGAVOCKS OF CARNTON PLANTATION

Elizabeth Crockett (1795-1862), wife of Lysander McGavock (1800-1855) of Midway Plantation, Brentwood, Tennessee. Portrait from about 1850. Like Colonel John of Carnton, Elizabeth, of the celebrated American Crockett family, is related—through blood or marriage—to the founders of nearly every historical home in Middle Tennessee. The Crocketts were among the earliest settlers in Williamson County. (Image © The Tennessee Historical Society)

THE MCGAVOCKS OF CARNTON PLANTATION

Frederick Douglass (1818-1895), former *Northern* slave, civil rights leader, author, editor, and abolitionist. One of the thousands of black servants who purchased his freedom, Douglass is living proof that true slavery was never practiced in America, for under authentic slavery an individual cannot buy his liberty. Pro-North writers tell us that Douglass was a "trusted advisor" and "friend" of Abraham Lincoln. Yet the president refused to seriously consider any of Douglass' suggestions, such as his sage advice that blacks should be enlisted as soldiers in the Union army—even when Douglass told him (correctly) that the Confederacy already had black soldiers on the field (Lincoln waited two years before he reluctantly allowed black enrollment). The two did share one conviction: unlike the majority of other whites and blacks, both believed in using violence in an effort to disturb servitude in the South. Despite this one commonality, Douglass had little love for Lincoln, publicly stating that the president's policies regarding blacks showed nothing but "contempt for Negroes" and lacked "the genuine spark of humanity." On April 14, 1876, the brilliant African-American orator gave a speech at Washington, D.C. where, gazing out at the blacks in the audience, he revealed how most of them actually felt about "Honest Abe" after the War: "Abraham Lincoln was not our man or our model. In his interests and in his prejudices he was a white man. He was preeminently the white man's President, entirely devoted to the welfare of the white man. The race to which we belong were not the special objects of his consideration." (Photo courtesy Library of Congress)

THE MCGAVOCKS OF CARNTON PLANTATION

Cemetery for the servants who worked at Midway Plantation. It is located not far from Midway, in Brentwood, Tennessee. Known to traditional Southerners as a servant cemetery, scallywags and Yankees misleadingly refer to the location as a "slave cemetery." (Photo © Lochlainn Seabrook)

THE MCGAVOCKS OF CARNTON PLANTATION

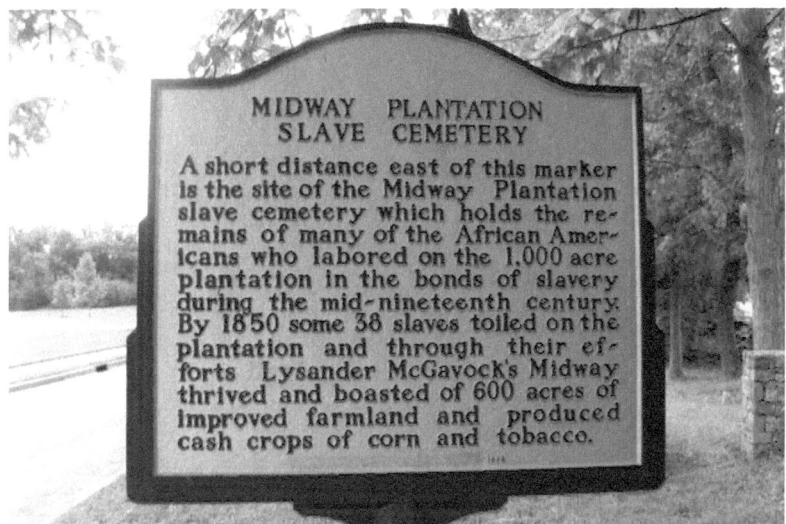

Disinformative anti-South slanted historical marker at Midway Plantation Servant Cemetery, Brentwood, Tennessee. The uninformed writer is incorrect: "slavery" was never known in the American South. As "slaves" could marry, bear children, attend church, hunt and fish, purchase their freedom, draw a paycheck, hire themselves out, own their own homes, gardens, and businesses, take off holidays, and had innumerable civil, social, religious, and legal rights, the institution as it was practiced in Dixie is more correctly called servitude. While the South continues to be unfairly punished for accepting the forced introduction of the Northern invented institution (the American slave trade got its start in Massachusetts in 1638), these same critics fail to mention the fact that authentic slavery is still being practiced in Africa, just as it was prior to the arrival of Arab, European, and later Yankee slave traders. They also conveniently neglect to note that the American abolition movement began in the South, that the Confederacy never traded in slaves, and that tens of thousands of African-Americans and Native-Americans were also slave owners. All of this is precisely why the great 19th-Century black civil rights leader W. E. B. Dubois said: "I shall forgive the white South much in its final judgement day: I shall forgive its slavery, for slavery is a world-old habit . . ." (Photo © Lochlainn Seabrook)

THE MCGAVOCKS OF CARNTON PLANTATION

Thomas Pointer (1826-1904), husband of Sally E. McGavock (1828-1899), daughter of Lysander McGavock and Elizabeth Crockett of Midway Plantation. Thomas and Sally married in 1852, eventually moving back to Midway. Portrait is from about 1858. (Image © The Tennessee Historical Society)

THE MCGAVOCKS OF CARNTON PLANTATION

Thomas Pointer Hayes (1858-1862) and dog, son of Oliver Bliss Hayes, II (1825-1868), and Emily McGavock (1830-1920) of Boxwood Hall. This portrait, probably by Washington B. Cooper, was made just before Thomas' death at a little under four years of age (as was the Victorian custom with very young children's portraits, the boy has been intentionally aged). Thomas is the grandson of Lysander McGavock (1800-1855) and Elizabeth Crockett (1795-1862), and the 1st cousin twice removed of Colonel John of Carnton. (Image © The Tennessee Historical Society)

THE MCGAVOCKS OF CARNTON PLANTATION

Gravestone of William White (1768-1815), William White Family Cemetery, Franklin, Tennessee. After the Battle of Franklin II the body of Confederate General States Rights Gist (1831-1864) was taken to White's house on Boyd Mill Road (now Boyd Mill Pike, a few miles west of Franklin center), and buried under a cedar tree. A few days later, on December 2, 1864, Gist's loyal body servant, "Uncle" Wiley Howard, took the general's body back to his home in Columbia, South Carolina, where he was laid to rest at the Trinity Episcopal Church. The White and Maury families intermarried and both were instrumental in developing the town of Franklin. William White's brother, Chapman White (b. about 1768), for example, married Martha Maury (1772-1845), a sister of Abram Maury (1766-1825), the founder of Franklin. (Photo © Lochlainn Seabrook)

THE MCGAVOCKS OF CARNTON PLANTATION

Gravestone of Lusinda Ewing (1792-1848), unmarked cemetery, Franklin, Tennessee. Lusinda is the wife of James McGavock (1790-1841), who was murdered near Nashville in 1841. James is the son of David McGavock (1763-1838)—the surveyor who laid out the lines of Davidson County, Tennessee, and the grandson of James "Dada" McGavock (1728-1812) of County Antrim, Ireland, the founder of the Mansion House at Max Meadows, Wythe County, Virginia. Lusinda's father is Captain Alexander Ewing (b. about 1751), famed Revolutionary War officer. Her husband James is the 1st cousin of Colonel John of Carnton Plantation. There are over a dozen other graves at this lonesome deteriorating cemetery, only a few that I am able to identify. It appears, however, to be the graveyard of James and Lusinda and their children, their children's spouses, and their grandchildren. (Photo © Lochlainn Seabrook)

THE MCGAVOCKS OF CARNTON PLANTATION

Gravestone of Alexander Ewing McGavock (1820-1833), located next to his mother Lusinda Ewing's grave (previous page), unmarked cemetery, Franklin, Tennessee. Alexander is the great-grandson of the famous Irishman James "Dada" McGavock (1728-1812). Like so many 19th-Century children, Alexander, the author's cousin, died before reaching adulthood. Alexander is the 1st cousin once removed of Colonel John of Carnton. (Photo © Lochlainn Seabrook)

THE MCGAVOCKS OF CARNTON PLANTATION

Thomas Hart Benton (1782-1858), one of Tennessee's most celebrated and accomplished statesmen. Born in North Carolina he later moved to Nashville, after which he became a successful attorney in Franklin. The author of the noted work *Thirty Years' View*, Benton went on to become a U.S. senator, an aide-de-camp to General Andrew Jackson, and a military officer, among dozens of other prestigious positions too numerous to mention. Nicknamed "Old Bullion," he was the father of the aristocratic author and Southern belle Jessie Ann Benton (1824-1902), who married U.S. presidential nominee (in 1856 and 1864) and Yankee Civil War officer General John Charles Frémont (1813-1890). When General Frémont liberated slaves in Missouri, white separatist and black colonizationist Abraham Lincoln angrily relieved him of his command. Jessie bravely stood up to our bigoted sixteenth president, but he cruelly dismissed her and immediately rescinded Frémont's emancipation proclamation. Thomas Hart Benton's wife is Elizabeth Preston McDowell (1794-1854), the granddaughter of Virginia Governor James McDowell (1738-1771) and Elizabeth Cloyd (1739-1796), making Jessie a close cousin of both the McGavocks and the author. Benton descendants also married into the author's Bowling (Bolling) family out of southeastern Virginia. (Photo courtesy Library of Congress)

THE MCGAVOCKS OF CARNTON PLANTATION

The crumbling ruins of the home of Thomas Hart Benton (1782-1858), Leiper's Fork, Tennessee. The historical marker at the site reads: "On the foundations of this house was the home of Thomas Hart Benton, whose family came from North Carolina in 1799. In 1809 he was state senator. Moving to Missouri in 1815, he became U.S. Senator in 1821, and remained in the senate 30 years. Dying at the age of 76 in 1858, he left a record of outstanding statesmanship." Benton is related to the McGavocks of Carnton Plantation through his wife Elizabeth Preston McDowell (1794-1854). (Photo © Lochlainn Seabrook)

THE MCGAVOCKS OF CARNTON PLANTATION

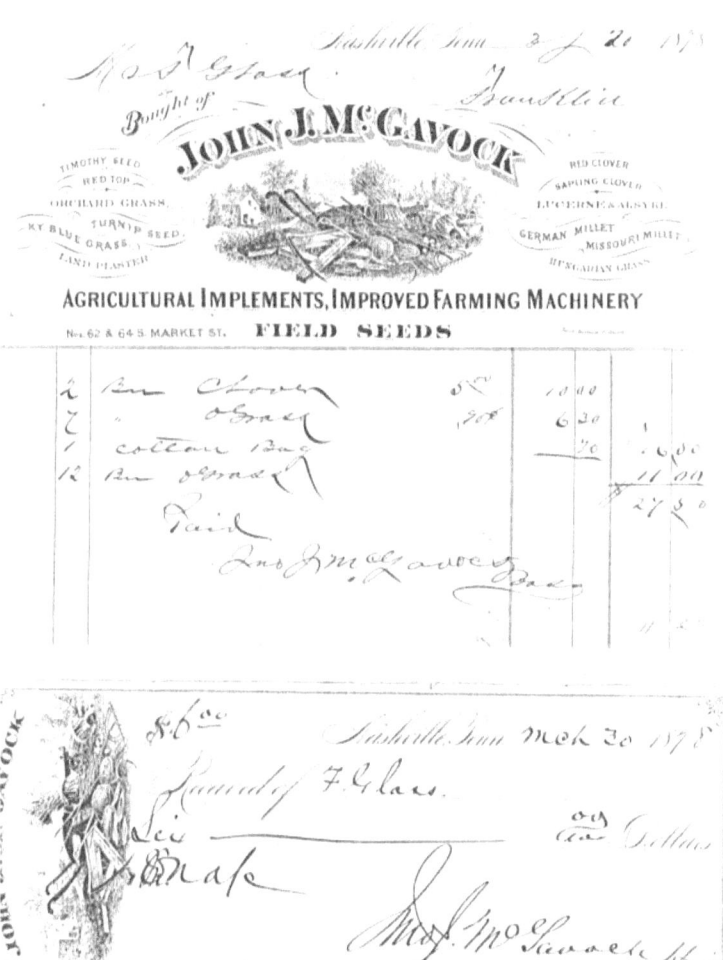

A bill of sale from the company of John Jacob McGavock (b. 1835), son of Jacob McGavock (1790-1878) and Louisa Caroline Grundy (1798-1878). The address of the company is 62 and 64 South Market Street, Nashville, Tennessee. On the receipt can be seen such items as clover, a cotton bag, and twelve bushels of grass seed. The total is $27.50, the date is March 20, 1878. Below it is what appears to be a check (or another receipt) for $6.00 from John, who is the 1st cousin once removed of Colonel John of Carnton Plantation. (Image courtesy Williamson County Public Library)

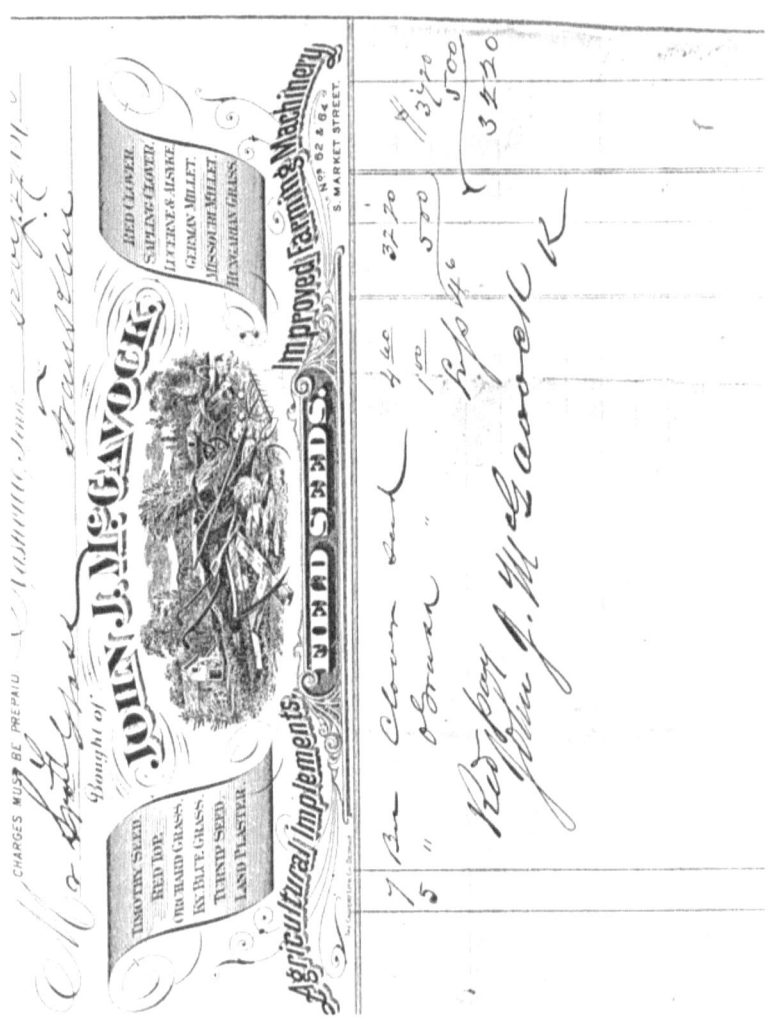

Another bill of sale written out by John Jacob McGavock (b. 1835). The total is $32.20, for several bushels of clover and grass seed. (Image courtesy Williamson County Public Library)

THE MCGAVOCKS OF CARNTON PLANTATION

From Lindsley's *Historical Series*, a composite engraving of the officers of the Tenth Tennessee Infantry Regiment, Confederate States of America. Clockwise from top center: Lieutenant Colonel Randal William McGavock (1826-1863), Captain Thomas Gibson, Dr. Joseph M. Plunkett, Captain Saint Clair M. Morgan, Captain Lewis R. Clark. Center: Colonel Adolphus Heiman. (Image © The Tennessee Historical Society)

THE MCGAVOCKS OF CARNTON PLANTATION

Hugh Lysander McGavock (1833-1852), born at Midway Plantation, Brentwood, Tennessee. Nineteen year old Hugh, the son of Lysander McGavock (1800-1855) and Elizabeth Crockett (1795-1862), and the 1st cousin once removed of Colonel John of Carnton, died unexpectedly of pneumonia while attending Cumberland University (now the University of Nashville). Portrait date about 1852. Artist possibly Washington B. Cooper. (Image © The Tennessee Historical Society)

THE MCGAVOCKS OF CARNTON PLANTATION

Autographed image of Jeremiah George Harris (1808-1901), husband of Lucinda McGavock (1817-1847), the 1st cousin once removed of Colonel John of Carnton. Harris was an influential newspaper editor who helped get McGavock friend James Knox Polk (1795-1849) elected both governor and U.S. president. (Image © The Tennessee Historical Society)

THE MCGAVOCKS OF CARNTON PLANTATION

Mary Louise McGavock (b. 1838), wife of James Todd (1821-1890), an early Nashville settler. Mary is the daughter of Jacob McGavock (1790-1878) and Louisa Caroline Grundy (1798-1878), and the 1st cousin once removed of Colonel John of Carnton (1815-1893). Date and creator of image unknown. (Image courtesy TSLA)

THE MCGAVOCKS OF CARNTON PLANTATION

Randal William McGavock (1826-1863). Portrait from 1858, during his term as mayor of Nashville, Tennessee. Lincoln's War was only three years away. (Image courtesy TSLA)

THE MCGAVOCKS OF CARNTON PLANTATION

Confederate Lieutenant Colonel Randal William McGavock (1826-1863) in uniform. Portrait done sometime between 1861 and 1863. Randal was killed at the Battle of Raymond while courageously leading his Irish unit, the Tenth Tennessee Regiment. He is buried at the McGavock Family Mausoleum, Mount Olivet Cemetery, Nashville, Tennessee. (Image courtesy TSLA)

THE MCGAVOCKS OF CARNTON PLANTATION

A signed illustration of Randal William McGavock (1826-1863), with signature. Portrait probably from the late 1850s. Note the Scottish manner in which he spells his surname: "Mac Gavock." (Image courtesy TSLA)

The McGavocks of Carnton Plantation

My 3rd cousin, Edmund Winchester Rucker (1835-1924), commander of Rucker's Brigade (Chalmer's Division, Forrest's Cavalry), which was organized in September 1864. Rucker fought with Forrest at Franklin II, and lost his left arm two weeks later at the Battle of Nashville. The two were close friends and went into the railroad business together after the War (from 1869-1874). I am the 4th great-grandson of Phoebe Rucker, who was the 1st cousin of Colonel Rucker. His 1924 obituary reads: "The death of Gen. E. W. Rucker, at his home in Birmingham, Ala, on the night of Sunday, April 13, 1924, takes another from the fast-dwindling list of gallant Confederate leaders and one of the patriotic upbuilders of the South since the war. He had reached the advanced age of eighty-eight years, but was still an outstanding figure in the business and social life of that city. After the war, and before removing from his native Tennessee, he built a forty-mile stretch of the Memphis and Little Rock Railroad. Later he was president of the Salem, Marion and Memphis Railroad following his removal to Birmingham, and had also been prominently connected with large manufacturing interests in that city. Edmund Winchester Rucker was born July 22, 1835, at Murfreesboro, Tenn., the son of Edmund and Louisa Winchester Rucker, and a grandson of Gen. James Winchester." General Winchester was a pioneer, an officer in the War of 1812, and along with Andrew Jackson (of the Hermitage) and John Overton (of Travellers Rest), one of the founders of Memphis, Tennessee. Winchester's home, Cragfont, can still be seen at Castalian Springs, Tennessee. (Photo courtesy the Ronny Mangrum Collection)

THE MCGAVOCKS OF CARNTON PLANTATION

From left to right: an unidentified admiral; center, Stanley F. Horn (pro-South author and president of the Tennessee Historical Society); and right, General Jacob McGavock Dickinson, Jr. (b. 1891), commander of the Tennessee State Guard. Jacob is the son of U.S. Secretary of War Jacob McGavock Dickinson, Sr. (1851-1928) and Martha Overton (1853-1917) of Travellers Rest. Date of photo: June 8, 1945. Location: the Hermitage, the tomb of President Andrew Jackson. Occasion: 100th anniversary of Jackson's death. Harry Truman was U.S. president at the time. Jacob is the 1st cousin three times removed of Colonel John of Carnton Plantation. (Photo © The Tennessee Historical Society)

The McGavocks of Carnton Plantation

Lysander McGavock (1800-1855) of Midway Plantation, Brentwood, Tennessee. This portrait is from the 1850s. Artist, unknown. (Image © The Tennessee Historical Society)

THE MCGAVOCKS OF CARNTON PLANTATION

Confederate General Charles Sidney Winder (1829-1862), the 2nd cousin once removed of Caroline E. "Carrie" Winder (1829-1905), the wife of Colonel John of Carnton Plantation. Charles, the 2nd cousin of Confederate General John Henry Winder (1800-1865), was imbued with greatness from birth: he is the grandson of Maryland Governor Levin Winder (1757-1819), and the great-grandson of General William Winder (1714-1792)—a noted officer in the American Revolutionary War. Born in Talbot County, Maryland, Charles was considered one of the most talented and valuable officers in the Confederate army. He astutely led the Stonewall Brigade under Rebel General Stonewall Jackson during the Shenandoah Valley Campaign, and fought at the Battles of Seven Days and Gaines' Mill. Charles was killed by cannon fire at the Battle of Cedar Mountain on August 9, 1862, and was buried at Wye House, just outside Easton, Maryland. Both Lee and Jackson mourned his untimely death. (Image courtesy Library of Congress)

THE MCGAVOCKS OF CARNTON PLANTATION

Edward Jacob McGavock (1828-1880), son of Jacob McGavock (1790-1878) and Louisa Caroline Grundy (1798-1878), and 1st cousin once removed of Colonel John of Carnton. Edward is a brother of Lieutenant Colonel Randal William McGavock (1826-1863), C.S.A. Date of image and creator unknown. (Image courtesy TSLA)

THE MCGAVOCKS OF CARNTON PLANTATION

Felix Grundy McGavock (1832-1897), son of Jacob McGavock (1790-1878) and Louisa Caroline Grundy (1798-1878), and the 1st cousin once removed of Colonel John of Carnton. After Lincoln's War, in 1867, Felix worked with Confederate General Nathan Bedford Forrest (1821-1877), in Memphis, Tennessee. Date of painting unknown. Artist, possibly Washington B. Cooper. (Image courtesy TSLA)

THE MCGAVOCKS OF CARNTON PLANTATION

Mary Manoah Bostick (d. 1862), wife of Dr. Felix Grundy McGavock (1832-1897). Mary was born in Triune, just east of Franklin, Tennessee. She died at age thirty in Memphis and is buried at Mount Olivet Cemetery, Nashville. Date and artist unknown. (Image courtesy TSLA)

THE MCGAVOCKS OF CARNTON PLANTATION

Historical marker in front of the old Bostick Female Academy, Triune, Tennessee. The aforementioned Mary Manoah Bostick is the 1st cousin once removed of Dr. Jonathan Smith Bostick (b. 1794), referenced in the sign above. During Lincoln's War, just as they did in Franklin and in thousands of other Southern towns, Yankee troops unnecessarily, cruelly, and illegally burned down the original school located here, known as Porter Female Academy. Due to the generosity of McGavock relation Dr. Bostick, it was rebuilt after the War and renamed in his honor. (Photo © Lochlainn Seabrook)

THE MCGAVOCKS OF CARNTON PLANTATION

Hugh Albert McGavock (1842-1854), youngest child of Jacob McGavock (1790-1878) and Louisa Caroline Grundy (1798-1878), and 1st cousin once removed of Colonel John of Carnton. Date of portrait and artist unknown. (Image courtesy TSLA)

THE MCGAVOCKS OF CARNTON PLANTATION

Carnton Mansion, front view, from a newspaper, probably in the early 1900s. Note the large tall trees on either side of the front walkway. (Image courtesy Williamson County Public Library)

THE MCGAVOCKS OF CARNTON PLANTATION

A photo of some of the American members of the Northern branch of the McGavocks. It is not known for sure how the Southern branch of the McGavocks connects with them, but there can be no doubt that they are linked: both come from County Antrim, Ireland, and both descend from an ancestor named Hugh McGavock (a rare name in any country). This makes both branches integrally related. It is my theory that the Northern branch descends from a man named Randal McGavock, who was probably the brother of James "Dada" McGavock, Sr. (1728-1812). Both men then would have been the sons of Hugh McGavock (b. about 1700) of Galloway, Scotland, the great-grandfather of Colonel John W. McGavock (1815-1893) of Carnton Plantation. While the Southern McGavock branch came from Ireland through Pennsylvania, moved to Virginia, then branched out into Tennessee, the Northern McGavock branch came to America from Ireland and went directly west, settling in Fox Lake, Illinois. They then spread out into Minnesota, Wisconsin, and Nebraska. The elderly gentleman at the front center of this photo (with the cane) is Hugh McGavock (son of Alexander McGavock and Sarah Ann Devlin), born 1828 in County Antrim, Ireland; he died at Beloit, Rock County, Wisconsin in 1908. If my genealogical theory is correct, Hugh of Beloit would be the 2nd cousin once removed of Colonel John of Carnton. Lincoln's War was truly one of "brother against brother": all of the eligible members of the Northern McGavock branch fought on the Union side, while all of the eligible members of the Southern McGavock branch fought on the Confederate side. Photo from the late 1800s or early 1900s. (Image courtesy the Van Rens family)

THE MCGAVOCKS OF CARNTON PLANTATION

Sons of Hugh McGavock (1828-1908)—shown in previous photo—and Catherine Buckley of Beloit, Wisconsin, members of the Northern branch of the American McGavocks. From left to right: Alexander, John, Hugh, Patrick, William, Thomas, James, and Edward. Many of these same first names can be found among the males of the Southern McGavock branch, such as Colonel John of Carnton, indicating a common and traditional family naming pattern. (Image courtesy the Van Rens family)

THE MCGAVOCKS OF CARNTON PLANTATION

The Northern McGavocks were an industrious and prosperous lot, giving their name to countless areas, regions, businesses, and locations across the Midwest and northern Midwest, such as McGavock's Camp, Minnesota City, Minnesota, shown here. According to their descendants, the Northern McGavocks "worked railroad grading and construction from the 1840s through the turn of the century. They followed the work from Chicago west and as far south as South Carolina." (Image courtesy the Van Rens family)

THE MCGAVOCKS OF CARNTON PLANTATION

One of the many McGavock street signs in and around Nashville, Tennessee. Behind this one, at Opry Mills Mall, can be seen the Cumberland River, which played such an important part in Lincoln's War. The Cumberland continues to heavily influence the region: in May of 2010 the river crested, flooding many areas along its banks, including parts of downtown Nashville. Opry Mills Mall itself was deluged, forcing its closure for several years. (Photo © Lochlainn Seabrook)

McGavock street sign in Nashville. (Photo © Lochlainn Seabrook)

Another McGavock street sign in Nashville. (Photo © Lochlainn Seabrook)

THE MCGAVOCKS OF CARNTON PLANTATION

Another Yankee-oriented historical marker, Franklin, Tennessee, this one denoting the site of one of the Union lines at the Battle of Franklin II. "Breastworks" are temporary fortified trenches dug to the depth of a man's chest (about four or five feet), allowing soldiers to take cover or stand and fire over the edge while protecting the lower body. (Photo © Lochlainn Seabrook)

THE MCGAVOCKS OF CARNTON PLANTATION

Gravestone of Confederate Private John Byars Womack (1839-1864) of the Sixteenth Tennessee Regiment, McGavock Confederate Cemetery, Carnton Plantation, Franklin, Tennessee. John, a close cousin of the author and of country artist Lee Ann Womack, gave his life at the Battle of Franklin II on November 30, 1864, trying to preserve the original confederate government and confederate Constitution of the Founding Fathers. (Photo © Lochlainn Seabrook)

THE MCGAVOCKS OF CARNTON PLANTATION

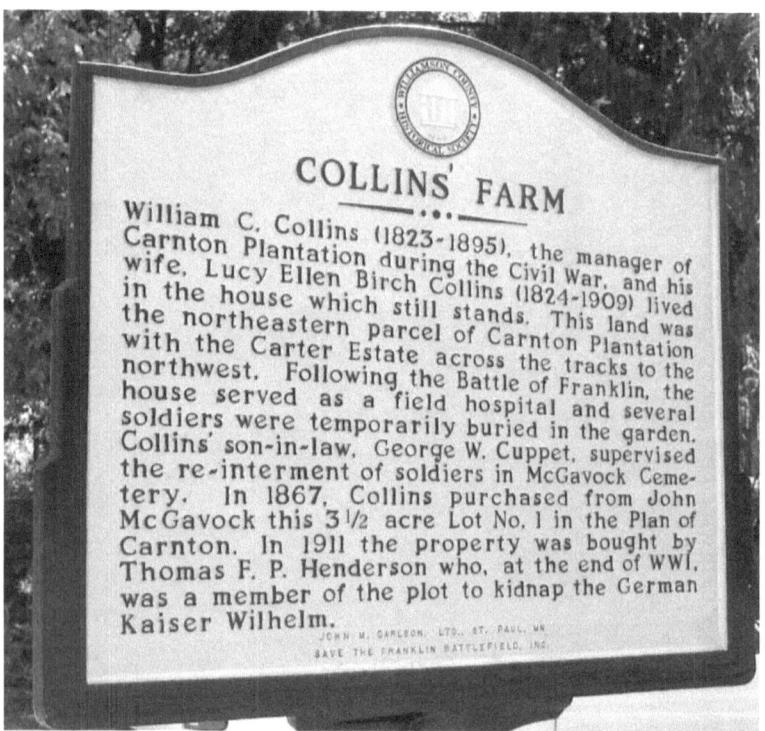

Historical marker at the site of the Collins' Farm, Franklin, Tennessee, since removed, but which contains valuable information, and so is included here. The homestead was once connected to the McGavocks and Carnton Plantation. (Photo © Lochlainn Seabrook)

THE MCGAVOCKS OF CARNTON PLANTATION

Restored remnants of Collins' Farm (located within walking distance of Carnton), Franklin, Tennessee, which played a role in both the history of Carnton Plantation and the War for Southern Independence. (Photo © Lochlainn Seabrook)

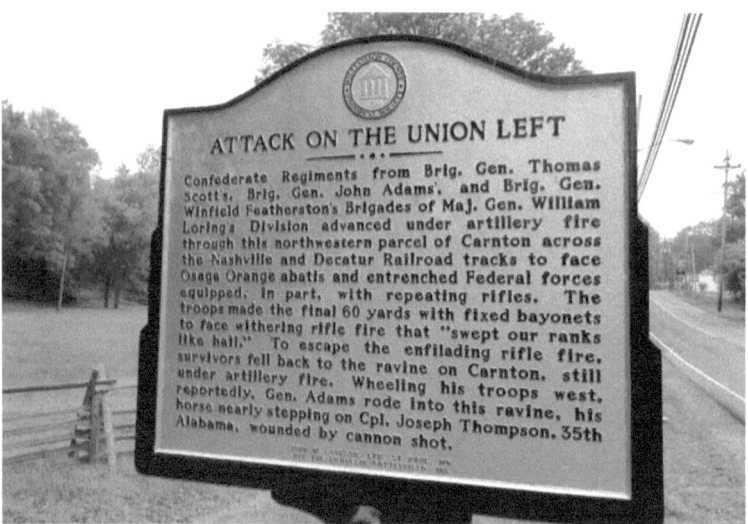

Current historical marker at Collins' Farm, describing the movements of Confederate forces around the property during the Battle of Franklin II, November 30, 1864. (Photo © Lochlainn Seabrook)

THE MCGAVOCKS OF CARNTON PLANTATION

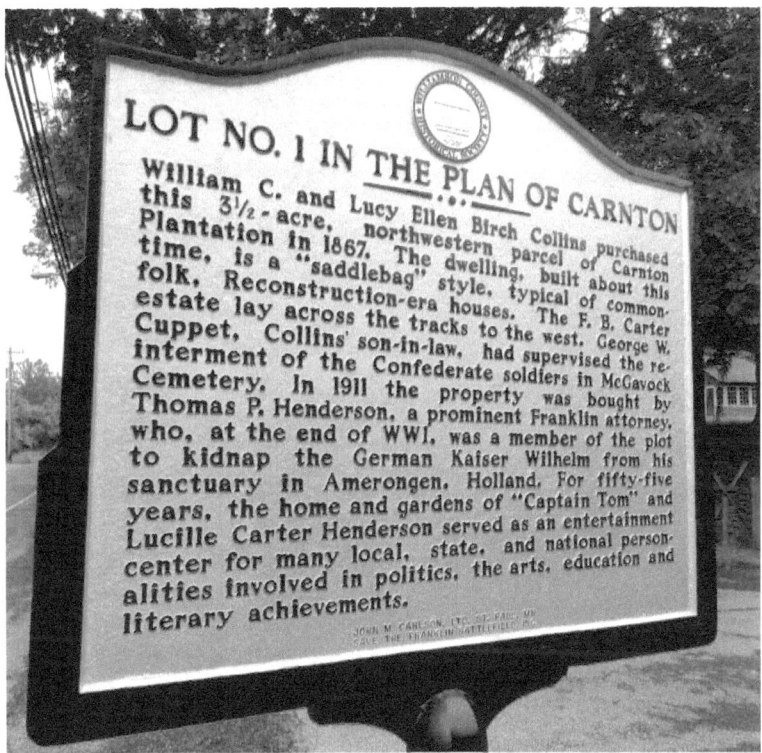

Reverse side of previous historical marker, located in front of Collins' Farm. (Photo © Lochlainn Seabrook)

THE MCGAVOCKS OF CARNTON PLANTATION

Franklin, Tennessee, with three bloody battles to her name, is steeped in Civil War history. With some 298 engagements fought on her soil during the conflict, the Volunteer State has the second highest number of officially recognized engagements of all the states (though Southern historians believe that Tennessee may have hosted as many as 1,000 between 1861 and 1865). Only Virginia has more officially recognized engagements, at 519. Unlike many Southern regions, Middle Tennessee, where Carnton Plantation is located, hosted major battles and campaigns every year of the War. (Photo © Lochlainn Seabrook)

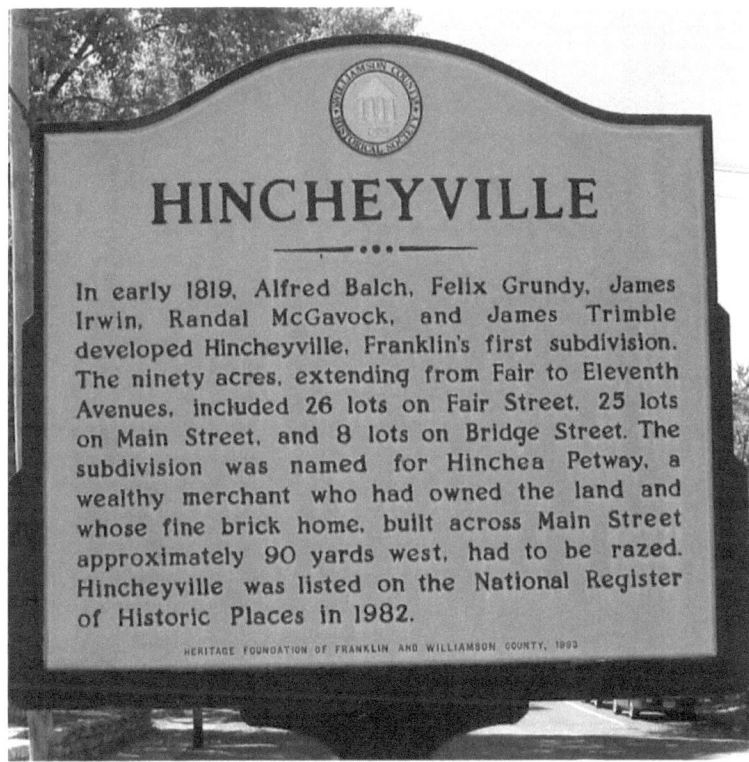

Historical marker describing the area of Hincheyville, Franklin, Tennessee. As the text notes, Franklin's first subdivision was developed in 1819 by a group of men that included Randal McGavock (1766-1843), founder of Carnton Plantation and the eleventh mayor of Nashville, Tennessee. Hincheyville is one of four existing historic districts in Franklin. The other three are the Natchez Street district, the Adams Street district, and the Lewisburg Ave. district. (Photo © Lochlainn Seabrook)

Stone marker, Franklin, Tennessee, at the location of Yankee General Nathan Kimball's right flank at the Battle of Franklin II. (Photo © Lochlainn Seabrook)

THE McGAVOCKS OF CARNTON PLANTATION

Historical marker in Franklin, Tennessee, indicating the location of Harpeth Academy, which was owned by Randal McGavock (1766-1843), founder of Carnton, in the 1820s. The school would probably still be in existence today had it not suffered the fate of so many other Southern educational facilities: in 1863, during Lincoln's War, it was pilfered and laid waste by marauding Yankee troops. Though Carnton Plantation was spared, this was only because Colonel John W. McGavock took Lincoln's illegal, anti-South "Oath of Allegiance." In fact, according to the North's own *Official Records*, numerous homes in and around Franklin were also burned to the ground around this time. There was no purpose for these war crimes (it is against international law and the Geneva Conventions for an army to disturb civilian property). It was sheer malice and vengeance. (Photo © Lochlainn Seabrook)

Historical marker at the Old Factory Store, Franklin, Tennessee, one of the forty-four buildings in Franklin used as a field hospital during the Battle of Franklin II in the Fall of 1864. (Photo © Lochlainn Seabrook)

THE MCGAVOCKS OF CARNTON PLANTATION

The Old Factory Store is today the home of Franklin's most popular bookstore. (Photo © Lochlainn Seabrook)

THE MCGAVOCKS OF CARNTON PLANTATION

Historic Saint Paul's Episcopal Church, Franklin, Tennessee. (Photo © Lochlainn Seabrook)

THE MCGAVOCKS OF CARNTON PLANTATION

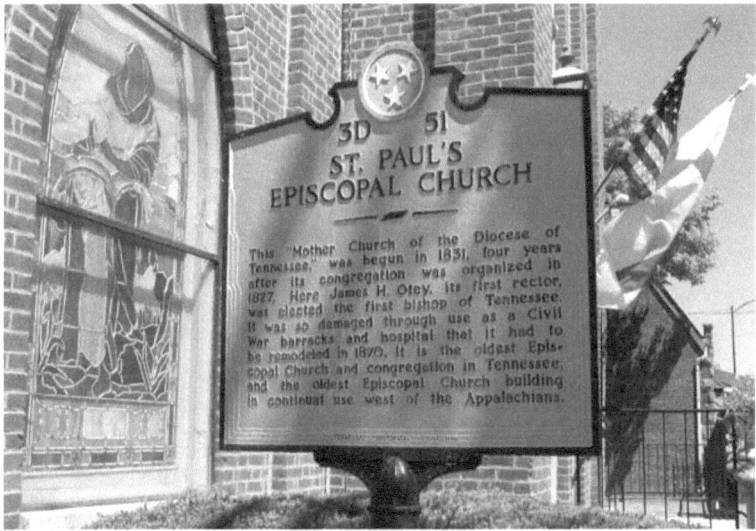

Historical marker at Saint Paul's Episcopal Church, Franklin, Tennessee. Along with Carnton Plantation, Saint Paul's was one of forty-four buildings in town that was used as a field hospital during the Battle of Franklin II. (Photo © Lochlainn Seabrook)

THE MCGAVOCKS OF CARNTON PLANTATION

Historic Franklin Presbyterian Church, Franklin, Tennessee. The Carnton McGavocks, whose ancestors were Presbyterians as far back as 17th-Century Scotland, worshiped here, and after death their funeral services were held here. This church has had many incarnations and several locations. The current site is its second location, moved from its original home near the town's City Cemetery in 1842. Known at the time as the First Presbyterian Church, during the Battle of Franklin II it suffered serious damage, after which it was used as a field hospital by the Yankees. The structure was rebuilt several more times over the years, most notably in 1888 and 1908. (Photo © Lochlainn Seabrook)

THE MCGAVOCKS OF CARNTON PLANTATION

Gravestone of Andrew Crockett (1793-1852), Crockett Cemetery, Brentwood, Tennessee. Andrew, the son of famed rifle maker Samuel Crockett, III (1772-1827) of Forge Seat—and the grandson of one of Williamson County's first settlers, Revolutionary War hero Lt. Andrew Crockett (1745-1821)—was born in Wythe County, Virginia, the same county that the author's McDowell ancestors are from. The Tennessee McGavocks, who intermarried into both the Crockett and the McDowell families, also got their start in Wythe County. Andrew is the 1st cousin once removed of Elizabeth Crockett (1795-1862), the wife of Lysander Crockett (1800-1855) of Midway Plantation, the 1st cousin of Colonel John of Carnton. The seemingly unfinished sentence at the bottom of the stone continues on the next side. It reads: "Andrew Crockett was Married to Catherine W. Bell Apr. 2, 1818." (Photo © Lochlainn Seabrook)

THE MCGAVOCKS OF CARNTON PLANTATION

Winder McGavock, Jr. (1894-1948), son of Winder McGavock (1857-1907) and Susan Lee "Susie" Ewing (1863-1931), and grandson of Colonel John W. McGavock (1815-1893) and Caroline Elizabeth "Carrie" Winder (1829-1905) of Carnton Plantation. Winder was an army sergeant in World War I, serving with the One-Hundred-Fifteenth Field Artillery. (Image courtesy Williamson County Public Library)

THE MCGAVOCKS OF CARNTON PLANTATION

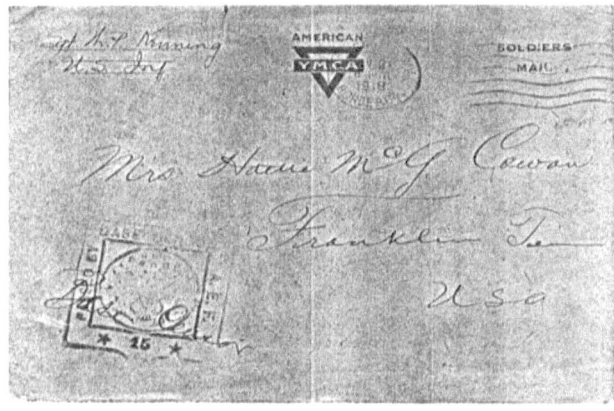

Letter addressed to Harriet Young "Hattie" (McGavock) Cowan (1855-1932), wife of Confederate officer George Limerick Cowan (1842-1919), and daughter of Colonel John of Carnton Plantation. The missive is from a World War I soldier, McGavock friend, and probable relative named Sergeant Winder P. Kenning—who resided in the Nashville, Tennessee, area. The letter is from Bordeaux, France, dated November 12, 1918, U.S. Infantry. It reads: "Dear Mrs. Cowan, I am now spending my furlough in this place. It is a wonderful place right at foot of Alps mountains. I was last in big Argonne drive and came out without a scratch. Great peace is here at last and I hope to be on way home soon. Sincerely, Winder P. Kenning." A relative of Winder's named Henry Kenning served as a pallbearer at Colonel John's funeral in 1893. Another relation is Winder P. Kenning, Jr., born June 3, 1918, died February 7, 1980, at Cedar Hill, Robertson County, Tennessee. (Image courtesy Williamson County Public Library)

The McGavocks of Carnton Plantation

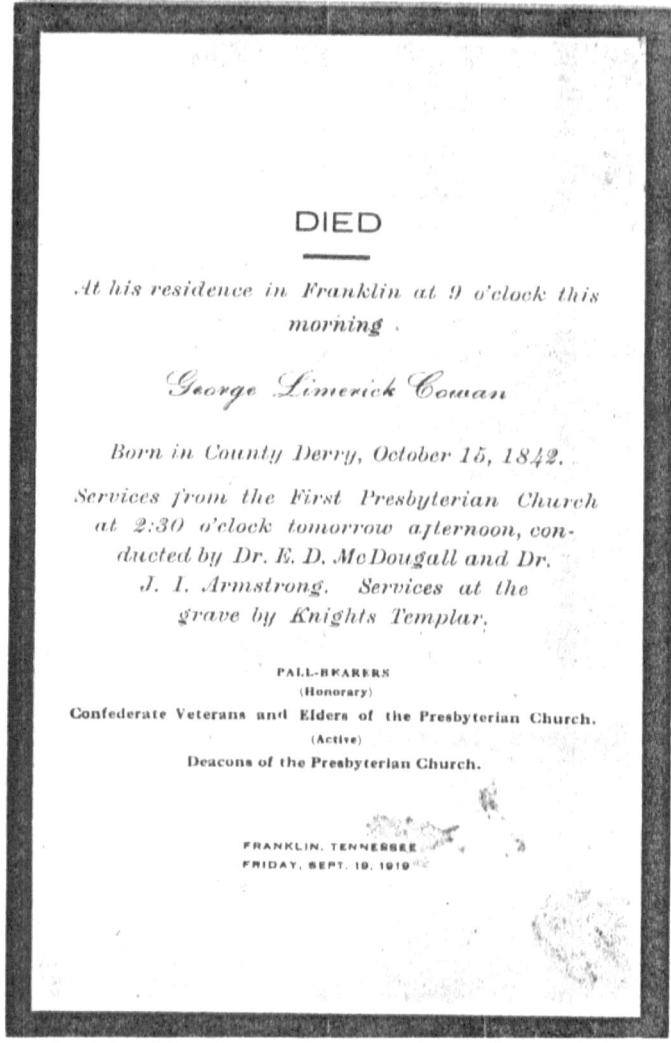

Funeral card of Confederate Lieutenant George Limerick Cowan, born in Ireland in 1842, died at Windermere in Franklin, Tennessee, in 1919. George, the husband of Hattie McGavock (daughter of Colonel John of Carnton), served in General Nathan Bedford Forrest's famous cavalry band known as Forrest's Escort. Among George's pallbearers were members of the United Confederate Veterans (UCV), the forerunner of today's Sons of Confederate Veterans (SCV). Note the mention of the Knights Templar, the controversial secret Christian order said to be in charge of protecting "the bloodline of Jesus," and which has long been connected to the Divine Feminine, Goddess-worship, and King Arthur and the Holy Grail. (Image courtesy Williamson County Public Library)

THE MCGAVOCKS OF CARNTON PLANTATION

Carnton Mansion's front walkway and driveway, looking south across one of the plantation's original crop fields. (Photo © Lochlainn Seabrook)

THE MCGAVOCKS OF CARNTON PLANTATION

Carnton, front of the Mansion looking west. This forlorn muddy road is all that is left of the plantation's once magnificent cedar-lined driveway, which ran all the way around the house. (Photo © Lochlainn Seabrook)

THE MCGAVOCKS OF CARNTON PLANTATION

Cultural signage, Franklin, Tennessee. The Harpeth River runs just to the right, behind the line of trees. (Photo © Lochlainn Seabrook)

THE MCGAVOCKS OF CARNTON PLANTATION

Bishop Charles Todd Quintard (1824-1898), who served as a chaplain for the Army of Tennessee, CSA, during Lincoln's War. Originally a physician and a professor of anatomy, Quintard led many a funeral service for fallen Rebels, including Cleburne, Granbury, and Strahl—all who perished at the Battle of Franklin II. When these three officers were buried too near the graves of Union soldiers, the clergyman objected and had them moved to a more South-friendly location. For his devotion to Dixie, Quintard—a Yankee from Connecticut—continues to be held up as a Southern patriot and hero. (Photo from Ridley's *Battles and Sketches of the Army of Tennessee*)

THE MCGAVOCKS OF CARNTON PLANTATION

Franklin, Tennessee, street signs named after Confederate General Nathan Bedford Forrest (1821-1877). They are located near the area where he forded the Harpeth River while cutting down Yankees during the Battle of Franklin II. To this day this part of Franklin is called Forrest Crossing. (Photo © Lochlainn Seabrook)

THE MCGAVOCKS OF CARNTON PLANTATION

Signage, Franklin, Tennessee. (Photo © Lochlainn Seabrook)

Signage, Franklin, Tennessee. (Photo © Lochlainn Seabrook)

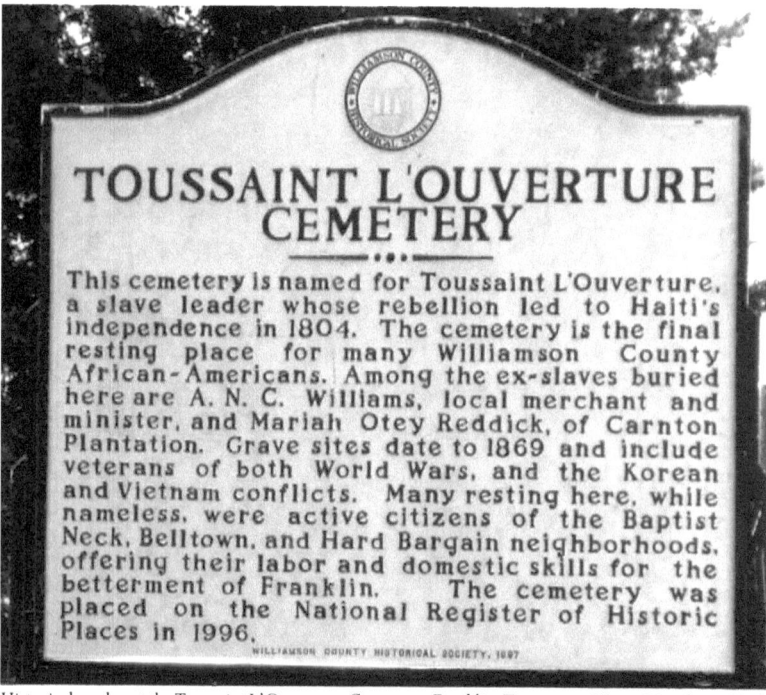

Historical marker at the Toussaint L'Ouverture Cemetery, Franklin, Tennessee. Maria (Mariah) Reddick and Carnton Plantation are mentioned. (Photo © Lochlainn Seabrook)

THE MCGAVOCKS OF CARNTON PLANTATION

Reddick family plot, Toussaint L'Ouverture Cemetery, Franklin, Tennessee. (Photo © Lochlainn Seabrook)

THE MCGAVOCKS OF CARNTON PLANTATION

Gravestone of Maria (Mariah) Otey Reddick (1832-1922), Toussaint L'Ouverture Cemetery, Franklin, Tennessee. Maria worked for the McGavocks from age sixteen to eighty-seven, first as a servant, then later as an employee. She outlived all of the Carnton McGavocks by many years, even giving the eulogy at Carrie McGavock's funeral in 1905. While today Maria is referred to as a lowly "slave" by the uneducated, the McGavocks regarded her as a household domestic, a friend, and even a member of their family. Indeed, this is why Maria voluntarily, and happily, returned to Carnton after Lincoln's War to continue working for the McGavocks. This is not the action of an oppressed, abused, and downtrodden "slave." (Photo © Lochlainn Seabrook)

Gravestone of Maria's husband, Bolling Reddick (his surname is also sometimes spelled Redick), Toussaint L'Ouverture Cemetery, Franklin, Tennessee. (Photo © Lochlainn Seabrook)

THE MCGAVOCKS OF CARNTON PLANTATION

A Franklin, Tennessee, street named after Carnton Plantation. (Photo © Lochlainn Seabrook)

Decorative street banner, Franklin, Tennessee, this one promoting the city's annual rodeo. (Photo © Lochlainn Seabrook)

The McGavocks of Carnton Plantation

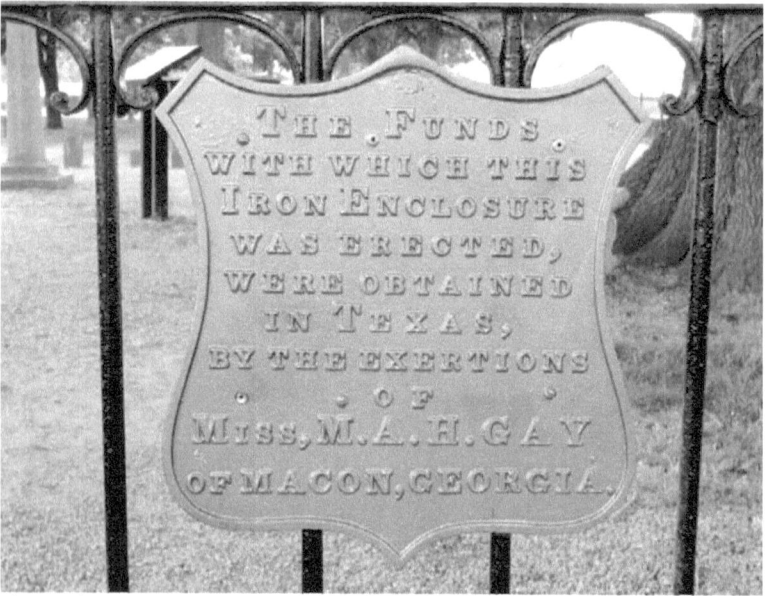

Plaque at the west entrance to the McGavock Confederate Cemetery commemorating Mary Ann Gay, whose dedicated fund-raising efforts made the iron fence and gates surrounding the graveyard possible. (Photo © Lochlainn Seabrook)

THE MCGAVOCKS OF CARNTON PLANTATION

Cultural sign, Franklin, Tennessee. (Photo © Lochlainn Seabrook)

THE MCGAVOCKS OF CARNTON PLANTATION

Cultural sign, Franklin, Tennessee. (Photo © Lochlainn Seabrook)

THE MCGAVOCKS OF CARNTON PLANTATION

McLemore House, site of the African American House Museum, Franklin, Tennessee. Of the 4 million Southern blacks alive during Lincoln's War (500,000 free, 3.5 million in servitude), at least 95 percent (some 3.8 million) supported the Confederacy. At the same time, Lincoln was vigorously campaigning for black colonization, a largely *Northern* effort to have all freed blacks deported back "to their own native land" (Africa), as he phrased it in a public speech at Peoria, Illinois, on October 16, 1854. Both of these facts are regularly suppressed by anti-South organizations and pro-North writers. (Photo © Lochlainn Seabrook)

THE MCGAVOCKS OF CARNTON PLANTATION

Sign in front of the McLemore House, African American House Museum, Franklin, Tennessee. While African-Americans served in the Confederate armies from day one of Lincoln's War (April 9, 1861), the Yankee president prohibited black enlistment in the Union armies for two full years, only permitting it after he reluctantly issued his fake and illegal Final Emancipation Proclamation on January 1, 1863. By then, most blacks, recognizing Lincoln's overt racism, decided they did not want to fight for the Union and had to be coerced at gunpoint to "enlist." Those who were unlucky enough to have to serve under Lincoln were then forced to perform slave-like duties, were segregated from white soldiers, and were given half the pay of whites. After the War they were often denied their military pensions, and were prohibited from marching in Union victory parades or even attending Lincoln's funeral. Blacks in the Southern military, however, were being (unofficially) signed up even before the start of the War, at which time they were given guns, drilled as soldiers, fully integrated with whites, and given equal pay. After the War they received their pensions and were openly and heartily welcomed at Confederate reunions and parades, as well as at Confederate funerals (such as General Nathan Bedford Forrest's). In part of what I call the Great Yankee Coverup, America's history books have been purged of these and other important facts that exonerate the South of all her alleged crimes (secession, racism, slavery, etc.). Afraid of the truth—that Lincoln was a white separatist and a black colonizationist, that his War was illegal, pointless, and unnecessary, and that the vast majority of Southern blacks supported the Confederacy—many Southern Civil War sites, historic places, museums, bookstores, and schools refuse to carry pro-South books such as this one. It is hoped that this unfortunate situation will change as these individuals are re-educated concerning authentic Southern history. (Photo © Lochlainn Seabrook)

THE MCGAVOCKS OF CARNTON PLANTATION

An interracial group of modern day Southern belles (one sporting a pipe) on the front porch of General Nathan Bedford Forrest's boyhood home, Chapel Hill, Tennessee. Southern females of all races, ethnicities, nationalities, and ages, supported the Confederate Cause throughout Lincoln's War—and in a myriad of ways. Some held bake sales to raise money for their hometown troops, while others, posing as men, donned butternut or Confederate gray and joined the fight on the battlefield alongside their fathers, husbands, brothers, and sons. Just as importantly, most, like Carrie (Winder) McGavock, remained at home, where they selflessly and courageously maintained their families, farms, and businesses, not to mention Southern society itself. While Lincoln was doing his best to ignore the women's rights movement in the North, every Southern male of note, from President Jefferson Davis on down, rightly hailed Dixie's hardy but fetching women as the backbone of the Confederacy and the Southern War effort. (Photo © Lochlainn Seabrook)

THE MCGAVOCKS OF CARNTON PLANTATION

Travellers Rest, Nashville, Tennessee. The plantation was established in 1799 by Judge John Overton (1766-1833) of Louisa County, Virginia, who, like the McGavocks, was a good friend of Andrew Jackson (1767-1845). Judge John's granddaughter, Martha Overton (1853-1917), married Jacob McGavock Dickinson, Sr. (1851-1928), the 1st cousin twice removed of Colonel John of Carnton Plantation (1815-1893). (Jacob went on to become U.S. assistant attorney general under President Stephen Grover Cleveland and secretary of war under President William Howard Taft.) Along with Jackson and General James Winchester (1751-1826)—the grandfather of my 3rd cousin, Confederate Colonel Edmund Winchester Rucker (1835-1924)—Judge Overton was one of the founders of Memphis, Tennessee, in 1819. He passed away at Travellers Rest in 1833. Between the Battle of Franklin II (November 30, 1864) and the Battle of Nashville (December 15-16, 1864), Confederate General John Bell Hood (1831-1879) used the plantation house as his Army of Tennessee headquarters. (Photo © Lochlainn Seabrook)

THE MCGAVOCKS OF CARNTON PLANTATION

Debate raged over the establishment of this particular battlefield park, located next to Carnton Plantation. For though the McGavocks' property was on the Confederate rear lines (of the eastern flank) during the Battle of Franklin II, the core battlefield—where the most intense action took place—was several miles to the northwest. (Photo © Lochlainn Seabrook)

THE MCGAVOCKS OF CARNTON PLANTATION

The Southern Confederacy's five primary flags. Moving clockwise, top: the Battle Flag; right: the First National Flag (the "Stars and Bars"); lower right: the Second National Flag (the "Stainless Banner"); lower left: the Bonnie Blue Flag; left: the Third National Flag (the "Blood Stained Banner"). Each has its own fascinating history. Each is an emblem of America's multiracial Southern heritage and the South's dedication to the Constitution and self-determination. None are in any way connected to slavery or racism, as enemies of the South and the uninformed teach.

The McGavocks of Carnton Plantation

The Parthenon, Nashville, Tennessee. This stunning replica of the famous temple at Athens, Greece—constructed in 1897 for the Tennessee Centennial Exposition—is illustrative of the great love traditional Southerners, like the McGavocks, have always had for Classical culture, many of whose architectural elements were later incorporated into Carnton Plantation during its modernization period in the 1840s and 1850s. (Photo © Lochlainn Seabrook)

THE MCGAVOCKS OF CARNTON PLANTATION

Northern slave owner Benjamin Franklin (1706-1790), after whom the town of Franklin, Tennessee, was named. The McGavocks are related to the Franklins through marriage: during Lincoln's War, Alberta Pugsley McGavock (1841-1878)—the 1st cousin once removed of Colonel John of Carnton—married Dr. Dallas Bache (1838-1902), Benjamin's great-grandson. (Image courtesy Library of Congress)

THE MCGAVOCKS OF CARNTON PLANTATION

The Cumberland River at Nashville, Tennessee. This body of water played an important role in the history of the McGavock family, the city of Nashville, and Lincoln's War. (Photo © Lochlainn Seabrook)

Franklin street sign honoring Confederate General John Carpenter Carter (1837-1864), who lost his life at the Battle of Franklin II. John is not related to the Carters of the famous Carter House nearby. (Photo © Lochlainn Seabrook)

THE MCGAVOCKS OF CARNTON PLANTATION

Grave site of President James Knox Polk (1795-1849) and his wife Sarah Childress (1803-1891), State Capitol grounds, Nashville, Tennessee. The location is said to be extremely haunted. Not only were the Polks friends of the Carnton McGavocks, but the two families were related to one another (through marriage). (Photo © Lochlainn Seabrook)

THE MCGAVOCKS OF CARNTON PLANTATION

The Confederate Seal, with George Washington (1733-1799), "the Father of the Confederacy," at the center. The Latin phrase *Deo Vindice* means: "God will vindicate us." The Seal is still proudly displayed by traditional Southerners—and always will be.

THE MCGAVOCKS OF CARNTON PLANTATION

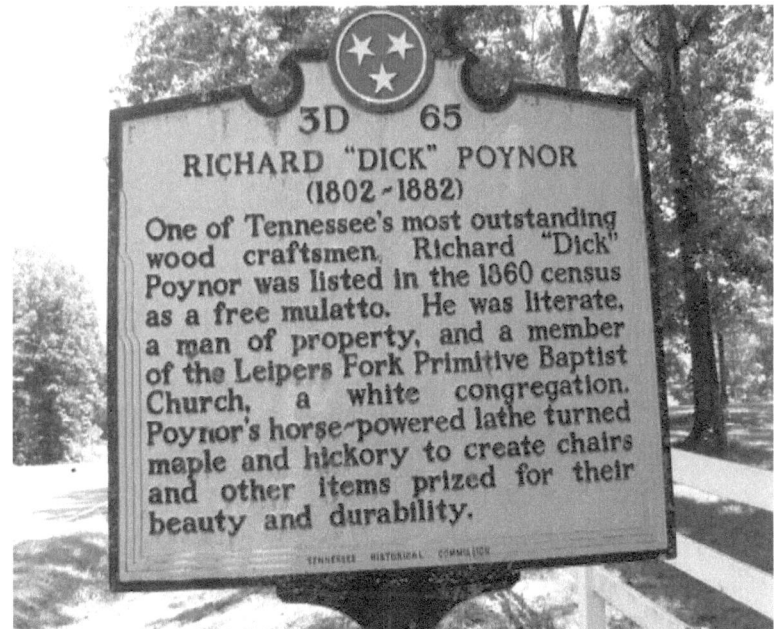

Historical maker, Leiper's Fork, Tennessee, memorializing Richard "Dick" Poynor (1802-1882), famed black local craftsman. One of his chairs is on display at Carnton Plantation. (Photo © Lochlainn Seabrook)

THE MCGAVOCKS OF CARNTON PLANTATION

Natchez Trace Parkway Bridge, Williamson County, Tennessee. Located about nine miles northwest of Franklin, the structure—the first segmentally constructed concrete arch bridge in the U.S.—is part of the nearly 450 mile long Natchez Trace, an 18th-Century land route that connects Natchez, Mississippi, with Nashville, Tennessee. The trail—instigated by President Thomas Jefferson (1743-1826)—was used by early Americans, including, no doubt, the Tennessee McGavocks, some who owned land in Alabama and Louisiana. My cousin Meriwether Lewis (1774-1809)—one-half of the Lewis and Clark Expedition—died October 11, 1809, on the Trace near what is now the town of Hohenwald, Tennessee (sixty miles southwest of Franklin). The county in which Hohenwald sits was named Lewis County after Meriwether, and his grave and monument can still be seen in the area. Natchez Trace has been preserved as a modern but largely unspoiled, beautiful rural highway. The road running under the bridge is Route 96. (Photo © Lochlainn Seabrook)

THE MCGAVOCKS OF CARNTON PLANTATION

Isola Bella, Brentwood, Tennessee. Built around 1840 (on land that was originally part of Nashville) by James Johnston and his wife Narcissa Merritt, Confederate General John Bell Hood is said to have stopped here after the Battle of Franklin II in December 1864. Meeting with his staff, Hood drew up plans for his next move, which would result in the Battle of Nashville on the 15th. Both Confederate and Union soldiers marched their wagons and cannon across the house's yards, and after that conflict Isola Bella served as a field hospital. The 10,000 square foot mansion and surrounding land (worth an estimated $3.5 million dollars), is as impressive today as it was in the Victorian Era. The mantle in the house's parlor is believed to be from Victor Hugo's home in Paris, France. Like Carnton, Isola Bella went through a period of neglect and vacancy, at which time it was used to store crops such as tobacco and hay. Since the 1940s the landmark home has been owned and restored by several different families dedicated to preserving this important piece of Williamson County history. (Photo © Lochlainn Seabrook)

The McGavocks of Carnton Plantation

Cultural signage, Franklin, Tennessee. (Photo © Lochlainn Seabrook)

THE MCGAVOCKS OF CARNTON PLANTATION

One of our greatest Southern heros, Jefferson Davis (1808-1889), who was named after another Southern icon, Thomas Jefferson. Mr. Davis is the Southern Confederacy's first and only president. Many Southerners are looking forward to our second president. (Photo courtesy Library of Congress)

THE MCGAVOCKS OF CARNTON PLANTATION

McGavock Confederate Cemetery, the largest privately owned military graveyard in the U.S., as it looked in 2011. Carnton's rear upper porch is just visible on the ridge of the hill near the center of the frame. A complete list of the dead is included in the author's book *Carnton Plantation Ghost Stories*. (Photo © Lochlainn Seabrook)

The McGavocks of Carnton Plantation

One of the South's sacred flags, known as the Second National. In the upper right corner of the banner is the Confederate Battle Flag, patterned on Scotland's St. Andrew's Cross and Ireland's Saint Patrick's Cross. At least half of the U.S. once supported this Christian symbol (note the crucifix at the top of the flagpole), and untold thousands of Southern men and women, of all races and creeds, died for what it represents: the original constitutional government of the U.S.—known as "the Confederacy" from 1781 to 1789, created primarily by the Southern Founding Fathers. The flag's thirteen stars, signifying the thirteen Southern states that supported the new Confederacy, were an intentional allusion to America's original thirteen colonies, a true confederacy formed under the Articles of Confederation, our nation's first Constitution. The above engraving, probably made around 1867, bears the inscription: "The warrior's banner takes its flight to greet the warrior's soul." Around the outer edge are scenes commemorating "A charge in the wilderness," "The crater," "The fight in Hampton Roads," and "After the surrender." (Image courtesy Library of Congress)

THE MCGAVOCKS OF CARNTON PLANTATION

Main Street in Franklin Center, or Old Franklin, as it is called by the locals. The town's Confederate Monument is visible at the end of the street. (Photo © Lochlainn Seabrook)

THE MCGAVOCKS OF CARNTON PLANTATION

Carnton Plantation in the morning. (Photo © Lochlainn Seabrook)

THE MCGAVOCKS OF CARNTON PLANTATION

McGavock Confederate Cemetery, with Carnton Mansion in the background. (Photo © Lochlainn Seabrook)

Notes on the Bibliography

❧ NORTHERN BIAS & MYTHOLOGY

Those readers who are interested in authentic Southern history will want to take great care when selecting books on the topic of the "Civil War." At least 99.99 percent of all books on this subject have been written from a Northern or New South—that is, from an anti-South—point of view. Some are shockingly vitriolic. All are preposterously biased and full of errors.

By and large these books are penned by individuals who have never forgiven the South for having the gumption to legally break away from the Union in 1860 and 1861, and for what they, in their ignorance, completely misperceive as the region's "reluctance to give up slavery." As such, you will find these types of works brimming with a hatred toward the South and her sons and daughters that is so overt, so strange, so unfounded on fact, that it would be laughable if it were not for the serious damage they have inflicted.

❧ DISINFORMATION & ANTI-SOUTH STEREOTYPES

Filling the world's homes, bookstores, schools, universities, and public libraries with works based on Northern mythology, Yankee wartime propaganda, and New South political correctness is bad enough, but many of these writers go one step further by knowingly and purposefully disseminating both misinformation and disinformation about the South.

One of the most vile, ridiculous, and patently false of these absurdities is that "the Confederate Flag is a symbol of slavery, and therefore of racism." This idea would have certainly surprised the 300,000 African-Americans who fought and died for the Confederacy, and the countless millions of other blacks who remained in Dixie throughout the War in support of what they regarded as their one and only true homeland.

This effort to promote the North's perspective of American history while disregarding, and even maligning, the South's, has indeed had dire

The McGavocks of Carnton Plantation

effects, for it has painted the South and her people as cowardly villains, treasonous rebels, illiterate hicks, and naive fools, images still very much alive to this day. The South, for example, continues to be mocked on TV and in films using absurd stereotypes that make us look like a dilapidated region of inbred hillbillies, racist rednecks, violent zombies, and corn-fed ignoramuses living in run-down shacks. Is this the image of the South we want to leave the world?

❧ THE TRUTH ABOUT DIXIE

How surprised many non-Southerners be would be to learn that Dixie is a land of breathtaking vistas, that her farms and cities produce fabulous wealth (and lifestyles to go with it), and that her people are among the most humane, most literate, most civilized, and best-educated on the planet. Fourteen of America's top fifty schools, for example, are in the South.

Besides, not only is the South family-friendly, her taxes are lower, her climate is better, her men are handier, and her women are prettier, than anywhere else in the nation. Perhaps some of those belonging to the anti-South movement are simply jealous, for we also have the highest quality of life and the lowest cost of living of any region in the U.S.

Thankfully more authors are coming forward with books like this one, *The McGavocks of Carnton Plantation*, that promote a Southern view of American history, and that show the South and her people in a positive, honest, historically accurate, and respectful light.

❧ CAVEAT EMPTOR

Well over 95 percent of the books listed in my bibliography are anti-South in nature, most of which are obvious from their titles or the names of their well-known, South-hating, North-loving authors. A majority of the creators of these hateful and highly inaccurate works are uninformed liberals, and even socialists and Marxists, who detest the U.S.A., our Constitution, our freedoms, and Western capitalism.

In particular, many of this ilk would like to eliminate the concept of free speech; that is, for everyone but themselves. This, of course, was the goal of socialist Adolf Hitler and of every other dictator before and since, including white supremacist and arch liberal, Abraham Lincoln. No wonder progressives feel such an affinity for the "Great Emancipator"!

THE MCGAVOCKS OF CARNTON PLANTATION

While pro-South writers like myself strive to integrate a combination of Southern and Northern works into their own, not surprisingly, the bibliographies of anti-South writers are 100 percent pro-North.[1692] Thus I caution anyone wishing to learn the *truth* about the War for Southern Independence to take great care in deciding which books they read. For you will only find the full set of facts in pro-South books, written by pro-South authors, published by pro-South publishers.

On the other hand, a working knowledge of the Northern perspective is important if one wants a thorough understanding of the conflict, and of how Yankee propaganda was used, and is still used, in an effort to justify Lincoln's unjustifiable War. This is why, as a Southern historian, I use both pro-South *and* pro-North books in my research.

My point is this: nearly everything one reads in pro-North works is suspect due to the extreme bias, lack of real scholarship, overt Northern-skewed perspective, and often wholly subjective approach of their authors. Reader beware.

⁂ SOUTHERN HISTORIES OF THE WAR

Lastly, I am very often asked to recommend a history of the "Civil War" that is written from the Southern point of view. Northern, New South, and liberal slanted publishers, libraries, museums, bookstores, colleges, gift shops, Civil War sites, and authors have made sure that such works are difficult if not impossible to find by suppressing early out of print works and by refusing to publicize (or publish or sell) modern ones. Still, they do exist.

As discussed in Appendix E, for sheer pro-South writing at its sharpest and most politically incorrect (that is, factual), none can compare with Edward A. Pollard's hard-hitting two-volume treatise, *Southern History of the War*. This is the traditional Southerner's ideal "Civil War" book. Begun while the War was still underway and printed shortly after (in 1866), Pollard's work should be in every Southern household and should be required reading in every Southern high school.[1693]

1692. Anti-South writers seem oblivious to the fact that there are now many dozens of pro-South books (like this one) available. More likely, they are aware of them but refuse to purchase or research them.
1693. Pollard's work *The Lost Cause* is also highly recommended.

The McGavocks of Carnton Plantation

Also already recommended is one of the most detailed, factual, and eloquent histories of Lincoln's War ever written. I am speaking here of President Jefferson Davis' fantastic two-volume work entitled: *The Rise and Fall of the Confederate Government*. This book ought to be carried in all Civil War and museum gift shops; not merely for its vast educational value, but as an alternative to the stale, slanted, predictable, misleading, revisionist, South-loathing history books usually found on our nation's bookshelves.[1694]

A tamer and more mainstream Southern history, the three-volume *The Civil War: A Narrative,* was penned by the wonderful late Shelby Foote. The noted author even takes the time to defend my cousin General Nathan Bedford Forrest, something you will never find in pro-North books on Lincoln's War.

For those who want to get as deep as possible into the Southern perspective on the War, there is the twelve-volume tome, *Confederate Military History*, published in 1899 by Colonel John W. McGavock's beloved "band of brothers," the United Confederate Veterans, an organization that later became the Sons of Confederate Veterans (SCV), the organization to which I belong.

If one wants to read the actual words of those Southerners who participated in the War Against Northern Aggression that have not been overly tampered with by anti-South advocates, another good source is the massive multi-volume discourse entitled, *The War of the Rebellion: A Compilation of the Official Records of the Union and Confederate Armies*, more commonly known as the *Official Records (ORA)*.

As one can tell from the title, this work was put together by the U.S. government, and charges of bias against the South have been rightfully noted over the decades. Still, most of the Confederacy's original records (those that were discovered, collected, and saved) remain intact here, making the world's truly gargantuan flood of Northern mythology, Yankee propaganda, and New South disinformation, much easier to sift through.

L.S.

[1694]. I would also strongly suggest Davis' *A Short History of the Confederate States of America*.

Bibliography

Abbott, John Stevens Cabot. *The Life of General Ulysses S. Grant*. Boston, MA: B. B. Russell, 1868.
Acklen, Jeannette Tillotson (ed.). *Tennessee Records: Tombstone Inscriptions and Manuscripts*. Westminster, MD: Heritage Books, 2009.
———. *Tennessee Records: Bible Records and Marriage Bonds*. Baltimore, MD: Clearfield, 2009.
Adams, Charles. *When in the Course of Human Events: Arguing the Case for Southern Secession*. Lanham, MD: Rowman and Littlefield, 2000.
Adams, Francis D., and Barry Sanders. *Alienable Rights: The Exclusion of African Americans in a White Man's Land, 1619-2000*. 2003. New York, NY: Perennial, 2004 ed.
Adams, Henry (ed.). *Documents Relating to New-England Federalism, 1800-1815*. Boston, MA: Little, Brown, and Co., 1877.
Adams, Nehemiah, Rev. *A Southside View of Slavery: Three Months at the South in 1854*. Boston, MA: T. R. Marvin, 1855.
Aiken, Leona Taylor. *The McGavocks of Two Rivers*. Kingsport, TN: East Tennessee Printing Co., 1975.
———. *The Descendants of James McGavock, Sr. and the McGavock Mansions, Fort Chiswell, VA, and Carnton, Franklin, Tenn*. Rogersville, TN: East Tennessee Printing Co., 1986.
Alexander, William T. *History of the Colored Race in America*. Kansas City, MO: Palmetto Publishing, 1887.
Allen, James Egert. *The Negro in New York*. New York, NY: Exposition Press, 1964.
Alotta, Robert I. *Civil War Justice: Union Army Executions Under Lincoln*. Shippensburg, PA: White Mane, 1989.
An Appeal From the Colored Men of Philadelphia to the President of the United States. N.p.: Philadelphia, PA, 1862.
Anderson, John Q. (ed.). *Brokenburn: The Journal of Kate Stone, 1861-1868*. 1955. Baton Rouge, LA: Louisiana State University Press, 1995 ed.
Andrews, Elisha Benjamin. *The United States in Our Own Time: A History From Reconstruction to Expansion*. 1895. New York, NY: Charles Scribner's Sons, 1903 ed.
Andrews, Sidney. *The South Since the War: As Shown by Fourteen Weeks of Travel and Observation*. Boston, MA: Ticknor and Fields, 1866.
Angle, Paul M. (ed.). *The Complete Lincoln-Douglas Debates of 1858*. Chicago, IL: University of Chicago Press, 1991.
Annunzio, Frank (chairman). *The Capitol: A Pictorial History of the Capitol and of the Congress*. Washington, D.C.: U.S. Joint Committee on Printing, 1983.
Anonymous. *Life of John C. Calhoun: Presenting a Condensed History of Political Events, From 1811 to 1843*. New York, NY: Harper and Brothers, 1843.
Applebome, Peter. *Dixie Rising: How the South Is Shaping American Values, Politics, and Culture*. New York, NY: Harvest, 1997.
Appleman, Roy Edgar (ed.). *Abraham Lincoln: From His Own Words and Contemporary Accounts*. Washington, D.C.: U.S. Department of the Interior, National Park Service, 1942.
Aptheker, Herbert. *American Negro Slave Revolts*. New York, NY: International Publishing Co., 1969.
Arnold, Isaac Newton. *The History of Abraham Lincoln, and the Overthrow of Slavery*. Chicago, IL: Clarke and Co., 1866.
Ashdown, Paul, and Edward Caudill. *The Myth of Nathan Bedford Forrest*. 2005. Lanham, MD: Rowman and Littlefield, 2006 ed.
Ashe, Captain Samuel A'Court. *A Southern View of the Invasion of the Southern States and War of 1861-1865*. 1935. Crawfordville, GA: Ruffin Flag Company, 1938 ed.
Ashmore, Richard D., Lee Jussim, and David Wilder (eds.). *Social Identity, Intergroup Conflict, and Conflict Reduction*. New York, NY: Oxford University Press, 2001.
Ashworth, John. *Slavery, Capitalism, and Politics in the Antebellum Republic*. 2 vols. New York, NY: Cambridge University Press, 2007.
Astor, Gerald. *The Right to Fight: A History of African Americans in the Military*. Cambridge, MA: Da Capo, 2001.
Baepler, Paul (ed.). *White Slaves, African Masters: An Anthology of American Barbary Captivity Narratives*. Chicago, IL: University of Chicago Press, 1999.
Baigent, Michael. *The Jesus Papers: Exposing the Greatest Cover-Up in History*. New York, NY:

HarperSanFrancisco, 2007.
Baigent, Michael, Richard Leigh, and Henry Lincoln. *Holy Blood, Holy Grail: The Secret History of Christ, The Shocking Legacy of the Grail.* 1982. New York, NY: Bantam Dell, 2004.
Bailey, Anne C. *African Voices of the Atlantic Slave Trade: Beyond the Silence and the Shame.* Boston, MA: Beacon Press, 2005.
Bailey, Hugh C. *Hinton Rowan Helper: Abolitionist-Racist.* Tuscaloosa, AL: University of Alabama Press, 1965.
Bailey, Thomas A. *A Diplomatic History of the American People.* 1940. New York, NY: Appleton-Century-Crofts, 1969 ed.
Bailyn, Bernard, Robert Dallek, David Brion Davis, David Herbert Donald, John L. Thomas, and Gordon S. Wood. *The Great Republic: A History of the American People.* 1977. Lexington, MA: D. C. Heath and Co., 1992 ed.
Baker, George E. (ed.). *The Works of William H. Seward.* 5 vols. 1861. Boston, MA: Houghton, Mifflin and Co., 1888 ed.
Ballagh, James Curtis. *White Servitude in the Colony of Virginia: A Study of the System of Indentured Servitude in the American Colonies.* Whitefish, MT: Kessinger Publishing, 2004.
Bancroft, Frederic. *The Life of William H. Seward.* 2 vols. New York, NY: Harper and Brothers, 1900.
Bancroft, Frederic, and William A. Dunning (eds.). *The Reminiscences of Carl Schurz.* 3 vols. New York, NY: McClure Co., 1909.
Bardsley, Charles Wareing. *English Surnames: Their Sources and Significations.* London, UK: Chatto and Windus, 1889.
Barnes, Gilbert H., and Dwight L. Dumond (eds.). *Letters of Theodore Dwight Weld, Angelina Grimké Weld and Sarah Grimké, 1822-1844.* 2 vols. New York, NY: D. Appleton-Century Co., 1934.
Barney, William L. *Flawed Victory: A New Perspective on the Civil War.* New York, NY: Praeger Publishers, 1975.
Barrow, Charles Kelly, J. H. Segars, and R. B. Rosenburg (eds.). *Black Confederates.* 1995. Gretna, LA: Pelican Publishing Co., 2001 ed.
———. *Forgotten Confederates: An Anthology About Black Southerners.* Saint Petersburg, FL: Southern Heritage Press, 1997.
Barton, William E. *The Soul of Abraham Lincoln.* New York, NY: George H. Doran, 1920.
Basler, Roy Prentice (ed.). *Abraham Lincoln: His Speeches and Writings.* 1946. New York, NY: Da Capo Press, 2001 ed.
——— (ed.). *The Collected Works of Abraham Lincoln.* 9 vols. New Brunswick, NJ: Rutgers University Press, 1953.
Bateman, William O. *Political and Constitutional Law of the United States of America.* St. Louis, MO: G. I. Jones and Co., 1876.
Baxter, Maurice G. *Henry Clay and the American System.* Lexington, KY: University Press of Kentucky, 2004.
Beard, Charles A., and Birl E. Schultz. *Documents on the State-Wide Initiative, Referendum and Recall.* 2 vols. in one. New York, NY: Macmillan, 1912.
Beard, Charles A., and Mary R. Beard. *The Rise of American Civilization.* 1927. New York, NY: Macmillan, 1930 ed.
Beck, Glenn. *Glenn Beck's Common Sense: The Case Against an Out-of-Control Government, Inspired by Thomas Paine.* New York, NY: Threshold, 2009.
Bedwell, Randall (ed.). *May I Quote You, General Forrest? Observations & Utterances from the South's Great Generals.* Nashville, TN: Cumberland House, 1997.
Bell, Lily Cartwright. *History of Dickinson Road.* Goodlettsville, TN: Robert Cartwright Chapter, DAR, 1936.
Bennett, Lerone. *Forced into Glory: Abraham Lincoln's White Dream.* Chicago, IL: Johnson Publishing Company, 2000.
Benton, Thomas Hart. *Thirty Years View; or A History of the Working of the American Government for Thirty Years, From 1820 to 1850.* 2 vols. New York, NY: D. Appleton and Co., 1854.
Bergeron, Paul H., Stephen V. Ash, and Jeanette Keith. *Tennesseans and Their History.* Knoxville, TN: University of Tennessee Press, 1999.
Bergh, Albert Ellery (ed.). *The Writings of Thomas Jefferson.* 20 vols. Washington, D.C.: Thomas Jefferson

Memorial Association of the U.S., 1905.
Bergman, Peter M. *The Chronological History of the Negro in America.* Chicago, IL: Harper and Row, 1969.
Berlin, Ira. *Slaves Without Masters: The Free Negro in the Antebellum South.* New York, NY: Pantheon, 1975.
Bernhard, Winfred E. A. *Political Parties in American History* (Vol. 1: 1789-1828). New York, NY: G. P. Putnams' Sons, 1973.
Berry, Wendell. *The Gift of Good Land: Further Essays Cultural and Agricultural.* Berkeley, CA: Counterpoint, 1981.
———. *The Unsettling of America: Culture and Agriculture.* San Francisco, CA: Sierra Club Books, 1996.
———. *The Art of the Commonplace: The Agrarian Essays of Wendell Berry.* Berkeley, CA: Counterpoint, 2003.
———. *Bringing It to the Table: On Farming and Food.* Berkeley, CA: Counterpoint, 2009.
Berwanger, Eugene H. *The Frontier Against Slavery: Western Anti-Negro Prejudice and the Slavery Extension Controversy.* 1967. Urbana, IL: University of Illinois Press, 1971, ed.
Beschloss, Michael R. *Presidential Courage: Brave Leaders and How They Changed America, 1789-1989.* New York, NY: Simon and Schuster, 2007.
Beveridge, Albert Jeremiah. *The Life of John Marshall.* 2 vols. Boston, MA: Houghton Mifflin Co., 1916.
———. *Abraham Lincoln: 1809-1858.* 2 vols. Boston, MA: Houghton Mifflin Co., 1928.
Bingham, Emily S., and Thomas A. Underwood (eds.). *The Southern Agrarians and the New Deal: Essays after I'll Take My Stand.* Charlottesville, VA: University Press of Virginia, 2001.
Black, Chauncey F. *Essays and Speeches of Jeremiah S. Black.* New York, NY: D. Appleton and Co., 1886.
Black, Col. Robert W. *Cavalry Raids of the Civil War.* Mechanicsburg, PA: Stackpole, 2004.
Blackerby, Hubert R. *Blacks in Blue and Gray.* New Orleans, LA: Portals Press, 1979.
Blassingame, John W. *The Slave Community: Plantation Life in the Antebellum South.* 1972. New York, NY: Oxford University Press, 1974 ed.
Bledsoe, Albert Taylor. *An Essay on Liberty and Slavery.* Philadelphia, PA: J. B. Lippincott and Co., 1856.
———. *A Theodicy; or a Vindication of the Divine Glory, as Manifested in the Constitution and Government of the Moral World.* New York, NY: Carlton and Porter, 1856.
———. *Is Davis a Traitor; or Was Secession a Constitutional Right Previous to the War of 1861?* Richmond, VA: Hermitage Press, 1907.
Blee, Kathleen M. *Women of the Klan: Racism and Gender in the 1920s.* 1991. Berkeley, CA: University of California Press, 1992 ed.
Blight, David W. *Frederick Douglass' Civil War: Keeping Faith in Jubilee.* 1989. Baton Rouge, LA: Louisiana State University Press, 1991 ed.
Bliss, William Dwight Porter (ed.). *The Encyclopedia of Social Reform.* New York, NY: Funk and Wagnalls, 1897.
Blumrosen, Alfred W., and Ruth G. Blumrosen. *Slave Nation: How Slavery United the Colonies and Sparked the American Revolution.* Napierville, IL: Sourcebooks, 2005.
Boatner, Mark Mayo. *The Civil War Dictionary.* 1959. New York, NY: David McKay Co., 1988 ed.
Bode, Carl, and Malcolm Cowley (eds.). *The Portable Emerson.* 1941. Harmondsworth, UK: Penguin, 1981 ed.
Boorstin, Daniel J. *The Discoverers: A History of Man's Search to Know His World and Himself.* 1983. New York, NY: Vintage, 1985 ed.
Bork, Robert H. *Slouching Towards Gomorrah: Modern Liberalism and American Decline.* 1996. New York, NY: ReganBooks, 1997 ed.
Bowen, Catherine Drinker. *John Adams and the American Revolution.* 1949. New York, NY: Grosset and Dunlap, 1977 ed.
Bowman, John S. *The Civil War Day by Day: An Illustrated Almanac of America's Bloodiest War.* 1989. New York, NY: Dorset Press, 1990 ed.
———. *Encyclopedia of the Civil War* (ed.). 1992. North Dighton, MA: JG Press, 2001 ed.
Bowman, Virginia McDaniel. *Historic Williamson County: Old Homes and Sites.* 1971. Franklin, TN: Territorial Press, 1989 ed.
Bradford, James C. (ed.). *Atlas of American Military History.* New York, NY: Oxford University Press, 2003.
Bradford, Ned (ed.). *Battles and Leaders of the Civil War* (one-vol. ed.). New York, NY: Appleton-Century-Crofts, 1956.

THE MCGAVOCKS OF CARNTON PLANTATION

Bradley, Michael R. *Tullahoma: The 1863 Campaign for the Control of Middle Tennessee*. Shippensburg, PA: White Mane, 1999.
——. *It Happened in the Civil War*. Augusta, GA: TwoDot, 2002.
——. *With Blood and Fire: Life Behind Union Lines in Middle Tennessee, 1863-65*. Shippensburg, PA: Burd Street press, 2003.
——. *Nathan Bedford Forrest's Escort and Staff*. Gretna, LA: Pelican Publishing Co., 2006.
——. *Myths and Mysteries of the Civil War: True Stories of the Unsolved and Unexplained*. Guilford, CT: The Globe Pequot Press, 2011.
Brady, Cyrus Townsend. *Three Daughters of the Confederacy*. New York, NY: G. W. Dillingham, 1905.
Brady, James S. (ed.). *Ronald Reagan: A Man True to His Word - A Portrait of the 40th President of the United States In His Own Words*. Washington, D.C.: National Federation of Republican Women, 1984.
Brandt, Robert S. *Touring the Middle Tennessee Backroads*. 1995. Winston-Salem, NC: John F. Blair, 2005 ed.
Brent, Linda. *The Deeper Wrong; or Incidents in the Life of a Slave Girl, Written by Herself*. London, UK: W. Tweedie, 1862.
Brinkley, Alan. *The Unfinished Nation: A Concise History of the American People*. 1993. Boston, MA: McGraw-Hill, 2000 ed.
Brockett, Linus Pierpont. *The Life and Times of Abraham Lincoln, Sixteenth President of the United States*. Philadelphia, PA: Bradley and Co., 1865.
Brooks, Gertrude Zeth. *First Ladies of the White House*. Chicago, IL: Charles Hallberg and Co., 1969.
Brooksher, William R., and David K. Snider. *Glory at a Gallop: Tales of the Confederate Cavalry*. 1993. Gretna, LA: Pelican Publishing Co., 2002 ed.
Brown, Dan. *The Da Vinci Code*. New York, NY: Anchor, 2003.
Brown, Dee. *Bury My Heart at Wounded Knee: An Indian History of the American West*. 1970. New York, NY: Owl Books, 1991 ed.
Brown, Rita Mae. *High Hearts*. New York, NY: Bantam, 1987.
Brown, William Wells. *The Black Man: His Antecedents, His Genius, and His Achievements*. New York, NY: Thomas Hamilton, 1863.
Browne, Ray B., and Lawrence A. Kreiser, Jr. *The Civil War and Reconstruction*. Westport, CT: Greenwood Publishing, 2003.
Browning, Robert, M., Jr. *Forrest: The Confederacy's Relentless Warrior*. Dulles, VA: Brassey's, Inc., 2004.
Bruce, Philip Alexander. *The Plantation Negro As a Freeman*. New York, NY: G. P. Putnam's Sons, 1889.
Bryan, William Jennings. *The Commoner Condensed*. New York, NY: Abbey Press, 1902.
Buchanan, James. *The Works of James Buchanan*. 12 vols. Philadelphia, PA: J. B. Lippincott Co., 1911.
Buchanan, Patrick J. *A Republic, Not an Empire: Reclaiming America's Destiny*. Washington, D.C.: Regenry, 1999.
Buckingham, James Silk. *The Slave States of America*. 2 vols. London, UK: Fisher, Son, and Co., 1842.
Buckley, Gail. *American Patriots: The Story of Blacks in the Military from the Revolution to Desert Storm*. New York, NY: Random House, 2001.
Bultman, Bethany. *Redneck Heaven: Portrait of a Vanishing Culture*. New York, NY: Bantam, 1996.
Burke, John. *Burke's Peerage: Genealogical and Heraldic History of the Baronetage and Knightage* (104th ed.). 1826. London, UK: Waterlow and Sons, 1967 ed.
Burke, Pauline Wilcox. *Emily Donelson of Tennessee*. 1941. Knoxville, TN: University of Tennessee Press, 2001 ed.
Burlingame, Michael. *The Inner World of Abraham Lincoln*. Champaign, IL: University of Illinois Press, 1997.
Burns, James MacGregor, and Jack Walter Peltason. *Government by the People: The Dynamics of American National, State, and Local Government*. 1952. Englewood Cliffs, NJ: Prentice Hall, 1964 ed.
Burns, James MacGregor, Jack Walter Peltason, Thomas E. Cronin, David B. Magleby, and David M. O'Brien. *Government by the People* (National Version, 2001-2002 ed.). 1952. Upper Saddle River, NJ: Prentice Hall, 2002 ed.
Burrill, Emily, Richard Roberts, and Elizabeth Thornberry. *Domestic Violence and the Law in Colonial and Postcolonial Africa*. Athens, OH: Ohio University Press, 2010.
Burton, Robert. *The Anatomy of Melancholy*. 3 vols. 1621. London, UK: George Bell and Sons, 1896 ed.
Bushnell, Horace. *The Census and Slavery, Thanksgiving Discourse, Delivered in the Chapel at Clifton Springs, New

York, November 29, 1860. Hartford, CT: L. E. Hunt, 1860.
Butler, Benjamin Franklin. *Butler's Book (Autobiography and Personal Reminiscences of Major-General Benjamin F. Butler: A Review of His Legal, Political, and Military Career)*. Boston, MA: A. M. Thayer and Co., 1892.
Butler, Lindley S., and Alan D. Watson (eds.). *The North Carolina Experience: An Interpretive and Documentary History*. Chapel Hill, NC: University of North Carolina Press, 1984.
Butler, Trent C. (ed.). *Holman Bible Dictionary*. Nashville, TN: Holman Bible Publishers, 1991.
Calvert, Thomas H. *The Federal Statutes Annotated*. 10 vols. Northport, NY: Edward Thompson, 1905.
Cannon, Devereaux D., Jr. *The Flags of the Confederacy: An Illustrated History*. Memphis, TN: St. Luke's Press, 1988.
Carey, Matthew, Jr. (ed.). *The Democratic Speaker's Hand-Book*. Cincinnati, OH: Miami Print and Publishing Co., 1868.
Carlton, Frank Tracy. *Organized Labor in America*. New York, NY: D. Appleton and Co., 1920.
Carpenter, Stephen D. *Logic of History: Five Hundred Political Texts, Being Concentrated Extracts of Abolitionism*. Madison, WI: Stephen D. Carpenter, 1864.
Cartmell, Donald. *Civil War 101*. New York, NY: Gramercy, 2001.
Cash, W. J. *The Mind of the South*. 1941. New York, NY: Vintage, 1969.
Catton, Bruce. *The Coming Fury* (Vol. 1). 1961. New York, NY: Washington Square Press, 1967 ed.
——. *Terrible Swift Sword* (Vol. 2). 1963. New York, NY: Pocket Books, 1967 ed.
——. *A Stillness at Appomattox* (Vol. 3). 1953. New York, NY: Pocket Books, 1966 ed.
Celeste, Sister Mary. *The Old World's Gifts to the New*. 1932. Long Prairie, MN: Neumann Press, 1999 ed.
Chambers, Robert (ed.). *The Book of Days: A Miscellany of Popular Antiquities in Connection with the Calender*. 2 vols. London, UK: W. and R. Chambers, 1883.
Channing, Steven A. *Confederate Ordeal: The Southern Home Front*. 1984. Morristown, NJ: Time-Life Books, 1989 ed.
Cheek, William F. *Black Resistance Before the Civil War*. Beverly Hills, CA: Glencoe Press, 1973.
Chesnut, Mary. *A Diary From Dixie: As Written by Mary Boykin Chesnut, Wife of James Chesnut, Jr., United States Senator from South Carolina, 1859-1861, and afterward an Aide to Jefferson Davis and a Brigadier-General in the Confederate Army*. (Isabella D. Martin and Myrta Lockett Avary, eds.). New York, NY: D. Appleton and Co., 1905 ed.
——. *Mary Chesnut's Civil War*. 1860-1865 (Woodward, Comer Vann, ed.). New Haven, CT: Yale University Press, 1981 ed.
Chodes, John. *Destroying the Republic: Jabez Curry and the Re-Education of the Old South*. New York, NY: Algora, 2005.
Christian, George L. *Abraham Lincoln: An Address Delivered Before R. E. Lee Camp, No. 1 Confederate Veterans at Richmond, VA, October 29, 1909*. Richmond, VA: L. H. Jenkins, 1909.
Cimprich, John. *Fort Pillow, a Civil War Massacre, and Public Memory*. Baton Rouge, LA: Louisiana State University Press, 2005.
Cisco, Walter Brian. *States Rights Gist: A South Carolina General of the Civil War*. 1991. Gretna, LA: Pelican Publishing Co., 2008 ed.
——. *War Crimes Against Southern Civilians*. Gretna, LA: Pelican Publishing Co., 2007.
Civil War Society, The. *Civil War Battles: An Illustrated Encyclopedia*. 1997. New York, NY: Gramercy, 1999 ed.
——. *The Civil War Society's Encyclopedia of the Civil War*. 1997. New York, NY: Wings Books.
Clark, L. Pierce. *Lincoln: A Psycho-Biography*. New York, NY: Charles Scribner's Sons, 1933.
Clarke, James W. *The Lineaments of Wrath: Race, Violent Crime, and American Culture*. 1998. New Brunswick, NJ: Transaction, 2001 ed.
Clayton, W. Woodford. *History of Davidson County, Tennessee, with Illustrations and Biographical Sketches of its Prominent Men and Pioneers*. Bristol, Avon, UK: J. W. Lewis and Co., 1880.
Clinton, Catherine. *The Plantation Mistress: Woman's World in the Old South*. New York, NY: Pantheon, 1982.
Cluskey, Michael W. (ed.). *The Political Text-Book, or Encyclopedia*. Philadelphia, PA: Jas. B. Smith, 1859 ed.
Cmiel, Kenneth. *Democratic Eloquence: The Fight Over Popular Speech in Nineteenth-Century America*. Berkeley, CA: University of California Press, 1990.

THE MCGAVOCKS OF CARNTON PLANTATION

Coe, Joseph. *The True American.* Concord, NH: I. S. Boyd, 1840.
Coffin, Charles Carleton. *Abraham Lincoln.* New York, NY: Harper and Brothers, 1893.
Coit, Margaret L. *John C. Calhoun: American Portrait.* Boston, MA: Houghton Mifflin/Sentry, 1950.
Collier, Christopher, and James Lincoln Collier. *Decision in Philadelphia: The Constitutional Convention of 1787.* 1986. New York, NY: Ballantine, 1987 ed.
Collins, Elizabeth. *Memories of the Southern States.* Taunton, UK: J. Barnicott, 1865.
Collins, John A. (ed.). *The Anti-Slavery Picknick: A Collection of Speeches, Poems, Dialogues and Songs Intended for Use in Schools and Anti-Slavery Meetings.* Boston, MA: H. W. Williams, 1842.
Commager, Henry Steele, and Erik Bruun (eds.). *The Civil War Archive: The History of the Civil War in Documents.* 1950. New York, NY: Black Dog and Leventhal, 1973 ed.
Conkin, Paul K. *The Southern Agrarians.* Nashville, TN: Vanderbilt University Press, 2001.
Connelly, Thomas Lawrence. *Army of the Heartland: The Army of Tennessee, 1861-1862.* 1967. Baton Rouge, LA: Louisiana State University Press, 2001.
———. *Autumn of Glory: The Army of Tennessee, 1862-1865.* 1970. Baton Rouge, LA: Louisiana State University Press, 2001.
Connelley, William Elsey, and Ellis Merton Coulter. *History of Kentucky.* 5 vols. Chicago, IL: The American Historical Society, 1922.
Conner, Frank. *The South Under Siege, 1830-2000: A History of the Relations Between the North and the South.* Newnan, GA: Collards, 2002.
Conway, Moncure Daniel. *Testimonies Concerning Slavery.* London, UK: Chapman and Hall, 1865.
Cooke, Alistair. *Alistair Cooke's America.* 1973. New York, NY: Alfred A. Knopf, 1984 ed.
Cooke, John Esten. *A Life of General Robert E. Lee.* New York, NY: D. Appleton and Co., 1871.
Cooley, Henry S. *A Study of Slavery in New Jersey.* Baltimore, MD: Johns Hopkins University Press, 1896.
Cooper, William J., Jr. *Jefferson Davis, American.* New York, NY: Vintage Books, 2000.
———. (ed.). *Jefferson Davis: The Essential Writings.* New York, NY: Random House, 2003.
Cornish, Dudley Taylor. *The Sable Arm: Black Troops in the Union Army, 1861-1865.* 1956. Lawrence, KS: University Press of Kansas, 1987.
Coulter, Ann. *Guilty: Liberal "Victims" and Their Assault on America.* New York, NY: Three Rivers Press, 2009.
Council, R. Bruce, Nicholas Honerkamp, and M. Elizabeth Will. *Industry and Technology in Antebellum Tennessee: The Archaeology of Bluff Furnace.* Knoxville, TN: University of Tennessee Press, 1992.
Cox, Jacob Dolson. *The Battle of Franklin Tennessee, November 30, 1864: A Monograph.* New York, NY: Charles Scribner's Sons, 1897.
Crallé, Richard Kenner. (ed.). *The Works of John C. Calhoun.* 6 vols. New York: NY: D. Appleton and Co., 1853-1888.
Craven, John J. *Prison Life of Jefferson Davis.* New York: NY: Carelton, 1866.
Crawford, Samuel Wylie. *The Genesis of the Civil War: The Story of Sumter, 1860-1861.* New York, NY: Charles L. Webster and Co., 1887.
Crocker, H. W., III. *The Politically Incorrect Guide to the Civil War.* Washington, D.C.: Regnery, 2008.
Cromie, Alice Hamilton. *A Tour Guide to the Civil War: The Complete State-by-State Guide to Battlegrounds, Landmarks, Museums, Relics, and Sites.* 1964. Nashville, TN: Rutledge Hill Press, 1990 ed.
Cromwell, John Wesley. *The Negro in American History: Men and Women Eminent in the Evolution of the American of African Descent.* Washington, D.C.: American Negro Academy, 1914.
Cross, F. L., and F. A. Livingston (eds.). *The Oxford Dictionary of the Christian Church.* 1957. London, UK: Oxford University Press, 1974 ed.
Crutchfield, James Andrew. *Williamson County: A Pictorial History.* Virginia Beach, VA: Donning Co., 1980.
———. *A Heritage of Grandeur.* Franklin, TN: Carnton Association, 1981.
———. *Tennesseans at War: Volunteers and Patriots in Defense of Liberty.* Nashville, TN: Rutledge Hill Press, 1988.
———. *On This Day: A Brief History of Nashville and Middle Tennessee.* Franklin, TN: Cool Springs Press, 1995.
———. *Franklin: A Photographic Recollection.* 2 vols. Franklin, TN: Canaday Enterprises, 1996.
———. *The Natchez Trace: A Pictorial History.* Nashville, TN: Rutledge Hill Press, 2000.
———. *It Happened in the Old South: Remarkable Events That Shaped History.* Guilford, CT: The Globe Pequot Press, 2009.
Crutchfield, James A., and Robert Holladay. *Franklin: Tennessee's Handsomest Town.* Franklin, TN: Hillsboro

Press, 1999.
Cummins, Joseph. *Anything For a Vote: Dirty Tricks, Cheap Shots, and October Surprises in U.S. Presidential Campaigns*. Philadelphia, PA: Quirk, 2007.
Cunningham, Horace Herndon. *Doctors in Gray: The Confederate Medical Service*. 1958. Baton Rouge, LA: Louisiana State University Press, 1993 ed.
Current, Richard N. *The Lincoln Nobody Knows*. 1958. New York, NY: Hill and Wang, 1963 ed.
———. (ed.) *The Confederacy (Information Now Encyclopedia)*. 1993. New York, NY: Macmillan, 1998 ed.
Curry, Leonard P. *Blueprint for Modern America: Nonmilitary Legislation of the First Civil War Congress*. Nashville, TN: Vanderbilt University Press, 1968.
Curti, Merle, Willard Thorpe, and Carlos Baker (eds.). *American Issues: The Social Record*. 1941. Chicago, IL: J. B. Lippincott, 1960 ed.
Curtin, Philip D. *The Atlantic Slave Trade: A Census*. Madison, WI: University of Wisconsin Press, 1969.
———. *The Rise and Fall of the Plantation Complex: Essays in Atlantic History*. 1990. Cambridge, UK: Cambridge University Press, 1999 ed.
Curtis, George Ticknor. *Life of James Buchanan: Fifteenth President of the United States*. 2 vols. New York, NY: Harper and Brothers, 1883.
Curtis, William Eleroy. *Abraham Lincoln*. Philadelphia, PA: J. B. Lippincott Co., 1902.
Cushman, Horatio Bardwell. *History of the Choctaw, Chickasaw and Natchez Indians*. Greenville, TX: Headlight Printing House, 1899.
Custer, George Armstrong. *Wild Life on the Plains and Horrors of Indian Warfare*. St. Louis, MO: Excelsior Publishing, 1891.
Dabney, Robert Lewis. *A Defense of Virginia and the South*. Dahlonega, GA: Confederate Reprint Co., 1999.
Dalrymple, Theodore. *Our Culture, What's Left of It*. Chicago, IL: Ivan R. Dee, 2005.
Dammann, Gordon. *Pictorial Encyclopedia of Civil War Medical Instruments and Equipment*. Missoula, MT: Pictorial Histories Publishing Co., 1983.
Daniel, John M. *The Richmond Examiner During the War*. New York, NY: John M. Daniel, 1868.
Daniel, John W. *Life and Reminiscences of Jefferson Davis by Distinguished Men of His Time*. Baltimore, MD: R. H. Woodward, and Co., 1890.
Daniel, Larry J. *Soldiering in the Army of Tennessee: A Portrait of Life in a Confederate Army*. Chapel Hill, NC: University of North Carolina Press, 1991.
Darwin, Charles. *On the Origin of Species By Means of Natural Selection*. London, UK: John Murray, 1866.
Daugherty, James. *Abraham Lincoln*. 1943. New York, NY: Scholastic Book Services, 1966.
Davenport, Robert R. *Roots of the Rich and Famous: Real Cases of Unlikely Lineage*. Dallas, TX: Taylor Publishing Co., 1998.
Davidson, Basil. *The African Slave Trade*. 1961. Boston, MA: Back Bay Books, 1980 ed.
Davie, Maurice R. *Negroes in American Society*. New York, NY: McGraw-Hill, 1949.
Davis, Jefferson. *The Rise and Fall of the Confederate Government*. 2 vols. New York, NY: D. Appleton and Co., 1881.
———. *A Short History of the Confederate States of America*. New York, NY: Belford, 1890.
Davis, Kenneth C. *Don't Know Much About the Civil War: Everything You Need to Know About America's Greatest Conflict But Never Learned*. 1996. New York, NY: HarperCollins, 1997 ed.
Davis, Michael. *The Image of Lincoln in the South*. Knoxville, TN: University of Tennessee Press, 1971.
Davis, William C. *Jefferson Davis: The Man and His Hour*. New York, NY: HarperCollins, 1991.
———. *An Honorable Defeat: The Last Days of the Confederate Government*. New York, NY: Harcourt, Inc., 2001.
———. *Look Away: A History of the Confederate States of America*. 2002. New York, NY: The Free Press, 2003 ed.
Davis, Varina. *Jefferson Davis: Ex-President of the Confederate States of America - A Memoir by His Wife*. 2 vols. New York, NY: Belford Co., 1890.
Dawson, Sarah Morgan. *A Confederate Girl's Diary*. London, UK: William Heinemann, 1913.
De Angelis, Gina. *It Happened in Washington, D.C.* Guilford, CT: The Globe Pequot Press, 2004.
Dean, Henry Clay. *Crimes of the Civil War, and Curse of the Funding System*. Baltimore, MD: William T. Smithson, 1869.
DeCaro, Louis A., Jr. *Fire From the Midst of You: A Religious Life of John Brown*. New York, NY: New York University Press, 2002.

Deems, Edward Mark. *Holy-Days and Holidays: A Treasury of Historical Material, Sermons in Full and Brief, Suggestive Thoughts, and Poetry*. New York, NY: Funk and Wagnalls, 1902.
De Forest, John William. *A Volunteer's Adventures: A Union Captain's Record of the Civil War*. 1946. North Haven, CT: Archon, 1970 ed.
DeGregorio, William A. *The Complete Book of U.S. Presidents*. 1984. New York, NY: Barricade, 1993 ed.
Delbanco, Andrew. *The Portable Abraham Lincoln*. New York, NY: Penguin, 1992.
Deloria, Vine, Jr. *Custer Died For Your Sins: An Indian Manifesto*. 1969. New York, NY: Avon, 1973 ed.
Denney, Robert E. *The Civil War Years: A Day-by-Day Chronicle of the Life of a Nation*. 1992. New York, NY: Sterling Publishing, 1994 ed.
Denson, John V. (ed.). *Reassessing the Presidency: The Rise of the Executive State and the Decline of Freedom*. Auburn, AL: Mises Institute, 2001.
Derosa, Marshall L. *The Confederate Constitution of 1861: An Inquiry into American Constitutionalism*. Columbia, MO: University of Missouri Press, 1991.
Desty, Robert. *The Constitution of the United States*. San Francisco, CA: Sumner Whitney and Co., 1881.
Diamond, Jared. *Guns, Germs, and Steel: The Fate of Human Societies*. 1997. New York, NY: W. W. Norton and Co., 1999 ed.
Dicey, Edward. *Six Months in the Federal States*. 2 vols. London, UK: Macmillan and Co., 1863.
DiLorenzo, Thomas J. "The Great Centralizer: Abraham Lincoln and the War Between the States." *The Independent Review*, Vol. 3, No. 2, Fall 1998, pp. 243-271.
——. *The Real Lincoln: A New Look at Abraham Lincoln, His Agenda, and an Unnecessary War*. Three Rivers, MI: Three Rivers Press, 2003.
——. *Lincoln Unmasked: What You're Not Supposed to Know About Dishonest Abe*. New York, NY: Crown Forum, 2006.
——. *Hamilton's Curse: How Jefferson's Archenemy Betrayed the American Revolution—and What It Means for America Today*. New York, NY: Crown Forum, 2008.
Dinkins, James. *1861 to 1865: Personal Recollections and Experiences in the Confederate Army, by an "Old Johnnie"*. Cincinnati, OH: Robert Clarke, 1897.
Doddridge, Joseph. *Notes on the Settlement and Indian Wars of the Western Parts of Virginia and Pennsylvania, From 1763 to 1783, Inclusive*. Albany, NY: Joel Munsell, 1876.
Donald, David Herbert. *Lincoln Reconsidered: Essays on the Civil War Era*. 1947. New York, NY: Vintage Press, 1989 ed.
——. (ed.). *Why the North Won the Civil War*. 1960. New York, NY: Collier, 1962 ed.
——. *Lincoln*. New York, NY: Simon and Schuster, 1995.
Dorward, David. *Scottish Surnames: A Guide to the Family Names of Scotland*. Glasgow, Scotland: HarperCollins, 1995.
Douglas, Henry Kyd. *I Rode With Stonewall: The War Experiences of the Youngest Member of Jackson's Staff*. 1940. Chapel Hill, NC: University of North Carolina Press, 1968 ed.
Douglass, Frederick. *Narrative of the Life of Frederick Douglass: An American Slave*. 1845. Reprint. New York, NY: Signet, 1997.
——. *The Life and Times of Frederick Douglass, From 1817 to 1882*. London, UK: Christian Age Office, 1882.
Doyle, Don H. *New Men, New Cities, New South: Atlanta, Nashville, Charleston, Mobile, 1860-1910*. Chapel Hill, NC: University of North Carolina Press, 1990.
Drescher, Seymour, and Stanley L. Engerman (eds.). *A Historical Guide to World Slavery*. New York, NY: Oxford University Press, 1998.
Du Bois, William Edward Burghardt. *Darkwater: Voices From Within the Veil*. New York, NY: Harcourt, Brace and Howe, 1920.
DuBose, John Witherspoon. *General Joseph Wheeler and the Army of Tennessee*. New York, NY: Neale Publishing Co., 1912.
Duff, Mountstuart E. Grant. *Notes From a Diary, 1851-1872*. 2 vols. London, UK: John Murray, 1897.
Duke, Basil W. *Reminiscences of General Basil W. Duke, C.S.A.* New York, NY: Doubleday, Page and Co., 1911.
Dunbar, Rowland (ed.). *Jefferson Davis, Constitutionalist: His Letters, Papers, and Speeches*. 10 vols. Jackson, MS: Mississippi Department of Archives and History, 1923.

THE MCGAVOCKS OF CARNTON PLANTATION

Durden, Robert F. *The Gray and the Black: The Confederate Debate on Emancipation.* Baton Rouge, LA: Louisiana State University Press, 1972.
Early, Jubal A. *A Memoir of the Last Year of the War for Independence in the Confederate States of America.* Lynchburg, VA: Charles W. Button, 1867.
Eaton, Clement. *A History of the Southern Confederacy.* 1945. New York, NY: The Free Press, 1966 ed.
———. *Jefferson Davis.* New York, NY: The Free Press, 1977.
Eaton, John, and Ethel Osgood Mason. *Grant, Lincoln and the Freedmen: Reminiscences of the Civil War, With Special Reference to the Work of the Contrabands and Freedmen of the Mississippi Valley.* New York, NY: Longmans, Green, and Co., 1907.
Edmonds, Franklin Spencer. *Ulysses S. Grant.* Philadelphia, PA: George W. Jacobs and Co., 1915.
Elliot, Jonathan. *The Debates in the Several State Conventions on the Adoption of the Federal Constitution, As Recommended by the General Convention at Philadelphia in 1787.* 5 vols. Philadelphia, PA: J. B. Lippincott, 1891.
Elliott, E. N. *Cotton is King, and Pro-Slavery Arguments: Comprising the Writings of Hammond, Harper, Christy, Stringfellow, Hodge, Bledsoe, and Cartwright, on this Important Subject.* Augusta, GA: Pritchard, Abbott and Loomis, 1860.
Elliott, Sam Davis. *Isham G. Harris of Tennessee: Confederate Governor and United States Senator.* Baton Rouge, LA: Louisiana State University Press, 2010.
Ellis, Joseph J. *American Sphinx: The Character of Thomas Jefferson.* 1996. New York, NY: Vintage, 1998 ed.
———. *Founding Brothers: The Revolutionary Generation.* 2000. New York, NY: Vintage, 2002 ed.
Eltis, David. *The Rise of African Slavery in the Americas.* Cambridge, UK: Cambridge University Press, 2000.
Eltis, David, Stephen D. Behrendt, David Richardson, and Herbert S. Klein (eds.). *The Trans-Atlantic Slave Trade: A Database on CD-ROM.* Cambridge, UK: Cambridge University Press, 1999.
Emerson, Bettie Alder Calhoun. *Historic Southern Monuments: Representative Memorials of the Heroic Dead of the Southern Confederacy.* New York, NY: Neale Publishing Co., 1911.
Emerson, Ralph Waldo. *The Complete Works of Ralph Waldo Emerson.* 12 vols. 1878. Boston, MA: Houghton, Mifflin and Co., 1904 ed.
———. *Journals of Ralph Waldo Emerson.* 10 vols. Edward Waldo Emerson and Waldo Emerson Forbes, eds. Boston, MA: Houghton, Mifflin and Co., 1910.
———. *The Journals and Miscellaneous Notebooks of Ralph Waldo Emerson.* 16 vols. Cambridge, MA: Belknap Press, 1975.
Emison, John Avery. *Lincoln Über Alles: Dictatorship Comes to America.* Gretna, LA: Pelican Publishing Co., 2009.
Encyclopedia Britannica: A New Survey of Universal Knowledge. 1768. Chicago, IL/London, UK: Encyclopedia Britannica, 1955 ed.
Escott, Paul D. (ed.). *North Carolinians in the Era of the Civil War and Reconstruction.* Chapel Hill, NC: University of North Carolina Press, 2008.
Essah, Patience. *A House Divided: Slavery and Emancipation in Delaware, 1638-1865.* Charlottesville, VA: University Press of Virginia, 1996.
Evans, Clement Anselm (ed.). *Confederate Military History: A Library of Confederate States History, in Twelve Volumes, Written By Distinguished Men of the South.* 12 vols. Atlanta, GA: Confederate Publishing Co., 1899.
Evans, Eli N. *Judah P. Benjamin: The Jewish Confederate.* 1988. New York, NY: The Free Press, 1989 ed.
Evans, Lawrence B. (ed.). *Writings of George Washington.* New York, NY: G. P. Putnam's Sons, 1908.
Ewing, James, and James A. Crutchfield. *A Treasury of Tennessee Tales: Unusual, Interesting, and Little-Known Stories of Tennessee.* 1985. Nashville, TN: Rutledge Hill Press, 1997 ed.
Faragher, John Mack. *Sugar Creek: Life on the Illinois Prairie.* New Haven, CT: Yale University Press, 1986.
Farrar, Victor John. *The Annexation of Russian America to the United States.* Washington, D.C.: W. F. Roberts, 1937.
Farrow, Anne, Joel Lang, and Jennifer Frank. *Complicity: How the North Promoted, Prolonged, and Profited from Slavery.* New York, NY: Ballantine, 2005.
Faulkner, William. *The Unvanquished.* 1934. New York, NY: Vintage, 1966 ed.
Faust, Patricia L. (ed.). *Historical Times Illustrated Encyclopedia of the Civil War.* New York, NY: Harper and

Row, 1986.
Fay, Edwin Hedge. *This Infernal War: The Confederate Letters of Edwin H. Fay*. Austin, TX: University of Texas Press, 1958.
Fehrenbacher, Don E. (ed.). *Abraham Lincoln: A Documentary Portrait Through His Speeches and Writings*. New York, NY: Signet, 1964.
———. *Lincoln in Text and Context: Collected Essays*. Stanford, CA: Stanford University press, 1987.
———. (ed.) *Abraham Lincoln: Speeches and Writings, 1859-1865*. New York, NY: Library of America, 1989.
———. *The Slaveholding Republic: An Account of the United States Government's Relations to Slavery*. New York, NY: Oxford University Press, 2002.
Fehrenbacher, Don E., and Virginia Fehrenbacher (eds). *Recollected Works of Abraham Lincoln*. Stanford, CA: Stanford University Press, 1996.
Ferris, Marcie Cohen, and Mark I. Greenberg (eds.). *Jewish Roots in Southern Soil: A New History*. Waltham, MA: Brandeis University Press, 2006.
Fields, Annie (ed.) *Life and Letters of Harriet Beecher Stowe*. Cambridge, MA: Riverside Press, 1897.
Findlay, Bruce, and Esther Findlay. *Your Rugged Constitution: How America's House of Freedom is Planned and Built*. 1950. Stanford, CA: Stanford University Press, 1951 ed.
Fineseth, Ian Frederick. *The American Civil War: An Anthology of Essential Writings*. New York, NY: Routledge, 2006.
Finger, John R. *Tennessee Frontiers: Three Regions in Transition*. Bloomington, IN: Indiana University Press, 2001.
Finkelman, Paul. *Dred Scott v. Sanford: A Brief History With Documents*. Boston, MA: Bedford Books, 1997.
Fisher, John E. *They Rode With Forrest and Wheeler: A Chronicle of Five Tennessee Brothers' Service in the Confederate Western Cavalry*. Jefferson, NC: McFarland and Co., 1995.
Fite, Emerson David. *Social and Industrial Conditions in the North During the Civil War*. New York, NY: Macmillan, 1910.
———. *The Presidential Election of 1860*. New York, NY: MacMillan, 1911.
Fleming, Walter Lynwood. *Civil War and Reconstruction in Alabama*. New York, NY: Macmillan, 1905.
Flood, Charles Bracelen. *1864: Lincoln At the Gates of History*. New York, NY: Simon and Schuster, 2009.
Fogel, Robert William. *Without Consent or Contract: The Rise and Fall of American Slavery*. New York, NY: W. W. Norton, 1989.
Fogel, Robert William, and Stanley L. Engerman. *Time on the Cross: The Economics of American Negro Slavery*. Boston, MA: Little, Brown, and Co., 1974.
Foley, John P. (ed.). *The Jeffersonian Cyclopedia*. New York, NY: Funk and Wagnalls, 1900.
Foner, Eric. *Free Soil, Free Labor, Free Men: The Ideology of the Republican Party Before the Civil War*. New York, NY: Oxford University Press, 1970.
———. *History of Black Americans: From Africa to the Emergence of the Cotton Kingdom*. Westport, CT: Greenwood Press, 1975.
———. *Reconstruction: America's Unfinished Revolution, 1863-1877*. 1988. New York, NY: Harper and Row, 1989 ed.
Foner, Philip S., and Robert James Branham (eds.). *Lift Every Voice: African American Oratory, 1787-1900*. Tuscaloosa, AL: University of Alabama Press, 1998.
Foote, Shelby. *The Civil War: A Narrative, Fort Sumter to Perryville, Vol. 1*. 1958. New York, NY: Vintage, 1986, ed.
———. *The Civil War: A Narrative, Fredericksburg to Meridian, Vol. 2*. 1963. New York, NY: Vintage, 1986, ed.
———. *The Civil War: A Narrative, Red River to Appomattox, Vol. 3*. 1974. New York, NY: Vintage, 1986, ed.
Ford, Paul Leicester (ed.). *The Works of Thomas Jefferson*. 12 vols. New York, NY: G. P. Putnam's Sons, 1904.
Ford, Worthington Chauncey (ed.). *A Cycle of Adams Letters*. 2 vols. Boston, MA: Houghton Mifflin, 1920.
Foreman, Amanda. *A World on Fire: Britain's Crucial Role in the American Civil War*. New York, NY: Random House, 2010.
Forman, S. E. *The Life and Writings of Thomas Jefferson*. Indianapolis, IN: Bowen-Merrill, 1900.
Förster, Stig, and Jörg Nagler (eds.). *On the Road to Total War: The American Civil War and the Germans Wars of Unification, 1861-1871*. 1997. Cambridge, UK: Cambridge University Press, 2002 ed.

Foster, John W. *A Century of American Diplomacy*. Boston, MA: Houghton, Mifflin and Co., 1901.
Fowler, John D. *The Confederate Experience Reader: Selected Documents and Essays*. New York, NY: Routledge, 2007.
Fowler, William Chauncey. *The Sectional Controversy; or Passages in the Political History of the United States, Including the Causes of the War Between the Sections*. New York, NY: Charles Scribner, 1864.
Fox-Genovese, Elizabeth. *Within the Plantation Household: Black and White Women of the Old South*. Chapel Hill, NC: University of North Carolina Press, 1988.
Fox, Gustavus Vasa. *Confidential Correspondence of Gustavus Vasa Fox, Assistant Secretary of the Navy, 1861-1865* (Vol. 1). 1918. New York, NY: Naval History Society, 1920 ed.
Franklin, Benjamin. *The Life and Writings of Benjamin Franklin*. 2 vols. Philadelphia, PA: McCarty and Davis, 1834.
———. *The Complete Works of Benjamin Franklin*. 10 vols. New York, NY: G. P. Putnam's Sons, 1887.
Franklin, John Hope. *Reconstruction After the Civil War*. Chicago, IL: University of Chicago Press, 1961.
Fredrickson, George M. *The Black Image in the White Mind: The Debate on Afro-American Character and Destiny, 1817-1914*. New York, NY: Harper and Row, 1971.
Freemon, Frank R. *Gangrene and Glory: Medical Care During the American Civil War*. 1998. Urbana, IL: University of Illinois Press, 2001 ed.
Fremantle, Arthur James. *Three Months in the Southern States, April-June, 1863*. New York, NY: John Bradburn, 1864.
Friedman, Saul S. *Jews and the American Slave Trade*. New Brunswick, NJ: Transaction, 2000.
Furguson, Ernest B. *Freedom Rising: Washington in the Civil War*. 2004. New York, NY: Vintage, 2005 ed.
Furnas, J. C. *The Americans: A Social History of the United States, 1587-1914*. New York, NY: G. P. Putnam's Sons, 1969.
Galenson, David W. *White Servitude in Colonial America*. Cambridge, UK: Cambridge University Press, 1981.
Garland, Hugh A. *The Life of John Randolph of Roanoke*. New York, NY: D. Appleton and Co., 1874.
Garlow, James L. *The Da Vinci Code Breaker*. Bloomington, MN: Bethany House, 2006.
Garraty, John A. (ed.). *Historical Viewpoints: Notable Articles from American Heritage* (Vol. 1 to 1877). 1970. New York, NY: Harper and Row, 1979 ed.
Garraty, John A., and Robert A. McCaughey. *A Short History of the American Nation*. 1966. New York, NY: HarperCollins, 1989 ed.
Garrett, William Robertson, and Albert Virgil Goodpasture. *History of Tennessee: Its People and Its Institutions, From the Earliest Times to the Year 1903*. Nashville, TN: Brandon Co., 1903.
Garrison, Webb B. *Civil War Trivia and Fact Book*. Nashville, TN: Rutledge Hill Press, 1992.
———. *The Lincoln No One Knows: The Mysterious Man Who Ran the Civil War*. Nashville, TN: Rutledge Hill Press, 1993.
———. *Civil War Curiosities: Strange Stories, Oddities, Events, and Coincidences*. Nashville, TN: Rutledge Hill Press, 1994.
———. *The Amazing Civil War*. Nashville, TN: Rutledge Hill Press, 1998.
Garrison, Wendell Phillips, and Francis Jackson Garrison. *William Lloyd Garrison, 1805-1879*. 4 vols. New York, NY: Century Co., 1889.
Garrison, William Lloyd. *Thoughts on African Colonization*. Boston, MA: Garrison and Knapp, 1832.
Gates, Henry Louis, Jr. (ed.) *The Classic Slave Narratives*. New York, NY: Mentor, 1987.
Genovese, Eugene D. *Roll, Jordan, Roll: The World the Slaves Made*. New York, NY: Pantheon, 1974.
Gentry, Jimmy. *An American Life*. Franklin, TN: Pleasantview Press, 2002.
Gerster, Patrick, and Nicholas Cords (eds.). *Myth and Southern History*. 2 vols. 1974. Champaign, IL: University of Illinois Press, 1989 ed.
Gerzina, Gretchen Holbrook. *Black London*. New Brunswick, NJ: Rutgers University Press, 1995.
Gilbert, Oliver. *Narrative of Sojourner Truth: A Bondswoman of Olden Time, Emancipated by the New York Legislature in the Early Part of the Present Century; With a History Drawn from Her "Book of Life."* Boston, MA: n.p., 1875.
Golay, Michael. *A Ruined Land: The End of the Civil War*. New York, NY: John Wiley and Sons, 1999.
Goodman, Nathan G. (ed.). *A Benjamin Franklin Reader*. New York, NY: Thomas Y. Crowell Co., 1945.
Gordon, Armistead Churchill. *Figures from American History: Jefferson Davis*. New York, NY: Charles

Scribner's Sons, 1918.
Gower, Herschel, and Jack Allen (eds.). *Pen and Sword: The Life and Journals of Randal W. McGavock.* Nashville, TN: Tennessee Historical Commission, 1959.
Gragg, Rod. *The Illustrated Confederate Reader: Extraordinary Eyewitness Accounts by the Civil War's Southern Soldiers and Civilians.* New York, NY: Gramercy Books, 1989.
Graham, John Remington. *A Constitutional History of Secession.* Gretna, LA: Pelican Publishing Co., 2003.
———. *Blood Money: The Civil War and the Federal Reserve.* Gretna, LA: Pelican Publishing Co., 2006.
Graham, Lloyd M. *Deceptions and Myths of the Bible.* 1975. New York, NY: Citadel Press, 1991 ed.
Grant, Arthur James. *Greece in the Age of Pericles.* London, UK: John Murray, 1893.
Grant, Ulysses Simpson. *Personal Memoirs of U. S. Grant.* 2 vols. 1885-1886. New York, NY: Charles L. Webster and Co., 1886.
Gray, Robert, Rev. (compiler). *The McGavock Family: A Genealogical History of James McGavock and His Descendants, from 1760 to 1903.* Richmond, VA: W. E. Jones, 1903.
Gray, Thomas R. *The Confessions of Nat Turner: The Leader of the Late Insurrection in Southampton, Virginia.* Richmond, VA: Thomas R. Gray, 1831.
Greeley, Horace (ed.). *The Writings of Cassius Marcellus Clay.* New York, NY: Harper and Brothers, 1848.
———. *A History of the Struggle for Slavery Extension or Restriction in the United States From the Declaration of Independence to the Present Day.* New York, NY: Dix, Edwards and Co., 1856.
———. *The American Conflict: A History of the Great Rebellion in the United States, 1861-1865.* 2 vols. Hartford, CT: O. D. Case and Co., 1867.
Green, Constance McLaughlin. *Eli Whitney and the Birth of American Technology.* Boston, MA: Little, Brown, and Company, 1956.
———. *Washington: A History of the Capital, 1800-1950.* 1962. Princeton, NJ: Princeton University Press, 1976 ed.
Greenberg, Martin H., and Charles G. Waugh (eds.). *The Price of Freedom: Slavery and the Civil War —Vol. 1, The Demise of Slavery.* Nashville, TN: Cumberland House, 2000.
Greene, Lorenzo Johnston. *The Negro in Colonial New England, 1620-1776.* New York, NY: Columbia University Press, 1942.
Greenhow, Rose O'Neal. *My Imprisonment and the First Year of Abolition Rule at Washington.* London, UK: Richard Bentley, 1863.
Grime, John Harvey. *History of Middle Tennessee Baptists.* Nashville, TN: Baptist and Reflector, 1902.
Grimké, Angelina Emily. *Letters to Catherine E. Beecher, in Reply to an Essay on Slavery and Abolitionism.* Boston, MA: Angelina Emily Grimké, 1838.
Grimsley, Mark. *The Hard Hand of War: Union Military Policy Toward Southern Civilians, 1861-1865.* 1995. Cambridge, UK: Cambridge University Press, 1997 ed.
Grissom, Michael Andrew. *Southern by the Grace of God.* 1988. Gretna, LA: Pelican Publishing Co., 1995 ed.
Groce, W. Todd. *Mountain Rebels: East Tennessee Confederates and the Civil War, 1860-1870.* Knoxville, TN: University of Tennessee Press, 1999.
Groom, Winston. *Shrouds of Glory - From Atlanta to Nashville: The Last Great Campaign of the Civil War.* New York, NY: Grove Press, 1995.
Guelzo, Allen C. *Abraham Lincoln as a Man of Ideas.* Carbondale, IL: Southern Illinois University Press, 2009.
Guy, Joe. *The Hidden History of East Tennessee.* Charleston, SC: The History Press, 2008.
Gwatkin, H. M., and J. P. Whitney (eds.). *The Cambridge Medieval History, Vol. 2: The Rise of the Saracens and the Foundation of the Western Empire.* New York, NY: Macmillan, 1913.
Hacker, Louis Morton. *The Shaping of the American Tradition.* New York, NY: Columbia University Press, 1947.
Hagerman, Edward. *The American Civil War and the Origins of Modern Warfare: Ideas, Organization, and Field Command.* Bloomington, IN: Indiana University Press, 1992.
Hale, Will Thomas, and Dixon Lanier Merritt: *A History of Tennessee and Tennesseans.* 8 vols. Chicago, IL: Lewis Publishing Co., 1913.
Hall, B. C., and C. T. Wood. *The South: A Two-step Odyssey on the Backroads of the Enchanted Land.* New York, NY: Touchstone, 1996.

Hall, Clifton Rumery. *Andrew Johnson: Military Governor of Tennessee*. Princeton, NJ: Princeton University Press, 1916.
Hall, Kermit L. (ed). *The Oxford Companion to the Supreme Court of the United States*. New York, NY: Oxford University Press, 1992.
Hamblin, Ken. *Pick a Better Country: An Unassuming Colored Guy Speaks His Mind About America*. New York, NY: Touchstone, 1997.
Hamilton, Alexander, James Madison, and John Jay. *The Federalist Papers*. New York, NY: Signet Classics, 2003.
Hamilton, Neil A. *Rebels and Renegades: A Chronology of Social and Political Dissent in the United States*. New York, NY: Routledge, 2002.
Hannity, Sean. *Let Freedom Ring: Winning the War of Liberty Over Liberalism*. New York, NY: HarperCollins, 2002.
Hansen, Harry. *The Civil War: A History*. 1961. Harmondsworth, UK: Mentor, 1991 ed.
Hanson, Victor Davis. *Fields Without Dreams : Defending the Agrarian Ideal*. New York, NY: The Free Press, 1996.
Harding, Samuel Bannister. *The Contest Over the Ratification of the Federal Constitution in the State of Massachusetts*. New York, NY: Longmans, Green, and Co., 1896.
Harper, William, James Henry Hammond, William Gilmore Simms, and Thomas Roderick Dew. *The Pro-Slavery Argument, As Maintained by the Most Distinguished Writers of the Southern States*. Charleston, SC: Walker, Richards and Co., 1852.
Harrell, David Edwin, Jr., Edwin S. Gaustad, John B. Boles, Sally Foreman Griffith, Randall M. Miller, and Randall B. Woods. *Unto a Good Land: A History of the American People*. Grand Rapids, MI: William B. Eerdmans, 2005.
Harris, Joel Chandler. *Stories of Georgia*. New York, NY: American Book Co., 1896.
Harris, Lee. *The Next American Civil War: The Populist Revolt Against the Liberal Elite*. New York, NY: Palgrave Macmillan, 2010.
Harris, Norman Dwight. *The History of Negro Servitude in Illinois*. Chicago, IL: A. C. McClurg and Co., 1904.
Harrison, Peleg D. *The Stars and Stripes and Other American Flags*. 1906. Boston, MA: Little, Brown, and Co., 1908 ed.
Hartzell, Josiah. *The Genesis of the Republican Party*. Canton, OH: n.p., 1890.
Harwell, Richard B. (ed.). *The Confederate Reader: How the South Saw the War*. 1957. Mineola, NY: Dover, 1989 ed.
Haskins, Susan. *Mary Magdalene: Myth and Metaphor*. New York, NY: Harcourt Brace, 1993.
Hattaway, Herman, and Archer Jones. *How the North Won: A Military History of the Civil War*. 1983. Champaign, IL: University of Illinois Press, 1991 ed.
Hawthorne, Julian (ed.). *Orations of American Orators*. 2 vols. New York, NY: Colonial Press, 1900.
Hawthorne, Julian, James Schouler, and Elisha Benjamin Andrews. *United States, From the Discovery of the North American Continent Up to the Present Time*. 9 vols. New York, NY: Co-operative Publication Society, 1894.
Hawthorne, Nathaniel. *The Works of Nathaniel Hawthorne*. 15 vols. 1860. Boston, MA: Houghton, Mifflin and Co., 1883 ed.
Haygood, Atticus G. *Our Brother in Black: His Freedom and His Future*. Nashville, TN: M. E. Church, 1896.
Haywood, John. *Civil and Political History of Tennessee*. 1981. Johnson City, TN: Overmountain Press, 1999 ed.
Hedrick, Joan D. (ed.). *The Oxford Harriet Beecher Stowe Reader*. New York, NY: Oxford University Press, 1999.
Heidler, David Stephen, and Jeanne T. Heidler (eds.). *Encyclopedia of the American Civil War: A Political, Social, and Military History*. New York, NY: W. W. Norton and Co., 2000.
Heiskell, Samuel Gordon. *Andrew Jackson and Early Tennessee History*. 2 vols. 1918. Nashville, TN: Ambrose Printing Co., 1920 ed.
Helper, Hinton Rowan. *The Impending Crisis of the South: How to Meet It*. New York, NY: A. B. Burdick, 1860.
———. *Compendium of the Impending Crisis of the South*. New York, NY: A. B. Burdick, 1860.

———. *Nojoque: A Question for a Continent*. New York, NY: George W. Carleton, 1867.
———. *The Negroes in Negroland: The Negroes in America; and Negroes Generally*. New York, NY: George W. Carlton, 1868.
———. *Oddments of Andean Diplomacy and Other Oddments*. St. Louis, MO: W. S. Bryan, 1879.
Henderson, George Francis Robert. *Stonewall Jackson and the American Civil War*. 2 vols. London, UK: Longmans, Green, and Co., 1919.
Henry, Robert Selph (ed.). *The Story of the Confederacy*. 1931. New York, NY: Konecky and Konecky, 1999 ed.
———. *As They Saw Forrest: Some Recollections and Comments of Contemporaries*. 1956. Wilmington, NC: Broadfoot Publishing Co., 1991 ed.
———. *First with the Most: Forrest*. New York, NY: Konecky and Konecky, 1992.
Henson, Josiah. *Father Henson's Story of His Own Life*. Boston, MA: John P. Jewett and Co., 1858.
Herndon, William H., and Jesse W. Weik. *Abraham Lincoln: The True Story of a Great Life*. New York, NY: D. Appleton and Co., 1909.
Hertz, Emanuel. *Abraham Lincoln: A New Portrait*. 2 Vols. New York, NY: H. Liveright, 1931.
———. *The Hidden Lincoln*. New York, NY: Blue Ribbon Works, 1940.
Hervey, Anthony. *Why I Wave the Confederate Flag, Written by a Black Man: The End of Niggerism and the Welfare State*. Oxford, UK: Trafford Publishing, 2006.
Hesseltine, William B. *Lincoln and the War Governors*. New York, NY: Alfred A. Knopf, 1948.
Hey, David. *The Oxford Guide to Family History*. Oxford, UK: Oxford University Press, 1993.
Hickey, William. *The Constitution of the United States*. Philadelphia, PA: T. K. and P. G. Collins, 1853.
Higginbotham, A. Leon, Jr. *In the Matter of Color: Race and the American Legal Process: The Colonial Period*. 1978. Oxford, UK: Oxford University Press, 1980 ed.
Highsmith, Carol M. and Ted Landphair. *Civil War Battlefields and Landmarks: A Photographic Tour*. New York, NY: Random House, 2003.
Hildreth, Richard. *The White Slave: Another Picture of Slave Life in America*. Boston, MA: Adamant Media Corp., 2001.
Hinkle, Don. *Embattled Banner: A Reasonable Defense of the Confederate Battle Flag*. Paducah, KY: Turner Publishing Co., 1997.
Hitler, Adolf. *Mein Kampf*. 2 vols. 1925, 1926. New York: NY: Reynal and Hitchcock, 1941 English translation ed.
Hoffer, Peter Charles. *The Great New York Conspiracy of 1741: Slavery, Crime, and Colonial Law*. Lawrence, KS: University Press of Kansas, 2003.
Hoffman, Michael A., II. *They Were White and They Were Slaves: The Untold History of the Enslavement of Whites in Early America*. Dresden, NY: Wiswell Ruffin House, 1993.
Hofstadter, Richard. *The American Political Tradition, and the Men Who Made It*. New York, NY: Knopf, 1948.
Holland, Jesse J. *Black Men Built the Capitol: Discovering African-American History in and Around Washington, D.C.* Guilford, CT: The Globe Pequot Press, 2007.
Holland, Josiah Gilbert. *The Life of Abraham Lincoln*. Springfield, MA: Gurdon Bill, 1866.
Holland, Rupert Sargent (ed.). *Letters and Diary of Laura M. Towne: Written From the Sea Islands of South Carolina, 1862-1884*. Cambridge, MA: Riverside Press, 1912.
Holzer, Harold (ed.). *The Lincoln-Douglas Debates: The First Complete, Unexpurgated Text*. 1993. Bronx, NY: Fordham University Press, 2004 ed.
Hood, John Bell. *Advance and Retreat: Personal Experiences in the United States and Confederate States Armies*. New Orleans, LA: G. T. Beauregard, 1880.
Horn, Stanley F. *Invisible Empire: The Story of the Ku Klux Klan, 1866-1871*. 1939. Montclair, NJ: Patterson Smith, 1969 ed.
———. *The Decisive Battle of Nashville*. 1956. Baton Rouge, LA: Louisiana State University Press, 1991 ed.
Horwitz, Tony. *Confederates in the Attic: Dispatches from the Unfinished Civil War*. 1998. New York, NY: Vintage, 1999 ed.
House Documents, 64th Congress, 1st Session, December 6, 1915, to September 8, 1916, Vol. 145. Washington, D.C.: Government Printing Office, 1916.
Howe, Daniel Wait. *Political History of Secession*. New York, NY: G. P. Putnam's Sons, 1914.

THE MCGAVOCKS OF CARNTON PLANTATION

Howe, Henry. *Historical Collections of Virginia.* Charleston, SC: William R. Babcock, 1852.
Howe, M. A. DeWolfe (ed.). *Home Letters of General Sherman.* New York, NY: Charles Scribner's Sons, 1909.
Hubbard, John Milton. *Notes of a Private.* St. Louis, MO: Nixon-Jones, 1911.
Hummel, Jeffrey Rogers. *Emancipating Slaves, Enslaving Free Men: A History of the American Civil War.* 1996. Peru, IL: Open Court, 2002 ed.
Hunt, John Gabriel (ed.). *The Essential Abraham Lincoln.* Avenel, NJ: Portland House, 1993.
Hurmence, Belinda (ed.). *Before Freedom, When I Can Just Remember: Twenty-seven Oral Histories of Former South Carolina Slaves.* 1989. Winston-Salem, NC: John F. Blair, 2002 ed.
Hurst, Jack. *Nathan Bedford Forrest: A Biography.* 1993. New York, NY: Vintage, 1994 ed.
Ingersoll, Thomas G., and Robert E. O'Connor. *Politics and Structure: Essential of American national Government.* North Scituate, MA: Duxbury Press, 1979.
Isaacson, Walter (ed.). *Profiles in Leadership: Historians on the Elusive Quality of Greatness.* New York, NY: W. W. Norton and Co., 2010.
Jahoda, Gloria. *The Trail of Tears: The Story of the American Indian Removals, 1813-1855.* 1975. New York, NY: Wings Book, 1995 ed.
Jaquette, Henrietta Stratton (ed.). *South After Gettysburg: Letters of Cornelia Hancock, 1863-1868.* Philadelphia, PA: University of Pennsylvania Press, 1937.
Jefferson, Thomas. *Notes on the State of Virginia.* Boston, MA: H. Sprague, 1802.
———. *Thomas Jefferson's Farm Book.* (Edwin Morris Betts, ed.). Charlottesville, VA: Thomas Jefferson Memorial Foundation, 1999.
Jenkins, John S. *The Life of James Knox Polk, Late President of the United States.* Auburn, NY: James M. Alden, 1850.
Jensen, Merrill. *The New Nation: A History of the United States During the Confederation, 1781-1789.* New York, NY: Vintage, 1950.
———. *The Articles of Confederation: An Interpretation of the Social-Constitutional History of the American Revolution, 1774-1781.* Madison, WI: University of Wisconsin Press, 1959.
Jimerson, Randall C. *The Private Civil War: Popular Thought During the Sectional Conflict.* Baton Rouge, LA: Louisiana State University Press, 1988.
Johannsen, Robert Walter. *Lincoln, the South, and Slavery: The Political Dimension.* Baton Rouge, LA: Louisiana State University Press, 1991.
Johnson, Adam Rankin. *The Partisan Rangers of the Confederate States Army.* Louisville, KY: George G. Fetter, 1904.
Johnson, Benjamin Heber. *Making of the American West: People and Perspectives.* Santa Barbara, CA: ABC-Clio, 2007.
Johnson, Clint. *The Politically Incorrect Guide to the South (and Why It Will Rise Again).* Washington, D.C.: Regnery, 2006.
Johnson, Ludwell Harrison. *North Against South: The American Iliad, 1848-1877.* 1978. Columbia, SC: Foundation for American Education, 1993 ed.
———. *Division and Reunion: America, 1848-1877.* New York, NY: John Wiley and Sons, 1978.
———. *Red River Campaign: Politics and Cotton in the Civil War.* Kent, OH: Kent State University Press, 1999.
Johnson, Michael, and James L. Roark. *Black Masters: A Free Family of Color in the Old South.* New York, NY: W.W. Norton, 1984.
Johnson, Oliver. *William Lloyd Garrison and His Times.* 1879. Boston, MA: Houghton Mifflin and Co., 1881 ed.
Johnson, Paul. *A History of the American People.* 1997. New York, NY: HarperCollins, 1999 ed.
Johnson, Robert Underwood (ed.). *Battles and Leaders of the Civil War.* 4 vols. New York, NY: The Century Co., 1884-1888.
Johnson, Thomas Cary. *The Life and Letters of Robert Lewis Dabney.* Richmond, VA: Presbyterian Committee of Publication, 1903.
Johnston, David Emmons. *A History of the Middle New River Settlements and Contiguous Territory.* Huntington, WV: Standard Printing and Publishing Co.,1906.
Johnston, Mary. *Pioneers of the Old South: A Chronicle of English Colonial Beginnings.* Boston, MA: IndyPublish,

2009.
Jones, John Beauchamp. *A Rebel War Clerk's Diary at the Confederate States Capital*. 2 vols. in 1. Philadelphia, PA: J. B. Lippincott and Co., 1866.
Jones, John William. *Personal Reminiscences, Anecdotes, and Letters of Gen. Robert E. Lee*. New York, NY: D. Appleton and Co., 1874.
Jones, Wilmer L. *Generals in Blue and Gray*. 2 vols. Westport, CT: Praeger, 2004.
Jordan, Don, and Michael Walsh. *White Cargo: The Forgotten History of Britain's White Slaves in America*. New York, NY: New York University Press, 2008.
Jordan, Ervin L. *Black Confederates and Afro-Yankees in Civil War Virginia*. Charlottesville, VA: University Press of Virginia, 1995.
Jordan, Thomas, and John P. Pryor. *The Campaigns of General Nathan Bedford Forrest and of Forrest's Cavalry*. 1868. Reprint. Cambridge, MA: Da Capo Press, 1996.
Julian, George Washington. *Speeches on Political Questions*. New York, NY: Hurd and Houghton, 1872.
Kane, Joseph Nathan. *Facts About the Presidents: A Compilation of Biographical and Historical Data*. 1959. New York, NY: Ace, 1976 ed.
Kaplan, Sidney. *The Black Presence in the Era of the American Revolution, 1770-1800*. Washington, D.C.: New York Graphic Society, 1973.
Katcher, Philip. *The Civil War Source Book*. 1992. New York, NY: Facts on File, Inc., 1995 ed.
——. *Brassey's Almanac: The American Civil War*. London, UK: Brassey's, 2003.
Kautz, August Valentine. *Customs of Service for Non-Commissioned Officers and Soldiers (as Derived from Law and Regulations and Practised in the Army of the United States)*. Philadelphia, PA: J. B. Lippincott and Co., 1864.
Keckley, Elizabeth. *Behind the Scenes, or Thirty Years a Slave, and Four Years in the White House*. New York, NY: G. W. Carlton and Co., 1868.
Keegan, John. *The American Civil War: A Military History*. 2009. New York, NY: Vintage, 2010 ed.
Kelly, Alfred H., Winfred A. Harbison, and Herman Belz. *The American Constitution: Its Origins and Development* (Vol. 2). 1965. New York, NY: W.W. Norton, 1991 ed.
Kennedy, James Ronald, and Walter Donald Kennedy. *The South Was Right!* Gretna, LA: Pelican Publishing Co., 1994.
——. *Why Not Freedom!: America's Revolt Against Big Government*. Gretna, LA: Pelican Publishing Co., 2005.
——. *Nullifying Tyranny: Creating Moral Communities in an Immoral Society*. Gretna, LA: Pelican Publishing Co., 2010.
Kennedy, Walter Donald. *Myths of American Slavery*. Gretna, LA: Pelican Publishing Co., 2003.
Kennett, Lee B. *Sherman: A Soldier's Life*. 2001. New York, NY: HarperCollins, 2002 ed.
Kettell, Thomas Prentice. *History of the Great Rebellion*. Hartford, CT: L. Stebbins, 1865.
Kinder, Hermann, and Werner Hilgemann. *The Anchor Atlas of World History: From the French Revolution to the American Bicentennial*. 2 vols. Garden City, NY: Anchor, 1978.
King, Charles R. (ed.). *The Life and Correspondence of Rufus King*. 6 vols. New York, NY: G. P. Putnam's Sons, 1897.
King, Edward. *The Great South: A Record of Journeys*. Hartford, CT: American Publishing Co., 1875.
King, Florence. *Reflections in a Jaundiced Eye*. New York, NY: St. Martin's Press, 1989.
Kinshasa, Kwando Mbiassi. *Black Resistance to the Ku Klux Klan in the Wake of the Civil War*. Jefferson, NC: McFarland and Co., 2006.
Kirkland, Edward Chase. *The Peacemakers of 1864*. New York, NY: Macmillan, 1927.
Klingaman, William K. *Abraham Lincoln and the Road to Emancipation, 1861-1865*. 2001. New York, NY: Penguin, 2002 ed.
Klinkner, Philip A., and Rogers M. Smith. *The Unsteady March: The Rise and Decline of Racial Equality in America*. 1999. Chicago, IL: University of Chicago Press, 2002 ed.
Knight, James R. *The Battle of Franklin: When the Devil Had Full Possession of the Earth*. Charleston, SC: The History Press, 2009.
Knox, Thomas Wallace. *Camp-Fire and Cotton-Field: Southern Adventure in Time of War - Life With the Union Armies, and Residence on a Louisiana Plantation*. New York, NY: Blelock and Co., 1865.
Kobrin, David. *The Black Minority in Early New York*. Albany, NY: New York State American Bicentennial

Commission, 1971.
Koger, Larry. *Black Slaveowners: Free Black Slave Masters in South Carolina, 1790-1860*. Columbia, SC: University of South Carolina Press, 1995.
Kuypers, Jim A., and Andrew King (eds.). *Twentieth-Century Roots of Rhetorical Studies*. Westport, CT: Praeger, 2001.
Lacey, Theresa Jensen. *Amazing Tennessee: Fascinating Facts, Entertaining Tales, Bizarre Happenings, and Historical Oddities about the Volunteer State*. Nashville, TN: Rutledge Hill Press, 2000.
Lamon, Ward Hill. *The Life of Abraham Lincoln: From His Birth to His Inauguration as President*. Boston, MA: James R. Osgood and Co., 1872.
———. *Recollections of Abraham Lincoln: 1847-1865*. Chicago, IL: A. C. McClurg and Co., 1895.
Lang, J. Stephen. *The Complete Book of Confederate Trivia*. Shippensburg, PA: Burd Street Press, 1996.
Lanning, Michael Lee. *The African-American Soldier: From Crispus Attucks to Colin Powell*. 1997. New York, NY: Citadel Press, 2004 ed.
Lapsley, Arthur Brooks (ed.). *The Writings of Abraham Lincoln*. 8 vols. New York, NY: The Lamb Publishing Co., 1906.
Lawrence, William. *Life of Amos A. Lawrence*. Boston, MA: Houghton, Mifflin, and Co., 1899.
Leech, Margaret. *Reveille in Washington, 1860-1865*. 1941. Alexandria, VA: Time-Life Books, 1980 ed.
Lee, Robert E., Jr. *Recollections and Letters of General Robert E. Lee*. New York, NY: Doubleday, Page and Co., 1904.
Lemay, J.A. Leo, and P.M. Zall (eds.). *Benjamin Franklin's Autobiography: An Authoritative Text, Backgrounds, Criticism*. 1791. New York, NY: W. W. Norton and Co., 1986 ed.
Lemire, Elise. *Black Walden: Slavery and Its Aftermath in Concord, Massachusetts*. Philadelphia, PA: University of Pennsylvania Press, 2009.
Lester, Charles Edwards. *Life and Public Services of Charles Sumner*. New York, NY: U.S. Publishing Co., 1874.
Lester, John C., and D. L. Wilson. *Ku Klux Klan: Its Origin, Growth, and Disbandment*. 1884. New York, NY: Neale Publishing, 1905 ed.
LeVert, Suzanne (ed.). *The Civil War Society's Encyclopedia of the Civil War*. New York, NY: Wings Books, 1997.
Lewis, Lloyd. *Myths After Lincoln*. 1929. New York, NY: The Press of the Reader's Club, 1941 ed.
Lincoln, Abraham. *The Autobiography of Abraham Lincoln* (selected from *Complete Works of Abraham Lincoln*, 1894, by John G. Nicolay and John Hay). New York, NY: Francis D. Tandy Co., 1905.
Lincoln, Abraham, and Stephen A. Douglas. *Political Debates Between Abraham Lincoln and Stephen A. Douglas*. Cleveland, OH: Burrows Brothers Co., 1894.
Lind, Michael (ed.). *Hamilton's Republic: Readings in the American Democratic Nationalist Tradition*. New York, NY: The Free Press, 1997.
Linderman, Gerald. *Courage: The Experience of Combat in the American Civil War*. New York, NY: The Free Press, 1987.
Littell, Eliakim (ed.). *The Living Age*. Seventh Series, Vol. 30. Boston, MA: The Living Age Co., 1906.
Litwack, Leon F. *North of Slavery: The Negro in the Free States, 1790-1860*. Chicago, IL: University of Chicago Press, 1961.
———. *Been in the Storm So Long: The Aftermath of Slavery*. New York, NY: Vintage, 1980.
Livermore, Thomas L. *Numbers and Losses in the Civil War in America, 1861-65*. 1900. Carlisle, PA: John Kallmann, 1996 ed.
Livingstone, William. *Livingstone's History of the Republican Party*. 2 vols. Detroit, MI: William Livingstone, 1900.
Locke, John. *Two Treatises of Government* (Mark Goldie, ed.). 1924. London, UK: Everyman, 1998 ed.
Lodge, Henry Cabot (ed.). *The Works of Alexander Hamilton*. 12 vols. New York, NY: G. P. Putnam's Sons, 1904.
Logan, John Alexander. *The Great Conspiracy: Its Origin and History*. New York, NY: A. R. Hart, 1886.
Logsdon, David R. (ed.). *Eyewitnesses at the Battle of Franklin*. 1988. Nashville, TN: Kettle Mills Press, 2000 ed.
———. *Tennessee Antebellum Trail Guidebook*. Nashville, TN: Kettle Mills Press, 1995.

THE MCGAVOCKS OF CARNTON PLANTATION

Long, Everette Beach, and Barbara Long. *The Civil War Day by Day: An Almanac, 1861-1865*. 1971. New York, NY: Da Capo Press, 1985 ed.
Lonn, Ella. *Foreigners in the Confederacy*. 1940. Chapel Hill, NC: University of North Carolina Press, 2002 ed.
Losson, Christopher. *Tennessee's Forgotten Warriors: Frank Cheatham and His Confederate Division*. Knoxville, TN: University of Tennessee Press, 1989.
Lott, Stanley K. *The Truth About American Slavery*. 2004. Clearwater, SC: Eastern Digital Resources, 2005 ed.
Lower, Mark Antony. *Patronymica Britannica: A Dictionary of the Family Names of the United Kingdom*. London, UK: John Russell Smith, 1860.
Lowry, Don. *Dark and Cruel War: The Decisive Months of the Civil War September-December 1864*. New York, NY: Hippocrene, 1993.
Lubbock, Francis Richard. *Six Decades in Texas, or Memoirs of Francis Richard Lubbock, Governor of Texas in War-Time, 1861-1863*. 1899. Austin, TX: Ben C. Jones, 1900 ed.
Ludlow, Daniel H. (ed.). *Encyclopedia of Mormonism: The History, Scripture, Doctrine, and Procedure of the Church of Jesus Christ of Latter-Day Saints*. New York, NY: Macmillan, 1992.
Luna, Kristin. *Tennessee Curiosities: Quirky Characters, Roadside Oddities and Other Offbeat Stuff*. Guilford, CT: Morris Book Publishing, 2011.
Lytle, Andrew Nelson. *Bedford Forrest and His Critter Company*. 1931. Nashville, TN: J. S. Sanders and Company, 1992 ed.
MacDonald, William. *Select Documents Illustrative of the History of the United States 1776-1861*. New York, NY: Macmillan, 1897.
Mackay, Charles. *Life and Liberty in America, or Sketches of a Tour in the United States and Canada in 1857-58*. New York, NY: Harper and Brothers, 1859.
MacLeod, Duncan. *Slavery, Race and the American Revolution*. London, UK: Cambridge University Press, 1974.
MacLysaght, Edward. *The Surnames of Ireland*. 1985. Dublin, Ireland: Irish Academic Press, 1999 ed.
Madison, James. *Letters and Other Writings of James Madison, Fourth President of the United States*. 4 vols. Philadelphia, PA: J. B. Lippincott and Co., 1865.
Maihafer, Harry J. *War of Words; Abraham Lincoln and the Civil War Press*. Dulles, VA: Brassey's, 2001.
Main, Jackson Turner. *The Anti-Federalists: Critics of the Constitution, 1781-1788*. 1961. New York, NY: W. W. Norton and Co., 1974 ed.
Malone, Laurence J. *Opening the West: Federal Internal Improvements Before 1860*. Westport, CT: Greenwood Press, 1998.
Mandel, Bernard. *Labor, Free and Slave: Workingmen and the Anti-Slavery Movement in the United States*. New York, NY: Associated Authors, 1955.
Manegold, C. S. *Ten Hills Farm: The Forgotten History of Slavery in the North*. Princeton, NJ: Princeton University Press, 2010.
Manning, Timothy D., Sr. (ed.) *Lincoln Reconsidered: Conference Reader*. High Point, NC: Heritage Foundation Press, 2006.
Mansfield, Stephen, and George Grant. *Faithful Volunteers: The History of Religion in Tennessee*. Nashville, TN: Cumberland House, 1997.
Marshall, Jessie Ames. *Private and Official Correspondence of General Benjamin F. Butler During the Period of the Civil War*. 5 vols. Norwood, MA: The Plimpton Press, 1917.
Marten, James. *The Children's Civil War*. Chapel Hill, NC: University of North Carolina Press, 1998.
Martin, Iain C. *The Quotable American Civil War*. Guilford, CT: Lyons Press, 2008.
Martineau, Harriet. *Retrospect of Western Travel*. 3 vols. London, UK: Saunders and Otley, 1838.
Martinez, James Michael. *Carpetbaggers, Cavalry, and the Ku Klux Klan: Exposing the Invisible Empire During Reconstruction*. Lanham, MD: Rowman and Littlefield, 2007.
Masur, Louis P. *The Real War Will Never Get In the Books: Selections From Writers During the Civil War*. New York, NY: Oxford University Press, 1993.
Mathes, Capt. J. Harvey. *General Forrest*. 1902. Reprint. New York, NY: D. Appleton and Co., 2003.
Maury, Dabney Herndon. *Recollections of a Virginian in the Mexican, Indian, and Civil Wars*. New York, NY:

The McGavocks of Carnton Plantation

Charles Scribner's Sons, 1894.
Mayer, David N. *The Constitutional Thought of Thomas Jefferson*. Charlottesville, VA: University of Virginia Press, 1995.
Mayer, Henry. *All on Fire: William Lloyd Garrison and the Abolition of Slavery*. New York, NY: St. Martin's Press, 1998.
McAfee, Ward M. *Citizen Lincoln*. Hauppauge, NY: Nova History Publications, 2004.
McCabe, James Dabney. *Our Martyred President: The Life and Public Services of Gen. James A. Garfield, Twentieth President of the United States*. Philadelphia, PA: National Publishing Co., 1881.
McClure, Alexander Kelly. *Abraham Lincoln and Men of War-Times: Some Personal Recollections of War and Politics During the Lincoln Administration*. Philadelphia, PA: Times Publishing Co., 1892.
———. *Our Presidents and How We Make Them*. New York, NY: Harper and Brothers, 1900.
McCullough, David. *John Adams*. New York, NY: Touchstone, 2001.
McDonald, Forrest. *States' Rights and the Union: Imperium in Imperio, 1776-1876*. Lawrence, KS: University Press of Kansas, 2000.
McDonough, James Lee, and Thomas L. Connelly. *Five Tragic Hours: The Battle of Franklin*. 1983. Knoxville, TN: University of Tennessee Press, 2001 ed.
McDougall, Walter A. *Throes of Democracy: The American Civil War Era 1829-1877*. New York, NY: HarperCollins, 2008.
McElroy, Robert. *Jefferson Davis: The Unreal and the Real*. 1937. New York, NY: Smithmark, 1995 ed.
McFeely, William S. *Yankee Stepfather: General O. O. Howard and the Freedmen - The Story of a Civil War Promise to Former Slaves Made—and Broken*. 1968. New York, NY: W. W. Norton and Co., 1994.
McGehee, Jacob Owen. *Causes That Led to the War Between the States*. Atlanta, GA: A. B. Caldwell, 1915.
McGuire, Hunter, and George L. Christian. *The Confederate Cause and Conduct in the War Between the States*. Richmond, VA: L. H. Jenkins, 1907.
McHenry, George. *The Cotton Trade: Its Bearing Upon the Prosperity of Great Britain and Commerce of the American Republics, Considered in Connection with the System of Negro Slavery in the Confederate States*. London, UK: Saunders, Otley, and Co., 1863.
McIlwaine, Shields. *Memphis Down in Dixie*. New York, NY: E. P. Dutton, 1848.
McKenzie, John L. *Dictionary of the Bible*. New York, NY: Collier, 1965.
McKissack, Patricia C., and Frederick McKissack. *Sojourner Truth: Ain't I a Woman?* New York: NY: Scholastic, 1992.
McKnight, Brian D. *Confederate Outlaw: Champ Ferguson and the Civil War in Appalachia*. Baton Rouge, LA: Louisiana State University Press, 2011.
McManus, Edgar J. *A History of Negro Slavery in New York*. Syracuse, NY: Syracuse University Press, 1966.
———. *Black Bondage in the North*. Syracuse, NY: Syracuse University Press, 1973.
McMaster, John Bach. *Our House Divided: A History of the People of the United States During Lincoln's Administration*. 1927. New York, NY: Premier, 1961 ed.
McMurry, Richard M. *John Bell Hood and the War For Southern Independence*. 1982. Lincoln, NE: University of Nebraska Press, 1992 ed.
McMurray, William Josiah. *History of the Twentieth Tennessee Regiment Volunteer Infantry, C.S.A.* Nashville, TN: The Publication Committee, 1904.
McPherson, Edward. *The Political History of the United States of America, During the Great Rebellion (from November 6, 1860, to July 4, 1864)*. Washington, D.C.: Philp and Solomons, 1864.
———. *The Political History of the United States of America, During the Period of Reconstruction, (from April 15, 1865, to July 15, 1870,) Including a Classified Summary of the Legislation of the Thirty-ninth, Fortieth, and Forty-first Congresses*. Washington, D.C.: Solomons and Chapman, 1875.
McPherson, James M. *The Struggle for Equality: Abolitionists and the Negro in the Civil War and Reconstruction*. 1964. Princeton, NJ: Princeton University Press, 1992 ed.
———. *The Negro's Civil War: How American Negroes Felt and Acted During the War for the Union*. 1965. Chicago, IL: University of Illinois Press, 1982 ed.
———. *Battle Cry of Freedom: The Civil War Era*. Oxford, UK: Oxford University Press, 2003.
———. *The Atlas of the Civil War*. Philadelphia, PA: Courage Books, 2005.
McPherson, James M., and the staff of the *New York Times*. *The Most Fearful Ordeal: Original Coverage of the Civil*

War by Writers and Reporters of the New York Times. New York, NY: St. Martin's Press, 2004.
McRae, Andrew. *God Speed the Plough: The Representation of Agrarian England, 1500-1660.* Cambridge, UK: Cambridge University Press, 1996.
McWhiney, Grady, and Judith Lee Hallock. *Braxton Bragg and Confederate Defeat.* 2 vols. Tuscaloosa, AL: University of Alabama Press, 1991.
McWhiney, Grady, and Perry D. Jamieson. *Attack and Die: Civil War Military Tactics and the Southern Heritage.* Tuscaloosa, AL: University of Alabama Press, 1982.
Meier, August, and Rudwick Elliott. *From Plantation to Ghetto: An Interpretive History of American Negroes.* New York, NY: Hill and Wang, 1970.
Melish, Joanne Pope. *Disowning Slavery: Gradual Emancipation and 'Race' in New England 1780-1860.* Ithaca, NY: Cornell University Press, 1998.
Meltzer, Milton. *Slavery: A World History.* 1971. New York, NY: Da Capo Press, 1993 ed.
Meriwether, Elizabeth Avery. *Facts and Falsehoods Concerning the War on the South, 1861-1865.* (Originally written under the pseudonym "George Edmonds".) Memphis, TN: A. R. Taylor, 1904.
Metzger, Bruce M., and Michael D. Coogan (eds.). *The Oxford Companion to the Bible.* New York, NY: Oxford University Press, 1993.
Miller, Brian Craig. *John Bell Hood and the Fight for Civil War Memory.* Knoxville, TN: University of Tennessee Press, 2010.
Miller, Francis Trevelyan. *Portrait Life of Lincoln.* Springfield, MA: Patriot Publishing Co., 1910.
Miller, John Chester. *The Wolf By the Ears: Thomas Jefferson and Slavery.* 1977. Charlottesville, VA: University Press of Virginia, 1994 ed.
Miller, Marion Mills (ed.). *Great Debates in American History.* 14 vols. New York, NY: Current Literature, 1913.
Miller, Nathan. *Star-Spangled Men: America's Ten Worst Presidents.* New York, NY: Touchstone, 1998.
Miller, Robert J. (ed.). *The Complete Gospels* (Annotated Scholars Version). 1992. Sonoma, CA: Polebridge Press, 1994 ed.
Mills, A. D. *Oxford Dictionary of English Place-names.* 1991. Oxford, UK: Oxford University Press, 1998 ed.
Min, Pyong Gap (ed.). *Encyclopedia of Racism in the United States.* 3 vols. Westport, CT: Greenwood Press, 2005.
Minor, Charles Landon Carter. *The Real Lincoln: From the Testimony of His Contemporaries.* Richmond, VA: Everett Waddey Co., 1904.
Mirabello, Mark. *Handbook for Rebels and Outlaws.* Oxford, UK: Mandrake of Oxford, 2009.
Mises, Ludwig von. *Human Action: A Treatise on Economics.* Auburn, AL: Ludwig von Mises Institute, 1998.
Mish, Frederick C. (ed.). *Webster's Ninth New Collegiate Dictionary.* Springfield, MA: Merriam-Webster, 1984.
Mitchell, Margaret. *Gone With the Wind.* 1936. Reprint. New York, NY: Avon, 1973.
Mitgang, Herbert (ed.). *Lincoln As They Saw Him.* 1956. New York, NY: Collier, 1962 ed.
Mode, Peter George. *Source Book and Bibliographical Guide for American Church History.* Menasha, WI: Collegiate Press, 1921.
Mode, Robert L. (ed.). *Nashville: Its Character in a Changing America.* Nashville, TN: Vanderbilt University, 1981.
Montagu, Ashley (ed.). *Man's Most Dangerous Myth: The Fallacy of Race.* New York, NY: Columbia University Press, 1946.
——. *The Concept of Race.* 1964. Toronto, Canada: Collier, 1969 ed.
Montefiore, Simon Sebag. *Stalin: The Court of the Red Star.* 2003. New York, NY: Vintage, 2004 ed.
Montgomery, David Henry. *The Student's American History.* 1897. Boston, MA: Ginn and Co., 1905 ed.
Moore, Frank (ed.). *The Rebellion Record: A Diary of American Events.* 12 vols. New York, NY: G. P. Putnam, 1861.
Moore, George Henry. *Notes on the History of Slavery in Massachusetts.* New York, NY: D. Appleton and Co., 1866.
Moore, Marijo (ed.). *Birthed From Scorched Hearts: Women Respond to War.* Golden, CO: Fulcrum, 2008.
Moorhead, James H. *American Apocalypse: Yankee Protestants and the Civil War, 1860-1869.* New Haven, CT: Yale University Press, 1971.

THE MCGAVOCKS OF CARNTON PLANTATION

Morgan, Sarah. *The Civil War Diary of a Southern Woman* (Charles East, ed.). Originally published as *A Confederate Girl's Diary* in 1913. New York, NY: Touchstone, 1992 ed.

Morris, Benjamin Franklin (ed.). *The Life of Thomas Morris: Pioneer and Long a Legislator of Ohio, and U.S. Senator from 1833 to 1839*. Cincinnati, OH: Moore, Wilstach, Keys and Overend, 1856.

Morris, Thomas D. *Free Men All: The Personal Liberty Laws of the North, 1780-1861*. Baltimore, MD: John Hopkins University Press, 1974.

Morton, John Watson. *The Artillery of Nathan Bedford Forrest's Cavalry*. Nashville, TN: The M. E. Church, 1909.

Moses, John. *Illinois: Historical and Statistical, Comprising the Essential Facts of Its Planting and Growth as a Province, County, Territory, and State* (Vol. 2). Chicago, IL: Fergus Printing Co., 1892.

Muhlenfeld, Elisabeth. *Mary Boykin Chesnut: A Biography*. 1981. Baton Rouge, LA: Louisiana State University Press, 2009, ed.

Mullen, Robert W. *Blacks in America's Wars: The Shift in Attitudes from the Revolutionary War to Vietnam*. 1973. New York, NY: Pathfinder, 1991 ed.

Muller, Herbert J. *The Uses of the Past: Profiles of Former Societies*. 1952. New York, NY: Mentor, 1960 ed.

Munford, Beverly Bland. *Virginia's Attitude Toward Slavery and Secession*. 1909. Richmond, VA: L. H. Jenkins, 1914 ed.

Murphy, Jim. *A Savage Thunder: Antietam and the Bloody Road to Freedom*. New York, NY: Margaret K. McElderry, 2009.

Murphy, Paul V. *The Rebuke of History: The Southern Agrarians and American Conservative Thought*. Chapel Hill, NC: University of North Carolina Press, 2001.

Napolitano, Andrew P. *The Constitution in Exile: How the Federal Government has Seized Power by Rewriting the Supreme Law of the Land*. Nashville, TN: Nelson Current, 2006.

Neely, Mark E., Jr. *The Fate of Liberty: Abraham Lincoln and Civil Liberties*. New York, NY: Oxford University Press, 1991.

Neilson, William Allan (ed.). *Webster's Biographical Dictionary*. Springfield, MA: G. and C. Merriam Co., 1943.

Neufeldt, Victoria (ed.). *Webster's New World Dictionary of American English* (third college edition). 1970. New York, NY: Prentice Hall, 1994 ed.

Nevins, Allan. *The Evening Post: A Century of Journalism*. New York, NY: Boni and Liveright, 1922.

Nicolay, John G., and John Hay (eds.). *Abraham Lincoln: A History*. 10 vols. New York, NY: The Century Co., 1890.

———. *Complete Works of Abraham Lincoln*. 12 vols. 1894. New York, NY: Francis D. Tandy Co., 1905 ed.

———. *Abraham Lincoln: Complete Works*. 12 vols. 1894. New York, NY: The Century Co., 1907 ed.

Nivola, Pietro S., and David H. Rosenbloom (eds.). *Classic Readings in American Politics*. New York, NY: St. Martin's Press, 1986.

Noe, Kenneth W., and Shannon H. Wilson (eds.). *The Civil War in Appalachia: Collected Essays*. Knoxville, TN: University of Tennessee Press, 1997.

Norwood, Thomas Manson. *A True Vindication of the South*. Savannah, GA: Citizens and Southern Bank, 1917.

Nye, Russel B. *William Lloyd Garrison and the Humanitarian Reformers*. Boston, MA: Little, Brown and Co., 1955.

Oakes, James. *The Ruling Race: A History of American Slaveholders*. New York, NY: W. W. Norton and Co., 1998.

Oates, Stephen B. *Abraham Lincoln: The Man Behind the Myths*. New York, NY: Meridian, 1984.

———. *The Approaching Fury: Voices of the Storm, 1820-1861*. New York, NY: Harper Perennial, 1998.

O'Brien, Cormac. *Secret Lives of the U.S. Presidents: What Your Teachers Never Told You About the Men of the White House*. Philadelphia, PA: Quirk, 2004.

———. *Secret Lives of the Civil War: What Your teachers Never Told You About the War Between the States*. Philadelphia, PA: Quirk, 2007.

Oglesby, Thaddeus K. *Some Truths of History: A Vindication of the South Against the Encyclopedia Britannica and Other Maligners*. Atlanta, GA: Byrd Printing, 1903.

Olmsted, Frederick Law. *A Journey in the Seaboard Slave States, With Remarks on Their Economy*. New York,

NY: Dix and Edwards, 1856.
———. *A Journey Through Texas; or a Saddle-Trip on the Western Frontier.* New York, NY: Dix and Edwards, 1857.
———. *A Journey in the Back Country.* New York, NY: Mason Brothers, 1860.
———. *The Cotton Kingdom: A Traveler's Observations on Cotton and Slavery in the American Slave States.* 2 vols. London, UK: Sampson Low, Son, and Co., 1862.
Olson, Ted (ed.). *CrossRoads: A Southern Culture Annual.* Macon, GA: Mercer University Press, 2004.
ORA (full title: *The War of the Rebellion: A Compilation of the Official Records of the Union and Confederate Armies.* (Multiple volumes.) Washington, D.C.: Government Printing Office, 1880.
ORN (full title: *Official Records of the Union and Confederate Navies in the War of the Rebellion*). (Multiple volumes.) Washington, D.C.: Government Printing Office, 1894.
Owsley, Frank Lawrence. *King Cotton Diplomacy: Foreign Relations of the Confederate States of America.* 1931. Chicago, IL: University of Chicago Press, 1959 ed.
Page, Thomas Nelson. *Robert E. Lee, Man and Soldier.* New York, NY: Charles Scribner's Sons, 1911.
Palin, Sarah. *Going Rogue: An American Life.* New York, NY: HarperCollins, 2009.
———. *America By Heart: Reflections of Family, Faith, and Flag.* New York, NY: HarperCollins, 2010.
Parker, Bowdoin S. (ed.). *What One Grand Army Post Has Accomplished: History of Edward W. Kinsley Post, No. 113.* Norwood, MA: Norwood, Press, 1913.
Parker, Star. *Uncle Sam's Plantation: How Big Government Enslaves America's Poor and What We Can Do About It.* 2003. Nashville, TN: Thomas Nelson, 2010 ed.
Parks, Aileen Wells. *Bedford Forrest: Horseback Boy.* 1952. Indianapolis, IN: Bobbs-Merrill Co., 1963 ed.
Parry, Melanie (ed.). *Chambers Biographical Dictionary.* 1897. Edinburgh, Scotland: Chambers Harrap, 1998 ed.
Patrick, Rembert W. *Jefferson Davis and His Cabinet.* Baton Rouge, LA: Louisiana State University Press, 1944.
Paul, Ron. *The Revolution: A Manifesto.* New York, NY: Grand Central Publishing, 2008.
Paull, Jennifer, and Christopher Culwell (eds.). *Fodor's Guide to the Da Vinci Code.* New York, NY: Fodor's Travel Publications, 2006.
Pearson, Henry Greenleaf. *The Life of John A. Andrew, Governor of Massachusetts, 1861-1865.* 2 vols. Boston, MA: Houghton, Mifflin and Co., 1904.
Perkins, Henry C. *Northern Editorials on Secession.* 2 vols. D. Appleton and Co., 1942.
Perry, James M. *Touched With Fire: Five Presidents and the Civil War Battles That Made Them.* New York, NY: Public Affairs, 2003.
Perry, John C. *Myths and Realities of American Slavery: The True History of Slavery in America.* Shippensburg, PA: Burd Street Press, 2002.
Perry, Mark. *Lift Up Thy Voice: The Grimké Family's Journey From Slaveholders to Civil Rights Leaders.* New York, NY: Penguin, 2001.
Peter, Laurence J., and Raymond Hull. *The Peter Principle: Why Things Always Go Wrong.* New York, NY: William Morrow and Co., 1969.
Peterson, Merrill D. (ed.). *James Madison, A Biography in His Own Words.* (First published posthumously in 1840.) New York, NY: Harper and Row, 1974 ed.
———. (ed.). *Thomas Jefferson: Writings, Autobiography, A Summary View of the Rights of British America, Notes on the State of Virginia, Public Papers, Addresses, Messages and Replies, Miscellany, Letters.* New York, NY: Literary Classics, 1984.
Peterson, Paul R. *Quantrill of Missouri: The Making of a Guerilla Warrior, The Man, the Myth, the Soldier.* Nashville, TN: Cumberland House, 2003.
Phelan, James. *History of Tennessee: The Making of a State.* Boston, MA: Houghton, Mifflin and Co., 1888.
Phillips, Michael. *White Metropolis: Race, Ethnicity, and Religion in Dallas, 1841-2001.* Austin, TX: University of Texas Press, 2006.
Phillips, Robert S. (ed.). *Funk and Wagnalls New Encyclopedia.* 1971. New York, NY: Funk and Wagnalls, 1979 ed.
Phillips, Ulrich Bonnell. *American Negro Slavery: A Survey of the Supply, Employment and Control of Negro Labor as Determined by the Plantation Régime.* New York, NY: D. Appleton and Co., 1929.
Phillips, Wendell. *Speeches, Letters, and Lectures.* Boston, MA: Lee and Shepard, 1894.

The McGavocks of Carnton Plantation

Piatt, Donn. *Memories of the Men Who Saved the Union.* New York, NY: Belford, Clarke, and Co., 1887.

Piatt, Donn, and Henry V. Boynton. *General George H. Thomas: A Critical Biography.* Cincinnati, OH: Robert Clarke and Co., 1893.

Pickett, George E. *The Heart of a Soldier: As Revealed in the Intimate Letters of General George E. Pickett, C.S.A..* 1908. New York, NY: Seth Moyle, 1913 ed.

Pickett, William Passmore. *The Negro Problem: Abraham Lincoln's Solution.* New York, NY: G. P. Putnam's Sons, 1909.

Picknett, Lynn, and Clive Prince. *The Templar Revelation: Secret Guardians of the True Identity of Christ.* New York, NY: Touchstone, 1997.

Pike, James Shepherd. *The Prostrate State: South Carolina Under Negro Government.* New York, NY: D. Appleton and Co., 1874.

Plano, Jack C., Milton Greenberg, Roy Olton, and Robert E. Riggs. *Political Science Dictionary.* Hinsdale, IL: The Dryden Press, 1973.

Pois, Robert, and Philip Langer. *Command Failure in War: Psychology and Leadership.* Bloomington, IN: Indiana University Press, 2004.

Pollard, Edward A. *Southern History of the War.* 2 vols. in 1. New York, NY: Charles B. Richardson, 1866.

———. *The Lost Cause.* 1867. Chicago, IL: E. B. Treat, 1890 ed.

———. *The Lost Cause Regained.* New York, NY: G. W. Carlton and Co., 1868.

———. *Life of Jefferson Davis, With a Secret History of the Southern Confederacy, Gathered "Behind the Scenes in Richmond."* Philadelphia, PA: National Publishing Co., 1869.

Post, Lydia Minturn (ed.). *Soldiers' Letters, From Camp, Battlefield and Prison.* New York, NY: Bunce and Huntington, 1865.

Potter, David M. *The Impending Crisis: 1848-1861.* New York, NY: Harper and Row, 1976.

Powell, Edward Payson. *Nullification and Secession in the United States: A History of the Six Attempts During the First Century of the Republic.* New York, NY: G. P. Putnam's Sons, 1897.

Powell, William S. *North Carolina: A History.* 1977. Chapel Hill, NC: University of North Carolina Press, 1988 ed.

Pratt, Harry E. *Concerning Mr. Lincoln: As He Appeared to Letter Writers of His Time.* Springfield, IL: The Abraham Lincoln Association, 1944.

Pritchard, Russ A., Jr. *Civil War Weapons and Equipment.* Guilford, CT: Lyons Press, 2003.

Putnam, Samuel Porter. *400 Years of Free Thought.* New York, NY: Truth Seeker Co., 1894.

Quaker Biographies. 5 vols. Philadelphia, PA: Representatives of the Religious Society of Friends for Pennsylvania, New Jersey and Delaware, 1916.

Quarles, Benjamin. *The Negro in the Civil War.* 1953. Cambridge, MA: Da Capo Press, 1988 ed.

Quintero, José Agustín, Ambrosio José Gonzales, and Loreta Janeta Velazquez. *Cubans in the Confederacy.* Jefferson, NC: McFarland and Co., 2002.

Quirk, William J., and R. Randall Bridwell. *Judicial Dictatorship.* Brunswick, NJ: Transaction, 1995.

Rable, George C. *The Confederate Republic: A Revolution Against Politics.* Chapel Hill, NC: University of North Carolina Press, 1994.

Radzinsky, Edvard. *Stalin: The First In-depth Biography Based on Explosive New Documents From Russia's Secret Archives.* New York, NY: Anchor, 1996.

Ramage, James A. *Rebel Raider: The Life of General John Hunt Morgan.* Lexington, KY: University Press of Kentucky, 1986.

Randall, James Garfield. *The Confiscation of Property During the Civil War.* Indianapolis, IN: Mutual Printing and Lithographing Co., 1913.

———. *Constitutional Problems Under Lincoln.* 1926. Urbana, IL: University of Illinois Press, 1951 ed.

———. *The Civil War and Reconstruction.* 1937. Lexington, MA: D. C. Heath and Co., 1969 ed.

———. *Lincoln the President: Springfield to Gettysburg.* 4 vols. New York, NY: Dodd, Mead and Co., 1945.

———. *Lincoln and the South.* 1946. Westport, CT: Greenwood Press, 1980 ed.

———. *Lincoln: The Liberal Statesman.* New York, NY: Dodd, Mead and Co., 1947.

Randall, James Garfield, and Richard N. Current. *Lincoln the President: Last Full Measure* (Vol. 4 of the above series). 1955. Urbana, IL: University of Illinois Press, 2000 ed.

Randolph, Thomas Jefferson (ed.). *Memoir, Correspondence, and Miscellanies, From the Papers of Thomas Jefferson.*

4 vols. Charlottesville, VA: F. Carr and Co., 1829.
Ransom, Roger L. *Conflict and Compromise: The Political Economy of Slavery, Emancipation, and the American Civil War*. Cambridge, UK: Cambridge University Press, 1989.
Rawle, William. *A View of the Constitution of the United States of America*. Philadelphia, PA: Philip H. Nicklin, 1829.
Rayfield, Donald. *Stalin and His Hangmen: The Tyrant and Those Who Killed For Him*. New York, NY: Random House, 2004.
Rayner, B. L. *Sketches of the Life, Writings, and Opinions of Thomas Jefferson*. New York, NY: Alfred Francis and William Boardman, 1832.
Reaney, P. H., and R. M. Wilson. *A Dictionary of English Surnames*. 1958. Oxford, UK: Oxford University Press, 1997 ed.
Reid, Richard M. *Freedom For Themselves: North Carolina's Black Soldiers in the Era of the Civil War*. Chapel Hill, NC: University of North Carolina Press, 2008.
Remsburg, John B. *Abraham Lincoln: Was He a Christian?* New York, NY: The Truth Seeker Co., 1893.
Reports of Committees of the Senate of the United States (for the Thirty-eighth Congress). Washington, D.C.: Government Printing Office, 1864.
Report of the Joint Committee on Reconstruction (at the First Session, Thirty-ninth Congress). Washington, D.C.: Government Printing Office, 1866.
Reports of Committees of the Senate of the United States (for the Second Session of the Forty-second Congress). Washington, D.C.: Government Printing Office, 1872.
Report of the Joint Select Committee to Inquire into the Condition of Affairs in the Late Insurrectionary States. Washington, D.C.: Government Printing Office, 1872.
Reuter, Edward Byron. *The Mulatto in the United States*. Boston, MA: Gorham Press, 1918.
Rhodes, James Ford. *History of the United States From the Compromise of 1850 to the Final Restoration of Home Rule at the South in 1877*. 7 vols. 1895. New York, NY: Macmillan Co., 1907 ed.
Rice, Allen Thorndike (ed.). *The North American Review*, Vol. 227. New York, NY: D. Appleton and Co., 1879.
———. (ed.). *Reminiscences of Abraham Lincoln, by Distinguished Men of His Time*. New York, NY: North American Review, 1888.
Richardson, James D. (ed.). *A Compilation of the Messages and Papers of the Confederacy*. 2 vols. Nashville, TN: United States Publishing Co., 1905.
Ridley, Bromfield Lewis. *Battles and Sketches of the Army of Tennessee*. Mexico, MO: Missouri Printing and Publishing Co., 1906.
Riley, Franklin Lafayette (ed.). *Publications of the Mississippi Historical Society*. Oxford, MS: The Mississippi Historical Society, 1902.
———. *General Robert E. Lee After Appomattox*. New York, NY: MacMillan Co., 1922.
Riley, Russell Lowell. *The Presidency and the Politics of Racial Inequality*. New York, NY: Columbia University Press, 1999.
Rives, John (ed.). *Abridgement of the Debates of Congress: From 1789 to 1856* (Vol. 13). New York, NY: D. Appleton and Co., 1860.
Roberts, Paul M. *United States History: Review Text*. 1966. New York, NY: Amsco School Publications, Inc., 1970 ed.
Roberts, R. Philip. *Mormonism Unmasked: Confronting the Contradictions Between Mormon Beliefs and True Christianity*. Nashville, TN: Broadman and Holman, 1998.
Robertson, James I., Jr. *Soldiers Blue and Gray*. 1988. Columbia, SC: University of South Carolina Press, 1998 ed.
Rogers, Joel Augustus. *Africa's Gift to America: The Afro-American in the Making and Saving of the United States*. St. Petersburg, FL: Helga M. Rogers, 1961.
———. *The Ku Klux Spirit*. 1923. Baltimore, MD: Black Classic Press, 1980 ed.
Rosen, Robert N. *The Jewish Confederates*. Columbia, SC: University of South Carolina Press, 2000.
Rosenbaum, Robert A. (ed.). *The New American Desk Encyclopedia*. 1977. New York, NY: Signet, 1989 ed.
Rosenbaum, Robert A., and Douglas Brinkley (eds.). *The Penguin Encyclopedia of American History*. New York, NY: Viking, 2003.

THE MCGAVOCKS OF CARNTON PLANTATION

Rothschild, Alonzo. *"Honest Abe": A Study in Integrity Based on the Early Life of Abraham Lincoln*. Boston, MA: Houghton Mifflin Co., 1917.

Rouse, Adelaide Louise (ed.). *National Documents: State Papers So Arranged as to Illustrate the Growth of Our Country From 1606 to the Present Day*. New York, NY: Unit Book Publishing Co., 1906.

Rowland, Dunbar (ed.). *Jefferson Davis, Constitutionalist: His Letters, Papers, and Speeches*. 10 vols. Jackson, MS: Mississippi Department of Archives and History, 1923.

Rozwenc, Edwin Charles (ed.). *The Causes of the American Civil War*. 1961. Lexington, MA: D. C. Heath and Co., 1972 ed.

Russell, Charles Wells (ed.). *The Memoirs of Colonel John S. Mosby*. Boston, MA: Little, Brown, and Co., 1917.

Rubenzer, Steven J., and Thomas R. Faschingbauer. *Personality, Character, and Leadership in the White House: Psychologists Assess the Presidents*. Dulles, VA: Brassey's, 2004.

Ruffin, Edmund. *The Diary of Edmund Ruffin: Toward Independence: October 1856-April 1861*. Baton Rouge, LA: Louisiana State University Press, 1972.

Rutherford, Mildred Lewis. *Four Addresses*. Birmingham, AL: The Mildred Rutherford Historical Circle, 1916.

——. *A True Estimate of Abraham Lincoln and Vindication of the South*. N.p., n.d.

——. *Truths of History: A Historical Perspective of the Civil War From the Southern Viewpoint*. Confederate Reprint Co., 1920.

——. *The South Must Have Her Rightful Place In History*. Athens, GA, 1923.

Rutland, Robert Allen. *The Birth of the Bill of Rights, 1776-1791*. 1955. Boston, MA: Northeastern University Press, 1991 ed.

Sachsman, David B., S. Kittrell Rushing, and Roy Morris, Jr. (eds.). *Words at War: The Civil War and American Journalism*. West Lafayette, IN: Purdue University Press, 2008.

Salley, Alexander Samuel, Jr. *South Carolina Troops in Confederate Service*. 2 vols. Columbia, SC: R. L. Bryan, 1913 and 1914.

Salzberger, Ronald P., and Mary C. Turck (eds.). *Reparations For Slavery: A Reader*. Lanham, MD: Rowman and Littlefield, 2004.

Samuel, Bunford. *Secession and Constitutional Liberty*. 2 vols. New York, NY: Neale Publishing, 1920.

Sancho, Ignatius. *Letters of the Late Ignatius Sancho, an African*. 1782. New York, NY: Cosimo Classics, 2005 ed.

Sandburg, Carl. *Abraham Lincoln: The War Years*. 4 vols. New York, NY: Harcourt, Brace and World, 1939.

——. *Storm Over the Land: A Profile of the Civil War*. 1939. Old Saybrook, CT: Konecky and Konecky, 1942 ed.

Sargent, F. W. *England, the United States, and the Southern Confederacy*. London, UK: Sampson Low, Son, and Co., 1863.

Scarlett, James D. *Tartans, of Scotland*. 1972. Cambridge, UK: The Lutterworth Press, 1996 ed.

Scharf, John Thomas. *History of the Confederate Navy, From Its Organization to the Surrender of Its Last Vessel*. Albany, NY: Joseph McDonough, 1894.

Schauffler, Robert Haven. *Our American Holidays: Lincoln's Birthday - A Comprehensive View of Lincoln as Given in the Most Noteworthy Essays, Orations and Poems, in Fiction and in Lincoln's Own Writings*. 1909. New York, NY: Moffat, Yard and Co., 1916 ed.

Schlüter, Herman. *Lincoln, Labor and Slavery: A Chapter from the Social History of America*. New York, NY: Socialist Literature Co., 1913.

Schurz, Carl. *Life of Henry Clay*. 2 vols. 1887. Boston, MA: Houghton, Mifflin and Co., 1899 ed.

Schwartz, Barry. *Abraham Lincoln and the Forge of National Memory*. Chicago, IL: University of Chicago Press, 2000.

Scott, Emmett J., and Lyman Beecher Stowe. *Booker T. Washington: Builder of a Civilization*. Garden City, NY: Doubleday, Page, and Co., 1916.

Scott, James Brown. *James Madison's Notes of Debates in the Federal Convention of 1787, and Their Relation to a More Perfect Society of Nations*. New York, NY: Oxford University Press, 1918.

Scruggs, Mike. *The Un-Civil War: Truths Your Teacher Never Told You*. Hendersonville, NC: Tribune Papers, 2007.

THE MCGAVOCKS OF CARNTON PLANTATION

Seabrook, Lochlainn. *The Goddess Dictionary of Words and Phrases: Introducing a New Core Vocabulary for the Women's Spirituality Movement*. 1997. Franklin, TN: Sea Raven Press, 2010 ed.
——. *Britannia Rules: Goddess-Worship in Ancient Anglo-Celtic Society - An Academic Look at the United Kingdom's Matricentric Spiritual Past*. 1999. Franklin, TN: Sea Raven Press, 2010 ed.
——. *The Book of Kelle: The Story of the Great Celtic Mother-Goddess, the Original Blessed Lady of Ireland*. 1999. Franklin, TN: Sea Raven Press, 2010 ed.
——. *The Caudills: An Etymological, Ethnological, and Genealogical Study - Exploring the Name and National Origins of a European-American Family*. 2003. Franklin, TN: Sea Raven Press, 2010 ed.
——. *Carnton Plantation Ghost Stories: True Tales of the Unexplained From Tennessee's Most Haunted Civil War House!* 2005. Franklin, TN: Sea Raven Press, 2010 ed.
——. *Nathan Bedford Forrest: Southern Hero, American Patriot: Honoring a Confederate Hero and the Old South*. 2007. Franklin, TN: Sea Raven Press, 2010 ed.
——. *Abraham Lincoln: The Southern View - Demythologizing America's Sixteenth President*. 2007. Franklin, TN: Sea Raven Press, 2010 ed.
——. *A Rebel Born: A Defense of Nathan Bedford Forrest - Confederate General, American Legend*. Franklin, TN: Sea Raven Press, 2010.
——. *Aphrodite's Trade: The Hidden History of Prostitution Unveiled*. Franklin, TN: Sea Raven Press, 2010.
——. *Everything You Were Taught About the Civil War is Wrong, Ask a Southerner! - Correcting the Errors of Yankee "History."* Franklin, TN: Sea Raven Press, 2010.
——. *Lincolnology: The Real Abraham Lincoln Revealed in His Own Words - A Study of Lincoln's Suppressed, Misinterpreted, and Forgotten Writings and Speeches*. Franklin, TN: Sea Raven Press, 2011 Civil War Sesquicentennial Edition.
Segal, Charles M. (ed.). *Conversations With Lincoln*. 1961. New Brunswick, NJ: Transaction, 2002 ed.
Segars, J. H., and Charles Kelly Barrow. *Black Southerners in Confederate Armies: A Collection of Historical Accounts*. Atlanta, GA: Southern Lion Books, 2001.
Seligmann, Herbert J. *The Negro Faces America*. New York, NY: Harper and Brothers, 1920.
Semmes, Admiral Ralph. *Service Afloat, or the Remarkable Career of the Confederate Cruisers Sumter and Alabama During the War Between the States*. London, UK: Sampson Low, Marston, Searle, and Rivington, 1887.
Sewall, Samuel. *Diary of Samuel Sewall*. 3 vols. Boston, MA: The Society, 1879.
Sewell, Richard H. *John P. Hale and the Politics of Abolition*. Cambridge, MA: Harvard University Press, 1965.
Shellenberger, John K. *The Battle of Franklin, Tennessee: November 30, 1864*. Hampton, VA: John K. Shellenberger, 1915.
Shenkman, Richard, and Kurt Edward Reiger. *One-Night Stands with American History: Odd, Amusing, and Little-Known Incidents*. 1980. New York, NY: Perennial, 2003 ed.
Sheppard, Eric William. *Bedford Forrest, The Confederacy's Greatest Cavalryman*. 1930. Dayton, OH: Morningside House, 1981 ed.
Sherman, William Tecumseh. *Memoirs of General William T. Sherman*. 2 vols. 1875. New York, NY: D. Appleton and Co., 1891 ed.
Shillington, Kevin. *History of Africa*. 1989. New York, NY: St. Martin's Press, 1994 ed.
Shorto, Russell. *Thomas Jefferson and the American Ideal*. Hauppauge, NY: Barron's, 1987.
Shotwell, Walter G. *Life of Charles Sumner*. New York, NY: Thomas Y. Crowell and Co., 1910.
Siepel, Kevin H. *Rebel: The Life and Times of John Singleton Mosby*. New York, NY: St. Martin's Press, 1983.
Simkins, Francis Butler. *A History of the South*. New York, NY: Random House, 1972.
Simmons, Henry E. *A Concise Encyclopedia of the Civil War*. New York, NY: Bonanza Books, 1965.
Simon, Paul. *Lincoln's Preparation for Greatness: The Illinois Legislative Years*. 1965. Chicago, IL: University of Illinois Press, 1971 ed.
Simpson, Lewis P. (ed.). *I'll Take My Stand: The South and the Agrarian Tradition*. 1930. Reprint. Baton Rouge, LA: University of Louisiana Press, 1977.
Skeat, Rev. W. Walter. *An Etymological Dictionary of the English Language*. New York, NY: Macmillan and Co., 1882.
Skidmore, Max J. *Presidential Performance: A Comprehensive Review*. Jefferson, NC: McFarland and Co., 2004.
Slotkin, Richard. *No Quarter: The Battle of the Crater, 1864*. New York, NY: Random House, 2009.

Smelser, Marshall. *American Colonial and Revolutionary History*. 1950. New York, NY: Barnes and Noble, 1966 ed.
——. *The Democratic Republic, 1801-1815*. New York, NY: Harper and Row, 1968.
Smith, Hedrick. *Reagan: The Man, The President*. Oxford, UK: Pergamon Press, 1980.
Smith, John David (ed.). *Black Soldiers in Blue: African American Troops in the Civil War Era*. Chapel Hill, NC: University of North Carolina Press, 2002.
Smith, Joseph. *The Pearl of Great Price*. Salt Lake City, UT: George Q. Cannon and Sons, 1891.
Smith, Kimberly K. *Wendell Berry and the Agrarian Tradition: A Common Grace*. Lawrence, KS: University Press of Kansas, 2003.
Smith, Mark M. (ed.). *The Old South*. Oxford, UK: Blackwell Publishers, 2001.
Smith, Page. *Trial by Fire: A People's History of the Civil War and Reconstruction*. New York, NY: McGraw-Hill, 1982.
Smith, Philip D., Jr. *Tartan for Me!: Suggested Tartan for 13,695 Scottish, Scotch-Irish, Irish and North American Names with Lists of Clan, Family, and District Tartans*. Bruceton, WV: Scotpress, 1990.
Smucker, Samuel M. *The Life and Times of Thomas Jefferson*. Philadelphia, PA: J. W. Bradley, 1859.
Snider, Denton J. *Lincoln at Richmond: A Dramatic Epos of the Civil War*. St. Louis, MO: Sigma, 1914.
Sobel, Robert (ed.). *Biographical Directory of the United States Executive Branch, 1774-1898*. Westport, CT: Greenwood Press, 1990.
Sorrel, Gilbert Moxley. *Recollections of a Confederate Staff Officer*. New York, NY: Neale Publishing Co., 1905.
Spaeth, Harold J., and Edward Conrad Smith. *The Constitution of the United States*. 1936. New York, NY: HarperCollins, 1991 ed.
Sparks, Jared. *The Works of Benjamin Franklin*. 10 vols. Chicago, IL: Townsend MacCoun, 1882.
Speer, William S. *Sketches of Prominent Tennesseans*. Nashville, TN: Albert B. Tavel, 1888.
Spence, James. *On the Recognition of the Southern Confederation*. Ithaca, NY: Cornell University Library, 1862.
Spooner, Lysander. *No Treason* (only Numbers 1, 2, and 6 were published). Boston, MA: Lysander Spooner, 1867-1870.
Stampp, Kenneth M. *The Peculiar Institution: Slavery in the Antebellum South*. New York, NY: Vintage, 1956.
Stanford, Peter Thomas. *The Tragedy of the Negro in America*. Boston, MA: published by author, 1898.
Stanton, Elizabeth Cady, Susan B. Anthony, and Matilda Joslyn Gage (eds.). *History of Woman Suffrage*. 2 vols. New York, NY: Fowler and Wells, 1881.
Starr, John W., Jr. *Lincoln and the Railroads: A Biographical Study*. New York, NY: Dodd, Mead and Co., 1927.
Staudenraus, P. J. *The African Colonization Movement, 1816-1865*. New York, NY: Columbia University Press, 1961.
Stebbins, Rufus Phineas. *An Historical Address Delivered At the Centennial Celebration of the Incorporation of the Town of Wilbraham, June 15, 1863*. Boston, MA: George C. Rand and Avery, 1864.
Stedman, Edmund Clarence, and Ellen Mackay Hutchinson (eds.). *A Library of American Literature From the Earliest Settlement to the Present Time*. 10 vols. New York, NY: Charles L. Webster and Co., 1888.
Steele, Joel Dorman, and Esther Baker Steele. *Barnes' Popular History of the United States of America*. New York, NY: A. S. Barnes and Co., 1904.
Steele, Shelby. *White Guilt: How Blacks and Whites Together Destroyed the Promise of the Civil Rights Era*. New York, NY: Harper Perennial, 2007.
Stein, Ben, and Phil DeMuth. *How To Ruin the United States of America*. Carlsbad, CA: New Beginnings Press, 2008.
Steiner, Bernard. *The History of Slavery in Connecticut*. Baltimore, MD: Johns Hopkins University Press, 1893.
Steiner, Lewis Henry. *Report of Lewis H. Steiner: Inspector of the Sanitary Commission, Containing a Diary Kept During the Rebel Occupation of Frederick, MD, September, 1862*. New York, NY: Anson D. F. Randolph, 1862.
Stephens, Alexander Hamilton. *Speech of Mr. Stephens, of Georgia, on the War and Taxation*. Washington, D.C.: J & G. Gideon, 1848.
——. *A Constitutional View of the Late War Between the States; Its Causes, Character, Conduct and Results*. 2 vols.

Philadelphia, PA: National Publishing, Co., 1870.
——. *Recollections of Alexander H. Stephens: His Diary Kept When a Prisoner at Fort Warren, Boston Harbour, 1865.* New York, NY: Doubleday, Page, and Co., 1910.
Stephenson, Nathaniel Wright. *Abraham Lincoln and the Union: A Chronicle of the Embattled North.* New Haven, CT: Yale University Press, 1918.
——. *Lincoln: An Account of His Personal Life, Especially of Its Springs of Action as Revealed and Deepened by the Ordeal of War.* Indianapolis, IN: Bobbs-Merrill, 1922.
Sterling, Dorothy (ed.). *Speak Out in Thunder Tones: Letters and Other Writings by Black Northerners, 1787-1865.* 1973. Cambridge, MA: Da Capo, 1998 ed.
Stern, Philip Van Doren (ed.). *The Life and Writings of Abraham Lincoln.* 1940. New York, NY: Modern Library, 2000.
Stewart, L. Lloyd. *A Far Cry From Freedom: Gradual Abolition (1799-1827): New York State's Crime Against Humanity.* Bloomington, IN: AuthorHouse, 2005.
Stonebraker, J. Clarence. *The Unwritten South: Cause, Progress and Results of the Civil War - Relics of Hidden Truth After Forty Years.* Seventh ed., n.p., 1908.
Stovall, Pleasant A. *Robert Toombs: Statesman, Speaker, Soldier, Sage.* New York, NY: Cassell Publishing, 1892.
Strain, John Paul. *Witness to the Civil War: The Art of John Paul Strain.* Philadelphia, PA: Courage, 2002.
Strode, Hudson. *Jefferson Davis: American Patriot.* 3 vols. New York, NY: Harcourt, Brace and World, 1955, 1959, 1964.
Sturge, Joseph. *A Visit to the United States in 1841.* London, UK: Hamilton, Adams, and Co., 1842.
Summers, Mark W. *The Plundering Generation: Corruption and the Crisis of the Union, 1849-1861.* New York, NY: Oxford University Press, 1988.
Sumner, Charles. *The Crime Against Kansas: The Apologies for the Crime - The True Remedy.* Boston, MA: John P. Jewett, 1856.
Swint, Henry L. (ed.) *Dear Ones at Home: Letters From Contraband Camps.* Nashville, TN: Vanderbilt University Press, 1966.
Sword, Wiley. *The Confederacy's Last Hurrah: Spring Hill, Franklin, and Nashville.* New York, NY: HarperCollins, 1992.
——. *Southern Invincibility: A History of the Confederate Heart.* New York, NY: St. Martin's Press, 1999.
Tarbell, Ida Minerva. *The Life of Abraham Lincoln.* 4 vols. New York, NY: Lincoln History Society, 1895-1900.
Tatalovich, Raymond, and Byron W. Daynes. *Presidential Power in the United States.* Monterey, CA: Brooks/Cole, 1984.
Taylor, Richard. *Destruction and Reconstruction: Personal Experiences of the Late War in the United States.* New York, NY: D. Appleton, 1879.
Taylor, Susie King. *Reminiscences of My Life in Camp With the 33rd United States Colored Troops Late 1st S. C. Volunteers.* Boston, MA: Susie King Taylor, 1902.
Taylor, Walter Herron. *General Lee: His Campaigns in Virginia, 1861-1865, With Personal Reminiscences.* Norfolk, VA: Nusbaum Book and News Co., 1906.
Tenney, William Jewett. *The Military and Naval History of the Rebellion in the United States.* New York, NY: D. Appleton and Co., 1865.
Terkel, Studs. *Hard Times: An Oral History of the Great Depression.* New York, NY: Avon, 1970.
Testimony Taken By the Joint Select Committee to Inquire Into the Condition of Affairs in the Late Insurrectionary States. 13 vols. Washington, D.C.: Government Printing Office, 1872.
Thackeray, William Makepeace. *Roundabout Papers.* Boston, MA: Estes and Lauriat, 1883.
Thatcher, Marshall P. *A Hundred Battles in the West: St. Louis to Atlanta, 1861-1865.* Detroit, MI: Marshall P. Thatcher, 1884.
The American Annual Cyclopedia and Register of Important Events of the Year 1861. New York, NY: D. Appleton and Co., 1868.
The American Annual Cyclopedia and Register of Important Events of the Year 1862. New York, NY: D. Appleton and Co., 1869.
The American Annual Cyclopedia and Register of Important Events of the Year 1863. New York, NY: D. Appleton and Co., 1864.

The Civil War Book of Lists. 1993. Edison, NJ: Castle Books, 2004 ed.
The Congressional Globe, Containing Sketches of the Debates and Proceedings of the First Session of the Twenty-Eighth Congress (Vol. 13). Washington, D.C.: The Globe, 1844.
The Great Issue to be Decided in November Next: Shall the Constitution and the Union Stand or Fall, Shall Sectionalism Triumph? Washington, D.C.: National Democratic Executive Committee, 1860.
The Oxford English Dictionary. Compact edition, 2 vols. 1928. Oxford, UK: Oxford University Press, 1979 ed.
The National Almanac and Annual Record for the Year 1863. Philadelphia, PA: George W. Childs, 1863.
The North British Review, February-May 1862, Vol. 36, Edinburgh, Scotland: T. and T. Clark, 1862.
The Quarterly Review, Vol. 111. London, UK: John Murray, 1862.
Thomas, Emory M. *The Confederate Nation: 1861-1865*. New York, NY: Harper and Row, 1979.
Thomas, Gabriel. *An Account of Pennsylvania and West New Jersey*. 1698. Cleveland, OH: Burrows Brothers Co., 1903 ed.
Thompson, Frank Charles (ed.). *The Thompson Chain Reference Bible* (King James Version). 1908. Indianapolis, IN: B. B. Kirkbride Bible Co., 1964 ed.
Thompson, Neal. *Driving With the Devil: Southern Moonshine, Detroit Wheels, and the Birth of NASCAR*. Three Rivers, MI: Three Rivers Press, 2006.
Thompson, Robert Means, and Richard Wainwright (eds.). *Confidential Correspondence of Gustavus Vasa Fox, Assistant Secretary of the Navy, 1861-1865*. 2 vols. 1918. New York, NY: Naval History Society, 1920 ed.
Thorndike, Rachel Sherman (ed.). *The Sherman Letters*. New York, NY: Charles Scribner's Sons, 1894.
Thornton, Brian. *101 Things You Didn't Know About Lincoln: Loves and Losses, Political Power Plays, White House Hauntings*. Avon, MA: Adams Media, 2006.
Thornton, Gordon. *The Southern Nation: The New Rise of the Old South*. Gretna, LA: Pelican Publishing Co., 2000.
Thornton, John. *Africa and Africans in the Making of the Atlantic World, 1400-1800*. 1992. Cambridge, UK: Cambridge University Press, 1999 ed.
Thornton, Mark, and Robert B. Ekelund, Jr. *Tariffs, Blockades, and Inflation: The Economics of the Civil War*. Wilmington, DE: Scholarly Resources, 2004.
Thruston, Gates P. *The Antiquities of Tennessee and the Adjacent States*. Cincinnati, OH: Robert Clarke and Co., 1890.
Tilley, John Shipley. *Lincoln Takes Command*. 1941. Nashville, TN: Bill Coats Limited, 1991 ed.
——. *Facts the Historians Leave Out: A Confederate Primer*. 1951. Nashville, TN: Bill Coats Limited, 1999 ed.
Tocqueville, Alexis de. *Democracy in America*. 2 vols. 1836. New York, NY: D. Appleton and Co., 1904 ed.
Tourgee, Albion W. *A Fool's Errand By One of the Fools*. London, UK: George Routledge and Sons, 1883.
Traupman, John C. *The New College Latin and English Dictionary*. 1966. New York, NY: Bantam, 1988 ed.
Trimpi, Helen P. *Crimson Confederates: Harvard Men Who Fought For the South*. Knoxville, TN: University of Tennessee Press, 2010.
Trumbull, Lyman. *Speech of Honorable Lyman Trumbull, of Illinois, at a Mass Meeting in Chicago, August 7, 1858*. Washington, D.C.: Buell and Blanchard, 1858.
Truth, Sojourner. *Narrative of Sojourner Truth*. 1850. Mineola, NY: Dover, 1997 ed.
Tucker, St. George. *On the State of Slavery in Virginia, in View of the Constitution of the United States, With Selected Writings*. Indianapolis, IN: Liberty Fund, 1999.
Turner, Edward Raymond. *The Negro in Pennsylvania, Slavery, Servitude, Freedom, 1639-1861*. Washington, D.C.: American Historical Association, 1911.
Tyler, Lyon Gardiner. *The Letters and Times of the Tylers*. 3 vols. Williamsburg, VA: N.P., 1896.
——. *Propaganda in History*. Richmond, VA: Richmond Press, 1920.
——. *The Gray Book: A Confederate Catechism*. Columbia, TN: Gray Book Committee, SCV, 1935.
Upshur, Abel Parker. *A Brief Enquiry Into the True Nature and Character of Our Federal Government*. Philadelphia, PA: John Campbell, 1863.
Vallandigham, Clement Laird. *Speeches, Arguments, Addresses, and Letters of Clement L. Vallandigham*. New York, NY: J. Walter and Co., 1864.

Vanauken, Sheldon. *The Glittering Illusion: English Sympathy for the Southern Confederacy*. Washington, D.C.: Regnery, 1989.
Van Buren, G. M. *Abraham Lincoln's Pen and Voice: Being a Complete Compilation of His Letters, Civil, Political, and Military*. Cincinnati, OH: Robert Clarke and Co., 1890.
Van Loon, Hendrik Willem. *The Story of America*. 1927. Cleveland, OH: World Publishing Co., 1942 ed.
Van West, Carroll (ed.). *The Tennessee Encyclopedia of History and Culture*. Nashville, TN: Rutledge Hill Press, 1998.
———. *Tennessee History: The Land, the People, and the Culture*. Knoxville, TN: University of Tennessee Press, 1998.
Vaux, Roberts. *Memoirs of the Life of Anthony Benezet*. London, UK: Darton, Harvey, and Co., 1817.
Ver Steeg, Clarence Lester, and Richard Hofstadter. *A People and a Nation*. New York, NY: Harper and Row, 1977.
Villard, Henry. *Memoirs of Henry Villard, Journalist and Financier, 1835-1900*. 2 vols. Boston, MA: Houghton, Mifflin and Co., 1904.
Voegeli, Victor Jacque. *Free But Not Equal: The Midwest and the Negro During the Civil War*. Chicago, IL: University of Chicago Press, 1967.
Wade, Wyn Craig. *The Fiery Cross: The Ku Klux Klan in America*. 1987. New York, NY: Touchstone, 1988 ed.
Walker, Barbara G. *The Woman's Encyclopedia of Myths and Secrets*. New York, NY: Harper and Row, 1983.
Wallcut, R. F. (pub.). *Southern Hatred of the American Government, the People of the North, and Free Institutions*. Boston, MA: R. F. Wallcut, 1862.
Wallechinsky, David, Irving Wallace, and Amy Wallace. *The People's Almanac Presents The Book of Lists*. New York, NY: Morrow, 1977.
Walsh, George. *"Those Damn Horse Soldiers": True Tales of the Civil War Cavalry*. New York, NY: Forge, 2006.
Ward, Andrew. *River Run Red: The Fort Pillow Massacre in the American Civil War*. New York, NY: Viking, 2005.
Ward, John William. *Andrew Jackson: Symbol for an Age*. 1953. Oxford, UK: Oxford University Press, 1973 ed.
Waring, George Edward, Jr. *Whip and Spur*. New York, NY: Doubleday and McClure, 1897.
Warner, Ezra J. *Generals in Gray: Lives of the Confederate Commanders*. 1959. Baton Rouge, LA: Louisiana State University Press, 1989 ed.
———. *Generals in Blue: Lives of the Union Commanders*. 1964. Baton Rouge, LA: Louisiana State University Press, 2006 ed.
Warren, Robert Penn. *Who Speaks for the Negro?* New York, NY: Random House, 1965.
Warshauer, Matthew. *Connecticut in the American Civil War: Slavery, Sacrifice, and Survival*. Middletown, CT: Wesleyan University Press, 2011.
Washington, Booker T. *Up From Slavery: An Autobiography*. 1901. Garden City, NY: Doubleday, Page and Co., 1919 ed.
Washington, Henry Augustine. *The Writings of Thomas Jefferson*. 9 vols. New York, NY: H. W. Derby, 1861.
Watkins, Samuel Rush. *"Co. Aytch," Maury Grays, First Tennessee Regiment; or, A Side Show of the Big Show*. 1882. Chattanooga, TN: Times Printing Co., 1900 ed.
Watson, Harry L. *Andrew Jackson vs. Henry Clay: Democracy and Development in Antebellum America*. New York, NY: St. Martin's Press, 1998.
Watts, Peter. *A Dictionary of the Old West*. 1977. New York, NY: Promontory Press, 1987 ed.
Waugh, John C. *Surviving the Confederacy: Rebellion, Ruin, and Recovery - Roger and Sara Pryor During the Civil War*. New York, NY: Harcourt, 2002.
Way, George, and Romilly Squire. *Scottish Clan and Family Encyclopedia*. Glasgow, Scotland: HarperCollins, 1994.
Weeks, Michael. *The Complete Civil War Road Trip Guide*. Woodstock, VT: Countryman Press, 2009.
Weintraub, Max. *The Blue Book of American History*. New York, NY: Regents Publishing Co., 1960.
Welles, Gideon. *Diary of Gideon Welles, Secretary of the Navy Under Lincoln and Johnson* (Vol. 1). Boston, MA: Houghton Mifflin, 1911.
White, Charles Langdon, Edwin Jay Foscue, and Tom Lee McKnight. *Regional Geography of Anglo-America*.

1943. Englewood Cliffs, NJ: Prentice-Hall, 1985 ed.
White, Henry Alexander. *Robert E. Lee and the Southern Confederacy, 1807-1870*. New York, NY: G. P. Putnam's Sons, 1897.
Whitman, Walt. *Leaves of Grass*. 1855. New York, NY: Modern Library, 1921 ed.
——. *Complete Prose Works*. Philadelphia, PA: David McKay, 1892.
Wilbur, Henry Watson. *President Lincoln's Attitude Towards Slavery and Emancipation: With a Review of Events Before and Since the Civil War*. Philadelphia, PA: W. H. Jenkins, 1914.
Wilder, Craig Steven. *A Covenant With Color: Race and Social Power in Brooklyn*. New York, NY: Columbia University Press, 2000.
Wiley, Bell Irvin. *Southern Negroes: 1861-1865*. 1938. New Haven, CT: Yale University Press, 1969 ed.
——. *The Life of Johnny Reb: The Common Soldier of the Confederacy*. 1943. Baton Rouge, LA: Louisiana State University Press, 1978 ed.
——. *The Plain People of the Confederacy*. 1943. Columbia, SC: University of South Carolina, 2000 ed.
——. *The Life of Billy Yank: The Common Soldier of the Union*. 1952. Baton Rouge, LA: Louisiana State University Press, 2001 ed.
Wilkens, J. Steven. *America: The First 350 Years*. Monroe, LA: Covenant Publications, 1998.
Wilkerson, Lyn. *Roads Less Traveled: Exploring America's Past on Its Back Roads*. San Jose, CA: Writers Club Press, 2000.
Williams, Charles Richard. *The Life of Rutherford Birchard Hayes, Nineteenth President of the United States*. 2 vols. Boston, MA: Houghton Mifflin Co., 1914.
Williams, George Washington. *History of the Negro Race in America: From 1619 to 1880, Negroes as Slaves, as Soldiers, and as Citizens* (2 vols. in 1). New York, NY: G. P. Putnam's Sons, 1885.
——. *A History of the Negro Troops in the War of the Rebellion 1861-1865*. New York, NY: Harper and Brothers, 1888.
Williams, James. *The South Vindicated*. London, UK: Longman, Green, Longman, Roberts, and Green, 1862.
Williams-Meyers, A. J. *Long Hammering: Essays on the Forging of an African American Presence in the Hudson River Valley to the Early Twentieth Century*. Trenton, NJ: Africa World Press, 1994.
Williams, Oscar. *African Americans and Colonial Legislation in the Middle Colonies*. New York, NY: Garland Publishing, 1998.
Williams, William H. *Slavery and Freedom in Delaware, 1639-1865*. Wilmington, DE: Scholarly Resources, 1996.
Wills, Brian Steel. *The Confederacy's Greatest Cavalryman: Nathan Bedford Forrest*. Lawrence, KS: University Press of Kansas, 1992.
Wills, Ridley W., II. *The History of Belle Meade: Mansion, Plantation, and Stud*. Nashville, TN: Vanderbilt University Press, 1991.
Wilson, Charles Reagan, and William Ferris. *Encyclopedia of Southern Culture* (Vol. 1). New York, NY: Anchor, 1989.
Wilson, Clyde N. *Why the South Will Survive: Fifteen Southerners Look at Their Region a Half Century After I'll Take My Stand*. Athens, GA: University of Georgia Press, 1981.
——. (ed.) *The Essential Calhoun: Selections From Writings, Speeches, and Letters*. New Brunswick, NJ: Transaction Publishers, 1991.
——. *A Defender of Southern Conservatism: M.E. Bradford and His Achievements*. Columbia, MO: University of Missouri Press, 1999.
——. *From Union to Empire: Essays in the Jeffersonian Tradition*. Columbia, SC: The Foundation for American Education, 2003.
——. *Defending Dixie: Essays in Southern History and Culture*. Columbia, SC: The Foundation for American Education, 2005.
Wilson, Henry. *History of the Rise and Fall of the Slave Power in America*. 3 vols. Boston, MA: James R. Osgood and Co., 1877.
Wilson, Joseph Thomas. *The Black Phalanx: A History of the Negro Soldiers of the United States in the Wars of 1775-1812, 1861-'65*. Hartford, CT: American Publishing Co., 1890.
Wilson, Woodrow (President). *Division and Reunion: 1829-1889*. 1893. New York, NY: Longmans, Green,

and Co., 1908 ed.
———. *A History of the American People.* 5 vols. 1902. New York, NY: Harper and Brothers, 1918 ed.
Wirzba, Norman (ed.) *The Essential Agrarian Reader: The Future of Culture, Community, and the Land.* Lexington, KY: University Press of Kentucky, 2003.
Wood, W. J. *Civil War Generalship: The Art of Command.* 1997. New York, NY: Da Capo Press, 2000 ed.
Woodard, Komozi. *A Nation Within a Nation: Amiri Baraka (LeRoi Jones) and Black Power Politics.* Chapel Hill, NC: University of North Carolina Press, 1999.
Woodburn, James Albert. *The Life of Thaddeus Stevens.* Indianapolis, IN: Bobbs-Merrill, 1913.
Woods, Thomas E., Jr. *The Politically Incorrect Guide to American History.* Washington, D.C.: Regnery, 2004.
Woodson, Carter G. (ed.). *The Journal of Negro History* (Vol. 4). Lancaster, PA: Association for the Study of Negro Life and History, 1919.
Woodward, William E. *Meet General Grant.* 1928. New York, NY: Liveright Publishing, 1946 ed.
Woodworth, Steven E. *Jefferson Davis and His Generals: The Failure of Confederate Command in the West.* Lawrence, KS: University Press of Kansas, 1990.
Wright, Donald R. *African Americans in the Colonial Era: From African Origins Through the American Revolution.* Wheeling, IL: Harlan Davidson, 2000.
Wright, John D. *The Language of the Civil War.* Westport, CT: Oryx, 2001.
Wyeth, John Allan. *Life of General Nathan Bedford Forrest.* New York, NY: Harper and Brothers, 1899.
———. *That Devil Forrest* (redacted modern version of Wyeth's *Life of General Nathan Bedford Forrest*). 1959. Baton Rouge, LA: Louisiana State University Press, 1989 ed.
Young, Bennett Henderson. *Confederate Wizards of the Saddle.* 1914. Lanham, MD: J. S. Sanders and Co., 1999 ed.
Young, John Russell. *Around the World With General Grant.* 2 vols. New York, NY: American News Co., 1879.
Zaehner, R. C. (ed.) *Encyclopedia of the World's Religions.* 1959. New York, NY: Barnes and Noble, 1997 ed.
Zall, Paul M. (ed.). *Lincoln on Lincoln.* Lexington, KY: University Press of Kentucky, 1999.
Zavodnyik, Peter. *The Age of Strict Construction: A History of the Growth of Federal Power, 1789-1861.* Washington, D.C.: Catholic University of America Press, 2007.
Zinn, Howard. *A People's History of the United States: 1492-Present.* 1980. New York, NY: HarperCollins, 1995.

INDEX

NOTES:
- *Only the primary McGavocks and Winders in the McGavock and Winder family trees are listed in the Index.*
- *The information contained in the captions under the illustrations is not listed in the Index.*
- *An automatic indexer was used to assist in the preparation of this Index, which may have resulted in some irregularities.*

abatis, 329, 333, 351, 353, 455
Aberdeenshire, Scotland, 522
abolition, 9, 14, 69, 74, 86, 88, 95, 101, 164, 179, 180, 185, 187, 189, 190, 192, 194, 198, 204, 207, 244, 249-251, 259, 293, 394, 972, 979, 986, 988
abolition movement, 14, 86, 185, 187, 189, 198, 207, 259
abolition of slavery, 179, 293, 979
abolitionism, 68, 227, 270, 965, 972
abolitionist hypocrisy, 182
abolitionist sentiment, 69, 85
abolitionist-racists, 67
abolitionists, 68, 69, 72, 73, 86, 97, 98, 108, 119, 121, 128, 163, 172, 179, 180, 183, 185, 188, 190, 207, 245, 246, 249-251, 255, 257, 264, 270, 293, 295, 319, 979
abolitionists, Southern, 185
abolitionization, of whites, 96
Abraham Lincoln: The Southern View (Seabrook), 144, 196, 596
Abraham Lincoln's white dream, 962
Abraham, of the Bible, 211, 321
absenteeism levels, in Confederate military, 311
abuse of servants, myth of, 142
abuses, 118, 142
accordion, 478
ACS, 121, 207, 262-264
Adam, of the Bible, 217
Adams, Charles F., Jr., 190
Adams, Charles F., Sr., 190
Adams, John, 190, 194, 197, 374, 375, 379, 415
Adams, Nehemiah, 120, 189
Adams, Shelby Lee, 1044
Adamu, the Sumerian "Adam", 217
Adapa, the Babylonian "Adam", 217
Advance and Retreat (Hood), 351
Africa, 12, 14, 66, 68, 76, 80, 83, 87, 90-92, 96, 97, 100, 108, 112, 113, 115-117, 119, 126, 127, 135, 141, 144, 146, 150-156, 162, 163, 165, 167-171, 173, 175, 176, 179, 181, 182, 185, 188, 190, 193, 197, 198, 203, 205-207, 214-216, 220, 222, 227-231, 249, 253-255, 259, 263, 264, 266, 268-270, 279, 285, 291, 294-297, 300, 318, 344, 362, 390, 394, 398, 400, 440, 448-450, 479, 494, 594, 595, 957, 961, 962, 964, 966, 967, 969-971, 974, 977, 984-987, 989, 991, 992
  slavery in, 116
  slavery in today, 117
Africa's role in slavery, 169
African domestic slavery, 169
African immigrants, and postbellum South, 83
African Iron Age, 169
African Methodist Episcopal Church, 163
African peoples, 171, 216
African servitude, 127, 203, 269
African slave owners, 167
African slave trade, 171, 967
African slavers, 116, 168, 216
African slavery, 127, 167, 185, 190, 206, 969
African-American Confederate soldiers, 106, 595
African-American slave owners, 126, 149-152, 206
African-American superstitions, 448
African-American war effort, 112
African-Americans, cultural contributions, 227
Africanization, of whites, 96
Africans, who practiced slavery, 170
African-American culture, 119
African-American servants, 440, 479
African-Americans, 12, 14, 66, 83, 87, 91, 92, 97, 108, 135, 153, 154, 163, 188, 220, 227, 229-231, 249, 253, 254, 291, 294-296, 300, 318, 344, 390, 595, 957
Aiken, Sally, 559
Alabama, 30, 112, 135, 142, 151, 161, 221, 271, 289, 317, 377-380, 401, 503, 593, 962, 970, 980, 986, 1045
Alaska, 30, 263
Albany, NY, 174
Alcott, Louisa May, 89
Alexander, James L., 598
Alexander, King of Troy, 37, 589
Alexandria, VA, 449

THE MCGAVOCKS OF CARNTON PLANTATION

Alfonzo IX, King, 42, 590
Alfred the Great, King, 37, 589
Algiers, LA, 299
all-black churches, 163
allegiance to nation, 239
allegiance to state, 239
Allen family, of West Virginia, 1044
Allen, Felix G., 597
Allen, Richard, 163
Allison, Elizabeth, 285, 538
Allisona, TN, 285, 538, 1044
Alston, R. A., 234
Alton, IL, 72, 77, 99
amalgamation, 194, 223, 224
Amburgey, Irene E., 355
Amburgey, Lloyd F., 355
Amburgey, Opal J., 355
America, 2, 4, 11-15, 27-30, 32-36, 38-41, 44-47, 49, 51, 52, 54-57, 61, 62, 66-69, 72-74, 76-83, 85-92, 94-97, 103, 106-108, 112, 113, 115-119, 121-127, 129, 132, 135, 138, 141-146, 148, 150-155, 157, 158, 160, 162, 163, 165-178, 181, 182, 184, 187, 188, 190, 191, 193-198, 200-202, 205-213, 215-220, 222, 224, 225, 227-236, 238-241, 243, 247, 249, 250, 253-257, 259, 260, 262-274, 276-281, 288, 291, 292, 294-297, 300, 302, 303, 306-315, 317, 318, 321, 323, 333, 343-345, 348, 351, 362, 367, 369, 371, 376, 377, 382, 385, 390, 394, 398-401, 403, 405, 416, 426, 427, 435, 437, 438, 440, 448, 450, 455, 456, 467-471, 473, 477, 479, 483, 486, 494, 514, 526, 527, 532-534, 552, 554, 563, 569, 578, 581, 584, 588, 594, 595, 957, 958, 960-982, 984-992, 1040, 1047
    slavery in today, 116
American abolition movement, 14, 86, 187
American apartheid, 14, 144, 262
American Bond, 440
American branches of the McGavocks, 32
American Colonization Society, 207, 213, 262
American Confederacy, 39, 196, 215, 233, 240, 277
American McGavocks, 29, 33
    Northern branch, 32, 33
    Southern branch, 29, 33
American Revolutionary War, 39, 45, 51, 56, 57, 188, 255, 527, 533, 552, 569, 588
American slave industry, 167
American slave traders, 117

American slavery, 14, 66, 72, 79, 81, 85, 127, 144, 146, 153, 168, 169, 172, 174, 184, 197, 230, 263, 279, 970, 976, 978, 982
American System, 76, 95, 103, 236, 240, 241, 273, 276, 312, 486, 962
America's true slave capital, 182
Americo-Liberians, 264
ammunition runners, 111
amputations, 488
An Essay on Liberty and Slavery (Bledsoe), 211
Anaconda Plan, 362, 491
anarchy, 307, 397
Anderson, Liz, 355
Anderson, Robert T., 593
Andrew Crockett House, Brentwood, TN, 563
Andrew, Prince, 43, 589
Andrews, Frank M., 598
Andrews, John, 598
Anglin, Daniel, 598
Anglo-Puritanism, in the North, 235
Anglo-Saxon culture, in the North, 234
Anglo-African, 156
antebellum houses, 287
antebellum plantation system, 383
Antenor IV, King, 37, 590
Anthony, Marc, 37
Anthony, Susan B., 257
anti-abolitionism, and Lincoln, 144
anti-Confederate mind set, 281
anti-Confederate societies, Southern, 310
anti-Federalism, 186
anti-Lincoln Yankees, 315
anti-personnel entanglements, 351
anti-South abolitionist tracts, 118
anti-South authors, 114
anti-South Civil War propaganda, 13
anti-South crusaders, 80
anti-South groups, 594
anti-South propagandists, 244
anti-South scholars, 114
Antifederalism, 236
Antifederalists, 238
Antigua, 178
Antioch, TN, 449
antislavery leaders, Southern, 189
antisocial personality disorder, 122
antiwar sentiment, 302, 303, 305, 311
anti-abolitionists, 72
anti-South folklore, 202
anti-South partisans, 129
anti-South propaganda, 80, 85, 397, 438
anti-South proponents, 199, 230, 344
anti-South whites, 84
anti-South writers, 146, 220, 250, 450, 595, 959

994

THE MCGAVOCKS OF CARNTON PLANTATION

apartheid, 14, 144, 262
apartheid, American, 144, 262
Aphrodite (goddess), 449
Aphrodite's Trade (Seabrook), 424
apocryphal texts, 423
Appalachia, 40
apple toddy, 462
Appomattox Court House, 367
Appomattox, NC, 231
Appomattox, VA, 16, 46, 244, 274, 311, 362
apprenticeship, 144
apprenticeship, servitude as a form of, 144
apprenticing, black servants, 144
Aquinas, Saint Thomas, 202
Arabian slave traders, 116, 117
Arabian slavery, 209
Arabic slave trade, 169
archaeologists, 47, 436, 449
archaeology, 435, 436, 445, 452, 966
archaeology, Native-American, in Franklin, TN, 47
architects, 137, 228, 277
Argyll, Scotland, 523
Argyllshire, Scotland, 523, 524
aristocratic planters, 200
Aristotle, 210, 213
Arizona, 30, 55
Arkansas, 30, 317, 379, 599
Arlington Cemetery, 382
Arlington House, 382
Armistead, George H., 420
Armistead, W. H., 426
Armstrong, Ben F., 598
Armstrong, George Washington, 535, 555
Armstrong, J. I., 422
Armstrong, William, 535
Army of Tennessee, 23, 327, 335, 336, 340, 346, 351, 352, 354-356, 359, 368, 378, 503, 966-968, 984, 1043
Army of the Ohio, 327, 333, 336, 339
Army of the Potomac (U.S.), 292
Arthur, Chester A., 343
Articles of Confederation, 195, 196, 239, 369, 470, 975
Asante, 216
Asbury, A. E., 506
ash floors, at Carnton, 461
ash tree wood, 441, 461
Ashanti, 216
Ashby, Turner, 364
Ashe, Sam, Private (black Confederate), 109
Ashe, Samuel A'Court, 318
Asian-American Confederate soldiers, 107, 595
asparagus, 463
Association of Lt. Gen. Nathan Bedford Forrest Escort and Staff, 283
Assyrian slavery, 209
Assyrian slaves, 209
astrology, 424
Asylum for the Blind, intentionally destroyed by Yanks, 340
atheism, 205
Athelred II, King, 37, 589
Athena (goddess), 449
Athens, GA, 449
Athens, Greece, 449
Atkins, Chet, 1041
Atkinson, Mary A., 502
Atlanta campaign, 343
Atlanta, GA, 174, 330, 349, 352, 358, 364
Atlantic slave trade, 962, 967, 969
Atorkor, Africa, 216
Attucks, Crispus, 255
Atwood, John, 411
Auberjonois, René, 43, 590
Augusta County, VA, 35, 36
Aulson, John, 47
Austen, Jane, 589
Australian Confederate soldiers, 595
Avery, Mary, 536, 556, 573
Ayres, Elijah Hanes, Sr., 571, 582
Ayres, Lawrence, 422
Ayrshire, Scotland, 522, 523
Babylonian creation myth, 217
Babylonian slavery, 209
Babylonian slaves, 209
Bache, Alexander Dallas, 41, 589
Bache, Caroline P., 565
Bache, Dallas, 41, 565, 589
Bache, Richard, Jr., 41, 565
Bache, Richard, Sr., 41
Bachmann, Michele, 15
Back to Africa movement, 266
bacon, 462
bacteria, 489
bacterial infections, 491
Balch, Alfred, 49
balusters, 447
balustrade, 447
banjo, 228
Banks, Nathaniel Prentiss, 216, 295, 297
baptism, 205, 214
barbed wire, 455
Barber, Captain, 605
Barnicot, Nigel, 593
Bartherus, King, 37, 590
Barton, Edward, 506
basement, Carnton's, 454
Basin Springs, TN, 598, 600, 601
Basina, Queen, 424

THE MCGAVOCKS OF CARNTON PLANTATION

Bass, John M., 408, 410, 418
Bateman, Elizabeth, 533
Bateman, Jonathan, 533, 553
Bateman, William, 533, 553
Batte, Emily, 557
Batte, Thomas, 557
Battery Donaldson, 340
Battle of Antietam, 95, 221
Battle of Atlanta, 368, 369, 596, 599, 601
Battle of Barbourville, 289
Battle of Baxter Springs, 325
Battle of Bean's Station, 325
Battle of Bennington, 256
Battle of Bethel Church, 109
Battle of Blackburn's Ford, 289
Battle of Brandywine, 256
Battle of Brentwood, 325
Battle of Brices Cross Roads, 326
Battle of Brown's Mill, 326
Battle of Buckland Mills, 325
Battle of Bull's Gap, 326
Battle of Calcasieu Pass, 325
Battle of Camden, 51
Battle of Cane Hill, 324
Battle of Carthage, 288
Battle of Cedar Mountain, 57, 324
Battle of Chancellorsville, 325, 353
Battle of Charleston Harbor, 325
Battle of Charlestown, 325
Battle of Chester Station, 325
Battle of Chickamauga, 325, 344, 348, 390, 598, 600-604
Battle of Chustenahlah, 289
Battle of Chusto-Talasah, 289
Battle of Clark's Mill, 324
Battle of Cold Harbor II, 326
Battle of Columbia, 326
Battle of Concord, 39, 256
Battle of Corinth, 600
Battle of Corydon, 325
Battle of Cumberland Church, 366
Battle of Dandridge, 325
Battle of Deep Bottom II, 326
Battle of Dinwiddie Courthouse, 366
Battle of Dry Wood Creek, 289
Battle of Fair Oaks and Darbytown Road, 326
Battle of Fairfield, 325
Battle of Fishing Creek, 599-604
Battle of Fort Donelson, 50, 285, 355, 367
Battle of Fort Fisher I, 366
Battle of Fort Pillow, 325, 388, 391, 393
Battle of Fort Pillow, and Forrest, 391
Battle of Fort Sumter I, 93, 140, 275, 280, 288
Battle of Fort Sumter II, 325
Battle of Franklin I, 21, 329, 378, 381, 484

Battle of Franklin II, 7, 12, 21, 232, 288, 327, 333, 334, 336, 341, 346, 348, 350, 353, 354, 358-360, 364-366, 368, 370, 371, 374, 375, 378-380, 386, 394, 395, 401, 414, 425, 455, 463, 487, 489, 493, 494, 501, 505, 507-509, 514, 517, 596, 598, 599, 603, 1042, 1044
Battle of Franklin II, statistics, 335
Battle of Franklin III, 21, 345, 378
Battle of Fredericksburg I, 324
Battle of Gainesville, 326
Battle of Gaines's Mills, 353
Battle of Galveston, 324
Battle of Germantown, 468
Battle of Gettysburg, 163, 189, 348, 353
Battle of Gladsville, 1043
Battle of Glasgow, 326
Battle of Greenbrier River, 289
Battle of Harpers Ferry, 324
Battle of Hartsville, 324
Battle of Hartville, 325
Battle of Hobkirk Hill, 51
Battle of Hoover's Gap, 598-601
Battle of Independence I, 324
Battle of Invernahaven, 28
Battle of Jackson, 324
Battle of Johnsonville, 326
Battle of Jonesboro, 600, 601, 603, 604
Battle of Kelly's Ford, 325
Battle of Kennesaw Mountain, 326, 603
Battle of Kernstown II, 326
Battle of Kessler's Cross Lanes, 289
Battle of Lawrence, 325
Battle of Leatherwood, 1043
Battle of Lebanon, 325
Battle of Lexington, 39, 256
Battle of Lexington I, 289
Battle of Lexington II, 326
Battle of Liberty, 289
Battle of Little Blue River, 326
Battle of Lone Jack, 324
Battle of Lovejoy's Station, 326
Battle of Manassas Gap, 325
Battle of Manassas I, 289
Battle of Manassas II, 324
Battle of Manassas Station Operations, 324
Battle of Mansfield, 325
Battle of Marks' Mills, 325
Battle of Memphis, 326
Battle of Mile Hill, 324
Battle of Mill Cliff, 1043
Battle of Mill Springs, 599, 601
Battle of Miskel Farm, 325
Battle of Missionary Ridge, 598, 603

THE MCGAVOCKS OF CARNTON PLANTATION

Battle of Monocacy, 326
Battle of Munfordville, 324
Battle of Murfreesboro I, 324, 598, 599
Battle of Nashville, 335, 344, 346, 368, 378, 394, 508, 596, 598, 600, 602, 603
Battle of Natural Bridge, 366
Battle of New Hope Church, 326, 599
Battle of New Market, 326
Battle of New Orleans, 256
Battle of Oak Hills, 289
Battle of Okolona, 325
Battle of Olustee, 325
Battle of Paducah, 325
Battle of Palmito Hill, 366
Battle of Palmito Ranch, 366
Battle of Parker's Cross Roads, 324
Battle of Parry Station, 377
Battle of Patients and Penitents, 326
Battle of Peach Tree Creek, 601
Battle of Petersburg I, 326
Battle of Petersburg II, 326
Battle of Pickett's Mill, 326
Battle of Poison Spring, 325
Battle of Poor Fork, 1043
Battle of Proctor's Creek, 326
Battle of Raymond, 286
Battle of Ream's Station I, 326
Battle of Resaca, 600, 603
Battle of Richmond, 324
Battle of Rio Hill, 325
Battle of Rogersville, 325
Battle of Round Mountain, 289
Battle of Sabine Pass II, 325
Battle of Sacramento, 289
Battle of Salem Church, 325
Battle of Saltville, 1043
Battle of San Jacinto, 55
Battle of Saratoga, 256
Battle of Savannah, 256
Battle of Sharpsburg, 95, 221, 345
Battle of Shepherdstown, 324
Battle of Shiloh, 598, 599, 601-604
Battle of Spring Hill, 346
Battle of Staunton River Bridge, 326
Battle of Sterling Bridge, 351
Battle of Stirling's Plantation, 325
Battle of Tampa, 324
Battle of the Alamo, 55
Battle of the Crater, 326, 986
Battle of Thompson's Station, 50, 325, 355
Battle of Thoroughfare Gap, 324
Battle of Ticonderoga, 256
Battle of Valverde, 324
Battle of Vicksburg, 57
Battle of Walkerton, 325

Battle of Wapping Heights, 325
Battle of Ware Bottom Church, 326
Battle of White Plains, 256
Battle of Whitesburg, 1043
Battle of Winchester II, 325
Battle of Yorktown, 256
battles, number of fought in TN, 327
Baumfree, Isabella (Sojourner Truth), 132
Beard, Francis, 549
beatings, Yankee, 294
Beauchamp, Louise, 509
Beauregard, P. G. T., 280, 404, 1044
Beck, Glenn, 487
Bedford County, TN, 385
Beech, Fred B., 598
Beech, Paul B., 598
beef, 463
Beethoven, Ludwig von, 478
beeves, 345
beggary, 320
Belcher, Jonathan, 177
Belchers, New England slaving family, 178
Belgian Confederate soldiers, 595
Belgium, 271
Bell, Alfred W., 491
Belle Meade Mansion, 1047
Belle Meade Plantation, 48, 146, 342, 446, 476, 503, 520, 558, 572, 1043, 1044
Belle Meade Plantation's (horse) race track, 342
Belmont Mansion, 1047
Ben Bolt (song), 330
Benjamin, Judah, 101, 112
Bennett, J. A., 598
Bennett, W. S., 598
Bennett, William, 598
Bentley, Judith Archer, 559
Benton, Jessie Ann, 42
Benton, Thomas Hart, 42, 47
Berry, Jane Campbell, 557
Berry, Johnson, 598
bias toward Southerners, 16
Bible, 12, 21, 27, 65, 88, 201-203, 205, 206, 211, 212, 301, 472, 473, 495, 515, 518, 569, 589, 961, 965, 972, 979, 980, 989
Bible, McGavock family, 301
Big Brother, 312
big government, 54, 76, 264, 275, 312, 976, 982
big house, 229, 437, 438, 443
bigotry, 66
Bill of Rights, 14, 985
Billups, Amanda, 551, 576
Billups, Cealy, 552, 576
Billy Yank, 333, 991
Birch, Lucy E., 507

997

THE MCGAVOCKS OF CARNTON PLANTATION

biscuits, 463
black caste system, 450
black civil rights, 88, 95, 105, 110, 153, 154, 164, 197, 214, 216, 224, 246, 252, 254, 256, 257, 259, 267, 269, 296, 298
Black Codes, 141, 153, 154, 156, 164, 222, 224, 225
black colonization, 216, 241, 264
black commerce, 133
black Confederate soldiers, 109, 115
black Confederate troops, 112
black Confederates, 108, 962, 976
black delegation, to see Lincoln, 267
black deportation, 179, 190, 223, 264
black deportation, compulsory, 269
black economy, the, 320
black enlistment, 254, 259, 260, 295
black equality, 259
black female Confederate soldiers, 111
black hate crimes, against whites, 398
black insurrections, 84
black labor, 138
black land giveaways, 105
Black Law, 71
black leaders, 251
black mammies, 230
Black Mammy of the South, 230
Black Mammy statue, 230
black men, 107, 160, 223, 295, 298, 974
black nationalism, 266
black officers, 297
black overseers, 152
black plantation foremen, 133
black plantation managers, 133
black pride, 266
black racism, 266
black separatism, 266
black separatists, 266
black servant economy, in South, 135
black servants, and apprenticeship, 144
black servitude, 130, 136, 144, 202, 232, 280, 435
black slave owners, 125, 149-152, 165, 230
black slaves, Northern, 106
black slaves, percentage of that stayed in Dixie during the War, 114
black soldiers, 107, 109, 112, 226, 255, 260, 261, 293-298, 316, 344, 984, 987
black soldiers defrauded, by U.S. government, 296
black soldiers, and Lincoln's racist pay scale, 297
black suffrage, 224, 225
black troops, 260, 293, 966
black Union soldiers, executed by Lincoln, 297
black wet nurses, 230
black-only state, idea of, 266

Blackburn, Mildred, 574
blacks, 67-69, 72-76, 80-87, 90-94, 96, 97, 102, 103, 105-111, 113-115, 119, 121-124, 127, 131-133, 135, 138-142, 144, 145, 147-150, 152-165, 168, 176, 178, 180, 183, 187, 188, 198, 205-207, 213-215, 218, 219, 221-228, 230, 231, 249-251, 253-257, 259-270, 290-294, 296-300, 309, 318-320, 328, 344, 350, 362, 383, 389, 390, 394, 396-398, 400, 405, 448, 506, 957, 963, 964, 981, 987
blacks, free, 149
blacks, freed, known as contraband in North, 296
blacks, Lincoln prohibits from enlisting, 253
blacks, Northern whites' fears of, 96
blacks, postwar, and quality of life, 318
blacksmiths, 137, 295
Blackwell, Catherine, 559
Blackwell, Hardin, 108
Bland, Anna, 373
Bledsoe, Albert Taylor, 211
Bleeding Kansas, 87
blockade, Lincoln's, 304, 362, 491, 492
Boadicea, Queen, 60, 416, 589
boar, 454
Board, Nancy, 544
bodark tree, 455
body servant, 147
boiled ham, 462
Bolling, Edith, 1044
bondage, 96, 116, 124, 128, 146, 170, 213, 252, 979
bondmaids, 212
bondmen, 212
bondservants, 173
Bondurant, Matilda, 543
Bonnie Blue Flag (song), 330
bookkeeping, at Carnton, 465
Boone, Daniel, 386
Boone, Nathan, 386
Boone, Pat, 386, 1041
Booth, John Wilkes, 265
Bostick Female Academy, 386, 539
Bostick, John C., 539
Bostick, Jonathan Smith, 381, 386, 539
Bostick, Mary Manoah, 386, 539
Boston Harbor, MA, 178, 285
Boston Massacre, 255
Boston, MA, 41, 67, 69, 71, 120, 158, 173, 263, 285, 478, 961-967, 969-975, 977, 980-982, 984-988, 990, 991
Boudicca, Queen, 589
bow and arrows, 455

998

THE MCGAVOCKS OF CARNTON PLANTATION

Bowers, George Philips, Jr., 560
Bowers, George Philips, Sr., 560
Bowman, Virginia M., 374, 445
Boxley, Philip H., 598
Boxwood Hall, 563, 1044
Boyd Mill Road, 376
Boyd, John, 598
Boyd, Nancy, 556
Boyd, Sallie, 557
Boyd, W. E., 598
Brace, C. Loring, 593
Bradenton, FL, 429
Bradford, William F., 391
Bradley, Michael R., 19, 23, 24, 594, 1045
Bragg, Braxton, 104, 355, 404
Bramlett, Byrd, 47
Branch, Patience, 519, 571
brandy, 463
Bransford, Thomas L., 539
Bransford, William S., 539
Bratton, Ann Christian, 574
Braveheart, Sir William Wallace, 351, 589
Brazil, 168
breastworks, 351
Breckinridge, John C., 598, 601, 1044
Bredesen, Phil, 1046
Brent, Linda, 116
Brent, Solomon, 47
Brentwood Hills, Brentwood, TN, 343
Brentwood, TN, 64, 301, 345, 385, 477, 602, 1044
Brereton, Elizabeth, 579
brickwork masonry, 439
Bridge Street, Franklin, TN, 49, 426
bridge, card game, 465
Briggs, George, 108
Briggs, Nathaniel, 176
Bristol County, MA, 173
Britain, 39, 57, 129, 177, 186, 190, 193, 238, 243, 261, 979
Britain, supports the Confederacy, 129
Britannia Rules (Seabrook), 424
British army, 404
British Empire, 236, 255, 313
British government, 173
British Isles, 28, 285
British myth, 423
British North America, 127
British tyranny, 39
Brooke, Edward W., 1041
Brookline, MA, 178
Brooks, Preston S., 79, 1044
brown slave owners, 167, 219, 230
brown slave ownership, 169
Brown University, connected to slavery, 178

Brown, John, 87-89, 91, 161, 164, 253, 438
Brown, John C., 334
Brown, William, 964
Brown, William J., 577
Brownlow, William G., 226, 258
browns (Hispanics and Latinos), 218, 266
Browns, New England slaving family, 178
Bruce family, 42
Bruce, Marjorie, 522
Bruce, Robert the, 522, 589
Bryan, Hardy S., 536, 573
Bryan, Hardy Wilkerson, 536, 555, 573
Bryant, America N., 534, 554
Bryant, William, 534
Bryant, William Cullen, 89
Buchanan, Bay, 15
Buchanan, Martha, 546
Buchanan, Mary, 532
Buchanan, Patrick J., 15, 1044
Buchanan, Thomas, 598
bucket rings, 489
Buckingham, James S., 158, 164
Buckley, Catharine, 578
Buckner, Simon B., Jr., 605
Buckner, Simon B., Sr., 605
Buddhism, 66
Buford, Henry, 574
Buford, Mary M., 574
Buford, Sarah, 567
Buford, William L., 553
bullet-forceps, 489
bullets, 489
bullets, Civil War, 492
Bureau of Printing and Engraving, 312
burial mounds, 47
Burnside, Ambrose E., 95
Butler, Andrew P., 1044
Butler, Benjamin F., 106, 216, 265, 296, 309, 394
Butler, Rhett, 358
Butler, William L., 380
butter, 462
butternut, 330
buttonhole molding patterns, 460
Butts, C. C., 598
Butts, Daniel, 598
Butts, J. L., 598
Byars, Mary E., 577
Bynum, Mary, 538
Byrd, Thomas H., 598
C.S. Navy, 50
C.S.A., 39, 74, 182, 197, 198, 215, 225, 243, 271, 276, 286, 306, 316, 362, 486, 502, 517, 518, 520, 527, 537, 560, 568, 570, 572, 581-583, 585, 587, 588, 968, 979, 983

999

The McGavocks of Carnton Plantation

Cabots, New England slaving family, 177
Cain, Herman, 15
Cain, mark of, 205
Cairnton House, 438
Cairntown, Ireland, 34, 40
Cairntun Manor, Ireland, 35
Cairntun, Ireland, 29, 34
Cairo, GA, 449
Calabar, Africa, 171
Calhoun, John C., 15, 55, 75, 186, 242, 384, 469
California, 30, 55, 77, 415, 418
Cameron, Ewen, 47, 435
Cameron, Simon, 291, 304
Camp Chimborazo Hospital, 58
Camp Douglas, Yankee POW prison, Chicago, IL, 380
Camp Winder Hospital, 58
Campbell, Andrew, 525
Campbell, Archibald, 523, 524
Campbell, Brown, 420
Campbell, Clara S., 524
Campbell, Colin, 523, 524
Campbell, Dugal, 524
Campbell, Duncan, 523-525
Campbell, Elizabeth, 574
Campbell, Hugh, 525
Campbell, James A., 598
Campbell, John, 525
Campbell, Margaret, 36, 38, 523, 526, 532
Campbell, Nancy, 586
Campbell, Patrick, 525, 583
Campbell, W. W., 416, 418
Campbell, Zacharias, 586
Canaan, land of, 212
Canaan, of the Bible, 205, 206
Canaanite slaves, 209
Canada, 224, 565
Canada, Allen, 599
Canada, Joseph A., 599
Canada, William C., 599
Canadian Confederate soldiers, 595
canned foods, 454
Cannon, Ann, 580
Cannon, Newton, Jr., 422
Canterbury, CT, 69-71
Cantor, Eric, 15
canvas, 461
Capital Square, Richmond, VA, 470
capitalism, 958, 961
capitol, Nashville's, 340
Caribbean islands, 168
Caribbean Islands, and Yankee slavery, 76
Carl, Betty Jane, 19
Carlisle, PA, 43
Carnlough, Ireland, 34

Carnton Association, 21, 429, 436, 446, 454, 966
Carnton Mansion, 49, 53, 56, 133, 228, 429, 437, 443, 446, 447, 458, 460, 483, 484, 488, 497, 498
Carnton Mansion, as a field hospital, 370
Carnton McGavocks, 50
Carnton Plantation, 1-4, 7-12, 14, 15, 17, 23, 24, 33, 34, 42, 44, 45, 48, 51, 53, 61, 65, 68, 78, 79, 82, 131, 133, 150, 172, 198, 214, 280, 284, 286, 327, 329, 333, 342, 381, 422, 431, 433, 437, 446, 468, 476, 496, 507-509, 513, 514, 517-521, 526, 527, 569-572, 581, 582, 594, 596, 958, 986, 1042, 1044
Carnton Plantation Ghost Stories (Seabrook), 431, 596
Carnton Plantation legend, regarding Ernest Hemingway, 333
Carnton Plantation sacked, by Union soldiers, 381
Carnton's attic, 497
Carnton's basement, 456
Carnton's carriage house, 444
Carnton's dining room, 462
Carnton's ell, 445
Carnton's exterior, 435
Carnton's family Bible, 473
Carnton's front driveway, 444
Carnton's front walkway, 443
Carnton's fruit orchards, 446
Carnton's garden, 453
Carnton's ghosts, 430, 431
Carnton's greenhouse, 445, 454
Carnton's interior, 458
Carnton's ladies' parlor, 471
Carnton's outbuildings, 449
Carnton's privy, 452
Carnton's root cellar, 454
Carnton's servant houses, 449
Carnton's smokehouse, 451
Carnton's springhouse, 450
Carnton's trees, 442
Carnton's windows, 441
Carnton's house servants, 79
Carntown, Ireland, 29, 34
Caroline, Princess, 589
Carpenter, Frank, 252
carpenters, 136, 295, 449
carpetbag-scallywag regime, 383
carpetbaggers, 396, 978
carpetbaggism, 396
Carson, Martha, 355, 1041
Carter cotton gin house, 332, 334, 375, 503
Carter House, 359, 376, 377, 502
Carter, Fountain Branch, 383, 502

The McGavocks of Carnton Plantation

Carter, Hattie, black female Confederate soldier, 111
Carter, Helena Bonham, 43, 590
Carter, Jessie Gidley, 70
Carter, Jimmy, 125
Carter, John C., 375, 377
Carter, Littleberry Walker, 125
Carter, Moscow B., 502, 597
Carter, Theodrick "Tod", 286, 383, 501, 505, 598
Carter, Wad, 599
Carthage, TN, 449
Cartwright, Joseph, 598
Cartwright, Thomas, 327
Caruthers family, 287
Caruthers, Robert, 47
Caruthers, Thomas, 599
Cash, Johnny, 1041
caste system, among black servants, 450
Castleman, Charles, 599
Castleman, James D., 599
castles, Irish, 35
Catholic Church, 214, 423
Catholic convents, Yankees burn down, 308
Catholicism, and early Goddess-worship, 424
Catholics, 293, 449
Catholics, Northern, racism among, 293
Caucasian, 86, 180, 209
Caucasians, 38, 209, 210
Caudill, Benjamin E., 1040, 1043
Caudill's Army, 274, 1043
Ceinneidigh, 589
Celtic ancestor-goddess, 34
Celtic combat methods, 351, 359
Celtic myth, 423
Celtic names, 27
Celtic nations, and England, 235
Celtic peoples, 28
Celto-cavalier culture, in the South, 235
Celts, 235, 351, 467
Central America, 267, 269, 270
central government, 196, 237, 238, 241, 311
Central Park, New York, NY, 160
central passageway, 429, 459, 460, 478
Chaffin, Alexander, 568
chair rails, 460, 467, 477
chamber pots, 452, 495
chambermaid, 147
champagne, 463
Champlains, New England slaving family, 178
Chapel Hill, TN, 378, 386
Chapel, Don, 355
Chapel, Donna, 355
Chapel, Jean, 355
chaplains, 107
Charlemagne, 37, 589

Charles, Prince, 43, 589
Charleston Harbor, 325
Charleston, SC, 84, 110, 150, 271, 377
Chase, Salmon P., 102, 179
Chattanooga, TN, 465
Cheairs, Nathaniel F., 50, 355, 1044
Cheatham County, TN, 602
Cheatham, Amanda, 559
Cheatham, Archer, 559
Cheatham, Benjamin F., 328, 332
Cheatham, Felix R., 332
Cheatham, John Long, 559
Cheatham, Mary D., 559
Cheatham, William Bolling, 559
checkers, 465
Chenault, Louisa C., 301, 473, 514, 550, 569
Chenault, Stephen, 515, 569
Cherokee, 46, 165-167
Cherokee capital, 46
cherry chest, 495
Cherry Hill Mansion, 174
cherry tree wood, 463, 479, 497
Chesnut family, 144, 186
Chesnut, James, Jr., 58, 112, 135, 145, 185, 360
Chesnut, Mary, 57, 58, 76, 81, 112, 115, 118, 122, 132, 135, 136, 139, 140, 142, 143, 145-147, 152, 161, 185, 186, 189, 213, 220, 229, 247, 259, 279, 284, 290, 291, 299, 309, 321, 336, 349, 358, 360, 376, 462, 485, 1044
Chicago Tribune, 253
Chicago, IL, 155, 346, 347, 359, 380
Chickasaw, 46, 165-167, 967
chicken salad, 462
chicken stock, 463
chickens, 429, 454, 463
chickens in jelly, 463
child labor, 257
child labor, and Lincoln, 257
Child, Lydia Maria, 251
Childeric I, King, 37, 590
children, 27, 33, 35, 39, 41, 45, 53, 61-63, 67, 78, 82, 84, 86, 96, 98, 113, 116, 117, 125, 131, 136, 140, 160, 161, 170, 191, 199, 210, 212, 221, 229, 230, 232, 257, 258, 260, 261, 274, 283, 284, 288, 290, 298, 300, 302, 306, 309, 329, 357, 373, 374, 389, 404, 413, 418, 420-422, 425, 427, 429, 452, 457, 464, 466, 475, 480, 482, 483, 497, 502, 514-527, 531-588, 1043, 1046
Childress, Sarah, 56
Childress, Stephen, 47
china set, 464

chloroform, 488
chocolate jelly cake, 462
Choctaw, 165-167, 967
Christ, 64, 203, 205, 214, 373, 423, 424, 504, 962, 978, 983
Christian Church, 424
Christian Church, and slavery, 202
Christian Church, Gnostic branch, 423
Christian denominations, number of, 425
Christian legends, 35
Christian mysticism, and the McGavocks, 424
Christian Oldenberg I, King, 42, 590
Christian, James R., 562
Christian, Randal McGavock, 562
Christianity, 2, 66, 202, 214, 280, 415, 423-425, 517, 984
Christianization, of Pagan figures, 424
Christians, 71, 202-204, 211, 212, 214, 218, 423, 424
Christians, early, and fish symbol, 424
Christmas, 2, 137, 373, 394, 423, 1041
Christmas Before Christianity (Seabrook), 423
Church Fathers, 202
Church of Jesus Christ of Latter-Day Saints, 205, 978
churches, Yankees burn down, 308
Churchill, Winston, 43, 589
cigars, 465
Cincinnati, OH, 118, 292, 465
citizenship, 188, 255, 259
City Cemetery, Franklin, TN, 51
civil liberties, Lincoln suppresses, 310
civil rights, 88, 94, 95, 105, 110, 114, 128, 153, 154, 164, 187, 197, 202, 214, 216, 224, 225, 246, 248, 249, 251, 252, 254, 256-259, 267, 269-271, 296, 298, 310, 311, 399, 982, 987, 1045
Civil Rights Act of 1964, 399
Civil War, 2, 9, 13, 16, 17, 66, 77, 85, 108, 116, 118, 129, 131, 146, 149, 165, 167, 175, 194, 196, 229, 243, 244, 250, 257, 270, 281, 282, 287, 304, 309, 312, 313, 324, 327, 330, 335, 344, 350, 356, 364, 405, 413, 419, 430, 431, 490, 491, 509, 517, 518, 541, 568, 594-596, 957, 959-992, 1040, 1045, 1046
civil war defined, 243
Civil War sites, 595
Civil War tourists, 281, 595
Civil War, was not over slavery, 243, 246, 250, 252
Claiborne, Mary Eliza Terrell, 49
Claiborne, Thomas, 408, 411
Clan Davidson, 28

Clan Davidson Association, 28
Clan Dhai, 28
clan of David, 27
claret cups, 452
claret soup, 463
Clark, L., 965
Clarke, Peleg, 176
Classical and Mathematical Seminary, 285
Classical European culture, 479
Claud, Eldrige N., 533, 552
Claud, Philip, 533, 553
Clay, Cassius M., 276
Clay, Henry, 236, 241, 262, 312, 469, 486
Clayton, Henry D., 334
cleaning, 136
Cleburne, Patrick R., 328, 346, 374, 375, 378, 379, 415, 430, 431, 447
Cleopatra VII, 38
clergymen, 304
Cleveland, Stephen Grover, 54, 537
Cliffe, Daniel, 598
Clifflawn Plantation, Nashville, TN, 558, 1044
cliometrics, 138
Clodion, King, 37, 424, 590
Clodius III, King, 37, 590
Clodomir III, King, 37, 590
Clodomir IV, King, 37, 590
Clopton, Elizabeth Hoggatt, 558
Clotaire I, King, 37, 590
clothes-warming closets, at Carnton, 482
Clouston, Elizabeth Field, 288, 483
Clover Bottom Mansion, 1047
Clovis I "the Great," King, 37, 590
Cloyd, 42
Cloyd, Cynthia M., 559, 577
Cloyd, David, 549, 559, 561, 577
Cloyd, David, Sr., 526, 532
Cloyd, Elizabeth, 552
Cloyd, Gordon, 574, 575, 577
Cloyd, James, 526
Cloyd, James McGavock, 549, 577
Cloyd, Joseph, 38, 532, 575, 577
Cloyd, Mary, 574
Cloyd, Mary "Sally", 36, 38, 39, 41-43, 526, 532
Cloyd, Nancy, 532
Cloyd, Thomas, 532, 561
coachmen, 137
Coal Creek, 391
Coalition to Abolish Slavery and Trafficking, 117
Cobb, Thomas R. R., 471
Cocke, Daniel F., 563
Cocke, Hortense, 563
Cockrell, Francis M., 335, 415
coffee, 463
Coles, Edward, 159

THE McGAVOCKS OF CARNTON PLANTATION

collard greens, 452
college campuses, Northern, racism at, 165
Collins, William C., 507
Collins' Farm, 507
Cologne, Germany, 224
Colonial Period, 172, 974
Colonial Williamsburg, 40
colonialism, 241
colonization, 96, 180, 207, 213, 216, 241, 259, 262-267, 971, 987
colonization of America, 265
colonization, black, 144, 266
colonization, black, and Abraham Lincoln, 121
colonization, black, and Harriet Beecher Stowe, 121
colonization, black, and Horace Greeley, 121
colonization, black, and William Lloyd Garrison, 121
colonizationists, 180
Colorado, 30
Colossae, Turkey, 203
Columbia Avenue, Franklin, TN, 375, 377
Columbia Pike, Franklin, TN, 502
Columbia Road, Franklin, TN, 334, 375
Columbia, TN, 331, 345, 365, 376-378
Columbus, Christopher, 118, 168
Combs family, of Kentucky, 1044
Combs, Bertram T., 1044
Combs, John, Sr., 49
commander-in-chief, rank created by Confederacy, 362
Committee on the Conduct of the War, 392
Common Bond, 187
Company Aytch (Watkins), 504
Company H, Twentieth Tennessee Regiment Voluntary Infantry CSA, 286, 332, 597, 599, 601, 604
comparative slavery, 169
compensated emancipation, 319
Compromise of 1850, 984
Comptroller of the Currency, 312
Concord, MA, 39, 178, 438
condiments, 453
Confederacy, 12, 14, 17, 19, 24, 39, 46, 55, 73, 77, 92, 95, 100, 102, 107-110, 115, 125, 129, 151, 166, 190, 196, 197, 210, 215, 226, 232, 233, 236, 238-244, 253, 254, 257, 260, 263, 273, 275-277, 280, 282-284, 296, 303-306, 310, 311, 318, 323, 324, 329, 334, 340, 342, 343, 345-348, 354, 356, 359, 361-364, 366-369, 373, 382, 403, 404, 413, 416, 419, 426, 427, 448, 469-471, 485-487, 508, 509, 594, 595, 957, 964, 965, 967, 969, 974, 978, 983-985, 990, 991, 1041, 1043
confederacy, defined, 196
Confederacy, early USA as the, 196, 239
confederal government, 237
Confederalists, 240
Confederate ancestors, 593
Confederate Army, 109-112, 126, 235, 254, 345, 347, 351, 358, 402, 502, 503, 595, 965, 967, 968
Confederate Battle Flag, 234, 280, 323, 327, 329, 593, 974
Confederate bonds, 108
Confederate Cause, 108, 114, 115, 282, 283, 360, 374, 377, 390, 410, 418, 979
Confederate cavalry, lack of horses, 382
Confederate Cemetery, Helena, AR, 379
Confederate cities, 67
Confederate Congress, 198
Confederate Constitution, 198, 968
Confederate deaths, statistics, 492
Confederate Flag, 11, 66, 67, 182, 198, 280, 281, 594, 957, 974
Confederate House of Representatives, 343
Confederate Indian troops, 166
Confederate Mary, 111
Confederate military, 58, 111, 112, 260, 328, 363, 490, 595, 960, 969
Confederate Military History (UCV), 960
Confederate money, 470
Confederate Movement, 283
Confederate Navy, 109, 595, 985
Confederate peace commissions, 308
Confederate Republic, 14, 95, 239, 240, 242, 983
Confederate Soldier's Home, 599, 604
Confederate Stadium, Mobile, AL, 593
Confederate State Association, 411
Confederate States of America, 4, 74, 197, 243, 303, 306, 377, 471, 960, 967, 969, 982
Confederate symbols, 593
Confederate Torpedo Bureau, 50
Confederate troops, 113, 333, 491
Confederate veterans, 8, 19, 282, 283, 329, 410, 411, 419, 422, 509, 593, 594, 596, 960, 965, 1046
Confederate victories, 323
confederation, 195, 196, 237-239, 277, 311, 369, 470, 975, 987
Confiscation Act, 248
Confiscation Acts, 248, 258
Congress, 4, 93, 97, 98, 100, 124, 162, 179-181, 188, 193, 195, 196, 198, 247, 258, 260, 263, 265, 268, 297, 308-310, 342, 343, 395, 397, 485, 961, 967,

1003

974, 984, 989
Conkling, James C., 295
Connecticut, 30, 69-72, 87, 118, 119, 165, 173, 183, 987, 990
Connecticut, racism in, 165
Conrad, Frances, 566
conservatism, 15, 73, 236, 282, 991
conservatives, 21, 58, 236, 280, 315, 443, 596
conservatives, percentage of in U.S., 281, 595
consolidation, 277
Constitution Day, 487
Constitutional Convention of 1787, 486, 966
constitutional law, 962
Constitutional Republic, 257
Constitutionalism, 237, 968
Constitutionalists, 258
containment, the U.S. policy of, 164
Continental Army, 124
contraband, 298, 304, 988
contraband camps, 298, 988
contraband, freed blacks as, 296
contrabands, 969
Contract Labor Act, 312
Conway family, of Virginia, 57
Conway, Moncure D., 292
Cook, N. P., 599
cooking, 105, 136, 229, 295, 451
cooks, 111, 114, 254
Cooper Union speech, Lincoln's, 89, 264
Cooper, Steve, 506
Cooper, Thomas, 236
Cooper, Washington B., 464
coopers, 136
Copperhead, 128
Corinth, MS, 449
corn, 453
cornbread, 10, 452
Cornett, Rachel, 274, 509, 1043
Cornish words, 29
corrals, 446
cotton, 9, 78, 79, 118, 124, 135, 137, 146, 160, 165, 168, 170, 175, 180, 181, 279, 289, 320, 332, 334, 338, 340, 357, 363, 375, 383, 446, 480, 503, 534, 554, 969, 970, 975, 976, 979, 982
cotton (Confederate), burned, 289
cotton gin, 78, 79, 332, 334, 338, 375, 503
cotton states, 383
Cotton Triangle, 180
cotton-export plan, Stephens', 363
country music artists, 285
County Antrim, Ireland, 29, 32, 33
County Derry, Ireland, 385
courthouses, Southern, bombed, 492
courthouses, Yankees burn down, 309

coverers, 136, 963
Cowan family plot, 428
Cowan, Carrie W., 425, 426, 518, 571
Cowan, George Limerick, 283, 385, 405, 406, 413, 422, 425, 427, 506, 507, 518, 570, 582
Cowan, John, 422, 427
Cowan, John McGavock, 425, 426, 518, 571
Cowan, Leah, 425, 426, 518, 571
Cowan, Robert, 385, 518, 571, 582
Cowan, Samuel Kincaid, 425-427, 518, 571
Cowan, Winder McGavock, 425-427, 518, 571
cowhide, 356
cows, 132, 137, 454, 466
Cox, Caroline A., 585
Cox, Jacob D., 502
Cox, N. N., 411
Cox, Samuel S., 223
craftsmen, 133, 137, 143, 144, 228, 460
craftswomen, 137
Craig, Mary, 575
cranberries, 462
Crandall, Prudence, 69-71
cream, 463
Credit Mobilier Scandal, 368
Creek, Indians, 165-167
Crenshaw, Hardin, 599
Crenshaw, Thomas, 599
Crete, 209
Crews, Milton, 543
Crews, Sally A., 543
cribbage, 465
criminals, 124, 206, 214, 227, 309, 368
crinoline skirts, 452
Crockett, Agnes, 566
Crockett, Andrew, 563
Crockett, Davy, 41, 55, 473, 477, 589
Crockett, Elizabeth, 301, 477, 562
Crockett, Elizabeth Malvina, 575
Crockett, James, 562, 566
Crockett, John, 575
Crockett, Joseph, 473
Crockett, Joseph McGavock, 575
Crockett, Mary, 573
Crockett, Mary Drake, 566
Crockett, Robert, 566
Crockett, Samuel Rush, 575
Crockett, Samuel, III, 47, 301, 562
Croly, David G., 223
croquet, at Carnton, 452
Cross and Bible Motif, 495
Crowe, James R., 395
Crowley, Monica, 15
Crowninshield Island, MA, 178
Crowninshields, New England slaving family, 178

cruciform design, 495
cruet set, 463
Cruise, Tom, 43, 590, 1044
Cuba, 168
Cuban Confederate soldiers, 595
Cumberland County, England, 29, 34
Cumberland Presbyterian Church, Memphis, TN, 400
Cumberland River, 44, 363
Cumberland University, 563
Cumbria County, England, 59
Cunningham, H. R., 599
Cunningham, Margaret, 545, 550, 577
Cuppet, George W., 496, 507
Cuppet, Marcellus, 507
Currin, R. P., 47
custard, 463
Custis, Mary Anna Randolph, 382
Cyprus, 209
Cyrus, Billy Ray, 1041
Cyrus, Miley, 1041
Dabóc, 28
Dahomey, Africa, 216
Daibheid, 27
Daibhidh, 27
dairy cows, 466
dairy maid, 147
dairying, 137
Dalles, Sophia Burrell, 41, 565
Dalton, GA, 349, 352
Daltry Calhoun (film), 354
Danzielstour, Joanna, 523
DAR, 39
Dare, Virginia, 165
Dashiel, Anne, 585, 587
Dashiel, George, 585
Dashiel, James, Jr., 580
Dashiel, James, Sr., 580
Dashiel, Jane, 222, 580
Daughters of the American Revolution, 39, 426
David Dubh of Invernahaven, 28
David Filius, 28
David I, King, 27, 37, 589
David II, King, 27
David, and McGavock surname, 27
David, King, of Israel, 27
Davidson County, TN, 45, 284, 467, 599
Davidson Tartan, 29
Davidson, family name, 28
Davidson, William, 599
Davidstow, England, 29
Davis, Buster, 599
Davis, Elizabeth, 538
Davis, James A., 599
Davis, Jasper, 599

Davis, Jefferson, 15, 16, 21, 75, 92, 101, 104, 110, 145, 182, 185, 239, 242, 260, 269, 270, 275, 276, 281, 287, 326, 346, 348, 353, 354, 357, 359, 361, 365, 369, 403, 471, 487, 596, 960, 1043
  allows civil liberties, 310
Davis, John, 599
Davisoun, 28
Daviyd, 27
Davock, 28
days off, among servants, 137
Daytona Beach, FL, 426
de Ayllón, Lucas V., 168
De Burgh, Cecilia, 522
De Ergadia, Isabel, 524
de Las Casas, Bartolomé, 169
de Santa Anna, Antonio Lopez, 55
de Vattel, Emerich, 309
Dean, Henry Clay, 307, 317
death, 9, 16, 36, 45, 53, 54, 56-58, 62, 63, 72, 79, 87, 90, 122, 139, 157, 158, 162, 181, 182, 193, 205, 206, 220, 224, 232, 254, 258, 271, 283, 297, 298, 301, 305, 311, 313, 328, 332-334, 355, 359, 368, 372, 376, 377, 380, 388, 391, 394, 402, 406, 408, 409, 411-413, 415, 417-420, 422, 424-427, 430, 453, 495, 497, 504, 517, 519, 571, 582, 1041, 1045
Deborah, of the Bible, 416
DeBow, James D. B., 200
Debro, Sarah, 320
Decatur, AL, 602
Declaration of Independence, 14, 15, 39, 58, 193-195, 207, 972
Deep South, 124, 150
deer, 454
Deery Family Home, 285
Deery, Seraphine, 285, 286, 538
Deery, William, 285, 538
defection, 254
Degataga, Chief, 46
DeGraffenreid family, 287
DeGraffenreid, M. Fount, 597
degrees, servants earning, 144
Deism, 66
Delany, Martin, 266
Delaware, 30, 183, 256, 969, 983, 991
Delaware River, 256
democracy, Northern, under Lincoln, 311
democracy, Southern, under Davis, 311
Democrat, 282, 409, 412, 469
Democratic National Convention, 443, 517
Democratic Party, 21, 240, 409, 413

THE MCGAVOCKS OF CARNTON PLANTATION

Democratic Party, switches platforms with the Republican Party, 236
Demonbruen, Timothy, 47
Denmark, 38, 271
Denmark Vesey Rebellion, 84
denominations, number of Christian, 425
Denwood, Prisilla, 581
Deo Vindice, 471
Department of Agriculture, 312
deportation, 14, 154, 156, 171, 179, 180, 190, 223, 225, 262-264, 269, 270
deportation, black, 262
depression, 80, 475, 988
desertion, 124, 254, 303, 311, 363, 366
desertion, Confederate, 311, 363, 366
desertion, under Washington, 124
desertion, Union, 252, 254, 292
Design Star (TV series), 355
Desire (ship), 173
despotism, 104, 307
Detroit, MI, 165
Devlin, Sarah Ann, 33, 578
Devonshire County, England, 56, 60
DeWolfs, New England slave trading family, 178
Dhabhóig, 27
Diana, Princess, 43
diaries, 118, 132, 165, 294
Dicey, Edward, 159
Dick (McGavock servant), 214, 215, 218, 219
Dickens, Charles, 272
Dickinson College, 43, 207
Dickinson, Henry, I, 54, 537
Dickinson, Jacob McGavock, Jr., 537
Dickinson, Jacob McGavock, Sr., 54, 410, 416, 418, 537
Dickinson, Louise Grundy, 537
Dickson, TN, 599, 600
Diffenbacher, B. E., 393
differences, between South and North, 233, 235
DiLorenzo, Thomas J., 15
Dinkins, James, 342
disease, 96, 122, 261, 311, 319, 320, 357, 384, 415, 455, 490-492, 604
District of Columbia Emancipation Act, 179
disunion, 272
Divine Feminine, 424
Divine Feminine, and early Christian goddess worship, 424
Division and Reunion (Wilson), 145
Dixie, 11, 16, 19, 73, 74, 76, 77, 83, 84, 91, 96, 105, 111, 113-115, 118, 120, 129, 147-150, 153, 164, 171, 183, 186, 187, 202, 227, 234-236, 239, 241, 242, 269, 272, 275, 280, 281, 284, 294, 299, 302, 314, 318, 330, 354, 374, 384, 394, 396, 398, 400, 405, 469, 593, 957, 958, 961, 965, 979, 991
Dixie (song), 330, 593
Dodson, Jacob, 291
Domesday Book, 34
Dominican Republic, 116
dominoes, 465
Donelson Creek Parkway, 468
Donelson family, 468
Donelson, John, 468
Donelson, Rachel, 453, 468, 469, 514
door casings, 460
door lock, 495
dormers, 441, 443, 446
Douglas, Edwin H., 516, 569
Douglas, Stephen A., 77, 99, 103, 194, 223, 246, 250
Douglass, Frederick, 88, 110, 134, 214, 251, 254, 255, 257, 261, 268, 298
Douglass' Monthly, 111, 255, 268
Doyle, Drury, 87
Doyle, James, 87
Doyle, William, 87
Dr. J. B. Cowan Camp #155, SCV, Tullahoma, TN, 24, 594
Dracula, Count, 43, 589
Drake, Mary, 562, 566
draughts, 465
Dred Scott case, 43
drillers, 137
drivers, 136
drivers, black, 125
droppers, 137
Drumboden, Kilmacrenan, County Donegal, Ulster Province, Ireland, 36
Drumnagreagh Port, Ireland, 34
Du Bois, William E. B., 216
duck, 454, 462
Duck River, Columbia, TN, 331, 345
Ducros Plantation, Houma, LA, 61-63, 474, 517, 1044
Dudley family, of England, 374
Dudley, Guilford, Sr., 51
Dumfries, Scotland, 34
Dumfriesshire, Scotland, 34
Dunbar, Euphemia, 42
Dunbartonshire, Scotland, 522, 524
Duncan I, King, 37, 589
Duncan School, 563
Dundonald Castle, 522
Durnford, Andrew, 151
Dury, George, 473
Dutch slavers, 215
Dutch, the, and slavery, 168

THE MCGAVOCKS OF CARNTON PLANTATION

Duvall, Robert, 1044
Dyersburg, TN, 379
Earl of Oxford, 1042
earthworks, 351
Eaton, Anna Bland, 51
Eben, Chesnut servant, 115
economic historians, 138
economics, 73, 126, 272, 970, 980, 989
Edgar the Peaceful, King, 37, 589
Edmondson, William, 47
Edmund I, King, 37, 589
Edmund II, King, 37, 589
Edney, Robert, 599
Edney, Turner, 599
Edward I, King, 37, 42, 50, 57, 589, 1042
Edward II, King, 42, 589
Edward III, King, 42, 589
Edwards, Jonathan, 109
Eelbeck, Frank, 599
Eelbeck, P. H., 597, 598
Efik, the, 171
Egbert, King, 37, 589
egg yolks, 463
Eggleston, J. F., 422
eggnog, 463
eggs, 462
Egypt, 38
Egyptian slavery, 209
Egyptian slaves, 209
Egyptians, 209, 279
Ehrlich, Paul R., 593
Eighth Tennessee Cavalry Battalion, 287
El Dorado wallpaper, 464
election of 1860, 314
election of 1864, 315, 317
Electoral College, 238, 314
electric light bulbs, 461
Elizabeth II, Queen, 43, 589
Ellerys, New England slaving family, 178
Ellison, William, black slave owner, 150
Emancipation Proclamation, 92, 94, 99, 100, 102, 103, 105, 113, 153, 156, 164, 180, 190, 195, 197, 249-255, 257, 260, 265, 266, 270, 292, 295, 296, 300, 309, 316, 319, 344, 390
Emancipation Proclamation, racism behind, 251
embrasures, 351
Emerson, Ralph Waldo, 89, 178, 438
empire, 209, 236, 240, 241, 255, 313, 964, 972, 974, 978, 991
Encyclopedia of Mormonism (Ludlow), 205
engineers, 6, 41, 137
England, 29, 34, 35, 37, 41, 42, 50, 56, 57, 59, 60, 69, 72, 76, 92, 97, 124, 129, 162, 173, 175-178, 190, 193, 207, 208, 213, 222, 235, 239, 263, 271, 304, 305, 522, 524, 536, 556, 564, 573, 579, 961, 972, 980, 985, 1042, 1047
English, 27-29, 37, 51, 56, 59, 60, 68, 120, 123, 140, 158, 159, 165, 168, 171, 176, 191, 206, 215, 235, 239, 272, 349, 424, 438-440, 446, 595, 962, 974, 975, 980, 981, 984, 986, 989, 990, 1040
English abolitionists, 164
English Bond, 440, 446
English Confederate soldiers, 595
English McGavocks, 29
English royals, 37
English, William, 176
Enlightenment, the, 192
Episcopal Church, 163, 378
Epistle of Philemon, 203
equal rights, 113, 154, 158, 257, 259
Eriksson, Knut, 589
erysipelas, 490
escapees, black servant, 147
Esclavon, Jacques, 108
Eskridge, Elizabeth Scott, 538
Essex County, MA, 173
étagère, 476
Ethelwulf, King, 37, 589
Europe, 2, 11, 32-34, 36, 38-43, 46, 47, 49, 51, 56, 57, 66-68, 82, 86, 92, 95, 96, 106, 115-117, 126, 128, 129, 132, 157, 162, 165-171, 173, 206, 207, 209-211, 213, 216, 220, 241, 266, 268, 271, 281, 285, 308, 323, 335, 357, 362, 395, 404, 435, 448-450, 473, 479, 513, 521, 531, 536, 556, 563, 573, 579, 594, 595, 986, 1042
European kings, 42
European slave industry, 167
European slave traders, 116, 117
European slavery, 209, 210
European support, 308, 362
European-America superstitions, 448
European-American Confederate soldiers, 106, 595
European-American slaves, 206
Europeans, 38-40, 46, 167-171, 207, 209, 268
European-Americans, 46, 47, 66, 96, 106, 165, 266, 435, 595
Evans, Augusta Jane, 447
Evans, Malachi, 535, 554
Everything You Were Taught About the CW is Wrong (Seabrook), 196, 594, 596
Ewin family, 287
Ewin, Theresa, 538

1007

The McGavocks of Carnton Plantation

Ewing, Alexander, 533
Ewing, Andrew, 577
Ewing, Andrew B., 51, 515, 550, 569, 577
Ewing, Andrew J., 550
Ewing, Ann Eliza, 551
Ewing, Carrie Eliza, 515
Ewing, Charles Andrew, 515
Ewing, F. G., 410, 418
Ewing, Francis McGavock, 416, 418, 515
Ewing, Herbert, 421, 519
Ewing, Hugh F., 564
Ewing, Hugh McGavock, 550
Ewing, James McGavock, 564
Ewing, John O., 564
Ewing, Joseph Love, 564
Ewing, Joseph William, 577
Ewing, Lucy Elizabeth, 577
Ewing, Lusinda, 533, 552
Ewing, Margaret, 550
Ewing, Randal Milton, 515, 550, 569
Ewing, Sarah Amanda, 551
Ewing, Susan Lee "Susie", 385, 421, 422, 428, 429, 475, 519, 571, 582
Ewing, Susan Mary, 551
Ewing, William, 550, 564, 577
Ewing, William F., 515
Examiner, the (Richmond), 127
Executive Order 9981, 260
Exodus, 212
expansion of slavery, 95-97
expansionism, 240, 241
exposure, to harsh weather, 491
Fair Labor Standards Act, 257
Fair Street, Franklin, 49
Fairfield County, CT, 173
Fall of Man, 202
family heirlooms, 382, 463, 467, 473, 477
Faneuil Hall, Boston, MA, 178
Faneuils, New England slaving family, 178
fanlight windows, 460
Fanti, 216
Farabert, King, 37, 590
farmers, 23, 103, 124, 135, 169, 172, 198, 199, 201, 235, 455
faro, card game, 465
Farragut, David G., 246
fascism, Union and, 276
Father of Mine Warfare, 50
Father of the Confederacy, George Washington, 470
Father-God, 205
Faulkner, William, 401
faux marble finish, 462
feather tick, 480
feather ticks, 480

Federal architectural features, at Carnton, 460
Federal architecture, 439, 459
Federal cavalry, at Nashville, 341
Federal design, 439
federal government, 75, 93, 111, 188, 237, 242, 251, 255, 312, 490, 981, 989
Federalism, 961
Federalists, 236, 240, 241, 978
feminism, 132
feminist leaders, 257
Ferdinand II, King, 42, 590
Ferguson Hall, 355
Ferguson, Sarah, Duchess, 43, 589
Fernandina, FL, 271, 297
Fernando III, King, 42, 590
Fernvale Springs, TN, 601
feudalism, 202
fiddle music, 452
field servants, 136, 450
Fifeshire, Scotland, 522, 523
Fifteenth Amendment, 257
Fifth Regiment Louisiana Volunteers, 112
Figuers family, 380
Figuers, Hardin P., 503
Figuers' Bluff, 327
Fillmore, Millard, 208
Final Emancipation Proclamation, 92, 190, 249, 250, 254, 266, 316, 319
Fincastle, VA, 38, 39
Finley, Robert, 262
fire-eater, 359
first black governor, was in a Southern state, 162
first black U.S. Congressmen, were in Southern states, 162
First Colored Brigade (U.S.), 344
First Inaugural Address, Lincoln's, 245
First North Carolina Infantry, 109
First Presbyterian Church, Franklin, TN, 51, 422
fish, 454
fish symbol, and Jesus, 424
Fisher, Rose, 585
Fisher, T. B., 411
Fitzhugh, George, 146
five-dollar bill, U.S., 318
Flein, Frank, 600
Flemish Bond, 439, 440, 446
floor cloth, Carnton's, 461
Florence, AL, 378
Florian, Laura Eugenia, 560
Florida, 30, 82, 271, 297, 317, 428, 429, 594, 601
flute, 478
Fon, 216
foot trails, 47
Foote, Shelby, 201, 960

THE McGAVOCKS OF CARNTON PLANTATION

Footner, Hulbert, 207
forced labor, 105, 217
forced labor, the rule in human societies, 217
Ford, Henry, 15
foreign-born Confederate officers, 595
Forest Stewardship Council, 4
Forge Seat, Brentwood, TN, 301, 563
Forrest Gump (Groom), 401
Forrest Park, Memphis, TN, 400
Forrest, Jesse, 400
Forrest, Nathan Bedford, 12, 50, 51, 83, 125, 151, 242, 260, 283, 329, 332, 341, 342, 344-346, 354, 355, 364, 365, 367, 373, 378, 385-398, 400-405, 416, 518, 570, 572, 582, 594, 960, 1042
Forrest's Escort, 283, 386, 570, 582
Fort Chiswell, VA, 35, 36, 473
Fort Garesché, 340
Fort Gillem, 340
Fort Granger, 327
Fort Harker, 340
Fort Houston, 340
Fort Johnson, 340
Fort McCook, 340
Fort Morton, 340
Fort Nashborough, 44, 468
Fort Negley, 340
Fort Sill, 340
Fort Sumter, 93, 140, 243, 275, 280, 288, 325, 970
Fort Warren, 285, 988
Fort-de-Joux, 222
fortifications, 351
forty acres and a mule, 105, 319
Foster family, 287
Foster, Captain, 359
Foster, Joseph A., 600
Founders, 14, 49, 72, 236, 237, 276, 277, 395, 468
Founders Pointe, Franklin, TN, 49
Founding Fathers, 14, 15, 73, 196, 236, 276, 311, 369, 469, 470, 486, 596
Founding Fathers, Southern, 236
Fourteenth Amendment, 257, 258
Fox and Geese, 465
Fox Lake, IL, 33
Fox, Bryant E., 599
Fox, Joe, 599
Fox, Rhoda, 543
fragmented plantations, 114
France, 57, 129, 177, 196, 222, 271, 304, 305, 348, 416, 423, 424
France, supports the Confederacy, 129
Franklin Chapter 14, UDC, 19, 283, 426, 427, 508, 509
Franklin Garden Club, 426
Franklin Pike, 342
Franklin Plain, 329, 502
Franklin, Benjamin, 41, 66-68, 565, 589
Franklin, Sarah "Sally", 41
Franklin, TN, 11, 12, 17, 44-47, 49, 51, 56, 61, 143, 148, 229, 232, 280, 285, 286, 288, 289, 327-333, 335, 336, 343, 345, 346, 350, 355, 356, 358, 359, 361, 364, 365, 367, 370, 378-382, 386, 401, 406, 422, 425, 428, 429, 435, 437, 454-457, 463, 473, 483, 484, 487, 494, 496, 501-503, 505, 506, 508, 526, 527, 598, 602, 603, 1044
Franklin's first subdivision, 49
free artisans, 134
free blacks, 86, 93, 110, 138-140, 145, 148-150, 155, 159, 162, 198, 215, 223-225, 263, 267, 320
free blacks, in the South, 149
free enterprise, 312
free labor, 98, 123, 138, 970
free laborers, 115, 138, 139, 141
free trade, 240
free Urban mail delivery, 312
free-soil position, 97
Free-Soilers, 97
Freedman's Village, 300
freedmen, 91, 93, 132, 319, 969, 979
freedmen, true meaning of, 296
freedmen, used by the North instead of freemen, 106
Freedmen's Bureau, 395-398
Freedmen's labor system, fraud and corruption in, 295
freedom of religion, 240
freedom of speech, 310
freedom of the press, 310
freedwomen, 91, 93
freemen, 135
Freemen of Fincastle County, Virginia, 39
freemen, as opposed to freedmen, 106
freemen, freed blacks not called, 296
Free-Soil party, 208
Frémont, John C., 42, 304
French and Indian War, 39
French Confederate soldiers, 595
French Jura, 222
French, Samuel G., 330
French's Division, 330
Frierson, William, 515, 569
frontier era, 54
fruit, 462

1009

THE MCGAVOCKS OF CARNTON PLANTATION

fruits, 465
Fugitive Slave Law, 93, 219, 298
fugitive slave laws, 81
Fulton, John H., 568
furnishings, at Carnton, 458
furniture makers, 137, 144
Gabriel Prosser Rebellion, 84
Gaelic culture, in the South, 234
Gaelic heritage, 34
Gaelic language, 27, 34
Gaelic McGavocks, 29
Gaelic words, 27
Gaines, Philip, 575
Gale, William D., 372
Gallgaidhill, 34
Galloway region of Scotland, 34
Galloway, Scotland, 32, 34
Gallup Poll, 281, 595
galvanized Yanks, 392
Games, J. N., 506
gangrene, 490
garden, at Carnton, 453
gardeners, 136
Gardners, New England slaving family, 178
Garfield, James A., 343
Garrett, W. R., 410
Garrett, Walsh, 600
Garrett, William R., 364
Garrison, William Lloyd, 69, 85, 88, 121, 161, 257
Garvey, Marcus, 266
Gavock, 27
Gay, Mary Ann, 507
Gayheart, Rebecca, 1044
Gee, W. H., 600
Gemmill, Hugh, 586
Geneva Convention, 309
George III, King, 52, 177, 193, 194, 238, 239
George, W. R., 600
Georges Island, MA, 285
Georgia, 30, 46, 53, 136, 168, 174, 271, 317, 330, 343, 348, 357-359, 439, 449, 459, 471, 507, 558, 600, 603, 973, 987, 991
Georgia Institute of Technology, 330
Georgian architecture, 439, 459
Georgian period, 53
German Confederate soldiers, 595
Germans, 67, 68, 970
Germany, 210, 224, 271, 273, 424, 1047
Gettysburg of the West, 336
Ghana, Africa, 216
ghosts, at Carnton Plantation, 12, 430, 442
Giant's Causeway, 35
Gilbert, Olive, 132

Giles, C. Y., 600, 604
Giles, Thomas J., 600
Gilkerson family, of West Virginia, 1044
Gillespie, Nancy R., 540
Gillis, Esther, 222, 581
Gillis, Thomas, 581
Gilmer, John A., 179
gingerbread designs, 460, 479
ginners, 136
gins, Yankees burned down Southern, 308
Gist plantation, SC, 376
Gist, Nathaniel, 377
Gist, States Rights, 374, 376, 415, 1042
Gist, William H., 376
Gist's Brigade, 1042
Givens, Ben M., 600
Givens, John, 600
Givens, Sharp, 600
glass cake stand, 463
Glass, E. F., 410
glazed ham, 452
Glenarm, County Antrim, Ireland, 29, 34, 438
Gnostic Christianity, 424
Gnosticism, 423
God, 64-66, 78, 84, 88, 98, 119, 129, 187, 202-206, 211, 212, 217, 219, 234, 252, 274, 309, 337, 338, 360, 361, 384, 406, 414, 470, 485, 486, 492, 972, 980
Goddess-worship, and Christianity, 424
Goddess-worship, 2, 424, 449, 986
Godiva, Lady, 589
Goff, Andrew, 47
gold, 157, 167
Gone With the Wind (Mitchell), 229, 358, 459
Good Friday, 137
Good Springs Post Office, 477
Goode, Bettie, 584
Goodlow, Daniel Reaves, 189
Goodpasture, Albert V., 365
Goodwyn, Philo Hiram, Jr., 560
Goodwyn, Philo Hiram, Sr., 560, 562
Goodwyn, William A., 302, 562
Gordon, Elizabeth, 532, 575, 577
Gordon, George W., 335, 395, 1042
Gordon, Nathaniel, 181, 300
Gordon, R. J., 410
Gorgas, Josiah, 351
Gospel of Mary, 423
Gospel of Philip, 423
government plantations, 298
Graham, John, 535, 555
Graham, John H., 535, 555
Graham, Levin, 108
Graham, Margaret, 474, 550, 551, 575

THE MCGAVOCKS OF CARNTON PLANTATION

Graham, Mary, 525
Graham, Nancy Agnes, 575
Graham, Robert, 575
Graham, William A., 535, 555
Granbury Cemetery, Granbury, TX, 379
Granbury, Hiram B., 374, 375, 378, 379, 415
Granbury, TX, 379
Granbury's Brigade, 359
Grand Invasion, 78
Grand Rapids, MI, 313
Granny White Pike, 342, 345
Grant, Ulysses S., 50, 201, 208, 215, 216, 246, 270, 309, 341, 343, 346, 347, 354, 355, 364, 367, 368, 392, 605
  war crimes of, 309
Grappe, Gabriel, 108
Grassland, TN, 601
Graves, Robert, 1040
graveyard decorations, 228
gravy, 463
greasers, Lincoln's word for Mexicans, 259
Great Britain, 177, 186, 190, 193, 238, 243, 261, 979
Great Depression, 80
Great Emancipator, 99, 227, 316, 321
Great Seal of the Confederacy, 470, 471
Greek culture, 448
Greek Revival, 53, 56, 439, 443, 446-449, 459, 477, 482, 497
Greek Revival fever, 448
Greek Revival style, 53, 56
Greek ruins, 449
Greek slavery, 209
Greek slaves, 209
Greeks, 209, 351, 449
Greeley, Horace, 89, 121, 216, 251, 266
Green County, TN, 41
green peas, 463
Green, E. E., 420
Greensboro, NC, 601, 603
Greenwood, Richard, 561
Greenwood, William Murphy, 561
Gregory, Eliza W., 558
Gresham, Joseph A., 600
Grey, Adeline, 319
Grierson, Benjamin H., 402
Grimké, Angelina, 189, 264
Grimké, Sarah, 189, 264
Groom, Winston, 401
Grundy family, 56
Grundy, Felicia, 419
Grundy, Felix, 38, 45, 49, 51, 53, 285, 301, 413, 418, 419, 425, 427, 443, 476, 514, 515, 537, 581
Grundy, Louisa Caroline, 285, 419, 537

Grundy, Martha Ann, 59, 222, 408, 517, 527, 570, 581
Grundy, Mary M., 408, 419
Guion, George S., 584
gumbo, 228, 462
gunpowder, 170
habeas corpus, 303, 307
habeas corpus, Lincoln suspends, 307
Hagen, Henry, 564
Hagen, Mary Wilson, 564
Hager, Elizabeth L., 551, 576
Hager, John W., 551
Haggard. W. T., 420, 421
Haiti, 116, 180, 222
Hale, John Parker, 264
Halifax County, NC, 51
Hall, Frances, 19
Halleck, Henry W., 367
Halloween, 308
hallway candle, 461
ham stand, 463
Ham, Fred, 600
Ham, Isaac, 600
Ham, Jesse D., 601, 604
Ham, of the Bible, 205
Hamilton, Alexander, 240
Hamilton, Melanie, 358
Hamiltonians, 236, 240
Hammond, James H., 402
Hampton Roads, VA, 244
Hampton, John, 600, 604
Hampton, Wade, III, 350
Handy, Anne, 585
Handy, Esther, 585
Handy, George Day Scott, 586
Handy, Harriet, 581
Handy, Henry Dashiel, 585, 586
Handy, Isaac, 585-587
Handy, Margaret Winder, 587
Handy, Peter, 586
Handy, Thomas Poultney, 586
Handy, Thomas Winder, 586
Handy, William Winder, 586
Hanks, Nancy, 321
Hanks, Tom, 321
Hanner, J. W., 414, 416, 418
Hanner, James P., 411
Hannity, Sean, 15
Harbison, W. J. Butch, 600
Hardenberghs, the, 132
Harding, Amanda P., 558
Harding, John, 410, 520, 558, 572
Harding, M. Louise, 232, 520, 572
Harding, Mary Elizabeth, 520, 572
Harding, Nancy Margaret, 49, 476

THE MCGAVOCKS OF CARNTON PLANTATION

Harding, Sarah Susan, 56, 520, 572
Harding, Selene, 342, 520, 572
Harding, Thomas, 49
Harding, William Giles, 48, 146, 342, 476, 520, 558, 572, 1044
Harding, William R., 63, 520, 572
Harding, Willie E., 476, 558
Hardscrabble Farm, 151
harems, and white slavery, 209
Harlem, NY, 165
Harmonson, Susannah, 584
Harness, John, 47
harp, 478
Harpers Ferry, VA, 87, 88
Harpeth Academy, Franklin, TN, 381
Harpeth River, 19, 45, 47, 301, 327, 330, 332, 339, 401, 454, 494, 514, 602
Harpeth River Watershed Association, 19
harpsichord, 478
Harris, Elijah, 557
Harris, Jeremiah George, 536, 556, 573
Harris, Richard, 536, 556, 573
Harris, Sarah, 70
Harrison Family Cemetery, 377
Harrison House, 377
Harrison, Benjamin, 343
Harrison, Dan, 600
Harrison, Dock, 600
Harrison, Harvey, 600
Harrison, James, 600
Harrison, William H., 15
harrowers, 136
Harry, Prince, 43, 589
Hart, John S., 557
Hartford County, CT, 173
Harvard Law School, 178, 285
Harvard University, 986
Harvey, Robert H., 600
Hatch, Edward, 309, 402
hate crimes, 165
Hawaii, 30
Hawthorne, Nathaniel, 89
Hay, Elizabeth, 546
Hay, Grizella, 525
Hay, Jesse K., 600
Hay, Patrick, 525
Hay, Sally, 532
Hay, William, 532, 546
Hayes, Elizabeth, 563
Hayes, Lysander McGavock, 563
Hayes, Margaret, 563
Hayes, Mary Elizabeth, 563
Hayes, McGavock, 563
Hayes, Oliver Bliss, Jr., 563
Hayes, Oliver Bliss, Sr., 563

Hayes, Rutherford B., 16, 343
Hayes, Thomas Pointer, 563
Hayesland, 563
Hayne, Robert Young, 158
Haynes, Almira, 532, 559, 577
Haynes, Elizabeth, 542
Haynes, Stephen, 559
Haynes, William, 542
Hays, Elizabeth, 543
headright system, 208
health care, and servitude, 138
Hebrew laws, and slavery, 212
Hebrew names, 27
Hebrew people, and slavery, 211
Hebrew slavery, 209
Hebrew slaves, 209
Hebrews, early, 204
hedge apple tree, 455
hedge fence, trees as a, 455
hedge tree, 455
Hedrick, Benjamin Sherwood, 189
height, as a measure of diet, 145
height, of Southern black servants, 145
heirlooms, 382, 463, 467, 473, 477, 494
Helena, AR, 379
Helper, Hinton Rowan, 189
Hemingway, Anson T., 333
Hemingway, Ernest, 333
hemp, 446
Henderson, John H., 420
Hennen family tomb, 357
Hennen, Anna M., 357
Henry Plantagenet II, King, 42, 589
Henry Plantagenet III, King, 42, 589
Henry the Navigator, 167
Henry the VIII, King, 589
Henry, Charlotte, 584, 587
Henry, John, 584
Henry, Matilda, 586
Henry, Patrick, 14, 234
Henson, Josiah, 120
Hepburn, Helen, 523
herbs, 453
Hermitage Gardens, 54
Hermitage, the, 45, 54, 220, 468, 1043
Herringbone Bond, 440, 443
HGTV, 355
Hickman County, TN, 601
Hickman, Ann, 540
Hickman, Thomas, 540
hickory nuts, 454
Hiernaux, Jean, 593
High School for Young Colored Ladies and Misses, 69
Hightower, Sarah C., 563

THE MCGAVOCKS OF CARNTON PLANTATION

Hilderic, King, 37, 590
Hill (Number) 210, 340
Hill of Slemish, Ireland, 35
Hill, Ambrose P., 95
Hilton Head Island, SC, 297
Hincheyville District, 49
Hincheyville, TN, 49, 50
Hindman, KY, 274
Hinduism, 66
Hines, Sally, 549
Hinton, Elizabeth B., 556
Hinton, Jeremiah, 557
Hispanic Europe, 168
Hispanic slave industry, 168
Hispanic slave owners, 167
Hispanic slavers, 168
Hispanic-American Confederate soldiers, 107, 595
Hispanic-Americans, 107, 595
Hispanic-Europeans, and slavery, 167
Hispanics, 167, 168
Hispanic-American slave owners, 206
Hispanic-Europeans, 167
Hispaniola, 168, 169
Historic Franklin Presbyterian Church, Franklin, TN, 51
historic homes, 595
History of Tennessee (Garrett and Goodpasture), 77, 509
Hite, Anne, 540
Hite, James H., 540
Hitler, 226
Hitler, Adolf, 211, 273, 958
hoe hands, 136
Hogben, Lancelot, 593
hogs, 132, 451, 454, 466
Holbrook family, of Kentucky, 1044
Holcombe, Martha, 551, 576
Holland, Cynthia R., 516, 570
Holm, Richard W., 593
Holstein River, VA, 36
Holy Blood of Jesus, the, 424
Holy Blood, Holy Grail (Baigent, Leigh, and Lincoln), 43
Holy Grail, 422
Holy Scriptures, 203
homelessness, 139, 141, 320, 484
homemade breads, 462
homes, Yankees burn down, 308
homestead act, 312, 319
Homo sapiens, and so-called "race", 218
Hood, John Bell, 327-329, 331, 334, 336-340, 342, 345, 348, 352, 353, 355-358, 360, 364, 365, 367-370, 378, 502, 505, 508, 537, 1042
Hood, Lydia, 357

Hood, Robin, 424
Hood's Retreat, 345, 378
Hooker, Joseph, 292
hooped skirts, 452
Horace Mann School, 563
Horn, Stanley F., 341, 343, 347
horse breeding farms, 48
Horton, Jane, 535, 555
hotcakes, 463
Hotchkiss shell, Union, found at Carnton, 456
Houma, Terrebonne Parish, LA, 62, 63, 406, 474, 517, 527, 570, 581
House of Burgesses, 193, 207
House of Representatives, 53, 162, 197, 343
house servants, 79, 117, 136, 260, 344, 390, 450
housekeeper, 147
Houston, Sam, 51, 55, 443, 476
Howard, Wiley, 376
Howe, Julia Ward, 89
huckleberries, 454
Huff, Sam, 601
Hughes, James, 600
Hughes, John, 293
Hughes, R. B., 600
Hughes, Sally, 519
Hughes, W., 600
Hughes, W. P., 600
Hulmey, William, 47
Hume, William M., 601
Humphreys County, TN, 603
Humphreys, Dan, 108
Hungarian Confederate soldiers, 595
Hunt, John, 975
Hunt, Mary, 572
Hunt, Zion, 47
Hunter, David, 304, 309
Hutchinson, Alfred, 600
Hutchinson, R. R., 506
Hyde, Mary T., 539
Hyre, Eliza, 557
ice cream, 463
ices, 10, 452, 463
ichthyology, and Jesus, 424
ichthys, 424
Idaho, 30, 46
illegal draft, of war industry workers in South, 362
Illinois, 30, 33, 69, 72, 77, 98, 99, 103, 154-156, 159, 183, 194, 205, 222-224, 242, 246, 250, 259, 263, 293, 318, 321, 333, 368, 963, 964, 969, 971-973, 979, 981, 983, 986, 989
Illinois license plate, 318
Illinoisans, 72, 154, 155, 224
imperialism, 241
income tax, 240, 241, 306, 312

1013

income, of servants, 143
Independence Day, 137
India, 116
Indian corn, 465
Indian massacres, 38
Indian slave owners, 166
Indian Territories, 166
Indiana, 30, 183, 336, 398, 399
Indianapolis, IN, 336
Indians, 38, 166, 167, 169, 291, 292, 308, 348, 352, 473, 526, 967
industrialism, 272, 313, 384
industrialism, Northern, 272
industrialists, 197
industrialization, 192
infant mortality, in Victorian era, 302
infections, 493
infections, from surgery, 490
inferior races, Lincoln's phrase for all non-whites, 259
inflation, 117, 288, 363, 364, 989
Ingraham, Laura, 15
inhumane slave owners, 122
Inman, Jeff, 601
Inman, Joseph, 601
Inman, Reuben, 601
integration, 155, 180, 256, 260
internal improvements, 240, 241, 469, 978
internal revenue, 306
Internal Revenue Service, 306
interracial business relationships, in the South, 153
interracial marriage, 259
intertribal raids, and slavery in Africa, 170
involuntary enlistment, of blacks into U.S. military, 294
Iowa, 30, 225
Ireland, 28, 29, 32-36, 40, 209, 235, 280, 285, 328, 331, 385, 438, 518, 525, 526, 531, 539, 541, 570, 578, 582
Irish, 27-29, 32, 34, 35, 37-40, 379, 462, 465-467, 474, 478, 479, 498, 595, 978, 987, 1040
Irish Confederate soldiers, 595
Irish kings, 37
Irish potatoes, 465
Irish Sea, 34
Irish-American architecture, 40
Ironclad Oath, 486
IRS, the, 306
Irwin, James, 49
Isabella Stewart Gardner Museum, 178
Isabella, Queen, 169, 172
Israel, 27, 416
Israelite slaves, 209
Italian Confederate soldiers, 595

Italy, 209, 210, 271
Ivy, A., 601
Ivy, John W., 601
Ivy, W. L., 601
Ivy, W. R., 601
IXOYE, 424
Jackson, Alexander, 572
Jackson, Andrew, 44, 46, 51, 54, 220, 256, 409, 443, 453, 468-470, 476, 495, 514, 537, 1043
Jackson, George W., 282
Jackson, Henry R., 1042
Jackson, Howell E., 408, 410, 520, 572
Jackson, Thomas "Stonewall", 57, 89, 109, 364, 381, 1044
Jackson, William H., 342, 408, 410, 520, 572
Jackson's Brigade, 1042
Jacob Summerlin Camp #1516, SCV, Kissimmee, FL, 594
Jacobs, Walter, 580
jails, Yankees burn down, 309
James Stewart I, King, 590
James Stewart II, King, 42, 590
James Stewart III, King, 42, 590
James VI, King, 589
James "Iron Belt" Stewart IV, King, 42, 590
James, Frank, 1044
James, Jesse, 1044
Jamestown, VA, 215, 1042
Jamison, Sam, 601
Japheth, of the Bible, 206
jazz, 228
Jefferson County, WV, 87
Jefferson, Thomas, 15, 38, 54, 57, 58, 144, 151, 172, 176, 181, 184, 186, 188, 189, 193, 196, 233, 237, 239, 240, 242, 257, 264, 277, 596, 1041, 1044
Jeffersonian Confederacy, 241
Jeffersonianism, 15, 236, 237, 311, 596, 1041
Jent, Elias, Sr., 274, 509, 1043
Jersey City, NJ, 165
Jerusalem, VA, 85
Jesus, 65, 88, 89, 202-205, 321, 423, 424, 495, 961, 978
Jesus Fish, 424
Jesus, and Satan are brothers according to Mormons, 205
Jewish creation myth, 217
Jewish slaves, 209
Jewish-American Confederate soldiers, 107, 595
Jewish-Americans, 107, 595
Jews, 211
jib window, 439, 482, 496, 497
jib windows, at Carnton, 482
Jim Crow Laws, 93, 153

THE MCGAVOCKS OF CARNTON PLANTATION

Jim Crow laws, in the North, 93
Jim Crow states, 154
Jingo, TN, 600
Joan of Arc, 60, 416
John Brown Slave Rebellion, 86
John Brown's Body (song), 89
John E. Stephens Post, American Legion, 426, 427
John "Lackland" I, King, 42, 590
Johnny Reb, 107, 288, 333, 356, 366, 491, 991
Johns Hopkins University, 1045
Johnson, Andrew, 16, 208, 226, 350
Johnson, Clint, 596
Johnson, Edward, 334
Johnson, Mathew, 47
Johnson, William, 151
Johnson's Division, 334
Johnston, Albert S., 339, 364, 367
Johnston, Joseph E., 349, 353, 354, 404, 600, 603, 604
Jomini, Baron Antoine-Henri, 363
Jones, Absalom, 163
Jones, Elizabeth, 581
Jones, George, 354
Jones, J. Calvin, 395
Jones, James, 601
Jones, John, 155, 601, 976
Jones, Roland W., 288
Joseph, of the Bible, 205
journals, 76, 152, 165, 219, 286, 294, 969, 972
Judaism, 66, 211
Judd, Ashley, 1041
Judd, Naomi, 1041
Judd, Wynonna, 1041
juleps, 452
Kansas, 30, 87
Kansas Territory, 87
Kautz, August V., 107
Keckley, Elizabeth, 134
Keith, Muriella, 523
Keith, William, 523
Kelly, Grace, 589
Kelly, John H., 377
Kendael, Hiram, 108
Kennard, S. M., 506
Kenneday, D. J., 420
Kenneday, Dave, 422
Kennedy, Frank, 358
Kennedy, John B., 395
Kennedy, John F., 399
Kennedy, Mark, 410
Kenning, Henry, 410, 416, 418, 420
Kent, Cynthia, 556, 574
Kent, David F., 575
Kent, Gordon C., 532, 577
Kent, Hugh McGavock, 574

Kent, Jacob, 572, 573
Kent, James R., 574
Kent, Jane D., 574
Kent, John Brown, 552, 576
Kent, Joseph, 536, 556, 572
Kent, Joseph F., 552, 576
Kent, Joseph Karolleman, 574
Kent, Margaret L., 574
Kent, Mary, 536, 555, 573
Kent, Nancy, 51, 473, 532, 576
Kent, Robert, 574
Kent, Sally, 574
Kentucky, 30, 49, 53, 274, 303, 323, 324, 347, 355, 367, 455, 598, 600, 602, 605, 606, 1040, 1042, 1044, 1045
Kentucky Cavalry, 13th, 274
Key, Anne Phoebe Charlton, 207
Key, Francis Scott, 207, 263
Key, Thomas J., 345
King of Spades, Lee's nickname, 351
King, Horace, black slave owner, 151
King, Nehemiah, 588
King, Robert, 601
King, William, 601
Kirby, Mack D., 601
Kirkcudbright, Scotland, 34
Kirkcudbrightshire, Scotland, 34
Kirkland, Mary, 290, 291
Kitchell, Joseph, 155
KKK, 205, 387, 394-399
KKK investigative committee, 395
KKK, and Mormons, 205
Knight, Thomas M., 601
Knights Templar, 11, 422, 423, 425
Knights Templar, and goddess-worship, 424
Knott County, KY, 274
Knoxville, Johnny, 354
Knoxville, TN, 465, 598, 602, 603
Ku Klux Klan, 394, 974, 976-978, 990
laborers, 73, 83, 107, 111, 115, 116, 127, 138, 139, 141, 209, 214, 254, 255, 264, 295, 298
Lady of the Lake (Scott), 88
Lafayette, Marquis de la, 57
laissez-faire economy, in South, 313
Lake Champlain, 178
land grants, 44
land management, 137
land redistribution program, 319
Lander, Eliza, 541
Lane, Jim, 304
Langhorne, John A., 574
lard, 451, 460, 461
Latin America, 168, 216
Latin words, 129

1015

THE MCGAVOCKS OF CARNTON PLANTATION

Latin-American colonies, 168
Latin-Americans, and slavery, 168
Latino slave owners, 167
Latinos, 167, 169
laudanum, 348
laundry, 105, 295, 451
laundry at Carnton, 451
Lavender, F. M., 597, 601
Lawrence, KS, 87
Lawrence, Margaret E., 537, 538
Lawrenceburg, TN, 600
LDS, 205
le Windere, John, 60
le Windere, surname, 60
Leake, Thomas, 547
Lebanon, TN, 564
Lee, Fitzhugh, 1044
Lee, Robert E., 57, 95, 145, 192, 238, 242, 274, 311, 339, 345, 351, 361, 362, 381, 382, 404, 405, 502, 509, 1043
Lee, Stephen D., 331, 334, 343, 596, 1042
Lee, William H. F., 1044
Lee's lost "Special Orders Number 191", 363
Lee's surrender, at Appomattox, 16
Legare family, 119
Legree, Simon, 119
lemonade, 463
Lester, Charles Edward, 245
Lester, John C., 395
lettuce, 453
lettuce salad, 452
Lewis and Clark Expedition, 46
Lewis, Addison, 544
Lewis, Juliette, 354
Lewis, Kelly, 601
Lewis, Lucy M., 544
Lexington, MA, 39
liberal left, 387
liberalism, 73, 277, 963, 973
liberals, 12, 21, 66, 227, 236, 469, 958
liberals, percentage of in U.S., 281, 595
Liberia, 72, 100, 180, 207, 262-264
Liberia, etymology of, 263
libertarian, 15, 21, 186, 277, 282, 363, 438
Libertarianism, 236, 237
libertarians, 58
liberty, 21, 39, 74, 92, 140, 158, 162, 193, 194, 211, 215, 262, 272, 276, 313, 318, 363, 371, 470
libraries, Yankees burn down, 308
life tenure, 469
Lightfoot, Mary, 541
Lightfoot, Philip, 541
Ligon, James, 559
Ligon, Pauline, 559

Limbaugh, Rush, 15
Limber, Jim, Pres. Jefferson Davis' adopted black child, 260
Limerick, Margaret, 385, 518, 571, 582
Lincoln apologists, 269
Lincoln scholars, 236
Lincoln, Abraham, 11, 13, 14, 16, 17, 21, 42, 43, 50, 52, 54, 57, 61, 68, 69, 72, 74-80, 88, 89, 91-93, 95-102, 104-106, 111, 113, 114, 116, 121, 129, 134, 144, 152, 154, 155, 163, 164, 168, 170, 179, 181, 183, 188, 190-192, 194, 197, 205, 207, 213, 216, 222, 223, 225, 226, 232, 236, 239, 241-243, 246, 250, 252, 256, 259, 261, 263-266, 268, 270, 273, 275, 276, 278, 280, 284, 287, 289, 291, 293-296, 300, 302, 304, 306, 307, 309, 317, 319, 321, 332, 340, 344, 360, 362, 363, 367, 368, 376, 380, 381, 386, 390, 392-394, 396, 399, 406, 438, 444, 469-471, 484-487, 490-492, 507, 596, 958, 1041
and 1860 and 1864 elections, 314
suppresses civil liberties, 310
war crimes of, 302, 308, 309
Lincoln's civil rights record, 256
Lincolnology (Seabrook), 144, 196, 438, 596
Lincolnshire County, England, 56, 60
Lincoln-Douglas Debates, 250
Lincoln's War, 7, 11, 16, 41, 47, 50, 52, 53, 57, 62, 69, 72, 78, 83, 84, 103, 106, 108, 116, 124, 125, 127, 136, 145, 146, 156, 172, 175, 181, 192, 196, 199, 208, 216, 220, 222, 231-233, 243, 249, 253, 259, 263, 269, 271, 272, 276, 278, 281, 286, 287, 291, 300, 319, 323, 324, 327, 334, 339, 343-345, 348, 360, 361, 364, 366, 369, 373, 382, 384, 386, 389, 393, 397, 402, 403, 435, 455, 490, 493, 507, 517, 539, 595, 960
Lincoln's white supremacist views, 247
Lindbergh, Charles, 15
Lindsley, John Berrian, 538
Lindsley, Philip, 537, 538
Lindsley, Randal McGavock, 539
Lipscomb, Thomas H., 559
liquor, 465
Little Tennessee River, 46
livestock, 35, 108, 128, 132, 133, 148, 155, 228, 260, 382, 383, 429, 451, 455, 462, 466, 520
Livingstone, Frank B., 593

THE McGAVOCKS OF CARNTON PLANTATION

Llewelyn, Elen Verch, 522
Lloyd, Elizabeth Taylor, 588
Lodge, Henry Cabot, Jr., 177
Lodge, Henry Cabot, Sr., 177
London Spectator, 92
London Standard, 92
London Times, 92, 276
London, England, 536, 556, 573
Longfellow, Henry Wadsworth, 89
longshoremen, 295
Longstreet, James, 1044
Longview Mansion, 1047
Lopez, Aaron, 176
lords of the lash and loom, 80
Loring, William W., 330
Loring's Division, 330
Lorton, Cumberland County, England, 56, 222
Los Angeles, CA, 117
Lost Cause, 283, 361, 427, 959, 983
Lott's Creek, KY, 274
Lotz House Museum, 10, 19, 502, 1047
Lotz, Johann Albert, 502
Lotz, Matilda, 1047
Louis the XIV, King, 589
Louisiana, 30, 56, 59, 61-63, 82, 150, 151, 154, 162, 222, 228, 271, 289, 317, 339, 357, 405, 413, 415, 418, 419, 421, 471, 474, 507, 595
Louisville, KY, 359
Love, Henry, 108
Love, Margaret, 564
Lovejoy, Elijah Parish, 72
Loveless, Patty, 1041
Lovell, Mansfield, 58
Lowell, James Russell, 89
loyal Southern blacks, 113
loyalty, between black servant and white owner, 221
Ludlow, Daniel H., 205
Lundy, Benjamin, 189
Luther, Martin, 213
Lutz, Charles, 108
Lyons, James, 188
Lytle, Andrew N., 272, 346, 401
Ma (goddess), 424, 449
Ma Ma (goddess), 424
Mac Dabhóc, 27
Macaria or Altars of Sacrifice (Evans), 447
MacArthur, Arthur, 332
MacArthur, Douglas, 332
MacCavock, 28
MacDade, 28
MacDaibheid, 28
MacDaid, 28
MacDavid, 28

MacDavitt, 28
MacDavock, 28
MacDavymore, 29
MacDevitt, 28
MacGavic, 28
MacGavick, 28
MacGavock, 32
MacGavock, Patrick, 33
Machiavellian Diplomacy, Lincoln's, 104
Mack, Wilhelm, 36
Mack's Meadows, VA, 36
Maclura pomifera, 455
MacMurchada, Erchad, 37
Macnee, Patrick, 43, 590
MacVicar, 28
Madeira, 463
Madison, James, 14, 120, 159, 188, 189, 208
Magnolia Cemetery, Mobile, AL, 377
mahogany wood, 494
Maid Marian, 424
Main Street, Franklin, TN, 49
Maine, 30
Malbones, New England slaving family, 178
Malcolm III, King, 27, 37, 589
malingering, 299
Mallory, Stephen R., 242
mammy, the, 125, 229, 230
Manassas, VA, 111, 255
Mangrum, John W., 602
Mangrum, Ronny, 19
Mangrum, W. B., 602
Mangrum, Wesley, 602
Mangrum, Wiley, 602
Manifest Destiny, 54
Manigault, Arthur M., 335, 1042
Manigault's Brigade, 1042
Mansion House, the, 36, 39, 40
manure carts, 489
Maplewood Cemetery, Pulaski, TN, 379
Mapother, Thomas Cruise, IV ("Tom Cruise"), 43, 590
Mar (goddess), 424, 449
Marblehead, MA, 173
Marc Antony, 589
March to the Sea, Sherman's, 359
Marcomir IV, King, 37, 590
mare, 424, 449
Margaret (wife of Hugh McGavock), 35
Maria (goddess), 424, 449
Mariah (goddess), 424
Mariam (goddess), 424, 449
Marie (goddess), 424, 449
Marina (goddess), 424, 449
Marmaduke, Linneus V., 506
Marr, Ben F., 601

1017

The McGavocks of Carnton Plantation

Marshall family, 287
Marshall, Eliza M., 515
Marshall, John, 602
Marshall, John (1), 14
Marshall, John (2), 505
Martin, James, 540
Martin, Sally D., 540
Martin, W. W., 563
Martineau, Harriet, 120, 159
Marvin, Lee, 502, 1044
Marxism, 958
Mary Magdalene, 423, 973
Mary, mother of Jesus, 423
Maryland, 30, 52, 57, 88, 120, 207, 222, 263, 306
Mason, George, 14
Masonic Lodge, Franklin, TN, 370
Masonry and Mormonism, 205
masons, 137, 295, 449
Mason-Dixon Line, 96, 153, 313
mass execution, largest under Lincoln, 308
Massachusetts, 30, 39, 41, 69, 89, 90, 109, 153, 173-178, 181, 183, 208, 215, 245, 263, 285, 300, 438, 478
Massachusetts Bay, 208
Massachusetts Bay Colony, 208
Massachusetts, and slavery, 175
Massachusetts, first state to legalize slavery, 174
massed frontal assault, 351
Matilda, Lady, 522
Matthews, Harold Smythe, 568
Matthews, John P., 568
Mauley, James, 602
Maury County, TN, 49, 463, 599, 603, 1042
Maury Family Cemetery, 49
Maury, Abraham Poindexter, 49, 50, 463
Maury, Abram Poindexter, 47, 49, 1042
Maury, Matthew Fontaine, 50
Maury, Susan, 49
Max Meadows, VA, 36, 39, 40, 514, 526, 532
Maxwell House Hotel, Nashville, TN, 537
Maxwell, Harriet V., 537
May, Samuel J., 72, 75
McAllister, James M., 602
McClellan, George B., 89, 95, 298, 316, 317, 369
McConnell, Lewis, 108
McCook, Dan, 340
McCord, Frank O., 395
McCoy, Mary, 525
McCulloch, Robert, 506
McDaniel, Elizabeth L., 377
McDavid, 28
McDougall, E. D., 422
McDowell family, 42, 43
McDowell, Elizabeth, 42-44, 552, 573, 574
McDowell, Elizabeth Preston, 42

McDowell, James, 552
McDowell, Uchtred, 42
McEwen Bivouac, 282, 408, 411
McEwen, John B., 410
McEwin family, 287
McEwin, David, 47
McFadden, Robert, 601
McFerrin, James, 557
McFerrin, John Berry, 557
McGaffick, 32
McGavic, 32
McGavick, 32
McGavock Cemetery in Chiswell, Wythe County, VA, 39
McGavock Confederate Cemetery, 8, 10, 12, 53, 379, 414, 457, 505, 506, 508, 509, 528
McGavock Confederate Cemetery Corporation, 508
McGavock Creek, 450, 451, 454
McGavock emigration, 29
McGavock family, 8, 9, 23, 24, 29, 33, 42-44, 53, 63, 66, 75, 144, 222, 286, 300, 301, 329, 407, 410, 426, 428, 443, 452, 454, 456, 474, 484, 506, 513, 514, 517-519, 521, 526, 527, 531, 972, 1042
McGavock Family Cemetery, 53, 63, 301, 407, 456, 506, 514, 517, 518, 526, 527
McGavock family plot, 286, 428, 519
McGavock family tartan, 29
McGavock Family Tree, 513
McGavock Family Vault, 53
McGavock genealogy, 513
McGavock House, the, 40
McGavock servant period, 79
McGavock surname, etymology of, 27
McGavock, Albert, 566
McGavock, Albert Pugsley, 41, 565
McGavock, Alexander, 33, 578
McGavock, Alexander Ewing, 534, 553
McGavock, Amanda, 559
McGavock, Amanda M., 534, 553
McGavock, Andrew J., 568
McGavock, Ann Louise, 301, 516, 569
McGavock, Anne Eliza, 54, 537
McGavock, Anne Rooke, 566
McGavock, Annie Lou, 557
McGavock, Caroline Pugsley, 565
McGavock, Catherine Blackwell, 560
McGavock, Catherine Louisa, 557
McGavock, Charles Alexander, 546
McGavock, Charles Pugsley, 565
McGavock, Cloyd, 545
McGavock, Cynthia, 563, 566, 568

1018

THE MCGAVOCKS OF CARNTON PLANTATION

McGavock, Cynthia E., 473, 551, 575
McGavock, Cynthia Holland, 516, 570
McGavock, Cynthia Tennessee, 557
McGavock, David, 42, 44, 46, 467, 476, 514, 549, 552, 573, 574
McGavock, David Albert, 566
McGavock, David Cloyd, 541
McGavock, David Ella, 566
McGavock, David Harding, 45, 410, 476, 558, 1044
McGavock, David Shall, 559, 577
McGavock, David Turner, 41, 564
McGavock, Edward Jacob, 538
McGavock, Edwin A., 557
McGavock, Eliza Jane, 535, 555
McGavock, Eliza L., 564
McGavock, Eliza McDowell, 51, 515, 550, 569, 577
McGavock, Elizabeth, 556, 568, 574, 575
McGavock, Elizabeth C., 547
McGavock, Elizabeth Harding, 515, 569
McGavock, Elizabeth Irwin, 48, 56, 63, 232, 342, 476, 520, 572
McGavock, Elizabeth McDowell, 532, 561
McGavock, Elizabeth Virginia, 559
McGavock, Ella Young, 538
McGavock, Emily, 562, 563, 1044
McGavock, Ephraim, 567
McGavock, Ephraim C., 563
McGavock, Felix Grundy, 386, 539
McGavock, Felix Hugh, 537
McGavock, Frances A., 549
McGavock, Frances E. H., 541
McGavock, Francis, 568, 1044
McGavock, Francis Ella, 567
McGavock, Francis F., 410, 416, 418, 545, 550, 577
McGavock, Francis Hargrave, 568
McGavock, Frank, 538
McGavock, Frank Owens, 558
McGavock, Frank W., 558
McGavock, George Shall, 562
McGavock, Gordon Cloyd, 544
McGavock, Harriet Russel, 302, 562
McGavock, Harriet Young "Hattie", 61, 283, 288, 371, 372, 385, 415, 420, 421, 423, 425, 426, 457, 473, 475, 505, 518, 527, 570, 582
McGavock, Hattie, 519, 571
McGavock, Henry Bentley, 560
McGavock, Hugh, 32, 33, 35, 51, 473, 526, 531, 532, 546, 576
McGavock, Hugh (2), 578
McGavock, Hugh Albert, 540
McGavock, Hugh Ewing, 551, 576

McGavock, Hugh Felix, 537
McGavock, Hugh Frank, 564
McGavock, Hugh L. White, 564
McGavock, Hugh Lysander, 563
McGavock, Hugh W., 557
McGavock, Jacob, 284, 419, 536, 542
McGavock, Jacob Cloyd, 551, 576
McGavock, James, 533, 536, 552, 573
McGavock, James H., 543
McGavock, James Hampton, 567
McGavock, James Randal (1), 301, 473, 514, 550, 569, 1044
McGavock, James Randal (2), 516, 569
McGavock, James Randal (3), 516, 570
McGavock, James Randal (4), 560
McGavock, James W., 548
McGavock, James, Jr., 566
McGavock, James, Sr., 32, 35, 36, 38-43, 526, 532, 578
McGavock, Jane, 540
McGavock, Jane B., 548
McGavock, Jane Ellen, 562
McGavock, Jane Lewis, 567
McGavock, John, 519, 556, 574
McGavock, John Augustus, 557
McGavock, John Fulton, 567
McGavock, John Harding, 558
McGavock, John Hickman, 544
McGavock, John Jacob, 539
McGavock, John Randal, 61, 63, 481, 518, 570, 582
McGavock, John William, 557
McGavock, John Williamson, 567
McGavock, John, Col., 11, 43, 45, 48, 52, 53, 56, 61-64, 78, 79, 82, 215, 218, 232, 280-282, 286, 288, 300, 332, 371, 372, 381, 382, 406, 407, 409-416, 418, 419, 421, 424-426, 437, 442, 446, 449, 457, 460, 464, 466, 467, 473-477, 480, 483-485, 494, 495, 497, 506, 509, 517, 527, 570, 581, 594, 960, 1044
McGavock, John, Jr., 457
McGavock, Joseph, 473, 532, 545, 550, 551, 575
McGavock, Joseph Cloyd, 568
McGavock, Joseph Kent, 536, 556, 573
McGavock, Joseph Randal, 551, 576
McGavock, Lawrence, 419
McGavock, Lida Carey, 558
McGavock, Lillie Hite, 541
McGavock, Louisa, 516
McGavock, Louisa G., 547
McGavock, Louisa Grundy, 538
McGavock, Lucinda, 536, 556, 573
McGavock, Lucinda Elizabeth, 534

1019

THE MCGAVOCKS OF CARNTON PLANTATION

McGavock, Lucinda Ewing, 535, 555
McGavock, Lucy Nancy, 552, 576
McGavock, Lula A., 550, 577
McGavock, Lysander, 64, 301, 477, 562, 1044
McGavock, Manoah, 539
McGavock, Margaret, 536, 549, 556, 568, 572, 575
McGavock, Margaret E., 564
McGavock, Margaret Jane, 537
McGavock, Margaret K., 536, 555, 573
McGavock, Margaret Lucinda, 550, 577
McGavock, Margaret M., 568
McGavock, Maria Louisa, 515, 569
McGavock, Martha, 288, 457, 532
McGavock, Martha H., 548
McGavock, Martha Shall, 560
McGavock, Martha Winder, 61, 301, 481, 517, 570, 581
McGavock, Martha Winder (2), 519, 571
McGavock, Martha Winder (3), 540, 583
McGavock, Mary, 457, 532, 566, 568, 575
McGavock, Mary Ann Kent, 557
McGavock, Mary Ann Scott, 561
McGavock, Mary Cloyd, 300, 301, 519, 571
McGavock, Mary Elizabeth, 61, 63, 232, 480, 517, 570, 581
McGavock, Mary Ellen, 515, 516, 550, 569, 570
McGavock, Mary Haller, 575
McGavock, Mary Jouet, 568
McGavock, Mary Kent, 536, 556, 573
McGavock, Mary Louisa, 539
McGavock, Mary Louise, 539
McGavock, Mary T., 564
McGavock, Melinda Winder, 533, 553
McGavock, Myra, 562
McGavock, Myra Lee, 560
McGavock, Nancy Crockett, 575
McGavock, Nancy Kent, 533, 552
McGavock, Nancy M., 546
McGavock, Oscar Hugh, 534, 535, 554
McGavock, Oscar W., 541
McGavock, Patrick, 578
McGavock, Pauline Archer, 560
McGavock, Randal, 35, 39, 43, 44, 46, 48, 50, 51, 54, 55, 59, 63, 78, 82, 148, 198, 200, 207, 285, 379, 381, 407, 436-438, 440, 446, 453, 457, 464, 466-468, 473, 474, 476, 478, 480, 514, 515, 526, 551, 559, 569, 576, 577
    and the Northern McGavock branch, 32
McGavock, Randal (2), 515
McGavock, Randal (Northern McGavock branch), 578

McGavock, Randal Ewing, 516, 570
McGavock, Randal H., 540
McGavock, Randal William, 39, 284, 286, 537, 1044
McGavock, Reed, 551
McGavock, Robert, 540
McGavock, Robert Emmet, 543
McGavock, Rosa Delia, 541
McGavock, Sallie Ewing, 519
McGavock, Sallie Pointer, 516, 570
McGavock, Sally, 549, 552, 559, 564, 577
McGavock, Sally Cloyd, 575
McGavock, Sally E., 563
McGavock, Sally M., 551, 576
McGavock, Samuel Pointer, 516, 570
McGavock, Sara Ewing, 422, 571, 582
McGavock, Sarah, 515, 568
McGavock, Sarah "Sallie", 301, 473, 538, 569
McGavock, Sarah A., 557
McGavock, Sarah H., 547
McGavock, Sarah Jackson, 567
McGavock, Sarah Jane, 536, 556, 573
McGavock, Sarah M., 533, 553
McGavock, Stephen, 568
McGavock, Stephen Chenault, 516, 569
McGavock, Susan R., 549
McGavock, Susannah Elizabeth, 559
McGavock, Thomas Cloyd, 541
McGavock, Thomas Elmore, 540
McGavock, Thomas Pointer, 516, 570
McGavock, Van Winder, Jr., 516, 570
McGavock, Van Winder, Sr., 516, 569
McGavock, Wiley, 536, 556, 573
McGavock, William, 50, 517, 568, 570
McGavock, William Chenault, 515, 569
McGavock, William Ligon, 560
McGavock, William McGavock, 516, 570
McGavock, Winder, 61, 288, 372, 385, 413, 415, 418, 420, 457, 475, 518, 571, 582
McGavock, Winder, Jr., 519, 571, 583
McGavock's Grove, 442
McGavocks, 1-5, 7-17, 21, 23-25, 27-30, 32-34, 36, 38, 39, 42-44, 47, 50, 54, 55, 63, 65, 66, 68, 75, 79, 80, 83, 94, 106, 131, 144, 147, 150, 172, 185, 201, 211, 214, 216-220, 222, 232, 235, 236, 259, 277, 278, 280, 284, 286-289, 300, 323, 330, 357, 377, 381-384, 386, 396, 405, 407, 419, 422, 424, 425, 429, 430, 435, 445, 447, 452-454, 458, 460-464, 466-468, 470-473, 476-481, 483, 484, 487, 494-498, 501, 521, 558, 578, 589, 594, 596, 958, 961, 993, 1042

THE MCGAVOCKS OF CARNTON PLANTATION

McGavocks distribution list, 30
McGavocks, and Lincoln's War, 278, 323
McGavocks, and their servants, 219
McGavocks, Celtic heritage, 235
McGavocks, Northern branch, 280
McGavocks, sue Lincoln, 277
McGavocks' servants, 82
McGavock's Grove, 286, 442, 443
McGinty, Ewing P., 557
McGinty, William A., 557
McGuffock, 28, 32
Mcintosh, John, 601
McKay, R. H., 602
McKay, Thomas, 47
McKinley, William, 343
McKissack, Jessie H., 355
McKissack, Susan P., 355
McMillan, W. J., 414, 416, 418, 420, 421
McMurray family, 287
McMurray, William J., 287, 597
McNair, Louise, 583
McNari, Rev., 56
McNeal, Young, 601
McNeilly, James H., 328, 413, 414, 416, 418
McNutt, Frances E., 549, 577
McNutt, Hugh McGavock, 549
McNutt, James A., 549
McNutt, Margaret, 549
McNutt, Maria, 549
McNutt, Mary, 549
McNutt, Robert, 549
McNutt, Samuel, 549, 577
McNutt, Samuel D., 549
McNutt, Sarah K., 549
McWhirter, Louis B., 539
Meade, George, 368
Meador, Bridget, 222, 579
Medford, MA, 178
medical officers, Confederate, 490
medical supplies, shortage of in South, 490
Meigs, Montgomery C., 113, 114
Mein Kampf (Hitler), 273
melodeon, 478
melons, 452, 453, 463
Melting Pot, U.S. as a, 271
Memoir of the Last Year of the War for Independence, A (Early), 969
Memphis, TN, 61, 386, 389, 393, 400, 449, 465, 537
merchants, 73, 75, 171, 175
Meriwether family, of Virginia, 327
Meriwether, Elizabeth A., 1044
Meriwether, Minor, 1044
Merovech, 43
Merovée, 43, 423, 590

Merovingian heritage, 425
Merovingians, the, 423
Merrill, Hannah, 560
Mesopotamians, 209
Metairie Cemetery, 357
Methodist Church, Franklin, TN, 421
Metoyer family (black slave owners), 150
Mexican Confederate soldiers, 595
Mexican-American War, 55, 56, 97
Mexicans, 55, 259
Mexicans, Lincoln's attitude toward, 259
Mexico, 30, 55, 97, 305, 984
Michigan, 30, 183, 224, 313
Middle Ages, 210
Middle Eastern slave industry, 169
Middle Passage, 171
Middle Tennessee, 23, 45-47, 53, 121, 222, 226, 280, 355, 365, 406, 419, 421, 426, 440, 468, 479, 964, 966, 972, 1041, 1045
Middle Tennessee Basin, 47
Midway Plantation, 64, 301, 477, 562-564, 1044
Milan, Italy, 202
military districts, in South during Reconstruction, 339
military draft, 163, 362
military draft, Northern, 163
military forces, 324, 361
military measure, 102
military necessity, 251
milkmaids, 136
millers, 142
Milligan, Sarah E., 549
mills, Yankees burn down, 308
Minié ball, 502
Minié, Claude-Etienne, 502
Minnesota, 30, 33
Minor, Sarah, 544
minorities, and Lincoln, 257
minstrel shows, U.S., 294
mint julep recipe, 605, 606
mint juleps, 10, 452
miscegenation, 223
Mississippi, 30, 54, 57, 59, 60, 82, 151, 162, 174, 185, 188, 221, 222, 286, 317, 339, 340, 346, 357, 358, 401, 402, 419, 449, 507, 509
Mississippi River, 46, 57, 61, 357, 363, 391, 465
Missouri, 30, 42, 166, 205, 245, 306, 323, 324, 327, 506, 507
Missouri Compromise, 205
Missouri River, 46
Mitchell, Margaret, 229, 230, 358, 459
mixing stand, 463
Mobile, AL, 112, 271, 377, 379

The McGavocks of Carnton Plantation

moderates, percentage of in U.S., 281, 595
modern America, 54
Mona Lisa (da Vinci), 424
monarchists, 470
money order system, 312
mongrels, Lincoln's word for Mexicans, 259
Monroe Harding Children's Home, Nashville, TN, 426, 427
Monroe, James, 14, 15
Montagu, Ashley, 218, 593
Montana, 30, 46
Montgomery County, VA, 473
Montgomery, Margaret, 524
Montgomery, Mary Ann, 51, 400
Moon worship, and Christianity, 424
Moon-Goddess, worship of, and early Christianity, 424
Moore, Charles H., 548
Moore, Georgia A., 558
Moore, Joseph T., 558
Mooreland House, 1047
More, Thomas, 214
Morgan, John H., 1044
Morgan, Sarah, 190
Mormon beliefs, 205
Mormon groups, 205
Mormon law, and slavery, 205
Mormon laws, 205
Mormon ministers, 205
Mormon priesthood, 205
Mormon slave owners, 205
Mormon War, 339
Mormonism and Curse of Ham, 205
Mormonism and Goddess-worship, 205
Mormonism and Masonry, 205
Mormonism Unmasked (Roberts), 205
Mormons, 205
Mormons, and KKK, 205
Morrill Land-Grant College Act, 312
Morrill Tariff, 312
Morris, Jeremiah, 548
Morris, John, 548
Morris, Nathan E., 601
Morris, William, 547
Morton family, 287
Morton, John W., 1044
Mosby, Elizabeth Bacon, 1043
Mosby, John S., 242, 1043
Moses, of the Bible, 321
Mosley, Anne, 49
Moss, Newton J., 601
Mother Zion African Methodist Episcopal Church, 163
Mother-Goddess, 205
Mother-Goddess, and Mormonism, 205

Motlow College, 1045
Mount Olivet Cemetery, Nashville, TN, 53, 342
Mount Rushmore, 318
mourning portrait, 481
Mt. Hope Cemetery, Franklin, TN, 50, 420-423, 426, 428, 457
Mt. Pleasant, TN, 378
muffins, 462
Muir, Adam, 523
Muir, Elizabeth, 523
mulattoes, 223
mulberry family of trees, 455
mules, 105, 109, 132, 466
mumbo-jumbo, 228
Murchada, Erchad Mac, 589
murder, Yankee, 294
murderers, 86
Murfreesboro, TN, 341, 365, 378, 380
Murphy, John, 601
Murphy, Mary, 561
Murray, Anna, 88
Murray, Martha, 565
mushrooms, 454, 462
Music City, 45, 359
musicians, 137
mutiny, charges of, under Lincoln, 297
Myrrh (goddess), 424, 449
n word, the, 259, 293
NAACP, 266
Napoleon III, 594
Napolitano, Andrew, 15
Narragansett planters, and slavery in Rhode Island, 176
Narragansett, RI, 173
Narrative of Sojourner Truth (Truth), 132
NASCAR, 593
Nash, Francis, 35, 468
Nashville, TN, 35, 41, 44-46, 48-51, 53, 56, 284-286, 339, 340, 345, 346, 356, 359, 363-365, 367, 375, 380, 398, 446, 449, 464, 467, 468, 476, 484, 526, 527, 599, 600, 602, 1044
Nashville, TN, Union capture of, 226, 289
Nat Turner Rebellion, 85, 86
Natchez National Historical Park, 152
Natchez, MS, 59, 357, 413, 415
Nathan Bedford Forrest (Seabrook), 405
National Academy of Science, 312
National Agricultural Congress, 342
National Banking Acts, 312
National Cemetery, Murfreesboro, TN, 380
National Cemetery, Nashville, TN, 380
national debt, 469
national government, 238, 312, 362, 975
National Historic Landmark, 437

THE MCGAVOCKS OF CARNTON PLANTATION

National Intelligencer, 253
National Park Service, 437, 961
National Register of Historic Places, 49, 437
nation-states, 196, 237-239, 276, 311
Native-American Confederate soldiers, 595
Native-American slaves, in Rhode Island, 176
Native-Americans, as slaves, 169
Native-Americans, make slaves of early white settlers, 165
Native-American cities, 47
Native-American slave owners, 165, 166, 206
Native-Americans, 35, 36, 38, 39, 46, 66, 107, 165, 169, 172, 201, 224, 257, 292, 308, 309, 348, 435, 455, 595
natural law, 66
natural rights, 116, 212
natural selection, 967
naval blockade, 304, 362, 492
Nazi Germany, 210
Nazi slavery, 211
Nebraska, 30, 98, 979
Neely, George, 47
Neely, James, 411
negotiated peace talks, 244
Negro, 70, 83, 96, 98, 99, 110, 111, 127, 156, 157, 159, 161, 162, 168, 170, 190, 191, 219, 222-224, 247, 253, 255, 261, 270, 290, 292, 409, 961, 963, 964, 966, 970, 972, 973, 977, 979, 982, 983, 986, 987, 989-992
Negro Convention, 231
Negro Haitian Rebellion, 222
Negro kings, and African slavery, 170
Negroes, 70, 109-111, 120, 145, 151, 155-159, 169-171, 182, 189, 191, 194, 198, 224, 255, 256, 261, 265, 268, 290, 291, 293, 295, 320, 967, 974, 979, 980, 991
Negrophobia, 249
Nelson family, of West Virginia, 1044
Nelson, Louis Napoleon, 108, 594
Neo-Confederates, 508
Neon, Letcher County, KY, 355
neo-Confederate, 594
Netherlands, 208
Nevada, 30, 55, 308
Nevils, John M., 411
New Bern, NC, 271
New Deal, 312, 963
New Deal programs, 312
New England, 69, 76, 97, 124, 162, 173, 175-178, 213, 239, 263, 972, 980
New England bankers, and slavery, 175
New England slave industry, 173
New England, textile mills in, 181

New Englanders, 438
New Hampshire, 30, 173, 181, 183, 191
New Jersey, 30, 95, 175, 183, 188, 262
New London County, CT, 173
New Mexico, 30, 55
New Netherland, 174
New North, 388
New Orleans Seminary, 1045
New Orleans, LA, 61, 64, 112, 174, 256, 271, 299, 357, 363, 373, 406, 471, 485, 517, 527, 596
New River, VA, 36
New South, 13, 14, 16, 55, 65, 99, 113, 120, 127, 128, 132, 142, 163, 186, 227, 280, 281, 373, 388, 391, 596, 957, 959, 960, 968
New South authors, 142
New South disinformation, 960
New South folklore, 127
New South movement, 227
New South Southerners, 65, 281, 596
New South thought police, 14
New South values, 280
New South writers, 127, 132, 186
New Testament, 203, 204, 424
New Testament, and Goddess-worship, 424
New World, 167, 169, 173, 981
New York, 30, 71-73, 79, 90, 97, 101, 109, 132, 158-160, 163-165, 173-175, 181, 183, 208, 223, 225, 248, 253, 263, 264, 293, 297, 300, 313, 339, 350, 465, 561, 593
New York Draft Riots, 163
New York Evening Post, 297
New York Harbor, 174
New York State Militia, 109
New York Times, 253
New York, NY, 71, 158, 159, 175, 465
New York, racism in, 165
Newcomb, Nelson, 602
Newnan, GA, 601
Newport County, RI, 173
Newport, RI, 41, 176
Newton, Emma, 540
NHL, 437
Niall of the Nine Hostages, 37, 589
Nigeria, Africa, 216
Nightingale (ship), 181
Nineteenth Amendment, 258
Ninth Amendment, 237
Noah, of the Bible, 205, 206
Noah's Sacrifice, 473
Nolen, F. C., 602
Norfolk, VA, 207, 271
Norman, Jack A., 602

THE MCGAVOCKS OF CARNTON PLANTATION

Normandy, France, 57, 209
Normans, the, 34
Norse heritage, 34
North, 11, 12, 14, 16, 17, 21, 30, 34, 36, 38, 41, 44, 51, 55, 57, 58, 64, 66, 68, 69, 71-77, 80, 81, 83, 85, 88-98, 101-109, 113, 115, 117, 118, 121, 127, 128, 130, 131, 137, 141, 147, 149, 153, 156-166, 171-174, 177-180, 182, 183, 185, 187-189, 192, 193, 196, 198-202, 205, 208, 215, 219, 220, 225, 228-231, 233-236, 243, 249, 251, 253-255, 258, 261, 265, 266, 270-274, 276, 278, 279, 281, 284, 285, 287, 295, 296, 302, 304, 307, 311, 315, 317, 318, 320, 321, 323, 324, 330-332, 339, 345-347, 354, 359, 363, 366-368, 370, 373, 378, 380, 381, 384, 387-389, 391, 393, 394, 396, 397, 399, 402, 422, 456, 472, 474, 491, 496, 563, 571, 581, 582, 584, 591, 592, 596, 600, 958-960, 963, 965-971, 973, 975, 977-979, 981, 983, 984, 987-990, 992, 1041, 1042, 1045
North Africa, 117
North American Review, 984
North British Review (England), 156
North Carolina, 14, 30, 41, 44, 51, 109, 188, 189, 208, 231, 271, 287, 317, 320, 366, 474, 491, 600, 1042
North Dakota, 30
North Star (Douglass), 88
North Western Railroad, 602
North, contrasted with South, 233, 235
North, R. B., 422
North, slavery began in the, 172
North, the, as seen by the South, 233
North, whites' fears of blacks in the, 96
Northern abolitionists, 98, 119, 172, 245, 250, 264, 270
Northern arrogance, 16
Northern bias, 957
Northern Black Codes, 153
Northern blacks, 106, 159, 164, 253, 299, 300
Northern businessmen, 103, 183, 194
Northern distilleries, 181
Northern free labor farms, 138
Northern greed, 77
Northern historians, 90, 97, 202, 438
Northern history, 171
Northern industrialism, 313
Northern industrialists, 197
Northern Ireland, 29, 34, 36, 40, 525, 526, 531, 532, 578
Northern Ireland's American emigrants, 40
Northern merchants, 75
Northern myth, 123, 143, 148, 193, 199, 218, 263
Northern mythologists, 73, 125
Northern mythology, 13, 68, 185, 957, 960
Northern newspapers, 303, 315
Northern peace advocates, 315
Northern press, 387
Northern propaganda, 17, 118
Northern propagandists, 344
Northern publishers, 269
Northern Puritans, 235
Northern racism, 154, 163, 164, 296, 299
Northern racist beliefs concerning enlisting blacks, 253
Northern slave owners, 120, 132, 215
Northern slave traders, 183
Northern slavery, 106, 131, 132, 176, 182, 246, 300
Northern states, 71, 153, 156, 157, 159, 181, 183, 188, 196, 222, 224, 227, 305, 315
Northern states, years they abolished slavery, 183
Northern textbook publishers, 269
Northern view of Southern slavery, 146
Northern white society, 158
Northern whites, 69, 163, 165, 207
Northern-biased school texts, 80
Northerners, 14, 65-68, 75, 76, 78, 87-89, 95-97, 103, 105, 118, 119, 127, 134, 136, 143, 146, 154, 156, 163, 164, 176, 181, 188, 190, 199, 223, 226, 233, 236, 239, 246, 247, 250, 253-255, 264, 271, 275, 296, 307, 313, 315, 317, 319, 321, 339, 363, 368, 373, 387, 388, 391, 394, 400, 988
Northerners, as seen by Southerners, 233
Northerners, of Tennesseans, 392
Northernization, of Southerners, 16
Northernizing the South, 16
Northrop, Lucius B., 362
Northwest Ordinance, 183, 196
Northwest Territory, 183
North's illegal invasion of Dixie, 16
Notes on the State of Virginia (Jefferson), 195
Nugent, Ted, 1041
nullification, 469, 983
nurses, 137, 161
Nusom, Susan, 533, 553
nutrition, 491
Oaklawn Mansion, 354
Oath of Allegiance, 100, 303, 381, 484-487
Oath, Ironclad, 486
oats, 465

THE McGAVOCKS OF CARNTON PLANTATION

Obama, Barack H., 487
Odo (Star Trek), 43
Odomi, 37
Odomir, King, 590
Office of Immigration, 312
Ogles, Levi, 602
Ohio, 30, 35, 118, 183, 223, 246, 286, 292, 302, 369, 379, 465, 504
Ohio River, 347
Oklahoma, 30, 166
Old America, 54
Old City Cemetery, Dyersburg, TN, 379
Old Dixie, 148
Old Glory Chapter, DAR, 426
old maid, card game, 465
Old North, 225, 234, 388
Old South, 2, 9, 12, 16, 66, 127-129, 131, 185, 201, 213, 231, 234, 239, 260, 387, 470, 593, 594, 605, 965, 966, 971, 975, 986, 987, 989
Old Testament, 204, 205
Old Wild West, 46
Oliphant, Laurence, 135
olives, 462
Olmsted, Frederick Law, 160, 191, 228
Omagh, County Tyrone, Northern Ireland, 40
Onesimus, of the Bible, 203
onions, 453
operating theaters, at Carnton, 488
opium, 371
opossum, 454
oral histories, 80
Order of the Heroes of America, 310
Ordinance of Secession, SC, 376
Oregon, 30
Original Sin, 202
Ormes, William, 602
ornamental flowers, at Carnton, 454
Osage Nation, Native-American, 455
osage orange trees, 455
Otey, John H., 552
Otey, Mariah (Reddick), 221
outlaws, 980
Ovens Township, County Cork, Ireland, 328
overseers, black, 125
Overton Hill, 342
Overton, James, 602
Overton, John, Jr., 537
Overton, John, Sr., 537
Overton, Martha, 537
Owen, Joshua, 602
Owen, Sarah E., 515
Owsley, Frank Lawrence, 233, 397
oxen, 466
oysters, fried, 462

O'Brien, Dounough, King, 37, 589
O'Brien, Mortogh, King, 37, 589
O'Brien, Teige, King, 37, 589
O'Brien, Torlogh, King, 37, 589
O'Hara, Scarlett, 358, 368
packers, 136
paddocks, 446
Pagan traditions, and the Knights Templar, 423
Page, Jane, 567
painkillers, 490
Paisley, Scotland, 522
Pakistan, 116
paleoconservatism, 15, 236
paleoconservative republicanism, and the McGavocks, 282
Palin, Sarah, 15
paranormal activities, at Carnton, 12
Paris, France, 177
Park, John S., 410
Parker, D. C., 602
Parkes, James L., 410
Parkes, Thomas, 597, 602
Parrish, Susanna Caroline, 49
Parthenon, in Greece, 449
Parthenon, in Nashville, TN, 449
Parton, Dolly, 1041
partridge, 462
passage lamp, 461
Pathfinder of the Sea, 50
Patron Saint of Scotland, 327
Patron Saint of Wales, 27
patronage, 469
Paul, Ron, 15, 237
Paycheck, Johnny, 355
peace advocates, 315
Peace and Constitutional Society, 310
Peach Orchard Hill, skirmish at, 344
peacock feather fly brushes, 452
peasantry, servitude as, 136
pecan trees, at Carnton, 456
peculiar institution, 987
Pendleton, George H., 369
Pendleton, Gurdon H., 567
Pendleton, Jane Byrd, 567
Pennsylvania, 30, 33, 35, 41, 43, 67, 97, 123, 163, 183, 348, 463, 465, 468, 473
penny, U.S., 318
Pensacola, FL, 271
peonage, black, after emancipation, 320
Peoria, IL, 98
Pepin, King, 37
Pepperell, MA, 178
Pepperells, New England slaving family, 178
Pepsin, King, 590
Percy Warner Park, Nashville, TN, 539

1025

Perkins family, 287
Perkins, Nicholas, 47
Perkins, Samuel, 538
Perkins, Theresa Ewin, 538
Perkins, Thomas H., 47
Perkins, W. G. N., 410
Perry County, KY, 49
Perry County, TN, 602
Perthshire, Scotland, 523
Peter Principle, the, 349
Peters, George B., 355
Pettibone, Augustus Herman, 286
Pettigrew, James Johnston, 189
Petway, Hinchea, 49
Petway, W. J., 411
Peyton, Frances, 552, 576
Pharamond, King, 37, 590
Phelps, John W., 304
Phelps, Thomas A., 112
Philadelphia, PA, 35, 41, 71, 158, 159, 163, 165, 239, 463, 465
Philemon, of the Bible, 203
Philistine slaves, 209
Phillips, Anne, 514, 527, 569
Phillips, Wendell, 257
Phoenician slaves, 209
physical force, and slavery, 123, 126
piano-forte, 478
Pickerell, Julia Ann, 548
Pickett, Thomas J., 321
pickles, 463
Pierce, William, 173
Pierre-August, Jean Baptiste, 108
Pierre-August, Lufray, 108
Pike, Albert, 166
pillage, Yankee, 294
Pillow, Gideon J., 58, 104, 1044
Pinchback, Pinckney B. S., 162
Pinckney, Charles, 14
pineapple, symbol, and slavery, 177
Pinkerton Park, Franklin, TN, 328
Pinkerton, Allan, 88
Pinkerton, Jack, 602
pintle hinges, 442
Pisces, and Jesus, 424
Pitcher, Molly, 416
Pitts, Helen, 88
Plain of Franklin, 45, 333, 356, 505, 1042
plantation books, 126
plantation hands, postwar term for former servants, 115
plantation life, benefits of for some servants, 138
plantation management, and servants, 152
plantation, defined, 118
planters, wealthiest, 200

plowmen, 136
Plymouth County, MA, 173
Pointer, Cynthia Rodes, 516, 570
Pointer, Elizabeth, 567
Pointer, Samuel, 516, 570
Pointer, Thomas, 563
Pointer, William H., 567
police stations, Northern, racism at, 165
Polish Confederate soldiers, 595
political correctness, 66, 128, 204, 280, 957
politically correct, 12, 17, 172, 281, 387, 594, 595
Polk family, 52, 56
Polk House, 1043
Polk, Betsy, 588
Polk, Charlotte, 588
Polk, David, 587
Polk, Gertrude, 584, 587
Polk, Hetty, 588
Polk, James K., 15, 41, 50-52, 54, 55, 286, 443, 476, 517, 584, 587, 589, 1043
Polk, Josiah, 588
Polk, Leonidas, 1044
Polk, Lucius E., 1044
Polk, William, 378, 585, 587, 588
Pollard, Edward A., 17, 127, 144, 364, 596, 959
polygamy, 205
poor whites, 149
Poplar Grove, TN, 49
poplar tree wood, 462, 463, 479
Porter Female Academy, 381, 386, 539
Porter, Mary, 550
Portugal, 167, 176
Portugal, and slave trade, 167
Portuguese slave trade, 167
post offices, Northern, racism at, 165
postal service, sporadic, 362
Pottawatomie Creek, KS, 87
Potter family, of Kentucky, 1044
Poultney, Mary Ann, 586
pound cake, 462
pound cake pudding, 463
poverty, 311, 320
Powel, Anne, 566
Powell, Ferdinand, 563
Poynor, Richard "Dick", 144, 494
Preliminary Emancipation Proclamation, 156, 190, 249, 265
Presbyterian Church, Franklin, TN, 410, 415, 419, 421, 422, 426
Presbyterianism, 33
presentism, 13, 217
preserves, 463
Presley, Elvis, 1041
Preston family, of South Carolina, 360

THE MCGAVOCKS OF CARNTON PLANTATION

Prewitt, Adam, 602
Prewitt, Sarah, 540
Prewitt, Thomas, 602
Prewitt, William, 602
Price family, of Kentucky, 1044
Priest, Miles, 51
Priest, Moses, 51
Prince of Slavers, the, 181
Princeton University, 58
prisons, Yankees burn down, 308
Pritchard, Isaac, 602
Pritchard, John, 602
Pritchard, Wash, 602
private house servants, 117
private soldier, defined, 107
pro-North writers, 121
Proclamation of Amnesty and Reconstruction, Lincoln's, 16
profit sharing schemes, plantation, 134
Prosser, Gabriel, 84
prostitutes, 117
prostitution, 2, 320, 986
protectionism, 241
proto-peasants, servants as, 136
Providence Plantations, 118, 177
Providence, RI, 71
Provisional Congress of the Confederacy, 343
Provisional Detachment District of the Etowah (U.S.), 343
pro-North historians, 85, 162, 228, 255, 261, 270, 272, 321
pro-North writers, 121, 201, 307, 596
pro-states' rights, 87, 129
Prussia, 595
Prussian Confederate soldiers, 595
psychopathy, and slavery, 122
public opinion, 121, 156
Pugsley, Caroline Elizabeth, 41, 564
Pulaski, TN, 260, 379, 394
Purdue University, 399
Puritan abolitionists, 162
Puritans, 235
pyemia, 490
pyramidal mounds, 47
Quakers, 213
Quakers, racism among the, 213
Quantrill's Raid, 325
Quarles, Benjamin, 115
Quarles, Lucy, 574
Quarles, William A., 335, 373
Quartermaster Department, Confederate, 362
Quintard, Charles T., 377, 378
race track, at Belle Meade, 342
race, fallacy of the idea of, 217
racial cleansing, Lincoln and, 262

racial interbreeding, 223
racial purity, 67
racial separatism, 266
racism, 66-68, 72, 79, 141, 153, 154, 158, 159, 162-164, 180, 182, 205, 213, 251, 253, 255, 256, 258, 260, 290, 291, 293, 294, 296, 299, 593, 595, 957, 963, 980
and the South, 593
racism, in the North, 157, 158
racism, less severe in the South, 160
racism, towards blacks in the North, 158
racism, worst in the North, 153
Radicals, 264, 319
Ragsdale, Belle, 543
railroad lines, non-connecting, 362
railroad track widths, 362
railway mail service, 312
rail-splitters, 137
Rainey, Joseph H., 162
rakers, 136
Raleigh, NC, 208
Randall, James G., 236
Randolph, George W., 1044
Randolph, John, 186, 239
rape, 16, 122, 294, 297, 396
rape of black females, by Yankee soldiers, 294, 297
rapists, 392
Ratchford, Henry, 549
Rathberius, King, 37, 590
Ravensdale, Cassidy, 19
Raymond, Henry J., 101
Reading, Berkshire, County, England, 50
Reagan, Ronald, 1041
reality of Southern slavery, 146
Reams, W. R., 602
Rebel Born, A (Seabrook), 260, 405, 596
Rebels, 108-111, 129, 150, 248, 255, 327-331, 333, 334, 342, 343, 366, 378, 504, 958, 972, 973, 980
Reconstruction, 16, 226, 227, 251, 309, 339, 350, 367, 383, 387, 397-400, 484, 539
Reconstruction Acts, 16
red slave owners, 165, 166, 199, 230
Reddick, Bolling, 221
Reddick, Isaiah, 457
Reddick, Maria, 221, 457
Reddick, Theopolis, 372
Reddick, Winder, 457
Redford, James, 437
reds (Native-Americans), 218, 266
Reed, Maria, 551
Reed, Richard R., 395
refrigeration at Carnton, 451

THE MCGAVOCKS OF CARNTON PLANTATION

refugeeing, 289, 300
refugees, Southern, 484
regional pride, 74
Registrar of the Land Office, 45
Reid, J. W., 420
Reid, Louisa Trimble, 538
Reid, Peter H., 602
Reid, William, 410
relationships, between Southern whites and blacks, 220
Renfrew, Scotland, 523
Rennolds, Fielding, 108
Republic of Washington, the, 471
Republican, 21, 235-237, 240, 245, 277, 282, 409, 413, 964, 970, 973, 977
Republican Party, 21, 235, 236, 970, 973, 977
Republican Party, switches platforms with the Democratic Party, 236
Republicanism, 236
resources, the South's, 271
Rest Haven Cemetery, 505
reunion, 145, 602, 975, 991
Revels, Hiram R., 162
Revolutionary War, 39, 44-46, 51, 52, 56, 57, 124, 188, 243, 255, 351, 468, 527, 532, 533, 552, 569, 576, 588, 981, 1045
Reynolds, Burt, 1041
Rhine wine, 463
Rhode Island, 30, 41, 90, 173, 175-178, 183
Rhode Island and Providence Plantations, 118
Rhode Island slave industry, 175
Rhode Island, slavery in, 176
rice, 463
Rice, Harriet, 562
Richardson, Henry Woodson, 567
Richardson, John R., Jr., 566
Richardson, John R., Sr., 566, 567
Richemer, Edmund W., 37, 590
Richmond Examiner, 92, 127, 967
Richmond, VA, 50, 57, 58, 117, 182, 254, 354
Rider, Dorothy, 584
Rippavilla Plantation, 50, 355, 1043, 1044
rituals, 167
Riverside McGavocks, the, 473, 477, 480, 497, 550
Riverside Plantation, 301, 473, 494, 514, 550, 569, 1044
robbery, Yankee, 294
Roberson, Margaret, 563
Robert Stewart II, King, 36, 589
Robert the Bruce, 27, 37, 1042
Robert "the Regent" Stewart III, 36, 589
Roberts, R. Philip, 205
Roberts, Walter A., 410, 416, 418

Robertson, Walter H., 551, 576
Robertson, William H., 551, 576
Robinson, Charles D., 254
Robinson, Daniel, 108
Robinsons, New England slaving family, 178
Rockbridge County, VA, 35, 36, 42, 43
Rockingham County, NH, 173
Roderick, Forrest's warhorse, 401
Roderick, Forrest's War Horse Camp 2072, SCV, 19
Rodes, William G., 602
Rodgers family, 436, 438, 456, 462
Rodgers, Ann Phillips, 45, 59, 285, 301, 515, 537, 581
Rodgers, John, 45, 514, 526, 569
Rodgers, Mary Eleanor, 301, 515, 569
Rodgers, Sarah Dougherty, 45, 48, 59, 61, 63, 82, 229, 285, 436, 453, 457, 464, 468, 480, 495, 514, 515, 517, 526, 569
Roman Empire, and Lincoln, 313
Roman government, ancient, 424
Roman slavery, 204, 209
Roman slaves, 209
Rome, ancient, 423
Roosevelt, Franklin D., 257, 312
Roosevelt, Theodore, 313
root, pig, or perish emancipation plan, Lincoln's, 320
Roper's Knob, Franklin, TN, 47
Rose Hill Cemetery, Columbia, TN, 377, 378
Rose, S. E. R., 416
roses, 453
royal bloodline, of Jesus, 423, 425
royal European ancestry, 33
royal McGavock family tree, 521
royal Scots, 36
Royall family crest, 178
Royalls, New England slaving family, 178
Rucker, Edmund W., 394, 537, 1042
Rucker, Phoebe, 394
Rucker's Brigade, 394, 1042
Ruffin, Edmund, 140, 242
rum, 170, 181, 337, 347, 456, 980
rum, traded for slaves in Africa, 170
Running Bond, 440
Rush, Sarah, 50
Russell County, AL, 151
Russia, 68, 210, 276, 969, 983
Rutherford County, TN, 600
Sahara, the, 171
sails, ship, 461
Saint Ambrose, 202
Saint Andrew, 234, 280, 327
Saint Andrew's Cross, 234, 280, 327, 331
Saint Andrew's Cross, and Confederate battle flag,

THE MCGAVOCKS OF CARNTON PLANTATION

234
Saint Andrew's Day, 327
Saint Augustine, 202
Saint Edward II, 589
Saint George's Church, Philadelphia, PA, 163
Saint Gregory, of Nazianzus, 202
Saint John's Episcopal Church, 378
Saint Leger family, 57
Saint Patrick, 35, 235, 280
Saint Patrick's Cross, 235, 280, 331
Saint Paul, 88, 203-205, 213
Saint Peter, 204, 423
salad dressings, 462
Salem Witch Trials, 162
Salem, MA, 162, 173
Salomon, Edward, 291
Salonika, Greece, 209
San Antonio, TX, 55
Sanborn, Benjamin Franklin, 89
Sandburg, Carl, 345
Sanders family, of Kentucky, 1044
sandwiches, 462
sanitation unknown, 489
Sansom family, 60
Sansom, Emma, 60, 416
SAR, 39
Sarah, "daughter" of Jesus, 423
Satan, and Jesus are brothers, according to Mormons, 205
Saunders, Melissa, 559
sausages, 463
Savannah, GA, 271
Sayers, Harvey, 603
scallywag-carpetbag regime, 396
scallywags, 136, 199, 281, 373, 387, 396
Scarborough, Elizabeth, 535, 554
Schofield, John M., 327, 337, 339, 350, 354, 359, 365
Schurz, Carl, 224
Schuyler family, 174
Schuyler Mansion, 174
Scotia, 34
Scotland, 8, 9, 14, 27-29, 32, 34, 37, 42, 58, 59, 234, 235, 280, 327, 331, 419, 467, 477, 521-525, 531, 586, 968, 982, 985, 989, 990, 1042
Scots, 27, 29, 34, 36, 327, 446, 462, 466, 467, 479
Scots-Irish emigration, 29
Scots-Irish pioneers, 29
Scott, James W., 547
Scott, Thomas M., 335
Scott, Walter, Sir, 88
Scott, Winfield, 246, 362, 491
Scottish Confederate soldiers, 595

Scottish kings, 37
Scottish McGavocks, 28
Scottish people, 34
Scottish royals, 27
Scruggs, Earl, 1041
SCV, 24, 108, 282, 329, 508, 509, 594-596, 960, 989
Seabrook, Lochlainn, 17, 513, 521, 594, 1040, 1041, 1044
seamstresses, 137
Sears, Clyde, 445
secession, 9, 16, 39, 50, 74, 110, 177, 227, 240, 243, 272, 273, 280, 306, 307, 311, 315, 316, 376, 961, 963, 972, 974, 981-983, 985
secession, right of, 240
Second Colored Brigade (U.S.), 344
Second Revolutionary War, Civil War as, 243
sectionalism, 989
seed sowers, 136
segregated black brigades, U.S., 344
segregation, 153, 180, 260
self-determination, the South's true goal, 130, 256
self-government, 21, 39, 73-75, 130, 170
Sellars, Thomas S., 603
Selma, Marion, and Memphis Railroad, 394
Seminole, 165, 167
Semiramis, of Assyria, 416
Semmes, Thomas J., 471
separation of powers, 240
serfdom, 202
serfs, 202
servant, 17, 75, 79, 85, 115-117, 123, 133-140, 142, 143, 147, 150, 151, 160, 201, 204, 206-208, 211, 212, 214, 219-222, 228, 299, 319, 320, 344, 372, 376, 457, 494, 507, 594
servant owners, responsibilities of, 139
servants, 10, 12, 43, 48, 52, 65, 69, 75, 78-82, 84, 87, 90, 91, 93, 102, 104-106, 108, 111, 112, 114, 115, 117, 122, 126-129, 131-145, 147-150, 152, 155, 160-162, 183, 188, 190, 191, 198, 200, 203-208, 210, 214-216, 218-222, 225, 227, 228, 230, 247, 254, 258, 260, 266, 268, 288-290, 298-300, 320, 321, 344, 373, 383, 389, 390, 392, 394, 430, 440, 444, 446, 450, 452, 454, 460, 462, 466, 467, 479, 502
servants, and apprenticeship, 144
servants, and literacy, 143
servants, black, 65
servants, expense of keeping, 140
servants' income, 143

1029

THE MCGAVOCKS OF CARNTON PLANTATION

servants' quarters, 450
servants' cemetery, at Carnton, 457
servile laborers, 298
servitude, 88, 98, 124, 127-131, 134-136, 138, 139, 141, 144, 146, 147, 156, 158, 172, 191, 196, 202, 203, 205-207, 213, 216, 217, 232, 260, 269, 280, 320, 435, 962, 971, 973, 989
servitude, as a form of apprenticeship, 144
servitude, benefits of for some servants, 139
Settle, Lucinda, 539
Settle, Yorkshire County, England, 41
Seven Years War, 39
Seventh Tennessee, 393
Seventy-second Illinois Volunteer Infantry Regiment, 333
Sewall, Samuel, 162, 175, 207
Seward, AK, 263
Seward, William H., 89, 100, 129, 252, 263, 305
sewing stand, 473
Sexton, James, 603
Seymour, Horatio, 175
Shall, Sally, 556
Shannon, Amelia, 546
sharecropping, 91, 114, 383
Sharp, Susannah, 548
sharpshooters, 416
Shawnee, 46, 473
sheep, 96, 132, 454, 466
Shellenberger, John K., 503, 504
shelterbelt, trees as a, 455
Shelton, G. M., 603
Shem, of the Bible, 206
Shenandoah, Warren County, VA, 49, 476
Shepherd, Elizabeth, 585, 587
Shepherd, Heyward, 90
Sheridan, Philip, 309, 350, 368
Sherman, William, 87
Sherman, William T., 253, 256, 309, 342, 346, 359, 368, 369, 392, 394, 404, 509
sherry (drink), 463
shock troops, Northern blacks used as, 294
shoddy, defined, 284
shops, Yankees burn down, 308
Short History of the Confederate States of America (Davis), 960
Short, Henry M., 603, 604
Short, Jesse, 603
shrapnel, 489
Shute, Susannah, 520, 558, 572
Shy, W. M., 603
Shy's Hill, 343
Sicily, 209
sideboard, 463
Sidewell, Levi, 549

Sioux, 308
Sixth Annual Message, Jefferson's, 197
Skaggs, Ricky, 1041
Skillman, Elizabeth, 544
Skillman, Richard, 544
slave homes, 148
slave income, average annual, 133
slave insurrection, 89, 164
slave insurrections, 104
slave labor, 118, 146, 151, 167, 177
slave labor, in preconquest Africa, 169
Slave Narratives, 80, 971
slave owners, African-American, 149, 151, 152
slave owners, correct number of, 199
slave owners, Latin-American, 167-169
slave owners, Native-American, 165-167
slave owners, skewing number of by anti-South movement, 199
slave rebellions, 81, 84
slave revolt, 225, 309
slave revolts, 84, 961
slave ships, Yankee, 181
slavery, 7, 9, 14, 55, 65-67, 69, 72-85, 88-102, 113, 115-122, 127-129, 131, 132, 134, 144-147, 151, 153, 155-159, 162, 166-169, 171-175, 177-179, 181-194, 196-199, 201-206, 209-219, 223-227, 230, 231, 243-250, 252, 256, 259, 262, 263, 265-267, 269-272, 275, 278, 279, 293, 296, 298, 300, 304, 318, 319, 321, 389, 390, 407, 593, 957, 961, 963, 964, 966, 968-970, 972-982, 984, 985, 987, 989-991
slavery and servitude, differences between, 127
slavery began in the North, 172
slavery business, 72, 116, 174
slavery figures, skewing by anti-South advocates, 199
slavery scholars, 217
slavery statistics, in the South, 199
slavery today, 116
slavery, African-American, 149
slavery, and inheritance, 133
slavery, and marriage, 131
slavery, and the Christian Church, 202
slavery, as a "mild" institution, 144
slavery, as the domestic institution, 147
slavery, European-American, 206
slavery, in New England, 173
slavery, not practiced in South, 127
slavery, truth about Southern, 131
slavery, when it began in the South, 174
slavery, white, 206, 209
slavery, worldwide support of, 213

THE MCGAVOCKS OF CARNTON PLANTATION

slaves, 13, 14, 42, 65, 67, 70, 74-76, 78, 80, 82, 84, 86, 88-93, 99, 100, 102-104, 106, 110, 112, 113, 116, 118-121, 125-127, 129, 136, 139, 140, 142-146, 149-151, 153, 156, 158, 159, 162-177, 179-183, 186-188, 190-193, 195, 197-201, 203-207, 209-216, 219, 223, 225, 227, 230, 231, 243-246, 248, 252, 253, 257, 258, 260, 265, 268, 270, 279, 290, 294, 295, 300, 304, 320, 340, 344, 390, 396, 438, 485, 961, 963, 971, 974-976, 979, 991
slaves of the Lord, 204
slaves, and home ownership, 132
slaves, and personal wealth, 132
slaves, and property ownership, 132
slaves, as butlers, 147
slaves, as domestics, 147
slaves, as hands, 147
slaves, as maids, 147
slaves, as servants, 147
slaves, earnings and wages of, 132
slaves, Lincoln uses in Nashville, 340
slaves, Northern, 106
slaves, Northern, used to build White House, 179
slaves, wealthy, 132
Slavs, the, 209
Sloss, Mary Stoughton, 588
Slovakia, 209
Smart, Hiram, 603
Smith family, of Kentucky, 1044
Smith, Dub, 603
Smith, Ella Blanton, 563
Smith, George C., 603
Smith, Gerrit, 161
Smith, James, Jr., 533, 553
Smith, James, Sr., 533, 553
Smith, John C., 603
Smith, John E., 597
Smith, Joseph, 205
Smith, Joseph J., 603
Smith, Sally, 533
Smith, Sam, 603
Smith, Thomas Benton, 599
Smith, Turner, 534, 553
Smith, William Sooy, 350, 402
Smithson, George W., 411
smokehouse, 436, 451, 452
Smythe, Malvina, 568
Snyder, Carrie, 336-339, 358
soap, 489
socialism, 141, 240, 958
sociopathy, and slavery, 122
solar lamp, 477

soldiers, statistics, 302
Somerset County, MD, 52
Somerville, Elizabeth, 523
Somerville, John, 523
Sons of Confederate Veterans, 8, 19, 282, 329, 509, 593, 594, 596, 960, 1046
Sons of the American Revolution, 39
sorters, 136
South, 2, 6, 9, 11-17, 21, 23, 30, 33, 34, 45, 47, 51, 52, 55, 57, 65-67, 72-74, 76-86, 88-92, 94-97, 99, 101-103, 106-108, 110, 113-115, 117-122, 124, 127-136, 140-153, 156-165, 168, 169, 171, 172, 174, 177, 178, 181-187, 189-192, 196, 198-202, 204, 206, 208-211, 213, 216, 219, 220, 225-236, 239, 240, 242-245, 247, 249-251, 254, 256-258, 260, 264-266, 269, 271-276, 278-282, 284, 288, 289, 294, 297, 299, 300, 302, 304, 306, 307, 309-311, 313-315, 317-319, 321, 323, 324, 331, 334, 339, 341-347, 349, 354, 358, 361-363, 366, 367, 369, 373, 376, 377, 384, 387, 388, 390-403, 408, 412, 414, 416, 438, 439, 450, 462, 465, 468-471, 476, 485-488, 497, 505, 507, 519, 571, 572, 591-596, 602-605, 957-961, 963, 965-969, 971-977, 980, 981, 983-989, 991, 1040, 1044, 1045
South America, 144, 265
South and North, differences between, 233
South Carolina, 14, 16, 30, 57, 77, 79, 82, 84, 110, 119, 134-136, 145, 150, 151, 158, 162, 174, 189, 232, 236, 242, 271, 297, 299, 317, 319, 366, 376, 377, 470, 507, 1044
South Carolina College, 236
South Dakota, 30
South Harpeth, TN, 602
South, abolition began in the, 187
South, abolitionist movement in the, 187, 188
South, as a Northern colony, 236
South, begins using slavery, 174
South, contrasted with North, 233, 235
South, the, as seen by itself, 233
South-demeaning TV shows, 15
South-insulting TV commercials, 15
Southall, Joseph Branch, 519, 571
Southall, Josephine P., 300, 519, 572
Southall, Philip, 603, 604
Southall, Randal McGavock, 519, 571
Southern abolition movement, 185, 189
Southern and Northern statistics, 323

The McGavocks of Carnton Plantation

Southern Black Codes, 164
Southern black war effort, 106
Southern blacks, 83, 84, 87, 90, 91, 103, 106-109, 113, 114, 124, 133, 135, 139, 141, 142, 149, 153, 158, 165, 259, 260, 296, 298, 299, 309, 320
Southern blacks, try to escape Yanks, 298
Southern Cause, 150, 283, 284, 347, 470, 501, 595
Southern cavaliers, 235
Southern Confederacy, 14, 73, 109, 232, 243, 273, 282, 283, 361, 364, 413, 419, 470, 486, 487, 969, 983, 985, 990, 991
Southern culture, 448
Southern families, 75, 113, 172, 199, 397
Southern farmers, 235
Southern Founders, 15
Southern History of the War (Pollard), 596, 959
Southern peace movement, 310
Southern plantations, 81, 83, 126, 142, 152
Southern ports, 76, 304, 491
Southern pro-Unionists, 310
Southern senators, 230
Southern slave owners, 80, 122, 127, 151, 183, 199, 200
Southern states, 16, 50, 82, 99, 100, 102, 129, 166, 168, 175, 188, 200, 225, 236, 238, 239, 242, 243, 245, 250, 257, 268, 270, 275, 279, 296, 303-306, 314-317, 366, 507, 961, 966, 971, 973
Southern System, 242
Southern Truth, 16, 17, 193, 396
Southern whites, 87, 105, 113, 147, 199, 200, 227, 230, 396
Southern "slavery", 117
Southerners, 14-16, 58, 61, 65, 66, 68, 72-75, 78, 83, 86, 91, 104-107, 116, 117, 119, 122, 127, 129, 136, 140, 141, 143, 145, 147, 156, 161, 164, 185-189, 192, 196, 198, 199, 201, 202, 206, 210, 217, 219, 220, 222, 223, 229, 231, 233, 234, 236, 238-243, 247, 257, 259, 264, 269, 277, 278, 280, 281, 284, 304, 315, 318, 322, 326, 328, 329, 339, 341, 358, 367, 369, 377, 378, 380, 382, 387-389, 392, 393, 396, 400, 405, 412, 438, 449, 469-471, 486, 487, 491, 508, 594, 596, 958, 960, 962, 986, 991
Southerners, as seen by themselves, 233
Southerners, percentage of who owned servants, 199
Southside View of Slavery, A (Adams), 120

sovereignty, 77
Spain, 167, 271
Spanish Confederate soldiers, 595
Spanish Conquest of the Americas, 169
Spanish government, 168
spareribs, 463
Sparta, TN, 449
Speer, William S., 145
Spence, Lula, 558
Spencer repeating rifles, 343
Spencer, Diana, 589
spies, 58, 111, 295, 303
spittoon, 465
Spring Hill Affair, 331, 354, 365
Spring Hill Blunder, 354
Spring Hill, TN, 50, 331, 378, 1044
Springfield, IL, 194, 223
squash, 453
squatters camps, 438
Squier, David, 51
squirrel, 454
Stack Bond, 440
Stainless Banner, the, 281
Stalin, Joseph, 210
Stampp, Kenneth M., 199
Stand Watie, 46
Standard, the, 92
Stanley, David, 381
Stanley, John, black slave owner, 150
Stanton, Edwin M., 392
Stanton, Elizabeth Cady, 257
Star of the Sea, the, and the Virgin Mary, 424, 449
Star Spangled Banner (Key), 207
Star Trek: Deep Space Nine, 43, 590
Stars and Bars, 107
Stars and Stripes, 107, 263, 973
starvation, 139, 141, 261, 320
State Capitol, Nashville, TN, 56
States' Rights, 15, 48, 55, 77, 87, 92, 94, 95, 108, 129, 140, 184, 186, 226, 233, 240, 241, 256, 273, 275, 276, 281, 302, 326, 369, 443, 465, 469, 470, 487, 979
statistics, Southern and Northern, 323
Steedman, James B., 343
Steffe, William, 89
Stegar, T. M., 416, 418
Steger, T. M., 410
Stella Maris, 424, 449
Stephanie, Princess, 589
Stephens, Alexander H., 93, 242, 306, 361, 363
Stevens, Thomas, 603
Stevenson, Carter L., 334
stewards, 137
Stewart family, 42, 477

THE MCGAVOCKS OF CARNTON PLANTATION

Stewart I, King, 42
Stewart, Alexander P., 330, 332, 379, 1042
Stewart, Elizabeth, 524
Stewart, James, 522
Stewart, Jennie Lewis, 566
Stewart, John, 524
Stewart, Marjory, 523
Stewart, Robert, 522, 523
Stewart, Walter, 522
Stewart's Corps, 330, 1042
still operators, 137
stock minders, 136
Stockton, R. H., 506
stone graves, 47
Stonebraker, J. Clarence, 170
Stones River National Battlefield, Murfreesboro, TN, 380
Stonewall Jackson of the West, 328
Stovall, Martin, 603
Stovall, Thomas, 603
Stowe, Harriet Beecher, 12, 117, 119-121, 174, 185
Strahl, Otho F., 374, 375, 378, 379, 415
strawberries, 454, 463
Stretcher Bond, 440
string beans, 453
Stuart, Jeb (James Ewell Brown), 1044
stuffed peppers, 463
stuffed tomatoes, 463
Sturge, Joseph, 159
Sturgis, Samuel D., 402
Suffolk County, MA, 173
Sugar Creek, NC, 41
sugar plantations, 168, 182
sugar plantations, and slavery, 76
sugarplums, 463
Sugg, W. D., 429
Sullavan, Margaret, 502
Sullivan, Tom, 281, 595
Sumerian creation myth, 217
Sumerian slavery, 209
Summers, Elizabeth Anne, 552, 576
Sumner, Charles, 245
Sunno, King, 37, 590
support plans, 319
Supreme Court, 43, 207, 305, 308, 310, 362, 485, 486, 973
suprême de volaille, 463
surgeries, at Carnton, 489
Sustainable Forestry Initiative, 4
sutlers, 107
Swanson, R., 597, 598
Sweden, 38
Swedish Confederate soldiers, 595
sweet potatoes, 463, 465

Sweet, Benjamin J., 380
sweets, 463
Swope (Carnton architect), 48
Tacitus, 37, 589
Taft, William Howard, 54, 537
Talbot, Catherine, 564
Talbot, Martha, 543
Talbot, Williston J., 543
Tally, Thomas J., 603
Talmud, 212
Tanase, 46
Tanase River, 46
Tanasi, 46
Taney, Roger Brooke, 43, 207, 307
Tanner, Thomas A., 603
tariff war, between South and North, 235
Tarlton, Susan, 379
taverns, Yankees burn down, 309
Taylor, John, 186
Taylor, John McCandlass, Jr., 574
Taylor, John McCandlass, Sr., 574
Taylor, Richard, 111, 299, 349, 357, 1043, 1044
Taylor, Sarah K., 357, 1043
Taylor, William E., 603
Taylor, Zachary, 112, 1043
tea, 453, 462
tea parties, at Carnton, 452
Tea Partyism, 15, 58, 236, 237, 443
Team, James, 152
teamsters, 107, 137, 295
Ten Broeck Manor, 174
Ten Percent Plan, 100, 101
Tennessean Abroad, A (McGavock), 285
Tennesseans, 44, 46, 52, 226, 278, 279, 285, 340, 453, 962, 966, 972, 987
Tennessee, 2-4, 8, 10-12, 17, 19, 21, 23, 24, 29, 30, 33, 35, 39, 41, 42, 44-50, 52, 53, 56, 58, 59, 61, 66, 77, 79, 104, 110, 121, 143, 149, 174, 208, 210, 212, 220, 222, 225-227, 258, 260, 278, 280, 284-289, 301, 316, 317, 327, 329, 335, 336, 340-342, 345, 346, 351, 352, 354-359, 361, 363, 365, 367, 368, 372, 375, 377-380, 385, 386, 391, 393, 394, 400, 401, 405-407, 411-414, 417, 419, 421, 426, 427, 439, 440, 443, 449, 454, 462, 463, 465, 468, 469, 477, 479, 497, 503, 509, 526, 528, 533, 537, 553, 557, 591, 594, 597, 603, 604, 961, 962, 964-973, 977-982, 984, 986, 989, 990, 1041-1043, 1045-1047
Tennessee Bureau of Agriculture, 342
Tennessee Historical Society, 19

THE MCGAVOCKS OF CARNTON PLANTATION

Tennessee Home Guard, 285
Tennessee legislature, 44
Tennessee McGavocks, 39
Tennessee River, 46, 346
Tennessee State Board of Health, 287
Tennessee State Library and Archives, 19
Tennessee, first American state to enlist blacks, in June 1861, 226
Tennessee, secession of, 279
Tennessee, statehood, 44
Tennessee, whites, and black Confederates, 225
Tennessee's black soldiers, 226
Tennyson, Lord Alfred, 589
Tenth Amendment, 184, 237
Tenth Tennessee Regiment, 285
termites, 455
terrapin stew, 10, 452
Terrebonne Parish, LA, 61-63, 405
Terrell, William, 50
Terrill, TX, 601
Texas, 30, 51, 55, 166, 317, 339, 348, 357, 379, 405, 413, 507, 598-601
Texas Revolution, 55
textiles, 170
Thackeray, William M., 140, 191
Thailand, 116
Thanksgiving Day, 316
    Lincoln's creation of, 316
The Avengers (TV show), 43, 590
The Battle Hymn of the Republic (song), 89
The Blithedale Romance (Hawthorne), 89
The Book of Kelle (Seabrook), 424
The Christian Record, 56
The Civil War: A Narrative (Foote), 960
The Cotton Kingdom (Olmsted), 160
The Crisis, 988
The Da Vinci Code (Brown), 43
The Girl I Left Behind (song), 330
The Goddess Dictionary of Words and Phrases (Seabrook), 424
The House of the Seven Gables (Hawthorne), 89
The Last Supper (da Vinci), 424
The Liberator (Garrison), 69, 85
The Lost Cause (Pollard), 959
The McGavocks of Carnton Plantation (Seabrook), 14, 17, 596
The Memoirs of Uncle Tom (Henson), 120
The Politically Incorrect Guide to the South (Johnson), 596
The Rise and Fall of the Confederate Government (Davis), 269, 596, 960
The Scarlet Letter (Hawthorne), 89
The Selling of Joseph (Sewall), 175
The South, 6, 11-14, 16, 17, 21, 23, 30, 45, 47, 51, 52, 55, 72-74, 76-78, 81-84, 86, 88-92, 94-97, 99, 101-103, 106-108, 113-115, 118-122, 124, 128-133, 140-149, 152, 153, 156-162, 164, 168, 169, 171, 172, 174, 177, 178, 181, 183, 184, 186, 187, 189, 191, 192, 196, 198-202, 204, 206, 208, 220, 226, 228-230, 233-236, 240, 242-245, 247, 249, 251, 254, 256, 258, 260, 265, 269, 271-276, 278-282, 284, 288, 294, 302, 304, 306, 307, 309-311, 313, 314, 318, 321, 323, 324, 331, 334, 342, 344, 347, 349, 354, 358, 361-363, 366, 367, 369, 373, 384, 387, 392, 394, 396-403, 408, 412, 416, 439, 450, 465, 468-471, 476, 485-488, 497, 505, 593, 596, 957, 958, 960, 961, 965-967, 969, 972, 973, 975, 976, 980, 981, 983-986, 989, 991
The Star-Spangled Banner (Key), 263
The Templar Revelation (Picknett and Prince), 43
The Tennessee Historical Society, 19
The War of the Rebellion (U.S. Gov.), 960
The Yellow Rose of Texas (song), 357
Thessaloniki, Greece, 209
thievery, 320, 382
Thirteenth Amendment, 116, 128, 168, 183, 193, 197, 215, 216, 227, 246, 321, 344, 390
Thirteenth Kentucky Cavalry, 509
Thirty-ninth North Carolina Regiment, 491
Thirty-second Tennessee Regiment, 599
Thomas, Gabriel, 123
Thomas, George H., 246, 339, 342, 346, 359, 365, 367, 368
Thomas, Lorenzo, 111
Thompson, Absalom, 354
Thompson, Sue A., 19, 1047
Thoreau, Henry David, 89, 438
thoroughbred horse farms, 51
Thoroughgood, Adam, 207
Three Marys, the, 424
Tiberius, Octavia Major, 37, 589
ticking, 480
Tickmacrevan Parish, Ireland, 34
Tierce, J. P., 603
Tilden, Mary Frisby, 586
Timbuktu, Africa, 171
tin sheeting, 443, 446
Titcomb, Alex, 420
Tocqueville, Alexis de, 156-158
Todd, James, 539
Todd, Mary (Lincoln's wife), 246
toddies, 463
Tom, husband of Sojourner Truth, 132

1034

THE McGAVOCKS OF CARNTON PLANTATION

tomatoes, 453
Tomlin, George, 603
Toombs, Robert, A., 402
Toplovich, Ann, 19
Torah, 204
Torrington, CT, 87
torture, 16, 122, 167, 294, 299
torture, Yankee, 294
tourists, Civil War, most are conservative and traditional, 281, 595
Toussaint L'Ouverture Cemetery, Franklin, TN, 222
Toussaint, Francois Dominique, 222
Townsend, Almy, 588
Transcontinental Railroad land grants, 312
Travellers Rest, Nashville, TN, 537
treason, 88, 987
treaty of peace, Paris, 238
Treaty with Great Britain, 177
trench warfare, 351
Trigg, Alanson, 574
Trigg, Connally F., 286
Trigg, Jane, 574
Trimble, James, 49
Trinity Episcopal Churchyard, SC, 376
Triple-Goddess, 424
Triune, TN, 381, 386
Troublesome Creek, KY, 1043
Troup, Rebecca, 588
Troy, TN, 449
Truett, Frank, 603
Truett, James T., 603
truffles, 463
Truman, Harry, 260
Trumbull, Lyman, 97
Truth Is Stranger Than Fiction (Henson), 120
Truth, Sojourner, 88, 132, 257, 298, 300
Tubb, Ernest, 355
Tucker, St. George, 188
Tupelo, MS, 346, 356
Turkey, 203
turkey (bird), 454, 462
Turnberry Castle, 522
Turner, Josh, 285
Turner, Mary, 564
Turner, Mildred, 533, 553
Turner, Nat, 85, 86, 164
turtleback walkway, 443
turtles, 454
Tweed Ring Scandal, 368
Twentieth Tennessee Regiment Voluntary Infantry CSA, 286, 597
Twenty-fifth Alabama, 380
Twenty-fourth Wisconsin Volunteer Infantry, 332
Twenty-third Army Corps, USA, 502

Twitty, Conway, 355
Two Rivers Mansion, 45, 476
Two Rivers Plantation, 45, 1044
Tyler, John, 15, 317, 343
Tynes, Ellen B., 1044
tyranny, 17, 39, 236, 276, 346, 380, 384, 400, 470, 976
Tyson, Elizabeth, 586
U.S. army, 41, 253, 294, 295, 300, 347, 348, 605
U.S. army and navy, 253
U.S. Army Corps of Engineers, 41
U.S. Capitol, 179
U.S. Census, 82, 198, 200
U.S. Coast Guard stations, Northern, racism at, 165
U.S. Coastal Survey, 41
U.S. Confederacy, 196, 239, 242
U.S. Congress, 162, 181, 247, 258, 263, 297, 397
U.S. Constitution, 66, 73, 74, 77, 93, 177, 198, 215, 234, 237, 269, 315, 486, 487
U.S. flag, 300
U.S. government, 14, 128, 164, 236, 260, 267, 296, 298, 308, 313, 382, 383, 387, 390, 396, 960
U.S. government plantations, 298
U.S. military, 253-256, 291, 295, 297, 306, 390
U.S. navy, 50
U.S. Oath of Allegiance, 486
U.S. Supreme Court, 207, 310
U.S. threatens war on Great Britain, for aiding Confederacy, 190
U.S. Treasury, 404
U.S.A., 39, 182, 196, 198, 215, 242, 243, 276, 316, 362, 469, 486, 958
UCV, 282, 594
UDC, 283, 329, 508
Ulster American Folk Park, 40
Ulster Country, NY, 132
Ulster Province, Northern Ireland, 34, 526
unalienable rights, 194
Uncle Tom's Cabin (Stowe), 118, 119, 121
underground bombproofs, 351
Underground Railroad, 91, 141
unforced labor, 217
Union, 4, 14, 16, 42, 47, 49, 50, 61, 72, 77, 89, 92, 95, 100-102, 107, 109, 110, 114, 125, 128, 156-158, 163, 187, 190, 192, 196, 216, 221, 224-227, 233, 234, 236, 237, 242, 244, 246, 248, 249, 252, 255, 258, 260, 261, 264-267, 269-276, 278, 280, 285, 286, 290-299, 301, 302, 304, 306, 308, 316, 323, 324, 327, 331-333, 338-347, 350, 353, 354, 357, 359, 363, 367, 368, 370, 376-378,

1035

THE MCGAVOCKS OF CARNTON PLANTATION

380-383, 391-393, 395, 399, 400, 403, 404, 469, 470, 484-486, 492, 502, 503, 598, 603, 957, 960, 961, 964, 966, 968, 972, 976, 979, 982, 983, 988-991, 1043, 1045
Union army, 110, 227, 298, 380, 961, 966
Union City, TN, 603
Union deaths, statistics, 492
Union Oath of Allegiance, 484
Union officers, 285, 293, 341, 344, 354, 404
Union Valley, TN, 598
union, defined, 276
Union, on verge of collapse just before Battle of Nashville, 347
United Confederate Veterans, 282, 408, 594, 960
United Daughters of the Confederacy, 19, 24, 107, 283, 329, 426, 508, 509, 595
United States Colored Troops, 988
United States of America, 169, 198, 233, 239, 256, 278, 280, 303, 323, 376, 962, 979, 984, 987
universities, Yankees burn down, 308
University of Nashville, 285
University of Pennsylvania, 41
University of Tennessee, 563
Unmelted Pot, U.S. as an, 271
urbanization, 192
Utah, 31, 55, 205
Vallandigham, Clement L., 302, 315, 369
Valley of Death, the, 328
Van Buren, Cornelius M., 208
Van Buren, Martin, 45, 53, 207, 208
Van Dorn, Earl, 355
Van Loon, Hendrik W., 231
Van Rens family, 19
Van Rensselaer family, 174
Vance, Robert B., 1044
Vance, Zebulon, 1044
Vanderbilt University, 1045
Vanderslice, Jacob, 546
Vanderslice, Richardson, 546
Vaughan's Brigade, 1042
Vaughn, George W., 604
Vaughn, J. R., 604
Vaughn, Thomas R., 604
Vaught, G. M., 604
vegetables, 465
velouté, 463
Venables, Joseph, 580
Venetian blinds, 467
venison, 462
Vermont, 31, 77, 183
Vertrees, Peter, 108
Vesey, Denmark, 84, 134
Veterans Association, 283, 386

Vico, Perry County, KY, 49
Victoria, Queen, 495, 589
Victorian Christians, 203
Victorian era, 62, 302
Victorian era, infant mortality in, 302
Victorian Period, 255, 495
Victorian South, 117
Victorian Southern children, 125
Victorian Tennessee, 212
Victorian times, 302
Victorians, 13, 438, 448, 472, 480, 481, 494, 495
Vikings, the, 38, 209
Vinci, Leonardo da, 424
Virgin Mary, 321, 424, 449
Virgin-Moon-Triple-Goddess, and McGavocks, 424
Virgin-Mother-Goddess, 424
Virginia, 14, 30, 33, 35, 36, 38-43, 45, 48, 49, 51, 53, 57, 58, 60, 84-88, 95, 109, 110, 112, 117, 127, 134, 140, 144, 146, 149, 151, 159, 160, 162, 168, 182, 186-189, 191, 192, 195, 196, 207, 215, 221, 239, 244, 253, 254, 268, 271, 287, 297, 307, 315, 317, 327, 330, 339, 343, 354, 357, 366, 405, 449, 463, 468, 470, 473, 476, 509, 1042, 1043
Virginia Constitution, 195
Virginia McGavocks, 42
Virginia Reel, the, 452
Virginia, abolitionism in, 187
Virginia, American abolition movement started in, 187
Vlad III, 43
Volta region, Ghana, Africa, 216
Vonore, Monroe County, TN, 46
Vowel, Jones, 604
Wade-Gooch Report, 391
Wakeman, George, 223
Walden Pond, Concord, MA, 178, 438
Waldos, New England slaving family, 178
Waldron, Nathaniel, 176
Wales, 27, 29, 235, 522
Wall Street Boys, 197, 272
Wall, Edmund, 47
Wall, S. V., 411
Wallace, J. G., 410
Wallace, William, Sir, 351, 589
wallpaper, 54, 460, 464, 467, 472, 496, 498
walnut roof shakes, 446
Walter, King, of the Franks, 37
Walthall, Edward C., 330
Walthall's Division, 330
Wanton, Joseph, 177
war clubs, 455

THE MCGAVOCKS OF CARNTON PLANTATION

war crimes, Yankee, 297, 380
War Department, 175, 255, 291, 347, 396
War for Southern Independence, 7, 57, 179, 188, 227, 232, 243, 297, 343, 351, 387, 437, 492, 527, 537, 541, 560, 570, 581, 583, 587, 959, 979, 1042, 1043
war measure, 244, 251
War of 1812, 256, 532, 573
War of Secession, first, 39
war powers, and Lincoln, 303
Ward's Seminary, 563
Warmoth, Henry Clay, 162
Warner, James C., 539
Warner, Percy, 539
Warren, Joe, 108
Washburn, S. L., 593
Washburne, Elihu B., 270
washerwoman, 147
Washington County, RI, 173
Washington, Booker T., 142
Washington, D.C., 14, 16, 74, 76, 165, 178-180, 182, 230, 237, 253, 261, 262, 276, 292, 300, 347, 384, 565
Washington, George, 14, 15, 43, 44, 124, 151, 187, 256, 298, 382, 470, 471, 589
Washington's birthday, and the Confederacy, 471
watercress, 454
Waters, Mary, 580
Watie, Stand, 166, 292
Watkins, Anna, 543
Watkins, Sam, 332, 333, 349, 359, 360, 501, 504
Watkins, Virginia M., 557
Watson, Thomas J., 604
weavers, 137
Webb, R. C., 410
Webster, Daniel, 263, 469
Webster, MA, 263
Wells, Kitty, 355
Welsh, 27, 595, 1040
Welsh Confederate soldiers, 595
Welsh culture, 27
West Africa, 167
West African coast, 167
West Harpeth River, 454
West Harpeth, TN, 598, 599
West Indian Confederate soldiers, 595
West Indies, 168, 173
West Mark Street, Franklin, TN, 378
West Point Military Academy, 41, 57, 347, 350, 402
West Virginia, 31, 60, 87, 307, 315, 316, 1042
Western states, 46, 96, 158, 196
Western Territories, 55, 96, 97, 158, 196
Western Territory, 46, 196
Westphalia, Germany, 424

wet nurses, black, 230
whale oil, 460, 461
wheat, 465
Wheeler, Joseph, 602
Whigs, 227, 469
whip, 65, 111, 120, 123-126, 288, 355, 990
whipping, 123-125, 155, 175
whipping, and slavery, 123, 124
whipping, in England, 123
whiskey, 488
whiskey punches, 452
Whiskey Ring Scandal, 368
whist, card game, 465
white backlash, 399
white birth rates, 182
White Hall, 1047
white hegemony, 69
White House, 179, 241, 265, 267, 323
white labor, 79, 98, 172
white man's party, 97
white man's war, 255
white men, 89, 99, 109, 114, 223, 262
White Oak, TN, 600
white racism in Illinois, 154, 155
white racism, in U.S. army, 294
white racism, legalized, in Washington, D.C., 180
white sauce, 463
white servitude, 207, 962, 971
white sharecroppers, 114
white slave owners, 150, 166, 200, 205
white slavery, 206, 208-210
white slavery, in Medieval Europe, 209
white slaves, 139, 150, 172, 173, 207, 209-211, 961, 976
white supremacist ideas, and Lincoln, 278
white supremacy, 66, 209
white supremacy, and Lincoln, 247
white wet nurses, to black children, 230
white Yankee racism, 293
White, Ben E., 604
White, James H., 604
White, John, 422, 604
White, William, 376
Whitehead family, 86
Whitehead, Margaret, 86
whites, 38, 67-69, 74, 82-87, 91, 93, 96-98, 105-107, 113, 114, 118, 123, 132, 133, 135, 139, 142, 145, 147-149, 153, 155-158, 160, 162, 163, 165, 166, 170, 172, 180, 182, 187, 190, 199-201, 207-210, 218, 221, 223, 225, 227, 230, 231, 250, 253, 254, 256, 260, 266, 268, 293, 296, 300, 320, 324, 394, 396-399, 405, 974, 987, 1043

1037

THE MCGAVOCKS OF CARNTON PLANTATION

Whitfield, Thomas, 604
Whitman, Walt, 17
Whitney, Eli, 78
Whitside, Samuel Marmaduke, 565
Whitside, William H., 565
why the South lost Lincoln's War, 361
Wicca, 66
Wigfall, Louis T., 359
Wigtown, Scotland, 34
Wigtownshire, Scotland, 34
Wilcox, Albert Gallatin, 536, 556, 573
Wilcox, John Earl, 536, 573
wild foods at Carnton, 454
wild game, 454, 462
wild turkey, 462
Wilder, Lawrence Douglas, 162
Wilderness Road, 35
Wiley, Calvin A., 188
Wilkinson, Allen, 87
Wilkinson, Fannie E., 564
William Harrison House, 377
William the Conqueror, 37, 38, 589
William, Prince, 43, 589
Williams, America, 534
Williams, Cornelia, 584
Williams, Mary, 551
Williams, Mary Serena Chesnut, 58
Williams, Michael, 15
Williamson County Public Library, 19, 53, 62, 64, 374, 376, 406, 407, 428, 506
Williamson County, TN, 23, 44-47, 49, 58, 283, 373, 407, 408, 410, 412, 414, 416, 419, 425-427, 437, 443, 445, 451, 474, 501, 517, 598, 600
Williamson County, TX, 598
Williamson, Abbie Jouett, 567
Wilmington, NC, 271
Wilmot Proviso, 97
Wilmot, David, 97, 98
Wilson, Clyde, 15
Wilson, Henry, 208
Wilson, James, 14
Wilson, James H., 341
Wilson, Sheldon, 538
Wilson, Woodrow, 94, 97, 118, 145, 148, 187, 242, 260, 271, 277, 1044
Winbush, Nelson W., 108, 594
Winchester, James, 537
windbreak, osage orange tree as a, 455
Winder family, 56
Winder surname, etymology of, 60
Winder, Aurelia, 585, 588
Winder, Bridget, 580
Winder, Caroline E., 11, 23, 43, 56, 59, 61-63, 82, 221, 222, 229, 232, 280-283, 288, 301, 370-373, 375, 385, 405-407, 413, 414, 416, 420, 421, 425, 427, 446, 447, 457, 467, 473-475, 480, 482, 483, 496, 509, 517, 519, 527, 570, 581, 1044
Winder, Caroline Lucretia, 584
Winder, Charles S., 57, 588, 1044
Winder, Charlotte, 585, 588
Winder, Cumbria County, England, 59
Winder, Edward S., 588
Winder, Elizabeth, 579, 580
Winder, Elizabeth Rowan, 583
Winder, Esther, 585, 586
Winder, Felix Grundy, 57, 419, 583
Winder, George Guion, 583
Winder, Gertrude, 585, 587
Winder, Harriet Ann Grundy, 583
Winder, Jane, 585
Winder, John, 222, 580, 584
Winder, John "the Immigrant", 579
Winder, John Bay, 583
Winder, John C., 587
Winder, John Davidson Smith, 583
Winder, John H., 57, 58, 585, 587, 1044
Winder, John Jones, 581
Winder, Levin, 56, 57, 588
Winder, Louise McGavock, 415, 418, 583
Winder, Lucretia Perkins, 584
Winder, Malvina Bass, 61, 583
Winder, Margaret Rawlins, 583
Winder, Martha Ann Grundy, 62, 583
Winder, Meriam, 580
Winder, Miss, 57
Winder, Rachel, 580
Winder, Sallie Guion, 415, 418, 419, 584
Winder, Susan, 579
Winder, Thomas, 579, 580
Winder, Thomas Jones, 581
Winder, Thomas Levin, 415, 418, 419, 584
Winder, Thomas P., 585, 587
Winder, Van Perkins, Jr., 405, 406, 584
Winder, Van Perkins, Sr., 52, 62, 63, 222, 415, 417, 419, 517, 527, 570, 581
Winder, William, 222, 581, 584, 587, 588
Winder, William A., 585, 587
Winder, William H., Jr., 585, 588
Winder, William H., Sr., 584, 587
Winder, William Shields, 61, 584
Winder, William Sidney, 585, 587
Winder, William Tasker, 585, 588
Windermere, 385, 475, 527
window casings, 441
window jambs, 441
window muntins, 441
window sashes, 441

THE MCGAVOCKS OF CARNTON PLANTATION

window sills, 441
window stools, 441
Windsor chairs, 495
wine sauce, 462
Winstead Hill, 329, 377
Winstead Hill Park, 329
Winstead, Samuel, 330
Winthrop, John, 109
Winthrop, Theodore, 109
Wisconsin, 30, 33, 183, 291
Witch Trials, Salem, MA, 162
Withers, Ben, 604
Withers, James H., 604
Withers, John W., 550
Witherspoon, John (1), 58
Witherspoon, John (2), 58
Witherspoon, Reese, 58, 393, 1044
Witherspoon, William, 393
Wolseley, Garnet J., 404
Womack, John Byars, 1043
Womack, Lee Ann, 1041, 1043
Womack, Martha, 1043
women, 17, 39, 78, 84, 86, 98, 116, 121, 150, 160, 172, 174, 191, 199, 222, 223, 228, 230, 257, 258, 261, 274, 290, 294, 306, 309, 337, 358, 372, 404, 412, 416, 417, 419, 426, 452, 472, 474, 606, 958, 963, 964, 966, 971, 980
women's movement, and Lincoln, 257
women's rights, 257, 258, 596
Wood, Fernando, 175
Wood, Mary Agnes, 575
woodwork, at Carnton, 458
Work Projects Administration, 80
work week, for servants, 137
World War I, 563, 571, 582, 583
World War II, 319, 332, 571, 582, 605
worldwide slave industry, 116
Worsham family, 50
Worsham, Martha B., 49
wounding, 503
wounds, 80, 348, 374, 379, 417, 468, 489-493, 598
Wray, Frank, 604
Wray, Major I., 604
Wright family, of Kentucky, 1044
Wright, John Wesley, 1044
Wyatt Hall, Franklin, TN, 418
Wynette, Tammy, 354
Wyoming, 31, 46
Wythe County, VA, 35, 36, 39, 42, 45, 473
Wytheville, VA, 35, 44
Yankee atrocities, 289, 293, 299
Yankee bomb, found at Carnton, 456

Yankee brutality, against women, 294
Yankee devils, 78
Yankee folklore, 17, 395
Yankee military rule, of Middle TN, 484
Yankee myth, 161, 196
Yankee mythologists, 14
Yankee mythology, 171
Yankee propaganda, 97, 119, 281, 959, 960
Yankee racism, 159, 291, 293
Yankee reporters, 391
Yankee rule, 140
Yankee slave owners, 66
Yankee slave ships, 181, 448
Yankee soldiers, war crimes of, 290
Yankee Stadium, New York, NY, 593
Yankee tyranny, 39
Yankee war crimes, 274, 297, 380
Yankee war criminals, 368
Yankee, turning, 484
Yankee-slanted history books, 80
Yankeedom, 66, 225
Yankees, 6, 12, 67, 68, 89, 106, 109, 110, 112, 115, 168, 171, 216, 224, 231, 247, 263, 272, 279, 284, 288, 290, 299, 315, 320, 327, 358, 380, 381, 392, 393, 396, 469, 508, 596, 976
Yates, Richard, 156
Yellmann, John, 175
yellow fever, 63, 357
yellow journalism, Northern, 387
Yellowstone National Park, 46
yeoman farmers, 201
York, Thomas J., 604
Yoruba, 216
Yosemite nature reserve land grant, 312
Young, Alexander, 538
Young, Brigham, 205
Young, Catherine, 536, 573
Young, Ella, 538
Young, John, 556
Young, Napoleon, 556
Zollicoffer, Felix K., 1044
Zuber wallpaper company, 464
Zuber, Jean, 464
Zuber, Jean Henri, 464

About the Author

LOCHLAINN SEABROOK is an unreconstructed Southern historian, author, and a traditional agrarian of Scottish, English, Irish, Welsh, German, and Italian extraction. An encyclopedist and lexicographer, a musician, artist, graphic designer, and photographer, and an award-winning poet, songwriter, and screenwriter, he has a thirty year background in historical nonfiction writing.

(Illustration © Tracy Latham)

Due to similarities in their writing styles, ideas, and literary works, Seabrook is sometimes referred to as the "American ROBERT GRAVES," after the prolific English writer, historian, mythographer, poet, and author of the classic tome *The White Goddess*.

The grandson of an Appalachian coal-mining family, Seabrook is a seventh-generation Kentuckian, co-chair of the Jent/Gent Family Committee (Kentucky), founder and director of the Blakeney Family Tree Project, and a board member of the Friends of Colonel Benjamin E. Caudill. Seabrook's literary works have been endorsed by leading authorities, museum curators, award-winning historians, bestselling authors, celebrities, noted scientists, well respected educators, esteemed Southern organizations, and distinguished academicians from around the world.

As a professional writer Seabrook has authored some thirty popular adult books specializing in the following topics: the American Civil War, pro-South studies, Confederate biography and history, the anthropology of religion, genealogical monographs, Goddess-worship (thealogy), ghost stories, the paranormal, family histories, military encyclopedias, etymological dictionaries, ufology, comparative analysis of

THE MCGAVOCKS OF CARNTON PLANTATION

the origins of Christmas, and cross-cultural studies of the family and marriage.

Seabrook's seven children's books include a dictionary of religion and myth, a rewriting of the King Arthur legend (which reinstates the original pre-Christian motifs), two bedtime stories for preschoolers, a naturalist's guidebook to owls, a worldwide look at the family, and an examination of the Near-Death Experience.

Born with music in his blood, Seabrook is an award-winning, multi-genre, Nashville songwriter and lyricist who has composed some 3,000 songs (250 albums). A musician, producer, multi-instrumentalist, and renown performer—whose keyboard work has been variously compared to pianists from HARGUS ROBBINS and VINCE GUARALDI to ELTON JOHN and LEONARD BERNSTEIN—Seabrook has opened for groups such as the EARL SCRUGGS REVIEW, TED NUGENT, and BOB SEGER, and has performed privately for such luminaries as President RONALD REAGAN, BURT REYNOLDS, and Senator EDWARD W. BROOKE.

(Photo © Lochlainn Seabrook)

Seabrook's cousins in the music business include: JOHNNY CASH, ELVIS PRESLEY, BILLY RAY and MILEY CYRUS, PATTY LOVELESS, TIM MCGRAW, DOLLY PARTON, PAT BOONE, NAOMI, WYNONNA, and ASHLEY JUDD, RICKY SKAGGS, the SUNSHINE SISTERS, MARTHA CARSON, CHET ATKINS, and, as mentioned, LEE ANN WOMACK.

Seabrook lives with his wife and family in historic Middle Tennessee, the heart of the Confederacy, where his conservative Southern ancestors fought valiantly against liberal Lincoln and the progressive North in defense of Jeffersonianism, constitutional government, and personal liberty.

www.LochlainnSeabrook.com

The Author's Genealogy

A professional genealogist who has helped many people find their ancestors, Lochlainn Seabrook continues the lifelong research of his own family history. Of blue-blooded Southern stock through his Kentucky, Tennessee, Virginia, West Virginia, and North Carolina ancestors, he is a direct descendant of European royalty via his 6th great-grandfather, the EARL OF OXFORD, after which London's famous Harley Street is named. Among his celebrated male Celtic ancestors is ROBERT THE BRUCE, King of Scotland, Seabrook's 22nd great-grandfather. The 21st great-grandson of EDWARD I "LONGSHANKS" PLANTAGENET, King of England, Seabrook is also a thirteenth-generation descendant of the colonists of Jamestown, Virginia (1607).

Through these same families Seabrook is also closely connected to Carnton Plantation, the town of Franklin, the Battle of Franklin II, and the War for Southern Independence. He is related to the founder of Franklin, ABRAM POINDEXTER MAURY (after whom Maury County, Tennessee, is named), and is cousins with the McGavocks (who built Carnton); the Winders (who married into the McGavock family); General JOHN BELL HOOD (1831-1879)—commander of Confederate forces at Franklin II; Southern hero General NATHAN BEDFORD FORREST (1821-1877)—who led cavalry operations at Franklin II; General ALEXANDER PETER STEWART—who led Stewart's Corps at Franklin II; General ARTHUR M. MANIGAULT—who led Manigault's Brigade at Franklin II; GEORGE W. GORDON—who led Vaughan's Brigade at Franklin II; HENRY R. JACKSON—who led Jackson's Brigade at Franklin II; General STATES RIGHTS GIST—who led Gist's Brigade at Franklin II; and cavalry officer Colonel EDMUND WINCHESTER RUCKER (1835-1924)—who led Rucker's Brigade under the "Wizard of the Saddle" at the Battles of Franklin II, Spring Hill, and Murfreesboro.

(Photo © Lochlainn Seabrook)

Seabrook is also cousins with General STEPHEN DILL LEE (1833-1908), who led Lee's Corps under Hood at Franklin II (tragically, Hood initiated the fight before Lee's 9,700-man infantry showed up, seriously incapacitating Rebel forces and assisting in their defeat on the Plain of Franklin). Lee and Seabrook are both, in turn, cousins

THE MCGAVOCKS OF CARNTON PLANTATION

with the celebrated General ROBERT E. LEE (1807-1870), commander-in-chief of the Confederate armies and the South's most beloved officer. Among the Rebel commanders who reported to Lee was Seabrook's cousin, the daring partisan cavalry ranger Colonel JOHN SINGLETON MOSBY (1833-1916), who successfully terrorized the Yanks throughout the War (Seabrook's 6th great-grandmother is ELIZABETH BACON MOSBY, b. 1739 in VA).

In addition to having relatives who fought at Franklin II, Seabrook also has kin buried at the McGavock Confederate Cemetery. One of these is JOHN BYARS WOMACK (1839-1864), of

(Photo © Lochlainn Seabrook)

Warren Co., TN. Seabrook's 7th great-grandmother is MARTHA WOMACK (1680-1758) of Virginia, making him 5th cousins with John. Also related to both John and Lochlainn is Nashville country artist LEE ANN WOMACK.

Seabrook's other notable War relations include two of the children of the 12th US president, ZACHARY TAYLOR (1784-1850): SARAH KNOX TAYLOR (1814-1835)—the first wife of the Confederacy's president, JEFFERSON DAVIS (1808-1889), and her Confederate brother, Lieutenant General RICHARD TAYLOR (1826-1879)—who took over command of the tattered remains of the Army of Tennessee from Hood when he resigned after the Battle of Nashville (December 15-16, 1864). Seabrook is also closely related to the Cheairs family (who built Rippavilla Plantation in Spring Hill, TN), the Harding family (who built Carnton's sister plantation Belle Meade in Nashville, TN), President ANDREW JACKSON (who built the Hermitage in Nashville, TN), and President JAMES K. POLK (whose family built the Polk House in Columbia, TN).

(Photo © Lochlainn Seabrook)

The 2nd, 3rd, and 4th great-grandson of dozens of Confederate soldiers, one of Seabrook's closest connections to the War for Southern Independence is through his 3rd great-grandfather, ELIAS JENT, SR., who fought for the Confederacy in the 13th Cavalry KY under Seabrook's 2nd cousin, Colonel BENJAMIN E. CAUDILL (1830-1889). The 13th, also known as "Caudill's Army," fought in numerous conflicts, including the Battles of Saltville, Gladsville, Mill Cliff, Poor Fork, Whitesburg, and Leatherwood.

While on furlough, Elias and his wife RACHEL CORNETT (Seabrook's 3rd great-grandmother) were out for a walk when they were captured by Union soldiers and promptly hanged from a tree near Troublesome Creek, KY. This heinous war crime continues to haunt Seabrook's family to this day. Colonel Caudill was captured at

THE MCGAVOCKS OF CARNTON PLANTATION

Gladsville, July 7, 1863, along with another of Seabrook's relations, his 1st cousin, the infamous Kentucky lawman *and* outlaw, JOHN WESLEY "DEVIL JOHN" WRIGHT (1844-1931). Other Confederate ancestors include the surnames NELSON, ALLEN, GILKERSON, COMBS, PRICE, SMITH, SANDERS, POTTER, WRIGHT, and HOLBROOK.

Seabrook is also related to the following Confederates: STONEWALL JACKSON, JAMES LONGSTREET, JOHN HUNT MORGAN, JEB STUART, P. G. T. BEAUREGARD, JOHN H. WINDER, GIDEON J. PILLOW, JOHN C. BRECKINRIDGE, LEONIDAS POLK, WILLIAM GILES HARDING (of Belle Meade Plantation, Nashville, TN), ZEBULON VANCE, GEORGE WYTHE RANDOLPH (grandson of Thomas Jefferson), FELIX K. ZOLLICOFFER, FITZHUGH LEE, NATHANIEL F. CHEAIRS (of Rippavilla Plantation, Spring Hill, TN), JESSE JAMES, FRANK JAMES, ROBERT BRANK VANCE, RICHARD TAYLOR, CHARLES SIDNEY WINDER, JOHN W. MCGAVOCK (of Carnton Plantation, Franklin, TN), CARRIE (WINDER) MCGAVOCK (of Ducros Plantation, Houma, LA), DAVID HARDING MCGAVOCK (of Two Rivers Plantation, Nashville, TN), LYSANDER MCGAVOCK (of Midway Plantation, Brentwood, TN), JAMES RANDAL MCGAVOCK (of Riverside Plantation, Franklin, TN), RANDAL WILLIAM MCGAVOCK (of the Deery Family Home, Allisona, TN), FRANCIS MCGAVOCK (of Clifflawn Plantation, Nashville, TN), EMILY MCGAVOCK (of Boxwood Hall, Brentwood, TN), WILLIAM HENRY F. LEE, LUCIUS E. POLK, MINOR MERIWETHER (husband of noted pro-South author Elizabeth Avery Meriwether), ELLEN BOURNE TYNES (wife of Forrest's chief of artillery, Captain John W. Morton), South Carolina Senators PRESTON SMITH BROOKS and ANDREW PICKENS BUTLER, and famed South Carolina diarist MARY CHESNUT.

(Photo © Lochlainn Seabrook)

Seabrook's modern day cousins include: PATRICK J. BUCHANAN (conservative author), REBECCA GAYHEART (Kentucky-born actress), SHELBY LEE ADAMS (Letcher County, Kentucky, portrait photographer), BERTRAM THOMAS COMBS (Kentucky's fiftieth governor), EDITH BOLLING (wife of President Woodrow Wilson), and actors ROBERT DUVALL, REESE WITHERSPOON, LEE MARVIN, and TOM CRUISE.

About the Introduction Writer

MICHAEL R. BRADLEY is a native of the Tennessee-Alabama state line region near Fayetteville, Tennessee. He attended Samford University for his B.A., took a Masters of Divinity at New Orleans Seminary, and a M.A. and the Ph.D. from Vanderbilt University, graduating there in 1970.

For thirty-six years Dr. Bradley taught United States History at Motlow College, a Tennessee Board of Regents junior college near Tullahoma. He retired in May 2006. He has been pastor of two Presbyterian churches in Middle Tennessee, LaVergne Presbyterian from 1968 to 1976 and Clifton Presbyterian from 1977 to 2006. He served as Interim Pastor of the First Presbyterian Church in Manchester from January 2007 until June 2008.

(Photo © Michael R. Bradley)

During his teaching career Dr. Bradley received a National Endowment for the Humanities Grant and a National Sciences Foundation Grant. He also was made a Fellow of Johns Hopkins University.

Dr. Bradley is the author of several books on the War Between the States period including *Tullahoma: The 1863 Campaign*; *With Blood and Fire: Behind Union Lines in Middle Tennessee*; *Nathan Bedford Forrest's Escort and Staff*; *It Happened in the Civil War*, a second edition of which appeared in 2010; and *Home Fires in the Line of Fire*, published as part of an anthology titled *Sister States/Enemy States*, about the war in Tennessee and Kentucky.

Two recent articles have been published in *North & South* magazine; "Death Lists in Middle Tennessee," and "In the Crosshairs: Confederate Civilians Targeted for Death by the United States Army." "Tullahoma: The Wrongly Forgotten Campaign" was published in *Blue & Gray* magazine in 2010. He also writes on other topics including the Revolutionary War, the Great Smoky Mountains, and historical stories. Dr. Bradley has written for various reference works, including *The Civil Rights Encyclopedia*, *The Tennessee Encyclopedia,* and *Sports Encyclopedia*.

Dr. Bradley continues to research and write on Civil War history.

The McGavocks of Carnton Plantation

His current projects are a biography of David C. Kelley, a prominent Methodist minister who was a Colonel under Bedford Forrest, and a proposed volume which will give a short history of each regiment and artillery battery which served under Bedford Forrest. Another book for general readers, *Mysteries and Legends of the Civil War,* was released in April 2011. In 2006 Dr. Bradley was elected Commander of the Tennessee Division of the Sons of Confederate Veterans. He is a Life Member of that organization.

In February 2010 Dr. Bradley was appointed by Governor Phil Bredesen to the Tennessee Civil War Sesquicentennial Commission.

Dr. Bradley is married to Martha Rae Dobbins Bradley. They are the parents of two adult children, Nancy Todd Bradley Warren and Michael Lee Bradley. Dr. and Mrs. Bradley have two grandsons, William Andrew Warren and Michael Alexander Warren.

michaelrbradley@lighttube.net

About the Foreword Writer

SUE ARMSTRONG THOMPSON is the master curator and decorative arts director of the Lotz House Museum, 1111 Columbia Ave., Franklin, Tennessee. A professional antique and fine arts appraiser of note, she is often called the "One Woman Antiques Roadshow," as she has conducted numerous antique appraisal fairs for many years.

As an independent appraiser, Thompson has been involved in the art and antiques appraisal business for nearly five decades. She has been retained to do appraisals throughout the U.S., England, and Germany. She is also a former art instructor who worked in the Western Pacific Islands of Guam and Saipan.

(Photo © Lochlainn Seabrook)

Her international work and travel have enabled her to understand art on a global level. She is a noted antiquarian who works as a consultant to individuals and corporations, and lectures on the subjects of investment collecting, the art of Matilda Lotz, antique and art collecting, and the Lotz House Museum.

Thompson is an avid collector of American furniture and decorative arts, and was instrumental in locating and collecting many of the furnishings and decorative arts you see at the Lotz House today. She has also been involved in the restoration and preservation of many of Middle Tennessee's other famous historical homes, including the Mooreland House, Longview Mansion, Belmont Mansion, Belle Meade Mansion, Clover Bottom Mansion, White Hall and, of course, the Lotz House.

A student of nineteenth-century furnishings since childhood, Ms. Thompson's lifetime antique collection is now on loan at the Lotz House Museum. Here the guest will find the home's beautiful rooms populated with period pieces correct to the lifestyle of the South's great antebellum plantation families.

www.LotzHouse.com

(Photo © Lochlainn Seabrook)

The McGavocks of Carnton Plantation

(Photo © Lochlainn Seabrook)

www.ingramcontent.com/pod-product-compliance
Lightning Source LLC
Chambersburg PA
CBHW021216300426
44111CB00007B/332